Encyclopedia
of American
Family Names

Encyclopedia of American Family Names

H. Amanda Robb and Andrew Chesler

HarperCollins*Publishers*

In memory of Philip Slepian

ENCYCLOPEDIA OF AMERICAN FAMILY NAMES. Copyright © 1995 by H. Amanda Robb, Andrew Chesler, and New England Publishing Associates, Inc. All rights reserved. Printed in the United States of America. No part of this book may be used or reproduced in any manner whatsoever without written permission except in the case of brief quotations embodied in critical articles and reviews. For information address HarperCollins*Publishers*, Inc., 10 East 53rd Street, New York, New York 10022.

HarperCollins books may be purchased for educational, business, or sales promotional use. For information, please write to: Special Markets Department, HarperCollins*Publishers*, Inc., 10 East 53rd Street, New York, New York 10022.

FIRST EDITION

Library of Congress Cataloging Card Number 94-28719
ISBN 0-06-270075-8

95 96 97 98 99 ❖/RRD 10 9 8 7 6 5 4 3 2 1

CONTENTS

———●———

ACKNOWLEDGMENTS

———•———

We are indebted to Margaret Heinrich Hand and Larry E. Hand who contributed biographical information for use in this book.

The authors wish to thank Lamia Matta, Kate Swisher, and the librarians at the New York Public Library and the Library of Congress for their help with this book. We also are indebted to Elizabeth Attebery for her meticulous copyediting of a long and complex manuscript.

INTRODUCTION

———————•———————

T HE GENESIS FOR THIS BOOK was the posthumous discovery of
my grandfather's office files. For as long as I knew him, he refused to dis-
cuss the nature of his work, and as a child I thought he was a CIA opera-
tive. Apparently, however, instead of uncovering espionage plots, he uncovered
etymological roots of surnames.

From what we can gather from his files, it appears that between the 1950s
and 1980s, he compiled etymologies and biographies for about 20,000 surnames
and published them in a column called "Is Your Name...?", which appeared in
dozens of small newspapers in the northeastern and midwestern United States.
His sales pitch seems to have been particularly inspired and effective. He would
get a copy of his target publication and write a column about the surname of his
sales target—the paper's editor or publisher. It must have worked reasonably well,
as it appears he made about half his living for more than 30 years from the "Is
Your Name...?" columns.

When we first thought of publishing a book based on his columns, we
thought we would simply create a compilation of his work. There were, however,
shortcomings in this method. For example, his columns were written for local
newspapers. Therefore, the biographies often only listed regional personages.
And because his columns were written between the 1950s and 1980s, many
biographies were out of date. But most problematic was the fact that all of the
nearly 20,000 surnames he profiled were of western European origin.

A publisher, we realized, would want a more comprehensive sampling of
American surnames. But finding a comprehensive list of common surnames in
the United States proved problematic. The most obvious sources of lists available
were telephone directories, property deeds, and immigration records. All, however, have inherent shortcomings as a comprehensive methodology. Lists gathered from telephone directories and property deeds are skewed by regional
settlement patterns, and immigration records are skewed by historical emigration
patterns. Furthermore, utilzing these sources offered little hope of scientifically
determining which names were actually the most common.

Realizing this, we contacted the Social Security Administration and found
that every ten years it publishes the *Report of Distribution of Surnames in the Social
Security Number File*. The Report lists the surnames that appear in the Social

Security indexes with a frequency of more than 5,000. Though it is almost certainly the best available source for the actual distribution of surnames in the United States and is the one we chose to use, the Report does have some limitations that should be mentioned. First, although almost every American has a Social Security number, not everyone does. The Report does not account for the names of those who do not. Second, the Social Security files have never been purged. That means that the names in the Report account for every person issued a Social Security number between 1936 and 1984. In fact, although the Report lists the surnames of almost 350 million individuals, about 75 million more than that live in the United States today. Third, the Report provides only the first six letters of surnames, and these six letters are often the root of many names. In these cases, there is no way to know which among them are the most common.

All of this having been said, we remain confident that the *Report of Distribution of Surnames in the Social Security Number File* is the best source on surname distribution in the United States. We utilized the 1984 edition of the Report to compile this book. It is the most recent edition available. A 1994 edition was not produced, and plans for future editions are on hold, as the resources of the Social Security Administration are presently dedicated to completing a modernization program.

HOW SURNAMES DEVELOPED

———●———

THROUGHOUT THE WORLD, the vast majority of surnames developed in one of five ways: 1) from a father or grandfather's first name, 2) from an occupation, 3) from a place of residence, 4) from a nickname, or 5) from an ornamental word or phrase.

Surnames first appeared in China; the Emperor Fu Hsi obligated all Chinese to take them in 2852 B.C. In Europe, the Irish were the first to take surnames. The precursor of the surname, the byname (name formed by attaching a word meaning "son of" or "descendant of" to a first name), appeared in Ireland in the fourth century A.D. Surnames became common in England, France, Germany, Italy, and Spain between the eleventh and sixteenth centuries. Jews living in Germany were forced to take surnames in the late eighteenth and early nineteenth centuries. And many Turks took surnames for the first time in this century.

Most surnames in the United States are of English origin. Some families are actually from England and have long hereditary ties to a name, but others do not. Immigrants from eastern Europe and Russia, particularly Jews, either had their surnames Anglicized for them by an immigration officer or later Anglicized their names themselves. Most African Americans have the name of the family that had enslaved their ancestors.

Though it has occurred elsewhere in the world, this kind of nebulous, sometimes nefarious tie to the etymological root of one's surname is a particularly American phenomenon. It is also one reason that this book contains biographies of notable Americans with common surnames. Even if one is not a Taylor descended from actual English tailors, one can feel a kinship with other Americans who share this name.

Even today, surnames are by no means fixed. They are in constant flux, changed by politics, emigration patterns, language evolution, fashion, and even simple practicality. For example, in Ireland today there is a movement to take Gaelicized versions of names, while in Denmark the government is urging people to take new surnames to reduce confusion among the large numbers of people with the same last names.

In an effort to create a consistent methodology, the authors of this book list the earliest etymological root of each defined surname. Sometimes, however, the earliest etymological root may not be the actual word that inspired the name. It may be, instead, the precursor of the word that inspired the name.

HOW TO USE THIS BOOK

———————•———————

Each of the Encyclopedia's 5,000 alphabetically arranged entries contains the following elements:

Family Name(s): As appropriate, this includes the "root" name as well as derivatives and variants.

Ranking: That family name's rank in the Social Security Administration's frequency table.

Social Security Count: The number of individuals with this name found in the SSA database in 1980.

Origin: The national and etymological origin of the surname.

Famous Bearers: Prominent Americans who have shared this family name. We have included all such individuals profiled in the following standard biographical reference works: *Dictionary of American Biography*, *Webster's New Biographical Dictionary*, *Who Was Who in America*, *Notable American Women*, *Concise Dictionary of American Biography*, *National Cyclopedia of American Biography*, and *Webster's American Biographies*. In addition, to accommodate the interests of genealogists, we have included many early settlers and Revolutionary War officers who are not found in these sources. With a handful of exceptions (e.g. presidents of the United States), we have included only the deceased in these listings. To include well-known contemporary bearers, we believed, would require far too much space and add little to the research value of the book.

Genealogies: We have listed all genealogies published on the family found in the Library of Congress's card catalog of genealogical titles, which includes more than 100,000 items. Bear in mind that many of these genealogies were published by their authors. This accounts for the fact that many were never properly copyrighted and lack full bibliographic data; they often contain no data or incomplete data on place of publication and the like.

Encyclopedia of American Family Names

AARON

Ranking: 2367 **S.S. Count:** 19,166

Origin: English. Derived from the Hebrew first name Hairōn, meaning mountain of strength.

Famous **Aarons:** HENRY L. (HANK) AARON (1934–) of Alabama, in his 22-year baseball career, achieved several batting records, including most career home runs (755), extra-base hits (1,477), and times at bat (12,364). An Atlanta Brave, he hit his 715th home run April 8, 1974, in Atlanta, breaking a record that had been held by Babe Ruth since the 1930s. He was elected to the Baseball Hall of Fame in 1982.

Genealogies: *Aarons of Crates, Pennsylvania, from 1820–1980* was compiled by Catherine and Paul B. Shannon and published in Mayport, Pennsylvania, in 1984. *An Abbott Family: A Brief Account of the Antecedents and Descendants of Norman and Martha (Tidwell) Abbott* was compiled by Ruth Marcum Lind and published in Dinuba, California, in 1972.

ABBOTT

Ranking: 540 **S.S. Count:** 75,164

Origin: English. 1) derived from Middle English word "abbott" and the Old English word "abbod," both meaning priest. The name was given to those who worked with or near abbots or to those who had the characteristics of an abbot. 2) derived from the name Abb, a diminutive of the first name Abraham.

Famous **Abbotts:** JACOB ABBOTT (1803–1879) of Massachusetts, a clergyman and author, founded the Mount Vernon School for girls in Boston and was known for the writing of juvenile books, especially the 28-volume *Rollo* series that began in 1834. Jacob Abbott's son, LYMAN ABBOTT (1835–1922) of Massachusetts, followed in the clerical and literary footsteps as editor of *Illustrated Christian Weekly* and other endeavors. Brothers AUSTIN ABBOTT (1831–1896) and BENJAMIN VAUGHAN ABBOTT (1830–1890), both of Massachusetts, as law partners in New York City began publishing in 1855 a series of books called *Reports of Practice Cases Determined in the Courts of the State of New York,* and for 15 years afterward they published widely used legal texts, reports, and digests. CHARLES CONRAD ABBOTT (1843–1919) of New Jersey wrote more than 100 authoritative articles as a naturalist and archaeologist specializing in the Delaware Valley region. EMMA ABBOTT (1850–1891) of Illinois traveled to Europe to prepare as an opera singer, then formed her own company in New York City. She sang leading roles for the Abbott English Opera Company until her death. ROBERT SENGSTACKE ABBOTT (1868–1940) of Georgia founded in 1905 and edited until 1940 the *Chicago Defender,* a newspaper devoted to the interests of the black community. GRACE ABBOTT (1878–1939) of Nebraska was a social worker whose life's work was protecting children and immigrants. In 1921, she became head of the U.S. Children's Bureau, a post she held until 1934. She led an unsuccessful attempt at passing a constitutional amendment outlawing child labor.

Genealogies: *The Abbotts of West Virginia* was compiled by David A. Turner and published in Madison, West Virginia, in 1981.

ABEL

Ranking: 1733 **S.S. Count:** 25,833

Origin: Dano-Norwegian, English, French. Derived from the Hebrew first name Hevel, meaning breath or vanity.

Famous **Abels:** JOHN JACOB ABEL (1857–1938) of Ohio was a pharmacologist and physiological chemist who, through his research on endocrine glands, isolated the hormone adrenaline in 1897.

Genealogies: *The Abel Keller Genealogy* was compiled by Walter R. McCarley and Margaret Florence Poe McCarley and published in Greenwich, Ohio, in 1980.

ABELL

Ranking: 4785 **S.S. Count:** 9,359

Origin: English. Transformation of Abel.

Famous **Abells:** ARUNAH SHEPHERDSON ABELL (1806–1888) of Rhode Island was a newspaper publisher and editor who, with two partners, founded the *Philadelphia Public Ledger* (1836) and the *Baltimore Sun* (1837). He was editor of the *Sun* and became sole owner in 1868. His pioneering system of news gathering included the use of express riders, carrier pigeons, and the telegraph.

Genealogies: *The Abell Family of St. Mary's County, Maryland, and the American Revolution* was compiled by William Russell Abell and published in Des Moines, Iowa, in 1984. *Heirs of Eleanor Abell and Thomas Greenwell* was compiled by Tillie Whelan Onischak and published in Sacramento, California, in 1974.

ABERCROMBIE (S.S. Abbreviation: Abercr)

Ranking: 4949 **S.S. Count:** 9053

Origin: Scottish. Derived from the Brittonic word "aber," meaning confluence, and the Brittonic component "crom," meaning crooked. The name was given to those from Abercrombie, a place in Fife County, Scotland.

Famous **Abercrombies:** JOHN WILLIAM ABERCROMBIE (1866–1940) represented Alabama as a member of the House of Representatives for two terms and was president of the University of Alabama for nine years.

Genealogies: *A History of Cole, Shipman, and Allied Families* (including Abercrombie) was compiled by Pauline Callaway Sheriff and published in Hollis, Oklahoma, in 1982.

ABERNATHY (S.S. Abbreviation: Aberna)

Ranking: 1945 S.S. Count: 23,264

Origin: Scottish. Derived from the Brittonic word "aber," meaning confluence, and other components meaning at the narrow opening. The name was given to those from Abernathy, a place in Perthshire, Scotland.

Genealogies: None known.

ABNEY

Ranking: 3450 S.S. Count: 13,081

Origin: English. Uncertain etymology. The name was possibly given to those who lived at the Abney estate which is near a peak in Derbyshire, England.

Genealogies: *In Search of Kate* was compiled by Charlotte Ann Abney Metzger and published in St. Louis, Missouri, in 1978.

ABRAHAM, ABRAHAMS, ABRAHAMSSEN, ABRAHAMSSON (S.S. Abbreviation: Abraha)

Ranking: 1068 S.S. Count: 41,161

Origin: Abraham—Dutch, English, French, German, Hungarian, Jewish, et al.; Abrahams—Dutch, Jewish; Abrahamssen—Danish, Norwegian; Abrahamsson—Swedish. 1) derived from the Hebrew phrase "av hamon goyim," meaning father of a multitude of nations. 2) derived from the Hebrew first name Avraham, meaning high father.

Genealogies: None known.

ABRAMS, ABRAMSON

Ranking: 918 S.S. Count: 46,925

Origin: English. 1) derived from the first name Abraham, meaning high father. 2) transformation of Abraham.

Famous **Abramses:** ALBERT ABRAMS (1863–1924) of California was a physician who developed a system of universal diagnosis and treatment of disease called the Electronic Reactions of Abrams. He was a prolific writer whose published works included *Spondylotherapy: Spinal Concussion* (1913) and *New Concepts in Diagnosis and Treatment* (1916). However, much of his work was criticized as being more commercial than professional.

Genealogies: *The Abrams Family Genealogy, 1745–1979* was compiled by George Carter Abrams and published in Newberry, South Carolina, in 1979. *The Ancestors of Our Children (and Cousins, Too)* was compiled by Maynard Abrams and published in Delray Beach, Florida, in 1984.

ABREU

Ranking: 3906 S.S. Count: 11,543

Origin: Spanish, Portuguese. The name was given to those who came from Abreu, a place in Spain.

Genealogies: None known.

ACEVEDO (S.S. Abbreviation: Aceved)

Ranking: 863 S.S. Count: 49,834

Origin: Spanish. Derived from the Old Spanish "azevo," meaning holly. The name was given to those who worked with or lived near holly trees.

Genealogies: None known.

ACKER

Ranking: 3082 S.S. Count: 14,750

Origin: Dutch, English, German. Derived from the German word "acker" and the Old English word "acer," both meaning a tended field. The name was given to farmers.

Famous **Ackers:** CHARLES ERNEST ACKER (1868–1920) of Indiana was an inventor, manufacturer, and electrical engineer. He won the Elliott Cresson Gold Medal of the Franklin Institute in 1902 for using the electrolysis of molten salt to produce caustic soda and chlorine.

Genealogies: None known.

ACKERMAN, ACKERMANN (S.S. Abbreviation: Ackerm)

Ranking: 1129 S.S. Count: 38,954

Origin: English, German. Transformation of Acker.

Famous **Ackermans:** ERNEST R. ACKERMAN (1863–1931) of New Jersey was a member of the U.S. House of Representatives for 12 years.

Genealogies: *The Ackerman Family* was compiled by Barbara W. Tobey and published in Boiceville, New York, in 1980. *Ackerman Homesteads: A Saga of Ackerman Lives and Times* was compiled by Rosa Ackerman Livingston and published in Ho-Ho-Kus, New Jersey, in 1977.

ACKLEY

Ranking: 4660 S.S. Count: 9593

Origin: English. Derived from the Old English word "ac," meaning oak. The name was given to those from Acle, a place in Norfolk, England.

Genealogies: *The Eckler-Ackler-Ackley Family* was compiled by Ross A. Eckler and published in Morristown, New Jersey, in 1970. *Dewitt Clinton Ackley, Clarrissa Woodworth Ackley: Their Ancestors and Descendants* was compiled by Buel Clifford Ackley and published in Washington, D.C., in 1915.

ACOSTA

Ranking: 667 S.S. Count: 62,880

Origin: Spanish. Derived from the Portuguese words "da costa," meaning long coast. The name was given to those who lived near the sea.

Famous **Acostas:** BERTRAM BLANCHARD ACOSTA (1895–1954) of California was a barnstorming and racing pilot who took part in an aerial survey in 1927 that was used to set up the first transcontinental air-mail system. ROMANA

ACOSTA (BANUELOS) (1925–) was the 34th treasurer of the United States and is the founder of Romana's Mexican Food Products, Inc., in California.

Genealogies: None known.

ACUNA

Ranking: 4974 S.S. Count: 9013

Origin: Portuguese. Derived from the Portuguese word "acunar," meaning to coin or mint money. The name was given to those who came from Cunha or Acuna, the names of several places in Portugal.

Genealogies: None known.

ADAIR

Ranking: 1792 S.S. Count: 25,142

Origin: English: derived from the Old English first name Eadgār, which is derived from words meaning prosperity and spear. Irish, Scottish: 1) derived from the Gaelic words "ath" and "dare," meaning a shallow place in a river and oaks. The name was given to those who lived near such places. 2) transformation of the Scottish first name Edzear, which is equivalent to the English first name Edgar.

Famous **Adairs**: JAMES ADAIR (1709?–?1783), apparently born in Ireland but an emigrant to South Carolina, was a pioneer trader with American Indians and the author of *The History of American Indians*. JOHN ADAIR (1757–1840) of South Carolina was a soldier during the American Revolution, after which he migrated to Kentucky. There, he was elected to the state legislature a number of times, served as governor, and then represented Kentucky in the U.S. House of Representatives. WILLIAM P. ADAIR (1828?–1880) was assistant chief of the Cherokee nation. During the Civil War, he led a band of Native Americans in the Confederate Army and fought at the Battle of Pea Ridge. He later represented his tribe in government relations in Washington, D.C.

Genealogies: *The Descendants of James Adair* was compiled by Miriam Dabbs Adair and published in Clarksdale, Mississippi, in 1976.

ADAM

Ranking: 3276 S.S. Count: 13,858

Origin: English, Welsh. Derived from the Hebrew word "adama," meaning earth.

Genealogies: None known.

ADAMS

Ranking: 40 S.S. Count: 578,634

Origin: English, Welsh. Transformation of Adam.

Famous **Adamses**: One of the great dynasties in American history, the Adams family has produced many prominent figures. JOHN ADAMS (1735–1826) of Massachusetts and his son JOHN QUINCY ADAMS (1767–1848) both served as president of the United States. John Adams's second cousin SAMUEL ADAMS (1722–1803), of Massachusetts, was a member of the first and second Continental Congresses and a signer of the Declaration of Independence. CHARLES FRANCIS ADAMS (1835–1915), the grandson of John Quincy, was a prominent historian and social critic. ANDY ADAMS (1859–1935) of Indiana learned the cowboy's life in Texas, then settled in Colorado, where he wrote of the western life as he knew it. His novels, including *The Log of a Cowboy* (1903), dispelled the romanticized image of the cowboy. MAUDE ADAMS (1872–1953) of Utah was an actress who played the Peter Pan role more than 1500 times on stage. ANNETTE ABBOTT ADAMS (1877–1956) of California was the first woman to be a U.S. Attorney (1918), U.S. Assistant Attorney General (1920), and judge for the California Court of Appeals (1942). FRANKLIN PIERCE ADAMS (1881–1960) was a journalist and humorist who signed his columns "F.P.A." JAMES SEYBOLD ADAMS (1897–1976) of Indiana, whose business successes included the presidency of Standard Brands in New York, went at the request of Franklin Roosevelt in 1930 to help organize the Georgia Warm Springs Foundation. He is credited with launching the March of Dimes and is one of the founders of the American Cancer Society. ANSEL ADAMS (1902–1984) of California was the premier landscape photographer of his time and beyond. His images of the American southwest stand as artistic and technical achievements. JOEL E. ADAMS (1908–1977), born in Persia, was an orthopedic surgeon in California. As a consultant to the San Bernardino County School District, he made X-ray studies of the effects of strenuous sports on 132 Little League baseball players. His tests showed damage to 80 pitchers. He reported his findings to the American College of Surgeons and made recommendations that young athletes not be trained as professionals.

Genealogies: *Adams Family Records: A Genealogical and Biographical History of All Branches of the Adams Family* was compiled by J. T. Adams and published in Wise, Virginia, in 1929. *Adams, an American Dynasty* was compiled by Francis Russell and published in New York in 1976.

ADAMSON (S.S. Abbreviation: Adamso)

Ranking: 2112 S.S. Count: 21,732

Origin: English, Welsh. Transformation of Adam.

Famous **Adamsons**: WILLIAM CHARLES ADAMSON (1854–1929) represented a Georgia district in the U.S. House of Representatives, where he was the author of the Adamson Act (1916), which made eight hours the normal work day for railroad workers.

Genealogies: *The Adamsons as We See Them* was compiled by Jack Stambaugh and published in Dallas, Texas, in 1982.

ADCOCK

Ranking: 2586 S.S. Count: 17,604

Origin: English. Derived from the name Ad, a diminutive of Adam.

Genealogies: *Adcock Family and Allied Families* was compiled by Mrs. Jimmie Adcock and published in Canadian, Texas, in 1979. *Adcock Kinfolks* was compiled by Robert McClane Adcock and published in St. Petersburg, Florida, in 1981.

ADDISON (S.S. Abbreviation: Addiso)

Ranking: 2030 S.S. Count: 22,488

Origin: English, Scottish, Welsh. Derived from the name Addie, a diminutive of the first names Adam or Adda, the latter meaning noble cheer.

Famous Addisons: DANIEL DULANY ADDISON (1863–1936) of West Virginia was an Episcopal clergyman who spent most of his professional life in Massachusetts and Liberia. In 1904, the Liberian government knighted him for his work there. His first ancestor in the United States, Col. JOHN ADDISON, was a cousin of Joseph Addison, the English essayist and poet.

Genealogies: *The Family of John Addison and Elizabeth Stones* was compiled by Herbert J. Addison and published in Glen Ridge, New Jersey, in 1978.

ADKINS, ADKINSON

Ranking: 393 S.S. Count: 98,712

Origin: English. Derived from the name Ade, a diminutive of the first name Adam.

Famous Adkinsons: HOMER BURTON ADKINS (1892–1949) was awarded the Medal of Merit by President Harry Truman for his work as a chemist performing research in chemical warfare and other military matters.

Genealogies: *William H. Adkins Family of American Falls, Idaho, a Genealogy of Ancestors and Descendants of William Harmon Adkins and Linnie Lee Pennington of Elliott, Colorado* was compiled by Fred E. Sawyer and published in American Falls, Idaho, in 1977.

ADLER

Ranking: 1865 S.S. Count: 24,268

Origin: German. 1) derived from the German word "adler," meaning eagle. 2) derived from the Germanic component "adal," meaning noble.

Famous Adlers: DANKMAR ADLER (1844–1900), a native of Germany, was an architect in Chicago and Detroit who designed the Chicago Stock Exchange. FELIX ADLER (1851–1933), a native of Germany, founded and lectured at the New York Society for Ethical Culture and was an author of books, including *Creed and Deed* (1877) and *An Ethical Philosophy of Life* (1918). SARA ADLER (1858–1953), born in Russia, played leading roles in about 300 plays during her 30-year acting career in New York. CYRUS ADLER (1863–1940) of Arkansas served as president of Dropsie College (1908–1924) and as president of the Jewish Theological Seminary of America (1924–1940). He founded the American Jewish Committee in 1906 and worked as editor of the *Jewish Encyclopedia* and the *American Jewish Year Book.* ELMER ADLER (1884–1962) of New York was a typography consultant to the *New York Times* and *The New Yorker* in the 1920s. He, along with Bennett Cerf and Donald Klopfer, founded the publishing firm Random House in 1927. POLLY ADLER (1900?–1962) managed a prominent New York bordello and was a central figure in investigations of corruption in New York City. MORTIMER JEROME ADLER (1902–) of New York is co-originator of the Great Books Program, a seminar series based on Western literature and philosophy. He has published many philosophical books, the most popular of which are *How to Read a Book* and *How to Think About War and Peace.*

Genealogies: None known.

AGEE

Ranking: 3172 S.S. Count: 14,321

Origin: English, French. Derived from the first name Agnes, meaning pure.

Famous Agees: JAMES AGEE (1909–1955) of Tennessee was a versatile writer, with credits ranging from the film script *African Queen* (1951), to the nonfiction book *Let Us Now Praise Famous Men* (1941) to the Pulitzer Prize–winning novel *A Death in the Family* (1957).

Genealogies: *The Agee Register: A Genealogical Record of the Descendants of Mathieu Agee, a Huguenot Refugee to Virginia* was compiled by Louis N. Agee and published in Baltimore, Maryland, in 1982. *Our Missouri Ancestors in the Counties of Callaway, Osage, Polk, Dallas, Greene: Age-Agee: The Agee Family* was compiled by Barbara Agee and published in Park City, Kansas, in 1982.

AGNEW

Ranking: 3168 S.S. Count: 14,331

Origin: English. 1) derived from the Old French word "agneau," meaning lamb. 2) derived from the Gaelic word "O Gnimh," meaning son of Griomh, which means action.

Famous Agnews: ELIZA AGNEW (1807–1883) of New York was a missionary who taught in a female boarding school in Ceylon for 43 years without a furlough, except for a brief sojourn to southern India. Of the 1000 individuals in three generations she taught, more than 600 adopted the Christian faith. SPIRO THEODORE AGNEW (1918–) of Maryland was vice president of the United States (1969–1973) under President Richard Nixon. As vice president, he made many controversial remarks, such as saying that opponents of the war in Vietnam were encouraged by "an effete corps of impudent snobs." He resigned the vice presidency, then pleaded *nolo contendere* to a charge of tax evasion. He had previously served as governor of Maryland. His father was a Greek immigrant whose surname was originally Anagnostopoulos.

Genealogies: None known.

AGOSTO
Ranking: 3895 **S.S. Count:** 11,581
Origin: Italian. Derived from the Latin word "augere," meaning to grow.
Genealogies: None known.

AGUILAR (S.S. Abbreviation: Aguila)
Ranking: 593 **S.S. Count:** 70,541
Origin: Spanish. Derived from the Spanish word "aguila," meaning eagle. The name was given to those who came from Aguilas, meaning the place of eagles, in southern Spain.
Genealogies: None known.

AGUILERA (S.S. Abbreviation: Aguile)
Ranking: 3563 **S.S. Count:** 12,649
Origin: Spanish. Transformation of Aguilar.
Genealogies: None known.

AGUIRRE (S.S. Abbreviation: Aguirr)
Ranking: 1184 **S.S. Count:** 37,022
Origin: Spanish. Derived from the Basque word "ager," meaning easily visible. The name was given to those who lived in such places.
Genealogies: None known.

AHERN
Ranking: 3819 **S.S. Count:** 11,809
Origin: Irish. 1) derived from the Gaelic words "each" and "tigherna," meaning horse and master. 2) derived from the name Eachthighearna.
Famous **Aherns:** JAMES AHERN (1839–1901) changed his name to JAMES A. HERNE to perform on the stage. He became one of the most famous touring actors of the nineteenth century and also wrote many plays characterized by a blend of realism and sentimentality.
Genealogies: None known.

AHRENS, AHRENSDORF
Ranking: 2973 **S.S. Count:** 15,291
Origin: Dutch, Swedish. Dutch: cognate to Adler. Swedish: derived from the Swedish word "arende," meaning tenancy.
Genealogies: None known.

AIELLO
Ranking: 3743 **S.S. Count:** 12,093
Origin: Italian. Derived from the Latin word "ager,"

meaning field. The name was given to those from Aiello, the name of several places in Italy.
Genealogies: None known.

AIKEN
Ranking: 2530 **S.S. Count:** 17,924
Origin: English, Scottish. 1) transformation of Adkin. 2) derived from the Saxon word "acen," meaning oaken.
Famous **Aikens:** WILLIAM AIKEN (1806–1887) was governor of South Carolina (1844–1846). Aiken County was named for him. GEORGE L. AIKEN (1830–1876) of Massachusetts was an actor and playwright, best known for his stage adaptation of *Uncle Tom's Cabin*. The play ran first at the Troy Museum in Troy, New York, then at Purdy's Theater in New York City. CONRAD POTTER AIKEN (1889–1973) of Georgia was a poet, critic, and writer. His works include a number of volumes of verse and several novels, including *King Coffin* (1935). HOWARD HATHAWAY AIKEN (1900–1973) of New Jersey was a mathematician who was among the developers of early electronic digital computer technology.
Genealogies: None known.

AINSWORTH (S.S. Abbreviation: Ainswo)
Ranking: 3429 **S.S. Count:** 13,164
Origin: English. Derived from the Old English component "-ægen" and the Old English word "wor," meaning own and enclosure. The name was given to those who came from Ainsworth, a place in Lancashire, England.
Famous **Ainsworths:** JAMES EDWARD AINSWORTH (1830–1909) of Connecticut was a noted civil engineer and authority on building railroads. JOHN CHURCHILL AINSWORTH (1870–1943) was president of Ainsworth National Bank of Portland, Oregon.
Genealogies: *The Genealogy of the Ainsworth Families in America* was compiled by Francis J. Parker and published in Boston, Massachusetts, in 1894. *Our Ainsworth Heritage* was compiled by Lucille Dickinson Ainsworth and published in Winnsboro, Louisiana, in 1988.

AKERS
Ranking: 1317 **S.S. Count:** 33,795
Origin: English. Derived from the English word "acre," which is still today a measurement of land. The name was given to farmers or those who tended one acre.
Famous **Akerses:** BENJAMIN PAUL AKERS (1825–1861) of Maine was a sculptor whose work, including busts of national political figures, illustrates the neoclassicist style of his time. His wife for about a year (they married a year before he died) was ELIZABETH CHASE AKERS (1832–1911), also of Maine, who was an author and poet. She was among the favorite household poets of the day because her poetry expressed the emotions of ordinary people.
Genealogies: None known.

AKIN

Ranking: 3721 **S.S. Count:** 12,140

Origin: English, Scottish. 1) the name was given to those who were from the area near Akin, a strait in Scotland named for King Hakon of Norway. 2) transformation of Atkins.

Famous **Akins:** THOMAS RUSSELL AKIN (1867–1945) of Massachusetts, a descendant of John Akin, who came to the Massachusetts Bay Colony in 1670, established the Laclede Steel Company in St. Louis, Missouri. THERON AKIN (1855–1933) of New York was a member of the U.S. House of Representatives.

Genealogies: *Ancestors and Descendants of Justus H. Akin of Rensselaer County, New York* was compiled by Daphne M. Brownell and published in Florida in 1971.

AKINS

Ranking: 1916 **S.S. Count:** 23,586

Origin: English, Scottish. Transformation of Akin.

Famous **Akinses:** ZOE AKINS (1886–1958) of Missouri was the author of poetry, plays, and film scripts. Among her works was the 1935 play *The Old Maid,* which won a Pulitzer Prize.

Genealogies: None known.

ALANIZ

Ranking: 4088 **S.S. Count:** 11,059

Origin: Spanish. Transformation of Alanis.

Genealogies: None known.

ALBANEL, ALBANELLI (S.S. Abbreviation: Albane)

Ranking: 4714 **S.S. Count:** 9,494

Origin: Italian. Derived from the Latin word "alba," meaning dawn. The name was given to those from Alba, the name of several places in Italy and Spain.

Genealogies: None known.

ALBERS, ALBERSWERTH

Ranking: 3,126 **S.S. Count:** 14,542

Origin: Dutch, German. Derived from the first name Albert, which comprises the Germanic words "adal" and "berht," meaning noble and famous or bright.

Famous **Alberses:** JOSEF ALBERS (1888–1976), originally from Germany, was an abstract painter who won many awards. His work continues to be shown internationally.

Genealogies: None known.

ALBERT, ALBERTS, ALBERTSON

Ranking: 504 **S.S. Count:** 79,768

Origin: English. Derived from the Germanic components "adal" and "berht," meaning noble and famous or bright.

Famous **Alberts:** CARL BERT ALBERT (1908–) of Oklahoma served in the U.S. House of Representatives for a number of years, beginning in 1946, and was chosen Speaker of the House in 1971.

Genealogies: *Links with the Past: A Genealogical and Historical Account of the Albert and Related Families* was compiled by Ethel Evans Albert and published in Kingsport, Tennessee, in 1972.

ALBRECHT, ALBRECT (S.S. Abbreviation: Albrec)

Ranking: 1828 **S.S. Count:** 24,705

Origin: German. 1) transformations of Albert. 2) derived from the first name Albrecht.

Genealogies: None known.

ALBRIGHT, ALBRIGHTON (S.S. Abbreviation: Albrig)

Ranking: 1239 **S.S. Count:** 35,720

Origin: English. Derived from the name Aldbeorht and the Old English word "tūn," meaning settlement. The names were given to those from Albright, a place in Shropshire, England.

Famous **Albrights:** JACOB ALBRIGHT (1759–1808) of Pennsylvania was a minister who helped organize the Evangelical Association, a movement that broke away from traditional Methodists. WILLIAM FOXWELL ALBRIGHT (1891–1971), born in Chile of American parents, was a noted archaeologist and author. His books include *Archaeology of Palestine and the Bible* (1932), *From Stone Age to Christianity* (1940), and *The Bible and the Ancient Near East* (1961). IVAN LE LORRAINE ALBRIGHT (1897–1983) of Illinois was an artist whose paintings, including *The Door and the Window,* illustrated such concepts as obsession, corruption, and decay.

Genealogies: *The Albrights* was compiled by Shannon D. Albright and published in Richmond, Virginia, in 1981. *Ancestry of Albright and Holt Families of Clay County, Missouri* was compiled by Claribel Albright McClain and published in St. Joseph, Missouri, in 1984.

ALBRITTAIN, ALBRITTON (S.S. Abbreviation: Albrit)

Ranking: 4780 **S.S. Count:** 9,367

Origin: English. 1) transformations of Albright combined with the Old English word "tūn," meaning settlement.

Genealogies: None known.

ALCANTARA, ALCANTAR (S.S. Abbreviation: Alcant)

Ranking: 4967 **S.S. Count:** 9019

Origin: Portuguese, Spanish. Derived from the Arabic words "al qantara," meaning the arch or bridge. The name was given to those who came from Alcantara, the name of several places in Spain.

Genealogies: None known.

ALCORN

Ranking: 4153 S.S. Count: 10,892

Origin: English. Uncertain etymology. The name was given to those who came from Alchorne, a manor in the parish of Rotherfield in Sussex County, England.

Famous **Alcorns:** JAMES LUSK ALCORN (1816–1894), born in Illinois, was a deputy sheriff and state legislator in Kentucky, then practiced law in Mississippi, where he went on to become the legislator most responsible for establishing the levee system along the Mississippi River. He served as a Confederate officer in the Civil War. He was elected governor of Mississippi in 1869 and later served in the U.S. Senate.

Genealogies: None known.

ALDERMAN (S.S. Abbreviation: Alderm)

Ranking: 3295 S.S. Count: 13,769

Origin: English. Derived from the Old English word "ealdorman," meaning elder. The name was given to those who had judicial or military rank.

Famous **Aldermans:** EDWIN ANDERSON ALDERMAN (1861–1931) was president of three universities: the University of North Carolina (1896–1900), Tulane University (1900–1904), and the University of Virginia (1904–1931).

Genealogies: *Your Family and Mine* was compiled by Mattie Ellen Brown Trube and published in Houston, Texas, in 1973.

ALDERSMITH (S.S. Abbreviation: Alders)

Ranking: 4764 S.S. Count: 9396

Origin: English. Derived from the Old English words "ealdorman" and "smi," meaning elder and smith. The name was given to the oldest smith, someone who worked in metals, of a family.

Genealogies: None known.

ALDRICH (S.S. Abbreviation: Aldric)

Ranking: 1805 S.S. Count: 24,942

Origin: English. 1) derived from the first name Alderich, which is derived from the Old English word "eald," meaning old. 2) same derivation as in 1. The name was given to those who came from Aldridge, a place in Staffordshire, England.

Famous **Aldriches:** THOMAS BAILEY ALDRICH (1836–1907) of New Hampshire was a poet, writer, and editor. His best-known prose work was the book *The Story of a Bad Boy* (1870), and he was editor of the *Atlantic Monthly* from 1881 to 1890. NELSON WILMARTH ALDRICH (1841–1915) was a U.S. senator from Rhode Island for 30 years. He was the father-in-law of John D. Rockefeller Jr. WILLIAM FARRING-TON ALDRICH (1825–1925) of New York founded the town of Aldrich, Alabama, and was a three-term member of the U.S. House of Representatives. BESS GENEVRA ALDRICH (1881–1954) of Iowa wrote short stories and novels, including *The Rim of the Prairie* (1925) and *Song of Years* (1939).

Genealogies: The *George Aldrich Genealogy, 1605–1971* was compiled by Alvin James Aldrich and published in Decorah, Iowa, in 1972.

ALDRIDGE (S.S. Abbreviation: Aldrid)

Ranking: 1444 S.S. Count: 30,907

Origin: English. Meaning village among alder trees, the name was given to those who came from Aldridge in Staffordshire, England.

Famous **Aldridges:** IRA FREDERICK ALDRIDGE (1805–1867) of New York was an actor of African and European descent. He studied acting in England, where he played a range of Shakespearean characters at the Royalty Theater. The King of Prussia wrote him a personal letter when he conferred upon Aldridge a first-class medal of art and science.

Genealogies: *Aldridge Family Genealogy and History* was compiled by Franklin Rudolph Aldridge and published in Nashville, Tennessee, in 1960.

ALEJANDRO (S.S. Abbreviation: Alejan)

Ranking: 4892 S.S. Count: 9137

Origin: Spanish. Cognate to Alexander.

Genealogies: None known.

ALEMAN

Ranking: 3546 S.S. Count: 12,728

Origin: English, Spanish. Derived from the Spanish word "aleman," meaning German. The name was given to those who came from Germany.

Genealogies: None known.

ALEXANDER (S.S. Abbreviation: Alexan)

Ranking: 104 S.S. Count: 268,483

Origin: English, Scottish. Derived from the Greek words "alexein" and "andros," meaning to help or defend and man.

Famous **Alexanders:** ABRAHAM ALEXANDER (1717–1786), a Scotch–Irish immigrant, was one of the founding commissioners of Charlotte, North Carolina. He chaired the May 31, 1775, public meeting at which resolutions were adopted forming a Mecklenberg County government, the first step in any of the colonies toward establishing a government independent of the British Crown. BARTON STONE ALEXANDER (1819–1878) of Kentucky was a soldier and construction engineer instrumental in design and construction of the fort system around Washington, D.C. He personally designed Fort McPherson, next to Arlington

National Cemetery. EDWARD PORTER ALEXANDER (1835–1910) of Georgia, after an exemplary Confederate military career as an artillerist, wrote *Memoirs of a Confederate Soldier* (1907), which was recognized as a significant contribution to the history of the Civil War. WILLIAM DEWITT ALEXANDER (1833–1913) of Hawaii founded the Hawaiian Historical Society and wrote a grammar of the Hawaiian language. His *Brief History of the Hawaiian People* (1891) was a lasting reference tool. DEALVA STANWOOD ALEXANDER (1845–1925) of Maine, while representing a New York congressional district in the U.S. House of Representatives, began writing *Political History of the State of New York,* which became a highly regarded three-volume work (first two published in 1906, the third in 1909). JOHN WHITE ALEXANDER (1856–1915) of Pennsylvania was staff illustrator for *Harper's* and painted portraits of a number of prominent individuals, including President Grover Cleveland, Maude Adams, and Mark Twain (Samuel Clemens). GROVER CLEVELAND ALEXANDER (1887–1957) of Nebraska was considered one of the greatest right-handed baseball pitchers of his day. He pitched in the National League for Philadelphia, Chicago, and St. Louis and was elected to the Baseball Hall of Fame in 1938. FRANZ GABRIEL ALEXANDER (1891–1964), a Hungarian–Austrian immigrant, founded and directed the Chicago Institute for Psychoanalysis and wrote books, including *Fundamentals of Psychoanalysis* (1948) and *The Western Mind in Transition* (1960). HATTIE ELIZABETH ALEXANDER (1901–1968) of Maryland was a pediatrician and an early practitioner of microbiological genetics in the 1940s.

Genealogies: *The Alexander Family: Early Settlers of Giles County, Tennessee* was compiled by Naomah Elizabeth Alexander Lance and published in 1977. *The Alexanders and Descendants* was compiled by William A. York and published in Pittsburg, Kansas, in 1981.

ALFARO

Ranking: 3759 S.S. Count: 12,047
Origin: Spanish. Derived from the Arabic words "al faras," meaning horseman or cavalry. The name was given to those who came from Alfaro, a place in Logrono, Spain.
Genealogies: None known.

ALFONSO (S.S. Abbreviation: Alfons)

Ranking: 4158 S.S. Count: 10,879
Origin: Spanish. Derived from the first name Adafuns, which is derived from the Germanic words "adal" and "funs," meaning noble and ready.
Genealogies: None known.

ALFORD

Ranking: 1028 S.S. Count: 42,649
Origin: English. Derived from the Old English words
"eald" and "ford," meaning old and a shallow place in a river. The name was given to those who came from Alford, the name of several places in England.*

Famous **Alfords:** LEON PRATT ALFORD (1877–1942) of Connecticut was an editor who specialized in the subject of industrial management. He was editor of three publications: *Industrial Management, Management Engineering,* and *Manufacturing Industries.*

Genealogies: *The Alford-Drake Family of Middle Tennessee* was compiled by Naomi Hailey and published in Nashville, Tennessee, in 1982. *The Alford-Kennedy Family History* was compiled by Eileen Alford and published in San Antonio, Texas, in 1971.

ALI

Ranking: 3010 S.S. Count: 15,092
Origin: Arab. Derived from the first name Ali, meaning exalted.
Famous **Alis:** Heavyweight boxing champion MUHAMMAD ALI (1942–) of Kentucky was born CASSIUS MARCELLUS CLAY.
Genealogies: None known.

ALICEA

Ranking: 1894 S.S. Count: 23,879
Origin: Spanish. Derived from the first name Alicea, meaning noble and kind.
Genealogies: None known.

ALLAN

Ranking: 3104 S.S. Count: 14,643
Origin: English. Transformation of Allen.
Famous **Allans:** JOHN ALLAN (1746–1805) of Scotland, later of Nova Scotia, became sympathetic to the cause of the Massachusetts patriots and successfully commanded a northern outpost during the American Revolution. He is credited with keeping the U.S. northeast boundary at St. Croix, instead of at Kennebec. FRANK NATHANIEL ALLAN (1899–1977), born in Canada, worked as a physician in Canada, Minnesota, and Massachusetts but gave up his clinical duties to become full-time deputy editor of *The New England Journal of Medicine.*

Genealogies: *Military Operations in Eastern Maine and Nova Scotia During the Revolution* was a memoir of Col. John Allan and includes a geneaology of his family compiled by Frederick Kidder. It was published in 1867 and reprinted in 1971 in New York, New York.

ALLARD

Ranking: 3202 S.S. Count: 14,156
Origin: English, French. Derived from the first name Alard, meaning noble.
Genealogies: None known.

ALLEN

Ranking: 28 S.S. Count: 653,943

Origin: Danish, English, German, Scottish, Swedish. *Danish, German, Swedish: derived from the Germanic word "adal," meaning noble. English, Scottish: derived from the Gaelic word "ailin," meaning little rock.*

Famous **Allens:** ETHAN ALLEN (1738–1789) and IRA ALLEN (1751–1814) were brothers who worked to achieve independent statehood for Vermont. They and their other brothers had acquired 77,000 acres in what is now Vermont from New Hampshire. Because the British Crown had mistakenly given both New Hampshire and New York patents to the land, New York sought rights to the area. Ethan raised the Green Mountain Boys regiment to protect their property from New York. Vermont was granted statehood in 1791. ZACHARIAH ALLEN (1795–1882) of Rhode Island invented the first hot-air heating system for homes in 1821. HORATIO ALLEN (1802–1890) of New York was a civil engineer who designed the first American-built railroad locomotive. ELISHA HUNT ALLEN (1804–1884) served as U.S. consul to Hawaii, minister of finance under the king of Hawaii, and then Hawaiian minister to the United States. EDWARD TYSON ALLEN (1875–1942) was a pioneer forest ranger who helped set boundaries of, then helped administer, the national forests of the Pacific Northwest. He wrote the first contract for the sale of standing timber in a national forest, and that contract became a model for future contracts. FLORENCE ELLINWOOD ALLEN (1884–1966) of Utah, as a judge for the Ohio Supreme Court, was the first woman to sit on a court of last resort, and then, as a judge for the U.S. Circuit Court of Appeals, was the first woman to be chief judge of a federal appeals court. FORREST CLARE ALLEN (1885–1974), as basketball coach at the University of Kansas (1919–1956), won 770 games and lost 223. He succeeded in getting basketball added to the Olympic games in 1936 and coached a winning U.S. Olympic team in 1952. FREDERICK LEWIS ALLEN (1890–1954) of Massachusetts was editor of *Harper's* magazine (1941–1953) and author of four books. GRACIE ALLEN (1905–1964) of California made her debut as an entertainer at age 3. She and George Burns were later a team in comedy and marriage. Her career spanned stage, radio, and television, and she and Burns were pioneers in the field of domestic comedy.

Genealogies: *The Allen Family: Descendants of John and Amy Cox Allen with Allied Lines* was compiled by Lester M. Allen and published in Greensboro, North Carolina, in 1987. *Allen and Allied Families* was compiled by Dorris Allen O'Neal Dunn and published in Greenville, South Carolina, in 1978.

ALLEY

Ranking: 2395 S.S. Count: 18,945

Origin: English. *Derived from the first name Alli, meaning one who lived at the narrow pass.*

Genealogies: *Alley Highlights: Yesterday for Tomorrow* was compiled by Virginia Miller Carey and Garnet Alley Hampton in Prichard, West Virginia, and Comanche, Oklahoma, in 1983.

ALLISON (S.S. Abbreviation: Alliso)

Ranking: 571 S.S. Count: 72,327

Origin: English, Scottish. *Derived from the first name Alice, which is derived from the Germanic words "adal" and "haid," meaning noble and kind.*

Famous **Allisons:** WILLIAM BOYD ALLISON (1829–1908), who practiced law in Iowa before being elected to Congress, became one of the most powerful U.S. senators in the early 1900s. He was best known for his work in securing a compromise between freesilver supporters and traditional business interests.

Genealogies: *Early Osbornes and Alleys* was compiled by Rita Kennedy Sutton and published in New York, New York, in 1978. *Allison, Dewees, Johnson, Scruggs and Other Related Families* was compiled by Judith Allison Walters and published in Bothell, Washington, in 1976.

ALLMAN

Ranking: 3744 S.S. Count: 12,091

Origin: English, French, Jewish. *English, French: derived from the Anglo-Norman-French word "aleman," meaning German. Jewish: 1) derived from the Hebrew word "alman," meaning widower. 2) the name was given to those who came from Germany, the Baltic states, and Holland.*

Genealogies: *Allman-Allmon: Testament to the Future* was compiled by Thelma E. Kurtz and published in Kansas City, Missouri, in 1973.

ALLRED

Ranking: 2247 S.S. Count: 20,360

Origin: English. *1) derived from the Middle English first name Aldred, which is derived from two Old English names that are derived from the words "ald" or "ealh" and "red," meaning old or temple and counsel. 2) derived from the Middle English word "aldrett," meaning alder grove. The name was given to those who lived near such a place.*

Famous **Allreds:** JAMES V. ALLRED (1899–1959) was governor of Texas (1935–1939), then a U.S. district judge.

Genealogies: None known.

ALMEIDA (S.S. Abbreviation: Almeid)

Ranking: 3392 S.S. Count: 13,343

Origin: Portuguese. *Derived from the Arabic words "al ma'ida," meaning plateau. The name was given to those who came from Almeida, the name of several places in Spain.*

Genealogies: None known.

ALMOND

Ranking: 4789 S.S. Count: 9351

Origin: English. 1) derived from the Old English first name Æelmund, which is derived from the words "æel" and "mund," meaning noble and protection. 2) transformation of Alman.

Famous **Almonds**: JAMES LINDSAY ALMOND JR. (1898–1986) served in the U.S. House of Representatives, as governor of Virginia,, and as senior judge for the U.S. Court of Appeals.

Genealogies: None known.

ALONSO

Ranking: 3109 S.S. Count: 14,628

Origin: Spanish. 1) derived from the Spanish first name Alfonso, meaning noble and ready. 2) derived from the Spanish word "alonso," meaning a type of wheat. The name was given to those who lived in areas where wheat was grown.

Genealogies: None known.

ALONZO

Ranking: 3399 S.S. Count: 13,318

Origin: Spanish. Transformation of Alonso.

Genealogies: None known.

ALSTON, ALLSTON

Ranking: 1114 S.S. Count: 39,746

Origin: English. 1) derived from the Old English first name Alstan. 2) same derivation as 1. The name was given to those who came from Alston, the name of several places in England.

Famous **Alstons**: JOSEPH ALSTON (1779?-1816) was governor of South Carolina (1812–1814) and husband of Theodosia Burr, Aaron Burr's daughter. WASHINGTON ALLSTON (1779–1843) was a prominent romantic painter and writer. ROBERT FRANCIS ALLSTON (1801–1864) was an agriculturalist, educator, and politician in South Carolina. He served as governor of the state 1856–1858.

Genealogies: *The Alstons and Allstons of North Carolina and South Carolina* was compiled by Joseph Asbury Groves and published in 1901. It was republished in Easley, South Carolina, in 1976.

ALTMAN

Ranking: 1826 S.S. Count: 24,719

Origin: German. 1) derived from the Middle High German word "alt," meaning old, and other components meaning servant. 2) derived from the first name Aldman, meaning old man.

Famous **Altmans**: BENJAMIN ALTMAN (1840–1913) was a dry goods merchant and department store owner in New York City who donated his $20 million art collection to the Metropolitan Museum of Art.

Genealogies: None known.

ALVARADO (S.S. Abbreviation: Alvara)

Ranking: 630 S.S. Count: 65,614

Origin: Spanish. 1) derived from the Arabic words "al barrada," meaning a wall of small stones. The name was given to those who lived near such a structure. 2) derived from the Spanish word "albar," meaning white hilly area. The name was given to those who came from such places.

Famous **Alvarados**: JUAN BAUTISTA ALVARADO (1809–1882) was governor of Mexican California (1836–1841), which then included Los Angeles.

Genealogies: None known.

ALVARENGA, ALVARES, ALVAREZ (S.S. Abbreviation: Alvare)

Ranking: 278 S.S. Count: 129,573

Origin: Spanish. Derived from the first name Alvaro, meaning prudent.

Famous **Alvarezes**: LUIS W. ALVAREZ (1911–1988) of California was a physicist who won the Nobel Prize in 1968 for his work in elementary particle research. He worked on the development of radar and the atom bomb and was a proponent of the theory that asteroid(s) or comet(s) struck Earth 65 million years ago, causing the extinction of dinosaurs.

Genealogies: None known.

ALVES

Ranking: 3684 S.S. Count: 12,249

Origin: Portuguese. Derived from the Spanish first name Alvaro, meaning prudent.

Genealogies: None known.

AMADOR

Ranking: 3668 S.S. Count: 12,307

Origin: Spanish. Derived from the Spanish word "amor," meaning love. The name was given to lovers and sweethearts.

Genealogies: None known.

AMARAL

Ranking: 4487 S.S. Count: 9988

Origin: Portuguese. Derived from the Portuguese word "amaral," which is a kind of black grape. The name was given to those who came from Amaral, the name of several places in Portugal.

Genealogies: None known.

AMATO

Ranking: 2790 S.S. Count: 16,322

Origin: Italian. Derived from the Italian word "am∂re," meaning to love.

Genealogies: None known.

AMBROSE (S.S. Abbreviation: Ambros)

Ranking: 1349 S.S. Count: 32,841

Origin: English. Derived from the Greek word "ambrosios," meaning immortal.

Famous **Ambroses:** JOHN WOLFE AMBROSE (1838–1899), originally from Ireland, was responsible for developing and building much of New York City's infrastructure, including the Second Avenue elevated train and the Sixth Avenue line (75th to 155th streets). To facilitate passage for large ships, he advocated the construction of a straight channel from New York Harbor to the open sea. This channel, which bears his name, opened in 1914.

Genealogies: *The Blake-Ambrose Family History* was compiled by Irma Ruth M. Anderson and published in Santa Cruz, California, in 1966.

AMES

Ranking: 1407 S.S. Count: 31,599

Origin: English. 1) derived from the French word "amie," meaning friend. 2) derived from the first name Emma. 3) the name was given to those who lived near elm trees. 4) transformation of Amos.

Famous **Ameses:** FISHER AMES (1758–1808) was a Federalist Party leader and theoretician and a vigorous supporter of the adoption of the U.S. Constitution. EDWARD RAYMOND AMES (1806–1879) of Ohio founded a seminary in Illinois that later became McKendree College. SAMUEL AMES (1806–1865) was chief justice of the Supreme Court of Rhode Island. JAMES BARR AMES (1846–1910) of Massachusetts, as an educator at Harvard University and a legal writer, advanced the case-study method of law study offered by his teacher C. C. Langdell. JOSEPH SWEETMAN AMES (1864–1943) of Vermont was a physicist who taught at, then became president of, Johns Hopkins University. OAKES AMES (1804–1873) of Massachusetts was a member of the U.S. House of Representatives, which censured him in 1873 after a committee investigation into financial matters. His grandsons WINTHROP AMES (1871–1937) and OAKES AMES (1874–1950), both of Massachusetts, did not choose political careers. Winthrop Ames was a theater manager in Boston and New York, and he wrote and produced the first play (*Snow White*) in New York City directed especially for children. Oakes Ames was a noted botanist and served as director of the Harvard University botanical garden. OLIVER AMES (1831–1895) was a governor of Massachusetts.

Genealogies: *Ames Ancestry: Europe to Maine* was compiled by Agnes H. Ames and published in Brewer, Maine, in 1979. *Descendants of Benjamin and Dorcas Ames of Connecticut, 1786–1979: A Genealogy* was compiled by Kathy L. DeLong and published in Reseda, California, in 1980.

AMMONS

Ranking: 3724 S.S. Count: 12,132

Origin: English. Derived from the first name Ammons, meaning terror or guardian.

Famous **Ammonses:** ELIAS MILTON AMMONS (1860–1925) of North Carolina was governor of Colorado (1912–1915).

Genealogies: None known.

AMOS

Ranking: 1426 S.S. Count: 31,223

Origin: English. 1) Derived from Amos, the Biblical prophet. 2) Derived from the first name Ambrose, meaning immortal.

Famous **Amoses:** ISAIAH H. AMOS (1844–1915) of Oregon was one of the founders of the Prohibition Party and a nationally known temperance worker.

Genealogies: *Ancestry from A to Z: Amos Zoll and Related Families* was compiled by Eugene P. Amos and published in Shawnee, Kansas, in 1980. *Some Early Families of the Altamaha Delta* was compiled by Bessie Lewis and Minnie Tremere Martin and was published in McHenry, Illinois, sometime in the 1960s.

AMUNDSEN, AMUNDSON (S.S. Abbreviation: Amunds)

Ranking: 3808 S.S. Count: 11,850

Origin: Icelandic, Norwegian. Derived from the first name Amund, meaning forever and guardian.

Genealogies: None known.

ANAYA

Ranking: 3411 S.S. Count: 13,262

Origin: French, Spanish. Derived from the Basque word "anai," meaning brother.

Genealogies: None known.

ANDERSEN, ANDERSON, ANDERSSON (S.S. Abbreviation: Anders)

Ranking: 9 S.S. Count: 1,145,634

Origin: Andersen—Danish, Norwegian; Anderson—English; Andersson—Swedish. Transformations of Andrew.

Famous **Andersons** and **Andersens:** JOSEPH ANDERSON (1757–1837) was governor of Tennessee for six terms, U.S. senator, and controller of the U.S. Treasury under President James Madison. Anderson County, Tennessee, was named for him. ALEXANDER ANDERSON (1775–1870) of New York originated wood engravings in America. ROBERT ANDERSON (1805–1871) was commander of Fort Sumter in South Carolina when Confederate soldiers attacked it in 1861 in the first battle of the Civil War. JOSEPH REID ANDERSON (1813–1892) of Virginia served the Confederate Army as a soldier and officer, and (through his manufacturing plant) he supplied much of the heavy ordnance used. MARY ANDERSON (1859–1940) of California achieved fame as an actress in New York and London. CARL THOMAS ANDERSON (1865–1948) created the comic strip "Henry." SHERWOOD ANDERSON (1876– 1941) of Ohio was the author of several acclaimed books, including *Beyond Desire* (1932) and the autobiographical *Story Teller's Story* (1924). MAXWELL ANDERSON (1888–1959) of Pennsylvania was a playwright whose works included *White Desert* (1923) and *Both Your Houses,* which won a Pulitzer Prize in 1933. MARGARET CAROLINE ANDERSON (1893?-1973) of Indiana was founding editor of the *Little Review,* which published works of many well-known writers. ELDA EMMA ANDERSON (1899–1961) of Wisconsin was a health physicist and a member of the team that developed the atomic bomb during World War II. DOROTHY ANDERSEN (1901– 1963) of North Carolina was a pathologist and pediatrician. Through research at Columbia University, she discovered cystic fibrosis and advanced its diagnosis and treatment. EDDIE ANDERSON (1905– 1977) of California made his debut as "Rochester" on the Jack Benny radio show in 1936, then went on to many radio and subsequently television shows with the legendary comedian. Outside of his professional career, Eddie Anderson became the first black man to own a horse (Burnt Cork) running in the Kentucky Derby.

Genealogies: *The Andersons of Rowlett's Creek* was compiled by W. Clytes Anderson Cullar and Jerry M. Flook and published in Dallas, Texas, in 1973. *Descendants of Capt. Henry Anderson, Sr., of Newberry County, South Carolina* was compiled by Lucien L. McNees and published in Ebenezer, Missouri, in 1972.

ANDINO

Ranking: 4946 S.S. Count: 9057
Origin: Spanish. The name was given to those who came from the Andes, a place in Spain.
Genealogies: None known.

ANDRADE (S.S. Abbreviation: Andrad)

Ranking: 1441 S.S. Count: 30,968
Origin: Portuguese. Uncertain etymology.
Genealogies: None known.

ANDRE

Ranking: 4578 S.S. Count: 9762
Origin: French. Cognate to Andrew.
Famous **Andres:** LOUIS ANDRE (1631–1715), born in France, was a Jesuit missionary to wandering tribes around Lake Huron and around Green Bay. He is said to have baptized about 500 people, mostly children, over a 10-year period.
Genealogies: None known.

ANDREA, ANDREACCIO, ANDREAZZI, ANDREASEN, ANDREASSEN, ANDREAS, ANDREASON

Ranking: 3224 S.S. Count: 14,059
Origin: Andrea, Andreaccio, Andreazzi—Italian; Andreasen, Andreassen—Danish; Andreas—Greek; Andreason—Swedish. Cognates to Andrew.
Genealogies: None known.

ANDRES, ANDRESEN, ANDRESS, ANDRESSER

Ranking: 2077 S.S. Count: 22,078
Origin: Andres—German, Spanish; Andresen—Danish; Andress—English; Andresser—German. Cognates to Andrew.
Genealogies: None known.

ANDREW, ANDREWS

Ranking: 163 S.S. Count: 200,116
Origin: English. Derived from the Greek word "andreas," meaning manly, strong, or courageous.
Famous **Andrews:** JAMES OSGOOD ANDREW (1794–1871) of Georgia was a Methodist Episcopal bishop whose holding of slaves resulted in a split into North and South branches of the church. JOHN ALBION ANDREW (1818–1867), a native of Maine, served as governor of Massachusetts during the Civil War years and organized his state's troops prior to President Abraham Lincoln's request for volunteers. ALEXANDER BOYD ANDREWS (1841–1915) of North Carolina was a railroad promoter in the South after the Civil War. He is best known for completing the Western North Carolina Railroad almost to the western state line, opening up a mountainous region. CHARLES MCLEAN ANDREWS (1863–1943) was a recognized authority on the history of colonial America. ABRAM PIATT ANDREW (1873–1936) of Indiana was one of the founders of the American Legion and a member of Congress from Massachusetts. One of his books, *Colonial Period of American History, Vol. 1,* won a Pulitzer Prize. FRANK MAXWELL ANDREWS (1884—1943) of Tennessee was organizer and first commander of the U.S. Army's first air force unit. He succeeded Dwight D. Eisenhower as commander of European forces in February 1943, then was killed in a plane crash in Iceland in May 1943. ROY CHAPMAN ANDREWS (1884–1960) of Wisconsin led natural history expeditions to Asia and Alaska and is credited with significant discoveries in the study of evolution. He was the director of the American Museum of Natural History (1935–1942) and the author of several books.

Genealogies: *History of the Andrew Family* was compiled by Adelia Brown Elmer and published in Ansonia, Connecticut, in 1889. *Thomas Andrew, Immigrant: A Genealogy of the Posterity of Thomas Andrew, One of the Early Settlers of New England* was compiled by Laurence Clyde Andrew and published in Portland, Maine, in 1972.

ANDRUS, ANDRUSOV, ANDRUSYAK
Ranking: 2978 S.S. Count: 15,275
Origin: Andrus—Russian, Ukrainian; Andrusov—Russian; Andrusyak—Ukrainian. Cognates to Andrew.

Famous **Andruses:** REUBEN ANDRUS (1829–1887) was president of DePauw University. ETHEL PERCY ANDRUS (1884–1967) of California was founder of the National Retired Teachers Association and the American Association of Retired Persons. She was the first woman to be a high school principal in California. EDWIN COWLES ANDRUS (1896–1978) of New York was a physician and educator associated with Johns Hopkins University. He was a prolific writer and editor of medical journal articles and a member or officer of many professional organizations. He was awarded the Presidential Certificate for Merit in 1948 by President Harry Truman.

Genealogies: *Some Descendants of John and Grace (Rude) Andrus of Preston, Connecticut, Lebanon, New Hampshire, Chelsea, Vermont* was compiled by Elizabeth Duncan Lee and published in Lexington, Missouri, in 1978.

ANGEL
Ranking: 2459 S.S. Count: 18,459
Origin: English, French, Spanish. Derived from the Greek word "angelos" and the Latin word "angelus," both meaning messenger. The name was given to those with angelic demeanors or appearances.

Famous **Angels:** BENJAMIN FRANKLIN ANGEL (1815–1894) of New York served as U.S. consul in Hawaii, special envoy to China, and later as a diplomat in Norway and Sweden. FRANCISCO ANGEL (1914–) was president of New Mexico Highlands University from 1971 to 1975. He was the first Mexican-American to serve as an American university president.

Genealogies: None known.

ANGELICA (S.S. Abbreviation: Angeli)
Ranking: 4412 S.S. Count: 10,160
Origin: Italian. Transformation of Angel.
Genealogies: None known.

ANGELL
Ranking: 3359 S.S. Count: 13,494
Origin: English. Transformation of Angel.

Famous **Angells:** JAMES BURRILL ANGELL (1829–1916) of Rhode Island was president of the University of Vermont (1866–1871) and the University of Michigan (1871–1909), and he was a U.S. diplomat to China and Turkey. His son, JAMES ROWLAND ANGELL (1869–1949) of Vermont, was president of Yale University (1921–1937) and an author of books, including *American Education* (1937).

Genealogies: *141 Years of Mormon Heritage: Rawsons, Browns, Angells—Pioneers* was compiled by Archie Leon Brown and Charlene L. Hathaway and published in Oakland, California, in 1973.

ANGELOPOULOU, ANGELO (S.S. Abbreviation: Angelo)
Ranking: 2593 S.S. Count: 17,537
Origin: Angelopoulou—Greek; Angelo—Italian, Portuguese. Derived from the Greek word "angelos," meaning messenger.
Genealogies: None known.

ANGLIN
Ranking: 3539 S.S. Count: 12,764
Origin: Irish. Derived from the first name Anglonn, meaning hero or victor.

Famous **Anglins:** MARY MARGARET ANGLIN (1876–1958), a native of Canada, debuted as an actress in New York in 1894 and went on to other roles and to forming a repertory company.

Genealogies: None known.

ANTHONY (S.S. Abbreviation: Anthon)
Ranking: 595 S.S. Count: 70,141
Origin: Welsh. Derived from the Latin name Antonius, an ancient Roman surname of unknown origin.

Famous **Anthonys:** HENRY BOWEN ANTHONY (1815–1884) of Rhode Island became editor of the *Providence Journal* at age 23 and later was elected governor of and U.S. senator from Rhode Island. SUSAN B. ANTHONY (1820–1906) of Adams, Massachusetts, was a political activist. Her causes included temperance, a woman's right to own property, and a woman's right to guardianship of her children. She gained most of her fame from her advocacy of women's suffrage. She worked unsuccessfully to see the 14th Amendment, which granted the vote to "all male inhabitants," extended to women. The 19th Amendment, which did give women the right to vote, was passed 14 years after her death. GEORGE TOBEY ANTHONY (1824–1896) of New York was governor of Kansas. ANDREW VARICK STOUT ANTHONY (1835–1906) of New York was a well-known wood engraver. KATHARINE SUSAN ANTHONY (1877–1965) of Arkansas was a biographer and women's rights advocate. Her book *Mothers Who Must Earn* (1914) detailed her study of 370 tenement mothers who had to work to support their families.

Genealogies: None known.

ANTONELLI (S.S. Abbreviation: Antone)
Ranking: 3311 S.S. Count: 13,681
Origin: Italian. Cognate to Anthony.
Genealogies: None known.

ANTONIE, ANTONINI, ANTONIO (S.S. Abbreviation: Antoni)

Ranking: 2506 S.S. Count: 18,097
Origin: Italian. Cognates to Anthony.
Genealogies: None known.

APODACA (S.S. Abbreviation: Apodac)

Ranking: 3987 S.S. Count: 11,334
Origin: Spanish. Uncertain etymology. Possibly derived from the Spanish word "apodar," to ridicule.
Genealogies: None known.

APONTE

Ranking: 1600 S.S. Count: 28,038
Origin: Spanish. Derived from the Spanish word "puente," meaning bridge. The name was given to those who lived near bridges.
Genealogies: None known.

APPEL

Ranking: 3924 S.S. Count: 11,493
Origin: Dutch, German, Jewish, Swedish. Transformation of Apple.
Famous **Appels:** KENNETH ELLMAKER APPEL (1896–1979) of Pennsylvania was one of the first psychiatrists in the country to set up a practice outside of a hospital. His speech on becoming president of the American Psychiatric Association in 1954 was instrumental in the U.S. Congress's formation of the Joint Commission on Mental Illness and Health, which resulted in the Mental Health Study Act of 1955. Under Appel's leadership, the commission offered many proposals that were incorporated into President John F. Kennedy's special message on mental retardation February 5, 1963.
Genealogies: None known.

APPLE

Ranking: 4576 S.S. Count: 9763
Origin: English, German, Scottish. Derived from the Old English word "æppel," meaning apple. The name was given to those who lived near apple orchards or worked selling or harvesting apples.
Famous **Apples:** THOMAS GILMORE APPLE (1829–1898) of Pennsylvania was a theologian, educator, and writer. He was a minister in the Reformed Church and president of Franklin and Marshall College. He was a major contributor to the "Mercersberg Theology system."
Genealogies: None known.

APPLEBEE, APPLEBY, APPLEBAUM (S.S. Abbreviation: Appleb)

Ranking: 3108 S.S. Count: 14,629

Origin: Applebee, Appleby—English; Applebaum—German; Applebee, Appleby: derived from the Old Norse words "apall" and "br," meaning apple and farm. The names were given to those who came from Appleby, the name of several places in England; Applebaum: transformation of Apple combined with the German word "baum," meaning tree.
Famous **Applebys:** JOHN FRANCIS APPLEBY (1840–1917), while a Union soldier in the Civil War, invented a magazine and automatic feeder for rifles, and as a farmer in Wisconsin later, he invented a wire binder and knotter for grain reapers.
Genealogies: None known.

APPLEGARTH, APPLEGATE (S.S. Abbreviation: Appleg)

Ranking: 2460 S.S. Count: 18,421
Origin: English, Scottish. Derived from the Old Norse words "apall" and "garr," meaning apple and orchard. The names were given to those who lived near apple orchards.
Famous **Applegates:** JESSE APPLEGATE (1811–1888) of Kentucky was a surveyor, cattleman, and author who led wagon-train expeditions to Oregon and then became a political leader there. His story, "A Day With the Cow-Column" (1876), is a classic in western literature of that time.
Genealogies: *Skookum: An Oregon Pioneer Family's History and Lore* was compiled by Shannon Applegate and published in New York, New York, in 1988.

AQUINO

Ranking: 3227 S.S. Count: 14,044
Origin: Filipino. Aquino is the name of a town in the Philippines. 1) The name was possibly given to those who came from that town. 2) possibly derived from the Spanish word "aqui," meaning here.
Genealogies: None known.

ARAGON, ARAGONES

Ranking: 2346 S.S. Count: 19,331
Origin: Spanish. The name was given to those from Aragon, a region in northeastern Spain.
Genealogies: None known.

ARANDA

Ranking: 4716 S.S. Count: 9483
Origin: Spanish. 1) derived from the Basque word "aran," meaning valley. 2) derived from the Latin word "aranda," meaning fertile land.
Genealogies: None known.

ARCE

Ranking: 3613 S.S. Count: 12,502
Origin: Spanish. 1) derived from the Latin word "acer,"

meaning maple tree. The name was given to those who lived near maple trees. 2) derived from the Basque word "artze," meaning stony place.

Famous **Arces:** FRANCISCO ARCE (1822–1878) of California was secretary to Gen. Jose Castro in the California military forces. He was supposedly bringing horses belonging to the California government from Sonoma to the south when Capt. John C. Fremont, commanding an American surveying party, prodded settlers into taking the horses. The June 6, 1846, "Arce Affair" began the Bear Flag revolt and the seizure of California by the United States.
Genealogies: None known.

ARCHAMBAULT, ARCHAMBEAU (S.S. Abbreviation: Archam)
Ranking: 4945 S.S. Count: 9059
Origin: French. Derived from the first name Aircanbald, meaning bold or natural.
Genealogies: None known.

ARCHER, ARCHERD
Ranking: 930 S.S. Count: 46,329
Origin: English. Derived from the Middle English and Old French words "archer" and "arch(i)cher," both meaning bowman. The name was given to soldiers armed with bows and arrows.

Famous **Archers:** JOHN ARCHER (1741–1810) was a physician and captain of Maryland troops during the Revolutionary War. He served in the U.S. House of Representatives for three terms. His sons, STEVENSON ARCHER (1786–1848) and WILLIAM SEGAR ARCHER (1789–1810), were active in politics in Maryland and Virginia, respectively. BRANCH TANNER ARCHER (1790–1856) was a physician and politician in Virginia until he is said to have shot and killed a cousin in a duel. He migrated to Texas, where he became a leader in the efforts to gain independence from Mexico. GEORGE FROST ARCHER (1871–1935) of Massachusetts was an inventor who held numerous patents, including one for a telephone switchboard.
Genealogies: *The Archer Family Genealogical Record* was compiled by Julia Mallison Murden and published in 1941. *Growing up Black in Rural Mississippi: Memories of a Family, Heritage of a Place* was compiled by Chalmers Archer and published in New York, New York, in 1992.

ARCHIBALD (S.S. Abbreviation: Archib
Ranking: 3448 S.S. Count: 13,086
Origin: English, Scottish. Derived from the Germanic words "ercan" and "bald," meaning precious and bold.
Genealogies: *Archbold (also Archibald) Genealogy and Selected Family Records and Memorabilia* was compiled by John Dana Archbold and published in 1976.

ARCHIE
Ranking: 4857 S.S. Count: 9212
Origin: English, Scottish. Transformation of Archibald.
Genealogies: None known.

ARCHULETA (S.S. Abbreviation: Archul)
Ranking: 3015 S.S. Count: 15,069
Origin: Spanish. Derived from the Basque name Artxuleta, which is derived from the words "aritz" and "eta," meaning oak tree and place.
Genealogies: None known.

ARELLANO (S.S. Abbreviation: Arella)
Ranking: 2150 S.S. Count: 21,327
Origin: Spanish. Possibly derived from the Spanish word "arelar," which is a kind of sieve. The name was given to those from Arellano, a place in the province of Navarre, Spain.
Genealogies: None known.

ARIAS
Ranking: 2100 S.S. Count: 21,873
Origin: Jewish, Spanish. Derived from the Spanish word "arias," meaning songs. The name was given to those who came from Arias, a place in Spain.
Genealogies: None known.

ARMBRUSTER, ARMBRUST (S.S. Abbreviation: Armbru)
Ranking: 4828 S.S. Count: 9276
Origin: German. Derived from the Anglo-Norman-French word "arblaster," meaning crossbowman. The names were given to those who fought with or sold crossbows.
Genealogies: None known.

ARMENTROUT (S.S. Abbreviation: Arment)
Ranking: 2880 S.S. Count: 15,809
Origin: German. Transformation of Armend. The name was given to those who were considered friends of the poor.
Genealogies: *Armentrout Family History 1739–1978* was compiled by Russell S. Armentrout and published in Reston, Virginia, in 1980.

ARMOUR
Ranking: 3973 S.S. Count: 11,395
Origin: English. Derived from the Middle English and Old French word "armure," meaning one who made weapons and defensive clothing. The name was given to those who used or made such items.

Famous **Armours:** PHILIP DANFORTH ARMOUR (1832–1901) of New York founded the business that became Armour & Co., the well-known meat-processing firm. He also founded Armour Institute of Technology, which later became Illinois Institute of Technology. THOMAS DICKSON ARMOUR (1895–1968), born in Scotland, won 14 major titles as a professional golfer, including the Canadian Open three times. He was a charter member of the Professional Golfers Association Hall of Fame.

Genealogies: *A Brief Visit with the Old Folks* was compiled by George Taylor and published in 1975.

ARMSTEAD (S.S. Abbreviation: Armste)
Ranking: 4258 S.S. Count: 10,578
Origin: English, German. English: 1) derived from the Middle English words "(h)ermite" and "stede," maning hermit and place. 2) the name was given to those who lived near a recluse. German: the name was given to those who came from Armstedt, Germany.
Genealogies: None known.

ARMSTRONG (S.S. Abbreviation: Armstr)
Ranking: 184 S.S. Count: 185,278
Origin: English, Scottish. Derived from the Middle English words "arm" and "strong," meaning arm and strong. The name was given to those who were strong in battle.

Famous **Armstrongs:** JOHN ARMSTRONG (1755–1816) of New Jersey, after serving as an army officer in the Revolutionary War, was an explorer, then treasurer, of the Northwest Territory. Another JOHN ARMSTRONG (1758–1842), of Pennsylvania, also was a Revolutionary army officer. He later served in both houses of Congress and as a diplomat. As secretary of war, he was blamed for military failures during the War of 1812. SAMUEL CHAPMAN ARMSTRONG (1839–1893) of Hawaii was the founder and head of Hampton Normal and Industrial Institute. PAUL ARMSTRONG (1869–1915) of Missouri was a playwright whose popular works included *Heir to the Hoorah* (1905) and *Alias Jimmy Valentine* (1909). HENRY WORTHINGTON ARMSTRONG (1879–1951) was a composer who wrote the music to *Sweet Adeline.* EDWIN HOWARD ARMSTRONG (1890–1954) of New York was an electrical engineer with several inventions credited to him in the field of radio communications, including the development of the frequency-modulation system. HAMILTON FISH ARMSTRONG (1893–1973) was founder, managing editor, then editor of *Foreign Affairs* magazine. LOUIS DANIEL ARMSTRONG (1900–1971) of New Orleans, Louisiana, was a jazz trumpeter known as "Satchmo." He shaped jazz in the 1920s and was known for his improvisation and rhythmic flexibility. NEIL ALDEN ARMSTRONG (1930–) of Ohio was the first civilian to enter astronaut training, and, as commander of the *Apollo 11* mission in 1969, became the first person to set foot on the moon.

Genealogies: *Ancestry Descendants of Daniel F. Armstrong and Sarah Nutter* was compiled by Evelyn Crawford Fenton and published in Chewelah, Washington, in 1987.

Armstrong Ancestry: A Genealogy of the Descendants of Robert R. Armstrong was compiled by John Edward Armstrong and published in Madison, Wisconsin, in 1990.

ARNDT
Ranking: 2312 S.S. Count: 19,651
Origin: Danish, Dutch, German. Derived from the first names Arend and Arndt, meaning eagle and rule.
Famous **Arndts:** WALTER TALLMADGE ARNDT (1873–1932) of New York wrote more than 1000 articles on American history and biography and was political editor for a number of years of the *New York Evening Post.*
Genealogies: None known.

ARNETT
Ranking: 1749 S.S. Count: 25,613
Origin: English. Derived from the Norman first name Arnold, meaning eagle or powerful.
Genealogies: None known.

ARNOLD, ARNOLDE, ARNOLDSON
Ranking: 170 S.S. Count: 195,933
Origin: English, German. 1) derived from the Norman first name Arnold, which is derived from the Germanic words "ehre" and "hold," meaning honor and devoted. 2) derived from the Old English words "earn" and "weald," meaning eagle and power.

Famous **Arnolds:** BENEDICT ARNOLD (1741–1801) of Connecticut ran away from his home at the age of 15 to join the army to fight the French and Indian Wars. During the Revolutionary War, he led troops into Canada and fought the British heroically but was nonetheless passed over for promotion. After his first wife died, he married the 18-year-old daughter of a loyalist. This damaged his reputation with the American forces. After he was accused of misusing public property and authority, he offered his services to the British for large sums of money and unsuccessfully attempted to betray the American fortress at West Point on the Hudson to the British. After the war, he and his wife moved to London. RICHARD DENNIS ARNOLD (1808–1876) of Georgia was one of the founding physicians of the American Medical Association and its first secretary. He also was the mayor of Savannah, Georgia, and surrendered the town to General William Sherman in December 1864 to prevent more of the bloodshed that had marked Sherman's march through Georgia in the Civil War. ISAAC NEWTON ARNOLD (1815–1884) wrote *The Life of Benedict Arnold* (1880) but was better known for his *Life of Abraham Lincoln* (1884). HENRY HARLEY ARNOLD (1886–1950) had the distinction, because of his flying abilities at a time when the military air forces were forming, of being a general in both the army and the air force. THURMAN WESLEY ARNOLD (1891–1969) of Wyoming, as assistant U.S.

attorney general, was known for pursuing antitrust cases. He also was a judge for the U.S. Court of Appeals for the District of Columbia and the author of *The Folklore of Capitalism* (1937) and *Democracy and Free Enterprise* (1942).

Genealogies: *Ancestry and Descendants of John Chambers Arnold and Mary Elizabeth (Shepherd) Arnold: 1789–1967* was compiled by Marjorie Organ Regan and published in Ohio in 1967. *The Arnold, Best, Cullison and Herron Families* was compiled by Evelyn L. Strong and published in Massillon, Ohio, in 1980.

ARRENDONDO (S.S. Abbreviation: Arrend)

Ranking: 3151 **S.S. Count:** 14,421

Origin: Spanish. Derived from the Spanish word "redondo," meaning round. The name was given to those who came from Arredondo, Spain.

Genealogies: None known.

ARRINGTON (S.S. Abbreviation: Arring)

Ranking: 1592 **S.S. Count:** 28,106

Origin: English. 1) derived from the Old English words "earn" and "tūn," meaning eagle and settlement. The name was given to those from Arrington in Cambridgeshire, England. 2) transformation of Harrington.

Famous **Arringtons:** ALFRED W. ARRINGTON (1810–1867) of North Carolina, using the pseudonym Charles Summerfield, wrote the novels *The Desperadoes of the Southwest* (1847) and *The Tanaha* (1856).

Genealogies: None known.

ARROYO

Ranking: 992 **S.S. Count:** 44,147

Origin: Spanish. Derived from the Spanish word "arroyo," meaning watercourse or small stream. The name was given to those who lived near a brook or irrigation channel.

Genealogies: None known.

ARSENAULT (S.S. Abbreviation: Arsena)

Ranking: 3796 **S.S. Count:** 11,883

Origin: French. The name was given to those who supervised an arsenal.

Genealogies: None known.

ARTHUR

Ranking: 1082 **S.S. Count:** 40,876

Origin: English, Welsh. 1) derived from the Welsh word "arth" and the Gaelic word "art," both meaning bear. The name was given to those who were considered courageous or bear-like. 2) derived from the first name Artur, meaning son or follower of Tur, the Norse god of war.

Famous **Arthurs:** WILLIAM ARTHUR (1797–1875), born in Ireland, was a Baptist clergyman and antiquarian in Ver-

mont. He published a magazine and an etymological dictionary of family and Christian names. He was the father of CHESTER ALAN ARTHUR (1830–1886) of New York, who succeeded to the U.S. presidency after President James A. Garfield was assassinated in 1881. TIMOTHY SHAY ARTHUR (1809–1885) of New York wrote *Ten Nights in a Barroom and What I Saw There* (1854), which outsold all books that decade except for *Uncle Tom's Cabin*. JOSEPH CHARLES ARTHUR (1850–1942) was a botanist and editor (*Botanical Gazette*) noted for research and discoveries involving rust fungi.

Genealogies: *Genealogy and History of the Descendents and Ancestory of Richard Henry Arthur and Susanna Coad* was compiled by Fred E. Sawyer and published in American Falls, Idaho, in 1978. *The William Arthur Family* was compiled by Robert L. Arthur and published in Parson, West Virginia, in 1982.

ARTIS

Ranking: 3933 **S.S. Count:** 11,473

Origin: English, French. 1) derived from the first name Arthur, meaning courageous. 2) same derivation as in 1. The name was given to those who came from Arthus, a place in France.

Genealogies: None known.

ASBURY

Ranking: 3951 **S.S. Count:** 11,445

Origin: English. Derived from the Old English word "burh," meaning fort or secure town. The name was given to those from Asbury, the name of several places in England.

Famous **Asburys:** FRANCIS ASBURY (1745–1816), born in England, was a Methodist missionary to the United States. He was recalled to England, but he refused to return and became a citizen of Delaware. Instrumental in establishing the Methodist Episcopal Church in America, he assumed the title of bishop in 1785 and headed the denomination until his death. HERBERT ASBURY (1891–1963) was a journalist and author whose books included *A Methodist Saint* (a biography of Francis Asbury).

Genealogies: None known.

ASH

Ranking: 1543 **S.S. Count:** 28,920

Origin: English. Derived from the Old English word "æsc," meaning ash. The name was given to those who lived near an ash tree.

Genealogies: *Ash, Ashe, Stillwell: A Genealogy and History* was compiled by John Reid Ashe and published in Greensboro, North Carolina, in 1977.

ASHBY

Ranking: 1953 **S.S. Count:** 23,185

Origin: English. Derived from the Old English words "æsc" and "by," meaning ash tree and dwelling. The name was given to those who lived near an ash tree.

Famous **Ashbys:** GEORGE FRANKLIN ASHBY (1885–1950) worked for the Union Pacific Railroad for nearly 30 years and served as its president (1946–1949).

Genealogies: *The Ashby Book* was compiled by Lee Fleming Reese and published in San Deigo, California, in 1978.

ASHCRAFT (S.S. Abbreviation: Ashcra)

Ranking: 3324 **S.S. Count:** 13,634

Origin: English. Derived from the Old English words "æsc" and "croft," meaning ash and enclosure. The name was given to those who lived near a field of ash trees.

Genealogies: None known.

ASHE

Ranking: 4350 **S.S. Count:** 10,307.

Origin: English. Transformation of Ash.

Famous **Ashes:** JOHN ASHE (1720?–1781) of North Carolina was a commander in the Revolutionary army. His unit's defeat at Brair Creek, Georgia, gave the British control in that state and access to the Carolinas. JOHN BAPTISTA ASHE (1748–1802) held nearly every political post possible in the state of North Carolina except governor. He was elected governor in 1802 but died before taking office. He was a member of the Continental Congress from 1787 to 1788. He was the father of SAMUEL ASHE, who was a three-term governor of North Carolina and who married twice, both times to cousins. Samuel Ashe also was the first judge for the North Carolina Supreme Court. ARTHUR ASHE (1943–1993) of Virginia was the first African-American man to win the U.S. Open and Wimbledon tennis championships. With his tremendous serve and strong backhand, he was a dominant force on the professional tennis circuit from 1968 to 1975. He died of complications from AIDS, which he had contracted through a blood transfusion.

Genealogies: *Genealogy and Letters of the Strudwick, Ashe, Young and Allied Families* was compiled by Betsy Lawson Willis and published in Alexandria, Virginia, in 1971.

ASHER

Ranking: 2725 **S.S. Count:** 16,703

Origin: English, Jewish. English: transformation of Ash. Jewish: derived from the Hebrew personal name Asher, meaning blessed.

Famous **Ashers:** JOSEPH MAJOR ASHER (1872–1909), born in England, moved to New York and became well known for his eloquence as rabbi of two congregations in New York City.

Genealogies: None known.

ASHFORD (S.S. Abbreviation: Ashfor)

Ranking: 3678 **S.S. Count:** 12,256

Origin: English. Derived from the Old English words "æsc" and "ford," meaning ash and shallow place in a river. The name was given to those from Ashford, the name of several places in England.

Famous **Ashfords:** BAILEY KELLY ASHFORD (1873–1934) of Washington, D.C., was a surgeon in the army during the Spanish-American War and was responsible for discovering and campaigning against hookworm disease in Puerto Rico. He was instrumental in creating the Puerto Rico Anemia Commission, which treated 300,000 people in a decade when mortality from tropical anemia declined 90 percent from a previous 12,000 deaths annually.

Genealogies: None known.

ASHLEY

Ranking: 887 **S.S. Count:** 48,967

Origin: English. 1) derived from the Old English words "æsc" and "lēah," meaning ash and clearing. 2) derived from the Old English name Astley, meaning east field. The name was also given to those from Ashley, the name of several places in England.

Famous **Ashleys:** WILLIAM HENRY ASHLEY (1778–1838) of Virginia was a fur trader and explorer who led expeditions to the West and later served in the U.S. House of Representatives. JAMES MITCHELL ASHLEY (1824–1896) of Ohio was a newspaper editor and an outspoken opponent of slavery. He served in the House of Representatives for four terms, and on December 14, 1863, he introduced the first proposition to amend the Constitution to abolish slavery.

Genealogies: *Ashleys of the Old Colony: Based upon the Research of R. Eugene Ashley, et al.* was compiled by Robert E. Ashley and published in Baltimore, Maryland, in 1982.

ASHTON

Ranking: 2862 **S.S. Count:** 15,914

Origin: English. Derived from the Old English words "æsc" and "tūn," meaning ash and settlement. The name was given to those who came from Ashton, the name of several places in England.

Famous **Ashtons:** ALBERT AVEDIS ASHTON (1908–1975) was a Turkish-born engineer and inventor who eventually held 53 U.S. and foreign patents. For the oil-drilling industry, he invented the first all-steel slurry pump.

Genealogies: None known.

ASHWORTH (S.S. Abbreviation: Ashwor)

Ranking: 3195 **S.S. Count:** 14,206

Origin: English. Derived from the Old English words "æsc" and "wor," meaning ash and enclosure. The name was given to those from Ashworth, a place in Lancashire, England.

Genealogies: *Descendants of George Frazier, Joseph Journey, Patrick Calvert, Thomas Endicott, Sr., John Ashworth, Sr., as They Entered "into this Fruitful Valley"* was compiled by Gloria M. Cox and published in Evansville, Indiana, in 1971.

ASKEW

Ranking: 2427 S.S. Count: 18,682

Origin: English. Derived from the Old Norse components "eiki" and "skorgr," meaning oak and wood. The name was given to those who came from Askew in North Yorkshire, England.

Genealogies: None known.

ATCHISON (S.S. Abbreviation: Atchis)

Ranking: 3989 S.S. Count: 11,332

Origin: English, Scottish. Derived from the first name Adkin, a diminutive of Adam.

Genealogies: None known.

ATHERTON (S.S. Abbreviation: Athert)

Ranking: 4742 S.S. Count: 9446

Origin: English. Derived from the Old English first name Ædelhere. The name was given to those who came from Atherton in Lancashire, England.

Famous **Athertons:** CHARLES GORDON ATHERTON (1804–1853) of New Hampshire served in both houses of Congress—three terms as a representative and one term as a senator. GEORGE WASHINGTON ATHERTON (1837–1906) was president of Pennsylvania State College for 22 years, a period during which the school advanced from 33 students and two buildings to 1200 students and 30 buildings. GERTRUDE FRANKLIN ATHERTON (1857–1948) of California was a novelist whose books included *The Californians* (1898) and *The Horn of Life* (1942).

Genealogies: None known.

ATKINS, ATKINSON

Ranking: 259 S.S. Count: 141,538

Origin: English. Derived from the first name Ad, a diminutive of Adam.

Famous **Atkins/Atkinsons:** HENRY ATKINSON (1782–1842) of North Carolina was a commander of expeditions to the West and was army commander during the Black Hawk War in 1832. JEARUM ATKINS (1840–1880) of Vermont fell from a wagon in Illinois and received crippling spinal injuries. He lay on his back with a drawing board suspended above his head and designed a self-rake attachment for a reaper that imitated human arms. Patented as Atkins's automaton in 1852, the invention brought instant but short-lived success. Because of a bankrupcy of a reaper manufacturer, Atkins realized about $7000 for an invention considered at the time to have been worth $2 million.

GEORGE WESLEY ATKINSON (1845–1925) was governor of West Virginia and author of several books, including *Hand Book for Revenue Officers* (1881). ELEANOR ATKINSON (1863–1942) of Indiana was the author of *Johnny Appleseed* (1915) and other books. BROOKS ATKINSON (1894–1984) was a book and theater critic. Writing for the *New York Times* from 1925 through 1960, he became the most influencial drama critic in the country. TED ATKINSON (1916–), originally from Canada, is a former jockey who was called "the slasher" for the way he used his whip. He won 3795 of his 23,611 starts in his 21-year racing career. His mounts won a total of $17,499,360.

Genealogies: *The Atkinson Family Builders, the Eastern Shore of Maryland and Westward* was compiled by Virginia Atkinson Chatelain and published in Manhattan, Kansas, in 1979. *Early Settlers in the Ozarks: A Genealogy of Atkinson, Best, Hall, Phillips, Stokes and Webb Families* was compiled by Garner J. Phillips and published in Springfield, Missouri, in 1976.

ATWELL

Ranking: 4016 S.S. Count: 11,273

Origin: English. Derived from the Middle English words "at" and "well," meaning at and well. The name was given to those who lived near a source of water.

Genealogies: None known.

ATWOOD

Ranking: 1933 S.S. Count: 23,377

Origin: Derived from the Middle English words "at" and "wood," meaning at and wood. The name was given to those who lived near woods.

Famous **Atwoods:** DAVID ATWOOD (1805–1889) of New York was mayor of Madison, Wisconsin, then a member of Congress from Wisconsin. LEWIS JOHN ATWOOD (1827–1909) of Connecticut was an inventor who obtained more than 50 patents in the field of brass-lantern making. CHARLES B. ATWOOD (1849–1895) of Massachusetts was an architect and in 1891 was designer-in-chief of the Chicago World's Fair. WALLACE WALTER ATWOOD (1872–1949) of Illinois, a geologist and geographer, was president of Clark University and founder and editor of *Economic Geography*. ANN MARGARET ATWOOD (1913–) of California is a poet and filmmaker. Her work includes *The Gods Were Tall and Green*, which won the silver medal at the International Film and TV Festival in New York in 1972, and *Haiku: The Hidden Glimmering*, which won the gold medal at the Atlanta Film Festival in 1973.

Genealogies: *The Ancestry of One Atwood Family* was compiled by Charles A. Atwood and published in Antioch, Illinois, in 1965. *Genealogy of the Gilbert Atwood Family* was compiled by Raymond Thomas Atwood and published in Hopkinsville, Kentucky, in 1979.

AUGUSTE, AUGUSTO (S.S. Abbreviation: August)

Ranking: 991 S.S. Count: 44,165

Origin: Auguste—French; Augusto—Portuguese. Cognates to Agosto.

Genealogies: None known.

AULT

Ranking: 4229 S.S. Count: 10,664

Origin: English. Transformation of Old(s).

Genealogies: *The Ault Genealogy* was compiled by Garnet W. Ault and published in Washington, D.C., in 1980. *Daniel Knarr and Lucinda Ault* was compiled by Nellie Wallace Reeser and published in York, Pennsylvania, in 1955.

AUSTIN

Ranking: 222 S.S. Count: 158,034

Origin: English, French. Derived from the first name Austin, a form of the Latin first name Augustus, meaning to increase.

Famous **Austins**: STEPHEN FULLER AUSTIN (1793–1836) of Austinville, Virginia, founded Texas in 1822 after his father, MOSES AUSTIN (1761–1821), obtained a permit from the Spanish governor in San Antonio to establish a community there, but he died before he could implement his plan. Stephen Fuller Austin was imprisoned in Mexico City from 1833 to 1834 because he promoted statehood for Texas and independence from Coahuila. The city of Austin, Texas is named for him. JANE GOODWIN AUSTIN (1831–1894) was the author of popular stories and books about life in early New England, including a series of *Pilgrim Books* (1889–1890). MARY AUSTIN (1868–1934) was an author of novels, short stories, and her autobiography, *Earth Horizon* (1932). WARREN R. AUSTIN (1877–1962) represented Vermont in the U.S. Senate for 15 years. He was the first U.S. ambassador to the United Nations. He received the first annual award from the American Association for the United Nations as the American who contributed the most to the UN in 1947.

Genealogies: *The Austin Family of Bennington, Vermont* was compiled by Hugh S. Austin and published in West Palm Beach, Florida, in 1973. *Austin and Rich Genealogy* was published in Farmington, Michigan, in 1968.

AUTRY

Ranking: 4070 S.S. Count: 11,111

Origin: French. Derived from the first name Aldric, meaning old and powerful.

Genealogies: *Meet Our Ancestors: Culbreth, Autry, Maxwell-Bundy, Winslow, Henley, and Allied Families* was compiled by V. Mayo Bundy and published in Greensboro, North Carolina, in 1978.

AVALOS

Ranking: 3752 S.S. Count: 12,065

Origin: Spanish. Derived from the Spanish word "avalar," meaning the site of earthquakes.

Genealogies: None known.

AVERY

Ranking: 811 S.S. Count: 52,091

Origin: English. Derived from the Germanic first name Alberic, which comprises the components "alb" and "ric," meaning elf and rich or powerful.

Famous **Averys**: SAMUEL PUTNAM AVERY (1822–1904) of New York was a founder of the Metropolitan Museum of Art in New York and, with a donation of 15,000 volumes, established an architectural library at Columbia University. ISAAC WHEELER AVERY (1837–1897) of Florida was a Confederate soldier and editor-in-chief of the *Atlanta Constitution* for a number of years. JOHN AVERY (1837–1887) was a master of 15 languages and editor of *American Antiquarian* and *Oriental Journal* (1875–1887). SEWELL LEE AVERY (1874–1960) of Michigan, as president and chairman, transformed U.S. Gypsum Co. from a regional producer of plaster to one of the nation's dominant building-materials suppliers. OSWALD THEODORE AVERY (1877–1955), born in Canada, was a bacteriologist who is credited with discovering the role of deoxyribonucleic acid (DNA) in the transfer of heritable characteristics in bacteria. MILTON AVERY (1885–1965) of New York was a painter best known for landscapes and figures with flat color masses.

Genealogies: *A Family History, Gray—Avery and Related Families* was compiled by Lewis and Ruby Gray and published in Burkburnett, Texas, in 1980. *The Groton Averys, Christopher and James* was compiled by Elroy M. Avery and published in Cleveland, Ohio, in 1893.

AVILA

Ranking: 1011 S.S. Count: 43,237

Origin: Spanish. Derived from the Spanish word "avilar," meaning to watch vigilantly. The name was given those who came from Avila, a place in Spain.

Genealogies: None known.

AVILES

Ranking: 2091 S.S. Count: 21,948

Origin: Spanish. Transformation of Avila.

Genealogies: None known.

AYALA

Ranking: 740 S.S. Count: 57,251

Origin: Spanish. The name was given to those who came from Ayala, a place in Spain.

Genealogies: None known.

AYERS, AYER

Ranking: 787 **S.S. Count:** 53,564

Origin: English. Derived from the Middle English words "eir" and "eyr," both meaning heir. The name was given to those who would inherit money or a title.

Famous **Ayerses:** FRANCIS WAYLAND AYER (1848–1923) of Massachusetts was one of the pioneers of the advertising business, founding N.W. Ayer & Son. HOWARD AYERS (1855–1917) was president of the University of Cincinnati.

Genealogies: *Ancestors of Silas Ayers and Mary Byram Ayers* was compiled by Charles H. Ayers and published in Detroit, Michigan, in 1905. *The Ayers Family: Descendants of William Eayers of Londonderry, New Hampshire* was compiled by Azuba Ruth Ward in Bellevue, Washington, in 1980. *The Story of the Ayers Family: Pioneers in the Middle West* was compiled by Allan Joy Searle and published in Key Biscayne, Florida, in 1973.

AYRES

Ranking: 2673 **S.S. Count:** 17,051

Origin: English. Transformation of Ayers.

Famous **Ayreses:** ANNE AYRES (1816–1896), born in England, emigrated to the United States and was consecrated Sister Anne, the first woman in the country to be a Protestant sister. BROWN AYRES (1856–1919) was president of the University of Tennessee (1904–1919).

Genealogies: *Ayres Genealogy: Some of the Descendants of Capt. John Ayres of Brookefield, Massachusetts* was compiled by Thomas D. Ayres in Simsbury, Connecticut, in 1985. *Genealogy of the Ayres Family of Fairfield County, Connecticut* was compiled by James Noyes States and published in New Haven, Connecticut, in 1916.

BABB

Ranking: 2480   S.S. Count: 18,261

Origin: English. Derived from the Old English first name Babba. The name was given to those who came from places that had the component "Bab" in their names.

Genealogies: None known

BABCOCK   (S.S. Abbreviation: Babcoc)

Ranking: 1384   S.S. Count: 31,968

Origin: English. Transformation of Babb.

Famous **Babcocks:** GEORGE HERMAN BABCOCK (1832–1893) of New York invented two printing presses and, with Stephen Wilcox, formed the company now known as Babcock and Wilcox. ORVILLE BABCOCK (1835–1884) of Vermont, a Union Army officer during the Civil War, served as aide-de-camp to General U.S. Grant, then as private secretary to President Grant. Grant's deposition regarding Babcock's character led to Babcock's acquittal on charges of Whiskey Ring participation. STEPHEN BABCOCK (1843–1931) of New York, an agricultural chemist, devised the Babcock test for determining the amount of fat in milk. HAROLD BABCOCK (1882–1968) of Wisconsin, an astronomer, invented the solar magnetograph. F. HUNTINGTON BABCOCK (1886–1973) of Rhode Island was president of J. H. Lane and Co. (1929–62), a textiles firm. He helped found Morningside Heights Inc., a nonprofit firm that built housing in New York City. HOWARD E. BABCOCK (1889–1950) of New York helped found the New York Farm Bureau Federation and advanced the farm cooperative system.

Genealogies: *Record of the Ancestors and Descendants of Nathan Burch (1781–1858) and Damaris Babcock (1783–1869) of Brookfield, Madison County, New York* was compiled by Harold John Witter and published in Skaneateles, New York, in 1978. *Slade-Babcock Genealogy* was compiled by Carl Boyer in Newhall, California, in 1970.

BACA

Ranking: 1681   S.S. Count: 26,618

Origin: Spanish. Derived from the Latin word "vacca," meaning cow. The name was given to those who tended cattle and to those who had gentle dispositions.

Genealogies: None known.

BACH

Ranking: 2993   S.S. Count: 15,176

Origin: Catalan, Czech, English, German, Jewish, Polish. Catalan: derived from the Catalan word "obac," meaning dark. Czech, Polish: derived from the name Sebastian. English, German: derived from the Middle High German and the Middle English words "bach" and "bache," both meaning

stream. German: the name was given to those who worked as bakers. Jewish: derived from the first letters of the Hebrew phrase "ben chayim," meaning son of life.

Genealogies: None known.

BACHMAN, BACHMANN   (S.S. Abbreviation: Bachma)

Ranking: 1935   S.S. Count: 23,272

Origin: German. Transformation of the German definition of Bach.

Famous **Bearers:** JOHN BACHMAN (1790–1874) of New York was a Lutheran minister and naturalist. He wrote liberal theological works and collaborated with John James Audubon, the naturalist and painter, on the three volumes of *The Viviparous Quadrupeds of North America.* GEORGE W. BACHMANN JR. (1914–1959) of New York, an anesthesiologist, was an anesthetist for army evacuation units in China during World War II and served as a medical liaison with the Chinese on the front.

Genealogies: *Our Heritage, a History of the Bachmans of Lititz, Pennsylvania* was compiled by Pauline Bachman Mann and published in Des Moines, Iowa, in 1981.

BACK

Ranking: 4306   S.S. Count: 10,425

Origin: English. Derived from the Old English word "baec," meaning back. The name was given to those with hunched or twisted backs.

Genealogies: None known.

BACKUS

Ranking: 4608   S.S. Count: 9698

Origin: English. Derived from the Old English word "bāechūs," meaning bakehouse. The name was given to those who worked in such places.

Famous **Backuses:** ISAAC BACKUS (1724–1806) of Connecticut was a clergyman and author of *A History of New England, With Particular Reference to the Denomination of Christians Called Baptists* (1777–1796). TRUMAN J. BACKUS (1842–1908) of New York was president of Packer Collegiate Institute in Brooklyn, New York (1883–1908). JIM BACKUS (1913–1989) of Ohio was an actor and writer successful on radio, stage, screen, and television. He was widely known as one of the stranded individuals on the television show "Gilligan's Island" and as the voice of the television cartoon character "Mr. Magoo."

Genealogies: None known.

BACON

Ranking: 1026   S.S. Count: 42,694

Origin: English. 1) derived from the the Middle English

word "bacon" and from the Old French word "bacun," both meaning bacon and/or ham. The name was given to those who made and sold pork. 2) derived from the Germanic first name Bahho, which is derived from the Germanic word "bag," meaning to fight.

Famous **Bacons:** NATHANIEL BACON (1647–1676) was a colonial leader in Virginia. He led attacks on the Pamunkey, Susquhannocks, and Occaneechees Native American tribes. JOHN BACON (1738–1820) was a clergyman and politician who represented Connecticut in Congress (1801– 1803). LEONARD BACON (1802– 1881) of Michigan was a clergyman in Connecticut and author of *Slavery Discussed in Occasional Essays* (1846) and *The Genesis of the New England Churches* (1874). His sister, DELIA SALTER BACON (1811– 1859) of Ohio, was a writer who worked in England on the theory that Shakespearean plays were written by a group headed by FRANCIS BACON (1561–1626), an English philosopher and author. AUGUSTUS O. BACON (1839– 1914) was a U.S. senator from Georgia (1894–1914). HENRY BACON (1866–1924) of Illinois was an architect whose credits include the Lincoln Memorial in Washington, D.C. LEONARD BACON (1887–1954) of New York was a poet whose "Sunderland Capture and Other Poems" won a 1940 Pulitzer Prize. ERNST BACON (1890– 1990) of Illinois, a musician and composer, composed two symphonies, two piano concertos, and four orchestral suites.

Genealogies: *Three Bacon Brothers: Descendants of Theodore S. Back of Allegany County, New York* was compiled by Marian Fox Graves and published in Arkport, New York, in 1981.

BADER
Ranking: 3578 **S.S. Count:** 12,607
Origin: German, Jewish. Derived from the German word "bad," meaning bath. The name was given to those who worked in bathhouses.
Genealogies: *The Bader-Bauder Family of the Mohawk Valley* was compiled by Peg Bauder Nielsen and published in Lombard, Illinois, in 1976.

BADGER
Ranking: 3897 **S.S. Count:** 11,576
Origin: English. 1) derived from the Middle English word "bagge," meaning bag. The name was given to those who made purses and sacks. 2) same derivation as in 1. The name was given to those who came from Badger, a place in Shropshire, England.
Famous Badgers: GEORGE EDMUND BADGER (1795–1866) was a U.S. senator from North Carolina (1846–1855) and a prominent lawyer respected for arguing cases before the U.S. Supreme Court.

Genealogies: *Badger and Tankard Families of the Eastern Shore of Virginia* was compiled by Austin Kilham and Fannie Clark and published in Charlottesville, Virginia, in 1973. *The Daniel Gill Family of Rhode Island: with Allied Families* (including Badger) was compiled by Lorraine Gill Croswell and published in Washougal, Washington, in 1989.

BAER
Ranking: 1875 **S.S. Count:** 24,137
Origin: German. Cognate to Bear.
Famous Baers: GEORGE FREDERICK BAER (1842–1914) of Pennsylvania was a lawyer and industrialist active against the United Mine Workers of America during the strike of 1902. WILLIAM JACOB BAER (1860–1941) of Ohio was a painter famous for portraits and genre pictures. ARTHUR (BUGS) BAER (1886–1969) of Pennsylvania was a journalist well known as a sports columnist through Hearst King Features. MAXIMILIAN ADELBERT BAER (1909– 1959) of Nebraska was a boxer who won 65 of 79 fights during his career and was world heavyweight champion (1934–1935).

Genealogies: *The Genealogy of Henry Baer of Leacock, Pennsylvania* was compiled by Willis Nissley Baer and published in Allentown, Pennsylvania, in 1955.

BAEZ
Ranking: 2136 **S.S. Count:** 21,434
Origin: Spanish. 1) the name was given to those with a dark complexion. 2) derived from the first name Pelayo.
Famous Baezes: JOAN BAEZ (1941–) was a folk singer and icon of the pop counterculture during the 1960s.
Genealogies: None known.

BAGETT
Ranking: 2528 **S.S. Count:** 17,947
Origin: English. Transformation of Bacon.
Genealogies: None known.

BAGLEY
Ranking: 1891 **S.S. Count:** 23,910
Origin: English. Derived from the Old English first name Bacga, signifying a "bag-shaped" (H&H) beast, and the Old English word "lēah," meaning wood. The name was given to those who came from Bagley, the name of several places in England.
Famous Bagleys: WILLIAM CHANDLER BAGLEY (1874–1946) of Michigan was an educator and president of the American Council of Education (1931– 1937). He also wrote *The Educative Process* (1905), *Craftsmanship in Teaching* (1911), *School Discipline* (1915), and other books.
Genealogies: *The Ancestry of Marie Louise Harrington and Her Bagley Descendants* was compiled by David Harrington Bagley and published in Vienna, Virginia, in 1983.

BAGWELL (S.S. Abbreviation: Bagwel)

Ranking: 3171 S.S. Count: 14,324

Origin: English. Derived from the first name Bagga and the Old English word "well(a)," meaning spring.

Genealogies: *Bagwell: The Family History Book* was compiled by Pamela Murrell Bagwell and published in Duluth, Georgia, in 1976.

BAHR

Ranking: 4509 S.S. Count: 9927

Origin: German. Cognate to Bear.

Famous **Bahrs**: CARL WILLIAM BAHR (1900–1963) of South Dakota was an influential lumber executive with the National Lumber Manufacturers Association and president of the California Redwood Association.

Genealogies: None known.

BAILEY

Ranking: 64 S.S. Count: 377,187

Origin: English. 1) derived from the Old English words "bēg" and "lēah," meaning wood and clearing. The name was given to those who came from Bailey, a place in Lancashire, England. 2) derived from the Middle English word "bail(l)i," signifying an official person. 3) derived from the Middle English word "baile," meaning the outside of a castle wall.

Famous **Baileys**: GAMALIEL BAILEY (1807–1850) of New Jersey was editor of the *Cincinnati Philanthropist*, the first antislavery publication in the western United States, and then, as editor of *New Era*, a Washington, D.C., publication sponsored by the American and Foreign Anti-Slavery Society, serialized *Uncle Tom's Cabin*. JAMES ANTHONY BAILEY (1847–1906) of Michigan, whose original name was James McGinniss, started working in a circus as a boy, became a partner in the Cooper & Bailey Circus in 1871, and in 1881 combined that circus with one owned by P. T. Barnum to form what became the Ringling Bros./Barnum & Bailey Circus. SOLON IRVING BAILEY (1854–1931) of New Hampshire, as an astronomer for Harvard University, selected the site and supervised the work performed at Harvard's Arequipa, Peru, observatory from 1893 to 1931. LIBERTY HYDE BAILEY (1858–1954) of Michigan was a botanist, horticulturalist, and one of the world's leading authorities on garden plants. From 1903 to 1913, he was dean of the New York State College of Agriculture at Cornell. FLORENCE AUGUSTA BAILEY (1863–1948) of New York was an ornithologist whose published works included *Birds Through an Opera Glass* (1889) and *Handbook of Birds of the Western United States* (1902). CONSUELA NORTHROP BAILEY (1899–1976) of Vermont was the first woman to be admitted to practice before the U.S. Supreme Court. She was the first woman in Vermont to prosecute a murder case.

Genealogies: *The Bailey Family: History and Genealogy of Descendants of Richard Bailey of Rowley, Massachusetts who came to Michigan by way of Maine, New Hampshire, Vermont and New York: 1635–1990* was compiled by Jeanne Bailey Ransom and published in Ann Arbor, Michigan, in 1991. *Ancestors and Descendants of Augustus Rudophus Bailey and Lucy Hosmer Smith of Elmore, Vermont* was compiled by Mariam Parr and published in Palo Alto, California, in 1982.

BAIN

Ranking: 1899 S.S. Count: 23,854

Origin: English, French, Scottish. English: 1) derived from the Old English word "bān," meaning bone. The name was given to those with bony appearances. 2) derived from the Middle English word "beyn," meaning friendly. English, French: cognate to Bader. Scottish: derived from the Gaelic word "bán," meaning white. The name was given to those with a fair complexion.

Famous **Bains**: GEORGE L.S. BAIN (1836–1891), born in Scotland, as a merchant in Missouri helped to develop exporting of flour from St. Louis to foreign countries.

Genealogies: *The Life and Ancestry (including the Bain family) of John Thistlehwaite Baynes 1833–1891* was compiled by Richard C. Baynes and published in Irvine, California, in 1987.

BAIR

Ranking: 3001 S.S. Count: 15,139

Origin: German. 1) transformation of Bayer. 2) cognate to Bear.

Genealogies: None known.

BAIRD

Ranking: 874 S.S. Count: 49,448

Origin: Scottish. Transformation of Bard.

Famous **Bairds**: SPENCER FULLERTON BAIRD (1823–1887) of Pennsylvania, a zoologist, was assistant secretary, then secretary, of the Smithsonian Institution in Washington, D.C. He served as the first U.S. commissioner of fish and fisheries and was author of *Catalogue of North American Mammals* (1857), *Catalogue of North American Birds* (1858), and other works. HENRY CAREY BAIRD (1825–1912) of Pennsylvania established under his own name the first publishing company in the United States to specialize in technical and industrial topics. CORA EISENBERG BAIRD (1912–1967) of New York was a puppeteer who, with her husband, William Baird, helped revive the puppet theater in the United States. She appeared in television shows such as the "Bil Baird Show" in 1953 and "Art Carney Meets Peter and the Wolf" in 1958. She opened the Bil Baird Theatre in New York City in 1967.

Genealogies: *A Baird Family in America and Allied Lines*

was compiled by Joie Baird and Delila Baird and published in Rotan, Texas, in 1971. *Francis Baird's American Descendants from 1758* was compiled by James T. Baird and published in Baltimore, Maryland, in 1990.

BAKER

Ranking: 39   S.S. Count: 580,667

Origin: English. Derived from the Old English word "baecere," meaning bake. The name was given to those who baked.

Famous **Bakers**: GEORGE FISHER BAKER (1840–1931) of New York, a successful banker in New York City, endowed to Harvard University's graduate school of business administration. GEORGE PIERCE BAKER (1866–1935) of Rhode Island was an educator whose students in playwriting included Eugene O'Neill and Thomas Wolfe. He wrote *Development of Shakespeare as a Dramatist* (1907) and *Dramatic Technique* (1919). RAY STANNARD BAKER (1870–1946) of Michigan was a journalist and author who, along with Lincoln Steffens, Ida M. Tarbell, W. A. White, and others, founded *American Magazine*. His authorized biography of President Woodrow Wilson, the eight-volume *Woodrow Wilson: Life and Letters* (1927–1939), took 15 years to complete and won a Pulitzer Prize. SARA JOSEPHINE BAKER (1873–1945) of New York was a pediatrician who, by organizing the first government-controlled bureau of child hygiene, in New York City, helped establish the lowest infant mortality rate of any large city. She was also an author; her books include *Healthy Babies* (1920) and *Child Hygiene* (1925). GEORGE BAKER (1877–1965) of Georgia, a religious leader in Georgia and New York, was known as Father Divine. JOHN F. BAKER (1886–1963) of Maryland was a baseball player whose nickname was "Home Run Baker." He played with the Philadelphia Athletics in four World Series, then later with the New York Yankees. MILTON G. BAKER (1896–1976) of Pennsylvania founded the Valley Forge Military Academy in 1928 and served as its president and superintendent. JOSEPHINE BAKER (1906–1975) of Missouri, who changed her name from Freda Josephine McDonald, achieved fame as a jazz singer and dancer who wore exotic costumes. DOROTHY DODDS BAKER (1907–1968) of Montana was a novelist whose books include *Young Man and a Horn* (1938), which was made into a motion picture in 1950. BRUCE ALEXANDER BAKER (1913–1976) of Illinois, an advertising executive, devised a promotion involving the giveaway of 21 million deeds to square-inch plots of land in Alaska in 1955 to promote the radio program "Sgt. Preston of the Yukon." GEORGE BAKER (1915–1975) of Massachusetts was a cartoonist who, while working for *Yank* magazine during World War II, developed "Sad Sack" as a character depicting an enlisted man. HOWARD H. BAKER JR. (1925–) was a U.S. senator from Tennessee (1966–1985). He was considered a moderate Republican, and he served as senate majority leader from 1981 to 1985.

Genealogies: *A Baker Family Genealogy: Pioneers of North Carolina, Kentucky, Indiana, Missouri and Iowa* was compiled by Ralph D. Shipp and published in Boulder, Colorado, in 1980. *The Baker Family of Westbrookville, New York* was compiled by Howard E. Case and published in 1981.

BALDERSTON   (S.S. Abbreviation: Balder)

Ranking: 3180   S.S. Count: 14,279

Origin: English. Derived from the Old English words "beald" and "here," meaning brave and army. The name came from Balderstone or Balderstonee, the names of places in Lancashire, England.

Famous **Balderstons**: JOHN LLOYD BALDERSTON (1889–1954) of Pennsylvania was a playwright whose credits include *Dracula* (1927) and *Frankenstein* (1931).

Genealogies: *The Balderston Family, Colora Branch* was published in Colora, Maryland, in 1959. *Balderston Family History* was compiled by Marion Balderston and published in 1973.

BALDRIDGE   (S.S. Abbreviation: Baldri)

Ranking: 4853   S.S. Count: 9219

Origin: English. The name was given to those who came from mountains where little or no vegetation grew.

Genealogies: *Our Baldridge Forebears and Some of Their Collateral Lines* was compiled by Chester C. Kennedy and published in Coway, Arkansas, in 1981.

BALDWIN   (S.S. Abbreviation: Baldwi)

Ranking: 340   S.S. Count: 111,829

Origin: English. Derived from the Germanic words "bald" and "wine," meaning bold and friend.

Famous **Baldwins**: LOAMMI BALDWIN (1745–1807) of Massachusetts was a civil engineer for the construction of the Middlesex Canal and the creator of the Baldwin apple. His son, also LOAMMI BALDWIN (1780–1838), was a civil engineer who worked on the Union Canal in Pennsylvania and designed the Bunker Hill Monument in Boston. ABRAHAM BALDWIN (1754–1807) of Connecticut, one of the founders of the University of Georgia, was a U.S. representative and later a U.S. senator from Georgia. HENRY BALDWIN (1780–1844) of Connecticut represented a Pennsylvania district in the U.S. House of Representatives and later was an associate justice of the U.S. Supreme Court. FRANK STEPHEN BALDWIN (1838–1925) of Connecticut invented a calculator called the arithmometer in 1875 and the Baldwin calculator in 1902. JAMES MARK BALDWIN (1861–1934) of South Carolina was a psychologist who specialized in child and social psychology and author of

Handbook of Psychology (1889–1891) and *Mental Development in the Child and in the Race* (1895), among other titles. EDWARD R. BALDWIN (1864–1947) of Connecticut, a physician, researched and published more than 100 papers on tuberculosis. He also wrote the book *Tuberculosis: Bacteriology, Pathology and Laboratory Diagnosis* (1927). ROGER NASH BALDWIN (1884–1981) of Massachusetts was founder and director (1920–1950) of the American Civil Liberties Union. JAMES ARTHUR BALDWIN (1924–1987) was an author and civil rights advocate. His first novel, *Go Tell It on the Mountain*, is semiautobiographical and discusses his impoverished youth in the Harlem neighborhood of New York. He became a permanent resident of France because of what he considered the chronic state of racism in the United States.

Genealogies: *The Baldwins: From Virginia Westward* was compiled by Frank C. Baldwin and published in Oak Park, Illinois, in 1985. *The Descendants of Joseph Baldwin* was compiled by Donald J. Sublette and published in Kirksville, Missouri, in 1980.

BALES

Ranking: 2497 **S.S. Count:** 18,151
Origin: English. Transformation of Bailey.
Genealogies: *Passing the Words Along: A Continuing History of the Alonzo L. Bales Family* was compiled by Miriam Halbert Bales and published in Muncie, Indiana, in 1990.

BALL

Ranking: 335 **S.S. Count:** 112,889
Origin: English. Derived from the Middle English word "bal(l)e" and the Old Norse word "böller," both meaning ball. The name was given to those who were stout and plump.
Famous **Balls:** THOMAS BALL (1819–1911) of Massachusetts was a sculptor whose works include the equestrian George Washington statue in Boston's Public Garden and the Daniel Webster statue in New York City's Central Park. ALBERT BALL (1835–1927) of Massachusetts, an engineer, designed the diamond-core drill and other mining tools. FRANK C. BALL (1857–1943) of Ohio was president of Ball Brothers Co., the firm that produced "Ball jars" after the patent on "Mason jars" expired. LUCILLE BALL (1911–1989) of New York was one of the most successful actors of her day. She appeared in numerous movies but perhaps was best known for the television series "I Love Lucy," which debuted in 1951 and was a comedy version of her marriage to Desi Arnaz, who also starred in the show. Later, she starred in the television series "The Lucy Show."

Genealogies: *Ball Cousins: Descendants of John and Sarah Ball and of William and Elizabeth Richards of Colonial Philadelphia County, Pennsylvania* was compiled by Margaret B. Kinsey and published in Lamesa, Texas, in 1981. *Ball Family Chart* was compiled by Charles M. Noble and published in Ponte Vedra Beach, Florida, in 1977.

BALLANTINE, BALLANTYNE (S.S. Abbreviation: Ballan)

Ranking: 4475 **S.S. Count:** 10,005
Origin: Scottish. The name was given to those who came from Belenden, Scotland.
Famous **Ballantines:** THOMAS A. BALLANTINE (1902–1975) of Kentucky was a lawyer and businessman who helped found the Kentucky Independent College Foundation.
Genealogies: None known.

BALLARD (S.S. Abbreviation: Ballar)

Ranking: 480 **S.S. Count:** 84,398
Origin: English. Transformation of Ball.
Famous **Ballards:** BLAND WILLIAMS BALLARD (1759–1853) of Virginia was a frontiersman in Kentucky, active in the Indian wars, and a five-term Kentucky legislator.
Genealogies: *The Ballard History from 1420 to 1903* was compiled by the Ballard Family Association and published in Connecticut in 1903. *They Came to Texas: The Family History and Genealogy of Cecil Raymond Ballard and Maurice (Bradford) Ballard, 1734–1975* was compiled by C. R. Ballard and published in Seguin, Texas, in 1980.

BALLENDINE, BALLENTINE (S.S. Abbreviation: Ballen)

Ranking: 3157 **S.S. Count:** 14,384
Origin: Ballendine—Irish, Scottish; Ballentine—Scottish. Transformations of and cognates to Ballantine.
Genealogies: None known.

BALLEW

Ranking: 4090 **S.S. Count:** 11,051.
Origin: French. Derived from the Old French word "baller," meaning to move. The name was most likely given to those who were considered good dancers.
Genealogies: *William Ballew; His Ancestors and Descendants* was compiled by Violet Ann Ballew Walton and published in Utah in 1972.

BALLINTYNE

Ranking: 3225 **S.S. Count:** 14,051
Origin: Scottish. Transformation of Ballantine.
Genealogies: None known.

BANDY

Ranking: 3806 **S.S. Count:** 11,852
Origin: Uncertain etymology; perhaps German. The

name was possibly given to those who worked as hoop makers.

Genealogies: None known.

BANKS

Ranking: 263   S.S. Count: 139,039

Origin: English, Irish, Scottish. English, Scottish: derived from the Middle English word "bank(e)" and the Old Norse word "bakke," both meaning bank. The name was given to those who lived on or near the edge of a river. Irish: derived from the name Bruchán, which was given to those with large, protruding stomachs.

Famous **Bankses:** NATHANIEL PRENTICE BANKS (1816–1894) was Speaker of the U.S. House of Representatives and governor of Massachusetts. President Abraham Lincoln made him a major general when the Civil War broke out. He was badly defeated by Stonewall Jackson in the Shenandoah Valley but led the capture of Port Hudson, the last Confederate fortress on the Mississippi River.

Genealogies: *The Banks Family of Maine* was compiled by Charles Edward Banks and published in Boston, Massachusetts, in 1890. *Daniel Black Orrell and His Descendants with the Banks Family* was compiled by Robert Stanley Orrell and published in South Daytona, Florida, in 1991. *The Genealogical Record of the Banks Family of Elbert County, Georgia* was compiled by Elbert Augustin Banks and was reprinted in Danielsville, Georgia, in 1972.

BANKSTON

Ranking: 4668   S.S. Count: 9582

Origin: Uncertain etymology; perhaps English or Scottish. Most likely a transformation of Banks combined with the Old English word "tūn," meaning settlement.

Genealogies: None known.

BANNER (ALSO BANNERMAN)

Ranking: 4783   S.S. Count: 9363

Origin: Scottish. Derived from the Anglo-Norman-French word "banere," meaning flag or banner. The name was given to those who were standard bearers.

Famous **Banners:** BOB BANNER (1921–) is a television producer and director from Ennis, Texas. His television series include "Don Ho" and "Solid Gold."

Genealogies: None known.

BANNISTER   (S.S. Abbreviation: Bannis)

Ranking: 3896   S.S. Count: 11,579

Origin: English. Derived from the Anglo-Norman-French word "banastre," meaning basket. The name was given to those who made baskets.

Genealogies: None known.

BAPTIST, BAPTISTE, BAPTISTA   (S.S. Abbreviation: Baptis)

Ranking: 3397   S.S. Count: 13,321

Origin: Baptist—English; Baptiste—French; Baptista—Portuguese, Spanish. Derived from the Greek word "batein," meaning to wash.

Genealogies: None known.

BARAJAS   (S.S. Abbreviation: Baraja)

Ranking: 2848   S.S. Count: 16,024

Origin: Spanish. Possibly derived from the Late Latin word "vara," meaning fence. The name was given to those who came from Barajas, the name of several places in Spain.

Genealogies: None known.

BARBARA, BARBARIN, BARBARY, BARBARELLI, BARBARINO, BARBARC(C)I, BARBARULO   (S.S. Abbreviation: Barbar)

Ranking: 3966   S.S. Count: 11,410

Origin: Barbara, Barbarin, Barbary—English; Barbarelli, Barbarino, Barbarc(c)i, Barbarulo—Italian. Derived from the Latin word "barbarus" and the Greek word "barbaros," both meaning foreign(er).

Genealogies: None known.

BARBEE

Ranking: 2882   S.S. Count: 15,802

Origin: English, French. 1) derived from the place name Barby, which means "homestead in the hills" (ES) and is a place in Northamptonshire, England. 2) derived from the Late Latin word "barbōsa," meaning bearded. The name was given to those who wore beards.

Genealogies: *A Study of the Barbee Families of Chatham, Orange, and Wake Counties in North Carolina* was compiled by Ruth Shields and published in Boulder, Colorado, in 1971.

BARBER (ALSO BARBERO)

Ranking: 309   S.S. Count: 119,254

Origin: English, Jewish, Spanish. English, Spanish: derived from the Anglo-Norman-French word "barber," which signified those who cut hair and beards, practiced dentistry and performed surgery. Jewish: uncertain etymology.

Famous **Barbers:** DONN BARBER (1871–1925) of Washington, D.C., was an architect whose works include the U.S. Justice Department building in Washington and the Connecticut Supreme Court building in Hartford. SAMUEL BARBER (1910–1981) of Pennsylvania was a composer who is considered one of the best representatives of the American lyric and romantic styles. He wrote several symphonies and concertos.

Genealogies: *Ancestors and Descendants of Maj. Hezekiah Barber* was compiled by Irene Marshall Barber and published in Tucson, Arizona, in 1975. *Barber "Grandparents": 125 Kings, 143 Generations* was compiled by Bernard and Gertrude Barber Bernard and published in McKinney, Texas, in 1978.

BARBIE (ALSO BARBIER, BARBIERI)
Ranking: 4958 **S.S. Count:** 9033
Origin: French, Italian. Cognate to the English and Spanish definition of barber.
Genealogies: None known.

BARBOSA
Ranking: 3890 **S.S. Count:** 11,592
Origin: Portuguese. Derived from the Late Latin word "barbōsa," meaning bearded. The name was given to those who lived near or on an area overgrown with vegetation.
Genealogies: None known.

BARBOUR (S.S. Abbreviation: Barbou).
Ranking: 2178 **S.S. Count:** 21,057.
Origin: Irish, Scottish. Cognate to the English definition of barber.

Famous **Barbours:** JAMES BARBOUR (1775–1842) of Barboursville, Virginia, was governor of Virginia, U.S. senator, U.S. secretary of war, and U.S. minister to Great Britain. His brother, PHILIP PENDELTON BARBOUR (1783–1841), also from Barboursville, was a justice of the U.S. Supreme Court who was known for his advocacy of states' rights. Before being appointed to the high court, he had served as Speaker of the U.S. House of Representatives. He lost his seat to Henry Clay in 1823. CLARENCE A. BARBOUR (1867–1937) of Connecticut was president of Brown University from 1929 to 1937. HENRY CLAY BARBOUR (1886–1943) of Connecticut was a pharmacologist and author of the textbook *Experimental Pharmacology and Toxicology* (1932).
Genealogies: None known.

BARCLAY (S.S. Abbreviation: Barcla)
Ranking: 2182 **S.S. Count:** 16,199
Origin: English, Scottish. Derived from the Old English words "be(o)rc" and "lēah," meaning birch and wood. The name was given to those who came from Berkeley and Berkely, the name of several places in England.
Genealogies: None known.

BARFIELD (S.S. Abbreviation: Barfie)
Ranking: 2619 **S.S. Count:** 17,360
Origin: English. Derived from the Old English words "byrde" and "feld," meaning riverbank and farmed land. The

name was given to those who came from Bardfield, a place in Essex, England.
Genealogies: *The Family Directory* was compiled by Doris Barfield Sanders and was published in Burnet, Texas, in 1980.

BARGER
Ranking: 2114 **S.S. Count:** 21,693
Origin: Dutch, English, German. Dutch, German: cognate to Berger. English, German: the name was given to those who worked as sailors.
Genealogies: None known.

BARKER
Ranking: 303 **S.S. Count:** 120,259
Origin: English. 1) derived from the Middle English word "bark(en)," meaning to tan in the Middle Ages. The process of tanning leather involved using tree bark. The name was given to those who worked as tanners. 2) derived from the Anglo-Norman-French word "bercher," meaning ram. The name was given to those who tended sheep.

Famous **Barkers:** JAMES N. BARKER (1784–1858) of Pennsylvania was a dramatist whose *Indian Princess* (1858) was the first acted play by an American on an Indian theme. BENJAMIN FORDYCE BARKER (1818–1891) of Maine was a physician who is credited with introducing the use of the hypodermic syringe into U.S. medicine. MARY CORNELIA BARKER (1879–1963) of Georgia was a teacher in the Atlanta public schools for 40 years. She was an organizer of the Atlanta Public School Teachers Association and then a president of the American Federation of Teachers. ROBERT WILLIAM (BOB) BARKER (1923–) is a television personality from Darrington, Washington. He was master of ceremonies for the game show "Truth or Consequences" from 1957 to 1975 and has been host of "The Price Is Right" since 1972. He also has hosted several beauty pageants.
Genealogies: *Barker-Harland: A Genealogical Study* was compiled by Marjorie Harland Barker Diedrich and published in Siesta Key, Florida, in 1989. *Odyssey of the Barkers and the Russells* was compiled by Don W. Barker and published in Baltimore, Maryland, in 1984. *West, Barker, Hodges: New York to Wisconsin, 1836–1846* was compiled by Beatrice West Seitz and published in Janesville, Wisconsin, in 1971.

BARKLEY (S.S. Abbreviation: Barkle)
Ranking: 2590 **S.S. Count:** 17,566
Origin: Irish. Cognate to Barclay.
Famous **Barkleys:** ALBEN WILLIAM BARKLEY (1877–1956) of Kentucky was a U.S representative, a U.S. senator, and then a vice president of the United States (1949–1953).
Genealogies: None known.

BARKSDALE, BARKSDALLE (S.S. Abbreviation: Barksda)

Ranking: 3268   S.S. Count: 13,896

Origin: English. Derived from the Old English words "bo(o)rc" and "dæl," meaning birch and valley. The names were given to those who lived in a valley of birches.

Genealogies: *Genealogy of Part of the Barksdale Family of America* was compiled by Sarah Donelson Hubert and published in Atlanta, Georgia, in 1895.

BARLOW

Ranking: 1053   S.S. Count: 41,743

Origin: English. Derived from the Old English words "bere" and "hlāw," meaning barley and hill. The name was given to those who came from Barlow, the name of several places in England.

Famous **Barlows:** JOEL BARLOW (1754–1812) was a poet and author from Connecticut who served for three years as chaplain in the Revolutionary Army. He wrote the mock-heroic poem "The Hasty Pudding" and the nine-volume poetic paean "Vision of Columbus." JOHN W. BARLOW (1838–1914) of New York was an army engineer who led a detachment on the first government exploration of the Yellowstone region in 1871.

Genealogies: *Bunches of Barlows: The Descendants of John Barlow of Wilkes County, North Carolina* was compiled by Elizabeth H. Michaels and published in Patterson, North Carolina, in 1991. *Haley, Marshal, Betchell, Barlow Genealogy* was compiled by Elaine Vertz Smithers and published in Waukesha, Wisconsin, in 1986.

BARNARD

Ranking: 1583   S.S. Count: 28,258

Origin: English, French. Transformation of and cognate to Bernard.

Famous **Barnards:** FREDERICK AUGUSTUS PORTER BARNARD (1809–1889) of Massachusetts was president of the University of Mississippi (1856–1858) and president of Columbia University (1864–1889), at which he espoused opening Columbia to women. Barnard College at Columbia is named in his honor. HENRY BARNARD (1811–1900) of Connecticut was chancellor of the University of Wisconsin (1858–1860), president of St. John's College (1866–1867), and the first U.S. commissioner of education (1867–1870). EDWARD E. BARNARD (1857–1923) of Tennessee, an astronomer, discovered the fifth satellite of Jupiter and Barnard's star and advanced the science of celestial photography. GEORGE G. BARNARD (1863–1938) of Pennsylvania was a sculptor whose works included two groups of 31 statues for the Pennsylvania capitol. CHESTER I. BARNARD (1886–1961) of Massachusetts, a pioneer in studying business organization as a sociological entity, held the presi-

dent's title at New Jersey Bell Telephone Co., United Services Organization, and the Rockefeller Foundation. He was chairman of the National Science Foundation and author of *Functions of the Executive* (1938) and *Organization and Management* (1948). DANIEL P. BARNARD IV (1898–1973) of Delaware, an engineer, wrote or co-wrote 60 scientific papers on oils, lubricants, and fuels.

Genealogies: None known.

BARNES

Ranking: 95   S.S. Count: 296,538

Origin: English, Irish, Jewish. English: 1) The name was given to those who either worked for or were sons of the upper classes. 2) derived from the Old English word "bern," meaning barn. The name was given to those who lived near or worked in a barn. Irish: derived from the Gaelic name Ó Beáráin, meaning "descendant of Beárán" (H&H), meaning spear. Jewish: derived from the Yiddish word "parnes," meaning president of a Jewish community. The name was given to those who worked as such.

Famous **Barneses:** JOSEPH K. BARNES (1817–1883) of Pennsylvania was a military surgeon in three wars and the attending physician for Presidents Abraham Lincoln and James A. Garfield on their deathbeds. CHARLES REID BARNES (1858–1910) of Indiana, a botanist, wrote textbooks on experimental and morphological methods of botany. DJUNA BARNES (1892–1982) of New York was a writer best known for her avant-garde novel *Nightwood* (1936).

Genealogies: *Barnes and Related Families, Past and Present* was compiled by Raymond Curtis Barnes and published in San Antonio, Texas, in 1966. *Barnes Families of Manitowoc, Wisconsin, 1858–1909* was compiled by Marjorie Barnes Thompson and published in Albuquerque, New Mexico, in 1978. *Barnes: The Westward Migration of One Line of the Descendants of Thomas Barnes of Hartford and Farmington, Connecticut* was compiled by Clair Elmer Barnes and published in Long Beach, California, in 1966.

BARNET (ALSO BARNETT)

Ranking: 255   S.S. Count: 142,534

Origin: English. Derived from the Old English word "baeret," meaning an area that was cleared by burning. The name was given to those who came from Barnet, the name of many places in England.

Famous **Barnets:** WILL BARNET (1911–) is an artist from Beverly, Massachusetts. His work is in the collections of the Whitney Museum of American Art, the Guggenheim Museum, and the Boston Museum of Fine Arts.

Genealogies: None known.

BARNEY

Ranking: 2223   S.S. Count: 20,643

Origin: Irish. *Derived from the first name Barney, a diminutive of Barnabas, meaning "son of prophecy or consolation." (ES)*

Famous **Barneys:** JOSHUA BARNEY (1759–1818) of Maryland, a naval officer during the American Revolution, was captured three times by the British; then he captured the British frigate General Monk. He later served with the French navy, then fought as a privateer in the War of 1812, during which he was captured again. NORA STANTON BLATCH BARNEY (1883–1971), born in England, was the first woman to earn a civil engineering degree at Cornell University. She also was the first woman to be a member of the American Society of Civil Engineers.

Genealogies: *Descendants of Jacob Barney: Salem, Massachusetts, 1634* was compiled by Mary E. Wesbrook and published in East Barnard, Vermont, in 1982. *Genealogy of the Barney Family in America* was compiled by Eugene Dimon Preston and reprinted in Springfield, Virginia, in 1991.

BARNHAM   (S.S. Abbreviation: Barnha)
Ranking: 1379. S.S. Count: 32,061.

Origin: English. *Derived from the Old English words "beorna" and "hām," meaning warrior and homestead. The name was given to those who came from Barham, the name of several places in England.*

Genealogies: None known.

BARNHILL   (S.S. Abbreviation: Barnhi)
Ranking: 3517 S.S. Count: 12,828

Origin: Derived from the first name Beorn and the Old English word "hyll," meaning hill. The name was given to those who came from Barnhill, a place in Yorkshire, England.

Genealogies: *Crowe Family (including Barnhill line) History 1700–1972* was published in New York in 1972.

BARON
Ranking: 2162 S.S. Count: 21,241

Origin: English, French, Irish, Jewish. English, French: derived from the Middle English and Old French words "baron" and "barun," both meaning baron. The name was most likely given to those who worked for barons. Irish: derived from the Gaelic name Ó Bearáin, meaning "descendant of Bearán," (H&H), which means spear. Jewish: uncertain etymology. Possibly derived from the Hebrew phrases meaning "bar-Aharon" and "bar-on," meaning son of Aaron and son of strength.

Genealogies: *David and Deborah Barronett: Their Ancestors and Descendants (including the Baron Family)* was compiled by Eva Laughlin LeBlanc and published in Decorah, Iowa, in 1982.

BARONE
Ranking: 2698 S.S. Count: 16,847
Origin: Italian. Cognate to Baron.
Genealogies: None known.

BARR
Ranking: 656 S.S. Count: 63,796

Origin: English, Scottish, Irish. English: 1) derived from the Old French word "barre," meaning an obstruction. The name was given to the makers of such bars and to those who lived near an obstruction. 2) same derivation as 1. The name was given to those who came from Barr, the name of several places in England. Irish: transformation of Barry. Irish, Scottish: derived from the Gaelic word "barr," meaning hill. The name was given to those who came from places in Scotland that have the component "barr" in their names.

Famous **Barrs:** AMELIA E. HUDDLESTON BARR (1831–1919), who was born in England and moved to the United States in 1853, was a novelist whose books included *Remember the Alamo* (1888). STRINGFELLOW BARR (1897–1982) of Virginia was president of St. John's College and later president of the Foundation for World Government. JAMES W. BARR JR. (1920–1975) worked his way up from sales representative to president of Pneumafil Corp., a company that produces air filtration and dust control systems for textile mills.

Genealogies: *The Family of Adam and Mary Claycomb/Barr* was compiled by Stephan A. Barr and published in Louisville, Kentucky, in 1977. *The Family of Matthew Alexander Barr and wife Nancy Turrentine Barr* was compiled by Alma Fulton Kellum and published in Bogalusa, Louisiana, in 1969. *John Kendig Barr: His Ancestors and His Descendants* was compiled by Mary Alice Burchfield and published in Bayard, Nebraska, in 1984.

BARRERA   (S.S. Abbreviation: Barrer)
Ranking: 1491 S.S. Count: 29,785

Origin: Spanish. 1) derived from the Spanish word "barro," meaning clay or mud. The name was given to those who lived near a clay pit or to those who were the wives of potters. 2) derived from the the Spanish word "barrera," meaning barrier. The name was given to those who lived near an obstruction.

Genealogies: None known.

BARRETT   (S.S. Abbreviation: Barret)
Ranking: 238 S.S. Count: 149,372

Origin: English. 1) transformation of Bernard. 2) derived from the Middle English word "bar(r)et(t)e," meaning cheating, strife, or trouble. The name was given to those considered difficult or dishonest. 3) derived from the Old French word "barette," meaning cap. The name was given to those who made hats.

Famous **Barretts:** LAWRENCE BARRETT (1838–1891) of New Jersey was an actor well known for Shakespearean roles. CHARLES S. BARRETT (1866–1935) of Georgia was the leading organizer of the National Farmers Union in 1906. JOHN BARRETT (1866–1938) of Vermont, after serving as diplomat to Siam, Argentina, Panama, and Colombia, was director of the Pan American Union. KATE HARWOOD WALLER BARRETT (1857–1925) of Virginia was a physician who led the rescue-home movement for unwed mothers. She served as the president of the Florence Crittenton Mission, which operated 50 homes for unwed mothers. JANIE PORTER BARRETT (1865–1948) of Georgia was a teacher and social worker who was the prime force in organizing the Virginia State Federation of Colored Women's Clubs in 1908. She helped found the Virginia Industrial School for Colored Girls in 1915.

Genealogies: *John Clinton Barrett, Tennessee Settler in the Ozarks: The Life and Times of John C. Barrett, his Family and Descendants* was compiled by Ron Pyron and published in Greeneville, Tennessee, in 1980.

BARRIE
Ranking: 2486   S.S. Count: 18,238
Origin: Scottish. Cognate to Barry.
Genealogies: None known.

BARRINGER, BARRINGTON   (S.S. Abbreviation: Barrin)
Ranking: 2751   S.S. Count: 16,569
Origin: Barringer—English, German; Barrington—English, Irish. Barringer: the name was given to those who were descendants of Beringar, a name meaning bear and spear. Barrington—English: derived from the Old English words "bern" and "tūn," meaning barn and settlement. The name was given to those who came from Barrington, the name of several places in England. Irish: derived from the Gaelic name Ó Beáráin, meaning descendant of "Beárán" (H&H), which means spear.

Genealogies: *The Forebearers and Descendants of Henry and Abigail Barringer* was compiled by Ross Milo Curry and published in Wisconsin Dells, Wisconsin, in 1978. *John Paul Barringer, 1721–1807 of Mecklenburg and Cabarrus, North Carolina* was compiled by Sheridan Reid Barringer and published in Newport News, Virginia, in 1990.

BARRIO (ALSO BARRIOS)
Ranking: 2944   S.S. Count: 15,465
Origin: Spanish. Derived from the Arabic word "barr," meaning suburb, and the Spanish word "barro," meaning

spot. The name was given to those who lived on a town's outskirts.

Genealogies: None known.

BARRON
Ranking: 819   S.S. Count: 51,615
Origin: English, French. Transformation of Baron.

Famous **Barrons:** JAMES BARRON (1768–1851) was captain of the *Chesapeake* when the ship was captured by the British *Leopard* in 1807. CLARENCE WALKER BARRON (1855–1928) of Michigan, financial publisher and editor, founded *Barron's Financial Weekly*. JENNIE LOITMAN BARRON (1891–1969) of Massachusetts was a judge, lawyer, and suffragist. She was the first woman in Massachusetts to be a full-time judge; her career on the bench lasted 33 years. RALPH M. BARRON (1892–1964) of Texas was president of Midland National Bank when it grew from $400,000 in deposits in 1938 to $5.6 million in deposits in 1958.

Genealogies: None known.

BARROW (ALSO BARROWS)
Ranking: 1260   S.S. Count: 34,949
Origin: English. Derived from the Old English word "bearo," meaning grove. The name was given to those who lived near a grove or in Barrow, the name of several places in England.

Famous **Bearers:** SAMUEL J. BARROWS (1845–1909) of New York spurred the passage of New York's first probation law and influenced the development of federal parole law. JOHN HENRY BARROWS (1847–1902) of Michigan was president of Oberlin College (1898–1902). LEONIDAS T. BARROW (1895–1978) of Texas was chief geologist, then vice president, then chairman of Humble Oil & Refinery Co.

Genealogies: *The Barrow Family of Virginia* was compiled by Mae Belle Barrow North and published in Summerfield, North Carolina, in 1972. *Ancestry of Elihu B. Gifford (1830–1898) and Catherine Sandow Barrows (1835–1917) of Saratoga County, New York, Buffalo County, Wisconsin, and Spokane County, Washington* was compiled by Raymond L. Olson and published in Baltimore, Maryland, in 1989.

BARRY
Ranking: 1260   S.S. Count: 64,099
Origin: English, French, Irish, Scottish, Welsh. English, French: derived from the Anglo-Norman-Saxon word "barri," meaning rampart. Irish: derived from the Gaelic name Ó Beargha, meaning "descendant of B'eargh" (H&H), which means robber. Scottish: possibly derived from the Gaelic word "borrach," meaning rough, grass-covered hill. The name was

given to those who came from Barry, the name of several
places in England. Welsh: 1) derived from the Welsh word
"barr," meaning summit. The name was given to those who
came from places that had "barr" as a component of their
names. 2) derived from the first name Harry.

Famous **Barrys**: LENORA MARIE BARRY (1849–1930),
born in Ireland, was a labor organizer and leader who
organized female workers during the 1880s. PHILIP BARRY
(1896–1949) of New York was a playwright whose works
included *You and I* (1922) and *The Philadelphia Story*
(1939). IRIS BARRY (1895–1969), born in England, was a
film critic and historian who organized the film archives at
the Museum of Modern Art in New York. During her life,
she saw more than 15,000 films.

Genealogies: *Descendants of John Ambrose Rowe
(including the Barry Family), Weld County Pioneer, 1828–
1886* was compiled by Arliss S. Monk and published in
Greeley, Colorado, in 1975.

BARTEL, BARTELEMY, BARTELMY, BARTELET, BARTELLI

Ranking: 1416 S.S. Count: 31,382
Origin: Cognates to the English definition of
Bartholomew.
Genealogies: None known.

BARTH

Ranking: 2197 S.S. Count: 20,872
Origin: German. 1) cognate to the first definition of
Beard. 2) cognate to Bartholomew.
Genealogies: None known.

BARTHELET, BARTHELEMY (S.S. Abbreviation: Barthe)

Ranking: 4379 S.S. Count: 10,246
Origin: French. Cognate to English definition of
Bartholomew.
Genealogies: None known.

BARTHOLOMEW, BARTHOLOMIEU, BARTHOLOMAUS (S.S. Abbreviation: Bartho)

Ranking: 2197 S.S. Count: 20,872
Origin: Bartholomew—English, Irish; Bartholomieu,
Bartholomaus—French. English, French: from the Arabic
phrase "bar-Talmay," meaning son of Talmay, a first name
meaning rich in land. Irish: transformation of McFarlane.
Genealogies: *Record of the Bartholomew Family: Historical, Genealogical, Biographical* was compiled by George
Wells Bartholomew and published in Austin, Texas, in
1885.

BARTLET, BARTLEY (S.S. Abbreviation: Bartle)

Ranking: 440 S.S. Count: 90,559
Origin: English. Bartlet: transformation of Bartholomew.
Bartley: derived from the Old English words "bo(o)rc" and
"lēah," meaning birch and wood. The name was given to
those who lived in Bartley, the name of several places in Eng-
land.
Genealogies: *Pilgrim, Robert Bartlett, 1603–1676, and
Some of His Descendants* was compiled by Robert Merrill
Bartlett and published in Plymouth, Massachusetts, in
1980.

BARTOLOMEOTTI, BARTOLOMUCCI, BARTOLINI, BARTOLETTI, BARTOLOMEAZZI, BARTOLOME (S.S. Abbreviation: Bartol).

Ranking: 2491 S.S. Count: 18,196
Origin: Italian, Spanish. Cognates to the English defini-
tion of Bartholomew.
Genealogies: None known.

BARTON

Ranking: 414 S.S. Count: 95,275
Origin: English, Czech. English: derived from the Old
English words "bere" and "tūn," meaning barley and settlement. The name was given to those who came from near
grain fields or from Barton, the name of several places in England. Czech: cognate to the English definition of
Bartholomew.

Famous **Bartons**: BENJAMIN S. BARTON (1766–1815) of
Pennsylvania was a physician and botanist who wrote
Elements of Botany, the first text on botany written by an
American. CLARISSA HARLOWE (CLARA) BARTON (1821–
1912) of Massachusetts was known as the "angel of the battlefield" and the founder of the American Red Cross. She
organized the distribution of relief supplies to wounded
soldiers during the Civil War, the Franco-German War, and
the Spanish-American War. BRUCE BARTON (1886–1967) of
Tennessee founded an advertising agency in New York,
served in the U.S. House of Representatives, and wrote several books, including *More Power to You* (1917) and *On the
Up and Up* (1929). JAMES EDWARD BARTON (1890–1962) of
New Jersey, the son of minstrel performers James and
Clara Barton, started performing at the age of two with his
parents. He toured as "Topsy" and other roles in *Uncle
Tom's Cabin*, then went on to a career in vaudeville, and on
stage, screen, and television.

Genealogies: *Barton-Green and Related Families* was
compiled by Ruth Lincoln Kay and published in Alexandria, Virginia, in 1969.

BARTOS, BARTOSEK, BARTOSCH, BARTOSZ, BARTOSZEK, BARTOSIAK, BARTOSIK, BARTOZEWICZ, BARTOZEWSKI, BARTOSZINSKI

Ranking: 4363   S.S. Count: 10,271

Origin: Czech, German, Polish. Cognates to the English definition of Bartholomew.

Genealogies: None known.

BASHAM

Ranking: 3866   S.S. Count: 11,659

Origin: English. Derived from the Old English words "bār" and "hām," meaning wild boar and homestead. The name was given to those who came from Basham, the name of several places in England.

Genealogies: *Jerry Basham and Ellen Higgs: Their Descendants, Ancestors and Related Families* was compiled by Omeegene Powers Powell and published in Utica, Kentucky, in 1986.

BASILE

Ranking: 4403   S.S. Count: 10,186

Origin: Italian. 1) derived from the Greek name Basileios, meaning royal.

Genealogies: None known.

BASKIN

Ranking: 4021   S.S. Count: 11,261

Origin: Jewish. Derived from the Yiddish first name Basye, which is from the Hebrew feminine first name Batya, meaning daughter of God.

Famous Baskins: LEONARD BASKIN (1922–) of New Jersey is a graphic artist and sculptor. His work is in the collections of the National Gallery of Art and the Museum of Modern Art.

Genealogies: *The Baskin(s) Family, South Carolina—Pennsylvania* was compiled by Raymond Martin Bell and published in Washington, Pennsylvania, in 1975.

BASS

Ranking: 517   S.S. Count: 77,552

Origin: English, Jewish, Scottish. English: 1) derived from the Middle English and Old French word "bas(se)," meaning short or low. The name was given to those who were stout and to those who were poor. 2) derived from the Old English word "baes," meaning bass, a type of fish. The name was given to those who sold fish or were thought to look like fish. Jewish: unknown etymology. Scottish: most likely derived from the Gaelic word "bathais," meaning forehead. The name was given to those who came from Bas(s), Scotland.

Famous Basses: WILLIAM C. BASS (1831–1894) of Geor-

gia was president of Methodist Wesleyan Female College, Macon, Georgia (1874–1894). SAM BASS (1851–1878) of Indiana was a stagecoach and train robber before being killed at a young age by Texas Rangers. MARY ELIZABETH BASS (1876–1956) of Mississippi, along with five other women, established the New Orleans Hospital for Women and Children in 1905. She also was one of the first two female professors of medicine at Tulane University. CHARLOTTA S. BASS (1880?–1969) of South Carolina edited for more than 40 years *The California Eagle*, the oldest black-owned newspaper on the west coast. She was the first black to serve on a grand jury in Los Angeles County in 1943. She also was a city councilwoman and a founding member of the Progressive Party.

Genealogies: *Ancestors of Moses Belcher Bass, Born in Boston July 1735, Died January 31, 1817* was compiled by Susan Augusta Smith and published in Boston, Massachusetts, in 1896. *A Backwards Glance* was compiled by Jane Parker McManus and published in Pineville, Louisiana, in 1986.

BASSET, BASSETT, BASETTI

Ranking: 1461   S.S. Count: 30,501

Origin: Basset—English, French; Bassett—English; Basetti—Italian. Transformations of and cognates to the first English definition of Bass.

Famous Bassetts: RICHARD C. BASSETT (1745–1815) of Maryland was a U.S. senator from Delaware, then governor of that state. EDWARD M. BASSETT (1863–1948) of New York was a lawyer and a leader in city planning. He chaired the committee that produced New York City's first comprehensive zoning ordinance, which became a model for the nation. JOHN S. BASSETT (1867–1928) of North Carolina was a historian whose writings included *Life of Andrew Jackson* (1911) and *Short History of the United States* (1913).

Genealogies: *Joseph Bassett, Englishman and American* was compiled by Barbara M. Anderson and published in State College, Pennsylvania, in 1979.

BASTIAAN, BASTIAN, BASTIAEN, BASTIAELLI, BASTIANI (S.S. Abbreviation: Bastia)

Ranking: 4591   S.S. Count: 9736

Origin: Bastiaan—Dutch; Bastian—English, German; Bastiaen—Flemish; Bastiaelli, Bastiani—Italian. Cognates to and transformations of Sebastian.

Famous Bastians: WALTER M. BASTIAN (1891–1975) of Washington, D.C., was a federal judge in that city (1950–1967).

Genealogies: None known.

BATCHELDER, BATCHELDOR, BATCHELER, BATCHELLOR (S.S. Abbreviation: Batche)

Ranking: 2124 S.S. Count: 21,556

Origin: English. Transformations of Bachelor.

Famous **Batchelders**: ROBERT F. BATCHELDER (1895–1973) of Massachusetts worked his way through the ranks from navy reserve enlistee to inspector general of the U.S. Navy Supply Corps.

Genealogies: *The Ancestry of the Families (including Batcheldor) in Hancock County, Ohio* was compiled by Pauline Sterner and published in Findlay, Ohio, in 1976. *The Batchelor-Williams Families and Related Lines* was compiled by Lyle Keith Williams and published in Fort Worth, Texas, in 1976.

BATEMAN (S.S. Abbreviation: Batema)

Ranking: 1772 S.S. Count: 25,342

Origin: English. The name was given to those who were servants of people Bate or Bates.

Famous **Batemans**: HEZEKIAN L. BATEMAN (1812–1875) of Maryland gave up his own acting career to manage his daughters, ELLEN (1823–1881) and KATE JOSEPHINE (1842–1917), who performed as the Bateman Children in the United States and Great Britain. HARRY BATEMAN (1882–1946), born in England, was a mathematics expert associated with the California Institute of Technology. He was the author of *Partial Differential Equations of Mathematical Physics* (1932).

Genealogies: *Descendants of Dr. Elisha Bateman* was compiled by Paul Bateman and published in Fresh Meadows, New York, in 1980. *Bateman Family Genealogy and Related Lines* was compiled by Harris Bateman and published in Tulsa, Oklahoma, in 1979.

BATES

Ranking: 275 S.S. Count: 130,294

Origin: Transformation of Bartholomew.

Famous **Bateses**: FREDERICK BATES (1777– 1825) of Michigan was secretary of the Louisiana Territory, secretary of the Missouri Territory, then governor of Missouri. KATHERINE LEE BATES (1859–1929) of Massachusetts wrote the poem "America the Beautiful." BLANCHE BATES (1873–1941) of Oregon starred in a number of plays, including *Madame Butterfly* in 1900 and *Witness for the Defense* in 1913. MARSTON BATES (1906–1974) was a zoologist and author whose books included *The Nature of Natural History* (1950). THEODORE L. BATES (1901–1972) of Connecticut was an advertising executive. He is credited with spurring a change in television advertising in the 1950s toward local spot commercials rather than sole sponsorship of programs.

Genealogies: *The Bates Family in America* was compiled by Edward Everett Lanphere and published in Chapel Hill, North Carolina, in 1972. *Bates-Jacob and Thomas's Descendants* was compiled by Janice Jean Bates Miller and published in Vernon, Michigan, in 1983.

BATISTA (S.S. Abbreviation: Batist)

Ranking: 2255 S.S. Count: 20,245

Origin: Portuguese. Cognate to Baptist.

Genealogies: None known.

BATSON

Ranking: 3788 S.S. Count: 11,903

Origin: English. Transformation of Bartholomew.

Genealogies: None known.

BATTAGLIA, BATTAGLINI (S.S. Abbreviation: Battag)

Ranking: 3654 S.S. Count: 12,345

Origin: Italian. Derived from the Late Latin word "battālia," meaning military exercises. The name was given to those who were aggressive.

Genealogies: None known.

BATTEN

Ranking: 3840 S.S. Count: 11,728

Origin: English. Transformation of Batt(s).

Genealogies: None known.

BATTISFORD (S.S. Abbreviation: Battis)

Ranking: 3471 S.S. Count: 13,015

Origin: Derived from the Old English first name B: aetti and the word "ford," meaning a shallow place in a river. The name was given to those who came from Battisford, a place in Suffolk, England.

Genealogies: None known.

BATTLE

Ranking: 1007 S.S. Count: 43,499

Origin: English. The name was given to those who came from places where battles had occurred.

Famous **Battles**: BURRELL B. BATTLE (1838–1917) was a justice of the Arkansas Supreme Court (1885–1911). KEMP DAVIS BATTLE (1888–1973) of North Carolina was a lawyer known for fighting human rights cases, categorized later as civil rights cases.

Genealogies: *A History of the Battelle (also Battle) Family in England* was compiled by Lucy Catherine Battelle and published in Columbus, Ohio, in 1985.

BATTS

Ranking: 4036 S.S. Count: 11,221

Origin: English. 1) derived from the Middle English first

name Bate, a diminutive of Bartholomew. 2) possibly derived from the Old English first name Bata, which may be derived form the the word "batt," meaning cudgel. The name was most likely given to those who were short or belligerent.

Genealogies: None known.

BAUER

Ranking: 443 **S.S. Count:** 90,106

Origin: German, Jewish. German: derived from the Old High German word "gibūro," meaning neighbor. The name was given to those who were neighbors and/or peasants. Jewish: uncertain etymology.

Famous **Bauers:** LOUIS A. BAUER (1865–1932) was a physicist and magnetician who conducted a world magnetic survey. HAROLD BAUER (1873–1951), born in England, was a pianist who helped introduce the music of Debussy and Ravel to the United States. MARION EUGENIE BAUER (1887–1955) of Washington was a music educator and composer who wrote many music compositions and books on music history.

Genealogies: *Alsace to America: The History of the Bauer Family* was compiled by Stephen Francis Bauer and published in 1981. *The Bauer Family; Descendants of Johann Jacob Bauer (1796–1858) and His Wife Mary Elizabeth (Roehner) Bauer (1794–1856) of Union County, New Jersey* was compiled by Harriet Stryker-Rodda and published in Elizabeth, New Jersey, in 1969.

BAUGH

Ranking: 2686 **S.S. Count:** 16,974

Origin: Welsh. Derived from the Welsh word "bach," meaning little. The name was given to those who were small or short.

Genealogies: None known.

BAUGHMAN   (S.S. Abbreviation: Baughm)

Ranking: 2253 **S.S. Count:** 20,272

Origin: German, Scottish, Welsh. German: the name was given to those who were farmers. Scottish, Welsh: transformation of and cognate to Baugh.

Genealogies: None known.

BAUM

Ranking: 1882 **S.S. Count:** 24,055

Origin: German, Jewish. German: derived from the German word "baum," meaning tree. The name was given to those who lived near trees and to those who were tall. Jewish: same derivation as in 1. The name was taken ornamentally.

Famous **Baums:** LYMAN FRANK BAUM (1856–1919) of New York wrote the book *Wonderful Wizard of Oz*, as well as 60 other books, including 13 about the land of Oz. VICKI BAUM (1888–1960), born in Austria, wrote a number of

novels, including *Shangha* (1937), after emigrating to the United States.

Genealogies: None known.

BAUMAN

Ranking: 989 **S.S. Count:** 44,334

Origin: German. Transformation of Bauer.

Genealogies: None known.

BAUMGARDNER, BAUMGARTEN   (S.S. Abbreviation: Baumga)

Ranking: 1263 **S.S. Count:** 34,877

Origin: German, Jewish. Derived from the German word "baumgarten," meaning orchard. The name was given to those who worked in or owned orchards.

Genealogies: *The Baumgardner Family* was compiled by Winifred Beatty and published in Chicago, Illinois, in 1972. *A Baumgardner Family in America: An Historical Genealogy* was compiled by J.T. Baumgardner and published in Austin, Texas, in 1970.

BAUTISTA

Ranking: 2607 **S.S. Count:** 17,428

Origin: Spanish. Cognate to Baptist.

Genealogies: None known.

BAXLEY

Ranking: 4832 **S.S. Count:** 9262

Origin: English. Derived from the Old English words "box" and "lēah," meaning box tree and wood. The name was given to those came from Bexley or Bixley, the names of several places in England.

Famous **Baxleys:** HENRY W. BAXLEY (1803–1876) of Maryland was a physician and surgeon who co-founded Baltimore College of Dental Surgery (1839), the first formally organized institution of its type in the world.

Genealogies: None known.

BAXTER

Ranking: 609 **S.S. Count:** 68,690

Origin: English. Transformation of Baker.

Famous **Baxters:** ELISHA BAXTER (1827–1899) of North Carolina organized and commanded Union troops in Arkansas during the Civil War. His brother, JOHN BAXTER (1819–1886), led Union activity in Tennessee.

Genealogies: *Ancestors and Descendants of Jonathan Burris and Mary Jemima Boardman, with Allied Families (including the Baxter Family)* was compiled in Hendersonville, North Carolina, and published in Naperville, Illinois, in 1982. *Baxter-Short, Miller-Gill, and Related Families* was compiled by Mary Cynthia Baxter Harrell and published in St. Petersburg, Florida, in 1989.

BAYER

Ranking: 3145 S.S. Count: 14,446

Origin: German, Jewish. The name was given to those who came from Bavaria, which derives it name from Boii, the name of the Celtic tribe that resided there.

Genealogies: None known.

BAYLES (ALSO BAYLESS)

Ranking: 3513 S.S. Count: 12,839

Origin: English. Transformation of the first definition of Bailey.

Famous **Bayleses**: JAMES C. BAYLES (1845–1913) of New York was editor of *Iron Age* (1869–1889).

Genealogies: None known.

BEACH

Ranking: 1023 S.S. Count: 42,827

Origin: English. Transformation of Beech.

Famous **Beaches**: MOSES BEACH (1800–1868) of Connecticut, as editor and owner of the *New York Sun*, originated syndication of news stories. His son MOSES S. BEACH (1822–1892) invented a web press and cutter. Another son, ALFRED E. BEACH (1826–1896), was publisher of *Scientific American*. AMY MARCY BEACH (1867–1944) of New Hampshire was a pianist and composer who appeared with the Boston Symphony Orchestra and whose works included "Mass in E-flat Major" (1892). REX BEACH (1877–1949) of Michigan wrote adventure stories, including the novels *The Spoilers* (1906) and *Alaskan Adventures* (1933). SYLVIA WOODBRIDGE BEACH (1887–1962) of Maryland was the publisher of James Joyce's *Ulysses*, a highly controversial book in its time. JOSEPH WATSON BEACH (1888–1973) of Connecticut was mayor of Hartford (1933–1935).

Genealogies: None known.

BEAL

Ranking: 1591 S.S. Count: 28,129

Origin: English. 1) derived from the Old French word "bel," meaning fair. The name was given to those who were considered good-looking. 2) derived from the Old English words "bēo" and "hyll," meaning bee and hill. The name was given to those who came from Beal, the name of several places in England.

Famous **Beals**: GIFFORD R. BEAL (1879–1956) was a painter well known for landscapes and coastal scenes.

Genealogies: *Coombs-Beal-Higgins Family History* was compiled by Virginia L. Higgins Rose and published in Wollaston, Massachusetts, in 1977.

BEALE

Ranking: 4192 S.S. Count: 10,771

Origin: English. Transformation of Beal.

Famous **Beales**: JOSEPH H. BEALE (1861–1943) of Massachusetts founded the law school at the University of California. He wrote 27 books and numerous articles for law reviews.

Genealogies: *The Beale Family of Halifax County, Virginia* was compiled by Barkley DeRoy Beale and published in Richmond, Virginia, in 1978.

BEALL

Ranking: 3279 S.S. Count: 13,843

Origin: English. Transformation of Beal.

Famous **Bealls**: SAMUEL W. BEALL (1807–1868) of Maryland led an exploration to Pikes Peak in 1859 and helped found Denver, Colorado.

Genealogies: *Alexander Beall of Maryland, 1649–1744: One Line of Descent in America* was compiled by William Hunter McLean and published in Fort Worth, Texas, in 1977.

BEALS

Ranking: 4595 S.S. Count: 9730

Origin: English. Transformation of Beal.

Genealogies: *The Quaker Yeomen* was compiled by James E. Ballarts and published in Portland, Oregon, in 1973. *Memoranda of the Early Settlement of Friends in the North-West Territory, and Especially of Thomas Beals* was compiled by Gershom Perdue and edited by Willard Heiss and reprinted in Indianapolis, Indiana, in 1974.

BEAM

Ranking: 2280 S.S. Count: 19,925

Origin: English. Derived from the Old English word "beam," meaning beam (of a loom). The name was given to those who worked as weavers.

Genealogies: *A Branch of the Beam Family Tree* was compiled by Katerine Logan Conley and published in Rutherfordton, North Carolina, in 1978.

BEAN

Ranking: 834 S.S. Count: 51,065

Origin: English, Scottish. English: 1) derived from the Old English word "bēan," meaning beans. The name was given to those who sold or grew beans. 2) derived from the Middle English word "bēne," meaning friendly. The name was given to those who were considered nice. Scottish: derived from the first name Beathán, meaning life.

Famous **Beans**: ROY BEAN (1825?–1903) was a justice of the peace and a saloon keeper who considered himself the "law west of the Pecos." After blockade running during the Civil War and living in San Antonio, Texas, he established a saloon at a place he named Langtry. There he became a justice of the peace, even though he had no legal training.

LEON LENWOOD (L.L.) BEAN (1872–1967) of Maine, an avid outdoorsman, was seeking in 1911 a way to keep his feet warm and dry on hunting trips. He designed what became known as the "Maine hunting shoe," with leather uppers and rubber overshoe and bottoms. He obtained the names of Maine hunting-license holders and sent them a three-page brochure on the shoes, and they started selling. Fully guaranteed, the first 100 pairs developed cracks, and Bean had to refund the money for them. But the business, now known as the L.L. Bean Catalog, kept growing.

Genealogies: *Genealogy of the Family of William Watson and Nancy Hoty Bean Roberts* was compiled by Richard C. Roberts and published in Connecticut in 1981. *Over the Mountain* was compiled by Martha L. Crabb and published in Baltimore, Maryland, in 1990. *William Bean, Pioneer of Tennessee, and His Descendants* was compiled by Jamie Ault Grady and published in Knoxville, Tennessee, in 1973.

BEAR
Ranking: 4446 **S.S. Count:** 10,079
Origin: English. 1) derived from the Old English word "bera," meaning bear. The name was given to those who were considered scary and unstable. 2) transformation of Beer.
Genealogies: *The Genealogy of Henry Baer (also Bear Family) of Leacock, Pennsylvania* was compiled by Willis Nissley Baer and published in Allentown, Pennsylvania, in 1955.

BEARD
Ranking: 619 **S.S. Count:** 67,331
Origin: English. 1) derived from the Old English word "beard," meaning beard. The name was given to those who had beards. 2) same derivation as in 1. The name was given to those who came from Beard, a place in Derbyshire, England, the name of which is derived from the Old English word "brerd," meaning brim.
Famous Beards: DANIEL C. BEARD (1850–1941) of Ohio was an outdoorsman, illustrator, and author who helped organize the Boy Scouts of America and wrote *American Boys' Book of Camplore and Woodcraft* (1920). CHARLES A. BEARD (1874–1948) of Indiana was a prominent historian whose books include *An Economic Interpretation of the Constitution* (1913). His wife, MARY RITTER BEARD (1876–1958), also was a historian. Her books include *Woman as Force in History* (1946). MARY BEARD (1876–1946) of New Hampshire, a public health nurse, at the age of 62 became director of the nursing service of the American Red Cross. She directed a large program during World War II to recruit nurses.
Genealogies: *A Beard Mosaic: David Beard and His Descendants* was compiled by Virginia Beard Asterino and published in Urbana, Ohio, in 1973. *History of the Beard,*

Bedichek, Craven and Allied Families was compiled by Pauline Beard Cooney and published in Austin, Texas, in 1979.

BEARDE (ALSO BEARDEN)
Ranking: 2514 **S.S. Count:** 18,055
Origin: English? Uncertain etymology. Most likely a transformation of Beard.
Famous Bearers: ROMARE HOWARD BEARDEN (1914–1988) of North Carolina was an artist who became best known for his collages that depicted American black culture.
Genealogies: None known.

BEARDS
Ranking: 3698 **S.S. Count:** 12,219
Origin: English. Transformation of Beard.
Genealogies: None known.

BEASLEY   (S.S. Abbreviation: Beasle)
Ranking: 638 **S.S. Count:** 65,113
Origin: English. Derived from the Old English words "bēos," and "lēah," meaning bent grass and wood. The name was given to those who came from Beesley, a place in Lancashire, England.
Genealogies: *My Folks: Pritchard, Vaught, Beasley, Sargent* was compiled by Thelma Sargent and published in Mesa, Arizona, in 1984.

BEATTIE   (S.S. Abbreviation: Beatti)
Ranking: 3286 **S.S. Count:** 13,799
Origin: Irish, Scottish. Transformation of Beatty.
Famous Beatties: FRANCIS R. BEATTIE (1848–1906), born in Canada, was the author of *Apologetics* (1903) and was a Presbyterian clergyman.
Genealogies: None known.

BEATTY
Ranking: 1176 **S.S. Count:** 37,146
Origin: Irish, Scottish. Irish: derived from the Gaelic word "biadhtach," meaning hospital worker. Irish, Scottish: cognate to Bartholomew.
Famous Beattys: WILLARD W. BEATTY (1891–1961) of California, as director of the Bureau of Indian Affairs, was an early advocate of bilingual education programs. CLYDE RAYMOND BEATTY (1903–1965) of Ohio was a wild-animal trainer who became well known for his "fighting act." In one of his spectacles, he used 40 lions and tigers. He became a prime attraction with the Ringling Bros. Circus, then started his own. Over a 40-year span, he trained about 2000 lions and tigers.
Genealogies: *Descendants of George S. Carrier and*

Mariah Foresman (including the Beatty Family) was compiled by Wilma May Myers and published in Fort Myers, Florida, in 1975.

BEATY

Ranking: 2516 S.S. Count: 18,040
Origin: Irish, Scottish. Transformation of Beatty.
Famous **Beatys**: AMOS L. BEATY (1870–1939) of Texas was president of the Texas Co. and the American Petroleum Institute.
Genealogies: None known.

BEAUCHAM, BEAUCHAMP (S.S. Abbreviation: Beauch)

Ranking: 2047 S.S. Count: 22,334
Origin: English, French. Derived from the Old French words "beu" and "champ(s)," meaning fair and field. The names were given to those who came from Beauchamp, the name of several places in France.
Famous **Beauchamps**: WILLIAM M. BEAUCHAMP (1830–1925) of New York was an Episcopal clergyman and a historian. He was an authority on the history of the Iroquois and an archaeologist at the New York State Museum.
Genealogies: None known.

BEAUDOIN (S.S. Abbreviation: Beaudo)

Ranking: 4750 S.S. Count: 9426
Origin: French? Uncertain etymology. Most likely derived from the Old French word "beu," meaning fair.
Genealogies: None known.

BEAULIEU (S.S. ABBREVIATION BEAULI)

Ranking: 2817 S.S. Count: 16,172
Origin: French. Derived from the the Old French words "beu" and "lieu," meaning fair and place. The name was given to those who came from Beaulieu, the name of several places in France.
Genealogies: None known.

BEAVER

Ranking: 794 S.S. Count: 53,096
Origin: English. 1) derived from the Old French words "beu" and "voir," meaning fair and to see. The name was given to those who came from places with these elements in their names in Normandy, France. 2) derived from the Old English word "beofor," meaning beaver. The name was given to those who were considered hardworking or otherwise like a beaver.
Famous **Beavers**: JAMES A. BEAVER (1837–1914) was governor of Pennsylvania (1887–1891).
Genealogies: None known.

BECERRA (S.S. Abbreviation: Becerr)

Ranking: 3009 S.S. Count: 15,095
Origin: 1) derived from the Spanish word "bicerra," meaning moutain goat. 2) derived from the Spanish word "becerra," meaning a young cow. The name in both cases was given to those who tended such animals and to those with energetic dispositions.
Genealogies: None known.

BECHTEL (S.S. Abbreviation: Bechte)

Ranking: 4486 S.S. Count: 9989
Origin: German. 1) transformation of Bechtold. 2) the name means New Year celebration.
Genealogies: *The Bechtel Family Encyclopedia* was compiled by Barbara M. Dalby and published in 1974.

BECK

Ranking: 271 S.S. Count: 133,116
Origin: English, German, Jewish. English: 1) derived from the Old Norse word "bekkr," meaning stream. The name was given to those who lived near streams. 2) derived from the Old English word "becca," signifying a kind of axe. The name was given to those who used or made such axes. German: transformation of Bach. German, Jewish: derived from the German word "beck" and the Yiddish word "bek," both meaning baker. The name was given to those who baked. Jewish: derived from the Hebrew phrase "ben-kedoshim," meaning son of martyrs. The name was given to those who had a parent who had been martyred for his or her religion.
Famous **Becks**: CARL BECK (1856–1911), born in Germany, was a surgeon who advanced the use of X-rays in U.S. medicine. JAMES M. BECK (1861–1936) was a member of Congress from Pennsylvania (1927–1934) and author of *The Constitution of the United States* (1922) and *The Vanishing Rights of the States* (1926). MARTIN BECK (1868?–1940), Hungarian-born, managed and then was president of the Orpheum Vaudeville Circuit of 60 theaters in the West and Midwest. He built the Palace Theatre, a top vaudeville venue, in 1913, then the Martin Beck Theatre in 1924, both in New York City.
Genealogies: *The Anton and Rosina Koenig Beck Family and Their Descendants 1844–1979* was compiled by Lillie Beck Wassermann and published in Brenham, Texas, in 1979. *The Beck-Reinemer Family Tree* was compiled by Mrs. Clarence Beck and published in Pocahontas, Illinois, in 1976.

BECKER

Ranking: 272 S.S. Count: 130,898
Origin: German, Jewish. German: transformation of Bach. Jewish: transformation of Baker.
Famous **Beckers**: GEORGE FERDINAND BECKER (1847–

1919) of New York was a geologist who produced important theoretical work about the Earth's interior. He was the first director of the geophysical laboratory of the Carnegie Institution of Washington, D.C. CARL L. BECKER (1873–1945) of Iowa was a historian who wrote, among other books, *The Declaration of Independence* (1922).

Genealogies: *Becker Story* was compiled by Dorothy Elaine Hackman Grace and published in Palmyra, Pennsylvania, in 1977.

BECKET (ALSO BECKETT)

Ranking: 2755 **S.S. Count:** 16,520

Origin: English. 1) transformation of Beck. 2) derived from the Old English words "bēo" and "cot," meaning bee and shelter. The name was given to those who came from Beckett, the name of several places in England.

Famous **Beckets:** FREDERICK M. BECKET (1875–1942), a Canadian native, was a metallurgist who developed the silicon reduction process for mass production of low-carbon ferroalloys and stainless steels.

Genealogies: None known.

BECKHAM (S.S. Abbreviation: Beckha)

Ranking: 3255 **S.S. Count:** 13,965

Origin: English. Derived from the Old English words "becca" and "hām," meaning a kind of axe and homestead. The name was given to those who came from Beckham, a place in Norfolk, England.

Genealogies: *Beckham: With Basic Information on William Beckham, William Beckham, Jr., Simon Beckham, et al.* was compiled by Brainard Sherwin Ferrell and published in Bellaire, Texas, in 1978. *Beckhams Beckoning* was compiled by W. M. Davis and published in Seneca, Missouri, in 1983.

BECKLES, BECKLEY (S.S. Abbreviation: Beckle)

Ranking: 4130 **S.S. Count:** 10,949

Origin: English. Beckles: derived from the Old English words "bec(e)" and "l-æs," meaning stream and meadow. The name was given to those who came from Beccles, a place in Norfolk, England. Beckley: derived from the Old English words "becca" and "lēah," meaning a type of axe and wood. The name was given to those who came from Beckley, the name of several places in England.

Genealogies: None known.

BECKMAN (S.S. Abbreviation: Beckma)

Ranking: 1776 **S.S. Count:** 25,290

Origin: English, German, Jewish. Transformation of Beck.

Genealogies: *Descendants of Johann Bernard (Barney) Beckmann of Bishop Creek, Effingham County, Illinois*

was compiled by Rich Schumacher and published in 1977.

BECKNER (S.S. Abbreviation: Beckne)

Ranking: 4995 **S.S. Count:** 8979

Origin: German. Transformation of Becker.

Genealogies: None known.

BECKWITH

Ranking: 2615 **S.S. Count:** 17,370

Origin: English. Derived from the Old English word "bēce" and the Old Norse word "viðr," meaning beech tree and wood. The name was given to those who came from Beckwith, a place in Yorkshire, England.

Famous **Beckwiths:** JAMES CARROLL BECKWITH (1852–1917) of Missouri was a painter renowned for his portrait and genre works.

Genealogies: *Genealogical Sketches* was compiled by Nancy Stout Beckwith and published in Washington, West Virginia, in 1964. *A History of Descendants (including the Beckwith Family), Tomas Ansley, Warren County, Georgia* was compiled by Phyllis Ansley Griffin and published in Denton, Texas, in 1979.

BEDFORD (S.S. Abbreviation: Bedfor)

Ranking: 3623 **S.S. Count:** 12,439

Origin: English. Derived from the Old English words "bēd" and "ford," meaning prayer and a shallow place in a river. The name was given to those who came from Bedford, the name of several places in England.

Famous **Bedfords:** GUNNING BEDFORD (1742–1797) was governor of Delaware (1796–1797). His cousin GUNNING BEDFORD (1747–1812) was among the first federal judges in the United States.

Genealogies: *New England Bedfords, State by State* was compiled by Florance Belle Wight and published in West Springfield, Massachusetts, in 1965. *Bedfords from Virginia to Maryland and Delaware (some Pennsylvania)* was compiled by Florance Belle Wight and published in West Springfield, Massachusetts, in 1966.

BEDNAR, BEDNARZ (S.S. Abbreviation: Bednar)

Ranking: 2670 **S.S. Count:** 17,070

Origin: Bednar—Czech; Bednarz—Jewish, Polish. Derived from the Polish word "bednarz," meaning cooper. The name was given to those who worked as coopers.

Genealogies: None known.

BEEBE

Ranking: 2068 **S.S. Count:** 22,177

Origin: English? Uncertain etymology. Most likely

derived from the Old English word "bēo" and the Old Norse word "býr," meaning bee and settlement. The name was probably given to those who came from Beeby, the name of a place in Leicestershire, England.

Famous **Beebes:** CHARLES BEEBE (1877–1962) of New York was curator of ornithology for the New York Zoological Society and author of several books, including *Two Bird Lovers in Mexico* (1905) and *Book of Naturalists* (1944). LUCIUS M. BEEBE (1902–1966) of Massachusetts was a journalist and author of a number of books, including *Boston and the Boston Legend* (1935) and *Saga of Wells Fargo* (1949).

Genealogies: *A Monograph of the Descent of the Family of Beebe* was compiled by Clarence Beebe and published in New York in 1904. *A Harkrader-Hathaway History (including the Beebe Family)* was compiled by Charles Briggs Hathaway and published in Baltimore, Maryland, in 1991.

BEELER

Ranking: 4121   **S.S. Count:** 9133

Origin: German. Most likely derived from the Old High German word "berg," meaning hill. The name was given to those who lived near or on a hill.

Genealogies: None known.

BEEMAN

Ranking: 4893   **S.S. Count:** 9133

Origin: English. Derived from the Old English words "bēo" and "mann," meaning bee and man. The name was given to those who kept bees.

Genealogies: *The Descendants of Thomas Beeman of Kent, Connecticut* was compiled by Gwen Boyer Bjorkman and published in Seattle, Washington, in 1971.

BEERS

Ranking: 2834   **S.S. Count:** 16,086

Origin: Dutch. Cognate to Bear.

Famous **Beerses:** ETHEL LYNN BEERS (1827–1879) of New York, a poet, wrote "All Quiet Along the Potomac" and a volume of verse under the same title. CLIFFORD BEERS (1876–1943) of Connecticut, after studying his own mental breakdown, confinement in a sanitarium, and recovery, published *A Mind That Found Itself* (1908). He went on to found a number of mental hygiene organizations.

Genealogies: *The Beers Genealogy* was compiled by Mary Louise Regan and published in Palatine, Illinois, in 1972.

BEESON

Ranking: 4665   **S.S. Count:** 9586

Origin: English. 1) derived from the name Bee, meaning bee. 2) the name was given to those who came from Beeston,

which means "homestead where reed or rush grew" (ES) and is the name of several places in England.

Famous **Beesons:** CHARLES HENRY BEESON (1870–1949) of Indiana was a noted classical scholar, medievalist, and paleographer.

Genealogies: *Genealogy of the Daniels Family: Ancestors and Family of John Francis Daniels and Allied Families (including the Beeson Family)* was compiled by Hazel Marie McDaniel Daniels and published in Napa, California, in 1986.

BEGAY

Ranking: 2609   **S.S. Count:** 17,395

Origin: French? Uncertain etymology. Possibly derived from the French surname Bégue.

Genealogies: None known.

BEGLEY

Ranking: 4052   **S.S. Count:** 11,160

Origin: Irish. Derived from the Gaelic name Ó Beaglaoich, meaning "descendant of Beaglaoch" (H&H), which comprises the components "beag" and "laoch," meaning small and hero.

Famous **Begleys:** EDWARD JAMES BEGLEY (1901–1970) was an actor who rose to national prominence on network radio shows, then was successful as a Broadway actor in New York. He won an Academy Award for his performance in "Sweet Bird of Youth" in 1962.

Genealogies: None known.

BEHRENDS, BEHRENSEN, BEHREND   (S.S. Abbreviation: Behren)

Ranking: 1908   **S.S. Count:** 23,726

Origin: Behrends, Behrensen—Dutch; Behrend—German. Cognates to Bernard.

Famous **Behrends:** ADOLPHUS J.F. BEHRENDS (1839–1900), born in Holland, was a popular pastor of Central Congregational Church in Brooklyn, New York.

Genealogies: None known.

BELANGER

Ranking: 2341   **S.S. Count:** 19,378

Origin: French. Derived from the name of the god Ans and from the Old English word "gari," meaning spear. The name was given to those who came from Angres, a place in France.

Genealogies: None known.

BELCHEM, BELCHER   (S.S. Abbreviation: Belche)

Ranking: 1106   **S.S. Count:** 39,990

Origin: English. Belchem: derived from the Old English

words "balca" and "hām," meaning roof beam and homestead. The name was given to those who came from what is now called Belchamp, the name of a place in Essex, England. Belcher: derived from the Old French words "beu" and "chere," meaning fair and face. The name was given to those who were considered good-looking and to those who had good dispositions.

Famous **Belchers:** JONATHAN BELCHER (1682–1757) of Massachusetts was governor of both Massachusetts and New Hampshire in the 1730s. He was dismissed from the posts because of his disagreements with the English crown but later regained his royal favor and was made governor of New Jersey.

Genealogies: *Belcher-Henshaw and Other Ancestry of Richard Townsend Henshaw, 1882–1938, of Rye, New York* was compiled by Richard Townsend Henshaw and published in New Orleans, Louisiana, in 1983.

BELL

Ranking: 63 S.S. Count: 382,281

Origin: English, Jewish, Scottish. English: derived from the Old English word "belle," meaning bell. The name was given to those who worked with bells or lived near bells. English, Scottish: derived from the Old French word "beu," meaning fair or handsome. Jewish: transformation of many similiar-sounding Jewish names. Scottish: cognate to Mullen.

Famous **Bells:** SAMUEL BELL (1770–1850) was governor of New Hampshire (1819–1823) and U.S. senator from New Hampshire (1823–1835). JOHN BELL (1797–1869) of Tennessee was a Speaker of the U.S. House of Representatives, U.S. secretary of war, a U.S. senator, and presidential nominee of the Constitutional Union Party in 1860. LUTHER V. BELL (1806–1862) of New Hampshire was a physician who described a form of insanity dubbed Bell's Disease or Bell's Mania. ALEXANDER MELVILLE BELL (1819–1905), born in Scotland, later a resident of Washington, D.C., was the author of *Visible Speech: The Science of Universal Alphabetics* (1867). His son, ALEXANDER GRAHAM BELL (1847–1922), invented the telegraph multiplexing system, made the first intelligible telephonic voice transmission, and patented the telephone. He, with Gardiner G. Hubbard, founded the Bell Telephone Co. He also founded the journal *Science*. LAWRENCE D. BELL (1895–1956) of Indiana, an aircraft designer, was president of Bell Aircraft (1935–1956), where he is credited with building the first U.S. jet aircraft, the *P-59 Airacomet* (1942), and the first aircraft to break the sound barrier, the *Bell X-1* (1947).

Genealogies: *Ancestral Lines and Descendants of Frances Emily (Botsfor, Morse and Jean) (Botsford) Bell* was compiled by Doreen Potter Hanna and published in Skowhegan, Maine, in 1974. *Backward Glimpse* was compiled by Iris Bell and published in Venice, California, in 1986.

BELLAMY (S.S. Abbreviation: Bellam)

Ranking: 2037 S.S. Count: 22,451

Origin: Irish. Derived from the Old French words "beu" and "ami," meaning fair and friend. The name was given both literally and sarcastically to those who were said to be good friends.

Famous **Bellamys:** ELIZABETH WHITFIELD CROOM BELLAMY (1837–1900) of Florida wrote romatic novels of life in the South. EDWARD BELLAMY (1850–1898) of Massachusetts wrote *Looking Backward* (1888), a popular book describing an economic organization guaranteeing material equality.

Genealogies: None known.

BELLINGHAM

Ranking: 2602 S.S. Count: 17,463

Origin: English. Derived from the Old English words "belle" and "hām," meaning bell and homestead. The name was given to those who lived near bells and to those who came from Bellingham, the name of several places in England.

Genealogies: None known.

BELLO

Ranking: 4617 S.S. Count: 9672

Origin: Spanish. Derived from the Latin word "bellus," meaning beautiful. The name was given to those who were considered attractive and to those who came from Bello, the name of several places in Spain.

Genealogies: None known.

BELT

Ranking: 3701 S.S. Count: 12,203

Origin: English, German. The name was given to those who worked making and/or selling belts and girdles.

Genealogies: None known.

BELTON

Ranking: 4110 S.S. Count: 10,986

Origin: English. Uncertain first component. Second component derived from the Old English word "tūn," meaning settlement.

Genealogies: *The Family of Edmund Smith Belton in America* was compiled by Blair Belton and published in Norfolk, Virginia, in 1989.

BELTRAM, BELTRAMELLI, BELTRAMI (S.S. Abbreviation: Beltra)

Ranking: 1737 S.S. Count: 25,814

Origin: Beltram—German; Beltramelli, Beltrami—Italian. Transformation of and cognates to Bertram.

Genealogies: None known.

BENAVIDES (S.S. Abbreviation: Benavi)
Ranking: 1808 S.S. Count: 24,929
Origin: Spanish. 1) the name means saintly life. 2) derived from the first name Abidis. The name was given to those who came from Benavides, a place in Spain. 3) the name means son of slaves. 4) the name means the greedy son.

Famous **Benavideses:** ALONZO DE BENAVIDES (1600–1664) of Spain was a Franciscan priest who worked among Apache Indians in what is now New Mexico and converted more than 16,000 tribesmen.

Genealogies: None known.

BENDER
Ranking: 763 S.S. Count: 55,424
Origin: German. The name was given to those who worked as coopers and to those who made casks.

Famous **Benders:** GEORGE H. BENDER (1896–1961) was a U.S. representative, then U.S. senator from Ohio.

Genealogies: *The Tansill, Bender, Callan, Holmeand, and Other Early American Families* was compiled by Xavier Bender Tansill and published in 1971.

BENEDEN, BENEDEK, BENEDETTI (S.S. Abbreviation: Benede)
Ranking: 4865 S.S. Count: 9202
Origin: Beneden—Dutch; Benedek—Hungarian; Benedetti—Italian. Beneden: cognate to Nieder. Benedek, Benedetti: cognates to Bennett.

Genealogies: None known.

BENEDICT, BENEDICTO, BENEDIKSSON
Ranking: 1639 S.S. Count: 27,442
Origin: Benedict—English; Benedicto—Spanish; Benediksson—Swedish. Transformation of and cognates to Bennett.

Famous **Benedicts:** STANLEY ROSSITER BENEDICT (1884–1936) of Ohio was a biological chemist who developed Benedict's Solution, a reagent for testing sugar in urine. His wife, RUTH FULTON BENEDICT (1887–1947) of New York, was a poet and an anthropologist. As a poet, she wrote under the pseudonym Anne Singleton. As an anthropologist, she studied several Native American tribes and advocated her beliefs in judging a culture within its context.

Genealogies: None known.

BENEFIELD (S.S. Abbreviation: Benefi)
Ranking: 4314 S.S. Count: 10,402
Origin: English. Derived from the first name Bera and the Old English word "feld," meaning pasture. The name was given to those who came from Benefield, a place in Northamptonshire, England.

Genealogies: None known.

BENITES (S.S. Abbreviation: Benite)
Ranking: 2004 S.S. Count: 22,731
Origin: Spanish. Cognate to Benedict.
Genealogies: None known.

BENJAMIN, BENJAMINS, BENJAMENS, BENJAMINOV (S.S. Abbreviation: Benjam)
Ranking: 906 S.S. Count: 47,611
Origin: Benjamin—English, French, Jewish; Benjamins, Benjamens—Dutch; Benjaminov—Jewish. Derived from the Hebrew first name Binyamin, meaning "Son of the South" or "Son of the Right Hand" (H&H).

Famous **Bearers:** ASHER BENJAMIN (1773–1845) of Massachusetts was an architect whose books *American Builder's Companion* (1806) and *Practical House Carpenter* (1830) influenced building throughout New England. JUDAH BENJAMIN (1811–1884), born in the Virgin Islands, was a U.S. senator from Louisiana, then held three positions in Jefferson Davis's Confederate cabinet. His unpopular plan to arm slaves for Confederate service forced him to flee to England, where he developed his legal practice into serving as the queen's counsel in 1872–1873. JULIEN E. BENJAMIN (1889–1973) of Ohio was a cardiologist who introduced the electrocardiograph machine to the United States while practicing medicine in Cincinnati.

Genealogies: *The Benjamin Families from Columbia County, New York* was compiled by R. M. Benjamin and published in Bloomington, Illinois, in 1911. *The Benjamin Family in America* was compiled by Gloria Wall Bicha and published in Racine, Wisconsin, in 1977.

BENNER
Ranking: 2570 S.S. Count: 17,702
Origin: English. 1) derived from the Old English word "bēan," meaning bean. The name was given to those who worked selling beans. 2) the name was given to those who worked making baskets.

Genealogies: None known.

BENNET (ALSO BENNETT)
Ranking: 73 S.S. Count: 344,913
Origin: English. Derived from the first name Benedict, which is derived from the Latin name Benedictus, meaning blessed.

Famous **Bearers:** JAMES G. BENNETT (1795–1872), born in Scotland, started the *New York Herald* in 1835 and served as its editor until he retired. He was a leader in publishing financial and society news. His son, JAMES G. BENNETT (1841–1918), succeeded him and established the *New York Evening Telegram* and the Paris edition of the *Herald*. CHARLES E. BENNETT (1858–1921) of Rhode Island, a Latin scholar, wrote *A Latin Grammar* (1895) and *Appendix to Bennett's Latin Grammar* (1895). RICHARD BENNETT (1872–1944) of Indiana was a successful actor and the father of actresses Constance and Joan Bennett. EDWARD BENNETT (1874–1954), born in England, designed city plans for Minneapolis, Detroit, and other cities and helped design the U.S. Capitol grounds. GRANVILLE G. BENNETT (1882–1975) of South Dakota was a nationally known Episcopal minister and an early radio preacher. He was bishop of Duluth (Minnesota) (1922–1933) and bishop of Rhode Island (1946–55). FLOYD BENNETT (1890–1928) was a pilot with Richard Byrd during the expedition to the North Pole in 1926. ROBERT BENNETT (1894–1981) of Missouri, a musician, was the orchestrator of about 300 Broadway musicals, including *Show Boat* (1920) and *Camelot* (1960). CONSTANCE CAMPBELL BENNETT (1904–1965) of New York was one of the highest-paid actors in Hollywood during the late 1920s and early 1930s. EARL W. BENNETT (1880–1973) of Michigan rose from office boy to chairman of Dow Chemical Co. JOHN C. BENNETT JR. (1895–1970) of Tennessee organized the first air National Guard unit in 1920, during World War II, he flew a top-secret, 33,000-mile observation mission over American front lines in 16 countries, studying the need for air support.

Genealogies: *A Chart of Some of the Ancestors of Benjamin Holmes West, 1861–1919; and His Wife Josepheine Bennet, 1857–1921; and a Genealogy of Their Descendants* was compiled by William J. Harrison and published in Bloomfield, New Jersey, in 1970.

BENNINK, BENNING, BENNINCK (S.S. Abbreviation: Bennin)

Ranking: 3131 **S.S. Count:** 14,502

Origin: Bennink—Dutch; Benning, Benninck—Frisian. Cognates to Bennett.

Famous **Bennings:** HENRY LOUIS BENNING (1814–1875) of Georgia was a justice of the state supreme court.

Genealogies: None known.

BENOIT (ALSO BENOITON)

Ranking: 1871 **S.S. Count:** 24,202

Origin: French. Cognates to Bennett.

Famous **Benoits:** EMILE BENOIT (1909–1978) of New York was an economist, educator, and author whose books include *Europe at Sixes and Sevens* (1961) and *Defense and Economic Growth in Developing Countries* (1973).

Genealogies: None known.

BENSON

Ranking: 305 **S.S. Count:** 120,127

Origin: English, Jewish. English: 1) transformation of Bennett. 2) derived from the Old English place name Ben-

esingtūn, the first component of which is of uncertain etymology and the second component of which is "tūn," meaning settlement. The name was given to those who came from Bensingtūn, now called Benson, a place in Oxfordshire, England. Jewish: derived from the name Besenson, which is of uncertain etymology.

Famous **Bensons:** WILLIAM S. BENSON (1855–1932) of Georgia, a naval officer, was the first chief of U.S. naval operations (1915–1919). FRANK W. BENSON (1862–1951) of Massachusetts was a painter noted for his works depicting women and children.

Genealogies: *The Benson Family; Descendants of Isaac Benson and Mary Bumpas, and Allied Families* was compiled by Grace Hildy Croft and published in Provo, Utah, in 1973. *Eastmond Benson Genealogy and Biography* was compiled by T. L. Eastmond and published in 1979.

BENTLEY   (S.S. Abbreviation: Bentle)

Ranking: 775 **S.S. Count:** 54,224

Origin: English. Derived from the Old English words "beonet" and "lēah," meaning bent grass and wood. The name was given to those who came from Bentley, the name of several places in England.

Famous **Bentleys:** ARTHUR BENTLEY (1870–1957), a political scientist and philosopher, wrote *The Process of Government* (1908), *Inquiry Into Inquiries* (1954), and other books. ELIZABETH TERRILL BENTLEY (1908–1963) of Connecticut was a courier for Communist agents employed by the U.S. government; then, when her Soviet lover died, she worked as an informant for the Federal Bureau of Investigation.

Genealogies: *Bente, Bentley* was compiled by Sylvia B. Lee and published in Cresco, Iowa, in the 1980s.

BENTON

Ranking: 802 **S.S. Count:** 52,556

Origin: English. Derived from the Old English words "beonet" or "bēan" and "tūn," meaning bent grass or beans and settlement. The name was given to those who came from Benton, the name of several places in England.

Famous **Bentons:** THOMAS HART BENTON (1782–1858) of North Carolina was a colonel under Gen. Andrew Jackson during the War of 1812. He moved to St. Louis, Missouri, and was elected to the U.S. Senate, where he fought against the national bank. His grandnephew THOMAS HART BENTON (1889–1975) of Missouri, a painter, was a leader in the American Regionalist school, noted for realistic portraiture of people in ordinary life and occupations in the Midwest. ALLEN R. BENTON (1822–1914) of New York organized the University of Nebraska in 1871. WILLIAM BENTON (1900–1973) founded, with Chester Bowles, the advertising firm of Benton and Bowles in 1929. He later was a U.S. senator from Connecticut and owner and publisher of *Encyclopaedia Britannica* (1942–1973).

Genealogies: *The Benton Family* was compiled by Talcott Sebastian Visscher and published in New York, New York, in 1912. *Bento-Graves Ancestry* was compiled by Blanche Benton Heller and published in Los Angeles, California, in 1953.

BERARD

Ranking: 3536   S.S. Count: 12,768
Origin: French. Transformation of Bernard.
Genealogies: None known.

BERG

Ranking: 579   S.S. Count: 71,227
Origin: German, Jewish, Swedish. German, Swedish: derived from the Old High German word "berg" and the Old Norse word "bjard," both meaning mountain. The name was given to those who lived near mountains. Swedes often took the name ornamentally. Jewish: derived from the German and Yiddish words "berg," meaning mountain or hill. The name was given to those who lived near mountains and was taken ornamentally.

Famous **Bergs:** GERTRUDE EDELSTEIN BERG (1899–1966) of New York was the author and star of the first successful radio show, "The Goldbergs," which was broadcast from 1929 to 1945. Variations of the show were developed into a Broadway play and a television show.

Genealogies: *The Hans Hanson Berg Family History* was compiled by Nancy Stout Larson and published in Brush Prairie, Washington, in 1980. *A Line of Descendants and Ancestors of Josiah Burge (including the Berg Family) a Revolutionary Patriot* was compiled by Joan A. Hoelaars and published in Royal Oak, Michigan, in the 1980s.

BERGEN

Ranking: 3952   S.S. Count: 11,444
Origin: Dutch, Swedish. Transformation of and cognate to Berg.

Famous **Bergens:** EDGAR JOHN BERGEN (1903–1978) of Chicago, Illinois, originally spelled his name Bergren and was a ventriloquist who gained fame through his shows with his dummy Charlie McCarthy. He had a long-running comic feud with W. C. Fields. His daughter CANDICE BERGEN (1946–) is an actress who stars in the television series "Murphy Brown," for which she won an Emmy Award.

Genealogies: None known.

BERGER

Ranking: 425   S.S. Count: 93,636
Origin: Dutch, German. Transformation of and cognate to Berg.

Famous **Bergers:** VICTOR L. BERGER (1860–1929), born in Transylvania, was the first Socialist elected to the U.S. Congress. He represented a Wisconsin district from 1911 to 1913, was elected again in 1918 and 1919, but was excluded by Congress on grounds of disloyalty. Then he was elected and served again from 1923 to 1929.

Genealogies: *The Genealogical Tree of Charles Berger* was compiled by Ruth Berger Blake and Mary Blake Dvorak and published in Marion, Iowa, in 1969.

BERGMAN, BERGMANN   (S.S. Abbreviation: Bergma)

Ranking: 1337   S.S. Count: 33,074
Origin: Bergman—Dutch, Swedish; Bergmann: transformation of and cognate to Berg.

Famous **Bearers:** CARL BERGMANN (1821–1944), born in Germany, conducted the New York Philharmonic Society (1858–1876). MAX BERGMANN (1886–1944), born in Germany, was a biochemist with the Rockefeller Institute for Medical Research and advanced the "carbonzoxy" method (which he and associates had devised earlier) for the synthesis of peptides.

Genealogies: *The Korn Legacy (including the Bergman Family)* was compiled by Jean Millicent Korn and published in Baltimore, Maryland, in 1990.

BERGSTEIN, BERGSTROM   (S.S. Abbreviation: Bergst)

Ranking: 2687   S.S. Count: 16,971
Origin: Bergstein—German; Bergstrom—Swedish. Bergstein: cognate to Berg combined with a German word meaning stone. Bergstrom: cognate to Berg combined with a Swedish word meaning river.
Genealogies: None known.

BERKOWITZ   (S.S. Abbreviation: Berkow)

Ranking: 3395   S.S. Count: 13,327
Origin: Jewish. Cognate to Bear.
Famous **Berkowitzes:** HENRY BERKOWITZ (1857–1924) of Pennsylvania was one of the first four rabbis ordained in the United States. He founded the Jewish Chautauqua Society in 1893.
Genealogies: None known.

BERLIN

Ranking: 2714   S.S. Count: 16,759
Origin: Jewish. The name was given to those who came from Berlin, a city in Germany which derives its name from a Wendish word that describes the scaffolding built over the Spree River in order to keep logs from jamming.
Famous **Berlins:** IRVING BERLIN (1888–1989), a Russian-born composer, was born Israel Baline. His first popular

hits were "Alexander's Ragtime Band" and "Everybody's Doin' It," although he had been somewhat successful before then with tunes for the Ziegfeld Follies. He was widely known for his writing, and sometimes producing, of musical comedies. Two enormously popular songs of his are "White Christmas" and "God Bless America."

Genealogies: None known.

BERMAN, BERMANN
Ranking: 1647 S.S. Count: 27,141
Origin: Berman—English; Bermann—German, Jewish. English: 1) derived from the Old English word "bæ rmann," meaning porter. The name was given to those who worked as porters. 2) possibly derived from the Old English words "beorn" and "protection," meaning warrior and protection. German, Jewish: cognate to Bear.

Genealogies: *Genealogy of the Berman and Related Families* was compiled by Julian Berman and published in Northbrook, Illinois, in 1980.

BERMUDEZ, BERMUDO (S.S. Abbreviation: Bermud)
Ranking: 2268 S.S. Count: 20,131
Origin: Spanish. Cognates to Berman.
Genealogies: None known.

BERNALDO (S.S. Abbreviation: Bernal)
Ranking: 2154 S.S. Count: 21,292
Origin: Spanish. Cognate to Bernard.
Genealogies: None known.

BERNARD, BERNARDI, BERNARDO
Ranking: 626 S.S. Count: 66,342
Origin: Bernard—Czech, English, French, Polish; Bernardi—Italian; Bernardo—Spanish. Derived from the Germanic words "ber" and "hard," meaning bear and brave.

Genealogies: *Bernard "Grandparents" Back to 300 B.C.* was compiled by Ted Butler Bernard and published in McKinney, Texas, in 1976. *Ellen Elizabeth Haynes: The New England Ancestry of Ellen Elizabeth Haynes (including the Bernard Family)* was compiled by Elizabeth Fjetland and published in Farmington, Minnesota, in 1990.

BERNDT
Ranking: 4989 S.S. Count: 8996
Origin: German. Cognate to Bernard.
Genealogies: None known.

BERNHAM (S.S. Abbreviation: Bernha)
Ranking: 2406 S.S. Count: 18,836
Origin: English. Derived from a word meaning stream and the Old English word "hām," meaning homestead. The name was given to those who came from Bernham, the name of several places in England.

Genealogies: None known.

BERNIER
Ranking: 3240 S.S. Count: 14,021
Origin: French. Cognate to Berner.
Genealogies: None known.

BERNSTEIN (S.S. Abbreviation: Bernst)
Ranking: 1330 S.S. Count: 33,248
Origin: German, Jewish. German: the name was given to those who came from Bernstein, the name of places in Bavaria and what used to be Prussia (now Poland). Jewish: derived from the Middle Low German words "bernen" and "stēn," meaning to burn and stone, which referred to the way amber was mistakenly thought to be created. The name was taken ornamentally.

Famous **Bernsteins**: HERMAN BERNSTEIN (1876–1935), a native of Russia, was a European correspondent for the *New York Times*, a translator of the writings of Chekhov, Gorki, and others, and later a diplomatic minister to Albania. LEONARD BERNSTEIN (1918–1990) of Massachusetts was a conductor and composer. He was the first American conductor at La Scala in Milan, Italy, and became permanent conductor of the New York Philharmonic, but he later resigned that post in order to devote more time to composing. His compositions include "Fancy Free," a ballet; "On the Town," a musical comedy; "The Age of Anxiety," a symphony; and "West Side Story," a movie.

Genealogies: *Family Matters, Sam, Jennie, and the Kids* was compiled by Burton Bernstein and published in New York, New York, in 1982. *It Began with Zade Usher: The History and Record of the Families Bernstein-Loyev/Lewis-Mazur* was compiled by Yaffa Draznin and published in Los Angeles, California, 1972.

BERRIOS (S.S. Abbreviation: Berrio)
Ranking: 2236 S.S. Count: 20,488
Origin: Spanish. Transformation of Barrio.
Genealogies: None known.

BERRY
Ranking: 179 S.S. Count: 187,694
Origin: English, French, Irish. English: derived from the Old English word "burh," meaning fortified place. French: the name was given to those who came from Berry, the former name of a central French province. Irish: transformation of Barry.

Famous **Berrys**: MARTHA BERRY (1866–1942) of Georgia founded schools for underprivileged families in Georgia. Berry College in Rome, Georgia, is named for her. EDWARD BERRY (1875–1945) of New Jersey was a premier paleobotanist of his time and the author of *Tree Ancestors* (1923) and *Paleontology* (1929). CHARLES EDWARD ANDERSON (CHUCK) BERRY (1926–) is a musician and singer. He began as a blues singer, worked in small black clubs, and became successful only when he signed a recording contract with Chess records. His biggest hits include "Maybellene," "Roll Over, Beethoven," and "Johnny B. Goode."

Genealogies: *Berry and Related Families* was compiled by Louis Ansel Duermyer and published in Staten Island, New York, in 1975. *Berry-Berrey Family: The Family of Elijah Berry, Virginia, Georgia, Alabama, and Texas, 1700–1980* was compiled by Lynn Berry Hamilton and published in Harlingen, Texas, in 1980.

BERRYMAN   (S.S. Abbreviation: Berrym)
Ranking: 4109   S.S. Count: 11,002

Origin: English. Derived from the Middle English word "buri," meaning manor, and the Old English word "mann," meaning man. The name was given to those who worked as servants in a manor.

Famous **Berrymans**: CLIFFORD K. BERRYMAN (1869–1949) of Kentucky was an editorial cartoonist whose 1902 cartoon in the *Washington Post* of Teddy Roosevelt refusing to shoot a bear cub spawned the "teddy bear" trend. JOHN BERRYMAN (1914–1972) of Oklahoma was a poet known for "77 Dream Songs" (1964), which won a Pulitzer Prize, and many other works.

Genealogies: None known.

BERTOLIN, BERTOLF   (S.S. Abbreviation: Bertol)
Ranking: 4181   S.S. Count: 10,810

Origin: Bertolin—Catalan; Bertolf—German. Bertolin: cognate to Bertel. Bertolf: derived from the Germanic words "berht" and "wolf," meaning bright and wolf.

Genealogies: None known.

BERTRAM   (S.S. Abbreviation: Bertra)
Ranking: 1615   S.S. Count: 27,724

Origin: English, French, German. Derived from the Germanic words "berht" and "hrabn," meaning bright and raven.

Genealogies: None known.

BESS
Ranking: 3564   S.S. Count: 12,646

Origin: Provençal. Derived from the Old Provençal word "bés," meaning birch. The name was given to those who lived near birch trees.

Genealogies: None known.

BEST
Ranking: 840   S.S. Count: 50,705

Origin: English, French, German. English. French: derived from the Middle English and Old French words "beste," meaning animal. The name was given to those who kept animals. German: 1) the name was given to those who lived near the Beste river or in Besten, the name of several places in Germany. 2) transformation of Sebastian.

Famous **Bests**: ROBERT D. BEST (1909–1976) of Washington was publisher of the Everett (Washington) *Daily Herald* and became a leader in the newspaper industry in 1966 when he computerized typesetting.

Genealogies: *The Arnold, Best, Cullison and Herron Families* was compiled by Evelyn Strong and published in Massillon, Ohio, in 1980. *A Genealogy of the Descendants of William Pinckney Best, Sr. (b. 1808 d. 1875) and Permelia Jane (Thomas) Best (b. 1810 d. unknown)* was compiled by Dale D. Best and published in Yorktown, Pennsylvania, in 1983.

BETANCOURT   (S.S. Abbreviation: Betanc)
Ranking: 2392   S.S. Count: 18,971

Origin: Spanish. Derived from the French word "Bethencourt," which refers to a Norman feudal estate.

Genealogies: None known.

BETHEA
Ranking: 3038   S.S. Count: 14,973

Origin: Scottish. Derived from the first name Bethea, meaning daughter or servant of Jehovah.

Genealogies: None known.

BETHELL   (S.S. Abbreviation: Bethel)
Ranking: 3789   S.S. Count: 11,900

Origin: English, Welsh. English: derived from the Old French word "bel," meaning fair, as it appears as a component of the first name Elizabeth. Welsh: derived from the first name Ithael, meaning "bountiful lord." (H&H)

Genealogies: *The Early Bethells and Their Descendants* was compiled by Virginia Mohler Garde and published in Edwardsville, Illinois, in the 1970s.

BETTENCOURT   (S.S. Abbreviation: Betten)
Ranking: 3874   S.S. Count: 11,635

Origin: French, Portuguese. Derived from the Germanic first name Betto, which is of uncertain etymology, and the Old French word "court," meaning farm.

Genealogies: None known.

BETTS
Ranking: 1660   S.S. Count: 26,956

Origin: English. Derived from Bartholomew and the first names Beatrice and Elizabeth, the latter two having the Old French word "bel," meaning fair, as a component.

Famous **Bettses:** SAMUEL ROSSITER BETTS (1786–1868) of Richmond, Massachusetts, served on the New York Supreme Court for 41 years, from 1826 to 1867.

Genealogies: *Wallace-Frierson and Allied Families (including the Best Family)* was compiled by Charles Hamilton Young and published in Kyle, Texas, in 1982.

BETZ

Ranking: 3095   S.S. Count: 14,671

Origin: German. 1) Cognate to Bernard. 2) Transformation of Berthold.

Genealogies: *The Ancestors and Descendants of Herman Buechele and Mary Rehklau and Michael Kirchner and Barbara Betz* was compiled by Ruth Buchele Doerr and published in Milford, Michigan, in 1991.

BEVERLEY   (S.S. Abbreviation: Beverl)

Ranking: 2504   S.S. Count: 18,119

Origin: Derived from the Old Engish word "beofor," meaning beaver. The name was given to those who came from Beverley, a place in Yorkshire, England.

Genealogies: None known.

BEYER

Ranking: 1774   S.S. Count: 25,302

Origin: German, Jewish. Transformation of Bayer.
Genealogies: None known.

BIANCHETTI, BIANCHI   (S.S. Abbreviation: Bianch)

Ranking: 3102   S.S. Count: 14,648

Origin: Italian. Transformations of Blanc(hard).
Genealogies: None known.

BIANCO

Ranking: 3867   S.S. Count: 11,657

Origin: Italian. Transformation of Blanc(hard).
Genealogies: None known.

BICKEL

Ranking: 3837   S.S. Count: 11,740

Origin: Jewish. Derived from the Yiddish word "bik," or the Polish and Russian word "byk," both meaning ox. The name was most often taken ornamentally.

Genealogies: *The Sheneman-Faust-Bickel-Machling Genealogy* was compiled by Allen D. Sheneman and published in Santa Ana, California, in 1978.

BICKFORD   (S.S. Abbreviation: Bickfo)

Ranking: 4053   S.S. Count: 11,160

Origin: English. Derived from the Old English words "becca" and "ford," meaning a kind of axe and a shallow place in a river. The name was given to those who came from Bickford, the name of several places in England.

Genealogies: *Three Hundred Years of Bickfords in New Hampshire* was compiled by Catherine Bickford Fahnestock and published in 1971.

BIDDLE (ALSO BIDDLECOMBE)

Ranking: 3181   S.S. Count: 14,278

Origin: English. Biddle: Most likely derived from the Old English first name Bita. Biddlecombe: Most likely derived from the Old English first name Bita and the Old English word "cumb," meaning valley. The name was given to those who came from Bittiscombe, a place in Somerset, England.

Famous **Biddles:** JAMES BIDDLE (1783–1848) of Pennsylvania, a naval officer, as commander of the *Ontario,* entered the Columbia River to claim Oregon for the United States. He also negotiated the first U.S. treaty with China. NICHOLAS BIDDLE (1786–1844) of Pennsylvania was president of the Bank of the United States and author of *History of the Expedition of Captains Lewis and Clark.* GEORGE BIDDLE (1885–1973) of Pennsylvania spurred the establishment of the Works Project Administration Federal Arts Program during the Depression to help artists on bread lines. He organized and headed a committee of 40 artists to produce a pictoral history of World War II. FRANCIS BIDDLE (1886–1968), born in France, was U.S. attorney general during World War II and a judge on the international military tribunal, the Nuremberg Trials, after the war. ANTHONY JOSEPH DREXEL BIDDLE JR. (1896–1961) of Pennsylvania was ambassador to Poland during the German invasion of 1939 and barely escaped to Romania. He then served as ambassador to refugee governments and later as ambassador to Spain.

Genealogies: *The Biddle Family* was compiled by Alexander Du Bin and published in Philadelphia, Pennsylvania, in 1950.

BIERMAN   (S.S. Abbreviation: Bierma)

Ranking: 4728   S.S. Count: 9466

Origin: German, Jewish. Derived from the German word "bier" and the Yiddish word "bir," both meaning beer. The name was given to those who were brewers.

Genealogies: None known.

BIGELOW   (S.S. Abbreviation: Bigelo)

Ranking: 2778   S.S. Count: 16,399

Origin: English. 1) the name was given to those who lived

near hills of barley. 2) the name was given to those who came from Baguley, which means "ram's woodland" (ES) and is the name of several places in England.

Famous **Bigelows:** JACOB BIGELOW (1786–1879) of Massachusetts was a physician and botanist who wrote authoritative works on botany. His son, HENRY JACOB BIGELOW (1818–1890), was a dominant New England surgeon for almost 40 years. WILLIAM STURGIS BIGELOW (1850–1926), son of Henry Jacob, was an authority on Japanese language, religion, art, and philosophy. ERASTUS B. BIGELOW (1814–79) of Massachusetts invented power looms for weaving commercial fabric and was a founder of the Massachusetts Institute of Technology. JOHN BIGELOW (1817–1911) of New York was co-editor and co-owner of the *New York Post* (1848–1861) and U.S. consul general and minister to France (1861–1865). In addition to writing books of his own, he discovered and edited Benjamin Franklin's autobiography. His son, POULTNEY BIGELOW (1855–1954), founded *Outing,* the first U.S. magazine for amateur sports, and was a correspondent for the *London Times* during the Spanish-American War. He wrote a number of historical books. HENRY B. BIGELOW (1879–1967) of Massachusetts, an oceanographer, was instrumental in establishing Woods Hole Oceanographic Institution in Massachusetts, of which he was director for 10 years.

Genealogies: *The Bigelow Family Genealogy* was compiled by Patricia Bigelow and published in Flint, Michigan, in 1986.

BIGGERSTAFF   (S.S. Abbreviation: Bigger)

Ranking: 2947   S.S. Count: 15,461

Origin: English. Transformation of the name Bicker combined with the Old English word "stæð," meaning landing site. The name was given to those who came from Bickerstaff or Biggerstaff, the names of several places in England.

Genealogies: *Biggerstaff 1978: Being an Updating of the Family History and Genealogy of the North Carolina Biggerstaffs and Related Families* was compiled by Ralph Lydron Biggerstaff and published in Mebane, North Carolina, in 1978. *Isaac Garinger Davis, His Davis and Biggerstaff Families* was compiled by Elizabeth Davis Thompson and published in Rolling Meadows, Illinois, in 1979.

BIGGS

Ranking: 1418   S.S. Count: 31,353

Origin: Irish. Cognate to Begg(s).

Famous **Biggses:** HERMANN M. BIGGS (1859–1923) was a New York health official who introduced the diptheria antitoxin to the United States in 1894.

Genealogies: *The Jesse Tree: History of Biggs-Dexter Families in America* was compiled by Rayma Leone Biggs and published in Luka, Mississippi, in 1980.

BILLINGHAM, BILLINGS, BILLINGSTON   (S.S. Abbreviation: Billin)

Ranking: 719   S.S. Count: 58,595

Origin: English. Billingham: derived from the Old English word "bil," meaning sword, as it was a component of the Germanic first name Billard combined with the Old English word "hām," meaning homestead. The name was given to those who came from Billingham, a place in Durham, England. Billings: derived from the Old English word "bil," meaning sword, as it was a component of the Germanic first name Billard. Billingston: derived from the Old English word "bil," meaning sword, as it was a component of the Germanic first name Billard combined with the Old English word "tūn," meaning settlement.

Famous **Bearers:** FREDERICK BILLINGS (1823–1890) of Vermont was a lawyer and railroad executive. Billings, Montana, is named for him. JOHN SHAW BILLINGS (1838–1913) of Indiana was a prominent librarian and surgeon. He planned Johns Hopkins Hospital, and he consolidated three libraries into the New York Public Library system.

Genealogies: *Nathaniel Billings and Certain of His Descendants* was compiled by Roger Billings and published in Delphos, Kansas, in the 1970s. *The Ryon-Billings Colonial Ancestry: A Compilation of the Forebears of the Author and His Wife Priscilla Alden Billingson Ryon* was compiled by William E. Ryon Jr. and published in Winter Haven, Florida, in 1969.

BILLS

Ranking: 3550   S.S. Count: 12,708

Origin: English. Transformation of Bill.

Genealogies: None known.

BINDER (ALSO BINDERMAN)

Ranking: 3173   S.S. Count: 14,319

Origin: German, Jewish. Derived from the German word "binder," meaning to bind. The name was given to those who worked as barrel makers, book binders, and coopers.

Genealogies: None known.

BINGHAM   (S.S. Abbreviation: Bingha)

Ranking: 1368   S.S. Count: 32,405

Origin: English. Derived from the Old Norse word "bingr" and the Old English word "hām," meaning manger and homestead.

Famous **Binghams:** WILLIAM BINGHAM (1752–1804) of Pennsylvania was a founder in 1781 of the first bank in the country. He served in the Continental Congress, was a state legislator, and was later a U.S. senator. He also founded the city of Binghamton, New York. HIRAM BINGHAM (1789–1869) of Vermont was a missionary to Hawaii

(1820–1840) who committed the Hawaiian language to writing. His son, HIRAM BINGHAM (1831–1908), accomplished the same goal as his father, but as a missionary to the Gilbert Islands. The next generation's HIRAM BINGHAM (1875–1956) of Hawaii was a world explorer who discovered the Inca capital of Vilcabamba and wrote books about his adventures. He was elected governor of Connecticut but resigned after a year to become a U.S. senator. GEORGE CALEB BINGHAM (1811–1879) of Virginia was a painter best known for his depictions of pioneer life and political events. He also served as Missouri state treasurer and adjutant general. EUGENE C. BINGHAM (1878–1945) of Vermont was a chemist and the founder of the science of rheology.

Genealogies: *Descendants of James Bingham of County Down, Northern Ireland* was compiled by James Barry Bingham and published in Baltimore, Maryland, in 1980. *Fathers and Sons, the Bingham Family and the American Mission* was compiled by Char Miller and published in Philadelphia, Pennsylvania, in 1982.

BINKLEY (S.S. Abbreviation: Binkle)

Ranking: 4414 **S.S. Count:** 10,152
Origin: English. Derived from a word meaning hill and the Old English word "lēah," meaning wood. The name was given to those who came from Binkley, a place in Yorkshire, England.

Famous **Binkleys:** WILFRID ELLSWORTH BINKLEY (1883–1965) of Ohio was a historian, political scientist, and author. His writings blended political analysis with historical causation. His books include *President and Congress* (1943).

Genealogies: *The Binkley Family* was compiled by Jonathan A. Binkley and published in Toledo, Ohio, in 1984.

BIRCH

Ranking: 2836 **S.S. Count:** 16,083
Origin: English. Derived from the Old English word "birce," meaning birch. The name was given to those who lived near birch trees.

Famous **Birches:** THOMAS BIRCH (1779–1851) was a painter noted for his works of sea battles during the War of 1812. REGINALD B. BIRCH (1856–1943) was a popular illustrator of magazines and books, including *Little Lord Fauntleroy* (1886).

Genealogies: None known.

BIRD

Ranking: 963 **S.S. Count:** 45,389
Origin: English. Derived from the Old English word "bridd," meaning young bird. The name was given to those

who were considered to be birdlike or those who worked catching birds.

Famous **Birds:** ROBERT M. BIRD (1806–1854) of Delaware wrote novels, including *The Infidel* (1835), and plays, such as *The Gladiator* (1831).

Genealogies: *The American Descendants of Robert Bird* was compiled by Katherine Moore Cushman and published in Belleville, Michigan, in 1976. *Genealogical Sketch of the Bird Family, Having Its Origin in Hartford, Connecticut* was compiled by Isaac Bird and published in Hartford, Connecticut, in 1855. *The Bird-Byrd Family* was compiled by Al Byrd and published in New Baltimore, Michigan, in 1985.

BISCHOP, BISCHOF, BISCHOFF (S.S. Abbreviation: Bischo)

Ranking: 3687 **S.S. Count:** 12,241
Origin: Bischop—Flemish; Bischof, Bischoff—German. Cognates to Bishop.
Genealogies: None known.

BISHOP

Ranking: 218 **S.S. Count:** 159,207
Origin: English. Derived from the Old English word "bisc(e)op," which referred to someone who oversaw a Christian community. The Old English word was derived from the Greek word "episkopos," meaning overseer. The name was given to those who worked for a bishop or to those who looked like a bishop.

Famous **Bishops:** JOEL P. BISHOP (1814–1901) was an author of classic treatises on legal subjects. JOHN P. BISHOP (1892–1944) of West Virginia was chief poetry reviewer for *The Nation* and author of his own books of verse. ELIZABETH BISHOP (1911–1979) of Boston, Massachusetts, was a poet and fiction writer. She published several volumes of poetry, including *North and South* and *Questions of Travel.*

Genealogies: *Ancestors and Descendants of David Bishop* was compiled by Virginia Miller Leasure and published in Hanley, Iowa, in 1969. *Ancestors and Descendants of Lewis Conley Bishop* was compiled by Winnie Branen and published in Marshall, Oklahoma, in 1980.

BISSON

Ranking: 4337 **S.S. Count:** 10,327
Origin: French. Derived from the Old French word "buisson," meaning bush. The name was given to those who lived near bushes.

Genealogies: None known.

BITTNER (S.S. Abbreviation: Bittne)

Ranking: 3413 **S.S. Count:** 13,254

Origin: German. *Derived from the Middle High German word "būte(n)," meaning cask. The name was given to those who worked as barrel makers.*

Genealogies: *The Bittinger, Bittner, Biddinger, and Bidinger Families and Their Kin of Garrett County, Maryland* was compiled by Wayne Bittinger and published in Parsons, West Virginia, in 1986.

BIVENS

Ranking: 3523 **S.S. Count:** 12,805
Origin: English. Transformation of Bevin(s).
Genealogies: None known.

BLACK

Ranking: 151 **S.S. Count:** 210,976
Origin: English, Irish, Jewish, Scottish. English: transformation of Blanc(h). English, Scottish: 1) derived from the Old English words "blac" and "blæc," meaning black. The name was given to those with dark complexions. 2) derived from the Old English word "blāc," meaning fair- or light-skinned. Irish, Scottish: transformation of Duff. Jewish: transformation of Schwarz.

Famous **Blacks:** JEREMIAH S. BLACK (1810–1883) of Pennsylvania was U.S. attorney general (1857–1860), then U.S. secretary of state (1860–1861). GREENE V. BLACK (1836–1915) was a dentist, a dentistry professor, and an author of books, including *Dental Anatomy* (1891). JAMES BLACK (1823–1893) of Pennsylvania founded the National Prohibition Party. HUGO LaFAYETTE BLACK (1886–1971) of Alabama was a justice of the U.S. Supreme Court. After serving 10 years in the U.S. Senate, he was appointed to the high court by President Franklin D. Roosevelt in 1937 and quickly confirmed, despite some controversy about his brief membership in the Ku Klux Klan. Protecting the Bill of Rights became his trademark on the Supreme Court. IRMA SIMONTON BLACK (1906–1972) of New Jersey was an educator, editor, and author. She wrote more than 20 children's books, three nonfiction books, and a number of articles. She also wrote and edited a series of books for children in grades 1–3, *The Bank Street Readers*, that are considered the first books of their kind to have a multicultural orientation.

Genealogies: *Black Family Record* was compiled by Doris Louise Black and published in White Heath, Illinois, in 1976. *Climbing Our Family Tree* was compiled by Edith Black and Lois Jones and published in Baltimore, Maryland, in 1988.

BLACKBURN, BLACKBURNE (S.S. Abbreviation: Blackb)

Ranking: 761 **S.S. Count:** 55,650
Origin: English. Derived from the Old English words

"blæc" and "burna," meaning black and stream. The names were given to those who came from Blackburn, the name of several places in England.

Famous **Bearers:** GIDEON BLACKBURN (1772–1838) of Virginia was a Presbyterian missionary to the Cherokee Indians, president of Centre College, and founder of Blackburn Theological Seminary in Carlinville, Illinois. JOSEPH CLAY STYLES BLACKBURN (1838–1918) was a U.S. senator from Kentucky active in investigating scandals in President Ulysses S. Grant's administration.

Genealogies: *Blackburn and Allied Descendants of John Blackburn, Sr., Who Came from Ireland to Pennsylvania in 1736* was compiled by Evelyn Gibson and published in Lincoln, Nebraska, in 1978. *Blackburns, Today and Yesterday* was compiled by Frances Blackburn Hilliard and published in Baltimore, Maryland, in 1978.

BLACKMAN, BLACKMUN (S.S. Abbreviation: Blackm)

Ranking: 748 **S.S. Count:** 56,876
Origin: English. Transformations of Black.

Famous **Blackmuns:** HARRY ANDREW BLACKMUN (1908–) of Nashville, Illinois, was a U.S. Supreme Court justice. He was appointed in 1970, after two of President Richard Nixon's previous nominees had been rejected by the Senate, and he retired in 1994.

Genealogies: *The Blackmans of Knight's Creek: Ancestors and Descendants of George and Maria (Smith) Blackman* was compiled by Henry James Young and published in Carlisle, Pennsylvania, in 1977.

BLACKSMITH (S.S. Abbreviation: Blacks)

Ranking: 1955 **S.S. Count:** 23,172
Origin: English. Derived from the Old English words "blæc" and "smið," meaning black and one who worked with metal. The name was given to those who worked with iron.
Genealogies: None known.

BLACKWOOD (S.S. Abbreviation: Blackw)

Ranking: 502 **S.S. Count:** 80,131
Origin: English. Derived from the Old English words "blæc" and "wudu," meaning black and wood. The names were given to those who came from Blackwood, the name of several places in England.
Genealogies: None known.

BLAINE

Ranking: 4745 **S.S. Count:** 9439
Origin: English, Scottish. Transformation of Blain.
Famous **Blaines:** JAMES GILLESPIE BLAINE (1830–1893) of Pennsylvania served in the U.S. House of Representatives and as a U.S. senator from Maine. A Republican, he chal-

lenged the presidential nominations of both Rutherford B. Hayes and James A. Garfield. Under President Garfield, he became secretary of state and was a leader of the Pan-American movement. JOHN J. BLAINE (1875–1934) was governor of Wisconsin (1921–1927) and a U.S. senator (1927–1932).

Genealogies: None known.

BLAIR
Ranking: 367 **S.S. Count:** 105,532
Origin: Irish, Scottish. Derived from the Gaelic word "blár," meaning field, particularly a battlefield. The name was given to those who lived near fields or battlefields.

Famous **Blairs:** JAMES BLAIR (1656–1743), a native of Scotland, was founder and first president of the College of William and Mary. JOHN BLAIR (1732–1800) of Virginia was a member of the Continental Congress and a U.S. Supreme Court justice. FRANCIS BLAIR (1791–1876) of Virginia was a member of President Andrew Jackson's "kitchen cabinet" and publisher of the *Congressional Globe.* He helped organize the Republican Party in 1856. His son FRANCIS PRESTON BLAIR JR. (1821–1875) helped organize the Free Soil Party in Missouri in 1848, then helped establish the Republican Party there in 1858. He served in the U.S. House of Representatives and the U.S. Senate. Another son, MONTGOMERY BLAIR (1813–1883) of Kentucky, was mayor of St. Louis, attorney for Dred Scott before the U.S. Supreme Court, and U.S. postmaster general during the Civil War. WILLIAM R. BLAIR (1874–1962), born in Ireland, was a physicist and inventor who received a patent for developing a radar-detection system for the army to detect approaching aircraft.

Genealogies: *The Blair Memorial* was compiled by Robert H. Blair and published in Bowie, Maryland, in 1991.

BLAKE
Ranking: 420 **S.S. Count:** 94,426
Origin: English, Irish. English: 1) transformation of Black. 2) derived from the Middle English words "blac" and "blāc," meaning dark and fair. In this case, it is impossible to say to which attribute the name originally referred. Irish: 1) derived from the Gaelic name Ó Bláthmhaic, meaning descendant of "Blaáthmahac," (H&H) which was derived from the words "bláth" and "mac," meaning flower or property, and son. 2) cognate to the English definitions of Black.

Famous **Blakes:** LILLIE DEVEREAUX BLAKE (1835–1913) of North Carolina was an author and reformer noted for her work for women's suffrage and economic rights. FRANCIS BLAKE (1850–1913) of Massachusetts invented a telephone transmitter. JAMES HUBERT (EUBIE) BLAKE (1883–1983) of Maryland was a show-tune and ragtime pianist

and composer. He and his longtime associate, Noble Sissle, were among the first African-American performers to work without minstrel makeup.

Genealogies: *The Blake-Ambrose Family History* was compiled by Irma Ruth M. Anderson and published in Santa Cruz, California, in 1966. *The Blakes of Bibb County, Alabama, 1819– 1988* was compiled by Chester Rankin Johnson Jr. and published in Cullman, Alabama, in 1988.

BLAKELEY, BLAKELY (S.S. Abbreviation: Blakel)
Ranking: 2196 **S.S. Count:** 20,893
Origin: English. Derived from the Old English words "blæc" and "lēah," meaning black and wood. The name was given to those who came from Blakeley or Blackley, both of which are places in England.

Famous **Bearers:** JOHNSTON BLAKELY (1781–1814) commanded two ships at different times during the War of 1812. GEORGE H. BLAKELEY (1865–1942) of New Jersey was an engineer credited with the introduction of thin-web, wide-flange girders, beams, and H-columns used in construction.

Genealogies: None known.

BLALOCK (S.S. Abbreviation: Blaloc)
Ranking: 2822 **S.S. Count:** 16,153
Origin: Irish? Uncertain etymology.

Famous **Blalocks:** ALFRED BLALOCK (1899– 1964) of Georgia was a surgeon who, with Dr. Helen Taussig, developed an artery bypass operation in 1944.

Genealogies: *Blalock and Related Families: Pioneers in Virginia, the Carolinas, Georgia, Alabama, and Texas, 1597–1988* was compiled by Delton D. Blalock and published in Montgomery, Alabama, in 1988. *The Blalocks and Related Families, Cass County, Texas* was compiled by Myreline Dailey Bowman and published in Atlanta, Texas, in 1977.

BLANCH, BLANCHE, BLANCHET, BLANCHETEAU, BLANCHETON, BLANCHONNET (S.S. Abbreviation: Blanch)
Ranking: 599 **S.S. Count:** 69,711
Origin: Blanch—Catalan; Blanche, Blanchet, Blancheteau, Blancheton, Blanchonnet—French. Derived from the Old High German word "blank," meaning bright, white, and/or beautiful. The name was given to those who were considered to have such characteristics.

Genealogies: None known.

BLANCO
Ranking: 1977 **S.S. Count:** 22,922
Origin: Spanish. Cognate to Blanc(he).
Genealogies: None known.

BLAND

Ranking: 1180 S.S. Count: 37,107

Origin: English. Derived from the Old English word "(ge)bland," meaning storm. The name was given to those who came from Bland, a place in Yorkshire, England.

Famous **Blands**: RICHARD P. BLAND (1835–1899) of Kentucky was a member of Congress from Missouri for 24 years. JAMES A. BLAND (1854–1911) of New York, a songwriter and member of the Original Georgia Minstrels, wrote "Carry Me Back to Old Virginny" and other tunes.

Genealogies: *A Vision of Unity: The Bland Family in England and America 1555–1900* was compiled by Charles L. Bland and published in Buffalo, New York, in 1982.

BLANK

Ranking: 2468 S.S. Count: 18,384

Origin: Dutch, German. Cognate to Blanc(he).

Genealogies: None known.

BLANKE

Ranking: 601 S.S. Count: 69,173

Origin: Dutch. Cognate to Blanc(he).

Genealogies: None known.

BLANKS

Ranking: 4862 S.S. Count: 9205

Origin: English. Cognate to Blanc(he).

Genealogies: *The Blanks Family* was compiled by John Human Wilson and published in Fort Worth, Texas, in 1971.

BLANTON (S.S. Abbreviation: Blanto)

Ranking: 1306 S.S. Count: 33,935

Origin: English? Uncertain etymology.

Genealogies: None known.

BLAYLOCK (S.S. Abbreviation: Blaylo)

Ranking: 3434 S.S. Count: 13,145

Origin: English. The name was given to those who had lead-colored hair.

Genealogies: None known.

BLEDSOE (S.S. Abbreviation: Bledso)

Ranking: 1747 S.S. Count: 25,621

Origin: English. Derived from the Old English word "bliðshlāw," meaning Blið's hill, Blið being a first name meaning cheerful. The name was given to those who came from Bedisloe, a place in Gloucestershire, England.

Famous **Bledsoes**: ALBERT T. BLEDSOE (1809–1877) of Kentucky edited *The Southern Review* for 10 years.

Genealogies: *The Bledsoe Family* was compiled by John T. Bledsoe and published in Pine Bluff, Arkansas, in 1973.

The Bledsoe's History was compiled by Pat Mercer Stephens and published in Bonham, Texas, in 1978.

BLESSING, BLESSINGTON (S.S. Abbreviation: Blessi)

Ranking: 4882 S.S. Count: 9157

Origin: English. Blessing: the name was given to those who portrayed the personified blessing in morality productions. Blessington: the name was given to those who came from Bletchingdon, which means "Blecces' hill" (ES) and is a place in Oxfordshire, England.

Genealogies: None known.

BLEVIN (ALSO BLEVINS)

Ranking: 894 S.S. Count: 48,652

Origin: Welsh. Derived from the Welsh word "blaidd," meaning wolf, and the diminutive component "yn." The name was given to those who were genuinely heroic and to those who acted as friends although they were truly enemies.

Genealogies: *Blevins Ancestry: A Historical and Genealogical Record of the Descendants of Richard Blevins and Rhoda Scott* was compiled by Bill Dwayne Blevins and published in Mountain Home, Arkansas, in 1972. *Jonathan Blevin, Sr. of Virginia and His Descendants* was compiled by Laccie W. Blevins and published in Powell, Tennessee, in 1982.

BLISS

Ranking: 2219 S.S. Count: 20,719

Origin: English, Jewish, Welsh. English: 1) derived from the Old English word "bliðs," meaning joy. The name was given to those who were considered joyful. 2) the name was given to those who came from Blay or Bliss, the names of several places in England. Jewish: uncertain etymology. Welsh: transformation of Ellis.

Famous **Blisses**: DANIEL BLISS (1823–1916) of Vermont was founder and first president of Syrian Protestant College (later American University) in Beirut, Lebanon. AARON T. BLISS (1837–1906) was governor of Michigan (1900–1904). TASKER HOWARD BLISS (1853–1930) of Pennsylvania was chief of staff of the U.S. Army under President Woodrow Wilson. He oversaw the army's quick growth when World War I broke out. ROBERT W. BLISS (1875–1962) of Missouri was a career foreign service officer who served in a variety of posts around the world, most notably as an ambassador to Argentina.

Genealogies: *Genealogy of the Bliss Family in America* was compiled by Aaron Tyler Bliss and published in Midland, Michigan, in 1982. *Genealogy of the Bliss Family in America, From About the Year 1550 to 1880* was compiled by John Homer Bliss and published in Middletown, Connecticut, in 1904.

BLOCK

Ranking: 1362   S.S. Count: 32,565

Origin: German. Derived from the Old High German word "bloh," meaning block of wood. The name was given to those who were big and blocklike. The name was often given to those who were criminals and frequently in the stocks.

Genealogies: None known.

BLOCKER   (S.S. Abbreviation: Blocke)

Ranking: 3716   S.S. Count: 12,156

Origin: German. The name was given to those who came from Blocker, the name of two places in Germany.

Famous **Blockers:** DAN BLOCKER (1929–1972) of Texas worked as a teacher in Texas, New Mexico, and California before becoming an actor playing the character of Hoss Cartwright on the television series "Bonanza," one of the longest-running television programs ever.

Genealogies: None known.

BLODGETT   (S.S. Abbreviation: Blodge)

Ranking: 4289   S.S. Count: 10,470

Origin: Welsh. Transformation of Lloyd.

Famous **Blodgetts:** LORIN BLODGETT (1823–1901) of New York was a statistician and climatologist associated with the Smithsonian Institution. He wrote the first major American work on climatology, *Climatology of the United States* (1857). THOMAS H. BLODGETT (1877–1964) of Iowa was president (1922–1950) and chairman (1950–1958) of American Chicle Co. He also was president of American Writing Paper Co. (1937–1952). KATHERINE BURR BLODGETT (1898–1979) of New York, a physicist and chemist, earned the first doctorate in physics awarded to a female by Cambridge University. She went on to invent nonreflecting glass, which is used in windshields, telescopes, and other products. She also invented a smoke screen that was widely used in World War II.

Genealogies: None known.

BLOOM

Ranking: 1172   S.S. Count: 37,300

Origin: English, Jewish. English: derived from the Old English word "blōma," meaning ingot of iron. The name was given to those who worked with iron. Jewish: transformation of Blum.

Famous **Blooms:** SOL BLOOM (1870–1949) was a member of Congress from New York (1924–1949).

Genealogies: None known.

BLOUNT

Ranking: 1672   S.S. Count: 26,720

Origin: English. Transformation of Blunt.

Famous **Blounts:** WILLIAM BLOUNT (1749–1800) of Bertie County, North Carolina, was the first territorial governor of Tennessee and one of the first two U.S. senators from the state.

Genealogies: *Reminiscences and Memoirs of North Carolina and Eminent North Carolinians* was compiled by John Hill Wheeler and published in Baltimore, Maryland, in 1966. *Parker and Blount in Florida* was compiled by Virginia Westergard and published in 1983.

BLUE

Ranking: 1433   S.S. Count: 31,168

Origin: English. Derived from the Old High German "blāo," meaning blue. The name was given to those with blue eyes, blue clothes, or a bluish complexion, or to those who were sickly.

Famous **Blues:** GERALD MONTGOMERY BLUE (1887?–1963) of Indiana was a major star of silent films in the 1920s. His career waned when sound came into movies, but he reestablished himself and worked through the 1950s.

Genealogies: *The Descendants of Jacob W. Blue/Blew, Born 10 September 1798, Died 25 October 1878, Ohio* was compiled by Jack V. Strickland and published in Universal City, Texas, in 1982. *Descendants of John Blaw (Blue)* was compiled by WIlliam H. Blue and published in Columbus, Ohio, in 1986.

BLUM

Ranking: 1689   S.S. Count: 26,436

Origin: Jewish. Derived from the Yiddish word "blum," meaning flower. The name was often taken ornamentally.

Famous **Blums:** ROBERT F. BLUM (1857–1903) was a noted painter in the Greenwich Village section of New York City at the turn of the century. IRVING BLUM (1915–1973) of Maryland founded Blum's Inc., a Baltimore capital firm that specialized in funding reorganized companies.

Genealogies: None known.

BLUMENFARB, BLUMENFIELD, BLUMENFRUCHT, BLUMENKOPF   (S.S. Abbreviation: Blumen)

Ranking: 2927   S.S. Count: 15,551

Origin: Jewish. Transformation of Blum, combined with other elements meaning, respectively: dyer, field, fruit, and head.

Genealogies: None known.

BLUNT

Ranking: 3995   S.S. Count: 11,319

Origin: English. 1) derived from the Anglo-Norman-French word "blunt," meaning blond. The name was given to those with blond hair. 2) derived from the Middle English

word "blunt," meaning dull. The name was given to those
who were considered unintelligent.

Famous **Blunts**: KATHERINE BLUNT (1876–1954) of
Pennsylvania was a chemistry professor and nutritionist
who helped establish home economics as a course of study.
She was president of Connecticut College for Women
(1929–1943).

Genealogies: *Reminiscences and Memoirs of North Carolina and Eminent North Carolinians; An Extract: Genealogy
of the Blount (also Blunt), Haywood and Phifer Families* was
compiled by John Hill Wheeler and published in Washington, D.C., in 1885. *Parker and Blount (also Blunt) in Florida*
was compiled by Virginia Westergard and published in
1983.

BLYTHE
Ranking: 3728   S.S. Count: 12,119
*Origin: English. 1) transformation of Bly. 2) same derivation as in 1. The name was given to those who came from
Blythe, the name of several places in England.*
Genealogies: None known.

BOARDMAN   (S.S. Abbreviation: Boardm)
Ranking: 4960   S.S. Count: 9028
*Origin: English. 1) derived from the Old English word
"board," meaning board. 2) derived from the Middle English
word "border," meaning border. The name was given to those
who lived at a border.*

Famous **Boardmans**: THOMAS DANFORTH BOARDMAN
(1784–1873) of Connecticut is considered the last pure
representative of the ancient tradition in pewter making.

Genealogies: *Boardman Genealogy, 1525–1895* was
compiled by Charlotte Goldthwaite and published in Hartford, Connecticut, in 1895.

BOATWRIGHT
Ranking: 4720   S.S. Count: 9472
*Origin: English. Derived from the Old English words
"bāt" and "wryhta," meaning boat and craftsman. The name
was given to those who worked making boats.*
Genealogies: None known.

BOBBITT   (S.S. Abbreviation: Bobbit)
Ranking: 4292   S.S. Count: 10,459
*Origin: French. 1) the name was given to those who stuttered. 2) the name was given to those who were thought to be
ostentatious.*

Genealogies: *Our Bobbitt Family: Genealogical and Historical Record of the Southern Branch* was compiled by Allen
Wade Mount and published in Prairie Village, Kansas, in
1972.

BOBO
Ranking: 3503   S.S. Count: 12,870
*Origin: Spanish. Derived from the Latin word "balbus,"
meaning stammering. The name was given to those who had
a speech impediment.*
Genealogies: None known.

BOCK
Ranking: 2351   S.S. Count: 19,298
Origin: German. Cognate to English definition of Buck.
Genealogies: *The Descendants of Frederick and Maria
(Reichard) Bock* was compiled by Melvin Bock and published in Franklin, North Carolina, in 1991.

BOEHM
Ranking: 3048   S.S. Count: 14,888
*Origin: German. The name was given to those who came
from Bohemia (which derives its name from Baii, the name of
the Celtic tribe that settled there) and the German word
"heim," meaning homeland.*

Famous **Boehms**: MARTIN BOEHM (1725–1812) of
Pennsylvania helped found the United Brethren in Christ
in Pennsylvania.

Genealogies: *Hiestand Family (including Boehm Family)
of Page County, Virginia* was compiled by David B. Trimble
and published in San Antonio, Texas, in 1974.

BOETTCHER   (S.S. Abbreviation: Boettc)
Ranking: 4841   S.S. Count: 9240
Origin: German. Cognate to Bodnar.
Genealogies: None known.

BOGAN
Ranking: 4232   S.S. Count: 10,651
*Origin: Irish. The name was given to the grandsons of
Bogan, which means soft or tender.*

Famous **Bogans**: LOUISE BOGAN (1897–1970) of Maine
was a poet and poetry critic. Her works include *Body of
This Death* (1923) and *Achievement in American Poetry*
(1951).

Genealogies: None known.

BOGART
Ranking: 4912   S.S. Count: 9109
*Origin: German. Derived from the Middle High German
word "boumgarte," meaning orchard. The name was given to
those who lived near, worked in, or owned an orchard.*

Famous **Bogarts**: JOHN BOGART (1836–1920) of New
York, an engineer, prepared the plans for the first subway
system in New York City and tunnels under the Hudson
River to New Jersey. HUMPHREY DEFOREST BOGART (1897–

1957) of New York City was an actor who started his career making westerns. He is best known for his role in *Casablanca,* and for the roles he played opposite Lauren Bacall, who became his wife, in such films as *To Have and Have Not* and *Key Largo.*

Genealogies: *The Flowering Orchard: Genealogy of an American Branch of the Bogaard (also Bogart) Family that Lived in the Medieval Dutch Town of Utrecht, Covering the Period from About 1320 to 1974* was compiled by P. H. Bogaard and published in De Meern, The Netherlands, in 1974. *Miscellaneous Bogarts* was compiled by Sue N. McLane and published in Cawker City, Kansas, in 1985.

BOGGS
Ranking: 1165   **S.S. Count:** 37,533
Origin: English. Derived from the Middle English word "boggish," meaning arrogant. The name was most likely given to those who were considered to be conceited.

Famous **Boggses:** CORINNE CLAIBORNE (LINDY) BOGGS (1916–) represented the second district of Louisiana as a member of the U.S. House of Representatives from 1973 to 1991. She originally ran for the office to fill the vacancy caused by the death of her husband, THOMAS HALE BOGGS (1914–1973).

Genealogies: *Carson-Bent-Boggs Genealogy* was compiled by Quantrille D. McClung and published in Denver, Colorado, in 1962. *Workbook of Lines Allied to Ewers and Boggs* was compiled by Dorothy Wood Ewers and published in 1977.

BOHANNAN, BOHANNON   (S.S. Abbreviation: Bohann)
Ranking: 2855   **S.S. Count:** 15,992
Origin: Irish. The name was given to the grandsons of little Buadhach, which means victorious.
Genealogies: None known.

BOHN
Ranking: 3472   **S.S. Count:** 13,012
Origin: German. 1) derived from the first name Bono, which is derived from the word "bon," meaning demand. 2) the name was given to those who worked growing or selling beans. 3) the name was given to those who came from Bohne, a place in Germany.
Genealogies: *The Families of Johann Martin Rau and Johann Conrad Bohne (also the Bohn Family)* was compiled by Nancy Ann Dietrich and published in Clarendon Hills, Illinois, in 1976.

BOLAND
Ranking: 2416   **S.S. Count:** 18,729

Origin: English, Irish. English: derived from the Old English words "boga" and "land," meaning bow and land. The name was given to those who came from Boland, the name of several places in England. Irish: derived from the Gaelic name Ó Beólláin, meaning "descendant of Beóllán" (H&H).
Genealogies: None known.

BOLDEN
Ranking: 1595   **S.S. Count:** 28,086
Origin: English. The name was given to those who came from Boldon, which means "hill with a homestead" (ES) and is a place in Durham, England.

Famous **Boldens:** CHARLES (BUDDY) BOLDEN (1877–1931) of Louisiana was a barber and a cornetist who is credited with being the founding father of jazz.
Genealogies: None known.

BOLEN
Ranking: 3670   **S.S. Count:** 12,305
Origin: English. The name was given to those who came from Boulogne, a place in France.
Genealogies: *Ancestors of Joseph Bolen and Mary Rea* was compiled by Todd Bolen and published in Wheaton, Illinois, in 1983. *Rhea County Relatives: a History of the Bolen, Fisher, Goad, Jewell, Knight, Purser, Ryan and Spence Families* was compiled by Virginia Knight Nelson and published in Knoxville, Tennessee, in 1982.

BOLES
Ranking: 2229   **S.S. Count:** 20,551
Origin: English. 1) derived from the Middle English word "bul(l)e," meaning bull. The name was given to those who were considered bull-like and/or pugnacious. 2) the name was given to those who came from Bole, which means "tree trunk" (ES) and is a place in Nottinghamshire, England. 3) the name was given to those who came from Bolas, which means "wood where bows were obtained" (ES) and is a place in Shropshire, England.
Genealogies: None known.

BOLIN
Ranking: 2585   **S.S. Count:** 17,619
Origin: Swedish. Derived from the Old Norse words "bú" and "maðr," meaning farm or domicile, and man. The name was given to those who lived in a faraway residence.
Genealogies: None known.

BOLINGBROKE   (S.S. Abbreviation: Boling)
Ranking: 2763   **S.S. Count:** 16,495
Origin: English. Derived from the Old English word "Bulingbrōc," meaning Bul(la)'s brook. The name was given to

those who came from Bolingbroke, a place in Lincolnshire, England.

Genealogies: None known.

BOLLINI

Ranking: 1654   **S.S. Count:** 27,066
Origin: Italian. Cognate to Jacob.
Genealogies: None known.

BOLT

Ranking: 4721   **S.S. Count:** 9472
Origin: English. 1) derived from the Old French word "beluter," meaning to sift. The name was given to those who worked as sifters. 2) derived from the Old English word "bolt," meaning arrow. The name was given to those who were strong. 3) derived from the Germanic word "bald," meaning bold. The name was given to those who were considered to be courageous. 4) derived from the Old English word "bōlð," meaning house. The name was given to those who worked in a well-known house.
Genealogies: None known.

BOLTON

Ranking: 979   **S.S. Count:** 44,763
Origin: English. Derived from the Old English words "bōlð" and "tūn," meaning house and settlement. The name was given to those who came from Bolton, the name of several places in England.

Famous **Boltons:** SARAH KNOWLES BOLTON (1841–1916) of Connecticut was an author, reformer, and active member of the temperance movement. HERBERT EUGENE BOLTON (1870–1953) of Wilton Township, Wisconsin, was an academic and historian who was among the first to advocate a hemispheric, rather than a nationalistic, concept of the Americas.

Genealogies: *Biographical Sketches and Records of the Ezra Olin Family (including the Bolton Family)* was compiled by George S. Nye and published in Chicago, Illinois, in 1892. *James Bolton of Bolton [England]* was compiled by Arthur T. Bolton and published in Clinton, Connecticut, in 1972.

BOND

Ranking: 586   **S.S. Count:** 70,867
Origin: English. Derived from the Old English words "bonda" and "bunda," both used to refer to peasant farmers and peasants who worked with animals.

Famous **Bonds:** THOMAS BOND (1712–1784) of Maryland helped, with Benjamin Franklin, to found Pennsylvania Hospital, the first hospital in the new American country, and taught there the first course of clinical lectures in the United States. WILLIAM BOND (1789–1859) of Maine, an astronomer, was in charge of construction and served as the first director of the Harvard Observatory. His son, GEORGE PHILLIPS BOND (1825–1865), also was an astronomer. The two worked as a team to develop photography as a mapping method. CARRIE JACOBS BOND (1862–1946) of Wisconsin wrote a number of successful songs, including "The End of a Perfect Day" and "Just A-Wearyin' for You." HUGH LENNOX BOND (1828–1893) of Maryland was the federal judge credited with breaking up a Ku Klux Klan reign of terror in South Carolina. JULIAN BOND (1940–) of Georgia was the first African-American to have his name placed in nomination for U.S. vice president by a major party, the Democrats. He began his career as a civil rights leader and was elected to the Georgia General Assembly. The body denied him his seat because he had endorsed a document critical of the Vietnam War. His constituents elected him twice again in special elections, but he was seated only when the U.S. Supreme Court ruled that denying him his seat was unconstitutional.

Genealogies: *The Bonds: An American Family* was compiled by Roger M. Williams and published in New York, New York, in 1971.

BONDS

Ranking: 2492   **S.S. Count:** 18,193
Origin: English. Transformation of Bond.
Genealogies: None known.

BONE

Ranking: 3199   **S.S. Count:** 14,183
Origin: English. 1) derived from the Old French word "bon," meaning good. The name was given to those who were considered to be good. 2) derived from the Old English word "bān," meaning bone. The name was given to those with bony appearances.

Genealogies: *History of the Bone Family of America: Descendants of William Bone I to the Mid-Nineteeth Century and Some of His Ancestors* was compiled by Robert Gehlman Bone and published in Normal, Illinois, in 1972.

BONHAM

Ranking: 4619   **S.S. Count:** 9671
Origin: English. Derived from those who were considered good men and those who were peasants.

Genealogies: *Bonham 1631–1973: Letters, Quotations, Genealogical Charts, Military Records, Directory Index* was compiled by Elmer Burt Hazie and published in Yucaipa, California, in 1973.

BONILLA   (S.S. Abbreviation: Bonill)

Ranking: 1538   **S.S. Count:** 28,953
Origin: Spanish. Derived from the Latin word "balneum,"

meaning *bath*. The name was given to those who came from *Bonilla*, the name of several places in Spain.

Genealogies: None known.

BONNER

Ranking: 976 **S.S. Count:** 44,869

Origin: English, Irish, Scottish, Welsh. English, Scottish: derived from the Middle English word "bonour," meaning gentle or handsome. Irish: derived from the Gaelic name Ó Cnáimhsighe, meaning "descendant of Cnáimhseach" (H&H), meaning midwife. Welsh: derived from the Welsh phrase "ab Ynyr," meaning son of Ynyr, a Welsh first name.

Famous Bonners: ROBERT BONNER (1824–1899), born in England, bought the *New York Ledger* and made it a successful newspaper.

Genealogies: *The Bonner Family Record* was compiled by Kathryn R. Bonner and published in Marianna, Arkansas, in 1979. *The Bonner Family History* was compiled by Sue Bonner Thornton and published in Waco, Texas, in 1972.

BONNET, BONNETT, BONNETTE

Ranking: 4118 **S.S. Count:** 10,972

Origin: French. 1) derived from the Latin word "bonus," meaning good. 2) derived from the Old French word "bon(n)et," meaning hat. The name was given to those who wore unusual things on their heads.

Genealogies: *Recollections of Lewis Bonnett, Jr. (1778–1850) and the Bonnett and Wetzel Families* was compiled by Jared C. Lobdell and published in Bowie, Maryland, in 1991.

BOOHER

Ranking: 4709 **S.S. Count:** 9507

Origin: German? Uncertain etymology.

Genealogies: None known.

BOOKER

Ranking: 859 **S.S. Count:** 50,029

Origin: English. 1) derived from the Old English word "bōcere," meaning a bookbinder or scribe. The name was given to those who worked with books. 2) derived from the Middle English word "bouken," meaning to bleach. The name was given to those who worked bleaching fabrics.

Genealogies: *The Bucher/Booker Family, 1686–1990* was compiled by Charles Lee Booker and published in 1990.

BOONE

Ranking: 582 **S.S. Count:** 50,029

Origin: Dutch, English. Dutch: cognate to Bean. English: transformation of Bone. The name was also given to those who came from Bohon, a place in La Manche, France.

Famous Boones: DANIEL BOONE (1734–1820) of Pennsylvania was a frontiersman. He blazed the Wilderness Road over the Cumberland Gap through the Allegheny Mountains, which led to the founding of three Kentucky settlements. He spent most of his time trapping and hunting, and fighting Native Americans. JOEL T. BOONE (1889–1974) of Pennsylvania was physician to Presidents Warren G. Harding and Calvin Coolidge.

Genealogies: *Boon (also Boone) Genealogy, 1984* was compiled by Rupert Farham Thompson and published in Studio City, California, in 1986. *Boone, Eller, Sledge, Vaughn and Related Families* was compiled by Jesse H. Boone and published in Middleboro, Massachusetts, in 1970.

BOOTH

Ranking: 585 **S.S. Count:** 70,596

Origin: English. Derived from the Middle English word "bōth(e)," meaning hut. The name was given to shepherds and others who lived in small temporary shelters.

Famous Booths: One Booth family had a long line of actors. JUNIUS BRUTUS BOOTH (1796–1852) emigrated from England in 1821 to take Shakespearean roles on the U.S. stage. His son JUNIUS BRUTUS BOOTH (1821–1883) was an actor and manager. Another son, EDWIN THOMAS BOOTH (1833–1893), toured internationally and was known for his performance of Hamlet. Another son, JOHN WILKES BOOTH (1838–1865), also was successful in Shakespearean roles, but he is best known as the assassin of President Abraham Lincoln. AGNES ROOKES BOOTH (1846–1910), an Australian immigrant who married the latter Junius Brutus Booth, also was an actress.

Genealogies: None known.

BOOTHE

Ranking: 3847 **S.S. Count:** 11,719

Origin: English. Transformation of Booth.

Genealogies: None known.

BORCHERS, BORCHERT (S.S. Abbreviation: Borche)

Ranking: 4361 **S.S. Count:** 10,277

Origin: French. Cognates to Burkette.

Genealogies: None known.

BORDEN

Ranking: 1928 **S.S. Count:** 23,417.

Origin: English. 1) derived from the Old English words "bār" and "denn," meaning boar and pasture. The name was given to those who came from Borden, a place in Kent, England. 2) transformation of Board.

Famous Bordens: GAIL BORDEN (1801–1874) of New York invented, among other things, condensed milk. She founded the New York Condensed Milk Co., which later became the Borden Co. LIZZIE ANDREW BORDEN (1860–1927) of Fall River, Massachusetts, was suspected of murdering her stepmother and father but was acquitted of the crime by a jury. She lived the remainder of her life ostracized by her community.

Genealogies: *Borden, Powers, Harvey, Wood, Peck* was compiled by Alexander Du Bin and published in Philadelphia, Pennsylvania, in 1950. *Historical and Genealogical Record of the Descendants as Far as Known of Richard and Joan Borden Who Settled in Portsmouth, Rhode Island, May, 1638* was compiled by Hattie Borden Weld and republished in Bethany, Oklahoma, in 1985.

BORDER
Ranking: 3011   S.S. Count: 15,086
Origin: English. Transformation of Board.
Genealogies: None known.

BOREN
Ranking: 4593   S.S. Count: 9731
Origin: German, Jewish. 1) derived from the Middle Low German word "bernen," meaning to burn. 2) the name is a shortened form of Bernstein or Borenstein.
Genealogies: None known.

BORGES
Ranking: 2937   S.S. Count: 15,502
Origin: Catalan, Portuguese. The name was given to those who came from Borges, a place in Tarragona, Spain.
Genealogies: None known.

BORN
Ranking: 4850   S.S. Count: 9225
Origin: English. Transformation of Bourne.
Genealogies: None known.

BOSCH
Ranking: 5000   S.S. Count: 8959
Origin: Catalan. 1) cognate to Bush. 2) derived from the Old French word "bois," meaning wood. The name was given to those who lived near woods.
Genealogies: None known.

BOSLEY
Ranking: 4671   S.S. Count: 9580
Origin: English. Derived from the first name Bosa and the Old English word "lēah," both meaning wood. The name was given to those who came from Bosley, a place in Cheshire, England.
Genealogies: None known.

BOSS
Ranking: 4128   S.S. Count: 10,954
Origin: English. Cognate to Bosse.
Famous **Bosses**: LEWIS BOSS (1846–1912) of Rhode Island was an astronomer who was well known for his star catalogues. He observed the northern stars from Albany, New York, and the southern stars from Argentina.
Genealogies: None known.

BOSTIC (ALSO BOSTICK)
Ranking: 1755   S.S. Count: 25,548
Origin: English. The name was given to those who came from Bostock, which means "Bota's cell" (ES) and is a place in Cheshire, England.
Genealogies: *Copeland, Bostick, Patton, and Allied Families* was compiled by Virginia Copeland Jantz and published in Waco, Texas, in 1981. *Our Family Circle* was compiled by Allie Elizabeth Miller and published in Linden, Tennessee, in 1975.

BOSTON
Ranking: 2212   S.S. Count: 20,748
Origin: English. The name was given to those who came from Boston, which means "Bōtwulf's stone" (H&H) and is a place in Lincolnshire, England.
Famous **Bostons**: CHARLES A. BOSTON (1863–1935) of Maryland was a lawyer and legal scholar active in the reform of judicial and professional ethics.
Genealogies: None known.

BOSWELL   (S.S. Abbreviation: Boswel)
Ranking: 1476   S.S. Count: 30,204
Origin: English, Scottish. The name was given to those who came from Beuzeville, a place in Seine Maritime, France, the name of which is derived from the Old French first name Beuze and the Old French word "ville," meaning settlement.
Genealogies: *The Boswells of Shelby County, Kentucky* was compiled by Eula Richardson Hasskarl and published in Ada, Oklahoma, in the 1970s. *Descendants of Edward Boswell: Prince William County, Virginia and Orange County, North Carolina* was compiled by Jean Boswell Pippenger and published in Baltimore, Maryland, in 1986.

BOTTOM
Ranking: 3968   S.S. Count: 11,409
Origin: Derived from the Old English word "btom," meaning valley bottom. The name was given to those who lived in the bottom of a valley.
Genealogies: None known.

BOUCHARD   (S.S. Abbreviation: Boucha)

Ranking: 2448   S.S. Count: 18,589

Origin: French. Cognate to Burkette.

Genealogies: None known.

BOUCHE (ALSO BOUCHERD, BOUCHER, BOUCHERON, BOUCHEY)

Ranking: 1451   S.S. Count: 30,730

Origin: French. Cognates to Butcher.

Famous **Bearers:** RENE R. BOUCHE (1905–1963), born in Austria-Hungary, was an illustrator and painter known for his fashion illustrations in *Vogue* (1938–1962).

Genealogies: None known.

BOUDREAU   (S.S. Abbreviation: Boudre)

Ranking: 1308   S.S. Count: 33,897

Origin: French. Derived from the first name Botthar, meaning messenger and army.

Genealogies: None known.

BOUNDS

Ranking: 4152   S.S. Count: 10,897

Origin: English. Transformation of Bond.

Genealogies: *The Bounds of Maryland* was compiled by Ruth T. Dryden and published in San Diego, California, in 1983.

BOURGEAT, BOURGEL, BOURGEOIS, BOURGET, BOURGEY   (S.S. Abbreviation: Bourge)

Ranking: 2308   S.S. Count: 19,692

Origin: French. Bourgeat, Bourgel, Bourget, Bourgey: cognates to Burke. Bourgeois, Bourgey: cognates to Burgess.

Genealogies: None known.

BOURNE

Ranking: 3579   S.S. Count: 12,599

Origin: English. Derived from the Old English word "burne," meaning stream. The name was given to those who lived near a stream.

Famous **Bournes:** RANDOLPH SILLIMAN BOURNE (1886–1918) of New Jersey was an essayist and literary critic who was considered a spokesman for young radicals just before the outbreak of World War I. He himself was disfigured from forceps used at his birth and was hunchbacked and stunted from spinal tuberculosis at age four. His book *Youth and Life* was a collection of essays stating his belief that young people should eliminate what he considered antiquated and bad ways of American life.

Genealogies: *The Bourne Genealogy* was compiled by Helen Bourne Joy Lee and published in Chester, Connecti-cut, in 1972. *Old Letters, Old Biographies and Old Family Trees of Bourne, Carr, Darden and Allied Families of Virginia, Tennessee and Other States* was compiled by Gertrude Morton Price Katz and published in Tampa, Florida, in 1976.

BOURQUE, BOURQUEL, BOURQUIN   (S.S. Abbreviation: Bourqu)

Ranking: 3417   S.S. Count: 13,240

Origin: French. Bourque, Bourquel: derived from the French word "bourrique," meaning ass. Bourquin: the name is a French version of a German name meaning peasant.

Genealogies: None known.

BOWDEN

Ranking: 1314   S.S. Count: 33,818

Origin: English, Irish. English: 1) derived from various components and the Old English word "dūn," meaning hill. 2) possibly also derived from the Gaelic phrase "both an duin," meaning "house on the hill" (H&H). Irish: derived from the Gaelic name Ó Buadáin, meaning "descendant of Buadách" (H&H), a first name meaning victorious.

Famous **Bowdens:** JOHN BOWDEN (1751–1817), born in Ireland, was an Anglican clergyman who held rectorates in Connecticut and served as the first principal of Episcopal Academy in Cheshire, Connecticut (1796–1802). He taught philosophy and logic at Columbia University (1802–1817).

Genealogies: None known.

BOWEN

Ranking: 352   S.S. Count: 108,041

Origin: Welsh. Transformation of Owen.

Famous **Bowens:** NORMAN L. BOWEN (1887–1956), born in Canada, advanced the study of petrology, particularly silicate systems. He wrote *Evolution of the Igneous Rocks* (1928). IRA S. BOWEN (1898–1973) of New York, an astronomer, was director of the Mount Wilson and Mount Palomar observatories and was noted for his work in atomic structure and nebular spectra. CATHERINE DRINKER BOWEN (1897–1973) of Pennsylvania was a magazine writer and biographer. Her *Beloved Friend* (1937), a biography of composer Peter Ilich Tchaikovsky, sold more than 150,000 copies.

Genealogies: *Bowens of Virginia and Tennessee: Descendants of John Bowen and Lily McIlhaney* was compiled by Jamie Ault Grady and published in Knoxville, Tennessee, in 1969. *Ancestry and Descendants (including the Bowen Family) of Isaac Applin Sheppard and Caroline Mary Holmes, His Wife* was compiled by Walter Lee Sheppard and published in Havertown, Pennsylvania, in 1973.

BOWENS

Ranking: 3780   S.S. Count: 11,939
Origin: Welsh. Transformation of Owen.
Genealogies: None known.

BOWER

Ranking: 1493   S.S. Count: 29,760
Origin: English. 1) derived from the Old English word "būr," meaning alcove or cottage. The name was given to those who came from Bower, the name of several places in England. 2) transformation of Bow(e).
Genealogies: *The Family Band: From the Missouri to the Black Hills, 1881–1900* was compiled by Lauran Bower Van Nuys and published in Lincoln, Nebraska, in 1961.

BOWERS

Ranking: 399   S.S. Count: 97,717
Origin: English. Transformation of Bower.
Famous **Bowerses**: ELIZABETH CROCKER BOWERS (1830–1895) of Connecticut was an actress who played leading roles in the United States and in England. LLOYD BOWERS (1859–1910) of Massachusetts was U.S. solicitor general (1909–1910).
Genealogies: *Hill Family of Early Central Texas—Bowers, Cole, McGehee, Michel, Roessler, Shelby* was compiled by Yates Michel Hill and published in Poughkeepsie, New York, in 1990.

BOWIE

Ranking: 2908   S.S. Count: 15,635
Origin: Irish, Scottish. Derived from the Gaelic word "buidhe," meaning blonde-haired.
Famous **Bowies**: ROBERT BOWIE (1750–1818) was governor of Maryland (1803–1807 and 1811–1812). JAMES BOWIE (1796–1836) was a Texas revolutionary leader. He fell ill during the siege at the Alamo and was found dead by General Santa Anna's troops. The "Bowie knife," a short hunting knife, was named after him or his brother, Rezie Bowie. RICHARD J. BOWIE (1807–1881) of Washington, D.C., was a member of Congress from Maryland (1849–1853) and then a distinguished chief justice of the Maryland Court of Appeals (1861–1881). ODEN BOWIE (1826–1894) of Maryland was president of the Baltimore & Potomac Railroad (1860–1894) and governor of Maryland (1867–1872). WILLIAM BOWIE (1872–1940) of Maryland, a geologist, was chief of geodesy with the U.S. Coast and Geodetic Survey and was known for developing formulas and tables showing the relationship between topography and isostatic compensation to the intensity of gravity.
Genealogies: None known.

BOWLES

Ranking: 1301   S.S. Count: 34,146
Origin: English. 1) transformation of Bowler. 2) derived from the Old Norman French word "boelle," meaning enclosure. The name was given to those who came from Bouelles, a place in Seine Maritime, France.
Famous **Bowleses**: SAMUEL BOWLES II (1826–1878) of Springfield, Massachusetts, was a newspaper editor. His father, SAMUEL BOWLES (1797–1851), was the owner of the *Springfield Republican*, a weekly. He put his son in charge of a daily evening edition, which became a widely acclaimed and independent newspaper. When Samual Bowles II died, his son, SAMUEL BOWLES (1851–1915), took over the *Republican* and ran the paper for almost 40 years. CHESTER B. BOWLES (1901–1986) of Massachusetts, after serving in administrative positions in the federal government, became governor of Connecticut, ambassador to India and Nepal, and a member of Congress from Connecticut.
Genealogies: *The Boyle-Bole-Boles (also Bowles) Descendants of James Boyle of Westmoreland County, Pennsylvania* was compiled by David B. Boles and published in Menands, New York, in 1986. *A Journey with the Bowles Family: Some Memories Along the Way* was compiled by Charles A. Bowles and published in 1983.

BOWLIN (ALSO BOWLING)

Ranking: 990   S.S. Count: 44,206
Origin: English. 1) derived from the word "bowling," meaning a dip at the foot of a hill. The names were given to those who came from Bowling, a place in Yorkshire, England. 2) the names were given to those who lived near a pasture for bulls.
Genealogies: None known.

BOWMAN

Ranking: 251   S.S. Count: 144,305
Origin: English, German. English: derived from the Old English words "boga" and "mann," meaning bow and man. The name was given to those who worked as archers. German: transformation of Bauer.
Famous **Bowmans**: JOHN BRYAN BOWMAN (1824–1891) of Kentucky was a founder of Kentucky University. ISAIAH BOWMAN (1878–1950), born in Canada, was a geographer and author of many articles and 17 books, including *Geography in Relation to the Social Sciences* (1934). He was also president of Johns Hopkins University (1935–1948).
Genealogies: *Baumann/Bowman Family of the Mohaw, Susquehanna and Niagara Rivers* was compiled by Maryly Barton Penrose and published in Franklin Park, New Jersey, in 1977. *Before the Bowman Boys: Being the Known American Ancestry of Alan, John and Ruel Bowman* was

compiled by Jane Belknap Bowman and published in Decorah, Iowa, in 1976.

BOWSER

Ranking: 2315   S.S. Count: 19,604

Origin: English. Derived from the polite greeting "beau sire," meaning good sir. The name was given to those who used the greeting often.

Genealogies: *The Bowsers and Claypool(e)s* was compiled by Evelyn Claypoole Bracken and published in Indiana, Pennsylvania, in 1981.

BOX

Ranking: 3233   S.S. Count: 14,030

Origin: English. Derived from the Old English word "box," meaning box tree. The name was given to those who lived near box trees, worked with wood, or had a yellowish complexion, like boxwood, and to those who came from Box, the name of several places in England.

Genealogies: *The Box Book with McElroy and Floyd* was compiled by Mrs. Jeff Wade and published in Bragg City, Missouri, in 1975.

BOYCE

Ranking: 1195   S.S. Count: 36,741

Origin: English, Irish. English: 1) derived from the Old French word "bois," meaning wood. 2) derived from the Middle English word "boy," meaning servant and/or boy. Irish: transformation of Bow(e).

Famous **Boyces:** JAMES P. BOYCE (1827–1888) of South Carolina was a founder of the Southern Baptist Theological Seminary in Greenville, South Carolina.

Genealogies: *Boyce Family History* was compiled by E. Daniel Boyce and published in Provo, Utah, in 1973. *The Genealogical Record of One Branch of the Boyce Family in America* was compiled by Earnest Boyce and published in Ann Arbor, Michigan, in 1972.

BOYD

Ranking: 149   S.S. Count: 211,337

Origin: Irish, Scottish. Uncertain etymology. Possibly the name was given to those who came from the island of Bute.

Famous **Boyds:** LINN BOYD (1800–1859) of Tennessee was a member of Congress from Kentucky for 18 years and was Speaker of the House for four years. DAVID F. BOYD (1834–1899) of Virginia was president of Louisiana State University (1865–1880). RICHARD H. BOYD (1843–1922) of Mississippi was a leader among African-American Baptists in Texas. He organized the National Baptist Publishing Board in 1897. BELLE BOYD (1844–1900) of Virginia was a Confederate spy and actress. She published her story in

Belle Boyd in Camp and Prison (1865). THOMAS BOYD (1854–1932) of Virginia was president of Louisiana State University (1896–1927). JAMES BOYD (1888–1944) of Pennsylvania was a novelist whose works included *Drums* (1925). WILLIAM BOYD (1898–1972) of Hendrysburg, Ohio, was an actor best known for his role of Hopalong Cassidy in several western movies and later in a television series.

Genealogies: *The Boyds of Albany: Three Generations* was compiled by Joanna B. Newton and published in 1978. *The Boyds of Boyds Tank* was compiled by Frank Ewell Boyd and William Taylor Boyd and published in 1970.

BOYER

Ranking: 578   S.S. Count: 71,298

Origin: French. Derived from the Late Latin word "bovārius," meaning herdsman. The name was given to those who worked as herdsmen.

Genealogies: *American Boyers* was compiled by Donald Arthur Boyer and published in York, Pennsylvania, in 1984. *Ancestral Lines: 144 Families in England, Germany, New England, New York, New Jersey and Pennsylvania* was compiled by Carl Boyer and published in Newhall, California, in 1975.

BOYETT (ALSO BOYETTE)

Ranking: 3617   S.S. Count: 12,478

Origin: French? Uncertain etymology. Possibly a transformation of Boyer or Boykin.

Genealogies: *Minnie Mallory Boyett and Mallory, Hagan, Pullen, Radford, Goggans, Peterson, and Richardson Kin* was compiled by Woodrow W. Boyett and published in Tuscaloosa, Alabama, in 1987.

BOYKIN

Ranking: 1614   S.S. Count: 27,752

Origin: English. Derived from the Germanic first names Boio and Bogo.

Famous **Boykins:** FRANK W. BOYKIN (1885–1969) was a member of Congress from Alabama (1935–1963).

Genealogies: *Dr. John McCaa of Camden, South Carolina, 1793–1859, His Descendants (including the Boykin Family)* was compiled by John McCaa and published in Anniston, Alabama, in 1975.

BOYLAN, BOYLAND   (S.S. Abbreviation: Boylan)

Ranking: 4129   S.S. Count: 10,950

Origin: English. Derived from the first name Boia. The names were given to those who came from Boyland, a place in Norfolk, England.

Genealogies: None known.

BOYLE

Ranking: 738   **S.S. Count:** 57,501

Origin: Irish, Scottish. Irish: derived from the Gaelic name Ó Baoighill, meaning "descendant of Baoigheall" (H&H), which may be derived from the Gaelic words "baoth" and "geall," meaning rash and pledge. Scottish: derived from the Germanic first name Boio and the Old French word "ville," meaning settlement. The name was given to those who came from Boyville, a place in England.

Famous **Boyles:** EDWIN BOYLE JR. (1923–1978) of South Carolina was a medical researcher who studied heart disease among ethnic groups in Charleston County, South Carolina (1959–1966), and developed a method of measuring cholesterol and breaking it down into different types.

Genealogies: *The Boyle-Bole-Boles Descendants of James Boyle of Westmoreland County, Pennsylvania* was compiled by David Boles and published in Menands, New York, in 1986.

BOYLES

Ranking: 2863   **S.S. Count:** 15,908

Origin: Irish, Scottish. Transformation of Boyle.

Genealogies: None known.

BOYNTON   (S.S. Abbreviation: Boynto)

Ranking: 4335   **S.S. Count:** 10,331

Origin: English. Derived from the Old English first name Boia and the word "tūn," meaning settlement. The name was given to those who came from Boyton, the name of several places in England.

Famous **Boyntons:** CHARLES B. BOYNTON (1806–1883) of Massachusetts was a long-time minister in Cincinnati, Ohio, and author of *A Journey Through Kansas* (1855) and other works.

Genealogies: *A Family Tree in America: Being a Genealogical Story of the Families of Deane, Putnam, Boynton, Gager, Bull, and Allied Families from the Year 1630* was compiled by Frank Putnam Deane and published in Richmond, Virginia, in 1979. *Genealogy of Dr. John Butler, William Boynton or Byington and Allied Families* was compiled by Opal Hinsey White and published in Dallas, Texas, in 1975.

BOZEMAN   (S.S. Abbreviation: Bozema)

Ranking: 4772   **S.S. Count:** 9383

Origin: English. The name was given to those who tended cattle.

Famous **Bozemans:** JOHN BOZEMAN (1835–1867) of Georgia was a pioneer who blazed a Rocky Mountain path now known as the Bozeman Trail.

Genealogies: *Sketches of the Bozeman Family* was compiled by Joseph W. Bozeman and published in Meridian, Michigan, in 1981.

BRACKEN, BRACKENRIDGE   (S.S. Abbreviation: Bracke)

Ranking: 1383   **S.S. Count:** 31,979

Origin: Bracken—English, Irish; Brackenridge—Scottish. Bracken—English: the name was given to those who came from Bracken, which means fern and is a place in Yorkshire, England. Bracken—Irish: derived from the Gaelic name Ó Breacáin, meaning "descendant of Breacán" (H&H), which is a first name meaning spotted. Brackenridge: derived from the Old Norse words "brækni" and "rigg," meaning bracken and ridge.

Famous **Bearers:** HUGH H. BRACKENRIDGE (1748–1816), born in Scotland, was a jurist and author who helped to establish the *Pittsburgh Gazette* in 1786. He was a justice of the Pennsylvania Supreme Court and author of the novel *Modern Chivalry*, which was published in parts between 1792 and 1815. His son, HENRY M. BRACKENRIDGE (1786–1871), was a lawyer and author as well. His books include *Voyage to South America* (1819). WILLIAM D. BRACKENRIDGE (1810–1893), born in Scotland, was a botanist on Charles Wilkes's expedition to the West (1838–1842) and wrote a report on ferns.

Genealogies: *The Brackin Family in the Southeastern United States* was compiled by Henry B. Brackin and published in Nashville, Tennessee, in 1979.

BRADBURY   (S.S. Abbreviation: Bradbu)

Ranking: 2954   **S.S. Count:** 15,403

Origin: English. Derived from the Old English words "brād" and "burh," meaning broad and fort. The name was given to those who came from Bradbury, the name of several places in England.

Famous **Bradburys:** JAMES W. BRADBURY (1802–1901) was a U.S. senator from Maine (1846–1852).

Genealogies: None known.

BRADEN

Ranking: 2479   **S.S. Count:** 18,266

Origin: Irish. Derived from the Gaelic name Ó Bradáin, meaning "descendant of Bradán" (H&H), a first name meaning salmon.

Genealogies: None known.

BRADFORD   (S.S. Abbreviation: Bradfo)

Ranking: 573   **S.S. Count:** 61,776

Origin: English. Derived from the Old English words "brād" and "ford,"meaning broad and a shallow place in a river. The name was given to those who came from Bradford, the name of several places in England.

Famous **Bradfords**: WILLIAM BRADFORD (1590–1657), born in England, was a signer of the Mayflower Compact and governor of Plymouth Colony. WILLIAM BRADFORD (1663–1742) emigrated from England to Pennsylvania, established a printing press in Philadelphia, and then set up operations in New York. There, he printed the first published legislative proceedings in America, the first New York paper money, and the first New York newspaper, the *New York Gazette*. His son ANDREW BRADFORD (1686–1742) founded and published the first newspaper in Philadelphia, the *American Weekly Mercury*. Andrew's nephew and William's grandson, WILLIAM BRADFORD (1721?–1791) of New York, founded and edited the *Weekly Advertiser* and in 1775 became printer to the Continental Congress, which earned him the title of "patriot printer of 1776." His son, THOMAS BRADFORD (1745–1838), founded and published the *Merchants Daily Advertiser* in Philadelphia and was a trendsetter in publishing financial news. AUGUSTUS W. BRADFORD (1806–1881) was the Unionist governor of Maryland during the Civil War. EDWARD H. BRADFORD (1848–1926) of Massachusetts, an orthopedic surgeon, founded the first school for handicapped children in the United States in Boston in 1893. GAMALIEL BRADFORD (1863–1932) of Massachusetts was a biographer whose books include *Lee the American* (1912) and *Darwin* (1926). ROARK W. BRADFORD (1896–1948) of Tennessee wrote a number of books, including *Ol' Man Adam an' His Chillun* (1928). ROBERT D. BRADFORD (1903–1973) of Utah rose from junior metallurgist to president of American Smelting & Refinery Co., a major international mining company.

Genealogies: *Bradford Roots and Branches* was compiled by Nancy Vashti Anthony Jacob and published in Louisiana in 1975. *Bradford: From the Mayflower and Plimouth Colony to Missouri with Related Families* was compiled by Sophia Freeland Kennedy and published in Kansas City, Missouri, in 1975.

BRADLEY   (S.S. Abbreviation: Bradle)
Ranking: 189   **S.S. Count:** 183,750
Origin: English, Irish, Scottish. English, Scottish: derived from the Old English words "brād" and "lēah," meaning broad and wood. The name was given to those who came from Bradley, the name of several places in England. Irish: transformation of Brawley.

Famous **Bradleys**: JOSEPH P. BRADLEY (1813–1892) of New York was a U.S. Supreme Court justice (1870–1892). LYDIA MOSS BRADLEY (1816–1908) of Indiana was a successful businesswoman who founded Bradley Polytechnic Institute. OMAR BRADLEY (1893–1981) of Missouri was a U.S. army general who, in World War II, led the largest force ever led by a field commander. He later became head of the Veterans Administration and chairman of the Joint

Chiefs of Staff. MILTON BRADLEY (1836–1911) of Maine was a game and toy manufacturer. His optic toy "The Wheel of Life" is said to have been the first moving-picture machine. Later in his life, he promoted the kindergarten movement.

Genealogies: *The Ancestors of Leland Shaw Bradley* was compiled by Leland Shaw Bradley and published in Putnam, Connecticut, in 1990. *The Bradley Family* was compiled by Frederick W. Bradley and published in New York, New York, in 1978.

BRADSHAW   (S.S. Abbreviation: Bradsh)
Ranking: 725   **S.S. Count:** 58,368
Origin: English. Derived from the Old English words "brād" and "sceaga," meaning broad and thicket. The name was given to those who came from Bradshaw, the name of several places in England.

Genealogies: *Ancestors and Descendants of John H. Bradshaw and Scythia Enfield Fritter of Stafford County Virginia and Allied Families* was compiled by J. Douglas Bradshaw and published in Richmond, Virginia, in 1991. *Clara Harmon Bradshaw; Her American Ancestors and Her Descendants* was compiled by Mary Frances Bradshaw Dittrich and published in Indiana in 1973.

BRADY
Ranking: 389   **S.S. Count:** 99,560
Origin: English, Irish. 1) derived from the Old English words "brād" and "eage," meaning broad and eyes. The name was given to those who had big or wide-set eyes. 2) derived from the Old English words "brad" and "eg," meaning broad and island. The name was given to those who came from a place called Broad Island. 3) derived from the Old English words "brad" and "(ge)haöege," meaning broad and enclosure. The name was given to those who lived near a broad enclosure. Irish: derived from the Gaelic name Ó Brádaigh, meaning "descendant of Brádach."

Famous **Bradys**: MATHEW BRADY (1823?–1896) of New York accompanied Union soldiers as a photographer during the Civil War and, in his Brady's National Photographic Collection, gave a lasting pictoral history of the war. JOHN G. BRADY (1848–1906) of New York was governor of Alaska (1897–1906). JAMES BUCHANAN (DIAMOND JIM) BRADY (1856–1917) of New York, New York, made his fortune as the sole U.S. agent for the Fox Pressed Steel Car Truck Company of England. He was known for being generous and lavish, as well as for collecting and wearing diamond jewelry. During his lifetime he bought more than $2 million worth of diamonds. WILLIAM A. BRADY (1863–1950) of California was a successful theatrical producer who served as president of the National Assembly of the Motion Picture Industry (1915–1920). His wife, GRACE GEORGE BRADY (1879–1961), was a popular actress in New York. His daughter, ALICE BRADY (1892–1939), also was a succesful stage actress. MILDRED ALICE EDIE BRADY (1906–1965) of Arkansas was a consumer advocate and editor. After editing columns for *McCall's* and *Consumer Reports*, she became editorial director, then senior editor at *Consumer Reports*.

Genealogies: *John Brady and His Descendants: (1813—County Caven, Ireland—Fort Dodge, Iowa, USA 1900)* was compiled by Margaret Mahan Goetz and published in Iowa City, Iowa, in the 1970s.

BRAGG

Ranking: 1460 **S.S. Count:** 30,515

Origin: English. Derived from the Middle English word "bragge," meaning merry. The name was given to those considered lively.

Famous **Braggs:** THOMAS BRAGG (1810–1872) of North Carolina was governor of North Carolina (1855–1859) and a U.S. senator (1859–1861). He was Confederate attorney general during part of the Civil War. His brother, BRAXTON BRAGG (1817–1876), was a Confederate army general and military advisor to Confederate President Jefferson Davis. EDWARD S. BRAGG (1827–1912) of New York was a member of Congress from Wisconsin (1877–1883).

Genealogies: None known.

BRAMLETT, BRAMLETTE, BRAMLEY (S.S. Abbreviation: Bramle)

Ranking: 4236 **S.S. Count:** 10,644

Origin: English. Bramlett, Bramlette: derived from the first name Bram, a form of Abraham, which means "father of a multitude" (ES). Bramley: derived from the Old English words "brōm" and "lēah," meaning broom and wood. The name was given to those who came from Bramley, the name of several places in England.

Famous **Bearers:** MILTON BRAMLETTE (1896–1977) of Texas, a geologist, was an authority on sedimentary petrology, submarine geology, and micropaleontology.

Genealogies: *The Ancestors of Harriett Chrisman Ross (including the Bramlett Family)* was compiled by John Hal Connor and published in 1976.

BRANCH (ALSO BRANCHE)

Ranking: 839 **S.S. Count:** 50,786

Origin: English, Finnish, Swedish. Derived from the Old French and Middle English word "branche," meaning branch.

Famous **Branches:** JOHN BRANCH (1782–1863) of North Carolina was a tireless politician. He was governor of North Carolina (1817–1820); U.S. senator from North Carolina (1823–1829); U.S. secretary of the navy (1829–1831), then governor of Florida (1843–1861). RUSSELL T. BRANCH (1889–1973) of New York, as vice president of Stone & Webster

Engineering Corp. during World War II, was in charge of the construction of the $400 million uranium-hexafluoride separation atomic bomb plant in Oak Ridge, Tennessee, in connection with work for the Manhattan Engineer District project, which developed the atomic bomb.

Genealogies: *Cousins by the Dozens* was compiled by Dorothy Sturgis Pruett and published in Macon, Georgia, in 1975. *Thomas Taylor and Benjamin Branch of Nashville, Tennessee, and Related Families* was compiled by Ethel Taylor Ford and published in Amarillo, Texas, in 1972.

BRAND

Ranking: 1715 **S.S. Count:** 26,086

Origin: English, French, German. English, French, German: derived from the Germanic word "brand," meaning sword as it is a root in the first name Brando. German: derived from the Middle High German word "brant," meaning a burned-out area. The name was given to those who came from such a place.

Genealogies: None known.

BRANDEJS, BRANDEIS, BRANDEL, BRANDES   (S.S. Abbreviation: Brande)

Ranking: 1572 **S.S. Count:** 26,086

Origin: Brandejs—Czech; Brandeis—Jewish; Brandel, Brandes—German. Brandejs, Brandeis: the names were given to those who came from Brandeis, which is just north of Prague, Czechoslovakia. Brandel, Brandes: cognates to Brand.

Famous **Brandeises:** LOUIS DEMBITZ BRANDEIS (1856–1941) of Kentucky was the first Jewish justice of the U.S. Supreme Court. Before being appointed to the high court, he devised a plan for affordable life insurance that was enacted by the Massachusetts legislature.

Genealogies: None known.

BRANDO, BRANDONE, BRANDONI, BRANDON

Ranking: 1174 **S.S. Count:** 37,195

Origin: Brando, Brandone, Brandoni—Italian; Brandon—English, French. Brando, Brandone, Brandoni, Brandon (French): cognates to and transformations of Brand. Brandon (English): derived from the Old English words "brōm" and "dūn," meaning broom and hill. The name was given to those who came from Brandon, the name of several places in England.

Famous **Bearers:** GERARD C. BRANDON (1788–1850) was the first native-born Mississippian to be governor of that state (1855–1861).

Genealogies: *The Brandons of Halifax County, Virginia, Gaston County, North Carolina and York County, South Carolina* was compiled by Arlie Brandon Betts and published in Massachusetts in 1987.

BRANDT

Ranking: 837 **S.S. Count:** 50,876
Origin: German. Transformation of Brand.
Genealogies: *Brandt Family History, 1822–1977* was compiled by Dolores J. Colletti and published in Franklin Park, Illinois, in 1979. *Some Descendants of William Coulston, Line of Levi Coulson (to 1915), Some Descendants of Ludwig Brandt, Line of John Brandt* was compiled by Samuel B. Mayo and published in Edina, Minnesota, in 1980.

BRANHAM (S.S. Abbreviation: Branha)

Ranking: 2428 **S.S. Count:** 18,669
Origin: English. Derived from the first name Branta and the Old English word "hām," meaning homestead. The name was given to those who came from Brantham, a place in Suffolk, England.
Genealogies: None known.

BRANNAGH, BRANNAN (S.S. Abbreviation: Branna)

Ranking: 4008 **S.S. Count:** 11,296
Origin: Irish. Brannagh: derived from the Gaelic word "Breathnach," meaning Briton. Brannan: transformation of Brennan.
Famous Bearers: SAMUEL BRANNAN (1819–1889) of Saco, Maine, was a Mormon leader (he converted as a young man) who led a large group of Mormon emigrants who sailed around South America from New York to California. In California, he led a vigilante justice system but resigned his post as president of the Committee of Vigilance when his methods were judged excessive.
Genealogies: None known.

BRANNO

Ranking: 1783 **S.S. Count:** 25,230
Origin: Italian. Cognate to Brand.
Genealogies: None known.

BRANSOM, BRANSON (S.S. Abbreviation: Branso)

Ranking: 2969 **S.S. Count:** 15,320
Origin: English. Transformations of Brand.
Famous Bearers: PAUL BRANSOM (1885–1979) of Washington, D.C., worked as a professional illustrator for about 70 years, illustrating magazines such as the *Saturday Evening Post*, and books such as Jack London's *Call of the Wild*. He was known as the dean of animal artists.
Genealogies: *Ellis Branson of Romine Township, Marion County, Illinois* was compiled by Donald Ray Branson and published in St. Charles, Illinois, in 1980. *History of the Branson Family and Descendants* was compiled by Joy Branson Gibboney and published in Athens, Ohio, in 1965.

BRANT

Ranking: 3221 **S.S. Count:** 14,077
Origin: German. Transformation of Brand.
Famous Brants: JOSEPH BRANT (1742–1807) of Ohio was a Native American leader and the son of a Mohawk chief. He aided the British against Chief Pontiac during the French and Indian Wars. During the Revolution he sided with the British, but after the war he led an effort to pacify the Native American frontier.
Genealogies: None known.

BRANTL, BRANTLEY, BRANTLY

Ranking: 1574 **S.S. Count:** 28,390
Origin: Brantl—German; Brantley, Brantly—English. Brantl: transformation of Brand. Brantley, Brantly: derived from the Old English words "brōm" and "lēah," meaning broom and wood. The names were given to those who came from Bramley, the name of several places in England.
Genealogies: *Dear Grandchildren: A Genealogy of the Descendants of James Brantley and Elizabeth Kirven* was compiled by James Ivey Jackson Brantley and published in Grady, Alabama, in 1976.

BRASHEAR, BRASHEARS, BRASHER (S.S. Abbreviation: Brashe)

Ranking: 2358 **S.S. Count:** 19,241
Origin: English. Brashear, Brashears, Brasher: 1) derived from the Old English word "bræsian," meaning to cast in brass. The names were given to those who made brass objects. Brasher 2) derived from the Late Latin word "braciāre," meaning a brewer. The name was given to those who worked as brewers.
Famous Bearers: EDWIN L. BRASHEARS (1899–1973) of Missouri was president of National Realty and Investment Co. and owner of the Drake Hotel in Chicago and other hotels.
Genealogies: *Belt Brashear and Amelia Duvall: Their Ancestors and Descendants* was compiled by Sydney M. Kilpatrick and published in Louisiana in the 1970s. *Our Family Heritage of Sackett, Tunison, French and Wonser (also Brashear) Families with Appendix of Beekman's and Brasier's* was compiled by Ruth Wonser McCormick and published in 1981.

BRASWELL (S.S. Abbreviation: Braswe)

Ranking: 2412 **S.S. Count:** 18,786
Origin: English. The name was given to those who came from Braithwell, which means "broad stream" (ES) and is a place in Yorkshire, England.

Famous **Braswells:** EARL B. BRASWELL (1889–1978) of Georgia was publisher and general manager of the Athens (Georgia) *Banner-Herald* (1921–1965). As president of Athens Publishing Co., beginning in 1929, he was the youngest publishing-company president in Georgia.

Genealogies: *Following the Braswells on the Move Westward in America, 1600–1973* was compiled by Roy Bennett Braswell and published in Amarillo, Texas, in 1973.

BRATCHER　(S.S. Abbreviation: Bratch)

Ranking: 3812　**S.S. Count:** 11,838

Origin: English. Derived from the Old English word "bræc," meaning freshly farmed or plowed land. The name was given to those who lived near farms or near places that were named at the time they had just been cultivated.

Genealogies: None known.

BRATTON　(S.S. Abbreviation: Bratto)

Ranking: 3390　**S.S. Count:** 13,352

Origin: English. The name was given to those who came from Bratton, which means "newly culivated homestead" (ES) and is the name of several places in England.

Genealogies: None known.

BRAUN

Ranking: 951　**S.S. Count:** 45,623

Origin: German. Cognate to Brown.

Famous **Brauns:** EMMA LUCY BRAUN (1889–1971) of Ohio was a botanist who wrote classic texts from her research, including *Deciduous Forests of Eastern North America* (1950). WERNHER VON BRAUN (1912–1977), born in Germany, was a rocket scientist. He developed several rockets for the United States, including the Redstone, Jupiter-C, Juno, and Pershing. He also developed the Saturn V rocket used in Apollo space flights, and he wrote or co-wrote books on space exploration.

Genealogies: *The Ancestors and Descendants of Abraham (Braun) Brown, the Miller: The Ancestors and Descendants of Jacob (Braun) Brown, the Wagonmaker* was compiled by John Burgess Fisher and published in Charlotte, North Carolina, in 1983. *Footprints in the Sands of Time* was compiled by Karen M. Gomez and published in Commerce City, Colorado, in 1978.

BRAVO

Ranking: 2779　**S.S. Count:** 16,392

Origin: Portuguese, Spanish. Derived from the Portuguese and Spanish word "bravo," meaning fierce. The name was given to those considered to be fierce.

Genealogies: None known.

BRAXTON　(S.S. Abbreviation: Braxto)

Ranking: 2831　**S.S. Count:** 16,110

Origin: English. Derived from the Old English first name Bracc and the word "tūn," meaning settlement. The name was given to those who came from Braxton, a now unidentifiable place in England.

Famous **Braxtons:** CARTER BRAXTON (1736–1797) of Virginia was a member of the Continental Congress and a signer of the Declaration of Independence.

Genealogies: *A Braxton Family Genealogy: Descendants of John Braxton (1782–1860) and Mary "Polly" Love (1801–1844)* was compiled by Bonnie Woody Braxton and published in North Carolina in 1989. *The History of Blair, Banister, and Braxton Families Before and After the Revolution* was compiled by Frederick Horner and published in Philadelphia, Pennsylvania, in 1898.

BRAY

Ranking: 947　**S.S. Count:** 45,681

Origin: English. Derived from the Old French word "bray," meaning march. The name was given to those who came from Bray, the name of several places in England.

Genealogies: *Bray Family History* was compiled by Raymond Gary Taylor and published in Alexandria, Virginia, in 1980. *John Proctor of Ipswich and Some of His Descendants (including the Bray Family)* was compiled by Leland H. Procter and published in Springfield, Massachusetts, in 1985.

BRAZIL

Ranking: 4980　**S.S. Count:** 9002

Origin: Irish. Derived from the Gaelic name Ó Breasail, meaning "descendant of Breasal" (H&H), a first name meaning strife.

Genealogies: None known.

BREAUX

Ranking: 3029　**S.S. Count:** 15,009

Origin: French? Uncertain etymology. Most likely derived from the Old French word "beu," meaning fair.

Famous **Breauxs:** JOSEPH ARSENNE (1838–1926) of Louisiana, a jurist, is credited with reforming Louisiana school laws and practice. He was chief justice of the Louisiana Supreme Court (1904–1914).

Genealogies: None known.

BREEDE (ALSO BREEDER)

Ranking: 2934　**S.S. Count:** 15,552

Origin: English. Derived from the Old English word "brāe du," meaning breadth. The name was given to those who came from Breed, the name of several places in England.

Genealogies: None known.

BREEDLOVE (S.S. Abbreviation: Breedl)

Ranking: 3787   S.S. Count: 11,908

Origin: English. The name was given to those who lived near a wide pool.

Genealogies: None known.

BREEN

Ranking: 2515   S.S. Count: 18,050

Origin: Irish. Derived from the Gaelic name Ó Braion, meaning "descendant of Braon" (H&H), a first name meaning moisture.

Famous **Breens:** JOSEPH I. BREEN (1890–1954) of Pennsylvania, as a Hollywood film censor, exercised influence over motion pictures for 20 years.

Genealogies: None known.

BREMER

Ranking: 4453   S.S. Count: 10,064

Origin: German. The name was given to those who came from Bremen, which means "by the seashore" (ES) and is a place in Germany.

Genealogies: None known.

BRENNAN (S.S. Abbreviation: Brenna)

Ranking: 576   S.S. Count: 71,615

Origin: Irish. Derived from the Gaelic name Ó Braonáin, meaning "descendant of Braonán" (H&H), a first name meaning little drop of moisture.

Famous **Brennans:** ALFRED L. BRENNAN (1853–1921) of Kentucky was an illustrator known mostly for his pen-and-ink work. FRANCIS J. BRENNAN (1894–1968) of Pennsylvania was the first American appointed judge in the Sacra Rota, the Vatican's court of appeals. WILLIAM JOSEPH BRENNAN JR. (1906–) of New Jersey was a justice of the U.S. Supreme Court (1956–1990). Although he is a Democrat, he was appointed by President Eisenhower. He was considered a liberal jurist.

Genealogies: *A History of the Brennans of Idough, County Kilkenny* was compiled by Thomas A. Brennan and published in Eastchester, New York, in 1975. *I Thank God for All My Memories* was compiled by Mary Zacchaeus Ryan and published in Minneapolis, Minnesota, in 1983.

BRENNER (S.S. Abbreviation: Brenne)

Ranking: 1286   S.S. Count: 34,416

Origin: German, Jewish. Derived from the German word "brenner," meaning one who burns. The name was often given to those who distilled liquor and was also given to those who burned clearings in forests.

Famous **Brenners:** VICTOR DAVID BRENNER (1871–1924), a Russian native, was a sculptor who designed the Lincoln penny, issued in 1909 and still in use today.

Genealogies: *Brenner—Brenner: A Genealogical Study of the Brenner Family from Goldingen in Kurland* was compiled by Albert Gerard Gluckman and published in 1981.

BRENT

Ranking: 4223   S.S. Count: 10,679

Origin: English. Derived from the Middle English word "brent," meaning burned. The name was given to those who lived near a burnt area.

Famous **Brents:** MARGARET BRENT (1600?–1671?) is considered America's first feminist. She was the first woman to receive a land grant from the British Crown, and she emigrated from England to settle in St. Mary's, Maryland, where she became one of the most prominent landowners in the region.

Genealogies: None known.

BREWER

Ranking: 264   S.S. Count: 138,231

Origin: English. Derived from the Old English word "brē-owan," meaning to brew. The name was given to those who worked brewing beer and ale.

Famous **Brewers:** THOMAS M. BREWER (1814–1880) of Massachusetts was an ornithologist and oologist. He wrote *North American Oology* (1857). DAVID JOSIAH BREWER (1837–1910), born in Asia Minor, was a U.S. Supreme Court justice and a member of the Venezuelan boundary and arbitration commissions. MARK S. BREWER (1827–1901) was a member of Congress from Michigan for eight years.

Genealogies: *The Chauncey Marble Brewer Family of Marshall, Michigan* was compiled by James DeWolfe and published in Marshall, Michigan, in 1979. *The Genealogy of Daniel P. Brewer* was compiled by Buel Amos Langdon and published in Illinois in 1950.

BREWSTER (S.S. Abbreviation: Brewst)

Ranking: 1730   S.S. Count: 25,936

Origin: English. Transformation of Brewer.

Famous **Brewsters:** WILLIAM BREWSTER (1567–1644) sailed from England to America on the *Mayflower* and was a religious leader in Plymouth Colony. BENJAMIN H. BREWSTER (1816–1888) of New Jersey was the U.S. attorney general who prosecuted the Star Route frauds in the Post Office Department (1881–1884). RALPH O. BREWSTER (1888–1961) served Maine as governor (1924–1928), member of Congress (1934–1940), and U.S. senator (1940–1951).

Genealogies: *Mark Brewster of Hull, England and Allied Families in America* was compiled by Marcus V. Brewster and published in Manning, South Carolina, in 1990. *A Notebook on the Descendants of Elder Willliam Brewster of Plymouth Colony* was compiled by Milton E. Terry and published in Mountainside, New Jersey, in 1985.

BRICE

Ranking: 3061   S.S. Count: 14,823

Origin: English, French, Jewish. English, French: derived from a first name that was most likely of Celtic origin. Jewish: transformation of Briess, a family name of uncertain etymology.

Famous **Brices**: FANNY BRICE (1891–1951) of New York City was born Fannie Borach. She worked as a pianist and singer before landing a place in the Ziegfeld Follies, where her comedy routines and her rendition of the French torch song "My Man" made her a star.

Genealogies: History of the Brice Family was compiled by Agnes Brice and published in Fort Worth, Texas, in 1972.

BRICKETT   (S.S. Abbreviation: Bricke)

Ranking: 2422   S.S. Count: 18,708

D1

Origin: English. Derived from the Old English word "bircett," meaning a birch tree thicket. The name was given to those who lived near several birch trees.

Genealogies: None known.

BRIDGE, BRIDGEMAN, BRIDGENS, BRIDGER, BRIDGES, BRIDGEWATER

Ranking: 381   S.S. Count: 101,961

Origin: English. Bridge, Bridgeman, Bridgens, Bridger, Bridges: derived from the Old English word "brycg," meaning bridge. The name was given to those who worked at a bridge. Bridgewater: derived from the place name "Brigwaltier," meaning Walter's bridge. The name was given to those who came from this place in Somerset, England.

Famous **Bearers**: JAMES (JIM) BRIDGER (1804–1881) of Virginia was a pioneer, scout, and fur trapper. He is known as the first white man to reach Great Salt Lake. CALVIN BRIDGES (1889–1938) of New York was a geneticist. He helped prove the chromosome theory of heredity and initiated the process of mapping chromosomes. STYLES BRIDGES (1898–1961) of Maine was governor of New Hampshire (1934–1936) and led the state to be the first to qualify under the federal Social Security Act. He was also a U.S. senator from New Hampshire (1937–1961). THOMAS JEFFERSON DAVIS BRIDGES (1906–1968) of Tennessee, a major league baseball pitcher, won 194 games (including 33 shutouts) and lost 138 games during a 16-year career with the Detroit Tigers. He pitched in four World Series.

Genealogies: None known.

BRIGGS

Ranking: 505   S.S. Count: 79,696

Origin: English. Transformation of Bridge.

Famous **Briggses**: CHARLES A. BRIGGS (1841–1913) of New York was tried for heresy and suspended from the Presbyterian ministry in 1892, then became an Episcopal clergyman in 1900. LE BARON BRIGGS (1855–1934) of Massachusetts was president of Radcliffe College (1903–1923). LYMAN J. BRIGGS (1874–1963) of Michigan, a physicist, organized and chaired in 1939 the first government committee that investigated the feasibility of the military's using atomic energy. He was director of the National Bureau of Standards (1932–1945). The May 1954 issue of *Scientific Monthly* was devoted to him as an 80th-birthday present. CLARE A. BRIGGS (1875–1930) of Wisconsin was a cartoonist on the staff of the *Chicago Tribune*, then the *New York Tribune*.

Genealogies: A Harkrader-Hathaway (including the Briggs Family) History was compiled by Charles Briggs Hathaway and published in Baltimore, Maryland, in 1991. *John Briggs of Sandwich, Massachusetts and His Descendants* was compiled by Edna Anne Hannibal and published in California in 1962.

BRIGHAM (S.S. ABBREVIATION BRIGHA)

Ranking: 4836   S.S. Count: 9252

Origin: English. Derived from the Old English words "brycg" and "hām," meaning bridge and homestead. The name was given to those who came from Brigham, the name of several places in England.

Famous **Brighams**: MARY ANN BRIGHAM (1829–1889) of Massachusetts was named the first president of Mount Holyoke College, but she died before taking office. She was associate principal at Brooklyn Heights Seminary (1863–1889).

Genealogies: From Whence We Came: A History of the Thomas Brigham and Related Families was compiled by Elden L. Brigham and published in Ann Arbor, Michigan, in 1976.

BRIGHT

Ranking: 750   S.S. Count: 56,372

Origin: English. Derived from the Old English word "beorht," meaning bright. The name was given to those who were considered to be bright and attractive.

Famous **Brights**: JESSE D. BRIGHT (1812–1875) was a U.S. senator from Indiana who was expelled from the Senate for treason. JAMES W. BRIGHT (1852–1926) of Pennsylvania edited *Modern Language Notes* from 1886 to 1915.

Genealogies: Looking Back: A Family History (including the Bright Family) and Genealogy of and by Hazel Wise Huffman was compiled by Hazel Wise Huffman and published in 1985.

BRILL

Ranking: 3379   S.S. Count: 13,395

Origin: Dutch, German. The name was given to those who came from Brill, a place in the Netherlands.

Famous **Brills**: ABRAHAM A. BRILL (1874–1948), born in Hungary, was the first practicing psychoanalyst in the United States. ISADOR C. BRILL (1888–1975), born in Russia, was a cardiologist and educator. While on the staff at the University of Oregon medical school in Portland, he advanced the process of typing blood.

Genealogies: None known.

BRINK

Ranking: 2843   S.S. Count: 16,053

Origin: Danish, Dutch, German, Jewish. Danish, Dutch, German: derived from the Middle Low German word "brinc," meaning pasture or raised meadow. The name was given to those who lived near or in such places. Jewish: uncertain etymology. Possibly derived from the Hebrew word "bar," meaning son of.

Famous **Brinks**: LYMAN A. BRINK (1909–1972) was a prominent attorney in Minnesota.

Genealogies: None known.

BRINKEN, BRINKER   (S.S. Abbreviation: Brinke)

Ranking: 4139   S.S. Count: 10,935

Origin: German. Transformations of Brink.

Genealogies: *The Homecoming: A Celebration of the Wofford, Lottie and Brinker Families* was compiled by Dorothy Wofford Witherspoon and published in Baltimore, Maryland, in 1990.

BRINKLEY   (S.S. Abbreviation: Brinkley)

Ranking: 2449   S.S. Count: 18,531

Origin: English. Derived from the Old English first name Brynca and the Old English word "lēah," meaning wood. The name was given to those who came from Brinkley, a place in Cambridgeshire, England.

Genealogies: None known.

BRINKMAN, BRINKMANN   (S.S. Abbreviation: Brinkm)

Ranking: 2574   S.S. Count: 17,673

Origin: Brinkman—Dutch; Brinkmann—German. Transformations of Brink.

Genealogies: None known.

BRINSON   (S.S. Abbreviation: Brinso)

Ranking: 2809   S.S. Count: 16,244

Origin: English. The name was given to those who came from Brienon, a place in Normandy, France.

Genealogies: None known.

BRISCO (ALSO BRISCOE)

Ranking: 2012   S.S. Count: 22,689

Origin: English. 1) derived from the Old Norse word "Bretaskógr," meaning "wood of the Britons" (H&H). 2) derived from the Old Norse words "birki" and "skógr," meaning birch and wood. In both cases, the names were given to those who came from Briscoe, the name of several places in England.

Genealogies: *Wright-Briscoe Pioneers* was compiled by John C. Wright and published in 1974.

BRISTO, BRISTOE, BRISTOL, BRISTOW, BRISTOWE

Ranking: 2142   S.S. Count: 21,386

Origin: English. Derived from the Old English words "brycg" and "stōw," meaning bridge and place for assembly. The name was given to those who came from Bristol, a place in England.

Famous **Bristows**: BENJAMIN HELM BRISTOW (1832–1896) of Kentucky was an active Unionist during the Civil War. He was elected to the Kentucky legislature without his knowledge in 1863. As Kentucky attorney general he was successful in opposing the Ku Klux Klan. As secretary of the treasury under President Ulysses S. Grant, he eliminated widespread corruption.

Genealogies: *Bristol Genealogy* was compiled by Warren Edwin Bristol and published in Milford, Connecticut, in 1967.

BRITO

Ranking: 4904   S.S. Count: 9119

Origin: Portuguese, Spanish. Uncertain etymology. The name was given to those who came from Brito, the name of several places in Portugal.

Genealogies: None known.

BRITT

Ranking: 1035   S.S. Count: 42,275

Origin: English, German. English: transformation of Brett. German: cognate to Brice.

Genealogies: None known.

BRITTAN, BRITTAIN   (S.S. Abbreviation: Britta)

Ranking: 3486   S.S. Count: 12,935

Origin: English. 1) transformation of Brett. 2) the name was taken by those who emigrated to Great Britain.

Genealogies: *The Brittain Family in America* was compiled by Virginia Thompson Britain and published in Pasadena, California, in 1971.

BRITTON   (S.S. Abbreviation: Britto)

Ranking: 1076   S.S. Count: 40,988
Origin: English. Transformation of Brittain.
Famous **Brittons**: ELIZABETH GERTRUDE KNIGHT BRITTON (1858–1934) of New York City was a botanist famous for her studies of mosses and her efforts on behalf of wildflower conservation. NATHANIEL L. BRITTON (1859–1934) of New York, a botanist, was a founder and first director of the New York Botanical Garden.
Genealogies: *The Brittain Family (also the Britton Family) in America* was compiled by Virginia Thompson Britain and published in Pasadena, California, in 1971. *Britton Genealogy; Early Generations from Somersetshire, England to Staten Island, New York* was compiled by Elmer Garfield Van Name and published in Woodbury, New Jersey, in 1970.

BROADWAY, BROADWELL   (S.S. Abbreviation: Broadw)

Ranking: 2952   S.S. Count: 15,420
Origin: English. Broadway: the name was given to the people who came from Broadway, which means "wide road" (ES) and is the name of several places in England. Broadwell: the name was given to those who came from Broadwell, which means "wide stream" (ES) and is the name of several places in England.
Genealogies: None known.

BROCK

Ranking: 492   S.S. Count: 81,394
Origin: English, German, Jewish. English, German: transformation of and cognate to Brook. English: derived from the Old English word "brocc," meaning badger. The name was given to those who were thought to look like badgers. Jewish: uncertain etymology. Possibly derived from the Hebrew word "bar," meaning son of.
Famous **Brocks**: SAMUEL BROCK (1893–1974) of New York was a neuropsychiatrist and educator who practiced in New York City. He was an author of many articles and book chapters and co-author of *Basis of Clinical Neurology* (1945, 1963).
Genealogies: *Brief Outline of the Brock Family of Shenandoah Valley, Virginia* was compiled by Franklin A. Zirkle and published in New Market, Virginia, in 1971.

BROCKENSHAW, BROCKER (S.S ABBREVIATION: BROCKE)

Ranking: 4551   S.S. Count: 9816
Origin: Brockenshaw—English;   Brocker—German.

Brockenshaw: derived from the Old English word "burhmann," meaning one who lived in a fortified town. Brocker: transformation of Brock.
Genealogies: None known.

BROCKMAN, BROCKMANN   (S.S. Abbreviation: Brockm)

Ranking: 2252   S.S. Count: 20,306
Origin: Brockman—English; Brockmann—German. Transformations of Brock.
Genealogies: None known.

BRODER, BRODERSON

Ranking: 2245   S.S. Count: 20,384
Origin: German, Jewish. German: transformation of Brother. Jewish: transformation of Brodski.
Genealogies: None known.

BRODIE

Ranking: 4686   S.S. Count: 9548
Origin: Jewish, Scottish. Jewish: transformation of Brodski. Scottish: uncertain etymology. Most likely derived from the Gaelic word "brothach," meaning muddy place. The name was given to those who came from near Brodie Castle, a place in Scotland.
Genealogies: None known.

BRODY

Ranking: 4693   S.S. Count: 9535
Origin: Jewish. Transformation of Brodski.
Genealogies: None known.

BROGAN

Ranking: 4364   S.S. Count: 10,271
Origin: Irish. Derived from the Gaelic name Ó Brógáin, meaning "descendant of Brógán" (H&H), which is derived from the word "bróg," meaning shoe.
Famous **Brogans**: JOHN A. BROGAN JR. (1892–1974) of New Jersey, as vice president and foreign sales manager of the Hearst Corp. is credited with a major role in King Features Syndicate's becoming the world's largest feature news organization.
Genealogies: None known.

BRONSON   (S.S. Abbreviation: Bronso)

Ranking: 2951   S.S. Count: 15,427
Origin: England. Transformation of Brown.
Genealogies: *Bronson-Brownson-Brunson: Some Descendants of John Bronson of Hartford (1636) Who Migrated to Vermont, New Hampshire, New Jersey [and] Pennsylvania* was compiled by Eliza Howlett Tracy and published in La Jolla, California, in 1973.

BROOKE

Ranking: 2638 S.S. Count: 17,250
Origin: English. Transformation of Brook.
Famous **Brookes:** JOHN M. BROOKE (1826–1906) of Florida was a naval officer who invented a deep-sea sounding device that enabled the ocean bottom to be mapped topographically. JOHN R. BROOKE (1838–1926) of Pennsylvania was a Union Army commander during the Civil War; he later served as military governor of Puerto Rico.
Genealogies: None known.

BROOKING, BROOKINGS (S.S. Abbreviation: Brooki)

Ranking: 4889 S.S. Count: 9141
Origin: English. Transformations of Brook.
Famous **Bearers:** ROBERT SOMERS BROOKINGS (1850–1932) of Maryland became a millionaire through his real estate business. At the age of 46, he retired and devoted himself to philanthropy. As president of the corporation of Washington University, he improved the medical school to a world-class standing. He was an original trustee of the Carnegie Endowment for International Peace, and when the Institute for Government Research, the Institute of Economics, and the Graduate School of Economics and Government merged, the trustees voted to name the new graduate and research center the Brookings Institute.
Genealogies: None known.

BROOKS, BROOKSBANK

Ranking: 72 S.S. Count: 348,753
Origin: English. Brooks: transformation of Brook. Brooksbank: derived from the Middle English words "brokes" and "bank," meaning brook and bank. The name was given to those who came from Brooksbank, the name of several places in England.
Famous **Bearers:** PHILLIPS BROOKS (1835–1893) of Massachusetts was an Episcopal pastor in Pennsylvania and Massachusetts and author of the hymn "O Little Town of Bethlehem." WILLIAM BROOKS (1848–1908) of Ohio, a zoologist noted for his study of marine animals, founded the Chesapeake Zoological Laboratory and wrote *The Oyster* (1891). ALFRED H. BROOKS (1871–1924) of Michigan, a geologist with the U.S. Geological Survey who extensively explored Alaska, discovered Rainy Pass. He wrote *Geography and Geology of Alaska* (1906). VAN WYCK BROOKS (1886–1963) of New Jersey was a writer whose *Flowering of New England* (1936) won a Pulitzer Prize.
Genealogies: *Brooks Family History* was compiled by Bernice Brooks Casey and published in Stillwater, Oklahoma, in 1982. *The Brooks of Virginia* was compiled by Bruce Montgomery Edwards and published in Baltimore, Maryland, in 1985.

BROOME

Ranking: 3088 S.S. Count: 14,706
Origin: English. Derived from the Old English word "brōm," meaning broom. The name was given to those who came from Broom(e) or Brome, the names of several places in England.
Genealogies: *Children Meet Your Ancestors* was compiled by Genevieve Broome Jones and published in West Point, Georgia, in 1976.

BROPHY

Ranking: 4870 S.S. Count: 9189
Origin: Irish. Derived from the Gaelic name Ó Bróithe, meaning "descendant of Brōth" (H&H).
Genealogies: None known.

BROTHER, BROTHERS (S.S. Abbreviation: Brothe)

Ranking: 1858 S.S. Count: 24,370
Origin: English, Irish. English: derived from the Old English word "brōðor," meaning brother. The name was used to refer to fellow guild members or the brother of someone important or someone's younger son. Irish: the name Ó Bruadair has been transformed into Brothers, although it most likely was derived from the Gaelic word "bruadar," meaning dream.
Genealogies: None known.

BROUGH (ALSO BROUGHAM, BROUGHTON)

Ranking: 1817 S.S. Count: 24,830
Origin: English. Brough: derived from the Old English word "burh," meaning fortress. The name was given to those who came from Brough, the name of several places in England. Brougham: same derivation as Brough, combined with the Old English word "hām," meaning homestead. The name was given to those who came from Brougham, the name of several places in England. Broughton: derived from the Old English words "brōc," "burh," or "beorg" and "tūn," meaning brook, fortress or hill, and settlement. The name was given to those who came from Broughton, the name of several places in England.
Famous **Broughs:** JOHN BROUGH (1811–1865) was editor of the *Cincinnati Enquirer* and governor of Ohio (1864–1865). CHARLES H. BROUGH (1876–1935) of Mississippi was governor of Arkansas (1916–1918).
Genealogies: None known.

BROUSS

Ranking: 1232 S.S. Count: 3598
Origin: French. Derived from the Late Latin word "bruscia," meaning brushwood. The name was given to those who

lived near scrub brush and to those who worked making brushes.

Genealogies: None known.

BROWER

Ranking: 2183   **S.S. Count:** 21,020
Origin: Dutch. Cognate to Brewer.

Famous **Browers:** JACOB V. BROWER (1844–1905) was an archaeologist and explorer who discovered aboriginal mounds at Mille Lacs, Minnesota.

Genealogies: None known.

BROWN

Ranking: 4   **S.S. Count:** 1,958,106
Origin: English. Derived from the Old High German word "brūn," meaning brown. The name was given to those with brown hair, brown eyes, or brown skin, or to those who habitually wore brown clothes.

Famous **Browns:** NICHOLAS BROWN (1729–1791) of Rhode Island helped found Rhode Island College, which became Brown University. WILLIAM H. BROWN (1765–1793) of Massachusetts wrote *The Power of Sympathy* (1789), considered the first novel in America and long attributed falsely to Sarah Morton. CHARLES B. BROWN (1777–1810) of Pennsylvania was the first American novelist to achieve international recognition. JAMES BROWN (1800–1855) of Massachusetts, along with Charles Little, formed a publishing company now known as Little, Brown & Co. JOHN BROWN (1800–1859) of Connecticut was a drifter and a business failure who became a radical in the abolitionist movement. He and his followers murdered five settlers in Kansas for their pro-slavery beliefs. Later, he and 21 followers took control of the federal arsenal at Harper's Ferry, Virginia. He was captured by Col. Robert E. Lee's troops and hanged for promoting slave insurrection and treason against Virginia. BENJAMIN G. BROWN (1826–1885) of Kentucky was a U.S. senator from Missouri, governor of Missouri, and a vice-presidential nominee. OLYMPIA BROWN (1835–1926) of Michigan, the first woman to be ordained as a minister in a regular denomination (Universalist Church), was a founder and president of the Federal Suffrage Association. HENRY B. BROWN (1836–1913) of Massachusetts was a U.S. Supreme Court justice. MARTHA MCCLELLAN BROWN (1838–1916) of Maryland was one of the founders of the Prohibition Party and the National Women's Christian Temperance Union. CHARLOTTE HAWKINS BROWN (1883–1961) of North Carolina, the daughter of former slaves, founded Palmer Memorial Institute in Sedalia, North Carolina, in 1902 and modeled the school after the Hampton and Tuskegee industrial institutes. The schools merged with Bennett College in 1971.

CLARENCE JAMES BROWN (1893–1965) was a member of Congress from Ohio (1938–1965). DAYTON T. BROWN (1898–1978), vice president and chief engineer for Brewster Aeronautical Corp., designed, and his company produced, the first monoplane capable of landing on a ship. MARGARET WISE BROWN (1910–1952) of New York wrote more than 100 books in 15 years, plus the lyrics for 21 children's records.

Genealogies: *Burgess, Mullins, Browning, Brown, and Allied Families* was compiled by James A. Burgess and published in Parsons, West Virginia, in 1978. *Ancestors and Descendants of Henry Marion Murphy and Anna Jane Brown* was compiled by Lera Murphy Johnson and published in the 1980s. *Brown and Sayre Ancestry; Three Centuries in Northern New Jersey* was compiled by Mortimer Freeman Sayre and published in Columbus, Ohio, in 1971. *Brown (Browne) and the Descendants in Carolina Today* was compiled by Joseph Parsons Brown and published in North Carolina in 1965.

BROWNE

Ranking: 954   **S.S. Count:** 45,581
Origin: English. Transformation of Brown.

Famous **Brownes:** CHARLES F. BROWNE (1834–1867) of Maine, who used the pseudonym Artemus Ward, was a humorist whose writings and lectures were popular nationally.

Genealogies: *Brown (Browne) and the Descendants in Carolina Today* was compiled by Joseph Parsons Brown and published in North Carolina in 1965. *Browne-Schutt Ancestral Lines* was compiled by Jessie Bruce Smith Ornes and published in Los Angeles, California, in 1979.

BROWNING, BROWNINGS   (S.S. Abbreviation: Browni)

Ranking: 694   **S.S. Count:** 60,556
Origin: English. Transformation of Brown.

Famous **Brownings:** JOHN MOSES BROWNING (1855–1926) of Ogden, Utah, was an inventor and designer of firearms, including the Remington automatic-loading shotgun and rifle and the Colt automatic pistol, which was used by the U.S. army during World War I. TOD BROWNING (1880–1962) of Kentucky was among Universal Studios' most successful silent-film directors. He also directed sound films, including *Dracula* (1931).

Genealogies: *Burgess, Mullins, Browning, Brown, and Allied Families* was compiled by James A. Burgess and published in Parsons, West Virginia, in 1978. *The Browning Family History—David C. Browning and His Descendants, 1782–1990* was compiled by Dottie D. Elliot and published in Tulsa, Oklahoma, in 1990.

BROWNLEE, BROWNLEY, BROWNLIE, BROWNLOW (S.S. Abbreviation: Brownl)

Ranking: 2244   S.S. Count: 20,404

Origin: English. Brownlee, Brownley, Brownlie: derived from the Old High German word "brūn" and the Old English word "lēah," meaning brown and wood. The names were given to those who lived in or near brown woods. Brownlow: derived from the Old High German word "brūn" and the Old English word "hlāw," meaning hill. The name was given to those who lived near a brown hill.

Famous **Bearers:** WILLIAM BROWNLOW (1805–1877) of Virginia was an editor of Whig newspapers in Tennessee, then governor of and U.S. senator from that state.

Genealogies: *Genealogical Record of the McDonalds, Logans, Dicksons, Brownlees* was compiled by Daniel McDonald and published in New York, New York, in 1956.

BROYLES (S.S. Abbreviation: Broyle)

Ranking: 3264   S.S. Count: 13,932

Origin: French? Uncertain etymology. The name was possibly given to those who came from Broy or Broyes, the names of places in France.

Genealogies: *The Broyles Family Ties* was compiled by John Kenneth Broyles and published in Rockwood, Tennessee, between 1969 and 1971.

BRUBAKER (S.S. Abbreviation: Brubak)

Ranking: 3030   S.S. Count: 15,008

Origin: German, Swiss. German: the name was given to those who came from Brubach, which means "stream with lye or alkaline water" (ES), or Brubbach, which means "the sudsy, frothy stream" (ES), and are both places in Germany. German, Swiss: the name was given to those who came from Brubach, a place in Switzerland.

Genealogies: *A Brubaker Genealogy: The Descendants of Henry Brubaker 1775–1848 of Salem, Virginia* was compiled by Ethel Harshbarger Weddle and published in Elgin, Illinois, in 1970. *Descendants (including the Brubaker Family) of John Hess Brubacher, D-14, 1782–1863, of Juniata County and His Nephew "Cooper" John Sherk Brubacher, D-63, 1807–1887 of Ontario, Canada* was compiled by Landis Brubaker and published in Seven Valleys, Pennsylvania, in 1977.

BRUCE

Ranking: 551   S.S. Count: 74,176

Origin: English, Scottish. Uncertain etymology. The name was given to those who came from a place in Normandy, France.

Famous **Bruces:** BLANCHE KELSO BRUCE (1841–1898) of Farmville, Virginia, was born a slave and was elected to the U.S. Senate in 1874 to represent Mississippi. He was the first African-American to serve a full term in the U.S. Senate. WILLIAM CABELL BRUCE (1860–1946) was a U.S. senator from Maryland and author of the Pulitizer Prize–winnning biography *Benjamin Franklin: Self Revealed* (1917). LENNY BRUCE (1925–1966) of New York, born Leonard A. Schneider, was a comedian known for a sharp wit and tongue. He rose to fame largely based on dramatic skits in which he spoke all parts, often using profanity. Beginning in 1961, he was repeatedly arrested on obscenity charges but never convicted. He was convicted on a narcotics charge, however. His autobiography is titled *How to Talk Dirty and Influence People* (1965).

Genealogies: *Alexander Bruce of Southside Virginia and Some of His Descendants* was compiled by June A. Bruce Stubbs and published in Columbia, Missouri, in 1990. *The Ancestry and Descendants of Robert Bruce and Catherine Cearley* was compiled by Lawrence Little and published in Portales, New Mexico, in 1989.

BRUMBACK (S.S. Abbreviation: Brumba)

Ranking: 4396   S.S. Count: 10,201

Origin: German. The name was given to those who came from Brombach, which means "swampy brook" (ES) and is the name of several places in Germany.

Genealogies: None known.

BRUMFIELD (S.S. Abbreviation: Brumfi)

Ranking: 2980   S.S. Count: 15,260

Origin: English. Derived from the Old English words "brōm" and "feld," meaning broom and field or pasture. The name was given to those who came from Broomfield or Bromfield, which are both the names of several places in England.

Genealogies: *Fields of Broom: John Brumfield and Margaret Kelly, Their Ancestors and Descendants* was compiled by Alma Dell Magee Clawson and published in New Orleans, Louisiana, in 1982.

BRUMLEY (S.S. Abbreviation: Brumle)

Ranking: 4664   S.S. Count: 9589

Origin: English. Derived from the Old English words "brōm" and "lēah," meaning broom and wood. The name was given to those who came from Brumley, the name of several places in England.

Genealogies: None known.

BRUMMELL (S.S. Abbreviation: Brumme)

Ranking: 3156   S.S. Count: 14,387

Origin: English. Derived from the Old English words "brōm" and "halh," meaning broom and recess. The name was given to those who came from Bramall, the name of sev-

eral places in England, many of which at one time had gorse, also known as broom, growing nearby.

Genealogies: None known.

BRUNEL, BRUNELLISCHI, BRUNELLI

Ranking: 4489   S.S. Count: 9985

Origin: Brunel—French; Brunellischi, Brunelli—Italian. Cognates to Brown.

Genealogies: None known.

BRUNER

Ranking: 2110   S.S. Count: 21,740

Origin: German. 1) the name was given to those who worked digging wells. 2) derived from the first name Bruheri, which means brown and army. 3) the name was given to those who lived near a stream.

Genealogies: *Descendants of George Peter Bruner* was compiled by Harlan Keith Bruner and published in Hawesville, Kentucky, in 1981.

BRUNET, BRUNETTI

Ranking: 3551   S.S. Count: 12,707

Origin: Brunet—Catalan, English, French; Brunetti—Italian. Transformation of and cognates to Brown.

Genealogies: None known.

BRUNNER   (S.S. Abbreviation: Brunne)

Ranking: 1963   S.S. Count: 23,066

Origin: German. Cognate to Bourne.

Genealogies: *Joseph Brunner of Rothenstein, Schifferstadt, and Frederick* was compiled by Donald Lewis Osborn and published in Lee's Summitt, Missouri, in 1991.

BRUNO

Ranking: 1111   S.S. Count: 39,775

Origin: Italian, Portuguese. Cognate to Brown.

Genealogies: None known.

BRUNS

Ranking: 3062   S.S. Count: 14,821

Origin: Dutch. Cognate to Brown.

Genealogies: None known.

BRUNSON   (S.S. Abbreviation: Brunso)

Ranking: 2073   S.S. Count: 22,118

Origin: English. Transformation of Brown.

Genealogies: None known.

BRUSH

Ranking: 4731   S.S. Count: 9461

Origin: English. 1) derived from the Old French word "brosse," meaning brush. The name was given to those who

were thought to look like brushes or to those who worked making brushes. 2) possibly derived from the Old French word "bousche," meaning cut wood. The name may have been given to those who worked cutting wood.

Famous Brushes: CHARLES F. BRUSH (1849–1929) of Ohio was an inventor. His Brush electric arc light system was used in street lights in Philadelphia and New York City. GEORGE DE FOREST BRUSH (1855–1941) of Tennessee was a painter noted for portraits of Indians and family groups.

Genealogies: *The Descendants of Thomas and Richard Brush of Huntington, Long Island* was compiled by Stuart Brush and published in Baltimore, Maryland, in 1982. *Brush, Sammis, Kelsey, and Allied Families* was compiled by Fannie Neumann and published in New York, New York, in 1954.

BRYAN

Ranking: 522   S.S. Count: 77,112

Origin: English. Derived from the Celtic first name Brian, which was derived from the component "bre," meaning hill. The first name was probably given to those who were considered to have high status.

Famous Bryans: WILLIAM JENNINGS BRYAN (1860–1925) was a member of the U.S. House of Representatives from Nebraska. He received the Democratic party's nomination for U.S. president several times. Before World War I he advocated a policy of neutrality but later came to support President Woodrow Wilson's policies. In 1924, he drafted a resolution for the Florida legislature banning the teaching of evolution in public schools. He was later invited to prosecute John T. Scopes for teaching Darwinian theory in a Tennessee public school. JOHN S. BRYAN (1871–1944) of Virginia was president of the College of William and Mary (1934–1942). KIRK BRYAN (1888–1950), a geologist, was an authority on the evolution of land forms.

Genealogies: *History of the Bryan-Cole Family in America* was compiled by Winfred Bryan Cole and published in Arnold, Missouri, in 1962. *Thomas Bryan and Some of His Descendants* was compiled by Leslie Aulls Bryan and published in Dixon, Illinois, in 1979. *Bryans, Hortons, and Allied Families* was compiled by Elizabeth Cate Manly and published in Cleveland, Tennessee, in 1978.

BRYANT

Ranking: 112   S.S. Count: 256,228

Origin: English. Transformation of Bryan.

Famous Bryants: WILLIAM C. BRYANT (1794–1878) of Massachusetts, an editor and poet, was co-owner and editor of the *New York Evening Post* for 49 years. JOSEPH D. BRYANT (1845–1914) of Wisconsin was the surgeon who performed the sarcoma operation on President Grover Cleveland's jaw in 1893. PAUL (BEAR) BRYANT (1913–1983) of Arkansas coached football at five universities but is best known for his work at the University of Alabama, where he had 25 winning seasons, took his teams to 24 bowl games, and won six national championships. At the time he died, he had more wins than any other college football coach.

Genealogies: *Cradled in the Mountains: A Brief History: Bryant, Sheppard, and Related Families* was compiled by Barbara Bryant White and published in Newark, Delaware, in 1984.

BRYSON

Ranking: 1775 **S.S. Count:** 25,302
Origin: English, Irish. English: transformation of Brice. Irish: transformation of Morris(sey).
Genealogies: None known.

BUCHAN, BUCHANAN

Ranking: 406 **S.S. Count:** 96,865
Origin: Scottish. Buchan: uncertain etymology. Most likely derived from the Gaelic word "baegh," meaning cow, and the diminutive "an." The name was given to those who came from Buchan, the name of several places in Scotland. Buchanan: derived from the Gaelic words "buth" and "chanain," meaning house and of the canon. The name was given to those who came from Buchanan, a place in Scotland.

Famous **Bearers:** JAMES BUCHANAN (1791–1868) from near Mercersburg, Pennsylvania, was the 15th U.S. president. Before his election he had opposed slavery in principle but defended it under the Constitution. He was elected U.S. president in 1856 but was unable to temper the growing animosity between the North and South.

Genealogies: *The Buchanans of Ohio* was compiled by Jim Buchanan and published in Bowie, Maryland, in 1987. *Southwest Virginia Families (including the Buchanan Family)* was compiled by David B. Trimble and published in Texas in 1974.

BUCHER

Ranking: 3677 **S.S. Count:** 12,258
Origin: English, German. English: transformation of Butcher. German: derived from the Middle High German word "buohe," meaning beech. The name was given to those who lived near a beech tree or in a beech wood house.

Famous **Buchers:** WALTER H. BUCHER (1888–1965) of Ohio was a geologist and author of *Deformation of the Earth's Crust* (1933).

Genealogies: *The Bucher/Booker Family, 1686– 1990: From Klein Gartach Wurttemberg, Germany to Frederick County, Virginia, to Harrison and Jefferson Counties, Kentucky, to Knox and Sullivan Counties, Indiana, to the the Illinois counties of Jasper, Macon, Moultrie, Piatt, and*

Sangamon was compiled by Charles Lee Booker and published in 1990.

BUCHHOLTZ, BUCHHOLZ (S.S. Abbreviation: Buchho)

Ranking: 3432 **S.S. Count:** 13,147
Origin: German, Jewish. Transformations of and cognate to the German definition of Buch(er).
Genealogies: None known.

BUCK

Ranking: 688 **S.S. Count:** 60,919
Origin: Danish, English, German. Danish, German: cognate to Baugh. English: 1) derived from the Old English word "bucc(a)," meaning a male goat. The name was given to those who were thought to look like or act like goats. 2) derived from the Old English word "bōc," meaning beech. The name was given to those who lived near a beech tree. German: cognate to Burkett.

Famous **Bucks:** FRANK BUCK (1884–1950) of Texas supplied zoos and circuses with wild animals he captured around the world. He also was co-author of several books on his expeditions. PEARL S. BUCK (1892–1973) of West Virginia was one of the most notable writers of the 20th century. She won a Pulitzer Prize for *The Good Earth* (1931), and she was awarded the Nobel Prize for literature in 1938.

Genealogies: *John Buck of Cape May County, New Jersey (d. 1716) and Some of His Descendants* was compiled by Bryon Buck and published in Ridgewood, New Jersey, in 1981. *Schwerr-Niese, Buck-Tordsen: A Narrative Genealogy* was compiled by Harold Schwerr and published in Mankato, Minnesota, in 1985.

BUCKINGHAM (S.S. Abbreviation: Buckin)

Ranking: 3851 **S.S. Count:** 11,709
Origin: English. Derived from the Old English name Buccingham, meaning "water meadow of the people of Bucc(a)" (H&H). Bucca was a first name derived from the Old English word "bucc(a)," meaning male goat. The name was given to those who came from Buckingham, a place in England.

Famous **Buckinghams:** EARLE BUCKINGHAM (1887–1978) of Connecticut, a mechanical engineer and authority on gears and gear systems, wrote several books, including *Principles of Interchangeable Manufacturing* (1921).

Genealogies: *Looking Back: A Family History and Genealogy (including the Buckingham Family)* was compiled by Hazel Wise Huffman and published in 1985. *Prologue, a Family History and Genealogy of and by Richard Wm. Buckingham and His Wife Muriel Barbara Earl* was compiled by Richard William Buckingham and published in Baltimore, Maryland, in 1979.

BUCKLE, BUCKLEY

Ranking: 560 S.S. Count: 73,220

Origin: Buckle—English; Buckley—English, Irish. Buckle: 1) derived from the Old French word "bocle," meaning buckle. The name was given to those who worked making buckles. 2) derived from the Middle High German word "buckel," meaning shield. The name was given to those who worked making shields. Buckley (English): derived from the Old English words "bucc(a)" and "lēah," meaning male goat and wood. The name was given to those who came from Buckley or Buckleigh, the names of several places in England. Irish: derived from the Gaelic name Ó Buachalla, meaning "descendant of Buachaill" (H&H), which means cowherd.

Genealogies: *The Buckley Family Genealogy* was compiled by Shirley Gray Buckley and published in Bradford, Tennessee, in 1987.

BUCKMAN   (S.S. Abbreviation: Buckma)

Ranking: 3845 S.S. Count: 11,721

Origin: English. 1) transformation of Buck combined with the Old English word "mann," meaning man. 2) derived from the Old English words "bōc" and "mann," meaning book and man. The name was given to those who were considered scholars.

Genealogies: *The Buckman Family of Maryland and Kentucky* was compiled by Mary Louise Donnelly and published in Burke, Virginia, in 1979. *A Bucknam/Buckman Genealogy: Some Descendants of William Bucknam of Charlestown and Malden, and John Buckman of Boston* was compiled by Ann Thepold Chaplin and published in Baltimore, Maryland, in 1988.

BUCKNELL, BUCKNER   (S.S. Abbreviation: Buckne)

Ranking: 1254 S.S. Count: 35,106

Origin: Bucknell—English; Buckner—German. Bucknell: 1) transformation of the English definitions of Buck combined with the Old English word "hyll," meaning hill. 2) transformation of the Dutch and German definitions of Buck combined with the Old English word "healh," meaning hollow. The name in both cases was given to those who came from Bucknell or Bucknall, the names of several places in England. Buckner: 1) the name was given to those who lived near beech trees. 2) derived from the name Burghar, meaning stronghold and army.

Famous Bearers: SIMON BOLIVAR BUCKNER (1823–1914) of Kentucky was a Confederate general, editor of the *Louisville Courier*, and governor of Kentucky (1887–1891).

Genealogies: *History of Ellis, Buckner and Allied Families in America* was compiled by Janis H. Miller and published in Washington, D.C., in 1973.

BUDD

Ranking: 3904 S.S. Count: 11,546

Origin: English. Derived from the Old English first name Budde, which was given to those who were considered to be overweight.

Famous Budds: RALPH BUDD (1879–1962) of Iowa was president of the Great Northern Railroad, then president of the Chicago, Burlington and Quincy Railroad.

Genealogies: *Three Centuries of Budds in America* was compiled by the Budd Family Association and published in New Jersey in 1981.

BUELL

Ranking: 4680 S.S. Count: 9559

Origin: English. The name was given to those who came from Bueil, which means "field infested by crows" (ES) and is a place in France.

Famous Buells: ABEL BUELL (1742–1822) of Connecticut, a silversmith and engraver, made the first American type font and engraved and printed the first map showing U.S. boundaries after the Treaty of Paris.

Genealogies: *Ancestors of Our Grandchildren and Their Cousins, 1742–1977* was compiled by Harriet Frische and published in Scottsdale, Arizona, in 1977. *Descendants of William Buell Who Came to America from England about 1631* was compiled by Nathan Deloss Buell and published in Beaverton, Oregon, in 1989.

BUFFINGTON   (S.S. Abbreviation: Buffin)

Ranking: 3335 S.S. Count: 13,586

Origin: English. Derived from the name Bofa and the Old English word "tūn," meaning settlement. The name was given to those who came from Bovington, a place in Dorset, England.

Genealogies: None known.

BUFORD

Ranking: 3501 S.S. Count: 12,875

Origin: English. The name was given to those who came from Buford, which means "ford [shallow place in a river] at which bees are found" (ES) and is a place in Yorkshire, England.

Genealogies: None known.

BULL

Ranking: 2783 S.S. Count: 16,381

Origin: English. Derived from the Middle English word "bul(l)e," meaning bull. The name was given to those who were considered bull-like and/or pugnacious.

Famous Bulls: EPHRAIM W. BULL (1806–1895), a horticulturist, developed the Concord grape.

Genealogies: *Descendants of Josiah Bull, Jr. (1738–1813) of Dutchess County, New York and His Ancestry* was compiled by Mary Lynch Young and published in Baltimore, Maryland, in 1992. *Genealogical History of the Bull Family from England to New Frontiers* was compiled by Lola Constance Crites Smith and published in Littleton, Colorado, in 1986.

BULLAR, BULLARD
Ranking: 1351 **S.S. Count:** 32,822
Origin: English. Bullar: 1) derived from the Old French word "bulle," meaning letter. The name was given to those who worked as scribes. 2) most likely same derivation as in 1. The name was given to those who came from an unidentifiable place in Normandy, France. Bullard: The name was given to those who worked tending bulls.
Genealogies: *Ancestors of Henry Ward Beecher and His Wife Eunice White Bullard* was compiled by Josephine C. Frost and published in Brooklyn, New York, in 1927.

BULLIN, BULLINGTON (ALSO BULLINGTON)
Ranking: 4642 **S.S. Count:** 9629
Origin: English. Bullin: The name was given to those who came from Boulogne, the name of a port on the French Channel, the name of which was most likely derived from the Latin word "bonus," meaning good. Bullington: The name was given to those who came from Bullington, the name of several places in England, meaning "the homestead of Bula's people" (ES).
Genealogies: *All in Our Family. A Family Book of the Bullington, Balbert, Legg, Golden, Vickrey, Brackeen, Eastep and Other Related Families* was compiled by Lilla Bullington Brackeen and published in Decatur, Alabama, in 1976.

BULLOCK (S.S. Abbreviation: Bulloc)
Ranking: 680 **S.S. Count:** 61,330
Origin: English. Derived from the Old English word "bulluca," meaning a young bull. The name was given to those who were considered to be vigorous.
Famous **Bullocks:** RUFUS B. BULLOCK (1834–1907) was governor of Georgia (1868–1871).
Genealogies: *A Bullock Family History* was compiled by John Morgan Peirce and published in Quincy, California, in 1976.

BUMGARDENER (S.S. Abbreviation: Bumgar)
Ranking: 3074 **S.S. Count:** 14,778
Origin: German. Derived from the German word "baum" and the Old Northern French word "gardin," meaning tree

and garden. The name was given to those who worked tending trees.
Genealogies: None known.

BUNCH
Ranking: 1448 **S.S. Count:** 30,749
Origin: English. Derived from the Middle English word "bunche," meaning hump. The name was given to those who were hunchbacks.
Genealogies: *Parkes and Bunch on the Trail West, with Allied Families* was compiled by Alice Crandall Park and published in Baltimore, Maryland, in 1974.

BUNDY
Ranking: 2745 **S.S. Count:** 16,594
Origin: English. Transformation of Bond.
Famous **Bundys:** JONAS M. BUNDY (1835–1891) of New Hampshire was founder and editor of the *New York Evening Mail*.
Genealogies: None known.

BUNKER
Ranking: 4432 **S.S. Count:** 10,122
Origin: English. Derived from the Old French words "bon" and "cuer," meaning good and heart. The name was given to those who were considered to be good-hearted.
Famous **Bunkers:** ELLSWORTH BUNKER (1894–1984) of New York served in many diplomatic capacities, including ambassador to Argentina, Italy, India, Nepal, and South Vietnam. He also negotiated the Panama Canal treaties (1973–1978). ARTHUR H. BUNKER (1895–1964) of New York was president of Climax Molybdenum Co., the world's largest producer of molybdenum.
Genealogies: *Meet Our Ancestors, Clubreth, Autry, Maxwell-Bundy, Winslow, Henley and Allied Families* was compiled by Vivian Mayo Bundy and published in Greensboro, North Carolina, in 1978.

BUNN
Ranking: 2984 **S.S. Count:** 15,238
Origin: English. Transformation of Bone.
Genealogies: None known.

BUNNELL (S.S. Abbreviation: Bunnel)
Ranking: 4885 **S.S. Count:** 9153
Origin: English. 1) the name was was given to those who were considered to be attentive and small. 2) the name was given to those who came from Bunwell, which means "reed stream" (ES) and is a place in Norfolk, England.
Genealogies: *Bunnell and Allied Families* was compiled

by Joan England Murray and published in Palatine, Illinois, in 1990.

BUNTIN, BUNTINE, BUNTING

Ranking: 3118   S.S. Count: 14,573

Origin: English. Uncertain etymology, though there is a species of Bunting birds.

Genealogies: *Anthony Bunting and Ellen Barker of Matlock, England: Descendants of Sons in America* was compiled by Elizabeth Potts Koleda and published in Prineville, Oregon, in 1980.

BURCH

Ranking: 846   S.S. Count: 50,399

Origin: English. Transformation of Birch.

Famous **Burches:** RICHARD J. BURCH (1908–1977) of Oklahoma, an oral surgeon who held numerous military surgery posts, developed the first residency training program for Air Force oral surgeons.

Genealogies: *History of the Burch Family of Kentucky* was compiled by Frank Eugene Toon and published in California in 1970. *Record of the Ancestors and Descendants of Nathan Burch (1781–1858) and Damaris Babcock (1783–1869) of Brookfield, Madison County, New York* was compiled by Harold John Witter and published in Skaneateles, New York, in 1978.

BURCHALL, BURCHARD, BURCHARDT, BURCHATT   (S.S. Abbreviation: Burcha)

Ranking: 4062   S.S. Count: 11,129

Origin: English. Burchall: transformation of Birchall. Burchard, Burchardt, Burchatt: transformations of Burkett.

Genealogies: *The Burchetts (also the Burchard Family) of East Kentucky and Their Descendants* was compiled by Margette Sue Burchett Holden and published in Apple Valley, California, in 1983.

BURCHERT, BURCHETT   (S.S. Abbreviation: Burche)

Ranking: 2563   S.S. Count: 17,719

Origin: English. Burchert, Burchett: transformations of Burkett. Burchett: derived from the Old English word "bircett," meaning a grove of birch trees. The name was given to those who lived near such places.

Genealogies: *That They Live* was compiled by Geraldine S. Kelly and published in Arlington, Texas, in 1981.

BURCHFIELD   (S.S. Abbreviation: Burchf)

Ranking: 4674   S.S. Count: 9578

Origin: English. Derived from the Old English words "birce" and "feld," meaning birch and pasture. The name

was given to those who came from Burchfield, a place in England.

Famous **Burchfields:** CHARLES EPHRAIM BURCHFIELD (1893–1967) of Ashtabula, Ohio, was a painter who was known for his railroad and mining scenes in his early career and as a romantic watercolorist in his later career.

Genealogies: None known.

BURDEN

Ranking: 2664   S.S. Count: 17,112

Origin: English. 1) derived from the Old French first name Burdo. 2) derived from the Old French word "bourdon," meaning a pilgrim or one who walked with the staff of a pilgrim. 3) derived from the Old English word "burh" and "dūn," meaning fortress and hill. The name was given to those who came from Burdon, the name of several places in England.

Famous **Burdens:** HENRY BURDEN (1791–1871), born in Scotland, invented machines for making horseshoes and hook-head railroad spikes, and for rolling iron into cylindrical bars.

Genealogies: None known.

BURDETT, BURDETTE   (S.S. Abbreviation: Burdet)

Ranking: 2182   S.S. Count: 21,032

Origin: English, French. 1) the name was given to those who lived near a border. 2) the name was given to those who lived on a rented farm. 3) derived from the first name Borda, meaning shield.

Famous **Bearers:** ROBERT J. BURDETTE (1844–1914) of Pennsylvania was a humorist and preacher. Among his writings was *The Rise and Fall of the Mustache* (1877).

Genealogies: None known.

BURDICK   (S.S. Abbreviation: Burdic)

Ranking: 2226   S.S. Count: 20,609

Origin: English. 1) derived from the first name Borda, meaning shield. 2) the name was given to those who came from Bourdic, the name of several places in France.

Genealogies: *Routes to Roots: The Burdick Family Chronology: Over a Thousand Years* was compiled by Frank P. Mueller and published in Sarasota, Florida, in 1982.

BURGE

Ranking: 3110   S.S. Count: 14,625

Origin: English. 1) transformation of Bridge. 2) transformation of Burke.

Genealogies: *A Line of Descendants and Ancestors of Josiah Burge, a Revolutionary Patriot* was compiled by Joan A. Hoelaars and published in Royal Oak, Michigan, in the 1980s.

BURGER, BURGERS

Ranking: 1477 **S.S. Count:** 30,203

Origin: Burger—Dutch, Flemish, English, German; Burgers—Dutch, Flemish, German. Derived from the Middle High German word "burc" and the Middle English word "burg," both meaning fortified town. The name was usually given to those freemen who were members of a town council.

Genealogies: None known.

BURGES, BURGESS

Ranking: 377 **S.S. Count:** 102,544

Origin: English. Derived from the Old French word "burgeis," meaning inhabitant. The name was often given to those who were freemen or to those who had civil duties in a town.

Famous Bearers: HUGH BURGESS (1825?–1892), born in England, invented a process for turning wood pulp into paper and, with Morris L. Keen, founded the American Wood Paper Co. in Pennsylvania in 1863. JOHN W. BURGESS (1844–1931) of Tennessee founded the *Political Science Quarterly* and organized the political science department at Columbia University. GELETT BURGESS (1866–1951) of Massachusetts, a humorist and illustrator, wrote a popular "Purple Cow" jingle, plus books including *Why Men Hate Women* (1927). THORNTON BURGESS (1874–1965) of Massachusetts, a writer, was well known for his children's nature and animal stories that ran in daily newspapers as "Burgess Bedtime Stories." He was the author of a number of books and hundreds of "Peter Rabbit" stories.

Genealogies: *The Burgess Family* was compiled by Harol Donal Burgess and published in Cullman, Alabama, in 1981. *Burgess, Mullins, Browning, Brown and Allied Families* was compiled by James A. Burgess and published in Parson, West Virginia, in 1978.

BURGOS

Ranking: 1446 **S.S. Count:** 30,889

Origin: Spanish. 1) the name was given to those who came from Burgos, the name of several places in Spain and the one-time capital of Castile. 2) cognate to Burke.

Famous Burgoses: JULIA DE BURGOS (1914?–1953) was a prominent Puerto Rican poet and journalist whose life was an inspiration to other Puerto Rican women but less than pleasant for herself. Although she enjoyed freedom as a journalist in New York and Cuba, she suffered from isolationism. Her poetry reflected her feelings regarding social ills and injustice.

Genealogies: None known.

BURK

Ranking: 2070 **S.S. Count:** 22,163

Origin: English, German. English: transformation of Birch. German: cognate to Burkett.

Famous Burks: MARTHA (CALAMITY) JANE BURK or BURKE (1852?–1903), formerly Martha Jane Canary, of Missouri was an expert marksman and rider who dressed as a man. For much of her life she made her home in Deadwood, South Dakota, where she was "Wild Bill" Hickok's companion.

Genealogies: *Burk(e) Family of Southwest Virginia and the Valley* was compiled by John A. Kelly and published in Roanoke, Virginia, in 1973.

BURKE

Ranking: 200 **S.S. Count:** 175,372

Origin: English. Derived from the Middle English words "burc" and "burk," both meaning fort. The name was given to those who lived in a fortified place.

Famous Burkes: BILLIE BURKE (1886–1970) was an actress and the wife of Florenz Ziegfeld, in whose Ziegfeld Follies she starred. She also was a leading woman in other roles and appeared in the motion picture *The Wizard of Oz* (1939). OLIVER W. BURKE JR. (1910–1975) of Indiana, an inventor, developed alone or in collaboration many chemical processes. He held about 200 U.S. patents and about 200 foreign patents.

Genealogies: *Burk(e) Family of Southwest Virginia and the Valley* was compiled by John A. Kelly and published in Roanoke, Virginia, in 1973. *A Family Tree* was compiled by James Robert Harrington and published in Arlington, Virginia, in 1975.

BURKET, BURKETT

Ranking: 1593 **S.S. Count:** 28,106

Origin: English. Derived from the Old English first name Burgheard, which is derived from the words "burh" and "heard," meaning fort and strong or brave.

Famous Burkets: WALTER C. BURKET (1888–1974) of Kansas was a surgeon who researched and published papers on the spleen, on transplanting the trachea, and on suturing large arteries.

Genealogies: *Burket/Burkett/Burkhardt Family: Tales and Trails, 1649–1900* was compiled by Nina Deeter Ellis and published in Bountiful, Utah, in 1990. *The History of the Burkett-Gilliam Generations* was compiled by Maxine Burkett Seltzer and published in Fort Worth, Texas, in 1976.

BURKHARD, BURKHARDT (S.S. Abbreviation: Burkha)

Ranking: 983 **S.S. Count:** 44,569

Origin: German. Derived from the Old High German

word "burg" and the Germanic word "hard," meaning brave and strong.

Genealogies: *Burkett/Burkhardt Family: Tales and Trails, 1649–1900* was compiled by Nina Deeter Ellis and published in Bountiful, Utah, in 1990.

BURKHOFF   (S.S. Abbreviation: Burkho)
Ranking: 3727   S.S. Count: 12,120
Origin: German. Derived from Old High German words "berg" and "hoff," meaning fort and farm.
Genealogies: None known.

BURKS
Ranking: 1215   S.S. Count: 36,291
Origin: English. Transformation of Burke.
Famous **Burkses:** JAMES W. BURKS III (1911–1978) of Ohio was a dermatologist who advanced surgical techniques for removing scars from skin and repairing skin cancers. His books include *Wire Brush Surgery* (1956).
Genealogies: None known.

BURLESON   (S.S. Abbreviation: Burles)
Ranking: 2542   S.S. Count: 17,861
Origin: English. The name was given to those who were sons of men who worked as servants.
Famous **Burlesons:** RUFUS C. BURLESON (1823–1901) of New York was president of Baylor University (1851–1861), organized Waco University (1861), and was president of both when they consolidated (1886– 1897). ALBERT S. BURLESON (1863–1937) was a member of Congress from Texas who went on to be U.S. postmaster general.
Genealogies: None known.

BURLEY
Ranking: 3735   S.S. Count: 12,106
Origin: English. Derived from the Old English words "burh" and "lēah," meaning fort and wood. The name was given to those who came from Burley, the name of several places in England.
Genealogies: *The Families of Rubsamen, Spear, Dawson, Burley* was compiled by Neil N. Ruebsamen and published in Baltimore, Maryland, in 1987.

BURLINGAME   (S.S. Abbreviation: Burlin)
Ranking: 4541   S.S. Count: 9843
Origin: English. Uncertain etymology. Possibly a transformation of Burkett.
Famous **Burlingames:** ANSON BURLINGAME (1820–1870) represented Massachusetts in the U.S. House of Representatives. After he lost his seat in 1860, he was named minister to Vienna by President Abraham Lincoln. He was later

made minister to China, where he won the confidence of the Chinese government.

Genealogies: *The Ancestry of Clara Elizabeth Robbins (1864–1948) Together with a Register of the Descendants of Samuel Prince Robbins (1773–1823) and His Wife Martha Burlingame (1792–1872)* was compiled by John Marshall Raymond and published in Menlo Park, California, in 1974. *Palmer-Burlingham (also the Burlingame Family) Genealogy* was compiled by Dale Cosnett Kellogg and published in Elyria, Ohio, in 1974.

BURNET, BURNETT, BURNETTE
Ranking: 360   S.S. Count: 106,998
Origin: English. Transformations of Brown.
Famous **Bearers:** FRANCES ELIZA HODGSON BURNETT (1849–1924), born in England, wrote more than 40 novels, one of which was *Little Lord Fauntleroy* (1866). WHIT BURNETT (1899–1973) of Utah was a foreign correspondent in Europe, then founder and editor of *Story* magazine. He edited many literary anthologies.
Genealogies: *Burnett-Baker-Beaman and Related Families* was compiled by Blanche Miller Burnett and published in Salem, Indiana, in 1978. *Blue Ridge Heritage* was compiled by Dorothy Burnett Peterson and published in 1987.

BURNEY
Ranking: 3511   S.S. Count: 12,842
Origin: English, Irish. English: 1) the name was given to those who came from Bernay—which is derived from the Gaulic first name Brenno—in Normandy, France. 2) the name was given to those who came from Berney, a place in Norfolk, England. Irish: derived from the Old Norse word "björn," meaning warrior or bear cub.
Genealogies: *A Catalogue of the Burney Familily Correspondence 1749–1878* was compiled by Joyce Hemlow and published in New York, New York, in 1971.

BURNHAM   (S.S. Abbreviation: Burnha)
Ranking: 1987   S.S. Count: 22,795
Origin: English. Derived from the Old English words "burna" and "hām," meaning stream and homestead. The name was given to those who came from Burnham, the name of several places in England.
Famous **Burnhams:** SHERBURNE W. BURNHAM (1838–1921) of Vermont, an astronomer, is noted for discovering and cataloging 1290 double stars, in addition to cataloging all known 13,665 double stars visible in the northern hemisphere. DANIEL H. BURNHAM (1846–1912) of New York, an architect, was chief of construction for the 1893 Chicago World's Fair. He also designed Montauk Building, the first

skyscraper, in Chicago, and Union Station in Washington, D.C. FREDERICK R. BURNHAM (1861–1947) of Minnesota explored much of Africa, discovering ancient buried treasure in Rhodesia and scouting for the British during the Boer War. He also discovered Mayan remains in Mexico. He wrote of the expeditions in *Scouting on Two Continents* (1926) and *Taking Chances* (1944).

Genealogies: Burnam (also the Burnham) Family was compiled by Joan Venema and published in Salt Lake City, Utah, in 1986. *Burnham Family Lineage Charts* was compiled by Walter Jefferson Burnham and published in Pittsburgh, Pennsylvania, in 1966.

BURNS
Ranking: 123   S.S. Count: 235,813

Origin: English, Irish, Jewish, Scottish. English, Scottish: derived from the Middle English word "burn," meaning stream. The name was given to those who lived near streams. Irish: transformation of Byrne. Jewish: transformation of Bernstein. Scottish: derived from the Middle English words "burn" and "house," meaning stream and house.

Famous **Burnses:** ANTHONY BURNS (1834–1862) of Virginia was a fugitive slave when he was arrested in Boston on a theft charge in 1854, and protestors rioted against his return. He was returned, however, but then bought out of slavery. He studied at Oberlin College and became a Baptist minister. WILLIAM BURNS (1861–1932) of Maryland, as a Secret Service agent, solved major corruption and counterfeit cases. He also was head of the Federal Bureau of Investigation prior to J. Edgar Hoover's tenure. LUCY BURNS (1879–1966) of New York was a leader in the women's suffrage movement. With Alice Paul, she founded the Congressional Union for Woman Suffrage in 1913, an organization that later became the National Woman's Party.

Genealogies: The Burns Family and Allied Lines of North Carolina, Alabama and Texas was compiled by Estella Mae Burns Stewart and published in Huntsville, Texas, in 1969.

BURNSIDE   (S.S. Abbreviation: Burnsi)
Ranking: 3760   S.S. Count: 12,045

Origin: English. Derived from the Old English word "burna," meaning stream. The name was given to those who lived next to streams.

Famous **Burnsides:** AMBROSE E. BURNSIDE (1824–1881) of Indiana had a less than exemplary career in the army but later served as governor of and U.S. senator from Rhode Island.

Genealogies: Wilson, Burnside, Warnock Families in the United States of America 1660–1969 was compiled by Beverly E. Wilson and published in Baytown, Texas, in 1969.

BURR
Ranking: 2075   S.S. Count: 22,103

Origin: English. Uncertain etymology. Possibly derived from the Middle English word "bur(r)," meaning burr. The name was possibly given to those who clung to others.

Famous **Burrs:** AARON BURR (1756–1836) of Newark, New Jersey, served under Col. Benedict Arnold and Gen. George Washington in the Continental Army. In 1796, he was nominated for U.S. vice president but through confused voting wound up tied for the U.S. presidency with Thomas Jefferson. The election was decided in the U.S. House of Representatives, where Burr's candidacy was adamantly opposed by Alexander Hamilton. Burr lost and was made U.S. vice president under President Thomas Jefferson.

Genealogies: A General History of the Burr Family in America: with Genealogical Records from 1570 to 1878 was compiled by Charles Burr Todd and republished in Bethany, Oklahoma, in 1985.

BURREL
Ranking: 1333   S.S. Count: 33,194

Origin: English. 1) derived from the Old French word "bourrel," meaning cushion, collar, and headdress, among other things. The name was given to those who made or wore such items. 2) derived from the Old French word "boureau," meaning a court torturer. The name was given to those who worked legally as torturers of prisoners.

Genealogies: The Burrell/Burrill Genealogy was compiled by Ruth Burell-Brown and published in Baltimore, Maryland, in 1990. *From Lynn to Brooklyn: A Burrill [and Burrell] Family Chronicle, 1589–1982* was compiled by William Henry Burrill and published in the 1980s.

BURRIS
Ranking: 1135   S.S. Count: 38,717

Origin: English. Transformation of Burrow(s).

Genealogies: Burris Ancestors was compiled by Arthur Price Burris and published in Minneapolis, Minnesota, in 1974.

BURROUGH, BURROUGHS   (S.S. Abbreviation: Burrou)
Ranking: 1618   S.S. Count: 27,669

Origin: English. Transformations of Burrow(s).

Famous **Bearers:** JOHN BURROUGHS (1837–1921) of New York was a naturalist who wrote many essays and books, including *Wake-Robin* (1871) and *Under the Apple Trees* (1916). EDGAR RICE BURROUGHS (1875–1950) of Chicago, a writer, created the Tarzan character of movie and television fame. NANNIE HELEN BURROUGHS (1878?–1961), founded the National Trade and Professional School for Women and Girls in Washington, D.C., as a school to prepare black girls for homemaking and respectable careers. WILLIAM S. BURROUGHS (1855–1898) of Auburn, New York, invented the adding machine.

Genealogies: *Horry and the Waccamaw* was compiled by Franklin Burroughs and published in New York, New York, in 1992.

BURROW, BURROWES, BURROWS

Ranking: 1221   S.S. Count: 36,127

Origin: English. 1) derived from the Old English word "beorg," meaning hill. The name was given to those who lived on or near hills. 2) the name has become confused with many forms of names that are derived from the Old English word "burh," meaning fort.

Genealogies: *Burrow Family History* was compiled by James Rightman Blanks and published in Decorah, Iowa, in 1986. *Burris Ancestors (including the Burrows Family)* was compiled by Arthur Price Burris and published in Minneapolis, Minnesota, in 1974.

BURT

Ranking: 1182   S.S. Count: 37,031

Origin: English. Uncertain etymology. Most likely derived from the Germanic first name Berto, which is derived from the word "berht," meaning bright.

Famous **Burts:** WILLIAM A. BURT (1792–1858) of Massachusetts invented the forerunner of the typewriter, the typographer. He also invented a solar compass and an equatorial sextant. STRUTHERS BURT (1882–1954) of Maryland, a cattle rancher in Wyoming, wrote a number of books, including *Chance Encounters* (1921) and *Philadelphia* (1945).

Genealogies: *The Mathew Burt Family of Virginia and Deep South* was compiled by Robert B. Mathis and published in 1976.

BURTON

Ranking: 242   S.S. Count: 148,284

Origin: English. Derived from the Old English words "burh" and "tūn," meaning fort and settlement. The name was given to those who came from Burton, the name of several places in England.

Famous **Burtons:** WILLIAM BURTON (1865–1954) of Ohio, a chemist, developed a thermal process for cracking petroleum. He later was president of Standard Oil Co. HAROLD BURTON (1888–1964) of Massachusetts was a mayor of Cleveland, Ohio, a U.S. senator from Ohio, and then a U.S. Supreme Court justice.

Genealogies: *Family of John M. Burton and Sarah Whitmore Burton* was compiled by Broadus McAfee and published in Virginia in the 1970s. *Our Courageous Ancestors: Facts and Fables, 1600–1974* was compiled by Marie Erwin Detty and published in Austin, Texas, in 1975. *Notes on the Richard and John Burton Families, New York and Massachusetts, 1850–1973* was compiled by John Bradley Arthaud and published in Houston, Texas, in 1974.

BUSBY

Ranking: 2078   S.S. Count: 22,069

Origin: English. Derived from the Old Norse words "buski" and "býr," meaning bush and homestead. The name was given to those who came from Busby, a place in Yorkshire, England.

Genealogies: *A Compilation of Facts Regarding the Family of Isaac Busby of Monroe County, West Virginia, and Some of His Descendants* was compiled by Dorothy Bushby Riggs and published in Anderson, Indiana, in the 1970s. *Nicholas Busby* was compiled by James William Hawes and published in Yarmouthport, Massachusetts, in 1911.

BUSCH

Ranking: 1788   S.S. Count: 25,157

Origin: German. Cognate to Bush.

Famous **Busches:** ADOLPHUS BUSCH (1839–1913), who emigrated from Germany, joined Eberhard Anheuser in the brewing business now known as Anheuser-Busch. Busch advanced the pasteurization process for beer and introduced the Budweiser brand.

Genealogies: *Under the Influence* was compiled by Peter Hernon and published in New York, New York, in 1991.

BUSH

Ranking: 320   S.S. Count: 116,347

Origin: English, Jewish. English: derived from the Middle English word "bush(e)," meaning bush. The name was given to those who lived near bushes. Jewish: derived from the German word "busch," meaning bush. The name was taken as an allusion to the burning bush, through which God spoke to Moses.

Famous **Bushes:** VANNEVER BUSH (1890–1974) of Massachusetts, an electrical engineer, was president of the Carnegie Institution in Washington, D.C., and director of the Office of Scientific Research and Development. GEORGE HERBERT WALKER BUSH (1924–) was the 41st U.S. president (1989–1993). He previously served as a member of the U.S. House of Representatives from Texas; U.S. ambassador to the United Nations; chairman of the Republican National Committee; chief of the U.S. liaison office in Beijing, China; director of the Central Intelligence Ageny; and U.S. vice president (1981–1989) under President Ronald Reagan.

Genealogies: *Bush Heritage: of Fairfield and Pompton*

Lakes, New Jersey was compiled by Glen Pierce and published in Fairfield, New Jersey, in 1982. *Descendants of Daniel Bush, Sr: Hempfield Township, Westmoreland County, Pennsylvania, 1750–1990* was compiled by Elizabeth Bush McCown and published in Pittsburgh, Pennsylvania, in 1990.

BUSS

Ranking: 3711   **S.S. Count:** 12,164

Origin: English. 1) derived from the Middle English and Old French word "busse," meaning cask. The name was given to those who worked for a cooper and to those who were considered fat. 2) derived from the Middle English word "busse," which was also used to refer to a kind of ship. The name was possibly given to those who worked in such a ship.

Genealogies: *Genealogy of the Buss Family and Their Descendants* was compiled by Daniel Buss and published in Boston, Massachusetts, in 1970.

BUSSEY

Ranking: 4296   **S.S. Count:** 10,441

Origin: English. Derived from the Latin first name Buccius, as it forms components in the place name Bucé, Boucey, or Bucy, all of which are in Normandy, France.

Genealogies: None known.

BUSTAMENTE   (S.S. Abbreviation: Bustam)

Ranking: 3269   **S.S. Count:** 13,889

Origin: Spanish. The name was given to those who came from Bustament, which means "covered sepulcher" (ES) and is a place in Spain.

Genealogies: None known.

BUTCHER   (S.S. Abbreviation: Butche)

Ranking: 1414   **S.S. Count:** 31,456

Origin: English. Derived from the Middle English word "bo(u)cher" and the Old French word "bourchier," both meaning butcher. The name was given to those who worked as butchers.

Genealogies: *Every Name Index: Gibbens-Butcher Genealogy* was compiled by George Warren Archer and published in Arlington, Virginia, in 1982.

BUTLER

Ranking: 93   **S.S. Count:** 300,014

Origin: English, Irish, Jewish. English, Irish: Derived from the Anglo-Norman-French word "butuileer," meaning wine steward. The name was given to those who were chief servants in households, often a position of considerable responsibility that was not involved with wine. Jewish: uncertain etymology.

Famous Butlers: BENJAMIN FRANKLIN BUTLER (1818–1893) of Deerfield, New Hampshire, was a major general of the Union troops during the Civil War. While in command of Fort Monroe, Virginia, he refused to return fugitive slaves, stating that they were "contraband of war." After the war, he served in the U.S. House of Representatives as a Radical Republican who had a leading role in the impeachment of U.S. President Andrew Johnson. NICKOLAS BUTLER (1862–1947) of New Jersey was president of Columbia University, Barnard College, Bard College, and the New York Post-Graduate Medical School. He also was president of the Carnegie Endowment for International Peace and shared the 1931 Nobel Peace Prize with Jane Addams. PIERCE BUTLER (1866–1939) of Minnesota was a U.S. Supreme Court justice. ELLIS PARKER BUTLER (1869–1937) of Iowa was a humorist who launched his success with the book *Pigs Is Pigs* (1906). SELENA SLOAN BUTLER (1872?–1964) of Georgia organized the Georgia Colored Parent-Teacher Association, then went on to found and serve as president of the National Congress of Colored Parents and Teachers. JOHN MARSHALL BUTLER (1897–1978) was a U.S. senator from Maryland (1950–1963).

Genealogies: *The Ancestry of Blanche Butler Ames and Adelbert Ames* was compiled by Pauline Ames Plimpton and published in New York, New York, in 1977. *Della Elizabeth Butler Hudson "Beth": Her Family and Ancestors* was compiled by Martha Ann Butler Guenther and published in St. Petersburg, Florida, in 1991.

BUTTER, BUTTERFIELD

Ranking: 1303   **S.S. Count:** 34,007

Origin: English. Butter: 1) derived from the Old French word "butor," meaning bittern. The name was most likely given to those who were considered to have loud voices. 2) derived from the Old English word "butere," meaning butter. The name was given to those who worked as dairymen. Butterfield: derived from the Old English words "butere" and "feld," meaning butter and field. The name was given to those who lived near cattle pastures or dairy farms.

Famous Bearers: JOHN BUTTERFIELD (1801–1869) of New York formed a company that, after merging with two other companies, became American Express Co. He was mayor of Utica, New York, in 1865. VICTOR LLOYD BUTTERFIELD (1904–1975) of Rhode Island was president of Wesleyan University (1943–1967).

Genealogies: *Alice Butterfield of Johnson County, Missouri, 1871–1936* was compiled by Veda Goodnight Jones and published in Orem, Utah, in 1983. *The Butterfield Family of Standish, Brownfield, and Hiram, Maine* was compiled by Hubert W. Clemons and published in Hiram, Maine, in 1980.

BUTTON

Ranking: 4465   **S.S. Count:** 10,038

Origin: English. Derived from the Old French word

"bo(u)ton," meaning button. The name was given to those who worked making and/or selling buttons.

Famous **Buttons:** STEPHEN DECATUR BUTTON (1803–1897), an architect, advanced the use of metal frames in construction.

Genealogies: *Button Familes of America* was compiled by Robert Glen Nye and published in California in 1971.

BUTTS
Ranking: 1245   S.S. Count: 35,507
Origin: English, German. English: transformation of Butt. German: derived from first names that are derived from the word "berg," meaning hill, such as Burghard and Burcward.
Genealogies: *The Butts Family of Rhode Island* was compiled by Francis B. Butts and published in 1948.

BUXTON
Ranking: 4169   S.S. Count: 10,837
Origin: English. 1) derived from the Old English words "būgan" and "stances," meaning to bow and stones, and referring precariously balanced rocks. 2) derived from the Old English first name Bucc and the word "tūn," meaning settlement. The name was given to those who came from Buxton, the name of several places in England.
Genealogies: *The Buxtons of Warren* was compiled by J. J. Donovan and published in Rockland, Maine, in 1976.

BYARS
Ranking: 4525   S.S. Count: 9897
Origin: English, Scottish. Transformation of Byers.
Genealogies: *Byars Family History: With Information or Records on...Allied Lines* was compiled by Nell Byars Thaten and published in Fort Worth, Texas, in 1976.

BYERS
Ranking: 988   S.S. Count: 44,390
Origin: English. Derived from the Old English word "byre," meaning cattle shed. The name was given to those who lived near a cattle shed or who came from Byers, a place in Scotland.
Genealogies: None known.

BYNUM
Ranking: 2096   S.S. Count: 21,890
Origin: English. Derived from the first name Bynna and the Old English word "hām," meaning homestead. The name was given to those who came from Binham, a place in Norfolk, England.
Genealogies: *Bynum and Baynham Families of America*

1616–1850 was compiled by Robert William Baird and published in Baltimore, Maryland, in 1983.

BYRD
Ranking: 285   S.S. Count: 126,100
Origin: English. Transformation of Bird.
Famous **Byrds:** WILLIAM BYRD (1674–1744) founded the city of Richmond, Virginia. RICHARD E. BYRD (1888–1957) of Virginia, a naval officer and explorer, made pioneering flights over the North and South poles and made three expeditions to Antarctica. He also wrote four books. His brother, HARRY FLOOD BYRD (1887–1966), was governor of (1925–1929) and a U.S. senator (1932–1965) from Virginia.
Genealogies: *A Byrd Family History* was compiled by Robert Earl Byrd and published in 1975. *The Bird-Byrd Family* was compiled by Al Byrd and published in New Baltimore, Michigan, in 1985.

BYRNE
Ranking: 1077   S.S. Count: 40,933
Origin: Irish. Derived from the Gaelic name Ó Broin, meaning "descendant of Bran" (H&H), a first name most likely derived from the word "bran," meaning raven.
Famous **Byrnes:** BARRY BYRNE (1883–1967) of Illinois, an architect, studied under Frank Lloyd Wright but developed and advanced his own style. He was best known for school and church designs.
Genealogies: None known.

BYRNES
Ranking: 2661   S.S. Count: 17,122
Origin: Irish. Transformation of Byrne.
Famous **Byrneses:** JAMES FRANCIS BYRNES (1879–1972) of Charleston, South Carolina, was known as the "assistant president for domestic affairs" when he was director of war mobilization from 1943 to 1945. After World War II, he served as U.S. secretary of state. It was he who declared that the United States would maintain a military presence in western Europe to counter Soviet expansion.
Genealogies: None known.

BYRON
Ranking: 4796   S.S. Count: 9338
Origin: English. Derived from the Old English word "byrum," meaning "at the cattle sheds" (H&H). The name was given to those who lived and/or worked at such places.
Genealogies: *Byrams (also the Byron Family) in America* was compiled by John Arnold Byram and published in Baltimore, Maryland, in 1988.

CABALLE, CABALLER, CABALLERO, CABALLO (S.S. Abbreviation: Caball)

Ranking: 2680 S.S. Count: 17,029

Origin: Caballe, Caballer—Catalan; Caballero, Caballo—Spanish. Caballe, Caballer, Caballero: cognates to Chevalier. C´caballo: cognate to Cavallo.

Genealogies: None known.

CABAN

Ranking: 4276 S.S. Count: 10,517

Origin: Provençal. Derived from the Late Latin word "capanna," meaning cabin or hut. The names were given to those who lived in such places or who came from places called Caban or Cabane or something similiar.

Genealogies: None known.

CABLE

Ranking: 3381 S.S. Count: 13,386

Origin: English. Derived from the Anglo-Norman-French word "cable," meaning cable. The name was given to those who made rope.

Famous **Cables:** GEORGE WASHINGTON CABLE (1844–1925) of Louisiana was a writer who was a major figure in the "local color" movement. His stories often appeared in *Scribner's* magazine, and his novels and essays became known for their genuine New Orleans flavor and style. FRANK TAYLOR CABLE (1863–1945) of Connecticut was an electrical engineer who worked in early submarine construction.

Genealogies: *The Robert Cable Family Genealogy* was compiled by George Winthrop Cable and published in Oceanside, California, in 1968.

CABRAL, CABRALES

Ranking: 2216 S.S. Count: 20,732

Origin: Spanish. 1) derived from the Spanish word "cabra," meaning goat. The names were given to those who lived near goats. 2) derived from the Aragonese word "cabreo," meaning registered stock. The names may have been given to those who lived near places where important papers were kept.

Genealogies: None known.

CABRER

Ranking: 1058 S.S. Count: 41,697

Origin: Catalan. Derived from the Latin word "capra," meaning nanny goat. The name was given to those who were considered stubborn and to those who worked herding goats.

Genealogies: None known.

CADE

Ranking: 4001 S.S. Count: 11,310

Origin: English. 1) derived from the Old English first name Cada, which appears to have meant lump. The name was possibly given to those considered fat. 2) derived from the Old French word "cade," meaning cask. The name was given to those who worked for a cooper. 3) derived from the Middle English word "cade," meaning pet. The name was given to those who were considered gentle.

Genealogies: None known.

CADY

Ranking: 3385 S.S. Count: 13,337

Origin: Scottish. Derived from the first name Cadda, meaning battle.

Famous **Cadys:** DANIEL CADY (1773–1859) of New York was a jurist who specialized in equity and real property law. He was the father of Elizabeth Cady Stanton. SARAH LOUISE ENSIGN CADY (1829–1912) of Massachusetts was the principal of the West End Institute in New Haven, Connecticut (1870–1899).

Genealogies: *The Ancestors of Edna Frances Cady* was compiled by Robert Cady Gates and published in Springfield, Missouri, in 1991. *Cady Genealogy* was compiled by James W. Cady and published in Batimore, Maryland, in 1991.

CAGLE

Ranking: 1853 S.S. Count: 24,408

Origin: German. 1) the name was given to those born outside of marriage. 2) the name was given to those who were considered refined. 3) the name was given to those who came from Kagel, a place in Germany. 4) the name was given to those who made hooded cloaks.

Genealogies: *The Cagle Families of Cherokee and Pickens Counties, Georgia* was compiled by Charles O. Walker and published in 1970.

CAHILL

Ranking: 1531 S.S. Count: 29,046

Origin: Irish. Derived from the Gaelic name Ó Cathail, meaning "descendant of Cathal" (H&H), which is derived from the Celtic words "cad" and "valos," meaning battle and powerful.

Famous **Cahills:** THADDEUS CAHILL (1867–1934) of Iowa was an inventor. He is credited with the invention of the electric typewriter and the tekharmonium, and with trying to produce music electronically. MARIE CAHILL (1870–1933), believed to have been born in New York, was an actress in comedy and vaudeville.

Genealogies: *The Cahills of Cincinnati and Related Families* was compiled by Richardson Dougall and published in Portland, Oregon, in 1990.

CAIN

Ranking: 478 S.S. Count: 84,447

Origin: English. 1) derived from the Middle English and Old French word "cane," meaning cane or reed. The name was given to those who lived near reeds or worked gathering reeds and to those who were tall and thin. 2) same derivation as in 1. The name was given to who came from Caen, a place in Normandy, France.

Famous **Cains:** WILLIAM CAIN (1847–1930) of North Carolina was a pioneer in writing American civil engineering textbooks and was head of the department of engineering at the University of North Carolina (1888–1920). JAMES MALLAHAN CAIN (1892–1977) of Maryland was a journalist and novelist who wrote *The Postman Always Rings Twice, The Moth,* and *Rainbow's End,* among others. RICHARD HARVEY CAIN (1825–1887) of Virginia was a Methodist clergyman and politician affiliated with the African Methodist Episcopal church, with pastorates in Iowa, New York, and South Carolina. As a member of Congress from South Carolina, he was known for his work in striving to keep politics clean.

Genealogies: *A History of our Cain Family of Virginia, Alabama and Tennessee* was published in Whitewater, Wisconsin, in 1970.

CALABRESE, CALABRESI, CALABRI, CALABRIA (S.S. Abbreviation: Calabr)

Ranking: 2446 S.S. Count: 18,559

Origin: Italian. The names were given to those who came from Calabria, the name of a region in Italy.
Genealogies: None known.

CALDER, CALDERON, CALDERA, CALDERO

Ranking: 701 S.S. Count: 60,293

Origin: Calder—English, Scottish; Calderon—English, French, Jewish; Caldera, Caldero—Spanish. Calder (English): uncertain etymology. The name was given to those who came from Calder or lived near the River Calder, both of which are in England. (Scottish): 1) derived from the Old Norse words "kalf" and "dalr," meaning calf and valley. The name was given to those who came from Calder, the name of a place in Scotland. 2) the name was given to those who came from other places called Calder, Caldor, or Cawdor in Scotland, which are of uncertain etymologies. Calderon, Caldera, Caldero: derived from the Old French word "cauderon," meaning caldron. The name was given to those who made cooking pots.

Famous **Calders:** ALEXANDER MILNE CALDER (1846–1923), born in Scotland, was a stonecutter whose most famous work, the statue of William Penn, sits atop the dome of Philadelphia City Hall. ALEXANDER STIRLING CALDER (1870–1945) of Pennsylvania was a sculptor known for his statues of George Washington in Washing-

ton Square Arch, New York City, among others. ALEXANDER CALDER (1898–1976) of Pennsylvania was a sculptor who became famous for his abstract, brightly colored forms. He later worked on "mobiles" (named by Marcel Duchamp).
Genealogies: None known.

CALDWELL (S.S. Abbreviation: Caldwe)

Ranking: 276 S.S. Count: 129,881

Origin: English, Irish, Scottish. Derived from the Old English words "c(e)ald" and "well(a)," meaning cold and spring. The name was given to those who came from Caldwell, the name of several places in England.

Famous **Caldwells:** DAVID CALDWELL (1725–1824) of Pennsylvania was a well-known patriot during the Revolutionary War. JAMES CALDWELL (1734–1781) of Virginia was known as "Soldier Parson" of the Revolutionary War. CHARLES CALDWELL (1772–1853) of North Carolina founded and directed the Professor Louisville Medical Institute in Lexington, Kentucky. JOSEPH CALDWELL (1773–1835) of New Jersey was an educator and president of the University of North Carolina. ALEXANDER CALDWELL (?–1917) of Pennsylvania delivered stores to posts west of the Missouri in 1861 and was a promotor of the Kansas railroad in 1870. HENRY CLAY CALDWELL (1832–1915) was a judge in Arkansas. MARY GWENDOLIN CALDWELL (1863–1909) of Kentucky was a philanthropist and socialite. OTIS CALDWELL (1869–1947) of Indiana directed Lincoln School (1917–1927), which was affiliated with Columbia Teachers College in New York City. EUGENE WILSON CALDWELL (1870–1918) of Missouri was an inventor known for many improvements in X-ray equipment.

Genealogies: *Cook, Caldwell, Peoples, Stuart, and Other Families* was compiled by David Stuart Peoples and published in Baltimore, Maryland, in 1990. *David Caldwell, 1705–1781, and His Descendants in the United States of America* was compiled by William W. Caldwell and published in Parkdale, Arkansas, in 1987.

CALHOUN (S.S. Abbreviation: Calhou)

Ranking: 718 S.S. Count: 58,654

Origin: Irish, Scottish. Possibly derived from the Gaelic words "cúil," "cóil," or "coill(e)," and "cumhann," meaning corner, nook, or wood, and narrow. The name was given to those who came from Colquhoun, a place in Scotland.

Famous **Calhouns:** JOHN CALDWELL CALHOUN (1782–1850) was elected to the U.S. House of Representatives from South Carolina. He advocated going to war with Britain in 1812 and served as secretary of war under President James Monroe. In 1824, he successfully ran for U.S. vice president and was reelected in 1828. He resigned the office to take a seat in the U.S. Senate to fight against tariffs imposed on the South. He briefly served as secretary of state under U.S. President John Tyler but returned to the U.S. Senate in 1845 and remained until his death. WILLIAM BARRON CALHOUN (1795–1865) of Massachusetts was a lawyer, politician, and educator. WILLIAM JAMES CALHOUN (1848–1916) of Pennsylvania was a diplomat and lawyer who served as minister to China (1909–1913). PATRICK CALHOUN (1856–1943) of South Carolina was a lawyer and businessman and the grandson of John C. Calhoun.

Genealogies: *The Calhoun Family and Thomas Green Clemson: The Decline of a Southern Patriarchy* was compiled by Ernest McPherson Lander and published in Columbia, South Carolina, in 1983. *800 Years of Colquhoun, Colhoun, Calhoun, and A Cahoon Family History in Ireland, Scotland, England, United States of America, Australia, and Canada* was compiled by Orval Calhoun and published in Baltimore, Maryland, in 1976.

CALKIN, CALKINS

Ranking: 3283 **S.S. Count:** 13,811
Origin: English. Derived from the first name Caleb, meaning dog.

Famous **Bearers:** NORMAN ALLISON CALKINS (1822–1895) of New York was an educator and author of *Primary Object Lessons for a Graduated Course of Development* (1861). MARY WHITON CALKINS (1863–1930) of Connecticut was the first American woman to attain eminence in the field of philosophy. GARY NATHAN CALKINS (1869–1943) of Indiana was a zoologist and professor of protozoology at Columbia University. He was the leading protozoologist of his time and was known for his study of Uroleptus mobilis.
Genealogies: None known.

CALL

Ranking: 2469 **S.S. Count:** 18,381
Origin: English, Irish, Scottish. 1) derived from the first name Cathal, meaning "battle mighty" (ES). 2) Uncertain etymology. The name was given to those who often wore a woman's small, close-fitting hat.

Famous **Calls:** RICHARD KEITH CALL (1791–1862) of Virginia served under Andrew Jackson in the War of 1812; practiced law in Pensacola, Florida; was a territorial delegate from Florida (1823–1825); was the Democratic governor of Florida (1836–1839); and was the Whig governor of Florida (1841–1844). He worked to keep Florida part of the Union but went along with the state on secession.
Genealogies: *A Collection of Stones: History and Genealogy of Stone and Related Families (including the Call Family)* was compiled by Doris Burch Stone and published in Hixson, Tennessee, in 1984. *The Descendants of Ira Call* was compiled by Joseph C. Call and Lowell E. Call and published in Logan, Utah, in 1973.

CALLAGHAN (S.S. Abbreviation: Callag)

Ranking: 4952 **S.S. Count:** 9049
Origin: Irish. Derived from the Gaelic name Ó Ceallagcháin, meaning "descendant of Ceallanchán" (H&H), which is derived from words meaning contention and strife.
Genealogies: None known.

CALLAHAN (S.S. Abbreviation: Callah)

Ranking: 553 **S.S. Count:** 74,087
Origin: Irish. Transformaton of Callaghan.

Famous **Callahans:** PATRICK HENRY CALLAHAN (1865–1940) of Ohio instituted profit sharing in his Louisville, Kentucky, varnish company in 1915.
Genealogies: *A History of the Callam and Carwile Families (also the Callahan Family)* was compiled by Anna Deihls Callahan and published in Charlotte, North Carolina, in 1976.

CALLAN, CALLANDER

Ranking: 3871 **S.S. Count:** 11,649
Origin: Callan—Irish, Scottish; Callander—English, Scottish. Callan (Irish): derived from the Gaelic name Ó Cathaláin, meaning "descendant of Cathaláan" (H&H). (Scottish): derived from the Gaelic name Mac Ailin, which is derived from the word "ail," meaning rock. Callander (English): derived from the Old French word "calandrier," which refers to those who worked finishing cloth by pressing it through heavy rollers. The name was given to those who worked at such jobs. (Scottish): the name was given to those who came from Callander, the name of several places in Scotland.
Genealogies: *The Tansill, Bender, Callan, Holmead, and other Early American Families* was compiled by Xavier Bender Tansill and published in 1971.

CALLAWAY (S.S. Abbreviation: Callaw)

Ranking: 2257 **S.S. Count:** 20,225
Origin: English. Transformation of Calloway.

Famous **Callaways:** SAMUEL RODGER CALLAWAY (1850–1904), born in Ontario, was the first president of the American Locomotive Co. (1901–1904). MORGAN CALLAWAY (1862–1936) of Georgia was a professor of English at the University of Texas (1890–1936). CABELL (CAB) CALLOWAY (1907–1994) of New York was a jazz composer, singer, and bandleader who became famous for his work in Harlem's Cotton Club and was called the "King of Hi-De-Ho," after a song he composed. He appeared in the all–African-American musical *Hot Chocolates* in New York City.
Genealogies: *The Descendants of the "Connecticut Calaways" and Family Album* was compiled by Merle Leland Calaway and published in Conneaut, Ohio, in 1976.

CALLENDAR, CALLENDER (S.S. Abbreviation: Callen)

Ranking: 3605 S.S. Count: 12,524
Origin: English, Scottish. Transformations of Callander.
Genealogies: None known.

CALLIS, CALLISS, CALLISTER

Ranking: 3998 S.S. Count: 11,313
Origin: Callis, Calliss—English; Callister—Irish. Callis, Calliss: the names were given to those who came from Calais, which means "inlet or strait" (ES) and is a place in France. Callister: derived from the first name Alastar, the Gaelic cognate to Alexander.
Genealogies: None known.

CALLOW

Ranking: 1848 S.S. Count: 24,504
Origin: English. 1) derived from the Old English words "caul," "cald," and "hlāw," meaning bare, cold, and hill. The name was given to those who came from Callow, the name of several places in England. 2) may be a transformation of Calloway.
Genealogies: None known.

CALVER, CALVERD, CALVERLEY, CALVERT

Ranking: 1694 S.S. Count: 26,356
Origin: English. Calver: derived from the Old English words "c(e)alf" and "ofer," meaning calf and ridge. The name was given to those who came from Calver, the name of a place in Derbyshire, England. Calverley: derived from the Old English words "c(e)alfra" and "lēah," meaning calves and wood. The name was given to those who came from Calverley, a place in Yorkshire, England. Calverd, Calvert: derived from the Middle English word "calfhirde," meaning cattle herder. The names were given to those who worked herding cattle.
Famous **Bearers:** GEORGE CALVERT (1579?–1632), born in England, was the first Lord Baltimore, but he died before the charter of Maryland passed the Great Seal, which was then issued to his son CECILIUS CALVERT (1605–1675), who established the colony of Maryland. LEONARD CALVERT (1606–1647), born in England, son of George Calvert, was the second Lord Baltimore. He came to America with the colonists in March 1634. He set up the government at St. Mary's City, Maryland. His support of laws passed by the assembly over the veto of his brother led to the right of initiative in legislation passing to that body. He was governor from 1637 until his death in 1647. CHARLES CALVERT (1637–1715), born in England, was the proprietor of Maryland (1675–1715) and the son of Cecilius and the grandson of George Calvert. He became Baron Baltimore in 1675 upon the death of his father. Because of religious conflicts between the Catholics and the Protestants of the time, he lost his position in Maryland government. He

sailed to England to try to regain his title but died before he succeeded. GEORGE HENRY CALVERT (1803–1889) of Maryland was an author and the brother of CHARLES BENEDICT CALVERT (1808–1864), who helped to establish the federal Bureau (now Department) of Agriculture in 1862.
Genealogies: *The Descendants of George Fraizer, Joseph Journey, Patrick Calvert, Thomas Endicott, Sr., John Ashworth, Sr., as They Entered "Into This Fruitful Valley"* was compiled by Gloria M. Cox and published in Evansville, Indiana, in 1971. *"Heritage of Faith": The Calvert, Green, and Alvey Families Histories* was compiled by James H. Mosby and published in Evansville, Indiana, in 1976.

CALVIN, CALVINI, CALVINO

Ranking: 3332 S.S. Count: 13,600
Origin: Calvin—English, French; Calvini, Calvino—Italian. Derived from the Latin word "calvus," meaning bald. The name was given to those who were bald.
Famous **Bearers:** SAMUEL CALVIN (1840–1911), born in Scotland, was a geologist who did important work on fossils of the upper Mississippi Valley.
Genealogies: None known.

CAMACHO (S.S. Abbreviation: Camach)

Ranking: 982 S.S. Count: 44,635
Origin: Spanish. Uncertain etymology. Probably of French origin. The name was given to those who came from Camacho, a place in Spain.
Genealogies: None known.

CAMERON (S.S. Abbreviation: Camero)

Ranking: 528 S.S. Count: 78,341
Origin: Scottish. Derived from the Gaelic words "cam" and "srón" or "brun," meaning crooked and nose or hill. The name was given to those who came from Cameron, the name of several places in Scotland.
Famous **Camerons:** ANDREW CARR CAMERON (1836–1892), born in England, helped organize the National Labor Union. SIMON CAMERON (1799–1889) of Pennsylvania was a U.S. senator from Pennsylvania before and after the Civil War and secretary of war during the conflict. He was in and out of the political arena because of his corrupt practices. His son JAMES DONALD CAMERON (1833–1918) succeeded him in both posts. ROBERT ALEXANDER CAMERON (1828–1894) of New York, a Union soldier, along with Nathan C. Meeker, in post-Civil War times, colonized the West through the Union Colony Movement. He was active in the settling of Greeley and Colorado Springs, Colorado. JAMES DONALD CAMERON (1833–1918) of Pennsylvania was president of the North Central Railroad (1863–1874); secretary of war (1876–1877); and a U.S. senator from Pennsylvania (1877–1897). WILLIAM EVELYN CAMERON (1842–1927) of Virginia was a newspaper editor

and governor of Virginia (1882–1886). DONALDINA MACKENZIE CAMERON (1869–1968), a missionary born in New Zealand, rescued more than 2000 girls and women from the Chinese slave trade in San Francisco, California.

Genealogies: *The Cameron Family* was compiled by Louise Frances Cameron Rose and published in Baltimore, Maryland, in 1973. *A Family Hierarchy in Canada and the United States of America, 1619–1971: Cameron, Allied Kinze and Warth Families* was compiled by C. E. Cameron and published in Kent, Washington, in 1972.

CAMP

Ranking: 1042 **S.S. Count:** 42,054

Origin: French. Derived from the Old French word "champ," meaning field. The name was given to those who lived near fields.

Famous Camps: HIRAM CAMP (1811–1893) of Connecticut was a clock manufacturer and philanthropist. He was president of the New Haven Clock Co. (1853–1892) and founder of Mount Hermon School and Northfield Seminary. DAVID NELSON CAMP (1820–1916) of Connecticut, an educator, was the principal of the New Britain Seminary. JOHN LAFAYETTE CAMP SR. (1828–1891) of Alabama, a lawyer and planter, helped prepare the Texas constitution in 1876. He served on the state bench (1878–1884). His son, JOHN LAFAYETTE CAMP JR. (1855–1918) of Texas, was a state judge who was instrumental in preserving the Alamo. WALTER CHAUNCEY CAMP (1859–1925) of Connecticut was a promoter of American football. He was Yale University's athletic director and a long-time member of the Intercollegiate Football Rules Committee. He was appointed chairman of a commission charged with maintaining the physical fitness of naval personnel, and he developed the "daily dozen" exercise routine.

Genealogies: *Camp, Jones, and Related Families of Connecticut, Illinois, Missouri, Virginia, Carolina, Georgia, Alabama, Mississippi, Louisiana, Texas, and Points West* was compiled by Nell Jones Carter and published in Tallahassee, Florida, in 1977. *John Steel Camp and His Descendants* was compiled by Paul W. Camp and Paul K. Camp and published in Evansville, Indiana, in 1980.

CAMPANA (S.S. Abbreviation: Campan)

Ranking: 2930 **S.S. Count:** 15,535

Origin: Italian. 1) Uncertain etymology. The name was given to those who lived at or near a sign of the bell. 2) Uncertain etymology. The name was given to those who were deaf.

Genealogies: None known.

CAMPBELL (S.S. Abbreviation: Campbe)

Ranking: 43 **S.S. Count:** 512,879

Origin: Scottish. Derived from the Gaelic words "cam" and "beul," meaning crooked and mouth.

Famous Campbells: JOHN CAMPBELL (1653–1728), born in Scotland, was the postmaster in Boston and publisher of the *Boston News-Letter* (1704–1722). LORD WILLIAM CAMPBELL (?–1778) was the colonial governor of South Carolina. He fled to England after a failed attempt to rally the Indians and Tories to help the royal cause against the colonists. THOMAS CAMPBELL (1763–1854), born in Ireland, founded, with his son, ALEXANDER CAMPBELL (1778–1866), the Disciples of Christ. GEORGE WASHINGTON CAMPBELL (1769–1848), born in Scotland, was a Tennessee lawyer, member of Congress, senator, secretary of the Treasury, and minister to Russia. JOHN WILSON CAMPBELL (1782–1833) of Virginia was a member of Congress from Ohio and a U.S. district judge. CHARLES CAMPBELL (1807–1876) of Virginia was the author of *An Introduction to the History of the Colony and Ancient Dominion of Virginia* and editor of the *Bland Papers*. WILLIAM BOWEN CAMPBELL (1807–1867) of Tennessee was a member of Congress from Tennessee, then governor. WILLIAM HENRY CAMPBELL (1808–1890) of Maryland was the president of Rutgers College in New Jersey (1863–1882). JOHN ARCHIBALD CAMPBELL (1811–1889) of Georgia was a justice of the U.S. Supreme Court. He left the Union with his state and served the Confederacy as assistant secretary of state. He returned to practice law in New Orleans after the war and was involved in the "Slaughterhouse Cases" and *New York and New Hampshire vs. Louisiana*. JAMES CAMPBELL (1812–1893) of Pennsylvania was U.S. postmaster general (1853–1877). ALLEN CAMPBELL (1815–1894) of New York was a civil engineer who helped build railroads in Georgia, New York, and Chile. He was president of the Harlem Railroad. GEORGE WASHINGTON CAMPBELL (1817–1898) of New York was a horticulturist who devedoped the "Campbell Early," a type of grape. ANDREW CAMPBELL (1821–1890) of New Jersey was an inventor and manufacturer. He developed paper-feed mechanisms and automatic features for printing presses. He invented and manufactured the Campbell County Press and a two-revolution picture press. JAMES VALENTINE CAMPBELL (1823–1890) of New York was a justice of the Michigan Supreme Court. JOSIAH A. PATTERSON CAMPBELL (1830–1917) of South Carolina was a justice of the Mississippi Supreme Court. FRANCIS JOSEPH CAMPBELL (1832–1914) of Tennessee, blind since birth, became a music teacher and cofounder of the Royal Academy of Music for the Blind in London. HELEN STUART CAMPBELL (1839–1918) of New York was an author, reformer, and home economist. She wrote about the poverty of the New York slums. BARTLEY CAMPBELL (1843–1888) of Pennsylvania was a playwright who wrote, among other works, *The White Slave* and *The Virginian, My Partner*. THOMAS JOSEPH CAMPBELL (1848–1925) of New York was a Jesuit priest who became president of Fordham University. He was editor of *America* and author of *The Jesuits: 1534– 1921*

(1921). MARIUS ROBINSON CAMPBELL (1858–1940) of Iowa was a geologist who made studies of national coal resources. PRINCE LUCIEN CAMPBELL (1861–1925) of Missouri was president of the University of Oregon. WILLIAM WALLACE CAMPBELL (1862–1938) of Ohio helped to lay the foundation for the new science of astrophysics through his design of and work with the Mill spectrograph. He was also president of the University of California (1923–1930). CHARLES MACFIE CAMPBELL (1876–1943), born in Scotland, was a physician whose main contribution to medicine was a belief that mental illness was brought about by one's maladjustment to life. PERSIA CRAWFORD CAMPBELL (1898–1974), born in Australia, was an economist and consumer advocate. She worked for the federal government writing consumer pamphlets. She hosted a radio program titled "Report to Consumers" and the public-television show called "You, the Consumer." JOSEPH CAMPBELL (1904–1987) of New York wrote and lectured extensively on comparative mythology, the function of mythology, and myths as archetypes. His books include *The Masks of God*, *Flight of the Wild Gander*, and *Myths to Live By*.

Genealogies: *Campbell Family History* was compiled by Gwen Campbell and published in Keno, Oregon, in 1988.

CAMPOS

Ranking: 1029 **S.S. Count:** 42,569

Origin: Portuguese. Cognate to C(h)amp.

Famous **Camposes:** SANTIAGO CAMPOS (1926–) is a U.S. District Court judge in New Mexico.

Genealogies: None known.

CANADA (ALSO CANADAS)

Ranking: 2737 **S.S. Count:** 16,632

Origin: Spanish. Cognates to Cain.

Genealogies: None known.

CANADY

Ranking: 3827 **S.S. Count:** 11,777

Origin: Irish, Scottish. Transformation of Kennedy.

Genealogies: None known.

CANALES (S.S. Abbreviation: Canale)

Ranking: 2734 **S.S. Count:** 16,650

Origin: Spanish. Derived from the Old French word "chenal," meaning channel. The name was given to those who lived near a ditch.

Genealogies: None known.

CANCELLOR, CANCELIER, CANCELLARIO, CANCELLIERI (S.S. Abbreviation: Cancel)

Ranking: 4302 **S.S. Count:** 10,434

*Origin: Cancellor—English; Cancelier—French; Cancel-*lario, Cancellieri—Italian. Transformations of and cognates to Chancellor.*

Genealogies: None known.

CANDELA, CANDELIER, CANDELARI, CANDELARO, CANDELIERI, CANDELAS, CANDELARIO, CANDELORO (S.S. Abbreviation: Candel)

Ranking: 2003 **S.S. Count:** 22,735

Origin: Candela—Catalan, Spanish; Candelier—French; Candelari, Candelaro, Candelieri—Italian; Candelas, Candelario, Candeloro—Spanish. Candela, Candelier, Candelari, Candelaro, Candelieri, Candelas, Candelario, Candeloro: cognates to Chandler. Candelario, Candeloro: derived from the Latin word "candela," meaning candle. The names signify the Catholic feast of the Purification of the Virgin. The name may have been given to those born on this day.

Genealogies: None known.

CANFIELD (S.S. Abbreviation: Canfie)

Ranking: 2796 **S.S. Count:** 16,264

Origin: English. Derived from the first name Canna and the Old English word "feld," meaning pasture. The name was given to those who came from Canfield, a place in Essex, England.

Famous **Canfields:** JAMES HULME CANFIELD (1847–1909) of Ohio was president of Ohio State University (1895–1899). DOROTHY CANFIELD (1879–1958) of Kansas, a writer, was on the selection board of the Book of the Month Club and for 25 years the only female board member. She wrote fiction under the name Dorothy Canfield and nonfiction under Dorothy Canfield Fisher, her married name. She was the first woman appointed to the Vermont Board of Education.

Genealogies: None known.

CANN

Ranking: 8121 **S.S. Count:** 5191

Origin: English. Derived from the Old English word "canna," meaning can or deep valley. The name was given to those who lived in valleys or to those who came from Cann, a place in Dorset, England.

Genealogies: None known.

CANNADY (S.S. Abbreviation: Cannad)

Ranking: 4879 **S.S. Count:** 9158

Origin: Irish, Scottish. Transformation of Kennedy.

Genealogies: *Ancestral Families of Alison Cannady* was compiled by Bruce B. Cannady and published in Baltimore, Maryland, in 1990. *The History and Genealogy of the George W. Cannady Family* was compiled by Bruce B. Cannady and published in Gresham, Oregon, in 1973.

CANNON

Ranking: 408 S.S. Count: 96,742

Origin: English, Irish. English: derived from the Middle English word "canun," meaning a member of the clergy who lived in a religious community. The name was given to those who were members of the lower classes who were thought to carry themselves with dignity. Irish: 1) derived from the Gaelic name Mac Canannáin, meaning "son of Canannán" (H&H). 2) derived from the Gaelic name Ó Canáin, meaning "descendant of Canán" (H&H), which means wolf cub.

Famous **Cannons:** NEWTON CANNON (1781–1841) of North Carolina was a member of Congress from Tennessee and the first Whig governor of Tennessee. WALTER BRADFORD CANNON (1871–1945) of Wisconsin was a Nobel Prize winner who did research that established the theory of homeostasis. He developed the basic technique for securing X-rays of soft organs of the alimentary canal. HARRIET STARR CANNON (1823–1896) of South Carolina was the first mother superior of the Episcopal community of St. Mary. ANNIE JUMP CANNON (1863–1941) of Delaware was an astronomer who spent much of her professional life recording, classifying, and cataloging stars. She classified the spectra of all stars from the North to the South poles that are visible on the Harvard plates. They can be found in the *Henry Draper Catalogue* (1818–1824). Including two additional volumes of fainter stars, she classified a total of 350,000 stars in her lifetime. JAMES CANNON (1864–1944) of Maryland was a Methodist minister, best known as a temperance reformer and the most effective lobbyist of the Anti-Saloon League during and after the campaign for the passage of the 18th Amendment, which established Prohibition.

Genealogies: *The Cannon Family* was compiled by Edward Pugh Cannon and published in Poplar Bluff, Missouri, in 1974. *Cannon Family Historical Treasury* was compiled by Beatrice Cannon Evans and published in Salt Lake City, Utah, in 1967.

CANO

Ranking: 2700 S.S. Count: 16,837

Origin: Spanish. Derived from the Late Latin word "cānūtus," meaning white-haired. The name was given to those who had white hair or were considered to have the wisdom associated with old age.

Genealogies: None known.

CANTER, CANTERA, CANTERO

Ranking: 2729 S.S. Count: 16,676

Origin: Canter—English, Jewish, Scottish; Cantera, Cantero—Portuguese, Spanish. Canter (English, Scottish): derived from the Old Norman French word "cant," meaning song. The name was given to those who sang often. (Jewish):

transformation of Kantor. Cantera, Cantero: derived from the Portuguese and Spanish word "canto," meaning stone. The name Cantera was given to those who lived near or on a stony area, Cantero to those who worked cutting or placing stones.

Genealogies: None known.

CANTRELL (S.S. Abbreviation: Cantre)

Ranking: 896 S.S. Count: 48,287

Origin: French. Cognate to Canter.

Genealogies: *The Cantrill-Cantrell Genealogy: A Record of the Descendants of Richard Cantrill, Who Was a Resident of Philadelphia Prior to 1689, and of Earlier Cantrills in England and America* was compiled by Susan Cantrill Christie and published in New York in 1908. *Letters to My Grandchildren* was compiled by Sabra Phillips Cantrell and published in North East, Pennsylvania, in 1991.

CANTU

Ranking: 1208 S.S. Count: 36,475

Origin: Italian, Spanish. 1) transformation of and cognate to Cantera. 2) cognate to Canter.

Genealogies: None known.

CANTWELL (S.S. Abbreviation: Cantwe)

Ranking: 4788 S.S. Count: 9352

Origin: English. Derived from the Old English name Cant(a) and the word "well(a)," meaning Cant(a)'s well. The name was given to those who came from Cantwell, an unidentified place in England.

Genealogies: None known.

CANTY

Ranking: 4503 S.S. Count: 9944

Origin: English, Scottish. Transformation of Cant.

Genealogies: None known.

CAPPEL, CAPPELL, CAPPELLA, CAPELLO, CAPPELLARI, CAPPELLARO, CAPPELLE, ET AL.

Ranking: 3793 S.S. Count: 11,889

Origin: Cappel, Cappell—English; Cappella, Capello, Cappellari, Cappellaro, Cappelle, et al.—Italian. Cappel, Cappell, Cappella, Capelle: transformations of and cognates to Chapell. Cappello, Cappellari, Cappellaro, Cappelle, et al.: cognates to Capers.

Genealogies: None known.

CAPPS

Ranking: 1765 S.S. Count: 25,406

Origin: English. Derived from the Old English word "cæp," meaning cap. The name was given to those who wore a distinctive hat or who worked making hats.

Famous **Cappses:** WASHINGTON LEE CAPPS (1864–1935) of Massachusetts was a naval officer who devised the skeleton mast and the "all big gun" ship. EDWARD CAPPS (1866–1950) of Illinois was the founder and first president of the American Association of University Professors.

Genealogies: *The Capps was compiled by Joyce Ford and published in Houston, Texas, in 1989. William Ransom Capps and Eliza Jane Jones was compiled by Joyce Capps and published in Fredona, Texas, in 1988.*

CAPUTO

Ranking: 3455 **S.S. Count:** 13,067
Origin: Italian. Derived from the Latin word "caput," meaning "head." The name was given to those who were considered to have distinctive heads or to those who were in charge of something.
Genealogies: None known.

CARABAJAL, CARABALLO (S.S. Abbreviation: Caraba)

Ranking: 2097 **S.S. Count:** 21,890
Origin: Spanish. Derived from the Spanish word "carba," meaning thicket of oaks. The name was given to those who lived near a group of oak trees or to those who came from Carballo, a place in Spain.
Genealogies: None known.

CARAWAY (S.S. Abbreviation: Carawa)

Ranking: 4715 **S.S. Count:** 9492
Origin: English, Scottish. English: derived from the Middle English word "carewei," meaning caraway. The name was given to those who worked selling caraway and other spices. Scottish: the name was given to those who came from Carloway, which means "Karl's bay" (ES) and is a place in Scotland.
Famous **Caraways:** THADDEUS HORATIUS CARAWAY (1871–1931) of Missouri was a U.S. senator from Arkansas. HATTIE OPHELIA WYATT CARAWAY (1878–1950) of Tennessee, the wife of Thaddeus Caraway, was appointed to Senate seat upon his death. She was then elected to the post, becoming the first female U.S. senator ever elected.
Genealogies: None known.

CARBON, CARBONEL, CARBONELL, CARBONELLI, CARBONETTE, CARBONIN, CARBONINI

Ranking: 1803 **S.S. Count:** 25,007
Origin: Catalan, English, French. Derived from the Latin word "carbo," meaning charcoal. The names were given to those with dark hair or a dark complexion.
Genealogies: None known.

CARD

Ranking: 3500 **S.S. Count:** 12,879
Origin: English. Derived from the Old French word "card(e)," meaning a tool for untangling wool. The name was given to those who worked untangling wool.
Genealogies: None known.

CARDENAL, CARDENAS

Ranking: 912 **S.S. Count:** 47,295
Origin: Spanish. Cardenal: cognate to Cardinal. Cardenas: derived from the Spanish word "cárdeno," meaning blue or bluish purple. The name was given to those who came from places called Cardenas in Spain because these places were covered with blue or bluish purple plants.
Genealogies: None known.

CARDIN, CARDINALL, CARDING, CARDINAL, CARDINEAU, CARDINALE, CARDINALIETTI, CARDINALI

Ranking: 2549 **S.S. Count:** 17,824
Origin: Cardin, Cardinall, Carding—English; Cardinal—English, French; Cardineau—French; Cardinale, Cardinalietti, Cardinali—Italian. Cardin, Carding: derived from the Old Norman French word "cardon," meaning thistle. The names were given to those who lived near thistles and to those who worked carding (untangling) wool. Cardinal, Cardinall, Cardineau, Cardinale, Cardinalietti, Cardinali: derived from the Middle English and Old French word "cardinal," meaning a church official. The name was given to those who worked for cardinals, to those who wore red often or played the part of a cardinal in a ceremony or festival, and to those who were considered to be patronizing.
Genealogies: None known.

CARDON, CARDONA, CARDONE, CARDONI

Ranking: 1435 **S.S. Count:** 31,116
Origin: Cardon—English; Cardona—Catalan; Cardone, Cardoni—Italian. Cardon, Cardona, Cardone, Cardoni: transformation of and cognates to Carding. Cardona: the name was given to those who came from Cardona, a place in Catalonia.
Genealogies: None known.

CARDOZO (S.S. Abbreviation: Cardoz)

Ranking: 4263 **S.S. Count:** 10,566
Origin: Portuguese, Spanish. The name was given to those who came from Cardoso, which means "place where thistles grew" (ES) and is a place in Spain.
Famous **Cardozos:** JACOB NEWTON CARDOZO (1786–1873) of Georgia was an economist who drew up the first petition from the South on behalf of free trade. BENJAMIN NATHAN CARDOZO (1870–1938) of New York was

a justice of the U.S. Supreme Court. Although he served only six years, his opinions on the accountability of third parties for negligence and his ability to simplify confused legal precedents have had long-lasting and long-ranging effects.

Genealogies: None known.

CARDWELL (S.S. Abbreviation: Cardwe)

Ranking: 2760 S.S. Count: 16,508

Origin: English, Irish, Scottish. Transformation of Caldwell.

Genealogies: *The Cardwells of Virginia* was compiled by Allen Pendergraft and published in Sedona, Arizona, in 1973.

CAREY

Ranking: 506 S.S. Count: 79,269

Origin: Cornish, English, Irish, Welsh. Cornish, Welsh: derived from the Welsh words "caer" and "rhiw," meaning fort and hill. The name was given to those who came from Carew, the name of several places in Wales. English: 1) Uncertain etymology. Most likely derived from the Celtic component "car," meaning love. The name was given to those who came from places called Carey that are near the River Carey in England. 2) the name was given to those who came from the Manor of Carrey, a place in Normandy, France. Irish: derived from the Gaelic name Ó Ciardha, meaning "descendant of Ciardha" (H&H), which is derived from the word "ciar," meaning black or dark.

Famous **Careys**: MATHEW CAREY (1790–1839), born in Ireland, was publisher of the *Pennsylvania Herald* and *The American Museum*. He was the father of HENRY CHARLES CAREY (1793–1879) of Pennsylvania, who was an economist and sociologist who believed that *laissez-faire* economic policies produced wealth throughout society. His books included *Principles of Political Economy* (1837–1840). JOSEPH MAULL CAREY (1845–1924) of Delaware was a territorial representative in Congress for Wyoming. He introduced the bill for Wyoming statehood and became the state's first U.S. senator, then its governor.

Genealogies: *Branches of the John Carey Family of Bucks County, Pennsylvania to Virginia, Ohio, and on West* was compiled by Dorothy Carey Cragg Toennies and published in 1969. *Cary-Estes (also the Carey Family) Genealogy* was compiled by May Folk Webb and republished in Huntingdon Valley, Pennsylvania, in 1979.

CARGILL (S.S. Abbreviation: Cargil)

Ranking: 4729 S.S. Count: 9464

Origin: Scottish. Derived from the Old Welsh words "kaer" and "geall," meaning fort and wager or pledge. The

name was given to those who came from Cargill, a place in Scotland.

Famous **Cargills**: OSCAR CARGILL (1898–1972) of Maine was a New York University professor, a consulting editor for Macmillan Co., and a critic and author. Among his books are *Intellectual America* (1941) and *Toward a Pluralistic Criticism* (1965).

Genealogies: *Our Mother's People* was compiled by Marie Doan Enderton and published in San Diego, California, in 1972.

CARL

Ranking: 2850 S.S. Count: 16,013

Origin: English. Transformation of Charles.

Genealogies: *A Carl Family History* was compiled by Skip Carl and published in Baldwin, New York, in 1974.

CARLIN, CARLINI, CARLINO, CARLINER

Ranking: 2035 S.S. Count: 22,466

Origin: Carlin—Italian, Jewish; Carlini, Carlino—Italian; Carliner—Jewish. Carlin (Italian), Carlini, Carlino: cognates to Charles. Carlin (Jewish), Carliner: transformation of Karlin.

Genealogies: None known.

CARLISLE, CARLISI (S.S. Abbreviation: Carlis)

Ranking: 1484 S.S. Count: 29,933

Origin: Carlisle—English; Carlisi—Italian. Carlisle: derived from the British word "ker," meaning fort. The name was given to those who came from Carlisle, a place in Cumbria, England. Carlisi: cognate to Charles.

Famous **Bearers**: JOHN GRIFFIN CARLISLE (1835–1910) of Kentucky was a lawyer who served in government as a member of Congress, lieutenant-governor of Kentucky, and Speaker of the House. He resigned the speakership to accept appointment as a U.S. senator, and then served as secretary of the Treasury.

Genealogies: *A Family History of Zachariah and Jennie Colwill Carlisle* was compiled by Robert Z. Carlisle and published in Columbus, Ohio, in 1977.

CARLOS

Ranking: 4808 S.S. Count: 9326

Origin: Spanish. Cognate to Charles.

Genealogies: None known.

CARLSON (S.S. Abbreviation: Carlso)

Ranking: 198 S.S. Count: 179,496

Origin: Danish, Norwegian, Swedish. Cognate to Charles.

Famous **Carlsons**: EVANS FORDYCE CARLSON (1896–1947) of New York was a soldier and commander of a Marine battalion that became known as "Carlson's

Raiders." CHESTER F. CARLSON (1906–1968) of Washington invented xerography, now know as photocopying.

Genealogies: *Memories, Peter E. Johnson 1855–1926, and the Descendants of Emil Anton Carlson, 1881–1950* was compiled by Fritzene Carlson Moore and published in Winter Haven, Florida, in 1981.

CARLTON (S.S. Abbreviation: Carlto)

Ranking: 1520 **S.S. Count:** 29,254

Origin: English. Derived from the Old Norse word "karl" and the Old English word "tūn," meaning peasant and settlement. The name was given to those who came from Carlton, the name of several places in England.

Famous **Carltons:** EFFIE CROCKETT CARLTON (1857–1940), under the pen name of Effie Canning, was the author of the lullaby "Rock-a Bye Baby."

Genealogies: *Livingston and Carlton: Who Are We?* was compiled by Henry Newell Carleton and published in New York, New York, in 1966. *Cousins by the Dozens* was compiled by Dorothy Sturgis Pruett and published in Macon, Georgia, in 1975.

CARMAN (ALSO CARMANS)

Ranking: 2786 **S.S. Count:** 16,355

Origin: English, Flemish. English: derived the first name Karlmaðr, which is derived from the Old Norse words "karl" and "maðr," meaning male and man. English, Flemish: derived from the Anglo-Norman-French and Middle Low German word "car," meaning cart. The name was given to those who worked as carters.

Genealogies: *The Carman Family, 1631–1981* was compiled by Carrol Carman Hall and published in Springfield, Illinois, in 1981. *Carman Family Chart* was compiled by Walter F. Wright and published in Detroit, Michigan, in 1952. *John Lee Carman and His Descendants* was published in Baltimore, Maryland, in 1966.

CARMICHAEL (S.S. Abbreviation: Carmic)

Ranking: 1468 **S.S. Count:** 30,331

Origin: Scottish. Derived from the British word "ker," meaning fort, and the first name Michael. The name was given to those who came from Carmichael, a place in Scotland.

Famous **Carmichaels:** WILLIAM CARMICHAEL (?–1795) of Maryland was a diplomat who was responsible for Lafayette's leaving the French military to become a Revolutionary War officer under George Washington. LEONARD CARMICHAEL (1898–1973) of Pennsylvania was president of Tufts University, secretary of the Smithsonian Institution, and a vice president of the National Geographic Society. HOAGLAND HOWARD (HOAGY) CARMICHAEL (1899–1981) of Indiana was a pianist, singer, actor, and composer. He composed many of the biggest hits of the big-band era. His works include "Riverboat Shuffle," "Georgia on My Mind,"

and "In the Cool Cool Cool of the Evening," which won an Academy Award in 1951.

Genealogies: *The Carmichael Clan, Westbrook and Allied Families* was compiled by Opal Carmichael Phoenix and published in Decatur, Georgia, in 1963. *The Scottish Highlander Carmichaels of the Carolinas* was compiled by Roderick L. Carmichael and published in Washington, D.C., in 1978.

CARMONA (S.S. Abbreviation: Carmon)

Ranking: 2378 **S.S. Count:** 19,089

Origin: Portuguese, Spanish. Derived from the Latin word "carmen," meaning a country house. The name was given to those who came from Carmona, a place in Santander, Spain.

Genealogies: None known.

CARNAHAN (S.S. Abbreviation: Carnah)

Ranking: 4426 **S.S. Count:** 10,128

Origin: Irish. Derived from the Gaelic name Ó Ceallacáin, which is derived from the first name Ceallac.

Genealogies: None known.

CARNES

Ranking: 2198 **S.S. Count:** 20,861

Origin: Scottish. Transformation of Cairn(e)s.

Genealogies: None known.

CARNEY

Ranking: 935 **S.S. Count:** 46,149

Origin: Irish. Derived from the Gaelic name Ó Catharnaigh, meaning "descendant of Carthanach" (H&H), a name meaning warlike.

Famous **Carneys:** THOMAS CARNEY (1824–1888) of Ohio was governor of Kansas (1862–1864). ARTHUR WILLIAM MATTHEW (ART) CARNEY (1918–) of New York is an actor. He had television roles in the series "The Honeymooners" and "Jackie Gleason." His movie appearances include *Going in Style, Take This Job and Shove It,* and *Fire Starter.*

Genealogies: None known.

CARON

Ranking: 2496 **S.S. Count:** 18,157

Origin: French. Uncertain etymology. Most likely derived from the Celtic word "car," meaning to love.

Genealogies: None known.

CARPENTER, CARPENTIER, CARPENTIERE, CARPENTIERI, CARPENE, CARPENETO, CARPENETTI, ET AL. (S.S. Abbreviation: Carpen)

Ranking: 196 **S.S. Count:** 181,089

Origin: Carpenter—English; Carpentier—French; Car-

pentiere, Carpentieri, Carpene, Carpeneto, Carpenetti, et al.—Italian. Carpenter, Carpentier, Carpentiere, Carpentieri: derived from the Anglo-Norman-French word "carpentier," meaning someone who worked with wood. The names were given to those who were woodworkers. Carpene, Carpeneto, Carpenetti: derived from the Latin word "carp- inus," meaning a group of witch elm trees. The names were given to those who lived near such trees.

Famous **Carpenters:** CYRUS CLAY CARPENTER (1829–1898) of Pennsylvania was governor of Iowa (1871–1875). FRANCIS BICKELL CARPENTER (1830–1900) of New York was the portrait painter who did the painting of Abraham Lincoln reading the Emancipation Proclamation to his cabinet. The painting hangs in the U.S. Capitol. JOHN ALDEN CARPENTER (1876–1951) of Illinois was a composer who introduced jazz rhythms in orchestral music. His works include "Krazy Kat" and "Skyscrapers."

Genealogies: *Carpenter and Related Family Members Migrating from England* was compiled by James Carpenter and published in Bowling Green, Kentucky, in 1992. *Carpenters a Plenty* was compiled by Robert C. Carpenter and published in Baltimore, Maryland, in 1982.

CARR
Ranking: 214 **S.S. Count:** 166,284
Origin: English, Irish. English: transformation of Kerr. Irish: 1) derived from the Gaelic name Ó Carra, meaning "descendant of Carra" (H&H), a name meaning spear. 2) a transformation of the Gaelic name Mac Giolla Chathair, meaning "son of the servant Cathar" (H&H), a name derived from the word "cath," meaning battle.

Famous **Carrs:** THOMAS MATTHEW CARR (1750–1820), believed to have been born in Ireland, was an Augustinian friar who came to America in 1796 and founded the first monastery for his order at St. Augustine's Church, Philadelphia, 1796. BENJAMIN CARR (1769–1831), born in England, came to America and settled in Philadelphia, Pennsylvania, where he opened this country's first music store. He became a famous singer and promoter of music. DABNEY CARR (1773–1837) of Virginia was a justice of the Virginia Supreme Court of Appeals (1824–1837). DABNEY SMITH CARR (1802–1854) of Virginia was a diplomat and journalist and minister to Turkey (1843–1850). ELIAS CARR (1839–1900) of North Carolina was governor of North Carolina (1893–1897). EMMA PERRY CARR (1880–1972) of Ohio was noted for her work in the field of spectroscopy. EUGENE ASA CARR (1830–1910) of New York was a Union soldier who won the Medal of Honor for gallantry as division commander at Pea Ridge (1862). WILBUR JOHN CARR (1870–1942) of Ohio went to work as a clerk at the U.S. State Department in 1892 and rose through the ranks to become head of the Foreign Service. He also served as minister to Czechoslovakia.

Genealogies: *Ancestors and Descendents of Amasa Carr* was compiled by Charles Carr and published in Ormond Beach, Florida, in 1981.

CARRAN
Ranking: 3561 **S.S. Count:** 12,677
Origin: Irish. Derived from the name Mac Ciarain, which is derived from the Gaelic word "ciar," meaning colored.
Genealogies: None known.

CARRASCO, CARRASQUILLA, CARRASQUILLO, CARRASCAL (S.S. Abbreviation: Carras)
Ranking: 1313 **S.S. Count:** 33,823
Origin: Carrasco—Catalan, Portuguese, Spanish; Carrasquilla, Carraquillo—Portuguese, Spanish; Carrascal—Spanish. Derived from the Latin word "cerrus," meaning holm-oak tree. The names were given to those who lived near such trees.
Genealogies: None known.

CARREL, CARRELL, CARRELET
Ranking: 4864 **S.S. Count:** 9,021
Origin: Carrel, Carrell—English; Carrelet—French. 1) derived from the Old French word "quar(r)el," meaning bolt for a crossbow. The name was given to those who worked making such bolts and to those who were short. 2) derived from the Late Latin word "querella," meaning complaint. The name was given to those who were considered argumentative.

Genealogies: *Southern Kirk and Carrell Families* was compiled by Maudie Marie Holt Marshall and published in Houston, Texas, in 1971.

CARRER, CARRERE, CARRERI, CARRERO, CARRERA, CARRERAS
Ranking: 2572 **S.S. Count:** 17,695
Origin: Carrer—Provençal; Carrere, Carreri, Carrero—Italian; Carrera, Carreras—Spanish. Carrer, Carreri, Carrero: cognates to Carrier. Carreras, Carrere, Carreri: congates to Carriere.

Famous **Bearers:** JOHN MERVEN CARRERE (1858–1911), born in Brazil, was an architect who did extensive work in Washington, D.C., and New York City.
Genealogies: None known.

CARRICK (S.S. Abbreviation: Carric)
Ranking: 3353 **S.S. Count:** 13,528
Origin: Scottish. Transformation of Craig.
Famous **Carricks:** SAMMUEL CARRICK (1760–1809), born in Pennsylvania, organized the first Presbyterian church in Knoxville, Tennessee, and later was president of

Blount College, which became the University of Tennessee.

Genealogies: *Carrick/Karrick Genealogy* was compiled by Bett M. Mann and published in Lansing, Michigan, in 1983.

CARRIE, CARRIEZ, CARRIER, CARRIERE, CARRIERI

Ranking: 1821 S.S. Count: 24,790

Origin: Carrie, Carriez—French; Carrier—English, French; Carriere, Carrieri—Italian. Carrie, Carriez, Carrier, Carrieri: derived from the Late Latin word "carrārius," meaning one who transports goods. The names were given to those who worked as such. Carriere: derived from the Late Latin word "carrāria," meaning road. The name was given to those who lived near a well-traveled road.

Famous Bearers: WILLIS HAVILAND CARRIER (1876–1950) of New York was a mechanical engineer who developed the radical refrigerating machine, which became the modern air-conditioning unit. He headed the Carrier Corp. and held patents on air-conditioning systems.

Genealogies: *Descendants of George S. Carrier and Mariah Foresman* was compiled by Wilma May Myers and published in Fort Myers, Florida, in 1975. *Some Descendants of Thomas Carrier of Andover and Billerica, Massachusetts, Who Died in Colchester, Connecticut, May 16, 1735, and His Wife Martha (Allen) Carrier, Who, As a Result of the Infamous Witch Trials, Was Hung at Salem, Massachusetts on August 19, 1692* was compiled by George S. May and published in Fair Oaks, California, in 1978.

CARRIGY (S.S. Abbreviation: Carrig)

Ranking: 3629 S.S. Count: 12,411

Origin: Irish. Transformation of McCarrick.

Genealogies: None known.

CARRILLO (S.S. Abbreviation: Carril)

Ranking: 907 S.S. Count: 45,029

Origin: Spanish. Derived from a Spanish word that means cheek. The name was given to those with unusual cheeks.

Genealogies: None known.

CARRINGTON (S.S. Abbreviation: Carrin)

Ranking: 2567 S.S. Count: 17,714

Origin: English, Scottish. Derived from the Old English first names Cāra or Cōra and the word "tūn," meaning settlement. The name was given to those who came from Carrington, the name of several places in England.

Famous Carringtons: PAUL CARRINGTON (1733–1818) of Virginia was chief justice of the Virginia general court and a justice of the court of appeals. HENRY BEEBEE CARRINGTON (1824–1912) of Connecticut was a lawyer and sol-

dier and was responsible for the building of Fort Phil Kearney. He also wrote *Battles of the American Revolution.*

Genealogies: *A Brief Historical Sketch of the Carrington Family* was compiled by John Claiborne Carrington and published in New York City in 1947.

CARRIO, CARRION

Ranking: 3315 S.S. Count: 13,666

Origin: Carrio—Catalan; Carrion—Spanish. The names were given to those who came from Carrión, the name of several places in Spain.

Genealogies: None known.

CARROL, CARROLL

Ranking: 174 S.S. Count: 192,671

Origin: Irish. Derived from the Gaelic first name Cearbal, which is possibly derived from the word "cearbh," meaning hacking.

Famous Bearers: The Carroll family has a lengthy history in Maryland: CHARLES CARROLL (1737–1832) was the only Roman Catholic to sign the Declaration of Independence and was the longest-surviving signer of the document. He served briefly in the U.S. Senate. DANIEL CARROLL (1730–1796), a cousin of Charles, was a U.S. senator. JOHN CARROLL (1735–1815), brother of Daniel and cousin of Charles, was the first Roman Catholic bishop in the United States and the first archbishop of Baltimore. WILLIAM CARROLL (1788–1844) of Pennsylvania was governor of Tennessee (1821–1827 and 1829–1835). JOHN LEE CARROLL (1830–1911), great-grandson of Charles, was governor of Maryland (1875–1879). JAMES CARROLL (1854–1917), born in England, was a physician who did research on yellow fever, allowing himself to be infected with the disease by a mosquito in order to prove Dr. Carlos Finlay's theory of disease transmission. He also demonstrated that yellow fever was ultramicroscopic. EARL CARROLL (1893–1948) of Pennsylvania was a songwriter who was the author of 400 popular songs.

Genealogies: *Carroll Frontiersmen, From North Carolina 1805 to Arkansas 1987* was compiled by Elizabeth Carroll Foster and published in Charlotte Hall, Maryland, in 1987. *Daniel Carroll II, One Man and His Descendants, 1730–1978* was compiled by Sister May Virginia Geiger and published in Baltimore, Maryland, in 1979.

CARRUTH, CARRUTHERS (S.S. Abbreviation: Carrut)

Ranking: 3993 S.S. Count: 11,321

Origin: English. Derived from the British word "ker," meaning fort and other components that probably mean red and ruler. The names were given to those who came from Carruthers, a place in Scotland.

Famous Bearers: FRED HAYDEN CARRUTH (1862–1932)

of Minnesota was editor of *Woman's Home Companion* (1905–1917).

Genealogies: *From Whence Ye Came: Carruth, Craighead, Davis, Grant, Hawkins, Miller, Mills, Noblitt, Packwood, Tyler, Wood, and Related Families* was compiled by Lela Grant Carruth and published in Burnet, Texas, in 1982.

CARSON
Ranking: 496 S.S. Count: 80,787
Origin: Scottish. Uncertain etymology.

Famous **Carsons:** CHRISTOPHER "KIT" CARSON (1809–1868) of Kentucky was a trapper, guide, Indian agent, and soldier. He served as John Charles Fremont's guide on his first expedition. Although plain-spoken, modest, and uneducated, he had integrity as his best asset. JOHN RENSHAW CARSON (1886–1940) of Pennsylvania was an electrical engineer who invented the single-sideband carrier-suppressed method of high-frequency transmission. RACHEL LOUISE CARSON (1907–1964) of Pennsylvania was a biologist and author.

Genealogies: *Carson-Bent-Boggs Genealogy* was compiled by Quantrill McClung and published in Denver, Colorado, in 1962.

CARSTENS, CARSTEN, CARSTENSEN, CARSTENSON (S.S. Abbreviation: Carste)
Ranking: 4730 S.S. Count: 9462
Origin: Carstens—Dutch; Carsten, Carstensen, Carstenson—German. Cognates to Christian.
Genealogies: None known.

CARTAGENA (S.S. Abbreviation: Cartag)
Ranking: 4127 S.S. Count: 10,955
Origin: Italian. The name was given to those who came from Cartagena, which means "new town" (ES) and is a place in Spain.
Genealogies: None known.

CARTER
Ranking: 44 S.S. Count: 505,864
Origin: English. Derived from the Anglo-Norman-French word "car(e)tier," meaning transporter. The name was given to those who worked transporting goods.

Famous **Carters:** ROBERT CARTER (1663–1732) of Virginia was a prominent member of the Virginia Assembly. JOHN CARTER (1737–1781) of Virginia was one of the first settlers in North Carolina. LANDON CARTER (1760–1800) of Virginia, son of John Carter, was a Tennessee pioneer. JAMES GORDON CARTER (1795–1849) of Massachusetts was at the forefront of reform and improvement of New England common schools (1821–1840). SAMUEL

POWHATAN CARTER (1819–1891) of Tennessee was both an army and navy officer and the only American ever to be both a rear admiral and a major general. JAMES COOLIDGE CARTER (1827–1905) of Massachusetts was prominent in movements for municipal reform and a leader of the fight against codification of the common law as proposed by David Dudley Field. FRANKLIN CARTER (1837–1919) of Connecticut was president of Williams College (1881–1901). HENRY ALPHEUS PEIRCE CARTER (1837–1891) of Hawaii was the Hawaiian minister to the United States (1883–1891). HENRY ROSE CARTER (1852–1925) of Virginia conducted the first U.S. campaign for malaria control. CAROLINE LOUISE CARTER (1862–1937) of Kentucky was an actress. ALVIN PLEASANT CARTER (1891–1960) of Virginia was popularly known as A.P. He formed the Carter Family singers, who were responsible for preserving much Appalachian folk music. BOAKE CARTER (1898–1944), born in Russia, was a journalist who was best known for his emotional coverage of the kidnapping of Charles Lindbergh's son and the subsequent trial of Bruno Richard Hauptmann. EUNICE HUNTON CARTER (1899–1970) of Georgia was a lawyer and community leader. HODDING CARTER (1907–1972) of Louisiana was a journalist and author. He won a Pulitzer Prize in 1946. JAMES EARL (JIMMY) CARTER JR. (1924–) of Georgia was the 39th U.S. president. His mediation of the Camp David accords between Egyptian President Anwar el-Sadat and Israeli Prime Minister Menachem Begin ended the war between Egypt and Israel that had been declared in 1948.

Genealogies: *A Brief History and Genealogy of the Carter and Some Allied Families* was compiled by Lyle Carter and published in Lake Worth, Florida, in the 1970s. *The Carter and Fulcher Families* was compiled by Jane Chapman Whitt and published in Falls Church, Virginia, in 1985.

CARTWRIGHT (S.S. Abbreviation: Cartwr)
Ranking: 1475 S.S. Count: 30,222
Origin: English. Derived from the Old English words "cræt" and "wyrhta," meaning cart and craftsperson. The name was given to those who worked making carts.

Famous **Cartwrights:** PETER CARTWRIGHT (1785–1872) of Virginia was a traveling preacher. He ran for Congress against Abraham Lincoln in 1846 and was defeated.

Genealogies: *Cartwright and Shipp Families of Lower Norfolk, Princess Anne and Surry Counties, Virginia and North Carolina* was compiled by Alice Granbery Walter and published in Lawrence, New York, in 1968.

CARUSO, CARUSONE
Ranking: 1586 S.S. Count: 28,206

Origin: Italian. Derived from the Italian word *"caruso,"* meaning close-cropped. The name was used to mean *"boy,"* because in the Middle Ages it was fashionable for young men to wear their hair much shorter than older men.

Genealogies: None known.

CARVALHAL, CARVALHEIRA, CARVALHO (S.S. Abbreviation: Carval)

Ranking: 4438 **S.S. Count:** 10,999
Origin: Portuguese. Cognates to *Car(a)ballo.*
Genealogies: None known.

CARVER

Ranking: 1016 **S.S. Count:** 43,025
Origin: English. 1) derived from the Old English word *"ceorfan,"* meaning to carve. The name was given to wood carvers and sculptors. 2) derived from the Anglo-Norman-French word *"caruier,"* meaning ploughman. The name was given to those who worked as such.

Famous **Carvers:** JOHN CARVER (1576–1621), born in England, was the first governor of Plymouth. He is responsible for a treaty signed in March 1621 with Massasoit. JONATHAN CARVER (1710–1780) of Massachusetts was an explorer who traveled the northern areas of the Mississippi River. GEORGE WASHINGTON CARVER (1860?–1943) of Missouri, the son of a slave woman, became an agricultural chemist who devoted his life to preparing rural African-Americans for their lives as free men. Through his Tuskegee Institute in Alabama, he developed more than 300 food and industrial products from sweet potatoes, thus aiding the social and economic situation of the newly freed slaves.

Genealogies: *Carver Family, 1769–1977* was compiled by John Bradley Arthaud and published in Columbia, Missouri, in 1978. *Genealogy of the Rev. Eleazer Carver Family* was compiled by Fred E. and Margaret R. Carver and published in Yakima, Washington, in 1971.

CARY

Ranking: 2733 **S.S. Count:** 16,659
Origin: Cornish, English, Irish, Welsh. Transformation of *Carey.*

Famous **Carys:** ARCHIBALD CARY (1721–1787) of Virginia was a member of all the Virginia revolutionary conventions. LOTT CARY (1780–1828) of Virginia, a slave, purchased freedom for himself and his family around 1813. He moved to Freetown, Liberia, where he became pastor of the first Baptist church. MARY ANN SHADD CARY (1823–1893) of Delaware was a teacher, journalist, and lawyer. She was the oldest of 13 children born to Abraham Doras and Harriett Parnell Shadd. Both of her parents were free Negroes. She helped slaves escape to Canada, established and edited a weekly paper called the *Provincial Freeman,* taught school, and earned her law degree. ALICE

CARY (1820–1871) and PHOEBE CARY (1824–1871) of Ohio were both poets. The two sisters together published the *Poems of Alice and Phoebe Cary.* Alice Cary wrote far more than her sister, and her work was praised by Edgar Allan Poe. She is best known for her hymn "Nearer Home." ANNIE LOUISE CARY (1841–1921) of Maine, a contralto, was one of the first American singers to acquire an international reputation. ELIZABETH LUTHER CARY (1867–1936) of New York was an author and an art critic.

Genealogies: *Senior Line of Virginia Carys* was compiled by Boyd Balford Cary and published in 1956.

CASANOVA, CASANOVAS (S.S. Abbreviation: Casano)

Ranking: 4510 **S.S. Count:** 9927
Origin: Casanova—Catalan, Italian, Spanish; Casanovas—Catalan. Derived from the Latin words *"casa"* and *"nova,"* meaning house and new. The names were given to those who lived in a new home.

Genealogies: None known.

CASARES (S.S. Abbreviation: Casare)

Ranking: 4549 **S.S. Count:** 9817
Origin: Basque, Portuguese, Spanish. 1) cognate to *Casale.* 2) derived from the Latin word *"cassare,"* meaning to destroy. 3) possibly derived from the Spanish word *"casada,"* meaning married.

Genealogies: None known.

CASAS

Ranking: 4406 **S.S. Count:** 10,178
Origin: Spanish. Derived from the Latin word *"casa,"* meaning house. The name was most likely given to those who lived in a particularly luxurious home.

Genealogies: None known.

CASE

Ranking: 772 **S.S. Count:** 54,472
Origin: English, Italian, Provençal. English: derived from the Anglo-Norman-French word *"cas(s)e,"* meaning case. The name was given to those who worked making chests, boxes, and/or cases. Italian: cognate to *Cheese(man).* Provençal: cognate to *Casa(s).*

Famous **Cases:** LEONARD CASE (1820–1880) of Ohio used his inheritance to serve the public as a philanthropist. SHIRLEY JACKSON CASE (1872–1947), born in Canada, a historian and clergywoman, developed the "Chicago School" method of historical research, which calls for examination of all dimensions of a given culture prior to working with documents on specific events within that culture. ADELAIDE TEAGUE CASE (1887–1948) of Missouri was an Episcopal educator.

Genealogies: *The Case Family, Descendants of Jonathan*

J. and Lucy Simmons Case, Pioneer Settlers in Ontario County, New York was compiled by Charles Richmond Case and published in Canandaigua, New York, in 1915. *The Descendants of Captain Stephen Case of Marlboro, New York* was compiled by Lynn Marshall Case and published in Havertown, Pennsylvania, in 1971.

CASEY

Ranking: 435 **S.S. Count:** 91,353

Origin: Irish. Derived from the Gaelic name Ó Cathassaigh, meaning "descendant of Cathasch" (H&H), a name meaning vigilant or noisy (H&H).

Famous **Caseys:** SILAS CASEY (1807–1882) of Rhode Island was a Union soldier who served on the midwestern front, in the Seminole War, and in Mexico. He was the author of *Casey's Tactics* (1862). JOSEPH CASEY (1814–1879) of Maryland was a jurist and a member of Congress from Pennsylvania, and editor of "Casey's Reports." THOMAS LINCOLN CASEY (1831–1896) of New York was an army engineer who completed construction in 1884 of the Washington Monument. WILLIAM HENRY CASEY (1918–1976) of New York was an engineer who designed the largest floating lifting crane in the world. It was used to drive pilings to construct the William Preston Lane Jr. Memorial Bridge over the Chesapeake Bay.

Genealogies: *A Bakers Dozen: We Were Thirteen, The Caseys of Tuscola, Taylor County, Texas* was compiled by Clifford Casey and published in Seagraves, Texas, in 1974. *Casey Family History* was compiled by Alvin Harold Casey and published in Stillwater, Oklahoma, in 1980.

CASH

Ranking: 1103 **S.S. Count:** 40,101

Origin: English. Transformation of Case.

Famous **Cashes:** WILBUR JOSEPH CASH (1900–1941) of South Carolina wrote *The Mind of the South* (1941), which was an analysis of the feelings of the white people of the South. It was used to improve race relations.

Genealogies: *Cash and Buffington: Being the Family of Reuben Cash (son of Howard) and His Wife, Elizabeth Buffington* was compiled by Ben LeGrande Cash and published in Albuquerque, New Mexico, in 1979.

CASILLO, CASILLAS (S.S. Abbreviation: Casill)

Ranking: 2945 **S.S. Count:** Number: 15,463

Origin: Casillo—Italian; Casillas—Spanish. Transformations of Casa(s).

Genealogies: None known.

CASON

Ranking: 2741 **S.S. Count:** 16,614

Origin: Italian. Transformation of Casa(s).

Genealogies: None known.

CASPER, CASPERS, CASPERRI

Ranking: 2227 **S.S. Count:** 20,581

Origin: Casper, Caspers—German; Casperri—Italian. Transformations of and cognates to Kasper.

Genealogies: *The American Ancestry of Harriet Matilda Casper Marchant* was compiled by Barbara S. Stoutner and published in Arlington, Virginia, in 1978.

CASS

Ranking: 4076 **S.S. Count:** 11,093

Origin: English. Derived from the first name Cassandra.

Famous **Casses:** LEWIS CASS (1782–1866) of New Hampshire was governor of the Michigan territory for 18 years. He also served as a U.S. senator, minister to France, secretary of war, and secretary of state. In 1848, he was the Democratic nominee for U.S. president.

Genealogies: *Our Southern Ancestors: Cain, Cash, Cooper, Hughes, Martin, Moore, Prince, Sanders, Sorrells, Still, Williams, Wright Families* was compiled by Thelma Faye Cain Prince and published in Baltimore, Maryland, in 1985.

CASSEL, CASSELL, CASSELLS, CASSELS

Ranking: 1724 **S.S. Count:** 25,999

Origin: English. Transformations of Castle.

Genealogies: None known.

CASSIDY (S.S. Abbreviation: Cassid)

Ranking: 1160 **S.S. Count:** 37,680

Origin: Irish. Derived from the Gaelic name Ó Caiside, meaning "descendant of Caiside" (H&H), a name derived from the word "cas," meaning curly.

Famous **Cassidys:** BUTCH CASSIDY (1866–1909?) of Utah was born Robert LeRoy Parker. He was an outlaw and leader of the Wild Bunch, a group of train and bank robbers. He first teamed up with Elzy Lay, but when his friend was imprisoned, he took up with Harry Longabaugh, who became known as the Sundance Kid. The place and time of their deaths are unknown.

Genealogies: None known.

CASTAN

Ranking: 1142 **S.S. Count:** 38,486

Origin: French. Derived from the Old French word "catan(h)," meaning chestnut tree. The name was given to those who lived near a chestnut tree or may have been given to those who had chestnut-colored hair.

Genealogies: None known.

CASTEEL, CASTEELS (S.S. Abbreviation: Castee)

Ranking: 3671 **S.S. Count:** 12,296

Origin: French. *Cognates to Castle.*
Genealogies: None known.

CASTEL, CASTELE, CASTELLETTI, CASTELLETTO, CASTELLINI, CASTELLARI, CASTELLARO, ET AL.

Ranking: 872 **S.S. Count:** 49,544

Origin: Castel—Catalan, Jewish; Castele—Dutch; Castelletti, Castelletto, Castellini, Castellari, Castellaro, et al.—Italian. Castel, Castele, Castelletti, Castelletto, Castellini: cognates to Castle. Castellari, Castellaro: derived from the Latin word "castellāre," meaning small castle. The names were given to those who came from Chatelier or places with similiar names in France and elsewhere.
Genealogies: None known.

CASTEROT, CASTEROU (S.S. Abbreviation: Caster)

Ranking: 5873 **S.S. Count:** 7501
Origin: Provençal. Cognates to Castle.
Genealogies: None known.

CASTILLE, CASTILLOU, CASTILLION, CASTILLEJO, CASTILLA, CASTILLO, CASTILLOS (S.S. Abbreviation: Castil)

Ranking: 311 **S.S. Count:** 118,459
Origin: Castille—French; Castillou—Provençal; Castillion—Provençal, Spanish; Castillejo, Castilla, Castillo, Castillos—Spanish. Castilla, Castille: derived from the Latin word "castellum," meaning fort. The names were given to those who came from Castilla, a region in Spain. Castillejo, Castillo, Castillion, Castillos, Castillou: cognates to Castle.
Genealogies: None known.

CASTLE, CASTLEMAN, CASTLES

Ranking: 940 **S.S. Count:** 45,999
Origin: English. Derived from the Anglo-Norman-French word "castel," meaning castle or home of a feudal lord or a fortified building or group of buildings. The name was given to those who lived in or near or worked in such a place.
Famous **Bearers:** VERNON BLYTHE CASTLE (1887–1918), born in England, was the husband and dance partner of Irene Castle. He revolutionized papular dancing between 1912 and 1914, creating the one-step, turkey-trot, and others. IRENE CASTLE (1893–1969) of New York was half of a famous dance team with her husband, Vernon Castle. After his death she founded Orphans in the Storm in Deerfield, Illinois.
Genealogies: None known.

CASTO

Ranking: 4682 **S.S. Count:** 9555
Origin: Italian?, German?, Spanish? Uncertain etymol-

ogy. Possibly derived from the Latin name Castor, which refers to the secretion of a beaver.
Genealogies: None known.

CASTOR, CASTORENO

Ranking: 4038 **S.S. Count:** 11,214
Origin: Castor—English?; Castoreno—Spanish. Castor: Uncertain etymology. The name was most likely given to those who came from Caister, the name of several places England. Castoreno: derived from the Spanish word "castor" and the component "eno," meaning beaver and of superiority. The name was given to those who built excellent homes and to those who lived near beavers.
Genealogies: *Benjamin Castor (1741– 1825) and Descendants* was published in Richmond, Texas, in 1984.

CASTRO

Ranking: 346 **S.S. Count:** 109,566
Origin: Italian, Jewish, Portuguese, Spanish. Derived from the Latin word "castrum," meaning military camp. The name was given to those who lived near a fortified town or a castle.
Famous **Castros:** RAUL HECTOR CASTRO (1916–), originally from Cananea, Mexico, has served as a judge in Arizona and as U.S. ambassador to El Salvador, Bolivia, and Argentina.
Genealogies: *The Castro Family: A Genealogical History of the Castro Family* was compiled by Karen Bonds Mitchell and published in Commerce City, Colorado, in 1990. *Castro of California: A Genealogy of a Colonial Spanish California Family* was compiled by Kenneth M. and Doris Castro and published in Murphys, California, in 1975.

CASWELL (S.S. Abbreviation: Caswel)

Ranking: 3348 **S.S. Count:** 13,537
Origin: English. Derived from the Old English words "cærse" and "well(a)," meaning cress and well. The name was given to those who came from Creswell and similarly named places in England.
Famous **Caswells:** RICHARD CASWELL (1729–1789) of Maryland was a Revolutionary War soldier and governor of North Carolina (1776–1780 and 1785–1787).
Genealogies: None known.

CATALA, CATALANI, CATALANO, CATALANOTTI, CATALAO, CATALAN, CATALANO

Ranking: 2610 **S.S. Count:** 17,395
Origin: Catala—Catalan; Catalani, Catalano, Catalanotti—Italian; Catalao—Portuguese; Catalan—Provençal; Catalano—Spanish. The names were given to those who came from Catalonia, a region in northeastern Spain.
Genealogies: None known.

CATES
Ranking: 1751 S.S. Count: 25,592
Origin: English. Derived from the Old Norse word "káti,"
meaning boy.
Genealogies: *The Cates Chain: The Hiram Cates Family:*
From Tennessee to Texas and Around the World, 1814–1988
was compiled by Greta Cates Leard and published in Wolfe
City, Texas, in 1988. *Cates-Hess-Phinney and Allied Lines*
was compiled by Florence Cates and published in King-
man, Kansas, in 1980.

CATHCART (S.S. Abbreviation: Cathca)
Ranking: 6702 S.S. Count: 6452
Origin: Scottish. Uncertain etymology. Possibly derived
from the British word "cad" and the Gaelic word "cath," both
meaning battle, or the British word "ker," meaning fort. The
name was given to those who lived near the River Cart in
Scotland.
Famous **Cathcarts:** James Leander Cathcart
(1767–1843), born in Ireland but brought to America at an
early age, served with distinction in the military and later
became consul at Madeira and Cadiz. William Cathcart
(1826–1908), born in Ireland, was editor of the *Baptist*
Encyclopedia.
Genealogies: None known.

CATHEY
Ranking: 3756 S.S. Count: 12,059
Origin: Scottish. Derived from the first name Cathan.
Genealogies: *Cathey Cousins* was compiled by Myrtice
Adell Cathey and published in Covington, Kentucky, in 1968.

CATO
Ranking: 4209 S.S. Count: 10,735
Origin: French? Uncertain etymology. Possibly derived
from the first name Catherine.
Genealogies: None known.

CAUDILL (S.S. Abbreviation: Caudil)
Ranking: 1752 S.S. Count: 25,583
Origin: English. Transformation of Caldwell.
Genealogies: None known.

CAUDLE
Ranking: 4120 S.S. Count: 10,969
Origin: English. Transformation of Caldwell.
Genealogies: None known.

CAUSEY
Ranking: 3040 S.S. Count: 14,962
Origin: English. Derived from the Middle English word
"cacey," meaning causeway or path. The name was given to
those who lived near a path.

Genealogies: None known.

CAVALIERE, CAVALIERO, CAVALIE, CAVALIER (S.S. Abbreviation: Cavali)
Ranking: 4969 S.S. Count: 901
Origin: Cavaliere, Cavaliero—Italian; Cavalie, Cava-
lier—Provençal. Cognates to Chevalier.
Genealogies: None known.

CAVALLAR, CAVALLARO, CAVALLIERE, CAVELLIERO, CAVALLI, ET AL., CAVALLO; CAVALLIE, CAVALLIER (S.S. Abbreviation: Cavall)
Ranking: 3261 S.S. Count: 13,945
Origin: Cavallar, Cavallaro, Cavalliere, Cavelliero, Cav-
alli, et al.—Italian; Cavallo; Cavallie, Cavallier—Provençal.
Cavallar, Cavallaro, Cavalliere, Cavelliero, Cavallie, Caval-
lier: cognates to Chevalier. Cavalli, Cavallo: derived from the
Late Latin word "caballus," meaning horse. The names were
given to those who worked with horses and may have been
given to those who looked like a horse.
Genealogies: None known.

CAVANA, CAVANAGH, CAVANAUGH
Ranking: 1345 S.S. Count: Number: 32,904
Origin: Cavana—Italian; Cavanagh, Cavanaugh—Irish.
Cavana: derived from the Late Latin word "capanna," mean-
ing hut. The name was given to those who lived in a tempo-
rary shelter. Cavanagh, Cavanaugh: transformations of
Kavanaugh.
Genealogies: None known.

CAVAZO, CAVAZOS
Ranking: 3309 S.S. Count: 13,687
Origin: Italian?, Mexican? Uncertain etymology. Italian:
possibly derived from the Italian name Iacava. Mexican: pos-
sibly derived from the Spanish word "cava," to dig, or a room
in a palace where wine and water were stored. The name was
possibly given to those who came from Cavazas, a place in
Nuevo Leon, Mexico.
Genealogies: None known.

CAVE
Ranking: 3859 S.S. Count: 11,679
Origin: English, French. English: 1) derived from the Old
English word "cáf," meaning swift. The name was given to those
who came from Cave, a place in England. 2) transformation of
Chaff. French: derived from the Old French word "cave," mean-
ing cave or basement. The name was given to those who worked
in a wine cellar and to those who lived near a cave.
Genealogies: None known.

CECIL

Ranking: 2886 S.S. Count: 15,780

Origin: Welsh. Derived from the Old Welsh first name Seisyllt.

Genealogies: *300 Years of Cecils in America, 1665–1971* was compiled by Alta Cecil Koch and published in West Terre Haute, Indiana, in 1971. *The Revolutionary Soldiers: Charles Andrews, Thomas Archbold, and Joshua Cecil, and Their Descendants* was compiled by Electa Iantha Batlzell Lochner and published in 1963.

CENTENO (S.S. Abbreviation: Centen)

Ranking: 4193. S.S. Count: 10,767.

Origin: Spanish. Derived from the Spanish word "centeno," meaning rye. The name was given to those who worked growing or selling rye.

Genealogies: None known

CERDA

Ranking: 4845 S.S. Count: 9230

Origin: Spanish. Derived from the Spanish word "cerda," meaning hair or bristle. The name was given to those who had peculiar protruding patches of hair.

Genealogies: None known.

CERVANTES (S.S. Abbreviation: Cervan)

Ranking: 1369 S.S. Count: 32,345

Origin: Spanish. The name was given to those who came from Cervantes, a place in Spain.

Genealogies: None known.

CHACON

Ranking: 2833 S.S. Count: 16,106

Origin: Latin American, Spanish. Uncertain etymology. Latin American: possibly derived from the Mayan word "chac," meaning grand. Spanish: 1) possibly derived from the Spanish word "jaconas," a kind of muslin. 2) possibly derived from the Spanish component "chac," which is used to connote laughter or music.

Genealogies: None known.

CHADWICK (S.S. Abbreviation: Chadwi)

Ranking: 2008 S.S. Count: 22,707

Origin: English. Derived from the first names Ceadel and Ceadda and the Old English word "wic," meaning a faraway settlement that was dependent on a larger settlement. The name was given to those who came from Chadwick, the name of several places in England.

Famous **Chadwicks:** JAMES READ CHADWICK (1844–1905) of Massachusetts established the Boston Medical Library. GEORGE WHITEFIELD CHADWICK (1854–1931) of Massachusetts was a composer. His work is noted for its romanticism. He composed three symphonies, two cantatas, five concert overtures, and many other pieces.

Genealogies: *Genealogy of Chadwick, King, and Allied Familes* was compiled by Darline Chadwick Smith and published in North Kansas City, Missouri, in 1982. *A Genealogy of the Chadick and Chaddick (also the Chadwick Family) Family Lines of the United States* was compiled by William D. Chadick and published in Yonkers, New York, in 1979.

CHAFFE, CHAFFEE

Ranking: 4707 S.S. Count: 9509

Origin: English. Derived from the Old French word "chauf," meaning bald. The names were given to those who were bald.

Famous **Bearers:** JEROME B. CHAFFEE (1825–1886) of New York was the founder and president of First National Bank in Denver, Colorado. He promoted Colorado for statehood, then served as its first U.S. senator. ANDA ROMANZA CHAFFEE (1842–1914) of Ohio was chief of staff for the U.S. army (1904–1906). His son, ANDA ROMANZA CHAFFEE (1884–1941) of Kansas, was a leader in the development of U.S. armored forces.

Genealogies: None known.

CHAFFIN (S.S. Abbreviation: Chaffi)

Ranking: 3045 S.S. Count: 14,922

Origin: English. Transformation of Chaff(e).

Genealogies: None known.

CHAMBERLAIN, CHAMBERS (S.S. Abbreviation: Chambe)

Ranking: 193 S.S. Count: 182,267

Origin: English. Chamberlain: derived from the Anglo-Norman-French word "Camberlanc," meaning chamberlain, one who was in charge of a noble's private chambers. The name was given to those who worked as such. Chambers: derived from the Middle English and Old French word "cha(u)mbre," meaning chamber. The name was given to those who worked in the private areas of a manor.

Famous **Bearers:** JOHN CHAMBERS (1780–1852) of New Jersey was a member of Congress from Kentucky and governor of Iowa Territory. JOSHUA LAWRENCE CHAMBERLAIN (1828–1914) of Maine received the Medal of Honor for gallantry at the Civil War battle at Gettysburg, Pennsylvania. He was governor of Maine (1866–1870). DANIEL HENRY CHAMBERLAIN (1835–1907) of Massachusetts settled in South Carolina and served as governor (1874–1876). He then moved to New York to practice law. JAMES JULIUS CHAMBERS (1850–1920) of Ohio explored the headwaters of the Mississippi River. GEORGE EARLE CHAMBERLAIN (1854–1928) of Mississippi settled in Oregon, where he was governor (1902–1909) and a U.S. senator

(1909–1921). CHARLES JOSEPH CHAMBERLAIN (1863–1943) of Ohio was a botanist whose books have been called "the keystones in the arch of morphological literature." ALEXANDER FRANCIS CHAMBERLAIN (1865–1914), born in England, was the editor of *Journal of American Folklore*.

Genealogies: *Descendants of William Chambers* was compiled by John Phillips and published in Cabin John, Maryland, in 1987. *Tales from the Past: Our Family (the Chambers Family) in America* was compiled by Frank Griffin and published in Gardnerville, Nevada, in 1975.

CHAMBLY (S.S. Abbreviation: Chambl)

Ranking: 2364 S.S. Count: 19,193

Origin: *English. Derived from the Old English first name Cēolmund, which is derived from the words "ceol" and "mund," meaning ship and protection, and the word "lēah," meaning wood. The name was given to those who came from Cholmondeley, a place in Cheshire, England.*

Genealogies: None known.

CHAMPAGNE, CHAMPAIGNE, CHAMPAIN (S.S. Abbreviation: Champa)

Ranking: 2568 S.S. Count: 17,711

Origin: *French. Champagne, Champaigne: derived from the Anglo-Norman-French word "champeneis," meaning someone who came from Champagne, France. Champain: transformation of C(h)amp.*

Genealogies: None known.

CHAMPION (S.S. Abbreviation: Champi)

Ranking: 1728 S.S. Count: 25,968

Origin: *English. Transformation of the first definition of Campion.*

Genealogies: *Champion Families: The Champion Trails in America* was compiled by Bonnie Duff Neal Smith and published in Cleveland, Texas, in 1976.

CHAN

Ranking: 996 S.S. Count: 44,033

Origin: *Chinese. The name means old.*

Genealogies: None known.

CHANCE, CHANCELLOR

Ranking: 1492 S.S. Count: 29,764

Origin: *Chance—English; Chancellor—English, Scottish. Chance: derived from the Anglo-Norman-French word "chea(u)nce," meaning good fortune. The name was given to those who gambled often and to those who were considered lucky. Chancellor: derived from the Anglo-Norman-French word "c(h)ancelier," meaning administrative official. The name was given to those who held such posts.*

Genealogies: *Chance Family, England to America, 1668 to 1972, in Forty Eight States* was compiled by Hilda Nancy Ersula Snowberger Chance and published in Liberty, Pennsylvania, in 1974.

CHANDLER, CHANDLISH (S.S. Abbreviation: Chandl)

Ranking: 975 S.S. Count: 107,056

Origin: *Chandler—English; Chandlish—Irish. Chandler: derived from the Late Latin word "candēlārius," meaning a maker or seller of candles. The name was given to those who worked as such. Chandlish: transformation of McCandless.*

Famous Bearers: THOMAS BRADBURY CHANDLER (1726–1790) of Connecticut was a leading advocate for an American episcopacy and author of several pamphlets on the episcopal question. JOHN CHANDLER (1762–1841) of New Hampshire was a Revolutionary War soldier and a U.S. senator from Maine. JOHN RIPLEY CHANDLER (1792–1880) of Massachusetts was a member of Congress from Pennsylvania (1849–1855) and U.S. minister to Naples (1858–1861). ELIZABETH MARGARET CHANDLER (1807–1834) of Delaware was an author of verse and prose and a contributor to the *Genius of Universal Emancipation*. ZACHARIAH CHANDLER (1813–1879) of New Hampshire was a U.S. senator from Michigan who felt that the Reconstruction acts were too lax. PELEG WHITMAN CHANDLER (1816–1889) of Maine was a lawyer who was considered the best jury pleader of his time in Massachusetts. WILLIAM EATON CHANDLER (1835–1917) of New Hampshire was a U.S. senator from New Hampshire (1887–1901). CHARLES FREDERICK CHANDLER (1836–1925) of Massachusetts was an industrial chemist and was co-founder of the Columbia School of Mines in 1864. He was a recognized authority on water supplies and sanitation and used his expertise to help the New York City Board of Health to improve conditions. JULIAN ALVIN CARROLL CHANDLER (1872–1934) of Virginia was president of the College of William and Mary (1919–1934). RAYMOND THORNTON CHANDLER (1888–1959) of Illinois was a detective-fiction writer. He was the creator of the private detective Philip Marlowe. His novels and short stories are all set in Los Angeles, California. His novels include *The Big Sleep, The Long Goodbye*, and *Farewell, My Lovely*.

Genealogies: *Chancler Ancestry of Kate (Chandler) Rhodes* was compiled by Dorothy Keen and published in Manhattan, Kansas, in 1989.

CHANEY

Ranking: 975 S.S. Count: 44,879

Origin: *English. Transformation of Chene(y).*

Famous Chaneys: ALONSO (LON) CHANEY (1883–1930) of Colorado was an actor who was known as the "Man of a Thousand Faces" for his work on the silent screen. He appeared in roles in the films *Hell Mor-*

gan's Girl, The Miracle Man, and The Hunchback of Notre Dame.

Genealogies: *The Chaney Family Register: Southern Branch* was compiled by Carolyn Cloud Stanley and published in Falls Church, Virginia, in 1991.

CHANG

Ranking: 1001 **S.S. Count:** 43,718

Origin: Chinese, Korean. The name means constantly, mountain, open, and draw-bow.

Genealogies: None known.

CHAPA

Ranking: 3739 **S.S. Count:** 12,098

Origin: Basque, Spanish. Basque: derived from the Basque word "chapar," meaning an ever-green oak grove. Spanish: derived from the Spanish word "capa," meaning cloak or cap. The name was given to those who wore distinctive outerwear.

Genealogies: None known.

CHAPIN

Ranking: 3049 **S.S. Count:** 14,886

Origin: French. The name was given to those who sold low shoes.

Famous **Chapins:** CALVIN CHAPIN (1763–1851) of Massachusetts was a Congregational clergyman and a founder of the American Board of Foreign Missions. SARAH FLOURNOY MOORE CHAPIN (1830?–1896) of South Carolina was a temperance reformer. AUGUSTA JANE CHAPIN (1836–1905) of New York was a Universalist minister. CHARLES VALUE CHAPIN (1856–1941) of Rhode Island was a public-health officer who helped establish the first (1888) municipal bacteriological laboratory in the United States and made its work the practical basis of his fight to control disease. HENRY DWIGHT CHAPIN (1857–1942) of Ohio was a pediatrician whose zeal for proper infant nutrition led him to recognize the inability of some infants to digest protein, and to determine the intestinal origin of acidosis. His and his wife's work to place foundlings and neglected children led to the establishment of the Alice Chapin Nursery, which after 1943 was known as the Spence-Chapin Adoption Service. ROY DIKEMAN CHAPIN (1880–1936) of Michigan was an automobile manufacturer and the president of the Hudson Motor Car Co. when the Essex car was introduced to the public.

Genealogies: *A Genealogy of Henry Judson Chapin: His Ancestors, His Descendants* was compiled by Gretchen E. Engel and published in Southbury, Connecticut, in 1970.

CHAPLIN (S.S. Abbreviation: Chapli)

Ranking: 4458 **S.S. Count:** 10,054

Origin: English, French. Derived from the Middle English

and Old French word "chapelain," meaning chantry priest, the priest who sang the daily mass on behalf of the dead souls. The name was given to those who worked as chantry priests and to those who worked for chantry priests.

Famous **Chaplins:** JEREMIAH CHAPLIN (1776–1841) of Massachusetts was president of Waterville College in Maine (1817–1833).

Genealogies: None known.

CHAPMAN (S.S. Abbreviation: Chapma)

Ranking: 202 **S.S. Count:** 175,106

Origin: English. Derived from the Old English word "cēapman," meaning a merchant. The name was given to those who worked as merchants.

Famous **Chapmans:** JOHN CHAPMAN (1774–1845) of Massachusetts was known as "Johnny Appleseed." He sold or gave away thousands of seeds of vegetables and herbs and apple seedlings to pioneers. He was considered a great medicine man by the Indians. NATHANIEL CHAPMAN (1780–1853) of Virginia was the first president of the American Medical Association (1848). REUBEN CHAPMAN (1802–1890) of Virginia was governor of Alabama (1847–1851). MARIA WESTON CHAPMAN (1806–1885) of Massachusetts was an abolitionist who joined with 12 other women in organizing the Boston Female Anti-Slavery Society. As the society's leader, she edited the annual report, titled "Right & Wrong in Boston." JOHN GADSBY CHAPMAN (1808–1889) of Virginia taught and practiced wood engraving, painted, and illustrated publications. His *American Drawing Book* (1847) is considered by some to be the best drawing book ever published. ALVAN WENTWORTH CHAPMAN (1864–1945) of New Jersey was the author of the pioneering manual *Flora of the Southern States* (1860).

Genealogies: *Chapman and Allied Families* was compiled by Lena E. Sweet and published in Saranac, Michigan, in 1980. *Chapman and Pugh Family History and Allied Lines* was compiled by Minnie May Pugh and published in Birmingham, Alabama, in 1976.

CHAPPE

Ranking: 1061 **S.S. Count:** 41,466

Origin: French. Derived from the Late Latin word "cappa," meaning hood, cloak, cape, or hat. The name was given to those who worked making such items or to those who wore these items habitually or distinctively.

Genealogies: None known.

CHARBONELL, CHARBONEL, CHARBONNEAU, CHARBONNEAUX (S.S. Abbreviation: Charbo)

Ranking: 4535 **S.S. Count:** 9862

Origin: Charbonell—English; Charbonel, Charbonneau, Charbonneaux—French. Transformations of Carbonell.

Genealogies: None known.

CHARLES, CHARLESWORTH (S.S. Abbreviation: Charle)

Ranking: 597 **S.S. Count:** 69,997

Origin: Charles—*English, French, Welsh;* Charlesworth—*English. Charles (English, French, Welsh): derived from the Germanic first name Carl, meaning man. Charles (English): derived from the Old English word "ceorl," meaning peasant. The name was given to those who worked as peasant farmers. Charlesworth: derived from the Old English words "cealf" and "worð," meaning jaw and enclosure. The name was given to those who came from a place in Derbyshire known as Chauelisworth in the 13th century.*

Famous **Bearers:** WILLIAM CHARLES (1776–1820), born in Scotland, was an engraver in Pennsylvania known for his etched caricatures of events of the War of 1812. RAY CHARLES (1930–) of Georgia was born Ray Charles Robinson. He was completely blind by the age of 7 and studied music at the State School for the Blind in St. Augustine, Florida. He is credited with the development of soul music, a mix of rhythm and blues, gospel, and jazz music. His biggest hits include "I've Got a Woman," "What'd I Say," and "Hit the Road Jack." He has received 10 Grammy Awards.

Genealogies: None known.

CHARLTON (S.S. Abbreviation: Charl)

Ranking: 3214 **S.S. Count:** 14,110

Origin: English, Irish. English: derived from the Old English word "Ceorlatūn," meaning "settlement of the peasants" (H&H). The name was given to those who came from Charlton, the name of several places in England. Irish: derived from the Gaelic name Ó Cearbhalláin, meaning "descendant of Cearbhallán" (H&H).

Genealogies: None known.

CHASE

Ranking: 565 **S.S. Count:** 72,707

Origin: Provençal. Cognate to Casa.

Famous **Chases:** SAMUEL CHASE (1741–1811) of Maryland was a Revolutionary leader and justice of the U.S. Supreme Court. SALMON PROTLAND CHASE (1808–1873) of New Hampshire was a statesman who defended escaped slaves and was called the "attorney-general for runaway negroes." In 1849 he was elected to the U.S. Senate. He was President Abraham Lincoln's secretary of the Treasury and the originator of the national banking system that became law in 1863. WILLIAM MERRITT CHASE (1849–1916) of Indiana was a painter whose use of color and bravura technique greatly influenced 20th-century American painting. MARY AGNES CHASE (1869–1963) of Illinois worked as a botanist and contributed greatly to what is known about

grasses. With Albert Hitchcock, she became famous for her work in North American agrostology.

Genealogies: *Charles Gardner Chase: His Ancestry and His Descendants* was compiled by Frederick Earl Chase and published in Cottonport, Louisiana, in 1973. *The Chase Family: Genealogy and History* was compiled by Hubert Hendricks Chase and published in Richardson, Texas, in 1982.

CHASTAIN, CHASTAN, CHASTAND, CHASTANET, CHASTANG (S.S. Abbreviation: Chasta)

Ranking: 2276 **S.S. Count:** 19,974

Origin: French. Transformations of Castan.

Genealogies: *Chastain Kith and Kin, 1700–1980* was compiled by Mary Avilla Abel Hall Farnsworth-Milligan and published in Owensboro, Kentucky, in 1980.

CHATMAN (S.S. Abbreviation: Chatma)

Social Security Count: 19,367

Origin: English. Transformation of Chapman.

Genealogies: None known.

CHAVARRI, CHAVARRIA (S.S. Abbreviation: Chavar)

Ranking: 4703 **S.S. Count:** 9513

Origin: Basque, Spanish. Transformations of Echevarri(a).

Genealogies: None known.

CHAVEZ

Ranking: 308 **S.S. Count:** 119,315

Origin: Portuguese, Spanish. Derived from the Latin word "clavis," meaning key.

Famous **Chavezes:** CESAR ESTRADA CHAVEZ (1927–1993) of Arizona worked as a farm laborer and created the National Farm Workers Association, which later became the United Farm Workers of America. Among other labor events, he led a grape pickers' strike in 1965.

Genealogies: *Chavez: A Distinctive American Clan of New Mexico* was compiled by Angelico Chavez and published in Santa Fe, New Mexico, in 1989.

CHAVIS

Ranking: 2649 **S.S. Count:** 17,177

Origin: French. The name was given to those who came from Chavis, which means "hollow" and is a place in France.

Genealogies: None known.

CHEATHAM (S.S. Abbreviation: Cheath)

Ranking: 2413 **S.S. Count:** 18,782

Origin: English. Most likely derived from the British word "ceto" and the Old English word "hām," meaning wood and homestead. *The name was given to those who came from Cheetham, a place in Lancashire, England.*

Famous **Cheathams:** BENJAMIN FRANKLIN CHEATHAM (1820–1886) of Tennessee was a Confederate major general.

Genealogies: *Descendants of Thomas Cheatham of Chesterfield County, Virginia* was compiled by Lucille Cheatham Mosely and published in Richmond, Virginia, in 1981.

CHEEK

Ranking: 2041 S.S. Count: 22,398

Origin: English. Derived from the Old English word "cē(a)ce," meaning cheek. The name was given to those who had an unusual cheek or jaw or a scar in those areas.

Genealogies: None known.

CHEN

Ranking: 1327 S.S. Count: 33,340

Origin: Chinese. The name means to attend or arrange.

Genealogies: None known.

CHENEY

Ranking: 2489 S.S. Count: 18,199

Origin: English. Derived from the Late Latin word "caxinus," meaning oak. The name was given to those who lived near an oak tree.

Famous **Cheneys:** JOHN CHENEY (1801–1885) of Connecticut was an engraver and the brother of Seth and Ward Cheney. SETH WELLS CHENEY (1810–1856) of Connecticut was a crayon artist and engraver in Boston, Massachusetts. He was the husband of Ednah Cheney. WARD CHENEY (1813–1876) of Connecticut was a pioneer silk manufacturer who was known for his concern for his employees. OREN BURBANK CHENEY (1816–1903) of Holderness, New Hampshire, helped found Bates College, Maine. EDNAH DOW LITTLEHALE CHENEY (1824–1904) of Massachusetts was a writer, reformer, supporter of the antislavery movement, and philanthropist. PERSON COLBY CHENEY (1828–1901) of New Hampshire was governor of New Hampshire (1875–1877). JOHN VANCE CHENEY (1848–1922) of New York was an author and librarian in San Francisco and Chicago.

Genealogies: *The Cheney Genealogy* was compiled by Charles Henry Pope and republished in Bethany, Oklahoma, in 1985. *George Cheney (1771–1829) of Manchester, Connecticut* was compiled by Edward H. Little and published in Farmington, Connecticut, in 1984.

CHENG

Ranking: 3150 S.S. Count: 14,424

Origin: Chinese. The name means journey and to complete.

Genealogies: None known.

CHERRY, CHERRYMAN

Ranking: 878 S.S. Count: 49,207

Origin: English. Cherry: derived from the Middle English word "cheri(e)," meaning cherry. Cherryman: transformation of Cherry combined with the Old English word "mann," meaning man. The names in both cases were given to those who worked growing or selling cherries or to those who lived near a cherry tree.

Genealogies: None known.

CHESTER, CHESTERS, CHESTERTON (S.S. Abbreviation: Cheste)

Ranking: 1967 S.S. Count: 23,038

Origin: Chester, Chesters: derived from the Old English word "ceaster," meaning Roman fort. The names were given to those who came from the region of Cheshire, England, or any of the other places named Cheshire in England. Chesterton: transformation of Chester combined with the Old English word "tūn," meaning settlement. The name was given to those who came from Chesterton, the name of several places in England.

Famous **Bearers:** JOSEPH LEMUEL CHESTER (1821–1882) of Connecticut was a genealogist and journalist. COLBY MITCHELL CHESTER (1844–1932) of Connecticut was a naval officer whose 1922 "Chester Claims" to trade concessions in Turkey aroused agitation against "dollar diplomacy." GEORGE RANDOLPH CHESTER (1869–1924) of Ohio was the author of, among other works, *Get-Rich-Quick Wallingford* (1908).

Genealogies: None known.

CHESTNUT (S.S. Abbreviation: Chestn)

Ranking: 3699 S.S. Count: 12,209

Origin: English. Transformation of Chesnut.

Genealogies: None known.

CHEUNG

Ranking: 4358 S.S. Count: 10,289

Origin: Chinese. The name means sedate.

Genealogies: None known.

CHEW

Ranking: 3932 S.S. Count: 11,478

Origin: English. 1) Uncertain etymology. Possibly derived from the Welsh word "cyw," meaning young animal. The name was given to those who lived near the River Chew or a place called Chew, both of which are located in Somerset, England. 2) derived from the Old English word "cēo," literally meaning fish gill but used to refer to a ravine. The name was given to those who came from Chew, the name of places in Lancashire and Yorkshire, England. 3) derived from the Old English word "cēo," as it referred to a bird now called a chough, a relative of the crow.

Famous **Chews:** BENJAMIN CHEW (1722–1810) of Maryland was chief justice of the Pennsylvania Supreme Court (1774–1776) and president of the Pennsylvania high court of errors and appeals (1791–1808).

Genealogies: *Genealogy of the Chew Family* was compiled by Robert L. Chew and published in Woodbury, New Jersey, in 1982.

CHILDE, CHILDERHOUSE, CHILDERS

Ranking: 1051 **S.S. Count:** 41,769

Origin: English. Childe: transformation of Child. Childers, Childerhouse: derived from the Old English words "cildra" and "hūus," meaning children and house as they appeared in Childerhouse, a now-unknown place in England.

Famous **Bearers:** JOHN CHILDE (1802–1858) of Massachusetts was a civil engineer who solved many engineering problems for new railroad lines.

Genealogies: *Genealogy of the Child, Childs, and Childe Families: of the Past and Present in the United States and the Canadas, from 1630 to 1881* was compiled by Elias Child and published in Utica, New York, in 1881. *Harris, Vredenburg, Child and Allied Families* was compiled by Marian J. Newell and published in Aurora, Illinois, in 1983.

CHILDRESS (S.S. Abbreviation: Childr)

Ranking: 1156 **S.S. Count:** 37,868

Origin: English. Transformation of Childers.

Genealogies: *Notes on the Childress, Hickman, Smith and Cabler Families* was compiled by William Cabler Moore and published in Stamford, Connecticut, in 1967.

CHILDS

Ranking: 1146 **S.S. Count:** 38,293

Origin: English. Transformation of Child.

Famous **Childses:** CEPHAS GRIER CHILDS (1793–1871) of Pennsylvania was an engraver, editor, and publisher and a pioneer in commercial lithography. THOMAS CHILDS (1796–1853) of Massachusetts was a soldier who served with distinction in the War of 1812. GEORGE WILLIAM CHILDS (1829–1894) of Maryland was a publisher and proprietor of the Philadelphia *Public Ledger* (1864–1894).

Genealogies: *Genealogy of the Child, Childs, and Childe Families: of the Past and Present in the United States and the Canadas, from 1630 to 1881* was compiled by Elias Child and published in Utica, New York, in 1881. *Harris, Vredenburg, Child and Allied Families (including the Childs Fam-*

ily) was compiled by Marian J. Newell and published in Aurora, Illinois, in 1983.

CHIN

Ranking: 1607 **S.S. Count:** 27,865

Origin: Chinese, Korean. The name means true, to grasp, and to increase.

Genealogies: None known.

CHING

Ranking: 4455 **S.S. Count:** 10,060

Origin: Chinese. Uncertain etymology.

Genealogies: *Ancestors: 900 Years in the Life of a Chinese Family* was compiled by Frank Ching and published in New York, New York, in 1988.

CHINN

Ranking: 4906 **S.S. Count:** 9117

Origin: English. Derived from the Old English word "cin," meaning chin. The name was given to those who were clean shaven or to those who had a prominent chin.

Genealogies: *The Chinn Book* was compiled by Ruth Wilson Dillon and published in Cottonport, Louisiana, in 1972.

CHISHOLM, CHISHOLME (S.S. Abbreviation: Chisho)

Ranking: 2483 **S.S. Count:** 18,250

Origin: Scottish. Derived from the Old English words "cēse" and "holm," meaning cheese and dry land at least partly surrounded by water. The name was given to those who came from Chisholme, a place in Scotland.

Genealogies: *The Chisz: A History of the Chisholme/Chism Family* was compiled by John D. Chism and published in Fredericksburg, Virginia, in 1989.

CHISM

Ranking: 4085 **S.S. Count:** 11,061

Origin: Scottish. Transformation of Chisholm.

Genealogies: *The Chisz: A History of the Chisholme/Chism Family* was compiled by John D. Chism and published in Fredericksburg, Virginia, in 1989.

CHITWOOD (S.S. Abbreviation: Chitwo)

Ranking: 4950 **S.S. Count:** 9053

Origin: English. Derived from the first name Chit, meaning child.

Genealogies: *1988 Update of the Family of Squire and Mary Wray Chitwood* was compiled by Margaret C. Pope and published in Dyersburg, Tennessee, in 1988. *Chitwood Family (and Related Lines)* was compiled by Jean Cragun Tombaugh and published in Rochester, Indiana, in 1976.

CHMIEL, CHMIELA, CHMIELECKI, CHMIELEWSKI, CHMIELINSKI, CHMIELOWIEC

Ranking: 4621 S.S. Count: 9669

Origin: Polish. Derived from the Polish work "chmiel," meaning hops, and the suffixes "ew" and "ski," denoting a place name and a local surname. The name was given to those who came from places that derived their names from chmiel.

Genealogies: None known.

CHO

Ranking: 3166 S.S. Count: 14,336

Origin: Chinese. The name means to draw a bow and to establish.

Genealogies: None known.

CHOATE

Ranking: 2889 S.S. Count: 15,759

Origin: English. The name was given to those who were considered overweight.

Famous **Choates**: RUFUS CHOATE (1799–1859) of Massachusetts was a lawyer and statesman who helped organize the Whig Party in Massachusetts. JOSEPH HODGES CHOATE (1832–1917) of Massachusetts was a lawyer and diplomat whose most important cases were in the Income Tax cases before the U.S. Supreme Court in 1895.

Genealogies: None known.

CHOI

Ranking: 2656 S.S. Count: 17,138

Origin: Chinese. The name means tortoise.

Genealogies: None known.

CHONG

Ranking: 3611 S.S. Count: 12,509

Origin: Chinese. The name means hanging bell.

Genealogies: None known.

CHOW

Ranking: 3427 S.S. Count: 13,167

Origin: Chinese. The name means everywhere.

Genealogies: None known.

CHRISMAN, CHRISMAS (S.S. Abbreviation: Chrisma)

Ranking: 4248 S.S. Count: 10,601

Origin: Chrisman—German; Chrismas—English. Chrisman: derived from the name Christianus, meaning "follower of Christ" (ES). Chrismas: transformation of Christmas.

Genealogies: *The Ancestors of Harriet Chrisman Ross* was compiled by John Hal Connor and published in 1976. *A Chrisman/Christman Genealogy: The Descendants of Jacob Christman I, of Frederick County, Virginia* was compiled by Glen Christman and published in 1984.

CHRISTIANSEN, CHRISTENSEN, CHRISTOFFELS, CHRISTMAS, CHRISTOPHER, CHRISTIAN, CHRISTINE, CHRISTAEN, CHRISTAUFFOUR, CHRISTOFE, CHRISTOFFE, CHRISTALLER, CHRISTLER, CHRISTOFFER, CHRISTOPHERSEN, CHRISTOL (S.S. Abbreviation: Christ)

Ranking: 59 S.S. Count: 393,332

Origin: Christiansen, Christensen—Danish, Norwegian; Christoffels—Dutch; Christmas, Christopher—English; Christian, Christine—English, French; Christaen—Flemish; Christauffour, Christofe, Christoffe—French; Christaller, Christler, Christoffer—German; Christophersen—Norwegian; Christol—Provençal. Christiansen, Christensen, Christian, Christine, Christaen, Christaller, Christler: derived from the Latin word "christiānus," meaning "follower of Christ" (H&H). Christmas: derived the Old English word "Chīstemæse," meaning festival of Christ. The name was given to those born on Christmas day. Christauffour, Christofe, Christoffe, Christoffer, Christoffels, Christol, Christopher, Christophersen: derived from Latin name Chrīstopherus and the Greek name Khristophoros, both meaning carrier or bearer of Christ as they developed into first names in many countries.

Famous **Bearers**: LEW FARR CHRISTENSEN (1909–1984) of Utah was a dancer and choreographer who performed with the American Ballet and Ballet Caravan. He choreographed more than 50 dances, the most significant of which were for the San Francisco Ballet.

Genealogies: None known.

CHU

Ranking: 2482 S.S. Count: 18,255

Origin: Chinese. The name means bamboo, every, vermilion, and to bless.

Genealogies: None known.

CHUN

Ranking: 3872 S.S. Count: 11,647

Origin: Chinese. The name means stupid, foolish, and clumsy.

Genealogies: None known.

CHUNG

Ranking: 1835 S.S. Count: 24,634

Origin: Chinese. The name means hanging bell.

Genealogies: None known.

CHURCH, CHURCHER, CHURCHMAN, CHURCHILL, CHURCHARD, CHURCHYARD

Ranking: 525 **S.S. Count:** 76,808

Origin: English. Church, Churcher: derived from the Old English word "cyrice," meaning church or house of the Lord. The names were given to those who lived near a church. Churchman: transformation of Church combined with the Old English word "mann," meaning man. The name was given to those who lived near churches. Churchill: transformation of Church combined with the Old English word "hyll," meaning hill. The name was given to those who came from Churchill, the name of several places in England. Churchard, Churchyard: transformation of Church combined with the Old English word "geard," meaning yard. The name was given to those who lived near churchyards.

Famous **Bearers:** BENJAMIN CHURCH (1639–1718) of Massachusetts was a soldier and captain of a Plymouth company. He fought in King Philip's War and was wounded at the "Great Swamp Fight" (1675). BENJAMIN CHURCH (1734–1778?) of Rhode Island was a physician, author, traitor, and the grandson of Benjamin Church. He was a paid informant of the British authorities in Boston and was court-martialed in October 1775. ALONZO CHURCH (1793–1862) of Vermont was an educator and president of the University of Georgia (1829–1859). THOMAS JAMES CHURCHILL (1824–1915) of Kentucky was a Confederate soldier and became the governor of Arkansas in 1880. FREDERICK EDWIN CHURCH (1826–1900) of Connecticut was a romantic landscape painter and one of the best-known members of the Hudson River School. JOHN ADAMS CHURCH (1843–1917) of New York was a metallurgist who introduced American mining methods in China. JENNIE JEROME CHURCHILL (1854–1921) of New York was a social leader, the wife of Lord Randolph Churchill, and the mother of Sir Winston Churchill. WILLIAM CHURCHILL (1859–1920) of New York was a philologist and ethnologist who began a study of Polynesian languages as consul general to Samoa (1896–1899). WINSTON CHURCHILL (1871–1947) of Missouri was a novelist and political reformer. His writings were influenced by his political interests.

Genealogies: The Man Who Owned the Pistols: John Barker Church and His Family was compiled by Helene C. Phelan and published in Almond, New York, in 1981. A Record of an Old-Established Retail and Glass Business was compiled by Wilfrid Spencer Church and published in Northampton, Massachusetts, in 1967. The Browns and Churchmans of Nottingham: Chester County, Pennsylvania and Cecil County, Maryland was compiled by Amos Day Bradley and published in Hastings-on-Hudson, New York, in 1977.

CINTRON (S.S. Abbreviation: Cintro)

Ranking: 1868 **S.S. Count:** 24,243

Origin: Portuguese, Spanish. The name was given to those who came from Cintra, which means "curvature of a bow" (ES) and is a place in Portugal.

Genealogies: None known.

CISNEROS (S.S. Abbreviation: Cisner)

Ranking: 2021 **S.S. Count:** 22,614

Origin: Spanish. Derived from the Spanish word "cisne," meaning swan. The name was given to those who came from a similarly named place in Palancia, Spain.

Genealogies: None known.

CLANCY

Ranking: 2576 **S.S. Count:** 17,651

Origin: Irish. Derived from the Gaelic name Mac Fhlaithimh, which is derived from the first name Flaitheamh, meaning prince.

Genealogies: None known.

CLANTON (S.S. Abbreviation: Clanto)

Ranking: 4226 **S.S. Count:** 10,675

Origin: English. The name was given to those who came from Clandon, which means "hill free of weeds" (ES) and is a place in Surrey, England.

Genealogies: None known.

CLAPP

Ranking: 3256 **S.S. Count:** 13,960

Origin: English. Derived from the Old English word "clop," meaning lump. The name was given to those who were considered big and/or clumsy.

Famous **Clapps:** WILLIAM WARLAND CLAPP (1826–1891) of Massachusetts was a journalist and author of plays. CORNELIA MARIA CLAPP (1849–1934) of Massachusetts was a professor of zoology at Mount Holyoke College and worked at what is now Woods Hole Oceanographic Institution (Massachusetts) after it opened in 1888. CHARLES HORACE CLAPP (1883–1935) of Massachusetts was a geologist and president of Montana State University (1921–1935). MARGARET ANTOINETTE CLAPP (1910–1974) of New Jersey was president of Wellesley College and a U.S. cultural attaché to India. She won a Pulitzer Prize for *Forgotton First Citizen: John Bigelow.*

Genealogies: The German Clapps in America was compiled by Elmo F. Clapp and published in Evansville, Indiana, in 1978. Josiah and Mercy Bennet of Herkimer County, New York, and 574 Descendants (including the Clapp Family) 1798 to 1975 was compiled by George Wirt Clapp and published in Canoga Park, California, in 1975.

CLARK

Ranking: 19 S.S. Count: 776,273

Origin: English. Derived from the Old English word "cler(e)c," meaning priest. The name was given to those who worked as secretaries or scribes or to those who were in religious orders, some of whom were permitted to marry.

Famous **Clarks:** ABRAHAM CLARK (1726–1794) of New Jersey was a surveyor, lawyer, farmer, and signer of the Declaration of Independence. He was a member of the New Jersey provincial congress (1775) and the Continental Congress (1776). He served as a member of Congress (1791–1794). GEORGE ROGERS CLARK (1752–1818) of Virginia, a surveyor, in 1773 explored the Ohio River; in 1774, he took part in Dunmore's War. He spent the majority of his life exploring and protecting the American frontier. He was the brother of William Clark of the Lewis and Clark expedition. JOHN CLARK (1766–1832) of North Carolina was governor of Georgia (1819–1823). WILLIAM CLARK (1770–1838) of Virginia, with Meriwether Lewis, gained fame for his expedition to the Pacific Northwest (1804–1806). On the expedition, he served as mapmaker and artist. JAMES CLARK (1779–1839) of Virginia was governor of Kentucky (1836–1839). ALVAN CLARK (1804–1887) of Massachusetts was an astronomer and renowned maker of astronomical lenses. MYRON HOLLEY CLARK (1806–1892) of New York was governor of New York (1854–1858). CHARLES CLARK (1810–1877) of Ohio was a Confederate brigadier general and governor of Mississippi. ALVAN GRAHAM CLARK (1832–1897) of Massachusetts was the son of Alvan Clark and also an astronomer and a maker of astronomical lenses. WILLIAM ANDREWS CLARK (1839–1925) of Pennsylvania was a merchant and mine operator and the governor of Montana (1901–1907). CHARLES EDGAR CLARK (1843–1922) of Vermont was the commander of the U.S.S. *Oregon* as it rounded Cape Horn in 1898. JOHN BATES CLARK (1847–1938) of Rhode Island was an economist who wrote numerous books on economic analysis. CHARLES HOPKINS CLARK (1848–1926) of Connecticut was editor of the *Hartford Courant* (1900–1926). CHAMP (JAMES BEAUCHAMP) CLARK (1850–1921) of Kentucky was a lawyer and politician. He was a member of Congress and served as Speaker of the House (1911–1919) and minority leader (1919–1921). He opposed the Selective Draft Act of 1917. MARGUERITE CLARK (1883–1940) of Ohio was a prominent stage and screen actress.

Genealogies: *Adam's Ancestors (including the Clark Family)* was compiled by Thomas Nathan Clark and published in two volumes in Naperville, Illinois, in 1981 and 1984.

CLARKE

Ranking: 437 S.S. Count: 91,222

Origin: English. Transformation of Clark.

Famous **Clarkes:** JOHN CLARKE (1609–1676) of England, along with William Coddington, founded Newport, Rhode Island, in 1639. He was largely instrumental in securing the royal charter for Rhode Island in 1663. WALTER CLARKE (1638–1714) of Rhode Island was deputy governor of Rhode Island (1679–1686 and 1700–1714), then governor (1676–1677, 1686, and 1696–1698). GEORGE CLARKE (1676–1760), born in England, was the secretary of the Province of New York (1703–1743) and lieutenant governor (1736–1743). MARY FRANCIS CLARKE (1803–1887) of Dublin, Ireland, was the founder and first mother superior of the Sisters of Charity of the Blessed Virgin Mary at Philadelphia, Pennsylvania (1833). MARY BAYARD DEVEREUX CLARKE (1827–1886) of North Carolina was an author and editor. EDITH CLARKE (1833–1959) of Maryland was an electrical engineer who worked with large electrical power systems, making detailed charts that other engineers could use to predict the systems' behavior. REBECCA SOPHIA CLARKE (1833–1906) of Maine wrote children's books under the name Sophie May. Among her titles were *Little Prudy* and *Dotty Dimple*. FRANCIS DEVEREUX CLARKE (1849–1913) of North Carolina was an educator of the deaf in Arkansas and Michigan. JAMES PAUL CLARKE (1854–1916) of Mississippi was governor of Arkansas (1893–1895) and a U.S. senator from Arkansas (1903–1916). JOHN HESSIN CLARKE (1857–1945) of Ohio was a justice of the U.S. Supreme Court.

Genealogies: *The Descendants of Daniel Clarke of Windsor, Connecticut* was compiled by Frances Bruce Todd and published in Maple Falls, Washington, in 1970.

CLARKSON, CLARKSTON, CLARKSTONE
(S.S. Abbreviation: Clarks)

Ranking: 3222 S.S. Count: 14,065

Origin: English. Transformations of Clark.

Famous **Bearers:** MATTHEW CLARKSON (1758–1825) of New York was a Revolutionary soldier and a prominent citizen of New York City. COKER FIFIELD CLARKSON (1811–1890) of Maine was editor of the *Iowa State Register* (1870–1890). JOHN GIBSON CLARKSON (1861–1909) of Massachusetts was a baseball pitcher who played on teams in Chicago, Illinois; Boston, Massachusetts; and Cleveland, Ohio.

Genealogies: *Descendants of of Thomas Clarkston (1787–1858)* was compiled by Gloria Kay Vandiver Inman and published in Pasco, Washington, in 1980.

CLARY

Ranking: 2890 S.S. Count: 15,756

Origin: English. Uncertain etymology. Possibly derived from the Medieval Latin word "sclarea," meaning clary sage.

Genealogies: None known.

CLAUDIN, CLAUDINO, CLAUDIO (S.S. Abbreviation: Claudi)

Ranking: 4299 **S.S. Count:** 10,439

Origin: French. Derived from the Latin surname Claudius, which is derived from the word "claudus," meaning lame.

Genealogies: *The Maternal Ancestry of Barbara Ellen Stanfield (including the Claudio Family) in the United States* was compiled by Barbara Ellen Stansfield Pace and published in Jersey City, New Jersey, in 1975.

CLAUSEN (S.S. Abbreviation: Clause)

Ranking: 2580 **S.S. Count:** 17,641

Origin: Danish, German. Derived from the first name Klaus, which is a form of the first name Niklaus, which is derived from the Greek words "nikān" and "laos," meaning to conquer and people.

Famous Clausens: CLAUS LAURITZ CLAUSEN (1820–1892) of Denmark was the founder of St. Ansgar, Iowa.

Genealogies: None known.

CLAWSON (S.S. Abbreviation: Clawso)

Ranking: 3248 **S.S. Count:** 13,984

Origin: English. 1) derived from the first name Clac. The name was given to those who came from Clawson, a place in Leicestershire, England. 2) transformation of Nicholas.

Genealogies: *Lady Eleanor, or Begotten but Not Forgotten* was compiled by Francis A. Knaus and published in Decorah, Iowa, in 1985. *Pi on the Floor* was compiled by Watson Swartz Clawson and published in Exeter, California, in 1967.

CLAY

Ranking: 633 **S.S. Count:** 65,477

Origin: English. Derived from the Old English word "clæg," meaning clay. The name was given to those who lived near clay or worked with clay.

Famous Clays: JOSEPH CLAY (1741–1804), born in England, was a Revolutionary officer and member of the Continental Congress. He was one of the "fathers" of the University of Georgia. MATTHEW CLAY (1754–1815) of Virginia was a Revolutionary soldier and member of Congress from Virginia. HENRY CLAY (1777–1852) of Virginia was known as "The Great Compromiser" and "The Great Pacificator." He served in the U.S. House of Representatives and the U.S. Senate for nearly 30 years. He was a major proponent of the Missouri Compromise and was well known as a gifted orator. He was nominated by the Whig Party for U.S. president in 1832 and 1844. EDWARD WILLIAMS CLAY (1799–1857) of Pennsylvania was an engraver, etcher, and caricaturist. CASSIUS MARCELLUS CLAY (1810–1903) of Kentucky was an abolitionist and the U.S. minister to Russia (1861–1862 and 1863–1869). CLEMENT CLAIBORNE CLAY (1816–1882) of Alabama served as a member of Congress, U.S. senator, and governor of Alabama. VIRGINIA CAROLINE TUNSTALL CLAY-CLOPTON (1825–1915) of North Carolina was an antebellum society leader and Alabama suffragist. At age 75 she published a book of antebellum memories called *A Belle of the Fifties.* LAURA CLAY (1849–1941) of Kentucky was a women's suffrage leader.

Genealogies: *History and Genealogy of the Hoskins, Clay and Related Families United in Cole County, Missouri* was compiled by Clarence E. Hoskins and published in St. Louis, Missouri, in 1972.

CLAYTON (S.S. Abbreviation: Clayto)

Ranking: 507 **S.S. Count:** 79,101

Origin: English. Derived from the Old English words "clæg" and "tūn," meaning clay and settlement.

Famous Claytons: JOSHUA CLAYTON (1744–1798) of Maryland was a Revolutionary soldier, president-governor of Delaware (1789–1796), and U.S. senator (1798). THOMAS CLAYTON (1777–1854) of Maryland served as secretary of state, attorney general, and chief justice in Delaware and was a U.S senator for 14 years. AUGUSTIN SMITH CLAYTON (1783–1839) of Virginia was the circuit judge in Georgia who ruled that the state had jurisdiction over Cherokee Indians. The U.S. Supreme Court later declared his ruling unconstitutional, and Clayton then became a strong advocate of state's rights as a member of Congress. JOHN MIDDLETON CLAYTON (1796–1856) served in the U.S. House of Representatives from Delaware and as secretary of state under President Zachary Taylor. He is best known for negotiating the Clayton-Bulwer Treaty, which concerned U.S. and British canal rights in Central America. POWELL CLAYTON (1833–1914) was a Union soldier and governor of Arkansas (1868–1871). He also was a U.S. senator and ambassador to Mexico.

Genealogies: *The Normans, 1720–1976, and Information on the Walker, Clayton and Weir Families of Mississippi* was compiled by Maggie Laurie Carson and published in Tuscaloosa, Alabama, in 1976. *The Quaker Yeomen: A Genealogy of Clayton, Reynolds, Beals, Brown and Descended and Related Lines* was compiled by James E. Bellarts and published in Portland, Oregon, in 1973.

CLEARY

Ranking: 2045 **S.S. Count:** 22,356

Origin: Irish. Derived from the Gaelic word "cléirach," meaning clerk. The name was given to those who worked as clerks.

Genealogies: *Clary (also Cleary) Genealogy* was compiled by Ralph Shearer Rowland and published in Fairfax, Virginia, in 1980.

CLEAVE, CLEAVER

Ranking: 3664 S.S. Count: 12,324

Origin: English. Cleave: derived from the Old English word "clif," meaning cliff or slope. The name was given to those who lived in hilly areas or on a bank. Cleaver: derived from the Old English word "clēfan," meaning to cut. The name was given to those who chopped wood or worked as butchers.

Famous **Bearers:** JOHN COURTNEY CLEAVER (1906–1976) pioneered in the development of packaged, preassembled boiler equipment, which enabled highway contractors to heat asphalt and road oils in tank cars. He also was instrumental in making desalinization of sea water commercially viable.

Genealogies: *A Fair and Happy Land (a Genealogy including the Cleaver Family)* was compiled by William A. Owens and published in New York, New York, in 1975.

CLEGG

Ranking: 4201 S.S. Count: 10,752

Origin: English. Derived from the Old Norse word "kleggi," meaning haystack. The name was given to those who came from Clegg, a place in Lancashire, England.

Genealogies: *The Cleggs of Old Chatham* was edited by W. Harold Broughton and published in Durham, North Carolina, in 1977.

CLEM

Ranking: 3876 S.S. Count: 11,630

Origin: English. Transformation of Clement.

Genealogies: *Descendants of Adam and Rachel Clem, 1788–1978* was compiled by Anna Clem Williams and published in the 1970s.

CLEMEN, CLEMENS, CLEMENT, CLEMENTS, CLEMENTSON, CLEMENCE, CLEMENDOT, CLEMENTE, CLEMENTI, CLEMENZA

Ranking: 306 S.S. Count: 119,661

Origin: Clemen, Clemens—Flemish; Clement—Cornish, Dutch, English; Clements, Clementson—English; Clemence, Clemendot—French; Clemente—Portuguese, Spanish; Clementi, Clemenza—Italian. Derived from the Latin first name Clēmens, meaning merciful.

Famous **Bearers:** JEREMIAH CLEMENS (1814–1865) of Alabama was a soldier in the war for Texas's independence and the Mexican War and later served as a U.S. senator. He also wrote historical novels, including *The Rivals* (1860). SAMUEL LANGHORNE CLEMENS (1835–1910) of Missouri was a humorist and novelist, better known by his pen name of Mark Twain, under which he wrote such classics as *The Celebrated Jumping Frog of Calaveras County, and Other Sketches* (1867) and *Huckleberry Finn* (1883). FREDERIC EDWARD CLEMENTS (1874–1945) of Nebraska was a botanist and pioneer ecologist. He has been described as "the greatest individual creator of the modern science of vegetation." ROBERTO CLEMENTE (1934–1972) of Puerto Rico was a professional baseball player who spent the majority of his career with the Pittsburgh Pirates. He batted more than .300 in 13 seasons, scored 1416 runs, and had 3000 hits. He was killed in a plane crash en route to provide relief supplies to victims of a Nicaraguan earthquake.

Genealogies: *The Ancestry of Samuel Clemens, Grandfather of Mark Twain* was compiled by Raymond Martin Bell and published in Washington, Pennsylvania, in 1980. *The Account Book of the Clemens Family of Lower Salford Township, Montgomery County, Pennsylvania, 1749–1857* was translated from German by Raymond E. Hollenbach and published in Breinigsville, Pennsylvania, in 1975.

CLEMMO, CLEMMOW

Ranking: 4119 S.S. Count: 10,971

Origin: English. Transformation of Clement.

Genealogies: None known.

CLEMONS, CLEMONTS (S.S. Abbreviation: Clemon)

Ranking: 1223 S.S. Count: 10,971

Origin: English. Transformation of Clement.

Genealogies: None known.

CLENDENNEN, CLENDENNING (S.S. Abbreviation: Clende)

Ranking: 4880 S.S. Count: 9158

Origin: Scottish. Uncertain etymology. The names were given to those who came from a place in England called Glendonwyne in the 14th century.

Genealogies: None known.

CLEVELAND, CLEVELEY (S.S. Abbreviation: Clevel)

Ranking: 1032 S.S. Count: 42,354

Origin: English. Cleveland: derived from the Old English words "clif" and "land," meaning cliff and land. The name was given to those who came from Cleveland, a place in England. Cleveley: derived from the Old English words "clif" and "lēah," meaning cliff and wood. The name was given to those who came from Cleveley, a place in Lancashire, England.

Famous **Clevelands:** BENJAMIN CLEVELAND (1738–1806) of Virginia was a Revolutionary soldier and a frontier judge. CHAUNCEY FITCH CLEVELAND (1799–1887) of Connecticut was the governor of Connecticut (1842–1843).

STEPHEN GROVER CLEVELAND (1837–1908) was elected the 22nd U.S. president after serving as governor of New York. He was well known for his efforts to cut tariffs and nullify fraudulent federal grants as well as for invoking the Monroe Doctrine to protect U.S. interests in Latin America. FRANCES FOLSOM CLEVELAND (1864–1947) of New York was the wife of President Cleveland.

Genealogies: *An Account of the Lineage of General Moses Cleaveland of Canterbury (Windham County) Connecticut, the Founder of the City of Cleveland, Ohio* was compiled by Horace Gillette Cleveland and published in Cleveland, Ohio, in 1885.

CLEVENT (S.S. Abbreviation: Cleven)
Ranking: 2584 **S.S. Count:** 17,634
Origin: French. Derived from the Latin word "lavus," meaning nail, peg, or plug.
Genealogies: None known.

CLIFFORD (S.S. Abbreviation: Cliffo)
Ranking: 1432 **S.S. Count:** 31,170
Origin: English. Derived from the Old English words "clif" and "ford," meaning cliff and a narrow place in a stream. The name was given to those who came from Clifford, the name of several places in England.
Famous **Cliffords:** NATHAN CLIFFORD (1803–1881) of New Hampshire was Maine attorney general and a member of Congress from Maine. In 1846, President James K. Polk appointed him U.S. attorney general. In 1858, he became a U.S. Supreme Court justice.
Genealogies: *The Family Histories of the Cliffords and Rollins* was compiled by Leslie G. Perry and published in Bangor, Maine, in 1964.

CLIFTON (S.S. Abbreviation: Clifto)
Ranking: 1281 **S.S. Count:** 34,539
Origin: English. Derived from the Old English words "clif" and "tūn," meaning cliff and settlement. The name was given to those who came from Clifton, the name of several places in England.
Genealogies: *A Genealogy of the Clifton, Leaton, Rourke, and Secord Families* was compiled by Richard Lee Secord and published in Arizona in 1988. *Our Clifton Ancestors and Their Descendants* was compiled by Nell M. Wright and published in Chillicothe, Ohio, in 1982.

CLINE
Ranking: 600 **S.S. Count:** 69,624
Origin: Jewish. Transformation of Klein.
Famous **Clines:** MAGGIE CLINE (1857–1934) of Massachusetts was a vaudeville singer. She was called one of the "golden dozen" of vaudeville's early years and was the first female Irish comedy singer. GENEVIEVE ROSE CLINE

(1878–1959) of Ohio was the first woman appointed as a federal judge.
Genealogies: *Cline-Kline Family* was compiled by Paul G. Kline and published in Dayton, Virginia, in 1971. *Descendants and Family of William Cline (1746–1853)* was compiled by William Du Bois and published in Muncie, Indiana, in 1990.

CLINTON (S.S. Abbreviation: Clinto)
Ranking: 2095 **S.S. Count:** 21,894
Origin: English. 1) most likely derived from Glympton, which means "settlement on the River Glyme" (H&H) and is a place in Oxfordshire, England. 2) possibly derived from Glinton, which is derived from a now-unknown Old English word that was a cognate to the Middle Low German word "glinde," meaning fence, and the Old English word "tūn," meaning settlement, and is a place in Northants, England.
Famous **Clintons:** GEORGE CLINTON (1686–1761) of England served as governor of New York (1741–1753) but was weak in that position. His administration permanently weakened the royal government in New York and increased the demand for popular control. JAMES CLINTON (1733–1812) of New York was a Revolutionary soldier who commanded a brigade at Yorktown. His brother, GEORGE CLINTON (1739–1812) of Little Britain, New York, was a Revolutionary soldier, statesman, and a delegate from New York to the Second Continental Congress. In 1804 and 1808, he was elected vice president of the United States. James Clinton's son, DEWITT CLINTON (1769–1828) of New York, was a statesman, philanthropist, man of letters, and U.S. senator. WILLIAM JEFFERSON (BILL) CLINTON (1946–) of Arkansas is the 42nd U.S. president. He served as governor of Arkansas (1979–1981 and 1983–1992).
Genealogies: None known.

CLOSE
Ranking: 3462 **S.S. Count:** 13,033
Origin: English. 1) derived from the Old French word "clos" and the Middle English word "clos(e)," both meaning closed or enclosed. The name was given to those who lived in an enclosure of some kind. 2) same derivation as in 1. The name was given to those who were considered secretive.
Genealogies: *The Closes, 1700–1982, from Ohio-Kansas* was compiled by Bernice Close Shackelton and published in Pittsburgh, Kansas, in 1983. *John Clowes, Jr., 1730–1790 (including the Close Family Genealogy)* was compiled by Hazel Brittingham and published in Wilmington, Delaware, in 1989.

CLOUD
Ranking: 2369 **S.S. Count:** 19,163

Origin: English, French. English: derived from the Old English word "clūd," meaning rock. The name was given to those who lived near a hill. French: derived from the Germanic first name Hlodald, which is derived from the words "hlōd" and "wald," meaning fame and rule.

Genealogies: The Martin-Cloude Families was compiled by Lewis Sasse and published in La Jolla, California, in 1982.

CLOUGH
Ranking: 3017 S.S. Count: 15,061
Origin: English. Derived from the Old English word "clōh," meaning ravine. The name was given to those who lived near a precarious slope.
Famous **Cloughs:** JOHN EVERETT CLOUGH (1845–1916) of New York was a Baptist clergyman and a missionary in India.
Genealogies: Clauw, Klauw, Klaw, Claw, Clow, Clough, Clowe: A Holland Dutch Name of the Upper Hudson Valley was compiled by Wilson Ober Clough and published in Laramie, Wyoming, in 1964.

CLOUSEL (S.S. Abbreviation: Clouse)
Ranking: 2990 S.S. Count: 15,193
Origin: French. Cognate to Close.
Genealogies: None known.

CLOUTIER (S.S. Abbreviation: Clouti)
Ranking: 4061 S.S. Count: 11,130
Origin: French. Derived from the Latin word "clāvus," meaning nail. The name was given to those who made or sold nails, particularly those kinds of nails used for horse shoes.
Genealogies: None known.

COATES
Ranking: 1338 S.S. Count: 33,031
Origin: English, Scottish. English: 1) derived from the Old English word "cot," meaning cottage. The name was given to those who lived in such a place. 2) possibly the same derivation as in 1. The name was given to those who came from any of the several places called Coates or other similarly named places in England. Scottish: derived from the Gaelic word "coillte," meaning woods. The name was given to those who came from Cults, a place in Scotland.
Famous **Coateses:** SAMUEL COATES (1748–1830) of Pennsylvania was a merchant and a philanthropist and a director of First United States Bank. GEORGE HENRY COATES (1849–1921) of Vermont was an inventor and manufacturer who developed a flexible shaft for transmission of power to drilling and grinding machinery. FLORENCE VAN LEER EARLE NICHOLSON COATES (1850–1927) of Pennsylvania wrote poetry and was published in the magazines of the day.

Genealogies: Robert Coates of Lynn, Massachusetts, and Some of His Descendants was compiled by Evelyn Coates Aherin and published in Syracuse, New York, in 1970.

COATS
Ranking: 2167 S.S. Count: 21,180
Origin: English. Transformation of Coates.
Genealogies: Coats Kin: from North Carolina to Tennessee to Arkansas was compiled by D. A. Tucker and published in Houston, Texas, in 1987.

COBB
Ranking: 429 S.S. Count: 92,713
Origin: English. 1) derived from the Middle English names Cobbe or Cobba, both of which are derived from a word meaning lump. The name was given to those who were considered to be large. 2) transformation of Jacob.
Famous **Cobbs:** HOWELL COBB (1815–1868) of Georgia, a lawyer and politician, was elected governor of Georgia on a Unionist platform in 1851 after serving eight years as a member of Congress. He returned to Congress (1855–1857) after failing to be reelected governor, then was secretary of the Treasury (1857–1860). After Abraham Lincoln was elected president, however, Cobb worked for secession. He chaired the convention in Montgomery, Alabama, to organize the Southern Confederacy and was a Confederate major general during the Civil War. His son, ANDREW JACKSON COBB (1857–1925) of Georgia, was a state supreme court justice who rendered the decision in the first U.S. "right of privacy" case. THOMAS READE ROOTES COBB (1823–1862) of Georgia, a lawyer and brother of Howell Cobb, codified Georgia's laws in 1851. He was a brigadier general in the Civil War who died in battle. IRVIN SHREWSBURY COBB (1876–1944) of Kentucky was a newspaper and magazine journalist who also was a widely read short-story writer. He was staff humorist for the *New York Evening World*, then a staff contributor to the *Saturday Evening Post* and *Cosmopolitan*. He also wrote many best-selling books and worked as a scriptwriter and actor in Hollywood. TYRUS RAYMOND (TY) COBB (1886–1961) of Georgia was a professional baseball player known as "The Georgia Peach." He is considered the best defensive player in baseball history, and he spent most of his career with the Detroit Tigers.
Genealogies: Cobb and Cobbs, Early Virginians was compiled by John E. Cobb and published in Alexandria, Virginia, in 1976.

COBBS
Ranking: 4847 S.S. Count: 9229
Origin: English. Transformation of Cobb.
Genealogies: Cobb and Cobbs, Early Virginians was

compiled by John E. Cobb and published in Alexandria, Virginia, in 1976.

COBLE

Ranking: 3437 S.S. Count: 13,133

Origin: English. Derived from the Middle English word *"cobel,"* meaning rowboat. The name was given to those who worked as sailors.

Genealogies: None known.

COBURN

Ranking: 2408 S.S. Count: 18,811

Origin: Scottish. Derived from the Old English words *"cocc"* and *"burna,"* meaning cock and stream. The name was given to those who came from Cockburn, the name of a place in the Borders region between Scotland and England.

Famous **Coburns:** ABNER COBURN (1803–1885) of Maine was the governor of Maine (1863–1866). FOSTER DWIGHT COBURN (1846–1924) of Wisconsin was an agricultural editor and the author of *Swine in America* (1909).

Genealogies: *Ancestors and Descendants of James William Coburn, 1850–1929* was compiled by Raymond H. Coburn and published in Parson, West Virginia, in 1982. *Genealogy of the Descendants of Edward Colburn [or] Coburn* was compiled by George Augustus Gordon and published in Lowell, Massachusetts, in 1913.

COCHRAN, COCHRANE (S.S. Abbreviation: Cochra)

Ranking: 417 S.S. Count: 94,793

Origin: Scottish. Uncertain etymology. Possibly derived from the Welsh word *"coch,"* meaning red. The names were given to those who came from an area in the parish of Paisley, Scotland.

Famous **Bearers:** JOHN COCHRAN (1730–1807) of Pennsylvania, a physician during the Revolution, was the director-general of the Continental Army hospitals (1777–1783). JOHN COCHRANE (1813–1889) of New York was a member of Congress from New York and the grandson of John Cochran. ALEXANDER SMITH COCHRAN (1874–1929) of New York was a manufacturer and philanthropist who was a benefactor of the Metropolitan Museum of Art and Yale University. WELKER COCHRAN (1897–1960) of California was a billiards player who, along with Wille Hoppe and Jake Shaefer Jr., dominated the game in the first half of the 20th century. He won the three-cushion title four times.

Genealogies: *The Cochrans of Horseshoe Bend* was compiled by Kathrine Hedges Evers and published in New York, New York, in 1969. *Early Cochran Marriages, 1600–1899* was compiled by Larry and Cynthia Cochran Scheuer and published in Warsaw, Indiana, in 1989.

COCKER, COCKERELL, COCKERILL, COCKERHAM

Ranking: 4348 S.S. Count: 10,311

Origin: English. Cocker: derived from the Middle English word "cock," meaning to fight. The name was given to those who were prone to fighting. Cockerell, Cockerill: derived from the Old English word "cocc," meaning cock. The names were given to those who strutted to those who were considered aggresive, and to those who lived near or in a house that bore the sign of a cock. Cockerham: Uncertain etymology. Possibly derived from the British word "kukro," meaning winding, and the Old English word "ham," meaning homestead. The name was given to those who came from Cocker, a place in Lancashire, England, and to those who lived near the River Cocker.

Famous **Bearers:** JOHN ALBERT COCKERILL (1845–1896) of Ohio was a well-known journalist who died while a special correspondent for the *New York Herald*. THEODORE DRU ALISON COCKERELL (1866–1948), born in England, was a naturalist who lectured and taught at the University of Colorado for 30 years. He was a specialist in entomology and the taxonomy of bees, and a pioneer in the classification of fossil fish. He wrote almost 4000 papers and notes.

Genealogies: None known.

COCKRELL (S.S. Abbreviation: Cockre)

Ranking: 3215 S.S. Count: 14,099

Origin: English. Transformation of Cock(erell).

Famous **Cockrells:** FRANCIS MARION COCKRELL (1834–1915) of Missouri was a Confederate soldier, lawyer, and U.S. senator from Missouri.

Genealogies: *The Early Cockrells in Missouri* was compiled by Monroe F. Cockrell and published in Illinois in the 1960s.

CODY

Ranking: 1736 S.S. Count: 25,840

Origin: Irish. 1) derived from the Gaelic name Ó Cuidighthigh, meaning "descendant of Cuidightheach" (H&H), meaning helpful person. 2) derived from the Gaelic came Mac Óda, meaning "son of Óda" (H&H).

Famous **Codys:** WILLIAM FREDERICK CODY (1846–1917) of Iowa rode for the Pony Express, scouted Native Americans during the Civil War, and provided buffalo meat for the Kansas Pacific Railroad construction workers, which is how he got his nickname, "Buffalo Bill." He then gained great fame as a showman in his traveling show, "Buffalo Bill's Wild West."

Genealogies: *Cody* was compiled by Peggy M. Winston and published in Vancouver, Washington, in 1990. *Philip and Martha, Their Sons and Daughters* was compiled by Aldus Morrill Cody and published in Kissimee, Florida, in 1981.

COE

Ranking: 1811 S.S. Count: 24,896

Origin: English. Derived from the Old Norse word "ká," meaning jackdaw.

Famous Coes: ISRAEL COE (1794–1891) of Connecticut was a brass manufacturer and a pioneer in the brass-rolling industry. GEORGE SIMMONS COE (1817–1896) of Rhode Island was a banker who helped establish the New York Clearing House.

Genealogies: *A Folk History of the Coe Ridge Negro Colony* was compiled by William Lynwood Montell and published in Bloomington, Indiana, in 1964.

COFFEE

Ranking: 4907 S.S. Count: 9117

Origin: Irish. Transformation of Coffey.
Genealogies: None known.

COFFEY

Ranking: 845 S.S. Count: 50,444

Origin: Irish. Derived from the Gaelic name Ó Cobhthaigh, meaning "descendant of Cobhthach" (H&H), meaning victorious.

Famous Coffeys: JAMES VINCENT COFFEY (1846–1919) of New York was a judge of probate in San Francisco County for 36 years.

Genealogies: *The Coffeys of Wayne County* was compiled by Jacqueline Coffey Sexton and published in Monticello, Kentucky, in 1974. *Lizzie's Legacy and Our Coffey Cousins* was compiled by Mary Elizabeth Coffey Self and published in Kiowa, Oklahoma, in 1984.

COFFIN, COFFINEL, COFFINET, COFFINIER

Ranking: 3234 S.S. Count: 14,028

Origin: Coffin—English, French; Coffinel, Coffinet, Coffinier—French. Derived from the Old French word "cof(f)in," meaning basket. The names were given to those who worked making baskets.

Famous Bearers: LEVI COFFIN (1789–1877) was considered the president of the Underground Railroad, which aided slaves to freedom in the North before the Civil War. CHARLES CARLETON COFFIN (1823–1896) of New Hampshire was a Civil War correspondent and an author. CHARLES FISHER COFFIN (1823–1916) of North Carolina was a banker and Quaker minister and one of the leading Quakers of the time. LORENZO COFFIN (1823–1915) of North Carolina was responsible for legislation requiring self-couplers and air brakes on freight trains. CHARLES ALBERT COFFIN (1844–1926) of Maine was the president of General Electric Co. HOWARD EARLE COFFIN (1873–1937) of Ohio was a car manufacturer who contributed to the standardization of the car and aircraft industries.

Genealogies: *Gatherings Toward a Genealogy of the Coffin Family* was compiled by W. S. Appleton and published in Decorah, Iowa, in 1984. *Genealogy of the Early Generations of the Coffin Family in New England* was compiled by Sivanus Jenkins Macy and published in Boston, Massachusetts, in 1870. *The Long Years* was compiled by Jean M. Maire and published in Jacksonville, Florida, in 1967.

COFFMAN (S.S. Abbreviation: Coffma)

Ranking: 1268 S.S. Count: 34,799

Origin: German. Cognate to Chapman.

Famous Coffmans: LOTUS DELTA COFFMAN (1875–1938) of Indiana was president of the University of Minnesota (1920–1938).

Genealogies: *Genealogy of Joseph and Rebecca Miller Coffman, and Early References about Kauffmanns* was compiled by Ruth Perdiue and published in Indiana in 1961.

COGGIN, COGGINS

Ranking: 3553 S.S. Count: 12,695

Origin: Jewish. Transformation of Cohen.
Genealogies: None known.

COHEN

Ranking: 243 S.S. Count: 143,864

Origin: Irish, Jewish. Irish: derived from the Gaelic name Ó Cadhain, meaning "descendant of Cadhan" (H&H), which is derived from the word "cadham," meaning barnacle goose. Jewish: derived from the Hebrew word "kohen," meaning priest. Traditionally, all Cohens descended from Aaron, the brother of Moses. When the Russian army forced Jews to join its ranks, many changed their names to Cohen because members of the clergy were exempt from service.

Famous Cohens: MENDES COHEN (1831–1915) of Maryland was active in many civic and historical societies. JACOB DA SILVA SOLIS COHEN (1838–1927) of New York was a physician who was considered an expert in the use of the laryngoscope. JOHN SANFORD COHEN (1870–1935) of Georgia was a well-known journalist and editor with the *Atlanta Constitution*. MORRIS RAPHAEL COHEN (1880–1947), born in Russia, was a prominent philosophy professor in New York who wrote *Reason and Nature: An Essay on the Meaning of Scientific Method* (1931).

Genealogies: None known.

COHN

Ranking: 2527 S.S. Count: 17,951

Origin: Irish, Jewish. Transformation of Cohen.

Famous Cohns: FANNIE MARY COHN (1885?–1962), born in Russia, was a labor educator and leader who worked within the International Ladies' Garment Workers' Union to educate the workers. HARRY COHN (1891–1958) of New York was president and head of production of Columbia Pictures. Under his leadership, the studio produced such classics as *It Happened One Night, It's a Wonderful Life,* and *All the King's Men.*

Genealogies: None known.

COKER

Ranking: 1424 **S.S. Count:** 31,295

Origin: English. The name was given to those who came from Coker, the name of a place in Somerset, England.

Famous **Cokers:** JAMES LIDE COKER (1837–1918) of South Carolina was a manufacturer and the founder of Coker College for women in Hartsville, South Carolina. His son, DAVID ROBERT COKER (1870–1938) of South Carolina, was an agriculturist who improved the strains of short-staple cotton.

Genealogies: None known.

COLBERT   (S.S. Abbreviation: Colber)

Ranking: 1391 **S.S. Count:** 31,875

Origin: English. Derived from the first name Colbert, meaning cool or bright.

Genealogies: None known.

COLBURN, COLBURNE   (S.S. Abbreviation: Colbur)

Ranking: 3304 **S.S. Count:** 13,708

Origin: English. Most likely derived from the Old English words "cōl" and "burna," meaning cool and stream. The name was given to those who came from Colburn and other similarly named places in England.

Famous **Bearers:** WARREN COLBURN (1793–1833) of Massachusetts was a teacher whose mathematics textbooks on the inductive method were revolutionary in this field. ZERAH COLBURN (1804–1839) of Vermont was a mathematical prodigy who wrote an autobiography. DANA POND COLBURN (1823–1859) of Massachusetts was an educator noted for teaching rational rather than memory methods of learning when he taught in Rhode Island. IRVING WIGHTMAN COLBURN (1861–1917) of Massachusetts invented machinery and the process for continuous production of sheets of glass.

Genealogies: *Genealogy of the Descendants of Edward Colburn [or] Coburn* was compiled by George Augustus Gordon and published in Lowell, Massachusetts, in 1913.

COLBY

Ranking: 2856 **S.S. Count:** 15,985

Origin: English. Derived from the Old Norse first name Koli, which is derived from the words "kol" and "býr," meaning coal and settlement. The name was given to those who came from Colby, the name of several places in England.

Famous **Colbys:** GARDNER COLBY (1810–1879) of Maine was a merchant and philanthropist who helped to finance a school, later called Colby College, at Waterville,

Maine. CLARA DOROTHY BEWICK COLBY (1846–1916), born in England, was a suffragist who helped establish a free public library in Beatrice, Nebraska, in 1873; edited a women's column in the *Beatrice Weekly Express;* and in 1881 helped organize the Nebraska Woman's Suffrage Association. In 1883 she began publishing the *Woman's Tribune,* an important paper to the suffragists. She adopted two children. One was a three-year-old waif from New York City; the other was found by her husband. The latter child was a Sioux Indian baby left in his dead mother's arms after the battle of Wounded Knee. FRANK MOORE COLBY (1865–1925) of Washington, D.C., was editor of the *International Year Book* and *The New International Yearbook.* He also wrote essays, many of which were published in *Vanity Fair* and *The New Republic.* BAINBRIDGE COLBY (1869–1950) of Missouri helped to found the Progressive Party in 1912. WILLIAM GEORGE COLBY (1907–1975), an agronomist and educator, developed the hardy late-maturing orchard grass called Mass Hardy.

Genealogies: *The Colby Family in Early America: Early Generations of the Descendants of Anthony Colby of Boston, Cambridge, Salisbury and Amesbury, Massachusetts, 1595–1661* was compiled by Frederick Lewis Weis and published in Concord, Massachusetts, in 1970.

COLE

Ranking: 107 **S.S. Count:** 264,284

Origin: English, Irish, Scottish. English: 1) transformation of Nicholas. 2) derived from the Old English name Cola, which is derived from the word "col," meaning coal. The name was most likely given to those with dark skin. Irish, Scottish: derived from the Gaelic names Mac Gille Chomhghaill and Mac Giolla Chombhghaill, both meaning "son of the servant of (St.) Comhghall" (H&H).

Famous **Coles:** THOMAS COLE (1801–1848), originally from England, was a romantic landscape painter and the founder of the Hudson River school. CHESTER CICERO COLE (1824–1913) of New York was a justice of the Iowa Supreme Court (1864–1876). ANNA VIRGINIA RUSSELL COLE (1846–1926) of Georgia was a social leader and philanthropist in Nashville, Tennessee. FRANK NELSON COLE (1861–1926) of Massachusetts was a mathematician and editor of *American Mathematical Society Bulletin* (1897–1925). CHARLES WOOLSEY COLE (1906–1978), at the age of 40, became the youngest president ever of Amherst College in Massachusetts. He was president there from 1946 to 1960.

Genealogies: *Cole Foot Prints* was compiled by Camellia T. Denys and published in Provo, Utah, in 1983.

COLEMAN   (S.S. Abbreviation: Colema)

Ranking: 96 **S.S. Count:** 289,289

Origin: English, Irish, Jewish. English: 1) derived from the

Middle English word "coleman," meaning one who burned charcoal. The name was given to those who worked as such. 2) Uncertain etymology. The name was given to those who were servants for someone named Cole. English, Irish: derived from the Old Irish first name Colmán, which is derived from the Latin name Columba, meaning dove. Irish: derived from the Gaelic name Ó Clumháin, meaning "descendant of Clumhán" (H&H). Jewish: derived from the Yiddish name Kloynemes, which is ultimately derived from the Greek words "kaols" and "kallos," meaning lovely and beauty.

Famous **Colemans**: WILLIAM COLEMAN (1766–1829) of Massachusetts was a Federalist journalist and editor of the *New York Evening Post*, and a supporter of Alexander Hamilton. LYMAN COLEMAN (1796–1882) of Massachusetts, a Congregational clergyman, taught classics at Amherst College, Princeton University, and Lafayette College. LEIGHTON COLEMAN (1837–1907) of Pennsylvania was an Episcopal bishop of Delaware. CHARLES CARYL COLEMAN (1840–1928) of New York was a painter of landscapes. ALICE BLANCHARD MERRIAM COLEMAN (1858–1936) of Massachusetts was a leader in church work.

Genealogies: *Coleman Family History* was compiled by George Simpson and published in Tama, Iowa, in 1980. *Colemans of Greene County: a Bit of Alabama History* was compiled by Stephen Beasley Coleman and published in Birmingham, Alabama, in 1984.

COLES
Ranking: 2292 S.S. Count: 19,872
Origin: English. Transformation of Nicholas.
Famous **Coleses**: EDWARD COLES (1786–1868) of Virginia was an abolitionist; secretary to President James Madison (1809–1815); and governor of Illinois (1822–1826).
Genealogies: None known.

COLEY
Ranking: 2230 S.S. Count: 20,543
Origin: English. Derived from the Old English word "colig," meaning dark. The name was given to those who had dark complexions.
Genealogies: None known.

COLLAZZO (S.S. Abbreviation: Collaz)
Ranking: 2131 S.S. Count: 21,482
Origin: Italian. Cognate to Nicholas.
Genealogies: None known.

COLLET, COLLETT
Ranking: 1905 S.S. Count: 23,773
Origin: Collet—English; Collett—French. Transformation of and cognate to Nicholas.

Genealogies: None known.

COLLEY
Ranking: 3658 S.S. Count: 12,338
Origin: English. Transformation of Coley.
Genealogies: None known.

COLLIE
Ranking: 498 S.S. Count: 80,700
Origin: English. Transformation of Coley.
Genealogies: None known.

COLLIN, COLLING, COLLINGS, COLLINGWOOD, COLLINGWORTH, COLLINS, COLLINSON, COLLINET, COLLINOT
Ranking: 49 S.S. Count: 465,489
Origin: Collin, Colling, Collings, Collingwood, Collingworth—English; Collins, Collinson—English, Irish; Collinet, Collinot—French. Collin, Colling, Collins, Collinson, Collinet, Collinot: transformations of and cognates to Nicholas. Colling, Collings: derived from the Old Norse name Koli, meaning dark. Collingwood, Collingworth: derived from the Middle English and Old French word "challenge," meaning dispute or challenge. The names were given to those who came from a wood, the ownership of which was disputed. Collins—Irish: derived from the Gaelic names Ó Coileáin and Mac Coileáin, both of which mean puppy.

Famous **Bearers**: JOHN COLLINS (1717–1795) was governor of Rhode Island (1786–1790). EDWARD KNIGHT COLLINS (1802–1878) of Massachusetts owned a line of transatlantic ships. JOHN ANDERSON COLLINS (1810–1879) of Vermont, an abolitionist and social reformer, was general agent for the Massachusetts Anti-Slavery Society. NAPOLEON COLLINS (1814–1875) of Pennsylvania was a naval officer who captured the Confederate raider *Florida* in 1864. ELLEN COLLINS (1828–1912) of New York City was a philanthropist and housing reformer who used her money to demonstrate the influence of a landlord over the lives of poor tenants in housing projects. JENNIE COLLINS (1828–1887) of New Hampshire was a labor reformer and a welfare worker. PATRICK ANDREW COLLINS (1844–1905), originally from Ireland, was mayor of Boston, Massachusetts (1901–1905). FRANK SHIPLEY COLLINS (1848–1920) of Massachusetts was a botanist who wrote *The Green Algae of North America* (1909). GUY N. COLLINS (1872–1938) was a geneticist who concentrated on the study of maize. MARION COLLINS (1906–1977) started Medic Alert, an international system of informing emergency medical personnel of a person's allergies and other afflictions. His idea came from his daughter's adverse reaction to being tested for a tetanus antitoxin.

Genealogies: *Collins Ancestry* was compiled by Mabel

Thacher Rosemary Washburn and published in New York, New York, in the 1940s. *The Collins and Travis Families and Their Allies* was compiled by Mary Collins Landin and published in Utica, Mississippi, in 1982. *Collison and Cohee Families: Maryland and Delaware to Many States* was compiled by Hilda Chance and published in Aston, Pennsylvania, in 1977.

COLLIS
Ranking: 4859 S.S. Count: 9211
Origin: English, Irish. Transformation of Collins.
Genealogies: None known.

COLOMB, COLUMBET, COLOMBEL, COLOMBEAU, COLOMBIER, COLOMBA, COLUMBO, COLOMBARI, COLUMBERI
Ranking: 4057 S.S. Count: 11,144
Origin: Colomb, Columbet, Colombel, Colombeau, Colombier—French; Colomba, Columbo, Colombari, Columberi—Italian. 1) derived from the Latin word "columbus," meaning dove. The name was given to those who worked keeping doves. 2) derived from the first names Columbus and Columba, which are of the same derivation as in 1.
Genealogies: *The Ancestry and Descendants of Christopher Columbus* (including the Columbo Family) was compiled by Charles Maduell and published in New Orleans, Louisiana, in 1975.

COLON
Ranking: 287 S.S. Count: 125,480
Origin: Spanish. Transformation of Colomb.
Genealogies: *The Ancestry and Descendants of Christopher Columbus* (including the Colon Family) was compiled by Charles Maduell and published in New Orleans, Louisiana in 1975.

COLSON
Ranking: 3481 S.S. Count: 12,959
Origin: English. Transformation of Coll.
Genealogies: None known.

COLVIN
Ranking: 1445 S.S. Count: 30,897
Origin: English, Irish, Scottish. 1) transformation of Calvin. 2) derived from the first name Ceolwin, which is derived from words meaning ship and friend. 3) derived from the first name Anluan, meaning great hero. 4) derived from the first name Col. The name was given to those who came from Colleville, a place in Normandy, France.
Famous **Colvins:** STEPHEN SHELDON COLVIN (1869–1923) of Rhode Island was an educational psychologist and author of *The Learning Process* (1911).

Genealogies: *The Colvins of Fayette: Some Descendants of Dr. William Colvin of Glasgow, Scotland* was compiled by Richard Hathaway and published in Pomona, California, in 1986. *The Colvins, Oregon Pioneers* was compiled by Stephen O. Stout and published in Brush Prairie, Washington, in 1982.

COLWELL (S.S. Abbreviation: Colwel)
Ranking: 3196 S.S. Count: 14,196
Origin: English. Derived from the Old English words "col" or "cōl" and "well(a)," meaning coal or cool and spring. The name was given to those who came from Colwell, the name of several places in England.
Famous **Colwells:** STEPHEN COLWELL (1800–1871) of Virginia, a political economist and lawyer, was a specialist on the social implications of Christian doctrine.
Genealogies: None known.

COMBS
Ranking: 568 S.S. Count: 72,638
Origin: English. Transformation of Coombs.
Famous **Combses:** MOSES NEWELL COMBS (1753–1834) of New Jersey, a manufacturer and philanthropist, was known as the "father of Newark [New Jersey] industries." He founded one of the first night schools in Newark in 1794. LESLIE COMBS (1793–1881) of Kentucky was a soldier, Unionist, politician, and lawyer.
Genealogies: *Combs Family* was compiled by Patricia Combs O'Dell and published in 1971.

COMEAU
Ranking: 2876 S.S. Count: 15,818
Origin: French. Cognate to Coombs.
Genealogies: None known.

COMER
Ranking: 1921 S.S. Count: 23,510
Origin: English. Derived from the Old English word "camb," meaning comb. The name was given to those who worked making or selling combs and to those who used combs in their work.
Famous **Comers:** BRAXTON BRAGG COMER (1848–1927) of Alabama, as governor of that state (1907–1911), obtained unprecedented levels of funding for schools and colleges.
Genealogies: None known.

COMPTON (S.S. Abbreviation: Compto)
Ranking: 876 S.S. Count: 49,394
Origin: English. Derived from the Old English words "cumb" and "tūn," meaning short valley and settlement. The name was given to those who came from Compton, the name of many places in England.

Famous **Comptons:** KARL TAYLOR COMPTON (1887–1954) of Ohio worked on the development of the atomic bomb and radar through his positions in the National Military Establishment and the Office of Scientific Research and Development. His brother, ARTHUR HOLLY COMPTON (1892–1962), won the Nobel Prize for physics with C.T.R. Wilson for a discovery that explained why X-ray wavelengths change when they collide with electrons.

Genealogies: *The Comptons of Grove Lake: A Story of the Ancestors Back to the Mayflower and Their Descendants to the Pacific* was compiled by Mildred Blair Hawkins and published in Albany, Oregon, in 1975. *Family Record of James Compton and Clarissa Cleveland-Compton* was compiled by Murat Compton and published in 1901.

COMSTOCK   (S.S. Abbreviation: Comsto)
Ranking: 2970 **S.S. Count:** 15,320
Origin: English. 1) the name was given to those who came from Comstock, which means "monastery in a narrow valley" (ES) and is a place in England. 2) the name was given to those who lived in a valley.

Famous **Comstocks:** GEORGE FRANKLIN COMSTOCK (1811–1892) of New York started Syracuse University. ELIZABETH LESLIE ROUS COMSTOCK (1815–1891), born in England, was a Quaker minister and reformer. HENRY TOMPHINS PAIGE COMSTOCK (1820–1870), born in Canada, was a prospector in Nevada on whose land the Comstock Lode was discovered. ANTHONY COMSTOCK (1844–1915) of Connecticut was responsible for postal regulations banning the mailing of obscene materials. However, he had difficulty distinguishing between obscenity and art. JOHN HENRY COMSTOCK (1849–1931) of Wisconsin was an entomologist and a professor at Cornell University. He pioneered in the classification of scale insects, moths, and butterflies and wrote, among other works, *Introduction to Entomology* (1888) and *Manual for the Study of Insects* (1895). His wife, ANNA BOTSFORD COMSTOCK (1854–1930) of New York, was a naturalist and wood engraver who also taught at Cornell. She wrote books, including *Ways of the Six-Footed* (1903), and was editor of *Nature Study Review* (1917–1923). GEORGE CARY COMSTOCK (1855–1934) of Wisconsin, an astronomer, showed that stars of faint light may simply be stars of low light and not stars that are far away. IDA LOUISE COMSTOCK (1876–1973) of Minnesota was the first full-time president of Radcliffe College.

Genealogies: *Comstock-Haggard and Allied Families* was compiled by Mary Jane Comstock and published in Chicago, Illinois, in 1973. *The Family of John Everett Comstock* was compiled by Roger Henry Comstock and published in Syracuse, New York, in 1981.

CONAWAY   (S.S. Abbreviation: Conawa)
Ranking: 4005 **S.S. Count:** 11,303
Origin: Welsh. Transformation of Conway.
Genealogies: None known.

CONCEPCION
Ranking: 2950 **S.S. Count:** 15,445
Origin: Spanish. Derived from the Late Latin word conceptio, meaning conception as it evolved into a first name alluding to the immaculate conception of Christ.
Genealogies: None known.

CONDON
Ranking: 2329 **S.S. Count:** 19,486
Origin: Irish. Uncertain etymology. Most likely derived from the Gaelic name Condún, which is derived from the Old English first name Calunðd, which is derived from the words "calu" and "nōd," meaning bold and daring, and the word "tūn," meaning settlement.

Famous **Condons:** THOMAS CONDON (1822–1907), born in Ireland, was a Congregational clergyman and missionary in Oregon.

Genealogies: *Condon* was compiled by Mae Bissinnar Condon and published in Greenville, Mississippi, in 1982.

CONE
Ranking: 3034 **S.S. Count:** 14,991
Origin: German. Cognate to Cohen.

Famous **Cones:** MOSES HERMAN CONE (1857–1908) of Tennessee was a prominent manufacturer of denim at Greensboro, North Carolina. ETTA CONE (1870–1949) of Maryland and CLARIBEL CONE (1864–1929) of Tennessee were sisters who amassed a large collection of modern art, with special emphasis on the art of Matisse. HUTCHINSON INGHAM CONE (1871–1941) of New York, a career naval officer, was fleet engineer for the Atlantic Fleet's around-the-world cruise and later served in a number of government capacities.

Genealogies: *Cone: Ancestors and Descendants of Henry Clay Cone* was compiled by Marion Abbott Gunderson and published in Rolfe, Iowa, in 1992. *Faulk-Cone and Allied Families* was compiled by Eleanor Faulk Cone and published in Baltimore, Maryland, in 1983.

CONGER
Ranking: 4501 **S.S. Count:** 9951
Origin: English. Derived from the first name Congar, meaning bold and spear.
Genealogies: *The Conger Family of America* was compiled by Maxine Crowell Leonard and published in Janesville, Iowa, in 1972.

CONKLIN, CONKLING (S.S. Abbreviation: Conkli)

Ranking: 1178 **S.S. Count:** 37,131

Origin: Dutch. 1) derived from the Dutch word "konkelen," meaning a conspirator. 2) the names were given to those who were the descendants of a minor ruler.

Genealogies: *The Conklin Family: Nicholas Conklin of Cochecton, New York, and His Descendants* was compiled by Richard O. Eldred and published in Baltimore, Maryland, in 1991.

CONLEY

Ranking: 548 **S.S. Count:** 74,547

Origin: Irish. Transformation of Connolly.

Genealogies: *The Conley Family: Descendants of Nicholas* was compiled by Jean A. Curran and published in 1976. *Conley-Connelly, Descendants of Thomas Connelly of Northern Lancaster and York Counties, Pennsylvania* was compiled by Frances Wise Waite and published in Doylestown, Pennsylvania, in 1980.

CONLON

Ranking: 4022 **S.S. Count:** 11,260

Origin: Irish. Transformation of Quinlan.

Genealogies: None known.

CONN

Ranking: 2125 **S.S. Count:** 21,548

Origin: Irish. Transformation of any of the Irish names beginning with Con.

Genealogies: None known.

CONNELL, CONNELLAN, CONNELLY (S.S. Abbreviation: Connel)

Ranking: 604 **S.S. Count:** 68,849

Origin: Irish. Connell, Connellan: transformations of Quinlan. Connelly: transformation of Connolly.

Famous Connellys: MARCUS COOK (MARC) CONNELLY (1890–1980) of Pennsylvania was a playwright best known for his play *Green Pastures,* a folk version of the Old Testament that told its story through the lives of African-Americans.

Genealogies: None known.

CONNER, CONNERS, CONNERNY, CONNERY

Ranking: 398 **S.S. Count:** 98,083

Origin: Conner, Conners—English; Connerny, Connery—Irish. Conner, Conners: derived from the Middle English word "connere," meaning inspector of weights and measures. The names were given to those who worked as such.

Connerny: transformation of McNairn. Connery—transformation of Conroy.

Famous Conners: DAVID CONNER (1792–1856) of Pennsylvania was a naval officer who was awarded two Congressional medals for service on the *Hornet.* JAMES CONNER (1829–1883) of South Carolina was a Confederate soldier and a lawyer who established the legality of Wade-Hampton government.

Genealogies: *A Family of the Bagaduce: The Ancestry and Genealogy of William Conner, Jr. (1807–1884)* was compiled by Albert E. Myers and published in Harrisburg, Pennsylvania, in 1976.

CONNOLLY (S.S. Abbreviation: Connol)

Ranking: 1014 **S.S. Count:** 43,192

Origin: Irish. Derived from the Gaelic name Ó Conghalaigh, meaning "descendant of Conghalach" (H&H), meaning valiant.

Famous Connollys: JOHN CONNOLLY (1750–1825), born in Ireland, was a Dominican priest and bishop in New York who established an orphan asylum.

Genealogies: *James C. Connolly: Parents and Descendants, 1805–1974* was compiled by Nancy Christensen Manley and published in Alvordton, Ohio, in 1974.

CONNOR, CONNORS

Ranking: 559 **S.S. Count:** 73,223

Origin: Irish. Derived from the Gaelic name Ó Conchobhair, meaning "descendant of Conchobhar," which is probably derived from the Gaelic words "cúu" and "cobhar," meaning dog and desiring.

Famous Bearers: PATRICK EDWARD CONNOR (1820–1891), born in Ireland, was a pioneer, soldier, Indian fighter, and a leader of the anti-Mormons in Utah. HENRY GROVES CONNOR (1852–1924) of North Carolina, as a federal district judge, overcame the prejudice of postbellum North Carolina against federal courts. ROBERT DIGGES WIMBERLY CONNOR (1878–1950) of North Carolina, as the first archivist of the United States, organized the National Archives.

Genealogies: *The American Descendants of Henry Connor of County Antrim, Ireland* was compiled by Robert Stephens Hand and published in Chaddsford, Pennsylvania, in 1971.

CONOVER (S.S. Abbreviation: Conove)

Ranking: 3502 **S.S. Count:** 12,873

Origin: Dutch. The name was given to those who lived near a "cool garden or a court" (ES).

Famous Conovers: OBADIAH MILTON CONOVER (1825–1884) of Ohio, a lawyer and educator, was a reporter for the Wisconsin Supreme Court and a state librarian.

Genealogies: *Conover Pioneers and Pilgrim: Celebration* *of a Family* was compiled by Elizabeth Conover Kelley and published in Canton, Michigan, in 1982.

CONRAD, CONRADSEN
Ranking: 691 **S.S. Count:** 60,672
Origin: Conrad—French; Conradsen—Danish. Derived from a Germanic first name that is derived from the words "kuoni" and "rad," meaning brave and counsel.

Famous **Bearers:** CHARLES MAGILL CONRAD (1804–1878) of Virginia was a member of Congress, U.S. senator, and secretary of war prior to the Civil War. ROBERT TAYLOR CONRAD (1810–1858) of Pennsylvania, a dramatist and jurist, was a respected journalist, judge of city criminal court, and the Know-Nothing mayor of Philadelphia (1854–1856). FRANK CONRAD (1874–1941) of Pennsylvania was an electrical engineer who broadcast from an amateur radio station in his home. When a local department store advertised wireless sets to receive his transmissions, Westinghouse Electrical and Manfacturing Company, his employer, applied for a commercial license and created the first commercial radio station.

Genealogies: *A Conrad Genealogy: Being a Direct-Line Compilation of 34 Surnames in America* was compiled by John R. Conrad and published in Bloomington, Indiana, in 1979. *Our Coulter Clan and Allied Families* (including the Conrad Family) was compiled by Steven Early Coulter and published in Des Moines, Iowa, in 1970.

CONROY
Ranking: 1914 **S.S. Count:** 23,621
Origin: Irish. Derived from the Gaelic name Ó Conaire, meaning "descendant of Conaire" (H&H), meaning "Keeper of the Hound" (H&H).
Genealogies: None known.

CONSTABLE, CONSTANTINE, CONSTANCE, CONSTANS, CONSTANT, CONSTATIN, CONSTANTINO, CONSTANY (S.S. Abbreviation: Consta)
Ranking: 1471 **S.S. Count:** 30,290
Origin: Constable, Constantine—English; Constance—English, French; Constans, Constant, Constatin—French; Constantino—Italian, Portuguese; Constany—Provençal. Constable: derived from the Middle English word "conestable" and the Old French word "cunestable," meaning law-enforcement officer. The name was given to those who worked as such. Constance: 1) derived from the Latin first name Constatia, meaning steadfastness. 2) possibly the same derivation as in 1. The name was given to those who came from Coutances, a place in Normandy, France. Constans, Constant: derived from the Latin name Constans, meaning steadfast and faithful. Constantine, Constatin, Constantino, Constany: 1) derived from the Latin name Costantinus, which is a deriva-

tive of the name Constans, meaning steadfast and faithful. 2) Uncertain etymology. The name was given to those who came from Coutances, a place in Normandy, France.
Genealogies: None known.

CONTE
Ranking: 4173 **S.S. Count:** 10,831
Origin: English, French, Portuguese, Provençal, Spanish. Congate to and transformation of Conde.
Genealogies: None known.

CONTI
Ranking: 3155 **S.S. Count:** 14,388
Origin: Italian. Cognate to Conde.
Genealogies: None known.

CONTREIRAS, CONTRERAS (S.S. Abbreviation: Contre)
Ranking: 758 **S.S. Count:** 56,043
Origin: Contreiras—Portuguese; Contreras—Spanish. Derived from the Late Latin word "contrāria," meaning surrounding area. The names were given to those who came from Contreras, a place in Spain.
Genealogies: None known.

CONVERS, CONVERSE, CONVERT, CONVERY (S.S. Abbreviation: Conver)
Ranking: 4569 **S.S. Count:** 9775
Origin: Convers, Converse, Convert—English; Convery—Irish. Convers, Converse, Convert: derived from the Middle English and Old French word "convers," meaning convert. The names were given to Jews who became Christians.

Famous **Bearers:** HARRIETT MAXWELL CONVERSE (1836–1903) of New York was an author, folklorist, and defender of Indian rights. JOHN HERMAN CONVERSE (1840–1910) of Vermont was a builder of locomotives and president of Baldwin Locomotive Works. EDMUND COGSWELL CONVERSE (1849–1921) of Massachusetts invented the lock-joint for gas and water pipes. FREDERICK SHEPHERD CONVERSE (1871–1940) of Massachusetts was a composer known for his romantic and impressionistic works. His compositions include the opera *The Pipe of Desire* and six symphonies.
Genealogies: None known.

CONWAY
Ranking: 669 **S.S. Count:** 62,727
Origin: Irish, Scottish, Welsh. Irish: derived from the Gaelic names Mac Connmhaigh, meaning "son of Conmhach" (H&H), meaning head smashing, and Ó Conbhuide, meaning "descendant of Conbuhuidhe" (H&H), which is derived from the words "cú" and "buidle," meaning dog and yellow. Scottish: most likely derived from the Gaelic word

"coinmheadh," meaning free quarters, and referring to the lodging of a local lord's troops. The name was given to those who came from Conway, a place in Scotland. Welsh: possibly derived from a British word meaning "reedy" (H&H). The name was given to those who came from Conwy, a place in Wales.

Famous **Conways**: THOMAS CONWAY (1735–1800), originally from Ireland, was a Revolutionary War general who advocated that Gen. George Washington be replaced by Horatio Gates as commander in chief of the army. He wrote Washington a letter of full apology for the incident and returned to France. JAMES SERIER CONWAY (1798–1855) of Tennessee was the first governor of Arkansas (1836–1840). His brother, ELIAS NELSON CONWAY (1812–1892) of Tennessee, also was governor of Arkansas (1852–1860). FREDERICK BARTLETT CONWAY (1819–1874), born in England, was an actor who played in stock theater in New York, Massachusetts, and Ohio.

Genealogies: None known.

CONYER, CONYERS

Ranking: 4521 S.S. Count: 9906
Origin: English. Transformation of Coyne.
Genealogies: None known.

COOK

Ranking: 56 S.S. Count: 420,450
Origin: English: derived from the Old English word "cūc," meaning cook. English, Jewish: The name was given to those who worked as cooks or sold meat or owned a restaurant. Jewish: transformation of the name Kuk, which is of uncertain etymology.

Famous **Cooks**: ZEBEDEE COOK (1786–1858) of Massachusetts founded the Massachusetts Horticultural Society. ISAAC COOK (1810–1886) of New Jersey was a politician and wine merchant and president of the American Wine Co., St. Louis, Missouri (1859–1886). GEORGE HAMMELL COOK (1818–1889) of New Jersey was a geologist who wrote the *Geology of New Jersey*. CLARENCE CHATHAM COOK (1828–1900) of Massachusetts was an art critic and journalist who wrote a *New York Tribune* column, edited a journal called *The Studio*, and wrote a book called *The House Beautiful*. ALBERT STANBURROUGH COOK (1853–1927) of New Jersey, a scholar who specialized in Old and Middle English, organized the English Department at Johns Hopkins University. FREDERICK ALBERT COOK (1865–1940) of New York was a surgeon and ethnologist on the 1891–92 expedition of Robert C. Perry to the North Pole. WILL MARION COOK (1869–1944) of Washington, D.C., a musician and composer, over a 10-year period composed much of the music for a series of black musicals featuring the team of Bert Williams and George Walker. One of the musicals, *In Dahomey* (1903), was a European and Ameri-

can success. He studied at Oberlin Conservatory of Music and in Berlin, Germany, and New York, but because of racial prejudice's limiting his chances in classical violin and composition, he chose to pursue a career in writing for popular audiences. GEORGE CRAM COOK (1873–1924) of Iowa was the founder and director of the Provincetown (Massachusetts) Players, the originator of the Playwright's Theater in New York City, and a novelist whose works include *The Chasm* (1911).

Genealogies: *The Cook Family Geneaelogical Record and Their Family Connections* was compiled by Bill J. Cook and published in Glendale, Ohio, in 1971. *The Cook Family in America: A Family History of Thomas and Milly (Marcum) Cook and Their Descendants of Bedford County, Tennessee (c. 1770– 1973)* was compiled by Jerry Wayne Cook and published in Normandy, Tennessee, in 1973. *Cook's Crier, the Franklin Fireplace; Surname Index* was compiled by Betty Harvey Williams and published in Warrensburg, Missouri, in 1973.

COOKE

Ranking: 891 S.S. Count: 48,818
Origin: English, Jewish. Transformation of Cook.

Famous **Cookes**: JAY COOKE (1821–1905) of Ohio was a prominent financier who, among other things, marketed government bonds to fund the Civil War. He also financed construction of a western railroad, the failure of which led to the financial panic of 1873. ROSE TERRY COOKE (1827–1892) of Connecticut, an author, wrote *The Mormon's Wife*, which is considered a valuable record of life in 19th-century New England because of the vernacular in which it was written. ANNA CHARLOTTE RICE COOKE (1853–1934) of Hawaii founded the Honolulu Academy of Arts. FLORA JULIETTE COOKE (1864–1953) of Ohio was an educator who became a leader in the progressive education movement as the principal of the Francis W. Parker School in Chicago, Illinois. JOHN ESTEN COOKE (1783–1853), born in Bermuda, was a physician who wrote *Treatise on Pathology*, considered the earliest American systematic textbook on medicine. His brother JOHN ROGERS COOKE (1788–1854), also born in Bermuda, was a prominent Virginia lawyer who earned distinction as a delegate to the Virginia constitutional convention. Another brother, PHILIP ST. GEORGE COOKE (1809–1895) of Virginia, was a West Point graduate who served on the western frontier in the Mexican War, was a Union general in the Civil War, and was the author of *Cavalry Tactics* (1861) and *The Conquest of New Mexico and California*.

Genealogies: *The Family of Elisha Cooke* was compiled by Florence Adeline Newberry and published in Blairstown, New Jersey, in 1934. *Things That Count—The Story of the Cooke Family* was compiled by Velma Cooke and published in 1974.

COOKSEY (S.S. Abbreviation: Cookse)

Ranking: 4527 S.S. Count: 9892

Origin: English. Derived from the Old English first name Cucu, which is probably derived from the word "cwicu," meaning lively, and the word "ēeg," meaning island. The name was given to those who came from Cooksey, a place in Worcestershire, England.

Genealogies: *Cooksey of Maryland* (1832) was compiled by James B. McCurley and published in Louisville, Kentucky, in 1980.

COOLEY

Ranking: 960 S.S. Count: 45,459

Origin: English, Irish. 1) transformation of Nicholas. 2) Uncertain etymology. The name was given to those who were the descendants of servants to St. Mochuille.

Famous **Cooleys**: THOMAS MCINTYRE COOLEY (1824–1898) of New York was a justice of the Michigan Supreme Court (1864–1885), a professor of law at the University of Michigan, a chairman of the Interstate Commerce Commission, and the author of authoritative legal books, including *General Principles of Constitutional Law* (1880). His son CHARLES HORTON BENTON (1864–1929) of Michigan was a sociologist who wrote, among other works, *Human Nature and the Social Order* (1902). Another son, THOMAS BENTON COOLEY (1871–1945) of Michigan, was a pediatrician who identified in 1925 a familial anemia that bears his name. MORTIMER ELWYN COOLEY (1844–1944) of New York, an engineering professor and a college dean in Illinois, developed procedures for utilities surveys that became a model for later surveys. His brother, LYMAN EDGAR COOLEY (1850–1917) of New York, was a civil engineer who established the feasibility of a Great Lakes/Atlantic Ocean canal. EDWIN GILBERT COOLEY (1857–1923) of Iowa was an educator and the superintendent of Chicago, Illinois, schools, where he accomplished many reforms.

Genealogies: *My Cooley-Walters Ancestry from Fairchance, Pennsylvania, and Surrounding Areas* was compiled by Kathryn Mercedes Cooley Miller and published in Houston, Texas, in 1987.

COOMBS

Ranking: 3515 S.S. Count: 12,830

Origin: English. Derived from the Old English word "cumb," meaning a short, curveless valley. The name was given to those who came from the many places in England with this component, such as Combe, in their names.

Genealogies: *The Antecedents and Descendants of James Witherell Coombs and His Wife Lucretia Getchell Coombs of Maine* was written by William Carey Coombs and published in Bloomfield, New Jersey, in 1969. *Coombs-Beal-Higgins Family History* was compiled by Virginia L. Higgins

Rose and published in Wollaston, Massachusetts, in the 1970s.

COON

Ranking: 1872 S.S. Count: 24,181

Origin: German. 1) derived from words meaning bold and keen. 2) cognate to Conrad.

Genealogies: *Coon Family Genealogy and Anecdotes* was compiled by George Christian Coon and published in 1970. *Coon-Gohn Descendants from Chanceford Township, York County, Pennsylvania* was compiled by Frances Davis McTeer and published in Holiday, Florida, in 1979. *A Tale of Two Continents: Pages from the History of the Families Coon, Feurstein, Leser, Maubach, Merrill, and Wittekind* was compiled by Will Schaber and published in New York, New York, in 1977.

COONEY

Ranking: 2240 S.S. Count: 18,607

Origin: Irish. Derived from the Gaelic name Ó Cuana, meaning "descendant of Cuana" (H&H), which is derived from the word "cuanna," meaning elegant.

Genealogies: None known.

COONS

Ranking: 3679 S.S. Count: 12,555

Origin: German. Transformation of Coon.

Genealogies: None known.

COOPER, COOPERMAN

Ranking: 61 S.S. Count: 383,923

Origin: Cooper—English, Jewish; Cooperman—Jewish. Cooper (English): derived from the Middle English word "couper," meaning one who made or repaired barrels and casks. The name was given to those who worked as such. Cooper, Cooperman (Jewish): transformation of names with the word "kuper," meaning copper, in them.

Famous **Bearers**: WILLIAM COOPER (1754–1809) of Pennsylvania settled the land that became Cooperstown, New York. His son, JAMES FENIMORE COOPER (1789–1851) of New Jersey, was the first major U.S. novelist. His books were about frontier adventures and were known as the Leatherstocking Tales. Among his most famous books are *The Last of the Mohicans* (1826) and *The Deerslayer* (1841). His oldest child to survive, SUSAN AUGUSTA FENIMORE COOPER (1813–1894) of New York, was also an author. She wrote *Rural Hours* (1850), a synoptic diary on nature over a year's period, and a biography of her father, published in 1861. THOMAS COOPER (1759–1839), born in England, a scientist and educator in Pennsylvania and South Carolina, engaged in frequent philosophical arguments with the clergy over his biblical criticism and materialistic beliefs. He wrote several books, including a pioneering textbook,

Lectures on the Elements of Political Economy (1826). PETER COOPER (1791–1883) of New York was an inventor of, among other things, "Tom Thumb," the first American-built steam engine. He also founded Cooper Union, a New York City college offering free courses in science, chemistry, electricity, engineering, and art. SARAH BROWN INGERSOLL COOPER (1836–1896) of New York was the founder of the kindergarten class. HENRY ERNEST COOPER (1857–1929) of Indiana was a lawyer who helped to organize the Hawaiian revolution. ANNA JULIA HAYWOOD COOPER (1859?–1964) of North Carolina, a teacher and school principal, worked on behalf of her students to have them admitted to colleges and universities on the basis of their abilities and not because of their color or sex. MERIAN C. COOPER (1895–1973) of Florida was a writer and motion-picture producer whose credits include *King Kong* (1933), *Fort Apache* (1948), and *The Quiet Man* (1952).

Genealogies: *A Confederate Soldier and His Descendants* was compiled by Norman Lee Cooper and published in Bowie, Maryland, in 1982. *Cooper Family History, 1730–1982* was compiled by Thomas R. Bryan and published in 1982.

COPE
Ranking: 1794 **S.S. Count:** 25,137

Origin: English. Derived from the Old English word "cāp," meaning cloak or cap. The name was given to those who worked making such items or to those who wore distinctive outerwear.

Famous **Copes:** THOMAS PYM COPE (1768–1854) of Pennsylvania was a merchant and philanthropist who established the first ship line between Philadelphia and Liverpool. EDWARD DRINKER COPE (1840–1897) of Pennsylvania, a zoologist and paleontologist, was an authority on fossil species, of which he discovered more than 1000. He was the owner and editor of *American Naturalist*. WALTER COPE (1860–1902) of Pennsylvania was an architect who designed buildings in the English Collegiate Gothic style for several colleges.

Genealogies: *Darlington Cope and His Descendants, 1815–1967* was compiled by Walter A. Cope and published in Columbus, Ohio, in the 1960s. *A History of Awbury* (including the Cope Family) was compiled by Mary C. Scattergood and published in Three Oaks, Michigan, in 1972.

COPELAND (S.S. Abbreviation: Copela)
Ranking: 530 **S.S. Count:** 76,226.

Origin: English, Scottish. Derived from the Old Norse word "kaupland," meaning bought land. The name was given to those who came from Copeland and Coupland, the names of places in England.

Famous **Copelands:** CHARLES W. COPELAND

(1815–1895) of Connecticut, a naval engineer, designed the engine of the first steam warship (the *Fulton*) built under navy supervision. ROYAL SAMUEL COPELAND (1868–1938) of Michigan was a physician, teacher, and medical writer, as well as a U.S. senator from New York.

Genealogies: *Copeland, Bostick, Patton, and Allied Families* was compiled by Virginia Copeland Jantz and published in Waco, Texas, in 1981. *The Copeland/Coplen and Allied Families* was compiled by Herman L. Coplen and published in Baltimore, Maryland, in 1983.

COPPOLA, COPPOLARO, COPPOLELLI, COPPOLETTA, COPPOLETTI ET AL. (S.S. Abbreviation: Coppol)
Ranking: 3568 **S.S. Count:** 12,639

Origin: Italian. Derived from the Neopolitan term "copola," meaning a kind of beret that is common in the region. The name was given to those who often wore such a hat or to those who worked making such hats.

Genealogies: None known.

CORBET, CORBETT, CORBETTI
Ranking: 1162 **S.S. Count:** 37,640

Origin: Corbett—English; Corbetti—Italian. Derived from the Anglo-Norman-French word "corbet," meaning little crow.

Famous **Bearers:** HENRY WINSLOW CORBETT (1827–1903) of Massachusetts was a merchant, banker, and railroad promoter, and a U.S. senator from Oregon (1867–1873). JAMES JOHN CORBETT (1866–1933) of California, known as "Gentleman Jim," was a boxer who defeated John L. Sullivan in 1892, then lost to Robert Fitzsimmons in 1897.

Genealogies: *The Corbett Family in England and America* was compiled by Henry R. Corbett and published in Kenilworth, Illinois, in 1915. *The Descendants of Robert Corbett of Weymouth, Massachusetts* was compiled by Melvin C. Corbett and published in Darien, Connecticut, in 1957.

CORBIN, CORBINI
Ranking: 1204 **S.S. Count:** 36,556

Origin: French. Derived from the Latin word "corvus," meaning raven. The name was given to those with shiny black hair or piercing voices.

Famous **Bearers:** MARGARET COCHRAN CORBIN (1751–1800) of Pennsylvania was a Revolutionary War heroine. She fought and was wounded on November 16, 1776, at the battle of Fort Washington, where she replaced her husband at his cannon when he was killed. She was one of the first women to take part in the war. She was also the first woman pensioner of the United States. Her father was killed by the Indians and her mother was taken captive. AUSTIN CORBIN (1827–1896) of New Hampshire was a capitalist and prominent railroad executive in New York. His brother, DANIEL CHASE CORBIN (1832–1918) of New Hampshire, built railroads in the Pacific Northwest and was the developer of Spokane, Washington. HENRY CLARK CORBIN (1842–1909) of Ohio was a soldier and an adjutant general during the Spanish-American War.

Genealogies: *Corbin-Waite-Cooper of Baltimore County and City* was compiled by Dorothy Cooper Knoff and published in Baltimore, Maryland, in 1983. *The David Corbin Family of St. Clair County, Missouri* was compiled by R. Corbin Pennington and published in Colorado Springs, Colorado, in 1970.

CORCORAN (S.S. Abbreviation: Corcor)

Ranking: 1768 **S.S. Count:** 25,380

Origin: Irish. Derived from the Gaelic name Ó Corcra, meaning "descendant of Corcra" (H&H), which is derived from the word "corcair," meaning purple.

Famous **Corcorans:** WILLIAM WILSON CORCORAN (1798–1888) of Washington, D.C., was a banker and a philanthropist who was responsible for the Corcoran Gallery of Art in Washington, D.C. JAMES ANDREW CORCORAN (1820–1889) of South Carolina was a Roman Catholic clergyman who devised the "Spaulding formula" on the pope's infallibility.

Genealogies: None known.

CORDEL, CORDELET, CORDELETTE, CORDELLE, CORDELL

Ranking: 3646 **S.S. Count:** 12,371

Origin: Cordel, Cordelet, Cordelette, Cordelle—French; Cordell—English, French. Derived from the Old French word "corde," meaning string. The names were given to those who worked making cord or string or to those who often wore distinctive ribbons.

Genealogies: *Cordell-Ryan, Hicks-Bradford Families* was compiled by John Cordell Hicks and published in Van Nuys, California, in 1978. *My Family, My Ancestors [the Cordell Family], Myself* was compiled by Robert Rikel Cordell and published in Toms River, New Jersey, in the 1980s.

CORDER, CORDEREY, CORDEROY, CORDERY, CORDERO

Ranking: 1097 **S.S. Count:** 40,262

Origin: Corder, Corderey, Corderoy, Cordery—English; Cordero—Spanish. Corder: transformation of Cordell. Corderey, Corderoy, Cordery: derived from the Old French phrase "cuer de roi," meaning king's heart. The name was given to those who were considered proud. Cordero: derived from the Spanish word "cordero," meaning young lamb. The name was given to those who worked as shepherds or to those who were thought to be lamblike.

Genealogies: None known.

CORDOVA, CORDOVES (S.S. Abbreviation: Cordov)

Ranking: 1372 **S.S. Count:** 32,302

Origin: Spanish. Derived from the Phoenician word "carta-tuba," which is of uncertain meaning. The names were given to those who came from Córdoba, Spain, and may have been taken by those who came from places called Córdoba in Argentina, Columbia, and Spain.

Genealogies: None known.

COREY

Ranking: 2173 **S.S. Count:** 21,087

Origin: English, Irish. Transformation of Cory.

Famous **Coreys:** MARTHA COREY (?–1692) was a victim of the Salem, Massachusetts, witchcraft hysteria. She was hanged on September 22, 1692, with seven others. She was accused by 12-year-old Ann Putnam and the Putnams' maid, Mercey Lewis. Ann Putnam recanted her story in 1706. Corey was buried in a common unmarked grave on Gallows Hill. WILLIAM ELLIS COREY (1866–1934) of Pennsylvania was a steel manufacturer who developed a way to toughen armor plate. He was also the president of U.S. Steel Corp.

Genealogies: *The American Corys* (also the Coreys) was compiled by Vernon Cory and published in Bowie, Maryland, in 1991. *The Corys* (also the Coreys) was compiled by Charles E. Cory and published in Green Valley, Arizona, in 1980.

CORLEY

Ranking: 1863 **S.S. Count:** 24,279

Origin: Irish. Transformation of Curley.

Genealogies: *The Southern Sojourners: Corley-Sanford and Allied Lines* was compiled by Rosemary Corley Neal and published in 1991. *William Corley and David Nolen Descendants of Tennessee and Illinois, 1730–1982* was compiled by Lynette Nolen McCarthy and published in Normal, Illinois, in 1982.

CORMIEAU, CORMIEAUD, CORMIER (S.S. Abbreviation: Cormie)

Ranking: 2060 **S.S. Count:** 22,226

Origin: French. Derived from the Old French word "cormier," meaning sorb tree. The names were given to those who lived near such trees.

Genealogies: None known.

CORN

Ranking: 4537 **S.S. Count:** 9850

Origin: Czech, German, French, Jewish. Czech, German, Jewish: transformation of Korn. French: derived from the Old French word "corne," meaning horn. The name was given to those who worked as horn blowers.

Genealogies: *Corn Stalks and Preachers: A Story of the Corn Family* was compiled by Lois Tincher Dorsey and published in Hendersonville, North Carolina, in 1981. *The Korn (also Corn) Legacy: Two Centuries* was compiled by Jean Millicent Corn and published in Baltimore, Maryland, in 1990.

CORNEL, CORNELL, CORNELS, CORNELIUSSEN, CORNELIS, CORNELISSE, CORNELIUS
Ranking: 605 **S.S. Count:** 68,814

Origin: Cornel, Cornell, Cornels—German; Corneliussen—Danish; Cornelis, Cornelisse—Dutch, Flemish; Cornelius—Swedish. Derived from the old Roman family name Cornēlius, which is most likely derived from the Late Latin word "corna," meaning horn.

Famous Bearers: EZEKIEL CORNELL (1733–1800) of Rhode Island was a Revolutionary War soldier who excelled at the battle of Rhode Island, August 28, 1778. EZRA CORNELL (1807–1874) of New York was a capitalist who, with Andrew D. White, founded Cornell University. ALONZO B. CORNELL (1832–1904) of New York, the son of Ezra Cornell, was governor of New York (1879–1883). KATHARINE CORNELL (1893–1974), a stage actress, was born in Germany to American parents. JOSEPH CORNELL (1903–1972) of New York was a sculptor associated with surrealists.

Genealogies: *A Cornell Family History: from County Essex, England to Winneshiek County, Iowa* was compiled by C. C. Cornell and published in Decorah, Iowa, in 1984. *A Cornell-Hartwell Genealogy: 1302 Years of Family History, Including 348 Years in Westchester County* was compiled by Stephen Wood Cornell and published in Baltimore, Maryland, in 1990.

CORNET, CORNETT, CORNETTE
Ranking: 1959 **S.S. Count:** 23,119

Origin: French. Derived from the Old French word "corne," meaning horn. The names were given to those who worked as horn blowers.

Genealogies: *The Cornett Family* was compiled by Essie Richardson Cornett and published in New York, New York, in 1971.

CORNISH (S.S. Abbreviation: Cornis)
Ranking: 3818 **S.S. Count:** 11,810

Origin: English. Derived from the Old English word "cornisc," meaning Cornish. The name was given to those who came from Cornwall, England.

Genealogies: None known.

CORNWELL (S.S. Abbreviation: Cornwe)
Ranking: 2583 **S.S. Count:** 17,635

Origin: English. Derived from the Old English tribal name Cornwealas, which is derived from the name Kernow, by which Cornish people referred to themselves, and the Old English word "wealas," meaning strangers.

Famous Cornwells: DEAN CORNWELL (1892–1960) of Kentucky was an illustrator and painter.

Genealogies: None known.

CORONA
Ranking: 1431 **S.S. Count:** 31,171

Origin: Italian, Spanish. Derived from the Italian and Spanish word "corona," meaning crown. The name was given to those who lived in a house with the sign of a crown and to those who had shaved a spot on their heads or wore small caps as part of a religious rite.

Genealogies: None known.

CORRAL, CORRALES
Ranking: 2752 **S.S. Count:** 16,564

Origin: Spanish. Derived from the Spanish word "corral," meaning an area for livestock. The names were given to those who lived near such a place.

Famous Bearers: PATRICK CORRALES (1941–) of California was a professional baseball player (1959–1978) and a professional baseball manager of the Texas Rangers, Philadelphia Phillies, and Cleveland Indians.

Genealogies: None known.

CORREA, CORREAS
Ranking: 1341 **S.S. Count:** 32,933

Origin: Spanish. Uncertain etymology. Possibly derived from the Spanish word "correa," meaning leather belt or strap. The names may have been given to those who worked making such items.

Genealogies: None known.

CORREIA (S.S. Abbreviation: Correi)
Ranking: 3878 **S.S. Count:** 11,627
Origin: Portuguese. Cognate to Correa.
Genealogies: None known.

CORRELL (S.S. Abbreviation: Correl)
Ranking: 4561 **S.S. Count:** 9797
Origin: English? Uncertain etymology.
Genealogies: None known.

CORRIGAN (S.S. Abbreviation: Corrig)
Ranking: 2827 **S.S. Count:** 16,132
Origin: Irish. Derived from the Gaelic name Ó Corra, meaning "descendant of Corra" (H&H), which is derived from the word "corr," meaning spear.
Genealogies: None known.

CORTES, CORTESI, CORTESINI

Ranking: 1175 S.S. Count: 37,177

Origin: Cortes—Catalan, Spanish; *Cortesi, Cortesini*—*Italian. 1) cognates to Curtis. 2) Uncertain etymology. The names were given to those who came from Cortes, the name of many places in Spain. 3) Uncertain etymology. The names were given to those who were considered polite and to those who were in the king's court.*

Genealogies: None known.

CORTEZ

Ranking: 897 S.S. Count: 48,267

Origin: Spanish. 1) Uncertain etymology. The name was given to those who came from Cortes, the name of many places in Spain. 2) Uncertain etymology. The name was given to those who were considered polite and to those who were in the king's court.

Genealogies: None known.

CORWIN

Ranking: 4493 S.S. Count: 9977

Origin: English. Uncertain etymology. The name was given to those who lived near a white enclosure or castle.

Famous **Corwins:** THOMAS CORWIN (1794–1865) of Kentucky was a member of the U.S. House of Representatives and secretary of the Treasury who foresaw the imminent conflicts that would cause the Civil War and worked to avert hostilities. EDWARD SAMUEL CORWIN (1878–1963) of Michigan was a political scientist who was an expert on U.S. constitutional law. He wrote several law reviews and books.

Genealogies: *Corwin Ancestry* was compiled by Robert Gillespie Corwin and published in Minneapolis, Minnesota, in 1975.

COSBY

Ranking: 3205 S.S. Count: 14,151

Origin: English. Derived from the Old English first name Cossa and the Old Norse word "býr," meaning farm. The name was given those who came from Cosby, a place in Leicestershire, England.

Famous **Cosbys:** BILL COSBY (1937–) of Pennsylvania is a comedian and actor. He is well known for his nightclub comedy routines, his movie and television performances, and his television series "The Cosby Show." He has received four Emmy Awards and eight Grammy Awards.

Genealogies: *Cosby Family Records* was compiled by Don Simmons and published in Melber, Kentucky, in 1981. *Cosby Genealogy* was compiled by Frank Carvill Cosby.

COSGROVE (S.S. Abbreviation: Cosgro)

Ranking: 3200 S.S. Count: 14,166

Origin: English, Irish. English: derived from the Old English name Cōfesgrāf, meaning "grove of Cōf," which is most likely a first name. Irish: derived from the Gaelic name Ó Coscraigh, meaning "descendant of Coscrach" (H&H), which is derived from the word "coscur," meaning victory.

Genealogies: None known.

COSTA

Ranking: 995 S.S. Count: 44,126

Origin: Catalan, Italian, Portuguese, Provençal, Spanish. 1) derived from the Latin word "costa," meaning side or rib. The name was given to those who lived on a shore or on a hillside. 2) derived from the Latin word "costa," meaning cost or price. 3) derived from the Latin word "costare," meaning to exist.

Genealogies: None known.

COSTANTI, COSTANZO, COSTANZI, COSTANTINO (S.S. Abbreviation: Costan)

Ranking: 2324 S.S. Count: 19,531

Origin: Costanti, Costanzo, Costanzi—Italian; Costantino—Italian, Portuguese. Costanti, Costanzo, Costanzi: cognates to Constant. Costantino: cognate to Constantine.

Genealogies: None known.

COSTEL, COSTELLE, COSTELLO, COSTELLOE, COSTELLOW

Ranking: 889 S.S. Count: 48,875

Origin: Costel, Costelle—French; Costello, Costelloe, Costellow—Irish. Costel, Costelle: derived from the Latin word "costa," meaning side or rib. The names were given to those who lived on a shore or on a hillside. Costello, Costelloe, Costellow: Uncertain etymology. 1) Possibly cognates to Costel. 2) possibly derived from the Gaelic name Mac Oisdealbhaigh, meaning "son of Oisdealbhach" (H&H), which is derived from the words "os" and "dealbhadh," meaning deer and resembling.

Genealogies: None known.

COTA

Ranking: 4872 S.S. Count: 9183
Origin: Spanish. Uncertain etymology.
Genealogies: None known.

COTE

Ranking: 1499 S.S. Count: 29,715
Origin: French. Transformation of Costel.
Genealogies: None known.

COTTER, COTTERELL, COTTERILL, COTTEREL, COTTEREAU

Ranking: 2240 S.S. Count: 20,482

Origin: Cotter—English, Irish; Cotterell, Cotterill—English; Cotterel—English, French; Cottereau—French. Cotter (English), Cotterell, Cotterill, Cotterel, Cottereau: derived from the Middle English word "cotter," meaning a serf who earned his cottage through service rather than rent. Cotter (Irish): derived from the Gaelic name Mac Oitir, meaning "son of Oitir" (H&H), which is derived from the Old Norse name Óttarr, which is derived from the words "otti," and "herr," meaning fear and army.

Genealogies: None known.

COTTO

Ranking: 3415 S.S. Count: 13,244

Origin: Italian. The name was given to those who had names that ended with this component.

Genealogies: None known.

COTTON

Ranking: 904 S.S. Count: 47,716

Origin: English, French. English: derived from the Old English word "cot," meaning cottage. The name was given to those who came from Cotton, the name of several places in England. French: transformation of Cotte(net).

Famous **Cottons**: JOHN COTTON (1585–1652), an English Puritan clergyman, moved to Boston in 1633 and became the head of Congregationalism in America.

Genealogies: *The Cottons of Catahoula and Related Families* was compiled by William Davis Cotton and published in Rayville, Louisiana, in 1987. *The English Ancestry of Rev. John Cotton of Boston* was compiled by H. G. Somerby and published in Boston, Massachusetts, in 1868.

COTTREAU, COTTREL, COTTRELL (S.S. Abbreviation: Cottre)

Ranking: 2051 S.S. Count: 22,299

Origin: French. Cognates to the English definition of Cotter.

Famous **Bearers**: FREDERICK GARDNER COTTRELL (1877–1948) of California invented the electrostatic precipitator, which can remove suspended particles from streams of gas.

Genealogies: None known.

COUCH

Ranking: 1202 S.S. Count: 36,562

Origin: Cornish, English. Cornish: uncertain etymology. Possibly derived from the word "cough," meaning red. The name was most likely given to those who had red hair. English: derived from the Middle English and Old French word "couche," meaning bed. The name was given to those who worked making beds or bedding.

Genealogies: *Sang Branch Settlers [including the Couch Family]: Folksongs and Tales of a Kentucky Mountain Family* was compiled by Leonard Roberts and published in Austin, Texas, in 1974.

COUGHLAN, COUGHLIN (S.S. Abbreviation: Coughl)

Ranking: 1878 S.S. Count: 24,099

Origin: Irish. Derived from the Gaelic name Ó Cochláin, meaning "descendant of Cochlán" (H&H), which is derived from the word "cochal," meaning cloak.

Famous **Bearers**: CHARLES EDWARD COUGHLIN (1891–1979) of Canada was a Roman Catholic priest who hosted a popular radio show advocating radical and social reforms. A supporter of the Pro-Facist Christian Front, he was silenced by church leaders.

Genealogies: None known.

COULTER (S.S. Abbreviation: Coulte)

Ranking: 1555 S.S. Count: 28,645

Origin: Irish, Scottish. Derived from the Gaelic phrase "cúl tir," meaning back land. The name was given to those who came from Coulter, the name of places in Lanarkshire and Aberdeenshire, Scotland.

Famous **Coulters**: JOHN MERLE COULTER (1851–1928) was born in China to missionary parents. He was a botanist and the founder and editor of the *Botanical Gazette*. ERNEST KENT COULTER (1871?–1952) of Ohio was a lawyer who helped organize the Children's Court of New York and who founded the Big Brothers organization.

Genealogies: *The Coulter Family of Catawba County, North Carolina* was compiled by Victor A. Coulter and published in Oxford, Mississippi, in 1975. *Our Coulter Clan and Allied Families* was compiled by Steven Earl Coulter and published in Des Moines, Iowa, in 1970.

COUNCIL (S.S. Abbreviation: Counci)

Ranking: 4170 S.S. Count: 10,835

Origin: English. 1) derived from the Anglo-Norman-French word "counseil," meaning consultation or advice. The name was given to those who were considered thoughtful. 2) derived from the Anglo-Norman-French word "councile," meaning council or assembly. The name was most likely given to those who held a position on a council.

Genealogies: None known.

COUNTS

Ranking: 3343 S.S. Count: 13,550

Origin: English. The name was given to those who worked as accountants and treasurers.

Genealogies: *The Counts Family of Missouri* was

compiled by Hilde W. Beaty and published in Detroit, Michigan, in 1983. *History of the Descendants of John Koontz* (including the Counts Family) was compiled by Lowell Koontz and published in Parsons, West Virginia, in 1979.

COURTNEY (S.S. Abbreviation: Courtn)
Ranking: 1161 S.S. Count: 37,678
Origin: English, Irish. Transformation of Courtenay.
Famous **Courtneys**: CHARLES EDWARD COURTNEY (1849–1920) of New York was the rowing coach at Cornell University (1883–1916).
Genealogies: None known.

COUSIN, COUSINS, COUSINEY, COUSINOT
Ranking: 2109 S.S. Count: 21,758
Origin: Cousin—English, French; Cousins—English; Cousiney, Cousinot—French. Derived from the Old French and Middle English word "co(u)sin," meaning relative. The name was given to those who were related to someone renowned in the area.
Genealogies: None known.

COUTURE, COUTURIE, COUTURIER, COUTURIEAUX (S.S. Abbreviation: Coutur)
Ranking: 3188 S.S. Count: 14,232
Origin: French. 1) derived from the Old French word "cousture," meaning seam. The names were given to those who worked as tailors. 2) derived from the Old French word "couture," meaning small plot. The names were given to those who owned a small piece of land.
Genealogies: None known.

COVERT, COVERTON
Ranking: 3846 S.S. Count: 11,720
Origin: English. Derived from the name of the River Cover and the Old English word "tūn," meaning settlement.
Genealogies: None known.

COVEY
Ranking: 3651 S.S. Count: 12,355
Origin: Irish. Derived from the first name Cobthach, meaning victorious.
Genealogies: *Ancestors and Descendants of Walter Covery, Dutchess County, New York (1750–1834)* was compiled by Mary Lancaster Quist and published in 1961.

COVINGTON (S.S. Abbreviation: Coving)
Ranking: 1222 S.S. Count: 36,126
Origin: English, Scottish. English: derived from the Old English name Cōfingtūn, meaning "Cōfa's settlement"

(H&H), *as it evolved into Covington. The name was given to those who came from Covington, a place in Huntingdonshire, England. Scottish: derived from the Old English first name Colban and the word "tūn," meaning settlement. The name was given to those who came from Covinton, a place in Lanarkshire, Scotland.*
Genealogies: *Covington and Allied Families of the Northern Neck of Virginia* was compiled by Robert Edward Dungan and published in Fredericksburg, Virginia, in 1991. *Covington and Kin* was compiled by Elbert E. Covington and published in Owensboro, Kentucky, in 1980.

COWAN
Ranking: 902 S.S. Count: 47,935
Origin: Scottish. Often of uncertain etymology. In some cases derived from the Gaelic name Eōgann, which may mean "born of the yew" (H&H).
Famous **Cowans**: EDGAR COWAN (1815–1885) was a U.S. senator from Pennsylvania.
Genealogies: *Cowan/Lenox, and Next of Kin* was compiled by Mildred C. Siever and published in Adair, Illinois, in 1976. *The Cowans from County Down* was compiled by John Kerr Fleming and published in Raleigh, North Carolina, in 1971.

COWARD
Ranking: 4826 S.S. Count: 9281
Origin: English. Derived from the Old English word "cūhyrde," meaning one who herds cattle. The name was given to those who worked herding cattle.
Genealogies: None known.

COWART
Ranking: 2870 S.S. Count: 15,853
Origin: English. Transformation of Coward.
Genealogies: *The Ancestry and Descendants of John Cowart, 1816–1882* was compiled by Kyser Cowart Ptomey and published in New Orleans, Louisiana, in 1984.

COWELL
Ranking: 4968 S.S. Count: 9019
Origin: English. Derived from the Old English words "cū" and "hyll," meaning cow and hill. The name was given to those who came from Cowell, the name of several places in England.
Famous **Cowells**: HENRY DIXON COWELL (1897–1965) of California was an American composer who taught at the New School for Social Research and Columbia University. He developed tone clusters and a method of playing directly on piano strings.
Genealogies: *The Cowells of Wrentham* was compiled by Roger Barnes and published in Carmel, California, in 1972.

COWLES

Ranking: 4754 S.S. Count: 9422
Origin: English. Transformation of Nicholas.

Famous **Cowleses:** BETSY MIX COWLES (1810–1876) of Connecticut, a teacher for 40 years, was a champion of women's rights and felt that women deserved equal pay for equal work. She actively opposed prejudice in schools and worked to elevate the lives of African-Americans, women, and children. ALFRED HUTCHINSON COWLES (1858–1929) of Ohio was an engineer and a metallurgist. He and his brother, EUGENE COWLES (1855–1892), were pioneers in electric smelting. HENRY CHANDLER COWLES (1869–1939) of Connecticut was a pioneer in plant ecology who developed the idea of ecological succession.
Genealogies: None known.

COX

Ranking: 67 S.S. Count: 362,607
Origin: English, Flemish. English: derived from the Middle English suffix "-coke," which created pet forms of many names. Flemish: cognate to Cook.

Famous **Coxes:** LEMUEL COX (1736–1806) of Massachusetts was responsible for the construction of the Boston-Charlestown bridge across the Charles River. HENRY HAMILTON COX (1769–1821) of Ireland was a farmer, poet, and a Quaker in Pennsylvania. SAMUEL HANSON COX (1793–1880) of New Jersey was the founder of New York University. HANNAH PEIRCE COX (1797–1876) of Pennsylvania was an active abolitionist. SAMUEL SULLIVAN COX (1824–1889) of Ohio, a lawyer and a politician, was a member of Congress from both Ohio and New York. JACOB DOLSON COX (1828–1900) of Canada was a lawyer and a Union general. He was governor of Ohio (1866–1868) and U.S. secretary of the interior (1869–1870). WILLIAM RUFFIN COX (1832–1919) of North Carolina was a Confederate soldier and a member of Congress from North Carolina (1880–1886). PALMER COX (1840–1924) of Quebec was an illustrator and author of magazine articles and children's books. ROWLAND COX (1842–1900) of Pennsylvania was a patent lawyer who was an expert in trademark and copyright laws. GEORGE BARNSDALE COX (1853–1916) of Ohio helped build the Republican Party in Ohio and dominated it from 1888 to 1910. KENYON COX (1856–1919) of Ohio was the son of Jacob Dolson Cox and a painter and author of books about paintings. JAMES MIDDLETON COX (1870–1957) was a member of the U.S. House of Representatives and governor of Ohio who was known for his advocacy of a minimum wage and workmen's compensation. In 1920, he was the Democratic nominee for U.S. president.
Genealogies: *Ambrose N. Cox, Sr., Descendants, 1772–1972* was compiled by Elza B. Cox and published in Lexington, North Carolina, in 1973. *The Cox-Bates Family and Related Families* was compiled by Ruby Cox Eddleman and published in St. Louis, Missouri, in 1983.

COY

Ranking: 2811 S.S. Count: 16,211
Origin: English. Derived from the Middle English word "coi" and the Old French word "quei," meaning calm and quiet. The name was given to those who were considered to be quiet or understated.
Genealogies: None known.

COYLE

Ranking: 1551 S.S. Count: 28,690
Origin: Scottish, Irish. Transformation of Cole.

Famous **Coyles:** GRACE LONGWELL COYLE (1872–1962) of Massachusetts is best known for her work with settlement houses and other agencies that provided recreation and education for those in need.
Genealogies: None known.

COYNE

Ranking: 2821 S.S. Count: 16,164
Origin: English, Irish. English: derived from the Middle English word "coin," meaning money piece. The name was given to those who worked as coin minters or to those who were considered stingy. Irish: 1) derived from the Gaelic name Ó Cúán, meaning "descendant of Cadhan" (H&H), which is derived from the word "cú," meaning dog. 2) derived from the Gaelic name Ó Cadhain, meaning "descendant of Cadhan," which is derived from the word "cadhan," meaning barnacle goose.
Genealogies: *Coan (and Coyne) Genealogy, 1697–1982: Peter and George of East Hampton and Guilford, Connecticut* was compiled by Ruth Coan Fulton and published in Portsmouth, New Hampshire, in 1983.

CRABTREE (S.S. Abbreviation: Crabtr)

Ranking: 1234 S.S. Count: 35,927
Origin: English, Scottish. Derived from the Middle English word "crabbe," meaning crabapple tree. The name was given to those who lived near such a tree or to those who were considered crabby.

Famous **Crabtrees:** LOTTA (ORIGINALLY CHARLOTTE) CRABTREE (1847–1924) of New York was an actress who performed in American burlesque.
Genealogies: None known.

CRADDOCK (S.S. Abbreviation: Craddo)

Ranking: 3667 S.S. Count: 12,318
Origin: Welsh. Derived from an Old Welsh first name meaning amiable.
Genealogies: *Sketches and Genealogy of the Bailey-Craddock-Lawson Families of Virginia and North Carolina* was

compiled by Betsy Lawson Willis and published in Alexandria, Virginia, in 1974.

CRAFT

Ranking: 1045 **S.S. Count:** 42,013

Origin: English. Transformation of Croft.

Famous **Crafts:** ELLEN CRAFT (1826?–1897) of Georgia was born a slave to her master father and her slave mother. She escaped to the North with her husband, William. With her lighter-than-average skin, she dressed as an ailing, elderly master, and with her husband posing as her slave traveled by boat and train to Boston, Massachusetts, where they attended antislavery meetings. They were tracked down by agents of the plantation, and deportation was attempted but failed. They and their five children escaped to England via Portland, Maine, and Nova Scotia. After the Civil War, they returned to Byran County, Georgia, and bought a plantation. She died in Charleston, South Carolina.

Genealogies: *Our Washburn Heritage: Including Allied Lines Carpenter, Craft, Dickinson, Noble, Rogers* was compiled in Manhattan, Kansas, in 1986.

CRAIG

Ranking: 280 **S.S. Count:** 128,624

Origin: Scottish. Derived from the Gaelic word "crea," meaning steep or sheer rock. The name was given to those who lived near such a rock.

Famous **Craigs:** DANIEL H. CRAIG (1814–1895) of New Jersey was a journalist who used carrier pigeons to send his stories to his newspapers. He was also the president of the Associated Press (1861–66). AUSTIN CRAIG (1824–1881) of New Jersey was a clergyman and an educator and a recognized scholar of the New Testament. THOMAS CRAIG (1855–1900) of Pennsylvania was a college mathematics professor who edited the *American Journal of Mathematics* (1894–1899). MALIN CRAIG (1875–1945) of Missouri was a career army officer who succeeded Gen. Douglas MacArthur as chief of staff of the U.S. army. ELIZABETH MAY ADAMS CRAIG (1888–1975) of South Carolina was a journalist who wrote a political newspaper column under the name May Craig.

Genealogies: *Craig: A Genealogy of the Descendants of James Craig and Mary Blake* was compiled by Daniel Turner and published in Cranston, Rhode Island, in 1977.

CRAIN

Ranking: 1841 **S.S. Count:** 24,575

Origin: English. Transformation of Crane.

Genealogies: *Ten Sons of Oliver* was compiled by Solon P. Crain and published in San Angelo, Texas, in 1972.

CRAMER

Ranking: 1018 **S.S. Count:** 42,946

Origin: German, Irish, Jewish, Scottish. Irish, Scottish: transformation of Creamer. German, Jewish: transformation of Kramer.

Famous **Cramers:** MICHAEL JOHN CRAMER (1835–1898), born in Switzerland, was a Methodist minister and brother-in-law of President Ulysses S. Grant, who appointed him minister to Denmark and Switzerland.

Genealogies: *The Ancestors, Family, and Descendants of William Dickinson Cramer and Abby Springer Cramer* was compiled by Alfred S. Cramer and published in Big Rapids, Michigan, in 1980. *Ancestors of H. Jaquelyn (Sandy) Cramer and William S. Sandy* was compiled by William Allee Sandy and published in Bloomington, Indiana, in 1983. *The Cranes of Oego, Marengo and Monroe* was compiled by Paul R. Austin and published in Newark, Delaware, in 1969.

CRANDALL (S.S. Abbreviation: Cranda)

Ranking: 1903 **S.S. Count:** 23,775

Origin: English. 1) derived from the Old English word "cran(uc)," meaning crane. The name was given to those who came from valleys where cranes lived. 2) the name was given to those who came from Crondall, which means "hollow" (ES) and is a place in Hampshire, England.

Famous **Crandalls:** PRUDENCE CRANDALL (1803–1890) of Rhode Island was a schoolteacher and abolitionist who was jailed for her efforts to educate young African-American girls in Connecticut. CHARLES HENRY CRANDALL (1858–1923) of New York was a poet who wrote for magazines. ELLA PHILLIPS CRANDALL (1871–1938) of New York was a leader in the field of nursing. She worked to develop courses in district nursing. She traveled to lecture and keep in contact with nurses in rural areas.

Genealogies: None known.

CRANE

Ranking: 792 **S.S. Count:** 53,220

Origin: English. Derived from the Old English word "cran(uc)," meaning crane or heron. The name was given to those who were tall or had thin legs or who were considered to look like a crane or heron.

Famous **Cranes:** JOHN CRANE (1744–1805) of Massachusetts was a Revolutionary soldier and was associated with Boston's Sons of Liberty. WILLIAM MONTGOMERY CRANE (1784–1846) of New Jersey was a naval officer who served at Tripoli and in the War of 1812. JONATHAN TOWNLEY CRANE (1819–1880) of New Jersey was a clergyman and the father of Stephen Crane. ANNE MONCURE CRANE (1838–1872) of Maryland was an author whose works were considered immoral by the people of that time. THOMAS FREDERICK CRANE (1844–1927) of New York was a lawyer and teacher at Cornell University. WILLIAN HENRY

CRANE (1845–1928) of Massachusetts was an actor and a comedian. WINTHROP MURRAY CRANE (1853–1920) of Massachusetts was a paper manufacturer who developed the silk-threaded paper that is used to make U.S. currency. CAROLINE JULIA BARTLETT CRANE (1858–1935) of Wisconsin was a Unitarian minister and urban reformer who worked to improve health and sanitary conditions in Michigan. She was responsible for the Michigan legislature's legalization of meat inspection ordinances. She was known as "America's Public Housekeeper." CHARLES RICHARD CRANE (1858–1939) of Illinois was a businessman and a philanthropist. FRANK CRANE (1861–1928) of Illinois was a clergyman who wrote spiritual columns for newspapers. FREDERICK EVAN CRANE (1869–1947) of New York was a lawyer and judge and a justice of the New York court of appeals. STEPHEN CRANE (1871–1900) of New Jersey gave up a career in professional baseball to become a writer. He is best known for his short story "The Open Boat" and his novels *The Red Badge of Courage* (1895) and *Maggie: A Girl of the Streets* (1892). HAROLD HART CRANE (1899–1932) of Ohio was a poet.

Genealogies: None known.

CRANFORD (S.S. Abbreviation: Cranfo)

Ranking: 4202 **S.S. Count:** 10,746

Origin: English. Derived from the Old English word "cran(uc)" and "ford," meaning crane and a shallow place in a river. The name was given to those who came from Cransford, a place in Suffolk, England.

Genealogies: None known.

CRAVEN

Ranking: 1398 **S.S. Count:** 31,726

Origin: English. Uncertain etymology. Most likely derived from a British word meaning garlic. The name was given to those who came from Craven, a place in Yorkshire, England.

Famous Cravens: BRAXTON CRAVEN (1822–1882) of North Carolina was the first president of Trinity College, now Duke University. JOHN JOSEPH CRAVEN (1822–1893) of New Jersey was a physician and inventor. He invented cable insulation for underwater use. As a doctor, he treated Jefferson Davis during Davis's imprisonment at Fortress Monroe. Brothers TUNIS AUGUSTUS MACDONOUGH CRAVEN (1813–1864) of New Hampshire and THOMAS TINGEY CRAVEN (1808–1887) of Washington, D.C., were both naval officers of distinction. Tunis Craven commanded the *Tecumseh* (1863–1864) and went down with her in Mobile Bay. Thomas Craven retired as a rear admiral. JOHN FRANCIS CRAVEN (1875–1945) of Massachusetts was an actor and playwright who acted in his own plays. Among his works were *Too Many Cooks* (1914) and *This Way Out* (1917).

Genealogies: *History of the Beard, Bedichek, Craven and Allied Families* was compiled by Pauline Beard Cooney and

published in Austin, Texas, in 1979. *The House of Cravens* was compiled by Ruth H. McConathy and published in Charlottesville, Virginia, in 1972.

CRAWFORD, CRAWFORTH (S.S.
   Abbreviation: Crawfo)

Ranking: 131 **S.S. Count:** 226,859

Origin: English, Irish, Scottish. 1) derived from the Old English words "crāva" and "ford," meaning crow and a shallow place in a river. The names were given to those who lived in Crawford, the name of several places in England. 2) the names were given to those who had deformed feet.

Famous Bearers: WILLIAM CRAWFORD (1732–1782) of Virginia was a Revolutionary soldier who served on many fronts. JOHN CRAWFORD (1746–1813) of Northern Ireland was a physician in Maryland who felt that infections were caused by parasitic organisms. WILLIAM HARRIS CRAWFORD (1772–1834) of Virginia was a U.S. senator, minister to France, secretary of war, and secretary of the Treasury. GEORGE WALKER CRAWFORD (1798–1872) of Georgia served as governor of Georgia (1843–1847) and secretary of war (1849–1850). THOMAS CRAWFORD (1813–1857) of New York was a sculptor known for the equestrian monument to George Washington in the U.S. Capitol, and for the "Armed Liberty" capping of the Capitol dome. MARTIN JENKINS CRAWFORD (1820–1883) of Georgia was a lawyer, member of Congress, and later a judge on Georgia district and supreme courts. SAMUEL JOHNSON CRAWFORD (1835–1913) of Indiana was a lawyer, Union soldier, and the governor of Kansas (1864–1868). JOHN MARTIN CRAWFORD (1845–1916) of Pennsylvania was a physician who served as consul general in Russia and translated *Industries of Russia*. JOHN WALLACE (CAPTAIN JACK) CRAWFORD (1847–1917) of Ireland was called the "poet scout." He succeeded Buffalo Bill Cody as chief of the scouts in the Sioux Campaign in 1876. FRANCIS MARION CRAWFORD (1854–1909) of Italy was the son of Thomas Crawford and an American author of more than 40 novels, including the trilogy *Saracinesca*. JAMES PYLE WICKERSHAM CRAWFORD (1882–1939) of Pennsylvania was a professor of Romance languages. RUTH PORTER CRAWFORD-SEEGER (1901–1953) of Ohio was a composer and folk-music scholar and teacher. She was married to Charles Seeger and was the stepmother of Pete Seeger. JOAN CRAWFORD (1908–1977) of Texas was a movie actress and dancer who was born Lucille Lesueur. She won an Academy Award for her role in *Mildred Pierce*. Her other well-known movies include *Humoresque* and *Whatever Happened to Baby Jane?*

Genealogies: *Ancestors and Friends: A History and Genealogy* was compiled by William Lusk Crawford and published in Dallas, Texas, in 1978. *Byram-Crawford and Allied Families Genealogy* was compiled by Eunice Byram Roberts and published in Wichita Falls, Texas, in 1976.

CRAWLEY (S.S. Abbreviation: Crawle)

Ranking: 2575 S.S. Count: 17,670

Origin: English. Transformation of Crowley.

Genealogies: None known.

CREAMER (S.S. Abbreviation: Creame)

Ranking: 3800 S.S. Count: 11,878

Origin: English, Irish, German, Jewish, Scottish. English: derived from the Middle English and Old French word "creme," meaning cream. The name was given to those who sold dairy products. German, Jewish: transformation of Kramer. Irish, Scottish: cognate to Kramer.

Famous **Creamers**: DAVID CREAMER (1812–1887) of Maryland was a hymnologist who did a study of John and Charles Wesley's works and was the author of *Methodist Hymnology* (1848).

Genealogies: None known.

CREECH

Ranking: 2420 S.S. Count: 18,720

Origin: English, Scottish. 1) the name was given to those who came from Creech, which means hill and is the name of several places in England. 2) the name was given to those who came from Criech, which means boundary and is a place in Fifeshire, England. 3) Uncertain etymology. The name was given to those who lived near streams.

Genealogies: None known.

CREEL

Ranking: 3941 S.S. Count: 11,460

Origin: Irish. Uncertain etymology. Possibly derived from the first name Raghailleach.

Famous **Creels**: GEORGE EDWARD CREEL (1876–1953) of Missouri was head of the U.S. publicity bureau during World War I. Subsequent propaganda programs were based on his successful publicity campaigns.

Genealogies: *Anywhere I Wander I Find Facts and Legends Relating to the Creel Family* was compiled by Jame Adolphus Owens and published in Warrior, Alabama, in 1975.

CREIGHTON (S.S. Abbreviation: Creigh)

Ranking: 4056 S.S. Count: 11,149

Origin: Scottish. Uncertain etymology. Most likely derived from the Gaelic word "crioch" and the Middle English word "tune," meaning border and farm.

Famous **Creightons**: WILLIAM CREIGHTON (1778–1851) of Virginia was Ohio's first secretary of state. EDWARD CREIGHTON (1820–1874) of Ohio was a builder during the early days of the telegraph system of communication. He also provided the money necessary to found Creighton University in Omaha, Nebraska. He was the brother of JOHN ANDREW CREIGHTON (1831–1907)

of Ohio, who was a philanthropist. JAMES EDWIN CREIGHTON (1861–1924) of Nova Scotia was a philosopher who taught at Cornell University. He edited *Philosophical Review* (1902–1924).

Genealogies: None known.

CRENSHAW (S.S. Abbreviation: Crensh)

Ranking: 1893 S.S. Count: 23,888

Origin: English. Derived from the Old English words "cran(uc)" and "sceaga,"meaning crane and grove. The name was given to those who came from Cranshaw, a place in Lancashire, England.

Genealogies: None known.

CRESPO, CRESPON, CRESPOUL

Ranking: 1859 S.S. Count: 24,350

Origin: Crespo—Italian; Crespon, Crespoul—French. Cognates to Crisp.

Genealogies: None known.

CREWS

Ranking: 1355 S.S. Count: 32,736

Origin: English. Transformation of Cru(i)se.

Famous **Crews**: LAURA HOPE CREWS (1879–1942) of California was a stage and screen actress. She was playing a lead role in *Arsenic and Old Lace* in New York City when she became ill and died shortly thereafter.

Genealogies: None known.

CRIDER

Ranking: 3204 S.S. Count: 14,152

Origin: German. 1) Uncertain etymology. The name was given to those who were considered argumentative. 2) Uncertain etymology. The name was given to those who lived near a field that had been cleared for cultivation.

Genealogies: *Crider from Pennsylvania into Pittsylvania County, Virginia, 1788, Kentucky and Tennessee, Early 1800s* was compiled by Ruth Crider-Drake and published in Ault, Colorado, in 1980. *History of the Kryder [also the Crider] Family: John Kryder (1736–1803)* was compiled by Edward Hemington Kryder and published in Alexandria, Virginia, in 1987.

CRISP

Ranking: 2633 S.S. Count: 17,291

Origin: English. Derived from the Old English word "crisp," meaning curly. The name was given to those with curly hair.

Famous **Crisps**: CHARLES FREDERICK CRISP (1845–1896) of England was a lawyer, a Confederate soldier, and a member of Congress from Georgia.

Genealogies: *Ancestors and Descendants of James Milton Crisp (1834–1925) and wife, Sarah Catherine (James) Crisp*

(1841–1911) was compiled by Orville Bixler Hoy and published in Arvada, Colorado, in 1978.

CRIST

Ranking: 3047 S.S. Count: 14,891
Origin: English, German. Transformation of cognate to Christian.
Genealogies: None known.

CRISWELL (S.S. Abbreviation: Criswe)

Ranking: 3977 S.S. Count: 11,365
Origin: English. Transformation of Creswell.
Genealogies: None known.

CRITES

Ranking: 4511 S.S. Count: 9925
Origin: German. The name was given to those who came from Kreitz, a place in Germany.
Genealogies: *The Ancestors and Descendants of F. A. Marsh and Ivy Crites* was compiled by William R. Marsh and published in Baltimore, Maryland, in 1990. *John and Elizabeth Crites, Pioneer Family of Wisconsin: Their Ancestors and Descendants, 1753–1977* was compiled by Dean G. Crites and published in Elm Grove, Wisconsin, in 1977.

CRITTENDEN (S.S. Abbreviation: Critte)

Ranking: 3784 S.S. Count: 11,920
Origin: English. Derived from the first name Cridela. The name was given to those who came from Criddon, a place in Shropshire, England.
Famous **Crittendens:** JOHN JORDAN CRITTENDEN (1787–1863) of Kentucky was a lawyer and statesman. He served as a U.S. senator, U.S. attorney general, a member of Congress, and as governor of Kentucky. His greatest efforts were spent in trying to keep the Union together during the Civil War. A son, GEORGE BIBB CRITTENDEN (1812–1880) of Kentucky, was a career soldier who fought in the Black Hawk War, in the Mexican War, and on the Confederate side in the Civil War. Another son, THOMAS LEONIDAS CRITTENDEN (1819–1893) of Kentucky, was a lawyer and soldier who fought on the side of the Union in the Civil War. A nephew, THOMAS THEODORE CRITTENDEN (1833–1909) of Kentucky, was a lawyer and the governor of Missouri. He was responsible for breaking up the Jesse James gang.
Genealogies: None known.

CROCKER, CROCKETT (S.S. Abbreviation: Crocke)

Ranking: 675 S.S. Count: 62,062
Origin: Crocker—English; Crockett—English, Scottish. Crocker: 1) derived from the Old English word "croc(ca)," meaning pot. The name was given to those who worked as potters. 2) derived from the Old French words "creve(r)" and
"ceur" meaning to break and heart. The name in this case was given to those who came from places named from these words in Normandy, France. Crockett (English, Scottish): derived from the Middle English word "croket," meaning large curl. The name was given to those who wore their hair in a style with a large curl. (Scottish): derived from the Gaelic name Mac Riocaird, meaning "son of Richard" (H&H), which is derived from the Germanic words "ric" and "hard," meaning power and hardy or brave.
Famous **Bearers:** HANNAH MATHER CROCKER (1752–1829) of Massachusetts was a writer, the granddaughter of Cotton Mather, and an advocate of women's rights. DAVID (DAVY) CROCKETT (1786–1836) of Tennessee gained some recognition for his participation in the Creek War from 1813 to 1815. He served in the U.S. House of Representatives and later went to Texas, where he died when Gen. Santa Anna stormed the Alamo. ALVAH CROCKER (1801–1874) of Massachusetts was a railroad builder, politician, and manufacturer. He was also a member of Congress. CHARLES CROCKER (1822–1888) of New York was a merchant, railroad builder, and capitalist. He was one of the principal builders of the Central Pacific Railroad across the Sierra Nevada Mountains. LUCRETIA CROCKER (1829–1886) of Massachusetts was an educator and school administrator. FRANCIS BACON CROCKER (1861–1921) of New York was an electrical engineer. Known as the "father of American electrical standards," he was partly responsible for the formulation of the National Electric Code. WILLIAM CROCKER (1874?–1950) of Ohio was a plant physiologist who conducted studies on the effects of gases on plants. He also did work on the dormancy and germination of seeds.
Genealogies: None known.

CROFT

Ranking: 2571 S.S. Count: 17,702
Origin: English. 1) derived from the Old English word "croft," meaning an enclosed space often attached to a house. The name was given to those who lived near such a place or came from Croft, the name of several places in England. 2) derived from the Old English word "cræft," meaning craft. The name in this case was given to those who came from Croft, a place in Leicestershire, England.
Genealogies: *James Croft, His Antecedants* [sic] *and Descendants* was compiled by Carol Daun Croft and published in Tacoma, Washington, in 1983. *A Southern Legacy: The House of Croft* was compiled by Robert William Croft and published in Baltimore, Maryland, in 1981.

CROMER

Ranking: 4046 S.S. Count: 11,190
Origin: English? Uncertain etymology. Possibly derived from the Old English word "crumb," meaning crooked or bent.

Genealogies: *Our Fathers Before Us: A Family Journal* was compiled by Jan Sparkman and published in Berea, Kentucky, in 1980.

CROMWELL   (S.S. Abbreviation: Cromwe)

Ranking: 4075 S.S. Count: 11,095

Origin: English. Derived from the Old English words "crumb" and "well(a)," meaning crooked and stream.

Famous **Cromwells:** WILLIAM NELSON CROMWELL (1854–1948) of New York was a lawyer who specialized in giving advice on complex businesses. GLADYS LOUISE HUSTED CROMWELL (1885–1919) of New York was a poet who also did work for the American Red Cross.

Genealogies: *Cromwells of Maryland, Kentucky and Clay County, Indiana: 1667 to 1900* was compiled by Jean Cromwell Price and published in Poland, Indiana, in 1984. *Just Folk: The Crowell (and Cromwell) Family* was compiled by Joyce Parker Hervey and published in Texas in 1984.

CRONIN

Ranking: 1620 S.S. Count: 27,637

Origin: Irish. Derived from the Gaelic name Ó Cróinín, meaning "descendant of Cróinín" (H&H), which is derived from the word "crón," meaning swarthy.

Genealogies: *Descendants of Michael Cronin and Pricillah Pulley Cronin* was compiled by Daniel Cronin and published in Strasburg, Virginia, in 1972. *The Genealogy of John Cronin, Sr. (1862– 1945)* was compiled by Melinda Cronin and published in Mt. Vernon, New York, in 1975.

CROOK

Ranking: 2233 S.S. Count: 20,498

Origin: English. Derived from the Old Norse name and word "Krókr," meaning crook or bend. The name was given to those who were hunchbacks or physically challenged, to those who were considered devious, and to those who lived at a bend in a road.

Famous **Crooks:** GEORGE CROOK (1829–1890) of Ohio was a soldier who worked with the Indians and advocated granting them citizenship.

Genealogies: None known.

CROOKS, CROOKSON, CROOKSHANK, CROOKSHANKS

Ranking: 2788 S.S. Count: 16,338

Origin: Crooks, Crookson—English; Crookshank, Crookshanks—Scottish. Crooks, Crookson: transformations of Crook. Crookshank, Crookshanks: derived from the Scottish words "cruik" and "shank," meaning bend and leg. The names were given to those with a crooked leg and may have been given to those who lived near the river Cruik in Scotland.

Famous **Bearers:** RAMSAY CROOKS (1787–1859) of Scotland was a fur trader who started a trading post in Nebraska, became a partner in Astor's Fur Co., and served as president of the Northern Department. His letters contained a great deal of historical information. GEORGE RICHARD CROOKS (1822–1897) of Pennsylvania was a clergyman who wrote schoolbooks and theological works.

Genealogies: *Records of Stark, Hamilton, Duncan, Crooks, McConnell, Freytag, Seaver, Brandt Families* was compiled by Evelyn Potter Freytag and published in Laramie, Wyoming, in 1973.

CROSBY

Ranking: 769 S.S. Count: 54,743

Origin: English, Irish. English: derived from the Old Norse words "kross" and "býr," meaning cross and farm. The name was given to those who came from places in England that have these words in their names. Irish: transformation of Cross.

Famous **Crosbys:** FANNY CROSBY (1820–1915) of New York was a hymn writer and teacher of the blind at the New York Institution for the Blind. PIERCE CROSBY (1824–1899) of Pennsylvania was a naval officer and the commander of the U.S.S. *Pinola* at the Battle of New Orleans, 1862. HOWARD CROSBY (1826–1891) of New York was a Presbyterian clergyman and reformer. He founded the Society for the Prevention of Crime. JOHN SCHUYLER CROSBY (1839–1914) of New York was a Union soldier, the U.S consul in Florence, Italy, and the territorial governor of Montana (1882–1884). WILLIAM OTIS CROSBY (1850–1925) of Ohio was a geologist. He was the consulting engineer on dams that were built in Idaho, Texas, Iowa, and Mexico. ERNEST HOWARD CROSBY (1856–1907) of New York was an author and social reformer and the son of Howard Crosby. HARRY LILLIS (BING) CROSBY (1904–1977) of California was a singer, songwriter, and actor. He won an Academy Award for his performance in *Going My Way*. An avid golfer, he died on a golf course.

Genealogies: *Ancestors and Descendants of Timothy Crosby, Jr.* was compiled by Paul Wesley Prindle and published in Orleans, Massachusetts, in 1981. *Crosby, a Pictorial History and Genealogy* was compiled by Samuel N. Crosby and published in Mobile, Alabama, in 1982.

CROSS

Ranking: 371 S.S. Count: 104,711

Origin: English, Irish. English: derived from the Old Norse word "kross," meaning cross. The name was given to those who lived near a marketplace or a stone cross. Irish: derived from the Gaelic name Mac an Chrosáin, which is derived from the word "crosán," meaning satirist.

Famous **Crosses:** EDWARD CROSS (1798–1887) of Virginia was a jurist and a member of Congress from

Arkansas. CHARLES WHITMAN CROSS (1854–1949) of Massachusetts was a geologist and petrologist. He prepared the original collection of rocks that was the nucleus of the Smithsonian Institution's petrographic collection. WILBUR LUCIUS CROSS (1862–1948) of Connecticut was a scholar, educator, and governor of Connecticut. He served four terms and was considered a strong and humane leader during the Depression. HARDY CROSS (1885–1959) of Virginia was an engineer who developed the moment distribution method in 1830. SAMUEL HAZZARD CROSS (1891–1946) of Rhode Island was a government official and an educator. He was also a military officer in World War I.

Genealogies: *A Lineal Genealogy of the Wilson Cross Family and Allied Families* was compiled by Lillian E. Good and published in Spring Valley, New York, in 1982. *My Cross and Hand Families* was compiled by Jeanne Hand Henry and published in New Market, Alabama, in 1977.

CROSSLAND, CROSSLEY (S.S. Abbreviation: Crossl)

Ranking: 3096 **S.S. Count:** 14,670
Origin: English. Crossland: derived from the Middle English words "cross" and "land," meaning cross and land. The name was given to those who came from Crossland, a place in Yorkshire, England. Crossley: derived from the Middle English words "cross" and "lee," meaning cross and clearing. The name was given to those who came from Crossley, the name of two places in Yorkshire, England.
Genealogies: None known.

CROUCH, CROUCHER, CROUCHMAN

Ranking: 1212 **S.S. Count:** 36,340
Origin: English. Derived from the Old English word "crūc," meaning cross. The names were given to those who lived near a cross.
Genealogies: *Family Ties of Broyles and Related Families* (including the Crouch Family) was compiled by Mr. and Mrs. John A. Broyles and published in 1979. *Saints and Black Sheep* was compiled by Kenneth Crouch and published in Bedford, Virginia, in 1973.

CROUSE

Ranking: 2297 **S.S. Count:** 19,853
Origin: English. Transformation of of Cru(i)se.
Famous Crouses: RUSSEL CROUSE (1893–1966) of Ohio was a writer. He won a Pulitzer Prize for his play *State of the Union* (1946).
Genealogies: *A Krouse (also Crouse) Family in America* was compiled by Thomas E. Krouse and published in Baltimore, Maryland, in 1992.

CROW

Ranking: 1256 **S.S. Count:** 35,048
Origin: English, Irish. English: derived from the Old Eng-
lish word "crāwa," meaning crow. Irish: 1) derived from the Gaelic name Mac Conchradha, which is derived from the word "cú," meaning dog. 2) derived from the word "fiach," meaning raven.*
Genealogies: *Crowe (also Crow) Family History 1700 to 1972* was compiled by Marjorie Seward Cleveland and published in New York, New York, in 1972. *The Fireside Stories of the Jacob Crow Family* was compiled by James Homer Crow and published in Parsons, West Virginia, in 1979. *Some of the Descendants of Revolutionary Veteran, John Crow, 1740–1830* was compiled by Howard Crosby Smiley and published in Memphis, Tennessee, in 1975.

CROWDER (S.S. Abbreviation: Crowde)

Ranking: 1270 **S.S. Count:** 34,739
Origin: English. Transformation of Crowther.
Famous Crowders: ENOCH HERBERT CROWDER (1859–1932) of Missouri was an army officer, diplomat, and lawyer. He was ambassador to Cuba (1923–1927).
Genealogies: *The Crowder Family Collection, 1200–1982* was compiled by Fredrea Cook and published in Cullman, Alabama, in 1982.

CROWE

Ranking: 1067 **S.S. Count:** 41,290
Origin: English, Irish. Transformation of Crow.
Famous Crowes: FRANCIS TRENHOLM CROWE (1882–1946) of Canada was a civil engineer in charge of the construction of 19 dams in the western part of the United States, two of which were the Hoover and the Shasta.
Genealogies: *Crowe Family History 1700 to 1972* was compiled by Marjorie Seward Cleveland and published in New York, New York, in 1972. *People of Purpose* was compiled by Garland Crowe DuPree and published in Fitzgerald, Georgia, in 1990. *Some of the Descendants of Revolutionary Veteran, John Crow, 1740–1830 (including the Crowe Family)* was compiled by Howard Crosby Smiley and published in Memphis, Tennessee, in 1975.

CROWEL, CROWELL

Ranking: 1711 **S.S. Count:** 26,148
Origin: English. Derived from the Old English words "crāwa" and "well(a)," meaning crow and spring. The names were given to those who came from Crowell, a place in Oxfordshire, England.
Famous Bearers: LUTHER CHILDS CROWELL (1840–1903) of Massachusetts was an inventor who devised the brown paper bag with the square bottom that is used in grocery stores today. He also invented a machine to make the bags.
Genealogies: *Crowel History: or "Footprints in the Sands*

of Time" was compiled by H. Crowel and published in Dayton, Ohio, in 1899.

CROWLE, CROWLEY

Ranking: 984 **S.S. Count:** 44,556

Origin: Crowle—English; Crowley—English, Irish. Crowle: 1) derived from the Old English words "croh" or "crōh," meaning saffron or bend, and "lēah," meaning wood. The name was given to those who came from a now-unknown place in Worcestershire, England. 2) Uncertain etymology. The name was given to to those who lived near a river called Crull, meaning winding, in Lincolnshire, England. 3) cognate to Kroll. Crowley (English): derived from the Old English words "crāwe" and "lēah," meaning crow and wood. The name was given to those who came from Crowley, the name of several places in England. (Irish): derived from the Gaelic name Ó Cruadhlaoich, meaning "descendant of Cruadhlaoch" (H&H), which is derived from the words "cruadh" and "laoch," meaning hardy and hero.

Genealogies: None known.

CRUM

Ranking: 1823 **S.S. Count:** 24,761

Origin: English? Uncertain etymology. Most likely a transformation of Crump.

Genealogies: *Now and Then with Kropffs and Crums* was compiled by Ruth Crum Wells and published in Tucson, Arizona, in 1974.

CRUMP

Ranking: 1557 **S.S. Count:** 28,640

Origin: English. Derived from the Old English word "crumb," meaning bent. The name was given to those who were hunchbacks and phyically challenged.

Famous **Crumps:** WILLIAM WOOD CRUMP (1819–1897) of Virginia was a jurist and the assistant secretary of the Treasury in the Confederacy.

Genealogies: *Collection of the Genealogical Notes on Col. Johannes Snyder and Other Ancestors* (including the Crump Family) was compiled by Barbara Ann Grever and published in 1977. *A Crump on Every Stump: The Crump Family of New Kent County, Virginia* was compiled by Marius Randolph Barham and published in 1986.

CRUSE

Ranking: 3750 **S.S. Count:** 12,078

Origin: English, French. English: 1) derived from the Middle English word "cr(o)us(e)," meaning bold. 2) Uncertain etymology. Possibly derived from the Gaulic word "crodiu," meaning hard. The name in this case may have been given to those who came from Cruys-Straëte, the name of a place in Nord, France. French: derived from the Old French

word "creus(e)," meaning hollow. The name was given to those who lived near such a place.

Genealogies: None known.

CRUTCH, CRUTCHER, CRUTCHLEY

Ranking: 2011 **S.S. Count:** 22,694

Origin: English. Crutch, Crutcher: transformations of Crouch. Crutchley: derived from the Old English and British word "crūc," meaning cross and hill, and the Old English word "lēah," meaning wood. The names were given to those who came from Crutchley, a now-unidentifiable place in England.

Genealogies: *Crutcher Families* was compiled by William Greer Peck and published in Atascadero, California, in 1976. *Descendants of Thomas Crutcher, Died 1722, Essex County, Virginia* was compiled by Elizabeth W. McNamara and published in Baltimore, Maryland, in 1985.

CRUZ

Ranking: 205 **S.S. Count:** 172,602

Origin: Portuguese, Spanish. Cognate to Cross.

Genealogies: None known.

CRUZ R[1]

Ranking: 4101 **S.S. Count:** 11,017

Origin: Spanish. Cognate to Cross.

Genealogies: None known.

CUELLAR (S.S. Abbreviation: Cuella)

Ranking: 3524 **S.S. Count:** 12,799

Origin: Spanish. 1) derived from the Asturian word "collera," meaning wooden collar for cattle to tie them in a stable. 2) the name was given to those who came from the villa of Cuéllar, a place in Spain.

Genealogies: None known.

CUEVAS

Ranking: 1784 **S.S. Count:** 25,214

Origin: Spanish. Cognate to the French definition of Cave.

Genealogies: None known.

CULBERT, CULBERSON, CULBERTSON (S.S. Abbreviation: Culber)

Ranking: 1985 **S.S. Count:** 22,826

Origin: English. Derived from the first names Culbert and Colbert, which both mean cool or bright.

Genealogies: *Descendants and Ancestors of Washington Hardy and His Wife Sophia Culbertson* was compiled by Floyd R. Brisack and published in Tacoma, Washington, in 1971.

[1]The surname Cruz is often the first component in a compound surname, such as Cruz-Rodriguez. The Social Security Administration counts compound surnames as separate surnames anytime a different letter(s) appears within the first six spaces.

CULLEN

Ranking: 1454 S.S. Count: 30,659

Origin: English, Irish, Scottish. English: transformation of Culling. The name was also given to those who came from Cologne, a place in Germany. Irish: 1) derived from the Gaelic name Ó Cuilinn, meaning "descendant of Cuileann" (H&H), meaning holly. 2) derived from the Gaelic name Ó Coileáin, meaning "descendant of Coileán" (H&H), meaning puppy. Scottish: derived from the Gaelic word "cúilan," meaning little nook. The name was given to those who came from Cullen, a place in Banffshire, Scotland.

Famous **Cullens:** COUNTÉE PORTER CULLEN (1903–1946) of New York was considered one of best poets of the Harlem Renaissance. Among his best known works are "Color," "Copper Sun," and "The Ballads of the Brown Girl."

Genealogies: *The Cullens of Sheboygan County Wisconsin, 1850–1900* was compiled by Katherin Cullen King and published in Baltimore, Maryland, in 1986.

CULLIN, CULLINAN

Ranking: 4261 S.S. Count: 10,572

Origin: Cullin—English, Irish, Scottish; Cullinan—Irish. Cullin: transformation of Cullen. Cullinan: derived from the Gaelic name Ó Cuilinn, meaning "descendant of Cuileann" (H&H), meaning holly.

Genealogies: *The Descendants of Dennis T. Cullinan Ennis, County Clare, Ireland* was compiled by Richard D. Kelly and published in Augusta, Maine, in 1976.

CULP

Ranking: 2432 S.S. Count: 18,684

Origin: German, Scottish. 1) Uncertain etymology. The name was given to those who lived at or near a sign of the calf. 2) Uncertain etymology. The name was given to those who came from Colp, which means cow and is a place in Aberdeenshire, Scotland.

Genealogies: *Culp Family History: 1729–1990* was compiled by Barbarta Augspurger and published in Neosho, Missouri, in 1991.

CULPEPER, CULPEPPER (S.S. Abbreviation: Culpep)

Ranking: 3070 S.S. Count: 14,789

Origin: English. Derived from the Middle English word "cullen," meaning to pick or pluck. The names were given to those who worked with herbs or spices.

Famous **Bearers:** JOHN CULPEPER lived in the 17th century and was born in England. He was the surveyor general of Carolina colony in 1671. He led an uprising against the British trade laws in Albermarle colony in 1677, helped form the colonial government, and served as governor (1677–1679). He was tried for treason against the Crown but was acquitted. He planned the city of Charleston, South Carolina (1680). LORD THOMAS CULPEPER (1635–1689) of England was the royal governor of Virginia. At first fair in his rule, he became a tyrant and was removed from office in 1683 because he left the colony without permission. He returned to England and died in London.

Genealogies: None known.

CULVER, CULVERHOUSE

Ranking: 1650 S.S. Count: 27,092

Origin: English. Derived from the Old English word "culfre," meaning dove. The name was given to those who kept doves or to those who had some attribute of a dove.

Genealogies: *Colver-Culver Family Genealogy* was compiled by Valerie Dyer Giorgi and published in Santa Maria, California, in 1984. *Edward Culver, John Porter and Mary Estey: A Line of Descent from Two Puritans and a Salem Witch* was compiled by Marilyn V. Squires Mills and published in Cullman, Alabama, in 1988.

CUMMIN, CUMMINE, CUMMINGS, CUMMINS

Ranking: 258 S.S. Count: 141,735

Origin: Cummin, Cummine—English, Irish, Scottish; Cummings, Cummins—English. Derived from a Breton name that was derived from the component "cam," meaning bent.

Famous **Bearers:** JOHN CUMMINGS (1785–1867) of Massachusetts was a leather tanner who modernized the industry. THOMAS SEIR CUMMINGS (1804–1894) of England was a painter who taught at the University of the City of New York. JOSEPH CUMMINGS (1817–1890) of Maine was a Methodist clergyman and the president of several universities. GEORGE DAVID CUMMINS (1822–1876) of Delaware founded the Reformed Episcopal Church. MARIA SUSANNA CUMMINS (1827–1866) of Massachusetts was a successful author. CHARLES AMOS CUMMINGS (1833–1905) of Massachusetts was an architect. JONATHAN CUMMINGS (1850?–1860) organized the Advent Christian Church. ALBERT BAIRD CUMMINS (1850–1926) of Pennsylvania was the governor of Iowa (1901–1908) and a U.S. senator (1909–1926). EDWARD CUMMINGS (1861–1926), whose place of birth is unknown, was a Unitarian minister, student, and worker in social ethics whose work was centered in Boston. HOMER STILLE CUMMINGS (1870–1956) of Illinois was a lawyer and politician who drafted President Franklin Roosevelt's plan to "pack" the Supreme Court. EDWARD ESTLIN (E.E.) CUMMINGS (1894–1962) of Massachusetts was a poet known for his eccentric use of punctuation and phrasing. Among his best known books of verse are *Tulips and Chimneys* and *XLI Poems* and *&*.

Genealogies: Ancestors and Descendants [including the Cummings Family] of James Comins was compiled by Lucia B. Comins and published in Amenia, New York, in 1965. *The History and Genealogy of the Cummins (also Cummings) Family* was compiled by Nora B. Cummins and published in Seattle, Washington, in 1958.

CUNDIFF   (S.S. Abbreviation: Cundif)
Ranking: 4953 S.S. Count: 9048
Origin: English. Uncertain etymology. The name was given to those who lived in a valley or on a cliff.
Genealogies: None known.

CUNNINGHAM, CUNNINGHAME, CUNNINGTON   (S.S. Abbreviation: Cunnin)
Ranking: 175 S.S. Count: 191,384
Origin: Cunningham, Cunninghame—Irish, Scottish; Cunnington—English. Cunningham, Cunninghame (Irish): derived from the Gaelic name Ó Cuinneagáin, meaning "descendant of Cuinneagán" (H&H), which was derived from the first name Conn, meaning leader. (Scottish): Uncertain etymology. The name was given to those who came from Cunningham, the name of a place in Scotland. Cunnington: derived from the Old Norse word "kunung" and the Old English word "tūn," meaning king and settlement. The name was given those who came from Cunnington, the name of two places in England.

Famous **Bearers:** ANN PAMELA CUNNINGHAM (1816–1875) of South Carolina was a pioneer southern clubwoman and founder of the Mt. Vernon Ladies' Association of the Union. Because of a letter she wrote to the women of the South that was published in the *Charleston Mercury*, Mt. Vernon was bought and given as a gift to the people of Virginia. KATE RICHARDS O'HARE CUNNINGHAM (1877–1948) of Kansas was a social lecturer, organizer, and prison reformer who worked to improve prison conditions in California. MINNIE FISHER CUNNINGHAM (1882–1964) was born in Texas. She worked as a suffragist, politician, and community leader. She was the executive secretary of the National League of Women Voters and organized new chapters nationwide. IMOGEN CUNNINGHAM (1883–1976) of Oregon was a photographer known for pictures of plants.

Genealogies: The Cunningham Family: Descendants of John Cunningham, Born About 1782–1786 in Norfolk County, England was compiled by Mary Gene McCall Middleton and published in South Orange, New Jersey, in 1976. *The Descendants of Gabriel Cunningham* was compiled by Joan Pate and published in Troy, Michigan, in 1987.

CUPP
Ranking: 4472 S.S. Count: 10,009
Origin: English. Derived from the Middle English word "cuppe," meaning rounded shape. The name may have been given to those who worked as cup bearers.
Genealogies: None known.

CURLEY
Ranking: 2765 S.S. Count: 16,493
Origin: Irish. Derived from the Gaelic name Mac Toirdhealbhaigh, which is derived from Tor, the name of the Norse god of war, and the word "dealbhack," meaning shaped like.
Famous **Curleys:** MICHAEL JAMES CURLEY (1874–1958) of Massachusetts was a member of Congress, a mayor of Boston, and a governor of Massachusetts.
Genealogies: None known.

CURRAN
Ranking: 1219 S.S. Count: 36,206
Origin: Irish. Derived from the Gaelic name Ó Corraidhín, meaning "descendant of Corraidhín" (H&H), which is derived from the word "corradh," meaning spear.
Genealogies: A Curran Family History was compiled by Shirley Gilbert Mapes and published in 1985.

CURREN, CURRENS
Ranking: 4926 S.S. Count: 9086
Origin: Irish. Derived from the Gaelic name Ó Corraroín.
Genealogies: The Family of Michael Curren and Sarah Crawford of Columbiana County, Ohio was compiled by J. Douglas Bradshaw and published in Richmond, Virginia, in 1989.

CURRIE
Ranking: 1132 S.S. Count: 38,894
Origin: English, Irish, Scottish. Transformation of Curry.
Genealogies: None known.

CURRY
Ranking: 382 S.S. Count: 101,958
Origin: English, Irish, Scottish. English: Uncertain etymology. The name was given to those who lived near the river Curry in Somerset, England. Irish: 1) transformation of Cory. 2) derived from the Gaelic name Ó Corra, meaning "descendant of Corra" (H&H), which is derived from the word "corr," meaning spear. Scottish: 1) derived from the Gaelic word "coire," meaning cauldron. The name was given to those who came from Corrie, the name of several places in Scotland. 2) possibly derived from the Gaelic word "currach," meaning marsh. The name was given to those who came from Currie, a place in Scotland.
Famous **Currys:** GEORGE LAW CURRY (1820–1878) of Pennsylvania was the territorial governor of Oregon

(1854–1859). He also founded the *Oregon Free Press*. JABEZ LAMAR MONROE CURRY (1825–1903) of Georgia was a statesman, author, and educator who worked with the Peabody Fund, the Slater Fund, and as supervising director of the Southern Education Board. JOHN STEUART CURRY (1897–1946) of Kansas was a painter whose work is known for its portrayal of the social attitudes of the 1930s. One of his murals is in the state capitol in Topeka, Kansas.

Genealogies: A Compilation of the Data Relating to the Descendants of William Curry and Charity Lockwood was compiled by Margaret A. Knapp Stevenson and published in East Aurora, New York, in 1977. *Curry Cousins, 1785 to 1974* was compiled by Carolyn Reeves Ericson and published in Nacogdoches, Texas, in 1975.

CURTIN

Ranking: 3290 **S.S. Count:** 13,787
Origin: English, Irish, Scottish. English: derived from the Old French and Middle English word "curt," meaning short. The name was given to those who were short. Irish, Scottish: derived from the Gaelic name Mac Cruitín, meaning "son of Cruitín" (H&H), which means hunchback.

Famous **Curtins:** ANDREW GREGG CURTIN (1815?–1894) of Pennsylvania was a lawyer and politician. He was governor of Pennsylvania (1861–1867) and in 1869 was appointed minister to Russia by President Ulysses S. Grant. JEREMIAH CURTIN (1835–1906) of Michigan was a well-known linguist.

Genealogies: None known.

CURTIS, CURTISS

Ranking: 250 **S.S. Count:** 144,918
Origin: English. 1) derived from the Old French word "curteis" and the Middle English word "co(u)rtois," both meaning refined. The names were given to those who were considered refined. 2) derived from the Middle English words "curt" and "hose," meaning short and leggings. The name was given to those who were considered to be short or to those who wore short stockings.

Famous **Bearers:** GEORGE CURTIS (1796–1856) of Massachusetts was a banker who wrote the constitution for the New York Clearing House. His son, GEORGE WILLIAM CURTIS (1924–1892) of Rhode Island, was an author and orator who was editor of *Harper's Weekly* (1863–1892). SAMUEL RYAN CURTIS (1805–1866) of New York was a soldier, lawyer, and engineer. He contributed to many railroad and river construction projects; as a soldier, he was victorious at the battle of Pea Ridge in Arkansas against the Confederates. MOSES ASHLEY CURTIS (1808–1872) of Massachusetts was a botanist who made many contributions through his work with fungi. BENJAMIN ROBBINS CURTIS (1809–1874) of Massachusetts was a jurist. He was a member of the U.S. Supreme Court and dissented in the Dred Scott case.

GEORGE TICKNOR CURTIS (1812–1894) of Massachusetts was a lawyer who was associated with the Dred Scott case and was the author of *Constitutional History of the United States*. ALFRED ALLEN CURTIS (1831–1908) of Maryland was the Roman Catholic bishop of Wilmington, Delaware (1886–1896). CYRUS HERMANN KOTZSCHMAR CURTIS (1850–1933) of Maine was the publisher of *Ladies' Home Journal* and the *Saturday Evening Post*. NATALIE CURTIS (1851–1921) of New York was a student of Indian and Negro music. She recorded native Indian music, visited reservations, and had the ban lifted against the singing of Indian songs in reservation schools. She co-founded the Music School Settlement for Colored People in Harlem in 1911. CHARLES CURTIS (1860–1936) of the Kansas Territory was the 31st vice president of the United States under President Herbert Hoover. EDWARD SHERIFF CURTIS (1868–1952) of Wisconsin was a photographer, especially of American Indians. HEBER DOUST CURTIS (1872–1942) of Michigan was an astrophysicist who did research on extragalactic nebulas.

Genealogies: *Ancestors and Descendants of James Curtis of Bristol, Maine and Noah Curtis of Woodstock, Maine* was compiled by Harold Curtis Pickwick and published in Lisbon, New Hampshire. *A Family Named Curtis: Descendants of Thomas Curtis of Wethersfield, Connecticut, 1598–1982* was compiled by Rose Mary Goodwin and published in Sunland, California, in 1983.

CUSHING (S.S. Abbreviation: Cushin)

Ranking: 4177 **S.S. Count:** 10,818
Origin: English. Transformation of Cousin.

Famous **Cushings:** THOMAS CUSHING (1725–1788) of Massachusetts was a merchant and a politician. He was active in Massachusetts politics and was a member of the First and Second Continental congresses. WILLIAM CUSHING (1732–1810) of Massachusetts was a jurist. He administered the oath of office at President George Washington's second inauguration. JOHN PERKINS CUSHING (1787–1862) of Massachusetts was a merchant who made his fortune in China (1803–1830). CALEB CUSHING (1800–1879) of Massachusetts was a statesman who served in the House of Representatives (1835–1843). Although opposed to slavery, he sided with Massachusetts Whigs who believed that the North should not interfere with the affairs of the South. He felt that the Union was more important than the abolition of slavery. He worked for a compromise to keep the states as one. After the war, he worked as the head of the committee that codified the U.S. statutes and was the main negotiator of the Alabama claims. From 1873 to 1877 he served as minister to Spain. LUTHER STEARNS CUSHING (1803–1856) of Massachusetts was a jurist who served in the Massachusetts General Court. WILLIAM BARKER CUSHING (1842–1874) of Wisconsin was a Civil War naval officer. HARVEY WILLIAMS CUSHING (1869–1939) of Ohio was a neurological surgeon of great renown. He received a Pulitzer Prize in 1925 for the biography of his longtime associate Dr. William Osler, titled *The Life of Sir William Osler*.

Genealogies: *The Genealogy of the Cushing Family, an Account of the Ancestors and Descendants of the Matthew Cushing, Who Came to America in 1638* was compiled by James Stevenson Cushing and published in New York, New York, in 1979.

CUSHMAN   (S.S. Abbreviation: Cushma)
Ranking: 4244 S.S. Count: 10,609

Origin: English. Uncertain etymology. The name was given to those who worked making thigh armour or cuish.

Famous **Cushmans:** ROBERT CUSHMAN (1579–1625) of England, along with John Carver, financially arranged for the Pilgrims' migration to America. JOSHUA CUSHMAN (1761–1834) of Massachusetts was a clergyman who served as a member of Congress from both Massachusetts and Maine. GEORGE HEWITT CUSHMAN (1814–1876) of Connecticut was a painter of miniatures. CHARLOTTE SAUNDERS CUSHMAN (1816–1876) of Massachusetts was the first U.S.-born stage star. She starred in Mozart's opera *The Marriage of Figaro, Oliver Twist,* and *Macbeth*. SUSAN WEBB CUSHMAN (1822–1859) was an actress and the younger sister of Charlotte Cushman. PAULINE CUSHMAN (1833–1893) of Louisiana was an actress and a spy for the Union. ALLERTON STEWARD CUSHMAN (1867–1930) of Italy was a chemist and the founder and director of the Institute of Industrial Research in Washington, D.C. VERA CHARLOTTE SCOTT CUSHMAN (1876–1946) of Illinois was the organizer and leader of the Y.W.C.A. JOSEPH AUGUSTINE CUSHMAN (1881–1949) of Massachusetts was a micropaleontologist.

Genealogies: *Pilgrims of the Fruitbelt: A Cushman Genealogy* was compiled by Martelle L. Cushman and published in Lansing, Michigan, in 1980. *Farewell to Youth: The Diary of Margery Cushman* was compiled by Margery Cushman and published in Lafayette, Louisiana, in 1982.

CUSTER, CUSTERS, CUSTERSON
Ranking: 3063 S.S. Count: 14,816

Origin: Custer—German; Custers—Dutch; Custerson—English. Custer, Custers: derived from the German word "Küster," meaning church warden or sexton. The names were given to those who worked as such. Custerson: derived from Latin first name Constatia, meaning steadfastness. The name was given to those who came from Coutances, a place in Normandy, France.

Famous **Bearers:** GEORGE ARMSTRONG CUSTER (1839–1876) of Ohio distinguished himself as a Union officer during the Civil War. Later, his famous "last stand" took place at the Little Big Horn River in Montana in a battle against Sitting Bull's men.

Genealogies: None known.

CUTLER
Ranking: 2071
Origin: Number: 22,135
Origin: English, Jewish. English: derived from the Middle English and Old French words "co(u)tel" and "co(u)teau," both meaning knife. The name was given to those who worked making knifes. Jewish: cognate to Kessel.

Famous **Cutlers:** TIMOTHY CUTLER (1684–1765) of Massachusetts was a clergyman and the rector of Yale College (1719–1722) and of Christ Church, Boston (1723–1765). MANASSEH CUTLER (1752–1823) of Connecticut was a Congregational clergyman and a botanist. He prepared the first systematic account of New England flora. He also founded the Ohio Company, which bought 1.5 million acres of land at the junction of the Ohio and Muskingum rivers from Congress at a cost of about eight cents per acre. HANNAH MARIE CONANT TRACY CUTLER (1815–1896) of Massachusetts was a women's rights leader and physician. She is known for her work in the area of legal rights for married women. She worked with Lucy Stone to organize the American Woman Suffrage Association. CARROLL CUTLER (1829–1894) of New Hampshire was an educator and the president of Western Reserve College (now University). LIZZIE PETIT CUTLER (1831–1902) of Virginia wrote *Light and Darkness, a Story of Fashionable Life*. JAMES GOOLD CUTLER (1848–1927) of New York was the inventor of the mail chute used in modern office buildings. ELLIOTT CARR CUTLER (1888–1947) of Maine was a surgeon and educator who played a role in the development of the medical school at Western Reserve University.

Genealogies: None known.

CYR
Ranking: 2868 S.S. Count: 15,866

Origin: English. 1) derived from the first name Cyr, meaning teacher. 2) same derivation as in 1. The name was given to those who came from St. Cyr, a place in France.

Genealogies: *Madwaskan Heritage* was compiled by Leo G. Cyr and published in Washington, D.C., in the 1980s.

DABNEY

Ranking: 4336 S.S. Count: 10,328

Origin: English. Derived from the preposition "de," meaning from, and the Gallo-Roman first name Albinius. The name was given to those who came from places that obtained their names from the name Albinius.

Famous **Dabneys:** RICHARD DABNEY (1787–1825) of Virginia was a poet whose works were published in two volumes of *Poems* (1812, 1815). THOMAS SMITH GREGORY DABNEY (1798–1885) was a planter who moved to Hinds County, Mississippi, in 1835. He was a well-known example of the southern gentleman. ROBERT LEWIS DABNEY (1820–1898) of Virginia was a theologian who taught at Union Theological Seminary and the University of Texas. He was a great defender of the Confederate cause. VIRGINUS DABNEY (1835–1894) of Virginia was the son of Thomas. An author, he wrote *The Story of Don Miff* (1886). CHARLES WILLIAM DABNEY (1855–1945) of Virginia was the president of the University of Tennessee and the director of its agricultural experimentation station. Under his leadership the university became a modern coeducational institution.

Genealogies: The Descendants of John Bass Dabney and Roxa Lewis Dabney was compiled by Alice Forbes Howland and published in Milton, Massachusetts, in 1966.

DAGOSTINO, D'AGOSTINO (S.S. Abbreviation: Dagost)

Ranking: 3660 S.S. Count: 12,335

Origin: Italian. Derived from the first name Augustine, meaning majestic or exalted.

Genealogies: None known.

DAHL

Ranking: 1450 S.S. Count: 30,731

Origin: Danish, German, Swedish. Cognate to Dale.

Famous **Dahls:** THEODOR HALVORSON DAHL (1845–1923) of Norway was a Lutheran clergyman who became a missionary among the Norwegians of the Midwest. He was instrumental in the founding of the United Norwegian Lutheran Church of America. GEORGE DAHL (1881–1962) of Illinois was a professor of the Hebrew language and its literature. ROALD DAHL (1916–1990) of Wales was an author of both children's and adult literature, including *Charlie and the Chocolate Factory* and *Tales of the Unexpected.* He then branched out into writing plays and screenplays, including *Willie Wonka and the Chocolate Factory* and *Chitty Chitty Bang Bang.* THOMAS MOORE DAHL (1918–1986) of Minnesota was an engineering and construction company leader.

Genealogies: None known.

DAIGLE

Ranking: 2472 S.S. Count: 18,344

Origin: German. Derived from the first name Dago.

Genealogies: The Daigle Family: Acadia to Valence was compiled by Ethel Tregre Daigle and published in Thibodaux, Louisiana, in 1991.

DAILEY

Ranking: 956 S.S. Count: 45,437

Origin: Irish. Transformation of Daly.

Genealogies: None known.

DAILY

Ranking: 2968 S.S. Count: 15,324

Origin: Irish. Transformation of Daly.

Famous **Dailys:** JOSEPH EARL DAILY (1888–1965) of Illinois was the chief justice of the Illinois Supreme Court.

Genealogies: None known.

DALE

Ranking: 1066 S.S. Count: 41,317

Origin: English. Derived from the Middle English word "dale," meaning valley. The name was given to those who came from places that had Dale as part of their names.

Famous **Dales:** SIR THOMAS DALE (?–1619) was marshal of Virginia (1611–1616). He ruled with a stern hand and was not well liked by the colonists, but Virginia prospered under his rule. He died in India. RICHARD DALE (1756–1826) of Virginia was taken prisoner by the British during the Revolutionary War. He escaped in England and returned to the United States to continue his military service. SAMUEL DALE (1772–1841) of Virginia was a pioneer and a soldier. He was a guide for immigrants who wished to settle in Mississippi. Later in life he was a statesman from both Alabama and Mississippi. PORTER HINMAN DALE (1867–1935) was a U.S. representative and U.S. senator from Vermont. MAUD MURRAY THOMPSON DALE (1875–1953) of New York and her second husband CHESTER DALE (1883–1962) of New York were art collectors. He also served as trustee at the major art museums of the time.

Genealogies: The Dales of Eastern Shore, Maryland, and Tennessee was compiled by Clarice G. Neal and published in Austin, Texas, in 1986.

DALESSANDRO, D'ALESSANDRO (S.S. Abbreviation: Daless)

Ranking: 3954 S.S. Count: 11,438

Origin: Italian. Derived from the first name Alexander, meaning helper or defender of man.

Genealogies: None known.

DALEY

Ranking: 1388   **S.S. Count:** 31,936

Origin: Irish. Transformation of Daly.

Famous **Daleys:** JOHN JAY DALEY (1888–1976) of Washington, D.C., was drama editor for 10 years at the *Washington Post* and also wrote a humor column for the *Post.* But he is well known for a poem he wrote while he was editor at the *New Britain* (Connecticut) *Herald* called "Toast to the Flag." The poem was published in many textbooks for generations of schoolchildren to memorize. RICHARD JOSEPH DALEY (1902–1976) was mayor of Chicago from 1955 until his death. He was considered the last of the big-city bosses. His administration was criticized for sluggishness in halting racial segregation and its handling of the demonstrations during the Democratic National Convention in 1968. JOHN PHILLIPS DALEY (1910–1963) of Washington, D.C., was a career army officer who rose through the ranks to the level of lieutenant general. He taught at war colleges and the military academy and served overseas.

Genealogies: None known.

DALLAS

Ranking: 3769   **S.S. Count:** 12,021

Origin: English, Scottish. English: derived from the Old English words "dæl" and "hūs," meaning valley and house. The name was given to those who lived in a house in a valley and to those who came from places that obtained their names from these words. Scottish: possibly derived from the British words "dol" and "gwas," meaning meadow and dwelling. The name was given to those who came from Dallas, a place in Scotland.

Famous **Dallases:** ALEXANDER JAMES DALLAS (1759–1817), born in Jamaica to Scottish parents, was U.S. secretary of the Treasury, where he restored public credit, favored a national banking institution, and advanced the concept of a protective tariff. GEORGE MIFFLIN DALLAS (1792–1864) of Pennsylvania was a minister to Russia and Great Britian, a U.S. senator, and U.S. vice president under President James K. Polk. TREVANION BARLOW DALLAS (1843– ?) of Washington, D.C., served under General Bragg in the Civil War, rising to the grade of captain. He also fought in the Prussian army in the Prussian-Austrian War. Eventually he became a cotton manufacturer with mills in Nashville, Tennessee, and Huntsville, Alabama.

Genealogies: *Families of Dallas, Lourens, Rogers, and Some of Their Relatives* was compiled by Zella Rogers Dallas and published in Enon, Ohio, in 1984. *The Family Directory: With Listings on Barefield/Barfield, Dallas, Davis, Gilley, Holley, Newsom, Spinks, and Stark* was compiled by Doris Barfield Sanders and published in Burnet, Texas, in the 1980s.

DALRYMPLE   (S.S. Abbreviation: Dalrym)

Ranking: 4565   **S.S. Count:** 9781

Origin: Scottish. Possibly derived from the Gaelic phrase "dail chruim puill," meaning "field of the crooked stream" (H&H). The name was given to those who came from Dalrymple, a place in the former county of Ayrs.

Genealogies: None known.

DALTON

Ranking: 602   **S.S. Count:** 69,058

Origin: English, Norman. English: derived from the Old English words "dæl" and "tūn," meaning valley and settlement. The name was given to those who came from Dalton, the name of several places in England. Norman: derived from the preposition "de," meaning from, and the place name Autun.

Famous **Daltons:** JOHN CALL DALTON (1825–1889) of Massachusetts was a physician and the first one known to devote his life to experimental physiology. ROBERT DALTON (1867–1892) of Missouri, along with his brothers Grattan and Emmet, was a notorious train robber. He began as a horse thief in Kansas prior to 1890. As a group, the Daltons were as well known as the James gang. JOHN NICHOLS DALTON (1931–1986) of Virginia was a lawyer and a governor of Virginia.

Genealogies: *Dalton Gang Days* was compiled by Frank Forrest Latta and published in Santa Cruz, California, in 1976.

DALY

Ranking: 944   **S.S. Count:** 45,875

Origin: Irish. Derived from the Gaelic name Ó Dálaigh, meaning "descendant of Dálach" (H&H), which is derived from the word "dál," meaning assembly.

Famous **Dalys:** CHARLES PATRICK DALY (1816–1899) of New York was a judge and legal adviser to President Abraham Lincoln. JOHN AUGUSTIN DALY (1838–1899) of North Carolina was a playwright and the author of *Under the Gaslight.* He was the owner of Daly's Theater in New York, which had the reputation of showing only tasteful plays. MARCUS DALY (1841–1900), born in Ireland, was a successful miner in California. He founded the city of Anaconda, developed many businesses there, including the Anaconda Copper Mining Co., and published the *Anaconda Standard.* REGINALD ALDWORTH DALY (1871–1957) of Canada was a well-respected authority on geology, with his area of expertise being igneous rocks. He wrote several books on the subject. PETER CHRISTOPHER ARNOLD DALY (1875–1927) of New York was an actor involved with George Bernard Shaw's plays in the New York theater.

Genealogies: None known.

D'AMATO

Ranking: 4984   S.S. Count: 8998

Origin: Italian. Derived from the Old French first name Amé, meaning beloved.

Genealogies: None known.

DAMIAN, DAMIANI, DAMIANO

Ranking: 4779   S.S. Count: 9370

Origin: Damian—French, Italian, German; Damiani, Damiano—Italian. Derived from the Latin first name Damiānus, which was most likely derived from the Greek word "damān," meaning to take or kill.

Genealogies: None known.

D'AMICO

Ranking: 2485   S.S. Count: 18,247

Origin: Italian. Derived from the Old French first name Amis, meaning friend.

Genealogies: None known.

DAMON

Ranking: 4454   S.S. Count: 10,062

Origin: English. Transformation of Damian.

Famous **Damons:** RALPH SHEPHERD DAMON (1897–1956) of New Hampshire was a pioneer in the commerical airline industry. TERRY ALLEN DAMON (1930–1984) of Washington, D.C., was a naval officer who was decorated four times. CATHRYN DAMON (?–1987) of Washington was an actress of stage and screen. She is probably best remembered for her role in the TV soap opera spoof named "Soap."

Genealogies: *Genealogy of a Demmon (also Damon) and Allied Families* was compiled by Elwood Leonard Demmon and published in Asheville, North Carolina, in 1976.

DAMRON

Ranking: 4133   S.S. Count: 10,943

Origin: French. Uncertain etymology. The name was given to those who were young and feeble.

Genealogies: None known.

DANFORD, DANFORTH   (S.S. Abbreviation: Danfor)

Ranking: 4280   S.S. Count: 10,495

Origin: English. 1) derived from Old English words "denu" and "ford," meaning valley and a shallow place in a river. The names were given to those who came from Denford, a place in Berkshire, England. 2) derived from an uncertain first component meaning concealed, combined with the Old English word "ford," meaning a shallow place in a river. The names were given to those who came from Danford, a place in Suffolk, England.

Famous **Danforths:** THOMAS DANFORTH (1623–1699) of England was the deputy governor of Massachusetts and a supporter of Harvard College. THOMAS DANFORTH (1703–1786) was a pewterer and the ancestor of the pewter families of Danforth and Boardman in America. CHARLES DANFORTH (1797–1876) of Massachusetts was an inventor and manufacturer. He invented the cap spinner, which is used in spinning frames. He headed the Danforth locomotive building works.

Genealogies: None known.

DANG

Ranking: 4604   S.S. Count: 9708

Origin: Chinese. The name means equal, keep off, political party, and proper.

Genealogies: None known.

DANGEL, D'ANGELO, D'ANGELIS

Ranking: 2547   S.S. Count: 17,836

Origin: Dangel—German; D'Angelo, D'Angelis—Italian. Dangel: transformation of Daniel. D'Angelo, D'Angelis: cognates to Angel.

Genealogies: None known.

DANIEL, DANIELIAN, DANIELSEN, DANIELLS, DANIELS, DANIELLOT, DANIELI, DANIELIS, DANIELLI, DANIELUT, DANIELCZYK, DANIELSKI, DANIELSKY, DANIELKIEWICZ, DANIELSSON

Ranking: 84   S.S. Count: 319,637

Origin: Daniel—English, French, German, Jewish, Polish, Portuguese; Danielian—Armenian; Danielsen—Danish; Daniells, Daniels—English; Daniellot—French; Danieli, Danielis, Danielli, Danielut—Italian; Danielczyk, Danielski, Danielsky—Jewish; Danielkiewicz—Polish; Danielsson—Swedish. Derived from the Hebrew first name Daniel, meaning "God is my judge" (H&H).

Famous **Bearers:** PETER VIVIAN DANIEL (1784–1860) of Virginia was an associate justice of the U.S. Supreme Court. FRED GARRUS DANIELS (1853–1913) of New Hampshire was the inventor of devices for manufacturing steel rods and wire products that made production faster and less expensive. FRANK ALBERT DANIELS (1856–1935) of Ohio was a comedian who performed in the musical comedies of Victor Herbert. ANNIE STURGES DANIEL (1858–1944) of New York was a doctor and reformer who first noticed the relationship between sickness and social environment. She also was the attending physician to the Women's Prison Association of New York, where her reports led to an 1888 law requiring that matrons be employed to supervise female prisoners. JOSEPHUS DANIELS (1862–1948) of North

Carolina was a self-made man who was raised by his widowed mother. He was secretary of the U.S. navy during World War I. WINTHROP MORE DANIELS (1867–1944) of Ohio was a member of the Interstate Commerce Commission and published the textbook *The Elements of Public Finance* (1899). MABEL WHEELER DANIELS (1878–1971) of Massachusetts was the only female composer to have had three different works played by the Boston Symphony. They were "Exultate Deo," "Deep Forest," and "A Psalm of Praise." THOMAS L. DANIELS (1892–1977) of Ohio was a U.S. diplomat in Belgium, Brazil, and Italy from 1922 to 1929, then president and chairman of Archer-Daniels-Midland Co., a major processor of vegetable and marine oils. FRANK ARTHUR DANIELS (1904–1986) of North Carolina was a newspaper executive in North Carolina. DOMINICK VINCENT DANIELS (1908–1987) of New Jersey was a member of Congress from his home state. PRICE DANIEL JR. (1910–1988) of Texas was a justice of the Texas Supreme Court and a governor of Texas. He was the author of several books on Texas government. ELMER HARLAND DANIELS (1905–?) of Michigan was a sculptor and an architect with works to his credit throughout the country. He also designed floats for the Tournament of Roses parade.

Genealogies: *John Daniel, Sr., 1724– 1819, of Essex County, Virginia, and Laurens County, South Carolina: His Virginia Ancestry and Some of his Descendants* was compiled by Christine Gee and published in Columbia, South Carolina, most likely in 1970.

DANNER

Ranking: 3121 **S.S. Count:** 14,565

Origin: German. Cognate to the English definition of Tanner.

Famous **Danners:** EDWARD DANNER (1882–1952) was an internationally recognized inventor of machinery used in manufacturing glass tubing. He held more than 40 U.S. patents. HARRIS LESLIE DANNER (1888–1941) was a chief justice of the supreme court of Oklahoma.

Genealogies: None known.

DARBY

Ranking: 1748 **S.S. Count:** 25,621

Origin: English, Irish. English: derived from the Old Norse words "djúr" and "býr," meaning deer and farm. The name was given to those who came from Derby, the name of places in Derbyshire and Lancashire, England. Irish: 1) derived from the Gaelic name Ó Duibhdhíormaigh, meaning "descendant of Duibhdhíormach" (H&H), which is derived from the words "dubh" and "díormach," meaning black and trooper. 2) derived from the Gaelic name Ó Diarmada, meaning descendant of Difharmait, which is derived from the component "di" and the word "farmat," meaning without envy.

Famous **Darbys:** JOHN FLETCHER DARBY (1803–1880) was mayor of St. Louis and a member of Congress from Missouri. JOHN DARBY (1804–1877) was president of Kentucky Wesleyan College.

Genealogies: *Comfortably Fixed* was compiled by Judith Morgan Darby and published in Weston, Connecticut, in 1990. *A Patterson Family: Also Darby and Stamps* was compiled by Noel Douglas Patterson and probably published in Dallas, Texas, in 1966.

DARDEN

Ranking: 2465 **S.S. Count:** 18,402

Origin: English. Derived from an uncertain first component meaning animal and the Old English word "tūn," meaning settlement. The name was given to those who came from Darton, a place in Yorkshire, England.

Genealogies: *Old Letters, Old Biographies and Old Family Trees of Bourne, Carr, Darden and Allied Families of Virginia, Tennessee and Other States. Allied Families: Gardner, Wilkerson, Polk and Many Others* was compiled by Gertrude Morton Price Katz and published in Tampa, Florida, in 1976. *Spoonbread and Strawberry Wine: Recipes and Reminiscences of a Family* was compiled by Norma Jean Darden and published in Garden City, New York, in 1978.

DARLING, DARLINGTON (S.S. Abbreviation: Darlin)

Ranking: 1529 **S.S. Count:** 29,057

Origin: English. Darling: derived from the Old English word "dēorling," meaning darling or loved one. Darlington: derived from the Old English first name Dēornōd, which is derived from the words "dēor" and "nōð," meaning dear and darling. The names were given to those who came from a place in Durham, England, which was called Dearthingtun in the 11th century.

Famous **Bearers:** WILLIAM DARLINGTON (1782–1863) of Pennsylvania was a botanist who wrote *Florula Cestrica* (1826). HENRY DARLING (1823–1891) of Pennsylvania was a minister and the president of Hamilton College. FLORA ADAMS DARLING (1840–1910) of New Hampshire was an author and founder of women's patriotic societies, including the Daughters of the American Revolution, which she cofounded. She advocated more leisure time for the middle-class woman. SAMUEL TAYLOR DARLING (1872–1925) of New Jersey was an authority on tropical medicine. His knowledge of sanitation made possible the building of the Panama Canal. He also contributed to the world's knowledge of hookworm disease. JAY NORWOOD "DING" DARLING (1876–1962) of Michigan was a national cartoonist who won several Pulitzer Prizes for his work.

Genealogies: None known.

DARNELL (S.S. Abbreviation: Darnel)

Ranking: 1843   S.S. Count: 24,545

Origin: English. Uncertain etymology. The name was given to those who came from Darnall, which means "hidden nook" (ES) and is a place in Yorkshire, England.

Genealogies: Darnall (also Darnell), Spence, Steers, Spangler, Stuckey, Sill, and Brief Accounts of Families Into Which Some Members Married was compiled by Erma Dessie Stuckey and published in Piper City, Illinois, in 1983.

DA SILVA (S.S. Abbreviation: Dasilv)

Ranking: 3018   S.S. Count: 15,059

Origin: Portuguese. Uncertain etymology. The name was given to those who lived in a wood or thicket.

Famous **Da Silvas:** HOWARD DA SILVA (1904–1986) was an actor of both stage and screen who starred in *Oklahoma!, Two Years Before the Mast,* and *The Great Gatsby.* In 1978 he received an Emmy Award.

Genealogies: None known.

DAUGHERTY (S.S. Abbreviation: Daughe)

Ranking: 793   S.S. Count: 53,166

Origin: Irish, Scottish. Transformation of Doherty.

Famous **Daughertys:** JEROME DAUGHERTY (1849–1914) was president of Georgetown University, then chancellor of Fordham College. HARRY MICAJAH DAUGHERTY (1860–1941) of Ohio, a politician who ran Warren G. Harding's political career, is believed to have coined the phrase "smoke-filled room." He served as U.S. attorney general and was tried and acquitted on charges of conspiring to defraud the federal government.

Genealogies: None known.

DAUGHTERY, DAUGHTREY, DAUGHTRY, DAUGHTON (S.S. Abbreviation: Daught)

Ranking: 3474   S.S. Count: 13,001

Origin: English. Daughtery, Daughtrey, Daughtry: derived from the preposition "de," meaning from, and the Old French phrase "haute rive," meaning high river. The names were given to those who came from Hauterive, a place in Orne, France. Daughton: transformation of Dalton.

Genealogies: None known.

DAVENPORT (S.S. Abbreviation: Davenp)

Ranking: 538   S.S. Count: 75,407

Origin: English, Irish. English: derived from a first component most likely meaning to trickle and the Old English word "port," meaning market town. The name was given to those who came from Davenport, a place in Cheshire, England. Irish: derived from the Gaelic name Ó Donndubhartaigh, meaning "descendant of Donndubhartach" (H&H),

which is derived from the words "dubh" and "artach," meaning black and nobleman.

Famous **Davenports:** JOHN DAVENPORT (1597–1670) of England was an American clergyman who developed Puritan sympathies and sailed to Boston after fleeing to Holland. He cofounded New Haven colony in 1638 and with Theophilus Eaton drew up its code of laws. GEORGE DAVENPORT (1783–1845) of England was an American fur trader. He was a frontier settler, an agent of the American Fur Co., and one of the founders of Davenport, Iowa. THOMAS DAVENPORT (1802–1851) of Vermont invented an electric motor in 1834 that he used to power the first electric train. EDWARD LOOMIS DAVENPORT (1815–1877) of Massachusetts was an American actor known for his ability to perform well in both comedies and tragedies but was best known for his character portrayal in Shakespearean works. IRA ERASTUS DAVENPORT (1839–1911) and his brother, WILLIAM HENRY HARRISON DAVENPORT (1841–1877), were both from New York. They were both spiritualistic mediums who were known throughout Europe and the United States but were exposed by Harry Houdini as sleight-of-hand experts. FANNY LILY GYPSY DAVENPORT (1850–1898), the daughter of Edward Loomis Davenport, was born in England and raised in Boston. She was a well-known actress of her time. EUGENE DAVENPORT (1856–1941) of Michigan was the dean of the College of Agriculture at the University of Illinois. HERBERT JOSEPH DAVENPORT (1861–1931) of Vermont was an economist whose posthumous book, *The Economy of Alfred Marshall,* is among the distinguished works in the literature of economics. HOMER CALVIN DAVENPORT (1867–1912) of Oregon was a well-known cartoonist. CHARLES BENEDICT DAVENPORT (1866–1944) of Connecticut was a zoologist and eugenicist. He is responsible for the founding of the Carnegie Institution Station for Experimental Evolution and the Eugenics Record Office in Cold Spring Harbor, New York. RUSSELL WHEELER DAVENPORT (1899–1954) of Pennsylvania was a writer and editor whose works appeared in *Fortune* and *Life* magazines.

Genealogies: *The Davenport Genology: History and Genealogy of the Ancestors and Descendants of the Rev. John Davenport, Founder of New Haven, Connecticut, and of Yale College* was compiled by Robert Ralsey Davenport and published in Cambridge, Massachusetts, in 1982. *The Genealogical and Biographical Records of Hewitt Davenport 1608–1951* was compiled by Howard A. Loveless and published in New York, New York, in 1984. *The Marriage of Catherine & David: A History of Southwestern Pennsylvania Families* was compiled by LaVonne Rae Hanlon and published in Laurel, Maryland, in 1982.

DAVEY

Ranking: 3740   S.S. Count: 12,095

Origin: Scottish. Transformation of David.

Famous **Daveys:** JOHN DAVEY (1846–1923) of England, a tree surgeon who specialized in ornamental trees, was known as the founder of tree surgery. MARTIN LUTHER DAVEY (1884–1946) was a member of Congress and governor of Ohio.

Genealogies: None known.

DAVID

Ranking: 968   **S.S. Count:** 45,162

Origin: Czech, English, French, Jewish, Portuguese, Scottish, Welsh. Derived from the Hebrew first name David, meaning beloved.

Genealogies: None known.

DAVIDS, DAVIDSEN, DAVIDSON, DAVIDSOHN, DAVIDSSON

Ranking: 246   **S.S. Count:** 146,594

Origin: Davids—Dutch, English, Scottish; Davidsen— Danish; Davidson, Davidsohn—Jewish; Davidsson— Swedish. Cognates to and transformations of David.

Famous **Bearers:** WILLIAM LEE DAVIDSON (1746–1781) was a Revolutionary soldier. He was killed at Cowan's Ford in the Catawba River. Davidson College is named for him. LUCRETIA MARIA DAVIDSON (1808–1825) of New York and MARGARET MILLER DAVIDSON (1823–1838) of New York were sisters and child poets. They both died of tuberculosis at tender ages. GEORGE DAVIDSON (1825–1911) of England was a geodesist and a geographer. As an astronomer he operated the first observatory in California. ISRAEL DAVIDSON (1870–1939) of Russia was a professor of medieval Hebrew literature. JO DAVIDSON (1883–1952) of New York was a famous American sculptor known for his sculptures of Woodrow Wilson, General John Pershing, Will Rogers, and Walt Whitman, among others. HERBERT MARC DAVIDSON (1895–1985) of New York was an editor and publisher with a Daytona Beach, Florida, newspaper. IRWIN DELMORE DAVIDSON (1906–1981) of New York was a member of Congress and a justice of the New York Supreme Court. JOHN FREDERICK DAVIDSON (1908–1981) of New York was a naval officer and the superintendent of the U.S. Naval Academy.

Genealogies: *Davidson Family Research and Compilation 1972, Descendants of George and Margaret Dunne Davidson* was compiled by Margaret Davidson and others and published in 1972. *Davidson Genealogy* was compiled by George G. Davidson and published in New York, New York, in 1927. *Davison-Davidson Family Research* was compiled by Mildred F. Roberts and published in Orange, California, in 1971 and reprinted in 1975.

DAVIES

Ranking: 875   **S.S. Count:** 49,426

Origin: English, Scottish. Transformation of David.

Famous **Davieses:** SAMUEL DAVIES (1723–1761) of Delaware was an ordained minister who, with Gilbert Tennent, raised funds for the College of New Jersey (Princeton). He served as its president (1759–1761). ARTHUR BOWEN DAVIES (1862–1928) of New York was a painter of pastoral scenes and allegorical neo-romantic compositions. JOSEPH EDWARD DAVIES (1876–1958) of Wisconsin was the first chairman and vice chairman of the Federal Trade Commission and was also an ambassador to Russia. MARION CECILIA DAVIES (1897–1961) of New York was an actress who was a very close friend of William Randolph Hearst without the benefit of marriage, as he was unable to obtain a divorce from his wife. With him financing her career, she starred in many films of little literary merit. *Citizen Kane* is based on their lives together.

Genealogies: *From the Rhondda Valley to the Clinch River Valley and Beyond: A Genealogy of the Descendants of John Davies* was compiled by Billie Ruth McNamara and published in Knoxville, Tennessee, in 1982.

DAVILA

Ranking: 1121   **S.S. Count:** 39,226

Origin: Spanish. Transformation of Avila.

Genealogies: None known.

DAVIS

Ranking: 8   **S.S. Count:** 1,508,839

Origin: English, Scottish. Transformation of David.

Famous **Davises:** ALEXANDER JACKSON DAVIS (1803–1892) of New York was an architect who designed the New York Custom House. CHARLES HENRY DAVIS (1807–1877) of Massachusetts was a naval officer in the Civil War who commanded a Union gunboat flotilla on the Mississippi River. HENRY GASSETT DAVIS (1807–1896) of Maine was the physician responsible for initiating the use of traction in orthopedics. JEFFERSON DAVIS (1808–1889) of Kentucky was the president of the Confederacy. WILLIAM AUGUSTINE DAVIS (1809–1875) of Kentucky was the postmaster of St. Louis, Missouri, who devised the system of sorting the mail on the trains instead of waiting until the mail reached its destination, thus speeding the system of mail delivery. PAULINA KELLOGG WRIGHT DAVIS (1813–1876) of New York was one of two women who petitioned the New York state legislature for a married women's property law. She also helped to found the New England Woman Suffrage Association. DAVID DAVIS (1815–1886) of Maryland was active in the campaign to elect Abraham Lincoln president. He was a U.S. senator and an associate justice of the U.S. Supreme Court. HENRY WINTER DAVIS (1817–1865) of Maryland was a member of the U.S. House of Representatives and was responsible for Maryland's not joining the Confederacy. He opposed Lincoln's Reconstruction. VARINA ANNE HOWELL DAVIS (1826–1906) of Louisiana was the wife of Jefferson

Davis. After his death she worked as a staff writer on the N.Y. Sunday *World*, which was owned by Joseph Pulitzer, a relative of hers by marriage. JEFFERSON COLUMBUS DAVIS (1828–1879) of Indiana was a Union soldier who seemed headed for a successful career as a military officer until he killed his commanding officer in a Louisville hotel in 1862. ANDREW MCFARLAND DAVIS (1833–1920) of Massachusetts was the author of important papers on the history of banking in the Massachusetts colony. MOLLIE EVELYN MOORE DAVIS (1844–1909) of Alabama was an author of poetry and books, including the child's history of Texas, *Under Six Flags*, and *The Price of Silence*. WILLIAM MORRIS DAVIS (1850–1934) of Pennsylvania was a geographer and geologist who taught geology at Harvard and developed the Davisian system of landscape planning by its "cycle of erosion." ALICE BROWN DAVIS (1852–1935) of Oklahoma was the leader and very briefly the chief of the Seminole Indians. She worked as a liasion between the Seminoles and the U.S. government. CHARLES HAROLD DAVIS (1856–1933) of Massachusetts was an artist whose early works were influenced by the Barbizon school. He settled in Mystic, Connecticut, where his realistic landscapes captured the flavor of southeastern Connecticut. KATHARINE BEMENT DAVIS (1860–1935) of New York was a penologist and social worker who improved penal conditions by identifying offenders in need of separation from others. She abolished striped prison clothing and supressed the drug dealing that was epidemic in the prison structure. ARTHUR POWELL DAVIS (1861–1933) of Illinois was a hydraulic and irrigation engineer. As director of the U.S. Reclamation Service, he was responsible for the building of many dams and tunnels. Some of the dams were the tallest in the world at the time they were built. His works are described in *Irrigation Works Constructed by the United States Government*. JOHN VIPOND DAVIS (1862–1939) of Wales is best remembered as a pioneer in the building of tunnels in New York City. OSCAR KING DAVIS (1866–1932) of New York was a war correspondent during the Spanish-American War. He wrote both fiction and nonfiction and was the U.S. representative at the first Pan-American Postal Congress. ARTHUR VINING DAVIS (1867–1962) of Massachusetts was involved in the making of aluminum that would be inexpensive enough for commercial use. He was the president and chairman of the board of Alcoa Aluminum. JOHN STAIGE DAVIS (1872–1946) of Virginia was a plastic surgeon who developed the "Davis Graft," a technique of grafting that is still in use today. His book *Plastic Surgery: Its Principles and Practice* is a classic. Many of the illustrations in the book were drawn by his wife, Kathleen Gordon Bowdoin Davis. JAMES JOHN DAVIS (1873–1947) of Wales was the secretary of labor under President Warren G. Harding. As a U.S. senator from Pennsylvania he sponsored the Davis-Bacon Act of 1930, which required contractors of federal construction to pay the standard wages of the area. JOHN WILLIAM DAVIS (1874–1955) of West Virginia was a Democrat who ran against President Calvin Coolidge in 1924. OWEN GOULD DAVIS (1874–1956) of Maine was a playwright and the winner of a Pulitzer Prize for *Icebound*. BENJAMIN OLIVER DAVIS (1877–1970) of Washington, D.C., was the first black general in the U.S. army. NORMAN HEZEKIAH DAVIS (1878–1944) of Tennessee was an advisor to Franklin D. Roosevelt and the head of the American Red Cross. DWIGHT FILLEY DAVIS (1879–1945) of Missouri was a U.S. secretary of war, governor general of the Philippines, and the donator of the Davis Cup, an international lawn tennis competition. WILLIAM HAMMATT DAVIS (1879–1964) of Maine was a patent attorney and labor mediator who worked as the government's liaison on the National Defense Mediation Board to curtail slowdowns and strikes. HARVEY NATHANIEL DAVIS (1881–1952) of Rhode Island was a physicist and the president of Stevens Institute of Technology in Hoboken, New Jersey. FRANCES ELLIOTT DAVIS (1882?–1965) of North Carolina was the first black woman enrolled in the American Red Cross. PAULINE MORTON SABIN DAVIS (1887–1955) of Illinois was the first woman appointed to the Republican National Committee and was the director of volunteer services of the American Red Cross during World War II. She was the heir to the Morton Salt fortune. CHESTER C. DAVIS (1887–1975) of Iowa was commissioner of agriculture in Minnesota, then the first administrator of the Agricultural Adjustment Administration under President Franklin Roosevelt. He was in charge of the controversial program to limit agricultural production to raise and stabilize prices by offering subsidies to farmers for acreage not cultivated. STUART DAVIS (1894–1964) of Pennsylvania was an abstract painter known for his colorful paintings inspired by urban scenes. BENNY DAVIS (1895?–1979), possibly of New York, was an American songwriter and the author of "Carolina Moon," "Margie," and "Baby Face," among others. WATSON DAVIS (1896–1967) of Washington, D.C., was a science writer and editor. He was the news editor of *Science News Letter*, which later became *Science News*. Under his supervision the circulation grew 500 percent. He helped create the National Association of Science Writers. ADELLE DAVIS (1904–1974) of Indiana, born Daisie Adelle Davis, was a food writer whose books carried the nutritional message of the 1950s. RUTH ELIZABETH (BETTE) DAVIS (1908–1989) of Massachusetts was an actress. She is best known for her intense portrayals of neurotic women. Her best-known movies were *Of Human Bondage, Dangerous, Jezebel,* and *All About Eve*. She won two Academy Awards. STEPHEN SMITH DAVIS (1910–1977) of Pennsylvania, as dean of the school of engineering and architecture at Howard University, initiated that school's first graduate program in engineering and the first undergraduate program in chemical engineering of any predominantly black institution. HAMILTON SEYMOUR DAVIS (1920–1986) of Pennsylvania was a physician interested in wellness care for babies. He founded and was on the board of directors of the Chagrin Falls Park Well Baby Clinic. EDDIE DAVIS (1921–1986) of New York was a jazz tenor saxophonist who played with the great bands of the 1940s. ERNEST R. "ERNIE" DAVIS (1939–1963) of Pennsylvania was the first black football player to win the Heisman Trophy.

Genealogies: *From the Rhondda Valley to the Clinch River Valley and Beyond: A Genealogy of the Descendants of John Davies (also Davis)* was compiled by Billie Ruth McNamara and published in Knoxville, Tennessee, in 1982. *Amos Williams Davis: Family History, Including His Ancestors and Descendants* was compiled by Eunice Freese Payne and published in 1971. *Ancestors and Kin, Davis, Hicks, Kennedy* was compiled by Mary Kennedy Reynolds and published in Birmingham, Alabama, in 1991.

DAVISON (S.S. Abbreviation: Daviso)

Ranking: 1377   S.S. Count: 32,146
Origin: English, Scottish. Transformation of David.

Famous **Davisons:** GREGORY CALDWELL DAVISON (1871–1935) of Missouri was a naval officer who commanded torpedo boats and destroyers. He is credited with the invention of the balanced-turbine torpedo, nonrecoil guns for planes, and the Y-gun depth charge projector. GEORGE WILLETS DAVISON (1872–1953) of New York was president and then chairman of the board of the Hanover Bank. CLINTON JOSEPH DAVISON (1881–1958) of Illinois was the 1927 winner of the Nobel Prize for physics.

Genealogies: *Davison-Davidson Family Research* was compiled by Mildred F. Roberts and published in Orange, California, in 1971 and reprinted in 1975.

DAWKIN

Ranking: 2487   S.S. Count: 18,219
Origin: English. Transformation of David.
Genealogies: None known.

DAWSON

Ranking: 332   S.S. Count: 113,587
Origin: English. Transformation of David.

Famous **Dawsons:** JOHN DAWSON (1762–1814) of Virginia was a member of the Virginia House of Delegates. FRANCIS WARRINGTON DAWSON (1840–1889) of England was a journalist who came to the United States, volunteered for the Confederate army, and purchased the Charleston (South Carolina) *News*. It later merged with the *Courier*, and he served as its editor. WILLIAM MERCER OWENS DAWSON (1853–1916) was governor of West Virginia (1905–1909). WILLIAM LEVI DAWSON (1886–1970) of Georgia was a political power in Chicago and the only

black member of the U.S. Congress during his first term. He also was the first black elected vice chairman of the Democratic National Committee, and, as chairman of the House Committee on Government Operations, he was the first black to head a standing committee in Congress. CECIL FORREST DAWSON (1893–1960) of Missouri was a manufacturing expert who initiated his company's packaging of ice cream in paper cups in 1923, which led to the nationally advertised product Ice Cream Dixies. The company then was known as the Individual Drinking Cup Co. but later became the Dixie Cup Co., of which he became president.

Genealogies: *Dawsons in the Revolutionary War and Their Descendants* was compiled by Carol Ruth Dawson and published in Eau Claire, Wisconsin, in 1974. *The Families of Ruebsamen, Spear, Dawson, Burley* was compiled by Neil Newayne Ruebsamen and published in Collinsville, Illinois, in 1987.

DAY

Ranking: 247   S.S. Count: 145,506
Origin: English, Irish. English: 1) transformation of David. 2) derived from the Old English name Dey(e), which is most likely derived from the word "dæg," meaning day. Irish: derived from the Gaelic name Ó Deághaidh, meaning "descendant of Deághadh" (H&H).

Famous **Days:** STEPHEN DAY or DAYE (1594?–1668) of England was the first printer in the English colonies in Cambridge, Massachusetts. *The Bay Psalm Book* printed by him was the first book in English printed in the colonies. BENJAMIN HENRY DAY (1810–1889) of West Springfield, Massachusetts, founded The New York Sun, the first "penny" newspaper. JEREMIAH B. DAY (1773–1867) was president of Yale University for 30 years. BENJAMIN DAY JR. (1838–1916) invented the Ben Day process for shading and coloring in printing illustrations. WILLIAM RUFUS DAY (1849–1923) of Ohio was a professional diplomat and an associate justice of the U.S. Supreme Court. HOLMAN FRANCIS DAY (1865–1935) of Maine was a writer whose books included *Up in Maine, Pine Tree Ballads,* and *Ships of Joy,* among others. ARTHUR LOUIS DAY (1869–1960) of Massachusetts was the first director of the geophysical laboratory at the Carnegie Institution of Washington, D.C. CLARENCE SHEPARD DAY JR. (1874–1935) of New York was the grandson of Benjamin Day. He was a writer and the author of *The Simian World, The Crow's Nest, In the Green Mountain Country, Life with Father, Life with Mother,* and *Father and I.* GEORGE PARMLY DAY (1876–1959) of New York was the founder of Yale University Press. EDMUND EZRA DAY (1883–1951) of New Hampshire was an economist and educator. At the University of Michigan, he organized and was the first dean of the College of Business Administration. He also worked with the Rockefeller Foundation and the General Education Board and was president of Cornell University. DOROTHY DAY (1897–1980) of New York was a writer and reformer who, with Peter Maurin, founded the *Catholic Worker,* a monthly paper dedicated to a program of communalism, hospices, and education. She founded hospices in many cities.

Genealogies: *Day unto Day: A Study of the Day Family in America* was compiled by Margery Frances Day Hanson and published in Poultney, Vermont, in 1978. *Descendants of Christopher Day of Bucks County, Pennsylvania* was compiled by James Edward Day and published in Pontiac, Michigan, in 1976.

DAYTON

Ranking: 3791 **S.S. Count:** 11,892

Origin: English. Uncertain etymology. Possibly derived from the Middle English word "diche" and the Old English word "tūn," meaning ditch and settlement. The name was given to those who came from Deighton, the name of several places in England.

Famous Daytons: ELIAS DAYTON (1737–1807) of New Jersey was the colonel of the New Jersey troops in the Revolutionary War; he was promoted to brigadier general on the recommendation of George Washington and later served as a member of the U.S. House of Representatives. JONATHAN DAYTON (1760–1824) of New Jersey, son of Elias, served as a captain in the Revolutionary army and as a member of the Continental Congress and the Constitutional Convention. He also served in the U.S. House of Representatives as Speaker and in the U.S. Senate. The city of Dayton, Ohio, is named for him. WILLIAM LEWIS DAYTON (1807–1864) of New Jersey, was a U.S. senator and candidate for vice president in 1856. As U.S. minister to France, he was responsible for the French's not giving aid to the Confederates during the Civil War. ALSTON GORDON DAYTON (1857–1920) was a member of Congress from West Virginia.

Genealogies: *Family History of the Warren, Stone, Dayton, Routh, Wurster, Daggett, and Young Families* was compiled by Candy Daggett Young and published in Ferriday, Louisiana, in 1983. *Indiana Cousins* was compiled by Louise Axsom and published in Mesa, Arizona, in 1984.

DE LA

Ranking: 446 **S.S. Count:** 89,358

Origin: Spanish. Derived from the words "de la," meaning of the or from the. This is the first part of a surname and is most often followed by a singular noun (e.g., "cruz," meaning cross; "fuente," meaning fountain; "rosa," meaning rose; "torre," meaning tower).

Genealogies: *The Letters of Alfred Robinson to the De la Guerra Family of Santa Barbara, 1834–1873* was compiled

by Alfred Robinson and published in Los Angeles, California, in 1972.

DE LOS

Ranking: 3811 **S.S. Count:** 11,844

Origin: Spanish. Derived from the words "de los," meaning of the or from the. This is the first part of a surname and is most often followed by a plural noun (e.g., "reyes," meaning kings; "santos," meaning saints).

Genealogies: None known.

DEAL

Ranking: 1635 **S.S. Count:** 27,483

Origin: English. Transformation of Dale.

Genealogies: *Deal Family: Descendants of William Deal III, and Thirteen Allied and Collateral Family Lineages of Sherrill, Pepper, Woods, Kirkpatrick, Caldwell, Rutherford, Bayless, Champion, Bartlett, Ellis, Lindsay, Jack, Tipton* was compiled by Fern Woods Deal and published in Knoxville, Tennessee, in 1975. *The Deal Family of Hornbrook, California: Five Generations of Descendants From George Deal and Elizabeth Rexford Since He Came to California in 1851* was compiled by Joy Lehmann Deal and most likely published in Novato, California, in 1984.

DEAN

Ranking: 230 **S.S. Count:** 153,134

Origin: English. 1) derived from the Old English word "denu," meaning valley. The name was given to those who came from valleys and to those who came from places that had this word as a component in their names. 2) derived from the Old French word "d(e)ien," meaning dean, the head of the chapter of canons. The name was given to those who looked or acted like a dean and to those who worked for deans.

Famous Deans: BASHFORD DEAN (1867–1928) of New York was the curator of arms and armor at the Metropolitan Museum of Art in New York (1906–1927). VERA MICHELES DEAN (1903–1972) of Russia is best known for her work with the Foreign Policy Association and helped to form American opinion on international relations. WILLIAM HENRY DEAN JR. (1910–1952) worked on the staff of the United Nations. JAY HANNA DEAN (1911–1974) of Arkansas was popularly known as "Dizzy." He played baseball professionally and was elected to the Baseball Hall of Fame in 1953. His brother, PAUL DEE DEAN (1913–1981), was also a baseball player. He was known as "Daffy." Both brothers pitched with the St. Louis Cardinals. JOHN EDWARD DEAN (1918–1976) of Nebraska, as an executive with a Nebraska savings and loan association, conceived an automatic fund-transfer system that allowed customers to permit fund transfers from institution to institution; then he developed an electronic fund-transfer system for deposits and withdrawals via remote computer. After court decisions allowing such transactions to continue, the practice of using automated tellers spread nationally. JAMES BYRON DEAN (1931–1955) of Marion, Indiana, was a movie actor who came to epitomize the restless and emotionally lost youth of the 1950s. His best known movies were *Rebel Without a Cause* and *Giant*. He died in an automobile accident at the age of 24.

Genealogies: *A Family Tree in America: Being a Genealogical Story of the Families of Deane (also Dean), Putnam, Boynton, Gager, Bull, and Allied Families From the Year 1630* was compiled by Frank Putnam Deane and published in Richmond, Virginia, in 1979. *My Maternal Ancestry: Dean, Matlock, Hale, Gahr Families in Tennessee and Missouri* was compiled by Melba Wood and published in Godfrey, Illinois, in 1968.

DEANE

Ranking: 4965   **S.S. Count:** 9021
Origin: English. Transformation of the first definition of Dean.

Famous **Deanes:** SILAS DEANE (1737–1789) of Connecticut was one of the leaders of revolutionary unrest in Connecticut. He was a member of the Continental Congress; went to France for supplies and aid; and with Benjamin Franklin and Arthur Lee, formed a commission of three but was charged with embezzlement by Lee. Deane failed to vindicate himself before Congress and returned to France for documents supporting his case. From France he wrote suggesting that the states try to reconcile with England. He died on a return voyage to the colonies.

Genealogies: *A Family Tree in America: Being a Genealogical Story of the Families of Deane, Putnam, Boynton, Gager, Bull, and Allied Families From the Year 1630* was compiled by Frank Putnam Deane and published in Richmond, Virginia, in 1979.

DE ANGELIS   (S.S. Abbreviation: Deange)

Ranking: 2608   **S.S. Count:** 17,414
Origin: Italian. Transfromation of Angel.

Famous **De Angelises:** THOMAS JEFFERSON DE ANGELIS (1859–1933) of California was an actor who starred with Lillian Russell and Della Fox in *The Wedding Day*, his career highlight. He appeared in more than 100 operas, minstrel shows, vaudeville shows, and movies.

Genealogies: None known.

DEARING   (S.S. Abbreviation: Dearin)

Ranking: 4843   **S.S. Count:** 9234
Origin: English. Derived from the Old English name Dēora, meaning beloved.

Famous **Dearings:** JOHN LINCOLN DEARING (1858–1916) was a Baptist clergyman and missionary to Japan.

Genealogies: None known.

DEATON

Ranking: 2456   **S.S. Count:** 18,498
Origin: English. 1) transformation of Dayton. 2) derived from the first name Dudda and the Old English word "tūn," meaning settlement. The name was given to those who came from Ditton, a place in Shropshire, England.

Genealogies: None known.

DE BOER

Ranking: 4985   **S.S. Count:** 8998
Origin: Dutch. Cognate to Bauer.

Genealogies: None known.

DE CARLI, DE CARLO   (S.S. Abbreviation: Decarl)

Ranking: 4837   **S.S. Count:** 9252
Origin: Italian. Cognates to Charles.

Genealogies: None known.

DECKER

Ranking: 494   **S.S. Count:** 81,148
Origin: English, German. English: derived from the Old English word "dic," meaning dike. The name was given to those who lived near a dike. German: derived from the Middle High German word "decke," meaning covering. The name was given to those who worked making blankets.

Famous **Deckers:** SARAH SOPHIA CHASE PLATT DECKER (1852–1912) of Vermont was instrumental in the campaign in Colorado that won women's suffrage in that state. ALONZO G. DECKER (1868–1958) was cofounder, in 1910, of the Black & Decker Manufacturing Co.

Genealogies: *The Decker Genealogy: Some Descendants of the Dutch Immigrants, Johannes Gerretsen and Jan Broersen: A Compilation* was compiled by Benton Weaver Decker and published in 1980. *Ours, Then and Now: Anneke Jans Bogardus, Van Horn, Yates, Decker, and Allied Lines* was compiled by Elinor Randlemon and published in South Gate, California, in 1975.

DEES

Ranking: 3091   **S.S. Count:** 14,697
Origin: English, Irish, Scottish, Welsh. English, Scottish: derived from a British word meaning sacred. The name was given to those who lived near the River Dee. Irish: derived from the Gaelic name Ó Deáhaidh, meaning "descendant of Deághadh" (H&H). Welsh: derived from the Welsh word "du," meaning black or dark. The name was given to those with dark complexions.

Genealogies: None known.

DE FRANCESCO, DE FRANCISCI, DE FRANCISCIS, DE FRANCHIS, DE FRANCO, ET AL.   (S.S. Abbreviation: Defran)

Ranking: 3291   **S.S. Count:** 13,786

Origin: Italian. De Francesco, De Francisci, De Franciscis: cognates to Francis. De Franchis, De Franco: cognates to Frank.
Genealogies: None known.

DE HART
Ranking: 3441   S.S. Count: 13,111
Origin: English, Irish, Jewish. Transformation of Hart.
Genealogies: None known.

DE JESUS   (S.S. Abbreviation: Dejesu)
Ranking: 770   S.S. Count: 54,616
Origin: Portuguese. The name was given to those who were particularly devoted to Christ.
Genealogies: None known.

DELANEY   (S.S. Abbreviation: Delane)
Ranking: 952   S.S. Count: 45,623
Origin: English, Irish. English: derived from the article and preposition "del," meaning of the or from the, and the Old French word "aunaie," meaning alder grove. The name was given to those who came from the many places in Normandy that obtain their names from "aunaie." Irish: derived from the Gaelic name Ó Dubhshláine, meaning "descendant of Dubhshláine" (H&H), which is from the words "dubh" and "slán," meaning black and challenge.
Famous Delaneys: MATTHEW A. DELANEY (1874–1936) was White House physician during the administration of William Howard Taft. JOHN J. DELANEY (1878–1948) of New York was a member of the U.S. House of Representatives for 20 years.
Genealogies: Gone to Texas: A Compendium of the Dulany, Haddox, Heaton, Holland and Martin Families was compiled by Mary Rebecca Dulany Scott and published in Tomball, Texas, in 1989.

DE LEON, DE LEONE, DE LEONARDI, DE LEONARDIS, DE LEONIBUS
Ranking: 767   S.S. Count: 54,860
Origin: Italian. De Leon, De Leone, De Leonibus: cognates to the first two definitions of Lyon. De Leonardi, De Leonardis: cognates to Leonard.
Famous Bearers: DANIEL DE LEON (1852–1914), originally from the Netherlands Antilles, was a socialist and founder of the Industrial Workers of the World. He was considered a radical and divisive to the cause of socialism in America.
Genealogies: None known.

DELGADO, DELGADILLO   (S.S. Abbreviation: Delgad)
Ranking: 418   S.S. Count: 94,600

Origin: Portuguese, Spanish. Derived from the Portuguese and Spanish word "delgado," meaning thin or slender. The names were given to those who were considered to be thin.
Genealogies: None known.

DELL
Ranking: 4320   S.S. Count: 10,380
Origin: English. Derived from the Old English word "dell," meaning valley. The name was given to those who lived in a valley.
Famous Dells: FLOYD DELL (1887–1969) of Illinois was a writer and editor. He wrote Moon-Calf, The Liberator, Runaway, and The Golden Spike, among others.
Genealogies: The Descendants of Frederick Dell and Charles Dell, Two Brothers Who Immigrated from Germany to America in 1854 was compiled by Wolford and Rockey Dell and most likely published in Middletown, Ohio, in 1990.

DELLINGER   (S.S. Abbreviation: Dellin)
Ranking: 4058   S.S. Count: 11,140
Origin: German. Uncertain etymology. The name was given to those who came from Delling, the name of two places in Germany.
Genealogies: None known.

DELOACH   (S.S. Abbreviation: Deloac)
Ranking: 3478   S.S. Count: 12,980
Origin: English. Derived from the Middle English word "loch(e)," which means a kind of freshwater fish.
Genealogies: None known.

DE LONG, DE LONGE
Ranking: 1745   S.S. Count: 25,655
Origin: French. 1) derived from the Latin word "longus," meaning long or tall. The names were given to those who were tall. 2) same derivation as in one. The names were given to those who came from Long, which means "large place" (ES) and is the name of several places in France.
Famous Bearers: GEORGE WASHINGTON DE LONG (1844–1881) of New York was a naval officer who conducted an Arctic expedition. The ship was crushed by ice in Siberia; three teams tried to go for help. In the team led by De Long, all died of starvation attempting to walk to civilization.
Genealogies: The De Longs of New York and Brooklyn: A Huguenot Family Portrait was compiled by Thomas A. DeLong and published in Southport, Connecticut, in 1972.

DE LUCA
Ranking: 2036   S.S. Count: 22,454
Origin: Italian. Cognate to Lucas.

Genealogies: None known.

DEL VALLE (S.S. Abbreviation: Devall)

Ranking: 2605 S.S. Count: 17,431

Origin: Spanish. Derived from the Spanish word "valle," meaning valley. The name was given to those who lived in valleys.

Genealogies: None known.

DE MARCHI, DE MARCHIS (S.S. Abbreviation: Demarc)

Ranking: 2034 S.S. Count: 22,468

Origin: Italian. Cognates to the first English definition of Mark.

Genealogies: None known.

DE MARIA, DE MARINI, DE MARINIS (S.S. Abbreviation: Demari)

Ranking: 4908 S.S. Count: 9111

Origin: Italian. De Maria: derived from the Latin first name Maria, which was derived from the Hebrew first name Miryam. De Marini, De Marinis: cognates to the first French definition of Marin.

Genealogies: None known.

DE MARTINI, DE MARTINIS, DE MARTINO (S.S. Abbreviation: Demart)

Ranking: 3327 S.S. Count: 13,622

Origin: Italian. Cognates to Martin.

Genealogies: None known.

DEMERS

Ranking: 3493 S.S. Count: 12,908

Origin: English, Manx, Scottish. Transformation of Dempster.

Genealogies: *The De May, Quinlin, and Jorgensen (also Demers) Families* was compiled by Ida De May Wilson and published in Saint Helena, California, in 1986.

DEMPSEY, DEMPSTER (S.S. Abbreviation: Dempse)

Ranking: 1149 S.S. Count: 38,150

Origin: Dempsey—Irish; Dempster—English, Manx, Scottish. Dempsey: derived from the Gaelic names Ó Díomasaigh and Mac Díomasaigh, meaning "descendant" and "son of Díomasach" (H&H), which is derived from the word "díomas," meaning pride. Dempster: derived from the Old English word "dēm(e)stre," meaning a judge or arbiter. The name was given to those who worked as such.

Famous **Bearers:** SISTER MARY JOSEPH DEMPSEY (1856–1939) was born in New York and raised in Minnesota. Born Julia Dempsey, she became a Catholic nun, was trained as a teacher, and taught school for 12 years. The destruction of a tornado showed the sisters that a hospital was needed in their town of Rochester. She received training in nursing and then convinced Dr. William Worrell Mayo to staff the hospital. She became the hospital's head nurse and is credited with giving a high priority to nursing education and to improving nursing as a profession. Dr. W. W. Mayo was the father of Drs. Charles and William Mayo, who developed the Mayo clinic. WILLIAM HARRISON (JACK) DEMPSEY (1895–1983) of Manassa, Colorado, was U.S. world heavyweight boxing champion from 1919 until 1926. He was called the "Manassa Mauler."

Genealogies: None known.

DENHAM

Ranking: 4002 S.S. Count: 11,304

Origin: English. Derived from the Old English words "denu" and "dūnna," or the name Dunna and the word "hām," meaning valley, low hill, or brown, and homestead, respectively. The name was given to those who came from Denham, the name of several places in England.

Genealogies: None known.

DENISON, DENISOT, DENISOV, DENISOVICH (S.S. Abbreviation: Deniso)

Ranking: 4726 S.S. Count: 9467

Origin: Denison—English, French; Denisot—French; Denisov—Russian; Denisovich—Ukrainian. Denison, Denisot: transformations of and cognates to the first English definition of Dennis. Denisov, Denisovich: cognates to Dennis.

Famous **Bearers:** MARY ANN ANDREWS DENISON (1826?–1911) of Mississippi was an author who wrote more than 80 novels. She also contributed to *Harper's Weekly* and the *Peoples' Home Journal*, among others. She often used the pen names "Clara Vance" and "N.I. Edson." HENRY STRUGIS DENISON (1877–1952) of Massachusetts was a businessman who supported President Franklin D. Roosevelt's New Deal and served on the Business Advisory and Planning Council of the U.S. Department of Commerce, as chairman of the Industrial Advisory Board of the National Recovery Administration, and as deputy chairman of the Federal Reserve Bank of Boston. ROBERT HOWLAND DENISON (1911–1985) of Massachusetts was a paleontologist who was professionally involved with all of the major museums of his time.

Genealogies: *Denison Genealogy: Ancestors and Descendants of Captain George Denison* was compiled by Elverton Glenn Denison and published in Baltimore, Maryland, in 1978. *A Record of the Descendants of Capt. George Denison of Stonington, Connecticut: With Notices of His Father and Brothers, and Some Account of Other Denisons Who Settled in America in the Colony Times* was compiled by John Denison Baldwin and published in Bethany, Oklahoma, in 1985.

DENNEY

Ranking: 2573   S.S. Count: 17,683
Origin: English, Irish, Scottish. Transformation of Denny.
Genealogies: None known.

DENNING, DENNINGTON   (S.S. Abbreviation: Dennin)

Ranking: 3525   S.S. Count: 12,798
Origin: Denning—Irish; Dennington—English. Denning: derived from the Gaelic name Ó Duinnín, meaning "descendant of Duinnín" (H&H), which is derived from the word "donn," meaning brown. Dennington: derived from the Old English first name Denegifu, which is derived from the words "Dene" and "gifu," meaning Dane and gift, and the word "tūn," meaning settlement.
Genealogies: None known.

DENNIS, DENNISH, DENNISON, DENNISS, DENNISTON

Ranking: 284   S.S. Count: 126,141
Origin: Dennis—English, Irish; Dennish, Dennison, Denniss—English; Denniston—Scottish. Dennis (English), Dennison, Denniss: 1) derived from the medieval first name Den(n)is, which is derived from the Greek word "Dioysios," meaning "(follower) of Dionysus" (H&H). Dennis 2) derived from Old English word "denisc," meaning Danish. The name was given to those who came from Demark. Dennis (Irish): transformation of Donohoe. Denniston: derived from the first name Daniel and the Middle English word "tūn," meaning settlement. The name was given to those who came from Danzielstoun, a place in Scotland.
Famous **Bearers:** FREDERIC SHEPARD DENNIS (1850–1934) of New Jersey was the surgeon who introduced the antiseptic methods of Joseph Lister to the United States. He also founded Harlem Hospital in New York and persuaded Andrew Carnegie to fund the endowment of the Carnegie Laboratory of Medical Research. ALFRED LEWIS PINNEO DENNIS (1874–1930) was born in Syria to parents of old New Jersey stock. He was considered one of the leading historians in the field of modern history and international relations. He was the nephew of Frederic Shepard Dennis. EUGENE DENNIS (1905–1961) of Washington was a labor organizer and Communist who was imprisoned for violating the Smith Act, which forbids the advocation of the overthrow of the U.S. government.
Genealogies: *The Ancestors and Descendants of Nathan Dennis, 1650–1982* was compiled by Frederick W. Dennis and published in Chandler, Arizona, in 1982. *Dennis and Chorn Kin: A Short Genealogy of Their Connections and a Companion to "Lucy Jane Wylder and Kin"* was compiled by Jessye Ann High and published in 1976.

DENNY

Ranking: 1866   S.S. Count: 24,260
Origin: English, Irish, Scottish. English, Scottish: transformation of and cognate to Dennis. Irish: derived from the Gaelic name Ó Duibhne, meaning "descendant of Duibhne" (H&H), meaning ill-tempered and disagreeable (H&H). Scottish: the name was given to those who came from a town in the former county of Stirlings.
Famous **Dennys:** GEORGE HUTCHESON DENNY (1870–1955) was president of Washington and Lee University in Kentucky. GEORGE VERNON DENNY JR. (1899–1959) of North Carolina initiated the radio program "America's Town Meeting on the Air."
Genealogies: None known.

DENSON

Ranking: 2806   S.S. Count: 16,232
Origin: English. Transformation of the second definition of Dean.
Genealogies: *The Denson Family of Houston and Anderson Counties, Texas* was compiled by Lucile De Berry McCutcheon and published in West Columbia, Texas, in 1988. *Jordan Denson (?–1806), Some of His Ancestors and Descendants* and *"Beechwood," Denson-Pretlow-Darden Ancestral Home, Southampton County, Virginia* was compiled by Peggy S. Joyner and published in Portsmouth, Virginia, in 1978.

DENT

Ranking: 2239   S.S. Count: 20,483
Origin: English. 1) derived from a British word meaning hill. The name was given to those who came from Dent, the name of several places in England. 2) derived from the Old French word "dent," meaning tooth. The name was given to those with odd teeth or to those who were considered to be voracious.
Famous **Dents:** FREDERICK TRACY DENT (1821–1892), a West Point graduate and professional soldier, was Ulysses S. Grant's brother-in-law and his aide during the Civil War. He served as military secretary during Grant's presidency. HUBERT STANLEY DENT (1869–1938) was a member of Congress from Alabama for 12 years. JOHN HERMAN DENT (1908–1988) of Pennsylvania was a member of Congress from that state.
Genealogies: None known.

DENTON

Ranking: 1145   S.S. Count: 38,460
Origin: English, Scottish. Derived from the Old English words "denu" and "tūn," meaning valley and settlement. The name was given to those who came from Denton, the name of several places in England and Scotland.
Famous **Dentons:** MARY FLORENCE DENTON (1857–

1947) of California was a missionary teacher in Japan, where she taught English, the Bible, and Western-style cooking. She was famed for her marble cake and was once asked to make one for the Japanese emperor. She was also active in the Red Cross and the Y.W.C.A.

Genealogies: *The Plum(ly, lee, ley, blee) Family From Bucks to Buncombe, 1682–1982, and Allied Lines: Denton, Murray, Fletcher, Johnson, Gullick, Ballenger* was compiled by Millard Quentin Plumblee and published in Salisbury, North Carolina, in 1982.

DE ROSA
Ranking: 3398   S.S. Count: 13,320
Origin: Italian. Derived from the first names Rosa and Rose, meaning rose.
Genealogies: None known.

DERR
Ranking: 4024   S.S. Count: 11,256
Origin: French, German. Transformation of Durr.
Famous **Derrs**: CYRUS GEORGE DERR (1848–1933) was a prominent industrialist and attorney in Reading, Pennsylvania, who founded the Pennsylvania Trust Co. of Reading.
Genealogies: *The Derr Family, 1750–1986: With Allied Families of Baker, Flook, Hoover, Koogle, Long, Metzger, Smith, Templing, Toms, Yaste, and Youtsey* was compiled by Roy H. Wampler and published in Baltimore, Maryland, in 1987.

DERRICK   (S.S. Abbreviation: Derric)
Ranking: 2471   S.S. Count: 18,371
Origin: English. Derived from the Dutch first names Diederick and Dirck.
Famous **Derricks**: JACOB SIDNEY DERRICK (1867–1948) was president of Newberry College in Newberry, South Carolina, for 12 years. CALVIN DERRICK (1870–1938) was nationally recognized for his accomplishments as superintendent of the New Jersey State Home for Boys.
Genealogies: *Genealogy and History of the Derthicks and Related Derricks: Eight Centuries of the Derthicks and Related Derricks in America and England* was compiled by Jack Taif Spencer and published in DeKalb, Illinois, in 1986.

DE SANTI, DE SANTIS   (S.S. Abbreviation: De Sant)
Ranking: 1931   S.S. Count: 23,383
Origin: Italian. Transformations of Santo.
Genealogies: None known.

DESIMONE, DE SIMONI   (S.S. Abbreviation: Desimo)
Ranking: 4069   S.S. Count: 11,112

Origin: Italian. Cognates to Simon.
Genealogies: None known.

DESJARDINS   (S.S. Abbreviation: Desjar)
Ranking: 4988   S.S. Count: 8997
Origin: French. Cognate to Gardener.
Genealogies: None known.

DESMOND   (S.S. Abbreviation: Desmon)
Ranking: 4116   S.S. Count: 6406
Origin: Irish. Derived from the Gaelic name Ó Desasmhumhnaigh, meaning "descendant of the man from S(outh) Munster" (H&H).
Famous **Desmonds**: ROBERT WILLIAM DESMOND (1900–1985) of Wisconsin was a journalist with assignments in both the United States and overseas. He was also heard on regular news commentary radio shows. JOHNNY ALFRED DESMOND (1921–1985) of Michigan was a singer and actor working with all of the major big bands of the time. He also made many appearances on TV shows.
Genealogies: None known.

DE STEFANI, DE STEFANIS   (S.S. Abbreviation: Destef)
Ranking: 4106   S.S. Count: 11,008
Origin: Italian. Cognates to Stephen.
Genealogies: None known.

DEUTSCH   (S.S. Abbreviation: Deutsc)
Ranking: 2851   S.S. Count: 16,013
Origin: German, Jewish. German: derived from the German word "deutsch," meaning German. The name was given to those who spoke a Germanic language instead of a Slavic one. Jewish: the name was given to those who came from places where German was spoken.
Genealogies: None known.

DEVANE, DEVANEY
Ranking: 4927   S.S. Count: 9083
Origin: Irish. Devane: 1) derived from the Gaelic name Ó Damháin, meaning "descendant of Damhám" (H&H), a name meaning fawn. 2) derived from the Gaelic name Ó Duibáin, meaning "descendant of Dubhán" (H&H), which is derived from the word "dubh," meaning black. Devaney: derived from the Gaelic name Ó Duibheannaigh, meaning "descendant of Duibheannach" (H&H), which is derived from the word "dubh," meaning black, and possibly the word "eanach," meaning marsh.
Famous **Bearers**: JOHN PATRICK DEVANEY (1883–1941) of Iowa was the first president of the National Lawyers Guild and was appointed by President Franklin Roosevelt to handle labor disputes in the Pacific Northwest. He settled the disputes, thereby averting a strike of 30,000 employees of the Railway Express Agency.

Genealogies: None known.

DEVEREAUX, DEVEREU, DEVEREUX (S.S. Abbreviation: Devere)

Ranking: 4749   S.S. Count: 9431

Origin: English. Derived from the preposition "de" and the name Evreux, which is a place in Normandy, France, that was most likely the capital of a Gallic tribe called Eburovices.

Famous **Bearers:** JOHN HENRY DEVEREUX (1832–1886) of Massachusetts, a civil engineer, was manager and president of several midwestern railroads. WILLIAM C. DEVEREAUX (1874–1941), a meteorologist with the U.S. Weather Service in Ohio, earned a reputation as the nation's top flood forecaster.

Genealogies: *Devereux of the Leap, County Wexford, Ireland and of Utica, New York: Nicholas Devereux, 1791–1855* was compiled by Clifford Lewis 3rd and John Devereux Kernan and published in 1974.

DEVILL, DEVILLE, DE VILLE, DEVILLERS, DEVILLIERS, DEVILLETTE

Ranking: 4374   S.S. Count: 10,252

Origin: Devill—English; Deville, De Ville—English, French; Devillers, Devilliers, Devillette—French. Devill, Deville, De Ville: 1) possibly derived from the Latin phrase "dei villa," meaning "settlement of God" (H&H). The names were given to those who came from the Déville, a place in Normandy, France. 2) derived from the Old English word "dèofol," meaning devil. The name was given to those who were considered mischievous and to those who played the part of a devil in a ceremony. Deville, De Ville, Devillette: derived from the Old French word "ville," meaning settlement. The names were given to those who lived in a community, rather than on its outskirts. Devillers, Devilliers: derived from Vil(i)er(s), the name of many places in France that is obtained from the Late Latin word "villāre," meaning an area that is dependent on a central community or a faraway farm.

Genealogies: None known.

DEVINE

Ranking: 1300   S.S. Count: 34,157

Origin: English, French. Derived from the Middle English word "devin" and Old French word "divin," meaning excellent and perfect. The name was given in an ironic sense.

Famous **Devines:** JOSEPH MCMURRAY DEVINE (1861–1938) was a governor of North Dakota. EDWARD THOMAS DEVINE (1867–1948) of Iowa was a social worker who was a professor of social economy at Columbia University and at American University in Washington, D.C. He also served as the director of the New York School of Philanthropy.

Genealogies: *Our Divine/Wells (also Devine) Family History: Including Divine Related Lines of Aersen, Bennet,*

Brooks, Crose, Fanckboner was compiled by Carol Divine Briggs and published in Chicago, Illinois, in 1988.

DE VITO

Ranking: 4399   S.S. Count: 10,199

Origin: Italian. Derived from a first name that was derived from the Latin word "vita," meaning life.

Genealogies: None known.

DEVLIN

Ranking: 2478   S.S. Count: 18,284

Famous **Devlins:** ROBERT THOMAS DEVLIN (1859–1938) of California was nationally recognized for his accomplishments as U.S. attorney for the northern district of California.

Origin: Irish, Scottish. Derived from the Gaelic name Ó Dobh(a)iléin, meaning "descendant of Dobhailéan" (H&H).

Genealogies: None known.

DE VORE, DEVORE

Ranking: 3004   S.S. Count: 15,118

Origin: French? Uncertain etymology. The name was most likely given to those who came from Vors, a place in France.

Genealogies: None known.

DE VRIES, DE VRIENT (S.S. Abbreviation: Devrie)

Ranking: 2774   S.S. Count: 16,443

Origin: De Vries—Dutch; De Vrient—Dutch, Flemish. De Vries: cognate to the Jewish definition of Fried. De Vrient: cognate to Friend.

Genealogies: None known.

DEW

Ranking: 4899   S.S. Count: 9126

Origin: Cornish. Transformation of Duff.

Famous **Dews:** THOMAS RODERICK DEW (1802–1846) of Virginia was an economist who wrote *The Pro-slavery Argument*, which won him the admiration of the South's elitist class. He became the president of William and Mary College in 1836 and greatly increased its enrollment.

Genealogies: None known.

DE WEESE, DEWEESE (S.S. Abbreviation: Dewees)

Ranking: 3688   S.S. Count: 12,241

Origin: French. Uncertain etymology. The name was possibly given to those who came from Wez, a place in France.

Genealogies: *Allison, Dewees (also Deweese), Johnson, Scruggs and Other Related Families: Old Photographs, Letters, etc.* was compiled by Judith Allison Walters and published in Bothell, Washington, in 1976.

DEWEY

Ranking: 2463   S.S. Count: 18,412

Origin: Scottish, Welsh. Derived from the Welsh first name Dew, a cognate to David.

Famous **Deweys:** GEORGE DEWEY (1837–1917) of Vermont was a naval officer in the Civil War who served under Admiral David Farragut. He was the commander of the Asian forces during the war with Spain and the commander of American forces at the battle of Manila Bay. RICHARD SMITH DEWEY (1845–1933) of New York was a psychiatrist who introduced the idea called "cottage plan," in which massive institutions are replaced by small, more homelike residences or cottages. MELVIL DEWEY (1851–1931) of New York was the director of the New York State Library and the founder and director of the New York State Library School. He was responsible for the decimal classification system known as the Dewey decimal system. ALICE CHIPMAN DEWEY (1858–1927) of Michigan was born either Hattie or Harriet. She and her husband founded the Laboratory School at the University of Chicago. Later they were active in the suffrage movement in New York City. JOHN DEWEY (1859–1952) of Burlington, Vermont, was one of the founders of the pragmatism school of philosophy and a leader in the progressive movement in U.S. education. THOMAS EDMUND DEWEY (1902–1971) of Michigan was a lawyer and special prosecutor in organized-crime investigations; district attorney of New York City; governor of the state of New York; and the Republican nominee for president in 1944 and 1948.

Genealogies: *Families of Dr. Charles Carroll, 1691–1755, and Cornet Thomas Dewey, 160?-1648* was compiled by Douglas Carroll and published in Brooklandville, Maryland, in the 1960s.

DE WITT, DE WITTE

Ranking: 1192   S.S. Count: 36,774

Origin: Dutch, Flemish. Cognates to White.

Famous **Bearers:** SIMEON DE WITT (1756–1834) of New York was a surveyor and military mapmaker during the Revolutionary War. LYDIA MARIA ADAMS DEWITT (1859–1928) of Flint, Michigan, investigated the chemotherapy of tuberculosis. Her studies became the standard of subsequent investigations.

Genealogies: *Bennett-DeWitt and Related Families* was compiled by Paul W. Bennett and published in Vandalia, Missouri, in 1980. *Dewitt-Duett: Roots and Shoots* was compiled by Avis Williams Dewitt and published in Cullman, Alabama, in 1984

DEXTER

Ranking: 3292   S.S. Count: 13,785

Origin: English, Irish. Transformation of Dyer.

Famous **Dexters:** SAMUEL DEXTER (1726–1810) was from Massachusetts. He was a merchant and a Revolutionary patriot. SAMUEL DEXTER (1761–1816) was a Federalist member of Congress from Massachusetts; a U.S. senator; secretary of war (1800); and secretary of the Treasury (1801–1802). FRANKLIN DEXTER (1793–1857) was the son of Samuel and a lawyer. HENRY DEXTER (1806–1876) of New York was a blacksmith and a self-taught sculptor who did busts of Henry Wadsworth Longfellow and Charles Dickens, among others. HENRY DEXTER (1813–1910) of Massachusetts organized newspaper dealers into the American News Co. He then served as its president. FRANKLIN BOWDITCH DEXTER (1842–1920) of Massachusetts was a historian. His favorite subjects of Yale University and the city of New Haven are reflected in his writings.

Genealogies: *Genealogy of the Descendants of Benjamin Dexter, Fifth Generation Descendant of Thomas Dexter, Lynn, Massachusetts, 1630* was compiled by Ella C. Belz and published in Falls Church, Virginia, in 1979. *The Jesse Tree: History of Biggs-Dexter Families in America* was compiled by Rayma Leone and Mary Louise Biggs and published in Iuka, Mississippi, in 1980.

DE YOUNG

Ranking: 4451   S.S. Count: 10,070

Origin: Dutch. The name was given to those who were considered young and to those who were younger sons.

Famous **De Youngs:** MICHEL HARRY DE YOUNG (1849–1925) of Missouri, with his brother CHARLES (1847–1880), founded the *San Francisco Chronicle*.

Genealogies: None known.

DIAL

Ranking: 3357   S.S. Count: 13,503

Origin: English?, French?, Italian? Uncertain etymology. Possibly derived from the Middle Latin word "dialis," meaning daily.

Genealogies: None known.

DIAMOND, DIAMONT, DIAMONTSTEIN
(S.S. Abbreviation: Diamon)

Ranking: 1458   S.S. Count: 30,532

Origin: English, Jewish. English: the name was given to those who worked as servants to someone named Day. Jewish: derived from the Middle High German word "diemant," meaning diamond. In most cases the name was taken ornamentally. In some cases it was given to those who worked as jewelers.

Famous **Diamonds:** MARTIN DIAMOND (1919–1977) of New York was a prominent educator and author of numerous essays on the U.S. founding fathers, particularly the Federalists. ISADORE DIAMOND (1920–1988) of Romania was a screenwriter who was responsible for some of the best-known movies of the 1960s and 1970s.

For the movie *The Apartment*, she received an Academy Award.

Genealogies: *Genealogy of the Dymond (also Diamond), Williams, and Related Families* was compiled by Robert Herschel Dymond and published in Baltimore, Maryland, in 1981. *James Diamond, 1781–1849, and His Descendants* was compiled by Laura P. Marbut and published in Danielsville, Georgia, in 1970.

DIAS

Ranking: 2923   S.S. Count: 15,572

Origin: Portuguese, Spanish. 1) means son of Diego, a first name that is a Spanish form of Jacob, and also derived from the Latin word "dies," meaning day or daytime. 2) derived from the name of Santiago, the patron saint of Spain.
Genealogies: None known.

DIAZ

Ranking: 188   S.S. Count: 184,248

Origin: Spanish. 1) derived from the first name Diego, a first name that is considered a Spanish form of Jacob. 2) derived from the Latin word "dies," meaning day or daytime.

Famous **Diazes:** ABBY MORTON DIAZ (1821–1904) of Massachusetts was an author of children's books, with contributions in *Atlantic Monthly, Youth's Companion*, and *Wide Awake*. One of her most famous books is *The William Henry Letters*.

Genealogies: None known.

DIAZ R[1]

Ranking: 4278   S.S. Count: 10,504

Origin: Spanish. Transformation of Diaz.
Genealogies: None known.

DICK

Ranking: 1198   S.S. Count: 36,685

Origin: English, German, Jewish, Scottish. English, Scottish: transformation of Richard. German: derived from the Middle High German word "dic(ke)," meaning thicket. The name was given to those who lived near a thicket. German, Jewish: derived from the German word "dick" and the Yiddish word "dik," both meaning thick. The name was given to those who were considered to be heavy-set.

Famous **Dicks:** ELISHA CULLEN DICK (1762–1825) of Pennsylvania was a physician. He was called in to consult with Dr. James Craik during George Washington's last illness. ALBERT BLAKE DICK (1856–1934) was founder and president of the A. B. Dick Co. CHARLES DICK (1858–1945) of Ohio was a U.S. representative and a U.S. senator from Ohio. GEORGE FREDERICK DICK (1881–1967) of Fort Wayne, Indiana, with his wife, GLADYS ROWENA HENRY DICK (1881–1963) of Nebraska, discovered the cause of and developed a cure for scarlet fever.

[1]The surname Diaz is often the first component in a compound surname, such as Diaz-Rodriguez. The Social Security Administration counts compound surnames as separate surnames anytime a different letter(s) appears within the first six spaces.

Genealogies: *History of Peter and Christina Shutt Dick Family, Frederick Co.* was compiled by Muriel Martens Hoffman and published in Anchor, Illinois, in 1970. *Immigration to St. Joseph County, Indiana: Chronology of Four German-Catholic Families—Zaehnle, Dick, Lauber, Schmitt* was compiled by Howard John Schmitt and published in Benton Harbor, Michigan, in 1983.

DICKEN, DICKENS, DICKENSON, DICKENSTEIN

Ranking: 1291   S.S. Count: 34,299

Origin: Dicken, Dickens, Dickenson—English; Dickenstein—Jewish. Dicken, Dickens, Dickenson: transformations of Richard. Dickenstein: transformation of the German, Jewish definition of Dick.

Genealogies: *The Dickenson Families of England and America (Dickinson, Dickerson, Dickson, Dixon, etc.)* was compiled by Bonnie Sage Ball and published in Searcy, Arkansas, in 1972.

DICKER

Ranking: 512   S.S. Count: 78,264

Origin: English, German, Jewish. English: 1) derived from the Middle English words "diche" and "dike," meaning ditch and dike. The name was given to those who lived near such waterways or worked making them. 2) derived from the Middle English word "dyker," meaning a group or unit of ten. The name was given to those who came from "the Dicker," the name of a place in East Sussex, England. German, Jewish: transformation of Dick.

Genealogies: *A Jewish Family Trail: The Dickers and Their Mates* was compiled by Herman Dicker and published in New York, New York, in 1977.

DICKEY

Ranking: 1272   S.S. Count: 34,724

Origin: English, Irish. Transformation of and cognate to Richard.

Famous **Dickeys:** SARAH ANN DICKEY (1838–1904) of Ohio worked her way through school, taking loans to pay for her education to become a teacher. She then traveled to Mississippi to open a school for the recently freed slaves. She and her supporters were met with much opposition because of her chosen field. JAMES EDWARD DICKEY (1864–1928) was president of Emory University in Atlanta.

Genealogies: *Families and Kin of Elias Stockton, Moses Dickey, and James Upchurch, Cherokee County, Texas, Pioneers* was compiled by Mae Gean Pettit and published in Baltimore, Maryland, in 1991. *John Alexander Dickey, Immigrants, 1772* was compiled by Grover C. Dickey and published in Oklahoma City, Oklahoma, in 1976.

DICKIN, DICKINGS, DICKINS, DICKINSON

Ranking: 1109 **S.S. Count:** 39,857

Origin: English. Transformation of Dick.

Famous **Bearers:** JONATHAN DICKINSON (1688–1747) of Massachusetts secured the first charter for the College of New Jersey (Princeton University) and served as its first president. JOHN DICKINSON (1732–1808) of Maryland is called "the penman of the Revolution." He was a member of the Stamp Act Congress and the Continental Congress, principal author of "Declaration . . . Setting Forth the Causes and Necessity of Their Taking Up Arms," helped draft the Articles of Confederation, and served in the Continental army. His brother, PHILEMON DICKINSON (1739–1809), with a rank of major general, served as commander in chief of the New Jersey militia in the Revolutionary War, defeating General Charles Cornwallis in one battle, and played a part in the colonists' success at the battle of Monmouth. He was a member of the Continental Congress and a U.S. senator from Delaware. EMILY ELIZABETH DICKINSON (1830–1886) of Amherst, Massachusetts, was a poet who is often referred to as "the New England mystic." ANNA ELIZABETH DICKINSON (1842–1932) of Pennsylvania was an orator and lyceum lecturer and was referred to as the Joan of Arc of the Unionist cause. After the Civil War she took up other timely causes and continued on the lecture circuit. ROBERT LATOU DICKINSON (1861–1950) of New Jersey was the foremost gynecologist of the day. He developed new surgical techniques, including the use of electric cauterization in treating cervicitis and in intrauterine sterilizations. He also was a strong supporter of feminist causes, birth control, and sex education. EDWIN DEWITT DICKINSON (1887–1961) of Iowa was a professor of international law and the author of *Law and Peace*. (WILLIAM) PRESTON DICKINSON (1889–1930) of New York was an artist who favored pastels. His works hang in all the major U.S. galleries. JOHN DICKINSON (1894–1952) of Maryland was a law professor at the University of Pennsylvania and the principal spokesman for the New Deal in the business community. WILLIAM BOYD DICKINSON (1908–1978) of Missouri, as a reporter for United Press (International), covered World War II in Europe and the South Pacific. He was the first to report many events and the only reporter to land on Leyte from the same landing barge as Gen. Douglas MacArthur. He flew with MacArthur from Okinawa to Tokyo to witness the surrender by the Japanese aboard the *Missouri* in 1945. In 1972, he went with the first group of editors to enter China after Communist domination ended and wrote a book about the trip, called *China Today*.

Genealogies: *The Dickenson Families of England and America (Dickinson, Dickerson, Dickson, Dixon, etc.)* was compiled by Bonnie Sage Ball and published in Searcy, Arkansas, in 1972. *Dickerson and Dickinson Descendants of Philemon Dickerson of Southold, Long Island, N.Y. Also Long Island Descendants of Captain John Dickinson of Oyster Bay* was compiled by Wesley Logan Baker and published in Chicago, Illinois, in 1979. *Descendants of Nathaniel Dickinson* was compiled by Elinor V. Smith and published in 1978.

DICKMAN, DICKMANN (S.S. Abbreviation: Dickma)

Ranking: 4883 **S.S. Count:** 9157

Origin: Dickman—English, Jewish; Dickmann—Jewish. Dickman (English): derived from the Middle English words "diche" and "dike," meaning meaning ditch and dike. The name was given to those who lived near such waterways. Dickman (Jewish), Dickmann: transformation of Dick.

Famous **Bearers:** JOSEPH THEODORE DICKMAN (1857–1927) of Ohio was an army officer who commanded troups in Europe during World War I.

Genealogies: None known.

DICKSON (S.S. Abbreviation: Dickso)

Ranking: 884 **S.S. Count:** 49,087

Origin: English, Irish, Scottish. Transformation of and cognate to Richard.

Famous **Dicksons:** SAMUEL HENRY DICKSON (1798–1872) of South Carolina was the founder of the Medical College of South Carolina. DAVID DICKSON (1809–1885) of Georgia introduced methods of farming to the South, including the use of Peruvian guano as a fertilizer. THOMAS DICKSON (1824–1884) of England came to the United States as a child. He was a developer of the coal industry in Scranton, Pennsylvania. LEONARD EUGENE DICKSON (1874–1954) of Iowa was a mathematician known for his work in theory of numbers and groups. EARLE ENSIGN DICKSON (1892–1961) of Tennessee was the inventor of the adhesive bandage that was marketed as the Band-aid.

Genealogies: *Downeast Dicksons: 42 lines of Early New England Settlers and All the Descendants, as of 1987, of Captain Talbot Dickson and Susan Hayland of Harrington, Maine* was compiled by Katharine Dickson and published in Henniker, New Hampshire, in 1987. *Genealogical Record of the McDonalds, Logans, Dicksons, Brownlees* was compiled by Daniel McDonald and published in New York, New York, in 1956.

DIEHL

Ranking: 1652 **S.S. Count:** 27,076

Origin: German. Cognate to Derrick.

Famous **Diehls:** CHARLES SANFORD DIEHL (1854–1946) was co-owner and publisher of the San Antonio (Texas) *Light* newspaper. WALTER STUART DIEHL (1893–1976) of Tennessee, an aeronautical engineer, wrote *Engineering Aerodynamics*, a reference book used by aircraft designers.

Genealogies: *The Deal (also Diehl) Family of Hornbrook, California: Five Generations of Descendants From George Deal and Elizabeth Rexford Since He Came to California in 1851* was compiled by Joy Lehmann Deal and most likely published in Novato, California, in 1984. *The Diehl-Deal-Dill-Dale Families of America* was compiled by Harry A. Diehl and published in Wilmington, Delaware, in 1989. *Genealogy of the Descendants of Samuel Diehl and Margaretha Ritchey, His Wife, of Loudoun County, Va. and Bedford County, Pa., 1740–1828* was compiled by the Diehl Genealogy Publishers Committee and published in Holidaysburg, Pennsylvania, in 1976.

DIETRICH (S.S. Abbreviation: Dietri)
Ranking: 1766 **S.S. Count:** 25,404
Origin: Austrian, German. Cognate to Derrick.
Genealogies: *Dietrich Pleffner Roos Genealogy: Being an Account of the Descendants of John Dietrich and Theresa Metz, Who Immigrated From Bavaria to the United States in 1848* was compiled by Robert Ralsey Davenport and published in Washington, D.C., in 1982. *Early Families of Northampton County, Pennsylvania* was compiled by John T. Humphrey and published in Washington, D.C., in 1991.

DIETZ, DIETZE
Ranking: 1667 **S.S. Count:** 26,830
Origin: German. Cognate to Derrick.
Famous Bearers: PETER ERNEST DIETZ (1878–1947) of New York was a priest and an early leader of the Roman Catholic social reform movement. He organized the American Academy of Christian Democracy, which was a school to train young Catholic women to become professional social workers. HOWARD DIETZ (1896–1983) of New York was a songwriter/composer responsible for the lyrics to more than 500 songs. Some of his best known are "Dancing in the Dark," "You and the Night and the Music," and "That's Entertainment."
Genealogies: *Deets (also Dietz) Descendants* was compiled by Walter S. Olson and published in Scarsdale, New York, in 1975.

DIGGS
Ranking: 2267 **S.S. Count:** 20,140
Origin: English. Transformation of Richard.
Genealogies: None known.

DILL
Ranking: 1727 **S.S. Count:** 25,994
Origin: English. Derived from the first name Dill, meaning dull one.
Famous Dills: JAMES BROOKS DILL (1854–1910) of New York was a corporation lawyer and is considered the father of corporation law in New Jersey.

Genealogies: *Some Descendants and Kinsmen of William Dill, Sr., a Delaware Colonist* was compiled by Harry F. Dill and published in Alexandria, Louisiana, in 1992.

DILLARD (S.S. Abbreviation: Dillar)
Ranking: 1037 **S.S. Count:** 42,173
Origin: English. Transformation of Dill.
Famous Dillards: JAMES HARDY DILLARD (1856–1940) of Virginia was an educator responsible for social and educational causes, including the Child Welfare Association and the Free Kindergarten Association. As the president of the New Orleans public library system, he secured a branch for the African-Americans of the day to use. Two black colleges in New Orleans merged to become Dillard College. He was considered a "bridge builder" between different groups. STARK S. DILLARD (1894–1975) of Virginia was co-founder and president of Dillard Paper Co. in North Carolina (1926–1950).
Genealogies: None known.

DILLING (S.S. Abbreviation: Dillin)
Ranking: 3380 **S.S. Count:** 13,393
Origin: English. Transformation of Dowling.
Genealogies: None known.

DILLON
Ranking: 615 **S.S. Count:** 67,907
Origin: English, French, Irish, Jewish. English: Uncertain etymology. The name was given to those who came from Diwlwyn, the name of a place in England. English, French: derived from the Germanic first name Dillo. Irish: 1) cognate to English and French definitions of Lyon. 2) derived from the Gaelic name Ó Duilleáin, meaning "descendant of Duilleán" (H&H). Jewish: derived from the Latin word "leo," meaning lion. The name was given to those who were considered to be brave soldiers and also developed through the first name Leo(n).
Famous Dillons: SIDNEY DILLON (1812–1892) of New York was a railroad builder and the principal contractor of the Union Pacific Railroad. CLARENCE DILLON (1882–1979) of Texas, a financier, outbid the legendary J. P. Morgan & Co. in 1925 to buy the Dodge Brothers Automobile Co. for $146 million, the largest transaction in industrial history to that time. Dodge later merged with Chrysler Corp. JOHN JORDAN DILLON (1898–1944) was president of Providence College in Rhode Island. GEORGE HILL DILLON (1906–1968) of Florida was a poet who won a Pulitzer Prize for "The Flowering Stone" in 1931.
Genealogies: *The Chinn (also Dillon) Book* was compiled by Ruth Wilson Dillon and published in Cottonport, Louisiana, in 1972. *The Dillon Family* was compiled by Elaine Egenes and published in Springville, California, most likely in 1969.

DINGLE

Ranking: 4605   S.S. Count: 9707

Origin: English. Derived from the Middle English word "dingle," meaning wooded hollow. The name was given to those who lived in such places.

Genealogies: None known.

DION

Ranking: 4113   S.S. Count: 10,978

Origin: French. Most likely derived from the Gallic component "divon," meaning hallowed spring. The name was given to those who came from Dion, Dions, and Dionne, the names of several places in France.

Genealogies: None known.

DIONNE, DIONNET

Ranking: 4752   S.S. Count: 9425

Origin: French. Transformations of Dion.

Genealogies: None known.

DIX

Ranking: 3193   S.S. Count: 14,217

Origin: English. Transformation of Richard.

Famous **Dixes**: JOHN ADAMS DIX (1798–1879) of New Hampshire was the secretary of the U.S. Treasury who issued the following order to a Treasury officer in New Orleans, Louisiana: "If anyone attempts to haul down the American flag, shoot him on the spot." DOROTHEA LYNDE DIX (1802–1887) of Maine is best known for her work to improve the living conditions of the "criminally insane" confined to state homes and prisons. She also was the superintendent of women nurses in the army during the Civil War. JOHN HOMER DIX (1811–1884) of Massachusetts is credited with performing the first medical operation in the United States. He is also believed to have introduced the first apartment house to this country.

Genealogies: None known.

DIXON

Ranking: 150   S.S. Count: 211,189

Origin: English. Transformation of Richard.

Famous **Dixons**: JEREMIAH DIXON (?–1777) of England was a surveyor who, with Charles Mason, surveyed the boundary between Pennsylvania and Maryland that became known as the Mason-Dixon Line and the unofficial boundary between the North and the South. JOSEPH DIXON (1799–1869) of Massachusetts was an inventor who is credited with a method of casting in a graphite crucible; printing bank notes in color; and developing a wood-planing machine, a process for printing calico material that is colorfast, and a galvanic battery. WILLIAM DIXON (1850–1913) of West Virginia was a frontiersman who left home to become a mule skinner and a buffalo hunter. He

fought in the second battle at Adobe Walls in 1874 and won the Congressional medal for bravery. THOMAS DIXON (1864–1946) of Shelby, North Carolina, was a writer whose novels sympathetically depicted white supremacists. GEORGE DIXON (1870–1909), originally from Canada, was the first African-American to win a world boxing championship. ROLAND BURRAGE DIXON (1875–1934) of Massachusetts was an anthropologist who wrote several books on the subject.

Genealogies: *Downeast Dicksons (also Dixon): 42 lines of Early New England Settlers and All the Descendants, as of 1987, of Captain Talbot Dickson and Susan Hayland of Harrington, Maine* was compiled by Katharine Dickson and published in Henniker, New Hampshire, in 1987. *The Descendants of James A. Dickson (also Dixon), ca. 1820–1864, of Tennessee and Texas: Allied Families, Coleman, Fulbright, Harkey, Nall, Tippen* was compiled by Roy Shelton Dickson and published in Bartlesville, Oklahoma, in 1987. *The Descendants of Nicholas Dixon: A Compilation of the Known Descendants As They Are Discovered, Updated Periodically* was compiled by Joel Dixon Wells and published in Hampton, Georgia, most likely in 1979.

DOAN

Ranking: 3805   S.S. Count: 11,863

Origin: Irish. Transformation of the second definition of Devane.

Genealogies: None known.

DOANE

Ranking: 4790   S.S. Count: 9350

Origin: Irish. Transformation of the second definition of Devane.

Famous **Doanes**: GEORGE WASHINGTON DOANE (1799–1869) of New Jersey was a leader in the Episcopal church and the author of many hymns. THOMAS DOANE (1821–1897) of Massachusetts was a mechanical engineer. He worked on New England railroads and tunnels. WILLIAM CROSWELL DOANE (1832–1913) of Massachusetts was an Episcopal minister and the son of George Washington Doane.

Genealogies: *The Doane, Emmons, Lindner, Roney, and Stout Families: Which Includes Some Ancestors and Descendants of . . .* was compiled by Robert Harold Lindner and published in Empire, Michigan, in 1986.

DOBBIN, DOBBING, DOBBINGS, DOBBINS

Ranking: 1924   S.S. Count: 23,467

Origin: English. Transformation of Robert.

Famous **Bearers**: JAMES COCHRAN DOBBIN (1814–1847) of North Carolina was a politician who was responsible for the enlarging and reorganizing of the navy.

Genealogies: *Jackson: Hefton-Dobbins-Riggins/Reagon-*

Cooper Genealogy and Family History was compiled by Naomi Ruth Jackson Chasteen in Miami, Oklahoma, in 1988. *Some Dobbin(s), Skiles Lines From Pennsylvania to North Carolina and Tennessee. With Additional Lines of Coker, Cowan, Dailey, Graham, Hess, Palmer, Barekman, Lowarance, Newbill* was compiled by June Beverly Barekman and published in Chicago, Illinois, in 1966.

DOBBS

Ranking: 1759   **S.S. Count:** 25,508
Origin: English. Transformation of Robert.

Famous **Dobbses:** ARTHUR DOBBS (1689–1765) of Ireland was the colonial governor of North Carolina. His administration had difficulty because of conflicts in priorities between interests of the Crown and the welfare of North Carolina.

Genealogies: *Gone to Alabama: A History of the Dobbs and Gilbreath Families* was compiled by Edward Johnson Ladd and published in Fort Worth, Texas, in 1972.

DOBSON

Ranking: 1706   **S.S. Count:** 26,174
Origin: English. Transformation of Robert.

Famous **Dobsons:** JOHN DOBSON (1827–1911), born in England, emigrated to Pennsylvania and became, with his brother James, a major textile manufacturer in the United States.

Genealogies: None known.

DOCKER, DOCKERAY, DOCKERY, DOCKERTY

Ranking: 2976   **S.S. Count:** 15,281
Origin: Docker—Bavarian; Dockeray, Dockery—English, Irish; Dockerty—Irish, Scottish. Docker: cognate to Decker. Dockeray, Dockery (English): Uncertain etymology. Most likely derived from the Old Norse words "dokk" and "vrá," meaning valleys and isolated site. The names were given to those who came from Dockray, the name of several places in England. (Irish): derived from the Gaelic name Ó Dochraidh, meaning "descendant of Dochrach" (H&H), meaning "unlucky" or "hurtful" (H&H). Dockerty: transformation of Doherty.

Genealogies: *Dockerys of Dixie* was compiled by William Glenn Allen in Spartanburg, South Carolina, in 1991.

DODD

Ranking: 1013   **S.S. Count:** 43,220
Origin: English, Irish. English: Derived from the Old English first names Dodda and Dudda, which may have referred to someone who was considered to be short and stout. Irish: derived from the Gaelic name Ó Dubhda, meaning "descendant of Dubhda" (H&H), which is derived from the word "dubh," meaning dark.

Famous **Dodds:** FRANK HOWARD DODD (1844–1916) of New Jersey was a publisher responsible for the *New International Encyclopedia*. WILLIAM EDWARD DODD (1869–1940) of North Carolina was a historian who wrote about the South and Woodrow Wilson. MONROE ELMON DODD (1878–1952) of Tennessee was a Southern Baptist preacher and the founder of Dodd College in 1926. BELLA VISONO DODD (1904–1969) of Italy was a union representative who renounced Communism.

Genealogies: *The Fields Family: With Notes on Whitesell and Dodd* was compiled by Ruth Fields Lewis and published in Evansville, Indiana, in 1976. *Our Dodd Family: Ancestors and Descendants of James Dodd* was compiled by Marjorie Dodd Floyd and most likely published in Dayton, Ohio, in 1971.

DODDS

Ranking: 3518   **S.S. Count:** 12,824
Origin: English. Transformation of Dodd.

Famous **Doddses:** JOHNNY DODDS (1892–1940) of Louisiana was a jazz clarinetist in New Orleans. His brother, WARREN DODDS (1898–1959), known as Baby Dodds, was a jazz drummer.

Genealogies: None known.

DODGE

Ranking: 1395   **S.S. Count:** 31,786
Origin: English. 1) transformation of Roger(s). 2) derived from the Old English word "docga," meaning dog.

Famous **Dodges:** DAVID LOW DODGE (1774–1852) of Connecticut was the founder of the New York Peace Society in 1815. It was the first organization of that type in America. HENRY DODGE (1782–1867) of Indiana was a colonel in the army during the Black Hawk War; a governor of Wisconsin; a member of the U.S. House of Representatives; and then a member of the U.S. Senate. WILLIAM EARL DODGE (1805–1883) of Connecticut, son of David Low Dodge, was co-founder of Phelps, Dodge and Company, which became one of the "big three" U.S. mining companies. He also was one of the organizers of the Y.M.C.A. AUGUSTUS CAESAR DODGE (1812–1883) was the first U.S. senator from Iowa and a U.S. minister to Spain. He was the son of Henry Dodge. GRENVILLE MELLEN DODGE (1831–1916) of Massachusetts was the major general of volunteers during the Civil War. He was involved in railroad building in the Southwest and Cuba. MARY ELIZABETH MAPES DODGE (1831–1905) of New York was a writer who specialized in children's books and is best remembered for her classic *Hans Brinker; or, the Silver Skates*. She was the wife of William Dodge. MARY ABIGAIL DODGE (1833–1896) of Massachusetts was a writer. She was the author of *Gala Days, A New Atmosphere,* and *Woman's Worth and Worthlessness,* among others. JOSEPHINE MARSHALL JEWELL DODGE

(1855–1928) of Connecticut was an advocate of day-care nurseries for working mothers. She sponsored the Virginia Day Nursery in 1878 in the East Side slums of New York City. In 1888 she founded the Jewell Day Nursery, based on the principle of educating the immigrant children to the cultural ways of the American-born middle class. GRACE HOADLEY DODGE (1856–1914) was born in New York. The great-granddaughter of David Low Dodge, she developed a working girls' club, which would become the Working Girls' Association of Clubs, and helped found the New York Travelers Aid Society. HENRY CHEE DODGE (1860–1947) was a tribal chairman of the Navajo whose sensitivity to the plight of the Indians allowed him to work as a liaison between the federal government and the Navajo people. WILLIAM DE LEFTWICH DODGE (1867–1935) of Virginia was an artist whose murals are on display in the Folies Bergère Theatre and in many government buildings, including the Library of Congress. It is believed that he added the "De" to his name himself. RAYMOND DODGE (1871–1942) of Massachusetts was a psychologist who was the founder of the Yale Institute of Psychology. He co-invented the tachistoscope and did work in the study of eye movements in reading.

Genealogies: *Ancestral Lines: 144 Families in England, Germany, New England, New York, New Jersey and Pennsylvania* was compiled by Carl Boyer and published in Newhall, California, in 1975. *The Dozier (also Dodge) Family of Lower Norfolk County: A Reference* was compiled by Anne Maling and published in Norfolk, Virginia, in 1986.

DODSON

Ranking: 803   **S.S. Count:** 52,492
Origin: English. Transformation of Dodd.
Genealogies: *The Dodson (Dotson) Family of North Farnham Parish, Richmond County, Virginia: A History and Genealogy of Their Descendants* was compiled by Mrs. Sherman Williams and published in Easley, South Carolina, in 1988. *The Dodson Family of Warren County, Tennessee, and Allied Families* was compiled by Catherine Gaffin Lynn and published in Centerville, Tennessee, in 1974.

DOHERTY   (S.S. Abbreviation: Dohert)

Ranking: 1140   **S.S. Count:** 38,549
Origin: Irish, Scottish. Derived from the Gaelic name Ó Dochartaigh, meaning "descendant of Dochartach" (H&H), meaning "unlucky" or "hurtful" (H&H).
Famous **Dohertys:** HENRY LATHAM DOHERTY (1870–1939) of Ohio founded Cities Service Co., which came to own more than 200 oil and utility firms. In order to check his freewheeling business deals, Congress passed the Security Act of 1933 and the Public Utility Holding Company Act of 1935. ROBERT ERNEST DOHERTY (1885–1950)

was president of Carnegie Institute of Technology in Pennsylvania.
Genealogies: None known.

DOLAN

Ranking: 1102   **S.S. Count:** 40,111
Origin: Irish. 1) derived from the Gaelic name Ó Dubhshaáin, meaning "descendant of Dubhshlán," which is derived from the words "dubh" and "slán," meaning dark and defiance. 2) transformation of Devlin.
Famous **Dolans:** THOMAS DOLAN (1834–1914) of Pennsylvania was involved with the development of public utilities. He was involved in a 1905 Philadelphia gas company scandal.
Genealogies: *The Dolan Family, 1811–1983* was compiled by Ellen Urness and published in Platteville, Wisconsin, in 1984. *The Seeds of the Planter: Our Family Story from 1636 to 1975* was compiled by Geraldine D. Gallagher and published in Fullerton, California, in 1975.

DOLL

Ranking: 3425   **S.S. Count:** 13,183
Origin: English. Derived from the Old English word "dol," meaning foolish and/or dull. The name was given to those who were considered to be silly and uninteresting.
Famous **Dolls:** EDGAR ARNOLD DOLL (1889–1968) of Ohio was a psychologist who developed the theory that social competence was a reliable test for the extent of deficiency or sufficiency of the handicaps of people. He led efforts to establish special schools and classes within conventional schools for handicapped children to develop more social competence. He wrote many articles, papers, and books, including *The Measure of Social Competence* (1953).
Genealogies: *Our Family History* was compiled by Irene Doll and published in Lena, Illinois, in 1976.

DOLLAR

Ranking: 3594   **S.S. Count:** 12,552
Origin: Scottish. Uncertain etymology. The name was given to those who came from Dollar, which means "dale of plowed land" (ES) and is a place in Clackmannanshire, Scotland.
Famous **Dollars:** ROBERT DOLLAR (1844–1932) of Scotland moved to the United States in 1882 and settled in San Francisco, where he started a shipping line with trade concentrated in the Orient. He introduced around-the-world passenger service on ocean liners.
Genealogies: None known.

DOMBROVSKI, DOMBROVSKY, DOMBROWSKI, DOMBROWSKY   (S.S. Abbreviation: Dombro)

Ranking: 2726   **S.S. Count:** 16,698

Origin: Jewish. *Derived from the Polish word "dąbrowa," meaning oak grove. The names were given to those who came from Dabrowa, the name of several places in Poland.*
Genealogies: None known.

DOMINGOS, DOMINGUES, DOMINGO, DOMINGUEZ (S.S. Abbreviation: Doming)
Ranking: 598   **S.S. Count:** 69,853
Origin: Domingos, Domingues—*Portuguese;* Domingo, Dominguez—*Spanish. Cognates to Dominique.*
Genealogies: None known.

DOMINIK, DOMINIQUE, DOMINI, DOMINICACCI, DOMINICHINI, DOMINICI, DOMINICO, DOMINIAK, ET AL.
Ranking: 3125   **S.S. Count:** 14,543
Origin: Dominik—*Czech, Polish;* Dominique—*French;* Domini, Dominicacci, Dominichini, Dominici, Dominico, et al.—*Italian;* Dominiak—*Polish. Derived from the Latin first name Dominicus, which is derived from "dominus," meaning master or lord.*
Genealogies: None known.

DONAHUE (S.S. Abbreviation: Donahu)
Ranking: 987   **S.S. Count:** 44,417
Origin: Irish. *Transformation of Donohue.*
Famous Donahues: PETER DONAHUE (1822–1885) of Scotland was a capitalist who founded the Union Iron Works in San Francisco and was a pioneer in California public utilities. He organized the first streetcar line in San Francisco.
Genealogies: None known.

DONALD, DONALDSON
Ranking: 634   **S.S. Count:** 65,348
Origin: Irish, Scottish. *Derived from the Gaelic first name Domhnall, which is derived from the Celtic components "dubno" and "val," meaning world and might.*
Famous Bearers: HENRY HERBERT DONALDSON (1857–1938) of New York was a neurologist who wrote *Growth of the Brain: A Study of the Nervous System in Relation to Education* (1895). He also developed the "Wistar Strain" of albino rat that is used as the standard animal in laboratory studies. JESSE MONROE DONALDSON (1885–1970) of Illinois was a U.S. postmaster general who greatly improved the efficiency of the department. WALTER DONALDSON (1893–1947) of Brooklyn, New York, composed many popular songs, such as "My Mammy," "Yes Sir, That's My Baby," and "Love Me or Leave Me."
Genealogies: *Donaldson [Genealogical Notes on the Donaldson Family and Its Maternal Lines, Macfarland, Winchester, Johnston and Dorsey]* was compiled by John Wilcox

Donaldson and most likely published in 1930–1972 in New York, New York.

DONATO
Ranking: 4600   **S.S. Count:** 9717
Origin: Italian. *Derived from the Latin name Dōnātus, which is derived from the word "dōnare," meaning given.*
Genealogies: None known.

DONNELLY, DONNELL, DONNELLAN (S.S. Abbreviation: Donnel)
Ranking: 722   **S.S. Count:** 58,531
Origin: Donnelly—*Irish;* Donnell, Donnellan—*Irish, Scottish. Donnelly: derived from the Gaelic name Ó Donnghaile, meaning "descendant of Donnghal" (H&H), which is derived from the words "donn" and "gal," meaning brown and valor. Donnell, Donnellan: transformations of Donald.*
Famous Bearers: IGNATIUS DONNELLY (1831–1901) of Philadelphia, Pennsylvania, was a writer who advocated the belief that Francis Bacon was the true author of Shakespeare's plays. He also wrote *Atlantis*, which traced civilization's origin to the mythical submerged city of Atlantis, and *Ragnarok: The Age of Fire and Gravel*, which theorized about a near-collision between Earth and a large comet. LUCY MARTIN DONNELLY (1870–1948) of New York taught English at Bryn Mawr College.
Genealogies: *Genealogy in Convenient Form* was compiled by Ralph W. Cathell and published in Boylestown, Pennsylvania, in 1976.

DONOHUE (S.S. Abbreviation: Donohu)
Ranking: 2159   **S.S. Count:** 21,251
Origin: Irish. *Derived from the Gaelic name Ó Donnchadha, meaning "descendant of Donnchadh" (H&H), which is derived from the words "donn" and "cath," meaning brown and battle.*
Genealogies: None known.

DONOVAN (S.S. Abbreviation: Donova)
Ranking: 737   **S.S. Count:** 57,522
Origin: Irish. *Derived from the Gaelic name Ó Donndubháin, meaning "descendant of Donndubhán" (H&H), a first name derived from the word "dubh," meaning dark and/or black, and the diminutive suffix "án."*
Famous Donovans: JOHN JOSEPH DONOVAN (1858–1938) of New Hampshire was a railroad pioneer and builder of the Pacific Northwest. WILLIAM JOSEPH DONOVAN (1883–1959) of New York was known as WILD BILL DONOVAN. He was the head of the Office of Strategic Services (1942–1945) and ambassador to Thailand (1953–1954). JAMES BRITT DONOVAN (1916–1970) of New York was a lawyer and educator. He was the general counsel of

the U.S. Office of Scientific Research and Development and handled the legal matters relevant to the atomic bomb. He also was the assistant prosecutor at the International Military Tribunal in Nuremberg, Germany. He arranged the release of Francis Gary Powers, the U-2 pilot shot down and accused of espionage, and of 9700 American and Cuban prisoners of war after the Bay of Pigs invasion.

Genealogies: None known.

DOOLEY

Ranking: 1311   **S.S. Count:** 33,840

Origin: Irish. Derived from the Gaelic word Ó Dubhlaoich, meaning "descendant of Dubhlaoch" (H&H), which is derived from the words "dubh" and "laoch," meaning black and/or dark, and champion.

Famous **Dooleys:** THOMAS ANTHONY DOOLEY (1927–1961) of St. Louis, Missouri, was known as the "jungle doctor" for his efforts to bring medical assistance to people of underdeveloped countries.

Genealogies: None known.

DOOLITTLE   (S.S. Abbreviation: Dooli)

Ranking: 4544   **S.S. Count:** 9832

Origin: English. Derived from the Old English words "dón" and "lytel," which combined together refer to a lazy man.

Famous **Doolittles:** AMOS DOOLITTLE (1754–1832) of Connecticut was an engraver who made prints of battles and illustrations and maps for books. JAMES ROOD DOOLITTLE (1815–1897) of New York was an adviser to President Abraham Lincoln and a supporter of President Andrew Johnson, which ultimately doomed his own career. DUDLEY DOOLITTLE (1881–1947) was a member of Congress from Kansas for three terms and president of the College of Emporia in Kansas. HILDA DOOLITTLE (1886–1961) of Pennsylvania was a poet who wrote "Hedgehog" and "Bid Me Love," among others.

Genealogies: None known.

DORAN

Ranking: 4554   **S.S. Count:** 9832

Origin: English, Irish. English: transformation of Durant. Irish: derived from the Gaelic name Ó Deoradháin, meaning "descendant of Deoradhán" (H&H), which is derived from the word "deoadh," meaning stranger or pilgrim.

Famous **Dorans:** GEORGE HENRY DORAN (1869–1956) of Canada moved to Chicago and started a publishing company that later merged with F. N. Doubleday to form Doubleday, Doran & Co.

Genealogies: None known.

DORE

Ranking: 1877   **S.S. Count:** 24,123

Origin: English, French, Irish. English: derived from the Old English word "dor," meaning door, and referring to the site of passage between hills. The name was given to those who came from Dore, the name of several places in England. French: derived from the Old French word "doré," meaning golden. The name was given to those who had gold-colored hair and to those who worked as goldsmiths. Irish: derived from the Gaelic name Ó Doghair, meaning "descendant of Doghar" (H&H), meaning sadness.

Genealogies: None known.

DORMAN, DORMANN

Ranking: 2626   **S.S. Count:** 17,314

Origin: Dorman—English; Dormann—German. Dorman: transformation of Dear. Dormann: derived from the Old High German word "tor," meaning gate. The name was given to those who lived near a town's gates or to those who worked guarding the gates.

Famous **Bearers:** WILLIAM EDWIN DORMAN (1875–1936) was a member of Congress from Massachusetts. LOUIS HAROLD DORMAN (1900–1875) of New York was president (1939–1972) of N. Dorman & Co., one of the nation's largest cheese-making, importing, and marketing firms.

Genealogies: None known.

DORN

Ranking: 3122   **S.S. Count:** 14,562

Origin: German. Cognate to the English and Danish definition of Thorn.

Genealogies: None known.

DORRIS

Ranking: 4699   **S.S. Count:** 9517

Origin: Irish. Derived from the first name Dubhros, meaning "black Ros" (ES).

Genealogies: None known.

DORSEY

Ranking: 709   **S.S. Count:** 59,679

Origin: English. Derived from the preposition "de," meaning of or from, and the place name Orsay, which is derived from the Latin first name Orcius. The name was given to those who came from Orsay, the name of a place in Seine-et-Orne, France.

Famous **Dorseys:** SARAH ANNE ELLIS DORSEY (1829–1879) of Mississippi was an author but is best known as Jefferson Davis's benefactor, who invited him to her home at Beauvoir to write his memoirs. She willed her estate to him. Rumors suggested that there was more to their relationship than just friendship, but nothing was ever proven. JAMES OWEN DORSEY (1848–1895) of Maryland was an ethnologist who was a missionary to the Ponca Indians in the Dakota territory of the 1870s, then an agent of the U.S. Bureau of American Ethnology who studied the Omaha Indians. He wrote several books on the languages and traditions of the Indians and edited *The Dakota-English Dictionary and Dakota Grammar, Texts, and Ethnography* by Stephen Return Riggs. SUSAN ALMIRA MILLER DORSEY (1857–1946) of New York was an educator and the first female assistant superintendent of schools in Los Angeles, California. She was the second female superintendent of schools in the country, second only to Ella Flagg Young of Chicago. In 1937 she was the first living person ever to have a Los Angeles school named for her. GEORGE AMOS DORSEY (1868–1931) of Ohio was an anthropologist who believed that science should be interesting to the layman. He wrote *Why We Behave Like Human Beings* and *Man's Own Show: Civilization*. JAMES (JIMMY) DORSEY (1904–1957) and THOMAS (TOMMY) DORSEY (1905–1956), brothers from Pennsylvania, were both leaders of dance orchestras and were first prominent in white jazz circles.

Genealogies: *Grandparents Are Great* was compiled by Lois Colette Dorsey Bennington and published in Victorville, California, in 1982.

DOSS
Ranking: 1619 **S.S. Count:** 27,646
Origin: German. Derived from first names beginning with the word "diet," meaning people.
Genealogies: None known.

DOTSON
Ranking: 1049 **S.S. Count:** 41,775
Origin: English. Transformation of Dodd.
Genealogies: None known.

DOTY
Ranking: 1716 **S.S. Count:** 26,080
Origin: English. Transformation of Doughty.
Famous **Dotys:** JAMES DUANE DOTY (1799–1865) served as territorial governor of both Wisconsin and Utah.
Genealogies: *The Doty-Doten Family in America: Descendants of Edward Doty, An Emigrant By the Mayflower, 1620* was compiled by Ethan Allen Doty and published in Rutland, Vermont, in 1985. *The James Alfred Doty Descendants of Edward Doty, A Mayflower Passenger, 1620* was compiled by Ervin A. Doty and published in Angola, Indiana, in the 1970s.

DOUCET
Ranking: 2390 **S.S. Count:** 18,992
Origin: English. Derived from the Middle English words "douce" and "dowce," meaning sweet and pleasant. The name was given to those considered to have these attributes.
Genealogies: None known.

DOUGHERTY (S.S. Abbreviation: Doughe)
Ranking: 759 **S.S. Count:** 55,863
Origin: Irish, Scottish. Transformation of Doherty.
Famous **Doughertys:** DENNIS JOSEPH DOUGHERTY (1865–1951) of Pennsylvania was a Roman Catholic cardinal and archbishop of Philadelphia. RAYMOND PHILIP DOUGHERTY (1877–1933) of Pennsylvania was a missionary educator and Assyriologist who tried to prove in his book *The Sealand of Ancient Arabia* that the sealand of Babylonian literature extended across the Arabian Peninsula and was more important than scholars had originally thought.
Genealogies: *History of the Daugherty (also Dougherty) Family in America* was compiled by Jackson Temple Daugherty and published in Cullman, Alabama, in 1987.

DOUGHTERY, DOUGHTY (S.S. Abbreviation: Dought)
Ranking: 2466 **S.S. Count:** 18,400
Origin: English. Doughtery: derived from the preposition "de," meaning of or from, and the Old French phrase "haute rive," meaning high bank. The name was given to those who came from Hauterive in Orne, France. Doughty: derived from the Old English words "dohtig" and "dyhtig," meaning valiant and strong. The name was given to those who were considered to possess these attributes.
Genealogies: None known.

DOUGLAS, DOUGLASS (S.S. Abbreviation: Dougla)
Ranking: 229 **S.S. Count:** 153,296
Origin: Scottish. Derived from the Gaelic words "dubh" and "glais," meaning dark and/or black, and stream. The name was given to those who came from Douglas, the name of several places in Scotland.
Famous **Bearers:** SARAH MAPPS DOUGLASS DOUGLASS (1806–1882) of Pennsylvania was a teacher and an abolitionist. Born a free Negro in Philadelphia, she opened a school for the Negro children of that city. (Douglass was her maiden name. She then married Rev. William Douglass.) STEPHEN ARNOLD DOUGLAS (1813–1861) served in both the U.S. House of Representatives and the U.S. Senate from Illinois. As a leader of the Democratic Party, he advocated national expansion and popular sovereignty for the issue of slavery. He lost the 1860 presidential election to Abraham Lincoln. FREDERICK DOUGLAS (1817–1895) of Maryland was a runaway slave originally named Frederick Augustus Washington Bailey who settled in New Bedford, Massachusetts. At that time he changed his name to Douglass. He became connected with the Massachusetts Anti-Slavery Society and lectured in Europe. He used his earnings to buy his freedom, then settled in Rochester, New York, where he founded and edited the *North Star*, also called *Frederick Douglass's Paper*. Douglass helped recruit a

black regiment for the North at the outbreak of the Civil War and served as a U.S. marshal and a recorder of deeds in the District of Columbia and as U.S. minister to Haiti (1889–1891). AMANDA MINNIE DOUGLAS (1831–1916) of New York was a writer of children's books. She is best known for her *Kathie* series, *Little Girl* series, and *Helen Grant* series. ADELE CUTTS DOUGLAS (1835–1899) of Washington, D.C., was the wife of Stephen A. Douglas and a prominent Washington belle. JAMES DOUGLAS (1837–1918) was born in Quebec. He was a metallurgist and mining engineer and the co-inventor of the process for copper extraction known as the Hunt-Douglas process. He also built the El Paso and Southwestern Railroad. The town of Douglas, Arizona, is named for him. HENRY KYD DOUGLAS (1838–1903) of West Virginia was a Confederate soldier. His brigade of Lee's army was the last unit to surrender at Appomattox, Virginia. ANDREW ELLICOTT DOUGLASS (1867–1962) of Vermont was an astronomer and the director of the Stewart Observatory. He took the first picture of zodiacal light. He is best known for the dating of prehistoric ruins by tree rings. MABEL SMITH DOUGLASS (1877–1933) of New Jersey founded and was the dean of the New Jersey College for Women, which was later named Douglass College. LLOYD CASSEL DOUGLAS (1877–1951) of Indiana was the author of several books, including *The Robe, White Banners, Invitation to Live,* and *The Big Fisherman,* among others. BEVERLY DOUGLAS (1891–1975) of Tennessee was a plastic surgeon who developed a procedure to correct micrognathia, a condition in newborn infants whose jaws are so short they are likely to swallow their tongues. The procedure was credited with saving the lives of 2000 babies a year in the United States. DONALD WILLS DOUGLAS (1892–1981) of New York was an engineer. He built airplanes first at the Davis-Douglas Co., then at the Douglas Aircraft Co. The company eventually merged and became the McDonnell-Douglas Co. WILLIAM ORVILLE DOUGLAS (1898–1980) of Minnesota was an associate justice of the U.S. Supreme Court who was known for his consistently liberal viewpoint, especially with laws dealing with one's freedom of speech.

Genealogies: *A Branch of the Douglas Family With Its Maryland & Virginia Connections* was compiled by Harry Wright Newman and published in Garden City, New York, in 1967.

DOVE

Ranking: 2388 S.S. Count: 19,015

Origin: English, Irish, German, Scottish. English: derived from the Old English word "dūfe," meaning dove. The name was given to to those who were considered peaceful like a dove and to those who worked keeping doves. Irish: derived from the name Mac Calmáin, which is derived from an Old Irish first name meaing dove. German: derived from the Middle High

German word "toup," meaning deaf. The name was given to those who were deaf. Scottish: transformation of Duff.

Famous Doves: DAVID JAMES DOVE (1696?–1769) of England is believed to be the first person in the colonies to offer an education to women. He came to Philadelphia in 1750, teaching there and in Germantown, Pennsylvania. He remained in the area until his death. ARTHUR GARFIELD DOVE (1880–1946) of Canandaigua, New York, was one of the first American abstract artists.

Genealogies: None known.

DOVER

Ranking: 3702 S.S. Count: 12,202

Origin: English, German, Jewish. English: derived from the Welsh word "dwfr," meaning water. The name was given to those who came from Dover, a place in Kent, England. German: the name was given to those who came from Doveren, a place in the Rhineland, Germany. Jewish: uncertain etymology.

Genealogies: None known.

DOW

Ranking: 2087 S.S. Count: 21,993

Origin: English, Irish, Scottish. English: 1) transformation of David. 2) derived from the Middle English word "daw," meaning jackdaw bird. The name was given to those who were dark, loud or prone to stealing, like the bird. Irish: derived from the Gaelic name Ó Deághaidh, meaning "descendant of Deághadh" (H&H). Scottish: transformation of Duff.

Famous Dows: NEAL DOW (1804–1897) of Maine was the mayor of Portland, Maine, who introduced a prohibition law that came to be known as the "Maine Law." It passed the legislature and allowed the town to clean up its liquor problem. Dow gained national attention because of the success of the law. He was the unsuccessful candidate for president on the Prohibition Party ticket in 1880. CHARLES HENRY DOW (1851–1902) of Connecticut was the founder of Dow Jones and Company, a financial service company that in 1884 made its first compilation of the average of U.S. stock prices. This came to be known as the Dow Jones average. ALEX DOW (1862–1942) of Scotland was a manager and businessman in the public utilities field in Detroit. He originated the concept of different rates for different times of the day based on the demand of power, thereby giving 24-hour factories a break on the cost of the utilities. This enticed more companies to settle in Detroit. HERBERT HENRY DOW (1866–1930) of Canada was a chemist who founded the Dow Chemical Co.

Genealogies: *The Ancestry of Harvey Dunn (also Dow)* was compiled by Judith Miner Hine Luedemann and published in Chester, Connecticut, in 1972.

DOWD

Ranking: 2321   **S.S. Count:** 19,554

Origin: Irish. Derived from the Gaelic name Ó Dubhda, meaning "descendant of Dubhda" (H&H), which is derived from the word "dubh," meaning dark.

Famous **Dowds:** JOHN WORTHINGTON DOWD (1847–1926) was elected president of the University of Toledo in Ohio at the age of 78 and served for one year until his death. WILLIAM CAREY DOWD (1893–1949) of North Carolina was president and publisher of the Charlotte (North Carolina) *News* for 20 years.

Genealogies: None known.

DOWDY

Ranking: 2434   **S.S. Count:** 18,647

Origin: Irish, Scottish. Derived from first name Dubhda, meaning black.

Genealogies: None known.

DOWELL

Ranking: 2275   **S.S. Count:** 20,014

Origin: Irish, Scottish. Derived from the Gaelic first name Dubhgall, which is derived from the words "dubh" and "gall," meaning black and strangers. The name was often given to dark-haired Scandinavians.

Famous **Dowells:** GREENSVILLE DOWELL (1822–1881) of Virginia was a surgeon and is best remembered for suggesting that yellow fever was carried by mosquitoes. He developed a cure for a hernia and designed a number of medical instruments. CASSIUS C. DOWELL (1864–1940) was a member of the U.S. House of Representatives from Iowa for 22 years.

Genealogies: None known.

DOWLIN, DOWLING

Ranking: 1895   **S.S. Count:** 23,878

Origin: Dowlin—Irish; Dowling—English, Irish. Dowlin, Dowling (Irish): transformation of the first definitions of Dolan. Dowling (English): derived from the Old English word "dol," meaning dull and stupid. The name was given to those who were considered unintelligent.

Famous **Bearers:** NOEL THOMAS DOWLING (1885–1969) of Alabama wrote the most widely used law-school textbooks on constitutional law.

Genealogies: None known.

DOWNEY

Ranking: 1154   **S.S. Count:** 37,981

Origin: Irish, Scottish. 1) derived from the Gaelic name Ó Dúnadhaigh, meaning "descendant of Dúnadhach" (H&H), meaning fortress holder and derived from the word "dún," meaning fortress. 2) derived from the Gaelic name Mac Giolla Dhomnaigh, meaning "son of the servant of the Church" (H&H). 3) derived from the Gaelic word "dún," meaning hill. The name was given to those who came from Downie or Duny, the names of places in Scotland.

Famous **Downeys:** JUNE ETTA DOWNEY (1875–1932) of Wyoming was a pioneer in clinical psychology. She developed the Downey Will-Temperament Test and was an authority on handedness and handwriting. JAMES HENRY DOWNEY (1864–1937), a surgeon in Gainesville, Georgia, invented the Downey Fracture Table, a device used to treat bone fractures. SHERIDAN DOWNEY (1884–1961) of Wyoming territory was a U.S. senator.

Genealogies: *A Downey & Crawford Ancestry* was compiled by Roy H. Downey and published in Salem, Virginia, in 1981. *The Genealogy of Thomas Downey and Margaret Tracey* was compiled by Joyce V. Hawley Spires and published in Gallup, New Mexico, most likely in 1978.

DOWNING   (S.S. Abbreviation: Downin)

Ranking: 1072   **S.S. Count:** 41,111

Origin: English. Transformation of Dunn.

Famous **Downings:** ANDREW JACKSON DOWNING (1815–1852) of New York was a horticulturist who co-wrote *Fruits and Fruit Trees of America*, which today is considered a standard. WARWICK MILLER DOWNING (1875–1963) was a prominent parks commissioner in Denver, Colorado, and is known as the father of mountain parks, the boulevard system, and the playgrounds of Denver.

Genealogies: *The Downings of Europe and America, 1273–1973* was compiled by Anna May Cochrane Gregath and published in Cullman, Alabama, in 1980. *Thaddeus K. Smith and Bertah Heyne: Their Ancestors and Descendants, Including the Families of Bard, Downing, and Veach* was compiled by Margaret E. Herrick and published in La Granville, New York, in 1989.

DOWNS

Ranking: 916   **S.S. Count:** 47,051

Origin: English. Transformation of Dunn.

Genealogies: *The Downs Family of Virginia, Ohio & Indiana* was compiled by George Gilbert McCarthy and published in Murray Hill, New Jersey, in 1982.

DOYLE

Ranking: 362   **S.S. Count:** 106,908

Origin: Irish, Scottish. Transformation of Dowell.

Famous **Doyles:** SARAH ELIZABETH DOYLE (1830–1922) of Rhode Island was a respected educator in Providence and one of the founders of the Rhode Island School of Design. ALEXANDER DOYLE (1857–1922) of Ohio was a sculptor who designed many public monuments, including "Horace Greeley" in New York City, "National Revolutionary Monument" in Yorktown, Virginia, and "Thomas H. Benton," "Francis P. Blaire," and "John E. Kenna" in Washington, D.C.

Genealogies: *Patrick Doyle and Timothy Keane, Their Families and Descendants* was compiled by Clarke L. Neal and published in Selfridge Base, Michigan, in 1981.

DOZIER
Ranking: 2108   S.S. Count: 21,773

Origin: French. Derived from the preposition "de," meaning of or from, and the Old French word "osier," meaning willow. The name was given to those who lived near willow trees.

Genealogies: *The Dozier Family of Lower Norfolk County: A Reference* was compiled by Anne Maling and published in Norfolk, Virginia, in 1986.

DRAKE
Ranking: 476   S.S. Count: 84,660

Origin: English. 1) derived from the Old English and Old Norse names Draca and Draki, both meaning snake. 2) derived from the Middle English word "drake," meaning male duck. The name was given to those who were thought to look like such creatures.

Famous **Drakes**: JOSEPH RODMAN DRAKE (1795–1820) of New York was a poet whose best-known works were "The Culprit Fay," "Niagara," and "The American Flag." SAMUEL GARDNER DRAKE (1798–1875) of New Hampshire was a historian and an author. He was the editor of several classic books on New England. FRANCIS SAMUEL DRAKE (1828–1885) of New Hampshire was a historian and an author. His works include *Dictionary of American Biography* and *Tea Leaves*. FRANCIS MARION DRAKE (1830–1903) of Illinois was the governor of Iowa, a railroad builder in Iowa, a Union soldier, and the benefactor of Drake University. EDWIN LAURENTINE DRAKE (1819–1880) of Greenville, New York, drilled the first productive oil well in the United States. ALEXANDER WILSON DRAKE (1843–1916) of New Jersey was a leader in the development of illustrative art.

Genealogies: *The Alford-Drake Family of Middle Tennessee, With Ancestors, Descendants, and Allied Families* was compiled by Naomi M. Hailey and published in Nashville, Tennessee, in 1982. *Descendants of Jessee Shelton and Some Related Families: Drake, Foster, Gibson, Hamby, Keele, Martin* was compiled by Cecil and Louise Shelton and published in Fresno, California, in 1977.

DRAPER, DRAPERON
Ranking: 1375   S.S. Count: 32,166

Origin: English. Derived from the Anglo-Norman-French word "draper," meaning one who made or sold wool cloth. The name was given to those who worked as either.

Famous **Bearers**: JOHN DRAPER (1702–1762) of Boston was the publisher of the *Boston News-Letter*. RICHARD DRAPER (1726?–1774) of Massachusetts, the son of John Draper, inherited his father's publishing business. The newspaper continued to be published under different names, such as *The Boston Weekly News-Letter and New England Chronicle* and *The Massachusetts Gazette and Boston News-Letter*. MARGARET GREEN DRAPER (1750–1807) was the wife of Richard. She published the *News-Letter* after Richard's death. Being a strong Loyalist, she left Boston in 1776. JOHN WILLIAM DRAPER (1811–1882) of England was a scientist who worked in the field of radiant energy, photochemistry, photography, and electric telegraphy. He made the first photograph of the moon. LYMAN COPELAND DRAPER (1815–1891) of New York edited the first 10 volumes of *Wisconsin Historical Collections*. He was also the author of *King's Mountain and Its Heroes*. HENRY DRAPER (1837–1882) of Virginia was an astronomer who photographed stars and planets and was a pioneer in the field of spectrology. He was the son of John William Draper. *The Draper Catalogue*, a collection of stellar magnitudes done by Harvard University, is a memorial to him. MARY ANNA PALMER DRAPER (1839–1914) of Connecticut was the wife of Henry Draper. After his death she donated his telescope and contributed heavily to Harvard College Observatory so that *The Draper Catalogue* would be completed as a testimony to him. RUTH DRAPER (1884–1956) of New York was a well-known monologist and monodramatist who appeared on U.S. and European stages. DOROTHY DRAPER (1889–1969) of New York was an interior designer known for her use of vivid colors and total design coordination.

Genealogies: *Draper Families in America* was compiled by Ethel Nichols Anderson and published in Nashville, Tennessee, in 1964. *The Mormon Drapers* was compiled by Delbert Morley Draper and published in Salt Lake City, Utah, in 1958.

DRAYTON   (S.S. Abbreviation: Drayto)
Ranking: 4602   S.S. Count: 9712

Origin: English. Derived from the Old English words "dræg" and "tūn," meaning drag or slipway and settlement. The name was given to those who came from Drayton, the name of several places in England.

Famous **Draytons**: WILLIAM HENRY DRAYTON (1742–1779) of South Carolina represented South Carolina in the Continental Congress. JOHN DRAYTON (1766–1822) of South Carolina was the governor of that state and was responsible for the establishment of South Carolina College. PERCIVAL DRAYTON (1812–1865) of South Carolina was a naval officer. He served under Du Pont and Farragut in the Civil War, rising to the position of chief of the Bureau of Navigation.

Genealogies: None known.

DREW
Ranking: 1342   S.S. Count: 32,969

Origin: English. 1) transformation of Andrew. 2) derived from the Germanic first name Drogo. 3) derived from the Old

French word *"dru,"* meaning lover, and a Gallic word meaning strong. 4) Uncertain etymology. The name was given to those who came from places with similar names in France.

Famous **Drews:** DANIEL DREW (1797–1879) of New York was an industrialist who was responsible for the founding of Drew Theological Seminary in Madison, New Jersey. JOHN DREW (1827–1862) of Ireland was an actor who specialized in comedies. His wife, LOUISA LANE DREW (1820–1897) of England, also concentrated on comedy roles. JOHN DREW (1853–1927) of Pennsylvania was their son. Also an actor, he had roles that were more dramatic in nature. He toured with his brother-in-law, Maurice Barrymore, whom his sister, Georgiana Emma, married. CHARLES RICHARD DREW (1904–1950) of Washington, D.C., was the first African-American physician and surgeon known for developing techniques to preserve human blood for transfusion.

Genealogies: *Just Look At All My Families* was compiled by Lydia Drew Elisaesser and published in La Junta, Colorado, in 1981.

DREYER

Ranking: 4902   S.S. Count: 9122
Origin: German, Jewish. German: cognate to Dreher. German, Jewish: derived from the Middle High German word "dri(e)," meaning three.
Genealogies: *The Dreier (also Dreyer) Family, 1888* was compiled by Lois L. Bode and published in Gibbon, Minnesota, in 1980. *Dryer-Lauck-Payne-Scott Genealogy: Going Home* was compiled by Elizabeth Dryer Humphrey and published in Baltimore, Maryland, in 1991.

DRIGGES   (S.S. Abbreviation: Drigge)

Ranking: 4225   S.S. Count: 10,678
Origin: Dutch? Uncertain etymology.
Genealogies: None known.

DRISCOLL   (S.S. Abbreviation: Drisco)

Ranking: 1275   S.S. Count: 34,694
Origin: Irish. Derived from the Gaelic name Ó Heidirsceóil, meaning "descendant of the messenger" (H&H), which is derived from the word "edirsceól," meaning news bearer.
Famous **Driscolls:** MICHAEL EDWARD DRISCOLL (1851–1929) was a member of the U.S. House of Representatives from New York for seven years. CLARA DRISCOLL (1881–1945) of Texas had an important role in the preservation of the Alamo Mission in San Antonio, Texas.
Genealogies: None known.

DRIVER

Ranking: 2152   S.S. Count: 21,323
Origin: English. Derived from the Old English word "dri-

fan," meaning to drive. The name was given to those who drove horses or cattle.
Genealogies: *Descendants of Ludwig Treiber (Lewis Driver) and Barbara Sprenkic in the Shenandoah Valley of Virginia, The United States of America* was compiled by Carolyn Click Driver and published in Harrisonburg, Virginia, in 1980.

DRUMMOND   (S.S. Abbreviation: Drummon)

Ranking: 1832   S.S. Count: 24,661
Origin: Scottish. Derived from the Gaelic word "druim," meaning ridge. The name was given to those who came from places in Scotland that obtained their names from this word.
Genealogies: *James and Cecelia Drummond and Descendants* was compiled by Everett William Drummond and published in 1974.

DRURY

Ranking: 3078   S.S. Count: 14,765
Origin: English, French. 1) derived from the Old French word "druerie," meaning friendship and/or love. 2) derived from a Germanic first name that is derived from the words "triuwa" and "ric," meaning trust and power.
Famous **Drurys:** FRANCIS EDSON DRURY (1850–1932) of Massachusetts was founder and president of the Cleveland Foundry Co. in Ohio.
Genealogies: *The Early Drury Line of New England: Some Descendants to 1850 of Hugh Drury (c. 1617–1689)* was compiled by Linda Lightholder Kmiecik and published in Spartanburg, South Carolina, in 1990. *My Mother's Brown (also Drury) Family* was compiled by Cuma Drury Schofield and published in North Fork, California, in 1980.

DUARTE

Ranking: 2007   S.S. Count: 22,708
Origin: Spanish. Cognate to Edward.
Genealogies: None known.

DUBE

Ranking: 3566   S.S. Count: 12,641
Origin: French. The name was given to those who worked selling feather-legged pigeons and to those who lived near or at the sign of a feather-legged pigeon.
Genealogies: None known.

DUBOIS, DU BOIS

Ranking: 1346   S.S. Count: 32,873
Origin: French. Derived from the Old French word "bois," meaning wood. The name was given to those who lived or worked in a wood.
Famous **Bearers:** AUGUSTUS JAY DUBOIS (1849–1915) of Ohio was a civil engineer. He wrote *Elements of Graphical Statistics,* which was the first complete work on the subject.

WILLIAM EDWARD BURGHARDT DU BOIS (1868–1963) of Great Barrington, Massachusetts, was instrumental in the creation of the National Association for the Advancement of Colored People (NAACP). During his career as an academic and a sociological investigator, he came to believe that social change would result only from protest and agitation. GUY PÈNE DUBOIS (1884–1958) of New York was a painter known for his genre paintings and illustrations.

Genealogies: *The European Ancestry of Chretien du Bois of Wicres, France* was compiled by Matthew Hilt Murphy and published in New Paltz, New York, in 1987. *DuBose (also Dubois) Genealogy* was compiled by Dorothy Kelly MacDowell and published in Columbia, South Carolina, in 1972.

DU BOSE

Ranking: 2676   **S.S. Count:** 17,039
Origin: French. Transformation of Dubois.

Famous **Duboses:** WILLIAM PORCHER DUBOSE (1836–1918) of South Carolina was the foremost thinker of the Episcopal church in the United States.

Genealogies: *DuBose Genealogy—Supplement: Descendants of Isaac DuBose and Wife Suzanne Coillandeau* was compiled by Dorothy Kelly MacDowell and published in Aiken, South Carolina, in 1975.

DUCKET, DUCKETT

Ranking: 4150   **S.S. Count:** 10,907
Origin: English. 1) transformation of Duck. 2) derived from the Middle English words "duk(ke)" and "heved," meaning duck and head. 3) derived from the Old French word "ducquet," meaning owl. 4) derived from the Old English first name Ducca. 5) derived from the Irish first name Marmaduke.

Genealogies: *The Ducketts, from Maryland to Texas* was compiled by Margaret Johnson King and published in Cary, North Carolina, in 1989.

DUCKWORTH (S.S. Abbreviation: Duckwo)

Ranking: 2635   **S.S. Count:** 17,287
Origin: English. Derived from the Old English first name Ducca and the word "worð," meaning enclosure.

Genealogies: *German Burnett (G.B.) Kyle of Logan County, Arkansas, and His Wayne County, Tennessee, Ancestors: Duckworth, Kyle, Nesbitt, Staggs, Wilson and their Descendants and Allied Families* was compiled by Edith Madeline Replogle Raymond and published in Pullman, Washington, in 1990. *Zachary Taylor French and Rachel Evelyn Duckworth: Their Ancestors and Descendants* was compiled by Gene Lawrence Jackson and published in Fort Worth, Texas, in 1991.

DUDLEY

Ranking: 825   **S.S. Count:** 51,426

Origin: English. Derived from the Old English first name "Dudda," which may mean short and plump, and the word "lēah," meaning wood.

Famous **Dudleys:** THOMAS DUDLEY (1576–1653) of England was a colonial administrator. At the Massachusetts Bay Colony, he served as governor and deputy governor. He was a member of the founding committee of the college at Cambridge and one of the first overseers of Harvard. His son, JOSEPH DUDLEY (1647–1720), was the governor of Massachusetts, New Hampshire, and Rhode Island west of Narragansett Bay. He was detested by the colonists for his role in Sir Edmund Andros's administration. PAUL DUDLEY (1675–1751) of Massachusetts was the founder of the Dudleian lectures at Harvard. BENJAMIN WINSLOW DUDLEY (1785–1870) of Virginia was a surgeon known for his operation for bladder stones. He was the most successful surgeon in this field at the time. CHARLES BENJAMIN DUDLEY (1842–1909) was a chemist who made chemistry more efficient and safe. He was the founder and served as president of the American society for Testing and Materials. WILLIAM RUSSEL DUDLEY (1849–1911) of Connecticut was active in conservation; he was the founder of the Dudley Herbarium. HELENA STUART DUDLEY (1858–1932) of Nebraska was one of the most important leaders in the early settlement movement.

Genealogies: *The Dudley Family* was compiled by Claude William Dudley and published in Richmond, Virginia, in 1971. *The Dudley Genealogies* was compiled by James Henry Mason and published in Glendale, California, in 1987.

DUFF

Ranking: 1912   **S.S. Count:** 23,670
Origin: Irish, Scottish. Derived from the Gaelic word "dubh," meaning black and/or dark. The name was given to those who had dark hair and/or dark complexions.

Famous **Duffs:** MARY ANN DYKE DUFF (1794–1857) of England was an actress who played mostly in the southern United States. Tragedy was her forte. JAMES HENDERSON DUFF (1883–1969) of Pennsylvania was the governor of Pennsylvania, then a U.S. senator from Pennsylvania who opposed Senator Joseph McCarthy and his methods.

Genealogies: *The Forefathers and Families of Certain Settlers in Western Pennsylvania* was compiled by William Boyd Duff and published in Pittsburgh, Pennsylvania, in 1976.

DUFFEY

Ranking: 4990   **S.S. Count:** 8991
Origin: Irish, Scottish. Transformation of Duffy.
Genealogies: None known.

DUFFY

Ranking: 752   **S.S. Count:** 56,357
Origin: Irish, Scottish. Irish: derived from the Gaelic name

Ó Dubhthaigh, meaning "descendant of Dubhthach" (H&H), which is derived from the word "dubh," meaning black. Irish, Scottish: derived from the Gaelic name Mac Dhuibhshithe, meaning "son of Dubhshíth" (H&H), which is derived from the words "dubh" and "síth," meaning black and peace.

Famous **Duffys:** HUGH DUFFY (1866–1954) of Rhode Island was a baseball player and a pioneer in the newly formed American League. He was elected to the Baseball Hall of Fame in 1945. FRANCIS PATRICK DUFFY (1871–1932) of Canada was a Roman Catholic priest who was the chaplain to the "Fighting 69th" in World War I. EDMUND DUFFY (1899–1962) of New Jersey was a cartoonist on the staff of the *Baltimore Sun* and *Saturday Evening Post.* Several of his cartoons won the Pulitzer Prize.

Genealogies: *Philip A. Duffy and Sam Wilson with Allied Families, York County, Merrick County, Nebraska* was published in Park Ridge, Illinois, in 1971.

DUGAN
Ranking: 1462   S.S. Count: 30,500
Origin: Irish, Scottish. Transformation of Duggan.
Genealogies: *Thomas Hinds Duggan (also Dugan), Descendant and Ancestor* was compiled by Alice Duggan Gracy and published in Austin, Texas, most likely in 1976. *A Cameo Study of the Descendants of George William Dugan (1810–1885)* was compiled by Lucille Dugan and published in Springfield, Missouri, in 1983.

DUGAS
Ranking: 4701   S.S. Count: 9514
Origin: French. Transformation of Gast.
Genealogies: None known.

DUGGAN
Ranking: 2532   S.S. Count: 17,904
Origin: Irish, Scottish, Welsh. Irish, Scottish: derived from the Gaelic name Ó Dubhagáin, meaning "descendant of Dubhagán" (H&H), which is derived from the word "dubh," meaning black and/or dark. Welsh: derived from the first names Cadwgan and Cadogan, both of which may be derived from the word "cad," meaning battle.
Genealogies: *Thomas Hinds Duggan, Descendant and Ancestor* was compiled by Alice Duggan Gracy and published in Austin, Texas, most likely in 1976. *A Cameo Study of the Descendants of George William Dugan (1810–1885) (also Duggan)* was compiled by Lucille Dugan and published in Springfield, Missouri, in 1983.

DUGGER
Ranking: 3631   S.S. Count: 12,404
Origin: German. Derived from the first name Tuchard, meaning worth and hard.
Famous **Duggers:** BENJAMIN MINGE DUGGAR (1872–1956)

of Alabama was a botanist who wrote *Fungous Diseases of Plants* and *Plant Physiology.*
Genealogies: None known.

DUKE
Ranking: 900   S.S. Count: 48,092
Origin: English. 1) derived from the Middle English word "duk(e)," meaning duke. The name was given to those who were considered pretentious. 2) Uncertain etymology. Possibly derived from the Irish first name Marmaduke.
Famous **Dukes:** BASIL WILSON DUKE (1838–1916) of Kentucky was a Confederate soldier who served with John Hunt Morgan's "Lexington's Rifles." BENJAMIN NEWTON DUKE (1855–1929) and his brother JAMES BUCHANAN DUKE (1856–1925), both born in North Carolina, were industrialists who introduced the cigarette-making machine. Both brothers contributed heavily to Trinity College in Durham, which was renamed Duke University in their honor. VERNON DUKE (1903–1969), originally from Russia, was born Vladimir Aleksandrovich Dukelsky and was a composer. After George Gershwin advised him, "Do not be scared about going low-brow," Duke composed some of America's best-known show tunes, such as "April in Paris" and "I Can't Get Started." He also composed many celebrated classical pieces.
Genealogies: *The Dukes of Durham, 1865–1929* was compiled by Robert Franklin Durden and published in Durham, North Carolina, in 1975. *The Henning and Duke Families of Louisville, Kentucky: Including Genealogical Material* was compiled by Charles P. Stanton and published in Brooklyn, New York, in 1983.

DUKES
Ranking: 1545   S.S. Count: 28,888
Origin: English. Transformation of the first definition of Duke.
Famous **Dukeses:** CHARLES ALFRED DUKES (1872–1942) was a physician and surgeon in California known as a cancer specialist.
Genealogies: None known.

DUMAS
Ranking: 1969   S.S. Count: 23,023
Origin: Provençal. Derived from the Old Provençal and Catalan word "mas," meaning farm. The name was given to those who lived in the country.
Genealogies: *Notes on the Dumas Families of Union Parish, Louisiana* was compiled by John H. Wilson, Carine Dumas Nolan, and Lorena Craighead Dumas and published in Farmerville, Louisiana, in 1979. *Pierre Dumas: His Life and His Descendants 1756–1986* was compiled by Hallie Arden DeMass Sweeting and published in Sterling, New York, in 1986.

DUMONT

Ranking: 4538 **S.S. Count:** 9849

Origin: French. Derived from the Old French word "mont," meaning hill. The name was given to those who lived on or near a hill.

Famous **Dumonts:** MARGARET DUMONT (1889–1965) of New York was an actress best known for her supporting role of a well-to-do matron in many Marx Brothers movies.

Genealogies: None known.

DUNAWAY (S.S. Abbreviation: Dunawa)

Ranking: 3032 **S.S. Count:** 15,001

Origin: English. Uncertain etymology. Most likely derived from the Old English word "dun," meaning hill, combined with another component meaning road. The name was given to those who lived on a road that led to a hill.

Genealogies: None known.

DUNBAR

Ranking: 1224 **S.S. Count:** 36,081

Origin: Scottish. Derived from the Gaelic words "dún" and "barr," meaning fort and summit. The name was given to those who came from Dunbar, a place in Scotland.

Famous **Dunbars:** MOSES DUNBAR (1746–1777) of Connecticut was the only person ever executed in Connecticut for treason. The charge was recruiting for the British service. WILLIAM DUNBAR (1749–1810) of Scotland was a planter, scientist, and explorer. As a friend and correspondent of Thomas Jefferson's, he explored sections of the South and was the first to identify Hot Springs, Arkansas. ROBERT DUNBAR (1812–1890) of Scotland was an expert designer of grain elevators. He was raised in Canada but moved to Buffalo, New York, and contributed greatly to that city's becoming a major grain market. LAURENCE DUNBAR (1872–1906) of Dayton, Ohio, was the son of former slaves and was one of the first African-American writers to gain a wide audience. He wrote poetry, short stories, and novels. (HELEN) FLANDERS DUNBAR (1902–1959) of Illinois was a pioneer in psychology and the author of *Psychiatry in the Medical Specialities.*

Genealogies: *Paul Laurence Dunbar's Roots and Much More: A Scrapbook of His Life and Legacy* was compiled by Charles Marshall Austin and published in Dayton, Ohio, in 1989.

DUNCAN, DUNCANSON

Ranking: 182 **S.S. Count:** 185,877

Origin: Irish, Scottish. Duncan, Duncanson: derived from the Gaelic name Duinnchinn, which is derived from the words "donn" and "ceann," meaning brown and head. Duncan: derived from the Gaelic name ' Donnagáin, meaning "descendant of Donnagán" (H&H), which is derived from the word "donn," meaning brown.

Famous **Bearers:** JAMES DUNCAN (1857–1928) of Scotland was a labor official whose notable achievement was gaining an 8-hour workday after a strike in 1900. ISADORA DUNCAN (1877–1927) of California, born Angela Duncan, is considered one of the formative influences on interpretive and modern dance. She gave up her lifelong aversion to marriage in order to marry Sergey Aleksandrovich Yesnin, a Soviet poet, so that he could make a tour of the United States. They were unjustly accused of being Communist agents. They left the United States and never returned. MARION MONCURE DUNCAN (1913–1978) of Virginia was the youngest person ever elected national president general (1962) of the National Society of the Daughters of the American Revolution.

Genealogies: *Brown-Duncan and Associated Families: Kittery, Maine, Piscataqua and New Castle, N.H.* was compiled by Hazel May Standeven and published in Coos Bay, Oregon, most likely in 1981. *The Duncan Family: Memories and More* was compiled by B.J. Rone and published in Wolfe City, Texas, most likely in 1982.

DUNHAM

Ranking: 1339 **S.S. Count:** 33,011

Origin: English. Derived from the Old English first name Dunna or the word "dūn," meaning hill, and the word "hām," meaning homestead. The name was given to those who came from Dunham, the name of several places in England.

Genealogies: *The Dunhams of Callaway: A Genealogical History* was compiled by Ray Fields Dawson and published in Winter Park, Florida, in 1981. *Fuller-Dunham Genealogy: From Edward Fuller of the Mayflower* was compiled by Robert Wallace Dunham and published in Madison, Wisconsin, in 1990.

DUNKLEY (S.S. Abbreviation: Dunkle)

Ranking: 4876 **S.S. Count:** 9176

Origin: English. Possibly derived from a British name meaning fort and wood, combined with the Old English word "lēah," meaning wood. The name may have been given to those who came from Dinckley, a place in Lancashire, England.

Genealogies: None known.

DUNLAP

Ranking: 753 **S.S. Count:** 56,268

Origin: Irish, Scottish. Transformation of Dunlop.

Famous **Dunlaps:** JOHN DUNLAP (1747–1812) of Ireland published the first daily newspaper in the United States. ROBERT PICKNEY DUNLAP (1794–1859) of Maine was the governor of that state and was instrumental in gaining prison reforms, an insane asylum, and a survey of Maine. WILLIAM DUNLAP (1766–1839) of New Jersey was a painter, playwright, and historian who produced many plays in the United States.

Genealogies: *The Dunlap-Kimbrough-Gilbert Book* was compiled by Sara Ada Rasco Crumpton and published in Birmingham, Alabama, most likely in 1973.

DUNN
Ranking: 166 **S.S. Count:** 199,503
Origin: English, Irish, Scottish. English: derived from the Old English word "dunn," meaning dark. The name was given to those who had dark complexions. Irish, Scottish: derived from the Gaelic name Donn, which is derived from the word "donn," meaning brown. Scottish: the name was given to those who came from Dun, the name of a place in Scotland.

Famous **Dunns:** WILLIAMSON DUNN (1781–1854) of Kentucky was a soldier and a pioneer in Indiana. He moved to what is now Hanover, Indiana, and donated the land on which Hanover College and Wabash College stand. CHARLES DUNN (1799–1872) of Kentucky was the chief justice of the territory of Wisconsin. WILLIAM McKEE DUNN (1814–1887) of Indiana was a Union soldier and judge advocate general of the U.S. army.

Genealogies: *The Ancestry of Harvey Dunn* was compiled by Judith Miner Hine Luedemann and published in Chester, Connecticut, in 1972. *The Dunn Descendants* was compiled by Charlene Dunn Owens and published in San Antonio, Texas, in 1982.

DUNNE
Ranking: 3504 **S.S. Count:** 12,865
Origin: Dutch, English, German, Irish, Scottish. Dutch, German: derived from Old English word "pynne," meaning thin. The name was given to those who were thin. English, Irish, Scottish: transformation of Dunn.

Famous **Dunnes:** FINLEY PETER DUNNE (1867–1936) of Illinois was a humorist with Chicago newspapers who created the Irish saloonkeeper character known as Mr. Dooley.

Genealogies: None known.

DUNNING (S.S. Abbreviation: Dunnin)
Ranking: 2629 **S.S. Count:** 17,304
Origin: English, Irish, Scottish. English: transformation of Dunn. Irish: derived from the Gaelic name Ó Duinnín, meaning "descendant of Duinnín" (H&H), which is derived from the word "donn," meaning brown. Scottish: derived from the Gaelic word "dún," meaning fort. The name was given to those who came from a place in Scotland recorded as Dunyn.

Famous **Dunnings:** ALBERT ELIJAH DUNNING (1844–1923) of Connecticut was a Congregational clergyman and the editor of *The Congregationalist*. WILLIAM ARCHIBALD DUNNING (1857–1922) of New Jersey was a his-

torian and one of the first to academically look at the Civil War and Reconstruction.

Genealogies: None known.

DUPONT, DU PONT, DU PONT
Ranking: 3426 **S.S. Count:** 13,179
Origin: French. Derived from the Anglo-Norman-French and Old French word "pont," meaning bridge. The name was given to those who lived near a bridge.

Famous **Bearers:** VICTOR MARIE DU PONT (1767–1827) of France was unsuccessful in several business and management ventures. He eventually became a bank director in Philadelphia. SAMUEL FRANCIS DU PONT (1803–1865) of New Jersey, the son of Victor Marie, was a naval officer. Joining the navy in 1815, he worked his way up the ranks through outstanding service. ELEUTHERE IRENEE DU PONT (1771–1834) of France was the brother of Victor Marie. He manufactured gunpowder near Wilmington, Delaware. His sons, ALFRED VICTOR (1798–1856) and HENRY (1812–1889), both served as president of their father's manufacturing plant. Henry's son, HENRY ALGERNON (1838–1926), fought in the Civil War, winning the Medal of Honor for the battle of Cedar Creek. He also was involved in the family business and was a U.S. senator (1906–1917). ALFRED IRENEE DU PONT (1864–1935) of Delaware, who headed the Du Pont dynasty, amassing great wealth, left the bulk of his estate to the Nemours Foundation for the care of physically challenged children, the aged, and the indigent. PIERRE SAMUEL DU PONT (1870–1954) of Delaware headed the Du Pont family empire. He served on several government committees during the Depression, including the advisory board of the National Recovery Administration. FRANCIS IRENEE DU PONT (1873–1942) of Delaware was the founder and head of the Du Pont Company Experimental Station. He was a chemist and inventor, devising an improved nitrometer for measuring the amount of nitrogen and nitrocellulose, among other things. IRENEE DU PONT (1876–1963) of Delaware was an industrialist who worked within the Du Pont family empire. LAMMONT DU PONT (1880–1954) of Delaware was a Du Pont family industrialist who resented governmental regulation of morals and opposed Prohibition.

Genealogies: None known.

DUPRE
Ranking: 4397 **S.S. Count:** 10,201
Origin: French. Derived from the Old French word "pred," meaning meadow. The name was given to those who lived near a meadow.

Genealogies: None known.

DUPREE, DU PREE
Ranking: 2126 **S.S. Count:** 21,534
Origin: French. Transformations of Dupre.

Genealogies: None known.

DUPUIS

Ranking: 3823   S.S. Count: 11,797

Origin: French. Derived from the Old French word "puts," meaning well. The name was given to those who lived near a well.

Genealogies: None known.

DURAN

Ranking: 805   S.S. Count: 52,362

Origin: English. Transformation of Durant.

Genealogies: None known.

DURAND

Ranking: 3937   S.S. Count: 11,465

Origin: English. Transformation of Durant.

Famous **Durands**: ELIE MAGLOIRE DURAND (1794–1873) of France was a pharmacist with the most extensive collection of medicines in Philadelphia. ASHER BROWN DURAND (1796–1886) of New Jersey was one of the founders of the Hudson River school of landscape painting, but he began his professional life as an engraver. With his brother, CYRUS DURAND (1787–1868), he formed a banknote-engraving company. Cyrus invented engraving machines that revolutionized currency engraving, while Asher designed paper currency. WILLIAM FREDERICK DURAND (1859–1958) of Connecticut was a mechanical engineer who was a consultant on the Hoover and Grand Coulee dams.

Genealogies: *Durand Genealogy* was compiled by Samuel R. Durand and most likely published in Palo Alto, California, in 1965. *Genealogy of the Durand Family: A Record of the Descendants of Francis Joseph Durand* was compiled by Celia C. Durand and published in Oberlin, Ohio, in 1921.

DURANT

Ranking: 2224   S.S. Count: 20,632

Origin: English, French. Derived from the Old French word "durant," meaning enduring. The name was given to those who were considered loyal and to those who were considered stubborn.

Famous **Durants**: HENRY DURANT (1802–1875) of Massachusetts was a clergyman who served as the first president of the University of California, which he was instrumental in founding. THOMAS CLARK DURANT (1820–1885) of Massachusetts was the organizer and vice president of the Union Pacific Railroad Co. HENRY FOWLE DURANT (1822–1881) of New Hampshire was the founder of Wellesley College. WILLIAM CRAPO DURANT (1861–1947) of Massachusetts was an organizer of several automobile-manufacturing companies, including Buick and Chevrolet; was president of General Motors (1916–1920); and started

Durant Motors in 1921. WILLIAM JAMES DURANT (1885–1981) of Massachusetts and his wife, IDA KAUFMAN DURANT (1898–1981) of Russia, known as ARIEL DURANT, co-wrote an 11-volume series entitled *The Story of Civilization*, with one volume, *Rosseau and Revolution*, in 1967 winning them a Pulitzer Prize. THOMAS MORTON DURANT (1905–1977) of Illinois was a physician, educator, author, and a president of the American College of Physicians (1964–65). He was internationally recognized as a cardiologist and specialist in heart diseases.

Genealogies: *A Durant Family History, 1825–1972: A History of the English and American Descendants of Samuel and Amelia Durant of Bishop's Caundle, Dorset, England and of Their Descendants* was compiled by Alexander G. Rose and most likely published in Baltimore, Maryland, in 1972. *The Durant Genealogy: A History of the Descendants of George and Elizabeth Durant of Malden, Mass. and Middletown, Conn.* was compiled by William Durant and published in Baltimore, Maryland, in 1966.

DURBIN

Ranking: 2498   S.S. Count: 18,144

Origin: French. The name was given to those who came from Durban, a place in France.

Famous **Durbins**: JOHN PRICE DURBIN (1800–1876) of Kentucky was a methodist clergyman and secretary of the Missionary Society.

Genealogies: *Lima Bean and City Chicken: A Memoir of the Open Hearth* was compiled by Martina Durbin and published in New York, New York, in 1989. *Durbin and Logdson Genealogy with Related Families, 1628–1991* was compiled by Betty Jewell and published in Bowie, Maryland, in 1991.

DURDEN

Ranking: 4638   S.S. Count: 9643

Origin: English. Derived from the Old English word "dēor," meaning beast or deer. The name was given to those who came from Dearden, a place in Lancashire, England.

Genealogies: None known.

DURHAM

Ranking: 713   S.S. Count: 59,194

Origin: English. Derived from the Old English word "dūn" and the Old Norse word "holmr," meaning hill and island. The name was given to those who came from Durham, a place in England.

Famous **Durhams**: CARL THOMAS DURHAM (1892–1974) of North Carolina was a U.S. representative from North Carolina who was reelected 10 times with very little campaigning. He sponsored the act that created the Atomic Energy Commission.

Genealogies: None known.

DURKIN

Ranking: 3970   S.S. Count: 11,404

Origin: Irish. Derived from the Gaelic name Mac Duarcán, meaning "son of Duarcán" (H&H), which is derived from the word "duairc," meaning surly.

Famous **Durkins**: MARTIN PATRICK DURKIN (1894–1955) of Illinois was a labor leader and the secretary of labor under President Dwight D. Eisenhower.

Genealogies: None known.

DUTTON

Ranking: 1950   S.S. Count: 23,266

Origin: English. Derived from the Old English first name Dudd(a) and word "tūn," meaning settlement. The name was given to those who came from Dutton, the name of several places in England.

Famous **Duttons**: HENRY DUTTON (1796–1869) was a governor of Connecticut. EDWARD PAYSON DUTTON (1831–1923) of New Hampshire was a book publisher and a partner in Ide & Dutton, later reorganized as E. P. Dutton & Co., of which he was president. CLARENCE EDWARD DUTTON (1841–1912) of Connecticut was the geologist who developed the method for pinpointing the depth of the epicenter of an earthquake. SAMUEL TRAIN DUTTON (1849–1919) of New Hampshire was a national leader in the U.S. educational system. He served as the superintendent of schools in New Haven, Connecticut, and Brookline, Massachusetts, and as a professor at Teachers College, Columbia University.

Genealogies: None known.

DUVAL

Ranking: 3682   S.S. Count: 12,251

Origin: French. Derived from the Old French word "val," meaning valley. The name was given to those who lived in a valley.

Famous **Duvals**: WILLIAM POPE DUVAL (1784–1854) of Virginia was the first judge of the superior court in East Florida and territorial governor of Florida (1822–1834), and he is credited with the peaceful removal of the Seminole Indians to South Florida.

Genealogies: None known.

DUVALL, DUVALLET

Ranking: 1641   S.S. Count: 27,389

Origin: French. Transformations of Duval.

Famous **Bearers**: GABRIEL DUVALL (1752–1844) of Maryland was a Revolutionary soldier and was a U.S Supreme Court justice appointed by President James Madison in 1811.

Genealogies: *Belt Brasheas and Amelia Duvall: Their Ancestors and Descendants* was compiled by Sydney Kilpatrick and most likely published in Alexandria, Louisiana,

in 1971. *Brisbin/Rose, Sevenker, Hayden, DeVol, Ward Family History* was compiled by Virginia Hayden Hughes and published in Melbourne, Florida, most likely in 1991.

DVORAK

Ranking: 4365   S.S. Count: 10,271

Origin: Czech. Derived from the Czech word "dvůr," meaning manor. The name was given to those who worked in such a place and to those who were freeholders and beholden to no one but the king.

Genealogies: *The Dvoraks of Minnetonka Township, Minnesota* was compiled by Helen Mary Vavra and published in Minneapolis, Minnesota, in 1988.

DWYER

Ranking: 1115   S.S. Count: 39,640

Origin: Irish. Derived from the Gaelic name Ó Du(i)bhuidhir, meaning "descendant of Du(i)bhuidhir" (H&H), which is derived from the words "dubh" and "odhar," meaning dark and sallow.

Genealogies: None known.

DYE

Ranking: 1155   S.S. Count: 37,926

Origin: English. Derived from the first name Dennis, which was given to women in medieval ages.

Famous **Dyes**: WILLIAM MCENTYRE DYE (1831–1899) of Pennsylvania was a professional soldier who fought with the Union army during the Civil War. He served with great distinction.

Genealogies: *A Partial History of Certain Mastin-Rathbun-Dye Families* was compiled by Victor E. Mastin and published in Des Moines, Iowa, most likely in 1974. *The K.A.R.D. Files—Dye Data* was compiled by John and Judy Dye and published in Spokane, Washington, in 1983.

DYER

Ranking: 622   S.S. Count: 67,091

Origin: English. Derived from the Middle English word "dyer," meaning a cloth dyer. The name was given to those who worked as such.

Famous **Dyers**: MARY DYER (?–1660) of England was a Quaker who was hanged in Boston on the charge of sedition when she attempted to visit imprisoned Quakers. ELIPHALET DYER (1721–1807) of Connecticut was a member of the Continental Congress. ALEXANDER BRYDIE DYER (1815–1874) of Virginia was a professional soldier who rose to the rank of brigadier general in the army in 1864. ISADORE DYER (1865–1920) of Texas was a dermatologist who specialized in leprosy. In 1894 he founded the Louisiana Leper Home, which became known as the National Leprosarium. JOHN PERCY DYER (1902–1975) of Mississippi was a college dean and author of several books, including *Fightin' Joe Wheeler* (1941) and *The Gallant Hood* (1950), both biographies of Confederate generals.

Genealogies: *Dyer Family History from England to America, 1600's to 1980: Virginia and Southern Dyer Families. Their Descendants and Connecting Families* was compiled by Watson B. Dyer and published in Cedartown, Georgia, in 1980. *Hebron Dyer Descendants: Pioneer of Ohio* was compiled by Franklin Leallah and published in Baltimore, Maryland, in 1991.

DYKES

Ranking: 2263   **S.S. Count:** 20,182
Origin: English. Transformation of Dyke.

Genealogies: *The Dykes Line of East Tennessee* was compiled by John H. Dykes Jr. and published in Charlotte, North Carolina, in 1981.

DYSON

Ranking: 2819   **S.S. Count:** 16,167
Origin: English. Transformation of Dye.

Famous **Dysons:** JOHN ROSE DYSON (1874–1947) was a physician in Pennsylvania noted for his specialty in ear, nose, and throat diseases. He practiced medicine for 48 years.

Genealogies: None known.

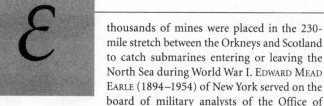

EADS

Ranking: 3696 S.S. Count: 12,221

Origin: English. 1) derived from the first name Edith. 2) derived from the first name Adam.

Famous **Eadses:** JAMES BUCHANAN EADS (1820–1887) of Lawrenceburg, Indiana, was an engineer whose idea to build a fleet of ironclad, steam-powered, shallow-draft warships for use on the Mississippi River gave the North its first victories in the Civil War. He also designed a triple-arch steel bridge over the Mississippi River.

Genealogies: None known.

EAGLE

Ranking: 3868 S.S. Count: 11,655

Origin: English. 1) derived from the Old French word "aigle" and the Middle English word "egle," both meaning eagle. The name was given to those who had good vision or were considered to be impressive and to those who came from Laigle, a place in Normandy, France. 2) derived from the Old Norse word "eik" and the Old English word "lēah," meaning oak and wood. The name was given to those who came from Eagle, a place in Lincolnshire, England.

Genealogies: None known.

EARL

Ranking: 2132 S.S. Count: 21,471

Origin: English. Derived from the Old English word "eorl," meaning earl. The name was given to those who worked in the house of a noble.

Famous **Earls:** RALPH EARL (1726–1808) of Massachusetts was a captain in the Massachusetts militia during the Revolutionary War. Privates DAVIL EARL (1756–1808) of New Jersey and THOMAS EARL (1762–1844) of Maryland also served their country in the war.

Genealogies: None known.

EARLE

Ranking: 3554 S.S. Count: 12,695

Origin: English. Transformation of Earl.

Famous **Earles:** RALPH EARLE (1751–1801) of Massachusetts was a designer of pictures of battles engraved by Amos Doolittle (see separate entry). PLINY EARLE (1762–1832) of Massachusetts invented a machine for making wool and cotton cards. PLINY EARLE (1809–1892) of Massachusetts, his son, was a pioneer in the treatment of the insane. ALICE MORSE EARLE (1851–1911) of Massachusetts was an author who specialized in books about colonial New England. RALPH EARLE (1874–1939) of Massachusetts was the naval officer responsible for implementing the North Sea Barrage, or the Northern Barrage, in which thousands of mines were placed in the 230-mile stretch between the Orkneys and Scotland to catch submarines entering or leaving the North Sea during World War I. EDWARD MEAD EARLE (1894–1954) of New York served on the board of military analysts of the Office of Strategic Services in Washington, D.C. He was appointed a fellow in military sciences at the Library of Congress and received the Presidential Medal of Merit.

Genealogies: *The Earles and the Birnies* was compiled by Joseph Earle Birnie and published in Richmond, Virginia, in 1974. *Oates-Earle and Related Families* was compiled by William L. Winebarger and published in Graham, Kentucky, in 1972.

EARLEY

Ranking: 3037 S.S. Count: 14,975

Origin: English, Irish. Transformation of Early.

Genealogies: None known.

EARLY

Ranking: 2251 S.S. Count: 20,313

Origin: English, Irish. English: 1) derived from the Old English words "earn" and "lēah," meaning eagle and wood. The name was given to those who came from places called Earley, Earnley, and Arley in England. 2) derived from the Old English word "eorlic," meaning noble and manly. The name was given to those who were considered to have such attributes. Irish: derived from the Gaelic name Ó Mochain, meaning "descendant of Mochán" (H&H), which is derived from the word "moch," meaning early.

Famous **Earlys:** PETER EARLY (1773–1817) of Virginia was the governor of Georgia (1813–1815). JOHN EARLY (1786–1873) of Virginia was a Methodist clergyman who helped to found Randolph-Macon College. JUBAL ANDERSON EARLY (1816–1894) of Virginia was a Confederate soldier who successfully fought against the Union forces, only to be stopped by General William T. Sherman. He remained loyal to the Confederacy after the war, refusing to accept Reconstruction. STEPHEN TYREE EARLY (1889–1951) of Virginia was press secretary to President Franklin D. Roosevelt.

Genealogies: *Descendants of John Early of Virginia (1729–1774)* was compiled by Margaret Woods Hampton and published in Fort Worth, Texas, in 1973. *The Early Families of Knox and Whitley Counties, Kentucky, with Allied Families* was compiled by Cleland Edward Early and published in Houston, Texas, in 1989.

EARNEST (S.S. Abbreviation: Earnes)

Ranking: 3962 S.S. Count: 11,418

Origin: German. Transformation of Ernst.

Genealogies: None known.

EASLEY

Ranking: 2061 **S.S. Count:** 22,217

Origin: English. Most likely derived from the Old English words "ēast" and "lēah," meaning east and wood. The name was given to those who came from Eastleigh and Astley, the names of places in England.

Famous **Easleys:** RALPH MONTGOMERY EASLEY (1856–1939) of Illinois was a reformer and the founder of the National Civic Federation.

Genealogies: *Now Living in Boone County, Missouri: Our Family Genealogies* was compiled by Virginia Easley DeMarce and published in Arlington, Virginia, in 1990. *A Tentative Outline of U.S. Easley Lines Primarily to the Year 1800* was compiled by Virginia Easley DeMarce and published in Maryville, Missouri, in 1970.

EASON

Ranking: 1968 **S.S. Count:** 23,027

Origin: English, Irish, Scottish. English: transformation of the English and Irish definitions of Eakin. Irish, Scottish: transformation of McKay.

Genealogies: None known.

EAST

Ranking: 2606 **S.S. Count:** 17,431

Origin: English. Derived from the Old English word "ēast," meaning east. The name was given to those who lived to the east of or in the eastern part of a town.

Famous **Easts:** EDWARD MURRAY EAST (1879–1938) of DuQuoin, Illinois, was a plant geneticist who helped develop hybird corn.

Genealogies: None known.

EASTER

Ranking: 1119 **S.S. Count:** 39,391

Origin: English. 1) transformation of East. 2) derived from the Old English word "ēastre," meaning Easter. 3) derived from the Old English word "eaowestre," meaning sheepfold. The name was given to those who came from Easter, a place in Essex, England.

Genealogies: None known.

EASTMAN (S.S. Abbreviation: Eastma)

Ranking: 1972 **S.S. Count:** 22,989

Origin: English. 1) transformation of East. 2) derived from the Old English first name Eastmund, which is derived from the words "ēast," meaning east or grace, and the word "mund," meaning protection.

Famous **Eastmans:** MARY HENDERSON EASTMAN (1818–1887) of Virginia was an author who wrote *Aunt Phillis's Cabin or Southern Life as It Is*, which is the best-known "anti-Uncle Tom" work. JOHN ROBIE EASTMAN (1836–1913) of New Hampshire was the astronomer responsible for the *Second Washington Catalogue of Stars* (1898). ANNIS BERTHA FORD EASTMAN (1852–1910) of Illinois, who took over the pastorship of Thomas K. Beecher's Park Church in Elmira, New York, was the mother of Max and Crystal. GEORGE EASTMAN (1854–1932) of New York founded the Eastman Kodak Company. He invented the first simple hand-held camera, which he called Kodak. In 1900, he introduced the Brownie camera, which had been intended for use by children. He gave away half his fortune before his death and was the first employer to offer profit sharing to his employees. He committed suicide. LINDA ANNE EASTMAN (1867–1963) of Ohio was the first woman to head a metropolitan library system in the United States. CRYSTAL EASTMAN (1881–1928) of Massachusetts was the sister of Max and the daughter of Annis. She was a social reformer of the time. Although married several times, she kept her maiden name. JOSEPH BARTLETT EASTMAN (1882–1944) of New York was a member of the U.S. Interstate Commerce Commission (1914–1944). MAX FORRESTER EASTMAN (1883–1969) of New York was a writer and editor. His works include *Enjoyment of Living* and *Love and Revolution*.

Genealogies: *The Eastmans from Lockport, New York* was compiled by Peter M. Rinaldo and published in Briarcliff Manor, New York, in 1992. *The Puritan Ancestors, in America, of Georgia Ann Eastman, Mrs. William Morris Bennett* was compiled by Russell White Bennett and published in Jacksonville, Florida, in 1929.

EASTON

Ranking: 3187 **S.S. Count:** 14,254

Origin: English, Scottish. 1) derived from the Old English words "ēast" and "tūn," meaning east and settlement. 2) derived from the Old English words "ēg" and "stān(as)," meaning island and stones. 3) derived from the Old English first names Æfric, meaning elf and power, and Aðelric, meaning noble and power. The name in all cases was given to those who came from Easton, the name of several places in England.

Famous **Eastons:** NICHOLAS EASTON (1593–1675) of Wales was a governor of Rhode Island and the first person to build a house in Newport, Rhode Island. JOHN EASTON (1625–1705), birthplace unknown, was the son of Nicholas. He also was a governor of Rhode Island.

Genealogies: None known.

EATON

Ranking: 625 **S.S. Count:** 66,685

Origin: English. Derived from the Old English words "ēa" or "ēg," and "tūn," meaning river or island, and settlement.

Famous **Eatons:** THEOPHILUS EATON (1590–1658) of England was one of the original patentees of the Massachusetts Bay Colony. He co-founded New Haven, Connecticut, in 1638 and served as the colony's governor until his death. With John Davenport, he wrote the code of laws for the colony. WILLIAM EATON (1764–1811) was a professional army officer and diplomat who spent much of his career in North Africa. AMOS EATON (1776–1842) of New York was a scientist who wrote *A Manual of Botany for the Northern States.* MARGARET O'NEALE EATON (1799–1879) of Washington, D.C., was known as Peggy. Her second husband was John H. Eaton. He became a member of President Andrew Jackson's cabinet during their marriage but, because of the snubbing she received from the wives of the other cabinet members, he was forced to resign his position. John C. Calhoun's wife was the one who refused to accept Margaret Eaton and led the snubbing of the other cabinet members' wives. This led to a rift between Calhoun and Jackson. DORMAN BRIDGMAN EATON (1823–1899) of Vermont drafted the National Civil Service Act and served as the head of the Civil Service Commission. JOHN EATON (1829–1906) of Sutton, New Hampshire, served as commisioner of the U.S. Bureau of Education for 16 years, beginning during the administration of President Ulysses S. Grant. He later served as the first U.S. superintendent of schools in Puerto Rico. BENJAMIN HARRISON EATON (1833–1904) was a governor of Colorado. DANIEL CADY EATON (1834–1895) was the grandson of Amos Eaton. He was a botany professor, like his grandfather, and the author of *The Ferns of North America.* WYATT EATON (1849–1896) of Canada was a painter and the founder in 1877 of the Society of American Artists. He excelled as a portrait painter, and one of his subjects was President James A. Garfield. CHARLES AUBREY EATON (1868–1953) of Canada spent 28 years in the U.S. House of Representatives; was chairman of the House Foreign Affairs Committee; was appointed a delegate to the UN Charter Conference in San Francisco; and signed the charter for the United States, which was a highlight of his career. CYRUS STEPHEN EATON (1883–1979) of Canada organized several power and light companies and worked to improve U.S.–Soviet relations.

Genealogies: *The Kiehl/Manwarren Genealogy* was compiled by Margery Kiehl Hughes and published in Fort Wayne, Indiana, in 1991.

EAVES

Ranking: 4172 **S.S. Count:** 10,833
Origin: English. Derived from the first name Eve, which is derived from the Hebrew first name Chava.
Genealogies: None known.

EBERHARD, EBERHARDT, EBERHART (S.S. Abbreviation: Eberha)

Ranking: 2279 **S.S. Count:** 19,947
Origin: German. Derived from a Germanic name that is derived from the words "eber" and "hard," meaning wild boar and hardy and/or brave.
Genealogies: None known.

EBERLE, EBERLEIN

Ranking: 4421 **S.S. Count:** 10,141
Origin: German. Transformation of Eberhard.
Famous Bearers: JOHN EBERLE (1787–1838) of Maryland was a physician and the founder of Jefferson Medical College (1824).
Genealogies: None known.

EBERT

Ranking: 2529 **S.S. Count:** 17,931
Origin: German. 1) transformation of Eberhard. 2) derived from a Germanic first name that is derived from the words "agi(l)" and "berht," meaning "edge or point (of a weapon)" (H&H) and bright.
Genealogies: None known.

ECHEVARRI, ECHEVARRIA (S.S. Abbreviation: Echeva)

Ranking: 3176 **S.S. Count:** 14,297
Origin: Basque, Spanish. Derived from the Basque name Etxeberria, which is derived from the words "etxe" and "berri," meaning house and new.
Genealogies: None known.

ECHOLS

Ranking: 2375 **S.S. Count:** 19,119
Origin: English, Scottish. Transformation of Eccles.
Famous Echolses: JOHN ECHOLS (1823–1896) of Virginia was a Confederate officer and an official in the Chesapeake & Ohio Railroad.
Genealogies: *Echols Notes* was compiled by Rebecca Echols Terry and published in Huntsville, Alabama, in 1977. *The Echols of Detroit: Genealogy* was compiled by James Echols and published in Port Jefferson Station, New York, in 1985.

ECK

Ranking: 4381 **S.S. Count:** 10,244
Origin: German, Jewish, Swedish. German: derived from several Germanic first names that are derived from the word "agil," meaning "edge or point (of a weapon)" (H&H). German, Jewish: derived from the German and Yiddish words "eck(e)" and "ek," both meaning corner. The name was given to those who lived on corners. Swedish: cognate to Oak.

Genealogies: None known.

ECKERT
Ranking: 1754 S.S. Count: 25,553
Origin: German. Transformation of Eckhardt.

Famous **Eckerts:** THOMAS THOMPSON ECKERT (1825–1910) of Ohio organized the U.S. military telegraph during the Civil War. From 1893 to 1900 he was the president of Western Union. GEORGE ARTHUR ECKERT (1889–1953) was chief surgeon at a number of U.S. navy hospitals, including the one at Pearl Harbor, Hawaii, during the Japanese attack in 1941. JOHN PRESPER ECKERT JR. (1919–) of Philadelphia, Pennsylvania, invented the first working electronic computer, which he called ENIAC (Electronic Numerical Integrator and Calculator).

Genealogies: *Eckert Record; Story of Georg Bernhardt Eckert and His Descendants, 1793–1957* was compiled by Estella Hartmann Orrison and published in San Angelo, Texas, in 1957. *The Eckerts in the Flush, Pottawatomie County, Kansas Area: The Descendants of George Eckert and Barbara Ebenhoh, the Descendants of Barbara Eckert and John Weixelman* was compiled by Anna Maria Eckart Ebert and published in St. George, Kansas, in 1981.

ECKHARDT (S.S. Abbreviation: Eckhar)
Ranking: 4186 S.S. Count: 10,795
Origin: German. Derived from a Germanic first name derived from the words "agi(n)" and "hard," meaning edge and/or point and hardy and strong.
Genealogies: None known.

EDDINGTON (S.S. Abbreviation: Edding)
Ranking: 3928 S.S. Count: 11,487
Origin: English, Scottish. English: derived from the Old English first name Eadifu, which is derived from the words "ead" and "gifu," meaning prosperity and settlement. English, Scottish: derived from several Old English first names and the word "tūn," meaning settlement. The name was given to those who came from Edington, the name of several places in England.
Genealogies: None known.

EDDY
Ranking: 1624 S.S. Count: 27,618
Origin: English. Derived from the Old English name Eadwig, which is derived from the words "ead" and "wig," meaning prosperity and war.

Famous **Eddys:** MARY BAKER EDDY (1821–1910) of Concord, New Hampshire, founded the Christian Science religion when she was healed from a chronic spinal problem after reading the New Testament. She also founded *The Christian Science Monitor,* which is still considered a leading U.S. newspaper. CLARENCE EDDY (1851–1937) of Massa-chusetts was an organist known for his recitals in the Chicago area. HARRISON PRESCOTT EDDY (1870–1937) of Massachusetts was a sanitary engineer and a leader in the development of water purification and sewage treatment in the United States. MANTON SPRAGUE EDDY (1892–1962) of Illinois was an army officer and field commander of the 9th Infantry Division. He led it through the North Africa, Sicily, and Normandy campaigns. NELSON EDDY (1901–1967) of Rhode Island was an actor and singer who gained fame in Hollywood.

Genealogies: *The Eddy Family in America, a Genealogy* was compiled by Ruth Story Devereux Eddy and published in Boston, Massachusetts, in 1930. *The Promised Land: The James Eaddy (also Eddy) Family in South Carolina* was compiled by Elaine Y. Eaddy and published in Hemingway, South Carolina, in 1976.

EDELMAN, EDELMANN (S.S. Abbreviation: Edelma)
Ranking: 4856 S.S. Count: 9213
Origin: Edelman—Jewish; Edelmann—German, Jewish. Edelman, Edelmann (Jewish): derived from the German word "edel" and the Yiddish word "eydl," both meaning noble. The names were taken ornamentally. Edelmann (German): derived from the Old High German word "edili," meaning noble. The name was given to those who were from the lowest class of free citizens.
Genealogies: None known.

EDEN
Ranking: 4834 S.S. Count: 9258
Origin: English, Frisian, Jewish. English: 1) derived from the Old English first name Eadhūn, which is derived from the words "ead" and "hūn," meaning prosperity and bear cub. 2) derived from a river called Ituna in the second century A.D. Frisian: derived from the first name Ede. Jewish: an ornamental name taken to refer the garden of Eden.

Famous **Edens:** CHARLES EDEN (1673–1722) of England was the colonial governor of North Carolina and the last person to receive the title "land grave." ROBERT EDEN (1741–1784) of England was the colonial governor of Maryland. He had a great many colonists as friends. He spent the Revolutionary years in England and returned to America sometime after the war.
Genealogies: None known.

EDGAR
Ranking: 2722 S.S. Count: 16,716
Origin: English, Jewish. English: derived from the Old English first name Eadgār, which is derived from the words "ēead" and "gār," meaning prosperity and spear. Jewish: uncertain etymology.

Famous **Edgars:** CHARLES EDGAR (1862–1922) of New Jersey invented the band saw with teeth on both sides. He also developed lumber areas of the Midwest and South.

Genealogies: *The Baker Family and the Edgar Family of Rahway, N.J. and New York City* was compiled by John Milnes Baker and published in Middletown, New York, in 1972.

EDGE
Ranking: 2966 S.S. Count: 15,329
Origin: English. Derived from the Old English word "ecg," meaning edge. The name was given to those who lived near an edge of a hill.

Famous **Edges:** WALTER EVANS EDGE (1873–1956) of Pennsylvania was the owner of the Atlantic City *Daily Press* and the Atlantic City *Evening Union.* He served as governor of New Jersey (1917–1919 and 1944–1947); as a U.S. senator (1919–1929); and as the ambassador to France (1929–1933).

Genealogies: None known.

EDMOND, EDMONDS, EDMONDSON
Ranking: 658 S.S. Count: 63,670
Origin: English, French. Derived from the Old English name Ēadmund, which is derived from the words "ēad" and "mund," meaning prosperity and protection.

Famous **Bearers:** SARAH EMMA EVELYN EDMONDS (1841–1898) was born in Canada. She served two years with the army of the Potomac "as a man" under the name of Franklin Thompson. She was a participant in the battles of Blackburn's Ford and the first battle of Bull Run. She also worked in a hospital, as a mail carrier, and twice as a spy, with the "disguise" in one mission of "being a woman." She eventually collected a pension of $12 a month. It is believed that as many as 400 women enlisted and served in the military during the Civil War. WILLIAM EDMONDSON (1882–1951) of Tennessee was the son of former slaves. He was a sculptor and the first black man given a show at the Museum of Modern Art for his work, which was known as "modern primitive" art. His most famous piece is titled "Mary and Martha."

Genealogies: None known.

EDMUND, EDMUNDS
Ranking: 3075 S.S. Count: 14,774
Origin: English. Transformations of Edmond.

Famous **Bearers:** GEORGE FRANKLIN EDMUNDS (1828–1919) served as a U.S. senator from Vermont for 25 years. He was influential in the impeachment proceedings against U.S. President Andrew Johnson and worked against polygamy and for antitrust laws. After he retired from the Senate, he successfully argued before the U.S. Supreme Court that income tax was illegal. CHARLES WALLIS EDMUNDS (1873–1941) of England came to the United States as a child. As a pharmacist he did much to establish drug standards.

Genealogies: None known.

EDWARD, EDWARDE, EDWARDES, EDWARDS, EDWARDSON
Ranking: 53 S.S. Count: 451,430
Origin: English. Derived from the Old English name Ēadward, which is derived from the words "ēad" and "w(e)ard," meaning prosperity and guard.

Famous **Bearers:** JONATHAN EDWARDS (1703–1758) of Connecticut entered Yale University at the age of 13. He later became a minister with his grandfather Solomon Stoddard at the Congregational Church in Northampton, Massachusetts. During his tenure, Edwards embellished his Calvinist sermons with demands that the members of his congregation profess their "regenerative experiences." He was later dismissed from his post. SARAH PIERPONT EDWARDS (1710–1758) of Connecticut was a Puritan mystic and the wife of Jonathan Edwards. JOHN EDWARDS (1748–1837) of Virginia played an important role in Kentucky's becoming a state and was one of its first two U.S. senators. His nephew was NINIAN EDWARDS (1775–1833), who was both a U.S. senator and the governor of Illinois. Ninian's son was NINIAN WIRT EDWARDS (1809–1889), who was the first school superintendent in Illinois and the one responsible for the state school system. He was a personal friend of Abraham Lincoln's, and it was at his home that Lincoln first met Mary Todd, who was Edwards's sister-in-law. Lincoln and Mary Todd were married in the Edwardses' home. CLARENCE RANSOM EDWARDS (1860–1931) of Ohio was an army officer who was awarded three Silver Stars and rose to the rank of brigadier general. RICHARD STANISLAUS EDWARDS (1885–1956) of Pennsylvania was a naval officer who attained the rank of admiral and received the Distinguished Service Medal for his wartime service.

Genealogies: None known.

EGAN
Ranking: 1347 S.S. Count: 32,867
Origin: Irish. Derived from the second Irish definition of Higgins.

Famous **Egans:** PATRICK EGAN (1841–1919) of Ireland was a political refugee to the United States. He served as the U.S. minister to Chile. MAURICE FRANCIS EGAN (1852–1924) of Pennsylvania was a journalist and diplomat and an advisor to Presidents William McKinley and Theodore Roosevelt, although unofficial in status. He was the minister to Denmark (1907–1918).

Genealogies: *Egan Ancestors: Hobart, 1574–1928* was

compiled by Clarence Edward Egan and published in Haverstraw, New York, in 1980.

EGGERS

Ranking: 3713 **S.S. Count:** 12,162
Origin: Dutch. Transformation of Eckhardt.
Genealogies: *Westward J-J* (the Eggers family) was compiled by Mildred Shirley and published in 1984.

EGGLESTON, EGGLESTONE (S.S. Abbreviation: Eggles)

Ranking: 3112 **S.S. Count:** 14,621
Origin: English. Derived from the Old English first name Ecgwulf and the word "tūn," meaning settlement. The names were given to those who came from Eggleston, the name of several places in England.
Famous **Bearers:** EDWARD EGGLESTON (1837–1902) of Vevay, Indiana, became a writer when poor health forced him to quit his post as a Bible agent. His novels, such as *The Hoosier Schoolmaster* and *The End of the World*, contributed to the realist literary movement. GEORGE CARY EGGLESTON (1839–1902) of Indiana was the brother of Edward. He was a journalist who worked on the newspapers of the day. He also wrote novels for boys, stories of post–Civil War life, and *The History of the Confederate War*. JOHN WILLIAM EGGLESTON (1886–1976) of Virginia was the judge who ruled that Virginia could not pay the private-school tuition of students who had left the public schools because of their having been integrated.
Genealogies: *Our Eggleston and Allied Families* was compiled by Elsie Eggleston Kempton and published in Saginaw, Michigan, in 1975.

EHLERS

Ranking: 4273 **S.S. Count:** 14,621
Origin: German. Derived from a Germanic first name that is derived from the words "agil" and "hard" or "ward," meaning "edge or point (of a weapon)" (H&H) and brave or guard.
Genealogies: *Germanic Roots of Chicagoans Harvey Metzger Ehlers & Evelynne Meiborg Ehlers: Baer-Ehlers-Jantzen-Meiborg-Metzger-Nielsen-Wagner-Wittum* was compiled by Harvey Metzger Ehlers and Evelynne Meiborg Ehlers and published in Villa Park, Illinois, in 1982.

EHRLICH (S.S. Abbreviation: Ehrlic)

Ranking: 4256 **S.S. Count:** 10,582
Origin: German, Jewish. German: derived from the German word "ehrlich," meaning honest and/or honorable, and the Yiddish word "erlekh," meaning honest. Jews took the name ornamentally.
Famous **Ehrlichs:** ARNOLD BAGUMIL EHRLICH (1848–

1919) of Polish Russia was a Hebrew scholar. His works were considered a valuable contribution to religious history.
Genealogies: None known.

EICHEL, EICHELBERG, EICHELE

Ranking: 4500 **S.S. Count:** 9956
Origin: Jewish. Transformation of Oak(s).
Genealogies: None known.

EISENBEIN, EISENBACH, EISENBAUM, EISENBERG (S.S. Abbreviation: Eisenb)

Ranking: 2499 **S.S. Count:** 18,143
Origin: Eisenbein—German; Eisenbach, Eisenbaum, Eisenberg—Jewish. Eisenbein: derived from the Old High German words "isan" and "bein," meaning iron and leg. The name was given to those who had an artificial leg and to those who worked with iron. Eisenbach, Eisenbaum, Eisenberg: derived from the Old High German word "isan," meaning iron, and words meaning stream, tree, and hill. The names were most often taken ornamentally.
Genealogies: None known.

EISENHOUWER, EISENHOWER, EISENHAUER, EISENHART, EISENHARDT, EISENHANDLER, EISENHENDLER (S.S. Abbreviation: Eisenh)

Ranking: 3628 **S.S. Count:** 12,413
Origin: Eisenhouwer—Dutch; Eisenhower—Dutch, German; Eisenhauer, Eisenhart—German; Eisenhardt—German, Jewish; Eisenhandler, Eisenhendler—Jewish. Eisenhouwer, Eisenhower, Eisenhauer: derived from the Old High German words "isan" and "houwan," meaning to chop or cut. The names were given to those who were iron workers. Eisenhart: derived from a Germanic first name that is derived from the words "isan" and "hard," meaning iron and brave or strong. Eisenhardt (German): transformation of Eisenhart. (Jewish): derived from the Old High German word "isan," meaning iron, and a word meaning hard. The name was most often taken ornamentally. Eisenhandler, Eisenhendler: the names were given to those who came from Ayznshtot, meaning "Iron City" (H&H), a town that used to be in Hungary but is now in Austria.
Famous **Bearers:** LUTHER PFAHLER EISENHART (1876–1965) of Pennsylvania is remembered as the father of differential geometry. DWIGHT DAVID (IKE) EISENHOWER (1890–1969) of Denison, Texas, was the 34th U.S. president. Previously, he had served as an army general. He was commander of U.S. forces in Europe and was later Allied commander during World War II. As president he was known as a moderate, nonideological Republican who worked well with Congress.

Genealogies: *Ancestry of the John Franklin Eisenhart Family* was compiled by Willis Wolf Eisenhart and published in Abottstown, Pennsylvania, in 1951. *Descendants of Peter and Anna Maria Eyster Eisenhart* was compiled by Ruth Madeline Eisenhart and published in Baltimore, Maryland, in 1971.

ELAM
Ranking: 2372 S.S. Count: 19,139
Origin: English. 1) derived from the Old English word "elm," meaning elm. The name was given to those who lived near elm trees. *2) uncertain etymology.* The name was given to those who came from Elham, which means "Homestead by a heathen temple" (ES) and is a place in Kent, England.
Genealogies: None known.

ELDER
Ranking: 1086 S.S. Count: 40,718
Origin: English. Derived from the Old English word "ealdra," meaning elder.
Famous **Elders**: WILLIAM HENRY ELDER (1819–1904) of Maryland was a Roman Catholic priest, a professor of theology, a bishop of Natchez, and the archbishop of Cincinnati. SUSAN BLANCHARD ELDER (1835–1923) of Louisiana was a writer of biographies, poems, and dramas. SAMUEL JAMES ELDER (1850–1918) was a lawyer and an expert on copyright laws.
Genealogies: *Maryland Elder Family and Kin: William Elder, 1707–1775* was compiled by Mary Louise Donnelly and published in Burke, Virginia, in 1975. *William Elder: Ancestors and Descendants* was compiled by Mary Louise Donnelly and published in Burke, Virginia, in 1986.

ELDRED
Ranking: 3575 S.S. Count: 12,609
Origin: English. 1) derived from the Middle English first name Aldred, which is derived from the Old English words "ead" or "æðel" and "ræd," meaning old or noble and counsel. 2) derived from the Middle English word "aldrett," meaning alder grove. The name was given to those who lived near an alder grove.
Genealogies: None known.

ELDRIDGE (S.S. Abbreviation: Eldrig)
Ranking: 1277 S.S. Count: 34,618
Origin: English. The name was given to those who came from Elbridge, which means "plank bridge" (ES) and is a place in Kent, England.
Famous **Eldridges**: GEORGE HOMANS ELDRIDGE (1854–1905) was a nationally recognized geologist through his work at the U.S. Geological Survey, where he worked for 21 years.

Genealogies: *The Ancestry of Marlen Eldredge (also Eldridge)* was compiled by Mark Eldredge and published in Santa Barbara, California, in 1970. *The Family of Clyde Mulford Eldridge and Other Descendants of William Eldred of Yarmouth* was compiled by Luella Eldridge and published in Silver Spring, Maryland, in 1983.

ELIAS
Ranking: 2370 S.S. Count: 19,157
Origin: French, German. Cognate to Ellis.
Genealogies: None known.

ELIZONDO (S.S. Abbreviation: Elizon)
Ranking: 4372 S.S. Count: 10,254
Origin: Spanish. The name was given to those who came from Elizondo, which means "adjacent to the church" (ES) and is a place in Spain.
Genealogies: None known.

ELKINS
Ranking: 1319 S.S. Count: 33,754
Origin: English. Transformation of Ellis.
Famous **Elkinses**: EARL C. ELKINS (1904–1977) of South Dakota was a physician who taught at the Mayo Clinic in Minnesota and was appointed to the President's Committee on Employment of the Handicapped.
Genealogies: *Leaves Folded Down* was compiled by Louise E. Sinkler and published in Wayne, Pennsylvania, in 1971. *Ancestors and Descendants of Robert Easley, Sr. & Elizabeth Earle Elkins of St. Helena Parish, Louisiana* was compiled by Austin Beverly Smith and published in 1981.

ELLENBERG, ELLENBERGER (S.S. Abbreviation: Ellenb)
Ranking: 4979 S.S. Count: 9003
Origin: German. Derived from the German place name Ellen, meaning elbow, and the Old High German word "berg," meaning hill.
Genealogies: None known.

ELLER
Ranking: 2490 S.S. Count: 18,199
Origin: German, Italian, Jewish. German: 1) derived from the names of two streams, Elera and Alira. 2) derived from the Middle Low German word "elre," meaning alder. The name was given to those who lived near an alder tree. *Italian: transformation of Hil(l)ary. Jewish: transformation of Heller.*
Genealogies: *Boone, Eller, Sledge, Vaughn and Related Families* was compiled by Jesse H. Boone and published in Middleboro, Massachusetts, in 1970.

ELLINGTON (S.S. Abbreviation: Elling)

Ranking: 1288 **S.S. Count:** 34,386

Origin: English. Derived from the Old English first names Ēdla and Ella and the word "hām," meaning homestead.

Famous **Ellingtons**: EDWARD KENNEDY (DUKE) ELLINGTON (1899–1974) of Washington, D.C., was one of the founders of big-band jazz. His band included many of jazz's greatest musicans and was known for its blend of orchestration and improvisation. He composed more than 1000 pieces of music, including "Satin Doll" and "Do Nothin' 'til You Hear from Me."

Genealogies: None known.

ELLIOT, ELLIOTT

Ranking: 162 **S.S. Count:** 201,218

Origin: English, Scottish. English: 1) transformation of Ellis. 2) derived from the Middle English first name Elyat, which is derived from the Old English word "aðel," meaning noble. Scottish: derived from the Gaelic word "eileach," meaning dam or mound.

Famous **Bearers**: JONATHAN ELLIOT (1754–1846) of England came to America and published the *Gazette* in Washington, D.C. It was the first evening paper in the country. JESSIE DUNCAN ELLIOT (1782–1845) of Maryland was a naval officer responsible for the capture of the British ships *Detroit* and *Caledonia* on Lake Erie in 1812. BENJAMIN ELLIOTT (1787–1836) of South Carolina was a lawyer who, with E. C. Holland, planned a defense of slavery called *A Refutation of the Calumnies, etc.* SARAH BARNWELL ELLIOTT (1848–1928) of Georgia was an author who wrote novels about Tennessee mountain people. MAUD HOWE ELLIOTT (1854–1948) of Massachusetts was an author and the winner of a Pulitzer Prize for a biography about her mother titled *Julia Ward Howe (1819–1910).* CHARLES BURKE ELLIOTT (1861–1935) of Ohio was a justice of the Minnesota Supreme Court and an associate justice of the supreme court of the Philippines appointed by President William Howard Taft. He wrote articles for various law publications. MAXINE ELLIOTT (1868–1940) was from Maine. She was an actress who appeared in Shakespearean theater and owned and managed the Maxine Elliott Theater in New York City. GERTRUDE ELLIOTT (1874–1950) of Maine was an actress and the sister of Maxine.

Genealogies: None known.

ELLIS

Ranking: 114 **S.S. Count:** 255,135

Origin: English. Derived from the first name Eliha, which is derived from the Hebrew name Eliyahu, meaning "Jehovah is God" (H&H).

Famous **Ellises**: CALVIN ELLIS (1826–1883) of Massachusetts was the dean of the Harvard Medical School. He

made many contributions to the field of medicine. JOHN WILLIS ELLIS (1820–1861) of North Carolina was the governor of that state. He was in favor of the South's leaving the Union and asked for "volunteers to resist the Northern invasion." EDWARD SYLVESTER ELLIS (1840–1916) of Ohio was the author of many dime-store novels, including *Seth Jones or the Captive of the Frontier.* HARVEY ELLIS (1852–1904) of Rochester, New York, was the best-known U.S. architect of his time. His best-known work was done in Minneapolis, Minnesota, and St. Louis, Missouri. CARLETON ELLIS (1876–1941) of New Hampshire was a chemist and inventor. He invented paint and varnish removers, then went on to invent 753 items for which patents were granted.

Genealogies: *Descendants of Charles Jones of New Brunswick from 1776 and Ellis Descendants from 1739* was compiled by Geneva Jones Emberley and published in Minneapolis, Minnesota, in 1972. *The Ellis Line from Surry-Sussex in Virginia* was compiled by Dixie L. McCrary and published in St. Petersburg, Florida, in 1978.

ELLISON (S.S. Abbreviation: Elliso)

Ranking: 706 **S.S. Count:** 59,916

Origin: English. Transformation of Ellis.

Famous **Ellisons**: RALPH WALDO ELLISON (1914–) of Oklahoma City, Oklahoma, wrote *Invisible Man,* a widely acclaimed novel about an African-American man who tries to fight white oppression. It was the only piece of fiction he ever wrote.

Genealogies: *Black Masters: A Free Family of Color in the Old South* was compiled by Michael P. Johnson and published in New York, New York, in 1984. *Arthur Ellison of Adams County, Ohio and Some of His Descendants and Relatives* was compiled by Floyd Vernon Ellison and published in Middletown, Ohio, in 1979.

ELLSWORTH (S.S. Abbreviation: Ellswo)

Ranking: 2457 **S.S. Count:** 18,479

Origin: English. Derived from the Old English first name Elli and the word "worð," meaning enclosure.

Famous **Ellsworths**: OLIVER ELLSWORTH (1745–1807) of Connecticut was a delegate to the Continental Congress and later, the Constitutional Convention, where he helped to secure the "Connecticut Compromise." His son, HENRY LEAVITT ELLSWORTH (1791–1858) of Connecticut, was also in government service. He was the first U.S. commissioner of patents and helped secure the first appropriation for agriculture, earning himself the name "father of the Department of Agriculture." ELMER EPHRAIM ELLSWORTH (1837–1861) of New York was a law clerk in Abraham Lincoln's office and worked on his presidential campaign. It is believed that he was the first man of note killed in the Civil War. LINCOLN ELLSWORTH (1880–1951) of Chicago, Illinois, led the first transarctic and transantarctic air crossings, in 1926 and 1935, respectively.

Genealogies: *Samuel Richardson, 1602–1658 and Josiah Ellsworth, 1629–1689, Some Descendants* was compiled by Ruth Ellsworth Richardson and published in 1974. *A Study of the Ancestry of Jonathan Ellsworth of Oneida County, New York* was compiled by Maxine Phelps Lines and published in Oneida County, New York, in 1965.

ELMORE

Ranking: 1258 **S.S. Count:** 35,028
Origin: English. Derived from the Old English words "elm" and "ofer," meaning elm and ridge. The name was given to those who came from Elmore, a place in Gloucestershire, England.
Genealogies: None known.

ELROD

Ranking: 2981 **S.S. Count:** 15,257
Origin: English, Jewish. 1) derived from the first name Aelred, meaning temple and counsel. 2) derived from the first name Elrawd, meaning "God is the ruler" (ES).
Genealogies: *The Elrod Family and Allied Lines of Douthit, Riddle, Douglas and Redenbaugh Families* was compiled by Pauline Walters and published in New Ross, Indiana, in 1971.

ELY

Ranking: 2333 **S.S. Count:** 19,464
Origin: English. Derived from the Old English words "æl" and "gē," meaning eel and district.
Famous **Elys:** RICHARD THEODORE ELY (1854–1943) of Ripley, New York, was an economist who was noted for his commitment to the social responsibility of economics. Among other groups, he founded the Association for Labor Legislation and the American Association for Agricultural Legislation. HANSON EDWARD ELY (1867–1958) of Iowa was an army officer. He was cited for heroism and was commandant of the Army General Service School and the Army War College. ZEBULON DEFOREST ELY III (1912–1971) of Pennsylvania was trained as a physician. He supplemented his income while in college by writing scripts for the radio show "Mr. District Attorney." He also wrote scripts for the radio shows "Reliving Dramas from the Bible," "Gang Busters," and "Dick Tracy."
Genealogies: *Descendants of William Ely and Richard Ely: Sons of Richard Ely, 1610–1685: With Some Account of the Elys of Wonston* was compiled by Moses S. Beach.

EMANUEL, EMANUELOV, EMANUELI, EMANUELE, EMANUELLI (S.S. Abbreviation: Emanue)

Ranking: 3929 **S.S. Count:** 11,484

Origin: Emanuel, Emanuelov—Jewish; Emanueli—Jewish, Italian; Emanuele, Emanuelli—Italian. Derived from the Hebrew first name Imanuel, meaning "God is with us" (H&H).
Genealogies: *Emanuel: Savoy to America* was compiled by Garvin R. Emanuel and most likely published in Huntsville, Alabama, in 1969.

EMBRY

Ranking: 4151 **S.S. Count:** 10,906
Origin: English. Transformation of Emery.
Genealogies: None known.

EMERIC, EMERICK

Ranking: 4516 **S.S. Count:** 9912
Origin: English. Transformation of Emery.
Genealogies: None known.

EMERSON (S.S. Abbreviation: Emerso)

Ranking: 1031 **S.S. Count:** 42,374
Origin: English. Transformation of Emery.
Famous **Emersons:** MARY MOODY EMERSON (1774–1863) of Massachusetts was a New England intellectual who greatly influenced her nephew Ralph Waldo Emerson. When her brother, Ralph's father, died, she moved in with her sister-in-law to help with the raising of the children. RALPH WALDO EMERSON (1803–1882) of Concord, Massachusetts, was a writer and control figure of the New England transcendentalism. Many of his most famous essays began as sermons he wrote while he worked as a Unitarian minister. His poetry, lectures, and essays were imbued with a great respect for nature and a questioning of established hierarchies. BENJAMIN KENDALL EMERSON (1843–1932) of New Hampshire was a geologist. He had an excellent collection of minerals, which he collected while on staff at Amherst University. He published many articles on the geology of the Northeast. ROLLINS ADAMS EMERSON (1873–1947) of New York was a pioneer in the field of genetics. He set up "The Maize Genetics Cooperation," where seeds were available for all in an exchange program and unpublished works could be circulated among interested scientists. HAVEN EMERSON (1874–1957) of New York was a public-health educator who was responsible for *Local Health Units for the Nation*, which is a standard on local health organization and which established the basic principle for the administration of local health services.
Genealogies: *English Roots of the Haverhill and Ipswich Emersons* was compiled by Ralph Stanton Emerson and published in Baltimore, Maryland, in 1985. *A Genealogy of the Emerson Family of Vallejo, California: A Branch of the Haverhill Emersons of Massachusetts and New Hampshire 1561–1975* was compiled by Robley Emerson Passalacqua and most likely published in California in 1975.

EMERY

Ranking: 1190 S.S. Count: 36,816

Origin: English. Derived from a Germanic first name derived from the words "amal" and "ric," meaning bravery and power.

Famous **Emerys**: ALBERT HAMILTON EMERY (1834–1926) of New York was an engineer and inventor who made considerable contributions in hydraulic pressure measuring devices. CHARLES EDWARD EMERY (1838–1898) of New York was an engineer and a consultant to the navy on steam engines. SARAH ELIZABETH VAN DE VORT EMERY (1838–1895) of New York was a reformer and a Greenbacker and Populist writer and campaigner. LUCILIUS ALONZO EMERY (1840–1920) of Maine introduced the theory of equity and chancery rules in Maine. STEPHEN ALBERT EMERY (1841–1891) of Maine was a music teacher at the New England Conservatory and Boston University. HENRY CROSBY EMERY (1872–1924) of Maine was the son of Lucilius. An economist, he taught at Yale University and was the chairman of the Tariff Board (1909–1913).

Genealogies: *Hemry (also Emery) Family History Book* was compiled by Larry H. Hemry and published in Fairfield, Washington, in 1985. *The Revised Genealogical Records of the Descendants of John Emery of Newbury, Massachusetts* was compiled by Judith Elaine Burns and published in Baltimore, Maryland, in 1982.

EMMONS

Ranking: 2310 S.S. Count: 19,670

Origin: English. Transformation of Emery.

Famous **Emmonses**: NATHANIEL EMMONS (1745–1840) of Connecticut was a Congregational clergyman. EBENEZER EMMONS (1799–1863) of Massachusetts was the North Carolina state geologist. GEORGE FOSTER EMMONS (1811–1884) was a naval officer. He was part of Wilkes's Exploring Expedition and actively part of the Gulf blockade in the Civil War. He also wrote a book called *The Navy of the United States. . . 1775–1853.* SAMUEL FRANKLIN EMMONS (1841–1911) of Massachusetts was a geologist. He took part in the geological exploration of the 40th parallel. Also an author, he wrote *Geology and Mining Industry of Leadville, Colorado.*

Genealogies: *An Ancestral Record of My Maternal Grandmother, Emma Jane (Emmons) Brown, Showing Her Descent from Governor William Bradford, 2nd Signer of the Mayflower Compact* was compiled by Lucy Ada Jewett Prescott and published in New Rochelle, New York, in 1965. *The Doane, Emmons, Lindner, Roney, and Stout Families* was compiled by Robert Harold Lindner and published in Empire, Michigan, in 1986. *An Emmons Genealogy* was compiled by Corwin J. Emmons and published in Southington, Connecticut, in 1983.

ENG

Ranking: 4141 S.S. Count: 10,934

Origin: Swedish. Derived from the Old Norse word "eng," meaning meadow. The name was given to those who lived near meadows and was also taken ornamentally.

Genealogies: None known.

ENGEL

Ranking: 1392 S.S. Count: 31,868

Origin: Dutch, German, Jewish. Dutch, German: 1) derived from several Germanic first names with the first component Engel that are derived from Ing, the name of a Germanic god. 2) derived from the Middle High German word "engel," meaning angel. Jewish: derived from the German word "engel," meaning angel. The name was taken ornamentally.

Famous **Engels**: CARL ENGEL (1883–1944) of France was the chief of the music division of the Library of Congress in Washington, D.C. ALBERT JOSEPH ENGEL (1888–1959) represented a Michigan district in the U.S. House of Representatives for eight terms.

Genealogies: *The Genealogy and History of the Ingalls (also Engel) Family in America: Giving the Descendants of Edmund Ingalls who Settled at Lynn, Mass. in 1629* was compiled by Charles Burleigh and published in Orlando, Florida, in 1984. *Upstream, Downstream: The Ancestors and Descendants of Peter and Hester Auter Engels* was compiled by Mary P. Engels and published in Forrest City, Arkansas, in 1978.

ENGELHARD, ENGELHARDT, ENGELHART (S.S. Abbreviation: Engelh)

Ranking: 3969 S.S. Count: 11,409

Origin: Engelhard—Dutch, English, German; Engelhardt, Engelhart—German. Derived from a German first name derived from the words "engel," referring to the Germanic god Ing, and "hard," meaning brave and strong.

Famous **Bearers**: ZEPHYRIN ENGELHARDT (1851–1934) of Germany was a Roman Catholic priest who was brought to the United States as an infant. He was a missionary to the Indians. He wrote *The Franciscans in California* and *Missions and Missionaries of California,* among others.

Genealogies: None known.

ENGLAND, ENGLANDER (S.S. Abbreviation: Englan)

Ranking: 1108 S.S. Count: 39,923

Origin: England—English; Englander—Jewish. England: derived from the Old French word "angleis," meaning English. Englander: transformation of Englisher.

Famous **Bearers**: JOHN ENGLAND (1786–1842) of Ireland was a Catholic priest who worked to reform the method used to transport convicts to Australia. He founded the first Catholic newspaper in the United States.

Genealogies: *Genealogies of Some England Families in America: With Miscellaneous England Marriages and Miscellaneous England Data* was compiled by Charles Walter England and published in Silver Spring, Maryland, in 1980. *Joseph England and His Descendants: An Historical Genealogy of the England Family as Descending from Joseph England, 1680–1748: A Quaker Family of Cecil County, Maryland* was compiled by Charles Walter England and published in Silver Spring, Maryland, in 1978.

ENGLE

Ranking: 1634 **S.S. Count:** 27,487

Origin: Dutch, German. Transformation of Engel.

Famous Engles: EARL T. ENGLE (1896–1957) was a physician, surgeon, and professor. During 18 years at the College of Physicians of Columbia University, he received numerous awards and wrote several books. CLAIR WILLIAM WALTER ENGLE (1911–1964) of California was a member of the House of Representatives and of the U.S. Senate.

Genealogies: None known.

ENGLER, ENGLERDING, ENGLERT

Ranking: 3134 **S.S. Count:** 14,490

Origin: German. Engler: transformation of the first Dutch and German definitions of Engel. Englerding, Englert: transformation of Engelhard.

Genealogies: *The Ancestral History of David Alan Engler, Born in Winona, Minnesota 14 Nov. 1949* was compiled by David Alan Engler and published in Woodbury, Minnesota, in 1985.

ENGLISH, ENGLISHER (S.S. Abbreviation: Englis)

Ranking: 648 **S.S. Count:** 64,246

Origin: English—English; Englisher—Jewish. Derived from the Old English word "Englisc," which orginally referred to an Angle rather than a Saxon but later referred to any resident of England.

Famous Bearers: GEORGE BETHUNE ENGLISH (1787–1828) of Massachusetts was a soldier and a linguist. He served in the marines, in the Egyptian army, and as a U.S. secret agent. JAMES EDWARD ENGLISH (1812–1890) of Connecticut was a clock and brass manufacturer in New Haven. He also served as a member of the House of Representatives, a U.S. senator, and governor of Connecticut. THOMAS DUNN ENGLISH (1819–1902) of Pennsylvania was a member of Congress from New Jersey. WILLIAM HAYDEN ENGLISH (1822–1896) of Indiana was a member of Congress from Indiana and the Democratic candidate for vice president in 1880.

Genealogies: *English Family History* was compiled by Nadine English Watson and published in Wichita Falls, Texas, in 1985. *English-Robertson Families in America* was compiled by Arthur Leslie Keith and published in Laguna Park, Texas, most likely in 1982.

ENGSTRAND, ENGSTROM

Ranking: 4467 **S.S. Count:** 10,029

Origin: Swedish. Transformation of Eng combined with components meaning shore and river.

Genealogies: None known.

ENNIS

Ranking: 1932 **S.S. Count:** 23,378

Origin: Irish. Derived from the Gaelic word "inis," meaning island, particularly in a river.

Genealogies: *The Name's the Same: The Ennis Family Genealogy* was compiled by Ellie Mayer and published in New York, New York, in 1987. *The Root Family of Bolivar, New York: A History of the Descendants of Abel Root, Sr., Who Settled Bolivar in Allegany County, New York: Related Families, Cook, Ennis, Holland, Hulbert, Johnson, Nichols, Nulsen, Richardson, Weatherell, Withey* was compiled by William Paquette and published in Baltimore, Maryland, in 1991.

ENOS

Ranking: 3917 **S.S. Count:** 11,509

Origin: English, French. Derived from the first name Enos, meaning mortal man.

Genealogies: *The Eno and Enos Family in America; Descendants of James Eno of Windsor, Conn.* was compiled by Douglas C. Richardson and published in Sacramento, California, in 1973.

ENRIGHT (S.S. Abbreviation: Enrigh)

Ranking: 4477 **S.S. Count:** 10,002

Origin: Irish. Derived from the Gaelic name Indreachtach, meaning attacker.

Genealogies: None known.

ENRIQUES, ENRIQUE, ENRIQUEZ (S.S. Abbreviation: Enriqu)

Ranking: 2278 **S.S. Count:** 19,951

Origin: Enriques—Portuguese; Enrique, Enriquez—Spanish. Cognates of the English and French definitions of Henry.

Genealogies: None known.

EPPERS

Ranking: 2597 **S.S. Count:** 17,500

Origin: German. Transformation of Egbert.

Genealogies: None known.

EPPS

Ranking: 1693 S.S. Count: 26,362

Origin: English. Derived from the Old English word "æps," meaning aspen. The name was given to those who lived near aspen trees and to those who were thought to tremble like aspen leaves.

Genealogies: None known.

EPSTEIN (S.S. Abbreviation: Epstei)

Ranking: 2014 S.S. Count: 22,661

Origin: German, Jewish. Derived from the Old High German words "ebur" and "stein," meaning wild boar and stone. The name was given to those who came from places that obtained their names from these words.

Famous **Epsteins:** JACOB EPSTEIN (1880–1959) of New York was a sculptor whose great works in nudity were ahead of their time. ABRAHAM EPSTEIN (1892–1942) of Russia was a pioneer in American insurance. He is credited with introducing European social insurance ideas to the United States. PHILIP G. EPSTEIN (1909–1952) of New York with his twin brother, JULIUS, and his other brother, MILTON, were playwrights responsible for *Yankee Doodle Dandy* and *Casablanca*.

Genealogies: None known.

ERB

Ranking: 3778 S.S. Count: 11,950

Origin: German. Derived from word "erbe," meaning inheritance, as it appears as a first component in many names.

Famous **Erbs:** DONALD MILTON ERB (1900–1943) was appointed president of the University of Oregon at the age of 38 and served in that capacity until his death.

Genealogies: *Descendants of David Erb* was compiled by Henry L. Erb and published in Blatic, Ohio, in 1990.

ERDMAN, ERDMANN

Ranking: 3006 S.S. Count: 15,108

Origin: German. The name was given to those who worked as farmers.

Famous **Bearers:** CHARLES ROSENBURY ERDMAN (1866–1960) of New York, an educator and theologian, was a very respected and popular theology professor at Princeton University.

Genealogies: None known.

ERICKSON (S.S. Abbreviation: Ericks)

Ranking: 293 S.S. Count: 121,959

Origin: Norwegian, Swedish. Derived from the first name Erik, meaning "ever king" (ES).

Famous **Ericksons:** JOHN E. ERICKSON (1863–1946) was governor of Montana and a U.S. senator from that state.

Genealogies: *The Norwegian-American Families of Hans Bredeson Haagenstad and Emma (Erickson) Haagenstad, His Wife, to the Fifth Generation, and Peder Erikson and Kari (Haagensdatter) Erikson, His Wife, to the Seventh Generation, Including the Families Whipple, Lundberg, Gulsvig, and Erickson* was compiled by Mrs. Lyle (Jean E.) Peterson and published in Dubuque, Iowa, in 1980. *Prairie Memories: A History of the Swanson, Erickson, and Lindberg Families of North Dakota* was compiled by Algot R. Swanson and published in Tucson, Arizona, in 1974.

ERICSON (S.S. Abbreviation: Ericks)

Ranking: 4932 S.S. Count: 9075

Origin: Norwegian, Swedish. Transformation of Erik.

Famous **Ericsons:** JOHN ERICSON (1803–1889) of Sweden was an engineer whose claim to fame is that he designed and built the Union ironclad the *Monitor*, which battled with the Confederate ironclad the *Merrimack*.

Genealogies: *No Stone Unturned: Genealogical Record of Descendants of Carl and Carolina Ericson, Immigrants from Sweden* was compiled by Martha Wreath Streeter and published in Manhattan, Kansas, in 1989.

ERNST

Ranking: 1679 S.S. Count: 26,653

Origin: Dutch, German, Jewish. Dutch, German: derived from the Germanic name Ernust, which is derived from the Middle High German word "ern(e)st," meaning seriousness. Jewish: derived from the German word "ernest," meaning serious and earnest.

Famous **Ernsts:** OSWARD HERBERT ERNST (1842–1926) of Ohio was a West Point graduate and an engineer who specialized in river and harbor improvements. He was involved with the digging of the Galveston, Texas, channel and was part of the Isthmian Canal Commission. HAROLD CLARENCE ERNST (1856–1922) was a bacteriologist and a professor at Harvard Medical School. RICHARD P. ERNST (1858–1954) was a U.S. senator from Kentucky. ALWIN CHARLES ERNST (1881–1948) founded, with his brother Theodore C. Ernst, the accounting firm of Ernst and Ernst, which had more than 40 offices by 1948.

Genealogies: *Friedrich Ernst of Industry: Research on Life, Family, Acquaintances, and Conditions of the Times* was compiled by Miriam Korff York and published in Giddings, Texas, in 1989.

ERVIN

Ranking: 1259 S.S. Count: 35,015

Origin: English, Irish, Scottish. Transformation of Irvine.

Famous **Ervins:** JOE W. ERVIN (1901–1945) was a U.S.

congressman from North Carolina. SAM J. ERVIN JR. (1896–1985) of Morgantown, North Carolina, served as a justice of the North Carolina Supreme Court (1948–1954) and as a U.S. senator from North Carolina (1954–1974). He gained fame as the chairman of the Senate Watergate Committee in 1973.

Genealogies: *Guide to 500 Early Irwin/Ervin etc. Families in the United States with Adult Children Prior to the 1850 Census* was compiled by L. M. Irwin and published most likely in Bloomington, Illinois, in 1991.

ERWIN

Ranking: 1328 **S.S. Count:** 33,298
Origin: English, Irish, Scottish. Transformation of Irvine.
Famous **Erwins:** WILLIAM ALLEN ERWIN (1856–1932) established Erwin Cotton Mills in North Carolina in 1893 and grew to become one of the most powerful textile manufacturers in the country.
Genealogies: None known.

ESCALA, ESCALANTE, ESCALADA

Ranking: 4933 **S.S. Count:** 9074
Origin: Spanish. Escala, Escalante: transformations of Escale. Escalada: uncertain etymology. Possibly a cognate to Escale. The name was given to those who came from Escalada, a place in Burgos, Spain.
Famous **Bearers:** SILVESTRE VELEZ DE ESCALANTE (1768?–1779) was born in Spain. He arrived in America (New Spain) in 1768 and served as a missionary to the Indians in New Mexico. While in the Southwest he explored much of the area and left reports on his journeys.
Genealogies: None known.

ESCAMILLA, ESCAMILLIA (S.S. Abbreviation: Escami)

Ranking: 4413 **S.S. Count:** 10,153
Origin: Spanish. The name was given to those who came from Escamilla, which means "small bench" (ES) and is a place in Spain.
Genealogies: None known.

ESCOBAR (S.S. Abbreviation: Escoba)

Ranking: 1965 **S.S. Count:** 23,056
Origin: Spanish. Derived from the Late Latin word "scopāre," meaning a place overgrown with broom, a shrubby plant. The name was given to those who came from Escobar, the name of several places in Spain.
Genealogies: None known.

ESCOBEDO (S.S. Abbreviation: Escobe)

Ranking: 3250 **S.S. Count:** 13,980
Origin: Spain. Transformation of Escobar.

Genealogies: None known.

ESPARZA (S.S. Abbreviation: Esparz)

Ranking: 2086 **S.S. Count:** 21,998
Origin: Spanish. Derived from the Latin word "sparsus," meaning scattered and referring to land where little grew. The name was given to those who came from Esparza, the name of several places in Spain.
Genealogies: None known.

ESPINO, ESPINOZA

Ranking: 508 **S.S. Count:** 78,855
Origin: Spanish. Derived from the Latin word "spinosus," meaning thorny. The names were given to those who came from Espinoza, the name of several places in Spain.
Genealogies: None known.

ESPOSI, ESPOSITO

Ranking: 1434 **S.S. Count:** 31,140
Origin: Italian. Derived from the Latin word "expositus," meaning exposed. The names were often given to those who had been abandoned as infants.
Genealogies: None known.

ESQUIVEL (S.S. Abbreviation: Esquiv)

Ranking: 2857 **S.S. Count:** 15,983
Origin: Spanish. Derived from the name Aizkibel, which is of uncertain eytmology but is possibly derived from the words "aitz" and "gibel," meaning rock and rear.
Genealogies: None known.

ESTEP

Ranking: 2444 **S.S. Count:** 18,576
Origin: Spanish. Cognate to Stephen.
Genealogies: *The Estep/Eastep Genealogy Estep/Eastep/Estepp/Esteb/Eastepp/Eastup* was compiled by Jane Farrell Burgess and published in Rockville, Maryland, in 1988.

ESTES

Ranking: 851 **S.S. Count:** 50,211
Origin: English. 1) possibly derived from the Old English word "ēast," meaning east. 2) derived from the first name Est, meaning gracious.
Famous **Esteses:** DANA ESTES (1840–1909) of Maine was a publisher and bookseller. He was the owner of Estes and Lauriat and Dana Estes and Co.
Genealogies: *Cary-Estes Genealogy* was compiled by May Folk Webb and published in Huntington Valley, Pennsylvania, in 1979. *The Estes Family of Virginia, Southern Kentucky, Iowa, Missouri, and Kansas and Their Ancestor Families—Yates, Marshall, Stockton* was compiled by Lucille Alexander and published in Wayne, New Jersey, in 1990.

ESTEVE

Ranking: 4711 S.S. Count: 9504
Origin: Catalan, Provençal. Transformation of Stephen.
Genealogies: None known.

ESTRADER, ESTRADA, ESTRADE, ESTRADERE, ESTRADIER (S.S. Abbreviation: Estrad)

Ranking: 711 S.S. Count: 59,235
Origin: Estrader—Catalan; Estrada—Catalan, Spanish; Estrade—Catalan, Provençal; Estradere, Estradier— Provençal. Cognates to Street.
Genealogies: None known.

ESTRELA, ESTRELLA (S.S. Abbreviation: Estrel)

Ranking: 4756 S.S. Count: 9419
Origin: Estrela—Portuguese; Estrella—Spanish. Cognates to Stella.
Genealogies: None known.

ETHERIDGE, ETHERINGTON (S.S. Abbreviation: Etheri)

Ranking: 2810 S.S. Count: 16,216
Origin: English. Etheridge: derived from the Old English first name Eadric, which is derived from the words "ead" and "ric," meaning prosperity and power. Etherington: Uncertain etymology. Possibly a transformation of Harrington.
Genealogies: *Ten Generations of the Etheredge-Etheridge-Ethridge Family in America* was compiled by Fae Alice Etheredge and published in Bossier City, Louisiana, in 1982.

ETHRIDGE (S.S. Abbreviation: Ethrid)

Ranking: 3921 S.S. Count: 11,505
Origin: English. Transformation of Etheridge.
Genealogies: None known.

EUBANK, EUBANKS

Ranking: 1267 S.S. Count: 34,829
Origin: English. The names were given to those who lived near yew trees.
Genealogies: *Our Eubanks Family and Related Families* was compiled by Lucille Dickinson Ainsworth and published in Winnsboro, Louisiana, in 1985.

EVANS

Ranking: 45 S.S. Count: 484,224
Origin: Welsh. Derived from the first name Ifan, a cognate of John.
Famous **Evanses**: OLIVER EVANS (1755–1819) of Delaware was an inventor who built the first high-powered

steam engine in America and the first powered vehicle that could run on roads. GEORGE HENRY EVANS (1805–1856) of England was an editor and reformer who worked for the Homestead Act. ANTHONY WALTON WHYTE EVANS (1817–1886) of New Jersey was a civil engineer who is best remembered as the builder of railroads in Chile and Peru. JOHN EVANS (1814–1897) of Ohio was the territorial governor of Colorado and the founder of Colorado Seminary, which became the University of Denver. Mt. Evans and Evanston, Illinois, are named in honor of him. ROBLEY DUNGLISON (FIGHTING BOB) EVANS (1846–1912) of Virginia was a professional naval officer who rose through the ranks and was the commander of the U.S. fleet on a voyage around the world. ELIZABETH GLENDOWER EVANS (1856–1937) of New York was a social reformer in the Massachusetts penal system. RUDOLPH EVANS (1878–1960) of Washington, D.C., was a sculptor famous for his statue of Thomas Jefferson in the Jefferson Memorial. ALICE CATHERINE EVANS (1881–1975) of Pennsylvania discovered the cause of brucillosis, and her discovery is considered one of the great medical achievements of the early 20th century. She served as the first female president of the Society of American Bacteriologists in 1928. HERBERT MCLEAN EVANS (1882–1971) of California was the scientist who discovered that humans have 48 chromosomes. He is also credited with the discovery of vitamin E. CHARLES (CHICK) EVANS (1890–1979) of Indiana was a golfer and the first to win both the U.S. Amateur and the U.S. Open in the same year. He is responsible for the Evans Scholarship Fund, which offers scholarships to qualified caddies. WALKER EVANS (1903–1975) of St. Louis, Missouri, was a photographer who was well known for his pictures of the rural poor that the Farm Security Administration employed him to take between 1935 and 1937. BERGEN (BALDWIN) EVANS (1904–1978) of Ohio was an educator, author, and a well-known TV and radio personality. OLIVER MARSHALL EVANS (1906–1975) of New Jersey was a humanitarian and businessman who devoted much of his life to the prevention of cruelty to animals, especially the type that resulted from the use of animals in experiments and the breeding of puppies and kittens in "puppy mills."

Genealogies: *American Family History: Fox, Ellicott, Evans* was compiled by Charles Worthington Evans and published in Cockeysville, Maryland, in 1976. *Anthony Evans of Colonial Southside Virginia: Lines of Banks, Blackwell, Bugg, Burnett, Davis, Evans, Fox, Ingram, Mathews, Smith, Walker: A Sourcebook for Related Materials* was compiled by June Banks Evans and published in New Orleans, Louisiana, in 1983.

EVERETT (S.S. Abbreviation: Everet)

Ranking: 687 S.S. Count: 60,957

Origin: English. Cognate to Eberhard.

Famous **Everetts**: DAVID EVERETT (1770–1813) of Massachusetts was a lawyer, journalist, and author of several works, including *Common Sense in Dishabille*, among others. ALEXANDER HILL EVERETT (1790–1847) of Massachusetts was the brother of Edward and the first ambassador to China. ROBERT EVERETT (1791–1875) of Wales was an abolitionist and a temperance leader. EDWARD EVERETT (1794–1865) of Massachusetts was a clergyman, statesman, and orator. He served his state and country as governor of Massachusetts, a member of Congress and senator, president of Harvard University, and as U.S. minister to Great Britain, but he is best known as the man who delivered the speech at the dedication of the national cemetery at Gettysburg, Pennsylvania on November 19, 1863, the day on which President Abraham Lincoln gave his famous Gettysburg Address. He was the brother of Alexander Hill Everett. CHARLES CARROLL EVERETT (1829–1900) of Maine was the dean of Harvard Divinity School (1878–1900).

Genealogies: *Stone, Grover, Ball and Everett Ancestry: Being The Ancestral Lines of John Wesley Stone, Delia Maria Theresa Grover Stone, Dan Harvey Ball and Emma Eugenia Everett Ball, All of Marquette, Michigan* was compiled by Frank Bush Stone and published in Summit, New Jersey, in 1990.

EVERHARD, EVERHART (S.S. Abbreviation: Everha)

Ranking: 2998 **S.S. Count:** 15,155
Origin: German. Transformations of Eberhard.
Genealogies: None known.

EVERS

Ranking: 3618 **S.S. Count:** 12,469
Origin: German. Transformation of Eberhard.

Famous **Everses**: (JAMES) CHARLES EVERS (1923–) and MEDGAR WILEY EVERS (1925–1963) of Decatur, Mississippi, were both civil rights activists. Charles worked in Philadelphia and other northern cities, and Medgar was the National Association for the Advancement of Colored People's (NAACP) first field secretary in Mississippi. When Medgar was killed in an ambush, he became a martyr for the cause of civil rights, and Charles took his place as field secretary of the Mississippi NAACP. In 1994, after three trials and 31 years, Medgar's killer was convicted of the crime.

Genealogies: None known.

EVERSON (S.S. Abbreviation: Everso)

Ranking: 2644 **S.S. Count:** 17,212
Origin: English. Transformation of E(a)ve(s).
Genealogies: None known.

EWING

Ranking: 917 **S.S. Count:** 47,020
Origin: Scottish. Derived from the Gaelic first name Eógann, which is most likely derived from the Latin name Eugenius, meaning well born.

Famous **Ewings**: FINIS EWING (1773–1841) of Virginia was the chief founder of the Presbyterian Church. CHARLES EWING (1780–1832) of New Jersey was the chief justice of the New Jersey Supreme Court (1824–1832). THOMAS EWING (1789–1871) was born in the area that was then Virginia but is now West Virginia. He served as a U.S. senator from Ohio, U.S. secretary of the Treasury, and as the first U.S. secretary of the interior. JAMES EWING (1866–1943) of Pennsylvania was the first pathologist at Cornell University. He specialized in the study of tumors and set up a tumor registry. WILLIAM MAURICE EWING (1906–1974) of Texas was a geophysicist known for his seismic studies of the ocean floor, including ocean-floor photography. He was the author of several books that dealt with this subject, including *Propagation of Sound in the Ocean* and *Elastic Waves in Layered Media*.

Genealogies: *Edley Ewing, the Texas Pioneer and His Descendants* was compiled by Milam Myrl Ewing and published in Tulsa, Oklahoma, in 1976. *From Whence We Came: Ancestors and Descendants of Gustavus H. Ewing, With Kindred Branches of the Ewing Families* was compiled by Vernon T. Ewing and published in Decorah, Iowa, in 1985.

EZELL

Ranking: 3021 **S.S. Count:** 15,047
Origin: English. The name was given to those who came from Isell, which means "Isa's corner" (ES) and is a place in Cumbria, England.
Genealogies: None known.

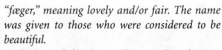

FABER

Ranking: 3314 **S.S. Count:** 13,672

Origin: English. Derived from the Latin word "faber," meaning craftsman. The name was given to those who worked as such.

Famous **Fabers:** JOHN EBERHARD FABER (1822–1879), originally from Bavaria (now Germany), at first imported pencils to and later manufactured pencils in the United States. He was the first to attach an eraser to the end of a pencil.

Genealogies: None known.

FABIAN

Ranking: 3052 **S.S. Count:** 14,871

Origin: Austrian, English, French, Italian, Polish. Derived from the Latin first name Fabiānus, which is derived from the word "faba," meaning bean.

Genealogies: *Faubion (also Fabian) and Allied Families* was compiled by Ann Faubion Armstrong and published in Georgetown, Texas, in 1982.

FAGAN

Ranking: 1833 **S.S. Count:** 24,645

Origin: Irish. Uncertain etymology.

Famous **Fagans:** JAMES FLEMING FAGAN (1828–1893) of Kentucky was a Confederate general who served in the western campaigns of the Civil War. He also fought in the Mexican War, attaining the rank of brigadier general.

Genealogies: None known.

FAHEY

Ranking: 3526 **S.S. Count:** 12,796

Origin: Irish. Derived from the Gaelic name Ó Fathartaigh, meaning "descendant of Fathartach" (H&H).

Genealogies: *The Descendants of Redmond Peter Fahey and Cecelia Haverty and John Sweeney and Mary Dineen, 1810–1984* was compiled by Verne Raymond Spear and published in West Springfield, Massachusetts, in 1984.

FAIN

Ranking: 3947 **S.S. Count:** 11,448

Origin: French. 1) the name was given to those who lived near a pagan temple. 2) the name was given to those who came from Fain (ES), which means "pagan temple" and is a place in France.

Genealogies: *Fain Family 1980* was compiled by Jeanette Fain Cornelius and published in Rockwall, Texas, in 1980.

FAIR

Ranking: 1738 **S.S. Count:** 25,802

Origin: English. Derived from the Old English word "fæger," meaning lovely and/or fair. The name was given to those who were considered to be beautiful.

Famous **Fairs:** JAMES GRAHAM FAIR (1831–1894) of Ireland came to the United States as a boy. He made his fortune in the Comstock Lode's Consolidated Virginia mine in 1849.

Genealogies: None known.

FAIRBAIRN, FAIRBAINS, FAIRBANK, FAIRBANKS (S.S. Abbreviation: Fairba)

Ranking: 2963 **S.S. Count:** 15,367

Origin: English. Fairbairn, Fairbains: derived from the Middle English words "fair" and "bairn," meaning lovely and child. The name was most likely given to those who were good-looking as children. Fairbank, Fairbanks: derived from the Middle English words "fair" and "bank," meaning lovely and bank or hill. The name was given to those who came from Fairbank, the name of several places in England.

Famous **Bearers:** ERASTUS FAIRBANKS (1792–1864) of Massachusetts was governor of Vermont and a business associate of his brother, Thaddeus. THADDEUS FAIRBANKS (1796–1886) of Massachusetts was an inventor who is responsible for the first platform scale. HENRY FAIRBANKS (1830–1918) of Vermont, the son of Thaddeus, was an inventor and manufacturer. He invented an alternating-current electric generator. CHARLES WARREN FAIRBANKS (1852–1918) of Ohio was a U.S. senator from Indiana and vice president of the United States (1905–1909). DOUGLAS ELTON FAIRBANKS (1883–1939) of Denver, Colorado, was born with the surname Ulman. He was a star and producer of many silent movies and was nearly worshipped by many of his fans. His best-known films include *The Mark of Zorro, The Three Musketeers,* and *Robin Hood.* He married and divorced the actress Mary Pickford. His son DOUGLAS FAIRBANKS JR. (1909–) was raised by his mother, Anna Beth Sully. He also became an actor and starred in several movies. He is best known for his roles in *Morning Glory* and *Catherine the Great.* He served with distinction in the U.S. navy during World War II.

Genealogies: *Down the Century from 1800* was compiled by Esther V.H. Cline and most likely published in Kalamazoo, Michigan, in 1963.

FAIRCHILD (S.S. Abbreviation: Fairch)

Ranking: 2396 **S.S. Count:** 18,940

Origin: English. Derived from the Middle English words "fair" and "child," meaning lovely and child. The name was given to those who were good-looking as children.

Famous **Fairchilds:** MARY SALOME CUTLER FAIRCHILD (1855–1921) of Massachusetts was a librarian and a leader in professional library training at the New York State

Library School. DAVID GRANDISON FAIRCHILD (1869–1954) of Michigan worked in the plant pathology section of the U.S. Department of Agriculture. He was responsible for the introduction of thousands of plants into the United States. BLAIR FAIRCHILD (1877–1933) of Massachusetts was a composer who lived in and was influenced by Paris, France. He published instrumental pieces and songs. FRANK LESLIE FAIRCHILD (1892–1978) of Connecticut was a businessman and artist. His artwork concentrated on circus life, and many of them are on display at the Ringling Museum of the American Circus. MUIR STEPHEN FAIRCHILD (1894–1950) of Washington was a professional army and air force officer and is considered the "father" of air force postgraduate professional officer education.

Genealogies: *Edward Eugene Fairchild, 1840–1911, and His Descendants* was compiled by David Fairchild Houston and published in El Cerrito, California, in 1979. *Ancestors and Descendants of Emma Tyas Horsfall: Largely a Chronicle of Two Families: Huxtable and Fairchild* was compiled by Emma Fairchild Patterson and most likely published in Maywood, Illinois, in 1964.

FAIRCLIFF, FAIRCLIFFE, FAIRCLOTH, FAIRCLOUGH (S.S. Abbreviation: Faircl)

Ranking: 3313 S.S. Count: 13,675
Origin: English. Derived from the Middle English words "fair" and "cloh," meaning lovely and ravine. The name was given to those who came from isolated ravines.
Genealogies: None known.

FAIRLEM, FAIRLEIGH, FAIRLEY, FAIRLIE (S.S. Abbreviation: Fairle)

Ranking: 4669 S.S. Count: 9581
Origin: Fairlem, Fairleigh—English; Fairley—English, Scottish; Fairlie—Scottish. Fairlem: derived from the Old English words "fæger" and "lamb," meaning lovely and lamb. The name was most likely given to those who came from Farlam, a place in Cumbria, England. Fairleigh, Fairley (English): derived from the Old English words "fearn" and "lēah," meaning fern and wood. The name was given to those who came from Farley, the name of several places in England. Fairley (Scottish), Fairlie: derived from the Old English words "fæger" and "lēah," meaning lovely and wood. The names were given to those who came from Fairle, a place in Scotland.

Famous **Bearers:** JOHN ARCHIBALD FAIRLIE (1872–1947) of Scotland came to the United States as a child and was raised in Jacksonville, Florida. He was graduated from Harvard University and taught at the college level in the field of political science. He was considered most knowledgeable on the subjects of state and local governments and was involved in reform movements of their administrations.

He was the founder of the American Political Science Association. *Municipal Administration* is his best-known book.
Genealogies: None known.

FAISON

Ranking: 4081 S.S. Count: 11,069
Origin: French. The name was given to those who worked raising and selling pheasants.
Genealogies: None known.

FALCON (ALSO FALCONAR, FALCONER, FALCONNAT, FALCONNET, FALCONNETTO, FALCONAT, FALCONE, FALCONI, FALCONIO, FALCONIERI, ET AL., FALCONNIER)

Ranking: 1481 S.S. Count: 30,036
Origin: Falcon—English, Provençal; Falconar, Falconer—English; Falconnat, Falconnet—French; Falconat, Falconnetto, Falcone, Falconi, Falconio, Falconieri, et al.—Italian; Falconnier—Provençal. Falcon, Falconnat, Falconnet, Falconetto, Falconat, Falcone, Falconi, Falconio: derived from the Latin word "falco," meaning falcon. The names were given to those who worked as falconers, to those who worked with a weapon named for the bird, and to those who were thought to look like falcons. Falconer, Falconar, Falconnier, Falconieri: transformations of and congates to Faulkner.

Famous **Bearers:** MARTHA PLATT FALCONER (1862–1941) of Ohio was a social worker. Appointed superintendent of the girls division of the House of Refuge in Philadelphia, she updated it with more homelike dorms, more humane treatment, and recreational and constructive training. Her school was later called Sleighton Farms.
Genealogies: None known.

FALK

Ranking: 2553 S.S. Count: 17,800
Origin: German. Cognate to Falcon.
Famous **Falks:** OTTO HERBERT FALK (1865–1940) of Wisconsin was a soldier and an industrialist. He was an army officer who fought in the Spanish-American War and rose to the rank of brigadier general in the Wisconsin National Guard. He excelled in business dealings after his retirement from the service. MAURICE FALK (1866–1946) of Pennsylvania was an industrialist and philanthropist. He was often referred to as "Little Carnegie," as he and his brother, LEON FALK JR., were exceedingly generous in helping those less fortunate, especially the Jewish community in Europe. HERBERT SEESHOLTZ FALK (1902–1975) of Virginia was a lawyer and a civic leader who had a special interest in fine arts and worked to bring more of the art world to his home town of Greensboro, North Carolina.
Genealogies: None known.

FALLON

Ranking: 2697 **S.S. Count:** 16,862

Origin: English, Irish. English: Transformation of Fuller. Irish: derived from the Gaelic name Ó Fallamhain, meaning "descendant of Fallamhan" (H&H), a name derived from the word "follamhnus," meaning supremacy.

Famous **Fallons:** JOHN FALLON (1901–1951) was a Massachusetts physician who earned national prominence in medical photography.

Genealogies: George Lawrence Fallon, 1888–1959: His Ancestors and Descendants was compiled by Kathleen Moore Fitzpatrick and published in Ellicott City, Maryland, in 1985.

FALLS

Ranking: 4370 **S.S. Count:** 10,259

Origin: English. Derived from the Old Norman French word "faleise," meaning cliff. The name was given to those who came from Falasie, a place in Calvados, France.

Genealogies: None known.

FANNIN (ALSO FANNING)

Ranking: 1815 **S.S. Count:** 24,840

Origin: Fannin—Irish; Fanning—English. Fannin: transformation of Finn. Fanning: transformation of Fenn.

Famous **Bearers:** EDMUND FANNING (1739–1818) of New York was a North Carolina loyalist who commanded the King's American Regiment of Foot in the Revolutionary War. He apparently returned to England sometime after the war, as he is known to have died in London, England. NATHANIEL FANNING (1755–1805) of Connecticut was a sea captain and the author of *Narrative of the Adventures of an American Naval Officer.* DAVID FANNING (1755–1825) of Virginia was a North Carolina loyalist and the author of *Narrative of Col. David Fanning.* EDMUND FANNING (1769–1841) of Connecticut, the brother of Nathaniel, was a sea captain and explorer. He discovered Fanning Island in the Pacific and was involved in trade in the South Pacific. ALEXANDER CAMPBELL WILDER FANNING (1788–1846) of Massachusetts was a soldier who served in the War of 1812 and the Seminole Wars of 1818 and 1835–1839. JAMES WALKER FANNIN (1804–1836) of Georgia was a colonel in the Texas army. During the battle near Goliad, he and his men were defeated by General Urrea's troops on March 19, 1836. Colonel Fannin and 330 of his men were shot by order of Santa Anna.

Genealogies: James Fanning of Hopkinton, Mass., and Some of His Descendants was compiled by Frederic L. Stafford and published in Hartford, Connecticut, in 1971.

FARBER, FARBERSOHN, FARBERSON

Ranking: 4297 **S.S. Count:** 10,440

Origin: German, Jewish. Derived from the German word "färber," meaning dyer. The names were given to those who worked as such.

Genealogies: Farber and Allied Families of Burkhart, Hildebrand, and Albaugh was compiled by Richard H. Dodge and published in Denver, Colorado, in 1976. *Farber Families of an Early Ohio Pioneer Who Settled Sandy Creek Valley, Tuscarawas County, Ohio, in 1806* was compiled by Samuel Edwin Weaver and published in Denver, Colorado, in 1978.

FARINA (ALSO FARINACCI, FARINARI, FARINARO, FARINASSO, FARINAZZO, FARINAUX)

Ranking: 4698 **S.S. Count:** 9518

Origin: Farina, Farinacci, Farinari, Farinari, Farinaro, Farinasso, Farinazzo—Italian; Farinaux—French. Derived from the Latin word "farina," meaning wheat flour. The names were given to those who milled or sold flour.

Genealogies: None known.

FARKAS, FARKASH

Ranking: 4490 **S.S. Count:** 9983

Origin: Hungarian, Jewish. Hungarian: derived from the Hungarian word "farkas," meaning wolf. Jewish: derived from the Yiddish first name Volf, meaning wolf. The names were taken ornamentally.

Genealogies: None known.

FARLEY

Ranking: 812 **S.S. Count:** 52,077

Origin: English, Irish. English: derived from the Old English words "fearn" and "lēah," meaning fern and wood. The name was given to those who came from Farley, the name of several places in England. Irish: derived from the Gaelic name Ó Fearghaile, meaning "descendant of Fearghal" (H&H), which is derived from the words "fear" and "gal," meaning man and valor.

Famous **Farleys:** HARRIET FARLEY (1813–1907) of New Hampshire was a mill worker and the editor of the *Lowell Offering.* She is best remembered as an example of the rural New England girls who found life in a mill town to be a liberating and broadening experience. JAMES ALOYSIUS FARLEY (1888–1976) of Grassy Point, New York, organized Franklin Delano Roosevelt's gubernatorial and presidential campaigns. He served as chairman of the national Democratic Party and as postmaster general. He and President Roosevelt had a falling out, and Farley resigned his cabinet position and ran against Roosevelt in 1940.

Genealogies: Francis Marion Farley and Lulu Cain Farley: Their Ancestors and Descendants was compiled by Lucille Farley Speer and published in Greenfield, Indiana, in 1973.

FARMER, FARMERY
Ranking: 409 S.S. Count: 96,706

Origin: English. Farmer: derived from the Middle English and Old French word "ferm(i)er," meaning farmer, usually referring to one who collected taxes and less frequently referring to one who rented land to farm. Farmery: derived from the Middle English and Old French word "enfermerie," meaning infirmary. The name was given to those who worked in infirmaries and to those who lived near infirmaries.

Famous **Bearers:** FERDINAND FARMER (1720–1786) of Germany was a Jesuit priest who came to America in 1752. Once here, he changed his name, as many immigrants did, from Steinmeyer to the "more English" Farmer. He served in several locations, and it is believed that he organized the first Roman Catholic church in New York City. JOHN FARMER (1798–1838) of Massachusetts was a genealogist whose best-remembered work was *A Genealogical Register of the First Settlers of New England* (1829). MOSES GERRISH FARMER (1820–1893) of New Hampshire was an inventor who specialized in the electronic field. He, with co-inventor W. F. Channing, invented the electric fire-alarm system. He also installed electric lights in a residence in Massachusetts and as the electrician at the U.S. Torpedo Station in Newport, Rhode Island, made improvements in torpedo warfare. His wife was HANNAH TOBEY SHAPLEIGH FARMER (1823–1891) of Maine. FANNIE MERRITT FARMER (1857–1915) of Massachusetts started the Miss Farmer's School of Cookery. It was designed to teach housewives how to cook.

Genealogies: *In America Since 1607: The Hollingsworth, Farmer, and Judkins Families, Their Ancestors, Descendants, and Many Related Families* was compiled by Walter Ings Farmer and published in Cincinnati, Ohio, in 1987. *Pioneer Fort Worth, Texas: The Life, Times and Families of South Tarrant County* was compiled by Lila Bunch Race and published in Dallas, Texas, in 1976.

FARNSWORTH (S.S. Abbreviation: Farnsw)
Ranking: 2964 S.S. Count: 15,361

Origin: English. Derived from the Old English words "fearn" and "worð," meaning fern and enclosure. The name was given to those who came from Farnsworth, the name of several places in England.

Famous **Farnsworths:** JOHN FRANKLIN FARNSWORTH (1820–1897), originally of Canada, was raised in Michigan. He was a Union soldier, a member of Congress from Illinois, and a radical during Reconstruction. ELON JOHN FARNSWORTH (1837–1863) of Michigan was a Union soldier who died gallantly near Gettysburg, Pennsylvania, in the Civil War. He was killed leading a cavalry charge near Little Round Top. PHILO TAYLOR FARNSWORTH (1906–1971) of Beaver, Utah, developed much of the technology needed to begin television communication. He later worked in the field of atomic energy.

Genealogies: *Hibbs-Farnsworth and Related Families* was compiled by Robert Glen Nye and published in San Diego, California, in 1968. *Farnsworth Memorial II: 2nd Edition of the Farnsworth Memorial Published in 1897 by Moses Franklin Farnsworth* was compiled by Moses Franklin Farnsworth and most likely published in La Mesa, California, in 1974.

FARR
Ranking: 1698 S.S. Count: 26,314

Origin: English, Scottish. Derived from the Old English word "fearr," meaning bull. The name was given to those who worked herding oxen and to those who were considered to be fierce.

Famous **Farrs:** JOHN RICHARD FARR (1857–1933) of Pennsylvania was a member of Congress for eight years. NEWTON CAMP FARR (1887–1967) was a prominent real estate executive in Chicago, Illinois. He was president of Chicago Railways Co., the Chicago Better Business Bureau, the Chicago Federation, and the Chicago Y.M.C.A.

Genealogies: *The Ancestors and Descendants of Julius E. Farr* was compiled by Mileta Farr Kilroy and published in 1986. *The Family of Willis Vernon Farr: Past and Present Including Descendants of His Grandfather, Ivah Newton Farr, and a Number of Female Lines* was compiled by Jayne E. Bickford and published in Lisbon Falls, Maine, in 1977.

FARRAR
Ranking: 2106 S.S. Count: 21,793

Origin: English. Derived from the Middle English and Old French words "ferreor" and "ferour," both meaning ironsmith. The name was given to those who worked as such.

Famous **Farrars:** TIMOTHY FARRAR (1788–1874) of New Hampshire was Daniel Webster's law partner and the writer of a report on the Dartmouth College Case of 1819. ELIZA WARE ROTCH FARRAR (1791–1870) was born in France to American parents. She was a writer of children's books, with her best-known work being a book of advice called *The Young Lady's Friend*. CYNTHIA FARRAR (1795–1862) of New Hampshire was the first single woman to be a missionary sent overseas. She served 34 years in Bombay, India, at the Marathi Mission. EDGAR HOWARD FARRAR (1849–1922) of Louisiana was a lawyer whose area of expertise was municipal corporate law. He reformed the New Orleans city government. GERALDINE FARRAR (1882–1967) of Massachusetts was a singer with the Metropolitan Opera in New York.

Genealogies: *The Farrar's Island Family and Its English Ancestry* was compiled by Alvahn Holmes and published in Baltimore, Maryland, in 1972. *Two Branches of the Farrar*

Family: with Ancestors and Descendants of William Clark Farrar and His Sister Mary Farrar Norwood was compiled by Montgomery Dell Thaxton and published in Little Rock, Arkansas, in 1981.

FARREL, FARRELL, FARRELLY
Ranking: 510 S.S. Count: 78,687
Origin: Irish. Derived from the Gaelic name Ó Fearghaile, meaning "descendant of Fearghal" (H&H), which is derived from the words "fear" and "gal," meaning man and valor.

Famous **Bearers**: JAMES AUGUSTINE FARRELL (1862–1943) of Connecticut was president of United States Steel Corp. for two decades. JAMES THOMAS FARRELL (1904–1979) of Chicago, Illinois, was a short-story writer. His work is known for its portrayal of the working-class Irish in Chicago.

Genealogies: *The Farrall (also Farell) and Frazell (Fraser) Families With Information on the Speck, Young, Alder, Myer, Buck and Knox Families: A History* was compiled by Arthur William Farrall and published in East Lansing, Michigan, in 1970.

FARRIN (ALSO FARRINGTON)
Ranking: 3179 S.S. Count: 14,282
Origin: Farrin—English, Irish; Farrington—English. Farrin (English): uncertain etymology. 1) possibly derived from the Old English words "fæger" and "hine," meaning handsome and servant. 2) possibly derived from the Old English words "fearr" and "hine," meaning bull and servant. The name may have been given to those who herded oxen. (Irish): derived from the Gaelic name O' Farachain, meaning "descendant of Faramund" (H&H), a first name possibly meaning thunder. Farrington: derived from the Old English words "fearn" and "tūn," meaning fern and settlement. The name was given to those who came from Farrington, a place in Somerset, England.

Famous **Bearers**: WALLACE RIDER FARRINGTON (1871–1933) of Maine was a newspaperman and the governor of Hawaii (1921–1929). JOSEPH RIDER FARRINGTON (1897–1954) of Washington, D.C., was the U.S. territorial delegate from Hawaii, where his first duty was to press for the restoration of civil liberties Hawaiians had lost after the Pearl Harbor bombing in 1941.

Genealogies: *Farrington and Kirk Family: Ancestors and Descendants of Abraham Farrington (1765–1845) of New Jersey and Ohio and Wife Deborah Kirk (1781–1829) of Chester, Co., Pennsylvania* was compiled by Herschel B. Rochelle and published in Hillsborough, North Carolina, in 1983. *The Farringtons, Colonists and Patriots: Descendants of John of Dedham, Massachusetts, Edmund of Lynn, Massachusetts, Edward of Flushing, New York* was compiled by Dorothy Farrington Parker and published in 1976.

FARRIS
Ranking: 1044 S.S. Count: 42,014
Origin: Irish, Scottish. Transformation of Fergus.

Famous **Farrises**: ROBERT PERRY FARRIS (1826–1903), a Presbyterian minister, was editor of the *St. Louis Presbyterian* for 29 years. HARRY ROSWELL FARRIS (1874–1923), a physician, was commended by the French government for his service as commanding officer of a Red Cross hospital in France.

Genealogies: *The Family of John Martin and Margaret Faris (also Farris) of Spartanburg County, South Carolina* was compiled by Judy L. Harvey and Marie R. Davis and published in Portland, Oregon, in 1982. *The Faris Family of Washington County, Indiana: A Genealogy of the Descendants of William Farrie Born in County Antrim, Ireland, About the Year 1745, Settled on Rocky Creek, Chester County, South Carolina in 1772* was compiled by David Faris and published in Baltimore, Maryland, in 1984.

FARROW
Ranking: 3143 S.S. Count: 14,449
Origin: English. Transformation of Farrar.

Genealogies: *A Genealogical History of the Farrow, Waters, and Related Families, With Personality Profiles and Brief Sketches of the Times and Experiences of Two Pioneer Virgina, South Carolina, and Mississippi Families* was compiled by Audrey Doris Goolsby Farrow and published in Ripley, Mississippi, in 1973.

FAULK
Ranking: 2957 S.S. Count: 15,387
Origin: English. Derived from the first name Fulk, meaning people.

Genealogies: *Faulk-Cone and Allied Families: Male and Female Lines to the Immigrant Ancestor* was compiled by Eleanor Faulk Cone and published in Falls Church, Virginia, in 1983.

FAULKNER, FAULKNOR (S.S. Abbreviation: Faulkn)
Ranking: 821 S.S. Count: 51,535
Origin: English, Scottish. Derived from the Latin word "falco," meaning falcon. The name was given to those who kept falcons for a lord or to those who operated a weapon named for the bird.

Famous **Bearers**: CHARLES JAMES FAULKNER SR. (1806–1884) of present-day West Virginia (then Virginia) served in Congress and as minister to France before the Civil War and as a staff officer to General T. J. Jackson in the Civil War. CHARLES JAMES FAULKNER JR. (1847–1929) of present-day West Virginia (now Virginia) was a senator from West Virginia who was responsible for the law against food and drug adulteration. BARRY FAULKNER (1881–1966) of New Hampshire was an artist who specialized in murals. WILLIAM CUTHBERT FAULKNER (1897–1962) of New Albany, Mississippi, was born with the surname Falkner. He won two Pulitzer Prizes and a Nobel Prize for literature. His characters, such as the Snopes family, have taken on mythic proportions in American literature. Among his best-known works are *The Sound and the Fury, As I Lay Dying*, and *Go Down, Moses*.

Genealogies: *A Collection of Facts and Recollections of the Descent Lines and the Relationships Among Some Descendants of William Herndon (also Faulkner) of England and New Kent Co., Va.* was compiled by Grace Y. Froom and published in Indianapolis, Indiana, in 1983. *The Early Ancestors and Descendants of the Burfords, Faulkners, Havens, Hursts, and their Related Families* was compiled by Ralph Edward Burford and published in Baltimore, Maryland, in 1983.

FAUST

Ranking: 1988 **S.S. Count:** 22,789

Origin: German, Jewish. German: derived from the Latin first name Faustus, meaning lucky. German, Jewish: derived from the Old High German word "füst," meaning fist. The name was given to those who had a club hand or to those who were considered to be argumentative.

Famous **Fausts:** CHARLES LEE FAUST (1879–1928) of Missouri was a member of the U.S. House of Representatives for eight years. FREDERICK SHILLER FAUST (1892–1944) of Washington was an author who wrote under the pen name of Max Brand, as well as numerous others. He also worked on motion-picture scripts and serious poetry. He was killed in action as a war correspondent in Italy during World War II. CLARENCE HENRY FAUST (1901–1975) of Iowa was an educator and an executive with the Ford Foundation Fund for the Advancement of Education.

Genealogies: *Descendants of John Faust, 1797–1887 and Elizabeth Bachart, 1801–1864* was compiled by Lillian and Leroy Faust and published in Weatherly, Pennsylvania, in 1977. *The Family of John Foust (also Faust) and Anna Barbara Albrecht and Allied Families* was compiled by Mozette Foust and most likely published in Thornton, Texas, in 1982. *Faust-Foust Family in America* was compiled by Howard M. Faust and published in Baltimore, Maryland, in 1976.

FAWCETT   (S.S. Abbreviation: Fawcet)

Ranking: 4858 **S.S. Count:** 9212

Origin: English. 1) derived from the Old English words "fag" and "side," meaning colored and slope. 2) derived from the Old English words "ford" and "(ge)sete," meaning a shallow place in a stream and house. In both cases, the name was given to those who came from Fawcett and Forcett, the names of places in England.

Genealogies: None known.

FAY

Ranking: 1990 **S.S. Count:** 22,778

Origin: English, Irish. English: 1) derived from the Middle English and Old French word "faie," meaning fairy. The name was given to those who were thought to have supernatural powers. 2) derived from the Middle English and Old French word "fei," meaning trust. The name was given to those who were considered to be trustworthy. 3) derived from the Old French word "faie," meaning beech. The name was given to those who came from places that obtain their names from this word. Irish: 1) transformation of Fee. 2) derived from the Gaelic name Ó Fathaigh, meaning "descendant of Fathach" (H&H), a first name probably meaning base.

Famous **Fays:** JONAS FAY (1737?–1818) of Massachusetts was active in the movement for statehood of Vermont from 1772 to 1785. THEODORE SEDGWICK FAY (1807–1898) of New York was an author and diplomat who served as minister to Switzerland and was the author of *Norman Leslie* (1835). EDWARD ALLEN FAY (1843–1923) of New Jersey was a teacher of the deaf and the author of several books, including *Marriages of the Deaf in America* (1898). EDWIN WHITFIELD FAY (1865–1920) of Louisiana was a classical scholar and professor at several universities. AMY FAY (1876–1928) of Louisiana was a pianist. She studied in Germany, and the letters she wrote home were saved by her family and published under the title *Music Study in Germany*. The work was said to have influenced hundreds of young students to flock to Germany for a musical education. SIDNEY BRADSHAW FAY (1876–1967) of Lexington, Massachusetts, was the first U.S. historian to challenge the notion that Germany alone instigated World War I. His work pointed out Serbian, Austrian, French, and British contributions to that conflict. FRANCIS ANTHONY "FRANK" FAY (1897–1961) of California was a vaudeville actor whose career began at the age of four. He appeared in movies and on stage and, as an author, wrote a collection of humorous stories in *How to Be Poor*.

Genealogies: *Edwin Fay of Vermont and Alabama, 1794–1876: His Origins from 1656 and His Descendants to 1987* was compiled by Mary Smith Fay and published in Houston, Texas, in 1988. *The History of the Bemis, Perkinson, Fay, and Lawrence Families: These Being the Four Ancestral Lines of the Compiler* was compiled by Ted Harrison Bemis and published in Stroudsburg, Pennsylvania, in 1980.

FAZIO

Ranking: 4896 **S.S. Count:** 9129

Origin: Italian. Derived from the Latin first name Bonifatius, which is derived from the words "bonum" and "fatum," meaning good and fate.

Genealogies: None known.

FEATHER, FEATHERSTON, FEATHERSTONE (S.S. Abbreviation: Feathe)

Ranking: 2441 **S.S. Count:** 18,604

Origin: English. Feather: derived from the Old English word "feðer," meaning feather. The name was given to those who worked making quills or trading feathers and to those who were very thin. Featherston, Featherstone: derived from the Old English word "feðerstān," meaning tetralith, a kind of prehistoric monument. The names were given to those who came from Featherstone, the name of several places in England.

Famous Bearers: WINFIELD SCOTT FEATHERSTON (1819–1891) of Tennessee was a Confederate soldier who led in the overthrow of the Ames Regime in Mississippi.

Genealogies: None known.

FEDERICI, FEDERICO, FEDERIGHI, FEDERGI, FEDERIGO (S.S. Abbreviation: Federi)

Ranking: 4997 **S.S. Count:** 8970

Origin: Italian. Cognates to Frederick.

Genealogies: None known.

FEE

Ranking: 4633 **S.S. Count:** 9648

Origin: Irish. Derived from the Gaelic name Ó Fiaich, meaning "descendant of Fiach" (H&H), a name meaning raven.

Famous Fees: JOHN GREGG FEE (1916–1901) of Kentucky was an abolitionist and the founder of Berea College in Kentucky.

Genealogies: *The Fee Family and the Daily Notes of Canonsburg, Pennsylvania: The Evolution of a Family, Its Newspaper, and Its Community* was compiled by William Warrell Fee and published in Apollo, Pennsylvania, in 1990. *A History of the Fee Family* was compiled by Ralph E. Pearson and published in Austin, Texas, in 1969.

FEENEY

Ranking: 3249 **S.S. Count:** 13,984

Origin: Irish. 1) derived from the Gaelic name Ó Fidhne, meaning "descendant of Fidhne," which is most likely derived from the word "fidh," meaning tree. 2) derived from the Gaelic name Ó Fiannaidhe, meaning "descendant of Fiannaidhe" (H&H), a name meaning warrior.

Genealogies: None known.

FELDER, FELDERER

Ranking: 2581 **S.S. Count:** 17,641

Origin: German. Cognates to Field.

Genealogies: *The David and Elizabeth Shuler Dantzler Family (also Felder)* was compiled by David Herber Dantzler and published in Orangeburg, South Carolina, in 1970. *The Felder Family of South Carolina* was published in 1899.

FELDMAN, FELDMANN (S.S. Abbreviation: Feldma)

Ranking: 1127 **S.S. Count:** 39,004

Origin: German, Jewish. Cognates to Field.

Genealogies: *A Packet of Letters* was compiled by Walter Feldman and published in Providence, Rhode Island, in 1988.

FELICI (ALSO FELICINI, FELICIOLI, FELICIONI, FELICIOTTI, ET AL., FELICIANO)

Ranking: 1118 **S.S. Count:** 39,418

Origin: Felici, Felicini, Felicioli, Felicioni, Feliciotti, et al.—Italian; Feliciano—Italian, Portuguese, Spanish. Cognates to Felix.

Genealogies: None known.

FELIX

Ranking: 1486 **S.S. Count:** 29,891

Origin: English, German, Jewish. English, German: derived from the Latin first name Fēlix, meaning lucky. Jewish: uncertain etymology. Possibly an adaptation of the gentile name Felix.

Genealogies: None known.

FELLER (ALSO FELLERER, FELLERMAN)

Ranking: 3676 **S.S. Count:** 12,266

Origin: Feller—English; Fellerer, Fellerman—German. Transformations of and cognates to Fell.

Genealogies: *The Descendants of Peter Etring (Etringer) of Luxemburg (also Feller)* was compiled by Theodore E. Rischard and published in Santa Ana, California, in 1972. *The Descendants of John Feller, Sr.: A History and Genealogy, 1798–1934* was compiled by Louis P. Dissly and published in Tulsa, Oklahoma, in 1982.

FELLOW, FELLOWES, FELLOWS

Ranking: 3916 **S.S. Count:** 11,512

Origin: English. Derived from the Middle English words "felagh" and "felaw," meaning partner and shareholder. The names were given to those who were fellow members of a trade union.

Famous Bearers: GEORGE EMORY FELLOWS (1858–1942)

was president of the University of Maine. GRANT FELLOWS (1865–1929) was a justice of the Michigan Supreme Court.

Genealogies: *Fellows Families of Onondaga County, New York and Their Ancestry* was compiled by Erwin W. Fellows and published in Zephyrhills, Florida, in 1991. *Obil Fellows of Onondaga County, New York: A Record of Ancestry and Descendants* was compiled by Erwin W. Fellows and published in Zephyrhills, Florida, in 1984.

FELTON
Ranking: 2122 S.S. Count: 21,594
Origin: English. Derived from the Old English words "feld" and "tūn," meaning field and settlement. The name was given to those who came from Felton, the name of several places in England.

Famous **Feltons**: CORNELIUS CONWAY FELTON (1807–1862) of Massachusetts was a professor of the classics who served as the president of Harvard University (1860–1862). SAMUEL MORSE FELTON (1809–1889) of Massachusetts was a builder of railroads. He built the Philadelphia, Wilmington & Baltimore Railroad, making it the best in the country in 1851. His railroads were invaluable to the Union troops during the Civil War. WILLIAM HARRELL FELTON (1823–1909) of Georgia was a physician and a reform politician in Georgia. CHARLES FELTON (1832–1914) was a U.S. senator from California. REBECCA ANN LATIMER FELTON (1835–1930) of Georgia became the first woman to hold a senatorial seat when she was appointed to fill a vacancy until an election could be held.

Genealogies: None known.

FELTS
Ranking: 4918 S.S. Count: 9100
Origin: Belgian, German. Belgian: derived from the first name Philibert, meaning bright and love. German: derived from the Old High German word "feld," meaning field. The name was given to those who lived near fields.

Genealogies: *The Feltz (also Felts) Family History: 150 Years* was compiled by Patricia Feltz Cohen and published in Huntington Beach, California, in 1990.

FENDERICO (S.S. Abbreviation: Fender)
Ranking: 4362 S.S. Count: 10,275
Origin: Italian. Cognate to Frederick.
Genealogies: None known.

FENNEL (ALSO FENNELL, FENNELLY)
Ranking: 2438 S.S. Count: 18,639
Origin: Fennel, Fennell—English, Irish; Fennelly—Irish. Fennel (English), Fennell (English): derived from the Old English word "finugle," meaning fennel. The name was given to those who worked growing or selling fennel. *Fennel (Irish), Fennell (Irish), Fennelly: derived from the Gaelic name Ó Fionnghail, meaning "descendant of Fionnghal" (H&H), which is derived from the words "fionn" and "gal," meaning white and valor.*

Genealogies: *My Fennell Chronicles* was compiled by Mrs. Raymond Ralston and published in Slippery Rock, Pennsylvania, in 1981.

FENNER
Ranking: 4185 S.S. Count: 10,796
Origin: English. Transformation of Fenn.
Famous **Fenners**: ARTHUR FENNER (1745–1805) of Rhode Island was an anti-Federalist governor of Rhode Island (1790–1805). JAMES FENNER (1771–1846) was the son of Arthur. He was a U.S. senator, then governor of Rhode Island on and off between 1807 and 1845. CHARLES ERASMUS FENNER (1834–1911) of Tennessee was a Confederate soldier and a member of the Louisiana Supreme Court (1880–1894).

Genealogies: *The Kiehl/Manwarren Genealogy (also Fenner)* was compiled by Margery Kiehl Hughes and published in Fort Wayne, Indiana, in 1991.

FENTON
Ranking: 2143 S.S. Count: 21,372
Origin: English, Irish, Jewish. English: derived from the Old English words "fenn" and "tūn," meaning marsh and settlement. The name was given to those who came from Fenton, the name of several places in England. Irish: derived from the Gaelic name Ó Fionnachta, meaning "descendant of Fionnachta" (H&H), which is derived from the words "fionn" and "sneachta," meaning white and snow. Jewish: derived from similiar-sounding Jewish names, such as Finkels and Finkelstein.

Famous **Fentons**: REUBEN EATON FENTON (1819–1885) of New York was a U.S. senator and governor of New York. Fentonville, a village in Chautauqua County, New York, is named for him.

Genealogies: None known.

FERGUS, FERGUSON, FERGUSSON
Ranking: 158 S.S. Count: 203,564
Origin: Irish, Scottish. Derived from the Gaelic first name Fearghus, which is derived from the words "fear" and "gus," meaning man and vigor.

Famous **Bearers**: ELIZABETH GRAEME FERGUSON (1737–1801) was from Pennsylvania. Because of her marriage to an English Loyalist, she was placed in compromising positions during the Revolutionary War but was never charged with treason and was sympathetic to the colonists' cause. ABBIE PARK FERGUSON (1837–1919) of Massachusetts opened a school in South Africa called the Huguenot Seminary at Wellington, later Huguenot College. WILLIAM JASON FERGUSON (1844–1930) was the only eyewitness to the assassination of President Abraham Lincoln. MARGARET CLAY FERGUSON (1863–1951) of New York was a botanist who did genetic research using the petunia as her subject. She was the first female president of the Botanical Society of America. JOHN CALVIN FERGUSON (1866–1945) was a missionary educator and public official in China, where he set up Nanking University. He owned a sizeable collection of Chinese art after his stay in China. SAMUEL FERGUSON (1874–1950) of New Hampshire was a utility company executive with the Hartford (Connecticut) Electric Co. JAMES EDWARD FERGUSON (1871–1944) of Texas was the governor of that state (1915–1917). He was impeached and removed from office in 1917. Then his wife, MIRIAM AMANDA WALLACE FERGUSON, also of Texas, ran for the office of governor, was elected, and held the position from 1925 to 1927 and 1933 to 1935. CLARENCE MEADD FERGUSON (1899–1977) of Canada was an educator and an advocate of educational programs for those involved in the business of agriculture.

Genealogies: *The Gold Rush Widows of Little Falls: A Story Drawn from the Letters of Pamelia and James Fergus* was compiled by Linda S. Peavy and published in St. Paul, Minnesota, in 1990.

FERNAN (ALSO FERNANDES, FERNANDEZ, FERNANDO)

Ranking: 227 **S.S. Count:** 153,547
Origin: Fernan—Spanish; Fernandes, Fernandez, Fernando—Portuguese, Spanish. Derived from a Spanish first name that is derived from the words "farð" and "nanð," meaning journey and daring.
Genealogies: None known.

FERRAN (ALSO FERRANS, FERRANTS, FERRAND, FERRANTE, FERRANTELLI, FERRANTELLO, FERRANTIN, FERRANTINI, ET AL., FERRANDEZ)

Ranking: 2693 **S.S. Count:** 16,899
Origin: Ferran—Catalan, English, Spanish; Ferrans, Ferrants—English; Ferrand—English, French; Ferrante, Ferrantelli, Ferrantello, Ferrantin, Ferrantini, et al.—Italian; Ferrandez—Spanish. Ferran, Ferrans, Ferrants, Ferrand, Ferrante, Ferrantelli, Ferrantello, Ferrantin, Ferrantini: cognates to the third and fourth English definitions of Farrer. Ferrandez: cognate to Fernan.
Genealogies: None known.

FERRAR (ALSO FERRARA, FERRARI, FERRARINI, FERRARIO, FERRARO, ET AL.)

Ranking: 868 **S.S. Count:** 49,595
Origin: Ferrar—English; Ferrara, Ferrari, Ferrarini, Ferrario, Ferraro, et al.—Italian. Ferrar, Ferrari, Ferrarini, Ferrario, Ferraro: transformation of and cognates to Farrar. Ferrara: cognate to Ferrers.
Famous Bearers: GERALDINE ANNE FERRARO (1935–) of New York was the first woman to be nominated for U.S. vice president by a major party. Before being the 1984 Democratic vice-presidential nominee, she served as district attorney for Queens County, New York, and in the U.S. House of Representatives.
Genealogies: None known.

FERREIR, FERREIRO (S.S. Abbreviation: Ferrei)

Ranking: 1860 **S.S. Count:** 24,329
Origin: Ferreir—English, French; Ferreiro—Portuguese, Spanish. Transformations of and cognates to Farrar.
Genealogies: None known.

FERREL (ALSO FERRELL, FERRELI)

Ranking: 865 **S.S. Count:** 49,692
Origin: Ferrel, Ferrell—Irish; Ferreli—Italian. Ferrel, Ferrell: transformation of Farrell. Ferreli: cognate to Farrar.
Famous Bearers: WILLIAM FERREL (1817–1891) of Pennsylvania invented a machine that calculated tidal maxima and minima. He is also known for his law of the deflection of air currents on the Earth. JOHN ATKINSON FERRELL (1880–1965) was a prominent North Carolina doctor who served as president of the American Public Health Association.
Genealogies: *Southwest Virginia Kin: A Genealogical and Historical Account of the Evans, Ferrell, Kelly, Counts, Stinson, and Related Families* was compiled by Ethel Evans Albert and published in Kingsport, Tennessee, in 1977.

FERRER (ALSO FERRERES, FERRERI, FERRERIO, FERRERO, FERRERA, FERRERAS)

Ranking: 1889 **S.S. Count:** 23,918
Origin: Ferrer—English; Ferreres—Catalan; Ferreri, Ferrerio, Ferrero—Italian; Ferrera—Catalan, Italian, Spanish; Ferreras—Spanish. Ferrer, Ferreri, Ferrerio, Ferrero: transformations of and cognates to Farrar. Ferreres, Ferrera, Ferreras: cognates to Ferrers.
Famous Bearers: EDWARD FERRERO (1831–1899) of Spain was a dancer and a Union soldier during the Civil War.
Genealogies: None known.

FERRIS

Ranking: 1423 **S.S. Count:** 31,301

Origin: Irish, Scottish. Transformation of Fergus.

Famous **Ferrises:** WOODBRIDGE NATHAN FERRIS (1853–1928) of New York was the founder of Ferris Institute in Michigan, the governor of Michigan, and a U.S. senator from Michigan. GEORGE WASHINGTON GALE FERRIS (1859–1896) of Illinois was an engineer remembered for building the Ferris wheel for the World's Columbian Exposition in Chicago in 1893. DEWARD OLMSTED FERRIS (1907–1977) of Canada was a surgeon at the Mayo Clinic in Minnesota who specialized in gynecologic, urologic, and general abdominal surgery.

Genealogies: *Ancestors and Descendants of James Edward McCreight and Barbara Jean Ferris* was compiled by James Edward McCreight and most likely published in Jonesville, Michigan, in 1990.

FERRY

Ranking: 3212

S.S. Count: 14,133

Origin: English, Irish. English: derived from the Old Norse word "ferja," meaning ferry. The name was given to those who worked on ferries and to those who lived near ferry crossings. Irish: derived from the Gaelic name Ó Fearadhaigh, meaning "descendant of Fearachach" (H&H).

Famous **Ferrys:** ORRIS SANFORD FERRY (1823–1875) of Connecticut was a Union soldier and a member of Congress from Connecticut. His views changed from radical to moderate on Reconstruction. ELISHA PEYRE FERRY (1825–1895) of Michigan was a Union soldier, governor of Washington territory, and the first governor of the state of Washington. THOMAS WHITE FERRY (1827–1896) of Michigan was president pro tempore of the U.S. Senate in 1877 during the Hayes-Tilden electoral count.

Genealogies: *The Charles Ferry Family in America (Feret, Ferry, Ferre, Fere, Ferrey, Ferree): An Account of Some of the Descendants of Charles and Sarah (Harmon) Ferry of Springfield, Massachusetts* was compiled by Edward M. Ferry and published in Amherst, Massachusetts, in 1978. *Ferree (also Ferry) Family Gunsmiths* was compiled by George Bennett Ferree and published in Fort Wayne, Indiana, in 1967.

FETTER, FETTERMANN

Ranking: 2398 **S.S. Count:** 18,907

Origin: Jewish. Derived from the Yiddish word "fet," meaning fat. The names were given to those who were considered to be overweight.

Famous **Bearers:** WILLIAM JUDD FETTERMAN (1833?–1866), birthplace unknown, was a soldier in Wyoming stationed at Fort Phil Kearny. He and the 80 soldiers he was leading were killed by Chief Red Cloud. The attack of the Indians on Fetterman was not considered strategically correct even at that time. FRANK ALBERT FETTER (1863–1949) of Indiana was an economist known for his capital theory, which highlighted time preference over physical productivity. His son Frank Whitson Fetter is an economic historian.

Genealogies: *The Michael Fetters Family: Westward Migration* was compiled by Mary Emma Curtis and published in Clearwater, Florida, in 1980.

FIEDLER (S.S. Abbreviation: Fiedle)

Ranking: 4307 **S.S. Count:** 10,425

Origin: German, Jewish. Derived from the German and Yiddish words "fiedler" and "fidler," both meaning fiddler. The name was given to those who played the fiddle.

Famous **Fiedlers:** ARTHUR FIEDLER (1894–1979) of Boston, Massachusetts, was maestro of the Boston Pops Orchestra for 50 seasons. He is the bestselling classical artist of all time. His Pops recordings sold 60 million copies.

Genealogies: None known.

FIELD

Ranking: 1171 **S.S. Count:** 37,335

Origin: English, Jewish. English: derived from the Old English word "feld," meaning field. The name was given to those who lived near a clear but not cultivated area. Jewish: transformation of many similar-sounding names, such as Feldbau, Feldbaum, Feldfisher, Feldharker, Feldhammer, and others.

Famous **Fields:** RICHARD STOCKTON FIELD (1803–1870) of New Jersey developed the educational system for New Jersey, was a senator from New Jersey, and was a federal judge for the New Jersey district. DAVID DUDLEY FIELD (1805–1895) of Connecticut was a lawyer. He prepared the Field Code of Civil Procedure for the state of New York, which was adopted by many other states. He is the brother of Cyrus and Stephen. ERASTUS SALISBURY FIELD (1805–1900) of Massachusetts was a painter who preferred historical and biblical subjects. STEPHEN JOHNSON FIELD (1816–1899) of Connecticut was an associate justice of the Supreme Court who rendered important decisions in constitutional law. CYRUS WEST FIELD (1819–1892) of Massachusetts was responsible for laying the first telegraph line between the United States and Europe. MARSHALL FIELD (1834–1906) of Conway, Massachusetts, was a department store owner. His firm, Marshall Field and Company, introduced the concept of customer returns, the one-price system, and the in-store restaurant. MARY CATHERINE KEEMLE FIELD (1838–1896) of Missouri was a journalist and a lyceum lecturer. EUGENE FIELD (1850–1895) of Missouri, a journalist and poet by trade, is probably best known for his children's poetry, such as "Dutch Lullaby" (better known as "Wynken, Blyken, and Nod") and "Little Boy Blue." FRED TARBELL FIELD (1876–1950) of Vermont was the chief justice of the supreme court of Massachusetts. SARA BARD FIELD (1882–1974) of Ohio was a suffragist and a poet. JOHN FIELD (1886–1979) of Wisconsin was a business executive in the Warner Co. and was instrumental in creating the innovative designs that made women's lingerie more comfortable and fashionable. MARSHALL FIELD III (1893–1956) was the president of the Child Welfare League of America; established the Field Foundation, which concentrated on general child welfare; and founded, with Eleanor Roosevelt, the U.S. Commission for the Care of European Children. He also founded the *Chicago Sun*. RACHAL LYMAN FIELD (1894–1942) of New York was a poet and writer of children's books. HENRY FIELD (1902–1986) of Illinois was associated with the Chicago Natural History Museum—now known as the Field Museum—and is best remembered as the man who discovered what is believed to be the oldest wheel. MARSHALL FIELD IV (1916–1965) of New York was a publisher. He bought the *Chicago Times* and merged it with the *Chicago Sun* to form the *Chicago Sun-Times*. He was the great-grandson of Marshall Field.

Genealogies: *Notes on Fields (also Field) and Congeneric Families of Ohio and Indiana, 1800–1982* was compiled by Elsie Fields Dawson and published in Winter Park, Florida, in 1982.

FIELDEN, FIELDER   (S.S. Abbreviation: Fielde)

Ranking: 3799 **S.S. Count:** 11,879
Origin: English. Transformations of Field.
Genealogies: None known.

FIELDS

Ranking: 252 **S.S. Count:** 144,155
Origin: English. Transformation of Field.

Famous **Fieldses:** JAMES THOMAS FIELDS (1817–1881) of New Hampshire was an author and publisher and the editor of *Atlantic Monthly* (1861–1870). His second wife, ANNIE ADAMS FIELDS (1834–1915) of Massachusetts, was an author who wrote books of verse. W. C. FIELDS (1880–1946) of Philadelphia, Pennsylvania, was born William Claude Dukenfield and was an actor. He ran away from home at the age of 11. He first worked as a juggler and performed for the Ziegfeld Follies. He starred in many movies, including *The Chemist, The Old-Fashioned Way*, and *David Copperfield*. DOROTHY FIELDS (1905–1974) of New Jersey was a lyricist who wrote for songs in Broadway shows and motion pictures. She is credited with writing "I Can't Give

You Anything But Love, Baby," "On the Sunny Side of the Street," "I'm in the Mood for Love," and "The Way You Look Tonight." EDWARD FIELDS (1912–1979) of New York was a carpet designer and manufacturer. He made several carpets for the White House, the first one depicting the symbols of the 50 states.

Genealogies: *The Fields Family: With Notes on Whitesell and Dodd* was compiled by Ruth Fields Lewis and published in Evansville, Indiana, in 1976. *Notes on Fields and Congeneric Families of Ohio and Indiana, 1800–1982* was compiled by Elsie Fields Dawson and published in Winter Park, Florida, in 1982.

FIERRO

Ranking: 3964 **S.S. Count:** 11,414
Origin: Italian. Transformation of Ferro.
Genealogies: None known.

FIFE

Ranking: 4993 **S.S. Count:** 8986
Origin: Scottish. Traditionally assumed to be derived from Fib, the name of one of the seven sons of Cruithe, father of the Pictish race. The name was given to those who came from Fife, a former kingdom in Scotland.

Genealogies: *Descendants of John and William Fife, Fifeshire, Scotland, Upper St. Clair, Penna., 1721–1890* was compiled by John V. Murphy and published in Carrier Mills, Illinois, in 1979. *Fife Family: Isaac Wade and Nancy's Children and Allied Families* was compiled by Clara Adrienne Sisk Wilson and published in Winnsboro, Louisiana, in 1983.

FIGUEROLA, FIGUERA, FIGUERAS, FIGUERE, FIGUERES, FIGUEREDO, FIGUEROA   (S.S. Abbreviation: Figuer)

Ranking: 370 **S.S. Count:** 104,739
Origin: Figuerola—Catalan; Figuera, Figueras—Catalan, Spanish; Figuere, Figueres—Provençal; Figueredo, Figueroa—Spanish. Derived from the Latin word "ficus," meaning fig. The names were given to those who grew or sold figs and to those who lived near a fig tree.
Genealogies: None known.

FINCH

Ranking: 1024 **S.S. Count:** 42,765
Origin: English. Derived from the Old English word "finc," meaning finch, a kind of bird. The name was given to those who caught or cooked finches and may have been given to those who were considered to be stupid, as finches were thought to be.

Famous **Finches:** FRANCIS MILES FINCH (1827–1907) of New York was a judge with the New York Court of Appeals.

He also wrote poetry. "Nathan Hale" and "The Blue and the Gray" are two poems of his that are best remembered.

Genealogies: *Finch and Ashley, American Frontiersmen, 1630–1977: A Finch and Ashley Genealogy, Including Allied Families of Main, Doe, Reynolds, Teneyck, Wagner, Low, Yoran, Shults, Snell, Bullis, et al., Plus Photographs, Obituaries, and Historical and Biographical Sketches* was compiled by Ralph D. Finch and published in Baltimore, Maryland, in 1978. *Finch Families of Dixie: 300 Years in the South* was compiled by Ruby Finch Thompson and published in Arlington, Virginia, in 1972.

FINCHER (S.S. Abbreviation: Finche)
Ranking: 3938 S.S. Count: 11,464
Origin: English. The name was given to those who worked trapping and selling finches.
Genealogies: *Fincher in the USA, 1683–1900* was compiled by Evelyn Davis and Ann Wilson Fincher and published in Ithaca, New York, in 1981.

FINDLEY (S.S. Abbreviation: Findle)
Ranking: 3480 S.S. Count: 12,961
Origin: Scottish. Transformation of Findlay.
Famous Findleys: WILLIAM FINDLEY (1741–1821) of North Ireland was a Revolutionary soldier who was active in the politics of the new nation. He is responsible for the first congressional committee, that of Ways and Means, being appointed. He represented the frontiersman and helped to settle the Whiskey Rebellion.
Genealogies: None known.

FINE
Ranking: 2641 S.S. Count: 17,235
Origin: English, Jewish. English: derived from the Old French word "fin," meaning fine or skilled. The name was given to those who were considered to be smart, sophisticated, or skilled. Jewish: uncertain etymology.
Famous Fines: HENRY BUCHARD FINE (1858–1928) of Pennsylvania was a professor of mathematics, then dean of the faculty and scientific departments at Princeton University.
Genealogies: *Vinett Fine and His Descendants* was compiled by Emerrett Goff Fine and published in Fayetteville, Arkansas, in 1971.

FINGER, FINGERHUT, FINGERMAN, FINGERREICH, FINGERYK
Ranking: 4250 S.S. Count: 10,597
Origin: English, German, Jewish. Derived from the Middle English, Middle High German, and Yiddish word "finger," meaning finger. The name may have been given to those with a deformed finger or to those who had lost a finger.

Genealogies: None known.

FINK
Ranking: 1003 S.S. Count: 43,700
Origin: English, German, Jewish. Derived from the Middle English, German, and Yiddish word "fink," meaning finch, a kind of bird. English, German: the name was given to those who were considered to have some attribute of the finch. Jewish: the name was most often taken ornamentally.
Famous Finks: MIKE FINK (1770?–1823) of Pennsylvania was an American frontiersman. He was an Indian scout and was known along the Mississippi and Ohio rivers as the "king of the keelboatmen." He was killed on a trapping expedition to the Rockies. A folk hero, he is best remembered for his boasting and fighting. ALBERT FINK (1827–1897), originally from Germany, designed and built the largest iron bridge in the country during his time. It crossed the Green River. As chief engineer of the Louisville and Nashville Railroad, he practiced sound economic policies through the Civil War and became known as the founder of railroad economics. ZERA SILVER FINK (1902–1979) of Nebraska was a professor of English at the university level. He was an expert in the literature of the romantic period and a Milton scholar. He was the author of several books on these subjects.
Genealogies: *Our Family Chronicle: Celebrating the 90th Birthday of Wilma Irene Van Horn Mattson Fink* was compiled by Charyl Mattson and published in Tulsa, Oklahoma, in 1982.

FINKEL (ALSO FINKELBERG, FINKELBRAND, FINKELKRAUT, FINKELMAN, FINKELSTEIN, ET AL.)
Ranking: 2748 S.S. Count: 16,585
Origin: Finkel—German, Jewish; Finkelberg, Finkelbrand, Finkelkraut, Finkelman, Finkelstein, et al.—Jewish. Finkel (German): transformation of Fink. Finkel (Jewish), Finkelberg, Finkelbrand, Finkelkraut, Finkelman, Finkelstein: derived from the Yiddish word "funk," meaning spark, and words meaning hill, torch, herb, man, and stone. The names were taken ornamentally.
Genealogies: None known.

FINLEY
Ranking: 806 S.S. Count: 52,299
Origin: Transformation of Finlay.
Famous Finleys: ROBERT FINLEY (1772–1817) of Princeton, New Jersey, was a Presbyterian minister who worked to try to repatriate the African slaves to Africa. MARTHA FINLEY (1828–1909) of Ohio was a writer of children's books, including the *Elsie Dinsmore* series. JOHN HUSTON FINLEY (1863–1940) of Illinois was an educator, editor, and

author. He was the president of Knox College in Illinois, editor of *Harper's Weekly*, president of City College of New York, and associate editor of the *New York Times*, and he worked to make the *Dictionary of American Biography* a reality, with the first 20 volumes published under his supervision. He became the editor-in-chief of the *New York Times* in 1937.

Genealogies: The Finley Clan, A Condensed Genealogy of the Finley Family at Home and Abroad was compiled by Herald Franklin Stout and published in Dover, Oregon, in 1940. *Our Book of Finleys and Their Kinfolk Families* was compiled by Leslie McLaughlin and most likely published in Jackson, California, in 1990.

FINN

Ranking: 1506 **S.S. Count:** 29,572

Origin: English, Irish, Jewish. English: derived from the Old Norse first name Finnr. Irish: derived from the Gaelic name Fionn, meaning white. Jewish: uncertain etymology.

Famous **Finns:** FRANCIS JAMES FINN (1859–1928) was a prominent Jesuit priest in Ohio and the author of many short stories, plays, and book reviews.

Genealogies: History of Our Moyer, Finn, Sutton, Russell & Related Families was compiled by William Finn Moyer and published in Garden City, New York, in 1979.

FINNEGAN (S.S. Abbreviation: Finneg)

Ranking: 3033 **S.S. Count:** 14,995

Origin: Irish. Transformation of Finn.

Genealogies: None known.

FINNERTY (S.S. Abbreviation: Finner)

Ranking: 4835 **S.S. Count:** 9257

Origin: Irish. Transformation of Fenton.

Genealogies: None known.

FINNEY

Ranking: 1827 **S.S. Count:** 24,707

Origin: English. Derived from the Old English word "finig," meaning heap. The name was given to those who came from Finney, the name of several places in Cheshire, England.

Famous **Finneys:** CHARLES GRANDISON FINNEY (1792–1875) of Connecticut is considered America's first professional evangelist. Although his revivals met with contempt in many areas, they were widely successful in big cities. He served as president of Oberlin College for 15 years. JOHN MILLER TURPIN FINNEY (1863–1942) of Mississippi worked at Johns Hopkins as a surgeon and was the first president of the American College of Surgeons. The Finney-Howell Research Foundation for the Investigation of Cancer was founded in his honor.

Genealogies: Rachel Barkely's Children: A History of the Finney Families (Southern Branch) was compiled by Edna B. Reece and published in Jonesville, North Carolina, in 1978. *Cates-Hess-Phinney (also Finney) and Allied Lines* was compiled by Florence Cates and published in Kingman, Kansas, in 1980.

FIORE

Ranking: 3586 **S.S. Count:** 12,574

Origin: Italian. Cognate to the first English definition of Flower.

Genealogies: The House of Flowers = La Casa di Fiore: 1890–1990 was compiled by Mary Palmer and published in Arlington, Virginia, in 1990.

FISCHEL, FISCHELOVITCH, FISCHELOVITZ, FISCHELSON, FISCHER, FISCHERS (S.S. Abbreviation: Fische)

Ranking: 365 **S.S. Count:** 106,155

Origin: Fischer—English, German; Fishers—German; Fischel—German, Jewish; Fischelovitch, Fischelovitz, Fischelson—Jewish. Fischer, Fischers: transformations of and cognates to Fisher. Fischelovitch, Fishelovitz, Fischelson—transformations of and cognates to Fish.

Famous **Bearers:** LOUISE FISCHER (1896–1970) of Pennsylvania was a journalist who wrote biographies of Russian leaders.

Genealogies: None known.

FISH

Ranking: 1241 **S.S. Count:** 35,577

Origin: English, Jewish. English: derived from the Old English word "fisc," meaning fish. The name was given to those who worked catching or selling fish and to those who were thought to look like a fish. Jewish: derived from the Yiddish word "fish," meaning fish. The name was given for the same reasons as in the English definition and for its associations with the Hebrew first name Yona (Jonah). In the Bible, Jonah is swallowed by a "great fish."

Famous **Fishes:** HAMILTON FISH (1808–1893) of New York served as secretary of state under President Ulysses S. Grant. He is credited with the highest achievements of the Grant administration, such as negotiations with England over North American land and keeping the United States out of the Cuban revolution. CARL RUSSELL FISH (1876–1932) of Rhode Island was a historian and the author of *The Development of American Nationality*, considered one of the most useful textbooks on American history.

Genealogies: The Ancestors and Descendants of Simeon Fish, Minuteman of Mason, N.H. and Pioneer of Lincoln County, Maine was compiled by Nathan Hale and published in Gardiner, Maine, in 1969. *Fish Families Records and Lines* was compiled by Laurine Mae Palmerton Logsdon and published in Spokane, Washington, in 1986.

FISHER (ALSO FISHERHOFER, FISHERMAN)
Ranking: 94 S.S. Count: 298,869

Origin: Fisher—English, Jewish; Fisherhofer, Fisherman—Jewish. Fisher (English): 1) derived from the Old English word "fiscere," meaning fisherman. The name was given to those who worked catching fish. 2) derived from the Middle English words "fisch" and "gere," meaning fish and gear. The name was given to those who lived near a fence set in a river to catch fish. Fisher (Jewish), Fisherman: derived from the Yiddish word "fisher," meaning fisherman. The names were given to those who worked catching fish. Fisherhofer: transformation of Fish.

Famous **Bearers**: MARY FISHER (1623?–1698) of England was a Quaker missionary and preacher who was refused admittance to the Massachusetts Bay Colony in 1656 on the basis of religion. Her granddaughter Sophia Hume became a noted Quaker preacher. WILLIAM ARMS FISHER (1861–1948) of California was a composer, music editor, and publisher. He wrote popular arrangements for old melodies like "Swing Low, Sweet Chariot" and "Deep River." He also wrote several anthologies of music in the United States. WALTER LOWRIE FISHER (1862–1935) of present-day West Virginia (then Virginia) was the secretary of the interior under President William Howard Taft. IRVING FISHER (1867–1947) of New York was an economist who started a company to make his index-card file system. CLARENCE STANLEY FISHER (1876–1941) of Pennsylvania was a Near East archaeologist who participated in the first Egyptian archaeological digs. He was insistent on careful mapping and surveying of everything that was excavated. FREDERIC JOHN FISHER (1878–1941) of Ohio was an automobile body maker and one of the Fisher brothers in the Fisher Body Co. DOROTHY CANFIELD FISHER (1879–1958) of Lawrence, Kansas, was a writer. Her best-known works include *The Home-Maker, Made-to-Order Stories,* and *Four Square.* FREDERICK BOHN FISHER (1882–1938) of Pennsylvania was a bishop in the Episcopal Church. HARRY CONWAY (BUD) FISHER (1885–1954) of Illinois was the cartoonist who created and drew the comic strip "Mutt and Jeff." It is considered the first regular comic strip. CHARLES T. FISHER (1880–1963) of Ohio and ALFRED T. FISHER (1882–1963) of Ohio were brothers who were carriage and automobile body makers. They formed the Fisher Body Co. RUTH FISHER (1895–1961) of Germany was a writer and an ex–Communist activist. HAMMOND EDWARD FISHER (1901?–1955) of Pennsylvania was the cartoonist who created the "Joe Palooka" comic strip.

Genealogies: *Blue Ridge Mountain Kinfolks: A Record of Ancestors, Descendants, and Relatives of the Author and Wife,*

Including Fisher-Gilbert-Hall-Hartley-Hill-King-Kirby-Lawson Families was compiled by Larry King and published in Manchester, Tennessee, in 1976. *The Descendants of Nathan Cramer—Alazana Fisher, Including Allied Families and Genealogical Notes: Applegate, Ball, Bean, Cheney, Cox, Cranmer, Fessenden, Hensley, Lyon, Mourning, Stookey, Wright* was compiled by Dolores Cramer Wolf and published in Odessa, Texas, in 1972.

FISHMAN (S.S. Abbreviation: Fishma)
Ranking: 4382 S.S. Count: 10,241

Origin: English. Transformation of the first English definition of Fisher.

Genealogies: None known.

FISK
Ranking: 3133 S.S. Count: 14,492

Origin: English. Derived from the Old Norse word "fiskr," meaning fish. The name was given to those who worked catching or selling fish and to those who were thought to look like a fish.

Famous **Fisks**: WILBUR FISK (1792–1839) of Vermont was responsible for changing the course of the Methodist religion in New England to a more intellectual and educational approach. He founded and headed Wesleyan Academy in Massachusetts and was the first president of Wesleyan University in Middletown, Connecticut. CLINTON BOWEN FISK (1828–1890) of New York was a Civil War army officer who reached the rank of brevetted major general in 1865, founded Fisk University in 1867, and was the Prohibition Party candidate for president in 1888. JAMES FISK (1834–1872) of Bennington, Vermont, was called the "Barnum of Wall Street" for his flashy financial techniques. He and Jay Gould tried to corner the gold market but failed, sending the market into a disastrous plummet known as "Black Friday." Many innocent investors and speculators were financially ruined.

Genealogies: *Random Recollections* was compiled by Brenton H. Dickson and published in Weston, Massachusetts, in 1977. *Stories of the Fisk Families* was compiled by Lalia Estey Fiske Corbett and published in Boynton Beach, Florida, in 1966.

FITCH
Ranking: 1656 S.S. Count: 26,983

Origin: English. Uncertain eytmology. Possibly derived from the Old French word "fiche," meaning stake and referring to one with an iron point. The name may have been given to those who used such a tool in their work.

Famous **Fitches**: THOMAS FITCH (1700?–1774) of Connecticut was the colonial governor of Connecticut. He was defeated when he sought reelection because he had supported the Stamp Act. In those days all were required to swear an oath stating that they supported it. He later wrote a pamphlet explaining the justification of the oath. JOHN FITCH (1743–1798) of Connecticut served in the Revolution, surveyed lands along the Ohio River, and secured the rights to run steamships on the waters of New Jersey, New York, Pennsylvania, Delaware, and Virginia. EBENEZER FITCH (1756–1833) of Connecticut was a clergyman and the first president of Williams College. ASA FITCH (1809–1879) of New York was an entomologist who studied the effects of insects on agriculture. WILLIAM CLYDE FITCH (1865–1909) of New York was a playwright who wrote mostly on the subject of society drama, such as *The Moth and the Flame.*

Genealogies: *A Fitch Family History: English Ancestors of the Fitches of Colonial Connecticut* was compiled by John T. Fitch and published in Camden, Maine, in 1990. *Henry Fitch of Maryland* was compiled by Deborah K. Small and published in Winter Park, Florida, in 1984.

FITZGERALD   (S.S. Abbreviation: Fitzge)
Ranking: 354 **S.S. Count:** 107,905
Origin: Irish. Derived from the Norman first name Gerald, which is derived from the Germanic words "geri" and "wald," meaning spear and rule, and the Anglo-Norman-French prefix "fitz," meaning son of.

Famous Fitzgeralds: THOMAS FITZGERALD (1819–1891) of New York was an editor, playwright, and the publisher of the *Philadelphia Evening City Item.* JOHN FRANCIS FITZGERALD (1863–1950) of Massachusetts was a political leader, a newspaper publisher, and the grandfather of President John F. Kennedy. As a politician he fought for the rights of immigrants and laborers. He was nicknamed "Honey Fitz." FRANCIS SCOTT KEY (F. SCOTT) FITZGERALD (1896–1940) of St. Paul, Minnesota, was a writer. His novels and short stories are considered brilliant portrayals of the jazz age. A relative on his father's side, for whom he was named, was the Francis Scott Key who wrote "The Star Spangled Banner." Fitzgerald and his wife, Zelda, were for a time considered the prince and princess of their generation. His best-known works include *The Great Gatsby, The Beautiful and Damned,* and *Tender Is the Night.*

Genealogies: *Proud Shoes: The Story of An American Family* was compiled by Pauli Murray and published in New York, New York, in 1978. *The Knights of Glin: A Geraldine Family (also Fitzgerald)* was compiled by J. Anthony Gaughan and published in Atlantic Highlands, New Jersey, in 1978.

FITZPATRICK, FITZPAYN   (S.S. Abbreviation: Fitzpa)
Ranking: 755 **S.S. Count:** 56,174

Origin: Irish. Fitzpatrick: 1) transformation of Kilpatrick. 2) possibly derived from the English first name Patrick, which means son of a noble, and the Anglo-Norman-French prefix "fitz," meaning son of. Fitzpayn: derived from the Middle English first name Pain(e), which is derived from the Latin word "pāgus," which first meant faraway village, then came to mean civilian as opposed to soldier, and later came to mean heathen, and the Anglo-Norman-French prefix "fitz," meaning son of.

Famous Bearers: THOMAS FITZPATRICK (1799?–1854), originally of Ireland, was an American frontiersman and a fur trader, trapper, and Indian scout. He was one of the organizers of the Rocky Mountain Fur Co. and was the guide for several well-known expeditions, including John C. Frémont's second expedition. BENJAMIN FITZPATRICK (1802–1869) of Georgia was the governor of Alabama, a U.S. senator, and a reformer of the banking system in Alabama. JOHN FITZPATRICK (1870–1946) of Ireland was a labor leader who brought mass-production workers into the craft-oriented American Federation of Labor (AFL). JOHN CLEMENT FITZPATRICK (1876–1940) of Washington, D.C., was a curator of manuscripts and a historical editor who worked in the Library of Congress. He is probably best known as the editor, for the George Washington Bicentennial Commission, of the collected writings of George Washington. DANIEL ROBERT FITZPATRICK (1891–1969) of Wisconsin was an editorial cartoonist for the St. Louis *Post-Dispatch.*

Genealogies: None known.

FITZSIMMONS, FITZSIMON, FITZSIMONS   (S.S. Abbreviation: Fitzsi)
Ranking: 2803 **S.S. Count:** 16,247
Origin: Irish. Derived from the biblical name Simōn and the Anglo-Norman-French prefix "fitz," meaning son of.

Famous Bearers: THOMAS FITZSIMMONS or FITZSIMONS (1741–1811) of Ireland was a Revolutionary soldier who also served in the Confederation Congress, the Pennsylvania legislature, and the Federal Convention of 1787. He was also a member of Congress from Pennsylvania after the war. He helped to establish the Bank of North America and was the founder of the Insurance Company of North America. ROBERT PROMETHEUS FITZSIMMONS (also called Bob or Ruby Robert) (1862–1917), originally from England and raised in New Zealand, made his mark as a prize fighter by winning the world's middleweight title from Jack Dempsey in 1891 in New Orleans. He also held the titles of world's heavyweight and world's light-heavyweight champion during his career. JAMES EDWARD FITZSIMMONS (1874–1966) of New York was one of the nation's leading horse trainers. He was nicknamed "Sunny Jim."

Genealogies: *The Fitzsimmons Family* was compiled by

John Phillips and published in Cabin John, Maryland, in 1983.

FLACK
Ranking: 4986 S.S. Count: 8998
Origin: German. The name was given to those who lived on a level field.
Genealogies: *On the Flach (also Flack) Family Trail* was compiled by Carolyn Lindemann Overstreet and published in Austin, Texas, in 1984.

FLAGG
Ranking: 4609 S.S. Count: 9697
Origin: English. Derived from the Old Norse words "flaga" and "flag," meaning slab and sod. The name was given to those who came from Flagg, the name of several places in England.
Famous Flaggs: JOSIAH FLAGG (1737–1795) of Massachusetts was a musician who was the author of several books of psalms and anthems. JOSIAH FOSTER FLAGG (1788–1853) of Massachusetts was a dentist who experimented with the use of dental porcelain. He developed traction apparatus and extracting forceps. AZARIAH CUTTING FLAGG (1790–1873) of Vermont was an editor and politician. He was the state comptroller of New York and the comptroller of New York City. He was said to be a man of "unassailable integrity." THOMAS WILSON FLAGG (1805–1884) of Massachusetts was a nationally recognized naturalist who wrote numerous books. ERNEST FLAGG (1857–1947) of New York was the architect who designed the buildings of the U.S. Naval Academy and the Corcoran Gallery in Washington, D.C., among others. JAMES MONTGOMERY FLAGG (1877–1960) of New York was a painter and illustrator best known for his wartime posters of Uncle Sam pointing at the viewer and saying, "I Want You."
Genealogies: *Genealogical Notes on the Founding of New England: My Ancestors' Part In That Undertaking* was compiled by Ernest Flagg and published in Baltimore, Maryland, in 1973. *The Flagg Correspondence: Selected Letters, 1816–1854* was compiled by Barbara Lawrence and Nedra Branz and published in Carbondale, Illinois, in 1986.

FLAHERTY (S.S. Abbreviation: Flaher)
Ranking: 1734 S.S. Count: 25,878
Origin: Irish. Derived from the Gaelic name Ó Flaithbhearaigh, meaning "descendant of Flaithbheartach" (H&H), meaning generous.
Famous Flahertys: ROBERT JOSEPH FLAHERTY (1884–1951) of Michigan was an explorer and a motion-picture director and writer. He explored eastern Canada and is probably best known as the director of the motion picture

Nanook of the North. He is considered the father of the documentary film. GERVASE STEPHEN FLAHERTY (1900–1975) of Wisconsin, a surgeon, was the chief of staff and chief of surgery at several hospitals in Milwaukee, Wisconsin. He was a founding member of the Wisconsin Surgical Society.
Genealogies: None known.

FLANAGAN, FLANAGHAN (S.S. Abbreviation: Flanag)
Ranking: 973 S.S. Count: 44,914
Origin: Irish. Derived from the Gaelic name Ó Flannagáin, meaning "descendant of Flannagán" (H&H), which is derived from the word "flann," meaning ruddy.
Famous Bearers: WEBSTER FLANAGAN (1832–1924) of Kentucky was a Confederate soldier and cattle breeder in Texas. He headed the Republican Party in Texas. EDWARD JOSEPH FLANAGAN (1886–1948) of Ireland was the Catholic priest who founded Father Flanagan's Home for Boys in Omaha, Nebraska. The incorporated village is now known as Boys Town. HATTIE MAE FERGUSON FLANAGAN (1890–1969) of South Dakota was a theater educator at several colleges and the dean of Smith College.
Genealogies: None known.

FLANDERS, FLANDER (S.S. Abbreviation: Flande)
Ranking: 3619 S.S. Count: 12,462
Origin: Flanders—English; Flander—German. Transformations of and cognates to Fleming.
Famous Bearers: HENRY FLANDERS (1824–1911) of New Hampshire was a practicing attorney in Philadelphia, specializing in maritime law, fire insurance, and legal biography. RALPH EDWARD FLANDERS (1880–1970) of Vermont was a mechanical engineer and a U.S. senator.
Genealogies: None known.

FLANIGAN (S.S. Abbreviation: Flanig)
Ranking: 4420 S.S. Count: 10,143
Origin: Irish. Transformation of Flanagan.
Genealogies: None known.

FLANNERY (S.S. Abbreviation: Flanner)
Ranking: 3073 S.S. Count: 14,783
Origin: Irish. Derived from the Gaelic name Ó Flannghaile, meaning "descendant of Flannghal" (H&H), a first name derived from the words "flann" and "gal," meaning ruddy and valor.
Famous Flannerys: JOHN FLANNERY (1835–1910) of Ireland was a Confederate soldier and the president of the Southern Bank and the Cotton Exchange.
Genealogies: None known.

FLECK

Ranking: 3857 **S.S. Count:** 11,689

Origin: German, Jewish. Derived from the German and Yiddish words "fleck" and "flek," both meaning spot. The name may have been given to those who used patches in their work, such as tailors and cobblers.

Famous **Flecks:** HENRY THOMAS FLECK (1863–1937), while a professor of music at Hunter College in New York for 23 years, was the founder of the Harlem Philharmonic Society and a composer of many songs and anthems.

Genealogies: None known.

FLEISCHHACK, FLEISCHHAUER, FLEISCH, FLEISCHER, FLEISCHMAN, FLEISCHMANN, FLEISCHNER (S.S. Abbreviation: Fleisc)

Ranking: 2383 **S.S. Count:** 19,064

Origin: Fleischhack, Fleischhauer—German; Fleisch, Fleischer, Fleischman, Fleischmann—German, Jewish; Fleischner—Jewish. Derived from the Middle English word "flescher," meaning butcher. The names were given to those who worked cutting meat.

Famous **Bearers:** CHARLES LOUIS FLEISCHMANN (1834–1897) of Hungary was a yeast manufacturer, capitalist, and philanthropist. NATHANIEL S. FLEISCHER (1887–1972) of New York was the editor of the boxing magazine *The Ring*. He was often the judge at championship fights.

Genealogies: None known.

FLEMING, FLEMINKS (S.S. Abbreviation: Flemin)

Ranking: 277 **S.S. Count:** 129,623

Origin: Fleminks—Dutch; Fleming—English. Derived from the Old French word "flamenc," meaning one who came from Flanders.

Famous **Bearers:** WILLIAM FLEMING (1729–1795) of Scotland arrived in America in 1755 and served in the Forbes and Abercromby campaigns, among others. He was wounded at the battle of Point Pleasant. From 1763 to 1768 he practiced medicine in Staunton, Virginia. He was a politician in Virginia state government. JOHN FLEMING (1764?–1800) of Scotland was a printer who arrived in the colonies in 1764. He was a Loyalist who published a Tory paper called the *Boston Chronicle* from late 1767 to mid-1770. He was "officially proscribed and banished" in 1778. JOHN FLEMING (1807–1894) of Pennsylvania was a missionary to the Indians and was the first to put the Creek Indians' language in writing. ARETAS BROOKS FLEMING (1839–1923) of present-day West Virginia (then Virginia) was the governor of West Virginia. ARTHUR HENRY FLEMING (1856–1940) of Canada was a lumber magnate and the chief financial benefactor of the California Institute of Technology. WILLIAMINA PATON STEVENS FLEMING (1857–1911) of Scotland was an astronomer on the staff of the Harvard observatory. She is credited with the discovery of new stars and variables; she also investigated stellar spectra. WALTER LYNWOOD FLEMING (1874–1932) was an educator and historian. He wrote books and articles on Reconstruction and founded *Documents Relating to Reconstruction*, a monthly publication. His most significant works include *Civil War and Reconstruction in Alabama* and *History of Reconstruction.* JOHN ADAMS FLEMING (1877–1956) of Ohio was a geophysicist and the director of the Carnegie Institution's Department of Territorial Magnetism. He developed magnetic observatories in Peru and Australia and assisted in perfecting a magnetic underwater mine that was used during World War I in the North Sea.

Genealogies: *Hamilton, Mullins, Fleming, and Related Lines (of Kentucky, West Virginia, North Carolina, and Tennessee)* was compiled by Verle Hamilton Parrish and published in Stamping Ground, Kentucky, in 1975. *Let the Deed Show: A Pictorial and Historical Record of the Fleming, Edwards and Woods Families Dating from 1700's to 1980* was compiled by James R. Fleming and published in Palos Verdes Estates, California, in 1981.

FLEMMING (S.S. Abbreviation: Flemmi)

Ranking: 4792 **S.S. Count:** 9345

Origin: Flemming—English, German. Cognate to and transformation of Fleming.

Genealogies: None known.

FLETCHER (S.S. Abbreviation: Fletch)

Ranking: 333 **S.S. Count:** 113,224

Origin: English. Derived from the Old French word "flech(i)er," meaning arrowsmith. The name was given to those who worked as such.

Famous **Fletchers:** BENJAMIN FLETCHER (1640–1703), probably born in London, was a soldier and colonial governor of New York. RICHARD FLETCHER (1788–1869) of Vermont was an outstanding lawyer of the day who challenged Harvard University's claim to ownership of the Charles River Bridge. CALVIN FLETCHER (1798–1866) of Vermont was the first lawyer in Indianapolis, Indiana. ROBERT FLETCHER (1823–1912) of England was a doctor who served in that capacity in the Civil War and worked as an assistant to John Shaw Billings in the surgeon general's office library preparing *Index-Catalogue of the Library of the Surgeon General's Office.* ALICE CUNNINGHAM FLETCHER (1838–1923) was born in Cuba to American parents. An ethnologist, she lived among the Indians of the American plains, studying their culture and music. ROBERT FLETCHER (1847–1936) of New York was an engineering educator who taught at the Thayer School, the engineering school connected with Dartmouth University. HORACE FLETCHER (1849–1919) of Massachusetts was a nutritionist who held the theory that the thorough chewing of one's food led to a long lifespan. He lectured often on the subject, until "fletcherism" and "to fletcherize" became part of the English language. DUNCAN UPSHAW FLETCHER (1859–1936) of Georgia was the mayor of Jacksonville, Florida, during the difficult period of the Great Fire of Jacksonville and was a U.S. senator from 1909 to 1936. While in the Senate, he was co-author of the Fletcher-Rayburn Act of 1934, which created the Securities and Exchange Commission. HENRY PRATHER FLETCHER (1873–1959) of Pennsylvania was a member of Teddy Roosevelt's Rough Riders. He served as ambassador to Cuba, Mexico, Chile, and Belgium, as well as in other diplomatic positions throughout his career. HARVEY FLETCHER (1884–1981) of Utah was a physicist who developed the system of stereophonic sound and reproduction. JOHN GOULD FLETCHER (1886–1950) of Arkansas was a poet first associated with the imagist group of poets, and later with the Fugitives.

Genealogies: *The Tackett-Fletcher Pioneers (and Supplement)* was compiled by Mae Elizabeth Lang and published in St. Joseph, Illinois, most likely in 1970.

FLICK
Ranking: 4195 **S.S. Count:** 10,765
Origin: German. Transformation of Fleck.
Famous **Flicks:** LAWRENCE FRANCIS FLICK (1856–1938) of Pennsylvania was the physician who realized that tuberculosis was a contagious, not inherited, illness and devoted his life to eradicating the disease.
Genealogies: None known.

FLINT
Ranking: 2156 **S.S. Count:** 21,269
Origin: English, Jewish, Welsh. English: derived from the Old English word "flint," meaning flint, a kind of stone used to make fire. The name was given to those who lived near such stones. Jewish: uncertain etymology. Welsh: possibly the same derivation as the English definition. The name was given to those who came from Flint, a place near Clwyd, England.
Famous **Flints:** TIMOTHY FLINT (1780–1840) of Massachusetts was a clergyman and author who became a missionary and a farmer in the Ohio River valley, where he wrote and edited the *Western Monthly Review*. AUSTIN FLINT (1812–1886) of Massachusetts was a physician and the founder of the Bellevue Hospital Medical College in New York. He brought the binaural stethoscope into popular use in the United States and discovered the Austin Flint heart murmur. His son AUSTIN FLINT (1836–1915) of Massachusetts was also a physician. He studied liver function

and taught at several major medical facilities. WESTON FLINT (1835–1906) of New York helped to organize the Civil Service Commission. CHARLES RANLETT FLINT (1850–1934) of Maine, a businessman, was responsible for bringing Brazilian rubber to the United States, and his company came to be known as the U.S. Rubber Co. He also consolidated many companies and was known as the "father of trusts." He was also known as the "rubber king of America." RICHARD FOSTER FLINT (1902–1976) of Michigan was a glaciologist who taught at Yale University and worked extensively on studies of the Pleistocene epoch.

Genealogies: *Flint Family History of the Adventuresome Seven* was compiled by Edward Francis Flint Jr. and published in Claremont, California, in 1984. *Flint, The Family Histories of Charles Edwin Flint, Junior, and Bessie Hazel Lee* was compiled by Rosalie Viola Matthews Flint and published in Quincy, Washington, in 1982.

FLOOD
Ranking: 1850 **S.S. Count:** 24,484
Origin: English, Irish, Welsh. English: derived from the Old English word "flōd(e)," meaning a small stream or spring. The name was given to those who lived near such places. Irish: derived from the Gaelic names derived or thought to be derived from the word "tuile," meaning flood. Welsh: transformation of Lloyd.
Genealogies: None known.

FLORA
Ranking: 4430 **S.S. Count:** 10,124
Origin: Spanish. 1) derived from the Latin word "fluor," meaning monthly menstrual flow. The name refers to the goddess of spring and fruits. 2) derived from the Latin word "flora," meaning flower.
Genealogies: *Flory, Flora, Fleury Family History, 1948,* was compiled by Walter Quinter Bunderman and published in Reading, Pennsylvania, in 1948. *Supplement to the Flory, Flora, Fleury Family History of 1948* was compiled by John P. Marcinkowski and published in 1973.

FLOREN (ALSO FLORENSA, FLORENCE, FLORENT, FLORENTIN, FLORENTY, FLORENZ, FLORENCIO)
Ranking: 2659 **S.S. Count:** 17,124
Origin: Floren—Swedish; Florensa—Catalan; Florence—English, French; Florent, Florentin, Florenty—French; Florenz—Jewish; Florencio—Portuguese. Floren: transformation of the first English definition of Flower. Forensa, Florence, Florenz, Florencio: derived from the Latin first names Flōrentius and Flōrentia. Florent, Florentin, Florenty: derived from the Latin name Floōrens, which is derived from the word "flōrre," meaning to flourish.

Famous **Bearers:** THOMAS BIRCH FLORENCE (1812–1875) of Pennsylvania was a Pennsylvania politician, a temperance reformer, and known to workmen as "the widow's friend." MALVINA PRAY FLORENCE (1830–1906) was the wife of William J. Florence. She was a dancer and a comic actress. WILLIAM JERMYN FLORENCE (1831–1891) of New York, who was born Bernard Conlin, was an actor who enjoyed great success in Irish-Yankee comedies, such as *The Irish Boy and the Yankee Girl.*

Genealogies: None known.

FLORES

Ranking: 153 **S.S. Count:** 210,115

Origin: Jewish, Spanish. Jewish, Spanish: cognate to and transformation of Florez. Spanish: cognate to Flower.

Famous **Floreses:** PATRICK F. FLORES (1929–) of Ganado, Texas, is archbishop of San Antonio, Texas.

Genealogies: None known.

FLOREZ

Ranking: 4441 **S.S. Count:** 10,093

Origin: Spanish. Derived from the first name Floro, which is derived from the Latin name Flōrus, which is derived from both the word "flōris," meaning flower, and the Germanic name Froila, which is derived from the word "fro," meaning lord.

Genealogies: None known.

FLOWER (ALSO FLOWERS)

Ranking: 513 **S.S. Count:** 77,920

Origin: Flower—English, Welsh; Flowers—English. Flower (English), Flowers: 1) derived from the Middle English word "flo(u)r," meaning flower. The names were originally used to show affection. Flower: 2) derived from the Middle English word "flo(u)r," meaning flour. The name was given to those who worked milling or selling flour and to those who had complexions that were considered to be as white as flour. 3) derived from the Old English word "flā," meaning arrow. The name was given to those who worked as arrowsmiths. Flower (Welsh): derived from the Welsh first name Llywerch.

Famous **Bearers:** RICHARD FLOWER (1761–1829) of England was a reformer and a pioneer in Illinois. He settled in Edwards County in 1819. His son George (below) was one of the county's co-founders. Richard probably started the first library in Illinois. GEORGE FLOWER (1788–1862) of England founded settlements in Edwards Co. with Morris Birkbeck. He resisted slavery's introduction in Illinois. LUCY LOUISA COUES FLOWER (1837–1921) was probably from Massachusetts. She was a social welfare leader in Illinois especially interested in child welfare. BENJAMIN ORANGE FLOWER (1858–1918) of Illinois was an editor who founded *American Spectator*, which merged with *Arena* in

1889, and who founded and edited *Twentieth Century Magazine.*

Genealogies: *Flowers Chronicles: Studies of Captain John Flower, II (1595–1657), Mariner of London, Bermuda and Virginia and Some of His Descendants in the American South* was compiled by Pugh B. Flowers and published in Baltimore, Maryland, in 1987.

FLOYD

Ranking: 447 **S.S. Count:** 89,281

Origin: Welsh. Transformation of Lloyd.

Famous **Floyds:** WILLIAM FLOYD (1734–1821) of New York was a member of the Continental Congress, a signer of the Declaration of Independence, and a member of the U.S. House of Representatives. JOHN FLOYD (1783–1837) of Kentucky was a surgeon and politician. He was the first to suggest territorial status for Oregon in 1821. He was also the governor of Virginia. JOHN BUCHANAN FLOYD (1806–1863) of Virginia was the governor of that state and a member of President James Buchanan's cabinet before the Civil War. He was a general in the Confederate army but was removed by Jefferson Davis. CHARLES ARTHUR (PRETTY BOY) FLOYD (1904–1934) of Akins, Oklahoma, was a bank robber whose machine gun was his trademark. He was gunned down by the FBI in Ohio.

Genealogies: *Descendants of Col. Mathew Floyd, Loyalist of South Carolina and his Son Abraham Floyd* was compiled by Marjorie Dodd Floyd and published in Dayton, Ohio, in 1980. *The Box Book With McElroy and Floyd* was compiled by Ophelia Richardson Wade and published in Bragg City, Missouri, in 1975.

FLYNN

Ranking: 442 **S.S. Count:** 90,197

Origin: Irish. Derived from the Gaelic name Ó Floinn, meaning "descendant of Flann" (H&H), a name derived from the word "flann," meaning ruddy.

Famous **Flynns:** WILLIAM JAMES FLYNN (1867–1928) of New York was the chief of the U.S. Secret Service and the director of the FBI. JOHN THOMAS FLYNN (1882–1964) of Maryland was a journalist and political commentator who saw freedom being threatened by the blacklisting in the 1940s and by the growth of the FBI. ELIZABETH GURLEY FLYNN (1890–1964) of New Hampshire was a labor organizer and a radical. She was a founder of the American Civil Liberties Union, from which she was expelled in 1940. EDWARD JOSEPH FLYNN (1891–1953) of New York was a political leader who dominated and controlled the Democratic Party in the Bronx, New York. He supported and was secretary of state for two governors of the state of New York, one of whom was Franklin D. Roosevelt. He supported FDR for president and was rewarded with political appointments. ERROL LESLIE THOMAS FLYNN (1909–1959), probably originally of Australia, was a movie actor. He was an instant star in his first motion picture, *Captain Blood.* His best-known roles include those he played in *The Adventures of Robin Hood, Dodge City,* and *Gentleman Jim.* His popularity greatly diminished when he was tried for (although acquitted of) statutory rape in 1942.

Genealogies: *The Flynn-Tolchard Families: An Ancestoral Genealogy Including Branches of the Hoskin, Hickok, and Foster Families* was compiled by Herman Halladay Flynn and published in Flushing, Michigan, in 1971. *Out of Grandfather's Trunk* was compiled by Elizabeth Blackshear Flinn and published in Decatur, Georgia, in 1986.

FOGARTY   (S.S. Abbreviation: Fogart)
Ranking: 3936 S.S. Count: 11,466
Origin: Irish. Derived from the Gaelic first name Fógartach, which is derived from the word "fógartha," meaning banished.

Genealogies: *They Called It Fogartyville; A Story of the Fogartys and Fogartyville* was compiled by Ollie Z. Fogarty and published in Brooklyn, New York, in 1972.

FOGLE
Ranking: 3142 S.S. Count: 14,450
Origin: Dutch, German. Transformation of Vogel.
Genealogies: None known.

FOLEY
Ranking: 547 S.S. Count: 74,590
Origin: Irish. 1) derived from the Gaelic name Ó Foghladha, meaning "descendant of Foghlaidh" (H&H), meaning pirate. 2) derived from the Gaelic name Mac Searraigh, which means son of the Gaelic form of Thomas.

Famous Foleys: FREDERICK CLEMENT FOLEY (1904–1955) was president of Providence College in Rhode Island.

Genealogies: *Our Foleys'* was compiled by Vivian E. Meissner Foley and published in Portland, Oregon, in the 1970s. *Notes on Andrews, Carlisle, Foley, and Hagarty Families of Washington County, Pennsylvania, 1790– 1870* was compiled by John Bradley Arthaud and published in Columbia, Missouri, in 1982.

FOLSOM
Ranking: 4092 S.S. Count: 11,044
Origin: English. Derived from the first name Foghel and the Old English word "hām," meaning homestead. The name was given to those who came from Foulsham, a place in Norfolk, England.

Famous Folsoms: NATHANIEL FOLSOM (1726–1790) of New Hampshire was a New Hampshire politician and a Revolutionary War soldier. CHARLES FOLSOM (1794–1872)

of New Hampshire was a Navy chaplain and instructor, a tutor and librarian at Harvard University, and the librarian at the Boston Athenaeum. GEORGE FOLSOM (1802–1869) of Maine was the editor and librarian at the American Antiquarian and New York Historical societies.

Genealogies: None known.

FOLTZ
Ranking: 3673 S.S. Count: 12,284
Origin: German. Derived from the first name Foltz, a form of Volk, meaning people. The name is a short form of many names with this component, such as Fuclger and Fulculf.

Famous Foltzes: CLARA SHORTRIDGE FOLTZ (1849–1934) of Indiana was the first female lawyer in California.

Genealogies: None known.

FONG
Ranking: 2307 S.S. Count: 19,705
Origin: Chinese. Uncertain etymology.
Genealogies: None known.

FONSECA   (S.S. Abbreviation: Fonsec)
Ranking: 2668 S.S. Count: 17,086
Origin: Portuguese, Spanish. Derived from the Latin words "fons" and "sicca," meaning spring and well. The name was given to those who lived near a well that dried up during hot periods.

Genealogies: None known.

FONTAINE   (S.S. Abbreviation: Fontai)
Ranking: 2835 S.S. Count: 16,085
Origin: French. Derived from the Old French word "fontane," meaning spring or well. The name was given to those who lived near a spring or well.

Genealogies: None known.

FONTANET, FONTANTEL, FONTANARI, FONTANAZZI, FONTANA   (S.S. Abbreviation: Fontan)
Ranking: 1901 S.S. Count: 23,824
Origin: Fontanet, Fontantel—French; Fontanari, Fontanazzi—Italian; Fontana—Italian, Spanish. Cognates to Fontaine.

Genealogies: None known.

FONTENAY, FORTENOY, FONTENET, FONTENEL, FONTENELLE ET AL., FONTENIILLE, FONTENIEU   (S.S. Abbreviation: Fonten)
Ranking: 1740 S.S. Count: 25,751
Origin: Fontenay, Fortenoy, Fontenet, Fonternel,

Fontenelle, et al: French; Fonteniille, Fontenieu—Provençal. Transformations of and cognates to Fontaine.

Genealogies: None known.

FOOTE

Ranking: 1923 **S.S. Count:** 23,478

Origin: English. Derived from the Old English word "fōt," meaning foot. The name was given to those who had a deformed foot.

Famous **Footes:** WILLIAM HENRY FOOTE (1794–1869) of Connecticut was a Presbyterian clergyman who organized and established many churches in spiritually impoverished communities. In the field of education, he founded several schools. He also wrote *The Huguenots, or Reformed French Church.* HENRY WILLIAM FOOTE (1804–1880) of Virginia was a lawyer and politician and both a personal and political enemy of Jefferson Davis. As both a U.S. senator and governor of Mississippi in the period before the Civil War, he was unable to quell the eventual secession of the state from the Union. He left Mississippi, resided in Europe for a time, and wrote several books about the war. ANDREW HULL FOOTE (1806–1863) of Connecticut was a professional naval officer who patrolled the coast of Africa, capturing slavers and trying to break up the slave trade. He distinguished himself during the Civil War by breaking the defenses of the Confederates along the upper Mississippi River. He ended his naval career with the rank of rear admiral. MARY ANNA HALLOCK FOOTE (1847–1938) of New York was an author and illustrator who gained fame through her accounts of western life as her husband's career sent them to different western locations. ARTHUR WILLIAM FOOTE (1853–1937) of Massachusetts composed church music and taught at the New England Conservatory. JOHN AMBROSE FOOTE (1874–1931) of Pennsylvania was a physician who wrote several pieces of medical literature for *National Geographic* magazine. He was interested in Children's Hospital in Washington, D.C., where the John A. Foote Memorial Library was established in his honor. WILLIAM JENKINS FOOTE (1905–1976) of Connecticut was a journalist who was an editorial writer for and editor of the *Hartford Courant.*

Genealogies: *Foote Family, Comprising the Genealogy and History of Nathaniel Foote of Wethersfield, Conn., and His Descendants* was compiled by Abram William Foote and published in Hughson, California, in 1981. *Chotankers, A Family History* was compiled by A. Edward Foote and published in Florence, Alabama, in 1982.

FORBES

Ranking: 957 **S.S. Count:** 45,524

Origin: Irish, Scottish. Irish: derived from the Gaelic name Mac Fearbhisigh, meaning son of Firbhigh, which is derived from Celtic words meaning man and prosperity. Scottish: derived from the Gaelic word "forba," meaning district or field. The name was given to those who came from Forbes, a place in Scotland.

Famous **Forbeses:** JOHN FORBES (1710–1759) of Scotland was a British officer who came to America in 1757 and cut a road through the Pennsylvania wilderness to Fort Duquesne, over which he raised the British flag upon the evacuation of the French. JOHN FORBES (1740?–1783) of Scotland was the first, and for many years the only, preacher in eastern Florida. JOHN FORBES (1769–1823) of Scotland was a merchant and trader with the Indians on the Spanish-Indian frontier. The procurement of the land grant on the Appalachicola River that is called the "Forbes purchase" is due to him. JOHN MURRAY FORBES (1771–1831) of Florida was President John Quincy Adams's commercial liaison in southern South America. ROBERT BENNET FORBES (1804–1889) of Massachusetts was a sea captain who invented the "forbes-rig" for boats, carried food to Ireland during the famine, and built Union warships during the Civil War. JOHN MURRAY FORBES (1813–1898) of France was a railroad builder in the Midwest who also organized black regiments from Massachusetts during the Civil War. STEPHEN ALFRED FORBES (1844–1930) of Illinois was a naturalist and the first writer and teacher to stress the study of ecology. He was also a pioneer in researching the foods of birds and fishes. WILLIAM CAMERON FORBES (1870–1959) of Massachusetts was the governor-general of the Philippines. He wrote *The Philippine Islands: A Political and Developmental History of the American Period.* BERTIE CHARLES (originally Robert Charles) FORBES (1880–1954) of Scotland was the founder, editor, and publisher of *Forbes* magazine. ESTHER FORBES (1891–1967) was a writer whose short story "Break-neck Hill" won an O. Henry Award in 1920. She was the first female member of the American Antiquarian Society.

Genealogies: *Forbes: An Ancestry Notebook* was compiled by William Albert Forbes and published in Chevy Chase, Maryland, in 1983. *The Forbes Family: The Descendants of Deacon Daniel Forbes of St. Lawrence County, New York (1789/90–1877)* was compiled by Allene Beaumont Duty and published in Cleveland, Ohio, in 1972.

FORD

Ranking: 115 **S.S. Count:** 252,940

Origin: English, Irish, Jewish. English: derived from the Old English word "ford," meaning a shallow place in a river. The name was given to those who lived near such places and to those who came from places that obtained their names from the word "ford." Irish: derived from the Gaelic names Mac Giolla na Naomh, meaning "son of Filla na Namh" (H&H), meaning "servant of the saints" (H&H); "Mac Con-

shámha," meaning "son of Conshnámha" (H&H), which is derived from the words "con" and "snámh," meaning dog and to swim; and Ó Fuar(th)áin, meaning "descendant of Fuar(th)án" (H&H), which is derived from the word "fuar," meaning cold. Jewish: transformation of a number of similar-sounding names.

Famous **Fords**: JACOB FORD (1738–1777) of New Jersey was a Revolutionary War soldier who, with his father, made shot and shell for General George Washington's army. JOHN BAPTISTE FORD (1811–1903) of Kentucky was a plate-glass manufacturer who made a fortune, lost it, and with his sons made it back again as the Pittsburgh Plate Glass Co. DANIEL SHARP FORD (1822–1899) of Massachusetts was a printer who edited and published *Youth's Companion* and who willed funds for the building of Boston's Ford Hall. JOHN THOMSON FORD (1829–1894) of Maryland was the owner of Ford's Theater in Washington, D.C., where President Abraham Lincoln was assassinated by John Wilkes Booth in 1865. WORTHINGTON CHAUNCEY FORD (1858–1941) of New York published *The Writings of George Washington*. He is the brother of Paul. HENRY FORD (1863–1947) of Michigan was the organizer and president of the Ford Motor Co. He used assembly-line production in the building of the Model T. He built Henry Ford Hospital in Detroit. PAUL LEICESTER FORD (1865–1902) of New York was a historian who edited many historical books, including *The Writings of Thomas Jefferson*. He is the brother of Worthington. GUY STANTON FORD (1873–1962) of Wisconsin was responsible for making the Mayo Clinic part of the graduate school at the University of Minnesota. HANNIBAL CHOATE FORD (1877–1955) of New York invented a system that controlled the speed of trains in the subways. Among his other inventions was a gyrostabilizer to counteract the rolling of ships on the high seas. GEORGE BURDETT FORD (1879–1930) of Massachusetts was the architect who worked on the Wisconsin state capitol. He was the city planner for hundreds of towns, including New Rochelle, New York, and the founder of the magazine *City Planner.* FRANCIS XAVIER FORD (1892–1952) of New York was a Catholic missionary who died a martyr in China. EDSEL BRYANT FORD (1893–1943) of Michigan worked in the Ford Motor Co. empire and did much to improve the automobile. He introduced improved brakes, balloon tires, all-steel bodies, enclosed cars, and a choice of colors. He was also instrumental in the overall design of the Model A and was responsible for the Lincoln-Zephyr and the Mercury. JOHN FORD (1895–1973) of Maine, originally named Sean Aloysius O'Feeney, was a motion-picture director who won Academy Awards for several of his movies. PAUL FORD of Maryland, originally named Paul Ford Weaver, was an actor of stage and screen and is best remembered for his role on "The Phil Silvers Show." GERALD RUDOLPH FORD JR.

(1913–) of Omaha, Nebraska, was the 38th U.S. president. He was born Leslie Lynch King Jr. but was renamed by his adoptive father (his mother's second husband) when he was still an infant. He rose to the position of minority leader of the U.S. House of Representatives. When Spiro Agnew resigned the vice presidency in 1973, President Richard Nixon named Ford vice president. When Nixon resigned because of the Watergate scandal the following year, Ford became president. He was widely criticized for granting Nixon a full pardon and lost his campaign for a full term to Jimmy Carter in 1976. He was the only non-elected U.S. president.

Genealogies: *The Fords of Dearborn* was compiled by Ford Richardson Bryan and published in Detroit, Michigan, in 1989. *The Genealogy of George Gillette, and of John Watts Ford* was compiled by Louise Dollison Marsh and published in Madison, Wisconsin, in 1978. *A History of Our Ford Family of Virginia, Kentucky, Indiana, Mississippi, Missouri, and Tennessee* was compiled by Stith Malone Cain and published in Whitewater, Wisconsin, in 1971.

FOREMAN (S.S. Abbreviation: Forema)
Ranking: 1163 **S.S. Count:** 37,602
Origin: English. Transformation of Forman.

Famous **Foremans**: CARL FOREMAN (1914–1984) of Illinois was a screenwriter who wrote many classics, including *The Bridge on the River Kwai,* which he wrote under a pen name after being blacklisted during the McCarthy hearings.

Genealogies: *The Genealogy of the Families Formon-Boisclair (also Foreman), Walker, Beers, Lacy* was compiled by Mary W. Meadows and published in Columbia, South Carolina, in 1980.

FOREST (ALSO FORESTER, FORESTIER)
Ranking: 2864 **S.S. Count:** 15,903
Origin: English. Transformation of Forrest.

Famous **Bearers**: CECIL SCOTT FORESTER (1899–1966) was born Cecil Lewis Troughton Smith in Egypt. He was a writer of more than 40 books and is best known for his *Hornblower* series.

Genealogies: None known.

FORMAN (ALSO FORMANEK, FORMANSKI, FORMANSKY)
Ranking: 2356 **S.S. Count:** 19,244
Origin: Forman—Czech, English, Jewish; Formanek—Czech; Formanski, Formansky—Jewish. Forman, Formanek, Formanski, Formansky (Czech, Jewish): derived from the Czech word "forman" and the Polish and Yiddish word "furman," both meaning driver. The names were given to those who worked driving horse-drawn vehicles. Forman (English):

1) derived from the Middle English word "foreman," meaning swine keeper. The name was given to those who worked tending pigs. 2) derived from the Old English words "fore" and "mann," meaning in front and man. The name was given to those who were considered leaders.

Famous **Bearers:** DAVID FORMAN (1745–1797) of New Jersey was a Revolutionary War soldier who commanded the Jersey militia at the battle of Germantown. JOSHUA FORMAN (1777–1848) of New York was a founder of Syracuse, New York, who was in favor of the building of the Erie Canal. PHILLIP FORMAN (1895–1978) of New York was a judge. He was an expert in antitrust and bankruptcy law.

Genealogies: None known.

FORNEY

Ranking: 4805 **S.S. Count:** 9320

Origin: Icelandic. Derived from the first name Forni, meaning ancient one.

Famous **Forneys:** JOHN WIEN FORNEY (1817–1881) of Pennsylvania was a journalist and the author of *Anecdotes of Public Men.* WILLIAM HENRY FORNEY (1823–1894) of North Carolina was a lawyer and a brigadier general in the Confederate army. His state of residency was Alabama. MATTHIAS NACE FORNEY (1835–1908) of New York was an inventor who in 1866 designed the tank locomotive, which is used on elevated trains in urban areas.

Genealogies: None known.

FORREST, FORRESTER, FORRESTIER, FORRESTOR (S.S. Abbreviation: Forres)

Ranking: 861 **S.S. Count:** 49,894

Origin: English. Derived from the Middle English word "forest," meaning forest. The names were given to those who lived near or worked in a royal forest, meaning a place reserved for the king and his court for hunting.

Famous **Bearers:** EDWIN FORREST (1806–1872) of Philadelphia, Pennsylvania, was an actor who caused two 19th-century scandals. After he hissed during a performance by the British actor William Macready in England, Macready performed at the Astor Place Opera House. During a show, Forrest fans stormed the theater, and the militia had to be called out. Twenty-two people were killed. Later, he caused another sensation when he sued his wife, Catherine Sinclair, for divorce on the grounds of adultery. He lost the case. NATHAN BEDFORD FORREST (1821–1877) of Tennessee was a Confederate army officer responsible for the massacre of 300 blacks at the surrender of Ft. Pillow, Tennessee, on April 12, 1864.

Genealogies: *The Browns and Forrests of Scotland, Who Came to Tennessee at the End of the Nineteenth Century, and Their Family* was compiled by Forrest David Brown and published in Lewisburg, Pennsylvania, in 1977.

FORSTER, FORSTEL (S.S. Abbreviation: Forste)

Ranking: 3271 **S.S. Count:** 13,875

Origin: Forster—English, German, Jewish; Forstel—German. Forster (English): 1) *derived from the Old French word "forcetier," meaning scissors. The name was given to those who used scissors in their work.* 2) *derived from the Old French word "fust(r)ier," meaning woodworker. The name was given to those who worked as such. Forster (English, German): derived from the Middle English word "forest," meaning forest. The name was given to those who lived near or worked in a royal forest, meaning a place reserved for the king and his court for hunting. Jewish: derived from the German word "forst," meaning forest. Forstel: derived from the Middle High German word "füerst," meaning prince. The name was given to those who were considered to be haughty.*

Genealogies: None known.

FORSYTHE, FORSYTH (S.S. Abbreviation: Forsyt)

Ranking: 1597 **S.S. Count:** 28,060

Origin: Forsythe—Irish; Forsyth—Scottish. Derived from the Gaelic first name Fearsithe, which is derived from the words "fear" and "sithe," meaning man and peace.

Famous **Bearers:** THOMAS FORSYTH (1771–1833) of Michigan was an explorer and an Indian agent. He was a fur trader in Michigan and Illinois and is credited with keeping the peace along the frontier. JOHN FORSYTH (1780–1841) of Virginia was a member of the U.S. House of Representatives and the Senate and a minister to Spain, where he was able to gain ratification of the Treaty of 1819, which ceded Florida to the United States. He also served as U.S. secretary of state and governor of Georgia.

Genealogies: *Genealogy of Newton-Forsyth* was compiled by Leo L. Lemonds and Zelma Newton Bose and published in 1978. *A Genealogical Record: Forsyth of Naydie* was compiled by Frederic Gregory Forsyth Vicomte de Fronsac and published in New Market, Virginia, in 1888.

FORT

Ranking: 3881 **S.S. Count:** 11,622

Origin: English, French. Derived from the Old French word "fort," meaning brave and/or strong. The name was given to those who were considered courageous, to those who lived near a fortress, and to those who worked in a fortress.

Genealogies: None known.

FORTE

Ranking: 3169 **S.S. Count:** 14,328

Origin: English, Italian. English: transformation of Fort. Italian: cognate to Fort.

Famous **Fortes:** FELIX FORTE (1895–1975) of Massachusetts was a judge, a reporter, and the youngest man admitted to the Massachusetts bar. He was the judge who presided over the trial resulting from the Brinks' robbery of $1.2 million in 1950.

Genealogies: None known.

FORTENBERRY, FORTENBERY, FORTENBURY (S.S. Abbreviation: Forten)
Ranking: 4547 S.S. Count: 9819

Origin: German. The names were given to those who came from Furtenbach, a place in Germany.

Genealogies: None known.

FORTIER (S.S. Abbreviation: Fortie)
Ranking: 4102 S.S. Count: 11,016

Origin: French. 1) derived from the Old French word "foret," meaning drill. The name was given to those who used a drill in their work. 2) derived from the Old French word "fort," meaning stronghold. The name was given to those who worked in a fortress.

Famous Fortiers: ALCÉE Fortier (1856–1914) of Louisiana was a professor of Romance languages at Tulane University in New Orleans. He wrote *History of Louisiana* and books on Creole history and customs.

Genealogies: None known.

FORTIN (ALSO FORTINI, FORTINO)
Ranking: 2911 S.S. Count: 15,607

Origin: Fortin—French; Fortini, Fortino—Italian. Cognates to Fort.

Genealogies: None known.

FORTNER (S.S. Abbreviation: Fortne)
Ranking: 2057 S.S. Count: 22,245

Origin: German. Cognate to the English definition of Ford.

Genealogies: *The Fortner Family* was compiled by Virginia Lobdell Jennings and published in Baton Rouge, Louisiana, in 1974.

FORTUNY, FORTUNE, FORTUNATI, FORTUNATO, FORTUNIO, FORTUNA, FORTUNAT (S.S. Abbreviation: Fortun)
Ranking: 1770 S.S. Count: 25,367

Origin: Fortuny—Catalan; Fortune—English, French; Fortunati, Fortunio—Italian; Fortuna—Italian, Portuguese; Fortunat—Provençal. Fortunat, Fortunati, Fortunato, Fortune: derived from the Latin first name Fortūnātus, which is derived from the word "fortūna," meaning luck or chance. Fortuna, Fortune, Fortunio, Fortuny (English): derived from the Old French and Middle English word "fortune," meaning luck or chance. The names were given to those who were gam-

blers. Scottish: derived from the Old English words "fōr" and "tūn," meaning hog and settlement. The name was given to those who came from Fortune, a place in Scotland.

Genealogies: None known.

FOSS
Ranking: 2290 S.S. Count: 19,887

Origin: Danish, English, French. Danish: derived from the Old Norse word "fors," meaning waterfall. The name was given to those who lived near waterfalls. English, French: derived from the Old English word "foss" and the Old French word "fosse," both meaning ditch. The name was given to those who lived near a ditch.

Famous Fosses: CYRUS DAVID FOSS (1834–1910) of New York was the president of Wesleyan University in Middletown, Connecticut, and a missionary to places around the world. SAM WALTER FOSS (1858–1911) of New Hampshire was an editor and writer. He was the author of the poem "House by the Side of the Road."

FOSTER
Ranking: 87 S.S. Count: 312,032

Origin: English, Jewish. English: 1) transformation of and cognate to Forster. 2) derived from the Middle English word "foster," meaning foster parent. The name was given to those who took in children. Jewish: uncertain etymology.

Famous Fosters: ABRIEL FOSTER (1735–1806) of Massachusetts was a Federalist, a supporter of the Revolution, and a member of Congress from New Hampshire after the war. HANNAH WEBSTER FOSTER (1758–1840) of Massachusetts was the author of *The Coquette* and *The Boarding School*. STEPHEN SYMONDS FOSTER (1809–1881) of New Hampshire worked for women's suffrage, temperance, peace, and reform. He was the husband of Abigail. ABIGAIL KELLEY FOSTER (1810–1887) of Pelham, Massachusetts, was an antislavery and women's rights activist. Her lectures gained her national prominence. STEPHEN COLLINS FOSTER (1826–1864) of Pennsylvania was a songwriter who wrote for the then-popular Negro minstrel troupes. Some of his classics are "My Old Kentucky Home," "O Susanna," "Camptown Races," and "Jeanie with the Light Brown Hair." JOHN WATSON FOSTER (1836–1917) of Indiana was a diplomat, with assignments as minister to Spain, Russia, and Mexico. He settled the boundary dispute between Alaska and Canada in 1903. JUDITH HELEN HORTON FOSTER (1840–1910) of Massachusetts was the first woman admitted to the Iowa bar. She was also a temperance leader. THOMAS JEFFERSON FOSTER (1843–1936) of Pennsylvania was a journalist and the founder of the International Correspondence Schools. FRANK HUGH FOSTER (1851–1935) of Massachusetts was a theologian best known for his published work. He wrote *A Genetic History of New England*

Theology. WILLIAM TRUFANT FOSTER (1879–1950) of Massachusetts was an economist concerned with the public as consumers. He was the chairman of the Committee on Consumer Credit and was also on the Consumers' Advisory Board of the National Recovery Administration. WILLIAM ZEBULON FOSTER (1881–1961) of Massachusetts organized steelworkers in 1919 for a major strike and was the Communist Party candidate for president of the United States in 1924, 1928, and 1932. HAROLD RUDOLF FOSTER (1892–1982) of Canada was a cartoonist who drew the "Tarzan" comic strip and created and produced the "Prince Valiant" comic strip. GEORGE VANCE FOSTER (1899–1974) of Canada was the first chief resident at Children's Hospital in Pittsburgh, Pennsylvania.

Genealogies: None known.

FOUNTAIN, FOUNTAINE (S.S. Abbreviation: Founta)

Ranking: 1539 **S.S. Count:** 28,947

Origin: English. Cognates to Fontaine.

Famous **Bearers:** RICHARD TILLMAN FOUNTAIN (1885–1945) was a prominent North Carolina attorney and state politician.

Genealogies: None known.

FOURNIE, FOURNIER (S.S. Abbreviation: Fourni)

Ranking: 2139 **S.S. Count:** 21,409

Origin: French. Derived from the Old French word "fo(u)rnier," meaning baker. The names were given to those who worked as such.

Famous **Bearers:** ALEXIS JEAN FOURNIER (1865–1948) was a landscape painter in Minnesota whose works were exhibited in leading art galleries in the United States and Europe.

Genealogies: None known.

FOUST

Ranking: 2696 **S.S. Count:** 16,873

Origin: German. Transformation of Faust.

Genealogies: *Faust-Foust Family in America* was compiled by Howard M. Faust and published in Baltimore, Maryland, in 1976. *The Family of John Foust and Anna Barbara Albrecht and Allied Families* was compiled by Mozette Foust and most likely published in Thornton, Texas, in 1982.

FOWLER

Ranking: 245 **S.S. Count:** 147,263

Origin: English. Derived from the Old English word "fugelere," meaning bird catcher. The name was given to those who worked as such.

Famous **Fowlers:** ORIN FOWLER (1791–1852) of Connecticut was a clergyman and politician who spoke in favor of temperance laws and cheap postage. GEORGE RYERSON FOWLER (1848–1906) of New York was a surgeon. He introduced the idea of classes in first-aid instruction. RUSSELL STORY FOWLER (1874–1959) of New York was a surgeon who wrote *The Operating Room and the Patient,* which ran through three editions. GENE FOWLER (1890–1960) of Colorado was an author and journalist. He wrote *Good Night, Sweet Prince,* a biography of the actor John Barrymore. It was a bestseller. LYDIA FOLGER FOWLER (1822–1879) of Massachusetts was a physician and reformer who was in favor of there being more female physicians.

Genealogies: *Immigrated to Tennessee: Chronicles of a Fowler Family* was compiled by Jane Cook Hollis and published in Memphis, Tennessee, in 1991. *Palmer, Fowler Genealogies* was published in 1991.

FOX

Ranking: 156 **S.S. Count:** 206,811

Origin: English, German, Irish, Jewish. English: derived from the Old English word "fox," meaning fox. The name was given to those who had red hair or another attribute of the animal. German: derived from the German name Fock, which is derived from the word "folk," meaning people. Irish: derived from the Gaelic name Mac an tSionnaigh, meaning "son of the fox" (H&H). Jewish: transformations of many similar-sounding names.

Famous **Foxes:** GILBERT FOX (1776–1807?) of England was an engraver, actor, and singer. He prodded Joseph Hopkinson into writing the song "Hail Columbia" in 1798. GUSTAVUS VASA FOX (1821–1883) of Massachusetts was a naval officer and assistant secretary of the navy. MARGARET FOX (1833?–1893) of Canada was a spiritualist who claimed to be in contact with the spirit world. Her sister, CATHERINE (1839?–1892), known as Kate, was a medium who toured Europe and the United States in that same line of work. Later in life she confessed, then recanted, that the show was an act. She claimed common-law marriage to Dr. Elisha Kent Kane, took his name, and wrote a book titled *The Love Life of Dr. Kane,* using his love letters to her as material. RICHARD KYLE FOX (1846–1922) of Ireland was the owner of *National Police Gazette,* a periodical of the day that sensationalized sex and crime. JOHN WILLIAM FOX (known as JOHN FOX JR.) (1863–1919) of Kentucky was a novelist. One of his many books was *The Kentuckians.* WILLIAM FOX (1879–1952), originally from Hungary, was born Wilhelm Fried. He controlled a large portion of the exhibition, distribution, and production of motion pictures during the silent-film era. He formed the Fox Film Corporation, which later became 20th Century–Fox Studios. FONTAINE TALBOT FOX JR. (1884–1964) of Kentucky was a cartoonist. He developed the "Toonerville Folks," which centered on the Toonerville Trolley. All of the characters were based on people he'd known as a child. One character, Mickey McGuire, was based on himself. This character was so popular that a child actor named Joe Yule Jr. tried to take the name as his own. The case went to court and it was decided that Fox owned the copyright to the character. The child actor eventually settled on another name, calling himself Mickey Rooney. DIXON RYAN FOX (1887–1945) of New York was the president of Union College in New York and the president of the New York State Historical Association. VIRGIL KEEL FOX (1912–1980) of Illinois was a well-known organist who played at Riverside Church in New York City and frequently toured the United States and Europe. LORRAINE FOX (1922–1976) of New York was an illustrator whose work was part of major advertising campaigns, books, and magazines. Much of her work can be seen at the Lorraine Fox Working library at the Parsons School of Design Library in New York.

Genealogies: *American Family History: Fox, Ellicott, Evans; Charles Worthington Evans, Martha Ellicott Tyson, G. Hunter Bartlett* was compiled by Charles Worthington Evans and published in Cockeysville, Maryland, in 1976. *Fox Family History, 1703– 1976* was compiled by John Franklin Vallentine and published in Ashland, Kansas, in 1976.

FOY

Ranking: 2655 **S.S. Count:** 17,145

Origin: French, Irish. French: 1) derived from the Old French word "foi," meaning faith. The name was given to those who were considered faithful and to those who used this word frequently. 2) derived from the first name Foy, which is derived from the Old French word "foi," meaning faith. Irish: transformation of Fah(e)y and Fee.

Famous **Foys:** EDDIE FOY (1856–1928) of New York was an entertainer originally named Edwin Fitzgerald. He had a successful career as a comedian on Broadway, in vaudeville, and in one motion picture that starred his children and was titled *The Seven Little Foys.*

Genealogies: None known.

FRALEY

Ranking: 2985 **S.S. Count:** 15,236

Origin: German. Derived from the Old High German word "frō," meaning happy. The name was given to those who were considered cheerful.

Famous **Fraleys:** FREDERICK FRALEY (1804–1901), a prominent Pennsylvania financier, was the founder and president of the Philadelphia Board of Trade and a founder and president of Girard College.

Genealogies: None known.

FRAME

Ranking: 3810 **S.S. Count:** 11,848.

Origin: Jewish, Scottish. Uncertain etymology.

Famous **Frames:** ALICE SEYMOUR BROUNE FRAME (1878–1941) was born in Turkey, where her parents were missionaries. She became a Congregational missionary and educator in China.

Genealogies: None known.

FRANCESC, FRANCESCH, FRANCES, FRANCESCO, FRANCESCHI, FRANCSECO, FRANCESCHETTI, FRANCESCHINO ET AL., FRANCY (S.S. Abbreviation: France)

Ranking: 1558 **S.S. Count:** 28,640

Origin: Francesc, Francesch—Catalan; Frances—English, Jewish, Provençal; Francesco, Franceschi, Francseco, Franceschetti, Franceschino et al.—Italian; Francy—Scottish. Transformations of and cognates to Francis.

Genealogies: None known.

FRANCIES, FRANCIS, FRANCIONE, FRANCIONI, FRANCILLO, FRANCINO, FRANCISKIEWICZ, FRANCIE, FRANCISCO (S.S. Abbreviation: Franci)

Ranking: 314 **S.S. Count:** 117,668

Origin: Francies, Francis—English; Francione, Francioni, Francillo, Francino, Franciskiewicz—Polish; Francie—Scottish; Francisco—Spanish. Derived from the Latin first name Franciscus, which developed into the Old French first name François, which came to mean Frenchman.

Famous **Bearers:** MILLY FRANCIS (1802?–1848) was a Creek Indian woman who was awarded a Congressional medal for saving the life of Duncan McKrimmon, a white captive who was a member of the Georgia militia. She died before receiving the medal, however; it was delayed because of Washington red tape. SAMUEL WARD FRANCIS (1835–1886) invented a number of devices. One invention was the "printing machine," a forerunner of the typewriter. CHARLES SPENCER FRANCIS (1853–1911) of New York was an editor and diplomat. He was the owner of the Troy *Times*, which he inherited from his father. He served as the U.S. minister to Greece, Romania, and Serbia. PAUL JAMES FRANCIS (1863–1940) of Maryland was an Episcopal clergyman, a Roman Catholic priest, and the founder of the Society of the Atonement. THOMAS FRANCIS JR. (1900–1969) of Indiana developed vaccines against influenza A and influenza B. KAY FRANCIS (1905–1968) of Oklahoma was born Katherine Edwina Gibbs. She was a well-known actress of her day.

Genealogies: *Captain William Upshaw, Gent., Planter of Virginia: Some of His Georgia Descendants and Allied Families, Francis, Wright, McAllen, Bardwell, Daves, Chalmers* was compiled by Sophie W. Upshaw and published in Baltimore, Maryland, in 1975. *Descendants of Joseph Francis of Maryland and Virginia* was compiled by L. M. Dickson and published in Montezuma, Iowa, in 1949.

FRANCO (ALSO FRANCOM, FRANCOMBE, FRANCOU, FRANCOUL, FRANÇOIS, FRANCONE, FRANCONI, FRANCOS)

Ranking: 768 **S.S. Count:** 54,769

Origin: Franco—Italian, Portuguese, Spanish; Francom, Francombe—English; Francou, Francoul, François—French; Francone, Franconi—Italian; Francos—Spanish. Franco, Francos, Francou, Francoul, Francone, Franconi: cognates to the English definitions of Frank. François: cognate to Francis. Francom, Francombe: derived from the Anglo-Norman-French word "franchomme," meaning free man. The names were given to those who were freemen.

Genealogies: None known.

FRANK

Ranking: 421 **S.S. Count:** 94,413

Origin: Czech, Danish, Dutch, Flemish, German, Hungarian, Jewish, Norwegian, English. Czech, Danish, Dutch, Flemish, German, Hungarian, Jewish, Norwegian: the name was given to those who came from Franconia, a place in southwest Germany that was originally settled by the Franks. English: 1) derived from the Norman first name Frank, which was originally an ethnic name for a Frank. 2) derived from the Middle English and Old French word "franc," meaning generous and/or liberal. The name was given to those who were considered unselfish.

Famous **Franks:** TENNY FRANK (1876–1939) of Kansas was a Classical scholar and a historian of ancient Rome. PHILLIP G. FRANK (1884–1966) of Austria was a mathematician, physicist, and philosopher of science. He was the first president of the Institute for the Unity of Science. He wrote *Einstein: His Life and Times*, an authorized biography. GLENN FRANK (1887–1940) of Missouri was an educator and editor and the president of the University of Wisconsin. WALDO DAVID FRANK (1889–1967) of New Jersey was the founder and editor of *The Seven Arts Magazine* and the author of many books, including *Birth of a World*. JEROME FRANK (1889–1957) of New York was a judge of the U.S. Circuit Court of Appeals for the 2nd Circuit, which included New York, Connecticut, and Vermont.

Genealogies: *Our Families and Kin, Now and Then: Blackburn, Franck (also Frank), Leake, and Thornton* was compiled by Arline Tatum Lorente and published in Richmond, Virginia, in 1985. *German-American Pioneers in Wisconsin and Michigan: The Frank-Kerler Letters, 1849–1864* was compiled by Louis Frederick Frank and published in Milwaukee, Wisconsin, in 1971.

FRANKE (ALSO FRANKEL, FRANKENHEIM, FRANKENSCHEIN, FRANKENSTEIN, FRANKENHAL)

Ranking: 1419 **S.S. Count:** 31,341

Origin: Franke—German; Frankel—German, Jewish; Frankenheim, Frankenschein, Frankenstein, Frankenhal—Jewish. Transformations of Frank.

Genealogies: None known.

FRANKL (ALSO FRANKLAND, FRANKLIN, FRANKLING, FRANKLYN, FRANKLE)

Ranking: 217 **S.S. Count:** 161,843

Origin: Frankl—Jewish; Frankland, Franklin, Frankling, Franklyn—English; Frankle—German, Jewish. Frankle, Frankl: transformations of Frank. Frankland: derived from the Anglo-Norman-French word "frank" and the Middle English word "land," meaning free and land. The name was given to those who owned their own land. Franklin, Frankling, Franklyn: derived from the Middle English word "frankelin," meaning franklin, meaning a freeman who owned land.

Famous **Bearers:** ANN SMITH FRANKLIN (1696–1763) of Massachusetts was the first female printer in New England and the second in British North America. She was the wife of James. JAMES FRANKLIN (1697–1735) of Massachusetts was the brother of Benjamin Franklin. He was a printer who had his business in Boston, where he founded and printed the *New England Courant*. He set up the first printing business in Rhode Island, then founded the *Rhode Island Gazette*, the state's first paper. BENJAMIN FRANKLIN (1706–1790) of Boston, Massachusetts, invented the lightning rod, bifocal spectacles, and the Franklin stove. He helped draft the Declaration of Independence, went to France in order to secure aid for the North American colonies against the British, and later negotiated a peace with England. He was also instrumental in the adoption of the U.S. Constitution. DEBORAH READ FRANKLIN (1707?–1774), birthplace unknown, was the wife of Benjamin Franklin. WILLIAM FRANKLIN (1731–1813) of Pennsylvania was the son, without benefit of marriage, of Benjamin Franklin. He was the governor of New Jersey (1763–1776). A Loyalist, he was arrested and returned to England around 1782. WILLIAM BUEL FRANKLIN (1823–1903) of Pennsylvania was an army officer who served in the Mexican War and the Civil War. He rose to the rank of major general but was defeated at the Battle of Fredericksburg in 1862 and was relieved of his command by General Ambrose Burnside, who held him responsible. He resigned from the army in 1866. FABIAN FRANKLIN (1853–1939) of Hungary was an editor of several newspapers and the writer of several books denouncing Prohibition. EDWARD CURTIS FRANKLIN (1862–1937) of Kansas was a chemist who was an expert on the ammonia system of compounds and liquid ammonia as an electrolytic solvent. PHILIP ALBRIGHT SMALL FRANKLIN (1871–1939) of Maryland is best remembered for his achievements in international shipping finance.

Genealogies: *Ancestors and Descendants of My Raymoure, Hubbell, Franklin, Osborne Grandparents: Includes 40+ Connecting Lines* was compiled by Dorothy Raymoure and published in Grand Rapids, Michigan, in 1982. *Cook's Crier, The Franklin's Fireplace* was compiled by Betty Harvey Williams and published in Warrensburg, Missouri, in 1973.

FRANKS
Ranking: 1036 S.S. Count: 42,188
Origin: English. Transformation of the first definition of Frank.

Famous **Frankses**: REBECCA FRANKS (1760?–1823) of Pennsylvania was a Revolutionary belle.

Genealogies: *The Lee Max Friedman Collection of American Jewish Colonial Correspondence: Letters of the Franks Family, 1733–1748* was compiled by Abigail Franks and published in Waltham, Massachusetts, in 1968.

FRANTZ (ALSO FRANTZEN)
Ranking: 2461 S.S. Count: 18,420
Origin: Frantz—German, Jewish; Frantzen—Dutch. Cognates to Francis.

Genealogies: *The Frans (also Frantz) Family of Grand Rapids* was compiled by John William Taylor and published in Moorestown, New Jersey, in 1984. *The Genealogy of the Matthias Frantz Family of Berks County, Pennsylvania* was compiled by E. Harold Frantz and published in Elizabethtown, Pennsylvania, in 1972.

FRANZ
Ranking: 2742 S.S. Count: 16,603
Origin: German, Jewish. Cognate to Francis.

Famous **Franzes**: SHEPHERD IVORY FRANZ (1874–1933) of New Jersey was a physiological psychologist known for his discoveries of different brain functions. He is also credited with being able to rehabilitate someone suffering from brain injuries.

Genealogies: None known.

FRANZEN, FRANZELINI, FRANZEWITCH
(S.S. Abbreviation: Franze)
Ranking: 3996 S.S. Count: 11,315
Origin: Franzen—Dutch, Swedish; Franzelini—Italian; Franzewitch—Jewish. Cognates to and transformations of Francis.

Genealogies: None known.

FRASER
Ranking: 1206 S.S. Count: 36,507
Origin: Irish, Scottish. The name was given to those who came from Friesland, a place in Holland.

Famous **Frasers**: JAMES EARLE FRASER (1876–1953) of Minnesota was a sculptor who created monuments of famous people but whose claim to fame was designing the U.S. buffalo five-cent piece (the buffalo nickel) and the World War I victory medal. CHARLES FRASER (1782–1860) was a painter of miniatures that were known for their subtle character. LEON FRASER (1889–1945) of Massachusetts was the president of the First National Bank of New York and the director of the Federal Reserve Bank of New York.

Genealogies: *Descendants of George Fraizer (also Fraser), Joseph Journey, Patrick Calvert, Thomas Endicott, Sr., John Ashworth, Sr., as They Entered "Into This Fruitful Valley"* was compiled by Gloria M. Cox and published in Evansville, Indiana, in 1971. *A Genealogical History of the Louis Defoy(e)/Fraser Family from Quebec to Redford, New York* was compiled by Richard Leon Provost and published in Creston, Iowa, in 1985. *Frazers (also Fraser), Baptists, Beatitudes: Descendants of James George Frazer (1799–1878) of Campbell County, Virginia and Highland County, Ohio* was compiled by Margaret (Gruse) Frazer and Elva (Frazer) Shelton and published in Vandalia, Ohio, in 1972. *The Heritage and Legacy of Francis Frazier II (also Fraser), A Blacksmith* was compiled by Zelda Schwarzkipf Frazier and published in Speedway, Indiana, in 1982.

FRASIER (S.S. Abbreviation: Frasie)
Ranking: 4385 S.S. Count: 10,234
Origin: Irish, Scottish. Transformation of Fraser.
Genealogies: None known.

FRAZER
Ranking: 3873 S.S. Count: 11,643
Origin: Irish, Scottish. Transformation of Fraser.

Famous **Frazers**: PERSIFOR FRAZER (1736–1792) of Pennsylvania was a merchant, iron worker, and Revolutionary War soldier. OLIVER FRAZER (1808–1864) of Kentucky was a portrait painter. His work showed simplicity of line and firmness of texture. JOHN FRIES FRAZER (1812–1872) of Pennsylvania was a scientist and professor of natural philosophy at the University of Pennsylvania. He was also the editor of the *Journal of the Franklin Institute*. PERSIFOR FRAZER (1844–1909) of Pennsylvania was the son of John F. He was a geologist and a metallurgist and a member of the Hayden Survey of Colorado and J. P. Lesley's geological survey of Pennsylvania.

Genealogies: *Frazers (also Fraser), Baptists, Beatitudes: Descendants of James George Frazer (1799–1878) of Campbell County, Virginia and Highland County, Ohio* was compiled by Margaret (Gruse) Frazer and Elva (Frazer) Shelton and published in Vandalia, Ohio, in 1972.

FRAZIER (S.S. Abbreviation: Frazie)
Ranking: 282 S.S. Count: 126,336
Origin: Irish, Scottish. Transformation of Fraser.
Famous **Fraziers:** JAMES BERIAH FRAZIER (1856–1937) was a governor of and U.S. senator from Tennessee. CHARLES HARRISON FRAZIER (1870–1936) of Pennsylvania was a neurological surgeon who, with William G. Spiller, founded the Public Charities Association of Pennsylvania. MAUDE FRAZIER (1881–1963) of Wisconsin was the superintendent of the Las Vegas schools and a member of the Nevada state legislature. Her greatest contribution was the reorganization of the Nevada school system. She also established Nevada Southern University, now known as The University of Nevada, at Las Vegas. LYNN JOSEPH FRAZIER (1874–1947) of Minnesota was a farmer and politician. He was elected governor of the state with farmers' rights as his platform. He pushed through a series of laws in favor of the farmer. He was elected several more times with the same policies. After his final election (1920), he faced much opposition and was recalled. He also passed laws to lessen the tax burden on individuals and grant suffrage to women. He was then elected to the U.S. Senate and was a co-author of the Frazier-Lemke Amendment to the Farm Bankruptcy Act of 1934. EDWARD FRANKLIN FRAZIER (1894–1962) of Maryland was a sociologist and an expert on racial interactions, especially those that dealt with the African American family. He was the author of several books on the subject. JOSEPH (JOE) FRAZIER (1944–) of Beaufort, South Carolina, was the world heavyweight boxing champion from 1970 to 1973.
Genealogies: *Descendants of George Fraizer (also Fraser), Joseph Journey, Patrick Calvert, Thomas Endicott, Sr., John Ashworth, Sr., as They Entered "Into This Fruitful Valley"* was compiled by Gloria M. Cox and published in Evansville, Indiana, in 1971. *The Heritage and Legacy of Francis Frazier II (also Fraser), A Blacksmith* was compiled by Zelda Schwarzkipf Frazier and published in Speedway, Indiana, in 1982. *Samuel Frazier, a Whig of 1776, one of the Framers of Tennessee's Constitution, 1796, First State Senator from Greene County, Tennessee, 1796–1801, His Wife Rebecca Julian and Their Descendants* was compiled by Virginia Knight Nelson and published in Knoxville, Tennessee, in 1978.

FREDERIKSEN, FREDERIKS, FREDERICK, FREDERICKS, FREDERIC, FREDERICH, FREDERICHSEN, FREDERICO, FREDERIKSSON (S.S. Abbreviation: Freder)
Ranking: 497 S.S. Count: 80,712

Origin: Frederiksen—Danish, Norwegian; Frederiks—Dutch; Frederick, Fredericks—English; Frederic—French; Frederich, Frederichsen—German; Frederico—Italian; Frederiksson—Swedish. Derived from a Germanic first name comprising the words "frid" and "ric," meaning peace and powerful.
Famous **Bearers:** GEORGE ALOYSIUS FREDERICK (1842–1921), a nationally prominent architect, designed the city hall of Baltimore, Maryland, in 1875, a model municipal building for its time. HAROLD FREDERIC (1856–1898) of New York was a journalist and a novelist. His books include *The Lawton Girl* and *March Hares*.
Genealogies: None known.

FREDRIC, FREDRICK, FREDRICH, FREDRICHS, FREDRICKSSON (S.S. Abbreviation: Fredri)
Ranking: 1616 S.S. Count: 27,681
Origin: Fredric, Fredrick—Flemish; Fredrich, Fredrichs—German; Fredricksson—Swedish. Cognates to Frederick.
Genealogies: None known.

FREE
Ranking: 3402 S.S. Count: 13,308
Origin: English. Derived from the Old English word "frēo," meaning free. The name was given to those who were not serfs.
Genealogies: None known.

FREED
Ranking: 3274 S.S. Count: 13,861
Origin: English, Jewish, Welsh, Scottish. English, Scottish: derived from the Old English word "firhðe," meaning woodland. The name was given to those who lived in or near such a place. Jewish: transformation of Fried. Welsh: derived from the Welsh words "ffrith" and "ffridd," meaning barren land and mountain pasture. The name was given to those who lived near such places.
Famous **Freeds:** ALAN J. FREED (1921–1965) of Pennsylvania was a nationally known disk jockey. He was known as the "father of rock 'n' roll." He was involved in a "payola" scandal that eventually destroyed his career.
Genealogies: *A Freed Family History: Ancestors and Descendants of Walter Curtin Freed and Dorothy Youngman Freed of Williamsport, Pennsylvania* was compiled by Joyce Wilcox Graff and published in Baltimore, Maryland, in 1981.

FREEDMAN (S.S. Abbreviation: Freedm)
Ranking: 3014 S.S. Count: 15,078
Origin: English, Jewish. English: derived from the Old English word "frēo," meaning free. The name was given to those who were not serfs. Jewish: transformation of Fried.

Famous **Freedmans:** ANDREW FREEDMAN (1860–1915) of New York was an organizer of insurance companies and also worked to make the New York subway system a reality.

Genealogies: None known.

FREELAND   (S.S. Abbreviation: Freela)
Ranking: 3596 **S.S. Count:** 12,549

Origin: English. Derived from the Old English words "frēo" and "land," meaning free and land. The name was given to those who lived on land they owned.

Genealogies: *A Freeland History: Being a Genealogical Record of the Descendants of Mary (Pollock) Freeland of Carlisle, Pennsylvania, 1746–1971* was compiled by Harry A. Focht and published in Hummelstown, Pennsylvania, in 1971.

FREEMAN   (S.S. Abbreviation: Freema)
Ranking: 132 **S.S. Count:** 226,369

Origin: English. Derived from the Old English word "frēo," meaning free. The name was given to those who were not serfs.

Famous **Freemans:** BERNARDUS FREEMAN (?–1741) of the Netherlands was a Dutch Reform clergyman who preached to the Mohawk Indians of New York and had religious texts translated into their native tongue. THOMAS FREEMAN (?–1821) of Ireland was a civil engineer and astronomer. He was an important member of Andrew Elliott's survey team that defined the boundary between the United States and Spanish land in North America in 1797. Also to his credit are the explorations of the Arkansas and Red rivers in 1806 and the mapping of the Tennessee-Alabama state lines. FREDERICK KEMPER FREEMAN (1841–1928) of Virginia was a Confederate soldier and a journalist. After the Civil War, he and his brother Leigh edited the *Frontier Index*, a newspaper published along the Union Pacific rail line. MARY ELEANOR WILKINS FREEMAN (1852–1930) of Massachusetts was a writer. The main theme of her novels was the frustrated lives led by the people of New England towns and villages. JOHN RIPLEY FREEMAN (1855–1932) of Maine was a member of engineering boards who advised the U.S. government on the construction of the Panama Canal. ALLEN WEIR FREEMAN (1881–1954) of Virginia was the dean of Johns Hopkins School of Hygiene and president of the American Public Health Association. DOUGLAS SOUTHALL FREEMAN (1886–1953) of Lynchburg, Virginia, won a Pulitzer Prize for his biography of Robert E. Lee. JOSEPH FREEMAN (1897–1965) of the Ukraine was a poet, radical journalist, publicist, and novelist. His best-known book was *Dollar Diplomacy: A Study in American Imperialism and the Social Worker.*

Genealogies: *Coppedge/Freeman and Next of Kin* was compiled by Mildred C. Siever and published in Clare-more, Oklahoma, in 1983. *Freeman-Palmer and Related Families* was compiled by Mary Ann Palmer-Schrepfer and published in Yakima, Washington, in 1972.

FREESE
Ranking: 4992 **S.S. Count:** 8987

Origin: English, German. Transformation of Fraser.

Genealogies: *Freese Families* was compiled by John Wesley Freese and published in Cambridge, Massachusetts, most likely in 1906.

FREITAG, FREITAS   (S.S. Abbreviation: Freita)
Ranking: 2373 **S.S. Count:** 19,129

Origin: Freitag—German, Jewish; Freitas—Portuguese. Freitag: derived from the German word "freitag," meaning Friday. The word refers to Freya, a pagan goddess of love. Freitas: derived from the Portuguese word "freitas," meaning broken. The name was given to those who lived in stony areas.

Genealogies: None known.

FRENCH
Ranking: 432 **S.S. Count:** 91,711

Origin: English. Derived from the Middle English word "frensche," meaning French person. The name was given to those who came from France.

Famous **Frenches:** WILLIAM HENRY FRENCH (1815–1881) of Maryland was a West Point officer who served in the Florida, Mexican, and Civil wars. LUCY VIRGINIA SMITH FRENCH (1825–1881) of Virginia was the author of romantic poems and novels. AARON FRENCH (1832–1902) of Ohio was an inventor who is credited with the invention of the coil and elliptic railroad-car springs. WILLIAM MERCHANT RICHARDSON FRENCH (1843–1914) of New Hampshire was the secretary and director of the Art Institute of Chicago. He was the brother of Daniel C. French. ALICE FRENCH (1850–1934) of Massachusetts used the pseudonym "Octave Thanet." She was raised in Arkansas and Iowa, and her novels had those states as their backdrops. DANIEL CHESTER FRENCH (1850–1931) of New Hampshire was among the first U.S. sculptors to gain a national reputation. His statue "The Minute Man" was commissioned by the town of Concord, Massachusetts. It became the symbol for war bonds and the posters of World War II. EDWIN DAVIS FRENCH (1851–1906) of Massachusetts was a silver engraver. SIDNEY JAMES FRENCH (1894–1979) of Wisconsin was an educator at the college level. He served as the dean of several universities and was the first dean at the University of South Florida in Tampa. PAUL COMLY FRENCH (1903–1960) of Pennsylvania was the executive director of Cooperative for American Remittances to Everywhere (CARE).

Genealogies: *Ancestors and Descendants of Frank Lusk*

Babbott, Jr., M.D., and His Wife Elizabeth Bassett French was compiled by Harriet M. Stryker-Rodda and published in Princeton, New Jersey, in 1974. *French and Related Family Genealogy: Treadway, Cummings, Blair, Hutton, Barker, Haynes, Jones, Barrows, Ward, Lobdell, Howland, and Brewster* was compiled by Mara Treadway French and published in San Jose, California, in 1982.

FREUND, FREUNDL, FREUNDLICH, FREUNDSCHAFT

Ranking: 4064 **S.S. Count:** 11,127

Origin: German, Jewish. Cognates to and transformations of Friend.

Famous **Bearers:** ERNEST FREUND (1864–1932) of New York was a lawyer and professor of law at several top law colleges in the United States. His area of expertise was in drafting statutes for legislatures to accept.

Genealogies: *A Short Family Story: Covering the Period from End of the 19th Century up to 1950* (Freund family) was compiled by Hilde Freund and published in the 1980s.

FREY

Ranking: 907 **S.S. Count:** 47,591

Origin: German. Cognate to Free(man).

Famous **Freys:** JOSEPH SAMUEL CHRISTIAN FREDERICK FREY (1771–1850) of Bavaria was a preacher for The American Society for Ameliorating the Condition of the Jews. He traveled all over the United States preaching his cause. JOHN PHILIP FREY (1871–1957) of Minnesota was a labor leader who was opposed to the Congress of Industrial Organizations (CIO) and worked to keep the CIO union members out of the American Federation of Labor (AFL). OLIVER W. FREY (1890–1939) was a member of Congress from Pennsylvania for three terms.

Genealogies: *Frey/Frei Family History* was compiled by Dottie Shimonek Schiefelbein and published in Wichita, Kansas, in 1975.

FRICK

Ranking: 3320 **S.S. Count:** 13,654

Origin: German. Cognate to Frederick.

Famous **Fricks:** HENRY CLAY FRICK (1849–1919) of West Overton, Pennsylvania, was instrumental in building the world's largest coke and steel operation, U.S. Steel, of which he was a director. Upon his death, he gave New York City $15,000 and his Fifth Avenue mansion to house his art collection, now known as the Frick Collection.

Genealogies: *Our Frick Ancestors in the United States and Allied Families* was compiled by Bernice Frick Clark and published in Baltimore, Maryland, in 1990.

FRICKE (ALSO FRICKEL, FRICKER)

Ranking: 4194 **S.S. Count:** 10,766

Origin: Fricke, Frickel—German; Fricker—English. Fricke, Frickel: cognates to Frederick. Fricker: uncertain etymology.

Genealogies: *Ledger of Anthony Fricker, Gunsmith, Womelsdorf, Heidelberg Township, Berks County, Pennsylvania, 1814–1821* was compiled by Anthony Fricker and published in Hershey, Pennsylvania, in 1985. *The Fricker Family: Berks County, Pennsylvania, 1750–Early 1800s* was compiled by Peggy S. Joyner and published in Portsmouth, Virginia, in 1976.

FRIDAY, FRIDAYE

Ranking: 4939 **S.S. Count:** 9066

Origin: English. Cognates to Freitag.

Famous **Fridays:** FRIDAY (1822?–1881) was an Arapaho sub-chief. He was born on the plains of the Midwest, either in Kansas or in Colorado. He was educated in St. Louis but returned to his Native American life, remaining friendly with the white man. He was famous for his great hunting and leadership abilities. DAVID FRIDAY (1876–1945) earned international prominence as an economist. He was president of Michigan Agricultural College, president of the National Bureau of Economic Research, and economic advisor to the U.S. Treasury Department.

Genealogies: None known.

FRIED

Ranking: 4309 **S.S. Count:** 10,418

Origin: German, Jewish. German: cognate to Frederick. Jewish: derived from the Yiddish word "frid," meaning peace. Most often it was taken ornamentally.

Genealogies: *Fried Cousins Club* was compiled by the Fried Cousins Club and published in New York, New York, most likely in the 1970s.

FRIEDE (ALSO FRIEDEL, FRIEDERICH, FRIEDERICHSEN, FRIEDEMAN, FRIEDENBERG, FRIEDENREICH, FRIEDENSTEIN, FRIENDENTHAL ET AL.)

Ranking: 3824 **S.S. Count:** 11,793

Origin: Friede, Friedel, Friederich, Friederichsen—German; Friedeman, Friedenberg, Friedenreich, Friedenstein, Friendenthal et al.—Jewish. Friede, Friedel, Friederich, Friederichsen: cognates to Frederick. Friedeman, Friedenberg, Friedenreich, Friedenstein, Friendenthal: transformations of Fried combined with words meaning man, hill, kingdom, stone, and valley. The names were taken ornamentally.

Genealogies: None known.

FRIEDLEIN, FRIEDLER, FRIEDLICH (S.S. Abbreviation: Friedl)

Ranking: 3007 **S.S. Count:** 15,105

Origin: Friedlein—German; Friedler, Friedlich—Jewish. Friedlein: cognate to Frederick. Friedler, Friedlich: transformations of Fried.

Genealogies: None known.

FRIEDMAN, FRIEDMANN (S.S. Abbreviation: Friedm)

Ranking: 697 **S.S. Count:** 60,410

Origin: Jewish. Transformations of Fried combined with a word meaning man.

Famous Bearers: WILLIAM FREDERICK FRIEDMAN (1891–1969) of Russia was a cryptologist who was chief of the Signal Intelligence Service (SIS). He wrote several books still considered to be standard references on the subject.

Genealogies: *Friedman Family Genealogical Record Booklet* was compiled by Steven D. Friedman and published in Columbus, Ohio, in 1980. *Friedman-Seidman Family Chart* was compiled by Judy Graf Klein and published in New York, New York, in 1978.

FRIEDREICHER, FRIEDRICH, FRIEDRICHS (S.S. Abbreviation: Friedr)

Ranking: 3706 **S.S. Count:** 12,179

Origin: German. Cognates to Frederick.

Famous Bearers: HANS RUDOLPH FRIEDRICH (1911–1958), a German native and a physicist, was perhaps the best-known rocket scientist in the United States. He is noted for his research in automatic control, flight mechanics, and design of guided missiles. Hours after his death, an intercontinental ballistic missile was launched from Cape Canaveral, Florida. A message in his memory was inscribed on the nose cone.

Genealogies: None known.

FRIEND

Ranking: 1799 **S.S. Count:** 25,031

Origin: English, Jewish. English: derived from the Old English word "frēond," meaning friend. The name was given to those who were considered friendly. Jewish: transformation of many similiar-sounding names, such as Freund or Freundlich.

Famous Friends: EMIL FRIEND (1878–1958) was financial editor of the Chicago *Herald-Examiner* for 13 years. CLARENCE LEWIS FRIEND (1878–1958) of Nebraska, an astronomer, is credited with the first sightings of four comets. Three of them are named for him.

Genealogies: *The Gelsinger, Friend, and Related Families* was compiled by Carol R. Gustafson and published in Oak Forest, Illinois, in 1990. *Chronicles of the Adventurous Friend Family* was compiled by the Friend Family Association of America and published in Fort Wayne, Indiana, in 1977.

FRIES

Ranking: 3747 **S.S. Count:** 12,085

Origin: German, Jewish, Swedish. 1) derived from the name Frisa, which refers to a now-unknown ethnicity. 2) the name was given to those who worked building dams and dikes. 3) cognate to Frederick.

Famous Frieses: JOHN FRIES (1750?–1818) of Pennsylvania was a local militia captain well liked by the area's residents. He led the people against the property tax of 1798 by ordering the assessors out of town, ejecting those who did not freely leave, and freeing federal prisoners. President John Adams sent in the cavalry, and Fries was arrested, tried for treason, and sentenced to death. Against the advice of his cabinet, Adams pardoned Fries. FRANCIS FRIES (1812–1863) of North Carolina was a manufacturer who brought industry to the South after the Civil War by building woolen and cotton mills in Salem, North Carolina.

Genealogies: None known.

FRIESE (ALSO FRIESEKE, FRIESEL)

Ranking: 4010 **S.S. Count:** 11,286

Origin: Friese, Frieseke—German; Friesel—Jewish. Transformations of Fries.

Famous Bearers: FREDERICK CARL FRIESEKE (1874–1939) of Michigan was an impressionistic painter well received by both colleagues and patrons.

Genealogies: None known.

FRISCH (ALSO FRISCHE, FRISCHMAN, FRISCHLER, FRISCHLING, FRISCHMANN, FRISCHWASSER)

Ranking: 4702 **S.S. Count:** 9512

Origin: Frisch, Frische—German; Frischman—German, Jewish; Frischler, Frischling, Frischmann, Frischwasser—Jewish. Frisch, Frische, Frischman (German): cognates to Frederick. Frischman (Jewish), Frischler, Frischling, Frischmann, Frischwasser: derived from the German word "frisch" and the Yiddish word "frish," both meaning fresh.

Famous Bearers: MARTIN FRISCH (1899–1959), a civil engineer, was the author of numerous articles on petroleum refining and the holder of many patents in that field.

Genealogies: *Some German-American Families, 1460–1975: A History and Genealogy of Families Who Settled in the Midwest, All Related Through Marriage With Members of the Reese Family of Pillenbruch, Germany—Arning, Bollman, Duwe, Frische, Reese, Schmidt* was compiled by Harriet R. Frische and published in Scottsdale, Arizona, in 1975.

FRITSCH, FRITSCHE, FRITSCHLER (S.S. Abbreviation: Fritsc)
Ranking: 4417 S.S. Count: 10,148
Origin: German. Cognates to Frederick.
Genealogies: None known.

FRITZ
Ranking: 925 S.S. Count: 46,683
Origin: German. Cognate to Frederick.

Famous **Fritzes**: JOHN FRITZ (1822–1913) of Pennsylvania was responsible for revolutionizing the American steel industry by using the Bessemer process. He also added the open-hearth furnace, the Thomas basic process, and the Whitworth forging press.

Genealogies: *The Fritts (Fritz) Family Heritage: A Historical, Genealogical, and Biographical Record of the Fritts (Fritz) and Allied Families from October 30, 1738* was compiled by Gregory A. and Patricia A. Fritts and published in Toledo, Ohio, in 1979. *The Noel Tree: A History of the Noel and Allied Families of Pennsylvania, Including Fevrier, Fritz, Dickey, Stepp, and Others* was compiled by Charles A. Noel and published in Laughlintown, Pennsylvania, in 1978.

FROST
Ranking: 747 S.S. Count: 56,885
Origin: Danish, English, German. Derived from the Old Norse, Old English, and Old High German word "frost," meaning frost. The name was given to those who were thought to be cold and to those who had white beards.

Famous **Frosts**: ARTHUR BURDETT FROST (1851–1928) of Pennsylvania was an illustrator who worked for magazines; he also illustrated *Uncle Remus* books. EDWIN BRANT FROST (1866–1935) of Vermont was an astronomer and the director of the Yerkes Observatory. His most important work dealt with the spectra of stars. After going blind and being no longer able to use the telescope, he developed extraordinary hearing. He then developed a mathematical chart showing the different crickets' chirps in relation to the temperature. ROBERT LEE FROST (1874–1963) of San Francisco, California, was a poet whose work celebrated quiet New England life. His best-known poems include "A Boy's Will," "Fire and Ice," and "Out, Out—." WADE HAMPTON FROST (1880–1938) of Virginia was an epidemiologist and part of the group of physicians that ended the yellow-fever epidemic by suppressing the breeding of the mosquito. He worked at the Hygienic Laboratory in Washington, D.C., which became the Microbiological Institute of the National Institutes of Health. HOLLOWAY HALSTEAD FROST (1889–1935) of New York was a naval officer. He developed tactics

that surface vessels and aircraft could use against submarines, and he was subsequently awarded the Navy Cross. He became an instructor at the Staff Command School of the army in Kansas.

Genealogies: *Benjamin Frost, a Texan from Tennessee* was compiled by Ruth Hollar Rickaway and published in Houston, Texas, in 1981. *The Descendants of John Frost, Jr. and Rebecca York Frost of Jackson County, Missouri,* was compiled by Earle W. Frost and published in Kansas City, Missouri, in 1975.

FRY
Ranking: 774 S.S. Count: 54,375
Origin: English. 1) transformation of Free(man). 2) derived from the Middle English word "fry," meaning child or small person. The name was given to those who were of small stature in adulthood.

Famous **Frys**: JOSHUA FRY (1700?–1754) of England was a mathematics professor, surveyor, and pioneer. He came to Virginia in 1720 and became a member of the House of Burgesses, commander of the militia, and co-author in 1751 of "Map of the Inhabited Parts of Virginia." WILLIAM HENRY FRY (1813–1864) of Pennsylvania wrote *Leonora*, the first grand opera ever written by a native American. FRANKLIN CLARK FRY (1900–1968) of Pennsylvania was a clergyman and the founder and president of the Lutheran World Relief. BIRKETT DAVENPORT FRY (1822–1891) of present-day West Virginia (then Virginia) was a cotton manufacturer and a brigadier general in the Confederate army. JAMES BARNET FRY (1827–1894) of Illinois was a West Point graduate. He organized the Bureau of the Provost-Marshal-General in 1863. As a soldier he was outstanding at the battles of the first Bull Run, Shiloh, and Perryville.

Genealogies: *Can You Find Me: A Family History* was compiled by Christopher Fry and published in New York in 1978. *Descendants of Peter Fry, Born 1787, York and Adams Counties, PA* was compiled by Nancy Fry Carter and published in Mendham, New Jersey, in 1976. *Some Descendants of John Fry, Late of Licking County, Ohio* was compiled by Charles Recker and published in Las Vegas, Nevada, in 1986.

FRYE
Ranking: 827 S.S. Count: 51,374
Origin: English. Transformation of Fry.

Famous **Fryes**: JOSEPH FRYE (1711?–1794) of Massachusetts was a soldier who survived the massacre of Fort William Henry in 1757; he also served in the Revolutionary War. The town of Fryeburg, Maine, is named for him. WILLIAM PIERCE FRYE (1831–1911) of Maine was a lawyer and the great-great-grandson of Joseph Frye. He was a member of Congress, then U.S. senator, from Maine, where he served his state's residents for 30 years and was one of the Old Guard under Presidents Theodore Roosevelt and William Howard Taft. WILLIAM JOHN "JACK" FRYE (1904–1959) of Texas was a pioneer in the airline industry. He concentrated on fast, comfortable, modern equipment and on devices that made all-weather operation safer.

Genealogies: *The Frye Family, Being a Record of the Descendants of Stephen Frye of Keokuk, Iowa & Sheridan Co., Kansas (1841–1917)* was compiled by Marian McCauley Frye and published in 1969. *Some Descendants of John Fry (also Frye), Late of Licking County, Ohio* was compiled by Charles Recker and published in Las Vegas, Nevada, in 1986.

FRYER

Ranking: 4241   S.S. Count: 10,632

Origin: English. Transformation of Freer.

Famous Fryers: DOUGLAS HENRY FRYER (1891–1960) of Connecticut was a pioneer in the field of applied psychology.

Genealogies: None known.

FUCHS

Ranking: 2274   S.S. Count: 20,015

Origin: German. Cognate to the English definition of Fox.

Famous Fuchses: EMIL FUCHS (1866–1929), a native of Vienna but a naturalized U.S. citizen, was a painter and sculptor whose works were shown in leading art galleries in the United States and Europe.

Genealogies: None known.

FUENTE, FUENTES

Ranking: 967   S.S. Count: 45,163

Origin: Spanish. Derived from the Latin word "fons," meaning spring. The names were given to those who lived near a spring and to those who came from Fuente or Fuentes, the names of several places in Spain.

Genealogies: None known.

FUGATE

Ranking: 3319   S.S. Count: 13,657

Origin: English. The name was given to those who lived near a "fowl gate," presumably the gate leading up to the pen where chickens were kept.

Genealogies: None known.

FUHRMANN, FUHRMAN   (S.S. Abbreviation: Fuhrma)

Ranking: 4482   S.S. Count: 9998

Origin: Fuhrmann—German, Jewish; Fuhrman—Jewish. German: derived from the Middle High German word "vüerer," meaning driver. The name was given to those who worked as drivers of horse-drawn vehicles. *Jewish: transformation of Forman.*

Genealogies: None known.

FULCHER   (S.S. Abbreviation: Fulche)

Ranking: 4773   S.S. Count: 9382

Origin: English. Derived from a Germanic first name derived from the words "folk" and "hari," meaning people and army.

Famous Fulchers: OSCAR HUGH FULCHER (1901–1978) of Virginia was a professor of neurological surgery at Georgetown, where he established an accredited training program in neurological surgery. He was a co-founder of the Washington Academy of Neurological Surgery.

Genealogies: None known.

FULKER

Ranking: 4722   S.S. Count: 9472

Origin: English. Transformation of Fulcher.

Genealogies: None known.

FULLER, FULLERTON

Ranking: 216   S.S. Count: 164,024

Origin: English. Derived from the Old English word "fullere," meaning a cloth dresser. The name was given to those who worked as cloth dressers, meaning those who cleaned and thickened raw cloth.

Famous Bearers: SARAH MARGARET FULLER (1810–1850) of Massachusetts was a social reformer and one of the most respected social critics of her time. She and all on board were lost at sea off the coast of Fire Island, New York. HIRAM FULLER (1814–1880) of Massachusetts was a journalist. He was a partner in the ownership of the *New York Mirror* and the owner and manager of the *Evening Mirror.* In the 1860s, when he spoke sympathetically of the southern cause, he fell out of favor with those in the North. He died in Paris, France. GEORGE FULLER (1822–1884) of Massachusetts was a painter known for the dreamlike figures in his landscapes. ANDREW FULLER (1828–1896) of New York was a horticulturist and a pioneer in the cross-breeding of strawberries. MELVILLE WESTON FULLER (1833–1910) of Maine was a chief justice of the U.S. Supreme Court. HENRY BLAKE FULLER (1857–1929) of Illinois was a novelist known for his realistic settings. MARIE LOUISE (LOIE) FULLER (1862–1928) of Illinois was a dancer and the inventor of the serpentine dance. GEORGE WARREN FULLER (1868–1934) of New York was an engineer who is credited with making many advances in the field of sanitary engineering. MINNIE URSULA OLIVER SCOTT RUTHERFORD FULLER (1868–1946) of Arkansas was a social reformer who was active in the fight for women's suffrage. LUCIA FAIRCHILD FULLER (1870–1924) of Massachusetts was a painter and miniaturist who was commissioned by some of the leading families of the time to do miniature portraits. META VAUX WARRICK FULLER (1877–1968) of Pennsylvania was a sculptor whose most memorable work is titled "The Crucifixion," done in memory of the four black girls killed in a church bombing in Birmingham, Alabama. CARL ALBERT FULLER (1885–1973) of Canada was the organizer in Hartford, Connecticut, of the company that would become the Fuller Brush Co. JOSEPH VINCENT FULLER (1890–1932) of Tennessee was a historical editor who worked within the Department of State in Washington, D.C. RICHARD BUCKMINSTER FULLER (1895–1983) of Milton, Massachusetts, was an architect and engineer who created the geodesic dome, the only large dome that sits on the ground as a complete structure. He is credited with saying that all human needs could be met through technology and planning.

Genealogies: *Fuller-Dunham Genealogy: From Edward Fuller of the Mayflower* was compiled by Robert Wallace Dunham and published in Madison, Wisconsin, in 1990. *Fullers, Sissons, and Scotts, Our Yeoman Ancestors: 46 New England and New York Families* was compiled by Carol Clark Johnson and published in Mobile, Alabama, most likely in 1976.

FULMER

Ranking: 3403 **S.S. Count:** 13,308

Origin: English, German. English: the name was given to those who came from Fulmer, which means "lake frequented by birds" (ES) and is a place in Buckinghamshire, England. German: derived from the first name Folcmar, meaning people and fame.

Genealogies: *Colonial Ancestors of the Fulmers of South Carolina and the Folmars of Alabama* was compiled by L. W. Folmar and published in Pelham, New York, in 1972.

FULTON

Ranking: 929 **S.S. Count:** 46,349

Origin: Irish, Scottish. 1) derived from the Old English words "fuglere" and "tūn," meaning bird catcher and settlement. The name was given to those who came from Fullerton, the name of several places in Scotland. 2) derived from the Old English words "fugol" and "tūn," meaning bird and settlement. The name was given to those who came from Fulton, the name of a place in the Borders region between England and Scotland.

Famous **Fultons:** ROBERT FULTON (1765–1815) of Pennsylvania was an inventor credited with inventing a machine that sawed marble, one for spinning flax, and one for twisting hemp into rope. He invented a submarine in 1797 but could not interest the government in it, then built the *Clermont*, the first economically feasible steamship. He also built the first steam warship. JUSTIN

DEWEY FULTON (1828–1901) of New York was a Baptist clergyman who had no tolerance for slavery, drinkers, women's suffrage, the theater, and Roman Catholics. MARY HANNAH FULTON (1854–1927) of Ohio was a medical missionary and pioneer in the medical education of Chinese women. WILLIAM SHIRLEY FULTON (1880–1964) of Connecticut was a business executive whose hobby of archaeology was his main interest. He participated in digs in Arizona and on the East Coast. WALLACE HERBERT FULTON (1896–1974) of California was an executive in the securities and investment banking business. JOHN FARQUHAR FULTON (1899–1960) of Minnesota was a pioneer in the field of neurophysiology.

Genealogies: *Fulton Genealogy, 1751–1986: Robert Fulton of Ireland; Boston, Massachusetts; Londonderry, New Hampshire; and Upper Canada, with His American and Canadian Descendants* was compiled by Ruth Coan Fulton and published in Portsmouth, New Hampshire, in 1986.

FULTZ

Ranking: 3053 **S.S. Count:** 14,871

Origin: German. Derived from the first name Fulco, which is a form of Volk, meaning people, as it appears in several names, such as Folcward and Fulculf.

Genealogies: None known.

FUNDERBURG, FUNDERS (S.S. Abbreviation: Funder)

Ranking: 3484 **S.S. Count:** 12,943

Origin: German. Derived from the German word "fund," meaning finding or discovery.

Genealogies: *Descendants of Jacob & Eve (Boone) Funderburgh (also Funderburg)* was compiled by Alvin K. Funderburg and published in Dallas, Texas, in 1978.

FUNK

Ranking: 1269 **S.S. Count:** 34,749

Origin: Jewish, Swedish. Derived from the Old High German word "funcho," meaning spark. The name was given to those who were considered particularly energetic.

Famous **Funks:** ISAAC KAUFFMAN FUNK (1839–1912) of Clifton, Ohio, was a Lutheran minister and a publisher. He founded I. K. Funk and Company, which later became Funk and Wagnalls, the publisher of *A Standard Dictionary of the English Language* and *A New Standard Dictionary of the English Language*. WILFRED JOHN FUNK (1883–1965) of New York was a publisher and lexicographer. He wrote poetry and won awards for his work. He first published "the ten most" lists with the ten most overused words and the ten most beautiful words. He was Isaac's son. CASIMIR FUNK (1884–1967) of Poland was a biochemist who is known for his research on vitamins (named by him); he isolated thiamine, later vitamin B_1. He also did research on hormones and cancer.

Genealogies: *Funk Forebears* was compiled by Norma J. Kinney and published in Spokane, Washington, in 1988. *A Tree Grows in Funks Grove: A History of the Funk-Stubblefield Families of McLean County, Illinois* was compiled by Stephen C. Funk and published in McLean, Illinois, in 1984.

FUQUA

Ranking: 3935 **S.S. Count:** 11,467

Origin: French. Derived from the first name Folc, meaning people, and the first name Fulcward, meaning people and guardian.

Genealogies: *Fuqua—a Fight for Freedom: Allied Families* was compiled by Alya Dean Smith Irwin and published in Houston, Texas, in 1974.

FURLONG, FURLONGE, FURLONGER (S.S. Abbreviation: Furlon)

Ranking: 4688 **S.S. Count:** 9545

Origin: English, Irish. Derived from the Old Middle English word "furlong," meaning a length of field. The names were given to those who lived near a measured field.

Genealogies: *Dulany-Furlong and Kindred Families* was compiled by Roland Dulany Furlong and published in Parsons, West Virginia, in 1975.

FURMAN (ALSO FURMANEK, FURMANSKY, FURMANSKI, FURMANIAK, FORMANCZYK)

Ranking: 3244 **S.S. Count:** 14,006

Origin: Furman, Furmanek, Furmansky—Jewish; Furmanek—Czech; Furmanski—Jewish, Polish; Furmaniak, Formanczyk, Furmanek—Polish. Transformations of and cognates to the Czech and Jewish definition of Forman.

Famous Bearers: RICHARD FURMAN (1755–1825) of Esopus, New York, converted to the Baptist faith as a young man. During his life he espoused the view that the South needed a Baptist college. After he died, an academy, later called Furman University, was opened. JAMES CLEMENT FURMAN (1809–1891) of South Carolina was the president of Furman College and the son of Richard Furman. BESS FURMAN (1894–1969) of Nebraska was a pioneer female journalist who covered the White House and women's activities for the *New York Times'* Washington bureau.

Genealogies: *"Gumption": Being a Genealogical and Historical Perspective of the Ancestors of Howard Remington Furman, Sr.* was compiled by Howard Remington Furman and published in Spokane, Washington, in 1979. *Kith and Kin: A Portrait of a Southern Family (1630–1934)* was compiled by Carolyn L. Harrell and published in Macon, Georgia, in 1983.

FURR

Ranking: 3914 **S.S. Count:** 11,517

Origin: English. The name was given to those who worked making or selling fur coats and other items made of fur.

Genealogies: None known.

FUSCO

Ranking: 3844 **S.S. Count:** 11,722

Origin: Italian. 1) derived from the Latin word "fuscus," meaning dark. The name was given to those who were dark or swarthy. 2) same derivation as in 1, but evolved from the Roman name Fuscus.

Genealogies: None known.

GABEL

Ranking: 4982 S.S. Count: 9000

Origin: German, Jewish. German: 1) derived from the Old High German word "gabala," meaning fork. The name was given to those who worked making and/or selling forks and to those who lived near a fork in a road. 2) derived from the Slavic word "jablo," meaning apple tree. The name was given to those who came from Gabel, a place in Germany. Jewish: uncertain etymology. Possibly a cognate to either of the above.

Genealogies: None known.

GABLE

Ranking: 3342 S.S. Count: 13,556

Origin: English. Derived from the Old Norse word "gafl," meaning gable, which is a triangular hill. The name was given to those who came from Gable, the name of several places in England.

Famous **Gables**: WILLIAM CLARK GABLE (1901–1960) of Ohio worked as a telephone repairman and an oil-field tool dresser before deciding on a career in acting. He became America's leading man during the period when talking pictures were just becoming popular. Among his best-known movies were *Gone with the Wind, The Misfits,* and *It Happened One Night,* for which he won an Academy Award.

Genealogies: *Mayflower to the Moon: Herveys & Gables* was compiled by Donald G. Hervey and published in Houston, Texas, in 1980.

GABRIE (ALSO GABRIELSEN, GABRIEL, GABRIELLI, GABRIELE, GABRIELI, GABRIELY, GABRIELSKI, GABRIELSSON)

Ranking: 1257 S.S. Count: 35,029

Origin: Gabrie—Provençal; Gabrielsen—Danish, Norwegian; Gabriel—English, French, German, Jewish, Portuguese, Scottish, Spanish; Gabrielli, Gabriele—Italian; Gabrieli—Italian, Jewish; Gabriely, Gabrielski—Jewish; Gabrielsson—Swedish. Derived from the Hebrew first name Gavriel, meaning "God has given me strength" (H&H).

Famous **Bearers**: GABRIEL (1776?–1800) of Virginia, whose slave name was Gabriel Prosser, planned the first major, but unsuccessful, slave rebellion in the United States. His goal of becoming king of an independent black state in Virginia was shattered when a severe summer storm scattered his forces in 1800. After arrest and trial, he was hanged.

Genealogies: None known.

GADDIS

Ranking: 3714 S.S. Count: 12,162

Origin: English. Derived from the first name Gadd, meaning comrade.

Genealogies: None known.

GADDY

Ranking: 4098 S.S. Count: 11,023

Origin: English. Transformation of Gadd(is).

Genealogies: None known.

GAFFNEY (S.S. Abbreviation: Gaffne)

Ranking: 2360 S.S. Count: 19,209

Origin: Irish. Derived from the Gaelic name Ó Gamhna, meaning "descendant of Gamhain" (H&H), meaning calf.

Genealogies: *Notes on George Washington Gaddy and Family* was compiled by Frank C. Rigler and published in Austin, Texas, in 1972. *A Springer Family History: Some Descendants of Dennis Springer and Ann Prickett, including Family Histories for Prickett, Gaddis, McIntire, et al.* was compiled by Ruth Beckey Irwin and published in Columbus, Ohio, in 1987.

GAGE

Ranking: 2038 S.S. Count: 22,426

Origin: English, French. 1) derived from the Middle English and Old French word "ga(u)ge," meaning measure. The name was given to those who worked checking the accuracy of measures. 2) derived from the Middle English and Old French word "gage," meaning surety. The name was given to those who worked as money lenders.

Famous **Gages**: THOMAS GAGE (1721–1787), born in England, was the last royal governor of Massachusetts. FRANCES DANA BARKER GAGE (1808–1884) of Ohio was a reformer and writer. After earning some fame as an author and lecturer, she presided over a statewide Ohio women's rights convention in 1853, then over a national convention in 1854, after which she began to lecture in many states. She was a speaker at the New York meeting of the newly organized American Equal Rights Association in 1864 and the author of *Poems*, a volume of poetry, and *Elsie Magoon*, a temperance novel. MATILDA JOSLYN GAGE (1826–1898) of New York was president of the National Woman Suffrage Association and founder of the Woman's National Liberal Union. LYMAN JUDSON GAGE (1836–1927) of New York was secretary of the Treasury under President William McKinley.

Genealogies: *Gage Families in the 1850 U.S. Census: Including a Gage Family Statistical Portrait and a Bibliography of Gage Genealogy* was compiled by Douglas W. Gage and published in San Diego, California, in 1992. *John Gage of Ipswich: His English Ancestry and Some American Descendants* was compiled by Duane Marshall Gage and published in North Truro, Massachusetts, in 1983.

GAGLIA (ALSO GAGLIANO, GAGLIARDI, GAGLIARDINI, GAGLIARDONE, GARLIARDUCCI)

Ranking: 3129 S.S. Count: 14,526

Origin: Italian. Derived from a Germanic first name that

is made up of the words "gail" and "hard," meaning joyous and brave.

Genealogies: None known.

GAGNE

Ranking: 3185 S.S. Count: 14,264

Origin: French. 1) the name was given to those who rented farm land. 2) the name was given to those who came from Gagne, which means "Gannus' estate" (ES) and is a place in France.

Genealogies: *A Genealogy of the French-Canadian Family Lines of Papineau, Dontigny-Lucas, Gaudin (Godin), Gagne* was compiled by Dorothy May Knudsen Chandler and published in Minneapolis, Minnesota, in 1978.

GAGNON

Ranking: 1480 S.S. Count: 30,056

Origin: French. The name was given to those who worked as peasant farmers.

Genealogies: None known.

GAINES

Ranking: 685 S.S. Count: 61,215

Origin: English. Derived from the Old French word "engaine," meaning ingenuity. The name was given to those who were considered clever.

Famous **Gaineses:** EDMUND PENDLETON GAINES (1777–1849) of Virginia was an army officer who fought in several wars. He was commander of the defense of Fort Erie during the War of 1812. JOHN POLLARD GAINES (1795–1857) of Virginia was governor of the Oregon territory. His term was one of constant turmoil over the location of the capital. MYRA CLARK GAINES (1805–1885) of Louisiana spent five decades trying to prove her claim to the substantial estate of her father, who had been married only secretly to her mother. Myra was raised as the daughter of a close friend of her father's. She first filed suit in 1835, but it wasn't until 1891—six years after her death—that the Supreme Court ordered that almost $600,000 be paid to her heirs. WESLEY JOHN GAINES (1840–1912) of Georgia was a promoter of African-American education and a bishop in the African Methodist Episcopal church. GEORGE STROTHER GAINES (1784–1873) of North Carolina was the Indian agent to the Choctaws, whom he treated with kindness and respect. Because of him, the settlers of the Mississippi territory were treated likewise by the Indians. He is the namesake of the town of Gainesville, Alabama. ARTHUR RAYMOND GAINES (1882–1977) of Pennsylvania was a physician and an army officer who was the chief of medical services at a hospital in France during World War I. FRANCIS PENDLETON GAINES (1892–1963) of South Carolina was a career university president. He first served in that capacity at Wake Forest University, then at Washington and Lee, where, under his direction, the assets of the university grew by 500 percent. IRENE MCCOY GAINES (1892?–1964) of Florida began her career as a community worker in Chicago, Illinois, where she was industrial secretary for the city's first African-American branch of the Y.W.C.A. She became a social worker for the Cook County Welfare Department and increased her activities in community and civic affairs to include serving as president (1939–1953) of the Council of Negro Organizations. She went on to become active in Illinois politics and was the first black woman to run—though unsuccessfully—for the Illinois state legislature. She was elected, however, president of the National Association of Colored Women's Clubs, in which capacity she was in great demand as a speaker.

Genealogies: *A Compilation of Gaines Family Data, With Special Emphasis on the Lineage of William and Isabella (Pendleton) Gaines* was compiled by Calvin E. Sutherd and published in Fort Lauderdale, Florida, in 1972. *Tinsley et al.: The Ancestry of My Four Honored Grandparents, William Julian Tinsley, Georgia Ann Gaines, William Henry Clarke, Jennie Elizabeth Lavender, Including the Families of Ballard* was compiled by William Eldon Tinsley and published in Pflugerville, Texas, in 1986.

GAINEY

Ranking: 4175 S.S. Count: 10,829

Origin: English? Uncertain etymology. Most likely a transformation of Gain(es).

Genealogies: None known.

GAITHER

Ranking: 3054 S.S. Count: 14,860

Origin: English. The name was given to those who tended goats.

Genealogies: None known.

GALARZA (S.S. Abbreviation: Galarz)

Ranking: 4388 S.S. Count: 10,229

Origin: Spanish. The name was given to those who came from Galarza, which means "stone mound" (ES) and is a place in Spain.

Genealogies: None known.

GALBRAITH (S.S. Abbreviation: Galbrai)

Ranking: 3442 S.S. Count: 13,108

Origin: Scottish. Derived from the Gaelic words "gall" and "Bhreathnach," meaning stranger and Briton. The name was given to the Britons' descendants living in Scotland.

Genealogies: *Galbreath* [also Galbraith] *Family Genealogy* was compiled by Joseph William Galbreath and published in Fairfield, Illinois, in 1976.

GALE

Ranking: 2083 S.S. Count: 22,019

Origin: English. 1) derived from the Middle English word "ga(i)le," meaning jovial. The name was given to those who were considered happy and lively. 2) derived from the Norman version of the Germanic first name Gal(on), which is derived separately from the words "gail" and "walh," meaning cheerful and stranger. 3) derived from the Old Northern French word "gaiole," meaning jail. The name was given to those who worked in a jail and to those who lived near a jail.

Famous **Gales:** BENJAMIN GALE (1715–1790) of New York was a physician who did important work with small-pox. GEORGE WASHINGTON GALE (1789–1861) of New York founded Oneida Institute and Knox College. Both schools were operated on a work/study principle. ELBRIDGE GALE (1824–1907) of Vermont is responsible for developing the Mulgoba mango. ZONA GALE (1874–1938) of Wisconsin was a fiction writer who won a Pulitzer Prize for her novel *Miss Lulu Bett*. She was considered an exponent of the realistic school.

Genealogies: *Genealogy of the Gale Family* was compiled by George Gale and published in Albany, New York, in 1863.

GALINDEZ, GALINDO (S.S. Abbreviation: Galind)

Ranking: 2285 S.S. Count: 19,895

Origin: Spanish. Derived from the first name Galindo.
Genealogies: None known.

GALL

Ranking: 3751 S.S. Count: 12,072

Origin: British, French, German. British: derived from the Celtic word meaning foreigner. French, German: derived from the Latin first name Gallus, which may have referred to the word "gallus," meaning cock, or to the Gauls.

Famous **Galls:** GALL (1840?–1894) of South Dakota, originally named Pizi, was a Sioux chieftain and warrior. He was war chief to Sitting Bull during the Battle of Little Big Horn (1876), where George Armstrong Custer was killed. Gall later opposed Sitting Bull, became a friend of whites, and urged education for Native Americans.

Genealogies: *Genealogy, Gall and Nothstine Families, 1730–1964* was compiled by Agnes Nothstine and published in Muskogee, Oklahoma, in 1965.

GALLAGHER (S.S. Abbreviation: Gallag)

Ranking: 391 S.S. Count: 98,914

Origin: Irish. Derived from the Gaelic name Ó Gallchobhair, meaning "descendant of Gallchobhar" (H&H), which is derived from the words "gall" and "cabhair," meaning foreign and support.

Famous **Gallaghers:** WILLIAM DAVIS GALLAGHER (1808–1894) of Pennsylvania was one of the first frontier-area poets. His works are collected in three sets of books. HUGH PATRICK GALLAGHER (1815–1882) of Ireland was a Roman Catholic priest who organized parishes, schools, orphanages, and hospitals in California. He also visited mining camps.

Genealogies: *The Seeds of the Planter: Our Family Story from 1635 to 1975* was compiled by Geraldine D. Gallagher and published in Fullerton, California, in 1975.

GALLAND, GALLANDON, GALLANT (S.S. Abbreviation: Gallan)

Ranking: 2904 S.S. Count: 15,675

Origin: French. Derived from the Old French word "galer," meaning to be enjoying and/or to be in good humor. The names were given to those who were considered to have good temperaments.

Genealogies: None known.

GALLARD, GALLARDO (S.S. Abbreviation: Gallar)

Ranking: 2690 S.S. Count: 16,928

Origin: Gallard—English; Gallardo—Spanish. English: derived from the Old French word "gaile," meaning cheerful. The name was given to those who were considered to have good temperaments. English, Spanish: derived from the Germanic first name Gailhard, which is derived from the words "gail" and "hard," meaning joyous and brave.

Genealogies: None known.

GALLEGO, GALLEGOS (S.S. Abbreviation: Galleg)

Ranking: 881 S.S. Count: 49,158

Origin: Spanish. Derived from the tribal name Gallaeci. The names were given to those who came from Galacia, a place in northwestern Spain.

Genealogies: *El Pueblo: The Gallegos Family's American Journey, 1503–1980* was compiled by Bruce Elliott Johansen and published in New York, New York, in 1983.

GALLO

Ranking: 1714 S.S. Count: 26,100

Origin: Italian, Spanish. 1) cognate to the French and German definition of Gall. 2) derived from the Latin word "gallus," meaning cock. The name was given to those who were considered to have one of the attributes of the bird, such as a nice voice or a large sexual appetite.

Genealogies: None known.

GALLOWAY (S.S. Abbreviation: Gallow)

Ranking: 888 S.S. Count: 26,10

Origin: Scottish. Derived from the Gaelic words "gall" and

"Gaidhel," meaning foreigner and Gaelic. The name was given to those who came from Galloway, a place in Scotland.

Famous **Galloways**: JOSEPH GALLOWAY (1731–1803) of Maryland was Speaker of the Pennsylvania legislature and a supporter of the British during the Revolutionary War. His 1774 plan to settle peacefully the differences between the colonies and the Crown narrowly failed in the Continental Congress. SAMUEL GALLOWAY (1811–1872) of Pennsylvania was an educator who redesigned the school system of the state of Ohio.

Genealogies: *Golladays* [also Galloway] *in America* was compiled by Ralph Jacob Golladay and published in Dayton, Virginia, in 1982. *Pioneer Families* was compiled by Becky Hardin and published in Mooresville, Indiana, in 1982.

GALVAN (ALSO GALVANI, GALVANO)
Ranking: 1636 **S.S. Count:** 27,478
Origin: Galvan—Spanish; Galvani, Galvano—Italian. Galvan: derived from the Latin first name Galbāanus, which is derived from the Roman name Galba. Galvani, Galvano: cognates to Gavin.
Genealogies: None known.

GALVIN
Ranking: 2772 **S.S. Count:** 16,461
Origin: French, Irish. French: derived from the Old French words "galer" and "vin," meaning to enjoy oneself or waste and wine. The name was given to those who were thought to drink too much. Irish: derived from the Gaelic name Ó Gealbháin, meaning "descendant of Gealbhán" (H&H), which is derived from the words "geal" and "bán," meaning bright and white.
Genealogies: None known.

GAMBLE, GAMBLES, GAMBLIN, GAMBLING
Ranking: 914 **S.S. Count:** 47,147
Origin: English. Derived from the Old Norse name Gamall, meaning old.
Famous **Bearers**: HAMILTON ROWAN GAMBLE (1798–1864) of Virginia was the judge at the first Dred Scott trial. He dissented in favor of Scott. Later, as governor of Missouri, he tried to keep the state pro-Union.
Genealogies: *The Descendants of Bradley Gambill* [also Gamble] was compiled by Louise G. Brown and published in Columbia, Tennessee, in 1979. *Early Families of Blount County, Alabama: Gamble, Sapp, Williams* was compiled by Carolina Nigg and published in Cullman, Alabama, in 1982.

GAMBOA
Ranking: 4466 **S.S. Count:** 10,038
Origin: Spanish. The name was given to those who came from Gaboa, which means quince (a kind of fruit) and is a place in Spain.

Genealogies: None known.

GAMBRELL (S.S. Abbreviation: Gambre)
Ranking: 4977 **S.S. Count:** 9005
Origin: French. Derived from the Latin word "gamba," meaning bend or knee.
Famous **Gambrells**: JAMES BRUTON GAMBRELL (1841–1921) of South Carolina was the president of Mercer College and the secretary of the Baptist General Convention of Texas.
Genealogies: *A Gambrell Album* was compiled by Esther Gambrell Deviney and published in Austin, Texas, in 1974.

GAMEZ
Ranking: 4504 **S.S. Count:** 9944
Origin: Spanish. Derived from the Spanish word "gamo," meaning fallow deer. The name was given to those who were considered to be shy.
Genealogies: None known.

GAMMON, GAMMOND
Ranking: 3986 **S.S. Count:** 11,341
Origin: English. 1) derived from the Old English word "gamen," meaning amusement. The names were given to those who were considered cheerful. 2) derived from the Anglo-Norman-French word "gambon," meaning ham.
Famous **Bearers**: ELIJAH HEDDING GAMMON (1819–1881) of Maine was a manufacturer of farm machinery and the partner of prominent industrialist William Deering. He was the founder of Gammon Theological Seminary in Atlanta. Most of his wealth went to religious and educational causes.
Genealogies: None known.

GANDY
Ranking: 3408 **S.S. Count:** 13,270
Origin: English. Uncertain etymology. Possibly derived from the Old French word "gant," meaning glove. The name may have been given to those who worked making gloves or to those who habitually wore gloves.
Genealogies: None known.

GANN
Ranking: 2604 **S.S. Count:** 17,433
Origin: German. The name means magic.
Genealogies: None known.

GANNON
Ranking: 2218 **S.S. Count:** 20,722
Origin: Irish. Derived from the Gaelic name Mag Fhionnán, which is derived from the word "fionn," meaning white.
Genealogies: None known.

GANT

Ranking: 2458 S.S. Count: 18,474

Origin: English. Derived from the Old French word "gant," meaning glove. The name was given to those who worked making or selling gloves.

Genealogies: None known.

GANTT

Ranking: 3590 S.S. Count: 12,567

Origin: English. Transformation of Gant.

Genealogies: *Gaunt-Gantt Family: Some of the Descendants of Peter Gaunt of Sandwich, Massachusetts* was compiled by Mary Chalfant Ormsbee and published in Boulder, Colorado, in 1983. *Peter Gaunt (also Gantt), 1610–1680 and Some of His Descendants* was compiled by David L. Gauntt and published in Woodbury, New Jersey, in 1988.

GARBER (ALSO GARBERDING)

Ranking: 2386 S.S. Count: 19,025

Origin: Garber—English, German, Jewish; Garberding—German. Garber (English): derived from the Middle English and Old French word "garbe," meaning wheat sheaf. The name was given to those who worked binding wheat into sheaves or to those who collected wheat sheaves. German: transformation of Garbering. Garber (German, Jewish): transformation of Gerber. Garberding: derived from the Norman first name Gerberht, which is derived from the Germanic words "geri" and "berht," meaning spear and famous.

Genealogies: *Ancestors of Jacob & Esther Garber and Their Descendants* was compiled by Dean K. Garber and published in Goshen, Indiana, in 1970.

GARCIA

Ranking: 30 S.S. Count: 641,404

Origin: Spanish. Uncertain etymology. The name is most likely pre-Roman and may in some cases be derived from the Basque word "(h)artz," meaning bear.

Famous **Garcias**: JEROME JOHN (JERRY) GARCIA (1942–) of California has been a guitarist for the band the Grateful Dead since 1966.

Genealogies: None known.

GARDIN (ALSO GARDINER, GARDINOR, GARDINIER))

Ranking: 2334 S.S. Count: 19,429

Origin: Gardiner, Gardinor—English; Gardinier, Gardin—French. Transformations of and cognates to Gardener.

Famous **Bearers**: LION GARDINER (1599–1663) of England was an engineer and a colonist. He was the builder of Saybrook Fort in what is now Old Saybrook, Connecticut. He also was the co-commander in the Pequot War.

SILVESTER GARDINER (1706–1786) of Rhode Island was a Loyalist and the founder of Pittston and Gardiner, Maine. JOHN GARDINER (1737–1793) of Massachusetts was a lawyer who zealously pursued legal reform in colonial courts. ROBERT HALLOWELL GARDINER (1782–1864) of England was the founder of Gardiner (Maine) Lyceum, which was the forerunner of the agricultural and technical schools to come. JAMES TERRY GARDINER (1842–1912) of New York was the chief topographer of the team that surveyed the 40th parallel. He also worked to have proper sewage treatment systems installed in New York.

Genealogies: *The Gardiner-Squires Connection: An Account of the Gardiner Family of Gardiner's Island, Long Island, New York, and the Squires Family of Squiretown, Long Island, New York and West Haven, Connecticut, Their Connections and Allied Families* was compiled by Tiger Gardiner and published in Baltimore, Maryland, in 1989.

GARDNER (S.S. Abbreviation: Gardne)

Ranking: 172 S.S. Count: 195,590

Origin: English. Transformation of Gardener.

Famous **Gardners**: CALEB GARDNER (1739–1806) of Rhode Island was a Revolutionary War soldier who piloted the French fleet into Newport, Rhode Island, in 1780. ALEXANDER GARDNER (1821–1882), born in Scotland, was a photographer noted for his images of the Civil War, railroad construction in the West, and Great Plains Native Americans. He had his own studio in Washington, D.C. ISABELLA STEWART GARDNER (1840–1924) of New York was a prominent art collector in Boston. Her collection of classical and contemporary works was left to the city of Boston on her death, along with her gallery, known as the Isabella Stewart Gardner Museum. MARY SEWALL GARDNER (1871–1961) of Massachusetts joined the public-health nursing service in its early years and helped to shape its future. She was active in the creation of and was later president of the National Organization of Public Health Nursing. Her book *Public Health Nursing* (1916) is considered a classic. HELEN GARDNER (1878–1946) of New Hampshire was the author of *Art Through the Ages*, a book that became a text for college courses in art history. She revised and published two later editions, the last of which was in galley proofs when she died. JULIA ANNA GARDNER (1882–1960) of Illinois was a prominent geologist with the U.S. Geological Survey (USGS). She was co-author of *Correlation of the Cenozoic Formations of the Atlantic and Gulf Coastal Plain and the Caribbean Region* (1943). Working with the USGS Military Geology Unit during World War II, she helped to pinpoint Japanese beaches from which balloon-borne incendiary bombs were launched toward U.S. Pacific Northwest forests. LEROY UPSON GARDNER (1888–1946) of Connecticut was a physician who found the connection between silica dust and tuberculosis. His work led to the implementation of safety measures in mining. ERLE STANLEY GARDNER (1889–1970) of Massachusetts was a lawyer and author of about 80 detective novels featuring the character Perry Mason. He also wrote two other series of books and other travel books.

Genealogies: *The Ancestors and Descendants of Henry Wood Gardner and Mary Brown Rathbone* was compiled by Ellen Gardner Brown and published in Atlantis, Florida, in 1985. *Gardner and Allied Families: Brown, Carson, Clyburn, Du Pont, Guerri, Guild, Ingram, Knight, Michau, Ogburn, Plyler, Rembert, Wells, Welsh* was compiled by William Leonard Gardner and published in Baltimore, Maryland, in 1979.

GARLAND, GARLANT (S.S. Abbreviation: Garlan)

Ranking: 1231 S.S. Count: 35,974

Origin: English. 1) derived from the Old English words "gāra" and "land," meaning triangular piece of land and land. The names were given to those who came from Garland, the name of a place in Devon, England. 2) the names were given to those who made garlands.

Famous **Bearers:** LANDON CABELL GARLAND (1810–1895) of Virginia was the president of several universities, including Randolph-Macon and the University of Alabama. HAMLIN GARLAND (1860–1940) of Wisconsin wrote a number of books, including *A Daughter of the Middle Border*, for which he won a Pulitzer Prize in 1921. JUDY GARLAND (1922–1969) of Minnesota was born Frances Gumm. She was an actress and a singer best known for her roles in the movies *The Wizard of Oz, Meet Me in St. Louis*, and *Judgment at Nuremberg*. The last 15 years of her life she fought alcoholism, drug addiction, and depression. She committed suicide in 1969. Her daughter Liza Minelli, whose father was the movie director Vincente Minelli, is also an actress and a singer.

Genealogies: *Warren and Ethel (Garland) Markwith, Their Ancestors, Descendants, and Related Families* was compiled by Joseph H. Vance and published in Lombard, Illinois, in 1982.

GARMAN

Ranking: 4034 S.S. Count: 11,225

Origin: English. Transformation of the first English definition of Gorman.

Famous **Garmans:** SAMUEL GARMAN (1843–1927) of Pennsylvania was an authority on sharks, skates, and rays. CHARLES EDWARD GARMAN (1850–1907) was a philosophy teacher at Amherst College.

Genealogies: *The Family of Samuel Garman in America: A Genealogical History* was compiled by Leo H. Garman and published in Elmhurst, Illinois, in 1977. *The Family of Johannes Germann (John Garman) in America: A Genealog-*

ical History was compiled by Leo H. Garman and published in Elmhurst, Illinois, in 1979.

GARNER

Ranking: 387 S.S. Count: 99,930

Origin: English. 1) transformation of Gardener. 2) transformation of the first definition of Warner. 3) derived from the Anglo-Norman-French word "gerner," meaning granary. The name was given to those who worked at a granary and to those who lived near a granary.

Famous **Garners:** JOHN NANCE GARNER (1868–1967) of Texas, known as "Cactus Jack," was U.S. vice president during President Franklin D. Roosevelt's first two terms. Although he served in the New Deal administration, he maintained deeply conservative political sentiments. JAMES WILFORD GARNER (1871–1938) was an authority on international law. He taught at the University of Illinois.

Genealogies: *Garner Genealogy: Record of the Descendants of Reverend James Garner II, Soldier of the American Revolution* was compiled by B. Irene Garner Mooney and published in Glendale, California, in 1977. *Southern Garners: Our Branch of the Garner-Keene Family* was compiled by Sam Garner and published in Rome, Georgia, in 1979.

GARNET, GARNETT

Ranking: 3039 S.S. Count: 14,969

Origin: English. 1) derived from the Old French word "(pome) grenate," meaning pomegranates. The names were given to those who sold pomegranates. 2) derived from the Old French word "carne," meaning hinge. The names were given to those who worked making or placing hinges. 3) transformations of Garner.

Famous **Bearers:** JAMES MERCER GARNETT (1770–1843) of Virginia was an agriculturist and an educator. He urged planters to use better methods in farming, including crop rotation, careful seed selection, and the use of fertilizers. He spoke in favor of a state school system. HENRY HIGHLAND GARNET (1815–1882) of Maryland, born a slave, was a leader in the abolitionist movement. In a New York speech, he urged slaves to kill their masters. He later served as U.S. minister to Liberia. JAMES MERCER GARNETT (1840–1916) of Virginia was a scholar and the first American to translate *Beowulf* from the Anglo-Saxon. He was the grandson of James Mercer Garnett (b. 1770). CHRISTOPHER BROWNE GARNETT JR. (1906–1975) of Virginia, a philosopher and professor, was a U.S. cultural officer in Germany immediately following World War II. He is credited with saving the public school records of East Germany by removing them from the Russian sector of Berlin two days before the Soviet blockade. He helped found the Free University and the American Memorial Library in Berlin. ALEXANDER YELVERTON PEYTON GARNETT (1818–1888) was the personal physician to Jefferson Davis. After the Civil

War he worked to improve standards of medical ethics. SARAH J. SMITH THOMPSON GARNET (1831–1911) of New York was the first African-American woman to become a principal in the New York City public-school system. She was principal at P.S. 80 from 1863 to 1900.

Genealogies: None known.

GARRETT, GARRETTS (S.S. Abbreviation: Garret)

Ranking: 228 **S.S. Count:** 153,315

Origin: English. 1) derived from the first name Gerard, which is derived from the Germanic words "geri" and "hard," meaning spear and brave. 2) derived from the first name Gerald, which is derived from the Germanic words "geri" and "wald," meaning spear and rule.

Famous **Bearers:** ROBERT GARRETT (1783–1857) of Ireland was a merchant who worked to build a better transportation system between Maryland and the West to better his chances of trade with that area of the continent. He also set up his own banking house for foreign trading. THOMAS GARRETT (1789–1871) of Delaware was an abolitionist who helped 2700 slaves escape to the North. JOHN WORK GARRETT (1820–1884) of Maryland was the son of Robert Garrett. He was the president of the B&O Railroad, which he used during the Civil War to transport 20,000 Union troops. This was the first time a railroad had been used in a war. EMMA GARRETT (1846?–1893) of Pennsylvania, a teacher of the deaf, was a strong advocate of the vocal approach in teaching, as opposed to just sign language. Her sister, MARY SMITH GARRETT (1839–1925) of Pennsylvania, also was an educator of the deaf. She worked with her sister, then succeeded her (after Emma's suicide) as principal of the Bala Home for the Deaf in Philadelphia.

Genealogies: *A Book of Garretts, 1600–1960,* was compiled by Hester Elizabeth Garrett and published in Lansing, Michigan, in 1963. *Garrett, Catlett, Ware, and Related Families* was compiled by Sunie Garrett Talbert Elliott Fisher and published in North Augusta, South Carolina, in 1989.

GARRISH, GARRISON (S.S. Abbreviation: Garris)

Ranking: 489 **S.S. Count:** 82,815

Origin: English. Garrish: transformation of the second English definition of Geary. Garrison: transformation of Garrett.

Famous **Bearers:** WILLIAM LLOYD GARRISON (1805–1879) of Massachusetts was an abolitionist who established *The Liberator,* one of the best-known antislavery journals. CORNELIUS KINGSLAND GARRISON (1809–1885) of New York was the mayor of San Francisco and a financier. WILLIAM RE TALLACK GARRISON (1834–1882) of Canada was responsible for the completion of the New York elevated railway system. LUCY MCKIM GARRISON (1842–1877) of Pennsylva-

nia was a musician and publisher of some of the earliest slave songs to be set to written words and music. She was co-author of *Slave Songs of the United States* (1867), which was reprinted in 1929 and 1951. LINDLEY MILLER GARRISON (1864–1932) of New Jersey was the U.S. secretary of war at the beginning of World War I. He told President Woodrow Wilson of the country's need for a larger army, and while Wilson verbally agreed with him, he did not act on the advice. Garrison resigned, but his actions brought the problem to light and were instrumental in the initiation of the National Defense Act of 1916.

Genealogies: *Descendants of Caleb Garrison Sr., and His Wife, Sarah Fleming, 1797–1966* was compiled by John Garrison Ross and published in Angleton, Texas, in 1967. *The Family of Isaac Garrison, 1732–1836: A Frontiersman and Soldier of the American Revolution* was compiled by The Isaac Garrison Family Association and published in Sentinel, Oklahoma, in 1980.

GARRIT

Ranking: 4023 **S.S. Count:** 11,259

Origin: English. 1) transformation of Garrett. 2) cognate to Garriga.

Genealogies: None known.

GARVEY

Ranking: 2942 **S.S. Count:** 15,476

Origin: Irish. Derived from the Gaelic first name Garbhith, which is derived from the word "garbh," meaning cruel.

Genealogies: None known.

GARVIN

Ranking: 2365 **S.S. Count:** 19,177

Origin: Irish. Derived from the Gaelic name Ó Gairbhín, meaning "descendant of Gairbhín" (H&H), a first name derived from the word "garbh," meaning cruel.

Famous **Garvins:** LUCIUS FAYETTE CLARK GARVIN (1841–1922) of Tennessee served for many years in Rhode Island politics and was governor of that state (1903–1905).

Genealogies: *The Garvin Genealogy: Descendants of Henry and Sarah McKee Garvin of Ireland and Pennsylvania* was compiled by Richard M. Cochran Sr. and published in South Bend, Indiana, in 1983. *Family Stories: The Garvins* was compiled by Robert Garvin and published in Albuquerque, New Mexico, in 1979.

GARY

Ranking: 1542 **S.S. Count:** 28,922

Origin: English. Transformation of the first English definition of Geary.

Famous **Garys:** JAMES ALBERT GARY (1833–1920) of Connecticut was a cotton manufacturer and banker and the U.S. postmaster general. ELBERT HENRY GARY (1846–

1927) of Illinois was chairman and chief executive officer of the U.S. Steel Corp. for 26 years. The city of Gary, Indiana, is named for him.

Genealogies: *Irish Roots: (A Genealogy of Ryan, Gary, and Allied Families)* was compiled by Mary Zacchaeus Ryan and published in Faribault, Minnesota, in 1980. *Our Jolly Granpas: The Jolly, Gary, Cockle, O[l]mstead, Vancleave, Demarest, and Allied Families* was compiled by Mrs. Iver Longeteig and published in Craigmont, Idaho, in 1974.

GARZA
Ranking: 337 **S.S. Count:** 112,312
Origin: Spanish. Transformation of Garcia.
Genealogies: *Origin of the Surnames Garza and Trevino in Nuevo Leon* was compiled by Tomas Mendirichaga Cueva, translated by Edna G. Brown, and published in Corpus Christi, Texas, in 1989. *Stolen Heritage: A Mexican-American's Rediscovery of His Family's Lost Land Grant* was compiled by Abel G. Rubio and published in Austin, Texas, in 1986.

GASKIN, GASKING
Ranking: 1941 **S.S. Count:** 23,295
Origin: English. Derived from the Old French word "Gascogne," meaning Gascony and referring to the Basques who lived in the area before the Middle Ages.
Genealogies: None known.

GASPARD (ALSO GASPARIN, GASPAROUX, GASPAR, GASPARY, GASPARDI, GASPARI, GASPARO, GASPARRI, GASPARRO, ET AL.)
Ranking: 2705 **S.S. Count:** 16,812
Origin: Gaspard, Gasparin, Gasparoux—French; Gaspar—French, Hungarian, Portuguese; Gaspary—German, Jewish; Gaspardi, Gaspari, Gasparo, Gasparri, Gasparro et al.—Italian. Cognates to and transformations of Kasper.
Genealogies: None known.

GASPERIN, GASPERI, GASPERINI, GASPERO, GASPERONI, GASPEROTTI ET AL. (S.S. Abbreviation: Gasper)
Ranking: 4624 **S.S. Count:** 9661
Origin: Gasperin—French; Gasperi, Gasperini, Gaspero, Gasperoni, Gasperotti et al.—Italian. Cognates to Kaspar.
Genealogies: None known.

GASS
Ranking: 4387 **S.S. Count:** 10,232
Origin: English, German, Jewish. English: derived from the Norman first name Wazo, which is most likely derived from the word "wad," meaning to go. German, Jewish: derived from the German word "gasse" and the Yiddish word "gas,"

both meaning street. The name was given to those who lived on a narrow road.

Famous Gasses: PATRICK GASS (1771–1870) of Pennsylvania was an explorer who wrote *Journal of the Voyages and Travels of a Corps of Discovery, etc.*, the first published journal of the Lewis and Clark expedition.

Genealogies: None known.

GASTON
Ranking: 1710 **S.S. Count:** 26,152
Origin: French. Derived from an Old French version of a Germanic first name derived from the word "gasti," meaning stranger.
Genealogies: *The Gaston, Howard, and Wilkinson Families: A Genealogical History of Three Inter-Married Families in the Black Belt of Alabama* was compiled by Kathleen Wilkinson Wood and published in Baltimore, Maryland, in 1976.

GATES
Ranking: 561 **S.S. Count:** 73,168
Origin: English. Derived from the Old English word "gatu," meaning gates. The name was given to those who lived near the gates of a town.

Famous Gateses: SIR THOMAS GATES (?–1621) of England was a governor of Virginia and the person responsible for laying the foundation for a prosperous government there before he returned to England. HORATIO GATES (1728?–1806), born in England, emigrated to Virginia and served as an officer under George Washington in the American Revolution. FREDERICK TAYLOR GATES (1853–1929) of New York was a Baptist minister whose fundraising efforts led John D. Rockefeller Sr. to donate $600,000 to open the University of Chicago. He later became president of 13 of Rockefeller's businesses. JOHN WARNE GATES (1855–1911) of Illinois, whose nickname was Bet-a-Million Gates, was a notorious speculator in the New York stock market. He made a fortune, lost it, then went into the oil business in Texas. CALEB FRANK GATES (1857–1946) was a missionary in Turkey who served as the president of several Turkish universities. THOMAS SOVEREIGN GATES (1873–1948) of Pennsylvania was a banker and president of the University of Pennsylvania, a position he took without salary to reorganize its finances. SAMUEL EUGENE GATES (1906–1979) of Indiana was a lawyer and an airline specialist who was instrumental in drafting the Civil Aeronautics Act of 1938.

Genealogies: *Gates Garden: Roots and Branches of Chester Gates and Maria Sheely* was compiled by Alice Gates Penrose and published in Warsaw, Indiana, in 1991. *My Gates Ancestry: Ancestry of Samuel Gates (1785–1841) of Bridgton, Maine, Waterford, Ohio, and Greene County, Illinois and Descendants of His Daughter, Phebe Gates*

Strawn of Jacksonville, Illinois was compiled by Margaret Tomlin Bellatti and published in Jacksonville, Illinois, in 1979. *Getz [also Gates] Genealogy* was compiled by O. E. Sunday and most likely published in Philadelphia, Pennsylvania, in 1961.

GATEWOOD   (S.S. Abbreviation: Gatewo)
Ranking: 3958 **S.S. Count:** 11,422
Origin: English. 1) the name was given to those who lived near the edge or entrance of a wood. 2) derived from the Old High German word "geiz," meaning goat. The name was given to those who lived in or near a wood that was home to goats.
Genealogies: *Atwell Bowcock Gatewood, His Ancestry and Descendants* was compiled by Gorden Jefferson Gatewood and most likely published in Tulia, Texas, in 1981. *Carr and Gatewood Families* was compiled by Emma Gatewood Samuel and published in Poteau, Oklahoma, in 1980.

GATLIN, GATLING
Ranking: 2624 **S.S. Count:** 17,324
Origin: English. The name was at first given to those who were considered to be companionable, and later to those who were considered idle.
Famous **Bearers:** RICHARD JORDAN GATLING (1818–1903) of North Carolina invented a hemp-breaking machine and other agricultural tools and the first practical machine gun for use by the North during the Civil War.
Genealogies: None known.

GAUDET, GAUDETTE
Ranking: 4159 **S.S. Count:** 10,873
Origin: French. Derived from the French first name Gaud, a cognate to Waldo, meaning ruler.
Genealogies: *The Gaudet Family* was compiled by Mr. and Mrs. Elmer L. Gaudet and published in Natchez, Mississippi, in 1970.

GAULT
Ranking: 4798 **S.S. Count:** 9336
Origin: English. Derived from the Old Norse word "goltr," meaning wild boar. The name was given to those who were thought to have some attribute of the boar or perhaps to those who hunted the animal.
Genealogies: None known.

GAUTHIER, GAUTHIEZ   (S.S. Abbreviation: Gauthi)
Ranking: 1980 **S.S. Count:** 22,888
Origin: French. Cognates to Walter.
Genealogies: *Genealogies* was compiled by Amesse A. Gauthier and George H. Gauthier and most likely published in New York, New York, in 1969.

GAVIN
Ranking: 2620 **S.S. Count:** 17,342
Origin: English. Derived from the Middle English first name Gawayne and the Old French first name Gauvin, both of which may be derived from an Old Welsh first name derived from the words "gwalch" and "gwyn," meaning hawk and white.
Genealogies: None known.

GAY
Ranking: 860 **S.S. Count:** 50,017
Origin: Catalan, English, French. Catalan: derived from the Latin first name Gauis, which may be of Etruscan origin. Catalan, English, French: the name was given to those who were considered cheerful. English: the name was given to those who came from Gaye, the name of several places in Normandy, France.
Famous **Gays:** EBENEZER GAY (1696–1787) of Massachusetts was a Congregational minister and a forerunner of the Unitarian movement in the United States. SYDNEY HOWARD GAY (1814–1888) of Massachusetts, the great-grandson of Ebenezer Gay, was a journalist. He edited *American Anti-Slavery Standard* and was the managing editor of the *New York Tribune* and the *Chicago Tribune.* WINCKWORTH ALLAN GAY (1821–1910) of Massachusetts was a landscape painter and one of the first Americans to be considered an artist of the new "naturalist" style of painting. FREDERICK PARKER GAY (1874–1939) of Massachusetts was responsible for the introduction of bacteriology and immunology as separate disciplines. LESLIE NEWTON GAY (1891–1978) of Pennsylvania was a physician and the founder of the allergy clinic at Johns Hopkins Hospital.
Genealogies: *John Gay of Wiltshire, England and the Town of Elba, Dodge County, Wisconsin and Some of His Descendants in America* was compiled by Grace Gay Sponem and published in Madison, Wisconsin, in 1990.

GAYLOR, GAYLORD
Ranking: 3634 **S.S. Count:** 12,397
Origin: English. Gaylor: transformation of the third definition of Gale. Gaylord: 1) derived from the Germanic first name Gailhard, which is derived from the words "gail" and "hard," meaning joyous and brave. 2) derived from the Old French word "gaile," meaning cheerful. The name was given to those who were considered robust and loud.
Genealogies: *Gaylords and Gildersleeves and Some Lateral Branches* was compiled by Helen Gaylord Gildersleeve and published in Decorah, Iowa, in 1989.

GEARHART   (S.S. Abbreviation: Gearha)
Ranking: 4114 **S.S. Count:** 10,977

Origin: German. Cognate to the first definition of Garrett.
Genealogies: None known.

GEARY
Ranking: 2640 **S.S. Count:** 17,237
Origin: English, Irish. English: 1) derived from a Germanic first name derived from the word "geri," meaning spear. 2) derived from the Middle English word "ge(a)ry," meaning fickle. The name was given to those who were thought to be capricious. Irish: derived from the Gaelic name Ó Gadhra, meaning "descendant of Gadhra" (H&H), which is derived from the word "gadhar," meaning hound.
Famous **Gearys:** JOHN WHITE GEARY (1819–1873) of Pennsylvania had a long career as a soldier and politician. He fought in the Mexican War and the Civil War. He was the first mayor of San Francisco, a territorial governor of Kansas, and a governor of Pennsylvania.
Genealogies: None known.

GEBHARD, GEBHARDT (S.S. Abbreviation: Gebhar)
Ranking: 2921 **S.S. Count:** 15,580
Origin: German. Derived from a Germanic first name that is derived from the words "geb" and "hard," meaning gift and brave.
Genealogies: None known.

GEE
Ranking: 1439 **S.S. Count:** 31,082
Origin: English. Uncertain etymology.
Genealogies: *Descendants of Solomon Gee of Lyme, Connecticut* was compiled by Charles E. Benjamin and most likely published in New Haven, Indiana, in 1981. *The Kin of Dr. Ned Gee, Lunenburg County, Virginia* was compiled by Samuel Edward Gee and published in Arlington, Virginia, in 1975.

GEER
Ranking: 3773 **S.S. Count:** 11,979
Origin: English. Transformation of Geary.
Genealogies: None known.

GEIGER
Ranking: 1425 **S.S. Count:** 31,291
Origin: German, Jewish. Derived from the Middle High German word "gige," meaning violin. The name was given to those who worked playing the fiddle.
Famous **Geigers:** ROY STANLEY GEIGER (1885–1947) of Florida was a Marine Corps officer and a naval pilot. He served in World Wars I and II.
Genealogies: *A Brief Digest of the Geiger Family in Mis-*

souri was compiled by Erwin J. Otis and published in Dearborn, Michigan, in 1959.

GELLER (ALSO GELLERMANN, GELLERT, GELLERMAN, GELLERSTEIN)
Ranking: 3999 **S.S. Count:** 11,314
Origin: Geller, Gellermann—German, Jewish; Gellert—German; Gellerman, Gellerstein—Jewish. Geller, Gellermann: derived from an ancient word meaning marshland. The names were given to those who came from Geldern, the name of a place in Germany, and to those who came from Gelderland, the name of a place in the Netherlands. Geller Gellert: derived from the Middle High German word "gellære," meaning town crier. The names were given to those who worked as such. Geller: derived from the Yiddish word "gel," meaning red. The name was given to those with red hair. Geller, Gellerman: transformations of Heller. Gellerstein: derived from the German words "gel" and "stein," meaning yellow and stone. The name was most often taken ornamentally.
Genealogies: None known.

GENTILE (ALSO GENTIL, GENTILLEAU, GENTILI, GENTILINI, GENTILLOTTI, GENTILLUCCI)
Ranking: 1939 **S.S. Count:** 23,303
Origin: Gentile—English, Italian; Gentil, Gentilleau—French; Gentili, Gentilini, Gentillotti, Gentillucci—Italian. Derived from the Middle English and Old French word "gent(il)," meaning well-born and/or noble. The names were given to those who were born into the upper classes and, in an ironic sense, to those who were born into the lower classes.
Genealogies: None known.

GENTRY
Ranking: 714 **S.S. Count:** 59,054
Origin: English. Transformation of Gentile.
Genealogies: None known.

GEORGE (ALSO GEORGESON, GEORGEL, GEORGELIN, GEORGEAU, GEORGEOT, GEROGEON ET AL., GEORGES, GEORGESCU)
Ranking: 209 **S.S. Count:** 169,643
Origin: George—English, French, German; Georgeson—English; Georgel, Georgelin, Georgeau, Georgeot, Gerogeon et al.—French; Georges—French, German; Georgescu—Romanian. Derived from the Greek first name Geōrgios, which is derived from the word "geōrgos," meaning farmer.
Famous **Bearers:** JAMES ZACHARIAH GEORGE (1826–1897) of Georgia was a soldier and U.S. Senator from Mississippi. He advocated the workers' right to organize. HENRY GEORGE (1839–1897) of Pennsylvania was a self-

taught economist whose idea of a single tax was popular during the 1873–1878 depression. HENRY GEORGE (1862–1916) of California was the son of Henry George (b. 1839). He was a journalist and the author of *Life of Henry George.* WILLIAM REUBEN GEORGE (1866–1936) of New York founded the George Junior Republic, which was an institution of self-government for teenagers. HENRY EDDY GEORGE (1927–1963) of New York was a pioneer in the manufacture of mobile homes.

Genealogies: *The DeMilles (also George): An American Family* was compiled by Anne Edwards and published in New York, New York, in 1988. *George Genealogy* was compiled by Keith H. George and published in Arizona in 1991.

GERARD (ALSO GERARDET, GERARDI)
Ranking: 2430 **S.S. Count:** 18,666
Origin: Gerard—English, French; Gerardet—French; Gerardi—Italian. Transformations of and cognates to the first definition of Garrett.

Famous **Bearers:** JAMES WATSON GERARD (1794–1874) of New York was the founder of the Society for the Reformation of Juvenile Delinquents. Its House of Refuge was the first one of its kind in the country.
Genealogies: None known.

GERBER (ALSO GERBERT, GERBERDING, GERBERICH)
Ranking: 1820 **S.S. Count:** 24,792
Origin: Gerber—German, Jewish; Gerbert—French, German; Gerberding, Gerberich—German. Gerber: derived from the Old High German word "(ledar)garawo," meaning leather preparer. The name was given to those who worked as tanners. Gerbert, Gerberding, Gerberich: derived from the Norman first name Gerberht, which is derived from the Germanic words "geri" and "berht," meaning spear and famous.

Genealogies: *A Genealogy of the Families of Michael and Anna Maria Gerber and Andrew and Anna Smith* was compiled by Gene Francis Noterman and most likely published in Adams, Minnesota, in 1977.

GERHARD, GERHARDT, GERHARTZ (S.S. Abbreviation: Gerhar)
Ranking: 2363 **S.S. Count:** 19,195
Origin: German. Cognates to the first definition of Garrett.

Famous **Bearers:** WILLIAM WOOD GERHARD (1809–1872) of Pennsylvania was the physician who discovered the difference between typhus and typhoid fever.
Genealogies: None known.

GERLACH, GERLACHER (S.S. Abbreviation: Gerlac)
Ranking: 4205 **S.S. Count:** 10,742

Origin: German. Uncertain etymology. Possibly derived from the Old English first name Gārlāc, which is derived from the words "gār" and "lāc," meaning spear and sport.

Genealogies: *Homer and Lillie Gerlach and Their Gerlach, Glick, Little, and Hempfield Ancestry* was compiled by Elmer K. Gerlach and published in McConnelsville, Ohio, in 1981.

GERMAIN, GERMAINE (S.S. Abbreviation: Germai)
Ranking: 4672 **S.S. Count:** 9580
Origin: English. Transformations of German.
Genealogies: None known.

GERMAN (ALSO GERMANN, GERMANEAU, GERMANI, GERMANINI, GERMANO, GERMANOFF, GERMANOV, GERMANOVITZ)
Ranking: 1474 **S.S. Count:** 30,235
Origin: German—English; Germann—English, German; Germaneau—French; Germani, Germanini, Germano—Italian; Germanoff, Germanov, Germanovitz—Jewish. German, Germann, Germaneau, Germani, Germanini, Germano (English): 1) derived from the Latin word "Germaānus," meaning German. The names were given to those who had come from Germany and to those who traded with Germans. 2) derived from the Middle English and Old French first name Germa(i)n, which is derived from Latin words meaning brother and/or cousin. Germann (German): cognate to the second English definition of Geary. Germanoff, Germanov, Germanovitz: cognates to Hermann.

Genealogies: *The Family of Johannes Germann (John Garman) in America: A Genealogical History* was compiled by Leo H. Garman and published in Elmhurst, Illinois, in 1979. *Nicholas German Family: Westward from New York, 1799–1978* was compiled by Leo and Rozetta Guess and published in Urbandale, Iowa, most likely in 1979.

GETZ
Ranking: 4049 **S.S. Count:** 11,173
Origin: German, Jewish. Derived from the German words "Gott" and "god," meaning God and good, as they appear as the first component in several names such as Gozbert, Gozhart, and Gotelieb.

Genealogies: *Getz (Gates) Genealogy* was compiled by O. E. Sunday and most likely published in Philadelphia, Pennsylvania, in 1961.

GEYER
Ranking: 3893 **S.S. Count:** 11,588
Origin: German. Transformation of Geier.
Genealogies: None known.

GIBBON, GIBBONS

Ranking: 985 S.S. Count: 44,519

Origin: English. 1) transformation of Gilbert, through Gibb(s). 2) derived from the Germanic first name Gebwine, which is derived from the words "geba" and "wine," meaning gift and friend.

Famous **Bearers:** THOMAS GIBBONS (1757–1826) of Georgia was a party to the landmark Supreme Court case of 1824 that declared monopolies null and void. WILLIAM GIBBONS (1781–1845) of Delaware was a proponent of the emancipation and education of African-Americans. ABIGAIL HOPPER GIBBONS (1801–1893) of Pennsylvania was a reformer active in New York antislavery, antipoverty, and prison-reform affairs. She worked in or headed numerous organizations. JOHN GIBBON (1827–1896) of Pennsylvania was a soldier and the author of *Artillerist's Manual.* JAMES SLOAN GIBBONS (1810–1892) of Delaware was an abolitionist and the author of the Civil War song "We Are Coming, Father Abraham." JAMES GIBBONS (1834–1921) of Maryland was an archbishop of Baltimore and the second Roman Catholic cardinal of North America. He was also the first chancellor of the Catholic University of America in Washington, D.C. HERBERT ADAMS GIBBONS (1880–1934) of Maryland was a journalist who worked as a foreign correspondent. FLOYD GIBBONS (1887–1939) of Washington, D.C., was a war correspondent and a radio commentator.

Genealogies: None known.

GIBBS

Ranking: 452 S.S. Count: 88,123

Origin: English, Scottish. Transformation of and cognate to the English definition of Gilbert.

Famous **Gibbses:** GEORGE GIBBS (1776–1833) of Rhode Island gave his valuable mineral collection to Yale University and inspired the founding of *The American Journal of Science.* JOSIAH WILLARD GIBBS (1790–1861) of Massachusetts taught sacred literature at Yale Divinity School. GEORGE GIBBS (1815–1873) of New York was an ethnologist who studied the languages and traditions of the American Indians. OLIVER WOLCOTT GIBBS (1822–1908) of New York was a chemist who modernized the chemical laboratory at Harvard University and brought the latest technological advances from Europe to the United States. He was the founder and president of the National Academy of Sciences. JAMES ETHAN ALLEN GIBBS (1829–1902) of Virginia, with his partner James Willcox, developed the Willcox and Gibbs sewing machine. JOSIAH WILLARD GIBBS (1839–1903) of Connecticut was a theoretical physicist and chemist. He received the first Ph.D. in engineering conferred in the United States and developed many theories on thermodynamics. He is considered by many to be one of the greatest scientists in American history. GEORGE GIBBS (1861–1940) of Illinois was an engineer who played a part in the devel-opment of electric trains. He developed the first all-steel subway car. WILLIAM FRANCIS GIBBS (1886–1967) of Pennsylvania was a naval architect who designed ships with watertight compartments that made them safe.

Genealogies: *Gibbs-Chilton-Evans: Families of Rockingham County, North Carolina* was compiled by Lizora Powell Harbour and published in Ruffin, North Carolina, in 1989. *The Gibbs Family History and Their Relatives of the Olden Times* was compiled by Vernon Lee Gibbs and published in Utica, Kentucky, in 1990.

GIBSON

Ranking: 113 S.S. Count: 255,784

Origin: English, Scottish. Transformation of Gilbert, through Gibb(s).

Famous **Gibsons:** JOHN GIBSON (1740–1822) was a frontier soldier and secretary of Indiana Territory (1800–1816). His brother, GEORGE GIBSON (1747–1791) of Pennsylvania was a Revolutionary War soldier. He arranged for the purchase of gunpowder from the Spanish in New Orleans for use by the Virginia and Continental troops. JOHN BANNISTER GIBSON (1780–1853) of Pennsylvania was a justice of the Pennsylvania Supreme Court and a man who greatly influenced Pennsylvania law. WALTER MURRAY GIBSON (1823–1888) was born at sea en route from England to the United States. He was an adventurer who eventually settled in Hawaii, became premier of the kingdom, and was deposed in an 1887 revolution. PARIS GIBSON (1830–1920) of Maine introduced sheep farming to northern Montana. He also planned the city of Great Falls, Montana. RANDALL LEE GIBSON (1832–1892) of Kentucky was a politician who worked to improve navigation on the Mississippi River. WILLIAM HAMILTON GIBSON (1850–1896) of Connecticut was an illustrator whose works appeared in the popular magazines of his time. CHARLES DANA GIBSON (1867–1944) of Massachusetts was an illustrator. His "Gibson girl" drawings that appeared in *Collier's* magazine came to be considered the standard of femininity at the beginning of the 20th century. JOSHUA GIBSON (1911–1947) of Georgia was a baseball player. An African-American, he played with the famed National Negro League, where he led in home runs for 10 consecutive years. He had a career batting average of .347 and was nicknamed the "Negro Babe Ruth." He was elected to the Baseball Hall of Fame in 1972.

Genealogies: *The Gibson and Related Families* was compiled by Penny Linder and published in Parsons, West Virginia, in 1991. *Gibson, McCormick, Turner Genealogy* was compiled by F. McCormick Moore and most likely published in Oxford, Pennsylvania, in 1980.

GIDDENS (S.S. Abbreviation: Gidden)

Ranking: 4628 S.S. Count: 9657

Origin: English. Transformation of Gideon.

Genealogies: *Genesis Four, "We Begat!": Giddens Family History* was compiled by Emily Woodall-Ivey and published in League City, Texas, in 1985.

GIESE

Ranking: 4694 S.S. Count: 9535

Origin: Danish, German. Cognate to the English definition of Gilbert.

Genealogies: None known.

GIFFORD (S.S. Abbreviation: Giffor)

Ranking: 1680 S.S. Count: 26,641

Origin: English. 1) derived from the Old French word "giffard," meaning bloated or round-faced. The name was given to those who were plump. 2) derived from the Old English word "Gyddingord," meaning Gydda's ford. The name was given to those who came from Giffords Hall, a place in Suffolk, England.

Famous Giffords: SANFORD ROBINSON GIFFORD (1823–1880) of New York was a landscape painter whose works were more subtle than those of the others of the Hudson River school. ROBERT SWAIN GIFFORD (1840–1905) of Massachusetts was a landscape painter and a teacher at Cooper Union. One of his best-known paintings is entitled *Dartmouth Moors.* EDWARD WINSLOW GIFFORD (1887–1959) of California was an anthropologist and the curator of the University of California Museum of Anthropology at Berkeley who was responsible for developing it into a major U.S. museum. SANFORD ROBINSON GIFFORD (1892–1944) of Nebraska, grandnephew of Sanford Gifford (b. 1823), was a well-respected ophthalmologist.

Genealogies: *The Genealogy of the Gifford Family from Massachusetts to Maine* was compiled by Christine R. Brown and published in Knoxville, Tennessee, in 1980. *Seitter-Gifford Family* was compiled by Audrey Seitter-Gifford and published in La Jolla, California, in 1991.

GIGLIO, GIGLIOLI, GIGLIONI, GIGLIOTTI

Ranking: 4437 S.S. Count: 10,100

Origin: Italian. Cognates to the second definition of Lilly.

Genealogies: None known.

GIL

Ranking: 4011 S.S. Count: 11,285

Origin: Catalan, Italian, Portuguese, Spanish. Cognate to the English definition of Gil.

Genealogies: None known.

GILBERD, GILBERS, GILBERT, GILBERTON ET AL. (S.S. Abbreviation: Gilber)

Ranking: 204 S.S. Count: 172,882

Origin: Gilberd, Gilberton—English; Gilbert—English,

French, German, Irish, Jewish, Scottish; Gilbers—German. Gilberd, Gilbert (English, French, German), Gilbers, Gilberton: derived from the Norman first name Gislebert, which is derived from the Germanic words "gisil" and "berht," meaning "hostage [or] noble youth" (H&H) and bright. Gilbert (Irish, Scottish): derived from Gaelic names meaning "son of the servant of (St.) Brigit" (H&H). Gilbert (Jewish): transformation of many similar-sounding names.

Famous Bearers: ANNE JANE HARTLEY GILBERT (1821–1904), born in England, was an actress known in the 1880s in New York as one of "The Big Four." The other three performers were Ada Rehan, John Drew, and James Lewis. RUFUS HENRY GILBERT (1832–1885) of New York patented the elevated railway system that was used in the building of the New York City system. LINDA GILBERT (1847–1895) of New York was a prison reformer who established her own organization, Gilbert Library and Prisoners' Aid Fund. CASS GILBERT (1859–1934) of Ohio was an architect. His designs include the U.S. Supreme Court building and the U.S. Treasury Annex, both in Washington, D.C., as well as the Woolworth Building in New York City. CHARLES HENRY GILBERT (1859–1928) of Illinois was a zoologist who worked in fish studies in the waters of the northern hemisphere. ALFRED CHARLES GILBERT (1884–1961) of Oregon invented the Erector Set toy kits, eventually adding chemistry kits and radio kits. He later bought the American Flyer Co. and made its electric trains popular throughout the country.

Genealogies: *Ancestry of the Jameson, Gilbert, Joy, Skinner, and Related Families* was compiled by Bradner Petersen and published in Pasadena, California, in 1986. *The Dunlap-Kimbrough-Gilbert Book* was compiled by Sarah Ada Rasco Crumpton and published in Birmingham, Alabama, in 1973.

GILCHRIST (S.S. Abbreviation: Gilchr)

Ranking: 2353 S.S. Count: 19,261

Origin: Scottish. Derived from the Gaelic first name Gille Críosd, meaning "servant of Christ" (H&H).

Famous Gilchrists: ROBERT GILCHRIST (1825–1888) of New Jersey was an authority on constitutional law. He interpreted the law in New Jersey that African-Americans of the state had the right to vote in elections. WILLIAM WALLACE GILCHRIST (1846–1916) of New Jersey was the founder and conductor of the Philadelphia Symphony Society.

Genealogies: *Alexander Gilchrist, 1721–1778, and His Descendants: Islay, Argylleshire, Scotland to Argyle, Washington County, New York, U.S.A.* was compiled by Frederick A. Gilchrist and published in Glens Falls, New York, in 1986.

GILES

Ranking: 781 S.S. Count: 53,869

Origin: English, Irish. English: derived from the Latin first name Ægidius, which is derived from the Greek word "aigidion," meaning young goat, kid. Irish: transformation of Gleason.

Famous **Gileses:** WILLIAM BRANCH GILES (1762–1830) of Virginia was a politician who allowed his personal feelings to interfere with his position in government. CHAUNCEY GILES (1813–1893) of Massachusetts was a teacher, clergyman, and editor. His parishes were located in Cincinnati, New York City, and Philadelphia.

Genealogies: None known.

GILL

Ranking: 439 S.S. Count: 90,718

Origin: Dutch, English, Irish, Jewish, Scottish. Dutch: cognate to Giles. English: 1) transformation of the names Giles, Julian, and Williams. 2) derived from the Middle English word "gil(l)," meaning ravine. The name was given to those who lived in a ravine. Irish, Scottish: 1) derived from the Gaelic name Mac An Ghoill, meaning son of Ghoill, which may be derived from a word meaning foreigner. 2) derived from the Gaelic names Mac Giolla (Irish) and Mac Gille (Scottish), which are derived from several first names and surnames for servants. Jewish: derived from the Hebrew word "gil," meaning joy. The name was taken ornamentally.

Famous **Gills:** JOHN GILL (1732–1785) of Massachusetts published the *Boston Gazette and Country Journal* with Benjamin Edes. The paper was known for its strong anti-British, proindependence stands. THEODORE NICHOLAS GILL (1837–1914) of New York was one of the foremost zoologists in the country. He was an expert in taxonomy and a writer of numerous books that made the subject easy for the lay reader. LAURA DRAKE GILL (1860–1926) of Maine started the first vocational bureau for college women. IRVING JOHN GILL (1870–1936) of California was an architect known for introducing to that state a geometrical style of architecture devoid of the ornate buildings of the past.

Genealogies: *Baxter-Short, Miller-Gill, and Related Families* was compiled by Mary Cynthia Harrell and published in Bainbridge, Georgia, in 1989. *The Descendants of Thomas & Sarah (Bennett) Gill and Related Families, Including English Emigrants, Palatines, Puritans, Mayflower Immigrants, and Royal Lineages* was compiled by Vivian York Simms and published in Murfreesboro, Tennessee, in 1988.

GILLEN

Ranking: 2526 S.S. Count: 17,956

Origin: Flemish. Cognate to the English definition of Giles.

Genealogies: None known.

GILLES (ALSO GILLESON, GILLESPEY, GILLESPIE, GILLESPY)

Ranking: 636 S.S. Count: 65,233

Origin: Gilles, Gilleson—French; Gillespey, Gillespie, Gillespy—Irish, Scottish. Gilles, Gilleson: cognates to the English definition of Giles. Gillespey, Gillespie, Gillespy: derived from the Gaelic names Mac Giolla Easbuig (Irish) and Mac Gille Easbuig (Scottish), which are derived from a name meaning servant of the bishop (H&H).

Famous **Bearers:** WILLIAM MITCHELL GILLESPIE (1816–1868) of New York was the first civil engineering professor at Union College. ELIZA MARIA GILLESPIE (1824–1887) of Pennsylvania was known as Mother Angela. She joined the French convent of the Sisters of the Holy Cross, returned to the United States, and started the American branch of the order. She is considered the founder of the Sisters of the Holy Cross in this country. She was also the director of St. Mary's College in Indiana, where she greatly improved the curriculum. MABEL EDNA GILLESPIE (1877–1923) of Minnesota was a labor leader and reformer who was executive secretary of the Boston Women's Trade Union League from 1909 until her death. She was the first woman on the executive board of the Massachusetts State Federation of Labor, and she was instrumental in administering the first minimum-wage law for women in the United States.

Genealogies: *Ancestry of Elizabeth Barrett Gillespie (Mrs. William Sperry Beincke)* was compiled by Paul W. Prindle and published in New York, New York, in 1976. *History and Descendants of James Gillespie, 1760–1990* was compiled by LaRoux K. Gillespie and published in Kansas City, Missouri, in 1990.

GILLETT (ALSO GILLETTE, GILLET)

Ranking: 1773 S.S. Count: 25,315

Origin: Gillett, Gillette—English; Gillet—English, French. Gillet, Gillett, Gillette (English): derived from the names Giles, Julian, and William. Gillett (English): derived from the Middle English words "gil(l)" and "heved," meaning glen and head. The name was given to those who lived at the top of a glen. Gillet (French): cognate to the English definition of Giles.

Famous **Bearers:** FRANCIS GILLETTE (1807–1879) of Connecticut helped to found the Republican Party. FREDERICK HUNTINGTON GILLETT (1851–1935) of Massachusetts was a member of the U.S. House of Representatives, a U.S. senator, and a leader in the reform of the method of appropriations, which resulted in the Budget Act of 1921. EMMA MILLINDA GILLETT (1852–1927) of Wisconsin, a lawyer and feminist, was the first woman appointed as a notary public in Washington, D.C. She was a co-founder of the Washington College of Law and founder of the Washington Wimodaughsis (Wives-Mothers-Daughters-Sisters), a club for helping young working women advance their education. The club was later absorbed into the Y.W.C.A. WILLIAM HOOKER GILLETTE (1855–1937) of Connecticut was an actor who is best known for his portrayal of Sherlock Holmes on stage. KING CAMP GILLETTE (1855–1932) of Wisconsin invented and manufactured the first safety razor and blade. After he made his fortune, he pursued socialist utopian ideals and even offered former U.S. President Theodore Roosevelt $1 million in 1910 to act as president of his "World Corporation," which he wanted to establish in the Arizona desert. HORACE WADSWORTH GILLETT (1883–1950) of New York was a metallurgist and the developer of the rocking arc electric furnace.

Genealogies: *The Jospeh Gillet/Gillett/Gillette Family of Connecticut, Ohio and Kansas* was compiled by Wilma Gillet Thomas and published in Chicago, Illinois, in 1970. *Our Pilgrim's Progress: A Genealogy; The Gillets, Gilletts, Gillettes of 1634 Windsor, Connecticut Down Thru Nine Generations to the Present, 1988* was compiled by Julius L. Ross and published in Beloit, Wisconsin, in 1988.

GILLEY

Ranking: 3203 **S.S. Count:** 14,155

Origin: Scottish. Transformation of Gillie.

Genealogies: *Gillis and Other Pioneer Families of Georgia* was compiled by Marvin B. Gillis and published in Glenview, Illinois, in 1988. *Scots and Their Kin* was compiled by Clayton G. Metcalf and published in Enterprise, Alabama, in 1984.

GILLIAM, GILLIAN, GILLIATT (S.S. Abbreviation: Gillia)

Ranking: 856 **S.S. Count:** 50,122

Origin: English. Gilliam: transformation of William. Gillian: transformation of Julian. Gilliatt: transformation of the first English definition of Gillett.

Genealogies: *The History of the Burkett-Gilliam Generations* was compiled by Maxine Burkett Seltzer and published in Fort Worth, Texas, in 1976.

GILLILAN, GILLILAND (S.S. Abbreviation: Gillil)

Ranking: 2190 **S.S. Count:** 20,915

Origin: Scottish. Derived from the Gaelic first name Gill Fhaoláin, meaning "servant of Saint Faolán" (H&H).

Genealogies: *A Family History, Gilliland-Danhauer of Lyndon, Osage County, Kansas: Their Ancestors and Collateral Lines* was compiled by Nadine Gilliland Howe and published in New Haven, Indiana, in 1978. *These Are My Roots: Gilliland & Jenkins Genealogy* was compiled by Matilda Jenkins Webb and published in Newport, Tennessee, in 1984.

GILLIS (ALSO GILLISON)

Ranking: 1228 **S.S. Count:** 36,023

Origin: Gillis—Flemish, Scottish; Gillison—Scottish. Gillis (Flemish): cognate to the English definition of Giles. Gillis (Scottish), Gillison: transformations of Gillies.

Genealogies: *The Gillis Family in the South* was compiled by Clayton G. Metcalf and published in Enterprise, Alabama, in 1975.

GILMAN

Ranking: 2562 **S.S. Count:** 17,737

Origin: English. 1) transformation of Gilbert. 2) transformation of Julian.

Famous Gilmans: JOHN TAYLOR GILMAN (1753–1828) of New Hampshire was a governor of that state. CAROLINE HOWARD GILMAN (1794–1888) of Massachusetts was an author who worked in a variety of literature forms, including novels, verse, and short stories. She also wrote about different regions of the country. *Recollections of a Housekeeper* (1834) was about home life in New England, and *Recollections of a Southern Matron* (1838) described a plantation girlhood. ARTHUR DELEVAN GILMAN (1821–1882) of Massachusetts was one of the first American eclectic architects. DANIEL COIT GILMAN (1831–1908) of Norwich, Connecticut, drew the plans for the scientific school at Yale University; was the first president of Johns Hopkins University in Baltimore, Maryland; was the first president of the Carnegie Institution of Washington, D.C.; and was president of the National Civil Service Reform League. CHARLOTTE ANNA PERKINS GILMAN (1860–1935) of Connecticut was a writer and a lecturer on feminism and socialism. She edited and published the monthly *Forerunner* and wrote verse and nonfiction. ELISABETH GILMAN (1867–1950) of Connecticut was a Socialist Party candidate for governor of Maryland in 1930 and Socialist Party candidate for U.S. senator in 1934 and 1938. LAWRENCE GILMAN (1878–1939) of New York was a music critic on the staff of the *New York Tribune*.

Genealogies: *The Gilmans of Connecticut* was compiled by Lloyd Gilman and published in Willmar, Minnesota, in 1984.

GILMER

Ranking: 4652 **S.S. Count:** 9612

Origin: Irish, Scottish. Transformation of Gilmore.

Famous Gilmers: NICHOLAS GILMER (1755–1814) of New Hampshire was a U.S. senator from that state. ELIZABETH MERIWETHER GILMER (1870–1951) of Tennessee was a writer who wrote under the name of Dorothy Dix. She was the editor of the women's section of the New Orleans *Picayune*, where she started writing her "advice to the lovelorn" column. She also was the author of several books.

Genealogies: None known.

GILMORE (S.S. Abbreviation: Gilmor)

Ranking: 606 S.S. Count: 68,746

Origin: English, Irish, Scottish. English: derived from the place name Gilling and the Old English word "mōr," meaning marsh. The name was given to those who came from Gillamoor, a place in Yorkshire, England. Irish, Scottish: derived from the Gaelic names Mac Giolla Mhuire (Irish) and Mac Gile Mhoire (Scottish), which are derived from first names meaning "servant of [the Virgin] Mary" (H&H).

Famous **Gilmores:** JOSEPH ALBREE GILMORE (1811–1867) of Vermont was a governor of New Hampshire. PATRICK SARSFIELD GILMORE (1829–1892), originally from Ireland, was a bandmaster and virtuoso cornetist. At 19, he took over the Boston Brigade Band, and it later became known as Gilmore's Band. The entire band enlisted in the Union army during the Civil War. He was known for his spectaculars, which included a piece with 10,000 performers and 100 firemen beating anvils in Verdi's "Anvil Chorus." JOSEPH HENRY GILMORE (1834–1918) of Massachusetts was a clergyman, college professor, and author of the hymn "He Leadeth Me."

Genealogies: *I Walk in the Light: The Ancestors and Descendants of John Smith Gilmore* was compiled by Walter S. and Florence F. Beanblossom and published in Hawkesville, Kentucky, most likely in 1969.

GILSON

Ranking: 4449 S.S. Count: 10,074

Origin: English. Transformation of Giles.

Famous **Gilsons:** HELEN LOUISE GILSON (1835–1868) of Massachusetts was a hospital worker during the Civil War who, without formal nursing or medical training, helped care for the Union's wounded troops in several different locations. Her last war assignment was at City Point, Virginia, after the battle of Petersburg. She was credited with taking the facility from a condition of filth and disease to a model of cleanliness.

Genealogies: None known.

GINN

Ranking: 4184 S.S. Count: 10,799

Origin: English, Irish. English: derived from the Middle English word "gin," meaning trick. The name was given to those who worked as trappers and to those who were considered to be clever. Irish: derived from the Gaelic name Mag Fhinn, which is possibly derived from a word meaning white.

Famous **Ginns:** EDWIN GINN (1838–1914) of Maine was the publisher of textbooks and founded Ginn & Co. He endowed the World Peace Foundation in 1910.

Genealogies: *The Ginns and Their Kin* was compiled by Marie Luter Upton and published in 1963.

GIORDA, GIORDAN, GIORDANO

Ranking: 1920 S.S. Count: 5263

Origin: Italian. Cognates to Jordan.

Genealogies: None known.

GIOVANARDI, GIOVANAZZI, GIOVANELLI, GIOVANNETTI, GIOVANNI ET AL. (S.S. Abbreviation: Giovan)

Ranking: 4515 S.S. Count: 9913

Origin: Italian. Cognates to John.

Genealogies: None known.

GIPSON

Ranking: 1701 S.S. Count: 26,280

Origin: English. Transformation of Gibb(s).

Genealogies: None known.

GIRARD (ALSO GIRARDEU, GIRARDET, GIRARDIN, GIRARDI, GIRARDINI)

Ranking: 1946 S.S. Count: 23,241

Origin: Girard, Girardeu, Girardet, Girardin—French; Girardi, Girardini—Italian. Cognate to the first definition of Garrett.

Famous **Bearers:** STEPHEN GIRARD (1750–1831), originally from France, built a worldwide trading fleet after the Revolutionary War. His purchase of government bonds financed the War of 1812 against Great Britain.

Genealogies: None known.

GIST

Ranking: 4910 S.S. Count: 9110

Origin: English. Derived from the Middle English word "g(h)est," meaning visitor or guest.

Famous **Gists:** CHRISTOPHER GIST (1706–1759?) of Maryland explored the Ohio Valley, western Maryland, and Kentucky. His journals are considered excellent descriptions of Native American and frontier life, as well as the events leading up to the French and Indian War. He spent his final years among the Cherokee tribes of the southern United States. MORDECAI GIST (1742?–1792) of Maryland was a Revolutionary War officer who rose to the rank of brigadier general. WILLIAM HENRY GIST (1807–1874) of South Carolina was the governor of that state who encouraged the its legislature to vote to secede from the Union.

Genealogies: *Our Guest Is Your Guess: With Related Families of Biss, Jones, Gimbel, and Gist: Including Over One Thousand Other Surnames* was compiled by Patricia Ann Guest and published in Oceanside, California, in 1984.

GIVENS

Ranking: 1358 S.S. Count: 32,645

Origin: English, Scottish. Transformation of Gilbert.

Genealogies: *Givens, Allen, Spawn, Roseberry, and Cal-*

hoon Families of Northern Missouri was compiled by Brenda E. Givens and published in Cullman, Alabama, in 1988.

GLADDEN   (S.S. Abbreviation: Gladde)
Ranking: 4445 S.S. Count: 10,087
Origin: English. Derived from several Old English first names that are derived from the word "glæd," meaning joyful.
Famous **Gladdens:** WASHINGTON GLADDEN (1836–1918) of Pennsylvania was a Congregational minister who advocated the Social Gospel movement. He exposed corruption in New York City's government and sought to solve social problems with "Christian law."
Genealogies: *John L. Gladden and Some of His Family* was compiled by Mrs. James M. Gladden and published in Casar, North Carolina, in 1978.

GLASER, GLASERMAN
Ranking: 3013 S.S. Count: 15,081
Origin: Jewish. Transformation of Glass.
Genealogies: None known.

GLASGOW   (S.S. Abbreviation: Glasgo)
Ranking: 3645 S.S. Count: 12,372
Origin: Irish, Scottish. Irish, Scottish: Transformation of McCluskey. Scottish: uncertain etymology. Most likely derived from British words that evolved into the Welsh words "glas" and "cau," meaning grey, green, or blue and hollows.
Famous **Glasgows:** ELLEN ANDERSON GHOLSON GLASGOW (1873–1945) of Virginia was a novelist. Beginning with *The Descendant* (1897), she wrote a series of novels dealing with realistic aspects of southern people. Her last book, however, was an account of her own life. *The Woman Within* (1954) was written over the last 10 years of her life and meant for posthumous publication.
Genealogies: *The Glasgow Family of Adams County, Ohio: A Genealogy of the Descendants of Robert Glasgow (1749–1839) and His Wife Rosanna of Bush Creek, Adams County, Ohio* was compiled by David Faris and published in Philadelphia, Pennsylvania, in 1990.

GLASS
Ranking: 712 S.S. Count: 59,229
Origin: English, Irish, Jewish, Scottish. English: derived from the Old English word "glæs," meaning glass. The name was given to those who worked as glassblowers and to those who worked fitting windows. Irish, Scottish: derived from the Gaelic word "glas," meaning gray, green, or blue. Jewish: derived from the German word "glas," meaning glass. The name was given to those who worked as glassblowers and to those who worked fitting windows.
Famous **Glasses:** HUGH GLASS (?–1833), birthplace unknown, was an American frontiersman. On a fur-trap-

ping expedition, he was mauled by a bear and left for dead by the rest of the trapping party. Glass crawled 100 miles to Fort Kiowa, where he healed and regained his health. He became the subject of legends about fur trapping and frontier life. CARTER GLASS (1858–1946) of Virginia was the owner of several Virginia newspapers and was a politican. He was a member of both the U.S. House and Senate. FRANKLIN POTTS GLASS (1858–1934) of Alabama was a strong, independent journalist in that state. MONTAGUE MARSDEN GLASS (1877–1934) of England was an author who developed the characters "Potash" and "Perlmutter."
Genealogies: *Glass: A Genealogist's Collection* was compiled by Lucille Barco Coone and published in Gainesville, Florida, in 1985.

GLAZE
Ranking: 4643 S.S. Count: 9629
Origin: English. Transformation of Glass.
Genealogies: None known.

GLEASON   (S.S. Abbreviation: Gleaso)
Ranking: 1227 S.S. Count: 36,025
Origin: Irish. Derived from the Gaelic name Ó Glasáin, meaning "descendant of Glasán" (H&H), which is derived from the word "glas," meaning gray, green, or blue.
Famous **Gleasons:** FREDERIC GRANT GLEASON (1848–1903) of Connecticut was a composer and organist who studied with Dudley Buck, a prominent American composer of organ music for church services. KATE GLEASON (1865–1933) of New York was a prominent business promoter and community developer. Her residential construction projects paralleled the shift of people from the city to the suburbs.
Genealogies: *Genealogy of the Descendants of Marcena Glezen* [also Gleason] *of Center Lisle, Broome County, NY* was compiled by J. Carver Glezen and published in Whitney Point, New York, in 1971. *The Gleason Family from Uriah of the Fourth Generation* was compiled by Ruth Marie Field and published in Hollywood, California, in 1964.

GLENN
Ranking: 590 S.S. Count: 70,600
Origin: English, Jewish, Scottish. English: derived from a British word meaning valley. The name was given to those who came from Glen, a place in Leicestershire, England. Jewish: transformation of many similar-sounding surnames. Scottish: derived from the Gaelic word "gleann," meaning valley. The name was given to those who lived in a valley and to those who lived in a place that obtained its name from the word "gleann."
Famous **Glenns:** HUGH GLENN (1788–1833) of Virginia was a partner of Jacob Fowler on the first successful trad-

ing expedition to the Mexican provinces. JOHN MARK
GLENN (1858–1950) was a social worker and foundation
director. He participated in the founding of the Russell
Sage Foundation. MARY WILLCOX BROWN GLENN (1869–
1940) was a prominent social worker in Maryland and
New York. She was the second woman to be elected president of the National Conference of Charities and Correc-
tion, and she was president of the Family Welfare
Association of America for 12 years.

Genealogies: None known.

GLICK

Ranking: 3669 S.S. Count: 12,306

Origin: Jewish. Derived from the German word "glück"
and the Yiddish word "glik," both meaning luck. The name
was taken ornamentally.

Genealogies: Homer and Lillie Gerlach and Their Gerlach, Glick, Little, and Hempfield Ancestry was compiled by
Elmer K. Gerlach and published in McConnelsville, Ohio,
in 1981. Genealogy of the Glick Family was compiled by
George H. Glick and published in Hanover, Indiana, in
1981.

GLOVER

Ranking: 436 S.S. Count: 91,293

Origin: English. Derived from the Middle English word
"glovere," meaning glove maker or seller. The name was given
to those who worked as such.

Famous Glovers: JOHN GLOVER (1732–1797) of Massachusetts was a Revolutionary War soldier. As a member of
the Continental army, he commanded the ships that
brought the soldiers from Long Island to the mainland. He
manned the boats and led the advance on Trenton, New
Jersey, on Christmas Day, 1776, against the Hessians.
SAMUEL TAYLOR GLOVER (1813–1884) of Virginia, a leading
lawyer of his time, was important in keeping the state of
Missouri in the Union during the Civil War.

Genealogies: The Heritage of White Hall was compiled
by William H. Davidson and most likely published in West
Point, Georgia, in 1970.

GLYNN

Ranking: 3371 S.S. Count: 13,445

Origin: Cornish, Scottish, Welsh. Cornish, Welsh: derived
from the Cornish word "glin" and the Welsh word "glyn," both
meaning valley. The name was given to those who lived in a
valley. Scottish: transformation of Glen(n).

Famous Glynns: JAMES GLYNN (1801–1871) of Pennsylvania was a naval officer who paved the way for Commodore Matthew Perry's mission to Japan. MARTIN HENRY
GLYNN (1871–1924) of New York was the governor of that
state who initiated its workmen's compensation law and
primary elections.

Genealogies: None known.

GOAD

Ranking: 3598 S.S. Count: 12,542

Origin: German? Uncertain etymology. Possibly derived
from the German surname Gode, meaning good.

Genealogies: None known.

GOBLE

Ranking: 3753 S.S. Count: 12,064

Origin: English. Derived from the Norman first name
Godebald, which is derived from the Germanic words "gōd" or
"god," and "bald," meaning good or God, and brave.

Genealogies: The Goble Family: Descended from Thomas
Goble of Charlestown, Massachusetts: Genealogy from 1634
was compiled by Norma Goble Boykiw and published in
State College, Pennsylvania, in 1976.

GODDARD   (S.S. Abbreviation: Goddar)

Ranking: 2103 S.S. Count: 21,839

Origin: English, French. Derived from the first name
Godhard, which is derived from the Germanic words "gōd" or
"god," and "bald," meaning good or God, and brave.

Famous Goddards: WILLIAM GODDARD (1740–1817) of
Connecticut was a pioneer printer in Rhode Island. SARAH
UPDIKE GODDARD (1700?–1770) of Rhode Island financed,
with £300, her son William Goddard's founding of the first
print shop and newspaper in Providence, Rhode Island: the
Providence Gazette. She then kept the print shop going after
William moved away and revived the newspaper after he
ceased publication. She sold the business for $550, then
joined her son in Philadelphia, Pennsylvania, where he was
publishing the Pennsylvania Chronicle. Sarah's daughter
and William's sister, MARY KATHERINE GODDARD (1738–
1816), born in Connecticut, was publisher of the Maryland
Journal, started by her brother as the first newspaper in
Baltimore. For much of the American Revolution, she ran
the only print shop in Baltimore. The first printed copy of
the Declaration of Independence with the names of its
signers came from her press. She later served as postmaster
in Baltimore, apparently the first woman to hold that position. JOHN GODDARD (1723?–1785) of Massachusetts was a
cabinetmaker who originated the "block front." PAUL BECK
GODDARD (1811–1866) of Maryland was the first person to
develop instant photographs by the heliographic process.
CALVIN LUTHER GODDARD (1822–1895) of New York
invented a machine for removing burrs and dust from
wool. LUTHER MARCELLUS GODDARD (1840–1917) of New
York was a Colorado judge who formed the laws of the
state during the days of mining and prospecting. MORRILL
GODDARD (1865–1937) of Maine was a journalist and the
developer of the "Sunday supplement," which contained
comics and pictures. PLINY EARLE GODDARD (1869–1928)

of Maine was an ethnologist with an interest in the Indian languages. ROBERT HUTCHINGS GODDARD (1882–1945) of Massachusetts is considered the father of modern rocketry. The world's first liquid-propelled rocket-engine flight took off from his Aunt Effie's farm in Auburn, Massachusetts.

Genealogies: *The Goddard Book* was compiled by John W. Harms and published in Baltimore, Maryland, in 1984. *Master Craftsmen of Newport: The Townsends and Goddards* was compiled by Michael Moses and published in Tenafly, New Jersey, in 1984.

GODFREE, GODFREY (S.S. Abbreviation: Godfre)

Ranking: 1123 **S.S. Count:** 39,153

Origin: English. Derived from the Norman first names Godefrei and Godefroi(s), which are both derived from the Germanic words "god" and "fred," meaning God and peace.

Famous **Bearers:** THOMAS GODFREY (1704–1749) of Pennsylvania was the inventor of Hadley's quadrant. His son, THOMAS GODFREY (1736–1763) of Pennsylvania was a poet and playwright and the author of *Prince of Parthia*. It was the first American play. BENJAMIN GODFREY (1794–1862) of Massachusetts was a sea captain and the maker and loser of several fortunes. He founded Monticello Female Academy in 1838. ARTHUR MORTON GODFREY (1903–1983) of New York was a radio and television entertainer. During the 1940s he had three entertainment programs, two daily and one weekly. He is credited with launching the careers of many performing artists of the era.

Genealogies: None known.

GODWIN

Ranking: 1459 **S.S. Count:** 30,532

Origin: English. Transformation of Goodwin.

Famous **Godwins:** PARKE GODWIN (1816–1904) of New Jersey was an author and editor. He collected the works of his father-in-law, William Cullen Bryant. BLAKE-MORE GODWIN (1894–1975) of Missouri was a museum director, art historian, and curator at the Toledo Museum of Art. Under him new programs were started. He also was the founder and trustee of the Toledo Educational TV Foundation.

Genealogies: *Godwin* was compiled by Jamie Ault Grady and published in Knoxville, Tennessee, in 1981. *The Godwin Ancestry* was compiled by Mrs. Millard Smith Trotter and published in Utica, New York, in 1972.

GOEBEL

Ranking: 3757 **S.S. Count:** 12,048

Origin: German. Derived from the first name Godbeald, meaning God and brave.

Famous **Goebels:** WILLIAM GOEBEL (1856–1900) of Kentucky was a politican who managed to make political enemies, one of whom murdered him on January 30, 1900, after he had been elected governor but before he had taken office. The legislature declared him legally to have been the governor.

Genealogies: None known.

GOETZ

Ranking: 2347 **S.S. Count:** 19,329

Origin: German. 1) the name was given to those who were considered beautiful. 2) derived from the first name Godizo, meaning God.

Genealogies: *Our Four Families: Prouty, Youngs, Krueger, Goetsch* [also Goetz] was compiled by Evelyn A. Krueger and most likely published in Clinton, Wisconsin, in 1985.

GOFF

Ranking: 965 **S.S. Count:** 45,223

Origin: English. Transformation of Gough.

Famous **Goffs:** JOHN WILLIAM GOFF (1848–1924) of Ireland was a jurist and the last recorder of New York (1894–1906). He also served as a New York Supreme Court justice. EMMET STULL GOFF (1852–1902) was a horticulturist who did research in plant pathology and physiology, and experiments using fungicides and insecticides.

Genealogies: *Common Ground: A Turbulent Decade in the Lives of Three American Families* was compiled by J. Anthony Lukas and published in New York, New York, in 1985. *The History and Genealogy of the Nathan P. Goff Family of Randolph County, West Virginia, Delaware County, Indiana and Madison County, Iowa* was compiled by Joseph Philip Barnes and published in St. Louis, Missouri, in 1972.

GOFORTH (S.S. Abbreviation: Gofort)

Ranking: 3722 **S.S. Count:** 12,138

Origin: English. The name was given to those who worked as messengers. It refers to the order to leave for one's destination.

Famous **Goforths:** WILLIAM GOFORTH (1766–1817) of New York was a physician in Cincinnati and the first doctor to vaccinate people in the Northwest Territory.

Genealogies: *The Goforth Genealogy: A History of the Descendants of George Goforth of Knedlington, England Together with Some Account of Other Families of the Name* was compiled by George Tuttle Goforth and published in Annandale, Virginia, in 1981.

GOINS

Ranking: 1483 **S.S. Count:** 29,988

Origin: French. Transformation of Going(s).

Genealogies: None known.

GOLD

Ranking: 1587 **S.S. Count:** 28,203

Origin: English, German, Jewish. English: 1) derived from

the Old English and Old High German word "gold," meaning gold. The name was given to those who worked with gold. 2) derived from the Old English first name Golda, which has the same derivation as in 1. English, German: same derivation as in 1. The name was given to those who had blonde hair. Jewish: derived from the German word "gold," meaning gold. The name was taken ornamentally.

Genealogies: None known.

GOLDBERG, GOLDBERGER (S.S. Abbreviation: Goldbe)

Ranking: 721 S.S. Count: 58,564

Origin: Jewish. Transformation of Gold combined with the German and Yiddish word "berg," meaning hill. The names were taken ornamentally.

Famous **Bearers:** JOSEPH GOLDBERGER (1874–1929) of Austria was a physician who identified and discovered the cure for pellagra, a disease that occurs in several different forms because of a deficiency of niacin.

Genealogies: None known.

GOLDEN (ALSO GOLDENBERG, GOLDENFARB, GOLDENHOLTZ, GOLDENROT, GOLDENTHAL ET AL.)

Ranking: 536 S.S. Count: 75,603

Origin: Golden—English, Irish; Goldenberg, Goldenfarb, Goldenholtz, Goldenrot, Goldenthal et al.—Jewish. Golden (English): transformation of and cognate to the English and German definition of Gold. Golden (Irish): derived from the Gaelic name Mag Ualghairg, which is derived from the first name Ualgharg, which is most likely derived from Celtic words meaning proud and fierce. Goldenberg, Goldenfarb, Goldenholtz, Goldenrot, Goldenthal et al.: transformations of Gold combined with German and Yiddish words meaning hill, color, wood, red, and valley. The names were taken ornamentally.

Famous **Bearers:** HARRY LEWIS GOLDEN (originally Golhirsch) (1903–1981) of New York was a writer and editor who settled in North Carolina, where he founded and edited the *Carolina Israelite* newspaper. He was a leader in the campaign against racial segregation.

Genealogies: *The Genealogy of the Golden Family Through Richard Golden (1746?–1796?) and His Descendants* was compiled by Rollin G. Golden and published in Sacramento, California, in 1983. *The Thompson Tree: Its Trunk and Twigs* [also Golden] was compiled by Virginia Biddle Thode and published in Tuscola, Illinois, in 1983.

GOLDIN (ALSO GOLDINGAY, GOLDING)

Ranking: 4448 S.S. Count: 10,076

Origin: Goldin—Jewish; Goldingay—English; Golding—English, Jewish. Goldin: derived from the Yiddish first name Golde, meaning gold. Goldingay: uncertain etymology. Most

likely derived from the Middle English words "golden" and "hey," meaning golden and enclosure. The name was probably given to those who came from Goldingay, a now-unknown place in England. Golding (English): derived from the Old English first name Golding, which is derived from the word "gold," meaning gold. Golding (Jewish): the name was given to those who came from Golding, the Yiddish name for Kuldiga, a place in Latvia.

Famous **Bearers:** HORACE GOLDIN (1873–1939) of Poland was a magician who devised the trick of "sawing a woman in half."

Genealogies: None known.

GOLDMAN, GOLDMANN (S.S. Abbreviation: Goldma)

Ranking: 1133 S.S. Count: 38,870

Origin: English, Jewish. Transformations of Gold.

Famous **Bearers:** EMMA GOLDMAN (1869–1940), originally from Lithuania, was an anarchist. She was associated with the Russian anarchist Alexander Berkman while both were living in New York. She was eventually deported from the United States for her activities. MAYER C. GOLDMAN (1874–1939) of Louisiana was a lifetime advocate of a public defender in criminal cases. EDWIN FRANKO GOLDMAN (1878–1956) of Kentucky was a composer and bandleader. He started the New York Military Band, which was later called the Goldman Band. His son, RICHARD FRANKO GOLDMAN (1910–1980), succeeded him as the leader of the band. HETTY GOLDMAN (1881–1972) of New York participated in four major archaeological excavations that revealed significant details about ancient Greek civilizations. Her three-volume *Excavations at Gozlu Kule, Tarsus* (1950, 1956, and 1963) document prehistoric and historical growth of that area.

Genealogies: *Genealogy of the Goldman, Levy, Wertheim, Kaufman, Fleishman, Haas, Koshland, Stern, Strauss, Meyer, and Newmark Families* was compiled by Douglas Edward Goldman and published in San Francisco, California, in 1978.

GOLDSBY (S.S. Abbreviation: Goldsb)

Ranking: 4587 S.S. Count: 9748

Origin: English. Most likely derived from the first name Gold and the Old Norse word "býr," meaning farm. The name was given to those who came from Goulceby, a place in Lincolnshire, England.

Genealogies: None known.

GOLDSMITH (S.S. Abbreviation: Goldsm)

Ranking: 1790 S.S. Count: 25,146

Origin: English. Derived from the Old English words "gold" and "smið," meaning gold and smith. The name was given to those who worked with gold.

Famous **Goldsmiths:** MIDDLETON GOLDSMITH (1818–1887) of Maryland was a surgeon who discovered a bromine treatment for gangrene. GRACE ARABELL GOLDSMITH (1904–1975) of Minnesota, a physician and nutritionist in Louisiana, conducted pioneer research into diseases related to nutritional deficiencies. She instituted the world's first nutritional training program for physicians at Tulane University in the 1940s. She wrote numerous articles, book chapters, and the book *Nutritional Diagnosis* (1959).

Genealogies: *The Goldsmiths of St. Mary's & Anne Arundel Counties, Maryland* was compiled by Timothy Campbell Burke and published in New York, New York, in 1992.

GOLDSTON, GOLDSTONE, GOLDSTEIN, GOLDSTERN, GOLDSTOFF (S.S. Abbreviation: Goldst)

Ranking: 686 **S.S. Count:** 61,189

Origin: Goldston—English; Goldstone—English, Jewish; Goldstein, Goldstern, Goldstoff—Jewish. Goldston, Goldstone (English): derived from the Old English first name Golda, which is derived from the word "gold," meaning gold, and the word "stan," meaning stone. The names were given to those who came from Goldstone, a place in Shropshire, England. Goldstone (English): derived from the Old English first name Goldstan, derived from the words "gold" and "stan," meaning gold and stone. Goldstone (Jewish): transformation of Goldstein. Goldstein, Goldstern, Goldstoff: transformations of Gold, combined with German and Yiddish words meaning stone, star, and fabric.

Famous **Bearers:** MAX AARON GOLDSTEIN (1870–1941) of Missouri, a physician interested in teaching the deaf, founded the Central Institute for the Deaf in 1914.

Genealogies: *Yesterday, Today and Tomorrow. A History of the Rottenberg, Rubin, Goldstein, Gralnick, Margulies, Klein, Levine, Gudelski, Tamarin, Cohen, Zinits, Schwartz, Mariansky, Vinshnupsky, Grapf, Sobel, Segal, Wiesenberg, Shapiro, Kirschbaum, Landerburg and Stern Families* was compiled by Daniel Jay Rottenberg and published in Philadelphia, Pennsylvania, in 1977.

GOMES

Ranking: 1961 **S.S. Count:** 23,076

Origin: Portuguese. Cognate to Gomez.

Genealogies: *The Gomez Family: A Genealogical History of the Gomez Family* was compiled by Karen Bonds Mitchell and published in Commerce City, Colorado, most likely in 1990.

GOMEZ

Ranking: 191 **S.S. Count:** 182,416

Origin: Spanish. 1) derived from the Spanish first name

Gomesano, meaning man or path, and the suffix "ez," meaning son of. The name was given to the sons of Gomesano, or Gomo, a shortened form. 2) derived from the Gothic word "guma," meaning man, and the suffix "ez," meaning son of.

Genealogies: None known.

GONSALVAS, GONSALVES (S.S. Abbreviation: Gonsal)

Ranking: 2168 **S.S. Count:** 21,178

Origin: Italian, Spanish. Derived from the first name Gonzalo, meaning battle and elf.

Genealogies: None known.

GONZALEZ, GONZALO, GONZALVEZ, GONZALVO (S.S. Abbreviation: Gonzal)

Ranking: 24 **S.S. Count:** 681,286

Origin: Spanish. Gonzalo, Gonzalvo: 1) derived from the Spanish first name Gonzalo, meaning battle or elf. 2) derived from the Latin first name Gundisalvus, which is derived from the word "gund," meaning battle. Gonzalez, Gonzalvez: transformations of Gonzalo combined with the suffix "ez," meaning son of.

Famous **Bearers:** RICHARD ALONZO (PANCHO) GONZALES (1928–) of California is a tennis player who won the U.S. professional championship in men's singles eight times, 1953–1959 and 1961.

Genealogies: None known.

GOOCH

Ranking: 2770 **S.S. Count:** 16,467

Origin: Welsh. Transformation of Gough.

Famous **Gooches:** SIR WILLIAM GOOCH (1681–1751) of England was a colonial governor of Virginia, well liked by the colonists.

Genealogies: None known.

GOOD

Ranking: 926 **S.S. Count:** 46,601

Origin: English. 1) derived from the Old English word "gōd," meaning good. The name was given to those who were considered to be good. 2) derived from the Old English first name Gōda, which is derived from the word "gōd," meaning good.

Famous **Goods:** JEREMIAH HAAK GOOD (1822–1888) of Pennsylvania was a German Reformed clergyman and the president of Heidelbery Theological Seminary. JOHN GOOD (1841–1908) of Ireland was an inventor and manufacturer of rope. He revolutionized the rope-making industry. JAMES ISAAC GOOD (1850–1924) of Pennsylvania was a German Reformed minister whose claim to fame was as a historian in the church. ADOLPHUS CLEMENS GOOD (1856–1894) of Pennsylvania was a missionary who went to Africa, worked with the Bulu, and translated the Gospels into their language.

Genealogies: *The Good Side of My Family* was compiled by Ruth Good Baker and most likely published in Kansas City, Missouri, in the 1960s. *Genealogy of the Tazewell and Allied Families: With Sketches of Tazewell, Bradford, and Goode* [also Good] was compiled by Calvert Walke Tazewell Sr. and published in Virginia Beach, Virginia, in 1990. *A Good Tree Grew in the Valley: The Family Record of Christian Good, 1842–1916* was compiled by Lewis Christian Good and published in Baltimore, Maryland, in 1974.

GOODALE, GOODALL (S.S. Abbreviation: Goodal)

Ranking: 3732 S.S. Count: 12,110

Origin: English. 1) derived from the Old English words "golde" and "halh," meaning marigold and recess. The names were given to those who came from Goodall or Gowdall, the names of several places in England. 2) derived from the Middle English words "gode" and "ale," meaning good and malt liquor.

Famous **Bearers:** STEPHEN LINCOLN GOODALE (1815–1897) of Maine was an agriculturalist and a scientific innovator in his field. GEORGE LINCOLN GOODALE (1839–1923) of Maine was a physician and a botanist. He developed the Harvard Botanical Garden and Museum.

Genealogies: *Goodale-Goodell Forebears* was compiled by Helena M. Goodale Hargrave and published in Walnut Creek, California, in 1971.

GOODE

Ranking: 1436 S.S. Count: 31,109

Origin: English. Transformation of Good.

Famous **Goodes:** JOHN GOODE (1829–1909) of Virginia was a Confederate soldier and president of the Virginia Constitutional Convention (1901–1902). GEORGE BROWN GOODE (1851–1896), birthplace unknown, was a world-respected ichthyologist. While in the employ of the Smithsonian Institution in Washington, D.C., he reorganized and recataloged the materials, then developed better ways to display the specimens. JOHN PAUL GOODE (1862–1932) of Minnesota was a geographer with a specialty in cartography. His book of maps, known as the *Goode Atlas*, is world known.

Genealogies: None known.

GOODEN, GOODENOUGH

Ranking: 2596 S.S. Count: 17,515

Origin: English. Gooden: derived from the Middle English greeting "gooden," meaning good evening. The name was given to those who said this phrase frequently. Goodenough: 1) derived from the Middle English words "gode" and "enoh," meaning good and enough. The name may have been given to those who had low expectations or to those who were thought to be low achievers. 2) uncertain etymology. Possibly derived

from the Old English words "gōd" and "cnafa," meaning good and boy. The name may have been given to those who were considered to be good boys.

Famous **Bearers:** FLORENCE LAURA GOODENOUGH (1886–1959) of Pennsylvania was a psychologist who contributed greatly to the field of child psychology. Her published works include *Anger in Young Children* (1931), *Developmental Psychology* (1934), and *Handbook of Child Psychology* (1931, 1933, and 1946).

Genealogies: None known.

GOODING, GOODINGE, GOODINGS (S.S. Abbreviation: Goodin)

Ranking: 2288 S.S. Count: 19,887

Origin: English. Transformations of the second definition of Good.

Genealogies: None known.

GOODMAN (S.S. Abbreviation: Goodma)

Ranking: 373 S.S. Count: 104,358

Origin: English, Jewish. English: 1) derived from the Middle English words "gode" and "man," meaning good and man. The name was given to those who were masters of a house or landowners. 2) derived from the Old English first name Gōdmann, which is derived from the words "gōd" or "god" and "mann," meaning good or God and man. 3) derived from the Old English first name Gūðmund, which is derived from the words "gūð" and "mund," meaning battle and protection. Jewish: transformation of many similar-sounding surnames, such as Goutmann, Gutterman, and Gitterman.

Famous **Goodmans:** CHARLES GOODMAN (1796–1835) of Pennsylvania was a stipple-engraver. KENNETH SAWYER GOODMAN (1883–1918) of Illinois was a playwright whose best-known works were in the form of one-act plays. BENJAMIN DAVID (BENNY) GOODMAN (1909–1986) of Chicago, Illinois, was a clarinetist and an orchestra leader known as the "King of Swing." His band helped popularize jazz among white listeners and launched the careers of many musical greats, such as Gene Krupa, Fletcher Henderson, and Teddy Wilson.

Genealogies: *Some Goodmans and McHughs* was compiled by Matthew Lee McHugh and published in Columbia, South Carolina, in 1968.

GOODRICH, GOODRICK, GOODRIDGE (S.S. Abbreviation: Goodri)

Ranking: 1408 S.S. Count: 31,571

Origin: English. Derived from the Old English first name Gōdric, which is derived from the words "gōd" and "rīc," meaning good and power.

Famous **Bearers:** CHAUNCEY GOODRICH (1759–1815) of Connecticut was a lawyer and politician. SARAH GOODRIDGE (1788–1853) of Massachusetts was a painter of miniatures whose works were exhibited widely in Boston. CHAUNCEY ALLEN GOODRICH (1790–1860) of Connecticut was part of the revision team for *Webster's Dictionary*. He also married Noah Webster's daughter. CHARLES AUGUSTUS GOODRICH (1790–1862) of Connecticut, brother of Chauncy Goodrich (b. 1759), was a writer of children's books. *History of the United States* was his biggest success. SAMUEL GRISWOLD GOODRICH (1793–1860) of Connecticut was an author who wrote under the name Peter Parley. More than 100 books were written under his name; however, it is not certain that all books were indeed written by him. CHAUNCEY GOODRICH (1798–1858) of Massachusetts was a horticulturist whose methods did much to improve the growing of fruit in Vermont and upstate New York. FRANK BOOTT GOODRICH (1826–1894) of Massachusetts was the author of dime-store novels. CHAUNCEY GOODRICH (1836–1925) of Massachusetts, nephew of Chauncy Goodrich (b. 1798), was a missionary to China, where he helped to translate the Bible into Mandarin. BENJAMIN FRANKLIN GOODRICH (1841–1888) of New York was a rubber manufacturer. He formed a partnership with J. P. Morris in the Hudson River Rubber Co., which eventually led to the B.F. Goodrich brand of automobile tires. ANNIE WARBURTON GOODRICH (1866–1954) of New Jersey, as superintendent of nurses at several New York hospitals, raised the standard of educational requirements for beginning nursing students. As a full-time nursing teacher at Teachers College, Columbia University, she became a national leader in nursing education, serving as president of the International Council of Nurses and the American Nurses Association. She later served as dean of the school of nursing at Yale University.

Genealogies: *Francis, Goodrich, Boardman* was compiled by William F.J. Boardman and published in Hartford, Connecticut, in 1898. *The Goodrich Family in America: A Genealogy of the Descendants of John and William Goodrich of Wethersfield, Connecticut* was compiled by Lafayette Wallace Case and was originally published in Chicago, Illinois, in 1889.

GOODSON (S.S. Abbreviation: Goodso)

Ranking: 2148 **S.S. Count:** 21,335

Origin: English. 1) derived from the Middle English words "gode" and "sune," meaning good and son. The name was given to those considered to be good sons. 2) derived from the Old English first name Gōdsunu, which is derived from the words "gōd" and "sunu," meaning good and son.

Genealogies: *Urquhart, Coffey, Boland and Allied Families of the South: Urquhart, Parker, Coffey, Kirk, Harris, Boland, Fussell, Barnes, Goodson, Strange: Genealogy and Family History With Photographs, Sketches and Maps* was compiled by Annie Velma Urquhart Klayder and published in Columbus, Georgia, in 1991.

GOODWILL, GOODWIN (S.S. Abbreviation: Goodwi)

Ranking: 372 **S.S. Count:** 104,446

Origin: English. Goodwill: derived from the Middle English words "gode" and "will," meaning good and desire. Goodwin: derived from the Old English first name Gōdwin, which is derived from the words "gōd" and "wine," meaning good and friend.

Famous Bearers: ICHABOD GOODWIN (1794–1882) of Maine was a New Hampshire businessman and politician who served as the governor of that state (1859–1861). ELIJAH GOODWIN (1807–1879) of Ohio was a pioneer preacher who traveled through Illinois and Indiana. DANIEL RAYNES GOODWIN (1811–1890) of Maine was the cofounder of the University of Chicago. JOHN NOBLE GOODWIN (1824–1887) of Maine was the territorial governor of Arizona, where he established a stable government. WILLIAM WATSON GOODWIN (1831–1912) of Massachusetts was a Hellenist who published a Greek grammar book and *Greek Reader*, both of which were well received. He was considered an authority in his chosen field. NATHANIEL CARLL GOODWIN (1857–1919) was an actor whose best productions were contemporary roles with his wife, Maxine Elliott.

Genealogies: *Godwin* [also Goodwin] was compiled by Jamie Ault Grady and published in Knoxville, Tennessee, in 1981. *Godwin-Hill and Related Families* was compiled by Ruth Godwin Gadbury and published in Lometa, Texas, in 1980.

GOOLSBY (S.S. Abbreviation: Goolsb)

Ranking: 4030 **S.S. Count:** 11,234

Origin: Scottish. 1) the name was given to those who came from Gaaseby, which means "Gasi's homestead" (ES) and is a place in Norway. 2) cognate to Gause.

Genealogies: None known.

GORDON (ALSO GORDONOFF, GORDONOWITZ)

Ranking: 232 **S.S. Count:** 152,825

Origin: Gordon—English, French, Irish, Jewish, Russian, Scottish; Gordonoff, Gordonowitz—Jewish. Gordon (English): derived from the Gallo-Roman first name Gordus. The name was given to those who came from Gourdon, the name of a place in Saône-et-Loire, France. Gordon (French): derived from the Old French word "gord," meaning fat. The name was given to those who were considered to be overweight. Gordon (Irish): derived from the Gaelic name Mag Mhuirneacháin, which is derived from the word "muirneach," meaning beloved. Gordon (Jewish, Russian), Gordonoff, Gordonowitz: uncertain etymology. The names were most likely given to those who came from Grodno, a place in Belorussia. Gordon (Scottish): uncertain etymology. Most likely derived from British words that evolved into the Welsh words "gor" and "din," meaning spacious and fort. The name was most likely given to those who came from Gordon, a place in Scotland.

Famous **Bearers:** GEORGE PHINEAS GORDON (1810–1878) of New Hampshire was a printer who invented and manufactured three presses known as the "Yankee," the "Firefly," and the "Franklin." The last of these was later referred to as the "Gordon." ANDREW GORDON (1828–1887) of New York was the founder of a mission in India for the Presbyterian church. JOHN BROWN GORDON (1832–1904) of Georgia was a Confederate officer in the Civil War and the leader of the last charge made at Appomattox before surrender. After the war he served as a U.S. senator from and governor of Georgia (1873–1897). LAURA DE FORCE GORDON (1838–1907) of Pennsylvania studied law while she worked as a newspaper journalist in California and became one of the first women to practice law in that state. She was president of the California Woman Suffrage Society for 11 years. ANNA ADAMS GORDON (1853–1931) of Massachusetts was a temperance reformer who rose to the presidency of the Women's Christian Temperance Union. KATE M. GORDON (1861–1932) and JEAN MARGARET GORDON (1865–1931) of Louisiana were sisters who were leaders in the women's suffrage movement. DOROTHY LERNER GORDON (1889–1970), born in Russia to American parents, was a singer, then a producer of radio and television programs. She presented one of the first radio programs for children on WEAF in New York in 1934. She became director of the CBS five-day-a-week program "American School of the Air," on which the first radio adaptation of James M. Barrie's *Peter Pan* aired. She also worked for the Mutual Broadcasting System and NBC. Her greatest achievement was to develop and run the Youth Forum programs, known first as the "New York Times Youth Forum" and then as "Dorothy Gordon Youth Forum." She worked on the broadcasts from 1945 until her death in 1970. RUTH GORDON (1896–1985) of Massachusetts was an actress of stage and screen, beginning on Broadway in 1915. She was still a favorite in her last several pictures, *Rosemary's Baby* (1968), for which she won an Academy Award, and *Harold and Maude* (1971). She also wrote screenplays. JOHN FRANKLIN GORDON (1900–1978) of Ohio was instrumental in the design and development of liquid-cooled aircraft engines during World War II. EDGAR STILLWELL GORDON (1906–1975) of Illinois was a physician and a specialist in endocrinology and metabolism. He was the first in Wisconsin to use radioactive iodine for thyroid disease.

Genealogies: *A Genealogical Study of the William Gordon Family in Indiana* was compiled by H. C. Gordon and published in Knightstown, Indiana, in 1961. *Gordon Kinship* was compiled by Nancy S. McBride and published in 1973.

GORE

Ranking: 1304 **S.S. Count:** 33,973

Origin: English, French. English: derived from the Old English word "gāra," meaning triangular piece of land. The name was given to those who came from Gore, the name of several places in England. French: derived from the Old French word "gore," meaning sow. The name was given to those who were considered somehow bovine.

Famous **Gores:** THOMAS PRYOR GORE (1870–1949) of Mississippi was a politician whose blindness at age 20 was never an obstacle to his career. He became a leader in politics in the Oklahoma territory and was elected to the U.S. Senate when Oklahoma was granted statehood.

Genealogies: *Family History With Name Origin and Lineage Lines, Gore: From Genealogical Records* was published in Carpinteria, California, most likely in 1975.

GORHAM

Ranking: 3782 **S.S. Count:** 11,928

Origin: English. Derived from the Old English words "gāra" and "hām," meaning triangular piece of land and homestead. The name was most likely given to those who came from Goreham, a now-unknown place in England.

Famous **Gorhams:** NATHANIEL GORHAM (1738–1796) of Massachusetts was a politician during the American Revolution and one of the signers of the Declaration of Independence. JOHN GORHAM (1783–1829) of Massachusetts was a professor of chemistry at Harvard University and the author of the textbook *Elements of Chemical Science.* JABEZ GORHAM (1792–1869) of Rhode Island was a silversmith and the founder of the Gorham Manufacturing Co.

Genealogies: *John Howland of the Mayflower* was compiled by Elizabeth Pearson White and published in Camden, Maine, in 1990.

GORMAN

Ranking: 923 **S.S. Count:** 46,756

Origin: English, Irish, Jewish. English: 1) derived from the Old English name Gārmund, which is derived from the words "gār" and "mund," meaning spear and protection. 2) transformation of Gore. Irish: derived from the Gaelic names Mac Gormáin and 'Gormáin, meaning son of and descendant of Gormán, which is derived from the word "gorm," meaning blue. Jewish: uncertain etymology.

Famous **Gormans:** WILLIS ARNOLD GORMAN (1816–1876) of Kentucky was the governor of the Minnesota territory and a Union brigadier general in the Civil War. ARTHUR PUE GORMAN (1839–1906) of Maryland was a U.S. senator from his home state. He was the co-author of the Wilson-Gorman Act of 1894.

Genealogies: *The Gorman Family History: Including the Genealogy of Their Rider and Armstrong Ancestors* was compiled by Edith Lynn Mlaker and published in San Ramon,

California, in 1984. *James Henry Gorman of Haverhill, Massachusetts, His Forebears, Family and Descendants* was compiled by Arthur Ellsworth Gorman and published in Ormond Beach, Florida, in 1974.

GORSKI

Ranking: 4383 S.S. Count: 10,240
Origin: Jewish, Polish. Derived from the Polish word "góra," meaning mountain, and the suffix "ski." The name was given to those who lived on a mountain.
Genealogies: None known.

GOSNELL (S.S. Abbreviation: Gosnel)

Ranking: 4330 S.S. Count: 10,353
Origin: English. Derived from the first name Gosa and a word meaning corner.
Genealogies: None known.

GOSS

Ranking: 1233 S.S. Count: 35,933
Origin: English, German. Derived from the Germanic first name Gozzo, which is derived from the words "gōd" and "god," meaning good and God.
Famous **Gosses:** ALBERT SIMON GOSS (1882–1950) of New York was a businessman and an agricultural leader who fought for the rights of farmers.
Genealogies: *All About Me and My Ancestors* was compiled by Laura Blanchard Simpson and published in Fort Collins, Colorado, in 1974. *Frederick Goss of Rowan County, North Carolina, and His Descendants* was compiled by Lois Ione Hotchkiss Heuss and published in Akron, Ohio, in 1968.

GOSSELIN, GOSSELK (S.S. Abbreviation: Gossel)

Ranking: 4639 S.S. Count: 9640
Origin: Gosselin—English; Gosselk—German. Gosselin: 1) derived from the Old French first names Goscelin, Goselin, and Joscelin, which are for the most part derived from the Germanic first name Gauzelin, which is derived from the word "gaut," meaning Scandinavians. 2) derived from the Middle English word "gosling," meaning young goose. The name was given to those who were considered to be in some way gooselike. Gosselk: transformation of Gottschalk.
Genealogies: None known.

GOSSET (ALSO GOSSETT)

Ranking: 2867 S.S. Count: 15,875
Origin: Gosset—English, French; Gossett—English. Transformations of and cognates to Goss(e).
Genealogies: *Chronicles of the Gossett Family* was compiled by Grace M. Jerkins and published in Gary, Indiana, in 1985. *The Family of Gossett* was compiled by Evangeline

Gossett Newcomer and published in Pico, California, in 1954.

GOTTLIB, GOTTLIEB (S.S. Abbreviation: Gottli)

Ranking: 3834 S.S. Count: 11,747
Origin: Gottlib—German; Gottlieb—German, Jewish. German: derived from a Germanic first name derived from the words "god" and "leoba," meaning God and love. German, Jewish: derived from the Yiddish first name Gotlib, which is derived from the words "got" and "lib," meaning God and love.
Famous **Bearers:** ADOLPH GOTTLIEB (1903–1974) of New York was a painter and a leader of the abstract expressionist school.
Genealogies: None known.

GOTTSCHLICH, GOTTSCHLING, GOTTSCHALK, GOTTSCHALL (S.S. Abbreviation: Gottsc)

Ranking: 4645 S.S. Count: 9626
Origin: Gottschlich, Gottschling—German; Gottschalk, Gottschall—German, Jewish. Derived from a first name that is derived from the Middle High German words "got" and "schalk," meaning God and court jester or servant.
Famous **Bearers:** LOUIS MOREAU GOTTSCHALK (1829–1869) of Louisiana was the first U.S. pianist to gain an international reputation. He was the first U.S. composer to imbue his music with Latin American and Creole rhythms and themes.
Genealogies: None known.

GOUGH

Ranking: 3730 S.S. Count: 12,114
Origin: English, Welsh. English: derived from the Gaelic word "gobha" and the Bretonic/Celtic word "goff," both meaning smith. The name was given to those who worked as smiths. Welsh: derived from the Welsh word "coch," meaning red. The name was given to those with red hair.
Genealogies: None known.

GOULD

Ranking: 733 S.S. Count: 57,886
Origin: English. Transformation of Gold.
Famous **Goulds:** BENJAMIN APTHORP GOULD (1824–1896) of Massachusetts was an astronomer of great renown. He founded *Astronomical Journal* and established observatories in several locations in South America. ROBERT SIMONTON GOULD (1826–1904) of North Carolina was a Confederate soldier, a justice of the Texas Supreme Court, and a law professor at the University of Texas. JAY GOULD (originally Jason Gould) (1836–1892) of New York was an American financier. As a wheeler and dealer, he engaged in some practices that were not on the "up and

up." His son GEORGE JAY GOULD (1864–1923) was born in New York. He inherited half of his father's fortune but overextended himself and lost it all. Another son, EDWIN GOULD (1866–1933), managed his half of the fortune well and became known as a philanthropist. ELGIN RALSTON LOVELL GOULD (1860–1915) of Canada was an economist who did studies for the U.S. Department of Labor on family budgets and wages. CHESTER GOULD (1900–1985) of Pawnee, Oklahoma, was a cartoonist who created "Dick Tracy." It was the first nonhumorous comic strip.

Genealogies: *The Gould Family and Allied Families: The Goulds and their 146 Great Grandparents* was compiled by Helen Weaver Gould and published in La Porte, California, in 1979.

GOULET
Ranking: 4909 S.S. Count: 9110
Origin: French. Derived from the Old French word "goulet," meaning gullet. The name was given to those who were considered greedy and to those who had a large appetite.
Genealogies: None known.

GOWER
Ranking: 4916 S.S. Count: 9104
Origin: English, Jewish, Welsh. English: 1) derived from the Old French place name Gohiere. The name was given to those who came from Gohiere, which is north of Paris, France. 2) derived from the Gallo-Roman first name Gaudius. The name was given to those who came from Gouy, the name of several places in France. 3) derived from the Norman first name Go(h)ier, which is derived from words meaning good and army. Jewish: uncertain etymology. Welsh: the name was given to those who came from Gŵyr, the name of a peninsula in South Wales, England.
Genealogies: None known.

GRABER (ALSO GRABERT, GRABERMAN)
Ranking: 3919 S.S. Count: 11,508
Origin: Graber—German, Jewish; Grabert—German; Graberman—Jewish. Graber, Grabert (German): derived from the Old High German word "graban," meaning to dig. The names were given to those who worked digging ditches or graves and to those who worked engraving seals. Graber, Graberman (Jewish): derived from the German word "gräber," meaning to dig. The names were given to those who worked as grave diggers.
Genealogies: *A History of the Greber, Graeber, Graber Family, 1680–1980* was compiled by Kathleen Neumann Graber and published in Oshkosh, Wisconsin, in 1981.

GRABOWSKI, GRABOWICZ (S.S. Abbreviation: Grabow)
Ranking: 2798 S.S. Count: 16,255

Origin: Grabowski—Jewish, Polish; Grabowicz—Polish. Derived from the Polish word "grab," meaning hornbeam, the wood used to make yokes. The names were given to those who lived in places that obtained their names from the word "grab" and to those who worked making yokes.
Genealogies: None known.

GRACE
Ranking: 1186 S.S. Count: 36,992
Origin: English. 1) derived from the Middle English and Old French word "grace," meaning charm. The name was given to those who were considered to be charming. 2) derived from the first name Grace, which is derived from the Germanic word "gris," meaning gray.
Famous **Graces:** WILLIAM RUSSELL GRACE (1832–1904), originally from Ireland, founded the shipping firm of W. R. Grace and Company, which for many years was a dominant force in the economies of several Latin American countries. Today, the firm continues to produce chemical and consumer products. Grace was twice elected mayor of New York City.
Genealogies: *Grace Family of Louisiana* was compiled by Desdemona Grace Redlich and published in Louisiana in 1970.

GRACIA
Ranking: 4869 S.S. Count: 9196
Origin: Catalan, Spanish. Cognate to Grace.
Genealogies: None known.

GRADY
Ranking: 1147 S.S. Count: 38,165
Origin: Irish. Derived from the Gaelic name Ó Gráda, meaning "descendant of Gráda" (H&H), meaning noble.
Famous **Gradys:** HENRY WOODFIN GRADY (1850–1889) of Georgia was editor and part owner of the Atlanta *Constitution.* He is famous for his speech called "The New South."
Genealogies: *From Ireland, Land of Pain and Sorrow: A Historical Chronicle of Two Cultures* was compiled by Joseph L. Grady and published in Phoenix, Arizona, in 1984. *William Bean, Pioneer of Tennessee, and His Descendants* was compiled by Jamie Ault Grady and published in Knoxville, Tennessee, in 1973.

GRAF
Ranking: 2327 S.S. Count: 19,497
Origin: German, Jewish. German: derived from the Old High German word "grāv(i)o," meaning count or magistrate. The name was given to those who were counts and/or magistrates. Jewish: same derivation as above. The name was taken by those enjoying its aristocratic implication.
Genealogies: None known.

GRAFF

Ranking: 2560 S.S. Count: 17,746

Origin: English, Jewish. English: derived from the Anglo-Norman-French word "grafe," meaning pen or quill. The name was given to scribes and clerks. Jewish: transformation of Graf.

Famous **Graffs:** FREDERICK GRAFF (1774–1847) of Pennsylvania was a civil engineer and the man responsible for the hydraulic system used in Philadelphia. FREDERICK GRAFF (1817–1890) continued his father's work as chief engineer of the Philadelphia Water Department.

Genealogies: *The Groff [also Graff] Book* was compiled by Clyde L. Groff and published in Ronks, Pennsylvania, in 1985.

GRAHAM, GRAHAME

Ranking: 100 S.S. Count: 275,799

Origin: Scottish. Uncertain first component. The last component is derived from the Old English word "hām," meaning homestead. The names were given to those who came from Grantham, a place in Lincolnshire, England.

Famous **Bearers:** JAMES GRAHAM (?–1700?), birthplace unknown, arrived in New York in 1678 and was involved in the politics of the province. ISABELLA MARSHALL GRAHAM (1742–1814) of Scotland was a teacher and philanthropist who settled in New York City. There she set up charitable organizations to help widows and orphans. SYLVESTER GRAHAM (1794–1851) of Connecticut was a reformer. He advocated temperance, vegetarianism, and the use of whole wheat unbolted and coarsely ground to make flour. This came to be known as Graham flour. JOHN ANDREW GRAHAM (1764–1841) of Connecticut was a lawyer in New York City, where he successfully worked to enact laws that protected clients' rights to counsel and declared inadmissable evidence gained without counsel. JOHN GRAHAM (1774–1820) of Virginia was Thomas Jefferson's spy against Aaron Burr. JAMES DUNCAN GRAHAM (1799–1865) of Virginia was the first person to discover a lunar tide on the Great Lakes. WILLIAM ALEXANDER GRAHAM (1804–1875) of North Carolina was a politician who opposed the secession of the southern states, remained loyal to his state, and worked for peace. DAVID GRAHAM (1808–1852) of England was raised in America and was the author of *Treatise on the Practice of the Supreme Court of New York.* GEORGE REX GRAHAM (1813–1894) of Pennsylvania was a journalist. He founded *Graham's Magazine.* ERNEST ROBERT GRAHAM (1868–1936) of Michigan was an architect. He was involved in the designing of many famous buildings, including Gimbel Brothers' store in New York City; Union Station and the post office in Washington, D.C.; Field Museum of Natural History, Civic Opera House, Shedd Aquarium, Marshall Field stores, and the Wrigley Building in Chicago; Pennsylvania Station and Wanamaker's in Philadelphia; and

Filene's in Boston. EDWARD KIDDER GRAHAM (1876–1918) of North Carolina made great advances at the University of North Carolina as its president. MARTHA GRAHAM (1893–1991) of Pittsburgh, Pennsylvania, was a dancer and choreographer. After working in the Denishaw company and the Greenwich Village Follies revue, she began her career as an independent artist. She danced for more than a half century and taught for nearly 75 years. She created more than 170 works and hoped that her dances would "reveal the inner man."

Genealogies: *The Gallant Grahams of America* was compiled by Joe C. Graham and most likely published in Birmingham, Alabama, in 1989. *Grahams of Noble Heritage: And Descendants [Scotland, England and America]: Descendants of Robert II [Stuart] 1316–1390 King of Scotland: Graham Family History, 1128–1990* was compiled by Joe C. Graham and published in 1992.

GRANADA, GRANADO, GRANADOS (S.S. Abbreviation: Granad)

Ranking: 3458 S.S. Count: 13,055

Origin: Spanish. Derived from the Spanish word "granata," meaning pomegranate. The names were given to those who worked growing or selling pomegranates and to those who came from Granada, a place in southern Spain.

Genealogies: None known.

GRANDE (ALSO GRANDEAU, GRANDEL, GRANDET)

Ranking: 4392 S.S. Count: 10,212

Origin: Italian, French. Grande—Italian. Grandeau, Grandel, Grandet—French. Cognates to Grant.

Genealogies: None known.

GRANGE (ALSO GRANGER))

Ranking: 1829 S.S. Count: 24,686

Origin: English, French. Grange: the name was given to those living near a granary. Granger: derived from the old French word "grangier," which was the official Anglo-Norman-French title given to those responsible for collecting the rent in the form of crops and animals and transferring these to the storehouses of the lord of the estate.

Famous **Bearers:** GIDEON GRANGER (1767–1822) of Connecticut was a politician and postmaster general (1801 1814). FRANCIS GRANGER (1792–1868) of Connecticut played a role in the anti-Masonic movement. GORDON GRANGER (1822–1876) of New York was a soldier whose suprise attack at Chickamauga forced the Confederate soldiers to retreat, thus saving the Union army of General George Henry Thomas from sure defeat. ALFRED HOYT GRANGER (1867–1939) of Ohio was an architect and the designer of the town of Euclid Heights, Ohio. WALTER GRANGER (1872–1941) of Vermont was a self-made paleontologist associated with the American Museum of Natural History, his area of expertise being the exploration of the Gobi Desert.

Genealogies: *The Bater Book and Allied Families: Shore-Ensley, Granger-Thomas* was compiled by A. L. Bowerman and published in Coldwater, Michigan, in 1987.

GRANT

Ranking: 185 S.S. Count: 185,130

Origin: English, Scottish. 1) derived from the Old French word "grand," meaning tall or large. The name was given to those who were of exceptional proportions or was used in addition to the first name when different members of the same family were given the same first names; often used to distinguish a younger member from an older one. 2) uncertain etymology. Probably a transformation of Grantham.

Famous **Grants:** JOHN THOMAS GRANT (1813–1887) of Georgia was a capitalist and the developer of Atlanta as a business center after the Civil War. ULYSSES SIMPSON GRANT (originally Hiram Ulysses Grant) (1822–1885) of Ohio was the 18th president of the United States. He took the name Ulysses Simpson after he was admitted to West Point under that name due to an error made by the congressman who appointed him. He served in the army through the Mexican War, at which time he resigned. At the beginning of the Civil War he volunteered for service and was appointed brigadier general of volunteers. He led the expedition that captured Fort Henry, Fort Donelson, and a Confederate troop of 15,000 under the command of General S. B. Buckner. Promoted to major general, he commanded at Battle of Shiloh; captured Vicksburg with 30,000 Confederate troops under General John Clifford Pemberton; became regular army major general; was victorious against General Braxton Bragg in Chattanooga; and was promoted to lieutenant general in charge of all of the Union armies. Despite the heavy losses at the Battle of the Wilderness and at Spotsylvania, the Union troops won and General Robert E. Lee surrendered. As a man Grant was honest; his terms as president, however, were marked by scandal. He retired in New York City and wrote his memoirs. CLAUDIUS BUCHANAN GRANT (1835–1921) of Maine was a Michigan judge known for his toughness toward the criminals brought before his court. JAMES BENTON GRANT (1848–1911) of Alabama was the first Democratic governor of Colorado. FREDERICK DENT GRANT (1850–1912) of Missouri was a soldier and the son of Ulysses S. Grant. ALBERT WESTON GRANT (1856–1930) of Maine was a naval officer who commanded the Atlantic submarine fleet and set up the submarine base in New London, Connecticut. HEBER JEDEDIAH GRANT (1856–1945) of Utah was a religious leader of the Council of Twelve, Church of Latter-Day Saints, and president of the church (1918–1945). CARY GRANT (originally Archibald Alexander Leach) (1904–1986) of

England was a well-known actor of his time. He starred in many movies and received a special Academy Award in 1970 for his lifetime of service to the film industry.

Genealogies: *Peter Grant, Scotch Exile, Kittery and Berwick, Maine: Genealogy* was compiled by Leola Grant Bushman and published in Arcadia, California, in 1976.

GRANTHAM   (S.S. Abbreviation: Granth)

Ranking: 3076 S.S. Count: 14,774

Origin: English. Uncertain etymology. 1) possibly derived from the Old English words "grand" and "hām," meaning gravel and homestead. 2) derived from the Old English name Granta, meaning snarler, and the Old English word "hām," meaning homestead. The name was given to those who came from Grantham, a place in Lincolnshire, England.

Genealogies: None known.

GRASSO (ALSO GRASSON, GRASSOT, GRASSOTTI)

Ranking: 4220 S.S. Count: 10,692

Origin: Grasson, Grassot—French; Grasso, Grassotti—Italian. 1) derived from the Middle English word "gras" or the German word "grass," both meaning grass or pasture. The names were often given to those who lived on a tract of grassland. 2) derived from the Anglo-Norman-French word "gras," meaning fat. The names were often given to those who were stocky or heavy. 3) derived from the Gaelic word "greusaiche," meaning shoemaker.

Famous **Bearers:** ELLA ROSA GIOVANNA OLIVA TAMBUSSI GRASSO (1919–1981) of Connecticut was a politician and the first woman in the United States to hold the office of governor (of Connecticut) without succeeding her husband.

Genealogies: None known.

GRAVEL (ALSO GRAVELEAU, GRAVELIN, GRAVELING, GRAVELLE ET AL.)

Ranking: 3473 S.S. Count: 13,011

Origin: Graveling—English; Gravel, Graveleau, Gravelin, Gravelle et al.—French. 1) derived from the Middle English word "greyve," meaning steward. The names were given to those who served as stewards of a manor or large estate. 2) transformations of and cognates to the first definition of Grove. 3) derived from the Old French word "grave," meaning gravel. The names were often given to those who lived on rocky soil. 4) cognates to Graf.

Genealogies: None known.

GRAVES (ALSO GRAVESEN, GRAVESON, GRAVESTON)

Ranking: 3473 S.S. Count: 117,306

Origin: Gravesen—Danish; Graves, Graveson, Graveston—English. Gravesen: cognate to Graf. Graves, Graveson, Graveston: transformations of the first definition of Grave(l).

Famous **Bearers:** ZUINGLIUS CALVIN GRAVES (1816–1902) of Vermont was the first president of Mary Sharp College in Virginia, where he held academics in the highest regard. JAMES ROBINSON GRAVES (1820–1893) of Vermont was a well-known Tennessee Baptist minister. ROSEWELL HOBART GRAVES (1833–1912) of Maryland was a missionary in South China. FREDERICK ROGERS GRAVES (1858–1940) of New York was a missionary in China and the bishop of Shanghai. WILLIAM SIDNEY GRAVES (1865–1940) of Texas was an army officer who commanded the American Expeditionary Force in Siberia. He was the author of *America's Siberian Adventure.* DAVID BIBB GRAVES (1873–1942) of Alabama was known as an effective and fair southern governor despite his personal affiliation with the Ku Klux Klan.

Genealogies: *Benton-Graves Ancestry* was compiled by Blanche Benton Heller and published in Los Angeles, California, in 1953. *Branching Out from Stephen Graves: (1759–1828)* was compiled by Jessie Wagner Graves and published in Knoxville, Tennessee, in 1991.

GRAY

Ranking: 75 **S.S. Count:** 341,759

Origin: English, Scottish. English: 1) derived from the Old English word "grœg," meaning gray. The name was often given to those who had gray hair or a gray beard. 2) derived from now-unknown Gaelic family names that were derived from the Gaelic word "riabhach," meaning gray. English and Scottish: derived from the Gallo-Roman first name Gratus, meaning "welcome or pleasing" (H&H). The name was given to those who came from Graye, the name of a place in the Calvados region of France.

Famous **Grays:** WILLIAM GRAY (1750–1825) of Massachusetts was a ship owner who made his fortune as a privateer during the American Revolution. He was one of the first to trade with Russia, China, and India. ROBERT GRAY (1755–1806) of Rhode Island was a navigator and fur trader. He is credited with carrying the American flag around the world for the first time and with exploring the Columbia River, which helped the United States in its claim to Oregon. ASA GRAY (1810–1888) of New York was the foremost botanist of his time. JOHN PURDUE GRAY (1825–1886) of Pennsylvania was the head of the New York State Lunatic Asylum, where he greatly improved the living conditions of those confined with a program of fresh air and exercise, and the abandonment of physical restraints and solitary confinement. HORACE GRAY (1828–1902) of Massachusetts was a member of the Massachusetts Supreme Court and the U.S. Supreme Court. ELISHA GRAY (1835–1901) of Ohio was an inventor. He invented, among other things, electro-harmonic telegraphy, which transmitted vocal sounds. On February 14, 1876, Gray filed a caveat with the patent office. Unfortunately he did this only a few hours after Alexander Graham Bell had filed a patent application for a speaking telephone. An infringement lawsuit ensued, with Bell the victor. Gray continued inventing, with his most important invention being the telautograph. JOHN CHIPMAN GRAY (1839–1915) of Massachusetts was a Union soldier and one of the foremost lawyers of his time. He was an authority on real property law. OSCAR [SOMERS] GRAY (1894–1977) of Texas was a nurseryman and pecan grower. He introduced six new varieties of papershell pecans to the market. WELLINGTON BURBANK GRAY (1919–1977) of New York was an artist and an educator. He taught art at the college level and is best remembered for his works in tempera and watercolor.

Genealogies: *Direct Ancestors of the Parker and Gray Families* was compiled by Elizabeth Gray Parker and published in Boston, Massachusetts, in 1967. *A Family History, Gray-Avery and Related Families* was compiled by Lewis and Ruby Gray and published in Burkburnett, Texas, in 1980.

GRAYSON (S.S. Abbreviation: Grayso)

Ranking: 1998 **S.S. Count:** 22,749

Origin: English. Transformation of the first definition of Grave(1).

Famous **Graysons:** WILLIAM GRAYSON (1736?–1790) of Virginia was an aide to George Washington during the Revolutionary War.

Genealogies: *Bateman, Grayson, Boyett, Carter, and Cole Families and Their Kin as They Marked the Way* was compiled by Cynthia E. Snider and published in Oakland, California, in 1985.

GRAZIA

Ranking: 3790 **S.S. Count:** 11,900

Origin: Italian. Cognate to Grace.

Genealogies: None known.

GREATHEAD (S.S. Abbreviation: Greath)

Ranking: 4060 **S.S. Count:** 11,132

Origin: English. Derived from the Old English words "grēat" and "hēafod," meaning large and head. The name was given to those who had large heads.

Genealogies: None known.

GRECO

Ranking: 1996 **S.S. Count:** 22,755

Origin: Italian. 1) derived from the Italian word "Greco," meaning Greek. The name was given to those who came from Greece. 2) same derivation as in 1. The name was given to those who were considered deceptive, as Greeks were often deemed in Italy.

Genealogies: None known.

GREEN

Ranking: 36 S.S. Count: 588,481

Origin: Danish, English, Irish, Jewish, Norwegian. Danish, Norwegian: derived from the Old Norse word "grein," meaning branch. The name may have been an allusion to the branches that make up a family tree. It was often attached to a suffix and was frequently taken ornamentally. English: derived from the Old English word "grēne," referring to the color. The name was given to those who often dressed in green, those who dressed as the "Green Man" (H&H) in May Day festivities, or those who lived near the town commons. Irish: derived from several, now-unknown Gaelic names that were derived from the words "uaithne" and "glas," meaning green and gray, green, or blue. Jewish: derived from the German word "grün" or the Yiddish word "grin," both meaning green. The name was most often taken ornamentally.

Famous **Greens**: BARTHOLOMEW GREEN (1666–1732) of Massachusetts was the chief printer of the *Boston News-Letter*. JAMES GREEN (1712–1767) of Massachusetts established the *Maryland Gazette* in 1745 and became a master typographer. ANNE CATHERINE HOOF GREEN (1720–1775) of Maryland, like her husband Jonas Green, was known as "printer to the Province." She published the *Maryland Gazette* after the death of her husband. THOMAS GREEN (1735–1812) of Connecticut was a printer. He founded the *Connecticut Courant* (now the *Hartford Courant*) in 1764. It is the oldest continuously published newspaper in the country. He also founded the *Connecticut Journal* and *New Haven Post Boy* (1791–1875) in 1767, now called the *New Haven Journal Courier*. ASHBEL GREEN (1762–1848) of New Jersey was outspoken against slavery and served as the president of Princeton University. DUFF GREEN (1791–1875) of Kentucky was a politician and a journalist. He bought the *St. Louis Enquirer* and founded the Jacksonian *United States Telegraph*. He failed in his attempt to purchase Texas, California, and New Mexico for the United States. ANDREW HASWELL GREEN (1820–1903) of Massachusetts was the planner of Central Park and the New York City comptroller who stablized the finances and set up the system of "Greater New York." BENJAMIN EDWARDS GREEN (1822–1907) of Kentucky was an active developer of Georgia. HENRIETTA HOWLAND ROBINSON GREEN (1834–1916) of Massachusetts was a financier. She inherited a great fortune from her family and increased it through shrewd business dealings. Considered the richest woman in the United States, she was often referred to as the "Witch of Wall Street." ANNA KATHARINE GREEN (1846–1935) of New York was an author of detective stories who wrote more than 35 novels. Her *Leavenworth Case* (1878) sold more than 500,000 copies and was made into a play. WILLIAM GREEN (1873–1952) of Ohio was a labor-union leader. He worked in the mines, working his way up the union ladder eventually to the position of president of the United Mine Workers and president of the American Federation of Labor (AFL). He was responsible for expelling Congress of Industrial Organization (CIO) unions from the AFL. PAUL ELIOT GREEN (1894–1981) of North Carolina was a playwright and a professor at the University of North Carolina. He served as the president of the American Folk Festival and wrote many plays, one of which, *In Abraham's Bosom*, won a Pultizer Prize. FLETCHER MELVIN GREEN (1895–1978) of Georgia was an educator and a historian. He was a professor of history at several major universities and the author of several books on the subject of southern history. CONSTANCE MCLAUGHLIN GREEN (1897–1975) of Michigan was an early scholar in the field of urban history as author of *Holyoke, Massachusetts: A Case History of the Industrial Revolution in America* (1939). Her book *Washington: Village and Capital, 1800–1878* (1962) won a Pulitzer Prize.

Genealogies: *A Branch from the Green Tree* was compiled by Robert M. Green and published in Baltimore, Maryland, in 1978. *The Descendants of John Segar of South Kingstown, Rhode Island: Including the Descendants of William Browning and Mary Hoxsie (Lewis) Greene* [also Green] *of Charlestown, Rhode Island* was compiled by William E. Wright and published in Houston, Texas, in 1992. *Green(e) Chronology 1600–1650 Virginia* was compiled by Dorothy H. Ward and published in Ft. Lauderdale, Florida, in 1982.

GREENACRE, GREENALF, GREENAWAY (S.S. Abbreviation: Greena)

Ranking: 4667 S.S. Count: 9584

Origin: Greenacre, Greenalf—English; Greenaway—English, Welsh. Greenacre: derived from the Old English words "grēne" and "œcer," meaning green and cultivated land. The name was given to those who lived near a stretch of lush, verdant land. Greenalf: transformation of Greenhalgh. Greenaway (English): derived from the Old English words "grēn" and "weg," meaning green and path. The name was given to those who lived by a grassy pathway. Greenaway (Welsh): transformation of the Welsh first name Goronwy, probably originating from a family name meaning "heron" (H&H).

Genealogies: None known.

GREENBAUM, GREENBERG, GREENBERGER, GREENBLAT, GREENBLATT, GREENBOM ET AL. (S.S. Abbreviation: Greenb)

Ranking: 867 S.S. Count: 49,601

Origin: Jewish. Greenbaum, Greenbom: derived from the German words "grün" and "baum," meaning green and tree. Greenberg, Greenberger: derived from the German words "grün" and "berg," meaning green and hill. Greenblat, Greenblatt: derived from the German words "grün" and "blat," meaning green and leaf.

Genealogies: None known.

GREENE

Ranking: 186 **S.S. Count:** 184,943

Origin: English. Transformation of Green.

Famous Greenes: NATHANAEL GREENE (1742–1786) of Rhode Island was a Revolutionary War officer. He led the left wing of the American forces at Trenton, New Jersey, on December 26, 1776. As a brigadier general, he led a series of assaults against the British, forcing them out of Georgia and the Carolinas. His wife, CATHERINE LITTLEFIELD GREENE (1755–1814) of Rhode Island, was a moral and financial supporter of Eli Whitney in his development of the cotton gin. SARAH PRATT MCLEAN GREENE (1856–1935) of Connecticut was a writer well known for her portrayal of real people in 11 editions of the fictional *Cape Cod Folks.* CHARLES SUMNER GREENE (1868–1957) of Missouri and his brother, HENRY MATHER GREENE (1870–1954) of Ohio, were architects who established their partnership in Pasadena, California, where they became famous for their bungalow-style house. Their best-known work is the Gamble House, which is now the Greene and Greene Library. BELLE DA COSTA GREENE (1883–1950) of Virginia was librarian and bibliographer for J. Pierpont Morgan. She traveled extensively around the world to procure books and manuscripts. EDWARD MELVIN GREENE (1904–1976) of Georgia was the president of the Dauphin Deposit Bank and Trust Co. in Harrisburg, Pennsylvania. During his presidency, the bank's size and assets grew. EDWARD JAMES GREENE (1908–1977) of New York was a management consultant and served as Dwight D. Eisenhower's personal assistant. GEORGE KENNETH GREENE (1911–1977) of Illinois was a nuclear physicist. He had a worldwide reputation as a designer and builder of atomic-particle accelerators.

Genealogies: *The Descendants of John Segar of South Kingstown, Rhode Island: Including the Descendants of William Browning and Mary Hoxsie (Lewis) Greene of Charlestown, Rhode Island* was compiled by William E. Wright and published in Houston, Texas, in 1992. *Ancestry and Descendants of Stephen Greene and Martha Mifflin Houston, His Wife* was compiled by Walter Lee Sheppard and published in the 1960s. *Green(e) Chronology 1600–1650 Virginia* was compiled by Dorothy H. Ward and published in Ft. Lauderdale, Florida, in 1982.

GREENFELD, GREENFIELD (S.S. Abbreviation: Greenf)

Ranking: 2368 **S.S. Count:** 19,164

Origin: Greenfield—English, Jewish; Greenfeld—Jewish. Greenfield (English): 1) derived from the Old English words "grēn" and "feld," meaning green and pasture. The name was often given to those who lived near a pasture or meadow. 2) derived from the Germanic first name "Guarin," meaning guard (a popular name in France taken from the Norman warrior Guérin de Montglave), *and the Old French word "ville," meaning settlement. The name was given to those who came from Greenfeld, the name of several places in Normandy. Greenfeld, Greenfield (Jewish): derived from the German words "grün" and "feld," meaning green and field.*

Famous Greenfields: ELIZABETH TAYLOR GREENFIELD (1817?–1876) of Mississippi was born of slave parents in the home of her owner, Elizabeth Greenfield, whose name she took as hers and used in conjunction with her own surname, Taylor. A self-taught musician and singer, she went on to become an international entertainer.

Genealogies: None known.

GREENHALL, GREENHALGH, GREENHAM, GREENHILL, GREENHORN, GREENHOUSE ET AL. (S.S. Abbreviation: Greenh)

Ranking: 3253 **S.S. Count:** 13,972

Origin: Greenhall, Greenhalgh, Greenham—English; Greenhill, Grenhouse—English, Jewish; Greenhorn—Scottish. Greenhall: derived from the Old English words "grēn" and "holh," meaning green and hollow. The name was given to those who came from Greenhall, the name of two places in Lancashire, England. Greenhalgh: derived from the Old English words "grēne" and "holh," meaning green and hollow. The name was given to those who lived in Greenhalgh, the name of several places in Lancashire, England. Greenham: 1) derived from the Old English words "grēne" and "hamm," meaning green and water meadow. The name was given to those who came from Greenham, a place in Berkshire, England. 2) derived from the Old English words "grēne" and "hām," meaning green and homestead. The name was given to those who came from Greenham, a place in Berkshire, England. Greenhill (English): derived from the Old English words "grēn" and "hyll," meaning green and hill. The name was given to those who came from Greenhill, the name of various places in England. Greenhill (Jewish): transformation of Green(berg). Greenhorn (Scottish): derived from the Old English words "grēne" and "hyrne," meaning green and corner. The name was given to those who came from Greenhorn, the name of a place in a now-unknown location. Greenhouse (English): derived from the Old English words "grēn" and "hūs," meaning green and house. The name was given to those who lived near the town commons and was not used to denote a room used to cultivate tender plants until the 17th century. Greenhouse (Jewish): derived from the German words "grün" and "haus," meaning green and house.

Famous Bearers: JACOB PEARL GREENHILL (1895–1975) of New York was a physician and an authority in the specialty field of obstetrics and gynecology.

Genealogies: None known.

GREENLAND, GREENLEE, GREENLEY, GREENLY (S.S. Abbreviation: Greenl)

Ranking: 1637 **S.S. Count:** 27,460

Origin: English. Greenland: derived from the Old English words "grēn" and "land," meaning green and land. The name was given to those who lived near communal pastures. Greenlee, Greenley, Greenly: derived from the Old English words "grēn" and "lēah," meaning green and wood. The name was given to those who came from Grindley, the name of various places in England.

Genealogies: None known.

GREENSLADE, GREENSMITH, GREENSPAN, GREENSPON (S.S. Abbreviation: Greens)

Ranking: 2918 **S.S. Count:** 15,595

Origin: Greenslade, Greensmith—English; Greenspan, Greenspon—Jewish. Greenslade: derived from the Old English words "grēn" and "slœd," meaning green and valley. The name was given to those who lived near a verdant dell. Greensmith: 1) derived from the Middle English words "grene" and "smith," meaning green and metalworker. The name was often given to coppersmiths and refers to the quality and color of oxidized copper. 2) same derivation as in Smith. The prefix Green refers to a metalworker who handles lead. Greenspan, Greenspon: derived from the German word "Grünspan," meaning verdigris, a green or bluish film which develops on copper, brass, or bronze after being exposed to the atmosphere for long periods of time. The name was often taken ornamentally.

Genealogies: None known.

GREENWALD, GREENWAY, GREENWELL, GREENWOOD (S.S. Abbreviation: Greenw)

Ranking: 631 **S.S. Count:** 65,542

Origin: Greenwell—English; Greenwood—English, Jewish; Greenwald—Jewish; Greenway—English, Welsh. Greenwell: 1) derived from the Old English words "grēn" and "well(a)," meaning green and stream or spring. The name was given to those who lived in a verdant meadow by a stream. 2) same derivation as 1. The name was given to those who came from Greenwell, the name of various places in Northumberland, England. Greenwood (English): derived from the Old English words "grēn" and "wudu," meaning green and wood. The name was given to those who lived in a lush forest. Greenwood (Jewish): derived from the German words "grün" and "holtz," meaning green and wood. Greenwald: derived from the German words "grün" and "wald," meaning green and forest. Greenway: transformation of and cognate to Greenaway.

Famous Bearers: ISAAC GREENWOOD (1702–1745) of Massachusetts was the author of the first American mathematics textbook by a native American, titled *Arithmetick, Vulgar and Decimal* in 1729. JOHN GREENWOOD (1760–1819) of Massachusetts was a dentist and the inventor of the foot-power drill, springs to hold artificial plates in position, and the use of porcelain for false teeth. He is the dentist who made a set of false teeth for George Washington. MILES GREENWOOD (1807–1885) of New Jersey owned the Eagle Iron Works in Cincinnati, where the first steam fire engine in the United States was made.

Genealogies: *Greenway Miscellany* was compiled by Carl Forrest Greenway and published in New York in the 1970s. *Greenwood Genealogies, 1154–1914: The Ancestry and Descendants of Thomas Greenwood of Newton, Mass., Nathaniel and Samuel Greenwood of Boston, Mass., John Greenwood of Virginia, and Many Later Arrivals in America, Also the Early History of the Greenwoods in England and the Arms They Used* was compiled by Frederick Greenwood and published in New York in 1914.

GREER

Ranking: 516 **S.S. Count:** 77,737

Origin: Scottish. Transformation of Gregory.

Famous Greers: JAMES AUGUSTIN GREER (1833–1904) of Ohio was a career naval officer and a graduate of the U.S. Naval Academy. DAVID HUMMELL GREER (1844–1919) of West Virginia was an Episcopal clergyman who had parishes in Kentucky and Rhode Island.

Genealogies: *Greer Family* was compiled by William Greer Peck and published in Atascadero, California, in the 1980s. *Greer-McNeill Family History* was compiled by Etta S. Greer and published in Greenville, South Carolina, in 1984.

GREGG

Ranking: 1200 **S.S. Count:** 36,581

Origin: English. Transformation of Gregory.

Famous Greggs: WILLIAM GREGG (1800–1867) of Virginia was an industrialist with huge fortunes from the cotton and watch industries. He promoted industrialization. JOSIAH GREGG (1806–1850) of Tennessee was a frontiersman. He was an army agent and a translator in the Southwest. MAXEY GREGG (1814–1862) of South Carolina was a Confederate general and a states' rights leader from his state of birth. DAVID MCMURTRIE GREGG (1833–1916) of Pennsylvania was a Union soldier in the Civil War. General Ulysses S. Grant considered him one of the best when he defeated J.E.B. Stuart's charge against General George Gordon Meade at Gettysburg. JOHN ROBERT GREGG (1867–1948) of Ireland is most famous for his invention of a new kind of shorthand system. He was the author of the *Gregg Shorthand Manual*.

Genealogies: *A Crane's Foot (or Pedigree) of Branches of the Gregg, Stuart, Robertson, Dobbs and Allied Families* was compiled by E. Stuart Gregg Jr. and published in Hilton Head Island, South Carolina, in 1975. *William Grigg I,*

Immigrant to the Virginia Colony: 340 Years of His Descendants, 1640–1980 was compiled by Cleo Grigg Johnson Gilchrist and published in Boise, Idaho, in 1980.

GREGOR (ALSO GREGORCZYK, GREGORETTI, GREGORIO, GREGORIOU, GREGORY ET AL.)

Ranking: 262 S.S. Count: 139,285

Origin: Gregory—English; Gregor—Czech, English, Jewish; Gregoretti—Italian; Gregorczyk—Polish; Gregorio—Spanish; Gregoriou—Greek. Derived from the Greek word "grēgorein," meaning to be watchful. The Latin form of the same word, "gregorius," was later interchanged colloquially with the Latin word "gregis," meaning flock, perhaps because Christian imagery refers to the good shepherd of the flock.

Famous **Bearers**: SAMUEL GREGORY (1813–1872) of Vermont was a pioneer in the medical education of women. JOHN MILTON GREGORY (1822–1898) of New York was the first president of the University of Illinois, where he worked to make it an academic, not vocational, institution. DANIEL SEELYE GREGORY (1832–1915) of New York was the managing editor of *Standard Dictionary of the English Language.* CASPER RENÉ GREGORY (1846–1917) of Pennsylvania was a New Testament scholar. STEPHEN STRONG GREGORY (1849–1920) of New York was a trial lawyer and the defense attorney for Eugene Debs and the American Railway Union in the Pullman strike. CHARLES NOBLE GREGORY (1851–1932) of New York was a professor of law at George Washington University. THOMAS WATT GREGORY (1861–1933) of Mississippi was the U.S. attorney general during World War I, when the U.S. Department of Justice greatly expanded. CLIFFORD VERNE GREGORY (1883–1941) of Iowa was a champion of the farmer and a spokesman for the farmer on federal committees. MENAS SARKAS BOULGOURJIAN GREGORY (1872–1941) of Turkey was one of the fathers of American psychiatry as a profession.

Genealogies: None known.

GREINER (S.S. Abbreviation: Greine)

Ranking: 3863 S.S. Count: 11,670

Origin: German. The name was given to a disagreeable, truculent person.

Genealogies: None known.

GRENIER (S.S. Abbreviation: Grenie)

Ranking: 4612 S.S. Count: 9688

Origin: French. The name was given to a person who ran a granary.

Genealogies: None known.

GRESHAM (S.S. Abbreviation: Gresha)

Ranking: 2781 S.S. Count: 16,383

Origin: English. Derived from the Old English words "græs" and "hām," meaning grass and homestead. The name was given to those who came from Gresham, a place in Norfolk, England.

Famous **Greshams**: WALTER QUINTIN GRESHAM (1832–1895) of Indiana was the Union major general of the volunteers during the Civil War, and this position opened many political doors for him after the war. RUPERT NEELY GRESHAM (1892–1976) of Texas was a lawyer who specialized in tax law and estate planning.

Genealogies: *A Family Named Gresham* was compiled by Virgil L. Gresham and published in Hutchinson, Kansas, in 1972.

GREY

Ranking: 2931 S.S. Count: 15,533

Origin: English. Transformation of Gray.

Famous **Greys**: ZANE GREY (1875–1939) of Ohio was a dentist who practiced in New York. He is best remembered for the stories he wrote about the American West.

Genealogies: None known.

GRICE

Ranking: 3479 S.S. Count: 12,973

Origin: English. 1) derived from the Old French word "gris," meaning gray. The name was given to those who had gray hair. 2) derived from the Middle English word "grise," meaning pig. The name was given to swineherds or was used as a nickname meaning pig.

Genealogies: None known.

GRIEGO

Ranking: 4917 S.S. Count: 9101

Origin: Spanish. The name means Greek.

Genealogies: *Good-Bye My Land of Enchantment: A True Story of Some of the First Spanish-Speaking Natives and Early Settlers of San Miguel County, Territory of New Mexico* was compiled by Alfonso Griego and published in 1981.

GRIER (ALSO GRIERSON)

Ranking: 2431 S.S. Count: 18,658

Origin: Scottish. Cognates to Gregory.

Famous **Bearers**: ROBERT COOPER GRIER (1794–1870) of Pennsylvania was an associate justice of the U.S. Supreme Court. BENJAMIN HENRY GRIERSON (1826–1911) of Pennsylvania was a Union soldier who rose through the ranks. He is credited with the famous charge from La Grange, Tennessee, to Baton Rouge, Louisiana, slicing through the Confederacy and destroying railroads and all in his way. "Grierson's Raid" was the main reason behind Vicksburg's fall. FRANCIS GRIERSON (1848–1927) of England was a musician and author who enjoyed musical success under the name of Jesse Shepard in Europe.

Genealogies: *The Griers: Pioneers in America and*

Canada, 1816–1991 was compiled by William Milton Grier Jr. and published in Denver, Colorado, in 1991. *The Grier, New Mexico Story* was compiled by Stanley Francis Louis Crocchiola and published in Pep, Texas, in 1965.

GRIFFE (ALSO GRIFFEY)

Ranking: 3351 **S.S. Count:** 13,534

Origin: Griffe—French; Griffey—Irish. Griffe: 1) derived from the Old French word "griffe," meaning claw. The name was given to those who were considered clutching or malevolent. 2) same derivation as 1. The name was used to refer jokingly to a person with an artificial hand. Griffey: transformation of Griffin.

Genealogies: None known.

GRIFFIN, GRIFFIS, GRIFFITH, GRIFFITHS
(S.S. Abbreviation: Griffi)

Ranking: 58 **S.S. Count:** 415,719

Origin: Griffin—English, Irish, Welsh; Griffis, Griffith, Griffiths—Welsh. Griffin (English): derived from the Middle English word "griffin," meaning griffin. The name was given to those who were considered violent or menacing. Griffin (Irish): derived from the Gaelic name Ó Gríiobhtha, meaning "descendant of Gríiobhtha" (H&H), meaning griffin. Griffin (Welsh): transformation of Griffith. Griffis, Griffith, Griffiths: derived from the Old Welsh first name Gruffydd, which is derived from the Old Welsh words "griff," of unclear significance, and "udd," meaning chief or lord.

Famous **Bearers:** BENJAMIN GRIFFITH (1688–1768) of Wales was a Baptist clergyman whose records became one of the best sources for the history of the Baptist Church. CYRUS GRIFFIN (1748–1810) of Virginia was the president of the Continental Congress and the judge who presided over Aaron Burr's trial for treason. JOHN WILLIS GRIFFITHS (1809–1882) of New York was a naval architect who developed the iron keelson, the bilge keel, and the twin and triple screws. EUGENE GRIFFIN (1855–1907) of Maine was an electrical engineer who pushed for the use of electric streetcars. ROBERT STANISLAUS GRIFFIN (1857–1933) of Virginia was responsible for the expansion of the navy in World War I. MARION LUCY MAHONY GRIFFIN (1871–1961) of Illinois and WALTER BURLEY GRIFFIN (1876–1937) of Illinois were partners in marriage and architecture. They worked together in the Oak Park, Illinois, studio of Frank Lloyd Wright, where she excelled at building designs and he at landscape architecture. Walter Griffin, with his wife's assistance, won the 1912 competition to design the city of Canberra, Australia, which began a 20-year period when they worked together in that country. DAVID LEWELYN WARK GRIFFITH (1875–1948) of Kentucky was a motion-picture director and producer. He was a pioneer in the film techniques of fade-in and fade-out, closeup, cross-cutting, pan shots, soft focus, and special framing. He introduced Mary Pickford, Dorothy and Lillian Gish, Lionel Barrymore, and Mack Sennett to the screen and was one of the founding members of the United Artists Co. EMILY GRIFFITH (1880?–1947) of Ohio, a teacher, founded the Denver (Colorado) Opportunity School as an institution where children and adults already working could attend and seek training for better opportunities.

Genealogies: *Gershom & Phoebe Griffin, Their Ancestors and Descendants* was compiled by Elaine Washburn Olney and published in Manhattan, Kansas, in 1976. *A Griffin and Related Families History* was compiled by Paul E. Griffin and published in Parsons, West Virginia, in 1987.

GRIGGS

Ranking: 1261 **S.S. Count:** 34,949

Origin: English. Transformation of Gregory.

Famous **Griggses:** JOHN WILLIAM GRIGGS (1849–1927) of New Jersey was the governor of that state; U.S. attorney general; and judge and permanent member of the Court of Arbitration, The Hague.

Genealogies: None known.

GRIGSBY (S.S. Abbreviation: Grigsb)

Ranking: 2782 **S.S. Count:** 16,382

Origin: English. Derived from the English name Grig, which is derived from the name Gregory. The name was given to those who resided at the home of a person named Grig.

Famous **Grigsbys:** HUGH BLAIR GRIGSBY (1806–1881) of Virginia was a newspaper editor and a historian who specialized in Virginia.

Genealogies: *Grigsby X Leonard: Bicentennial 1776–1976 Genealogy: Paternal Great Grand Fathers of Carroll Mendenhall Leonard* was compiled by Carroll Mendenhall Leonard and published in Stillwater, Oklahoma, in 1977. *Memorabilia, the Grigsby Family Reunion Book, 1779–1979* was compiled by Elizabeth M. Nicholson and published in Chestnut Hill, Massachusetts, in 1979.

GRILLO (ALSO GRILLON, GRILLONE, GRILLONI, GRILLOT)

Ranking: 4936 **S.S. Count:** 9069

Origin: Grillon, Grillot—French; Grillo, Grillone, Grillono—Italian. 1) the name was given to those who were considered to have a cricketlike quality. 2) the name was given to small, youthful men.

Genealogies: None known.

GRIM

Ranking: 4282 **S.S. Count:** 10,492

Origin: Dutch, English, Flemish. Transformation of and cognate to Grimm.

Famous **Grims:** DAVID GRIM (1737–1826) of Bavaria is

best known for his pen-and-ink sketches of New York City landmarks.

Genealogies: *Pennsylvania-German Settlers in Nebraska: Charles T. and Barbara Grim* was compiled by Jane Howard Dein and published in Lincoln, Nebraska, in 1988.

GRIMES
Ranking: 589 **S.S. Count:** 70,744

Origin: English. Derived from the Old English word "grima," meaning mask. The name took the form of "Grim" in Anglo-Scandinavian regions until the 12th century. It was often used as a nickname for those with the given name Woden, which means "masked person" or "shape changer" (H&H) and which was apparently given to male children in the hopes that the god Woden would provide them with protection.

Famous Grimeses: JAMES STANLEY GRIMES (1807–1903) of Massachusetts was an early evolutionist. JAMES WILSON GRIMES (1816–1872) of New Hampshire was a governor of Iowa and a U.S. senator. During the impeachment proceedings against President Andrew Johnson, Grimes suffered a stroke and had to be carried into the Senate chamber so that his vote for acquittal could be recorded. ABSALOM CARLISLE GRIMES (1834–1911) was a Mississippi River boat pilot, a Confederate mail runner, and a partner of Mark Twain in their band of a dozen or so wandering Confederate troops. He was captured and sentenced to death, a punishment that was commuted to imprisonment during the war by President Abraham Lincoln. He lived to marry twice.

Genealogies: *Genealogy of Myers and Grimes Families* was compiled by W. Oscar Grimes and published in Hillsboro, Indiana, 1969.

GRIMM
Ranking: 1455 **S.S. Count:** 30,624

Origin: German. Derived from the Old High German word "grimm," meaning austere. The name was often given to those who were considered dour and formidable.

Genealogies: None known.

GRIMME (ALSO GRIMMER, GRIMMERT)
Ranking: 4868 **S.S. Count:** 9198

Origin: Grimme—English; Grimmer—English, German; Grimmert—German. Grimme, Grimmer, Grimmert (German): transformations of and cognates to Grimm. Grimmer (English): derived from the Norman first name Grimier, which is derived from the Germanic words "grim" and "heri," meaning helmet or mask and army.

Genealogies: None known.

GRISHAEV, GRISHAGIN, GRISHAKIN, GRISHAKOV, GRISHANIN, GRISHANKOV, GRISHANOV (S.S. Abbreviation: Grisha)
Ranking: 4400 **S.S. Count:** 10,198

Origin: Russian. Cognates to Gregory.
Genealogies: None known.

GRISSOM, GRISSON (S.S. Abbreviation: Grisso)
Ranking: 2660 **S.S. Count:** 17,123

Origin: English. Transformations of the first definition of Grice.

Famous Bearers: VIRGIL IVAN (GUS) GRISSOM (1926–1967) of Indiana was an astronaut. He flew in a *Mercury* flight and a *Gemini* flight. He was killed in a flash fire during an *Apollo* training flight.

Genealogies: None known.

GRISWOLD (S.S. Abbreviation: Griswo)
Ranking: 2883 **S.S. Count:** 15,800

Origin: English. The name was given to those who lived in woods inhabited by pigs.

Famous Griswolds: MATTHEW GRISWOLD (1714–1799) of Lyme, Connecticut, was a Revolutionary War patriot, governor of Connecticut, and chief justice of the Connecticut Supreme Court. His son, ROGER GRISWOLD (1762–1812) of Lyme, Connecticut, was a member of Congress, then a governor of Connecticut. In 1798 he became famous for brawling on the House floor with Matthew Lyon of Vermont, for which a line from a poem was written: "a strange, offensive brute, too wild to tame, too base to shoot." STANLEY GRISWOLD (1763–1815) of Connecticut was a Congregational clergyman, a U.S. senator from Ohio, and a circuit judge of the Illinois territory. ALEXANDER VIETS GRISWOLD (1766–1843) of Connecticut was an Episcopal clergyman who was responsible for the church's spread throughout New England. RUFUS WILMOT GRISWOLD (1815–1857) of Vermont was a journalist and anthologist who is best remembered as Edgar Allan Poe's editor and literary executor, in which positions he made a great many errors. JOHN AUGUSTUS GRISWOLD (1818–1872) of New York was an iron manufacturer who made pieces of the ironclad the *Monitor*. WILLIAM MCCRILLIS GRISWOLD (1853–1899) of Maine was the son of Rufus. He edited his father's correspondence.

Genealogies: *The Griswold Family, England-America: Edward of Windsor, Connecticut, Matthew of Lyme, Connecticut, Michael of Wethersfield, Connecticut* was compiled by Glenn E. Griswold and published in Middleboro, Massachusetts, in 1935. *The Griswold Family: The First Five Generations in America* was compiled by Esther Griswold French and published in Wethersfield, Connecticut, in 1990.

GROFFMANN (S.S. Abbreviation: Groff)
Ranking: 3321 **S.S. Count:** 13,653

Origin: German. Derived from the Old High German

word "gerob," meaning coarse or crude. The name was given to those who were considered crass and ill-bred.

Genealogies: None known.

GROGAN

Ranking: 2767 S.S. Count: 16,484

Origin: Irish. 1) derived from the Gaelic name Ó Grúgáin, meaning "descendant of Grúagán" (H&H), which is derived from the Gaelic word "grúg," meaning anger and fierceness. 2) derived from the Gaelic name Ó Grugáin, meaning "descendant of Gruagán" (H&H), which is derived from the Gaelic word "gruag," meaning hair.

Genealogies: None known.

GROOMS

Ranking: 3101 S.S. Count: 14,656

Origin: English. 1) the name was given to male servants and sometimes to young boys who worked as servants. 2) the name was given to those who worked tending sheep.

Genealogies: None known.

GROSS

Ranking: 345 S.S. Count: 110,347

Origin: English, German, Jewish. English: 1) derived from the Old French word "gros," meaning large or stout. The name was given to large men. 2) derived from the Old English word "grēat," meaning great or large. The name was given to large men. German: derived from the Old High German word "grōz," meaning large or heavy. The name was given to large men. Jewish: same derivation as in the German definition.

Famous **Grosses:** SAMUEL DAVID GROSS (1805–1884) of Pennsylvania was a surgeon who wrote several books on the subject of surgery. SAMUEL WEISSELL GROSS (1837–1889) of Ohio was the son of Samuel David and also a surgeon. He co-developed the radical operation for cancer.

Genealogies: *A Family History and Genealogy; The Descendants of Johannes Fluck. . . Philip Christian Gross. . . John A. Greup. . . Giving Primary Consideration to the Lines of Their Descendants* was compiled by Laura Lydia Trumbower Price and published in Telford, Pennsylvania, in 1969. *The Family History of Friedrich Gross 1853–1968* was compiled by Charles and Eugenia Gross and published in Horsham, Pennsylvania, in 1969.

GROSSMAN, GROSSMANN (S.S. Abbreviation: Grossm)

Ranking: 1482 S.S. Count: 30,036

Origin: Jewish. Cognates to the German definition of Gross.

Famous **Bearers:** GEORG MARTIN GROSSMANN (1823–1897) of Germany was a Lutheran minister who helped to organize the German Lutheran Synod of Iowa. LOUIS

GROSSMANN (1863–1926) of Austria was a pioneer in the modernization of Jewish religious education.

Genealogies: None known.

GROTH

Ranking: 4823 S.S. Count: 9284

Origin: German. Transformation of the German definition of Gross.

Genealogies: *The Putzier-Vogel and Groth-Nielsen Families* was compiled by Clifford R. Putzier and published in Strafford, Missouri, in 1983.

GROVE

Ranking: 1428 S.S. Count: 31,201

Origin: English, German. English: 1) derived from the Old English word "grāf," meaning grove or wood. The name was often given to those who lived near a copse or wood. 2) derived from the Protestant French surname Le Groux or Le Greux of the 16th and 17th centuries, which is of uncertain derivation. German: transformation of Groff(man).

Genealogies: *A Backward Glance* was compiled by Jane Parker McManus and published in Pineville, Louisiana, in 1986. *Land of the Tamarack: Up-North Wisconsin* was compiled by Theodore Francis Groves and published in Berkeley, California, in 1986.

GROVER

Ranking: 1978 S.S. Count: 22,901

Origin: English. Transformation of the first definition of Grove.

Famous **Grovers:** LA FAYETTE GROVER (1823–1911) of Maine was influential in the presidential election of 1876 and represented Oregon in the House and Senate. He was feared and hated by the people of Oregon. His brother, CUVIER GROVER (1828–1885), was a career army officer who participated in the Civil War and the exploration of the far West.

Genealogies: *Stone, Grover, Ball and Everett Ancestry: Being the Ancestral Lines of John Wesley Stone, Delia Maria Theresa Grover Stone, Dan Harvey Ball and Emma Eugenia Everett Ball, All of Marguette, Michigan* was compiled by Frank Bush Stone and published in Summit, New Jersey, in 1990.

GROVES

Ranking: 1242 S.S. Count: 35,554

Origin: English. Transformation of the first definition of Grove.

Famous **Groveses:** LESLIE RICHARD GROVES (1896–1970) of New York was an army officer who commanded the Manhattan Engineer District (the atomic bomb project).

Genealogies: *Groves and Allied Families: 1982 Supplement Plus Complete New Genealogical Encyclopedia Plus*

Corrected and Expanded Basic Book of 1977 was compiled by James Groves and published in Decorah, Iowa, in 1982.

GRUBB

Ranking: 2149 S.S. Count: 21,328

Origin: English. Derived from the Middle English word "grub," meaning midget. The name was given to those who were considered short or dwarfish.

Genealogies: *Descendants of John Ambrose Rowe, Weld County Pioneer, 1828–1886: and Related Families of Barry, Grubb, McLeod, Morris, Palmer, Skinner and Southard* was compiled by Arliss S. Monk and published in Greeley, Colorado, in 1975.

GRUBBS

Ranking: 2046 S.S. Count: 22,345

Origin: English. 1) transformation of Grubb. 2) the name was often given to those who were considered crude or unrefined.

Genealogies: None known.

GRUBER

Ranking: 2221 S.S. Count: 20,671

Origin: German, Jewish. Derived from the German word "grube," meaning pit or hollow, which is derived from the Old High German word "graben," meaning to dig. The suffix "er" indicates habitation. The name was often given to those who lived in a basin or hollow.

Genealogies: *Grubn—Grube Couzins: Germany 1803 to Gallia County, Ohio* [also Gruber family] was compiled by Jane R. McCafferty and published in Fort Washington, Maryland, in 1981. *Gruber/Reissenweber, a Generation of Letters: Courtesy of the Ancestors* was compiled by Alice M. Gruber and published in Cuyahoga Falls, Ohio, in 1978.

GUAJAR

Ranking: 4352 S.S. Count: 10,304

Origin: Spanish. Uncertain etymology.

Genealogies: None known.

GUARINI, GUARINIELLO, GUARINO, GUARINONI (S.S. Abbreviation: Guarin)

Ranking: 4345 S.S. Count: 10,316

Origin: Italian. Cognates to Waring, an English name derived from the Norman first name Warin, which is derived from the Germanic word "warin," meaning guard.

Genealogies: None known.

GUENTHER, GUENTHNER (S.S. Abbreviation: Guenth)

Ranking: 3097 S.S. Count: 14,668

Origin: German. Derived from the first name Guntard, meaning bold or war.

Genealogies: None known.

GUERIN (ALSO GUERINI, GUERINO)

Ranking: 4618 S.S. Count: 9672

Origin: Guerin—English; Guerini, Guerino—Italian. Transformations of and cognates to Guarini et al.

Genealogies: None known.

GUERRA (ALSO GUERRAZZI)

Ranking: 934 S.S. Count: 46,189

Origin: Guerra—Italian, Portuguese, Spanish; Guerrazzi—Italian. 1) cognates to the English name Warr, which is derived from the Old French word "guerre," meaning war. The name was given to an argumentative or hostile person. 2) same derivation as in 1. The name was often given to a courageous soldier.

Genealogies: None known.

GUERRE (ALSO GUERREAU, GUERREIRO, GUERRERO, GUERRERU)

Ranking: 637 S.S. Count: 65,228

Origin: Guerre, Guerreau—French; Guerreru—Italian; Guerreiro—Portuguese; Guerrero—Spanish. Cognates to Guerra.

Genealogies: *The Guerreros of Ermita: Family History and Personal Memoirs* was compiled by Wilfrido Maria Guerrero and published in Detroit, Michigan, in 1988.

GUESS

Ranking: 4494 S.S. Count: 9972

Origin: English. Transformation of Guest.

Genealogies: *Guest-Guess, History and Lineage in America* was compiled by Alta Louise Biggs Martin and published in Atlanta, Texas, in 1981.

GUEST (ALSO GUESTIER)

Ranking: 3422 S.S. Count: 13,217

Origin: Guest—English; Guestier—French. Guest: derived from the Old English word "giest," meaning guest or visitor. The name was often given to those who were new to a town or community. Guestier: cognate to Waite.

Famous **Bearers:** EDGAR ALBERT GUEST (1881–1959) of England was on the staff of the *Detroit Free Press* and wrote books of poetry.

Genealogies: *Guest-Guess, History and Lineage in America* was compiled by Alta Louise Biggs Martin and published in Atlanta, Texas, in 1981. *Our Guest Is Your Guess: With Related Families of Biss, Jones, Gimbel, and Gist: Including Over One Thousand Other Surnames* was compiled by Patricia Ann Guest and published in Oceanside, California, in 1984.

GUEVARA

Ranking: 2681 S.S. Count: 17,028

Origin: Basque. Uncertain etymology. The name was given to those who came from a place in the province of Alava, in the Basque country.

Genealogies: None known.

GUFFEY

Ranking: 4800 S.S. Count: 9330

Origin: Irish, Scottish. Derived from the name Cobhthaigh, meaning victorious.

Genealogies: None known.

GUIDRY

Ranking: 1851 S.S. Count: 24,448

Origin: Italian? Uncertain etymology. Possible cognate to Guy.

Genealogies: None known.

GUILLE (ALSO GUILLELME, GUILLEM, GUILLEMET, GUILLERME, GUILLERMIC ET AL.)

Ranking: 2404 S.S. Count: 18,848

Origin: Guille, Guillelme, Guillemet, Guillerme, Guillermic—French; Guillem—Provençal. Guille: cognate to the first definition of Will. Guillelme, Guillem, Guillemet, Guillerme, Guillermic et al.: cognates to William.

Genealogies: None known.

GUILLON, GUILLONEAU, GUILLOT ET AL., GUILLOU, GUILLOUD ET AL. (S.S. Abbreviation: Guillo)

Ranking: 1732 S.S. Count: 25,898

Origin: French. Cognates to the first definition of Will.

Genealogies: None known.

GUINNARD, GUINNESS (S.S. Abbreviation: Guinn)

Ranking: 2493 S.S. Count: 18,188

Origin: Guinnard—French; Guinness—Irish. Guinnard: derived from an unknown Germanic first name that comprised the Germanic words "win" and "hard," meaning friend and robust. Guinness: transformation of McGuinness.

Genealogies: None known.

GULLEY

Ranking: 3406 S.S. Count: 13,282

Origin: English. 1) the name was often given to those who lived at the "sign of the little gull" (ES). 2) the name was often given to those who lived by a strait.

Genealogies: *John Gulley Genealogy: A Planter in Alabama and Arkansas and His Descendants: Also the Families of Bizzell, Godley, Lingon, Mendenhall, Purifoy and oth-*ers of England and Colonial America was compiled by John Paul and published in Houston, Texas, in 1991.

GUNDERSEN (S.S. Abbreviation: Gunder)

Ranking: 1778 S.S. Count: 25,280

Origin: Danish, Norwegian. Cognate to Gunter.

Genealogies: None known.

GUNN

Ranking: 1340 S.S. Count: 33,007

Origin: English, Scottish. English, Scottish: derived from the Old Norse first name Gunnr (feminine form: Gunne), which is derived from the word "gunn," meaning battle. English: 1) derived from the Middle English word "gunne," meaning cannon. The name was often given to a person who operated artillery machines. 2) same derivation as in 1. The name was often given to an aggressive person.

Famous **Gunns:** FREDERICK WILLIAM GUNN (1816–1881) of Connecticut was a schoolmaster and the founder of "The Gunnery" school. JAMES NEWTON GUNN (1867–1927) of Ohio perfected the tab-type index card and vertical file; he also helped in the organization of Harvard Business School. SELSKAR MICHAEL GUNN (1883–1944) of England was a public-health administrator involved with the Rockefeller Foundation. He worked mostly in China.

Genealogies: *Family Record of the Descendants of James and Harriett Gunn* was compiled by Bruce Alan Gunn and published in Atlanta, Texas, in in 1980. *My Findings* was compiled by Lilian Vesta Brown Johnson and published in Smyrna, Tennessee, in 1987.

GUNTER

Ranking: 1324 S.S. Count: 33,564

Origin: English. Derived from the Old French first name Gontier, which is derived from the Germanic words "gund" and "heri," meaning battle and army.

Famous **Gunters:** ARCHIBALD CLAVERING GUNTER (1847–1907) was a playwright and contemporary novelist. His best-known book was *Mr. Barnes of New York.*

Genealogies: *Gunter* was compiled by Edwin D. Gunter and published in Jacksonville, Texas, in 1983.

GUNTHER (S.S. Abbreviation: Gunthe)

Ranking: 3662 S.S. Count: 12,329

Origin: German. Cognate to Gunter.

Famous **Gunthers:** CHARLES FREDERICK GUNTHER (1837–1920) of Germany was a candy maker whose best-remembered confection is the caramel. JOHN GUNTHER (1901–1970) of Illinois was a journalist. He was a correspondent for several newspapers and the author of the famous "Inside" series, *Inside Europe, Inside Africa, Inside Russia Today,* etc.

Genealogies: None known.

GURLEY

Ranking: 3665 S.S. Count: 12,320

Origin: Manx. Derived from the name Toirdealbbhach, meaning "shaped like the god Thor" (ES).

Famous **Gurleys:** RALPH RANDOLPH GURLEY (1797–1872) of Connecticut was an agent, then a director, of the American Colonization Society, which was formed to colonize Liberia with African-Americans from the United States. He is the man credited with naming Liberia and its capital, Monrovia.

Genealogies: None known.

GUSTAFSEN, GUSTAFSSON (S.S. Abbreviation: Gustaf)

Ranking: 1055 S.S. Count: 41,715

Origin: Gustafsen—Danish, Norwegian; Gustafsson— Swedish. Derived from a now-unknown Old Norse first name that is derived from Gaut, the name of the Scandinavian tribe to which Beowulf belonged, and the Old Norse word "staf," meaning staff or club.

Genealogies: None known.

GUTHRIE (S.S. Abbreviation: Guthri)

Ranking: 924 S.S. Count: 46,712

Origin: Irish, Scottish. Irish: derived from the Gaelic name Ó Flaithimh, meaning "descendant of Flaitheamh" (H&H), which is a first name meaning prince. The name Guthrie came about when Ó Flaithimh was confused with the Gaelic word Laithigh, meaning mud, which was then associated with gutters. Scottish: 1) derived from the Gaelic word "gaothair," meaning windy place, and the regional suffix "ach." The name was given to those who lived near Forfar, in Tayside County in Scotland. 2) derived from the Gaelic name Mag Uchtre, meaning "son of Uchtre" (H&H), which is of uncertain etymology but may be related to the word "uchtlach," which means child.

Famous **Guthries:** SAMUEL GUTHRIE (1782–1848) of Massachusetts invented a "percussion pill" and a lock to explode it, replacing the flintlock musket. He discovered chloroform in 1831. JAMES GUTHRIE (1792–1869) of Kentucky was a railroad promoter who allowed the use of his railroad by Union troops during the Civil War. He also founded the University of Louisville. ALFRED GUTHRIE (1805–1882) of New York started the federal system of steamboat inspections. GEORGE WILKINS GUTHRIE (1848–1917) of Pennsylvania was a mayor of Pittsburgh and an ambassador to Japan, where he calmed the anti-American feelings brought about by the California Alien Land Bill. WILLIAM DAMERON GUTHRIE (1859–1935) of California was an authority on constitutional law. WOODROW WILSON (WOODY) GUTHRIE (1912–1967) of Oklahoma was an American folk singer. He composed more than 1000 songs, most with popular causes. "This Land Is Your Land" is one of his most famous.

Genealogies: *Guthery (also Guthrie): Henry-David-William and Their Descendants of Cullman County, Alabama* was compiled by Ima Gene Boyd and published in Akron, Ohio, in 1971. *Guthrie History* was compiled by Mable Hazel Guthrie and published in Huguley, Alabama, in 1981.

GUTIÉRREZ (S.S. Abbreviation: Gutier)

Ranking: 257 S.S. Count: 142,196

Origin: Spanish. Derived from the medieval first name Gutierre, which is derived from a now-unknown Visigothic name derived from the words "gunpi" and "hairus," meaning battle and sword.

Genealogies: None known.

GUY

Ranking: 1151 S.S. Count: 38,115

Origin: English, Jewish. English: 1) derived from a French form of the Germanic first name Wido, which has an uncertain etymology but is perhaps derived from either the Old English word "widu" or the Old High German word "witu," meaning wood, or the Old English word "wid" or the Old High German word "wit," meaning wide. The name was common among the Normans in the form Wi or Why, as well as in the rest of France in the form Guy. 2) derived from the Old French word "guider," meaning to guide. The name was often given to those who worked as guides. Jewish: uncertain etymology.

Famous **Guys:** SEYMOUR JOSEPH GUY (1824–1910) of England was a portrait painter best known for works that were childlike and genuine in sentiment.

Genealogies: None known.

GUYTON

Ranking: 4267 S.S. Count: 10,556

Origin: English. Derived from the Old English name Gœga, and the Old English word "tūn," meaning settlement. The name was often given to those who came from Gayton, a place in Norfolk, England.

Genealogies: *Guytons Galore: From French Huguenots to Oregon Pioneers* was compiled by Helen Guyton Rees and published in Portland, Oregon, in 1986.

GUZMÁN

Ranking: 474 S.S. Count: 84,866

Origin: Spanish. Derived from a now-unknown Visigothic first name that is derived from Gaut, the name of the Scandinavian tribe to which Beowulf belonged, and the word "man," meaning man.

Genealogies: None known.

HAAG

Ranking: 3316 S.S. Count: 13,665

Origin: Dutch. 1) the name was given to those who lived near an enclosure made of shrubs and hedges. 2) the name was given to those who tended hedges and fences. 3) the name was given to those who came from The Hague, a place in The Netherlands, meaning hedge.

Genealogies: None known.

HAAS

Ranking: 832 S.S. Count: 51,144

Origin: Dutch, German. 1) The name was given to those who lived near "the sign of the hare" (ES). 2) The name was given to those who were thought to have the qualities of a hare.

Genealogies: *Genealogy of the Goldman, Levy, Wertheim, Kaufman, Fleishman, Haas, Koshland, Stern, Strauss, Meyer, and Newmark Families* was compiled by Douglas Edward Goldman and published in San Francisco, California, in 1978. *Haas Family History* was compiled by Arthur Milton Haas and published in Fogelsville, Pennsylvania, in 1982.

HAASE

Ranking: 3529 S.S. Count: 12,786

Origin: Dutch, German. Transformation of Haas.

Genealogies: None known.

HACKER

Ranking: 2337 S.S. Count: 19,405

Origin: English, German, Jewish. English: derived from the Old English word "haccian," meaning to chop or cut. The name was given to butchers or, less often, to those who cut down trees and wood. German: derived from the Old High German word "hacchōn," meaning to chop or cut. The name was given to butchers or, less often, to those who cut down trees and wood. Jewish: uncertain etymology. 1) Possibly derived from the Yiddish words "heker," "holtsheker," or "valdheker," meaning butcher, woodcutter, and lumberjack, or the German word "hacker," meaning woodcutter. The name was given to butchers or, less often, to those who cut down trees and wood. 2) Possibly derived from either the Yiddish word "heker," which may mean retailer, or the Middle Low German word "höken," meaning to carry things around (on one's back). The name may have been given to those who sold their wares on the street.

Genealogies: *A German-American Hacker-Hocker Genealogy: 350 Years of Family History* was compiled by William O. Winegard and published in Harrisburg, Pennsylvania, in 1991.

HACKETT (S.S. Abbreviation: Hacket)

Ranking: 1528 S.S. Count: 29,072

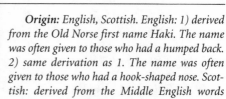

Origin: English, Scottish. English: 1) derived from the Old Norse first name Haki. The name was often given to those who had a humped back. 2) same derivation as 1. The name was often given to those who had a hook-shaped nose. Scottish: derived from the Middle English words "hauk" and "wude," meaning hawk and wood. The name was given to those who came from a region called Halkhead, a place in the former county of Renfrews in Scotland that is now part of the Strathclyde environs.

Famous **Hacketts:** JAMES HENRY HACKETT (1800–1871) of New York was an actor known for his roles as a character impersonator. His best-known performances were as Falstaff, Rip Van Winkle, and Nimrod Wildfire. His son, JAMES KETELTAS HACKETT (1869–1926) of Canada, was also an actor who is remembered for his roles as romantic heroes. His best-known portrayals were in *The Prisoner of Zenda, The Princess and the Butterfly,* and *The Fortunes of the King,* among others. HORATIO BALCH HACKETT (1808–1875) of Massachusetts was a clergyman who taught at area seminaries. He was part of the American Bible Revision Committee.

Genealogies: *Norris, Hackett, Prescott and Allied Families: Our Ancestors and Their Descendants, Including Adams, Andrews, Bachelder, Bartlett, Boulter, Brewer, Brown, et al.* was compiled by Hugh Albert Johnson and published in Annandale, Virginia, in 1976. *Reminiscences and Genealogy of the Joel Hinkley and Amos Hackett Families* was compiled by Margaret R. Carver and Kathryn H. Bowers and published in Tacoma, Washington, in 1971.

HACKNEY (S.S. Abbreviation: Hackne)

Ranking: 3235 S.S. Count: 14,026

Origin: English. 1) the name was given to those who came from Hackney, meaning "Haca's island" (ES), the name of a place in Middlesex, England. 2) the name was given to those who tended to the horses used by ladies.

Genealogies: None known.

HADDAD

Ranking: 4848 S.S. Count: 9228

Origin: Arabic, Syrian. The name was given to metalsmiths.

Genealogies: None known.

HADDOCK (S.S. Abbreviation: Haddoc)

Ranking: 4191 S.S. Count: 10,775

Origin: English. Uncertain etymology. 1) derived from the Middle English word "hadduc," meaning haddock. The name was given to fish vendors. 2) same derivation as in 1. The name was given to those who were thought to look like a fish. 3) derived from the Old English first name Ædduc, a diminutive of the name Æddi, the first element of which is "ēad," meaning wealth or fortune. The name endured into the medieval ages, at which time an initial "H" was added to it. 4) derived from the Old English words "hæþ" and "hōc," meaning heath and hook. The name was given to those who came from the Haydock, a place near Liverpool in England. 5) derived from the Welsh word "heiddog," meaning barley farm. The name was given to those who came from the Haydock, a place near Liverpool in England.

Famous **Haddocks:** CHARLES BRICKETT HADDOCK (1796–1861) of New Hampshire was a Congregational clergyman, the nephew of Daniel Webster, and a proponent of the public-school system in New Hampshire.

Genealogies: *Gone to Texas: A Compendium of the Dulany, Haddox (also Haddock), Heaton, Holland and Martin Families* was compiled by Mary Rebecca Scott and published in Tomball, Texas, in 1989. *Legends of the Haddock Family* was compiled by Hugh Ransom Haddock and Orpha Vaughan Haddock and published in Grants Pass, Oregon, in 1978.

HADLEY

Ranking: 1580 **S.S. Count:** 28,287

Origin: English. 1) derived from the Old English words "hōeð" and "lēah," meaning heath and wood. The name was given to those who came from Hadley, a place in Shropshire, England. 2) same derivation as in 1. The name was given to those who came from Hadleigh, a place in Essex, Suffolk, and other counties in England. 3) derived from the Old English first name "Hadda" (which is probably derived from the Old English word "heard," meaning brave or strong) and the Old English word "lēah," meaning woodland. The name was given to those who came from Hadley, a place in Worcestershire, England.

Famous **Hadleys:** JAMES HADLEY (1821–1872) of New York was the father of Arthur and a professor of Greek at Yale University. ARTHUR TWINING HADLEY (1856–1930) of Connecticut was an economist and educator who taught at and subsequently was the president of Yale University. He also wrote several books on economics. HENRY KINBALL HADLEY (1871–1937) of Massachusetts was a composer and conductor of many of the major orchestras in the country. HERBERT SPENCER HADLEY (1872–1927) of Massachusetts was a lawyer and the attorney general and governor of Missouri. He was responsible for starting a criminal justice reform movement that spread throughout the country.

Genealogies: *A History of American Descendants of George Hadley, Reydon Parish, Suffolk Shire, England, and Leo George Hadley, Sr., St. Louis, Missouri* was compiled by Willis Dean Hadley Sr. and published in St. Louis, Missouri, in 1986. *Our New England Hadley Family and Allied Families* was compiled by Elsie Eggleston Kempton and published in McLean, Virginia, in 1979.

HAGAN

Ranking: 1594 **S.S. Count:** 28,102

Origin: Irish. Derived from the Gaelic name Ó hÁgáin, meaning "descendant of Ogán" (H&H), which is a diminutive of the word "óg," meaning young.

Genealogies: *House of Hagan Re-visited* was compiled by Viola Hagan Carpenter and Imogene Hoover Hagan and published in Pulaski, Tennessee, in 1980. *Our Life— Our Times; The Gulbrand & Agnet Hagen Family Genealogy* was compiled by Olive Sorenson Severa and was most likely published in 1979.

HAGEMAN, HAGEMANN (S.S. Abbreviation: Hagema)

Ranking: 4443 **S.S. Count:** 10,091

Origin: Danish, Norwegian, Swedish. 1) derived from the Old Norse word "hagi," meaning enclosure. The name was given to those who came from Haig, the name of various places in northern France and in Lancashire and Yorkshire counties, England. 2) same derivation as in 1. The name was given to those who lived in an area enclosed by hedges. 3) same derivation as in 1. The name was given to those who cared for the village hedges.

Genealogies: None known.

HAGEN (ALSO HAGENAAR, HAGENSEN)

Ranking: 1364 **S.S. Count:** 32,520

Origin: Hagensen—Danish;   Hagenaar—Dutch; Hagen—Dutch, German. Hagensen: 1) derived from the Germanic last name Hagano, meaning hawthorn. 2) derived from the Old Norse last name Hagni, meaning hawthorn. Hagenaar, Hagen (Dutch): cognates to Hageman. Hagen (German): 1) derived from the Old High German word "hagan," meaning hawthorn or hedge. The name was given to those who lived by a stretch of enclosed meadowland. 2) cognate to Haagensen.

Famous **Bearers:** HERMANN AUGUST HAGEN (1817–1893) of Germany was an entomologist and the author of *Bibliotheca Entomologica.* WALTER CHARLES HAGEN (1892–1969) of New York was a champion golfer. He won 13 major championship tournaments in his career, with nine of those wins in the 1920s.

Genealogies: None known.

HAGER

Ranking: 1540 **S.S. Count:** 28,933

Origin: German. Cognate to Hageman.

Famous **Hagers:** JOHN SHARPENSTEIN HAGER (1818–1890) of New Jersey was a lawyer, judge, and U.S. senator from California, where he served as an antimonopoly Democrat.

Genealogies: *The Hager Family: Ancestors and Descendants of August and Mary Barbara (Reiter) Hager* was compiled by Ruth Ann Abels Hager and published in Florissant, Missouri, in 1983.

HAGGAR (ALSO HAGGARD, HAGGARTY)

Ranking: 3245 S.S. Count: 13,999

Origin: English. Derived from the Old French word "hagard," meaning savage or untamed. The name was probably given to falconers, as the word "hagard" in Middle English evolved into a technical term referring to a hawk that was already mature when it was captured and trained, as opposed to having been born and trained in captivity.

Genealogies: The Clabaughs: An Account of the Life and Times of Frederick Clabaugh of Maryland in 1742, and His Descendants who Migrated to East Tennessee, then on to Alabama and Texas: With a Special Chapter on Henry Haggard (1746–1842) a Frontier Baptist Preacher of Virginia, East Tennessee and Alabama, and His Family was compiled by Betty Harrell and published in Los Altos, California, in 1982. *Comstock-Haggard and Allied Families* was compiled by Mary Jane Comstock and published in Chicago, Illinois, in 1973.

HAGGER (ALSO HAGGERTY)

Ranking: 2627 S.S. Count: 17,309

Origin: Hagger—English; Haggerty—Irish. Hagger: transformation of Haggar. Haggerty: derived from the Gaelic name Ó hÉigceartaigh, meaning "descendant of Eigceartach" (H&H), which is a last name meaning unjust.

Famous **Bearers:** MELVIN EVERETT HAGGERTY (1875–1937) of Indiana was an educational psychologist who was a pioneer in the development and use of I.Q. tests. He was the dean of education at the University of Minnesota.

Genealogies: From Ireland, Land of Pain and Sorrow: A Historical Chronicle of Two Cultures was compiled by Joseph L. Grady and published in Phoenix, Arizona, in 1984.

HAHN

Ranking: 745 S.S. Count: 56,986

Origin: German, Jewish. German: 1) derived from the Old High German word "hano," meaning rooster. The name was given to a haughty or bawdy person. 2) same derivation as in 1. The name was given to those who lived at the sign of the rooster. 3) same derivation as in 1. The name was often given to chicken farmers. 4) transformation of Haagensen. Jewish: derived from the German word "hahn," meaning cock or rooster. The name was taken ornamentally.

Famous **Hahns:** GEORGE MICHAEL DECKER HAHN (1830–1886) of Bavaria came to the United States as a child and settled in Louisiana. He remained loyal to the Union cause during the Civil War and was the first Republican governor of Louisiana. DOROTHY ANNA HAHN

(1876–1950) of Pennsylvania was an organic chemist who taught at Mount Holyoke College.

Genealogies: People and Progenitors in My Pedigree was compiled by George Franklin Hahn and published in Mt. Pleasant, North Carolina, in 1982. *Rimmonim Bells, Ten Generations of the Behrman, Drucker, Hahn, Stockler, and Sztynberg Families Plus Ten Related Lines* was compiled by Richard Alperin and published in Philadelphia, Pennsylvania, in 1980.

HAIGHT

Ranking: 4613 S.S. Count: 9688

Origin: English. Cognate to Hageman.

Famous **Haights:** CHARLES COOLIDGE HAIGHT (1841–1878) of New York was a well-known architect of his time, designing buildings at Yale University and Hobart College.

Genealogies: Haight: A Family History of the Descendants of Stephen Haight and Matura Hubbs was compiled by Mary Lynch Young and published in San Francisco, California, in 1962. *A Genealogical History of the Hoyt, Haight, and Hight Families: With Some Account of the Earlier Hyatt Families, A List of the First Settlers of Salisbury and Amesbury, Mass.* was compiled by David W. Hoyt and published in Bethany, Oklahoma, in 1985.

HAILEY

Ranking: 4678 S.S. Count: 9563

Origin: English. Derived from the Old English words "hēg" and "lēah," meaning hay and wood. The name was given to those who came from Haley, a place in England.

Genealogies: None known.

HAINES

Ranking: 1008 S.S. Count: 43,429

Origin: English, Welsh. English: 1) derived from the Germanic last name Hagamo, meaning hawthorn. The name was made popular in England by the Normans. 2) uncertain etymology. Possibly derived from the name Hagenes. The name was given to those who lived in Haines, a place in Bedfordshire, England. Welsh: derived from the first name Einws, which is a diminutive of Einion, a name of uncertain etymology that is commonly confused with the Welsh word "einion," meaning anvil.

Famous **Haineses:** CHARLES GLIDDEN HAINES (1792–1825) of New Hampshire was a lawyer who wrote *United States Law Journal and Civilian Magazine*, one of the first American law journals. DANIEL HAINES (1801–1877) of New York was a New Jersey governor who improved both the educational and governmental systems of the state. He also served as a state supreme court justice. JACKSON HAINES (1840–1876) of New York was trained as a ballet dancer but turned to figure skating, using many of the techniques of ballet in skating. He is considered the "father of modern figure skating."

Genealogies: *The Sharp Family of Southern New Jersey: 300 Years in New Jersey 1682–1981* was compiled by Albert Stirling Adams and published in Vincentown, New Jersey, in 1981.

HAIR

Ranking: 4213 **S.S. Count:** 10,715

Origin: Scottish. Derived from the Gaelic name Ó hÁichir, meaning "descendant of Aichear" (H&H), a first name most probably derived from the Gaelic word "aichear," meaning violent or sharp.

Genealogies: None known.

HAIRSTON (S.S. Abbreviation: Hairst)

Ranking: 2187 **S.S. Count:** 20,974

Origin: English, Scottish. 1) The name was given to those who came from Hairstones, which means "standing stone" (ES) and is a place in Peeblesshire, England. 2) the name was given to those who came from Harston, which means "Heoruwulf's homestead or gray boundary stone" (ES) and is the name of several places in Cambridgeshire and Leicestershire counties, England.

Genealogies: None known.

HALBERSTAM, HALBERT (S.S. Abbreviation: Halber)

Ranking: 4700 **S.S. Count:** 9515

Origin: Halberstam—German; Halbert—English. Halberstam: uncertain etymology; the name was given to those who lived near a tree stump. Halbert: the name was given to the descendants of those named Halbert, which means estimable and intelligent.

Genealogies: None known.

HALE

Ranking: 310 **S.S. Count:** 188,511

Origin: English. 1) derived from the Old English word "hale," meaning niche. The name was given to those who lived in a recess or nook. 2) same derivation as in 1. The name was often given to those who came from Hale, the name of several places in England. 3) derived from the Old English first name Hæle, meaning hero. 4) derived from the Old English first name Hægel, meaning hawthorn.

Famous Hales: NATHAN HALE (1755–1776) of Connecticut was a Revolutionary War hero. He taught school and volunteered for the Continental army and to work as a spy behind the British lines. He was caught and hanged without the benefit of trial. It was strongly believed, although never proven, that his Tory cousin Samuel Hale was responsible for Nathan's capture. "I only regret that I have but one life to lose for my country" are said to be the last words he uttered. His nephew, NATHAN HALE (1784–1863) of Massachusetts, a newspaper editor, helped advance the use of editorial articles as regular features. SARAH JOSEPHA BUELL HALE (1788–1879) of New Hampshire was an editor of *Ladies Magazine* and the writer of children's poems and stories. "Mary's Lamb" is her best-remembered piece. ENOCH HALE (1790–1848) of Massachusetts was a physician and the brother of Nathan. He wrote *Observations on the Typhoid Fever of New England.* DAVID HALE (1791–1849) of Connecticut was the cousin of Nathan and a journalist who was responsible for new news-gathering techniques. BENJAMIN HALE (1797–1863) of Massachusetts was a clergyman and the president of Geneva (now Hobart) College. JOHN PARKER HALE (1806–1873) of New Hampshire was a member of Congress and U.S. senator and the first antislavery candidate elected to the Senate. He also was the Free-Soil candidate for president in 1852. HORATIO EMMONS HALE (1817–1896) of New Hampshire was an anthropologist who studied languages, especially that of the Iroquois. He was a member of Charles Wilkes's naval expedition and was the son of Sarah Josepha Buell Hale. LUCRETIA PEABODY HALE (1820–1900) of Massachusetts was a writer of children's books and is best known for the *Peterkin* series. She was the sister of Edward Everett Hale. Their father was Nathan Hale, the nephew and namesake of the Revolutionary War hero. EDWARD EVERETT HALE (1822–1909) of Massachusetts was a Congregational minister, U.S. senator, brother of Charles, and author of stories and novels, his best-known being "The Man Without a Country," considered one of the best short stories by an American. CHARLES HALE (1831–1882) of Massachusetts was the son of Nathan Hale (b. 1784) and the consul general to Egypt (1864–1870). EUGENE HALE (1836–1918) of Maine did much to develop the modern navy. GEORGE ELLERY HALE (1868–1938) of Illinois was an astronomer. He organized and directed several observatories, including the Yerkes and Mount Wilson in Washington. He started the planning and fund raising for the Palomar Observatory, which opened after his death. He invented the spectroheliograph, founded the *Astrophysical Journal,* and was the author of several books on astronomy. LOUISE CLOSSER HALE (1872–1933) of Illinois was an actress who played character roles. She also wrote travel books.

Genealogies: *Descendants From First Families of Virginia and Maryland: A Family History and Genealogy Covering 350 years, 1620–1970* was compiled by Maude Crowe and published in Fordsville, Kentucky, in 1978. *Spanning the Centuries With the Hale Family* was compiled by Muriel Nadine Hale Lynch and published in Independence, Missouri, in 1990.

HALES

Ranking: 4409 **S.S. Count:** 10,168

Origin: English, Scottish. English: 1) derived from the Welsh word "halog," meaning dirty. The name was given to those who came from Hailes, a place in Gloucester, England, that was named after the river Hailes (meaning polluted), which once flowed through parts of England. 2) derived from the Old English word "hale," meaning niche or hollow. Scottish: derived from the Middle English word "hall," meaning hall or manor. The name was given to those who came from Hailes, a place in Lothian, Scotland.

Genealogies: None known.

HALEY

Ranking: 799 **S.S. Count:** 52,739

Origin: Derived from the Old English words "hēg" and "lēah," meaning hay and wood. The name was given to those who lived in such a place.

Famous Haleys: MARGARET ANGELA HALEY (1861–1939) of Illinois was a teacher who worked to improve the lot of those in her profession. WILLIAM JOHN CLIFTON (BILL) HALEY (1925–1981) of Michigan was a pioneer in American rock 'n' roll music. He coined the term "rockabilly" and is known for such songs as "Rock Around the Clock" and "Shake, Rattle and Roll." He and his band were known as Bill Haley and the Comets.

Genealogies: *Haley, Marshall, Getchell, Barlow Genealogy* was compiled by Elaine Vertz Smithers and published in Waukesha, Wisconsin, in 1986.

HALL

Ranking: 25 **S.S. Count:** 675,028

Origin: Danish, English, German, Norwegian, Swedish. Danish, Norwegian, Swedish: 1) derived from the Old Norse word "holl," meaning hall or estate. The name was given to those who lived near a large house or estate or to those who worked at a large house or estate. 2) same derivation as in 1. The name was given to those who lived in one of the many towns called Hall. English: 1) derived from the Old English word "heall," meaning hall or estate. Same application as in 1 above. 2) derived from the Old English word "heall," meaning hall or estate. Same application as in 2 above. German: 1) derived from the Old High German word "halla," meaning hall or estate. Same application as in 1 above. 2) derived from the Old High German word "halla," meaning hall or estate. Same application as in 2 above.

Famous Halls: LYMAN HALL (1724–1790) of Connecticut was a Revolutionary War leader, a signer of the Declaration of Independence, and a governor of Georgia. DOMINICK AUGUSTIN HALL (1765?–1820), birthplace unknown, was a judge in Louisiana who once fined Andrew Jackson $1000 for overriding a writ of *habeas corpus.* ANNE HALL (1792–1863) of Connecticut was a miniaturist whose paintings were considered some of the best of the day. JAMES HALL (1793–1868) of Pennsylvania was an author and the first editor of the *Western Souvenir,* a literary annual. HILAND HALL (1795–1885) of Vermont was a governor of Vermont and the author of *The History of Vermont,* considered an important work. SAMUEL READ HALL (1795–1877) of New Hampshire was a writer of school textbooks. He established a training school for teachers in Concord, Vermont. BAYNARD RUSH HALL (1798–1863) of Pennsylvania was the author of *The New Purchase,* a frontier classic. HENRY BRYAN HALL (1808–1884) of England was an engraver. He started an engraving business called H. B. Hall & Sons and was the engraver of the portraits of many American historical figures. JAMES HALL (1811–1898) of Massachusetts was a geologist and paleontologist. He contributed to the development of the geosynclinal theory of mountain building and was the director of the New York Museum of Natural History for 27 years. CHARLES FRANCIS HALL (1821–1871) of New Hampshire was an explorer who led expeditions to the Arctic. FITZEDWARD HALL (1825–1901) of New York was the first American to edit a Sanskrit text. He was also a contributor to the *Oxford English Dictionary.* ABRAHAM OAKLEY HALL (1826–1889) of New York was the mayor of New York City and part of the Tammany Hall operation when the Tweed Ring was in force. He was tried for corruption and acquitted. THOMAS SEAVEY HALL (1827–1880) of New Hampshire was a pioneer in the development of signaling devices for railroads and drawbridges. His railroad signaling devices are still in use today. ASAPH HALL (1829–1907) of Connecticut was an astronomer who is credited with the discovery of two of the moons of Mars, which he named Deimos and Phobos. GRANVILLE STANLEY HALL (1844–1924) of Massachusetts was a psychologist and educator. He is considered the father of child psychology, educational psychology, and scientific psychology in the United States. EDWIN HERBERT HALL (1855–1938) of Maine discovered the "Hall Effect," which is the difference in potential of a current-carrying conductor when placed in a magnetic field. CHARLES MARTIN HALL (1863–1914), birthplace unknown, was involved in the electrolytic process of making aluminum inexpensively. ROSETTA SHERWOOD HALL (1865–1951) of New York was a physician and missionary in Korea. She founded a hospital in Seoul and helped to educate Korean women in the field of medicine. ALONZO C. HALL (1886–1979) of North Carolina, as a scholar, wrote *Outlines of American Literature* (1925) and *Grave Humor* (1940). He also was a pioneer in public-housing programs. As chairman of the Greensboro, North Carolina, Housing Authority, he spearheaded the building of a nine-story building exclusively for the elderly and handicapped. JAMES NORMAN HALL (1887–1951) of Iowa was an author and the co-author of the *Bounty* series, among others. ROBERT BURNETT HALL (1896–1975) of New Mexico was a geographer who directed expeditions to Haiti, Japan, and Latin America. He spurred the production of three educational films on Japan by the *Encyclopedia Britannica*. He also wrote or co-wrote a number of books and served on the Geographic Board of the Smithsonian Institution.

Genealogies: *An Alabama Newspaper Tradition: Grover C. Hall and the Hall Family* was compiled by Daniel Webster Hollis and published in University, Alabama, in 1983. *A Givens-Hall Family History From Pre-Revolutionary Times to 1970; Including Many Related Families Such as Alexander, Bowman, Black, Chapman, French, Green, Johnston, Phlegar, Ross, Snidow, Stafford, Welker and Others* was compiled by Dorothy Hall Givens and published in Radford, Virginia, in 1971.

HALLER

Ranking: 2910 **S.S. Count:** 15,609
Origin: German. Transformation of the German definition of Hall.
Genealogies: *The Haller Family History: Including the Descendants and Ancestors of Frank A. Haller and Anna Bellentin Haller of Erie, Pennsylvania* was compiled by Joan Erzer Behrens and published in Rancho Palos Verdes, California, in 1978. *Haller-Hollar-Holler Genealogy* was compiled by Amelia Cleland Gilreath and published in Nokesille, California, in 1981.

HALLMAN, HALLMANN (S.S. Abbreviation: Hallma)

Ranking: 2293 **S.S. Count:** 19,872
Origin: Hallman—English. Hallmann—German. Transformations of the English and German definitions of Hall.
Genealogies: None known.

HALPER (ALSO HALPERIN, HALPERN, HALPERT)

Ranking: 3709 **S.S. Count:** 12,165
Origin: Jewish. Derived from the Old High German words "heil(ag)" and "brunno," meaning holy and geyser or spring. The name was often given to those who came from Heilbronn, a place in Württemberg, Germany, where a large Jewish community once lived.
Famous Bearers: EDITH GREGOR HALPERT (1900?–1970) of Russia was an art dealer and collector who came to the United States as a child of six with her sister and widowed mother. She was raised in New York City. Through her galleries she introduced the American style of art to the public.
Genealogies: None known.

HALSEY

Ranking: 4180 **S.S. Count:** 10,814
Origin: English. Derived from the Old English words "hals" and "ēg," meaning channel of water and island. The
name was given to those who came from a now-unknown section of London and its environs.

Famous Halseys: JOHN HALSEY (1670–1716) of Massachusetts was a pirate of the South Seas. THOMAS LLOYD HALSEY (1776?–1855) of Rhode Island was the U.S. consul to Buenos Aires when he supplied arms to the South American rebels. He was dismissed from his post for his actions. FREDERICK ARTHUR HALSEY (1856–1935) of New York was a mechanical engineer and the developer of the profit-sharing plan called the Halsey premium payment plan. WILLIAM FREDERICK HALSEY JR. (1882–1959) of New Jersey was a naval officer during World Wars I and II, rising to the position of admiral of the fleet in 1945.

Genealogies: *One Branch of the Halsey Family* was compiled by Richard J. Halsey and published in Springfield, Missouri, in 1967.

HALSTEAD (S.S. Abbreviation: Halste)

Ranking: 3046 **S.S. Count:** 14,909
Origin: English. 1) derived from the Old English words "(ge)heald" and "stede," meaning shanty and site. The names were given to those who came from Halstead, the name of a place in several English counties, including Essex, Kent, and Leicestershire. 2) derived from the Old English words "h(e)al" and "stede," meaning hall and place. The names were often given to those who came from Halstead, a place in Burnley, England, so called because it was once the site of a large mansion or hall.
Famous Bearers: MURAT HALSTEAD (1829–1908) of Ohio was a journalist and war correspondent. He covered the Civil and the Franco-Prussian wars. WILLIAM STEWART HALSTED (1852–1922) of New York was a surgeon who administered the first blood transfusion in the country; discovered a method of anaesthesia by the injection of cocaine into particular nerves of the body; founded the first school of surgery in the country; stressed the idea of cleanliness during surgery with antiseptic procedures, rubber gloves, and other safeguards; and developed surgical techniques for most of the internal organs. GEORGE BRUCE HALSTEAD (1853–1922) of New Jersey was a mathematician. He worked to spread non-Euclidean geometry theories throughout the United States.
Genealogies: *Three Hundred and Fifty Years of Halsteads in America* was compiled by Gary Allen Halstead and published in Gering, Nebraska, in 1982.

HALTER

Ranking: 4325 **S.S. Count:** 10,361
Origin: German. Derived from the Old High German word "halda," meaning gradient or hillside. The name was given to those who lived high on a mountain range.
Genealogies: None known.

HALVERSON

Ranking: 2866 **S.S. Count:** 15,855

Origin: Norwegian. Derived from the name Halvor, meaning steadfast or judicious.

Genealogies: None known.

HALVORSON

Ranking: 3209 **S.S. Count:** 14,139

Origin: Norwegian. Transformation of Halverson.

Genealogies: None known.

HAM

Ranking: 2032 **S.S. Count:** 22,473

Origin: English, Scottish. English: derived from the Old English word "hamm," meaning water meadow. The name was often given to those who lived by a brook, on a stretch of flat, low-lying land made of sediment deposited by the flowing water of a river. Scottish: derived from the Old Norse word "hámi," meaning homestead. The name was given to those who came from a now-unknown place in what was once the county of Caithness, now a section of the Highland area.

Genealogies: None known.

HAMBRIC, HAMBRICK (S.S. Abbreviation: Hambri)

Ranking: 4288 **S.S. Count:** 10,472

Origin: German. Derived from the name Heimbrecht, which means radiant or home.

Genealogies: None known.

HAMBY

Ranking: 2473 **S.S. Count:** 18,342

Origin: English. The name was given to those who came from Hanby, which means "Hundi's homestead" (ES) and is located in Lincolnshire, England.

Genealogies: None known.

HAMEL

Ranking: 3167 **S.S. Count:** 14,332

Origin: Dutch, French, German, Jewish. Dutch: derived from the Middle Dutch word "hamel," meaning a gelded male sheep. The name was often given to shepherds. French: derived from the Old French word "hamel," meaning little homestead. The name was given to those who lived and worked on a farm that depended on the neighboring town but was located far away from it. German, Jewish: derived from the Germanic word "ham," meaning water meadow. The name was given to those who lived in the city of Hamlin, the spot where the river Hamel empties into the Weser River.

Genealogies: *Gunderman and Wullenjohn Cousins with Hampel (also Hamel) and Noll Families* was compiled by Barbara Chandler Spray and published in Amarillo, Texas, most likely in 1978. *Hammel-Laufer Families, 1600's to 1978*

was compiled by Martha Mae Schmidt and published in Marissa, Illinois, most likely in 1979.

HAMER

Ranking: 4705 **S.S. Count:** 9511

Origin: Dutch, English, Flemish, Jewish. Dutch, Flemish: derived from the Old German word "hamar," meaning stone. The name was given to those who either worked making hammers or used hammers as one of their principal occupational tools, such as laborers in a forge or foundry. English: derived from the Old English word "hamor," meaning cliff or boulder. The name was given to those who came from a now-unknown place in Lancashire. Jewish: 1) cognate of the Dutch and Flemish definition of Hamer. 2) derived from the Old German word "hamar," meaning stone. The name was given to those who were considered forceful or aggressive.

Famous **Hamers:** THOMAS LYON HAMER (1800–1846) of Pennsylvania was a soldier who died as the division commander in Mexico under Zachary Taylor. As a congressman from Ohio, he appointed Ulysses S. Grant to West Point. Hamer's error caused Grant to change his name from Hiram Ulysses.

Genealogies: None known.

HAMILTON (S.S. Abbreviation: Hamilt)

Ranking: 102 **S.S. Count:** 272,535

Origin: Irish, Scottish. 1) derived from the Old English words "hamel" and "dūn," meaning deformed and hill. The name was given to those who came from a now-deserted village in the parish of Barkby, in Leicestershire County, England, not to be confused with the town of Hamilton near Glasgow. 2) same derivation as in 1. The name may have been given to those who came from any number of towns founded by a notable Norman family called Hamilton.

Famous **Hamiltons:** ANDREW HAMILTON (ORIGINALLY TRENT) (1676–1741) of Scotland was the lawyer who defended John Peter Zenger, the publisher of the *New York Weekly Journal*, against the charge of seditious libel. ANDREW HAMILTON (?–1703) of Scotland came to America in 1686. He served as the governor of East and West Jersey and as the organizer of the first postal system in America. ALEXANDER HAMILTON (1712–1756) of Scotland was the author of *Itinerarium*, which described the northern colonies and the mannerisms of the people of 1744. It was not published, however, until 1907. ALEXANDER HAMILTON (1755–1804) of the Leeward Islands was an American politician during Revolutionary times. He was the first secretary of the Treasury, where he started a national fiscal system. He was the leader of the Federalists. A political enemy of Aaron Burr, Hamilton was killed by Burr in a duel. ELIZABETH SCHUYLER HAMILTON (1757–1854) of New York was the wife of Alexander Hamilton. JAMES HAMILTON (1786–1857) of South Carolina was a governor of that state and a political enemy of President John Quincy Adams's administration. He eventually left politics and South Carolina for Texas and was instrumental in the fight for Texas independence. FRANK HASTINGS HAMILTON (1813–1886) of Vermont was a surgeon who successfully healed old ulcers by skin grafting. EDWARD JOHN HAMILTON (1834–1918) of Ireland was a philosopher whose best-known published work was *The Human Mind.* EDITH HAMILTON (1867–1963) of Germany was the headmistress of Bryn Mawr College and an author. Her sister was Alice. ALICE HAMILTON (1869–1970) of New York was a toxicologist who worked with the government on industrial poisons and as a professor at Harvard Medical School. She was the sister of Edith. CLAYTON HAMILTON (1881–1946) of New York was the author of 11 books on the theater and fiction. (AMY) GORDON HAMILTON (1892–1967) of New Jersey was a social-work educator. As a member of the faculty of the New York School of Social Work, she inspired many to excel in the field of social work.

Genealogies: *Celena (Lena) Jane Russell Smith (also Hamilton), Her Ancestors, Descendants, and Collateral Kinsmen* was compiled by Matthew Lee McHugh and Celena Russell Smith McHugh and published in 1974. *Hamilton Kin of Martha "Mat" Tucker* was compiled by Duard Arnold Tucker and published in Houston, Texas, in 1987.

HAMLET (ALSO HAMLETT)

Ranking: 3741 **S.S. Count:** 12,095
Origin: English. Transformation of the first definition of Hammond.
Genealogies: None known.

HAMLIN

Ranking: 1753 **S.S. Count:** 25,571
Origin: Derived from the Anglo-Norman-French first name "Ham(b)lin," which is a diminutive of the English name Hammond.
Famous **Hamlins:** HANNIBAL HAMLIN (1809–1891) of Maine was a politician serving both as a member of Congress and a senator in Washington, D.C., and as a governor of Maine. He also served as Abraham Lincoln's first vice president (1861–1865). CYRUS HAMLIN (1811–1900) of Maine was a Congregational missionary in Turkey. EMMONS HAMLIN (1821–1885) of New York was an inventor and the maker of pianos and organs. He and Henry Mason formed the Mason & Hamlin Organ Co.

Genealogies: *History of the Hamlin Family with Genealogies of Early Settlers of the Name in America; 1639–1894, Part One* was compiled by Henry Franklin Andrews and published in Exira, Iowa, in 1894. *The Jacob Vernon Hamblin Family (also Hamlin): Jacob Vernon Hamblin, A Descendant of James Hamblin, Immigrant, Who Came From London, England, and Settled in Barnstable, 1639* was com-

piled by Vera Leib Miller and published in Tucson, Arizona, in 1975.

HAMM

Ranking: 1207 **S.S. Count:** 36,480
Origin: Transformation of the English definition of Hammer.
Famous **Hamms:** MARGHERITA ARLINA HAMM (1867–1907) of Canada was a journalist and author who wrote for the newspapers of the Northeast.
Genealogies: None known.

HAMMER

Ranking: 885 **S.S. Count:** 49,035
Origin: English, German, Jewish. English: derived from the Old English word "hamm," meaning water meadow. The name was often given to those who lived by a brook, on a stretch of flat, low-lying land made of sediment deposited by the flowing water of a river. German: derived from the Old High German word "ham," meaning water meadow. Same application as above. German, Jewish: 1) derived from the Old High German word "hamar," meaning stone. The name was given to those who either worked making hammers or used hammers as one of their principal occupational tools. 2) same derivation as in 1. The name was given to those who were considered forceful or aggressive.
Famous **Hammers:** WILLIAM JOSEPH HAMMER (1858–1934) of Pennsylvania was Thomas Edison's assistant during the invention of the light bulb. He worked in Europe on behalf of the Edison Co. and established the first central station in the world for incandescent electric lighting in London.

Genealogies: *The Hammer Story: Ancestors and Descendants of Anton Hammer* was compiled by Zada Hunter and published in Indialantic, Florida, in 1990. *John Hicks Hamer (also Hammer) 1765–1842: His Antecedents, Descendants and Collateral Families, 1744–1949; a Compilation* was compiled by Florie Janie Hamer Hooker and published in Hamer, South Carolina, most likely in 1949.

HAMMETT (S.S. Abbreviation: Hammet)

Ranking: 4171 **S.S. Count:** 10,834
Origin: English. Derived from the name Hamo, meaning home.
Famous **Hammetts:** SAMUEL ADAMS HAMMETT (1816–1865) of Connecticut was an author who wrote under the pen name Philip Paxton. His first novel, *A Stray Yankee in Texas*, was a boost to the literature of the Southwest. HENRY PICKNEY HAMMETT (1822–1891) of South Carolina was a cotton manufacturer and the founder of the Piedmont Manufacturing Co., whose success with his southern plant encouraged more cotton production in the pre–Civil War South. (SAMUEL) DASHIELL HAMMETT

(1894–1961) of Maryland was a writer and the founder of the hardline type of detective mysteries. His best-known book is probably *The Maltese Falcon*.

Genealogies: *Hammett Families: Descendants of John Hammett, Sr. (ca. 1735–1822) and Sarah (Underwood) Hammett (ca. 1740–1820) Named in Contemporary Family Letters and in Public and Family Records* was compiled by Wilbur Thomas Edwards and published in Atlanta, Georgia, in 1983.

HAMMOC (ALSO HAMMOCK)

Ranking: 4298 **S.S. Count:** 10,440

Origin: English. The name was given to those who lived near an oak tree, on grazing land lying below the water level.
Genealogies: None known.

HAMMON (ALSO HAMMOND)

Ranking: 270 **S.S. Count:** 134,631

Origin: English. 1) Derived from the Germanic name Haimo, which is derived from the word "haim," meaning home. Hammond 2): derived from the Old Norse first name Hámundr, which is derived from the words "há" and "mund," meaning high and protection. Hammond 3): derived from the Old Norse first name Amundr, which is derived from the prefix "á" and the word "mund," meaning great-grandfather and protection.

Famous **Bearers:** SAMUEL HAMMOND (1757–1842) of Virginia organized the first bank in St. Louis, Missouri. JAMES HENRY HAMMOND (1807–1864) of South Carolina was the governor of South Carolina and a Washington politician in the pre–Civil War years. As a U.S. senator he is famous for saying, "You dare not make war on cotton—no power on earth dares make war upon it. Cotton is king." WILLIAM ALEXANDER HAMMOND (1828–1900) of Maryland was a neurologist who wrote *Treatise on Diseases of the Nervous System*, which was the first textbook in English on the human nervous system. He was considered a forerunner in the treatment of mental and nervous disorders in the United States. WILLIAM GARDINER HAMMOND (1829–1894) of Rhode Island was one of the best lawyers of his time in the area of common law. GEORGE HENRY HAMMOND (1838–1886) of Massachusetts was a meat packer who was a pioneer in the use of refrigerated cars for the transport of the meat. JABEZ DELANO HAMMOND (1839–1913) of Massachusetts was the inventor of the Hammond Typewriter. JOHN HAYS HAMMOND (1855–1936) of California was a mining engineer in the California gold fields. His son, JOHN HAYS HAMMOND JR. (1888–1965), was an inventor of electronic devices. He developed radio remote-control devices, including a radio-controlled torpedo. LAURENS HAMMOND (1985–1973) of Illinois invented an electric organ. It is commonly referred to as the Hammond Organ.

Genealogies: *Can You Find Me: A Family History* was compiled by Christopher Fry and published in Oxford, New York, in 1978. *Lakes & Palmetters & Pines; the William B.B. and John W. Hammond Families of Orange and Lake Counties, Florida* was compiled by Frankie A. Hammond and published in Alachua, Florida, in 1991.

HAMPTON (S.S. Abbreviation: Hampto)

Ranking: 445 **S.S. Count:** 89,786

Origin: English. 1) derived from the Old English words "hām" and "tūn," meaning homestead and settlement. The name was given to those who came from a number of places in England called Hampton or a variation thereof, such as Southampton or Northampton. 2) derived from the Old English words "hamm" and "tūn," meaning water meadow and settlement. The name was given to those who came from a number of places in England called Hampton or a variation thereof, such as Southampton or Northampton. 3) derived from the Old English word "hēah" and "tūn," meaning high and settlement. The name was given to those who came from a number of places in England called Hampton or a variation thereof, such as Southampton or Northampton.

Famous **Hamptons:** WADE HAMPTON (1751?–1835) of Virginia was a Revolutionary War soldier and a member of the U.S. House of Representatives. WADE HAMPTON (1818–1902) of South Carolina was the grandson of Wade Hampton (1751?–1835). He was responsible for "Hampton's Legion." As a soldier, he compiled a record of victorious assaults and promotions during the Civil War. After the war he served as a Washington politician and the governor of South Carolina.

Genealogies: *The Venturers: the Hampton, Harrison, and Earle Families of Virginia, South Carolina, and Texas* was compiled by Virginia G. Meynard and published in Easley, South Carolina, in 1981. *Yesterday: the Hampton, McCracken, Longwith, Mabry & Wells Families* was compiled by Diana L. Mellen and published in Bowie, Maryland, in 1991.

HAMRICK (S.S. Abbreviation: Hamric)

Ranking: 2476 **S.S. Count:** 18,316

Origin: German. 1) cognate to the English and French definitions of Henry. 2) derived from the name Haimirich, which is composed of the German words "haimi" and "ricja," meaning home and rule.

Genealogies: *Genealogy and History of Thomas B. Hamrick, John Ray, Seaborn Mays, and E. Warbington, With Names of Many of Their Descendants* was compiled by Orville O. Ray Sr. and published in 1970. *The Hemrick [also Hamrick] and Allied Families [Germany to Georgia], 1727–1974* was compiled by Grace H. Jarvis and published in Jacksonville, Florida, in 1975.

HÀN (ALSO HANN)

Ranking: 3955 S.S. Count: 11,429

Origin: Hàn—Czech; Hann—English. Hàn: derived from the name Johannes, which is a German cognate to John. Hann: derived from the medieval first name Hann, which is a shortened form of Johann, a transformation of John.

Genealogies: None known.

HANCOCK (S.S. Abbreviation: Hancoc)

Ranking: 613 S.S. Count: 68,407

Origin: English. Derived from the Middle English first name Hann and the suffix "cock," which was used as a generic term for a youth or, more frequently, added to the end of a name as a term of endearment. This name was often taken by Gypsies living in Britain.

Famous **Hancocks:** JOHN HANCOCK (1737–1793) of Massachusetts was accused of smuggling by the Crown, which was one more piece of fuel for the fire of Revolution. The incident added to his popularity, and he was elected to political committees, serving as president of the second Continental Congress and as a signer of the Declaration of Independence. Congress's choice of George Washington over Hancock for the position of commander in chief upset Hancock so that he resigned his presidential position. He served as governor of Massachusetts on and off for a total of nine terms before he died. WINFIELD SCOTT HANCOCK (1824–1886) of Pennsylvania was a soldier who participated in the Mexican, Seminole, and Civil wars, winning fame as one of the top soldiers at Gettysburg. After the war he ran as the Democratic presidential candidate in 1880 but lost to James A. Garfield. CORNELIA HANCOCK (1840–1927) of New Jersey was a nurse who excelled during the Civil War in her chosen field. She was constantly in demand because of her gift of compassion for all with whom she came into contact.

Genealogies: *Anthony Hancock and Some of His Descendants: A Genealogy* was compiled by Harold H. Shepard and published in Arlington, Virginia, in 1986. *History of the Hancock and Barton Families: From Virginia to California: Allied Families, Corlews, Donahoos, and Holways* was compiled by the Hancock Family Organization and published in Castro Valley, California, in 1991.

HAND

Ranking: 1403 S.S. Count: 31,653

Origin: English, Irish, German. English: derived from the Old English word "hand," meaning hand. The name was often given to those who had a maimed hand or had lost one of their hands. Irish: Derived from the Gaelic name Ó Flaithimh, meaning "descendant of Flaitheamh" (H&H), which means prince. The name resulted from a confusion of the Gaelic name Ó Flaithimh with the word "lámh," meaning hand. German: derived from the Old High German

word "hand," meaning hand. The name was often given to those who had a maimed hand or had lost one of their hands.

Famous **Hands:** EDWARD HAND (1744–1802) of Ireland was a Revolutionary War soldier and a physician who was recognized for his outstanding service during the war. DANIEL HAND (1801–1891) of Connecticut made his fortune as a merchant in Georgia and South Carolina. Not forgetting his roots in colonial Connecticut, he sent back enough bricks and money to build a school in Madison. The school stands today on the town green as the elementary school and is called the Academy. The local high school carries his name. Besides the generosity to his town, in 1888 he established an educational fund for African Americans called the Daniel Hand Educational Fund for Colored People. (BILLINGS) LEARNED HAND (1872–1961) of New York was a judge with the U.S. Court of Appeals, 2nd District (1924–1951), who continued to hear special cases through 1961, making him the record holder of tenure on the federal bench. He is considered one of the greatest jurists of his time.

Genealogies: *Genealogy of the Hand Family and Related Families* was compiled by Dorothy Hand Dymond and published in Clarks Summit, Pennsylvania, in 1982. *Hand, Sisson, and Scott: More Yeoman Ancestors* was compiled by Carol Clark Johnson and published in 1981.

HANDLER, HANDLEY (S.S. Abbreviation: Handle)

Ranking: 2464 S.S. Count: 18,412

Origin: Handley—English, Irish; Handler—German, Jewish. Handley (English): derived from the Old English words "hēah" and "lēah," meaning high and wood. The name was given to those who came from Handley, the name of several places in Cheshire, Derbyshire, and Dorset, England, or from Hanley, the name of places in Staffordshire and Worcestershire, England. Handley (Irish): derived from the Gaelic name Ó hÁinle, meaning "descendant of Ainle" (H&H), which is a first name meaning champion. Handler (German, Jewish): derived from the Middle High German word "handeln," meaning to trade or deal. The name was given to those who worked as merchants or traders.

Genealogies: None known.

HANDY

Ranking: 2284 S.S. Count: 19,904

Origin: English. Uncertain etymology. 1) The name was often given as a nickname meaning "skillful with one's hands" (H&H), although this meaning probably did not develop until the 16th century, as that is the first known recording of the idiom. 2) derived from the Middle English word "hender," meaning courteous or gentle. The name was often given as a nickname to a considerate and congenial man.

Famous **Handys:** ALEXANDER HAMILTON HANDY (1809–1883) of Maryland was a Mississippi jurist. WILLIAM CHRISTOPHER HANDY (1873–1958) of Alabama was the first to publish songs called blues. His autobiography is called *Father of the Blues.*

Genealogies: None known.

HANES

Ranking: 3694 **S.S. Count:** 12,224

Origin: English, Welsh. Transformation of Haines.

Genealogies: *Blakesley Family and Allied Families of Hanes, White and Brees* was compiled by Wilda Mae Allan Sweigard and most likely published in Greeley, Colorado, in 1976.

HANEY

Ranking: 937 **S.S. Count:** 46,078

Origin: English, Irish. 1) the name was given to those who came from Hanney, which means "an island frequented by wild cocks" (ES) and is a place in Berkshire, England. 2) the name was given to the descendants of people who were named Eanna, which means bird.

Genealogies: None known.

HANKIN

Ranking: 1396 **S.S. Count:** 31,783

Origin: English, Jewish. English: derived from the Middle English first name Hankin, which is derived from the name Hann and the Low German suffix "-kin," which was frequently added to the end of a name as a term of endearment. Jewish: derived from the feminine name Khane, which is derived from the Hebrew name Chana, meaning "He [God] has favoured me [i.e., with a child]" (H&H), and the Slavic possessive suffix "-in."

Genealogies: *Plath (Plaat), Lenhart & Hankin From Germany, Illinois, Wisconsin and North Dakota* was compiled by Marion Plath Peterson and published in 1978. *Sullins-Hankins* was compiled by Michael S. Cole and published in Harrison, Arkansas, in 1979.

HANKS

Ranking: 2066 **S.S. Count:** 22,187

Origin: English. Derived from the Middle English first name Hank, which is derived from the name Hankin.

Famous **Hankses:** NANCY HANKS (1738–1818) was married to Thomas Lincoln in 1806. She was Abraham Lincoln's mother.

Genealogies: *Genealogy of the Hanks and Allied Families* was compiled by Gladys Hanks Johnson and most likely published in Llano, Texas, in 1965. *Hanks Family Records, Including References to the Following: Bartow Family, Chappell Family, Hale Family, Johnston Family, Shumway Family; a Consolidated Index to Show the Location of Records* was compiled by Stedman Shumway Hanks and published in 1971.

HANLEY

Ranking: 1673 **S.S. Count:** 26,702

Origin: English, Irish. Transformation of Handley.

Genealogies: None known.

HANLON

Ranking: 2924 **S.S. Count:** 15,569

Origin: Irish. Derived from the Gaelic name Ó hAnluain, meaning "descendant of Anluan" (H&H), which is a first name comprising the prefix "an-," denoting intensity, and the word "luan," meaning light or warrior.

Genealogies: None known.

HANNA

Ranking: 931 **S.S. Count:** 46,293

Origin: English, Irish, Scottish. English: derived from the medieval first name Hannah or Anna, which is derived from the Hebrew name Chana, meaning "He [God] has favoured me [i.e., with a child]" (H&H). In biblical tradition, the name was held by Samuel's mother (I Sam. I, 1–28), and it is popularly believed that this was also the name of the Virgin Mary's mother (H&H). Irish: derived from the Gaelic name Ó hAnnaigh, meaning "descendant of Annach" (H&H), which is a first name meaning transgression or immorality. Scottish: the name was given to those who lived in a now-unknown place. The first historical reference to this name is found in a 13th-century recording made in Wigtonshire, Scotland.

Famous **Hannas:** MARCUS ALONZO HANNA (1837–1904) of Ohio was a businessman who, realizing the importance of politics to the capitalist, became the backer and force behind an up-and-coming politician by the name of William McKinley, pushing him all the way to the White House. Hanna eventually became a U.S. senator from Ohio and remained a political advisor to McKinley, then to his successor, Theodore Roosevelt, after McKinley's assassination. EDWARD JOSEPH HANNA (1860–1944) of New York was a Roman Catholic priest who was one of the founders of the National Catholic Welfare Council (later called Conference). He excelled as a labor mediator in his California parish, where he worked to bridge the gap between different religious groups.

Genealogies: *The Gelsinger, Friend (also Hanna), and Related Families* was compiled by Carol R. Gustafson and published in Oak Forest, Illinois, in 1990. *The Hanna Family, 1744–1974, Laurens District, South Carolina, to Carroll County Indiana* was compiled by Betty A. Montoye and published in Knoxville, Tennessee, in 1974.

HANNAH

Ranking: 1668 **S.S. Count:** 26,812
Origin: English, Irish, Scottish. Transformation of Hanna.
Genealogies: None known.

HANNAN

Ranking: 4996 **S.S. Count:** 8971
Origin: Scottish. Transformation of the Scottish definition of Hanna.
Genealogies: None known.

HANNON

Ranking: 2647 **S.S. Count:** 17,186
Origin: Scottish. Transformation of the Scottish definition of Hanna.
Genealogies: None known.

HANSEL

Ranking: 4401 **S.S. Count:** 10,198
Origin: English, German. English: derived from a Germanic first name made up of the words "ans" and "helm," meaning god and protection. The name was common in Italy until it was brought to France and England in the 9th century by St. Anselm, who, in 1093, became the archbishop of Canterbury. German: derived from the name Johannes, which is a German cognate to John.*
Genealogies: None known.

HANSEN

Ranking: 177 **S.S. Count:** 189,171
Origin: Danish, German, Norwegian. Transformation of and cognate to the German definition of Hans(el).*
Famous **Hansens:** ALVIN H. HANSEN (1887–1975) of South Dakota was a highly influential economist during the Depression and World War II. He helped to draft full-employment legislation that took effect after the war. He was author of a number of books. MARCUS LEE HANSEN (1892–1938) of Wisconsin was a professor at the University of Illinois and a student of the patterns of human migration, especially of people coming to North America. NIELS EBBESEN HANSEN (1866–1950) of Denmark was a horticulturist who developed fruit, grain, and forage-crop hybrids suitable for growth in the North American prairies and plains. WILLIAM WEBSTER HANSEN (1909–1949) of California was a physics genius who was a pioneer in the development of radar.
Genealogies: *Ancestors and Kin* was compiled by Robert Walden Coggeshall and published in Spartanburg, South Carolina, in 1988. *The Genealogy of Dale Winslow Hansen* was compiled by Dale W. Hansen and published in New York, New York, in 1992.

HANSON

Ranking: 233 **S.S. Count:** 151,604
Origin: English, Jewish. English: transformation of Hann. Jewish: cognate to the English definition of Hanna.*
Famous **Hansons:** JOHN HANSON (1721–1783) of Maryland was a Revolutionary War–era politician who supported all of the Revolutionary ideals of the time. He was a member of the Continental Congress and the first president of the Congress under the Articles of Confederation. ALEXANDER CONTEE HANSON (1749–1806) of Maryland was the author of government legal writings, including "Remarks on the Proposed Plan of a Federal Government" in 1787. ALEXANDER CONTEE HANSON (1786–1819) of Maryland was the son of Alexander Contee Hanson (1749–1806). He was the founder of the *Federal Republican*, which was an extreme Federalist publication. As the result of an editorial that was critical of James Madison, a mob destroyed the newspaper building. A new building was purchased and when a member of a mob attempting to destroy that building was killed by someone in the building, a beating of Hanson and two of his allies resulted in public opinion's referring to the incident as "Republican terrorism." ROGER WEIGHTMAN HANSON (1827–1863) of Kentucky was a Confederate brigadier general who was killed at the battle of Murfreesboro, Tennessee. He was known by the nickname "Old Flintlock." JAMES CHRISTIAN MEINICH HANSON (1864–1943) of Norway was a librarian. He is credited with reorganizing the cataloguing system at the Library of Congress, devising a system agreeable to both the British and American systems. He is the author of *Catalogue Rules, Author and Title Entries* (1908). Hanson was elected to Congress in 1812 and the Senate in 1817. HAROLD C. HANSON (1892–1975) of Washington was a naval architect with worldwide clients. More than 17,000 vessels were built from his plans. HOWARD HAROLD HANSON (1896–1981) of Nebraska was a composer and the founder of the Eastman Philharmonia.
Genealogies: *Hans Hanson of Red Lyon Hundred, New Castle County, Delaware* was compiled by Baldwin Springer Maull and published in Princeton, New Jersey, in 1978. *Hanson Relatives: Ancestors and Descendants of Love, Susan, Nahum, and Charles Hanson, and Ancestors of Some of the Spouses of Hanson Descendants* was compiled by Charlotte A. Nicely and published in Baltimore, Maryland, in 1977.

HARBER (ALSO HARBERD, HARBERER, HARBERS, HARBERT)

Ranking: 4317 **S.S. Count:** 10,393
Origin: Harber, Harberd, Harberer—English; Harbert—English, French; Harbers—German. Harber, Harberer: derived from the Old English words "here" and "beorg,"*

meaning army and shelter. The names were given to those who worked managing an inn. Harberd, Harbert, Harbers: transformations of and cognates to Herbert.

Genealogies: None known.

HARBINSON (S.S. Abbreviation: Harbin)

Ranking: 3641 S.S. Count: 12,379
Origin: English. Transformation of Herbert.
Genealogies: None known.

HARDEN (ALSO HARDENBERG)

Ranking: 1130 S.S. Count: 38,954
Origin: Hardenberg—Dutch, German; Harden—English. Hardenberg: derived from the Middle Low German words "hard" and "berg," meaning unattainable and hill. The name was often given to those who came from Hardenberg, the name of several places in Holland and Germany. Harden: derived from the Old English words "hara" and "denu," meaning hare and valley. The name was given to those who came from Harden, the name of a place in West Yorkshire, England. This place is not to be confused with Harden, in Staffordshire, England, which has an altogether different etymology.
Genealogies: None known.

HARDER

Ranking: 3252 S.S. Count: 13,977
Origin: English. Derived from the Middle English word "hard," meaning hard or rigid. The name was often given to those who lived on a tract of land that was rocky or difficult to farm. The prepositions "de" or "le" were often added before the name of those who lived on such land.
Genealogies: *A Harder Family* was compiled by Katherine Block Wolpert and most likely published in Onawa, Iowa, in 1975.

HARDES

Ranking: 2932 S.S. Count: 15,529
Origin: English. 1) derived from either the Old English first name Heard or its Norman cognate, Hard(on), both of Germanic origin. The name was often given to those who were considered sturdy and courageous, and it was often used as the first element in a compound last name. 2) derived from the plural form of the Old English word "harað," meaning wood. The name was given to those who came from Hardres, the name of a place in Kent, England.
Genealogies: None known.

HARDIN (ALSO HARDING)

Ranking: 326 S.S. Count: 115,387
Origin: Harding—English; Hardin—French, Jewish. Harding: derived from the Old English first name Hearding,

which is a transformation of the first definition of Hard(es). Hardin (French): cognate to Harding. Hardin (Jewish): uncertain etymology.

Famous **Bearers:** SETH HARDING (1734–1814) of Massachusetts was a naval officer. In 1776, as the commander of the *Defence*, he captured three British ships that carried supplies badly needed by the Revolutionary soldiers. JOHN HARDIN (1753–1792) of Virginia was a Revolutionary War soldier and Indian fighter. He hunted Indians with the purpose of eradicating them. Justice prevailed and he was killed by the Miami Indians. MARTIN D. HARDIN (1780–1823) of Pennsylvania was the son of John Hardin. He was a lawyer in Kentucky and a politician at the state and national level. BEN HARDIN (1784–1852) of Pennsylvania was the nephew of John Hardin. He was active in Kentucky politics. CHESTER HARDING (1792–1866) of Massachusetts was a jack-of-all-trades until he settled on portrait painting, at which he excelled. Some of his subjects were Daniel Webster, Daniel Boone, and John C. Calhoun. JESPER HARDING (1799–1865) of Pennsylvania was a printer and newspaper publisher in Philadelphia. (The paper eventually became known as the *Philadelphia Inquirer*.) After 1829 he was the largest printer of Bibles in the country. ABNER CLARK HARDING (1807–1874) of Connecticut was a lawyer, railroad builder, and member of Congress from Illinois. JOHN J. HARDIN (1810–1847) of Kentucky was a lawyer and soldier. He was the son of Martin D. Hardin. He is best remembered as Abraham Lincoln's rival for Whig leadership in Illinois. GEORGE HARDING (1827–1902) of Pennsylvania was a patent lawyer. He was involved in cases dealing with the Morse telegraph and the McCormick reaper. He was a son of Jesper Harding. WILLIAM WHITE HARDING (1830–1889) of Pennsylvania was a son of Jesper Harding. He took over the position of publisher of the *Philadelphia Inquirer* from his father and built it into a top-rated paper. He was a pioneer in the first attempts at making paper from wood. FLORENCE KLING HARDING (1860–1924) of Ohio was the wife of President Warren G. Harding. She was called "Dutchess" by him. WARREN GAMALIEL HARDING (1865–1923) of Ohio was the 29th president of the United States. Some of Harding's appointees were less than honorable, and the administration suffered because of them.

Genealogies: *Thomas and Polly Hardin and Their Descendants* was compiled by Robert Allen Hardin and published in Norman, Oklahoma, in 1968. *Norris, Hackett, Prescott and Allied Families: Our Ancestors and Their Descendants, Including Adams, Andrews, Bachelder, Bartlett, Boulter, Brewer, Brown, Harding, Hinkley, Howard, Huntington, et. al.* was compiled by Hugh Albert Johnson and published in Annandale, Virginia, in 1976.

HARDISTY (S.S. Abbreviation: Hardis)

Ranking: 3372 S.S. Count: 13,438

Origin: English. Derived from the Old English first name Heardwulf (comprising the words "heard" and "wulf," meaning hardy and wolf) and the Old English word "stig," meaning path. The name was given to those who came from Hardolfsty, a place in Yorkshire, England.

Genealogies: None known.

HARDMAN

Ranking: 3548 S.S. Count: 12,724

Origin: English. 1) derived from the Middle English words "he(a)rde" and "mann," meaning flock or herd and man. The name was given to those who worked tending herds of animals. 2) derived from the Old English first name Heardmann, which comprises the words "heard" and "mann," meaning hardy and man.

Genealogies: *Thomas Powell, Colonial-Yeoman-Planter, Circa 1616–1687, Isle of Wight county, Virginia, and John Hardman, Colonial-Planter, circa 1725–1800; Progenitors with Thousands of Their Descendants Arranged in Chronological Order to 1985* was compiled by George Travis Powell Jr. and published in Macon, Georgia, in 1987. *The Wilhite Clan, 1539–1992: Herdman (also Hardman) and Haynes* was compiled by Julian G. Allen and published in Austin, Texas, in 1992.

HARDWICK, HARDWICKE, HARDWIG (S.S. Abbreviation: Hardwi)

Ranking: 2975 S.S. Count: 15,284

Origin: Hardwick, Hardwicke—English; Hardwig—German. Hardwick, Hardwicke: derived from the Old English words "heorde" and "wic," meaning herd and solitary farm. The name was given to those who came from Hardwick, the name of various places in England, including Buckinghamsire, Cambridgeshire, Norfolk, Northamptonshire, Worcestershire, and West Yorkshire counties. Hardwig: derived from a now-unknown Germanic first name comprising the words "hard" and "wig," meaning hardy or brave and war.

Famous **Bearers:** THOMAS WILLIAM HARDWICK (1872–1944) of Georgia was a member of Congress, then a U.S. senator from Georgia, then governor of Georgia (1921–1922).

Genealogies: None known.

HARDY

Ranking: 355 S.S. Count: 107,607

Origin: English, French. Derived from the Old French and Middle English word "hardi," meaning brave. The name was occasionally adopted by Jews, but the reason for this is unclear.

Famous **Hardys:** SAMUEL HARDY (1758?–1785) of Virginia was a statesman and Virginia delegate to the Conti-

nental Congress. WILLIAM HARRIS HARDY (1837–1917) of Alabama was the founder of Gulfport and Hattiesburg, Mississippi. He promoted southeastern railroads to further the development of the lands of the southern pinebelt. ANNA ELIZA HARDY (1839–1934) of Maine was a painter who is best known for her delicate still-life paintings. OLIVER NOWELL HARDY (1892–1957) of Georgia was the partner of Stan Laurel in the comedy team of Laurel and Hardy. They worked together in about 200 slapstick features.

Genealogies: *An American Family and Its Ancestor Predecessors; Back to Adam through Early American Immigrants of British Extraction According to Past and Present Records* was compiled by Vivian Higgins Morse and published in Baltimore, Maryland, in 1973. *The Eastern North Carolina Hardy-Hardee Family in the South and Southwest* was compiled by David Lydall Hardee and most likely published in Raleigh, North Carolina, in 1966.

HARE

Ranking: 2058 S.S. Count: 22,240

Origin: English, Irish. English: derived from the Old English word "hara," meaning hare. The name was often given to a fast sprinter. Irish: derived from the Gaelic name Ó hAichir, meaning "descendant of Aichear" (H&H), which was a first name presumably derived from the word "aichear," meaning cruel or cutting.

Famous **Hares:** ROBERT HARE (1781–1858) was a chemist who invented the oxyhydrogen blowpipe. GEORGE EMLEN HARE (1808–1892) of Pennsylvania was an Episcopal clergyman and the head of the school that came to be known as the Divinity School of Protestant Episcopal Church, Philadelphia. WILLIAM HOBART HARE (1838–1909) of New Jersey was the son of George E. Hare and an Episcopal minister. He served as a missionary bishop in Sioux country in an area located north of the Niobrara River. JAMES H. HARE (1856–1946) of England was a photographer who was a pioneer in using the hand-held camera and in aerial photography.

Genealogies: None known.

HARGIS

Ranking: 3803 S.S. Count: 11,867

Origin: English? Uncertain etymology. Possibly derived from the Old English word "hara," meaning hare.

Genealogies: None known.

HARGRAVE, HARGRAVES (S.S. Abbreviation: Hargra)

Ranking: 3153 S.S. Count: 14,392

Origin: English. Derived from the Old English words "hār" or "hara," and "grāf" or "grœ f," meaning gray or hare, and grove or thicket. The names were given to those who came from Hargr(e)ave, the name of several places in England, including Cheshire, Northamptonshire, and Suffolk counties. The names may also have been given to those who came from a parcel of land called Hargreves, located in Standen, in Lancashire County, England.

Genealogies: *Hargrave Forbears: A Genealogy and History of Some Descendants of Richard Hargrave, Sr. of Lower Norfolk County, Virginia, 1634–1968, With Notes on the English Family Background of Richard and on Other Hargrave Family Lines in America* was compiled by Helena M. Hargrave and published in Walnut Creek, California, in 1968.

HARGROVE, HARGROVES (S.S. Abbreviation: Hargro)

Ranking: 1560 S.S. Count: 28,590
Origin: *English. Transformation of Hargr(e)aves.*

Famous **Bearers:** ROBERT KENNON HARGROVE (1829–1905) of Alabama was the president of Vanderbilt University (1889–1905).

Genealogies: *Directory of Members and Their Ancestors with Allied Lines Indexed* was compiled by the Hargrove Family Association and published in Greensboro, North Carolina, in 1982.

HARKIN (ALSO HARKINS)

Ranking: 2437 S.S. Count: 18,640
Origin: *English. Derived from either the Old English first name Heard or its Norman cognate, Hard(on), both of Germanic origin. The names were often given to those who were considered sturdy and courageous, and they were often used as the first element in a compound last name.*

Genealogies: None known.

HARLAN (ALSO HARLAND)

Ranking: 2374 S.S. Count: 6847
Origin: *English. 1) derived from the Old English words "hār" and "land," meaning gray and land. The names were given to those who came from Harlan, the name of a number of places in England, mostly in Middlesbrough County. 2) derived from the Old English words "hara" and "land," meaning hare and land. The names were given to those who came from Harlan, the name of a number of places in England, mostly in Middlesborough County.*

Famous **Bearers:** THOMAS HARLAND (1735–1807) of England was a watch and clock maker and silversmith whose shop was in Norwich, Connecticut. RICHARD HARLAN (1796–1843) of Pennsylvania was a naturalist and physician. His interest in zoology and vertebrate paleontology is evident in his best-remembered work, *Fauna Americana.* JOSIAH HARLAN (1799–1871) of Pennsylvania was a secret agent and Asian explorer whose life's adventures are recalled in the book *A Memoir of India and Afghanistan.*

JAMES HARLAN (1800–1863) of Kentucky was a Civil War–era member of Congress from Kentucky who was opposed to secession. He also served in state politics. JAMES HARLAN (1820–1899) of Illinois was a politician who served as a U.S. senator and secretary of the interior. He is known as the person who terminated Walt Whitman from a clerk's job at the interior department, which generated considerable backlash from Whitman's literary friends. JOHN MARSHALL HARLAN (1833–1911) of Kentucky served in the Union army during the Civil War and was an associate justice of the U.S. Supreme Court, in which capacity he was known for his forceful dissents in civil rights cases. He once called the Consitution "color-blind." His grandson, JOHN MARSHALL HARLAN (1899–1971) of Illinois, was also an associate justice of the Supreme Court. HENRY HARLAND (1861–1905) of Russia, was a novelist. He was raised in New York City. Some of his works were under the pen name of Sidney Luska.

Genealogies: *Barker-Harland: A Genealogical Study* was compiled by Marjorie Harland Barker Diedrich and published in Siesta Key, Florida, in 1989.

HARLES

Ranking: 4627 S.S. Count: 9658
Origin: *English. Transformation of Earl.*
Genealogies: None known.

HARLEY

Ranking: 2892 S.S. Count: 15,741
Origin: *English. 1) derived from the Old English words "hœr" and "lēah," meaning rock and wood. The name was given to those who came from Harley, the name of several places in Shropshire and West Yorkshire, England. 2) derived from the Old English words "hara" and "lēah," meaning hare and wood. The name was given to those who came from Harley, the name of several places in Shropshire and West Yorkshire, England.*
Genealogies: None known.

HARLOW

Ranking: 2622 S.S. Count: 17,330
Origin: *English. 1) derived from the Old English words "hœr" and "hlāw," meaning rock and hill. The name was given to those who came from Harlow, in West Yorkshire, England. 2) derived from the Old English words "here" and "hlāw," meaning army (in the sense of gathering) and hill. The name was given to those who came from Harlow, the name of a place in Northumberland, England.*

Famous **Harlows:** JEAN HARLOW (1911–1937), originally Harlean Carpenter, was an actress who appeared in motion pictures in the 1920s and 1930s. She was known for being beautiful, sexy, and funny.

Genealogies: *The Cummington Harlows: Line of Ances-*

try From Sergeant William Harlow of Plymouth and Descendants of Matthew Harlow (1775–1847) of Sixth Generation was compiled by Cummington Harlows Association and published in Cummington, Massachusetts, in 1989. *Richard Penhallow (also Harlow): His Life and Descendants* was compiled by Aileen Smock DeLong and published in Rocky Hill, Connecticut, in 1983.

HARMAN (ALSO HARMAND, HARMANING, HARMANT)

Ranking: 2062 **S.S. Count:** 22,205

Origin: Harman, Harmand, Harmant—French; Harmaning—German. Transformations of and cognates to Hermann.

Genealogies: None known.

HARMON

Ranking: 380 **S.S. Count:** 101,998

Origin: English. Cognate to Hermann.

Famous **Harmons:** DANIEL WILLIAMS HARMON (1778–1845) of Vermont was a fur trader and explorer. He left a record of his experiences and journeys in the *Journal of Voyages and Travels in the Interiour of North America* (1820). JUDSON HARMON (1846–1927) of Ohio was a U.S. attorney general and governor of Ohio. MILLARD FILMORE HARMON (1888–1945) of California was a career army officer who was the ground and air commander of the army forces in the South Pacific. He was lost in flight during World War II.

Genealogies: *Clara Harmon Bradshaw: Her American Ancestors and Her Descendants* was compiled by Mary Frances Bradshaw Dittrich and most likely published in Ogden Dunes, Indiana, in 1973.

HARMS

Ranking: 2481 **S.S. Count:** 18,257

Origin: Dutch, English, German. Transformation of and cognate to Hermann.

Genealogies: *Biographical Notes and Genealogy of Descendants in Netherlands and America of Gert Harms and Grietje Raak Family Staphorst, Netherlands: Early 1700–early 1900* was compiled by Margaret Raak Vanderploeg and published in North Muskegon, Michigan, in 1978.

HAROLD

Ranking: 4867 **S.S. Count:** 9199

Origin: German. Derived from a now-unknown Germanic personal name composed of the words "heri" or "hari" and "wald," meaning army and rule. This evolved into the Old English form Hereweald, its Old Norse cognate Haraldr, or the modern English modification Herold.

Genealogies: None known.

HARP

Ranking: 2399 **S.S. Count:** 18,889

Origin: English, Scottish. Transformation of Harper.

Genealogies: None known.

HARPER

Ranking: 210 **S.S. Count:** 169,413

Origin: English, Scottish. Derived from the Middle English word "harp," meaning harp. The name was given to a harp player, one of the most significant figures in a medieval court—so much so that the position was sometimes hereditary.

Famous **Harpers:** ROBERT GOODLOE HARPER (1765–1825) of Virginia was a politician and a soldier in the War of 1812. He is best remembered for saying after the XYZ affair, "Millions for defense, but not a cent for tribute." WILLIAM HARPER (1790–1847) of Antigua was a South Carolina legislator who wrote *Memoir on Slavery*, considered to contain the most convincing proslavery arguments. FLETCHER HARPER (1806–1877) of New York, along with his brothers, JAMES HARPER (1795–1869), JOHN HARPER (1797–1875), and JOSEPH WESLEY HARPER (1801–1870), built the publishing business that became Harper & Brothers. They also started *Harper's Weekly* and *Harper's Bazar*. FRANCES ELLEN WATKINS HARPER (1825–1911) of Maryland was an African-American lecturer and author. She was an only child born to free Negro parents. Orphaned by the age of three, she was raised by her uncle. She spoke on the antislavery movement. With her concern for Negro morality she started Negro Sunday schools in the Philadelphia churches and became active in the National Association of Colored Women, and a suffragist. She wrote, much to her husband's dismay, for newspapers and magazines, mostly on women's issues. The marriage ended in divorce, and she took a full-time writing position with the *Terre Haute Daily News*. She was the official biographer of Susan B. Anthony. WILLIAM RAINEY HARPER (1856–1906) of Ohio was the first president of the University of Chicago. ROBERT ALMER HARPER (1862–1946) of Iowa was a biologist best known for his studies of cytology. JOHN LYELL HARPER (1873–1924) of New York was an engineer specializing in hydroelectric work. His best-remembered work was in the design and construction of the Niagara Falls Power Co. power plant located at the base of the falls. It was the largest at the time. JESSE HARPER (1884–1961), birthplace unknown, was a football coach at Notre Dame University. He developed the forward pass as an offensive strategy.

Genealogies: *The Harpers of Pulaski and Rockcastle Counties, Kentucky: A Genealogical and Historical Narrative* was compiled by Joseph Doyle Harper and published in Linvington, Montana, in 1990. *The Harpers of Virginia, West Virginia, and Mississippi* was compiled by Frank O'Beirne and published in Arlington, Virginia, in 1982.

HARREL (ALSO HARRELL)

Ranking: 487 S.S. Count: 83,132

Origin: English. 1) derived from a now-unknown Germanic personal name composed of the words "heri" or "hari" and "wald," meaning army and rule. This evolved into the Old English form Hereweald, its Old Norse cognate Haraldr, or the modern English modification Herold. 2) derived from the Old French word "herau(l)t," meaning herald. The name was given to those who worked as messengers.

Famous **Harrells:** JOHN HARRELL (1806–1876) of North Carolina was a Methodist clergyman who worked in western Arkansas and Indian territory.

Genealogies: *Under the Rainbow: The Harrells* was compiled by Wanda Frazier Harrell and published in Anton, Texas, in 1986.

HARRIGAN (S.S. Abbreviation: Harrig)

Ranking: 4262 S.S. Count: 10,570

Origin: Irish. Derived from a Gaelic name meaning "grandson of little Anradh" (ES), which means champion.

Famous **Harrigans:** EDWARD HARRIGAN (1845–1911) of New York was a playwright and actor. He wrote 39 plays and worked with Tony Hart in the famous firm of Harrigan and Hart.

Genealogies: None known.

HARRINGTON (S.S. Abbreviation: Harrin)

Ranking: 426 S.S. Count: 93,325

Origin: English, Irish. English: 1) derived from the Old English name Hœ feringtūn, meaning "settlement associated with 'Hœ fer'" (H&H), which is a nickname meaning male goat. The name was given to those who came from Harrington, in Cumberland, England. 2) derived from the Old English word "hœ r," meaning rock, and the suffix "ing." The name may have meant "settlement on stony ground" (H&H) and was given to those who came from Harrington, in Lincolnshire, England. 3) uncertain derivation. One of its elements may have been a word meaning heath. The name was given to those who came from Harrington, in Northamptonshire, England. Irish: derived from the Gaelic name Ó hArrachtáin, meaning "descendant of Arrachtán," a first name derived from the word "arrachtach," which means strong.

Famous **Harringtons:** MARK WALROD HARRINGTON (1848–1926) of Illinois was the first civilian chief of the U.S. Weather Bureau. He was the founder of the *American Meteorological Journal.* CHARLES HARRINGTON (1856–1908) of Massachusetts was an educator who was able to interest people in preventive medicine through his writings on the subject. THOMAS FRANCIS HARRINGTON (1866–1919) of Massachusetts was a pioneer of hygienic physical culture in public schools. JOHN LYLE HARRINGTON (1868–1942) of Kansas was a civil and mechanical engineer whose best-known work was the vertical lift bridge, which he invented

from a simpler invention of his partner, John A.L. Waddell.

Genealogies: *Harrington-Heath Heritage: Ancestors and Descendants (1600–1984) of Oramel Warren Harrington and Martha C. Heath* was compiled by Ruth Haddox Harrington and published in Philadelphia, Pennsylvania, in 1984. *The Ancestry of Marie Louise Harrington and Her Bagley Descendants* was compiled by David Harrington Bagley and published in Vienna, Virginia, in 1983.

HARRIS, HARRISMITH, HARRISON

Ranking: 11 S.S. Count: 1,087,838

Origin: Harrismith—English; Harris, Harrison—English, Jewish. Harrismith: derived from the Old English words "arwe" and "smið," meaning arrow and smith. The name was given to those who worked making metal arrowheads. Harris, Harrison (English): transformation of Harry. Harris, Harrison (Jewish): adopted as an Anglicized modification of similar-sounding Jewish names.

Famous **Bearers:** BENJAMIN HARRIS (1673?–1716) of England was a publisher and bookseller. He is credited with being the first American journalist. In 1690 he published the first newspaper that was printed in America, called *Publick Occurrences Both Forreign and Domestick,* but it contained nearly all American news. It was suppressed by the governor of Massachusetts because it was not licensed. He also published *The New England Primer,* a publication that was very well received. In 1695 he returned to London. PETER HARRISON (1716–1775) of England came to America and lived in Newport, Rhode Island, and New Haven, Connecticut. He was the foremost architect of his day. JOHN HARRIS (1726–1791) of Pennsylvania was a soldier in the Revolutionary War, a fur trader, and the founder of the town of Harrisburg, Pennsylvania. BENJAMIN HARRISON (1726?–1791) of Virginia was a Revolutionary War–era politician. He was one of the signers of the Declaration of Independence, the governor of Virginia, and a member of the Virginia political machinery of the times. His son, WILLIAM HENRY HARRISON (1773–1841), was the ninth president of the United States. He died from pneumonia one month after taking office. ANNA SYMMES HARRISON (1775–1864) of New Jersey was the wife of President William Henry Harrison. However, she never acted as first lady, because her husband died before she got to the White House. CHAPIN AARON HARRIS (1806–1860) of New York was a dentist and the co-founder of the first dental college, the Baltimore College of Dental Surgery. He was also the founder of the *American Journal of Dental Science.* GEORGE WASHINGTON HARRIS (1814–1869) was born in Pennsylvania and raised in eastern Tennessee. He was a humorist who wrote about the unique localisms of the people of the East Tennessee mountains. GABRIEL HARRISON (1818–1902) of Pennsylvania was an actor, author, and artist. He was an important part of art and theater life in Brooklyn, New York. He and Edgar Allan Poe were close friends. ISHAM GREEN HARRIS (1818–1897) of Tennessee was a Confederate soldier and a politician from his home state. CAROLINE LAVINIA SCOTT HARRISON (1823–1892) of Ohio was the first wife of the 23rd president of the United States, Benjamin Harrison. ELISHA HARRIS (1824–1884) of Vermont was a physician who devised a national system to record the deaths and burials of soldiers. JOSEPH HARRIS (1828–1892) was a scientific agriculturalist and editor. He wrote *Harris on the Pig* and *Talks on Manures*. BENJAMIN HARRISON (1833–1901) of Ohio was the 23rd president of the United States. He was the great grandson of Benjamin Harrison (b. 1726?) and the grandson of William Henry Harrison. CONSTANCE CARY HARRISON (1843–1920) of Virginia was a novelist whose works included *Flower de Hundred* (1890). His father was the nephew of Thomas Jefferson. JOEL CHANDLER HARRIS (1848–1908) of Georgia was an author who was famous for writing the *Uncle Remus* series of books. ELIZABETH HARRISON (1849–1927) of Kentucky was a kindergarten educator. In 1883 she co-founded the Chicago Kindergartners Club. She did much to make parents aware of the value of creative self-expression as a way of building children's mental, emotional, and moral abilities. MARY SCOTT LORD DIMMICK HARRISON (1858–1948) of Pennsylvania was the second wife of Benjamin Harrison, the 23rd president of the United States. She was also the niece of Harrison's first wife, Caroline. CHARLES KASSEL HARRIS (1865–1930) of New York was a songwriter who wrote "After the Ball," among others. CORRA MAY WHITE HARRIS (1869–1935) of Georgia was a novelist who wrote, among other works, *The Circuit Rider's Wife*, which became the movie *I'd Climb the Highest Mountain*. PAUL PERCEY HARRIS (1868–1947) of Wisconsin organized and served as the first president of the Rotary Clubs. SAM HENRY HARRIS (1872–1941) of New York was a movie executive who produced the Marx Brothers films as well as other popular movies of the day. MARY BELLE HARRIS (1874–1957) of Pennsylvania is best remembered as a prison administrator. A teacher, she was offered a position as superintendent of women and deputy warden of the Workhouse of Blackwell Island by Katharine Davis. Harris revolutionized the workhouse by creating a library, allowing leisure activities, and encouraging daily outdoor exercise. Her claim to fame is her record of common-sense administration. HAZEL HARRISON (1883–1969) of Indiana was a pianist of world renown. She was a descendant of runaway slaves who had made their way via the Underground Railroad to the Midwest and Canada. She faced many difficult situations in her chosen profession because of her race. A 1922 review of a Chicago recital ended with, "[s]he is extremely talented . . . it seems too bad that the fact that she is a Negress may limit her future plans." Despite the review she continued to

play, and she taught music at several institutes of higher learning. ROY ELLSWORTH HARRIS (1898–1979) of Oklahoma was a composer who wrote, among other songs, "When Johnny Comes Marching Home Again."

Genealogies: *Families of Elisha, Joseph and Woodruff Harris of Chenango County, New York and Geauga and Portage Counties, Ohio* was compiled by Gale Ion Harris and published in East Lansing, Michigan, in 1981. *Harris Index: A Biographical Index of Over 4500 American Descendants of Edward Harris and Flora Douglas of Scotland, 1730–1983* was compiled by Calsita V. Leonard and published in Santa Monica, California, in 1983. *The Venturers: The Hampton, Harrison, and Earle Families of Virginia, South Carolina, and Texas* was compiled by Virginia G. Meynard and published in Easley, South Carolina, in 1981.

HARRY

Ranking: 4217 **S.S. Count:** 10,704

Origin: English. Derived from the medieval first name Henry, which, in colloquial usage, took the form of Harry. The name was most common in Devon and Cornwall.

Genealogies: *Aristocratic and Royal Ancestors of Jane Harry* was compiled by Leslie Ray Tucker and published in Miami, Oklahoma, in 1991.

HART

Ranking: 180 **S.S. Count:** 187,522

Origin: English, Irish, Jewish. English: derived from the Old English word "heorot," meaning stag. The name was given to those who were thought to bear a likeness of some kind to the animal. Irish: derived from the Gaelic name Ó hAirt, meaning "descendant of Art" (H&H), which is a first name meaning bear or hero. Jewish: adopted as an Anglicized modification of similar-sounding Jewish names.

Famous Harts: JOHN HART (1711?–1779) of Connecticut was the New Jersey signer of the Declaration of Independence. He also represented New Jersey in the political assemblies of the day. NANCY HART (1735?–1830) was born either in Pennsylvania or North Carolina. Information is sketchy, but it is believed that she was Daniel Boone's first cousin, as was General Daniel Morgan the first cousin to both of them. Her claim to fame, however, is not in her relatives but in the folklore story of how she dealt with five Tories who had bullied their way into her Georgia home during the Revolutionary War, shooting one dead, wounding another, and holding the rest hostage until help arrived. EDMUND HALL HART (1839–1898) of New York was a Florida horticulturist and the fruit grower who introduced the Valencia orange to Florida. HASTINGS HORNELL HART (1851–1932) of Ohio was a social worker who introduced the idea of juvenile laws and juvenile court to Cook County, Illinois. They were the first of their kind in the country. EDWARD HART (1854–1931) of Pennsylvania was the founder of the Chemical Publishing Co. ALBERT BUSH-NELL HART (1854–1943) of Pennsylvania was a historian. He is the man responsible for making American history a respected academic subject. WILLIAM SURREY HART (1862?–1946) of New York was an actor of stage and screen who usually achieved fame and fortune as a cowboy star. LORENZ MILTON HART (1895–1943) of New York wrote musical lyrics. After 1918 he was the partner of Richard Rodgers. MOSS HART (1904–1961) of New York was a playwright of great renown. His movie script, *Gentlemen's Agreement*, won an Academy Award in 1947.

Genealogies: *The Harts of Randolph: or, Mostly Descendants of Edward and Daniel Hart, Sons of John Hart the Signer, With Some Allied Families* was compiled by Katherine Hart Frame and published in Parson, West Virginia, in 1976. *Heart (also Hart)-Diamond* was compiled by Kathy L. Greenwood and published in Denton, Texas, in 1990.

HARTER
Ranking: 3035 **S.S. Count:** 14,984
Origin: German. 1) the name was given to those who came from Hart, which means "willow wood" (ES) and is the name of several places in Germany. 2) the name was given to a person who tended to herds of animals.

Genealogies: *The Mohawk Valley Harters and Allied Families* was compiled by Marion Kofmehl and published in Herkimer, New York, in 1981.

HARTLE (ALSO HARTLEY)
Ranking: 843 **S.S. Count:** 50,550
Origin: English. Hartle: 1) derived from the Old English words "heorot" and "hyll," meaning stag and hill. The name was given to those who came from Harthill, the name of several places in Cheshire, Derbyshire, and West Yorkshire, England. 2) derived from the Old English first name Heortla and the word "burh," meaning fort. The name may be a shortened form of Hartlebury, a place in Worcestershire, England, and may have been given to those who lived there. Hartley: 1) derived from the Old English words "heorot" and "lēah," meaning stag and wood. The name was given to those who came from Hartley, the name of various places in England. 2) derived from the Old English words "heorot" and "hlāw," meaning stag and hill. The name was given to those who came from Hartley, the name of a place in Northumberland County, England. 3) uncertain etymology. Probably derived from the Old English words "heorot" and "clā," meaning stag and claw (in the sense of a piece of land lying between two rivulets). The name was given to those who came from Hartley, the name of a place in Cumberland County, England.

Famous Bearers: THOMAS HARTLEY (1748–1800) of Pennsylvania was a Revolutionary War soldier and the commander of the 1st Pennsylvania Brigade. JONATHAN SCOTT HARTLEY (1845–1912) of New York was a sculptor who was best known for his portraits of men. FRANK HARTLEY (1856–1913) of Washington, D.C., was a surgeon who perfected a surgical cure for trigeminal neuralgia. MARSDEN HARTLEY (1877–1943) of Maine was a painter and poet. He tried to no avail to copy the artistic styles of his day, finally developing his own style of Maine seascapes and landscapes in rich colors. FRED ALLEN HARTLEY JR. (1903–1969) of New Jersey was a member of Congress and the co-author of the Taft-Hartley Act.

Genealogies: *Blue Ridge Mountain Kinfolks: A Record of Ancestors, Descendants, and Relatives of the Author and Wife, Including Fisher-Gilbert-Hall-Hartley-Hill-King-Kirby-Lawson Families* was compiled by Larry King and published in Manchester, Tennessee, most likely in 1976. *Richardson-Hartley-Arender and Related Families; a List of the Known Descendants of Elijah Richardson of Tennessee and Frank Hartley of South Carolina, Both of Whom Moved to Mississippi About 1815* was compiled by Thomas F. Richardson and published in Poplarville, Mississippi, in 1969.

HARTMANN (S.S. Abbreviation: Hartma)
Ranking: 363 **S.S. Count:** 106,697
Origin: German. Cognate to the English definition of Hart.

Famous Hartmanns: CARL SADAKICHI HARTMANN (1867?–1944) was born in Japan to parents of Japanese and German descent. An author and critic, he worked for Walt Whitman before wandering about the country. He settled in southern California, supporting himself by lecturing and panhandling when necessary. His books, *Japanese Art* and *The Whistler Book*, were considered excellent.

Genealogies: *Christ and Anna, Descendants of Anton Bach, Jacob Damm, John Hartman, George Kremer and John Yocum: Including Local History and Memorabilia of Sandusky, Ohio and Surrounding Areas* was compiled by Patty Dahm Pascoe and published in Baltimore, Maryland, in 1980.

HARTNELL, HARTNETT (S.S. Abbreviation: Hartne)
Ranking: 3105 **S.S. Count:** 14,643
Origin: Hartnell: English. Uncertain etymology. 1) possibly derived from the Old English first name Heorta (a derivative of the word "heorot," meaning stag) and the word "hyll," meaning hill. The name was given to those who came from a now-unknown place or region in England. 2) possibly derived from the Old English first name Heorta (a derivative of the word "heorot," meaning stag) and the word "healh," meaning niche. The name was given to those who came from a now-unknown place or region in England. 3) possibly derived from the Old English first name Heorta (a derivative of the word "heorot," meaning stag) and the word "cnoll," meaning hill. The name was given to those who came from Hartnoll, a

place in Marwood, England. Harnett: Irish. Derived from the Gaelic name Ó hAirtnéada, meaning "descendant of Airtnéad" (H&H), which is a first name of uncertain etymology; the first element is most probably derived from the word "art," meaning bear or hero.

Genealogies: None known.

HARTSON (S.S. Abbreviation: Hartso)

Ranking: 4751 S.S. Count: 9426

Origin: English. Derived from the Old English word "heor(ot)," meaning hart, a kind of deer. The name was given as a nickname and to those who lived near a place with a sign of a hart.

Genealogies: None known.

HARTWELL (S.S. Abbreviation: Hartwe)

Ranking: 4539 S.S. Count: 9849

Origin: English. Derived from the Old English words "heorot" and "well(a)," meaning stag and spring or brook. The name was given to those who came from Hartwell, the name of several places in Buckinghamshire, Northamptonshire, and Stafforsdshire, England.

Genealogies: *A Cornell-Hartwell Genealogy: 1302 Years of Family History Including 348 Years in Westchester County* was compiled by Stephen Wood Cornell II and published in Carmel, New York, in 1990.

HARTWIG, HARTWIGER, HARTWIGSEN (S.S. Abbreviation: Hartwi)

Ranking: 3527 S.S. Count: 12,794

Origin: German. Derived from a Germanic first name composed of the words "hard" and "wig," meaning courageous and war.

Famous **Bearers:** JOHANN CHRISTOPH HARTWIG (1714–1796) of Germany was a Lutheran clergyman who had several parishes in New York before wandering up and down the eastern coast of America. He founded Hartwick Seminary.

Genealogies: None known.

HARTZER (S.S. Abbreviation: Hartze)

Ranking: 4235 S.S. Count: 10,648

Origin: German. Derived from the Old High German word "hard," which refers either to "a range of wooded hills" or to "a drovers' road for cattle" (H&H). The name was given to those who lived near such places.

Genealogies: None known.

HARVEY

Ranking: 221 S.S. Count: 158,492

Origin: English, Irish, Scottish. English, Scottish: derived from the Breton first name Aeruiu or Haerviu, which are both derived from the words "haer" and "vy," meaning combat or bloodshed and worthy. The name, which first appeared in England in the Gaelic form Hervé, was brought to the island by Breton followers of William the Conqueror. Irish: derived from the Gaelic name Ó hAirmheadhaigh, meaning "descendant of Airmheadhach" (H&H), a first name with an uncertain etymology; it is possibly derived from Airmheadh, the name of a mythical doctor.

Famous **Harveys:** SIR JOHN HARVEY (?–1646), possibly of England, was a sea captain and governor of Virginia (1630–1635, 1637–1639). He returned to England in 1641. HAYWARD AUGUSTUS HARVEY (1824–1893) of New York was an inventor who is best known for the Harvey process of treating armor plate. GEORGE BRINTON MCCLELLAN HARVEY (1864–1928) of Vermont was an editor of *North American Review* and *Harper's Weekly* and president of Harper & Brothers. He supported both Woodrow Wilson and Warren G. Harding for president, giving him friends in high political places. ETHEL BROUNE HARVEY (1885–1965) of Maryland was a cell biologist and embryologist who is best remembered for her work in cell division in sea urchin eggs.

Genealogies: *Adam's Ancestors* was compiled by Thomas Nathan Clark and published in Naperville, Illinois, in 1981. *Genealogy of the Harvey Family of Garrett County, Maryland* was compiled by Marshall G. Brown and published in Severna Park, Maryland, in 1975.

HARVIL

Ranking: 4987 S.S. Count: 8998

Origin: English?, Scottish? Uncertain etymology. Possibly derived from the Breton component "haer," meaning battle.

Genealogies: None known.

HARWEL

Ranking: 4323 S.S. Count: 10,366

Origin: English. The name was given to those who came from Harwell, which means "pleasant stream or stream flowing from the hill" (ES) and is a place in Berkshire and Nottinghamshire, England.

Genealogies: None known.

HARWOOD (S.S. Abbreviation: Harwoo)

Ranking: 2959 S.S. Count: 15,384

Origin: English, Scottish. 1) derived from the Old English words "hār" and "wudu," meaning gray and wood. The name was given to those who came from Harwood, the name of various places in Lancashire, Lothiam, Northumberland, and West Yorkshire, England, as well as parts of southern Scotland. 2) derived from the Old English words "hara" and "wudu," meaning hare and wood. The name was given to those who came from Harwood, the name of various places in Lancashire, Lothiam, Northumberland, and West Yorkshire, England, as well as parts of southern Scotland.

Genealogies: None known.

HASKEL (ALSO HASKELEVIC, HASKELL)

Ranking: 3099 S.S. Count: 14,658

Origin: Haskel, Haskell—English, Jewish; Haskelevic—Jewish. Haskel, Haskell (English): derived from the Old Norse first name Ásketill, which is composed of the words "óss" or "áss" and "ketill," meaning god and sacrificial cauldron (H&H). Haskel, Haskelevic, Haskell (Jewish): derived from the Hebrew first name Yechezkel, which means "God will strengthen" (H&H).

Famous **Bearers:** DUDLEY CHASE HASKELL (1842–1883) of Vermont was a politician from Kansas. CHARLES NATHANIEL HASKELL (1860–1933) of Ohio was the first governor of Oklahoma. ELLA LOUISE KNOWLES HASKELL (1860–1911) of New Hampshire was a lawyer who worked for equal rights for women. ERNEST HASKELL (1876–1925) of Connecticut was an artist who is best known as an etcher. DOUGLAS HASKELL (1899–1979), born in Turkey, was an editor who specialized in the subject of architecture. He worked for *Architectural Record, The Nation*, and *Architectural Forum.*

Genealogies: None known.

HASKIN (ALSO HASKING, HASKINGS, HASKINS)

Ranking: 1549 S.S. Count: 28,804

Origin: English. Derived from the Old Norse first name Ásketill, which is composed of the words "óss" or "áss" and "ketill," meaning god and sacrificial cauldron (H&H).

Famous **Bearers:** CHARLES HOMER HASKINS (1870–1937) of Pennsylvania was a historian and a member of the 1917 presidential advisory group called "The Inquiry."

Genealogies: *A Haskin History* was compiled by Joseph A. Haskin and published in Conroe, Texas, in 1981.

HASS

Ranking: 4814 S.S. Count: 9309

Origin: German, Jewish. German: 1) derived from the Old High German word "haz," meaning hatred. The name was given to men who were considered caustic and angry. 2) derived from a pet form of the German first name Hadubert, which is composed of the Germanic words "hadu" and "berht," meaning struggle or fight and illustrious. 3) derived from a German first name that begins with the Germanic word "hadu," meaning struggle or fight. Jewish: uncertain etymology. Possibly derived from the Old High German word "haz," meaning hatred. The name was most probably assigned to Jews by a non-Jewish government official who was enforcing the decree throughout central Europe that all individuals adopt last names.

Genealogies: None known.

HASSEL (ALSO HASSELBERG, HASSELBLAD, HASSELGREN, HASSELL)

Ranking: 2538 S.S. Count: 17,864

Origin: Hassell—English; Hassel, Hasselberg, Hasselblad, Hasselgren—Swedish. Hassell: 1) derived from the Old English first name Hæt and the word "halh," meaning hat and niche. The name was given to those who came from Hassall, a place in Cheshire, England. 2) derived from the Old English words "hætse" and "halh," meaning witch and niche. The name was given to those who came from Hassall, a place in Cheshire, England. Hassel, Hasselberg, Hasselblad, Hasselgren: cognates to Hazel.

Genealogies: None known.

HASTIN (ALSO HASTING, HASTINGS, HASTINS)

Ranking: 1089 S.S. Count: 40,610

Origin: English. Hastin, Hastins: transformations of Haskin. Hasting, Hastings: 1) derived from the Old English name H-æ stingas, meaning "people of H-æ sta" (H&H) and which is derived from the first name H-æ st, meaning violence. The name was given to those who came from Hastings, the name of a place in Sussex, England. 2) derived from the Norman first name Hastenc, which is derived from the Old Norse words "ha"' and "steinn," meaning high and stone.

Famous **Bearers:** THOMAS HASTINGS (1784–1872) of Connecticut was a hymn writer who has more than 1000 hymns to his credit. SERRANUS CLINTON HASTINGS (1814–1893) of New York was a jurist and the first chief justice of the supreme court of California. The funds to start Hastings College of Law in San Francisco came from him. CHARLES SHELDON HASTINGS (1848–1932) of New York was a physicist who is credited with making significant contributions to the microscope. THOMAS HASTINGS (1860–1929) of New York was an architect who combined the present and the past in his buildings. WILLIAM WIRT HASTINGS (1866–1938) of Oklahoma was a lawyer and a member of Congress from his state of birth. DANIEL OREN HASTINGS (1874–1966) of Maryland was a U.S. senator.

Genealogies: None known.

HASTY

Ranking: 4802 S.S. Count: 9329

Origin: English. Derived from the Middle English and Old French word "hasti," meaning swiftness. The name was given to those who were considered careless or abrupt.

Genealogies: *Hasty and Descendants* was compiled by Warren H. Hasty and published in Minneapolis, Minnesota, most likely in 1977. *The Hasty Family of York County, Maine* was compiled by Warren H. Hasty and most likely published in Minneapolis, Minnesota, in 1976.

HATCH

Ranking: 1323 **S.S. Count:** 33,648

Origin: English. Derived from the Old English word "hœ cce," meaning gate (often one that marks the entry to private grounds or other enclosed pieces of land). The name was given to those who lived by a gate.

Famous **Hatches:** JOHN PORTER HATCH (1822–1901) of New York was a Union soldier who received the Medal of Honor for actions at South Mountain. RUFUS HATCH (1832–1893) of Maine was a financier who is believed to have first used the phrase "lambs of Wall Street." EDWARD HATCH (1832–1889) of Maine was an officer in the Union army who rose to the rank of major general of the volunteers. WILLIAM HENRY HATCH (1833–1896) was the politician responsible for the Hatch Act, which gave federal aid to agricultural experiment stations. He also was the force behind the Department of Agriculture's status being raised to that of a cabinet position. CARL A. HATCH (1889–1963) of Kansas was a U.S. senator and a federal district judge. He is best remembered as the author of the Hatch acts of 1939 and 1940.

Genealogies: The Hatch Family: Descendants of Lewis Hatch of Lee, Massachusetts, and Granville, New York from Thomas Hatch of Barnstable, Massachusetts; Early Families of Washington County, New York was compiled by Azuba Ruth Ward and published in Bellevue, Washington, in 1985.

HATCHER (S.S. Abbreviation: Hatche)

Ranking: 820 **S.S. Count:** 51,609

Origin: English. Transformation of Hatch.

Famous **Hatchers:** WILLIAM ELDRIDGE HATCHER (1834–1912) of Virginia was the longtime pastor of the Grace Baptist Church in Richmond. ORIE LATHAM HATCHER (1868–1946) of Virginia was the founder and first president of the Virginia Bureau of Vocations for Women. (The name of the organization changed to reflect its change in growth and purpose, first to Southern Woman's Educational Alliance in 1920, and then to Alliance for Guidance of Rural Youth in 1937.) She helped give women more vocational choices than had ever been available to them before. ROBERT ANTHONY HATCHER (1868–1944) of Missouri was a pharmacologist who is best remembered for his work with digitalis.

Genealogies: None known.

HATFIELD (S.S. Abbreviation: Hatfie)

Ranking: 939 **S.S. Count:** 46,041

Origin: English. Derived from the Old English words "hœð" and "feld," meaning low shrubs and meadow. The name was given to those who came from Hatfield, the name of various places in Essex, Herefordshire, Hertfordshire, Nottinghamshire, Worcestershire, and East and West Yorkshire, England.

Famous **Hatfields:** EDWIN FRANCIS HATFIELD (1807–1883) of New Jersey was a Presbyterian minister and a hymnologist.

Genealogies: A Genealogical History of the Hatfield and Sherman Families of Utica, New York, was compiled by John Bennett Hatfield Sr. and published in 1981.

HATHAWAY (S.S. Abbreviation: Hathaw)

Ranking: 1781 **S.S. Count:** 25,242

Origin: English. 1) derived from the feminine Old English first name Heaðuwig, which is composed of the elements "heaðu" and "wig," meaning conflict and war. 2) derived from the Old English words "hæð" and "weg," meaning heath and way. The name was given to those who lived by a route across the way from a stretch of low shrubs.

Genealogies: A Harkrader-Hathaway History was compiled by Charles Briggs Hathaway and published in Baltimore, Maryland, in 1991. *Jesse Hathaway Family* was compiled by Gail Abner Hathaway and published in Hyattsville, Maryland, in 1972.

HATTEN

Ranking: 4831 **S.S. Count:** 9265

Origin: German. 1) the name was given to those who came from Hatten, which means swamp and is also a place in Germany. 2) the name was given to those who lived at or near a swamp or marsh.

Genealogies: None known.

HATTON

Ranking: 2852 **S.S. Count:** 16,008

Origin: English, French. English: derived from the Old English words "hæð" and "tūn," meaning low shrubs and settlement. The name was given to those who came from Hatton, the name of several places in Cheshire, Derbyshire, Lincolnshire, Old London, Shropshire, Staffordshire, and Warwickshire, England. French: derived from the Germanic first name Hatto, a shortened form of several Germanic names beginning with the word "hadu," which means conflict or dissension.

Famous **Hattons:** FRANK HATTON (1846–1894) of Ohio was a journalist who published the well-respected *Burlington Daily Hawk-Eye*. But his best-remembered achievement was his time working as assistant postmaster, then postmaster general, as it was he who created the special-delivery system.

Genealogies: Descendants of John Simmons and the Allied Families of Hatton, McGrew, Sherwood, Linthicum, and Cathcart was compiled by Ruth Maxwell Graham and published in Arlington, Virginia, in 1975.

HAUCK

Ranking: 3771 **S.S. Count:** 12,011

Origin: German. Derived from the Old French first name "hu(gh)e," which is a shortened form of Germanic names beginning with the word "hug," meaning soul or spirit.
Genealogies: None known.

HAUGEN
Ranking: 3538 S.S. Count: 12,765
Origin: German, Norwegian. 1) the name was given to those who lived near a burial hill or small knoll. 2) the name was given to someone who lived on or near a meadow. 3) the name was given to the descendants of those named Haug, a pet name of Hugo, which means soul or spirit.

Famous **Haugens:** NILS PEDERSON HAUGEN (1849–1931) of Norway, who as a child came to Wisconsin, was a member of Congress and, for many years, the Wisconsin tax commissioner. GILBERT NELSON HAUGEN (1859–1933) of Wisconsin was a member of Congress and the co-author of the McNary-Haugen Bill, which dealt with farm surpluses.
Genealogies: None known.

HAUGHTON (S.S. Abbreviation: Haught)
Ranking: 4567 S.S. Count: 9779
Origin: English. 1) derived from the Old English words "halh" and "tūn," meaning cranny or niche and settlement. The name was given to those who came from Haughton, the name of several places in Cheshire, Lancashire, Northumberland, Shropshire, and Staffordshire, England. 2) derived from the Old English words "hōh" and "tūn," meaning knob on a hill and settlement. The name was given to those who came from Haughton, the name of a place in Nottinghamshire, England.

Famous **Haughtons:** PERCY CUNCAN HAUGHTON (1876–1924) of New York was a college football player who went on to be one of the best college coaches.
Genealogies: None known.

HAUSER
Ranking: 1944 S.S. Count: 23,268
Origin: German. Derived from the Old English word "hūs," which means house. In the Middle Ages, the name referred to a person who was somehow connected to the most important building in the town, most often a religious edifice. The name also may have referred to a homeowner, a person who held the deed to his own cottage, as opposed to being a tenant.
Genealogies: *Alsatian-American Family Hauser* was compiled by Kenneth John Hauser Jr. and published in Winston-Salem, North Carolina, in 1977.

HAVENS
Ranking: 2794 S.S. Count: 16,290
Origin: English. The name was given to those who lived near a harbor or port.

Famous **Havenses:** JAMES SMITH HAVENS (1859–1927) of New York was a lawyer and a member of Congress.
Genealogies: *The Havens Family in Florida* was compiled by Elizabeth Haven Kocher and published in Tampa, Florida, in 1980. *The Havens Family in Suffolk County, New York; A Genealogical Survey of Some of the Descendants of William S. Havens, 17th Century Settler in Aquidneck, Rhode Island* was compiled by Barrington S. Havens and published in Scotia, New York, in 1975.

HAWES
Ranking: 3358 S.S. Count: 13,502
Origin: English. 1) derived from the Middle English first name Haw, which is a shortened form of the Middle English family name Hawkin. 2) derived from the Norman feminine first name Haueis, which is derived from the Germanic first name Haduwidis, which is composed of the Germanic words "hadu" and "widi," meaning dissension or conflict and wide.

Famous **Haweses:** GARRIET ANN BOYD HAWES (1871–1945) of Massachusetts was an archaeologist and the author of *Crete: The Forerunner of Greece.* CHARLES BOARDMAN HAWES (1889–1923) of New York was the author of adventure stories, including *The Dark Frigate.* ELIZABETH HAWES (1903–1971) of New Jersey, a fashion designer, supported day-care centers and issues that related to the oppressed, especially women. She was the first American of her profession to show her designs in Paris.
Genealogies: None known.

HAWK
Ranking: 1904 S.S. Count: 23,774
Origin: English. 1) derived from the Old English word "heafoc," meaning hawk. The name was given to those who worked training and raising hawks. 2) same derivation as in 1. The name may have been given to those who were thought to look or behave like hawks (those who had crooked noses or who were considered greedy). 3) may be derived from the Old English first name H(e)afoc, which means Hawk. 4) derived from the Old English word "halh," meaning cranny or niche. The name was given to those who lived in a secluded nook.
Genealogies: *Adam Hawkes (also Hawk) of Saugus, Massachusetts, 1605–1672; The First Six Generations in America* was compiled by Ethel Farrington Smith and published in Baltimore, Maryland, in 1980. *Early German Hawk Families of Westmoreland County, Pennsylvania* was compiled by Kenneth Hawk Slaker and published in Baltimore, Maryland, in 1990.

HAWKIN (ALSO HAWKING, HAWKINGE, HAWKINGS, HAWKINS)
Ranking: 168 S.S. Count: 197,250
Origin: English. Hawkin, Hawkings, Hawkins: 1) derived from the Middle English first name Hawkin, which is derived

from the name Hal, itself a term of endearment for Harry. 2) derived from the Middle English first name Hawkin, which is a pet form of the name Hawk. Hawking: 1) transformation of Hawkin. 2) transformation of Hawkinge. Hawkinge: derived from the Old English name Hafocing, which means "hawk place" (H&H). The name was given to those who came from Hawkinge, a place in Kent, England.

Famous **Bearers:** BENJAMIN HAWKINS (1754–1816) of North Carolina was a planter and Indian agent. He was responsible for treaties' being enacted between the federal government and the Cherokees, Chictaws, and the Chickasaws, and the Treaty of Coleraine with the Creeks. He was known as "Beloved Man of Four Nations." He was responsible for teaching modern agricultural methods to the Creeks and was well respected by them. The War of 1812, however, destroyed all that he had worked to achieve. DEXTER ARNOLD HAWKINS (1825–1886) of Maine was a lawyer and educator who helped establish a national Department of Education in 1867. RUSH CHRISTOPHER HAWKINS (1831–1920) of Vermont was the donator of a sizable art collection to the Annmary Brown Memorial in Rhode Island.

Genealogies: *Our Hawkins Cousins: Including the Ancestry and Descendants of John Hawkins (1813–1897) and the Women He Married, Eveline P. Goodlett (1815–1848) and Sarah Adeline Gaston (1817– 1897)* was compiled by Delores Hawkins McDonald and published in San Antonio, Texas, in 1980. *Appo, Fisher, Hawkins: Genealogy of Dr. Annette Hawkins Eaton and R. Walter Lincoln Hawkins* was compiled by Paul E. Sluby Sr. and published in Washington, D.C., in 1983.

HAWKS

Ranking: 3612 **S.S. Count:** 12,509

Origin: English. Transformation of Hawk.

Famous **Hawkses:** JOHN HAWKS (1731–1790) of England was an architect. He designed the governor's home in New Bern, North Carolina, which is considered one of the best of the colonial period. FRANCIS LISTER HAWKS (1798–1866) of North Carolina was the grandson of John Hawks. He was the first president of the University of Louisiana and, as an Episcopal minister, published materials on the history of the church in America.

Genealogies: None known.

HAWLEY

Ranking: 1688 **S.S. Count:** 26,482

Origin: English. 1) derived from the Old English words "hālig" and "lēah," meaning holy and wood. The name was given to those who came from Hawley, a place in Kent, England, which was most probably so named because it was once the location of a hallowed grove. 2) derived from the Old English word "h(e)all," meaning either manor or stone. The name

was given to those who came from Hawley, a place in Hampshire, England. 3) derived from the Old Norse word "haugr" and the Old English word "lēah," meaning mound and wood. The name was given to those who came from a place that no longer exists called Hawley, near Sheffield, England.

Famous **Hawleys:** JOSEPH HAWLEY (1723–1788) of Massachusetts was considered the "guiding spirit of the Revolution in the Connecticut Valley." GIDEON HAWLEY (1727–1807) of Connecticut was a Congregational missionary in Massachusetts. GIDEON HAWLEY (1785–1870) of Connecticut is best remembered as the first superintendent of public education in New York. There he set up the elementary educational school system. JOSEPH ROSWELL HAWLEY (1826–1905) of North Carolina was one of the organizers of the Republican Party in the state of Connecticut. He also was an editor at Hartford, Connecticut, newspapers, first at the *Evening Press*, then at the *Hartford Courant*. JAMES HENRY HAWLEY (1847–1929) of Iowa was the governor of Idaho and one of the best prosecuting attorneys in the nation. WILLIS CHATMAN HAWLEY (1864–1941) of Oregon was a politician and an expert in taxation and tariffs. He spoke strongly in favor of a protective tariff.

Genealogies: *A History of the Robinson and Hawley Families, Including Findings on the Morris, Putnam, Cary and Plummer Families* was compiled by Duane Robinson and published in Lombard, Illinois, in 1974. *Smith Hawley and His Descendants* was compiled by Marilyn Hawley Symonds and published in Lansing, Michigan, in 1961.

HAWTHORN, HAWTHORNE (S.S. Abbreviation: Hawtho)

Ranking: 1898 **S.S. Count:** 23,847

Origin: English. 1) derived from the Old English word "hægþorn," which refers to a thorn once used to make hedges and other kinds of fences or barriers. The name was given to those who lived by a hedge of hawthorn or a thicket. 2) same derivation as in 1. The name was given to those who came from Hawthorn, the name of several places in England.

Famous **Bearers:** NATHANIEL HAWTHORNE (1804–1864) of Massachusetts was a novelist who is noted for *The Scarlet Letter* and *The House of the Seven Gables.* SOPHIA AMELIA PEABODY HAWTHORNE (1809–1871) of Massachusetts was the wife of Nathaniel Hawthorne. She was an artist and writer herself, painting to help support them in the lean years. Original manuscripts of his novels show changes made in her handwriting. She was solicited to contribute to *Atlantic Monthly*, but, as Nathaniel Hawthorne wrote in a letter to publisher William D. Ticknor in 1857, "[h]er descriptions are the most perfect pictures that ever were put on paper; it is a pity they cannot be published; but neither she nor I would like to see her name on your list of female authors." JULIAN HAWTHORNE (1846–1934) was the son of Sophia and Nathaniel and also an author. CHARLES WEBSTER HAWTHORNE (1872–1930) of Illinois was a painter who founded the Cape Cod School of Art in Provincetown, Massachusetts.

Genealogies: *The Haythorne(s) (also Hawthorne): A History and Genealogy* was compiled by Dorothy Haythorn H. Collins and most likely published in New Jersey in 1982. *To Myself a Stranger: A Biography of Rose Hawthorne Lathrop* was compiled by Patricia Dunlavy Valenti and published in Baton Rouge, Louisiana, in 1991.

HAY

Ranking: 1814 **S.S. Count:** 24,847

Origin: English, Scottish. 1) *derived from the Middle English word "hey," meaning elevated or high. The name was given to those who were tall.* 2) *derived from the Old English word "(ge)hœg," meaning fence or boundary, which later came to mean enclosed forest. The name was given to those who lived near an enclosure or fence.* 3) *same derivation as in 2. The name was given to those who came from the many places with this appellation, such as, Les Hays and La Haye in Normandy.* 4) *derived from the medieval first name Hay, which was probably derived either from the Old English nickname Hēah, meaning tall, or from other names that contained the Old English word "hēah," meaning high.*

Famous Hays: GEORGE HAY (1765–1830) of Virginia was the son-in-law of President James Monroe and the prosecuting attorney of Aaron Burr in his trial for treason. JOHN MILTON HAY (1838–1905) of Indiana was President Abraham Lincoln's private secretary, adjutant general in the army assigned to the White House, a respected journalist, and author of *Abraham Lincoln: A History*, which was a 10-year effort in 10 volumes and a tribute to the 16th president. He returned to Washington, D.C., in 1878 as assistant secretary of state under President Rutherford B. Hayes. He continued his work there into the 1900s, working as a right-hand man to President William McKinley. OLIVER PERRY HAY (1846–1930) of Indiana was a paleontologist who was associated with the Field Museum. MARY GARRETT HAY (1857–1928) of Indiana was a suffragist and a temperance reformer. She is considered the driving force behind suffrage in the state of New York.

Genealogies: None known.

HAYDEN

Ranking: 841 **S.S. Count:** 50,625

Origin: English, Irish. English: 1) *derived from the Old English words "hēg" and "denu," meaning hay and valley. The name was given to those who came from Haydon, a place in Northumberland, England.* 2) *derived from the Old English words "hēg" and "dūn," meaning hay and hill. The name was given to those who came from Hayden, the name of several places in Dorset, Hertfordshire, Somerset, and Wiltshire counties in England.* 3) *derived from the Old English words "hege" and "dūn," meaning hedge and hill. The name was given to those who came from Hayden, the name of several places in England.* 4) *derived from the Old English words "(ge)hœg" and "dūn," meaning enclosure and hill. The name was given to those who came from Hayden, the name of several places in England. Irish: derived from the Gaelic names Ó hÉideáin and Ó hÉidín, meaning "descendant of Éidean" (H&H) or descendant of Éidín" (H&H), which are first names derived from the word "éideadh," meaning clothes or coat of mail.*

Famous Haydens: HORACE H. HAYDEN (1769–1844) of Connecticut founded the world's first dental college. JOSEPH SHEPARD HAYDEN (1802–1877) of Massachusetts was the inventor of the button-making machine. MOTHER MARY BRIDGET HAYDEN (1814–1890) of Ireland was a Catholic missionary among the Indians. She was born Margaret Hayden but took the name Mary Bridget when she became a nun. She taught at a missionary school for Indian girls in Kansas. Her duties included the teaching not only of academic subjects but also of household skills and the doctoring of the illnesses such a harsh environment produced. Because of her compassionate ways, she was referred to as "medicine woman." HIRAM WASHINGTON HAYDEN (1820–1904) of Massachusetts invented kettle-making machinery. FERDINAND VANDIVEER HAYDEN (1829–1887) of Massachusetts was responsible for the act of Congress that set aside for public use the western lands that would come to be known as Yellowstone National Park. EDWARD EVERETT HAYDEN (1858–1932) of Massachusetts was a meteorologist who, in working with barometric pressure and temperature, was able to devise a system of adjusting observatory time-signal transmissions to proper correctness. SOPHIA GREGORIA HAYDEN (1868–1953) was born in Chile to an American father and South American mother. She was raised by her paternal grandparents in Boston, Massachusetts. She was the first woman admitted to the Massachusetts Institute of Technology to study architecture. She became an architect of great ability who, because of her gender, met with obstacles that eventually defeated her. CHARLES HAYDEN (1870–1937) of Massachusetts was a philanthropist. He set up the Hayden Foundation for youth work and was the main contributor to the Hayden Planetarium in New York City.

Genealogies: *Hayden, Rapier, and Allied Families. Colonial Maryland, Kentucky, USA* was compiled by Mary Louise Donnelly and published in Ennis, Texas, in 1991. *Josiah Hayden of Williamsburg, Massachusetts: His Antecedents and Descendants* was compiled by Donald Bradford Macurda and most likely published in La Mesa, California, in 1984.

HAYES

Ranking: 106 **S.S. Count:** 265,424

Origin: English, French, Irish. English: 1) derived from the Middle English word "hay," meaning enclosure. The name was given to those who came from Hayes, the name of various places in Devon and Dorset counties in England. 2) derived from the Old English word "hœ (-)s," meaning brushwood. The name was given to those who came from Hayes, the name of several places in Kent County in England. 3) transformation of the fourth definition of Hay. French: cognate to the fourth definition of Hay. Irish: derived from the Gaelic name Ó hAodha, meaning "descendant of Aodh" (H&H), which is a first name meaning fire.

Famous **Hayeses:** AUGUSTUS ALLEN HAYES (1806–1882) of Vermont developed faster methods for smelting iron and refining copper. He is also credited with developing a method of manufacturing saltpeter that was used during the Civil War. RUTHERFORD BIRCHARD HAYES (1822–1893) of Ohio was the 19th president of the United States. LUCY WARE WEBB HAYES (1831–1889) of Ohio was the wife of Rutherford B. Hayes, the 19th president of the United States. Her detractors dubbed her "Lemonade Lucy" after she banned liquor in the White House. ISAAC ISRAEL HAYES (1832–1881) of Pennsylvania was a physician and an Arctic explorer. He wrote several books on his adventures, including one for children titled *Cast Away in the Cold.* EDWARD CARY HAYES (1868–1928) of Maine was a sociologist and the founder of the Department of Sociology at the University of Illinois.

Genealogies: *A Genealogical Record of the Descendants of Bazeal Hayes of Charley, Lawrence County, Kentucky* was compiled by Lora Thelma Chandler Walter and published in Lexington, Kentucky, in 1981. *Hayes and Allied Families of Gloucester County, Virginia: the Descendants of William Hayes and Elizabeth Foster* was compiled by Melinde Hatfield and published in Eugene, Oregon, in 1981.

HAYNES

Ranking: 312 **S.S. Count:** 117,912

Origin: English, Welsh. Transformation of and cognate to Haines.

Famous **Hayneses:** JOHN HAYNES (1594?–1653?) of England was the governor of Massachusetts. Banished by Roger Williams, he moved to Connecticut and became the first governor there. Under the "Fundamental Orders," he served every other year as the governor until his death. JOHN HENRY HAYNES (1849–1910) of Massachusetts was an archaeologist who worked at Nippur, a Sumerian settlement on the Euphrates River, and was the first American consul at Baghdad (1888). ELIZABETH ROSS HAYNES (1883–1953) of Alabama was the daughter of former slaves. She was a community and Y.W.C.A. leader who did much to help those less fortunate, regardless of color.

Genealogies: *The Wilhite Clan, 1539–1992: Herdman*

(also Hardman) and Haynes was compiled by Julian G. Allen and published in Austin, Texas, in 1992. *Ellen Elizabeth Haynes: The New England Ancestry of Ellen Elizabeth Haynes* was compiled by Elizabeth Fjetland and published in Farmington, Minnesota, in 1990. *Families of America: Where They Come From and How They Live* was compiled by George Sessions Perry and published in New York, New York, in 1949.

HAYNIE

Ranking: 4696 **S.S. Count:** 9532

Origin: English, Irish. English: the name was given to those who lived in Hanney, which means "island frequented by wild cocks" (ES) and is a place in Berkshire, England. Irish: derived from a Gaelic name meaning "grandson of Eanna" (ES), a traditional Irish saint.

Genealogies: None known.

HAYS

Ranking: 807 **S.S. Count:** 52,275

Origin: English. Transformation of the English definitions of Hayes.

Famous **Hayses:** ISAAC HAYS (1796–1879) of Pennsylvania was an ophthalmologist who is credited with the discovery of astigmatism. He also did studies on color blindness. JOHN COFFEE HAYS (1817–1883) of Tennessee was a soldier who served with distinction in the war in Texas, 1836. He went to California in 1849, served as the mayor of San Francisco, and went into business in the real estate field. ALEXANDER HAYS (1819–1864) of Pennsylvania was a soldier who fought in the Civil War and was killed in action at the Battle of the Wilderness. WILLIAM JACOB HAYS (1830–1875) of New York was an artist who is best remembered as a painter of animals. His most memorable work was entitled *The Wounded Buffalo.*

Genealogies: *The Bell-Hays Families in Greene County, Pennsylvania and Knox County, Ohio, 1750–1987* was compiled by John James Evans and published in Athens, Ohio, in 1987.

HAYWARD (S.S. Abbreviation: Haywar)

Ranking: 2089 **S.S. Count:** 21,986

Origin: English. Derived from the Middle English words "hay" and "ward," meaning enclosure and guardian. The name was given to those officials whose job it was to guard private land or enclosed forests from being marred by animals, trespassers, illegal hunters, or looters.

Famous **Haywards:** GEORGE HAYWARD (1791–1863) of Massachusetts was a physician and the first to use ether as an anesthesic in an operation. His medical writings are still considered important. NATHANIEL MANLEY HAYWARD (1808–1865) of Massachusetts invented a process of vulcanization of rubber-coated cloth. He sold his patented idea to Charles Goodyear for $1000. LELAND HAYWARD (1902–1971) of Nebraska was a theatrical producer and talent agent who represented such stars as Judy Garland, Gregory Peck, Henry Fonda, and James Stewart. Among his producton accomplishments was *State of the Union* (1945), which won a Pulitzer Prize. SUSAN HAYWARD (1917?–1975), an actress, was born Edythe Marrener in New York. She rose through the ranks of Hollywood beauties with a little luck and a lot of hard work.

Genealogies: *A Search for Haigwood-Hagwood-Haygood et cetera (also Hayward)* was compiled by John E. Haigwood and published in Rome, Georgia, in 1984.

HAYWOOD (S.S. Abbreviation: Haywoo)
Ranking: 1800 **S.S. Count:** 25,019
Origin: English. Derived from the Middle English words "hay" and "wudu," meaning enclosure and wood. The name referred to woodlands that were enclosed by the nobility for use as hunting grounds. The name was given to those who came from Haywood, the name of several places in Herefordshire, Nottinghamsire, Shropshire, and Staffordshire counties in England.

Famous **Haywoods:** JOHN HAYWOOD (1762–1826) of North Carolina was a self-taught lawyer. He moved to Tennessee, where he and Robert Cobbs wrote books on the state's laws and its history. WILLIAM DUDLEY HAYWOOD (1869–1928) of Utah was a labor agitator. He was tried and acquitted for the murder of an Idaho governor and convicted of sedition. He jumped bail and escaped to Russia, where he died.

Genealogies: *A Search for Haigwood-Hagwood-Haygood et cetera (also Hayward)* was compiled by John E. Haigwood and published in Rome, Georgia, in 1984. *Reminiscences and memoirs of North Carolina and Eminent North Carolinians: An Extract: Genealogy of the Blount, Haywood and Phifer Families* was compiled by John H. Wheeler and published in Washington, D.C., in 1885.

HAZEL
Ranking: 4459 **S.S. Count:** 10,050
Origin: English. Derived from the Old English word "hæ sel," meaning hazel. The name was given to those who lived near a hazel bush or orchard.
Genealogies: None known.

HAZEN
Ranking: 4230 **S.S. Count:** 10,655
Origin: English, Spanish. English: the name was given to those who came from Hazon, which means "enclosed sandy meadow" (ES) and is the name of a place in Northumberland County, England. Spanish: the name was given to someone who worked as a cantor in a synagogue.

Famous **Hazens:** MOSES HAZEN (1733–1803) of

Massachusetts was a Revolutionary War soldier. He also fought in the French and Indian War and was part of Richard Montgomery's attack on Quebec. HENRY ALLEN HAZEN (1849–1900) of India was a meteorologist who worked with the U.S. Weather Service. ALLEN HAZEN (1869–1930) of Vermont was a sanitary engineer who co-developed the Williams and Hazen pipeflow formula. ELIZABETH LEE HAZEN (1885–1975) of Mississippi was the co-discoverer of nystatin, an antifungal antibiotic cream.

Genealogies: *Descendants of Daniel Hazen, United Empire Loyalist* was compiled by Ross W. McCurdy and published in North Providence, Rhode Island, in 1986.

HEAD
Ranking: 1096 **S.S. Count:** 40,307
Origin: English. 1) derived from the Old English word "heafod," meaning head. The name was given to those who lived on top of a mountain, at the mouth of a brook, or at the head of a valley. 2) same derivation as in 1. The name was given to those who had abnormally shaped heads, whose heads were not proportionate to their bodies, or who had another similar irregularity.

Famous **Heads:** EDITH HEAD (1898?–1981) of California was a costume designer who won several Academy Awards for costumes she developed for films, including *All About Eve* (1950) and *The Sting* (1973).

Genealogies: *The Head Family According to Vital Records of New Hampshire* was compiled by Julia E. Head and published in Wolfeboro, New Hampshire, in 1983. *The Head Family According to Vital Records of Vermont* was compiled by Julia E. Head and published in Wolfeboro, New Hampshire, in 1983.

HEADLEY (S.S. Abbreviation: Headle)
Ranking: 3251 **S.S. Count:** 13,979
Origin: English. Derived from the Old English words "hœð" and "lēah," meaning shrubbery and wood. The name was given to those who came from Headley, the name of places in Hampshire, Surrey, Worcestershire, and West Yorkshire counties in England.

Famous **Headleys:** JOEL TYLER HEADLEY (1813–1897) of New York was the author of simple biographies, histories, and travel books. PHINEAS CAMP HEADLEY (1819–1903) of New York was a writer like his brother Joel. He wrote biographies similar in style to Joel's.

Genealogies: *George Lemley [also Headley] and Wife Catherine Yoho and Their Descendants for Two Centuries* was compiled by Alvah John Washington Headlee and published in Morgantown, West Virginia, in 1975. *Headlee (also Headley) Migrations* was compiled by Alvah John Washington Headlee and published in Morgantown, West Virginia, in 1971.

HEALEY

Ranking: 2894 **S.S. Count:** 15,736

Origin: English, Irish. English: derived from the Old English words "hēah" and "lēah," meaning high and wood. The name was given to those who came from Healey, a place near Manchester, England. The name may also have been given to those who came from several places called Healey in northern England. Irish: 1) derived from the Gaelic name Ó hÉilidhe, meaning "descendant of the claimant" (H&H), which is derived from the word "éilidhe," meaning claimant. 2) derived from the Gaelic name Ó hÉalaighthe, meaning "descendants of Éalathach" (H&H), which is a first name probably derived from the word "ealadhach," meaning ingenious.

Genealogies: None known.

HEALY

Ranking: 1421 **S.S. Count:** 31,313

Origin: English, Irish. Transformation of and cognate to Healey.

Famous **Healys:** GEORGE PETER ALEXANDER HEALY (1813–1894) of Massachusetts was a portrait painter. *Webster's Reply to Hayne* is his best-known work.

Genealogies: None known.

HEARD

Ranking: 1427 **S.S. Count:** 31,213

Origin: English. Derived from the Old English word "hi(e)rde," meaning herd. The name was given to cowherds, shepherds, or those who worked tending flocks of animals.

Famous **Heards:** AUGUSTINE HEARD (1785–1868) of Massachusetts was a sea captain. He and his import/export business, which was based in China, were highly respected by the Chinese. FRANKLIN FISKE HEARD (1825–1889) of Massachusetts was the author of many legal documents, including *A Treatise on Libel and Slander*, the first American work on the subject. DWIGHT BANCROFT HEARD (1869–1929) of Massachusetts moved to Arizona, where he became a leader in the governmental affairs of the state.

Genealogies: *Miscellaneous Collections of Heards* was compiled by Harold Heard and most likely published in Amarillo, Texas, in 1971. *Miscellaneous Heards, Addendum* was compiled by Harold Heard and published in Amarillo, Texas, in the 1970s. *Southern Heard Families* was compiled by Harold Heard and most likely published in Amarillo, Texas, in 1968.

HEARN

Ranking: 2204 **S.S. Count:** 20,828

Origin: English, Irish. English: 1) derived from the Old French word "hairon," meaning heron. The name was given to those who were gangly and skinny and were thought to look like herons. 2) derived from the Old English word "hær," meaning stone. The name was given to those who came from

Herne, a place in Bedfordshire, England. 3) derived from the Old English word "hyrne," which refers either to a curve in a river or to a hollow in a hill. The name was given to those who lived at a curve in a river or a hollow in a hill. 4) same derivation as in 3. The name was given to those who came from Herne, a place in Kent, England, or Hurn, a place in Dorset, England. 5) may also be derived from the Old English word "horn," meaning horn (in the sense of the spur of a hill, for example). Irish: derived from the Gaelic name Ó hEachthigheama, meaning "descendant of Eachthighearna" (H&H), which is a personal name composed of the words "each" and "tighearna," meaning horse and master. The name is most common in the southwestern region of Ireland.*

Famous **Hearns:** LAFCADIO HEARN (1850–1904) of Greece was a writer and journalist who worked his way up in his field, eventually producing some of the best prose of his time. He married a woman from Japan and moved there, leaving the United States.

Genealogies: None known.

HEATH

Ranking: 580 **S.S. Count:** 71,180

Origin: English. 1) derived from the Old English word "hæð," meaning heath. The name was given to those who lived on a heath. 2) same derivation as in 1. The name was given to those who came from Heath, the name of places in Bedfordshire, Derbyshire, Herfordshire, Shropshire, and West Yorkshire counties in England.

Famous **Heaths:** WILLIAM HEATH (1737–1814) of Massachusetts was involved with the pre-Revolutionary War committees of the day and served as a Revolutionary War soldier. His book, *Memoirs*, is considered an important work. JAMES EWELL HEATH (1792–1862) of Virginia was an author of *Edgehill, or The Family of the Fitzroyals*. PERRY SANFORD HEATH (1857–1927) was appointed by President William McKinley as the first assistant postmaster general. He started the rural free delivery of mail.

Genealogies: *Harrington-Heath Heritage: Ancestors and Descendants (1600–1984) of Oramel Warren Harrington and Martha C. Heath* was compiled by Ruth Haddox Harrington and published in Philadelphia, Pennsylvania, in 1984.

HEATON

Ranking: 2518 **S.S. Count:** 18,031

Origin: English. Derived from the Old English words "hēah" and "tūn," meaning high and settlement. The name was given to those who came form Heaton, the name of several places in Lancashire, Northumberland, and West Yorkshire counties in England.

Famous **Heatons:** JOHN LANGDON HEATON (1860–1935) of New York was a prominent editorial writer for the New York World (1900–1931).

Genealogies: *Gone to Texas: A Compendium of the Dulany, Haddox, Heaton, Holland and Martin Families* was compiled by Mary Rebecca Scott and published in Tomball, Texas, in 1989. *The Heaton Families: 350 Years in America* was compiled by Dean Heaton and published in Baltimore, Maryland, in 1982.

HÉBERT

Ranking: 795 **S.S. Count:** 53,034
Origin: French. Transformation of and cognate to Herbert.

Famous **Héberts:** Paul Octave Hébert (1818–1880) of Louisiana was a Confederate general and governor of Louisiana. His cousin Louis Hébert (1820–1901) of Louisiana was also a Confederate general.
Genealogies: *The Ancestry of Genevieve Jadot Anthon* was compiled by Marie Madeleine Genevieve Anthon and published in New York, New York, in 1901.

HECHT

Ranking: 4242 **S.S. Count:** 10,627
Origin: German, Jewish. German: 1) derived from the German word "hecht," meaning pike. The name was given to those who were considered greedy and selfish. 2) same derivation as in 1. The name may have been given to fishermen who caught pike. Jewish: derived from the German word "hecht" or the Yiddish word "hekht," both meaning pike. The name was taken ornamentally.

Famous **Hechts:** Selig Hecht (1892–1947) was born in Poland and emigrated to New York when he was six. He was a physiologist and biophysicist whose fellowships took him to do research in England, France, and the United States. He taught biophysics at Columbia University for 21 years.
Genealogies: None known.

HECK

Ranking: 2298 **S.S. Count:** 19,851
Origin: German. Cognate to Hedge(s).
Famous **Hecks:** Barbara Ruckle Heck (1734–1804) was born to German parents in Ireland. She is considered the "mother of American Methodism."
Genealogies: *Descendants of Daniel David Heck, a Settler in the Lower Part of the Shenandoah River Valley Near the Virginia Natural Bridge During the Latter Part of the 1700s* was compiled by Arch Oliver Heck and published in Columbus, Ohio, in 1970.

HECKER

Ranking: 4132 **S.S. Count:** 19,851
Origin: German. 1) cognate to Hedge(s). 2) transformation of and cognate to Hacker.
Famous **Heckers:** Isaac Thomas Hecker (1819–1888)

of New York was a Roman Catholic priest who founded the Paulists. He also founded *The Catholic World* in 1865.
Genealogies: None known.

HECKMANN (S.S. Abbreviation: Heckma)

Ranking: 3119 **S.S. Count:** 14,568
Origin: German. Cognate to Hedge(s).
Genealogies: None known.

HEDGES

Ranking: 3220 **S.S. Count:** 14,080
Origin: English. Derived from the Old English word "hocg," meaning hedge. The name was given to those who lived near a hedge.
Genealogies: None known.

HEDRICH, HEDRICK (S.S. Abbreviation: Hedric)

Ranking: 1657 **S.S. Count:** 26,978
Origin: German. The name was given to descendants of Haidrich, which means rule.
Genealogies: *A Hedrick Genealogy: The Descendants of William Alexander Hedrick, 1814–1890* was compiled by Allen Gardiner and published in Topeka, Kansas, in 1975.

HEFFER (ALSO HEFFERAN, HEFFERMAN, HEFFERNAN, HEFFERNON)

Ranking: 3367 **S.S. Count:** 13,466
Origin: Heffer, Hefferman—English; Hefferan, Heffernan, Heffernon—Irish. Heffer, Hefferman: derived from the Old English word "heahf(o)re," meaning young cow. The name was generally given to those who worked tending herds of cows. It may have also been given to those who were considered cowlike. Hefferan, Heffernan, Heffernon: derived from the Gaelic name Ó hÉigceartaigh, meaning "descendant of Eigceartach" (H&H), which is a nickname meaning unjust.
Genealogies: None known.

HEFFNER (S.S. Abbreviation: Heffne)

Ranking: 4322 **S.S. Count:** 10,368
Origin: German, Jewish. Derived form the Old High German word "havan," meaning pot or dish. The name was given to those who worked as potters. The name is most common in southern Germany and Austria.
Genealogies: None known.

HEFLIN

Ranking: 4043 **S.S. Count:** 11,195
Origin: German, French. The name was given to those who traded, bought, and sold oats.
Genealogies: None known.

HEFNER

Ranking: 4160 **S.S. Count:** 10,870
Origin: German, Jewish. Transformation of Heffner.
Genealogies: None known.

HEIL

Ranking: 4163 **S.S. Count:** 10,854
Origin: German. Derived from the name Heilo, which is a pet form of names beginning with Heil, meaning redemption or blessed.
Genealogies: None known.

HEILMAN, HEILMANN (S.S. Abbreviation: Heilma)

Ranking: 4384 **S.S. Count:** 10,236
Origin: German. 1) derived from the Jewish name Hell-mann, which is a cognate to the name Samuel, which means "God hath heard" (ES). 2) derived from the name Heilman, which means salvation. 3) the name was given to those who were healthy.
Genealogies: *Heil Heilman! Stand Proud!: The Story of the Heilmans* was compiled by Edith (Heilman) Medhurst and published in Ft. Myers, Florida, in 1984. *Early Carolina Heilmans (Hallmans-Holmans) 1736–1800* was compiled by Elmer Berley Hallman and published in Columbia, South Carolina, in 1972.

HEIM

Ranking: 3149 **S.S. Count:** 14,428
Origin: English, German, Jewish. English: derived from the Old English words "hēah" and "hām," meaning high and homestead. The name was given to those who came from Higham, the name of several places in England. German: cognate to the first definition of Hammond. Jewish: derived from the Hebrew name Chayim, meaning life.
Genealogies: None known.

HEIN

Ranking: 2614 **S.S. Count:** 17,373
Origin: German. Cognate to the English and French definitions of Henry.
Genealogies: None known.

HEINREICH, HEINRICH, HEINRICI, HEINRITZ, HEINRITZE (S.S. Abbreviation: Heinri)

Ranking: 3025 **S.S. Count:** 15,037
Origin: German. Cognates to the English and French definitions of Henry.
Famous **Bearers:** ANTONY PHILIP HEINRICH (1781–1861) of Germany was thought to be the first composer to express "Americanism" in music, using the people and places of America as his subjects. MAX HEINRICH

(1853–1916) of Germany was a pioneer in the German cheese industry. He also was a concert baritone.
Genealogies: None known.

HEINTZE, HEINTSCH (S.S. Abbreviation: Heintz)

Ranking: 3697
Origin: German. Cognates to the English and French definitions of Henry. **S.S. Count:** 12,221
Genealogies: None known.

HEINZ (ALSO HEINZE, HEINZEL)

Ranking: 3957 **S.S. Count:** 11,427
Origin: German. Cognates to the English and French definitions of Henry.
Famous **Bearers:** HENRY JOHN HEINZ (1844–1919) of Pennsylvania founded the F. and J. Heinz Co., which became the H. J. Heinz Co., a major food firm. He devised the advertising slogan "57 Varieties."
Genealogies: None known.

HELD

Ranking: 3734 **S.S. Count:** 12,107
Origin: English, Dutch, German, Jewish. English: derived from the Old English words "hylde" or "heilde," meaning incline. The name was often given to those who lived on a hillside. Dutch, German, Jewish: derived from the Middle High German and the Middle Dutch word "held," meaning hero. The name was often taken ornamentally by Jews.
Famous **Helds:** ANNA HELD (1865?–1918) of Poland was a musical-comedy star and the first wife of Florenz Ziegfeld, who discovered her in Europe and brought her to the United States.
Genealogies: None known.

HELLER (ALSO HELLERMAN, HELLERSTEIN)

Ranking: 1153 **S.S. Count:** 37,999
Origin: English, German, Jewish. English: derived from the Old English word "hyll," meaning hill. The name was commonly given to those who lived on or by a hill. German: derived from the German word "häller" or "heller," which was the name given to a small medieval coin first minted in the southwestern German town of Hall. Jewish: derived from the German word "hell" or the Yiddish word "hel," both meaning light or glowing. The name was often given to those with light-colored hair or a fair coloring.
Famous **Bearers:** MAXIMILLIAN HELLER (1860–1929), born in Bohemia, emigrated to the United States at age 19 and became a rabbi. He was pastor of Temple Sinai in New Orleans for 40 years and a leader in reform movements.
Genealogies: *The History of Louis Heller of Dunn County, Wisconsin, and His Descendants* was compiled by James L. Heller and published in Tallmadge, Ohio, in 1977.

HELM
Ranking: 2002 S.S. Count: 22,737

Origin: English, German. English: derived from the Middle English word "helm." The name was given to those who lived or worked at a crude, impermanent shelter built for animals. English, German: derived from the Old High German and Old English word "helm," which means helmet. The name was given to those who worked making helmets. German: the name is a shortened form of various family names, such as Helmold or Helmund, which begin with the German word "helm," meaning helmet.

Famous **Helms:** JOHN LARUE HELM (1802–1867) of Kentucky was governor of Kentucky, then president of the Louisville and Nashville Railroad. CHARLES JOHN HELM (1817–1868) of New York was a U.S. consul general, then a Confederate agent in Cuba.

Genealogies: *Vengeance!: The Saga of Poor Tom Cover (also Helm)* was compiled by Dan L. Thrapp and published in El Segundo, California, in 1988.

HELMER
Ranking: 4887 S.S. Count: 9149

Origin: German. Derived from the name Hildimar, which means battle or eminence.

Famous **Helmers:** BESSIE BRADWELL HELMER (1858–1927) of Illinois was a lawyer and editor who spurred the growth of the American Association of University Women.

Genealogies: *The Helmer Family: Phillip Helmer (the Pioneer) and His Descendants* was compiled by Pascoe W. Williams and most likely published in St. Johnsville, New York, in 1932.

HELMS
Ranking: 1065 S.S. Count: 41,403

Origin: English, German. English: transformation of the English definition of Helm. German: transformation of the German definition of Helm.

Genealogies: *Chronicles of a Virginia Family: the Klomans of Warrenton* was compiled by Erasmus Helm Kloman Jr. and published in Bowie, Maryland, in 1991. *Helms Descendants, 1720–1991* was compiled by Gerald C. Helms and published in Matthews, North Carolina, in 1992.

HELTON
Ranking: 1331 S.S. Count: 33,234

Origin: English. The name was given to those who came from Helton, which means "the homestead by the slope" (ES) and is the name of several places in England.

Genealogies: None known.

HEMBREY (S.S. Abbreviation: Hembre)
Ranking: 4777 S.S. Count: 9378

Origin: English. Derived from a now-unknown Germanic first name composed of the words "amal" and "ric," meaning courage or strength and power. The name is most common in Scotland and parts of Northumberland County in England.

Genealogies: None known.

HEMINGWAY (S.S. Abbreviation: Heming)
Ranking: 4315 S.S. Count: 10,398

Origin: English. Derived from the first name Hemming (see Hemming) and the Old English word "weg," meaning path. The name was given to those who came from a now-unknown place in West Yorkshire County, England.

Famous **Hemingways:** ERNEST MILLER HEMINGWAY (1899–1961) of Illinois was a novelist and a short-story writer. The author of *The Sun Also Rises* and *A Farewell to Arms*, he is one of the best of all American writers.

Genealogies: None known.

HEMMING, HEMMINGA, HEMMINGS, HEMMINGSEN, HEMMINGSSON, HEMMINGWAY (S.S. Abbreviation: Hemmin)
Ranking: 4920 S.S. Count: 9094

Origin: Hemming—Danish/Norwegian, Swedish; Hemmingsen—Danish, Norwegian; Hemmings, Hemmingway—English; Hemminga—Frisian; Hemmingsson—Swedish. Hemming, Hemminga, Hemmings, Hemmingsen, Hemmingsson: derived from the Old Norse first name Hemmingr, which stems from any number of first names having as their first element the Old Norse word "heim," meaning home. Hemmingway: transformation of Hemingway.

Genealogies: *The Sable Curtain* was compiled by Minnie Shumate Wooksson and published in Washington, D.C., in 1985.

HEMPHILL (S.S. Abbreviation: Hemphi)
Ranking: 2380 S.S. Count: 19,075

Origin: Scottish. Derived from the Old English words "henep" and "hyll," meaning hemp and hill. The name was given to those who came from an unidentified place in what is now the Strathclyde region of England.

Famous **Hemphills:** JOSEPH HEMPHILL (1770–1842) of Pennsylvania was a member of Congress from that state. JOHN HEMPHILL (1803–1862) of South Carolina, as chief justice of the Texas Supreme Court, earned a reputation as "the John Marshall of Texas" for his wisdom. He also was a U.S. senator from Texas.

Genealogies: None known.

HENDERSON (S.S. Abbreviation: Hender)
Ranking: 86 S.S. Count: 312,779

Origin: Scottish. 1) derived from the Scandinavian name

Hendry, which is a transformation of the name Henry. 2) transformation of the Scottish name Henryson.

Famous **Hendersons:** RICHARD HENDERSON (1735–1785) of Virginia was a North Carolina lawyer and judge who organized a series of colonizing projects to the west of the coastal state. The agent for his Richard Henderson & Co. was Daniel Boone, after whom a settlement established by Henderson was named. Another settlement in Tennessee, first called French Lick, grew to be Nashville. His son ARCHIBALD HENDERSON (1768–1822) of North Carolina was a prominent lawyer and member of Congress from North Carolina. Another son, LEONARD HENDERSON (1772–1833), was a lawyer who rose to chief justice of the North Carolina Supreme Court. THOMAS HENDERSON (1743–1824) of New Jersey was a doctor who also served as an acting governor and member of Congress from New Jersey. JOHN HENDERSON (1795–1857) of New Jersey was a U.S. senator from Mississippi. JAMES PINCKNEY HENDERSON (1808–1858) of North Carolina was the first governor of Texas and later was a U.S. senator from the state. PETER HENDERSON (1822–1890), born in Scotland, established the Peter Henderson & Co. seed and garden supply firm in New York and wrote many books, including *Gardening for Profit* (1866) and *Gardening for Pleasure* (1875, 1888). JOHN BROOKS HENDERSON (1826–1913) of Virginia, as a U.S. senator from Missouri, was one of President Andrew Johnson's critics. But in the Johnson impeachment trial, he put aside his political feelings to cast a vote for acquittal. DAVID BREMNER HENDERSON (1840–1906), born in Scotland, was a member of Congress from Iowa and Speaker of the U.S. House of Representatives (1899–1903). CHARLES RICHMOND HENDERSON (1848–1915) of Indiana was a clergyman and sociologist who wrote pioneering works on penology and industrial affairs. Among the works were *Introduction to the Study of the Dependent, Defective and Delinquent Classes* (1893) and *Industrial Insurance in America* (1907). WILLIAM JAMES HENDERSON (1855–1937) of New Jersey was a longtime New York music critic, first for the *New York Times*, then for the *New York Sun*. YANDELL HENDERSON (1873–1944) of Kentucky was a physiologist and toxicologist whose pioneering studies questioned and challenged theories concerning circulation and the heart. LAWRENCE JOSEPH HENDERSON (1878–1942) of Massachusetts was a biochemist and physiologist who made great contributions to the study of blood. He was the author of *Blood: A Study in General Physiology* (1928). RAY HENDERSON (1896–1970) of New York was a composer who is best remembered for "Five Foot Two, Eyes of Blue" and "I'm Sitting on Top of the World."

Genealogies: *The Olden Days* was compiled by LaVerne Hutchens Bish and published in Austin, Texas, in 1973. *The Joh Family; Plus Allied Lines of Runkle, Humbert, Wade,*

Henderson was compiled by Crystal Pauline Randel Walters and published in New Ross, Indiana, in 1972.

HENDRICHS, HENDRICK, HENDRICKS, HENDRIK, HENDRIKS, HENDRIKSEN, HENDRIX (S.S. Abbreviation: Hendri)

Ranking: 211 **S.S. Count:** 168,826

Origin: Hendrik, Hendriks, Hendrix—Dutch; Hendrick—English; Hendriksen—Flemish; Hendrichs—German; Hendricks—German, Swedish. Transformations of and cognates to the English and French definitions of Henry.

Famous **Bearers:** HENDRICK (1680–1755), whose Mohawk name was Tiyanoga, was a Mohawk spokesman whose friendship was pursued by English colonial governors. He was active in keeping Native Americans aligned with the English and against the French, and he died in battle. EUGENE RUSSELL HENDRIX (1847–1927) of Missouri, a Methodist clergyman, was the first president of the Federal Council of Churches of Christ in America. His brother, JOSEPH CLIFFORD HENDRIX (1853–1904) of New York, was a bank president and member of Congress from New York. BURTON JESSIE HENDRICK (1870–1949) of Connecticut wrote a number of biographies and American-history books popular for their accuracy, detail, and lack of criticism. WILLIAM HENDRICKS (1782–1850) of Pennsylvania was a member of Congress from, U.S. senator from, and governor of Indiana. His nephew THOMAS ANDREWS HENDRICKS (1819–1885) also was a member of Congress from, U.S. senator from, and governor of Indiana. He also was vice president of the United States in the first administration of Grover Cleveland. He died in office. JIMI HENDRIX (1942–1970) of Washington was a singer, songwriter, and guitarist. He was part of the Jimi Hendrix Experience, a popular musical group in the 1960s. In 1968 he was named Artist of the Year by the major trade publications and referred to as the "Black Elvis" (Presley). His death was indirectly caused by an overdose of drugs.

Genealogies: *Descendants of Albert(us) Hendricks(on), 1673–1984* was compiled by Florence Hendricks Moore and published in Charles Town, West Virginia, in 1985. *Copper for America: The Hendricks Family and a National Industry 1755–1939* was compiled by Maxwell Whiteman and published in New Brunswick, New Jersey, in 1971. *John and William, Sons of Robert Hendry* was compiled by Spessard Stone and published in Bradenton, Florida, in 1983.

HENDRY

Ranking: 4677 **S.S. Count:** 9568

Origin: French. Cognate to the English and French definitions of Henry.

Genealogies: None known.

HENKE

Ranking: 4433 S.S. Count: 10,119

Origin: Low German. Cognate to the English and French definitions of Henry.

Genealogies: None known.

HENKEL

Ranking: 4812 S.S. Count: 9312

Origin: German. Derived from the names Hagano or Heino, which mean "hedged place" (ES) and are shortened forms of longer names such as Haginold, Haginwarth, and Haganrich.

Famous **Henkels:** PAUL HENKEL (1754–1825) of North Carolina was the most prominent Lutheran clergyman of his time. He traveled perennially through Virginia, North Carolina, Tennessee, Kentucky, Ohio, and Indiana.

Genealogies: *Holcombe-Doane-Henke (also Henkel) Family History 1812–1983* was compiled by Mary Alice Henke and published in Enders, Nebraska, in 1983.

HENLEY

Ranking: 1561 S.S. Count: 28,586

Origin: English. 1) derived from the Old English words "hēah" and "lēah," meaning high and wood. The name was given to those who came from Henley, the name of various places in Oxfordshire, Suffolk, and Warwickshire counties in England. 2) derived from the Old English words "henn" and "lēah," meaning hen or wild fowl and wood. The name was given to those who came from Henley, the name of places in counties such as Ludlow and Shropshire in England.

Famous **Henleys:** ROBERT HENLEY (1783–1828) of Virginia was a naval officer known for his command of the brig *Eagle*.

Genealogies: *Hensley Family Records, and Allied Families of Other Spellings, Like Henley, Henlee, Hendly, etc.; Revolutionary Period, War of 1812, and Indian Wars, also Indian Land Claims* was compiled by Annie Walker Burns and published in Washington, D.C., in 1966.

HENNESEY, HENNESSEN, HENNESSEY, HENNESSY, HENNESY (S.S. Abbreviation: Hennes)

Ranking: 1523 S.S. Count: 29,232

Origin: Hennessen—German; Hennesey, Hennessey, Hennessy, Hennesy—Irish. Hennessen: transformation of the German definition of Hans(el). Hennesey, Hennessey, Hennessy, Hennesy: derived from the Gaelic name Ó hAonghusa, which means "descendant of Angus" (H&H), which is a name derived from the first name Aonghus, which is composed of the words "aon" and "ghus," meaning one and choice.

Famous **Bearers:** JOHN HENNESSEY (1825–1900), born in Ireland, a Roman Catholic priest, was bishop, then archbishop of Dubuque, Iowa. JOHN WILLIAM HENNESSEY

(1839–1917), born in Ireland, emigrated to the United States and became noted for his paintings and illustrations, particularly of the works of famous authors such as Alfred, Lord Tennyson and Henry Wadsworth Longfellow.

Genealogies: None known.

HENNIN

Ranking: 1216 S.S. Count: 36,244

Origin: French. 1) derived from the Old French word "hennins," which is derived from the Middle Low German word "hennick," meaning rooster. "Hennins" were the ornate and tall headdresses that women of the nobility wore during the Middle Ages, and they were similar in effect and appearance to the comb of the rooster. The name was given to those who worked creating or selling these ornamental accessories to women of the nobility. 2) derived from the Germanic first name Henno, which means rooster, and the Germanic suffix "-inum." The name was given to those who came from a now-unknown place in the Pas-de-Calais region of France.

Genealogies: *The Henning (also Hennin) and Duke Families of Louisville, Kentucky: Including Genealogical Material on the Following Families, Henning, Duke, Morgan, Hunt, Marshall, Randolph* was compiled by Charles P. Stanton and published in Brooklyn, New York, in 1983.

HENRIC (ALSO HENRICHS, HENRICHSEN, HENRICSSON)

Ranking: 2967 S.S. Count: 15,329

Origin: Henrichs—German; Henrichsen—Norwegian; Henric—Provençal; Henricsson—Swedish. Cognates to the English and French definitions of Henry.

Genealogies: None known.

HENRY

Ranking: 136 S.S. Count: 221,422

Origin: English, French, Irish. English, French: derived from a now-unknown Germanic first name composed of the words "haim" or "heim" and "ric," meaning home and power. The name became common in England during the Middle Ages. English: derived from a now-unknown Germanic first name that began with the element "hagan," meaning hawthorn. Irish: derived from the Gaelic name Ó hInnéirghe, meaning "descendant of Innéirghe" (H&H), which is a first name meaning desertion or decampment.

Famous **Henrys:** WILLIAM HENRY (1729–1786) of Pennsylvania was a Revolutionary War patroit and the first person to try to move a stern-wheel steamboat. PATRICK HENRY (1736–1799) of Virginia was a lawyer and Revolutionary War statesman, but he is best remembered as the man who said, "Give me liberty, or give me death." ALEXANDER HENRY (1739–1824) of New Jersey was a fur trader and explorer of the Great Lakes and the Northwest Territory. JOHN HENRY (1750–1798) of Maryland was the Maryland delegate to the Continental Congress, a state and U.S. senator, and the governor of Maryland. ANDREW HENRY (1775–1833) of Pennsylvania was a fur trapper and miner. He worked as the first American trapper in the western frontier and is remembered as a pioneer in his field. JOHN HENRY (1797–1878) of New York was the first director of the Smithsonian Institution. JOHN HENRY (1807–1820) was an adventurer. He wrote secret reports to the governor-general of Canada on U.S. public opinion, which were then sold to U.S. President James Madison. They were instrumental in the War of 1812. MORRIS HENRY HENRY (1835–1895) of England was a physician and a pioneer in the area of skin and venereal diseases. EDWARD LAMSON HENRY (1841–1919) of South Carolina was a historical painter. His paintings were of the life and customs of the American people and, done in oils, were accurate to the tiniest of details. ALICE HENRY (1857–1943) of Australia was a journalist and a women's trade union leader. While a resident of the United States, she was editor of the National Women's Trade Union League's publication, *Life and Labor*, and she was author of *The Trade Union Woman* (1915) and *Women and the Labor Movement* (1923).

Genealogies: *The François Henry Family* was compiled by Barbara P. Quealy and published in Denver, Colorado, in 1970. *A Genealogical and Biographical History of the Field Family of Massachusetts and Vermont and the French-Henry Families of Virginia and Texas: A Union of North and South* was compiled by Charles Kellogg Field III and published in Baltimore, Maryland, in 1985.

HENSLEY (S.S. Abbreviation: Hensle)

Ranking: 567 **S.S. Count:** 72,648

Origin: English. The name refers to those who lived in woods that were visited often by undomesticated birds.

Genealogies: *The Hensleigh (also Hensley) Family of Wembury: Thirty-Nine Generations, A Thousand Year History and Genealogy Follows the Family From France to Cornwall and Devonshire in England, and On to America and New Zealand* was compiled by Edith Pease and published in Fort Morgan, Colorado, in 1991. *Hensley Family Records, and Allied Families of Other Spellings, Like Henley, Henlee, Hendly, etc.; Revolutionary Period, War of 1812, and Indian Wars, also Indian Land Claims* was compiled by Annie Walker Burns and published in Washington, D.C., in 1966.

HENSON

Ranking: 659 **S.S. Count:** 63,657

Origin: English. 1) derived from the Old English word "henn," meaning hen or wild fowl. The name was often given to men who were considered finicky and fretful. 2) derived from the Middle English first name Henn(e), which is a shortened form of Henry.

Famous Hensons: JOSIAH HENSON (1789–1883) of

Maryland was a slave and the "Uncle Tom" in Harriet Beecher Stowe's book *Uncle Tom's Cabin*.

Genealogies: *A Henson Family History in Early America and Their Revolutionary War Soldiers, 1725–1850* was compiled by A. L. Henson and published in Independence, Missouri, in 1978. *The Story of Philip G. Henson of Wayne County, Illinois* was compiled by Beulah Reed May and published in Denver, Colorado, in 1977.

HERBERG, HERBERGER, HERBERT, HERBERTSON, HERBERTZ (S.S. Abbreviation: Herber)

Ranking: 1050 **S.S. Count:** 41,773

Origin: Herbert—English, French, German; Herbertson—English; Herberg, Herberger, Herbertz—German. Herbert, Herbertson, Herbertz: derived from a Germanic first name composed of the words "heri" or "hary" and "behrt," meaning army and renowned and resplendent. Herberg, Herberger: cognates to Harber.

Famous Bearers: HENRY WILLIAM HERBERT (1807–1858) of England was a writer who wrote under the name Frank Forester. HILARY ABNER HERBERT (1834–1919) of South Carolina was the secretary of the navy and was responsible for naval growth. VICTOR HERBERT (1859–1924) of Ireland was a musician of great renown. He was one of the founders of the American Society of Composers.

Genealogies: *Herbert in England & Virginia, 1399–1900s* was compiled by Alice Granbery Walter and published in Virginia Beach, Virginia, in 1977.

HERBST (ALSO HERBSTMAN)

Ranking: 3207 **S.S. Count:** 14,146

Origin: Herbst—German, Jewish; Herbstman—Jewish. German: derived from the Middle High German word "herb(e)st," which means harvest, especially of grains and grapes. The name evolved to mean fall, the time of harvest. The name was probably given to peasants who had to pay their lord a certain percentage of what they harvested. Jewish: derived from the modern German word "herbst," which means autumn. The name was taken ornamentally and may have been adopted during the fall season. It may also be one in a series of names that refer to the seasons and that were arbitrarily assigned to Jewish families by government officials.

Famous Bearers: JOSEPHINE HERBST (1892–1969) of Iowa was a journalist and writer who devoted her time to literature and radicalism.

Genealogies: None known.

HEREDIA (S.S. Abbreviation: Heredi)

Ranking: 4594 **S.S. Count:** 9731

Origin: Spanish. Derived from the Latin word "hērēdium," which means hereditary estate, a term which refers to property that is passed on to the heirs of its occupants rather than allowed to revert to its overseer. The name was given to those who came from Heredia, the name of various places in Spain.

Genealogies: None known.

HERMAN (ALSO HERMANN)
Ranking: 461 **S.S. Count:** 86,595

Origin: German. Derived from a now-unknown Germanic first name composed of the words "heri" or "hari" and "man," meaning army and man. The name is of an early origin, its first known recording having been made as early as the 1st century A.D. It has also been adopted by many Jews, probably as a modification of the modern German last name.

Famous **Bearers:** LEBRECHT FREDERICK HERMAN (1761–1848) of Germany was a highly influential clergyman in Pennsylvania.

Genealogies: *Germany to U.S.A.: Migration of the Matthew Herrmann Family* was compiled by Walter W. Herrmann and published in 1980. *Willard Adams Barber, His Ancestors and Descendants* was compiled by John W. Herrmann and published in Mountainside, New Jersey, in 1976.

HERNAMAN, HERNÁN, HERNÁNDEZ, HERNANDO, HERNANZ (S.S. Abbreviation: Hernan)
Ranking: 52 **S.S. Count:** 457,594

Origin: Hernaman—English; Hernán, Hernández, Hernando, Hernanz—Spanish. Hernaman: transformation of the third definition of Hearn. Hernán, Hernández, Hernando, Hernanz: derived from a Visigothic first name composed of the words "farð" and "manð," meaning journey and brave. The first name did not appear in Spain until the late 15th century, and the family name is, therefore, of recent period.

Genealogies: None known.

HERNDON (S.S. Abbreviation: Herndo)
Ranking: 1610 **S.S. Count:** 27,800

Origin: English. The name refers to those who lived in a cranny or corner near a hill or small mountain.

Famous **Herndons:** WILLIAM LEWIS HERNDON (1813–1857) of Virginia was a naval officer. He explored and wrote about the Amazon in a book called *Exploration of the Valley of the Amazon*. He was lost at sea off Cape Hatteras in 1857. WILLIAM HENRY HERNDON (1818–1891) of Kentucky was Abraham Lincoln's junior partner in his law firm. He eventually wrote a book called *Herndon's Lincoln: The True Story of a Great Life*. Although criticized at the time, the book proved true to facts.

Genealogies: *A Collection of Facts and Recollections of the Descent Lines and the Relationships Among Some Descendants of—William Herndon of England and New*

Kent County, Virginia was compiled by Grace Yager Froom and published in Indianapolis, Indiana, in 1983. *The Herndon and Inge Families: Genealogical, Historical, Biographical* was compiled by George B. Inge and published in Cullman, Alabama, in 1977.

HERR
Ranking: 2905 **S.S. Count:** 15,671

Origin: German, Jewish. German: 1) derived from the Old High German word "herro," meaning master or lord. The name was given to those who were employed in the service of the master of an estate. 2) same derivation as in 1. The name was given to a person who was affected and took on the mannerisms of the nobility. Jewish: uncertain etymology. It probably has the same derivation as in the German origin.

Famous **Herrs:** JOHN HERR (1781–1850) of Pennsylvania was the founder of the Mennonites. HERBERT THACKER HERR (1876–1933) of Colorado was the inventor of safety brakes for trains, among other things.

Genealogies: None known.

HERRERA, HERRERO, HERREROS (S.S. Abbreviation: Herrer)
Ranking: 424 **S.S. Count:** 93,762

Origin: Spanish. Herrera: derived from the Latin word "ferrāriae," which means "iron workings" (H&H). The name was given to those who came from Ferrières, the name of several places in Normandy, France. Herrero, Herreros: cognates to Farrar.

Genealogies: None known.

HERRICK (S.S. Abbreviation: Herric)
Ranking: 2559 **S.S. Count:** 17,767

Origin: English. 1) derived from the Old Norse first name Eiríkr, which is composed of the words "eir" and "rík," meaning mercy and power. 2) possibly derived from a now-unknown Germanic first name composed of the words "heri" or "hari" and "rík," meaning army and power.

Famous **Herricks:** MYRON TIMOTHY HERRICK (1854–1929) of Ohio was a diplomat who is best remembered as an effective ambassador to France. CHRISTINE TERHUNE HERRICK (1859–1944) of New Jersey was a writer on household affairs. Her articles appeared in the magazines of the day, and she had several books published on the subject. ROBERT WELCH HERRICK (1868–1938) of Massachusetts was the writer of a series of novels about middle-class life. ELINORE MOREHOUSE HERRICK (1895–1964) of New York was a journalist and a labor relations-specialist.

Genealogies: *The Herrick Family in England and America* was compiled by Edith Herrick Milhorat and published in Baltimore, Maryland, in 1984. *Herrick Genealogy: A Genealogical Register of the Name and Family of Herrick From the Settlement of Henrie Hericke in Salem, Massachu-*

setts, *1629 to 1846, With a Concise Notice of Their English Ancestry* was compiled by Jedediah Herrick and published in Columbus, Ohio, in 1885 and reprinted in 1985.

HERRING, HERRINGTON (S.S. Abbreviation: Herrin)

Ranking: 485 **S.S. Count:** 83,346

Origin: English. Herring: derived from the Old English word "hēring," meaning herring. The name was given to those who peddled the herring fish. In some places, the name came to be used as a nickname that referred to something trivial or inconsequential. Herrington: 1) derived from the Old English words "here" and "tūn," meaning army and settlement. The name was given to those who came from Herrington, the name of a place in Durham County, England. 2) the name may be a transformation of the family name Here, which itself is a shortened form of various family names beginning with the word "here," meaning army.

Famous **Bearers:** JAMES HERRING (1794–1867) of England was a portrait painter. SILAS CLARK HERRING (1803–1881) of Vermont was a safe manufacturer. AUGUSTUS MOORE HERRING (1867–1926) of Georgia was a pioneer in aviation who worked mostly with gliders.

Genealogies: *A Dutch Family in the Middle Colonies, 1660–1800* was compiled by Firth Haring Fabend and published in New Brunswick, New Jersey, in 1991.

HERRMANN (S.S. Abbreviation: Herrma)

Ranking: 2022 **S.S. Count:** 22,600

Origin: German. Transformation of Herman.

Famous **Herrmanns:** ALEXANDER HERRMANN (1844–1896) of France was a well-known magician of his time.

Genealogies: *Willard Adams Barber, His Ancestors and Descendants* was compiled by John W. Herrmann and published in Mountainside, New Jersey, in 1976.

HERRON

Ranking: 1229 **S.S. Count:** 35,999

Origin: English, Irish. English: derived from the Old French word "hairon," meaning heron. The name was given to those who were gangly and skinny and thought to look like a heron. Irish: 1) derived from the Gaelic name Ó hEaráin, meaning "descendant of Earán" (H&H), which is a first name derived from the word "earadh," meaning dread or suspicion. 2) derived from the Gaelic word Ó hUidhrín, meaning "descendant of Uidhrín" (H&H), which is probably derived from the word "odhar," meaning dun-colored or dark-skinned. 3) derived from the Gaelic name Mac Giolla Chiaráin, meaning "son of the servant of St. Ciarán" (H&H), a common name for early Irish saints derived from the word "ciar," which means dark or black.

Famous **Herrons:** FRANCIS JAY HERRON (1837–1902) of

Pennsylvania was the youngest major general in the Civil War. GEORGE DAVIS HERRON (1862–1925) of Indiana was a Congregational clergyman who was influential in the founding of Rand School in New York City.

Genealogies: *The Arnold, Best, Cullison and Herron Families* was compiled by L. Evelyn Strong and published in Massillon, Ohio, in 1980.

HERSHBEIN, HERSHBERG (S.S. Abbreviation: Hershb)

Ranking: 4844 **S.S. Count:** 9231

Origin: Jewish. Hershbein: derived from the German words "hirsch" (or its Yiddish cognate "hirsh") and "bein," meaning deer and leg. The name was taken ornamentally. Hershberg: 1) derived from the German words "hirsch" (or its Yiddish cognate "hirsh") and "berg," meaning deer and hill. The name was given to those who came from Hirschberg, the name of several places in the Thuringia and North Rhine–Westphalia regions of Germany, and in what is now called Jelenia Góra in western Poland. 2) same derivation as in 1. The name was taken ornamentally.

Genealogies: *Descendants of Emanuel J. Miller and Magdelena Weaver (also Hershberger): Family Records, 1776–1970* was compiled by Eli D. Mast and published in Apple Creek, Ohio, in 1970.

HERSHEL, HERSHENBAUM, HERSHENHAUS, HERSHENHORN, HERSHENSON, HERSHENSTRAUSS (S.S. Abbreviation: Hershe)

Ranking: 4717 **S.S. Count:** 9481

Origin: Jewish. Hershel: 1) derived from the Yiddish male first name Hirsh, which means deer. The name is common because the biblical figure Naftali, the son of Jacob, is at one point described as a female red deer. 2) derived from the German word "hirsch" or its Yiddish cognate "hirsh," both meaning deer. The name was taken ornamentally. Hershenbaum: derived from the German words "hirsch" (or its Yiddish cognate "hirsh") and "baum," meaning deer and tree. The name was taken ornamentally. Hershenhaus: derived from the German words "hirsch" (or its Yiddish cognate "hirsh") and "haus," meaning deer and house. The name was taken ornamentally. Hershenhorn: derived from the German words "hirsch" (or its Yiddish cognate "hirsh") and "horn," meaning deer and horn. The name was taken ornamentally. Hershenson: transformation of the first definition of Hershel. Hershenstrauss: derived from the German words "hirsch" (or its Yiddish cognate "hirsh") and "strauss," meaning deer and bouquet. The name was taken ornamentally.

Genealogies: None known.

HERZOG

Ranking: 2986 **S.S. Count:** 15,233

Origin: German, Jewish. German: derived from the Old High German word "herizoho," which is composed of the words "heri" and "ziohan," meaning army and to lead. The word evolved into Herzog, meaning duke, a title of nobility. The name was given either to those who worked in the service of a duke or to persons who were affected and took on the mannerisms of the nobility. Jewish: same derivation. The name was taken ornamentally.

Genealogies: None known.

HESS

Ranking: 490 **S.S. Count:** 82,531

Origin: German, Jewish. 1) derived from the Germanic word "Hassia," which was once a place in central western Germany and is now the state of Hesse. 2) transformation of Herman(n).

Famous **Hesses:** ALFRED FABIAN HESS (1875–1933) of New York was a pediatrician who was responsible for classic studies of scurvy in infants. He also worked to make pasteurized milk formulas plus orange juice a popular choice for certain infants. VICTOR FRANZ HESS (1883–1964) of Austria was a physicist and a pioneer in the field of X-rays and radiation.

Genealogies: Family History of Inter-Married Branches of the Families of Brown, Doane, Hess, Peck, Wintermute was compiled by Maurice E. Peck and published in Sarasota, Florida, in 1976. Descendants of John Hess 1809–1888: A Hess Genealogy Through Pioneer Hans Hess was compiled by James H. Hess et al. and published in Pennsylvania in 1981.

HESTER (ALSO HERSTERMAN)

Ranking: 838 **S.S. Count:** 50,800

Origin: Hersterman—Dutch; Hester—German. Derived from the Middle Low German word "hēster," meaning beech tree. The name was given to those who lived near a prominent beech tree.

Genealogies: Genealogy of the Bennington Family: Which Originated in Harford County, Maryland, with Notes on Other Bennington Families was compiled by William Hall and published in Scottsdale, Arizona, in 1991. Hester Genealogy; A Story of Some Descendants of John Hester, an Early Settler of Fleming County, Kentucky, Who arrived in America in the Year 1740. Including a Genealogy on Many Collateral Families was compiled by Hester Geraldine Lester Searl and most likely published in Patterson, California, in 1972.

HETRICK (S.S. Abbreviation: Hetric)

Ranking: 4793 **S.S. Count:** 9345

Origin: Uncertain etymology.

Genealogies: None known.

HEWITT

Ranking: 1052 **S.S. Count:** 41,765

Origin: English. 1) derived from the medieval first name Huet, which is a transformation of the name Hugh (see the English definition of Hugh[es]). 2) derived from the Old English word "hiewet," meaning to cut, fell, or hack. The name was given to those who lived in a newly made patch of felled forest land in the middle of a wood.

Famous **Hewitts:** ABRAM STEVENS HEWITT (1822–1903) of New York was an iron manufacturer and the owner of the first American open-hearth furnace. PETER COOPER HEWITT (1861–1921) of New York was a scientist and inventor. He was a pioneer in hydroplanes and high-speed motorboats but is best known for his 1903 invention of the mercury vapor lamp.

Genealogies: The Hewitts of Athens County, Ohio was compiled by Susan L. Mitchell and published in Westland, Michigan, in 1989. The Lineage of Lucy Waterman Hewitt and George Washburn was compiled by Philip Alan Wilcox and published in Durham, New Hampshire, in 1964.

HIATT

Ranking: 3174 **S.S. Count:** 14,308

Origin: English. The name was given to those who lived at "the high gate or gap in a chain of hills" (ES).

Genealogies: None known.

HIBBARD (S.S. Abbreviation: Hibbar)

Ranking: 4117 **S.S. Count:** 10,975

Origin: English. Derived from the Norman first name Hil(de)bert, which is composed of the Germanic words "hild" and "berht," meaning battle or conflict and renowned or resplendent.

Genealogies: None known.

HICKEY

Ranking: 999 **S.S. Count:** 43,761

Origin: Irish. Derived from the Gaelic name Ó hIcidhe, which means "descendant of Icidhe" (H&H), which is a first name meaning doctor or healer.

Genealogies: Hicklin (also Hickey) Families in America was compiled by Marjorie Abbott-Braswell and published in Hephzibah, Georgia, in 1986. Hicklin (also Hickey) was compiled by Pasha Palombi Smith and published in Mabton, Washington, in 1987.

HICKMAN (S.S. Abbreviation: Hickma)

Ranking: 741 **S.S. Count:** 57,162

Origin: English. Derived from the medieval first name Hicke, which is derived from the name Richard. The name was given to those who worked in the service of Hicke.

Genealogies: Descendants of Robert and Hannah Hickman Way of Chester County, Pennsylvania was compiled by

D. Herbert Way and published in Woodstown, New Jersey, in 1975. *Richard S. Hickman, Lydia Veal, and Their Descendants* was compiled by Paul and Alba Smith and published in Alpharetta, Georgia, in 1990.

HICKS
Ranking: 141 **S.S. Count:** 216,595
Origin: English. Derived from the medieval first name Hicke, which is derived from the name Richard.

Famous **Hickses:** ELIAS HICKS (1748–1830) of New York was a Quaker preacher and a leader of the 1827–1828 split among members of the Society of Friends. THOMAS HOLLIDAY HICKS (1798–1865) of Maryland was a Civil War–era governor of Maryland. He delayed the state's secession until the Union troops could arrive. He also served as a U.S. senator from Maryland. THOMAS HICKS (1833–1890) of Pennsylvania was a painter who is best remembered because of the well-known subjects he painted.

Genealogies: *Ancestors and Kin, Davis, Hicks, Kennedy* was compiled by Mary Kennedy Reynolds and published in Birmingham, Alabama, in 1991. *The Andrew Hicks and Charles Stone Families* was compiled by Lucille Kaufman Novak and published in Nashua, New Hampshire, in 1977.

HIDALGO (S.S. Abbreviation: Hidalg)
Ranking: 3509 **S.S. Count:** 12,850
Origin: Spanish. Derived from the Spanish word "hidalgo," which means nobleman and which was produced from an elision of the Spanish phrase "hijo de algo," meaning "son of something."
Genealogies: None known.

HIGDON
Ranking: 3485 **S.S. Count:** 12,941
Origin: English. The name refers to one who lives on or near a high hill or small mountain.
Genealogies: *The Higdons of Grayson County, Kentucky, 1810–1900* was compiled by Sarah Higdon Peyton and published in Arlington, Texas, in 1983. *Leonard Higdon of Anson County and His Descendants* was compiled by Jo Ann Smith and published in Raleigh, North Carolina, in 1982.

HIGGINBOTHAM, HIGGINBOTTAM, HIGGINBOTTOM, HIGGINS, HIGGINSON
(S.S. Abbreviation: Higgin)
Ranking: 266 **S.S. Count:** 137,646
Origin: Higginbotham, Higginbottam, Higginbottom, Higginson—English; Higgins—English, Irish. Higginbotham, Higginbottam, Higginbottom: uncertain etymology. Probably derived from the Old English words "œcen" and "botme," meaning oaken and broad valley. As the name evolved, it became associated with the words "hicken" or "higgen," both

meaning mountain ash. The name was given to those who came from a place in Lancashire, England, now known as Oakenbottom. Higgins (English), Higginson: derived from the medieval first name Higgin, which is a transformation of Hick(s). Higgins (Irish): derived from the Gaelic name Ó hUiginn, meaning "descendant of Uiginn" (H&H), which is a first name meaning Viking or sea rover.

Famous **Bearers:** FRANCIS HIGGINSON (1586–1630) of England was a clergyman who came with the Pilgrims to New England. He was the author of *New-Englands Plantation.* JOHN HIGGINSON (1616–1708) of England, also a clergyman, was the son of Francis. His pastorate was in Guilford, Connecticut. NATHANIEL HIGGINSON (1652–1708) of Connecticut was the son of John. He became a merchant in the East India Co. He died in England. STEPHEN HIGGINSON (1743–1828) of Massachusetts was a Revolutionary War privateer and a descendant of Francis. THOMAS WENTWORTH HIGGINSON (1823–1911) of Massachusetts was the grandson of Stephen. He was an early proponent of women's suffrage and an opponent of slavery. As a Union soldier, he served as a colonel in the first Negro regiment in the army. After the war he wrote for *Atlantic Monthly,* was one of the discoverers of Emily Dickinson, and wrote several books, including *Life in a Black Regiment.* FRANK WAYLAND HIGGINS (1856–1907) of New York was the governor of that state. He worked on behalf of insurance legislation and election and tax reform. MARGUERITE HIGGINS (1920–1966) of Hong Kong was the first woman to win a Pulitzer Prize as a journalist, for her coverage of the Korean War.

Genealogies: *Ancestors and Descendants of James Larkin Higginbotham of Noxubee County, Mississippi* was compiled by Rachel Hollingsworth Higginbotham and most likely published in California in 1977. *An American Family and Its Ancestor Predecessors; Back to Adam through Early American Immigrants of British Extraction According to Past and Present Records* was compiled by Vivian Higgins Morse and published in Baltimore, Maryland, in 1973.

HIGGS
Ranking: 3223 **S.S. Count:** 14,062
Origin: English. Transformation of Hick(s).
Genealogies: *The Higgs Family: Maryland to Missouri* was compiled by Betty Higgs Bridges and published in Webb City, Missouri, most likely in 1978.

HIGH
Ranking: 2443 **S.S. Count:** 18,592
Origin: English. 1) derived from the Old English word "hēah," meaning high or tall. The name was given to those who were unusually tall. 2) same derivation as in 1. The name was given to those who lived on a mountaintop or other high place.

Famous **Highs**: STANLEY HOFLUND HIGH (1895–1961) of Illinois was a writer and editor who contributed regularly to the magazines of the day.

Genealogies: *History of John High Family of Lancaster County, Pennsylvania, 1754–1977* was compiled by Levi High and published in Adamstown, Pennsylvania, in 1977. *My High Line* was compiled by Joseph and Jessye High and published in Sunnyvale, California, in 1980.

HIGHTON (S.S. Abbreviation: Highto)

Ranking: 1632 **S.S. Count:** 27,538

Origin: English. Derived from the Old English words "hēah" and "tūn," meaning high and settlement. The name was given to those who came from Hightown, the name of a place in southwest Lancashire County in England, or from another similarly named place in Salford Parish in England.

Genealogies: None known.

HILBER (ALSO HILBERING, HILBERS, HILBERT, HILBERTZ)

Ranking: 4530 **S.S. Count:** 9881

Origin: Hilbert—English, French, German; Hilber, Hilbering, Hilbers, Hilbertz—German. Transformations of and cognates to Hibbard.

Genealogies: None known.

HILDEBRAND, HILDEBRANDS (S.S. Abbreviation: Hildeb)

Ranking: 1655 **S.S. Count:** 26,994

Origin: English, French, German. Derived from a now-unknown Germanic first name composed of the words "hild" and "brand," meaning battle and burning sword.

Genealogies: *Farber and Allied Families of Burkhart, Hildebrand, and Albaugh* was compiled by Richard Howard Dodge and published in Denver, Colorado, in 1975.

HILDRETH (S.S. Abbreviation: Hildre)

Ranking: 4255 **S.S. Count:** 10,584

Origin: English. Derived from the name Hildefrith, which can mean either war or peace.

Genealogies: *The Heldreth (also Hildreth) Family* was compiled by Larry Heldreth and published in Dry Fork, Virginia, in 1978. *Hildreth Genealogy: Ancestors and Descendants of William and Joannah Chalker Hildreth of Glastonbury, Connecticut; With Information on Tuthill, Wells, Chalker, Coleman, Hurlbut, Stokely, and Riley Families* was compiled by Allen D. Sheneman and published in Defiance, Ohio, in 1982.

HILL

Ranking: 34 **S.S. Count:** 594,230

Origin: English, German, Jewish. English: 1) derived from the Old English word "hyll," which means hill. The name was very common in England and often given to those who lived on or near a hill. 2) derived from the medieval first name Hill, which is either a shortened form of the name Hilary or a shortened form of various Germanic names beginning with the word "hild," meaning battle or conflict. German: transformation of Hildebrand. Jewish: transformation of various similar-sounding Yiddish names.

Famous Hills: JAMES HILL (1734–1811) of Maine was a shipbuilder. He participated in the Revolutionary War. ISAAC HILL (1789–1851) of Massachusetts was a U.S. senator from and then a governor of New Hampshire. He also served as a member of President Andrew Jackson's "kitchen cabinet." FRANCES MARIA MULLIGAN HILL (1799–1884) of New York was an Episcopal missionary and the founder of educational institutions in Greece. DANIEL HARVEY HILL (1821–1889) of South Carolina was a brigadier general in the Confederate army. Before the war he was a university professor; after the war, he served as the president of several universities. BENJAMIN HARVEY HILL (1823–1882) of Georgia was a southerner who was opposed to secession but became the spokesman for Jefferson Davis in the Confederate senate (1861–1865). After the war he returned to U.S. politics as a member of Congress and then as a senator. AMBROSE POWELL HILL (1825–1865) of Virginia was a brigadier general in the Confederate army. He started the attack at Gettysburg. He was killed in action before Petersburg. GEORGE WILLIAM HILL (1838–1914) of New York was an American astronomer. He is best remembered for his work in celestial mechanics and mathematics. JAMES JEROME HILL (1838–1916) of Canada was a railroad magnate. GRACE LIVINGSTON HILL (1865–1947) of New York was a novelist and the author of *Matched Pearls* (1933), considered her best work. PATTY SMITH HILL (1868–1946) of Kentucky was a kindergarten educator who changed the curriculum concepts that had been in force in the kindergarten class, stressing realistic learning experiences. She also made two other contributions to the children of the future. The first was large-scale Patty Hill blocks, which allowed children to build in accordance with their motor-skill level. The second was a song for which she wrote the lyrics and her sister wrote the music. It originally was called "Good Morning to All," but the later version was titled "Happy Birthday to You." JOE HILL (1879–1915) was born in Sweden. He was a labor leader and a songwriter. He was considered a hero to the radical labor movement. GEORGE WASHINGTON HILL (1884–1946) of Pennsylvania was a businessman. He was the president of the American Tobacco Co. and was the person who introduced the Lucky Strike brand of cigarettes in 1917. He was largely responsible for the company's advertising slogans. JOHN WILEY HILL (1890–1977) of Indiana founded, with John Knowlton, the international public relations firm Hill and Knowlton. In addition to his public relations work, he wrote the books

Corporate Public Relations (1958) and The Making of a Public Relations Man (1963).

Genealogies: Blue Ridge Mountain Kinfolks: A Record of Ancestors, Descendants, and Relatives of the Author and Wife, Including Fisher-Gilbert-Hall-Hartley-Hill-King-Kirby-Lawson Families was compiled by Larry King and published in Manchester, Tennessee, most likely in 1976. Genealogy of Thomas Hill and Rebecca Miles; English Ancestors, Maryland Emigrants, Kentucky Pioneers, Americans, U.S.A. was compiled by Mary Louise Donnelly and published in 1971.

HILLARD, HILLARY (S.S. Abbreviation: Hillar)

Ranking: 4838 **S.S. Count:** 9251

Origin: Hillary—English; Hillard—French. 1) derived from a medieval first name that is derived from the Latin word "hilaris," which means joyful or happy. The name was chosen by early Christians to express their felicity and hope of salvation, and it was therefore the name of several early saints. 2) derived from the female first name Eulalie, which is derived from the Latin name Eulalia, meaning articulate or well spoken. The name was adopted by early Christians as an allusion to the ability to speak in tongues.

Genealogies: None known.

HILLER (ALSO HILLERBRAND, HILLERET, HILLERIN, HILLERY)

Ranking: 2845 **S.S. Count:** 16,044

Origin: Hiller, Hillery—English; Hillerbrand—English, French, German; Hilleret, Hillerin—French. Hiller: transformation of the first definition of Hill. Hillery: transformation of Hillary. Hillerbrand: transformation of and cognate to Hillerbrand. Hilleret, Hillerin: cognates to the first definition of Hillary.

Famous Bearers: WILLIAM FRANCIS HILLERBRAND (1853–1925) of Hawaii was a chemist who served with distinction as a member of the U.S. Geological Survey and the Bureau of Standards.

Genealogies: Descendants of Jonathan Hiller: From Old Dutchess to Chautauqua County, New York with Extensive Background History and Lineages on All Collateral Lines was compiled by Helen Traver Anderson and published in Livonia, New York, in 1983.

HILLIAR, HILLIARD (S.S. Abbreviation: Hillia)

Ranking: 1494 **S.S. Count:** 29,758

Origin: English. Hilliar: derived from the Old English word "helian," meaning to cover. The name was given to those who worked tiling or thatching roofs. Hilliard: derived from the Norman feminine first names Hildiarde or Hildegard, which are composed of the words "hild" and "gard," meaning battle or conflict and fortress.

Genealogies: None known.

HILLMAN, HILLMANN (S.S. Abbreviation: Hillma)

Ranking: 1999 **S.S. Count:** 22,746

Origin: Hillman—English; Hillmann—German. Hillman: transformation of the first English definition of Hill. Hillmann: transformation of the German definition of Hill.

Famous Bearers: THOMAS TENNESSEE HILLMAN (1844–1905) of Tennessee was an Alabama industrialist who was one of the builders of the first iron furnace in Birmingham. SIDNEY HILLMAN (1887–1946) of Lithuania was a labor leader and an organizer of textile workers.

Genealogies: Unto the Hills, Some Hillmans and Others: A Partial Genealogy of the Southwest Virginia Families of Carrico, Edwards, Hillman, Newberry, Stallard, Wells and Other Families was compiled by Belva Marshall Counts and published in Radford, Virginia, in 1979. Hillman, John, 1793–1879 and Rebecca, 1795–1879; His Ancestors, their Descendants was compiled by Endocen H. Hillman and published in Minneapolis, Minnesota, in 1980.

HILLS

Ranking: 2366 **S.S. Count:** 19,177

Origin: English. Transformation of the first and second definitions of Hill.

Famous Hillses: ELIJAH CLARENCE HILLS (1867–1932) of Illinois was a Romance philologist and an educator.

Genealogies: The Hills-Neet Story; Reminiscences by Jessie Hills Stewart was compiled by Dorothy Chapman and most likely published in Oregon in 1965.

HILTON

Ranking: 1117 **S.S. Count:** 39,504

Origin: English. 1) derived from the Old English words "hyll" and "tūn," meaning hill and settlement. The name was given to those who came from Hilton, the name of various places in England, including Cambridgeshire, Cleveland, Derbyshire, and Shropshire counties. 2) derived from the Old English words "hielde" and "tūn," meaning slope and settlement. The name was given to those who came from Hilton, the name of various places in Cumberland and Dorset counties in England. 3) derived from the Old English words "helde" and "tūn," meaning tansy plant and settlement. The name was given to those who came from Hilton, the name of various places in Cumberland and Dorset counties in England. 4) possibly derived from the Norman first name Hildun, which is composed of the Germanic words "hild" and "hūn," meaning battle or conflict and bear cub.

Famous Hiltons: CONRAD NICHOLSON HILTON (1887–1979) of Minnesota was a hotel magnate and the namesake of the Hilton hotels.

Genealogies: Blue Ridge Heritage: Burnett, Branscome,

Hylton (also Hilton), Cox, Slaughter, and Related Families was compiled by Dorothy Burnett Peterson and published in 1982. *Hylton-Hilton History* was compiled by Ernest Hilton and published in Madison, Maine, in Charlottesville, Virginia, in 1930.

HIMES

Ranking: 3718 S.S. Count: 12,153

Origin: English. Derived from the name Hyam, which means life.

Famous **Himeses:** JOSHUA VAUGHAN HIMES (1805–1895) of Rhode Island was an Adventist and Episcopal minister. CHARLES FRANCIS HIMES (1838–1918) of Pennsylvania was a university professor who was one of the first to teach photography as a course in college.

Genealogies: *The Himes Family History: The Descendants of John Himes and Catherine (Giesler) Himes of Lancaster County, Pennsylvania, and Washington County, Tennessee, 1797–1990* was compiled by Carolyn Joy Stafford and published in Brandon, Florida, in 1990.

HINDS

Ranking: 2361 S.S. Count: 19,208

Origin: English. 1) derived from the Old English word "hind," meaning female red deer. The name was given to those who were considered shy, mild, or apprehensive. 2) derived from the Middle English word "hine," meaning servant or youth. The name was given to those who worked as servants in a manor.

Famous **Hindses:** ASHER GROSBY HINDS (1863–1919) of Maine was a journalist and a politician. He served as the parliamentarian of Congress (1895–1911) and was the author of *Hinds' Precedents of the House of Representatives* (1907–1908).

Genealogies: None known.

HINES

Ranking: 403 S.S. Count: 97,006

Origin: English, Irish. English: derived from the Middle English word "hine," meaning servant or youth. The name was given to those who worked as servants in a manor. Irish: derived from the Gaelic name Ó hEidhin, meaning "descendant of Eidhin" (H&H), which is a first name of uncertain origin. It is possibly derived from the word "eidhean," meaning ivy, or it may be a transformation of Aidhne, the name of a place in Ireland.

Famous **Hineses:** WALKER DOWNER HINES (1870–1934) of Kentucky was a lawyer, railroad administrator, and the author of the book *War History of American Railroads.* FRANK THOMAS HINES (1879–1960) of Utah was an army officer. He is credited with transporting 2 million soldiers to and from Europe. He headed the Veterans' Bureau and reorganized the Veterans' Administration. DUNCAN HINES

(1880–1959) of Kentucky was an American food critic. He worked as a traveling salesman and kept a log of places worth noting where he had eaten in his travels. He published three books on the subject. EARL KENNETH HINES (1905–1983) of Pennsylvania was a big-band-era piano player. He was known as "Fatha" Hines.

Genealogies: *Hines and Allied Families: Some Descendants of William Hines of Sussex County, Virginia (ca. 1690–1760) and a Record of Their Principal Allied Families, Watson (Virginia, Mississippi); Shackelford (Virginia, South Carolina, Georgia); Nisbet (North Carolina, Georgia); and Kennon (Virginia)* was compiled by Benjamin McFarland Hines and published in 1981. *John William Hines, born c. 1600 in Londonderry, Ireland: His Descendants, Principally of North Carolina and Virginia, and their Associated Families* was compiled by William Neal Hurley and published in Bowie, Maryland, in 1992.

HINKLEY (S.S. Abbreviation: Hinkle)

Ranking: 1150 S.S. Count: 38,122

Origin: English. Derived from the Old English first name Hȳnca (itself derived from the Old English word "hūn," meaning bear cub) and the word "lēah," which means wood. The name was given to those who came from Hinckley, the name of a place in Leicestershire County in England.

Genealogies: *Norris, Hackett, Prescott and Allied Families: Our Ancestors and Their Descendants, Including Adams, Andrews, Bachelder, Bartlett, Boulter, Brewer, Brown, Harding, Hinkley, Howard, Huntington, et. al.* was compiled by Hugh Albert Johnson and published in Annandale, Virginia, in 1976. *Reminiscences and Genealogy of the Joel Hinkley and Amos Hackett Families* was compiled by Margaret R. Carver and Kathryn H. Bowers and published in Tacoma, Washington, in 1971. *Ancestors and Descendants of Martin V. Warren and Anna Elizabeth Hinkle* was compiled by Wallace Mock and most likely published in Ridgeville, Indiana, in 1981. *McLeod, Stovall, Hinkle, and Allied Families* was compiled by Daniel McLeod Peterson and published in Raleigh, North Carolina, in 1978.

HINOJO (ALSO HINOJOSA)

Ranking: 2232 S.S. Count: 20,506

Origin: Spanish. Hinojo: derived from the Latin word "fenuclum," which means hay. The name was given to those who worked growing or selling fennel, a popular plant used as an herb for food seasoning during the Middle Ages. The name may also have been given to those who lived on or near an area where fennel was grown, or it may have been given as a nickname to those who used the plant generously in their cooking. Hinojosa: derived from the Spanish word "hinojo," which means fennel. The name was given to those who came from Hinojosa, the name of various places in Spain.

Genealogies: None known.

HINSON

Ranking: 1663 S.S. Count: 26,908

Origin: English. Derived from a now-unknown medieval first name such as the Old English first names H[amy]nci or Hȳnca, which are derived from the Old English word "hūn," meaning bear cub.

Genealogies: None known.

HINTON

Ranking: 911 S.S. Count: 47,394

Origin: English. 1) derived from the Old English words "hēan" and "tūn," meaning high and settlement. The name was given to those who came from Hinton, the name of a place in several counties in England, including Berkshire, Dorset, Gloucestershire, Hampshire, Herefordshire, Somerset, and Wiltshire. 2) derived from the Old English words "hiwan" and "tūn," meaning household (of servants) or monastery and settlement. The name was given to those who came from Hinton, the name of a place in several counties in England, including Cambridgeshire, Dorset, Gloucestershire, Herefordshire, Northamptonshire, Shropshire, Somerset, Suffolk, and Wiltshire.

Genealogies: *The Hintons of Nash and Johnston Counties, North Carolina* was compiled by Judith Garner Hinton and published in Baltimore, Maryland, in 1990. *Hinton and Related Family History* was compiled by George Washington Hinton and most likely published in Everett, Washington, in 1971.

HINTZ

Ranking: 4478 S.S. Count: 10,002

Origin: German. Cognate to the English and French definitions of Henry.

Genealogies: *The Descendants of Gottfried & Wilhelmine Griepp & their Hintz & Rathke Kinships* was compiled by Frank R. and Muriel H. Griepp and published in Smithtown, New York, in 1980.

HIRSCH (ALSO HIRSCHBEIN, HIRSCHBERG, HIRSCHBERGER)

Ranking: 1054 S.S. Count: 41,728

Origin: Hirsch—German, Jewish. Hirschbein, Hirschberg, Hirschberger—Jewish. Hirsch (German): derived from the Old High German word "hir(u)z," which means deer. The name was given to those who owned or tended deer. It may also have been given to those who were thought to look like a deer in some way. Hirsch (Jewish): 1) derived from the Yiddish first name Hirsh, meaning deer. The name is common because the biblical figure Naftali, the son of Jacob, is at one point described as a female red deer. 2) derived from the German word "hirsch" or its Yiddish cognate "hirsh," meaning deer. The name was taken ornamentally. Hirschbein: derived from the German words "hirsch" (or its Yiddish cognate

"hirsh") and "bein," meaning deer and leg. The name was taken ornamentally. Hirschberg, Hirschberger: 1) derived from the German words "hirsch" (or its Yiddish cognate "hirsh") and "berg," meaning deer and hill. The name was taken ornamentally. 2) derived from the German and Yiddish family names Hirsch and Berg, meaning deer and hill. The name was given to those who came from Hirschberg, the name of several places in the Thuringia and North Rhine–Westphalia regions of Germany. The name was also common in what is now Jelenia Góra in western Poland.

Famous **Bearers:** SAMUEL HIRSCH (1815–1889) of Germany was an American clergyman and the author of *Religions Philosophie der Juden.* EMIL GUSTAV HIRSCH (1851–1923) of Luxembourg was a professor at the University of Chicago. He also was the editor of *The Jewish Encyclopedia.* ISAAC SETH HIRSCH (1880–1942) of New York was a physician who specialized in the field of radiology. At Bellevue Hospital in New York City, he is credited with making the radiology department one of the best in the country. MAXIMILLIAN JUSTICE HIRSCH (1880–1969) of Texas was a horse trainer. He was one of the best in his business in his day.

Genealogies: *Descendants of Joseph Nicholas Ammann, Franz Felchli, John Jacob Hirsch, and Joseph Marti* was compiled by Albert Oscar Felchlia and published in Highland, Illinois, in 1984.

HITCHCOCK, HITCHCOE, HITCHCOTT, HITCHCOX (S.S. Abbreviation: Hitchc)

Ranking: 2214 S.S. Count: 20,737

Origin: English. Transformation of Hick(s).

Famous **Bearers:** ENOS HITCHCOCK (1744–1803) of Massachusetts was a clergyman who served as a Revolutionary War army chaplain. He wrote several books after the war, including *Memoirs of the Bloomsgrove Family* and *The Farmer's Friend.* EDWARD HITCHCOCK (1793–1864) of Massachusetts was a geologist. He was responsible for a geological survey of Massachusetts, was the investigator of the dinosaur tracks in Connecticut, and was the state geologist of Vermont. He also wrote several books detailing his experiences. LAMBERT HITCHCOCK (1795–1852) of Connecticut was a furniture manufacturer. His pieces are known for their painted designs. HENRY HITCHCOCK (1829–1902) of Alabama was a Union soldier and the brother of Ethan Allen Hitchcock. He organized the Washington University law school and served as its first dean. PHINEAS WARRENER HITCHCOCK (1831–1881) of New York was a lawyer and politician. In politics, he represented Nebraska. ETHAN ALLEN HITCHCOCK (1835–1909) of Alabama was the brother of Henry Hitchcock. Ethan was influential in the American steel and glass manufacturing businesses. He entered the political field in 1897 as a foreign minister and diplomat and found it not to his liking.

It has been claimed and denied that President Theodore Roosevelt welcomed his resignation in 1907. EDWARD HITCHCOCK (1828–1911) of Massachusetts was the son of Edward (1793–1864). He was the first professor of physical education in an American college. The college was Amherst. GILBERT MONELL HITCHCOCK (1859–1934) of Nebraska was a politician who served as a member of Congress, then as a U.S. senator, from Nebraska. He supported the Treaty of Versailles. He was the son of Phineas. FRANK HARRIS HITCHCOCK (1869?–1935) of Ohio was a politician. He was President William Howard Taft's campaign manager and the postmaster general who initiated postal savings banks and parcel post and started the first air-mail service. THOMAS HITCHCOCK JR. (1900–1944) of South Carolina was considered one of the greatest polo players of his time. He was killed in a plane crash during World War II.

Genealogies: *Genealogy of John Drennen Hitchcock, His Brother and Sisters and Their Descendants, 1863–1983* was compiled by John H. Hitchcock and published in Princeton, Massachusetts, most likely in 1984. *Genealogy of Tidal Hitchock and His Descendants* was compiled by Francis E. Hitchcock and published in Princeton, Massachusetts, in 1982.

HITE

Ranking: 2679 **S.S. Count:** 17,035
Origin: English. Derived from the Old English word "hiêhðu," meaning summit. The name was given to those who lived on top of a hill or on a gradient.
Famous **Hites:** JOST HITE (?–1760) of Strasbourg, Alsace, arrived in America in 1710. He helped with settlements in New York and Pennsylvania before colonizing the Winchester, Virginia, area.
Genealogies: *Jost Hite—From the Neckar to the Shenandoah* was compiled by Ralph Connor and published in Chicago, Illinois, in 1980. *German Origins of Jost Hite, Virginia Pioneer, 1685–1761* was compiled by Henry Z. Jones and published in Edinburg, Virginia, in 1979.

HITTER, HITTLER (S.S. Abbreviation: Hitt)

Ranking: 4078 **S.S. Count:** 11,079
Origin: German. Hitter: derived from the German name Hüter, meaning protector, which is itself derived from the Old High German word "huotan," meaning to guard. The name was given to those who worked as watchmen, guards, or herdsmen. Hittler: derived from the Old High German word "huttea," meaning little hut. The name was probably given to those who lived in little huts, or, in Bavaria, it was given to those who worked as carpenters or builders.
Genealogies: None known.

HIXSON

Ranking: 4734 **S.S. Count:** 9456
Origin: English. Transformation of Hick(s).
Genealogies: *Ten Generations of Hixsons in America (1686–1976)* was compiled by William Amel Sausaman and published in Springfield, Illinois, in 1977.

HO

Ranking: 1956 **S.S. Count:** 23,170
Origin: Chinese. The name means what or to felicitate.
Genealogies: None known.

HOAG

Ranking: 4264 **S.S. Count:** 10,563
Origin: German, Norwegian. 1) the name was given to tall men. 2) the name was given to those who lived on or near a hill, a meadow, or a small burial mound. 3) derived from the name Haug, which is derived from the name Hugo, meaning soul or mind.
Famous **Hoags:** JOSEPH HOAG (1762–1846) of New York was a Quaker preacher who opposed the teachings of Elias Hicks, another Quaker preacher.
Genealogies: *Genealogical Charts of Descendants of John Tierney (born ca. Jan. 27, 1857) and of the Related Families (Barber, Hoag, etc.)* was compiled by Raymond Moran Tierney and published in Oceanport, New Jersey, in the 1970s.

HOAGLAND (S.S. Abbreviation: Hoagla)

Ranking: 4781 **S.S. Count:** 9367
Origin: Norwegian. The name was given to those who lived on a hill or on high, raised ground.
Famous **Hoaglands:** CHARLES LEE HOAGLAND (1907–1946) of Nebraska was a physician and a biochemist whose dedication to science led to his pioneering work in the area of the smallpox virus. He also was working on determining the cause of progressive muscular dystrophy when World War II interrupted his studies. Not being "soldier material," he served his country studying infectious hepatitis and treating the naval personnel suffering from the disease. He died of overwork in 1946. DENNIS ROBERT HOAGLAND (1884–1949) of Colorado was a plant physiologist and soil chemist. He made advances in the field of plant and soil interrelations.
Genealogies: *Dirck Jansen Hoogland Family History, 1657–1976. A Hoogland, Hogeland, Hoagland, Hoaglin Genealogy* was compiled by George Williams Hoagland and published in Cleveland, Ohio, in 1976.

HOANG

Ranking: 4407 **S.S. Count:** 10,171
Origin: Vietnamese. The name means yellow.
Genealogies: None known.

HOBBS

Ranking: 628 **S.S. Count:** 66,210

Origin: English. Derived from the medieval first name Hobb(e), which is derived from the name Robert.

Famous **Hobbses:** ALFRED CHARLES HOBBS (1812–1891) of Massachusetts was a machine-tool designer and an expert in locks.

Genealogies: *Hobbs and Related Families* was compiled by Ralph L. Hobbs and published in Winnsboro, South Carolina, in 1976. *The Joel Hobbs Family* was compiled by Ada Hobbs Linville and published in Poplar Bluff, Missouri, in 1990.

HOBSON

Ranking: 1943 **S.S. Count:** 23,276

Origin: English. Transformation of Hobb(s).

Famous **Hobsons:** EDWARD HENRY HOBSON (1825–1901) of Kentucky was the Union brigadier general who chased Confederate General J. H. Morgan for 900 miles through Kentucky and Ohio, capturing a large portion of his command. ELIZABETH CHRISTOPHERS KIMBALL HOBSON (1831–1912) of New York was one of the founders of the Bellevue Training School for Nurses. RICHARD PEARSON HOBSON (1870–1937) of Alabama was a career naval officer and a member of Congress from his state.

Genealogies: *Descendants of the May-Hobson-Lain Families* was compiled by Jeanette Lain Swafford and published in Fairfield Bay, Arkansas, in 1989.

HOCKENHULL, HOCKENSMITH (S.S. Abbreviation: Hocken)

Ranking: 4355 **S.S. Count:** 10,297

Origin: Hockenhull—English; Hockensmith—German. Hockenhull: the name was given to those who came from Hockenhull, which means "Hoca's hill" (ES) and is a place in Cheshire County, England. Hockensmith: the name was given to those who worked making hoes or short-handled axes.

Genealogies: None known.

HODGE

Ranking: 569 **S.S. Count:** 72,483

Origin: English. 1) derived from the medieval first name Hodge, which is derived from the name Roger. 2) derived from the Middle English word "hodge," meaning hog. The name was often given as a nickname to those who were thought to resemble hogs.

Famous **Hodges:** HUGH LENOX HODGE (1796–1873) of Pennsylvania was a designer of obstetrical instruments. He was the brother of Charles. CHARLES HODGE (1797–1878) of Pennsylvania was a scholar and theologian. He founded and edited the *Biblical Reportory and Princeton Review*. JOHN REED HODGE (1893–1963) of Illinois was an army officer called the "Patton of the Pacific."

He was a career army officer who attained the rank of general.

Genealogies: *Philo Hodge (1756–1842) of Roxbury, Connecticut* was compiled by Barbara Jean Mathews and published in Baltimore, Maryland, in 1992. *The Hodge/Hodges Book: Focus on Virginia-Tennessee-Arkansas Descendants of William Riley Hodge, M.G.* was compiled by Thomas Allen Bruce and published in Little Rock, Arkansas, in 1982.

HODGES

Ranking: 405 **S.S. Count:** 96,954

Origin: English. Transformation of Hodge.

Famous **Hodgeses:** HARRY FOOTE HODGES (1860–1929) of Massachusetts was a military engineer. He is remembered as the engineer who designed locks, dams, and regulating works on the Panama Canal. COURTNEY HICKS HODGES (1887–1966) of Georgia was a soldier whose dream of becoming a soldier led him to rise through the ranks eventually to become the commander who headed the invasion of Japan during World War II.

Genealogies: *The Family of Isham and Betsy Hodges from Virginia to Tennessee* was compiled by Juanita Maxine Patton and most likely published in Nashville, Tennessee, in 1990. *The Hodge/Hodges Book: Focus on Virginia-Tennessee-Arkansas Descendants of William Riley Hodge, M.G.* was compiled by Thomas Allen Bruce and published in Little Rock, Arkansas, in 1982.

HODGSON (S.S. Abbreviation: Hodgso)

Ranking: 3273 **S.S. Count:** 13,865

Origin: English. Transformation of Hodge.

Famous **Hodgsons:** WILLIAM BROWN HODGSON (1801–1871) of Washington, D.C., was a pioneer in the study of the Berber languages.

Genealogies: None known.

HOFER

Ranking: 4321 **S.S. Count:** 10,379

Origin: German. Derived from the Old High German word "hof," meaning far or settlement, and the suffix "er," which denotes human nouns. The name was given to those who lived at a now-unknown farmstead in Germany.

Genealogies: *Hofer-Donaldson History and Families by Marriage, 1700s–1979* was compiled by Fred Hoofer and published in Fremond, Nebraska, in 1979.

HOFF

Ranking: 1886 **S.S. Count:** 23,976

Origin: German. Transformation of Hofer.

Famous **Hoffs:** JOHN VAN RENSSELAER HOFF (1848–1920) of New York was the army medical officer who was responsible for the establishment of military rank and status for medical personnel in the service.

Genealogies: *Genesis, Hoffs & Hooffs of Virginia, 1730 to 1980* was compiled by Betty Hoff Lemons and published in Vienna, Virginia, in 1980.

HOFFER (ALSO HOFFERT)

Ranking: 3736 **S.S. Count:** 12,105

Origin: Hoffert—German; Hoffer—German, Jewish. *Hoffert, Hoffer (German): transformation of Hofer. Hoffer (Jewish): transformation of the Jewish definition of Hoffmann.*

Genealogies: *The History of the Daniel and Sarah (Heberling) Hoffer Family* was compiled by Giles Hoffer and published in Northglenn, Colorado, in 1975. *The Hoffer Families From Hoffer Hill, Rarden, Ohio, Scioto County* was compiled by Relva O. (Spears) Brown and published in Sardinia, Ohio, in 1984.

HOFFMAN, HOFFMANN (S.S. Abbreviation: Hoffma)

Ranking: 142 **S.S. Count:** 215,950

Origin: German, Jewish. *German: 1) derived from the Middle High German words "hof" and "mann," meaning settlement or farm and man. The name was given to farmers who were landowners instead of property renters or tenant farmers with obligations to the feudal lord. 2) same derivation as in 1. The name was given to the overseer or caretaker of an estate. Jewish: uncertain etymology. Possibly derived from the German word "hoffen" and its Yiddish cognate "hofn," meaning to hope. The name may have been taken as an expression of hope for a future free from tyranny. The name may also have been given to the overseer or caretaker of an estate.*

Famous Bearers: DAVID HOFFMAN (1784–1854) of Maryland was a lawyer whose grasp of the law in the study of statutes and forms was ahead of his time. DAVID MURRAY HOFFMAN (1791–1878) of New York was involved in the revision of the New York Code. OGDEN HOFFMAN (1793–1856) of New York was considered the outstanding criminal lawyer of his time. JOHN THOMPSON HOFFMAN (1828–1888) of New York was mayor of New York City, then governor of New York. He was involved in the corrupt government of New York known as Tammany Hall. FREDERICK LUDWIG HOFFMAN (1865–1946) of Germany was one of the founders of the American Cancer Society. MALVINA CORNELL HOFFMAN (1885–1966) of New York was a sculptor. Her greatest achievement was her series of racial types commissioned by the Field Museum of Natural History in Chicago. The series consisted of more than 100 figures that took five years of research and studio time to complete. PAUL GRAY HOFFMAN (1891–1974) of Illinois was an American businessman who worked with major American busi-

nesses and the UN as an adviser on economic affairs. P. BROWNING HOFFMAN (1937–1979), an educator, was a pioneer in integrating the study of law and psychiatry. He was the founding director of the Institute of Law, Psychiatry, and Public Policy at the University of Virginia. He also wrote or co-wrote many professional articles.

Genealogies: *The Hoffman-Schemel Families: Being a History and Genealogy of the Families of Jacob Hoffman (1808– 1869), Michael Schemel, Sr. (1812– 1882), and Related Families* was compiled by Larry Hoehn and published in 1982. *Hoffmans in America in the 18th and 19th Centuries: a Source Book About People Bearing the Name of Hoffman, Huffman, Hofmann, etc., with Emphasis on Those Who Resided in Virginia, West Virginia, Indiana, and Ohio* was compiled by Ruth Vernette McKee and published in Minneapolis, Minnesota, in 1989.

HOFMAN, HOFMANN (S.S. Abbreviation: Hofman)

Ranking: 2838 **S.S. Count:** 16,077

Origin: Hofman—German; Hofmann—Jewish. *Transformations of and cognates to Hoffmann.*

Famous Bearers: HEINRICH OSCAR HOFMAN (1852–1924) of Germany was a professor at Massachusetts Institute of Technology. A metallurgist, he wrote *Metallurgy of Lead and the Desilverization of Base Bullion*, which became a standard in his field. JOSEF CASIMIR HOFMANN (1876–1957) of Poland was a piano virtuoso and a child prodigy. He wrote concertos and piano pieces. HANS HOFMANN (1880–1966) of Germany was a painter in the United States. His was a modern style of painting with geometric shapes and splashes of color.

Genealogies: *Hoffmans in America in the 18th and 19th Centuries: a Source Book About People Bearing the Name of Hoffman, Huffman, Hofmann, etc., with Emphasis on Those Who Resided in Virginia, West Virginia, Indiana, and Ohio* was compiled by Ruth Vernette McKee and published in Minneapolis, Minnesota, in 1989.

HOGAN

Ranking: 463 **S.S. Count:** 86,571

Origin: Irish. *Derived from the Gaelic name Ó hÓgáin, meaning "descendant of Ógán" (H&H), which is a first name derived from the word "óg," meaning young.*

Famous Hogans: JOHN HOGAN (1805–1892) of Ireland was a Methodist minister and a Missouri politician.

Genealogies: None known.

HOGG

Ranking: 3948 **S.S. Count:** 11,448

Origin: English, Irish, Scottish. *English, Scottish: derived from the Middle English word "hog," meaning pig. The name was given to those who worked as swineherds, and it may have been given to those who were thought to look like pigs. It is notable that a pig in the Middle Ages was not necessarily considered unclean, and the nickname, therefore, made no reference to tidiness. Irish, Scottish: derived from the Gaelic name Mac an Bhfabh, which means "son of the hog" (H&H).*

Famous **Hoggs**: GEORGE HOGG (1784–1849) of England was a merchant, glass manufacturer, and operator of lake and river shipping. He was a pioneer in chain stores. JAMES STEPHEN HOGG (1851–1906) of Texas was the Texas attorney general who cleaned up the corruption in corporations, railroads, and land companies. IMA HOGG (1882–1975) of Texas was a philanthropist who put her money to use in the areas of mental health and music. Despite the stories, Ima did not have a sister named Ura. She had only three brothers. Her name came from the heroine of a poem that had been written by her uncle and had nothing to do with her father's wishing to keep her humble.

Genealogies: None known.

HOGUE

Ranking: 2107 **S.S. Count:** 21,789

Origin: English. 1) the name was given to those who lived on a small hill, at a burial mound, or near a fenced-in meadow where sheep were kept. 2) the name was given to those who were thought to resemble pigs. 3) the name was given to those who worked as swineherds. 4) the name was given to those who lived near the "sign of the hog" (ES).

Famous **Hogues**: WILSON THOMAS HOGUE (1852–1920) of New York was a minister and bishop in the Free Methodist Church. He also served as the president of Greenville College in Illinois.

Genealogies: None known.

HOKE

Ranking: 3726 **S.S. Count:** 12,126

Origin: English. The name was given to those who lived near a lateral ridge projecting from a mountain, or near a bend in a mountain.

Famous **Hokes**: ROBERT FREDERICK HOKE (1837–1912) of North Carolina was a Confederate soldier who served with and was well thought of by General Robert E. Lee.

Genealogies: *A History of the Hock, (anglicized) Hoke Family, 1405–1990* was compiled by Patricia A. Hoke and most likely published in New Carlisle, Ohio, in 1990.

HOLBERD, HOLBERT (S.S. Abbreviation: Holber)

Ranking: 4496 **S.S. Count:** 9969

Origin: English. Derived from the Middle English name Holbert, which is most probably derived from Holdbeorht, an unrecorded Old English name composed of the Germanic

words "hold" and "berht," meaning friendly and renowned or resplendent.

Genealogies: *The Root Family of Bolivar, New York: A History of the Descendants of Abel Root, Sr., Who Settled Bolivar in Allegany County, New York: Related Families, Cook, Ennis, Holland, Hulbert, Johnson, Nichols, Nulsen, Richardson, Weatherell, Withey* (also Holbert) was compiled by William A. Paquette and published in Baltimore, Maryland, in 1991.

HOLBROCK, HOLBROOK, HOLBROOKE (S.S. Abbreviation: Holbro)

Ranking: 1329 **S.S. Count:** 33,287

Origin: English. Derived from the Old English words "hol" and "brōc," meaning hollow and stream. The name was given to those who lived in Holbrook, the name of a place in various counties in England, including Derbyshire, Dorset, and Suffolk. The name was also common in Hanover, Germany.

Famous **Bearers**: JOSIAH HOLBROOK (1788–1854) of Connecticut was the originator of the American Lyceum movement. JONATHAN EDWARDS HOLBROOK (1794–1871) of South Carolina was a physician and a zoologist. He published *North American Herpetology* and *Ichthyology of South Carolina*. FREDERICK HOLBROOK (1813–1909) of Connecticut was a farmer and the governor of Vermont. ALFRED HOLBROOK (1816–1909) of Connecticut was a pioneer trainer of teachers. He founded Lebanon University in Ohio. STEWART HALL HOLBROOK (1893–1964) of Vermont was a journalist and a historian. Two of his books are titled *Holy Old Mackinaw: A Natural History of the American Lumberjack* and *The Story of American Railroads.*

Genealogies: *Colonial Holbrook Lines of America: An Overview of Research Findings With an Accounting of All Holbrook Found in the Records* was compiled by J. C. Holbrooks and published in Sterling, Connecticut, in 1982. *Pioneers: Five Families—Morse, Holbrook, Brown, Wright, Perrine* was compiled by Bianca Morse Federico and published in Washington, D.C., in 1977.

HOLCOM (ALSO HOLCOMB, HOLCOMBE)

Ranking: 814 **S.S. Count:** 51,945

Origin: English. Derived from the Old English words "hol" and "cumb," meaning depressed or sunken, and short, straight valley. The name was given to those who came from Holcombe, the name of a place in various counties in England, including Devon, Dorset, Gloucestershire, and Lancashire.

Famous **Bearers**: HENRY HOLCOMBE (1762–1824) of Virginia was a Baptist clergyman in South Carolina, Georgia, and Pennsylvania. AMASA HOLCOMB (1787–1875) of Massachusetts was a maker of telescopes. He also experimented with camera lenses. JAMES PHILEMON HOLCOMBE

(1820–1873) of Virginia was a lawyer, a writer of legal matters, a law professor at the University of Virginia, a Confederate politician, and a secret agent in Canada in 1864. WILLIAM HENRY HOLCOMBE (1825–1893) of Virginia was a homeopathic physician and an expert on yellow fever. CHESTER HOLCOMBE (1844–1912) of New York was a missionary to China who helped draft the treaty with China in 1880 and the 1882 treaty with Korea. SILAS ALEXANDER HOLCOMB (1858–1920) of Indiana was the governor of Nebraska and a state supreme court justice.

Genealogies: *Holcombe-Doane-Henke Family History 1812–1983* was compiled by Mary Alice Henke and published in Enders, Nebraska, in 1983. *Holcombe Ancestral Lineage* was compiled by Mabel Thacher Rosemary Washburn and most likely published in the 1930s.

HOLDEN
Ranking: 892 S.S. Count: 48,669
Origin: English. Derived from the Old English words "hol" and "denu," meaning depressed or deep and valley. The name was given to those who came from Holden, the name of a place in Lancashire and West Yorkshire counties in England.

Famous **Holdens:** OLIVER HOLDEN (1765–1844) of Massachusetts was a composer of hymns. *Union Harmony* contains 40 of his hymns. WILLIAM WOODS HOLDEN (1818–1892) of North Carolina was a governor of North Carolina who was impeached. LIBERTY EMERY HOLDEN (1833–1913) of Maine was a financier and mine owner. EDWARD SINGLETON HOLDEN (1846–1914) of Missouri was an astronomer and the director of the Lick Observatory. HALE HOLDEN (1869–1940) of Missouri was a lawyer and a railroad officer.

Genealogies: *John Holden of St. Armand, Quebec and Franklin, Vermont, The Family and Descendants* was compiled by Phyllis V. Owen and published in Alberta, Canada, in 1976. *Manuscript Genealogy of Holden Family* was compiled by F. A. Holden and published in 1870.

HOLDER (ALSO HOLDERBAUM, HOLDERER, HÖLDERLE, HOLDERMANN, HOLDERNESS)
Ranking: 796 S.S. Count: 52,997
Origin: Holderness—English; Holder—English, German, Jewish; Holderbaum, Holderer, Hölderle, Holdermann—German. Holder (German), Holderbaum, Holderer, Hölderle, Holdermann: derived from the Old High German word "holuntar" or "holantar," meaning elder tree. The name was given to those who lived near an elder tree. Holder (English): derived from the Old English word "h(e)aldan," meaning to guard or keep. The name was given to those who tended animals or to those who owned land in the feudal system. Holder (Jewish): derived from the German name Hol(un)der, which means elder tree. The name was taken ornamentally. Holder-

ness: derived from the Old Norse words "holdr" (a Danelaw title of nobility in the Middle Ages, directly under the title of earl) and "nœs," meaning nose or headland.

Famous **Bearers:** JOSEPH BASSETT HOLDER (1824–1888) of Massachusetts was a marine zoologist who made studies of coral formation. CHARLES FREDERICK HOLDER (1851–1915) of Massachusetts was the founder of the "Tournament of Roses" in Pasadena, California, and the developer of tuna fishing as a sport. He was the son of Joseph.

Genealogies: None known.

HOLGUIN (S.S. Abbreviation: Holgui)
Ranking: 4303 S.S. Count: 10,427
Origin: Spanish. Uncertain etymology.
Genealogies: None known.

HOLLAND, HOLLANDE, HOLLANDER, HOLLANDS (S.S. Abbreviation: Hollan)
Ranking: 225 S.S. Count: 156,655
Origin: Dutch, English, Flemish, German, Irish, Jewish. English: derived from the Old English words "hōh" and "land," meaning ridge and land. The name was given to those who came from Holland, the name of eight villages all over England. Dutch, Flemish, German, Jewish: derived from the Middle Low German words "hol" and "land," meaning depressed or deep and land. The name may be derived from another unknown initial word that makes reference to marshlands. The name comes from Holland, the name of a county of the Holy Roman Empire in The Netherlands. Irish: 1) derived from the Gaelic name Ó hUallacháin, meaning descendant of "Uallachán" (H&H), which is a first name derived from the word "úallach," meaning proud or arrogant. 2) derived from the Gaelic name Ó Maolchalann, meaning "descendant of the devotee of St. Calann" (H&H). 3) derived from the Gaelic name Ó Faoláin, meaning "descendant of Faolán" (H&H), which is a personal name derived from the word "faol," meaning wolf.

Famous **Bearers:** EDWIN CLIFFORD HOLLAND (1794?–1824) of South Carolina was an author of poetry. His *Odes, Naval Songs and Other Poems* in 1813 marked the beginning of the romantic period in South Carolina. JOSIAH GILBERT HOLLAND (1819–1881) of Massachusetts was an editor and author of popular books of the time. JOHN PHILIP HOLLAND (1840–1914) of Ireland was an inventor. His specialty was as a builder of submarines. WILLIAM JACOB HOLLAND (1848–1932) of Jamaica was director of the Carnegie Museum of Pittsburgh and the sponsor of fossil explorations in the West. He also wrote *The Butterfly Book* and *The Moth Book*. JACOB HARRY HOLLANDER (1871–1940) of Maryland was an economist who worked as a financial advisor on Puerto Rican finances and a financial advisor to the Dominican Republic. CLIFFORD

MILBRUN HOLLAND (1883–1924) of Massachusetts was a civil engineer and the builder of the New Jersey–New York tunnel under the Hudson River that bears his name.

Genealogies: *Gone to Texas: A Compendium of the Dulany, Haddox, Heaton, Holland and Martin Families* was compiled by Mary Rebecca Scott and published in Tomball, Texas, in 1989.

HOLLEN (ALSO HOLLENS, HOLLENZER)

Ranking: 2180 S.S. Count: 21,042

Origin: Hollen, Hollens—English; Hollenzer—Hungarian. Hollen, Hollens: transformation of Hollis. Hollenzer: cognate to the Dutch, Flemish, German, and Jewish definitions of Holland.

Genealogies: None known.

HOLLER

Ranking: 3648 S.S. Count: 12,366

Origin: German. The name was given to those who lived near an elder tree or in a low, unplowed valley.

Genealogies: *Haller-Hollar-Holler Genealogy* was compiled by Amelia Cleland Gilreath and published in Nokesille, California, in 1981.

HOLLEY

Ranking: 1057 S.S. Count: 41,699

Origin: English. Transformation of Hollis.

Famous **Holleys:** MYRON HOLLEY (1779–1841) of Connecticut was responsible for the formation of the Liberty Party. HORACE HOLLEY (1781–1827) of Connecticut was one of the great presidents of Transylvania University. He and Myron were brothers. Horace Holley's wife, MARY PHELPS AUSTIN HOLLEY (1784–1846) of Connecticut was a writer and land speculator in Texas. She was the cousin of Stephen F. Austin, the founder of Texas, and she was the author of *Texas: Observations Historical, Geographical and Descriptive.* SALLIE HOLLEY (1818–1893) of New York was the niece of Horace Holley. She was an abolitionist and a teacher of the newly freed slaves from the Civil War. Her school in Virginia was known as the Holley School. ALEXANDER LYMAN HOLLEY (1832–1882) of Connecticut was a mechanical engineer who applied his education to locomotives. He published *Holley's Railroad Advocate.* He became involved with the steel industry, buying the American rights to the Bessemer process. Today he is considered the "father of modern American steel manufacture." MARIETTA HOLLEY (1836–1926) of New York was an author, a humorist, and a speaker for women's rights and temperance.

Genealogies: None known.

HOLLIDAY (S.S. Abbreviation: Hollid)

Ranking: 1559 S.S. Count: 28,591

Origin: English, Scottish. Derived from the Old English word "hāligdœg," meaning holy day or spiritual festival. It is unclear why this became a family name; it may have been given to people who were born on religious holidays such as Christmas or Easter.

Famous **Hollidays:** CYRUS KURTZ HOLLIDAY (1826–1900) of Pennsylvania was the founder of the town of Topeka, Kansas. He also was responsible for the charter for the Atchison, Topeka & Sante Fe Railroad, of which he served as president and director. JUDY HOLLIDAY (1921–1965) of New York was an actress of great abilities whose career was cut short when she was blacklisted during the McCarthy hearings of the 1950s.

Genealogies: *The Holladay (also Holliday) Family* was compiled by Alvis Milton Holladay Sr. and published in Brentwood, Tennessee, in 1983. *In Search of the Hollidays; the Story of Doc Holliday and His Holliday and McKey Families* was compiled by Albert S. Pendleton Jr. and published in Valdosta, Georgia, in 1973.

HOLLING, HOLLINGS, HOLLINGSHEAD, HOLLINGSWORTH, HOLLINGTON, HOLLINS (S.S. Abbreviation: Hollin)

Ranking: 616 S.S. Count: 67,783

Origin: English. Holling, Hollings, Hollins: transformations of Hollis. Hollingshead: derived from the Old English words "hole(g)n" and "side," meaning holly and side of a hill. The name was given to those who came from a now-unknown place in Durham County, England, probably called Hollingside or Holmside. Hollingsworth: derived from the Old English words "hole(g)n" and "worð," meaning holly and enclosure. The name was given to those who came from Hollingworth, the name of places in Cheshire and Lancashire counties in England. Hollington: derived from the Old English words "hole(g)n" and "tūn," meaning holly and enclosure or settlement. The name was given to those who came from Hollington, the name of places in Derbyshire, Staffordshire, and Sussex counties in England.

Famous **Bearers:** GEORGE NICHOLS HOLLINS (1799–1878) of Maryland was a U.S. naval officer who resigned in favor of the Confederacy in 1861. He was the commander of the naval forces at New Orleans in 1861 and the upper Mississippi in 1862 when his advice on the defense of New Orleans was ignored.

Genealogies: *Burgard, Hollinger Families* was compiled by O. D. and Elizabeth Corbridge and published in Astoria, Illinois, in 1971.

HOLLIS (ALSO HOLLISS, HOLLISTER)

Ranking: 922 S.S. Count: 46,789

Origin: English. Derived from the Old English word "hole(g)n," meaning holly. The name was given to those who lived by a cluster of holly trees.

Famous **Bearers:** GIDEON HIRAM HOLLISTER (1817–1881) of Connecticut was a lawyer and the author of *Mount Hope* and *Kinley Hollow*. IRA NELSON HOLLIS (1856–1930) of Indiana was a naval engineer and educator. He graduated from the naval academy at Annapolis, taught at Harvard University, and was the president of Worcester Polytechnic Institute.

Genealogies: None known.

HOLLOMAN (S.S. Abbreviation: Hollom)

Ranking: 3801 S.S. Count: 11,868

Origin: English. Derived from the Old English words "halig" and "man," meaning holy and man. The name was most often given as a nickname.

Genealogies: None known.

HOLLY

Ranking: 3476 S.S. Count: 12,989

Origin: English. Transformation of Hollis.

Famous **Hollys:** JAMES THEODORE HOLLY (1829–1911) of Washington, D.C., was an Episcopal clergyman who led free blacks to Haiti in 1861.

Genealogies: None known.

HOLM

Ranking: 2425 S.S. Count: 18,696

Origin: Swedish. Cognate to Holme(s).

Genealogies: None known.

HOLMAN

Ranking: 978 S.S. Count: 44,793

Origin: Dutch, English, Flemish. Dutch, Flemish, English: derived from the Old English word "holh," meaning hole. The name was given to those who lived in a depression or hollow. English: derived from the Middle English words "holm" and "man," meaning holly and man. The name was given to those who lived by a holly tree or on an island.

Famous **Holmans:** JESSE LYNCH HOLMAN (1784–1842) of Kentucky was an Indiana pioneer and federal judge in Indiana. WILLIAM STEELE HOLMAN (1822–1897) of Indiana was a member of Congress from Indiana who was Jeffersonian in philosophy. His nicknames were many, including "hay-seed statesmanship," "The Watchdog of the Treasury," and "The Great Objector" to excessive spending.

Genealogies: *Early Carolina Heilmans (Hallmans-Holmans) 1736–1800* was compiled by Elmer Berley Hallman and published in Columbia, South Carolina, in 1972.

HOLMES

Ranking: 143 S.S. Count: 215,365

Origin: English, Scottish. 1) derived from the Middle English word "holm," which is derived from the Old English word "hole(g)n," meaning holly. The name was given to those who

lived by a holly tree. 2) derived from the Old Norse word "holmr," which refers to a mound of land lying in the middle of a bog or marsh. The name was given to those who lived at such a place or to those who lived on an island or a piece of land surrounded by streams. The name may have been given to someone who came from a now-unknown place whose name began with the Old Englsih word "holm," a cognate of the Old Norse word "holmr."

Famous **Holmeses:** ABIEL HOLMES (1763–1837) was a clergyman and the father of Oliver Wendell Holmes (1809–1894). He also wrote *American Annals*, the first well-done account of American history. DAVID HOLMES (1770–1832) of Pennsylvania was goveror of the territory, then the state, of Mississippi. He took part in the annexation of Mobile in 1812. EZEKIEL HOLMES (1801–1865) of Massachusetts was an agriculturalist. He started the first farm journal in Maine to promote scientific agriculture and was one of the founders of the University of Maine. OLIVER WENDELL HOLMES (1809–1894) of Massachusetts was a teacher and poet. He was the author of "Old Ironsides," which appeared in the *Boston Daily Advertiser* in 1830. He was the father of Justice Oliver Wendell Holmes of the U.S. Supreme Court. MARY JANE HAWES HOLMES (1825–1907) of Massachusetts was a romantic novelist. Her first novel was *Tempest or Sunshine; or, Life in Kentucky*, and her best-known was *'Lena Rivers*. She managed to produce a book a year, and her works were very popular in their time. OLIVER WENDELL HOLMES (1841–1935) of Massachusetts was the son of Oliver Wendell Holmes (1809–1894). As a justice of the U.S. Supreme Court, he was known for a number of well-written dissenting opinions, as well as many precedent-setting majority opinions. He formulated the "clear and present danger" test involving the right of free speech. His decisions are considered timeless. JOSEPH AUSTIN HOLMES (1859–1915) of South Carolina was a geologist and mining engineer. He is best remembered as a pioneer in accident prevention in coal mining and is credited with coining the phrase "safety first." JULIUS CECIL HOLMES (1899–1968) of Kansas was a soldier and a diplomat. He influenced many important policies.

Genealogies: *Falling Leaves: A History of the Holmes Family and Allied Lines* was compiled by Marjorie J. Caskey and published in Ozark, Missouri, in 1985. *Holmes Genealogy: a Compilation of Genealogical History About Adams Holmes (1720–1789) of New Braintree, Massachusetts* was compiled by John Albert Holmes and published in Concord Village, Missouri, in 1980.

HOLSTE

Ranking: 4334 S.S. Count: 10,335

Origin: Danish, Dutch, German. Derived from the Middle Low German word "holsäte," composed of the words "holdt" and "säte," meaning wood and tenant. The name was given to those who lived on a tract of woodland.

Genealogies: None known.

HOLT

Ranking: 299 S.S. Count: 120,634

Origin: English. Derived from the Old English word "holt," meaning wood or thicket. The name was given to those who lived in a wood or thicket. It may also have been given to those who came from Holt, the name of several places in England.

Famous **Holts**: JOHN HOLT (1721–1784) of Virginia was a Revolutionary War patroit. He owned pro-Revolutionary newspapers in New York City and Connecticut that the English destroyed during the war. After the war he returned to New York City and edited *The Independent New York Gazette*. He also tried to improve the delivery service of newspapers. JOSEPH HOLT (1807–1894) of Kentucky was the judge who presided over the trial of those accused in the conspiracy to assassinate President Abraham Lincoln. EDWIN MICHAEL HOLT (1807–1884) of North Carolina was a cotton manufacturer and the first to dye yarns. He invented the "Alamance Plaids." HENRY HOLT (1840–1926) of Maryland was an author and publisher who founded the Henry Holt & Co. publishing house. LUTHER EMMETT HOLT (1855–1924) of New York was a pediatrician and the founder of Babies Hospital in New York. He also published several books on the subject of pediatrics. WINIFRED HOLT (1870–1945) of New York dedicated her life to helping the blind. She founded "Lighthouse," which was a place where blind people could earn a living making wares to be sold. She also started a magazine for blind children called *Searchlight*. It was published in Braille. EDWIN BISSELL HOLT (1873–1946) of Massachusetts was a psychologist who believed that consciousness was controlled by one's physical and physiological processes. ARTHUR ERASTUS HOLT (1876–1942) of Colorado was a Congregational clergyman whose greatest concern was justice for those who lived a rural, agrarian life.

Genealogies: *Ancestors and Descendants of John and Isabel Holt, Williamson County, Tennessee* was compiled by Albert L. Cooper and published in Shelbyville, Tennessee, in 1971. *Ancestry of Albright and Holt Families of Clay County, Missouri* was compiled by Claribel Albright McClain and published in St. Joseph, Missouri, in 1984.

HOLTON

Ranking: 2768 S.S. Count: 16,483

Origin: English. 1) derived from the Old English words "hoh" and "tūn," meaning spur of a hill and enclosure or settlement. The name was given to those who came from Holton, the name of several places in Lincolnshire County, England.

2) *derived from the Old English words "halh" and "tūn," meaning cranny or alcove and enclosure or settlement. The name was given to those who came from Holton, the name of several places in Oxfordshire and Somerset counties, in England. 3) derived from the Old English words "holh" and "tūn," meaning hollow or depression and enclosure or settlement. The name was given to those who came from Holton, the name of several places in Dorset County in England. 4) derived from the Old English words "holt" and "tūn," meaning wood and enclosure or settlement. The name was given to those who came from Holton, the name of various places in Dorset County, England. 5) derived from the Old English word "hola" or the first name Hōla and the Old English word "tūn," meaning hollow and enclosure or settlement. The name was given to those who came from Holton, the name of a place in Suffolk County, England.*

Genealogies: None known.

HOLTZ

Ranking: 3409 S.S. Count: 13,269

Origin: German. Cognate to Holt.

Genealogies: None known.

HOMAN

Ranking: 3715 S.S. Count: 12,158

Origin: English. Transformation of and cognate to Holman.

Genealogies: None known.

HONEYCOMBE (S.S. Abbreviation: Honeyc)

Ranking: 1981 S.S. Count: 22,883

Origin: English. 1) derived from the Old English words "hunig" and "cumb," meaning honey and valley. The name was given to those who came from Honeycombe, the name of a place in Cornwall County, England. 2) same derivation as in 1. The name was used as a term of endearment.

Genealogies: None known.

HONG

Ranking: 2878 S.S. Count: 15,811

Origin: Chinese. The name is derived from the Hong dynasty.

Genealogies: None known.

HOOD

Ranking: 529 S.S. Count: 76,314

Origin: English, Irish. English: derived from the Old English word "hōd," meaning hood. The name was given to those who worked making hoods or to those who wore an unusual or flamboyant hood. The name may also have been given to those who lived in a place where the geography provided natural protection, such as, for example, rock formations that acted as shelters. Irish: derived from the Gaelic word Mac hUid, meaning "son of Ud," which is a first name with an uncertain etymology.

Famous **Hoods:** WASHINGTON HOOD (1801–1840) was a topographical engineer who mapped out the Oregon territory. JAMES WALKER HOOD (1831–1918) was an African Methodist Episcopal clergyman and the first black to preside over the Ecumenical Conference. He also served North Carolina as the assistant superintendent of schools. JOHN BELL HOOD (1831–1876) of Kentucky was a Confederate soldier who was a division commander at Gettysburg, was promoted to lieutenant general, and was defeated at Nashville because of strategically poor decisions and relieved of his command. RAYMOND MATHEWSON HOOD (1881–1934) of Rhode Island was an architect and one of the main contributors to the final form of Rockefeller Center in New York City. CLIFFORD F. HOOD (1894–1978) of Illinois was a longtime steel company executive who served as president of United States Steel Corp. (1953–1959).

Genealogies: None known.

HOOK

Ranking: 2326 **S.S. Count:** 19,498

Origin: English, Jewish. English: 1) derived from the Old English word "hōc," meaning hook. The name was given to those who lived by a "hooked" geographical formation such as a ridge projecting from a mountain range or a curve in a river's path. 2) same derivation as in 1. The name was given to those who made or sold hooks as farming tools or to those who used them in their daily work. 3) possibly same derivation as in 1 and 2 but most probably derived from a now-unknown Old English first name. The name was given as a nickname to those who had crooked noses or to those who had hunched backs. Jewish: uncertain etymology.

Genealogies: *Descendants and Ancestors of Benjamin and Ann Frizelle Hooker (also Hook), 1976, with 1977 and 1978, & 1979 Supplements and Revisions Added* was compiled by Malcolm D. Hooker and published in West Liberty, Ohio, in 1979. *William Henry Hooker (also Hook) and Descendants, 1793–1990* was compiled by Jerry Samuel Hooker and published in St. Petersburg, Florida, in 1990. *A Pride of Kin* was compiled by Callie Coe Wilson et al. and published in College Station, Texas, in 1985.

HOOKER

Ranking: 1883 **S.S. Count:** 24,022

Origin: English. Transformation of the first and second definitions of Hook.

Famous **Hookers:** THOMAS HOOKER (1586?–1647) of England was a Congregational clergyman who came to America with the Pilgrims. He settled in Boston, then led the majority of his congregation to Hartford, Connecticut, in the Connecticut Valley. He was one of the authors of the constitution of Connecticut. PHILIP HOOKER (1766–1836)

of Massachusetts was an architect who moved to Albany, New York, as a child. He architecturally transformed Albany from the frontier settlement it had been into a New England-like town. JOSEPH HOOKER (1814–1879) of Massachusetts was a West Point graduate and a career soldier. He was known as "Fighting Joe" and gained fame for his participation in the Civil War. ISABELLE BEECHER HOOKER (1822–1907) of Connecticut was a suffragist and advocate of women's rights. She was one of the founders of the New England Woman Suffrage Association. Her husband, John Hooker, sponsored a married woman's property bill in Connecticut that eventually passed. She was the sister of Harriet Beecher Stowe, the author of *Uncle Tom's Cabin.* DONALD RUSSELL HOOKER (1876–1946) of Connecticut was a physician and is considered a pioneer in the study of the circulatory system. JOHN JAY HOOKER (1903–1970) of Tennessee was a prominent Tennessee lawyer. His best-known cases involved the integration of the University of Tennessee and the prosecution of the noted union boss James R. Hoffa.

Genealogies: *Descendants and Ancestors of Benjamin and Ann Frizelle Hooker, 1976, with 1977 and 1978, & 1979 Supplements and Revisions Added* was compiled by Malcolm D. Hooker and published in West Liberty, Ohio, in 1979. *William Henry Hooker and Descendants, 1793–1990* was compiled by Jerry Samuel Hooker and published in St. Petersburg, Florida, in 1990.

HOOKS

Ranking: 2029 **S.S. Count:** 22,499

Origin: English. Transformation of the first and third definitions of Hook.

Genealogies: *A Pride of Kin* was compiled by Callie Coe Wilson et al. and published in College Station, Texas, in 1985.

HOOPER

Ranking: 882 **S.S. Count:** 49,150

Origin: English. Derived from the Middle English word "hoop," meaning hoop or band. The name was given to those who worked adjusting wooden or metal hoops on barrels or tubs. The name was most common in Devon County, England.

Famous **Hoopers:** WILLIAM HOOPER (1742–1790) of Massachusetts moved to North Carolina, where he practiced law. He also was a member of the Continental Congress and a signer of the Declaration of Independence. SAMUEL HOOPER (1808–1875) of Massachusetts was a member of Congress from his home state. He worked for the establishment of a national banking system, legal-tender notes, and the 1873 Currency Act. ELLEN STURGIS HOOPER (1812–1848) and her sister Caroline Sturgis Tappan were transcendentalist poets. They are best remembered for being part of the transcendentalist movement, which included Ralph Waldo Emerson and Henry David Thoreau. JOHNSON JONES HOOPER (1815–1862) of North Dakota was a journalist/humorist. He portrayed frontiersmen from the South. His stories were printed in the newspapers and in a collection called *Some Adventures of Captain Simon Suggs, Late of the Tallapoosa Volunteers.* FRANKLIN HENRY HOOPER (1862–1940) of Massachusetts was an editor of dictionaries and encyclopedias. JESSIE ANNETTE JACK HOOPER (1865–1935) of Iowa was a suffragist and a peace advocate. She was the founder of the first kindergarten and visiting nurses' program in Oshkosh and a tuberculosis sanitarium in Winnebago County, Wisconsin.

Genealogies: *The Hoopes (also Hooper) Family Record: A Genealogical Record of the Hoopes Family, Descendants of Daniel Hoopes of Westtown, Chester County, Pennsylvania* was compiled by Gerald Ralph Fuller et al. and published in Houston, Texas, in 1979. *We Travel With a Multitude; A History of the Hooper, Sharp, Adams, and Bonnifield Families and Twenty-Five Allied Families, ca. 1700 to 1970, From England, Ireland, France, Germany and Italy to the United States* was compiled by Virginia Sharp Hooper and published in Santa Clara, California, in 1970.

HOOVER

Ranking: 523 **S.S. Count:** 76,844

Origin: German. Transformation of the German and Dutch definitions of Huber.

Famous **Hoovers:** WILLIAM HENRY HOOVER (1849–1932) of Ohio bought a patent from James Murray Spangler for an electric cleaning machine and in 1908 started the Electric Suction Sweeper Co. He changed the name of the company in 1910 to the Hoover Suction Sweeper Co. CHARLES FRANKLIN HOOVER (1865–1927) of Ohio was a physician who specialized in cardiorespiratory, neurological, and hepatic diseases. HERBERT CLARK HOOVER (1874–1964) of Iowa was the 31st president of the United States (1929–1933). LOU HENRY HOOVER (1874–1944) of Iowa was the wife of Herbert Hoover, 31st president of the United States. She devoted part of her time to serving as national president of the Girl Scouts. JOHN EDGAR HOOVER (1895–1972) of Washington, D.C., is best remembered as the man who, as director of the Federal Bureau of Investigation, made the department the top-notch organization it was. He served as its director from 1924–1972.

Genealogies: *The Ancestors of Albina Johnson (Hoover) Lehr; Hoover, Houser, Johnson, Wood, Sharples* was compiled by Stephen J. Kennedy and published in Needham Heights, Massachusetts, most likely in 1980. *Descendants of Peter and Elizabeth Hoover* was compiled by Ruth Hoover Bowers and published in Wayne County, Indiana, in 1978.

HOPE

Ranking: 2005 **S.S. Count:** 22,721

Origin: English, Scottish. 1) derived from the Old English word "hop," which refers to a stretch of fenced-in territory or to an enclosed glen. The name was given to those who lived at or near such a place. 2) same derivation as in 1. The name was given to those who came from Hope, the name of a place in several counties in England, including Cheshire, Devon, Derbyshire, Herefordshire, Kent, Shropshire, and Sussex.

Famous **Hopes:** ROBERT HOPE-JONES (1859–1914) of England was a builder of organs. He founded his own company, called the Hope-Jones Organ Co., but later joined the Wurlitzer Co. JOHN HOPE (1868–1936) of Georgia was an educator of mixed racial background who could have "passed" for the easier life of a white person but chose to work for the education of black youth. He was a professor of the classics on the university level. He taught at Atlanta Baptist College, which became Morehouse College, and he eventually became its president, and then the president of Atlanta University. He was a strong advocate of equality for blacks. CLIFFORD RAGSDALE HOPE (1893–1970) of Iowa was a member of Congress who served 30 years representing the farmer.

Genealogies: *The Marlett Family in Southeast, Midwest, and Southwest United States, With Connections to the Ball, Humphries, Hope, and Cross Families* was compiled by Nadeen Cross Marlett and published in Modesto, California, in 1983. *More . . ., A Supplement in Two Parts to Receipt for An Inheritance* was compiled by Margery Day Hanson and published in Denver, Colorado, in 1983.

HOPKIN (ALSO HOPKINS, HOPKINSON)

Ranking: 265 **S.S. Count:** 137,774

Origin: English. Derived from a now-unknown medieval first name (which was a pet form of the family name Hobb) and the suffix "-kin."

Famous **Bearers:** EDWARD HOPKINS (1600–1657) of England came to Connecticut in 1637. He served as the governor or deputy governor for many years and supported educational institutions in New England. STEPHEN HOPKINS (1707–1785) of Rhode Island was governor of that state and a champion of colonial rights. His newspaper, the *Providence Gazette,* was his outlet for expressing his views on those rights. ESEK HOPKINS (1718–1802) of Rhode Island was the commander in chief of the Continental navy. A loyal patroit, he had difficulty dealing with Congress. SAMUEL HOPKINS (1721–1803) of Connecticut was one of the first Congregational ministers to speak against slavery. He was the man behind the philosophical thought called Hopkinsianism, which greatly influenced New Englanders. FRANCIS HOPKINSON (1737–1791) of Pennsylvania was a signer of the Declaration of Independence and the designer of the American flag in 1777. He also was the first ever to receive a diploma from the College of Philadelphia (1757). LEMUEL HOPKINS (1750–1801) of Connecticut was a physician and a satirist. He specialized in the treatment of tuberculosis with a method that was ahead of its time. As a satirist, he was known as one of the "Hartford Wits." JOSEPH HOPKINSON (1770–1842) of Pennsylvania was the author of "Hail Columbia," which was first performed in Philadelphia, his home town. JOHN HENRY HOPKINS (1792–1868), originally from Ireland, came to America as a child. He was an Episcopal clergyman who effectively brought about the reunion between the northern and southern factions of the church. JOHNS HOPKINS (1795–1873) of Maryland was a merchant and philanthropist who left his fortune for the establishment of a university and hospital. Today these institutions, located in the city of his death, bear his name. JULIET ANN OPIE HOPKINS (1818–1890) of Virginia was a Confederate hospital administrator. During the Civil War her likeness appeared on two denominations of Confederate currency. EDWARD AUGUSTUS HOPKINS (1822–1891) of Pennsylvania was responsible for the establishment of steam navigation on the Panama River and was the builder of a railroad between Buenos Aires and San Fernando. ISAAC STILES HOPKINS (1841–1914) of Georgia was responsible for technological instruction's being added at Emory College. He later became the first president of Georgia School of Technology. EMMA CURTIS HOPKINS (1853–1925) of Connecticut, a leader in the New Thought movement, published her own magazine, *Christian Metaphysician*, for 10 years. CYRIL GEORGE HOPKINS (1866–1919) of Minnesota was an agricultural chemist and an inventor. He devised the "Illinois System" of permanent soil fertility. HARRY LLOYD HOPKINS (1890–1946) of Iowa was a social worker who came to the attention of Franklin D. Roosevelt and became his right-hand man. He was one of the major designers of the New Deal and was such an effective policymaker during World War II that Winston Churchill referred to him as "Lord Root of the Matter." SAM HOPKINS (1912–1982) of Texas is considered one of the greatest country blues musician, and guitarist, in the world.

Genealogies: *Genealogies of the Moore & Hopkins Families of Rockingham & Guilford Counties in North Carolina* was compiled by Beatrice M. Caffey Reed et al. and published in High Point, North Carolina, in 1981. *Hopkins of Virginia and Related Families* was compiled by Walter Lee Hopkins and published in Harrisonburg, Virginia, in 1980.

HOPPE
Ranking: 3414 **S.S. Count:** 13,251
Origin: German. Derived from the Old High German word "hopfo," which means hop plant or hop flower, and the suffix "-er." The name was given to those who grew or traded hops or to brewers who used hops in the making of beer.

Famous **Hoppes:** WILLIAM FREDERICK HOPPE (1887–1959) of New York was known by the name of Willie. He was a billiards player and the world's champion at the 18.1 and 18.2 balkline game and the three-cushion game for many of the years between 1906 and 1952.
Genealogies: None known.

HOPPER
Ranking: 1093 **S.S. Count:** 40,422
Origin: German. Derived from the Middle Low German word "huppen," meaning to hop, skip, or jump. The name was given to professional acrobats or gymnasts at a fair. It may also have been given to someone who was nervous or fidgety and therefore moved about a lot.

Famous **Hoppers:** ISAAC TATEM HOPPER (1771–1852) of New Jersey was a major "conductor" on the Underground Railroad. DE WOLF HOPPER (1858–1935) of New York was an actor and singer best remembered for his rendition of "Casey at the Bat." EDWARD HOPPER (1882–1967) of New York was a painter whose realist paintings include the well-known *House by the Railroad*. HEDDA HOPPER (1885–1966), born Elda Furry in Pennsylvania, was an actress and gossip columnist.

Genealogies: *Ancestors and Descendants of Patty Backburn Davis: Davis, Hopper, Mays, Smith, Terrel, Blackburn, Bolton, Hale: Including Local History and Memorabilia of Barbourville, Kentucky, and Surrounding Areas* was compiled by Patty Dahm Pascoe and published in Baltimore, Maryland, in 1984. *A Study of the West-Hopper and Allied Families* was compiled by George Henry West and published in Durham, North Carolina, in 1973.

HOPSON
Ranking: 2900 **S.S. Count:** 15,693
Origin: English. Transformation of Hobb(s).

Famous **Hopsons:** HOWARD COLWELL HOPSON (1882–1949) of Wisconsin was a utilities executive who was ruined by the stock market crash of 1929. He was found guilty of fraud and sent to prison.
Genealogies: *Some Very Fine Folks; Hopson* was compiled by George Royalty Hopson and published in San Angelo, Texas, in the 1970s.

HORAN
Ranking: 3036 **S.S. Count:** 14,981
Origin: Irish. 1) derived from the Gaelic name Ó hUghróin, meaning "descendant of Ughrón" (H&H), which is a first name derived from the word "ughrach," meaning warlike. 2) derived from the Gaelic name Ó hOdhráin, meaning "descendant of Odhrán" (H&H), which, according to local tales, was the name of St. Patrick's charioteer and is a first name derived from the word "odhar," which means dark-colored.
Genealogies: None known.

HORN

Ranking: 532 S.S. Count: 76,063

Origin: Danish, English, German, Jewish, Norwegian. Danish/Norwegian, English, German: 1) derived from the Old English, Old High German, and Old Norse word "horn," meaning horn. The name was given to those who made small objects, such as spoons, combs, or boxes, out of the horns of mammals. 2) same derivation as in 1. The name was given to those whose job it was to play a musical instrument made out of the actual horn of an animal, either for entertainment purposes, during warfare, or for security reasons. 3) same derivation as in 2. The name was given to those who lived by a hornlike geographical formation such as a ridge projecting from a mountain range or a patch of land jutting out of a curve in a river. 4) same derivation as in 3. The name was given to those who came from any number of places in England whose names begin with the word "horn" and that were so called because they were built on a hornlike geographical formation. 5) same derivation as in 4. The name may have referred to the hornlike attributes of a person's appearance or it may have been given to a cuckold, a man whose wife had been adulterous. Jewish: derived from the German word "horn," meaning horn. The name may have been taken ornamentally, or it may have been adopted as a reference to the ram's horn that is blown in the synagogue before and after important religious celebrations.

Famous **Horns:** GEORGE HENRY HORN (1840–1897) of Pennsylvania was an authority on coleoptera, about which he wrote a book. TOM HORN (1860–1903) of Missouri was a government scout who was instrumental in arranging the surrender of Geronimo in 1886.

Genealogies: *Family History of Horn Ancestors & Descendants of Elisha Thomas Horn of Zion Hill, Mississippi* was compiled by the Horn History Book Committee and published in Carnegie, Oklahoma, in 1984.

HORNBERG, HORNBERGER (S.S. Abbreviation: Hornbe)

Ranking: 4251 S.S. Count: 10,594

Origin: German. Derived from the German words "horn" and "berg," meaning horn and hill. The name was given to those who came from Hornberg, which means "horn-shaped mountain" (ES) and is the name of several places in Germany.

Genealogies: None known.

HORNE

Ranking: 823 S.S. Count: 51,460

Origin: English. Transformation of and cognate to the Danish/Norwegian, English, and German definitions of Horn.

Genealogies: *The Hornes: An American Family* was compiled by Gail Lumet Buckley and published in New York, New York, in 1986. *The Horne Family of Bloomingdale Road* was compiled by Philip Field Horne and published in Bronxville, New York, in 1974.

HORNER

Ranking: 1325 S.S. Count: 33,555

Origin: English, German, Jewish. Transformation of and cognate to the Danish/Norwegian, English, German, and Jewish definitions of Horn.

Famous **Horners:** WILLIAM EDMONDS HORNER (1793–1853) of Virginia was a physician who wrote *A Treatise on Pathological Anatomy*, the first of its kind in America. HENRY HORNER (1878–1940) was an effective governor of Illinois during the Depression.

Genealogies: *The Ancestors, Families and Descendants of George Edward Richardson and His Wife, Eva Horner* was compiled by Helen Richardson Kluegel and published in New Orleans, Louisiana, in 1976. *Our Horner Ancestors, William of Fayette County, Pa., Son of Thomas of Baltimore County, Md., Family Genealogy ca. 1700–1973. Allied Lines: Preston-Gilbert-Mitchell-West-Snively-Bumgarner-Swearingen-Moore* was compiled by Virginia Horner Hinds and published in Waverly, Ohio, in 1974.

HORNSBY (S.S. Abbreviation: Hornsb)

Ranking: 4402 S.S. Count: 10,192

Origin: English. Derived from the Old Norse first name Ormr, meaning serpent, and the Old Norse word "býr," meaning farm or settlement. The name was given to those who came from Hornsby, the name of a place in Cumberland County in England.

Famous **Hornsbys:** ROGER HORNSBY (1896–1963) of Texas was a baseball player who is considered the greatest right-handed batter of all time, with a batting average of .358. He is a member of the Baseball Hall of Fame.

Genealogies: None known.

HOROWITZ (S.S. Abbreviation: Horowi)

Ranking: 2875 S.S. Count: 15,825

Origin: Jewish. Derived from the Slavic word "gora," meaning hill. The name was given to those who came from Ho[afr]ovice, the name of a place in Bohemia, a region in the western part of former Czechoslovakia.

Genealogies: None known.

HORST

Ranking: 4523 S.S. Count: 9899

Origin: German. Cognate to Hurst.

Genealogies: *The Brockemeier-Horst Family Tree* was compiled by Agnella Scheerger and published in Battle Creek, Nebraska, most likely in 1977.

HORTON

Ranking: 318 S.S. Count: 116,918

Origin: English. 1) derived from the Old English words "horh" and "tūn," meaning mire or muck and enclosure or settlement. The name was given to those who came from Horton, the name of various places in England. 2) derived from the Old English words "heorot" and "dūn," meaning stag and hill. The name was given to those who came from Horton, the name of a place in Gloucester County, England.

Famous **Hortons**: VALENTINE BAXTER HORTON (1802–1888) of Vermont was a lawyer and a pioneer in the bituminous coal business. He is credited as the man responsible for "Condor" towboats. SAMUEL DANA HORTON (1844–1895) of Ohio is best remembered as the man who tried to have the importance of silver restored as the basis for international currency. ROBERT ELMER HORTON (1875–1945) of Michigan was a hydraulic engineer who devised rules for natural drainage systems. He also invented a water-level gauge. EDWARD EVERETT HORTON JR. (1886–1970) of New York was an actor of stage and screen. His most memorable roles were in Fred Astaire and Ginger Rogers dance films, usually as Astaire's best friend, and in the television show "F Troop," as Roaring Chicken, the medicine man.

Genealogies: Descendants of David Horton of North Carolina was compiled by Reta M. Evans and published in Backsburg, Virginia, in 1987. Descendants of Thomas Horton of Springfield; and Including Some Descendants of Phineas Pratt was compiled by Carl W. Fischer and published in Bayside, New York, in 1976.

HORVAT (ALSO HORVÁT, HORVÁTH)

Ranking: 1741 S.S. Count: 25,725

Origin: Hungarian, Jewish. Hungarian: derived from the Slavic word "Hrvat" and its Hungarian cognate "Horváth," which refers to a Croat, one of the Slavonic people living in the former Yugoslavia, now partitioned into the Republic of Croatia, the Federation of Yugoslavian Republics, the Republic of Bosnia-Hercegovina, and the Republic of Slovenia. Jewish: same derivation as in 1. The name indicated that the bearer's family came from Croatia.

Genealogies: None known.

HOSKIN

Ranking: 1062 S.S. Count: 41,457

Origin: English. Derived from the Middle English first name Oekin, which derived from various other first names that begin with the Old English word "ōs" or its Old Norse cognate "ās," meaning god.

Genealogies: Genealogy of One Branch of the Hoskinson Family (also Hoskin); Descendants of George Washington Hoskinson was compiled by Alice H. Woolridge and published in Myrtle Point, Oregon, in 1963. Hoskins of Virginia

and Related Families was compiled by Charles Willard Hoskins Warner and published in Tappahannock, Virginia, in 1971.

HOSTETLER, HOSTETTER (S.S. Abbreviation: Hostet)

Ranking: 2564 S.S. Count: 17,719

Origin: German. The name was given to those who came from Hofstadt, Hofstatt, or Hofstetten, which all mean "place of the farms or manors" (ES) and which are places in Germany.

Genealogies: The Descendants of Christian J. and Magdalena Hershberger Hostetler was compiled by Larry L. Hostetler and published in Washburn, Illinois, in 1992.

HOTCHKIN, HOTCHKINS, HOTCHKIS, HOTCHKISS (S.S. Abbreviation: Hotchk)

Ranking: 4695 S.S. Count: 9533

Origin: English. Transformations of Hodge.

Famous **Bearers**: BENJAMIN BERKELEY HOTCHKISS (1826–1885) of Connecticut was the inventor of two guns known as the Hotchkiss machine gun in 1872 and the Hotchkiss magazine rifle in 1875.

Genealogies: The Hotchkiss Family: Descendants of Samuel Hotchkiss (ca. 1622–1663) of New Haven, Connecticut was compiled by Nellie Cowdell and published in Prospect, Connecticut, in 1985. John Hodgkin (Hotchkin; also Hotchkiss) of Guilford, Connecticut and His Descendants was compiled by Geoffrey Brown and published in New York, New York, in 1988.

HOUCK

Ranking: 2502 S.S. Count: 18,127

Origin: English, German. Derived from the name Hue, which stems from Hugo, meaning soul or mind.

Genealogies: Huyck, Howk, Houck in America, 1600s–1982 was compiled by Sylvia E. Wilson and published in Medina, Washington, in 1982.

HOUGH

Ranking: 2064 S.S. Count: 22,196

Origin: English. Derived from the Old English word "hōh," which refers to a ridge projecting from a hillside. The name was given to those who came from Hough, the name of a place in various counties in England, such as Cheshire and Derbyshire.

Famous **Houghs**: FRANKLIN BENJAMIN HOUGH (1822–1885) of New York was a forester. His work laid the foundation for the conservation movement that would arise many years later. GEORGE WASHINGTON HOUGH (1836–1909) of New York was an inventor of astronomical and meteorological instruments. As an astronomer he studied Jupiter and double stars. EMERSON HOUGH

(1857–1923) of Iowa was an author and a journalist. He wrote many novels and spoke in favor of conservation and national parks. WALTER HOUGH (1859–1935) of West Virginia was an anthropologist and the curator of the U.S. National Museum for many years. THEODORE HOUGH (1865–1924) of Virginia was a physiologist. He was an authority on the medical school curriculum.

Genealogies: *Hough and Huff Families of the U.S.* was compiled by Granville W. Hough and most likely published in Laguna Hills, California, in 1972. *Hough in Bucks County, Pennsylvania, 1683–1850* was compiled by Orville Louis Hough and published in Denver, Colorado, in 1975.

HOUGHTON (S.S. Abbreviation: Hought)

Ranking: 2118 S.S. Count: 21,631

Origin: English. 1) derived from the Old English words "hōh" and "tūn," meaning ridge and settlement or enclosure. The name was given to those who came from Houghton, the name of various places in England, or Haughton, the name of a place in Nottinghamshire County, England. 2) derived from the Old English words "halh" and "tūn," meaning niche or alcove and settlement or enclosure. The name was given to those who came from Houghton, the name of various places in Lancashire and West Yorkshire counties in England. 3) possibly derived from the Old English first names Huhha and Hofa, the meanings of which are unclear, and the Old English word "tūn," meaning settlement or enclosure. The name was given to those who came from Houghton, the name of places in Devon and East Yorkshire counties in England.

Famous **Houghtons:** DOUGLASS HOUGHTON (1809–1845) of New York was the surgeon/botanist on the expedition to find the source of the Mississippi River in 1831. GEORGE HENDRIC HOUGHTON (1820–1897) of Massachusetts was an Episcopal clergyman who founded the New York City parish of the Transfiguration, which came to be known as "The Little Church around the Corner." HENRY OSCAR HOUGHTON (1823–1895) of Vermont was a publisher who first started Houghton & Co., in 1852. The company later came to be known as Houghton Mifflin and Company, in 1880. ALANSON BIGELOW HOUGHTON (1863–1941) of Massachusetts was a glass manufacturer in the family business of Corning Glass Co. and a member of Congress from New York. He gave up his congressional seat to accept diplomatic appointments. DALE NEELY HOUGHTON (1893–1975) of Indiana, while a professor at New York University, conducted a 10-year study of the effectiveness of advertising and marketing. The study was printed in a series of articles in *Printer's Ink*. He also co-wrote books on marketing and sales promotion.

Genealogies: *Houghton Ancestry: With Houghton Family Supplement* was compiled by Mabel Tacher R. Washburn and published in New York, New York, in 1939.

HOUSE

Ranking: 736 S.S. Count: 57,661

Origin: English. 1) derived from the Old English word "hūs," meaning house. In the Middle Ages, the name referred to a person who was somehow connected to the most important building in the town, most often a religious edifice. The name also may have referred to a homeowner, a person who held the deed to his own cottage, rather than being a tenant. 2) transformation of Howes.

Famous **Houses:** ROYAL EARL HOUSE (1814–1895) of Vermont was an inventor who made a printing telegraph. He was the first to use standed wire. HENRY ALONZO HOUSE (1840–1930) of New York was the inventor of a machine to make buttonholes. He also designed a steam motor car. EDWARD MANDELL HOUSE (1858–1938) of Texas was a presidential advisor who was known as "Colonel House." He was the closest advisor to President Woodrow Wilson.

Genealogies: *House-Brown and Related Families: The Lineages of Charles Staver House (1908–) and Virginia Brown (1911–) Who were Married August 5, 1938* was compiled by Charles Staver House and published in Manchester, Connecticut, in 1984. *The House Family Tree and Some of It's [sic] Branches* was compiled by Ardis Phillips Rasperger and published in Independence, Missouri, in 1990.

HOUSER

Ranking: 1525 S.S. Count: 29,171

Origin: English. Transformation of the first definition of House.

Genealogies: *Descendants of John House, 1709–1763* was compiled by Elmer A. Houser and published in Tamarac, Florida, in 1991. *The Houser Family: Directory Listing, Memorable Dates, and Genealogical Data: The Family of Charles Franklin Houser and Fannie Jane Murphey* was compiled by E. A. Houser Jr. and published in 1983.

HOUSTON, HOUSTOUN (S.S. Abbreviation: Housto)

Ranking: 544 S.S. Count: 74,786

Origin: Scottish. 1) derived from the medieval first name Hugh (see the English, Irish, and Scottish definitions of Hugh[es]) and the Middle English word "tune" or "toun," meaning settlement or hamlet. The name was given to those who came from Houston, the name of a place near Glasgow. 2) derived from the Gaelic name Mac Uistean, which is derived from the first name Uisdean, a cognate to the English, Irish, and Scottish definitions of Hugh(es).

Famous **Bearers:** JOHN HOUSTOUN (1744–1796) of Georgia was a Revolutionary War leader and a governor of Georgia. WILLIAM CHURCHILL HOUSTON (1746?–1788), birthplace unknown, was a Revolutionary War leader in New Jersey. He taught at Princeton University and practiced law in Trenton, New Jersey. SAMUEL HOUSTON (1793–1863) of Virginia was the governor of Tennessee, an Indian trader, and confidante and a commander of the Texas army, which he expanded and improved. Elected as the Texas president, then U.S. senator from Texas and then governor of Texas, he opposed secession and resigned when Texas left the Union. He refused to take the Confederacy oath of allegiance. GEORGE SMITH HOUSTON (1811–1879) of Tennessee was raised in Alabama. He opposed secession and refused to serve in the Confederate army. He was the governor of Alabama, then U.S. senator from Alabama after the war. EDWIN JAMES HOUSTON (1847–1914) of Virginia was an educator and an electrical engineer. He was a pioneer in the laboratory method of teaching the sciences and the co-inventor of an improved arc-lighting system. CHARLES HAMILTON HOUSTON (1895–1950) of Washington, D.C., was a lawyer and an advocate of civil rights. He was special counsel for the NAACP and argued many of its cases before the U.S. Supreme Court.

Genealogies: *The History of John Huson From North Carolina to Alabama, His Huson/Huston/Houston Descendants, and the Allied Pioneer Families of Clepper, Robinson, Deen and Gilmore* was compiled by Margarette Hall Wood and published in Baltimore, Maryland, in 1990. *Ancestry and Descendants of Stephen Greene and Martha Mifflin Houston, His Wife* was compiled by Walter Lee Sheppard and most likely published in the 1960s.

HOWARD

Ranking: 69 S.S. Count: 357,697

Origin: English, Irish. English: 1) derived from the Anglo-Scandinavian first name Hāward, which is composed of the Old Norse words "há" and "varðr," meaning high and guardian. 2) derived from the Norman first names Huart or Heward, which are composed of the Germanic words "hug" and "hard," meaning heart, soul, or essence and courageous or robust. 3) derived from the Middle English word "ewehirde," which is composed of the Old English words "eowu" and "hierde," meaning ewe and herdsman. The name was given to shepherds. 4) derived from the Old English words "ēa" and "worð," meaning river and enclosure. The name was given to those who came from Ewart, a place in Northumberland, England, which is enclosed on three sides by rivers. 5) a Norman transformation of the first name Edward. Irish: derived from the Gaelic first name Fógartach, which is derived from the word "fógartha," meaning exiled or banned.

Famous Howards: JACOB MERRITT HOWARD (1805–1871) of Vermont was one of the founders of the Republican Party. WILLIAM TRAVIS HOWARD (1821–1907) of Virginia was a gynecologist. He was the first in the United States to successfulley use Tarnier's forceps; he also invented the bivalve, or Howard, speculum. ADA LYDIA HOWARD (1829–1907) of New Hampshire was the first president of Wellesley College. CAROLINE EMILY FOX HOWARD (1829–1908) of Massachusetts was an actress and dancer and the mother of Cordelia Howard. OLIVER OTIS HOWARD (1830–1909) of Maine was a Union soldier and a teacher at West Point in the area of mathematics. He was an officer in the war, but speculation exists as to how well he commanded in several key battles. BRONSON CROCKER HOWARD (1842–1908) of Michigan was a journalist, then a playwright. He was responsible for many of the plays between the years 1870 and 1900. BLANCHE WILLIS HOWARD (1847–1898) of Maine was an author who lived in Europe. Her main contribution to her homeland was the novels she wrote that gave Americans an insight into European life. CORDELIA HOWARD (1848–1941) of Rhode Island was the actress who played Little Eva in *Uncle Tom's Cabin*. LELAND OSSIN HOWARD (1857–1950) of Illinois was an entomologist who was interested in biological control and in insects as disease carriers. He wrote many books and papers on the mosquito and the housefly. ROY WILSON HOWARD (1883–1964) of Ohio was a newspaper executive closely associated with Robert Scripps in the running of the New York City papers. WILLIE HOWARD (1886–1949) of Germany was a comedian and an impersonator. He was one of the stars of the Ziegfeld Follies. SIDNEY COE HOWARD (1891–1939) of California was a playwright. He is best remembered as the man who wrote the screenplay for *Gone With the Wind*. LESLIE HOWARD (1893–1943) of England was an actor who is best remembered for his portrayal of Ashley Wilkes in the movie *Gone With the Wind*. His plane was shot down in service to his homeland during World War II.

Genealogies: *Norris, Hackett, Prescott and Allied Families: Our Ancestors and Their Descendants, Including Adams, Andrews, Bachelder, Bartlett, Boulter, Brewer, Brown, Harding, Hinkley, Howard, Huntington, et. al.* was compiled by Hugh Albert Johnson and published in Annandale, Virginia, in 1976. *Ancestors and Descendants of Matthew A.B. Howard, Georgia–Florida, 1793–1978, with Allied Families* was compiled by Norma Slater Woodward and published in Lake Butler, Florida, in 1979. *The Dukes of Norfolk: A Quincentennial History* was compiled by John Martin Robinson and published in Oxford, New York, in 1982.

HOWE

Ranking: 698 S.S. Count: 60,391

Origin: English, Jewish. English: 1) derived from the Old Norse word "haugr," meaning small hill. The name was given to those who lived by a small hill or burial mound. The name may also have been given to those who came from Howe, the name of a place in Norfolk and West Yorkshire counties, England. 2) transformation of the English definition of Hugh(es).

Jewish: transformation of several similar-sounding Jewish family names.

Famous **Howes:** GEORGE AUGUSTUS HOWE (1724?–1758) of England was an English soldier who fought against the French in New York. He is remembered for increasing the efficiency of the English by making them less conspicuous in their hats and coats. He was killed in a skirmish near Lake George, New York. SAMUEL GRIDLEY HOWE (1801–1876) of Massachusetts was a pioneer in the education of the blind, with his program at Perkins Institute in Massachusetts serving as a model. WILLIAM HOWE (1803–1852) of Massachusetts was an inventor who developed the Howe truss bridge, which he built over the Connecticut River at Springfield, Massachusetts. TIMOTHY OTIS HOWE (1816–1883) of Maine was a politician, serving as a senator, judge, and the U.S. postmaster general. He also spoke in favor of emancipation. HENRY HOWE (1816–1893) of Connecticut wrote *Historical Collections* of New York, New Jersey, Virginia, and Ohio which contained firsthand narratives on each particular area. ELIAS HOWE (1819–1867) of Massachusetts was the inventor of the sewing machine. JULIA WARD HOWE (1819–1910) of New York was the author of "The Battle Hymn of the Republic." FREDERICK WEBSTER HOWE (1822–1891) of Massachusetts was the inventor of the milling machine in 1850. WILLIAM F. HOWE (1828–1902) of Massachusetts was a corrupt lawyer in partnership with Abraham H. Hummel. Hummel fled the country; Howe died in New York City. PERCY ROGERS HOWE (1864–1950) of Rhode Island was a dentist who was convinced that nutrition played an important part in dental health. He is best remembered as the contributor of chemotherapeutic treatment of cavities. MARK DE WOLFE HOWE (1906–1967) of Massachusetts was a legal historian. He was the author of several books on legal American history and an opponent of Senator Joseph McCarthy.

Genealogies: None known.

HOWELL

Ranking: 224 **S.S. Count:** 157,134

Origin: English, Welsh. English: derived from the Old English first name Huna, which is a shortened form of several names composed of the Old English words "hūn" and "well(a)," meaning bear cub and spring or brook. The name was given to those who came from Howell, the name of a place in Lincolnshire County in England. Welsh: derived from the first name Hywel, meaning illustrious.

Famous **Howells:** EVAN PARK HOWELL (1839–1905) of Georgia was a Confederate soldier and the force that made the *Atlanta Constitution* the most important Southern newspaper of his time. His son, CLARK HOWELL (1863–1936) of South Carolina was a newspaper editor associated with the *Atlanta Constitution*, which was owned

by his father. He was politically active and was an advocate of southern industrialization, diversification of agriculture, and educational improvements. He worked closely with Presidents Warren G. Harding, Herbert Hoover, and Franklin D. Roosevelt. JOHN ADAMS HOWELL (1840–1918) of New York was a naval officer who invented the Howell torpedo in 1885 and a torpedo-launching device, among other things of military interest. WILLIAM HENRY HOWELL (1860–1945) of Maryland was a physiologist and the dean of the medical school at Johns Hopkins University. HARRY E. HOWELL (1900–1979), born in England, began work in the United States as a bookkeeper and rose to considerable prominence as an accountant and owner of Howell and Co. in Washington, D.C. He was involved in many international projects.

Genealogies: None known.

HOWERT

Ranking: 4622 **S.S. Count:** 9669

Origin: English? Uncertain etymology. Most likely a transformation of Howard.

Genealogies: None known.

HOWES

Ranking: 4753 **S.S. Count:** 9424

Origin: English. 1) derived from the Old Norse word "haugr," meaning small hill. The name was given to those who lived by a small hill or burial mound. 2) transformation of the English definition of Hugh(es).

Genealogies: None known.

HOWLAND (S.S. Abbreviation: Howlan)

Ranking: 3394 **S.S. Count:** 13,339

Origin: English. Transformation of the English definition of Holland.

Famous **Howlands:** GARDINER GREENE HOWLAND (1787–1851) of Connecticut was a merchant and railroad promoter. EMILY HOWLAND (1827–1929) of New York was an educator, reformer, and philanthropist. When she was a child her family was one of the "stops" on the Underground Railroad. Her main interest in life was the education of African-Americans. She monetarily supported their education and left part of her estate to the cause when she died at age 101. JOHN HOWLAND (1873–1926) of New York was a pediatrician who opened the first pediatric clinic in the country at Johns Hopkins University.

Genealogies: *John Howland of the Mayflower* was compiled by Elizabeth Pearson White and published in Camden, Maine, in 1990.

HOY

Ranking: 3436 **S.S. Count:** 13,134

Origin: Irish. Derived from the Gaelic name Ó

hEochaidh, meaning "descendant of Eochaidh" (H&H), which is a name derived from the first name Eachaidh, meaning horseman.

Genealogies: None known.

HOYLE

Ranking: 3567 **S.S. Count:** 12,640

Origin: English. Derived from the Old English word "holh," meaning hole, recess, or depression. The name was given to those who lived in or near a cranny or low-lying patch of land.

Genealogies: None known.

HOYT

Ranking: 1526 **S.S. Count:** 29,147

Origin: Dutch, Irish. 1) derived from the name Hoyte, which means spirit or soul. 2) derived from the name Ud.

Famous **Hoyts:** ALBERT HARRISON HOYT (1826–1915) of New Hampshire was an antiquarian and a contributor to the *Register* of the New England Historic Genealogical Society. HENRY MARTYN HOYT (1830–1892) of Pennsylvania was a Union soldier and the governor of Pennsylvania, where he reduced the state debt and opened institutions to help youthful offenders. JOHN WESLEY HOYT (1831–1912) of Ohio was governor of the Wyoming territory and the first president of the University of Wyoming.

Genealogies: *A Genealogical History of the Hoyt, Haight, and Hight Families: With Some Account of the Earlier Hyatt Families, A List of the First Settlers of Salisbury and Amesbury, Mass.* was compiled by David W. Hoyt and published in Bethany, Oklahoma, in 1985. *Genealogy of the Family of William Watson and Nancy Hoyt (Bean) Roberts* was compiled by Richard C. Roberts and published in Connecticut in 1981.

HSU

Ranking: 4849 **S.S. Count:** 9226

Origin: Chinese. The name means to promise. It may also mean poised.

Genealogies: None known.

HUANG

Ranking: 3602 **S.S. Count:** 12,535

Origin: Chinese. The name means yellow. It may also mean principal or sovereign, as yellow is the color of the aristocracy.

Genealogies: None known.

HUBBARD (S.S. Abbreviation: Hubbar)

Ranking: 397 **S.S. Count:** 98,093

Origin: English. Transformation of and cognate to Hubert.

Famous **Hubbards:** WILLIAM HUBBARD (1621?–1704) of England was brought to America as a child. He was a Congregational clergyman and historian who wrote *Narrative of the Troubles with the Indians* and *A General History of New England*. JOHN HUBBARD (1794–1869) of Maine was the governor of that state who signed the Maine Law of 1851, which prohibited liquor traffic. He set up schools of agriculture and reform and increased education opportunities for women. GURDON SALTONSTALL HUBBARD (1802–1886) of Vermont was a fur trader and manager of the American Fur Company's posts in Illinois. He was the last fur trader in Illinois to barter for furs. HENRY GRISWOLD HUBBARD (1814–1891) of Connecticut was the first rubber manufacturer to make the product into thread and weave it into webbing by machine. LUCIUS FREDERICK HUBBARD (1936–1913) of Minnesota was a governor of that state who fought corruption in wheat freight pricing and grading. FRANK MCKINNEY HUBBARD (1868–1930) of Ohio was a humorist and caricaturist. He was known as "Kin" and was the creator of the character "Abe Martin." BERNARD ROSECRANS HUBBARD (1888–1962) of California was a Jesuit priest, explorer, and lecturer. He worked as a missionary, explorer, and lecturer in Alaska. WYNANT DAVIS HUBBARD (1900–1961) of Missouri was a naturalist, author, and expert on Africa. He wrote books about the wildlife of Africa.

Genealogies: *The Genealogy of the Hubbard and Bogel Families of Presidio County, Texas: Their Ancestors and Descendants, 1660–1989* was compiled by Harry J. Hubbard Jr. and published in 1990. *McBride, Hubbard Family History, 1773–1979* was compiled by Peggy Arnold and published in Bloomfield, Iowa, in 1979.

HUBBELL (S.S. Abbreviation: Hubbel)

Ranking: 4842 **S.S. Count:** 9238

Origin: English. Derived from the names Hubbald or Hubald, which mean mind or intrepid.

Famous **Hubbells:** JOHN LORENZO HUBBELL (1853–1930) of New Mexico was a trader on the Navajo Reservation who was considered a friend of both the Navajos and the Hopis.

Genealogies: *Ancestors and Descendants of My Raymoure, Hubbell, Franklin, Osborne Grandparents: Includes 40+ Connecting Lines* was compiled by Dorothy Raymoure and published in Grand Rapids, Michigan, in 1982. *History and Genealogy of the Hubbell Family* was compiled by Harold Berresford Hubbell Jr. et al. and published in Brooklyn, New York, in 1980.

HUBER

Ranking: 831 **S.S. Count:** 51,164

Origin: German, Jewish. German: derived from the Old High German word "huoba," which refers to a measure of land of considerable size, usually much larger than what a

common peasant could own. The name was given to a
landowner who owned such an amount of land and who was
therefore a prominent member of his community. The name
may also have been given to wage earners who worked on
such a property and who did not own their own land. Jewish:
derived from the Yiddish word "hober," which means oats.
The name was usually taken ornamentally but may have
been given to a seller or grower of oats.

Famous **Hubers:** GOTTHELP CARL HUBER (1865–1934)
was born in India to a Swiss missionary family. He was an
anatomist and an authority on the sympathetic nervous
system. He came to the United States in 1871 and is considered the first American to use Ehrlich's methylene blue
technique.

Genealogies: *Genealogical History of John Francis Huber
From Bucks County, Pennsylvania and His Descendants,
With Related Families, 1751–1983* was compiled by Gloria
C. Hartzell and published in Gilbertsville, Pennsylvania, in
1983.

HUBERT
Ranking: 2858 **S.S. Count:** 15,983
*Origin: English, French, German. Derived from a Ger-
manic first name composed of the words "hug" and "berht,"
meaning heart or soul and renowned or resplendent. The
name became popular in Germany after the 8th century.*

Famous **Huberts:** CONRAD HUBERT (1885–1928) of
Russia was an inventor of electrical devices and is probably
best known as the man who founded the American Ever-
Ready Co.

Genealogies: *A Remarkable Negro Family: Reprint From
the Southern Workman, October 1925* was published by the
Association for the Advancement of Negro Country Life in
1926.

HUCKABAY, HUCKABONE, HUCKABY (S.S.
   Abbreviation: Huckab)
Ranking: 3242 **S.S. Count:** 14,012
*Origin: English? Uncertain etymology. Possibly derived
from the Old English name Hucca.*
Genealogies: None known.

HUDDLE (ALSO HUDDLESTON,
   HUDDLESTONE)
Ranking: 1629 **S.S. Count:** 27,560
*Origin: English. Huddle: derived from the medieval first
name Hudde, which is of an uncertain etymology. It may be a
pet form of the names Hugh or Richard. It may also be
derived from the Old English first name Hūda. The name is
common in England, especially in Bristol and its surrounding
areas and in Yorkshire County. Huddleston, Huddlestone:
derived from the Old English first name Hūdel and the Old
English word "tūn," meaning settlement or enclosure. The*

name was given to those who came from Huddleston, the
name of a place in West Yorkshire and in what was once
Dumfries County, England.

Genealogies: *Jarriott Morgan Huddleston Family, 1775–*
was compiled by Tim Huddleston and published in Oolte-
wah, Tennessee, in 1982. *Josiah Dunn Huddleston, 1782–
1865: Ancestors and Descendants* was compiled by Irma
Huddleston Bloom and published in Mountain Home,
Arkansas, in 1979.

HUDGIN (ALSO HUDGINS)
Ranking: 2552 **S.S. Count:** 17,802
*Origin: English. 1) derived from the name Hudd, which is
a pet form of the name Hugh, meaning soul or spirit. 2)
derived from the name Hudd, which is a pet form of the name
Richard, meaning edict or rigid.*
Genealogies: None known.

HUDSON
Ranking: 192 **S.S. Count:** 182,377
Origin: English. Transformation of Hudd(le).

Famous **Hudsons:** HENRY HUDSON (?–1611) of England
was a navigator. He made several voyages in an attempt to
find a northeast passage to the Orient. His "Third Voyage"
was in the spring of 1609 on the ship known as the *Halve
Maen*, which translates to the *Half Moon*. He sailed for the
Dutch East India Co. from Amsterdam with a mixed crew
of Dutch and English. Rounding the North Cape, he discovered icebergs and snowstorms and became depressed
with the weather conditions. He and the crew chose to
head west to America instead. Buffeted by storms, the ship
made repairs upon reaching Maine, then set about to
explore the coast. He explored the Chesapeake Bay, then
the Delaware Bay and River, but surmised that they would
not lead to the Orient. He continued northward into New
York harbor and his namesake, the Hudson River, exploring all the way to present-day Albany, New York. He then
returned to England, where those who received him were
not pleased with his accomplishments. He was forbidden
to sail for any English company in the future. His ship's
logs and papers were published, and he became a sort of
local hero to the people. He was financed by a group of
businessmen and, in April 1610, he sailed on the ship *Discovery* westward. He explored Hudson Bay late in the year
and could not travel again until the spring. Lack of food
and supplies, coupled with a disagreement between Hudson and his followers and the majority of the crew, resulted
in a mutiny. Hudson, his son, and seven loyal crew members were set adrift on June 23, 1611. WILLIAM SMITH HUD-
SON (1810–1881) of England was a mechanical engineer
and an inventor who was responsible for many locomotive
inventions, such as the radius bar and the double-end locomotive. MANLEY OTTNER HUDSON (1886–1960) of Missouri

was a jurist and a member of the Paris Peace Conference (1919). Most of his years were spent at Harvard University, where he taught law (1919–1954).

Genealogies: *Della Elizabeth Butler Hudson "Beth": Her Family and Ancestors* was compiled by Martha Ann Butler Guenther and published in St. Petersburg, Florida, in 1990. *Genealogy and History of the Garmire-Dunmire and Hudson Families: Also Some Family Lines, Snedeker, Wyckoff, Van Voorhies, Gutshall, Shockar, Addleman, Jacob Parker of Chester Co., Penn., Frey, and Frankhouser* was compiled by Live M. Garmire-Parker and published in Wichita, Kansas, in 1972.

HUEBNER (S.S. Abbreviation: Huebne)
Ranking: 4492 **S.S. Count:** 9978
Origin: German. The name was given to crop farmers who worked a "hube," which is a parcel of land consisting of approximately 120 acres.
Genealogies: None known.

HUERTA
Ranking: 1879 **S.S. Count:** 24,091
Origin: Spanish. Derived from the Old Provençal word "ort," meaning garden. The name was given to gardeners or to those who lived near a fenced-in garden.
Genealogies: None known.

HUEY
Ranking: 3236 **S.S. Count:** 14,026
Origin: Irish. Transformation of Hoy.
Genealogies: *Huey Family History: Many Families, Connected by Marriage. . .* was compiled by V. H. Huey and published in Birmingham, Alabama, in 1963.

HUFF
Ranking: 524 **S.S. Count:** 76,828
Origin: English. Derived from the Old English word "hōh," which literally means heel and refers to a ridge projecting from a hillside. The name was given to those who lived near such a natural formation.
Genealogies: *Hough and Huff Families of the U.S.* was compiled by Granville W. Hough and published in Laguna Hills, California, in 1972. *A Huff Genealogy: Descendants of Engelbert Huff of Dutchess County, New York* was compiled by George Lockwood Trigg and published in Bowie, Maryland, in 1992.

HUFFMAN (S.S. Abbreviation: Huffma)
Ranking: 574 **S.S. Count:** 71,757
Origin: German. The name was given to crop farmers who worked a "hube," which is a parcel of land consisting of approximately 120 acres.
Genealogies: *Stuckey-Huffman Cousins* was compiled

by Opal L. Streiff and published in Burwell, Nebraska, in 1978.

HUGGIN (ALSO HUGGINS)
Ranking: 1478 **S.S. Count:** 30,153
Origin: English. Transformation of the English definition of Hugh(es).
Genealogies: *The Descendants of James Huggins (1752–1819) of Granby, Connecticut* was compiled by Seth P. Holcombe and published in North Granby, Connecticut, in 1979. *Huggins Families of Western Pennsylvania and Northern West Virginia* was compiled by Charles E. Huggins and published in Chattanooga, Tennessee, in 1987.

HUGHES
Ranking: 79 **S.S. Count:** 326,063
Origin: English, Irish, Scottish. English: derived from the Old French first name Hu(gh)e. The name was originally a shortened form of various longer Germanic names that began with the word "hugh," meaning heart, soul, or mind. The name was made popular in England by the fame of St. Hugh of Lincoln and St. Hugh of Cluny. Irish, Scottish: derived from the Gaelic name Mac Aodha, which is derived from the first name Aodh, meaning fire.

Famous Hugheses: JOHN JOSEPH HUGHES (1797–1864) of Ireland was a Roman Catholic priest and a champion of the mass of immigrants that had come to the United States. He helped them become viable members of the community. ROBERT BALL HUGHES (1806–1868) of England was a sculptor and was the first to use marble and bronze as media for statues in the United States. DAVID EDWARD HUGHES (1831–1900) of England was an inventor who came to the United States as a child, settling in Virginia and Kentucky. He invented a printing telegraph that was combined with the one invented by Royal E. House. Hughes is also the inventor of the microphone. DUDLEY MAYS HUGHES (1848–1927) of Georgia was a member of Congress and the co-author of the Smith-Hughes Bill, which is better known as the Vocational Education Act. CHARLES EVANS HUGHES (1862–1948) of New York was the governor of New York and a U.S. Supreme Court justice. On the bench he was a champion of civil liberties and rights. EDWIN HILT HUGHES (1866–1950) was a Methodist minister who was responsible for the reunion of the Methodist Protestant Church, the Methodist Episcopal Church, and the Methodist Episcopal Church, South, in 1939. ADELLE PRENTISS HUGHES (1869–1950) of Ohio was the founder and manager of the Cleveland Orchestra. JAMES LANGSTON HUGHES (1902–1967) of Missouri was a poet, playwright, and novelist. He was honored for his writings and was considered one of America's great poets. HOWARD ROBARD HUGHES (1905–1976) of Texas was an industrialist and aviator who produced films in Hollywood and formed the

Hughes Aircraft Co., designing his own plane that broke speed and distance records. He is famed for the designing and building of an all-wooden airplane named the *Spruce Goose*. After 1950 he shut himself away from the world, becoming a recluse.

Genealogies: *The Families of Benjamin (1816– 1903)* [and] *Margaret Evans (1825– 1879) Hughes and Evan (1808– 1877)* [and] *Jane Davies (1817– 1858) James* was compiled by David Wendell Hughes and most likely published in Lincoln, Nebraska, in 1969. *Genealogy of Chadwick, King, and Allied Families: McKee, Callahan, Hughs/Hughes, Mock, Roberts, Langston* was compiled by Darline Chadwick Smith and published in North Kansas City, Missouri, in 1982.

HUGHEY

Ranking: 4377 **S.S. Count:** 10,249

Origin: English, Scottish. The name was given to those who came from Hughley, which means "Hugh's gorve" (ES) and is the name of a place in Shropshire, England.

Genealogies: None known.

HULL

Ranking: 689 **S.S. Count:** 60,914

Origin: English. 1) transformation of the English definition of Hill. 2) transformation of the English definition of Hugh(es).

Famous **Hulls:** JOHN HULL (1624–1683) of England came to Massachusetts at the age of 9, eventually becoming a minter of coins. He coined the first Massachusetts shillings and served as treasurer of the Massachusetts Colony. WILLIAM HULL (1753–1825) of Connecticut was a Revolutionary War soldier. He became the governor of the Michigan territory. ISAAC HULL (1773–1843) of Connecticut was a naval officer. He was the commander of the U.S.S. *Constitution* and was outstanding in his service to his country. CORDELL HULL (1871–1955) of Tennessee was a member of Congress, U.S. senator, secretary of state, and the author of several bills, including the federal income tax law of 1913 and its revision in 1916. He was responsible for the Good Neighbor Policy with Latin American countries and was the main planner of the United Nations, for which he received a Nobel Peace Prize in 1945. HANNAH HALLOWELL CLOTHIER HULL (1872–1958) of Pennsylvania was a pacifist active in the peace movement. She succeeded Jane Addams as the president of the Women's International League for Peace and Freedom. ALBERT WALLACE HULL (1880–1966) of Connecticut discovered the powder method of producing X-rays. CLARK LEONARD HULL (1884–1952) of New York was a behavioral psychologist who was the author of *Aptitude Testing* and *A Behavior System*.

Genealogies: *Hulls' Heritage: A Genealogical History* was compiled by Carolyn Hull Estes and published in Fort Worth, Texas, in 1986. *Hulls in 1850: A Directory of Persons Surnamed Hull in the U.S. in 1850* was compiled by Robert Hull Taylor and published in Lumberville, Pennsylvania, in 1983.

HULSE

Ranking: 4689 **S.S. Count:** 9542

Origin: English. Derived from the Old English word "holh," meaning cavity or depression. The name was given to those who came from Hulse, the name of several places in Cheshire, England, that may have also taken the form of Holis, Holes, and Holys.

Genealogies: None known.

HULSEY

Ranking: 3640 **S.S. Count:** 12,388

Origin: English? Uncertain etymology. Possibly derived from the Old English word "hole(g)n," meaning holly.

Genealogies: None known.

HUMBER (ALSO HUMBERDOT, HUMBERSTON, HUMBERSTONE, HUMBERT)

Ranking: 4807 **S.S. Count:** 9319

Origin: Humber, Humberston, Humberstone—English; Humberdot—French; Humbert—French, German. Humber: derived from the name Humber, which was commonly given to prehistoric rivers and which is of uncertain etymology. The name was given to those who lived on or near a river or stream with this name. Humberston, Humberstone: 1) derived from the river name Humber and the Old English word "stān," meaning stone. The name was given to those who came from Humberstone, the name of a place in Leicestershire, England. 2) derived from the first name Hūnbeorht (which is composed of the Old English words "hūn" and "berht," meaning cub bear and renowned or resplendent) and the word "stān," meaning stone. The name was given to those who came from Humberstone, the name of a place in Lincolnshire County, England. Humbert, Humberdot: derived from a now-unknown Germanic first name composed of the words "hūn" and "berht," meaning bear cub and renowned or resplendent.

Famous **Bearers:** JEAN JOSEPH AMABLE HUMBERT (1755–1823) of France was a general who was exiled by Napoleon, settled in New Orleans, and served under Andrew Jackson in the Battle of New Orleans.

Genealogies: *The Joh Family; Plus Allied Lines of Runkle, Humbert, Wade, Henderson* was compiled by Crystal Pauline Randel Walters and published in New Ross, Indiana, in 1972.

HUME

Ranking: 4596 **S.S. Count:** 9725

Origin: English, Scottish. Transformation of Holme(s).

Famous **Humes:** Sophia Wigington Hume (1702–1774) of South Carolina was a Quaker minister and writer. She preached publicly because of a divine calling to go to Charleston, South Carolina, and convince the residents to give up their self-indulgent ways. William Hume (1830–1902) of Maine was a pioneer in the salmon industry along the Sacramento and Columbia rivers.

Genealogies: *A Hume Chronicle: Andrew Hume of Fauquier County, Virginia, His Scottish Heritage and American Descendants* was compiled by O. Clyde Donaldson and published in Hopkins, Minnesota, in 1982. *The Ancestors of Robert Hume North, 1907–1974, A Descendant of Andrew Bloomfield, 1716–1796, and Anna Hude of Woodbridge, New Jersey* was compiled by Robert Hume North and published in 1974.

HUMMEL
Ranking: 1927 **S.S. Count:** 23,459
Origin: German. 1) derived from the Middle Low German word "hommel," meaning bee. The name was given to those who were often engaged in a flurry of activities. The name may also have been given to beekeepers. 2) transformation of Humbert. 3) derived from a now-unknown Germanic first name composed of the words "hūn" and "bald," meaning bear cub and bold or fearless.

Famous **Hummels:** Abraham Henry Hummel (1850–1926) of Massachusetts was a corrupt lawyer in partnership with William F. Howe. After his conviction for conspiracy and one year of jail, he fled to England, where he died.

Genealogies: None known.

HUMPHREY, HUMPHREYS, HUMPHRIES, HUMPHRIS, HUMPHRY, HUMPHRYS (S.S. Abbreviation: Humphr)
Ranking: 324 **S.S. Count:** 115,554
Origin: Humphrey, Humphry—English, Irish; Humphreys, Humphries, Humphris, Humphrys: English. English: derived from the Old French first name Humfrey, which is composed of the Germanic words "hūn" and "frid" or "fred," meaning bear cub and peace. It was the name of a 9th-century English saint. Irish: derived from the Old Norse first name Óleif, which was composed of the words "ans" and "leift," meaning god and relic. The name was introduced into Ireland and Scotland by Scandinavian colonists living there.

Famous **Bearers:** James Humphreys (1748–1810) of Pennsylvania published the first American *Works of Laurence Sterne*. Joshua Humphreys (1751–1838) of Pennsylvania was a shipbuilder and naval architect. He owned the ships that were captained by Ekel Hopkins. Humphreys's new design for ships was used in the building of the *United States, Constitution, Chesapeake, Constellation, President,* and *Congress*. The ships were a great improvement and became known for their speed and accomplishments. He served as the first U.S. naval contractor. David Humphreys (1752–1818) of Connecticut was a soldier in the Revolutionary War, where he served as aide-de-camp to George Washington and became his close friend. After the war he continued in a life of diplomatic service to his country, retiring to take up sheep breeding in his native Connecticut, where he joined up with his friends of youth in the literary group known as the "Hartford Wits." Herman Humphrey (1779–1861) of Connecticut was an advocate of temperance and was the president of Amherst College. West Hughes Humphreys (1806–1882) of Tennessee was a federal judge who was impeached and convicted for accepting a Confederate commission as a district judge. Andrew Atkinson Humphreys (1810–1883) of Pennsylvania was a soldier who rose to become chief of staff of the Army of the Potomac. He also served as the Chief of Engineers, U.S. Army. Alexander Crombie Humphreys (1851–1927) of Scotland came to the United States as a child. He was a mechanical engineer and the designer of gas plants worldwide. He was the president of Stevens Institute of Technology (1902–1927). George Magoffin Humphrey (1890–1970) of Michigan was a lawyer, industrialist, and the secretary of the Treasury under President Dwight D. Eisenhower. George Rolfe Humphries (1894–1969) of Pennsylvania was a poet, translator, and scholar. He wrote several volumes of poems and sonnets. Doris Batchelder Humphrey (1895–1958) of Illinois was a choreographer who, with Martha Graham, is best remembered as a creator of the form of American dance that uses movement to communicate feelings. Hubert Horatio Humphrey Jr. (1911–1978) of South Dakota was a mayor of Minneapolis, U.S. senator from Minnesota, vice president of the United States (1965–1969) under President Lyndon B. Johnson, and the Democratic candidate for the presidency in 1968.

Genealogies: *The Marlett Family in Southeast, Midwest, and Southwest United States, With Connections to the Ball, Humphries, Hope, and Cross Families* was compiled by Nadeen Cross Marlett and published in Modesto, California, in 1983. *That Humphrey Family and Others* was compiled by Donna Humphrey Metzger and published in Susanville, California, in 1991. *Fundy Family (also Humphrey)* was compiled by William Henry Irving and published in Durham, North Carolina, in 1972.

HUNDLEY (S.S. Abbreviation: Hundle)
Ranking: 3587 **S.S. Count:** 12,571
Origin: English. The name was given to those who came from Handley, which means "high grove" (ES) and is a place in Northamptonshire, England.
Genealogies: None known.

HUNT

Ranking: 146 **S.S. Count:** 213,475

Origin: English. Derived from the Old English word "hunta," meaning to hunt. The name was given to hunters, both those of the nobility who hunted game such as deer and boars for diversion and those who hunted fowl for food.

Famous **Hunts:** ROBERT HUNT (1568?–1608), possibly of England, was the chaplain of the Jamestown expedition. The rough lifestyle of the New World proved too much for him, and he died. WALTER HUNT (1796–1859) of New York was the inventor of a sewing machine that he never patented. He can best be remembered, though, as the inventor of the safety pin in 1849. HARRIOT KEZIA HUNT (1805–1875) of Massachusetts was a physician and reformer. She is considered the first woman to practice medicine in the United States. WILLIAM MORRIS HUNT (1824–1879) of Vermont was a painter whose best works hang at the capitol in Albany, New York. RICHARD MORRIS HUNT (1827–1895) of Vermont was an architect of great ability. His greatest achievement was "Biltmore" in North Carolina. MARY HANNAH HANCHETT HUNT (1830–1906) of Connecticut was a leader in the campaign for temperance education, which she managed to have incorporated into the classroom. And although the generation that was taught the evils of alcohol eventually voted for Prohibition, the amendment authorizing it was repealed, and her influence on the American drinking habits appeared to be short-lived. CARLETON HUNT (1836–1921) of Louisiana was the founder of the American Bar Association. ROBERT WOOSTON HUNT (1838–1923) of Pennsylvania founded the Cambria Iron Co. and was a pioneer in the manufacture of Bessemer steel in America. CHARLES WALLACE HUNT (1841–1911) of New York was a mechanical engineer who developed the automatic coal-handling system, which he patented in 1872. BENJAMIN WEEKS HUNT (1847–1934) of New York was a horticulturist who developed a livestock farm, worked to eradicate the tick, and worked with a variety of fruits. ALFRED EPHRAIM HUNT (1855–1899) of Massachusetts was involved in the development of the Hall process for reduction of aluminum. GEORGE WYLIE PAUL HUNT (1859–1934) of Missouri was the governor of Arizona and a legend in the Southwest. REID HUNT (1870–1948) of Ohio was a pharmacologist. He organized a division of pharmacology at the Hygienic Laboratory of the U.S. Public Health and Marine Hospital Service in Washington, D.C. HAROLDSON LAFAYETTE HUNT (1889–1974) of Illinois was the founder of the Hunt Oil Co. in 1936, which became the largest independent oil company in the country. He also was the founder of Facts Forum and Life Line in the 1950s. ELGIN FRASER HUNT (1895–1978) of Connecticut, an educator, was the co-author or editor of several books, including *Fundamentals of Economics* (1948) and *Modern Economic Problems*

(1950). He was author of *Social Science: An Introduction to the Study of Society* (1953).

Genealogies: *The Henning [also Hennin] and Duke Families of Louisville, Kentucky: Including Genealogical Material on the Following Families, Henning, Duke, Morgan, Hunt, Marshall, Randolph* was compiled by Charles P. Stanton and published in Brooklyn, New York, in 1983. *Ambiguous Lives: Free Women of Color in Rural Georgia, 1789–1879* was compiled by Adele Logan Alexander and published in Fayetteville, Arkansas, in 1991. *A History of the Hunt Family From the Norman Conquest, 1066 A.D., to the Year 1890: Early Settlement in Oregon; Mining Experience in California in 1849; Incidents of Pioneer Life and Adventures Among the Indian Tribes of the Northwest* was compiled by G. W. Hunt and published in Boston, Massachusetts, in 1890.

HUNTER

Ranking: 140 **S.S. Count:** 217,355

Origin: English. Transformation of Hunt.

Famous **Hunters:** ROBERT HUNTER (?–1734) of Scotland was a well-liked colonial governor of New York and New Jersey. He started the first postal service in the colonies. He also served as the governor of Jamaica, which is where he died. ANDREW HUNTER (1751–1823) of Pennsylvania was a Presbyterian chaplain of both the army and the navy. He was commended by George Washington for his conduct at the Battle of Monmouth (New Jersey). He was the first chaplain-schoolmaster in the Navy. DAVID HUNTER (1802–1886) of Washington, D.C., was the son of Andrew. He was the head of the military commission that tried those who had conspired in the assassination of President Abraham Lincoln. ROBERT MERCER TALIAFERRO HUNTER (1809–1887) of Virginia was a member of Congress, Speaker of the House, and a U.S. senator before the Civil War. He served as the secretary of state of the Confederacy, as a Confederate senator during the war, and as one of the negotiators at the Hampton Roads Conference in 1865. He completed his political career as the treasurer of Virginia (1874–1880). THOMAS HUNTER (1831–1915) of Ireland was a teacher at P.S. 35 in New York City, started the first evening high school, and founded Normal College of New York City, which came to be known as Hunter College. ROBERT HUNTER (1874–1942) of Indiana was responsible for the first statewide child labor law in New York. CROIL HUNTER (1893–1970) of North Dakota was an airline executive who was instrumental in the initiation of the Great Circle Route.

Genealogies: *From Ayr to Thurber: Three Hunter Brothers and the Winning of the West* was compiled by William Hunter McLean and published in Fort Worth, Texas, in 1978. *The Hunters of Bedford County, Virginia; Notes and Documents on the Family of James Hunter, Regulator Leader* of North Carolina, Including Forebearers in Pennsylvania, Virginia, North Carolina, Louisiana and Texas was compiled by Walter Marvin Hunter and published in Cottonport, Louisiana, in 1973.

HUNTINGDON, HUNTINGTON, HUNTINTON (S.S. Abbreviation: Huntin)

Ranking: 3841 S.S. Count: 11,728

Origin: English. 1) derived from the Old English words "hunta" and "tūn," meaning hunter and enclosure or settlement. The name was given to those who came from Huntington, the name of several places in England. 2) derived from the Old English words "hunta" and "dūn," meaning huntsman and hill. The name was given to those who came from Huntingdon, the name of a major town in Cambridgeshire County in England.

Famous **Bearers**: SAMUEL HUNTINGTON (1731–1796) of Connecticut was one of the signers of the Declaration of Independence. He was a member and president of the Continental Congress and was the governor of Connecticut for 10 years. COLLIS POTTER HUNTINGTON (1821–1900) of Connecticut was a railroad magnate and part of the group that built the Central Pacific Railroad. EMILY HUNTINGTON (1841–1909) of Connecticut was a teacher and welfare worker. She developed courses to teach domestic, household duties to disadvantaged young children. From that grew the "kitchen garden" movement, the "kitchen" coming from its emphasis on elementary domestic training and the "garden" coming from her inspiration from kindergarten observations. HENRY EDWARDS HUNTINGTON (1850–1927) of New York was the nephew of Collis and was involved in railroads. He built urban railway systems in Los Angeles and San Francisco. ARCHER MILTON HUNTINGTON (1870–1955) of New York City was the founder of the Hispanic Society of America. ANNA VAUGHN HYATT HUNTINGTON (1876–1973) of Massachusetts was a sculptor known for her use of animals in her works of art. ELLSWORTH HUNTINGTON (1876–1947) of Illinois was a geographer and explorer. He was an explorer of the Euphrates River valley and wrote many books on the beginnings of civilization.

Genealogies: Norris, Hackett, Prescott and Allied Families: Our Ancestors and Their Descendants, Including Adams, Andrews, Bachelder, Bartlett, Boulter, Brewer, Brown, Harding, Hinkley, Howard, Huntington, et. al. was compiled by Hugh Albert Johnson and published in Annandale, Virginia, in 1976. The Huntington Letters, In the Possession of Julia Chester Wells . . . Printed For Private Distribution was compiled by William Denison McCrakan and published in New York, New York, in 1897.

HUNTLEY (S.S. Abbreviation: Huntle)

Ranking: 2592 S.S. Count: 17,555

Origin: English, Scottish. English: derived from the Old English words "hunta" and "lēah," meaning hunter and wood. The name was given to those who came from Huntley, the name of a place in Gloucestershire, England. Scottish: same derivation as in 1. The name was given to those who came from Huntlie, the name of a no longer extant place in the former county of Berwickshire, England.

Genealogies: *Thomas Huntley, Sr. of Anson County, North Carolina: His Descendants in the Carolinas and Elsewhere* was compiled by Virgil W. Huntley and published in Mystic, Connecticut, in 1988. *John Huntley, Immigrant of Boston & Roxbury, Massachusetts and Lyme, Connecticut, 1647–1977, and Some of His Descendants* was compiled by Virgil W. Huntley and published in Mystic, Connecticut, in 1978.

HURD

Ranking: 1504 S.S. Count: 29,631

Origin: English. Transformation of Heard. The name is common in the central (Midlands) region of England.

Famous **Hurds**: NATHANIEL HURD (1730–1777) of Massachusetts was a silversmith and engraver of bookplates. DATE CAMPBELL HURD-MEAD (1867–1941) of Canada was a physician and a historian of women in medicine. She wrote *Medical Women of America* and *A History of Women in Medicine from the Earliest Times to the Beginning of the Nineteenth Century*. PETER HURD (1904–1984) of New Mexico was an artist. He was the war artist during World War II for *Life* magazine.

Genealogies: *Miscellaneous Heards, Addendum*, was compiled by Harold Heard and published in Amarillo, Texas, in the 1970s.

HURLBURT, HURLBUT, HURLBUTT (S.S. Abbreviation: Hurlbu)

Ranking: 4461 S.S. Count: 10,044

Origin: English. 1) derived from the name Hurlbert, which means army or radiant. 2) the name was given to those who were adept at using a hurlebatte, a broad-bladed, netless stick used in the medieval game of hurling—a sport that slightly resembles today's game of lacrosse. 3) the name was given to those who used a hurlbat, a stick-shaped weapon, in battle.

Famous **Bearers**: STEPHEN AUGUSTUS HURBUT (1815–1882) of South Carolina was a lawyer and a major general in the Union army. He was accused of corruption while in command of Louisiana and was considered incompetent in his diplomatic duties in Colombia and Peru. He served as the first commander of the Grand Army of the Republic. JESSE LYMAN HURLBUT (1843–1930) of New York was a Methodist minister, editor, and author. After 1875, he was connected with the Chautauqua movement.

Genealogies: *Nathaniel Hurlbutt Descendants* was compiled by Edith H. Hurlbutt and published in 1970. *Hildreth Genealogy: Ancestors and Descendants of William and Joannah Chalker Hildreth of Glastonbury, Connecticut; With Information on Tuthill, Wells, Chalker, Coleman, Hurlbut, Stokely, and Riley Families* was compiled by Allen D. Sheneman and published in Defiance, Ohio, in 1982.

HURLEY

Ranking: 762 S.S. Count: 55,501

Origin: English, Irish. English: derived from the Old English word "hyrne," which refers either to a curve in a river or to a hollow in a hill, and the Old English word "lēah," meaning wood. The name was given to those who came from Hurley, the name of a place in Berkshire and Warwickshire counties in England. Irish: derived from the Gaelic name Ó hIarfhlatha, meaning "descendant of Iarfhlatih" (H&H), which is a first name describing a medieval underlord.

Famous **Hurleys:** EDWARD NASH HURLEY (1864–1933) of Illinois was an industrialist. He was the organizer of Standard Pneumatic Tool Co. As president of the Emergency Fleet Corporation, he made possible the U.S. army's transportation to Europe in World War I. JOSEPH PATRICK HURLEY (1874–1967) of Ohio was a Roman Catholic priest who helped to shape the church in Florida. PATRICK JAY HURLEY (1883–1963) of Oklahoma was an American diplomat who served as secretary of war, ambassador to several countries, and President Franklin D. Roosevelt's personal representative in the Near and Middle East.

Genealogies: *The Ancestry of William Neal Hurley 111 [sic]; A Record of Many of His Ancestors and Present Day Relatives Who Share The Common Ancestry* was compiled by William Neal Hurley and published in Chelsea, Michigan, in 1985.

HURST

Ranking: 690 S.S. Count: 60,896

Origin: English. 1) derived from the Old English word "hyrst," meaning wooded hill. The name was given to those who lived at such a spot. 2) same derivation as in 1. The name was given to those who came from Hurst, the name of places in Berkshire, Kent, Somerset, and Warwickshire counties in England. It may also have been given to those who came from Hirst, the name of a place in Northumberland and West Yorkshire counties in England.

Famous **Hursts:** JOHN FLETCHER HURST (1834–1903) of Maryland was the founder of American University in Washington, D.C. FANNIE HURST (1889–1968) of Ohio was a writer whose main interests were oppressed Jews in eastern Europe, social and medical help for homosexuals, and women's issues, including equal pay for equal work and a woman's choice to retain her own name after marriage.

Genealogies: None known.

HURT

Ranking: 1567 S.S. Count: 28,473

Origin: English. Transformation of the English definition of Hart.

Genealogies: *Tidewater to Texas: The Hurt Family, A History* was compiled by Ronald Wayne Hurt and published in Dallas, Texas, in 1990.

HURTAD

Ranking: 3423 S.S. Count: 13,202

Origin: Spanish. Derived from the Spanish word "hurtar," meaning to steal. The name was given to either the child of an illicit union or to a child who had been abducted.

Genealogies: None known.

HUSKEY

Ranking: 4921 S.S. Count: 9093

Origin: English? Uncertain etymology. Possibly derived from the Middle English name Osekin.

Genealogies: *Smoky Mountain Clans* was compiled by Donald B. Reagan and published in Knoxville, Tennessee, in 1978.

HUSSEY

Ranking: 3387 S.S. Count: 13,366

Origin: English, Irish. English: 1) derived from the Middle English word "husewif," which is composed of the Old English words "hūs" and "wif," meaning house and woman. The name was given to a woman who managed her own household. 2) derived from the Old French word "hous," meaning holly. The name was given to those who lived in Houssaye, the name of a place in Seine-Maritime in Normandy, France. 3) derived from the Old French word "h(e)usé," meaning booted. The name was given to those who had boots of a novel design. It may also have been given to a person who owned boots as an indication of his wealth—most peasants could not afford such luxury. Irish: derived from the Gaelic name Ó hEodhusa, meaning "descendant of Eodhus" (H&H), which is a first name given to a person belonging to an ancient Celtic order of singing poets or bards who composed and recited verses on the legends and history of their tribes.

Famous **Husseys:** OBED HUSSEY (1792–1860) of Maine, an inventor, was actually the first to invent and develop the reaper. A bitter rivalry ensued between Hussey and Cyrus McCormick. Both men made improvements to their machines, but Hussey refused to buy inventions of others that would ultimately make his reaper superior to McCormick's, which led to the decline of Hussey's. He sold his business in 1858 and died two years later. CURTIS GRUBB HUSSEY (1802–1893) of Pennsylvania opened the first copper mine on Lake Superior. WILLIAM JOSEPH HUSSEY (1862–1926) of Ohio was an astronomer who is credited with the discovery of about 1400 double stars.

Genealogies: None known.

HUSTON
Ranking: 1869 S.S. Count: 24,232
Origin: Scottish. Transformation of the first definition of Houston.

Famous **Hustons**: CHARLES HUSTON (1822–1897) of Pennsylvania was a physician and partner in a steel mill. He was one of the first steel manufacturers to perform scientific studies on the product. WALTER HUSTON (1884–1950) of Canada, born Walter Houghston, was a successful stage and film actor in New York. He received an Academy Award for his performance in *The Treasure of Sierra Madre* (1948), a movie for which his son, John Huston, won an Oscar for directing and writing.

Genealogies: *The Descendants of James Huston, With Related Families of the Berard, Johnson, Trowbridge, Rugg, Case, Brigham, Fiske, Newton, and McKitrick* was compiled by Edith H. Hurlbutt and published in Faribault, Minnesota, in 1967. *The History of John Huson From North Carolina to Alabama, His Huson/Huston/Houston Descendants, and the Allied Pioneer Families of Clepper, Robinson, Deen and Gilmore* was compiled by Margarette Hall Wood and published in Baltimore, Maryland, in 1990.

HUTCHEON, HUTCHERSON, HUTCHESON (S.S. Abbreviation: Hutche)
Ranking: 1315 S.S. Count: 33,816
Origin: English, Scottish. Transformations of Hutchin.
Genealogies: None known.

HUTCHIN, HUTCHINGS, HUTCHINGSON, HUTCHINS, HUTCHINSON, HUTCHISON (S.S. Abbreviation: Hutchi)
Ranking: 240 S.S. Count: 148,948
Origin: English, Scottish. Derived from the medieval first name Huchin, which is a transformation of Hugh(es).

Famous **Bearers**: ANNE HUTCHINSON (1591?–1643) of England was the head of the first organized attack on Puritans in the Massachusetts Bay Colony. She was expelled from the colony and finally settled in what is now Pelham Bay Park in the Bronx, New York. The Hutchinson River near there was named in her honor. THOMAS HUTCHINS (1730–1789) of New Jersey was a cartographer appointed by Congress to be the "geographer to the United States." He was responsible for the surveying of the lands in the Northwest Territory. THOMAS HUTCHINSON (1711–1780) of Massachusetts, the great-great-grandson of Anne, was a colonial official who represented Massachusetts in England. He held various positions in the colonial government until he appointed too many salaried people to positions. Although opposed to the Stamp and Sugar acts, he fell out of grace with the people, and an angry mob ransacked his home on August 26, 1765. He served as the governor of the colony until 1774. His *History of the Colony of Massachusetts Bay* is considered outstanding. WOODS HUTCHINSON (1862–1930) of England came to Iowa as a boy. He was a physician who emphasized preventive medicine. GRACE HUTCHINS (1885–1969) of Massachusetts was a social reformer and a member of the Communist Party, on whose ticket she unsuccessfully ran in New York state elections. ROBERT HUTCHINS (1899–1977) of New York was an educator who introduced the "Great Books" program. He was the founder of the Center for the Study of Democratic Institutions.

Genealogies: *Hudgins, Virginia to Texas* was compiled by Edgar H. Hudgins and published in Houston, Texas, in 1983.

HUTSON
Ranking: 2145 S.S. Count: 21,358
Origin: English. Transformation of Hudd(le).

Famous **Hutsons**: RICHARD HUTSON (1748–1795) of South Carolina was a Revolutionary War patroit and a justice of the state chancery court.

Genealogies: None known.

HUTTO
Ranking: 3777 S.S. Count: 11,961
Origin: Bavarian. Derived from the Germanic first names Odo and Otto.

Genealogies: *The Family of Lonard Vernadeau and Sarah Hutto, Three Generations—Compiled and Published By a Committee of the Descendants of Leonard Vernadeau: William W. Varnedoe, Jr., Chairman* was most likely published in Huntsville, Alabama, in 1971.

HUTTON
Ranking: 1735 S.S. Count: 25,865
Origin: English, Scottish. Derived from the Old English word "hōh," which literally means heel and refers to a ridge projecting from a hillside, and the Old English word "tūn," meaning enclosure or settlement. The name was given to those who came from Hutton, the name of various places in England.

Famous **Huttons**: LAURENCE HUTTON (1843–1904) of New York was an editor and author of biographies. FREDERICK REMSEN HUTTON (1853–1918) of New York was the head of the Mechanical Engineering Department at Columbia University. He wrote textbooks on the subject. LEVI WILLIAM HUTTON (1860–1928) of Iowa was a philanthropist and the founder in 1917 of the Hutton Settlement for underprivileged children.

Genealogies: *History and Genealogy of the Hutton Family* was compiled by Harold Hutton and published in Broken Bow, Nebraska, in 1983.

HUYNH

Ranking: 2657 S.S. Count: 17,131

Origin: Vietnamese. 1) derived from the Vietnamese word "huýnh," meaning to show off or boast. 2) derived from the Vietnamese word "huynh," meaning brothers.

Genealogies: None known.

HYATT

Ranking: 1721 S.S. Count: 26,036

Origin: Jewish, Scottish. Jewish: derived from the Hebrew word "chayat," meaning tailor. The name was given to those who worked as tailors. Scottish: derived from the Old English words "hēah" and "geat," meaning high or tall and gate. The name was given to those who came from Highgate, the name of a place in what was once Ayrshire County, now part of the Strathclyde region, in England.

Famous **Hyatts:** JOHN WESLEY HYATT (1837–1920) of New York was an inventor and a pioneer in what was to become the plastics industry. He also is credited with inventing a sugarcane mill and a multiple-stitch sewing machine. ALPHEUS HYATT (1838–1902) of Washington, D.C., was a zoologist and a palaeontologist. He was one of the founders of the Peabody Academy of Sciences, *American Naturalist*, and Woods Hole Marine biological laboratories. ANNA VAUGH HYATT (1876–1973) of Massachusetts was a sculptor. She is remembered for her ability to represent the forms of animals.

Genealogies: *A Genealogical History of the Hoyt, Haight, and Hight Families: With Some Account of the Earlier Hyatt Families, A List of the First Settlers of Salisbury and Amesbury, Mass.* was compiled by David W. Hoyt and published in Bethany, Oklahoma, in 1985.

HYDE

Ranking: 1087 S.S. Count: 40,712

Origin: English. 1) derived from the Old English word "hī(gi)d," meaning hide and referring to a substantial measure of land, ranging at different times from 60 to 120 acres and usually considered to be an amount adequate for one free family and its dependents. The name was given to those who lived on and worked land that was at one time demarcated as a hide. 2) derived from the Germanic first name Ida, which is composed of the word "id," meaning to work, perform, or labor.

Famous **Hydes:** EDWARD HYDE (1650?–1712) was a colonial official who served as governor of Virginia. HENRY BALDWIN HYDE (1834–1899) of New York was the founder of Equitable Life Assurance Society. JAMES NEVINS HYDE (1840–1910) of Connecticut was a pioneer in the field of dermatology. IDA HENRIETTA HYDE (1857–1945) of Iowa was a physiologist who fought the prejudices of the day to achieve her goals. Her main interest was working with circulation, respiration, nervous function, and embryological development. She was one of the first to apply the micro methods of studying individual cells. HELEN HYDE (1868–1919) of New York was an artist who is best known for her woodblock prints. Her work was influenced by Japanese art. ARTHUR MASTICK HYDE (1877–1947) of Missouri was the governor of that state, in which position he improved rural schools, made technical information available to farmers, and built more than 7500 miles of highways.

Genealogies: None known.

HYLAND

Ranking: 3786 S.S. Count: 11,913

Origin: English, Irish. English: derived from the Middle English words "hegh" or "hie" and "land," meaning high or tall and land. The name was given to those who lived on a piece of high-lying ground. Irish: derived from the Gaelic name Ó Faoláin, meaning "descendant of Faolán" (H&H), which is a first name derived from the word "faol," meaning wolf.

Genealogies: *The Hyland Family History* was compiled by Lloyd Ernest Hyland and published in 1974.

HYLTON

Ranking: 4681 S.S. Count: 9558

Origin: English. Transformation of Hilton.

Genealogies: None known.

HYMAN

Ranking: 2658 S.S. Count: 17,128

Origin: English, Jewish. English: derived from the Old English words "hēah" and "hām," meaning high or tall and homestead. The name was given to those who came from Higham, the name of various places in England. Jewish: derived from the Yiddish first name Khayim, which is derived from the Hebrew word "chaim," meaning life.

Genealogies: None known.

HYNES

Ranking: 3831 S.S. Count: 11,761

Origin: Irish. Derived from the Gaelic name Ó hEidhin, meaning "descendant of Eidhin" (H&H), which is a first name with an uncertain etymology. It may be derived from the word "eidhean," meaning ivy, or it may stem from a transformation of the place name Aidhne.

Genealogies: None known.

IBARRA

Ranking: 2146 S.S. Count: 21,356
Origin: Basque. Derived from the word "ibar," meaning meadow. The name was given to those who lived near meadows.
Genealogies: None known.

INGALL

Ranking: 4598 S.S. Count: 9723
Origin: English. 1) derived from the Old English first name Ing(a) and the word "holh," meaning hollow. The name was given to those from Ingol, a place in England. 2) derived from the Old Norse first name Ingialdr, which is derived from the words "ing" and "gialdr," the latter meaning tribute.
Genealogies: *The Genealogy and History of the Ingalls Family in America* was compiled by Charles Burleigh and published in Malden, Massachusetts, in 1903. *Saundersville, an English Settlement in Vanderburgh County* was compiled by Ken McCutchan and published in Evansville, Indiana, in 1978.

INGERS, INGERSOLL (S.S. Abbreviation: Ingers)

Ranking: 4063 S.S. Count: 11,129
Origin: Ingers—English, Jewish; Ingersoll—English. Ingers (English): derived from the Old Norse first name Ingvarr, which is derived from the words "ing" and "varr," the latter meaning guard. (Jewish:) 1) Uncertain etymology. Possibly a transformation of the surname Hunger. 2) possibly derived from the Yiddish word "Yinger," meaning younger. The name was given to a younger son. Ingersoll: derived from Inkersall, meaning "the Monks' field" (ES). The name was given to those from Inkersall, a place in England.
Famous **Bearers**: JARED INGERSOLL (1722–1781) of Connecticut was London's agent in the Connecticut colony. He opposed the Stamp Act, but he accepted the position of stamp master for Connecticut, from which he was forced to resign. He later served as vice-admiralty judge in Pennsylvania. His son, JARED INGERSOLL (1749–1822) of Connecticut, was a lawyer who was a member of the Continental Congress and served as counsel in many early prominent cases before the U.S. Supreme Court. He also was attorney general of Pennsylvania. His son, CHARLES JARED INGERSOLL (1782–1862) of Pennsylvania, also was a lawyer and legislator, but he was well known as a writer. Among his works were plays and a history of the War of 1812. SIMON INGERSOLL (1818– 1894) of Connecticut invented and patented the Ingersoll rock drill in 1871. ROBERT GREEN INGERSOLL (1833–1899) of New York, a lawyer, orator, and author, was popular as an agnostic lecturer. He wrote several books, including *Some Mistakes of Moses* (1879) and *Why I Am an Agnostic* (1896). ROBERT

HAWLEY INGERSOLL (1859–1928) of Michigan developed a mail-order and chain-store business. ROYAL EASON INGERSOLL (1883–1976) of Washington, D.C., a naval officer, was commander of the U.S. Atlantic Fleet and the Western Sea Frontier. WILLIAM BROWN INGERSOLL (1908–1977) of Utah was a dentist. He was the founder and head of the Department of Periodontia and Endodontia at Georgetown University.
Genealogies: None known.

INGLE

Ranking: 3231 S.S. Count: 14,041
Origin: English. Transformation of Ingall.
Genealogies: None known.

INGRAHAM (S.S. Abbreviation: Ingrah)

Ranking: 4632 S.S. Count: 9654
Origin: Derived from the German first name Engil (see Engel) and the word "hraban,"meaning raven.
Famous **Ingrahams**: JOSEPH INGRAHAM (1762–1800) of Massachusetts, as captain of the *Hope* in 1791–93, discovered the Washington Islands in the Marquesas. His nephew, DUNCAN NATHANIEL INGRAHAM (1802–1891) of South Carolina, was an officer in the Confederate navy. JOSEPH H. INGRAHAM (1809–1860) of Maine, an Episcopal clergyman and author, wrote a number of novels, including *Lafitte* (1836). He also wrote *The South-West, by a Yankee* (1835) and religious romances. His son, PRENTISS INGRAHAM (1843–1904) of Mississippi, also wrote many novels but perhaps was best known as the literary friend of Buffalo Bill (William Cody).
Genealogies: None known.

INGRAM (ALSO INGRAMS)

Ranking: 422 S.S. Count: 94,389
Origin: English. Transformation of Ingraham.
Genealogies: *The Descendants of Jonas Ingram and Melinda Butler* was compiled by James Barry Bingham and published in Baltimore, Maryland, in 1991. *Rhodes-Barnett and Mitchusson-Ingram* was compiled by Norma Rhodes Ladd and published in Calvert City, Kentucky, in 1991.

INMAN

Ranking: 1359 S.S. Count: 32,634
Origin: English. Derived from the Middle English word "innmann," which is derived from the Old English words "inn" and "mann," meaning lodging and man. The name was given to innkeepers.
Famous **Inmans**: HENRY INMAN (1801–1846) of New York was a leading portrait painter of his time. His subjects included Martin Van Buren and Clara Barton. His son, HENRY INMAN (1837–1899) of New York, wrote *The Old*

Santa Fe Trail (1897) and other frontier adventures. JOHN INMAN (1805–1850) of New York was editor of the *New York Mirror*, the New York *Commercial Advertiser*, and other publications. Brothers SAMUEL M. INMAN (1843–1915) of Georgia and JOHN H. INMAN (1844–1896) of Tennessee were prominent cotton merchants and financiers in the South. Samuel helped organize the Southern Railway system and donated to many educational institutions. John was noted for his work in industrial development.

Genealogies: *Daniel Inman of Connecticut, Ontario, N.Y. and Sugar Grove, Ill.* was compiled by Charles Gordon Inman and published in 1978.

IRBY

Ranking: 2792 **S.S. Count:** 16,301

Origin: English. Derived from the Old Norse word "Irabýr," meaning "Settlement of the Irish" (H&H). The name was given to those who came from Irby, the name of several places in England.

Genealogies: None known.

IRELAND (S.S. Abbreviation: Irelan)

Ranking: 2105 **S.S. Count:** 21,795

Origin: English, Scottish. Derived from the Old English word "Iraland," which was derived from "Iras" and "land," meaning Irishmen and land. The name was given to those from Ireland.

Famous **Irelands:** JOHN IRELAND (1827–1896) of Kentucky was governor of Texas (1883–1887). JOSEPH NORTON IRELAND (1817–1898) of New York wrote *Records of the New York Stage: 1750–1860* (1866–1867). JOHN IRELAND (1838–1918), born in Ireland, was a Catholic priest in the United States who was instrumental in the founding of Catholic University in Washington, D.C.

Genealogies: *Genealogies of the Caffey, Iseley & Ireland Families* was compiled by Beatrice M. Caffey Reed and published in High Point, North Carolina, in 1981. *The Irelands in America* was compiled by Everett B. Ireland and published in Falls Church, Virginia, in 1989.

IRISH

Ranking: 4687 **S.S. Count:** 9547

Origin: English. Transformation of Ireland.

Genealogies: *John Irish, His Life and Ancestors, 1086–1677* was compiled by George E. Irish and published in Baltimore, Maryland, in 1991.

IRIZARRY, IRIZARRI (S.S. Abbreviation: Irizar)

Ranking: 1569 **S.S. Count:** 28,432

Origin: Spanish. Uncertain etymology. The name was given to those from the an village.

Genealogies: None known.

IRONS

Ranking: 4474 **S.S. Count:** 10,007

Origin: English. Derived from the name "Airaines," which was derived from the Latin word "harēnas," meaning sands. The name was given to those from Airaines, a place in France.

Genealogies: None known.

IRVIN

Ranking: 1452 **S.S. Count:** 30,691

Origin: English, Irish, Scottish. English: derived from the Old English first name Eoforwine, which was derived from the words "eofor" and "wine," meaning wild boar and friend. Irish: derived from the Gaelic "Ó hEireamhón" (H&H), a first name of unknown origin. Scottish: derived from the name of a Celtic river, possibly derived from the words "wiryr" and "afon," meaning fresh and water. The name was given to those from Irving and Irvine, places in Scotland.

Genealogies: None known.

IRVINE

Ranking: 3254 **S.S. Count:** 13,972

Origin: English, Irish, Scottish. Transformation of Irvin.

Famous **Irvines:** WILLIAM IRVINE (1741–1804), born in Ireland, was a surgeon, legislator, and soldier in Pennsylvania. He served in the Continental and federal congresses and commanded troops that quelled the Whiskey Rebellion in 1794.

Genealogies: None known.

IRVING

Ranking: 2242 **S.S. Count:** 20,450

Origin: English, Irish, Scottish. Transformation of Irvin.

Famous **Irvings:** WASHINGTON IRVING (1783–1859) is well known as the author of the essays "Rip Van Winkle" and "The Legend of Sleepy Hollow." His life, however, involved a broad range of work. He served on the staff of U.S. diplomats in Spain and England and as U.S. minister to Spain. He also wrote a number of books, including *A Chronicle of the Conquest of Granada* (1829) and *Companions of Columbus* (1831). His brother WILLIAM IRVING (1766–1821) of New York was a member of Congress from New York and a poet. Another brother, PETER IRVING (1771–1838) of New York, was owner of the New York *Morning Chronicle* and *The Corrector*. Washington's nephew and William's son, PIERRE M. IRVING (1803–1876) of New York, a lawyer, was an assistant to and financial manager for Washington Irving. JOHN BEAUFAIN IRVING (1825–1877) of South Carolina was a prominent portrait, genre, and historical painter in New York after the Civil War. ROLAND DUER IRVING (1847–1888) of New York was a geologist and professor who conducted important iron and copper surveys in the Lake Superior area. He also was an early developer of genetic petrography. His son, JOHN DUER IRVING

(1874–1918) of Wisconsin, followed in his footsteps as a geologist and university professor.

Genealogies: *Fundy (also Irving) Family* was compiled by William Henry Irving and published in Durham, North Carolina, in 1972.

IRWIN
Ranking: 829 **S.S. Count:** 51,302
Origin: English, Irish, Scottish. Transformation of Irvin.

Famous **Irwins:** AGNES IRWIN (1841–1914) of Washington, D.C., was the first dean of Radcliffe College. She served in that capacity from 1883 to 1909, but she was bypassed for the presidency of Radcliffe in 1903 when trustees chose LeBaron Russell Briggs, the dean of faculty at Harvard University, for the top Radcliffe post. MAY IRWIN (1862–1938), born in Canada, was a vaudeville actress in New York who also toured with a Massachusetts company. INEZ LEONORE HAYNES GILLMORE IRWIN (1873–1970) was a writer and activist in the women's suffrage movement. Among her books was *Story of the Woman's Party* (1921), a history of the suffrage campaign. She also wrote *Angels and Amazons: A Hundred Years of American Women* (1933). GEORGE LE ROY IRWIN (1868–1931) of Michigan was a soldier noted for the use and development of field artillery. WILLIAM HENRY (WILL) IRWIN (1873–1948) of New York was a journalist and author. His books include *The Confessions of a Con Man* (1909) and *Propaganda and the News* (1936). ELISABETH ANTOINETTE IRWIN (1880–1942) of New York, a progressive educator, developed an experimental school program for New York City schools in which the school curriculum was designed to meet the students' abilities. When public funds evaporated during the Depression, private funding was obtained for her to start (1932) her own school, The Little Red School House, which she directed until her death.

Genealogies: *Darrtown to Fairfield and Beyond: The Descendants of John and Mary Welsh Irwin* was compiled by Lyndon N. Irwin and published in Bois D'Arc, Missouri, in 1991. *Guide to 500 Early Irwin/Ervin etc. Families in the United States* was compiled by L. M. Irwin and published in Bloomington, Illinois, in 1991.

ISAAC
Ranking: 2258 **S.S. Count:** 20,209
Origin: English, French, Jewish. Derived from the Hebrew first name Yitschak, which is derived from the word "tschak," meaning to laugh.
Genealogies: None known.

ISAACS (ALSO ISAACSON)
Ranking: 1400 **S.S. Count:** 31,694
Origin: Isaacs—English, French, Jewish; Isaacson—English. Transformations of Isaac.

Famous **Isaacses:** SAMUEL M. ISAACS (1804–1878), born in England, was a prominent New York rabbi and founder and editor of the *Jewish Messenger*. His son, ABRAM SAMUEL ISAACS (1851–1921) of New York, took over as editor of the *Jewish Messenger* after his father's death. EDITH JULIET RICH ISAACS (1878–1956) of Wisconsin was editor of *Theatre Arts* magazine and the editor or author of books on the theater.
Genealogies: None known.

ISBELL
Ranking: 3239 **S.S. Count:** 14,022
Origin: English. Derived from the first name Isabel, which is derived from the first name Elizabeth, meaning "Oath of God" (ES).
Genealogies: None known.

ISOM
Ranking: 3625 **S.S. Count:** 12,422
Origin: English. Derived from the word "Isham," meaning "a village on the Ise River" (ES). The name was given to those from Isham, a place in England.

Famous **Isoms:** MARY FRANCES ISOM (1865–1920) of Tennessee, as a librarian in Portland, Oregon, greatly expanded the public library mission and made books more available in rural areas.
Genealogies: None known.

ISRAEL (ALSO ISRAELASHVILI, ISRAELER, ISRAELEVITCH, ISRAELEWICZ, ET AL.)
Ranking: 3000 **S.S. Count:** 15,141
Origin: Jewish. Derived from the Hebrew first name Yisrael, meaning "Fighter of God" (H&H).
Genealogies: None known.

IVERSON (S.S. Abbreviation: Iverso)
Ranking: 2166 **S.S. Count:** 21,189
Origin: Danish, Norse, Swedish. Derived from the word "Iver," meaning archer. The name was given to "the sons of Iver" (ES).

Famous **Iversons:** ALFRED IVERSON (1798–1873) of Georgia was a U.S. senator from Georgia and an early advocate of secession during the pre–Civil War era.
Genealogies: None known.

IVES
Ranking: 3795 **S.S. Count:** 11,885
Origin: English. Derived from the Norman first name Ivo, which is derived from the Old Norse word "ýr," meaning yew and bow.

Famous **Iveses:** ELI IVES (1778–1861) of Connecticut, a graduate of and professor at Yale University, helped establish the Yale medical school. JAMES MERRITT IVES

(1824–1895) of New York was a partner in a lithography business with Nathaniel Currier. They produced the famous Currier & Ives prints. JOSEPH CHRISTMAS IVES (1828–1868) of New York explored the Colorado River in 1857–58 and wrote a report that was characterized as a classic description of the area. HALSEY COOLEY IVES (1847–1911) of New York started a free drawing class that developed into the St. Louis Museum and School of Fine Arts. He also was art director for the Chicago and St. Louis world's fairs (1893 and 1904). FREDERIC EUGENE IVES (1856–1937) of Connecticut was an inventor whose contributions included developments that led to the modern processes for printing photographs. NORMAN SEATON IVES (1923–1978) was born in the Panama Canal Zone. He was an artist and professor of art at Yale and is best known for his collages of squares made up of triangles.

Genealogies: *The Migrating Ives and their Descendants, 1639–1988* was compiled by Dorothy Gilmore and published in Bethany, Oklahoma, in 1988.

IVEY
Ranking: 3795 **S.S. Count:** 31,707
Origin: English. 1) derived from the Old French word "ivoie," which was derived from "if," meaning yew tree. The name was given to those from Ivoy, a place in England. 2) transformation of Ive(s).
Genealogies: None known.

IVORY
Ranking: 4874 **S.S. Count:** 9180
Origin: English. Derived from the Gallo-Roman first name Eburius, which was derived from the Latin word "ebur," meaning ivory. The name was given to those from Ivry-la-Bataille, a place in England.
Genealogies: None known.

IVY
Ranking: 2706 **S.S. Count:** 16,806
Origin: English. Transformation of Ivey.
Genealogies: None known.

JABLONSKI, JABLONSKY (S.S. Abbreviation: Jablon)

Ranking: 3270 **S.S. Count:** 13,878

Origin: Polish. Derived from the word "jablon," meaning apple tree, and the surname suffix "ski." The name was given to those living near an apple orchard or who sold or grew apples.

Famous **Bearers:** HARVEY JULIUS JABLONSKY (1909–1989) of Missouri held many positions of authority as an officer in the U.S. army, including assistant division commander, 82nd Airborne Division, and director of the Office of Personnel, Department of the Army.

Genealogies: None known.

JACK

Ranking: 2435 **S.S. Count:** 18,642

Origin: English, Jewish, Scottish. English, Scottish: 1) derived from the name John. 2) derived from the Old French first name Jacques. Jewish: cognate to any of several Jewish names of similar sound.

Genealogies: *A Brief History of Our Cook Family and Our Sharp Family* was compiled by Violet Sharp Cook and published in Pacifica, California, in 1985. *John Jack of Cecil County, Maryland* was compiled by A. Lucille Harney and published in Baltimore, Maryland, in 1988.

JACKMAN

Ranking: 4499 **S.S. Count:** 9958

Origin: English, Jewish. English: 1) derived from Jack (see Jack) and the word "man," meaning man. The name was given to the servant of persons named Jack. 2) cognate to the French Jacquéme, which is a cognate to Jack. Jewish: derived from any of several Jewish surnames that sound similar.

Famous **Jackmans:** WILBUR SAMUEL JACKMAN (1855–1907) of Ohio was a pioneer in the teaching of nature studies in the elementary grades.

Genealogies: *Walking Through the Shadows with the Jackmans* was compiled by Etta C. Jackman and published in Cullman, Alabama, in 1982.

JACKS

Ranking: 4648 **S.S. Count:** 9617

Origin: English. Transformation of Jack.

Genealogies: None known.

JACKSON

Ranking: 15 **S.S. Count:** 931,594

Origin: English. Transformation of Jack.

Famous **Jacksons:** HALL JACKSON (1739–1797) of New Hampshire was chief surgeon of the New Hampshire Continental Army troops. He also was one of the first to raise foxglove, from which digitalis is derived. DAVID JACKSON (1747?–1801) of Pennsylvania was a Revolutionary patriot and the first graduate in medicine of the school that became the University of Pennsylvania. JAMES JACKSON (1757–1806) of England came to Georgia to start a new life and served his newly adopted country as a Revolutionary soldier, a U.S. senator, and as the governor of Georgia. WILLIAM JACKSON (1759–1828) was born in England and came to America as a child. He served as a Revolutionary soldier and as the personal secretary to George Washington (1789–1791). ANDREW JACKSON (1767–1845) of South Carolina was the seventh president of the United States. He was a lawyer, a member of Congress, a senator, a justice of the Tennessee Supreme Court, and a major general in both the Tennessee militia and the U.S. army. He captured Pensacola, Florida, and successfully defended New Orleans, which made him a national hero. As president, he completely paid off the national debt. He also served as governor of the Florida territory in 1821. RACHEL DONELSON ROBARDS JACKSON (1767–1828) of Virginia was the wife of President Andrew Jackson, but she never lived in the White House. Displeased with his continuing his public career, she refused to move to Washington when he was elected. Just prior to his leaving Tennessee to assume the presidency, she suffered a heart attack and died a few days later. JOHN GEORGE JACKSON (1777–1825) of what is now West Virginia was a Virginia politician, the first U.S. judge in western Virginia, and one of the developers of Virginia's natural resources. He also was the brother-in-law of President James Madison. JAMES JACKSON (1777–1867) of Massachusetts was a physician and one of the first to scientifically study the vaccination theory. He was one of the founders of the Massachusetts General Hospital. PATRICK TRACY JACKSON (1780–1847) of Massachusetts was one of the founders of the first factory that made cloth from raw cotton within one building. He was also one of the founders of Lowell, Massachusetts, and the builder of the Boston & Lowell Railroad. CHARLES THOMAS JACKSON (1805–1880) of Massachusetts was a physician, chemist, and geologist. It is rumored that he taught Samuel F.B. Morse the basic principles of the electric telegraph and that it was his suggestion to W.T.G. Morton that ether be used as an anesthetic for the removal of teeth. THOMAS JONATHAN JACKSON (1824–1863) of what is now West Virginia is best known as Stonewall Jackson. He was a soldier in the U.S., then the Confederate, army. He received the name Stonewall because of his resistance to the Union army at Bull Run. He died after being accidentally wounded by his troops at Chancellorsville, Virginia. ABRAHAM REEVES JACKSON (1827–1892) of Pennsylvania was the founder of the Woman's Hospital of Illinois and the one after whom Mark Twain patterned his witty doctor in *Innocents Abroad*. HELEN MARIA FISKE HUNT JACKSON (1830–1885) of Massachusetts was a writer who researched and wrote *A Century of Dishonor* (1881) as a documentation of the government's poor conduct in managing Native American affairs. HOWELL EDMUNDS JACKSON (1832–1895) of Tennessee was a lawyer and judge. He served as the first presiding judge of the U.S. Circuit Court of Appeals in Cincinnati, then as a justice of the U.S. Supreme Court. SHELDON JACKSON (1834–1909) of New York was a missionary in the western mountain states and Alaska. He served as the first superintendent of schools in Alaska and is credited with being the man who introduced domesticated reindeer to the state (1892). WILLIAM HENRY JACKSON (1843–1942) of New York was a photographer who traveled across the United States and was on his return to the East when he set up his shop in Omaha, Nebraska, and spent the next years canvassing the West, taking historical shots of Indians, frontiersmen, settlers, and the progress in the building of the transcontinental railroad. EDWARD JACKSON (1856–1942) of Pennsylvania was an opthalmologist who was instrumental in raising standards in the training of opthalmologists. JOHN BRICKERHOFF JACKSON (1862–1920) of New Jersey was a diplomat who served in Germany, Greece, Cuba, and Romania, among other countries. ROBERT R. JACKSON (1870–1942) of Illinois was a black political and civic leader who was a protégé of Edward Wright in turn-of-the-century Chicago politics. He felt that blacks should work within the system. CLARENCE MARTIN JACKSON (1875–1947) of Iowa was an anatomist and, as the head of the department of anatomy at the University of Minnesota Medical School, was responsible for the reorganization of that department, which included graduate and research work. He is himself remembered for his research on the effects of continual malnutrition, as cited in his paper "Effects of Inanition and Malnutrition Upon Growth and Structure" (1925). DUNHAM JACKSON (1888–1946) of Massachusetts was a mathematician who taught at the university level. LEE or LEO JACKSON (1891–1974) of Ohio was the president of Firestone Tire and Rubber Co. during its period of expansion and growth. MAHALIA JACKSON (1911–1972) of Louisiana was a gospel singer who refused to compromise her beliefs in music. One of her greatest achievements was the singing of an old slave spiritual during the 1963 March on Washington with Martin Luther King Jr. HENRY MARTIN JACKSON (1912–1983) of Washington was a politician known as Scoop Jackson. He made a career out of service to his country, serving as a member of Congress, then senator, from his home state. He twice ran unsuccessfully for the Democratic presidential nomination. SHIRLEY HARDIE JACKSON (1916–1965) of California was a writer whose novels depicted houses as symbols of their inhabitants. In her best-selling *We Have Always Lived in the Castle* (1962), the house becomes ill as the main character is rejected by her mother.

Genealogies: *Jacksons of Perry or Those Descendants and Ascendants of James Jackson born 1796* was compiled by Daniel L. Jackson and published in Morton Grove, Illinois,

in 1985. *Nicholas Jackson of Rowley, Massachusetts, and his Descendants, 1635–1976* was compiled by Blake Smith Jackson and published in Belchertown, Massachusetts, in 1977. *Pioneers West of Appalachia* was compiled by Jane Parker McManus and published in New Orleans, Louisiana, in 1976.

JACOB
Ranking: 1888 S.S. Count: 23,921
Origin: *English, Jewish, Portuguese. Derived from the Hebrew first name Yaakov.*
Famous **Jacobs**: RICHARD TAYLOR JACOB (1825–1903) of Kentucky was a Kentucky soldier and a Unionist.
Genealogies: *History of the Jacob Family in England, Ireland, and America* was compiled by Caroline Nicholson Jacob and published in West Chester, Pennsylvania, in 1964.

JACOBS (ALSO JACOBSEN, JACOBSKIND, JACOBSOHN, JACOBSON)
Ranking: 110 S.S. Count: 257,942
Origin: *Jacobs, Jacobson—English. Jacobs, Jacobskind, Jacobsohn—Jewish. Jacobsen—Danish, Dutch, Flemish, Norwegian. Transformations of Jacob.*
Famous **Bearers**: WILLIAM PLUMER JACOBS (1842–1917) of South Carolina was the founder of Thornwell Orphanage (1875) and the school that came to be Presbyterian College of South Carolina. FRANCES WISEBART JACOBS (1843–1892) of Kentucky was a leader of charity organizations in Denver, Colorado. JOSEPH JACOBS (1859–1929) of Georgia was a pharmacist and the owner of a chain of drugstores. He also was a collector of Robert Burns's works. PATTIE RUFFNER JACOBS (1875–1935) of West Virginia was a leader in Alabama and national women's suffrage activities. ALBERT CHARLES JACOBS (1900–1976) of Michigan was the president of Trinity College in Hartford, Connecticut. JOHN THEODORE JACOBS (1903–1975) of Colorado was a physician. He started the first amputation clinic in Denver and operated one of the largest clinics for physically impaired children in the state of Colorado.
Genealogies: *History of the Jacobson Family in Norway and America* was compiled by Harriet Martinson Sybilrud and published in New Richland, Minnesota, in 1990. *A History and Genealogy of the Pritchett, Rimmer, Jacobs, et al.* was compiled by Dorothy Symmonds and published in Bellaire, Texas, in 1985.

JACOBY
Ranking: 3457 S.S. Count: 13,057
Origin: *English. Transformation of Jacob.*
Famous **Jacobys**: LUDWIG SIGMUND JACOBY (1813–1874) of Germany was a Methodist clergyman who worked among the Germans in the Midwest.

Genealogies: None known.

JACQUE (ALSO JACQUEAU, JACQUEL, JACQUELAIN, JACQUELET)

Ranking: 1911 S.S. Count: 23,677

Origin: Jacques—English. Jacqueau, Jacquel, Jacquelain, Jacquelet—French. Transformations of Jack.

Genealogies: None known.

JAEGER

Ranking: 2543 S.S. Count: 17,857

Origin: Danish. Cognate to the German surname Jager, which was derived from the word "jagen," meaning to hunt. The name was given to those whose occupation was hunting.

Genealogies: *The Yeager Family Circle from Hither to Yonder* was compiled by Daphne Yeager McPherson and published in Cullman, Alabama, in 1991.

JAFFE

Ranking: 4767 S.S. Count: 9388

Origin: Jewish. Derived from the nickname Jaffe, which was derived from the name Japheth, meaning increase.

Famous Jaffes: HANS JAFFE (1909–1977), born in Germany, was a physicist in Connecticut and Ohio who specialized in research into piezoelectricity.

Genealogies: None known.

JAMES

Ranking: 89 S.S. Count: 310,625

Origin: English. Transformation of Jacob.

Famous Jameses: THOMAS CHALKLEY JAMES (1766–1835) of Pennsylvania was a pioneer in bringing to America the most updated material in the field of obstetrics. Because of his efforts, a strong foundation was laid for the scientific practice of this discipline. THOMAS JAMES (1782–1847) of Maryland was a trapper and trader on the frontier. He was the author of *Three Years Among the Indians and Mexicans* (1846), considered a good reference on frontier life. EDWIN JAMES (1797–1861) of Vermont was a physician, explorer, and naturalist. He was a participant in the Stephen H. Long western exploration of the lands between the Mississippi River and the Rocky Mountains, from which he wrote the official record of the journey, titled *Account of an Expedition from Pittsburgh to the Rocky Mountains* (1822–1823). THOMAS POTTS JAMES (1803–1882) of Pennsylvania was a pharmacist and botanist and the co-author of *Manual of North American Mosses* (1884). CHARLES TILLINGHAST JAMES (1805–1862) of Rhode Island was a U.S. senator from his home state. HENRY JAMES (1811–1882) of New York was a philosopher and author and the father of the Henry James born in 1843. DANIEL WILLIS JAMES (1832–1907) was born in England to American parents. He was the son of Arthur Curtiss James and continued his father's donations to char-

ities and institutions through the James Foundation. WILLIAM JAMES (1842–1910) of New York City was a psychologist and philosopher who taught at Harvard University. He founded the first psychology laboratory in the United States. HENRY JAMES (1843–1916) of New York City was an author who wrote *Daisy Miller*, among other works. JESSE WOODSON JAMES (1847–1882) of Missouri was an outlaw who, with his brother Frank and the Younger brothers, formed a gang of bank and train robbers. He was murdered by Robert Ford, one of his gang, for reward money. ALICE JAMES (1848–1892) of New York, sister of the novelist Henry James and the psychologist William James, kept her thoughts in a journal, published posthumously as *Alice James: Her Brothers, Her Journal* (1934). The journal is regarded as a significant family document. EDMUND JANES JAMES (1855–1925) of Illinois was an economist and the president of several universities. ARTHUR CURTISS JAMES (1867–1941) of New York was a financier and, at one time, the controller of over 40,000 miles of railroad lines. He also was a philanthropist and, through the James Foundation, gave more than $144 million to children's and educational institutions. OLLIE MURRAY JAMES (1871–1918) of Kentucky was a U.S. senator and one of the most popular speakers of the day. MARQUIS JAMES (1891–1955) of Missouri was a journalist and author. He won the Pulitzer Prize twice, once for *The Raven*, a biography of Sam Houston, and once for *Portrait of a President*, the second volume of a biography on Andrew Jackson. WILL RODERICK JAMES (1892–1942) of Canada was an author and artist who, unhappy with his name and family life, changed both. He was born Joseph Ernest Nephtali Dufault and lived in Montreal, where his father owned a hotel. James's version had his father as a Texas cattleman who had died, leaving him to be raised by a nomadic trapper in Canada. He left Canada in 1907 and wandered around western North America, killing a man, cattle rustling, and working as a Hollywood stuntman. The cattle rustling earned him a year in jail. In 1918 he joined the army but one year later was attending the California School of Fine Arts in San Francisco. A fan of the work of Frederic Remington and Charles Russell, he did publish sketches and earned a scholarship to Yale Art School, but he dropped out and returned to Nevada, where he began writing and illustrating. Finding his creative niche, he was published in magazines and then in books by Charles Scribner's Sons, mostly on the subject of cowboys. *Smoky* (1926) was his autobiography. Once published, he kept his true past life hidden until 1967. DANIEL JAMES JR. (1920–1978) of Florida, nicknamed Chappie, was a member of the Army Air Corps. He served as a pilot and instructor and saw combat in Korea and Vietnam. He was the first black four-star general in the U.S. military.

Genealogies: *James Families of America Since 1630* was

compiled by Wynne James and published in Bethesda, Maryland, in 1981. *The James Family of Wales and Bucks County, Pennsylvania, 1638–1974* was compiled by Wynne James and published in Arlington, Virginia, in 1974.

JAMESON
Ranking: 2551 **S.S. Count:** 17,806
Origin: English. Transformation of James.

Famous **Jamesons:** HORATIO GATES JAMESON (1778–1855) of Pennsylvania was the founder of the Washington Medical College in Baltimore. JOHN ALEXANDER JAMESON (1824–1890) was a jurist and the author of the historical account *The Constitutional Convention.* JOHN FRANKLIN JAMESON (1859–1937) of Massachusetts was a historian and the founder of the American Historical Association. He also wrote several books on the subject.

Genealogies: *Ancestry of the Jameson, Gilbert, Joy, Skinner, and Related Families* was compiled by Bradner Petersen and published in Pasadena, California, in 1986.

JAMIESON
Ranking: 4099 **S.S. Count:** 11,023
Origin: English. Transformation of James.

Genealogies: *The Jamieson Family, 1747– 1978* was compiled by the Jamieson Family Reunion Committee and published in 1978.

JAMISON
Ranking: 1214 **S.S. Count:** 36,297
Origin: English. Transformation of James.

Famous **Jamisons:** DAVID JAMISON (1660–1739) of Scotland was a lawyer who defended Francis Makemie for preaching without a license (1707). He was chief justice of the New Jersey Supreme Court (1711–1723) and one of the founders of the Church of England in New York. DAVID FLAVEL JAMISON (1810–1864) of South Carolina was a South Carolina politician and the president of the South Carolina secession convention. CECILIA VIETS DAKIN JAMISON (1837–1909) was born in Nova Scotia and moved to Massachusetts as a young child. She was the author of romance novels and juvenile stories.

Genealogies: *The Jamison Family, 1647–1960* was compiled by Henry Downs Jamison and published in Nashville, Tennessee, in 1960. *A Statistical History of the Descendants of William Andrew Jamison* was compiled by Ruth Jamison and published in 1978.

JANES
Ranking: 3807 **S.S. Count:** 11,852
Origin: English. Transformation of John.

Famous **Janeses:** LEWIS GEORGE JANES (1844–1901) of Rhode Island was a lecturer associated with the Ethical Association, a free religious group. He wrote *Health and a Day* (1901).

Genealogies: *History of the Janes-Peek Family* was compiled by Reba Neighbors Collins and published in Edmond, Oklahoma, in 1975. *Rendezvous in Racine* was compiled by Ralph M. Colburn and published in Decatur, Illinois, in 1980.

JANKOWICZ, JANKOWITZ, JANKOWSKI (S.S. Abbreviation: Jankow)
Ranking: 3008 **S.S. Count:** 15,104
Origin: Jewish, Polish. Derived from the Yiddish first name Yankev, which was derived from the Hebrew first name Yaakov.

Genealogies: None known.

JANSEN (ALSO JANSENS)
Ranking: 2231 **S.S. Count:** 20,517
Origin: Dutch, Flemish. Cognate to John.

Famous **Bearers:** REINER JANSEN (?–1706) of Holland came to America and worked for the Society of Friends in Philadelphia as a printer.

Genealogies: *The Cornelius Jansen Family History* was compiled by Betty Ann Miller and published in Berlin, Ohio, in 1974.

JANSSEN, JANSSENS (S.S. Abbreviation: Jansse)
Ranking: 3067 **S.S. Count:** 14,794
Origin: Flemish. Transformation of Jansen.

Famous **Bearers:** FRANCIS JANSSENS (1843–1897) of the Netherlands was a Roman Catholic priest who came to the United States in 1868 and served the communities of Richmond, Virginia; Natchez, Mississippi; and New Orleans, Louisiana.

Genealogies: None known.

JARAMILLO
Ranking: 2044 **S.S. Count:** 22,366
Origin: Spanish. Derived from the place name Jaramillo, meaning "a place where Orach grew" (ES). The name was given to those who came from Jaramillo, a place in Spain.

Genealogies: None known.

JARRELL, JARRELLS (S.S. Abbreviation: Jarrel)
Ranking: 2283 **S.S. Count:** 19,907
Origin: English. Transformations of Gerald.

Famous **Bearers:** HELEN IRA JARRELL (1896–1973) of Georgia was the superintendent of schools in Atlanta. There she appointed male principals to the elementary schools, something unheard of up to that point. RANDALL

JARRELL (1914–1965) of Tennessee was a college professor and a writer of verse and novels.

Genealogies: None known.

JARRET (ALSO JARRETT)

Ranking: 1579 S.S. Count: 28,294

Origin: Jarrett—English; Jarret—French. Jarrett: transformation of Garrett. Jarret: derived from the Old French word "jarre," meaning clay pots. The name was given to potters.

Famous Bearers: MARY CROMWELL JARRETT (1877–1961) of Maryland was a social worker who was a leader in developing psychiatric social work as a specialty.

Genealogies: *Morris & Jarretts of West Virginia* was compiled by Flora M. Beeler and published in Knoxville, Tennessee, in 1974.

JARVIS

Ranking: 927 S.S. Count: 46,443

Origin: English. 1) derived from Jervaulx, the name of a place in Yorkshire, England which was derived from the Anglo-Norman-French river Ure and the Anglo-Norman-French word "vaulx," meaning valley. The name was given to those from Jervaulx, a place in England. 2) derived from the Norman first name Gervase, which is derived from the Germanic component "gari," meaning spear, and another uncertain component.

Famous Jarvises: ABRAHAM JARVIS (1739–1813) of Connecticut was an Episcopal clergyman and the bishop of Connecticut. WILLIAM JARVIS (1770–1859) of Massachusetts was the U.S. consul to Portugal and the person responsible for the introduction of merino sheep to the United States in great numbers. JOHN WESLEY JARVIS (1780–1840) was born in England but came to America as a child. He was a painter and is best known for his portraits. EDWARD JARVIS (1803–1884) of Massachusetts was responsible for reorganizing the U.S. census. THOMAS JORDAN JARVIS (1836–1915) of North Carolina was a Confederate soldier, governor of North Carolina, and minister to Brazil. WILLIAM CHAPMAN JARVIS (1855–1895) of Virginia was a physician and the inventor of the famous "snare," which was considered a great advancement in the treatment of intranasal tumors. He was considered a pioneer in the diagnosis and treatment of nose and throat illnesses. ANNA M. JARVIS (1864–1948) of West Virginia campaigned for and won the national observance of Mother's Day.

Genealogies: *The Hemrick and Allied Families* was compiled by Grace H. Jarvis and published in Jacksonville, Florida, in 1975.

JASPER (ALSO JASPERS, JASPERSEN)

Ranking: 3093 S.S. Count: 14,676

*Origin: English, German. Derived from the central Euro-*pean first name Kaspar, which was derived from the Persian word "kaspar," meaning treasurer.*

Famous Bearers: WILLIAM JASPER (1750–1779) of South Carolina was a Revolutionary soldier best remembered as the one who picked up the American flag that had been shot down and remounted it during the battle and in heavy fire, June 1776, at the fort that would be renamed Fort Moultrie. He died attempting another flag hanging during the 1779 assault on Savannah, Georgia.

Genealogies: None known.

JAY

Ranking: 3449 S.S. Count: 13,085

Origin: English, French. Derived from the Middle English word "jay(e)" or the Old French word "gai," both meaning jay, the name of the bird.

Famous Jays: SIR JAMES JAY (1732–1829) was a physician, a brother of John Jay (1745–1829), and a suspected Loyalist, working against American independence. JOHN JAY (1745–1829) of New York City was a member of both the first and second Continental Congress, drafted New York's constitution, was the first chief justice of the U.S. Supreme Court, and was a governor of New York. PETER AUGUSTUS JAY (1776–1843) of New Jersey was the son of John Jay. He was a New York lawyer and his father's secretary on his 1794 mission to England. WILLIAM JAY (1789–1858) of New York City was another of John Jay's sons. He was involved in the antislavery movement and was an author. One of his books was *The Life of John Jay* (1833). JOHN JAY (1817–1894) of New York was the grandson of John Jay, an active participant in the antislavery movement, and one of the organizers of the New York Republican Party. He served as the U.S. minister to Austria (1869–1874).

Genealogies: *The Jays of Bedford* was compiled by Jennifer P. McLean and published in Katonah, New York, in 1984.

JEAN

Ranking: 3842 S.S. Count: 11,727

Origin: English, French. Cognate to John.

Genealogies: None known.

JEFFERIES, JEFFERIS, JEFFERS, JEFFERSON, JEFFERY (S.S. Abbreviation: Jeffer)

Ranking: 325 S.S. Count: 115,525

Origin: English. Derived from the Middle English first name Geffrey.

Famous Bearers: THOMAS JEFFERSON (1743–1826) of Virginia was the third president of the United States. He was the main writer of the Declaration of Independence and one of its signers. He served as governor of Virginia and as a member of the Continental Congress, designed the U.S. decimal coinage system, and was vice president of the United States and a member of Congress. As president, he purchased Louisiana, sent Meriwether Lewis and William Clark west, and prohibited the importation of slaves. After his presidency he was instrumental in the founding of the University of Virginia. JOHN JEFFERIES (1744?–1819) of Massachusetts was a Loyalist during the Revolution. He returned to England, where he became interested in aerostation. He made two ascents, the second one over the English Channel, where he took measurements of temperature and humidity. At an altitude of 9309 feet, the first scientific data were taken of the free air. Around 1790 he returned to Boston and continued his life. JOSEPH JEFFERSON (1774–1832) of England came to America in 1795 as an actor. He was famous in Philadelphia's Chestnut Street Theater. WILLIAM NICHOLSON JEFFERS (1824–1883) of New Jersey was a naval officer and the commander of the U.S.S. *Monitor* after its famous battle with the Confederate *Merrimack*. JOSEPH JEFFERSON (1829–1905) of Pennsylvania was an actor in Laura Keene's company. His most famous role was that of Rip Van Winkle in Dion Boucicault's play of the same name. He was the grandson of Joseph Jefferson. EDWARD TURNER JEFFERY (1843–1927) was born in England and came to the United States as a child. As a railroad executive, he was the general manager of the Illinois Central, the president of the Denver & Rio Grande, and part of the Western Pacific fiasco. MARK SYLVESTER WILLIAM JEFFERSON (1863–1949) of Massachusetts was a geographer and a professor at Michigan State Normal School, where so many students (15,000) took his course that the school earned the nickname "nursery of American geographers." He was the chief cartographer at the U.S. Peace Commission in Paris at the end of World War I. JOHN ROBINSON JEFFERS (1887–1962) of Pennsylvania was a poet and playwright. His poems reflect bitter contempt for humanity and love of nature.

Genealogies: *Collected Papers to Commemorate Fifty Years of the Monticello Association of the Descendants of Thomas Jefferson* was compiled by George Green Shackelford and published in Charlottesville, Virginia, in 1965. *A Genealogical Record of the Descendants of James Jeffery* was compiled by Dale Hanks and published in Glen Allen, Virginia, in 1976.

JEFFREE, JEFFREES, JEFFREY, JEFFREYS (S.S. Abbreviation: Jeffre)

Ranking: 2208 S.S. Count: 20,789
Origin: *English. Transformations of Jefferies.*
Genealogies: *The Jeffrey Family* was compiled by Mrs. Clarence Jeffrey and published in New Hampshire in 1974. *Marmaduke Norfleet Jeffreys* was compiled by Louise Jeffreys Andrew and was published in Springfield, Virginia, in 1983.

JEFFRIES

Ranking: 1335 S.S. Count: 33,140
Origin: *English. Transformation of Jefferies.*
Famous **Jeffrieses:** JOHN JEFFRIES (1745–1819) of Massachusetts was a Loyalist who left the United States for England at the start of the Revolutionary War. He was a balloonist and the first to cross the English Channel in a balloon. JAMES JACKSON JEFFRIES (1875–1953) of Ohio was a boxer. He was the world's heavyweight champion from 1899 to 1905. He won the title by defeating Bob Fitzsimmons. BENJAMIN JAY JEFFERIES (1833–1915) of Massachusetts was a physician and the writer of a paper on color blindness that was long considered a standard.

Genealogies: *Marmaduke Norfleet Jeffreys* (also Jeffries) was compiled by Louise Jeffreys Andrew and published in Springfield, Virginia, in 1983.

JENKIN

Ranking: 91 S.S. Count: 303,387
Origin: *English. Derived from the Middle English first name Jenkin, which is derived from the first name John and the Germanic suffix "kin."*
Genealogies: *Greenberry Jenkins of Cherokee County, Texas* was compiled by Jack S. Jenkins and published in San Antonio, Texas, in 1983. *The Jenkins Family of Virginia and North Carolina* was compiled by Antoinette Cornelia Bowen and published in Raleigh, North Carolina, in 1966.

JENKS

Ranking: 4431 S.S. Count: 10,123
Origin: *English. Transformation of Jenkin.*
Famous **Jenkses:** JOSEPH JENKS (1602–1683) of England was an inventor and the first to cut dies for the first coins minted in Boston. He also built the first fire engine and made a new type of scythe that is still in use today. TUDOR STORRS JENKS (1778–1866) of Massachusetts was a pioneer in the spiritual guidance of seamen. GEORGE CHARLES JENKS (1850–1929) of England was one of the writers of dime-store novels that followed the adventures of the imaginary Nick Carter and Diamond Dick. JEREMIAH WHIPPLE JENKS (1856–1929) of Michigan was the first American academic economist to sit on government boards and committees.

Genealogies: *Genealogy of the Jenks Family of Newport, N.H.* was compiled by George Edwin Jenks.

JENNINGS, JENNINS (S.S. Abbreviation: Jennin)

Ranking: 290 S.S. Count: 124,372
Origin: *English. Derived from the Middle English first name Janyn, which is a transformation of John.*
Famous **Bearers:** JOHN JENNINGS (1738?–1802), probably from Pennsylvania, was a Revolutionary soldier who

was instrumental in keeping settlers from Connecticut from coming to Pennsylvania in the Pennimite War. JONATHAN JENNINGS (1784–1834) of either New Jersey or Virginia was a member of Congress and the first governor of Indiana. JAMES HENNEN JENNINGS (1854–1920) of Kentucky initiated a process for removing gold from South Africa's Rand district. HERBERT SPENCER JENNINGS (1868–1947) of Illinois was a zoologist known for his studies of the behavior and physiology of some organisms and of genetics.

Genealogies: *A Family History* was compiled by Mildred King Whitten and published in Tupelo, Mississippi, in 1980.

JENSEN
Ranking: 239 S.S. Count: 149,308
Origin: Danish, Norwegian. Transformation of John.

Famous Jensens: JENS JENSEN (1860–1951) of Denmark was a landscape architect. He was responsible for the establishment of the Cook Co. (Illinois) Forest Preserve system. He also worked with Frank Lloyd Wright.

Genealogies: *The Sogndalers* was compiled by Ted Lawrence Bartlett and published in Chicago, Illinois, in 1969.

JERNIGAN (S.S. Abbreviation: Jernig)
Ranking: 2135 S.S. Count: 21,441
Origin: English. Uncertain etymology. Possibly derived from the Old Teutonic first name Gerwig.

Genealogies: *Jernigan Reunion* was compiled by Lillian Jernigan Worley and published in Clinton, North Carolina, in 1971.

JEROME
Ranking: 4582 S.S. Count: 9754
Origin: English. 1) derived from the Norman first name Gerram, which is derived from the Germanic words "geri" and "hraban," meaning spear and raven. 2) derived from the Greek first name Hieronymos, which is derived from the words "hieros" and "onyma," meaning sacred and name.

Famous Jeromes: CHAUNCEY JEROME (1793–1868) of Connecticut was an inventor and clockmaker. He is best remembered as the inventor of the one-day brass movement, which made mass production of the clocks possible. WILLIAM TRAVERS JEROME (1859–1934) of New York City was a foe of Tammany Hall and an effective district attorney of New York City.

Genealogies: *The Greer, Sabin, Elliot, and Jerome Ancestry* was compiled by Olive Daniels and published in Madison, Wisconsin, in 1969.

JESSUP
Ranking: 4563 S.S. Count: 9788

Origin: English. Transformation of Joseph.

Famous Jessups: HENRY HARRIS JESSUP (1832–1910) of Pennsylvania was a Presbyterian missionary and one of the founders of the American University of Beirut. WALTER ALBERT JESSUP (1877–1944) of Indiana was the president of the Carnegie Foundation for the Advancement of Teaching, then took on the duties of president of the Carnegie Corporation.

Genealogies: *John Kendig Barr* was compiled by Mary Alice Burchfield and published in Bayard, Nebraska, in 1984. *The Sixtieth Wedding Anniversary of Frank Pierson Jessup and Marie Barr Jessup* was compiled by Mary Alice Burchfield and published in Bayard, Nebraska, in 1977.

JESTER
Ranking: 4279 S.S. Count: 10,502
Origin: English, German. Derived from the word "jester," meaning "the professional fool in attendance at the king or baron" (ES) or one who "recited romances or acted the buffoon at fair and festival" (ES).

Genealogies: None known.

JETER
Ranking: 2637 S.S. Count: 17,277
Origin: English. Uncertain etymology. Possibly derived from the word "jester" refering to a court fool. The name was given to those who were considered ostentatious.

Famous Jeters: JEREMIAH BELL JETER (1802–1880) of Virginia was a leader of the Southern Baptist Convention.

Genealogies: *Hulls' Heritage* was compiled by Carolyn Hull Estes and published in Fort Worth, Texas, in 1986. *The Jeter Mosaic* was compiled by Grata Jeter Clark and published in Fort Worth, Texas, in 1987.

JETT
Ranking: 2953 S.S. Count: 15,413
Origin: English. Transformation of Jeter.

Genealogies: *The Jett and Allied Families* was compiled by Jeter Lee Jett and published in Baltimore, Maryland, in 1977.

JEWELL
Ranking: 1394 S.S. Count: 31,799
Origin: English. Derived from the Old Breton first name Iudicael, which comprises components meaning lord and generous.

Famous Jewells: HARVEY JEWELL (1820–1881) of New Hampshire was a lawyer appointed by President Ulysses S. Grant to the court of commissioners of Alabama. MARSHALL JEWELL (1825–1883) of New York was the governor of Connecticut, a U.S. minister to Russia, and the postmaster general of the United States.

Genealogies: *Fluhart-Jewell Genealogy* was compiled

by Donald J. Sublette and published in Birmingham, Michigan, in 1982. *The Jewell Register* was compiled by Pliny Jewell and published in Paint Rock, Alabama, in 1974.

JEWETT

Ranking: 3656 **S.S. Count:** 12,344
Origin: English. Derived from the Middle English first name Jowet, which is a transformation of Julian.

Famous **Jewetts:** MILO PARKER JEWETT (1808–1882) of Vermont was an educator who founded Judson Female Institute in Alabama and persuaded Matthew Vassar to endow a woman's college (Vassar College) with Jewett as its first president. JOHN PUNCHARD JEWETT (1814–1884) of Maine was the publisher of *Uncle Tom's Cabin*. CHARLES COFFIN JEWETT (1816–1868) of Maine was a biographer and librarian and the first to publish extended collections of statistics on libraries in the United States. WILLIAM CORNELL JEWETT (1823–1893) of New York City attempted to end the Civil War through the intervention of the Europeans. SARAH ORNE JEWETT (1849–1909) of Maine was a writer whose *Country of the Pointed Firs* (1896) is considered a classic in American prose. FRANK BALDWIN JEWETT (1879–1949) of California was a telephone engineer and one of the people responsible for the 1915 transcontinental telephone service.

Genealogies: *An Ancestral Record of My Paternal Grandfather* was compiled by Lucy Ada Jewett Prescott and published in New Rochelle, New York, in 1971.

JIMENEZ

Ranking: 343 **S.S. Count:** 110,823
Origin: Spanish. Uncertain etymology. Possibly derived from the first name Simon, meaning "gracious hearing" (ES).
Genealogies: None known.

JOBE

Ranking: 4094 **S.S. Count:** 11,037
Origin: English. 1) uncertain etymology. Possibly derived from the Middle English word "jube," meaning "a long woolen garment" (H&H). The name was given to those who sold or made or wore such a garment. 2) derived from the Middle English word "jobbe," meaning a "vessel containing four gallons" (H&H). The name was given to coopers. 3) derived from the Hebrew first name Iyov. 4) derived from the Old French word "job," referring to the biblical Job.
Genealogies: None known.

JOE

Ranking: 4673 **S.S. Count:** 9580
Origin: English. Transformation of Joseph.
Genealogies: None known.

JOHANN (ALSO JOHANNES, JOHANNESEN, JOHANNESSON)

Ranking: 2787 **S.S. Count:** 16,342
Origin: Johannesen—Danish; Johann, Johannes—German; Johannesson—Swedish. Cognates to John.
Genealogies: *Minne Johannis (also Johann) and Some of His Descendants* was compiled by Alice Minnerly Runyon and published in North Tarrytown, New York, in 1978.

JOHANSEN, JOHANSSEN, JOHANSSON (S.S. Abbreviation: Johans)

Ranking: 1633 **S.S. Count:** 27,492
Origin: Johansen—Danish, Dutch; Johanssen—German; Johansson—Swedish. Cognates to John.
Genealogies: None known.

JOHN

Ranking: 1565 **S.S. Count:** 28,515
Origin: English. Derived from the Hebrew first name Yochanan, meaning "may Jehovah favour (this child)" (H&H).
Genealogies: None known.

JOHNS

Ranking: 587 **S.S. Count:** 70,823
Origin: English. Transformation of John.

Famous **Johnses:** KENSEY JOHNS (1759–1848) of Maryland served as the chief justice of the supreme court of Delaware (1799–1830). JOHN JOHNS (1796–1876) of Delaware was an Episcopal clergyman, the assistant bishop of Virginia, and the president of the College of William and Mary.

Genealogies: *The Chronicles of John Clark Johns and His Descendants* was compiled by David Lamar Taylor and published in Costa Mesa, California, in 1990. *Mt. Comfort Plantation* was compiled by Richard L. Guild and published in Appomattox, Virginia, in 1983.

JOHNSEN (S.S. Abbreviation: Johnse)

Ranking: 3572 **S.S. Count:** 12,628
Origin: Danish. Cognate to John.

Famous **Johnsens:** ERIK KRISTIAN JOHNSEN (1863–1923) of Norway was a theologian and a professor at several seminaries.

Genealogies: None known.

JOHNSON (S.S. Abbreviation: Johnso)

Ranking: 2 **S.S. Count:** 2,593,837
Origin: English. Transformation of John.

Famous **Johnsons:** THOMAS JOHNSON (1732–1819) of Maryland was a Revolutionary War leader and the man who nominated George Washington for commander in chief. He served as the first governor of Maryland and as an associate justice of the U.S. Supreme Court. RICHARD MENTOR JOHNSON (1780–1850) of Kentucky was the vice president of the United States in the 1836 election, the only one in which no candidate gained the majority of the vote in the Electoral College. The election was decided by the U.S. Senate. ELIJAH JOHNSON (1780?–1849) of probably New Jersey was one of the founders of Liberia. CAVE JOHNSON (1793–1866) of Tennessee was a long-time member of Congress and the postmaster general under President James K. Polk. REVERDY JOHNSON (1796–1876) of Maryland was the defense attorney in the Dred Scott case. Responsible for keeping Maryland in the Union, he served as U.S. senator and U.S. attorney general and earned himself the nickname "the Trimmer" because of his work as a mediator and compromiser. ANDREW JOHNSON (1808–1875) of North Carolina was the 17th president of the United States, taking office on the assassination of President Abraham Lincoln. He served as governor of Tennessee and as a member of Congress and U.S. senator before the Civil War. His differences with the Congress led to impeachment proceedings, of which he was acquitted by one vote. After his presidency Johnson briefly served again in the U.S. Senate. JONATHAN EASTMAN JOHNSON (1824–1906) of Maine was a painter. He is best known for his portraits and scenes such as *My Kentucky Home.* ELLEN CHENEY JOHNSON (1829–1899) of Massachusetts was a prison reformer who was largely responsible for Massachusetts' establishing separate permanent institutions for women. ALEXANDER JOHNSON (1847–1941) of England was an educator and social worker who was a pioneer in educating the public about the abilities of the mentally handicapped. TOM LOFTIN JOHNSON (1854–1911) of Kentucky was the inventor of the streetcar fare box. He also served as a member of Congress and as the mayor of Cleveland, Ohio. GEORGE FRANCIS JOHNSON (1857–1948) of Massachusetts was a shoe manufacturer who left school at the age of 13 to work in a shoe factory that was then bought by Henry B. Endicott. Johnson became a partner of Endicott's in 1899. Under Johnson, innovative reforms were put into place, including high salaries, profit sharing, and other benefits. The company's name was changed to Endicott-Johnson. ADELAIDE JOHNSON (1859–1955) of Illinois was the sculptor of the monument to the women's movement that is in the U.S. Capitol. EDWARD AUSTIN JOHNSON (1860–1944) of North Carolina, the son of slave parents, was graduated from Atlanta University. He was elected to the state assembly of New York in 1917, the first black to do so. He wrote *A School History of the Negro Race in America: 1619–1890.* BYRON BANCROFT JOHNSON (1864–1931) of Ohio was known as Ban. He was a baseball player, the organizer of the American League in 1900, and the man who had the idea for the World Series as a way of ending each season. He was elected to the Baseball Hall of Fame in 1937. HIRAM WARREN JOHNSON (1866–1945)

of California was the governor of California (1911–1917) and former President Theodore Roosevelt's running mate in the 1912 election on the Bull Moose progressive ticket. He served as a U.S. senator (1917–1945). ELDRIDGE REEVES JOHNSON (1867–1945) of Delaware was the inventor of a spring-driven motor for use in a gramophone. He founded the Victor Talking Machine Co., which produced the leading American phonograph. JAMES WELDON JOHNSON (1871–1938) of Florida was an author. He wrote books pertaining to African-Americans' music, poetry, and place in American culture and literature, and he was an influential member of the National Association for the Advancement of Colored People (NAACP). Among his books was *The Autobiography of an Ex-Colored Man* (1912). ALVIN SAUNDERS JOHNSON (1874–1971) of Nebraska was an economist and the founder of the New School for Social Research in New York City. JOHN ARTHUR (JACK) JOHNSON (1878–1946) of Texas was the first black world heavyweight champion in the sport of boxing. MARTIN ELMER JOHNSON (1884–1937) of Illinois was an explorer and naturalist. With his wife, OSA HELEN LEIGHTY JOHNSON (1894–1953) of Kansas, he produced films in Africa about life there. WALTER PERRY JOHNSON (1887–1946) of Kansas was a baseball player nicknamed "Big Train." He pitched in the American League and was one of the first five players elected to the Baseball Hall of Fame. HALL JOHNSON (1888–1970) of Georgia was the director of the Hall Johnson Negro Choir, which appeared in concert and in motion pictures. CHARLES SPURGEON JOHNSON (1893–1956) of Virginia was a sociologist who studied the social ramifications of being black in America. He wrote several books on the subject. CLAUDIUS OSBORNE JOHNSON (1894–1976) of Virginia was a politician, scientist, and educator. His field of expertise was civil liberties. HOWARD DEERING JOHNSON (1896?–1972) of Massachusetts started the Howard Johnson restaurant/motel business. His chain eventually spread across the nation, making it the largest commercial food supplier in the country. PHILIP JOHNSON (1898–1976) of West Virginia was a physician who specialized in surgery of the spleen and gunshot wounds. LYNDON BAINES JOHNSON (1908–1973) of Texas, the 36th president of the United States, took office when President John F. Kennedy was assassinated in 1963. Johnson completed Kennedy's term and was then elected to a full term of his own. His administration is best remembered for the "Great Society" social welfare reform and for the country's involvement in the war in Vietnam.

Genealogies: *The Johnson Family* was compiled by Ruby Wiedeman and published in Huntsville, Arkansas, in 1972. *Some Johnsons of Southern Maryland* was compiled by Leona A. Cryer and published in Spring Hill, Florida, in 1991. *Those Handy Nordics* was compiled by Ethel Marie Johnson Taylor and published in Cimarron, Kansas, in

1977. *The Descendants of William and John Johnson* was compiled by Lorand Victor Johnson and published in Cleveland, Ohio, in 1940.

JOHNSTON, JOHNSTONE (S.S. Abbreviation: Johnst)

Ranking: 160 **S.S. Count:** 202,676

Origin: Scottish. Derived from the first name John and the Middle English word "tūn," meaning settlement. The name was given to those from Johnston, the name of several places in Scotland.

Famous **Bearers:** HENRIETTA JOHNSTON (1728?–?) is believed to have been the first female painter in North America. Her specialty was pastel portraits of colonial South Carolinians. DAVID CLAYPOOLE JOHNSTON (1799–1865) of Pennsylvania was a caricaturist and lithographer who published an annual series called *Scraps*. HARRIET LANE JOHNSTON (1830–1903) of Pennsylvania was mistress of the White House during the administration of her uncle, James Buchanan, a bachelor. SAMUEL JOHNSTON (1835–1911) of New York was an inventor whose patented rake and reel improvements for harvesters were employed throughout the world. JOSEPH F. JOHNSTON (1843–1913) of North Carolina was governor of Alabama (1896–1900), then a U.S. senator. ALEXANDER JOHNSTON (1849–1889) of New York, a professor, wrote *History of American Politics* (1879). ANNIE FELLOWS JOHNSTON (1863–1931) of Indiana wrote almost 50 children's books, one of which was *The Little Colonel* (1895). FRANCES BENJAMIN JOHNSTON (1864–1952) of West Virginia was a pioneer as a photographer and photojournalist and is best remembered for her professionalism. MARY JOHNSTON (1870–1936) of Virginia was an author. Her novel *To Have and to Hold* (1900), about the women of Jamestown, sold a half million copies and was made into films. EDWARD R. JOHNSTONE (1870–1946), born in Canada and raised in Ohio, improved the system of education for mentally disadvantaged people through his work at the Vineland (New Jersey) Home for the Education and Care of Feeble-Minded Children (1898–1944). WILLIAM HUGH JOHNSTON (1874–1937), born in Canada, was a U.S. labor leader. He was president of the International Association of Machinists (1912–1926). JOHN FRANCIS JOHNSTON (1900–1977) of Indiana was a dentist and was considered an authority on crowns and bridge prosthodontics.

Genealogies: *Ancestors and Descendants of James and Althea Johnston* was compiled by Aaron Montgomery Johnston and published in Knoxville, Tennessee, in 1983. *Eight Children of the Winged Spur* was compiled by Helen Johnston and published in Birmingham, Alabama, in 1980.

JOINER (ALSO JOINERS)

Ranking: 2088 **S.S. Count:** 21,989

Origin: English. Derived from the Old French word "joinre," meaning to join. The name was given to those who built wooden furniture.

Genealogies: *Joyner (also Joiner) of Southampton* was compiled by Ulysses P. Joyner and published in Orange, Virginia, in 1975. *The Woodbine Twineth* was compiled by Shirley Joiner Thompson and published in Jacksonville, Florida, in 1972.

JOLLEY

Ranking: 3689 **S.S. Count:** 12,240

Origin: English. Derived from the Middle English and Old French word "joli(f)," meaning happy. The name was given to those "of a cheerful disposition" (H&H).

Genealogies: None known.

JOLLY

Ranking: 2161 **S.S. Count:** 21,244

Origin: English, French, Scottish. Transformation of Jolley.

Genealogies: *Nelson Jolly, Sr., and His Family* was compiled by Nellie Fern Baker and published in Brandon, Texas, in 1983.

JONAS

Ranking: 4040 **S.S. Count:** 11,209

Origin: English, French, Jewish. English, French: derived from the Hebrew first name Yona, meaning dove. Jewish: cognate to any of several Jewish surnames that sound similar.

Genealogies: None known.

JONES

Ranking: 5 **S.S. Count:** 1,930,318

Origin: English, Jewish, Welsh. Transformation of John.

Famous **Joneses:** JOHN JONES (1729–1791) of New York, a surgeon, was author of the first surgical textbook written in the American colonies, *Plain Remarks on the Treatment of Wounds and Fractures*. JOHN PAUL JONES (1747–1792) of Scotland was born John Paul and added the "Jones" to his name when he moved to Virginia around 1773. During the Revolutionary War, as commander of the *Bonhomme Richard*, he is rumored to have said, "I have not yet begun to fight," as he defeated the British ship *Serapis*. ANSON JONES (1798–1858) of Massachusetts was the last president of the Republic of Texas, before it became a state. GEORGE JONES (1811–1891) was co-founder of the *New York Times* in 1851. ALEXANDER JONES (1802?–1863) of North Carolina was the first news reporter to file a message by telegraph, from New York to Washington, D.C., in 1846. He was instrumental in organizing a cooperative press service by wire among American cities. CATESBY AP ROGER JONES (1821–1877) of Virginia was the commander of the *Merrimack* during its battle with the *Monitor* on March 9, 1862.

MARY HARRIS JONES (1830–1930), originally of Ireland, came to America as a young child. Known as Mother Jones, she was active in labor circles and was one of the founders of the Industrial Workers of the World. AMANDA THEODOSIA JONES (1835–1914) of New York invented the Jones preserving process for fruit and meat. CHARLES JESSE JONES (1844–1918) of Illinois was a buffalo hunter before 1872. He then became a breeder of a buffalo/cattle mix called a cattalo. After 1902 he served as the game warden at Yellowstone National Park. RUFUS MATTHEW JONES (1863–1948) of Maine was a philosopher and author whose published works include *Social Law in the Spiritual World* (1904) and *Studies in Mystical Religion* (1909). JOHN LUTHER JONES (1864–1900) of Kentucky, nicknamed Casey, was the railroad engineer on the "Cannonball Express," which crashed on April 30, 1900. He was immortalized in the ballad "Casey Jones." HARRY C. JONES (1865–1916) of Maryland set up the nation's first specialized physical chemistry department at Johns Hopkins University in 1895. MATILDA SISSIERETTA JOYNER JONES (1869–1933) of Virginia broke new ground as an African-American opera singer. Among her venues was the White House, at the invitation of President Benjamin Harrison. SAM HOUSTON JONES (1897–1978) of Louisiana was the governor of Louisiana after Huey P. Long's corrupt tenure. He reorganized and stabilized the state government. THOMAS ELSA JONES (1888–1973) of Indiana was president of Fisk College. He stabilized the finances of the college and was also the founder of the United Negro College Fund. DONALD FORSHA JONES (1890–1963) of Kansas was a geneticist and the developer of a double-cross hybrid corn and the first hybrid sweet corn. THOMAS HUDSON JONES (1892–1969) of New York was a sculptor. Two of his best-known works are the Tomb of the Unknown Soldier in Arlington National Cemetery and a bust of Ulysses S. Grant. HOWARD MUMFORD JONES (1892–1980) of Michigan was an educator and writer and the author of the Pulitzer Prize–winning book *O Strange New World*. BENJAMIN CLARKE JONES (1896–1974) of Pennsylvania was a lawyer and the publisher of the Tyrone (Pennsylvania) *Daily Herald* and the Williamsburg (Pennsylvania) *Journal*. THOMAS BANFORD JONES (1898–1977) of New York was a surgeon. He headed a study on the use of the camera in operating theaters to help with the teaching of operating procedures. The program was sponsored by Eastman Kodak Co. ROBERT TYRE JONES (1902–1971) of Georgia, known as Bobby, was a golfer and the winner of many U.S. and British amateur and open tournaments. He was the first man ever to win the "Grand Slam," which involved winning both the open and amateur tournaments in both the United States and Great Britain. He was one of the founders of the Masters tournament. MARGO JONES (1912–1955) of Texas was a pioneer of regional theater and theater-in-the-round. A[RCHIBALD] QUINCY JONES (1913–1979)

of Missouri was an architect. He emphasized the importance of preserving the natural landscape.

Genealogies: *Camp, Jones, and Related Families* was compiled by Nell Jones Carter and published in Tallahassee, Florida, in 1977. *Captain Roger Jones of London and Virginia* was compiled by L. H. Jones and published in Albany, New York, in 1891. *Climbing Our Family Tree* was compiled by Edith Black and published in Baltimore, Maryland, in 1988.

JORDAN (ALSO JORDANA, JORDANET, JORDANEY, JORDANOV)

Ranking: 105 **S.S. Count:** 265,919

Origin: Jordanov—Bulgarian; Jordana—Catalonian; Jordan—English; Jordanet—French; Jordaney—Jewish. Derived from the name of the river called Jordan, which is derived from the Hebrew word "yarad," meaning to descend.

Famous Jordans: DAVID STARR JORDAN (1851–1931) of New York was a biologist and an educator. He served in academic positions at several universities and wrote many books on the animals of North America. ELIZABETH GARVER JORDAN (1865–1947) of Wisconsin was a prominent journalist on the staff of the New York *World*, then editor of *Harper's Bazaar*. She also wrote a number of novels. SARA CLAUDIA MARRAY JORDAN (1884–1959) of Massachusetts was a doctor and the head of the department of gastroenterology at the Lahey Clinic in Boston.

Genealogies: *These Jordans Were Here* was compiled by Octavia Perry and published in Provo, Utah, in 1969. *Yesterday in the Texas Hill Country* was compiled by Gilbert John Jordan and published in College Station, Texas, in 1979.

JORDON

Ranking: 3175 **S.S. Count:** 14,302

Origin: English. Transformation of Jordan.

Genealogies: None known.

JORGENSEN (S.S. Abbreviation: Jorgen)

Ranking: 1167 **S.S. Count:** 37,474

Origin: Danish, German. Transformation of George.

Genealogies: *The DeMay, Quintin, and Jorgensen Families* was compiled by Ida DeMay Wilson and published in Saint Helena, California, in 1986.

JOSEPH (ALSO JOSEPHI, JOSEPHOFF, JOSEPHOV, JOSEPHS)

Ranking: 458 **S.S. Count:** 87,284

Origin: Joseph, Josephs—English, French, Jewish; Josephi—German; Josephoff, Josephov—Jewish. Derived from the Hebrew first name Yosef, meaning "may He (God) add (another son)" (H&H).

Famous Josephs: JOSEPH (1840–1904) of Oregon was a

Nez Perce chief who was considered one of the greatest strategists among the Indians.

Genealogies: *An Account of the Joseph and Abrahams Families in America* was compiled by Marc Allan Austen and published in New York, New York, in 1978.

JOSLIN (ALSO JOSLING)
Ranking: 4735 **S.S. Count:** 9456
Origin: English, Jewish. English: Derived from an Old French first name of uncertain etymology. Jewish: transformations of Joseph.
Genealogies: None known.

JOY
Ranking: 2674 **S.S. Count:** 17,047
Origin: English. Derived from the Old French word "joie," meaning happy. The name was given to those who were cheerful.
Famous **Joys:** THOMAS JOY (1610?–1678) of England was an architect who designed and built the first state house in Boston and was a major influence on early Boston architecture. JAMES FREDERICK JOY (1810–1896) of New Hampshire was a financier and the creator of the "Joy system," which was the first large western railroad combination.
Genealogies: *Ancestry of the Jameson, Gilbert, Joy, Skinner, and Related Families* was compiled by Bradner Petersen and published in Pasadena, California, in 1986. *Thomas Joy and His Descendants* was compiled by James Richard Joy and published in New York, New York, in 1900.

JOYCE
Ranking: 893 **S.S. Count:** 48,658
Origin: English, Irish. Derived from the Brettonic first name Iodoc, which was derived from the word "iudh," meaning lord.
Famous **Joyces:** ISAAC WILSON JOYCE (1836–1905) of Ohio was a well-known preacher and revivalist.
Genealogies: None known.

JOYNER
Ranking: 1128 **S.S. Count:** 38,967
Origin: English. Transformation of Joiner.
Genealogies: *Joiner-Joyner* was compiled by Ransey Joiner and published in Mayfield, Kentucky, in 1973. *A Joyner in Every Corner* was compiled by Walter Joe Moore and published in Oronoco, Minnesota, in 1988.

JUAREZ
Ranking: 1376 **S.S. Count:** 32,154
Origin: Spanish. Transformation of Suarez.
Genealogies: *From Mission to Majesty* was compiled by Barbara Juarez Wilson and published in Baltimore, Maryland, in 1983. *The Past Is the Father of the Present* was compiled by Viviene Juarez Rose and published in Vallejo, California, in 1974.

JUDD
Ranking: 1900 **S.S. Count:** 23,838
Origin: English. Transformation of Jordan.
Genealogies: *In America Since 1607* was compiled by Walter I. Farmer and published in Cincinnati, Ohio, in 1987.

JUDGE
Ranking: 3114 **S.S. Count:** 14,610
Origin: English, Irish. English: derived from the Old French word "juge," which is derived from the Latin words "ius" and "dicere," meaning law and to say. The name was given to justice officials and to those considered judge-like. Irish: derived from the Gaelic word "breitheamhnach," meaning judge.
Famous **Judges:** WILLIAM QUAN JUDGE (1851–1896) of Ireland founded branches of the Theosophical Society in major cities. THOMAS AUGUSTINE JUDGE (1868–1933) of Massachusetts was a Roman Catholic clergyman and the founder of the Missionary Servants of the Most Holy Trinity.
Genealogies: None known.

JUDY
Ranking: 4915 **S.S. Count:** 9106
Origin: English? French? Uncertain etymology. Most likely derived from the Hebrew first name Yehuda (Judah).
Genealogies: *Juday and Judy in the Pacific Northwest* was compiled by Bill Lee and published in Smithfield, Utah, in 1989. *Three Centuries of the Franz Josef Tschudi-Judy Family* was compiled by Richard P. Judy and published in Lisle, Illinois, in 1990.

JULIAN
Ranking: 1743 **S.S. Count:** 25,704
Origin: English, French, German. Derived from the Latin first name Iulius.
Famous **Julians:** PERCY LAVON JULIAN (1899–1975) of Alabama was a research chemist and a prominent chemistry professor. He was known particularly for his soybean research that yielded medical products which reduced the cost of treating patients who suffered from diseases such as arthritis.
Genealogies: *The Julian Family* was compiled by Frances Julian Hine and published in Winston-Salem, North Carolina, in 1974. *The Julians* was compiled by Elizabeth Cate Manly and published in Cleveland, Tennessee, in 1972.

JUNG

Ranking: 17,091 **S.S. Count:** 2667
Origin: German, Jewish. Cognate to Young.
Genealogies: None known.

JUSTICE

Ranking: 1079 **S.S. Count:** 40,901
Origin: English. Derived from the Latin word "ius," meaning law. The name was given to those who worked as judges or to those considered just.

Genealogies: *Justice Genealogy* was compiled by Rara Avis Justice and published in Pikeville, Kentucky, in 1971. *The Justice Family in Virginia* was compiled by O. Neil Justice and published in Dallas, Texas, in 1988.

JUSTUS

Ranking: 4970 **S.S. Count:** 9016
Origin: English. Transformation of Justice.
Genealogies: None known.

KACZMAR, KACZMARCZYK, KACZMAREK, KACZMARKIEWICZ, KACZMARSKI (S.S. Abbreviation: Kaczma)

Ranking: 4634 S.S. Count: 9647

Origin: Kaczmar—German; Kaczmarczyk, Kaczmarek, Kaczmarkiewicz, Kaczmarski—Polish. Derived from the German word "kretscham," meaning inn. The name was given to innkeepers.

Genealogies: None known.

KAHN

Ranking: 2076

S.S. Count: 22,095

Origin: Jewish. Transformation of Cohen.

Famous **Kahns**: JULIUS KAHN (1861–1924) of Germany was brought to California as a child. He was a member of Congress for 12 terms and the author of the Selective Draft Act of 1917. FLORENCE PRAG KAHN (1866–1948) of Utah was elected in 1925 to fill a seat in the U.S. House of Representatives from California left vacant when her husband, Julius Kahn, died. She was reelected for five full successive terms. OTTO HERMANN KAHN (1867–1934) of Germany was a banker and a patron of the arts. He was one of the biggest contributors to the arts in the history of the United States. ALBERT KAHN (1869–1942), originally of Germany, came to the United States as a teenager. A noted architect, he designed factories for the manufacture of automobiles, including the Packard plant and one of the Ford Motor Co. plants. He won the silver medal of the Architectural League of New York in 1929 for his Fisher Building. GUSTAV GERSON KAHN (1886–1941) of Germany was a songwriter who composed lyrics for both Broadway and Hollywood. LOUIS ISADORE KAHN (1901–1974) of Estonia was an architect whose works include powerful massive forms. HERMAN KAHN (1922–1983) of New Jersey was a social theorist who founded the Hudson Institute, which predicts and solves the problems of the nation and world. They accurately foretold, among other things, the economic growth of Japan over the United States.

Genealogies: None known.

KAISER (ALSO KAISERMAN)

Ranking: 943 S.S. Count: 45,891

Origin: Kaiser—German, Jewish; Kaiserman—Jewish. Kaiser (German): derived from the Latin word "caesar," which was the title of the emperor. Jewish: derived from the German name Kaiser. The names was taken ornamentally. Kaiserman: derived from the German name Kaiser. The names was taken ornamentally.

Famous **Kaisers**: ALOIS KAISER (1840–1908) of Hungary came to Baltimore as a young man and became a cantor and a leader in the modification of Jewish musical tradition. JOHN HENRY KAISER (1882–1967) of New York, an industrialist, founded the Kaiser Foundation, which provided health care to his employees and the public. He was also involved in the aluminum, steel, and automobile industries.

Genealogies: *Idaho Homestead* was compiled by William J. Kiser and published in Huntsville, Alabama, in 1982. *Sandy Ridge-Powers Kinfolks* was compiled by Esther Kiser and published in Cleveland, Virginia, in 1986.

KAMINSKI, KAMINSKY (S.S. Abbreviation: Kamins)

Ranking: 1571 S.S. Count: 28,429

Origin: Jewish, Polish. 1) derived from the Polish word "kamie'n," meaning stone, and the surname suffix "-ski." The name was given to stonecutters or to those who worked in quarries.

Genealogies: None known.

KAMMER (ALSO KAMMERER, KAMMERLING, KAMMERMAN)

Ranking: 3991 S.S. Count: 11,324

Origin: Kammer—German; Kammerer—German; Kammerling—German; Kammerman—German. Kammer: 1) derived from the Old English word "camb," meaning comb. Most likely the name was given to those who made or sold combs or to those who used combs in textile work. 2) cognate to Chambers. Kammerer: cognate to Chambers. Kammerling: cognate to Chamberlain. Kammerman: cognate to Chambers.

Genealogies: None known.

KANE

Ranking: 575 S.S. Count: 71,638

Origin: English, Irish, Manx. 1) transformation of Cain. 2) transformation of Keane.

Famous **Kanes**: JOHN KINTZING KANE (1795–1858) of New York was a jurist and an assistant to President Andrew Jackson in the preparation of legal papers. ELISHA KENT KANE (1820–1857) of Pennsylvania was an Arctic explorer on two expeditions in search of Sir John Franklin on the Grinnell Expedition. JOHN KANE (ORIGINALLY CAIN) (1860–1934) of Scotland was a painter who favored primitive landscapes of Pennsylvania and Scotland and skylines of Pittsburgh as his subject material.

Genealogies: None known.

KANG

Ranking: 3765 S.S. Count: 12,029

Origin: Chinese, Korean. Uncertain etymology. The name was given to those living near rivers and bays.

Genealogies: None known.

KAPLAN

Ranking: 908 S.S. Count: 47,553

Origin: Czech, German, Jewish. Czech, German: cognates to Chaplin. Jewish: translation of the Jewish name Cohen, meaning priest.

Genealogies: None known.

KARR

Ranking: 3435 S.S. Count: 13,139

Origin: Irish? Uncertain etymology. Most likely a transformation of Carr.

Genealogies: *Karr Family Record* was compiled by Nola M. Karr and published in Port Tobacco, Maryland, in 1977.

KASPER

Ranking: 2749 S.S. Count: 16,585

Origin: German, Polish. Transformation of and cognate to Jasper.

Genealogies: None known.

KATZ

Ranking: 895 S.S. Count: 48,449

Origin: Jewish. Derived from the Hebrew phrase "kohen TSedek," meaning "priest of righteousness" (H&H).

Genealogies: *The New Yorker's Family History of Jacob Katz* was compiled by Alexander Jack Katz and published in Tampa, Florida, in 1974.

KAUFFMAN, KAUFFMANN (S.S. Abbreviation: Kauffm)

Ranking: 1585 S.S. Count: 28,252

Origin: Kauffman—Jewish; Kauffmann—German, Jewish. Cognates to Chapman.

Famous Kauffmans: CALVIN HENRY KAUFFMAN (1869–1931) of Pennsylvania was a botanist and mycologist and the author of *The Agaricaceae of Michigan* (1918).

Genealogies: *Descendants of John J. Bontrager IV and Fanny Kauffman* was compiled by Edna O. Yoder and published in Middlebury, Indiana, in 1984. *Ellen Virginia Kauffman* was compiled by Patricia Jean Minger Vorenberg and published in Lexington, Massachusetts, in 1980.

KAUFMAN, KAUFMANN (S.S. Abbreviation: Kaufma)

Ranking: 674 S.S. Count: 62,266

Origin: Kaufman—Jewish; Kaufmann—German, Jewish. Cognates to Chapman.

Famous Kaufmans: GEORGE SIMON KAUFMAN (1889–1961) of Pennsylvania was a playwright. He won a Pulitzer Prize for the play *You Can't Take it with You* (1936).

Genealogies: None known.

KAVANAGH (S.S. Abbreviation: Kavana)

Ranking: 2888 S.S. Count: 15,770

Origin: Irish. Derived from the Gaelic first name Caomh'anach, meaning "follower of St. Caomh'an," a first name that was derived from the Gaelic word "caomh," meaning gentle.

Famous Kavanaghs: EDWARD KAVANAGH (1795–1844) of Maine was the governor of that state and helped to set the Maine boundary with Secretary of State Daniel Webster and Lord Ashburton.

Genealogies: None known.

KAY

Ranking: 1367 S.S. Count: 32,456

Origin: English. 1) derived from the Middle English and Old French word "kay(e)," meaning quay. The name was given to those who lived near or worked on a wharf. 2) derived from the Old English word "cæg," meaning key. The name was given to those who made keys or to bearers of keys. 3) derived from the letter "k." The name was given to those with non-English surnames beginning with the letter "k." 4) derived from the Middle English word "kay," meaning jackdaw. 5) derived from the Danish word "kei," meaning left. The name was given to those who were left-handed.

Famous Kays: EDGAR BOYD KAY (1860–1931) of Pennsylvania was a sanitary engineer and educator and the inventor of the U.S. Standard Incinerator.

Genealogies: *The Ancestors of Robert Kay of South Carolina* was compiled by Carl B. Kay and published in Choctaw, Oklahoma, in 1991. *The Four Children of James Kay of Essex County, VA* was compiled by Kent Kay Freeman and published in Tacoma, Washington, in 1978.

KAYE

Ranking: 3745 S.S. Count: 12,089

Origin: English. Transformation of Kay.

Famous Kayes: FREDERICK BENJAMIN KAYE (1892–1930) of New York was a scholar, author and an authority on neoclassical English literature.

Genealogies: None known.

KEANE

Ranking: 3065 S.S. Count: 14,811

Origin: English, Irish. English: transformation of Keen. Irish: derived from the Gaelic name Ó Catháin, which was derived from the first name Cathán, which was derived from the word "cath," meaning battle.

Famous Keanes: JOHN JOSEPH KEANE (1839–1918) of Ireland was a Roman Catholic priest who came to the United States as a child. He was active in the founding of Catholic University in Washington, D.C., and was appointed as the university's first rector. He attained the rank of archbishop. JAMES JOHN KEANE (1857–1929) of Illinois was a Roman Catholic priest who attained the rank of archbishop and served the Church in Dubuque, Iowa (1911–1929).

Genealogies: *Patrick Doyle and Timothy Keane* was compiled by Clarke L. Neal and published in Selfridge ANG Base, Michigan, in 1981. *Southern Garners (also Keane)* was compiled by Sam Garner and published in Rome, Georgia, in 1979.

KEARNEY (S.S. Abbreviation: Kearne)

Ranking: 1510 **S.S. Count:** 29,475

Origin: Irish. Derived from the Gaelic name Ó Ceithearnaigh, which was derived from the first name Ceithearnach, meaning soldier.

Famous **Kearneys:** DENIS KEARNEY (1847–1907) of Ireland was a labor agitator and the leader of the Kearney movement. BELLE KEARNEY (1863–1939) of Mississippi was a temperance reformer and the first woman from the South to hold the office of U.S. senator.

Genealogies: *Midwest Families* was compiled by Michael John Kearney and published in Park Ridge, Illinois, in 1979.

KEARNS

Ranking: 2129 **S.S. Count:** 21,487

Origin: Irish. Derived from the Gaelic name Ó Céirín, which was derived from the word "cia," meaning dark or black.

Genealogies: None known.

KEATING (S.S. Abbreviation: Keatin)

Ranking: 1862 **S.S. Count:** 24,283

Origin: English, Irish. English: derived from the Old English first name Cȳting, which was derived from "cȳta," meaning kite or bird of prey. The name was given to predatory persons. Irish: derived from the Gaelic name Ó Céatfhadha, which was derived from the word "céat(fhadh)ach," meaning refined or rational.

Famous **Keatings:** WILLIAM HYPOLITUS KEATING (1799–1840) of Delaware was a mineralogical chemist and the geologist on Stephen H. Long's 1823 expedition, from which he wrote *Narrative of an Expedition to the Source of St. Peter's River* (1824). He was involved with the beginnings of the Franklin Institute in Pennsylvania. JOHN MCLEOD KEATING (1830–1906) of Ireland was a journalist and an editor at the *Memphis Appeal*. JOHN MARIE KEATING (1852–1893) of Pennsylvania was a physician who practiced in the fields of obstetrics and children's diseases.

Genealogies: None known.

KEATON

Ranking: 3861 **S.S. Count:** 11,676

Origin: English. Uncertain etymology. The name was given to those from Ketton, a place in England.

Famous **Keatons:** JOSEPH FRANCIS KEATON (1895–1966) of Kansas was an actor better known to the public as BUSTER KEATON. His career started in vaudeville when he was a child and continued through 1963 in the comedy film *It's a Mad, Mad, Mad, Mad World*. He is best remembered for his deadpan expression and the difficulty he had with machines.

Genealogies: None known.

KECK

Ranking: 2846 **S.S. Count:** 16,039

Origin: German. Uncertain etymology. The name was given to those who were lively or daring.

Famous **Kecks:** CHARLES KECK (1875–1951) of New York was a sculptor who is best remembered for his full-body sculptures and busts of famous Americans in history.

Genealogies: *Down in the Barns* was compiled by Virginia Billingsley Fletcher and published in Fort Lauderdale, Florida, in 1983. *Family Record of Isaac Plank and Catherine Keck* was compiled by W. H. Stutzman and published in Arthur, Illinois, in 1979. *More Kecks of Claiborne County, Tennessee* was compiled by Virginia Billingsley Fletcher and published in Fort Lauderdale, Florida, in 1992.

KEE

Ranking: 4012 **S.S. Count:** 11,282

Origin: Scottish. Derived from the first name Aedh or Aodh, meaning fire.

Genealogies: *The 1868–73 Journals of Emma Celinda Howe* was compiled by Ralph M. Kee and published in Springfield, Virginia, in 1975.

KEEFE

Ranking: 2743 **S.S. Count:** 16,599

Origin: Irish. Derived from the Gaelic name Ó Caoimh, which was derived from the first name Caomh, meaning gentle.

Genealogies: None known.

KEEFER (S.S. Abbreviation: Keefe)

Ranking: 3366 **S.S. Count:** 13,476

Origin: German. Cognate to Cooper.

Genealogies: *Genealogy of Hans Adam Kefer [also Keefer] Family* was compiled by Eugene R. Keffer and published in Warrensburg, Missouri, in 1984.

KEEGAN

Ranking: 3159 **S.S. Count:** 14,371

Origin: Irish. 1) *derived from the Gaelic name Mac Thadhgáin, which was derived from the name Tadhg, meaning poet.* 2) *derived from the Gaelic first name Aodhagán, which was derived from the name Aodh, meaning fire.*

Genealogies: Out of the Isle of Destiny *was compiled by Teresa Murphy and published in Falls Church, Virginia, in 1985.*

KEEL

Ranking: 3978 **S.S. Count:** 11,363
Origin: English. Transformation of Keeler.
Genealogies: None known.

KEELER

Ranking: 2791 **S.S. Count:** 16,315
Origin: English. Derived from the Old English word *"kele," meaning ship. The name was given to those who built or worked on a boat.*

Famous **Keelers:** RALPH OLMSTEAD KEELER (1840–1873) of Ohio was a journalist and the author of *Vagabond Adventures* (1870), an autobiography. He died at sea. JAMES EDWARD KEELER (1857–1900) of Illinois was an astronomer and an expert in the field of spectroscopy. WILLIAM HENRY KEELER (1872–1923) of New York was a baseball player known by the name "Wee Willie." He was elected to the Baseball Hall of Fame in 1939.

Genealogies: *Keeler Family* was compiled by Wesley B. Keeler and published in Castleton, New York, in 1985. *Ralph Keeler of Norfolk, Ct* was compiled by Wesley B. Keeler and published in Albany, New York, in 1980.

KEELIN (ALSO KEELING)

Ranking: 3717 **S.S. Count:** 12,156
Origin: English. Uncertain etymology. Most likely derived *from the Old English word "cēol," meaning ship.*

Genealogies: *The History of the Keeling Family of New York State* was compiled by Stanley Harvey Keeling and published in Syracuse, New York, in 1978.

KEEN

Ranking: 1884 **S.S. Count:** 24,000
Origin: English, Irish. English: 1) *derived from the Middle English first name Kene, which was derived from several Old English first names with the first component "cēne," meaning royal.* 2) *derived from the Middle English word "kene," meaning brave.*

Famous **Keens:** MORRIS LONGSTRETH KEEN (1820–1883) of Pennsylvania was the inventor of several paper-making techniques and the founder of American Wood Paper Co. (1863). WILLIAM WILLIAMS KEEN (1837–1932) of Pennsylvania was a surgeon and a pioneer in brain surgery who is said to have performed the first success-

ful operation to remove a brain tumor in the United States.

Genealogies: *The John Keen(e): 1578–1649* was compiled by Archie Timother Keene and published in 1971.

KEENAN

Ranking: 1598 **S.S. Count:** 28,044
Origin: Irish. Derived from the Gaelic word *"cian," meaning ancient.*

Famous **Keenans:** JAMES FRANCIS KEENAN (1858–1929) of Iowa was best known as Frank. He was an actor and is best remembered as a traveling performer, but he also worked in motion pictures.

Genealogies: None known.

KEENE

Ranking: 1834 **S.S. Count:** 24,643
Origin: English, Irish. Transformation of Keen.

Famous **Keenes:** LAURA KEENE (1820?–1873) of England was an actress and the first prominent woman theater manager in America. Some sources list her birth date as circa 1826. She is best remembered because her production of *Our American Cousin* was playing at Ford's Theater in Washington, D.C., the night that President Abraham Lincoln was shot and killed there. It was she who recognized John Wilkes Booth as the assassin, and she who held Lincoln's head in her lap as he lay dying. JAMES ROBERT KEENE (1838–1913) of England came to the United States as a boy and made his fortune as a stock market speculator. THOMAS WALLACE KEENE (1840–1898) of New York City was a Shakespearean actor who toured the country playing his parts.

Genealogies: None known.

KEENER

Ranking: 2558 **S.S. Count:** 17,771
Origin: English?, German? Uncertain etymology. English: *1) possibly given to those who lived near a parish named for St. Keyne. 2) possibly derived from the Old English word "céne," meaning bold or sharp. German: possibly a transformation of Koontz.*

Famous **Keeners:** WILLIAM ALBERT KEENER (1856–1913) of Georgia was a lawyer and educator and one of the reorganizers of the teaching methods of law schools. He was the author of a series of textbooks.

Genealogies: None known.

KEETON

Ranking: 3627 **S.S. Count:** 12,415
Origin: English? Uncertain etymology. Possibly a trans-*formation of Keaton.*

Famous **Keetons:** WILLIAM TINSLEY KEETON (1933–

1980) of Virginia was a biology professor and chairman of neurobiology and behavior for Cornell University's Biology Department.

Genealogies: None known.

KEHOE
Ranking: 3920 **S.S. Count:** 11,507
Origin: English, Irish. English: derived from the Norman name Caieu, once a place in France. Irish: derived from the Gaelic name Mac Eochaidh, which was derived from the first name Eochaidh, meaning each horse.
Genealogies: None known.

KEISER
Ranking: 4615 **S.S. Count:** 9675
Origin: German, Jewish. Transformation of Kaiser.
Genealogies: None known.

KEITH
Ranking: 632 **S.S. Count:** 65,523
Origin: Scottish. Derived from the British component "cet," meaning wood. The name was given to those from Keith, a place in Scotland.
Famous **Keiths:** SIR WILLIAM KEITH (1680–1749) of Scotland was the governor of Pennsylvania and Delaware and a royal customs official. After his return to England, he acted as an agent for the British, advising them on colonial business. GEORGE KEITH (1638?–1716) of Scotland was the founder of "Christian Quakers," a spinoff of the Quakers. After he was disowned by the Quakers, he became an Anglican missionary in America. JAMES KEITH (1839–1918) of Virginia was president of the state (Virginia) supreme court of appeals (1895–1916). WILLIAM KEITH (1839–1911) of Scotland came to the United States as a boy and settled in California. He was a landscape painter. BENJAMIN FRANKLIN KEITH (1846–1914) of New Hampshire was a theatrical manager and the owner of 400 vaudeville theaters across the country. MINOR COOPER KEITH (1848–1929) was a builder of railroads in Central America, a banana planter, and one of the founders of the United Fruit Co. ARTHUR KEITH (1864–1944) of Missouri was a geologist and a respected authority on the Appalachian Mountains. He was the head of the U.S. Geological Survey's national mapping program from 1906 to 1912.
Genealogies: *Keith Kinfolks* was compiled by Larry King and published in Hendersonville, Tennessee, in 1979. *Descendants of the Bates, Jackson, and Keith Families* was compiled by Loni Gardner and published in Bountiful, Utah, in 1981.

KELLEHER (S.S. Abbreviation: Kelleh)
Ranking: 3247 **S.S. Count:** 13,988
Origin: Irish. Derived from the Gaelic name Ó

Céileachair, which was derived from the name Céileachar, meaning uxorious.
Genealogies: None known.

KELLER (ALSO KELLERMAN)
Ranking: 248 **S.S. Count:** 145,034
Origin: German, Jewish. German: derived from the Old High German word "kellari," meaning cellar. The name was given to those who managed wine cellars in large houses. Jewish: derived from the Yiddish word "keln," meaning Koln or Cologne. The name was given to those from Cologne, a place in Germany.
Famous **Bearers:** MATHIAS KELLER (1813–1875) of Germany was a composer and songwriter and the author of several Civil War anthems. ARTHUR IGNATIUS KELLER (1867–1924) of New York City was a painter and a book and magazine illustrator. FLORENCE ARMSTRONG KELLER (1875–1974) of Missouri was a physician who traveled to Australia and New Zealand doing missionary work as a Seventh Day Adventist. She was not allowed to practice medicine in Australia because of her nationality and her sex but became the first woman to practice medicine in New Zealand. She also was the first woman elected to the board of governors of the Auckland General Hospital and the first foreigner, male or female, to join the teaching staff of the University of Auckland. Eventually she returned to Los Angeles and entered private practice. KARL FREDERIC KELLERMAN (1879–1934) was born in Germany to American parents. He was a plant physiologist and the originator of the *Journal of Agricultural Research*. He is credited with developing a program to contain and eradicate oriental citrus canker disease in the United States. This was the first case of control and eradication of a disease. HELEN ADAMS KELLER (1880–1968) of Alabama, deaf, blind, and mute since the age of 19 months, learned to communicate with the help of her tutor, Anne Sullivan.
Genealogies: *Kith and Kin of James and Mary Young* [also Keller] was compiled by Miriam Young Pack and published in Wichita, Kansas, in 1984. *Musgrave to Mosgrave* [also Keller] was compiled by Glenna James Mosgrave and published in Mansfield, Illinois, in 1979.

KELLEY
Ranking: 155 **S.S. Count:** 207,144
Origin: English, Irish, Scottish. Transformation of Kelly.
Famous **Kelleys:** ALFRED KELLEY (1789–1859) of Connecticut was the founder of Ohio's canal system and was the author of its banking and taxation system. HALL JACKSON KELLEY (1790–1874) of New Hampshire was a surveyor and teacher who became obsessed with the colonization of Oregon. He failed in his attempt to reach Oregon and had to be transported back to Boston, where he wrote a memoir. Considered a fanatic, he nonetheless

did alert the country to the possibilities of Oregon occupation. WILLIAM DARRAH KELLEY (1814–1890) of Pennsylvania was a member of Congress (1861–1890) and was nicknamed the "Iron Pig." OLIVER HUDSON KELLEY (1826–1913) of Massachusetts was one of the founders of the National Grange of the Patrons of Husbandry. JAMES DOUGLAS JERROLD KELLEY (1847–1922) of New York City was a naval officer, a writer on maritime history, and a pioneer in the development of wireless telegraphy. EDGAR STILLMAN KELLEY (1857–1944) of Wisconsin was a composer, music critic, and educator who composed music in the form of light opera and music for plays. FLORENCE KELLEY (1859–1932) of Pennsylvania was a social reformer who worked to improve the working conditions for women and to eliminate child labor.

Genealogies: *The History of Five Southern Families* was compiled by Ethel Evans Albert and published in Baltimore, Maryland, in 1970. *History of James and Catherine Kelly* was compiled by Richard Thomas Kelly and published in Springfield, Ohio, in 1900.

KELLOG (ALSO KELLOGG)

Ranking: 1986 **S.S. Count:** 22,816

Origin: English, Irish, Welsh. English: derived from the Middle English words "kellen" and "hog," meaning to kill and pig. The name was given to those who butchered pigs. Irish: transformation of Kelly. Welsh: uncertain etymology. Possibly derived from the Welsh word "ceiliog," meaning cock.

Famous Bearers: EDWARD KELLOGG (1790–1858) of New York was a financial reformer and a backer of greenbackism. ELIJAH KELLOGG (1813–1901) of Maine was a Congregational clergyman and author. He wrote "Lion Ben," a boys' adventure story, and "Spartacus to the Gladiators." ALBERT KELLOGG (1813–1887) of Connecticut wrote the first botanical account of California's silvas. WILLIAM PITT KELLOGG (1830–1918) of Vermont was a Union soldier and what one might have termed a carpetbagger after the Civil War: He moved to Louisiana, where he represented his adoptive state in the U.S. Senate and as its governor. CLARA LOUISE KELLOGG (1842–1916) of South Carolina was a soprano singer and the first American prima donna to be well received in Europe. JOHN HARVEY KELLOGG (1852–1943) of Michigan was a physician at the Battle Creek (Michigan) Sanitarium. He also founded the Battle Creek College and the Miami–Battle Creek Sanitarium in Florida. He and his brother developed a dry cereal that could be used in the sanitarium. FRANK BILLINGS KELLOGG (1856–1937) of New York was a lawyer and had, as his client, the U.S. government in antitrust suits against several major corporations. He was a U.S. senator and the co-author of the Kellogg-Briand Pact. He was the recipient of the Nobel Peace Prize in 1929. WILL KEITH KELLOGG (1860–1951) of Michigan was the brother of John Harvey

Kellogg. He helped his brother with nutritional experiments at the sanitarium. He started the W. K. Kellogg Co., which became one of the biggest manufacturers of breakfast cereals. (EVA) LOUISE PHELPS KELLOGG (1862–1942) of Wisconsin was considered one of the best historians of her time.

Genealogies: None known.

KELLY

Ranking: 65 **S.S. Count:** 364,413

Origin: English, Irish, Scottish. English: derived from a Cornish cognate to the Gaelic word "coille," meaning wood. The name was given to those from Kelly, a place in Devon, England. Irish: derived from the Gaelic name Ó Ceallaigh, which was derived from the personal name Ceallach, meaning belligerent. Scottish: derived from the Gaelic component "coille," meaning wood. The name was given to those from Kelly, the name of several places in Scotland.

Famous Kellys: EUGENE KELLY (1808–1894) of Ireland was the founder and benefactor of Catholic University. WILLIAM KELLY (1811–1888) of Pennsylvania was an inventor who is best remembered for inventing the Bessemer converter for making steel. FANNY WIGGINS KELLY (1845–1904) of Canada was held captive by the Sioux Indians, during which time she learned their language, mannerisms, and customs. She published an account of her time with them in *Narrative of My Captivity among the Sioux Indians*. LUTHER SAGE KELLY (1849–1928) of New York was an army scout who was nicknamed "Yellowstone Kelly." An account of his scouting and life in the West was published in 1926. MICHAEL J. KELLY (1857–1894) of New York was a Chicago White Sox baseball player who was nicknamed "King Kelly" and "Ten Thousand Dollar Beauty." HOWARD ATWOOD KELLY (1858–1943) of New Jersey was a physician and a pioneer in the area of gynecology, performing the first cesarean section under sanitary conditions in Philadelphia. FLORENCE FINCH KELLY (1858–1939) of Illinois was a journalist who struggled to the top of her profession without the use of "feminine wiles." ALOYSIUS OLIVER JOSEPH KELLY (1870–1911) of Pennsylvania was a professor of medicine at the University of Pennsylvania and a writer and editor of material for medical journals. MYRA KELLY (1876–1910) of Ireland came to the United States as a child and became a teacher of immigrant children in New York City. She wrote stories detailing the children she had known. Two of her more popular books were *Little Citizens* (1904) and *Little Aliens* (1910). EDWARD JOSEPH KELLY (1876–1950) of Illinois was a politician in Chicago associated with Patrick A. Nash, and their association was referred to as the "Kelly-Nash machine." He remained mayor for 14 years, restoring the city's financial stability and initiating a series of improvements, including public housing that was deemed free of discrimination. His tenure was not without its problems, however, for the Chicago police force was ineffective and the school system was substandard. GEORGE KELLY (1887–1974) of Pennsylvania was an actor and a playwright and the winner of a Pulitzer Prize in 1925 for *Craig's Wife*. ALVIN ANTHONY KELLY (1893–1952), birthplace unknown, was a famous stuntman who went by the name Shipwreck Kelly. He is best remembered for sitting atop a flagpole in Atlantic City, New Jersey, for 177 hours in 1930. GEORGE KELLY (1895–1954) of Tennessee was originally named George Kelly Barnes. He was a gangster with the nickname Machine Gun Kelly. EMMETT LEE KELLY (1898–1979) of Kansas was a clown. He created many characters, especially Weary Willie, the sad tramp in tattered business clothes. He is responsible for raising the role of the clown to an art form. WALTER CRAWFORD KELLY (1913–1973) of Pennsylvania was a cartoonist and an illustrator. He created the "Pogo" comic strip. COLIN P. KELLY (1915–1941) of Florida was an army pilot who attacked the Japanese battleship *Haruna* two days after the Japanese attack on Pearl Harbor. With his plane damaged, he ordered his crew to bail out. He died in the crash. ERNEST BYRON KELLY JR. (1915–1978) of Illinois was an investment banker and was active in civic and philanthropic work. He served as chairman of the United Foundation Torch Drive in Detroit and as a worker with Little League baseball teams. STEPHEN EUGENE KELLY (1919–1976) was a publisher and advertising executive involved with some of the major magazines of his day, including *Time*, *Sports Illustrated*, the *Saturday Evening Post*, and *McCall's*. GRACE KELLY (1929–1982) of Pennsylvania was an actress who wed Prince Rainier of Monaco, making her Princess Grace of Monaco.

Genealogies: None known.

KELSEY

Ranking: 2357 **S.S. Count:** 19,244

Origin: English. Derived from the Old English first name Cēnel, meaning brave, and the Old English word "ēg," meaning island. The name was given to those from Kelsey, a place in Lincolnshire, England.

Famous **Kelseys:** FRANCIS WILLEY KELSEY (1858–1927) of New York was a professor of Latin at the University of Michigan and an archaeologist. RAYNER WICKERSHAM KELSEY (1879–1934) of Illinois was a Quaker minister and professor of history on the university level.

Genealogies: *Brush, Sammis, Kelsey and Allied Families* was compiled by Fannie M. Neumann and published in New York, New York, in 1954. *A Genealogy of the Descendants of William Kelsey* was compiled by Edward A. Claypool and published in New Haven, Connecticut, in 1928.

KELSO

Ranking: 3666 **S.S. Count:** 12,319

Origin: Irish, Scottish. Uncertain etymology. Possibly derived from the Old English words "cealc" and "hōh," meaning chalk and ridge. The name was given to those from Kelso, a place in Scotland.

Genealogies: None known.

KEMP

Ranking: 654 **S.S. Count:** 63,904

Origin: English. Derived from the Middle English word "kempe," meaning warrior. The name was given to those who were victors at wrestling or jousting.

Famous **Kemps:** JOHN KEMP (1763–1812) was an educator in the areas of mathematics, geography, and the sciences. He advised DeWitt Clinton on the Erie Canal project. JAMES KEMP (1764–1827) of Scotland was an Episcopal minister and the bishop of Maryland. ROBERT H. KEMP (1820–1897) of Massachusetts was the leader of the "Old Folks Concerts" of Reading, Massachusetts.

Genealogies: *Hiestand* [also Kemp] *Family History* was compiled by Barbara Hiestand Moore and published in New Braunfels, Texas, in 1990. *Kemp Family Records* was compiled by Thomas J. Kemp and published in Stamford, Connecticut, in 1985.

KEMPER

Ranking: 3058 **S.S. Count:** 14,836

Origin: Dutch. Cognate to Kemp.

Famous **Kempers:** JACKSON KEMPER (1789–1870) of New York was an Episcopal clergyman who became a missionary in the Northwest. He was the missionary bishop of the area, establishing seven dioceses and three colleges for the training of clergymen. He was the single most effective person in rooting the Episcopal church in the Northwest. JAMES LAWSON KEMPER (1823–1895) of Virginia was a Confederate major general and the governor of Virginia after the Civil War.

Genealogies: None known.

KENDAL (ALSO KENDALL)

Ranking: 1059 **S.S. Count:** 41,665

Origin: English. Derived from the British river named Kent, which was derived from the Old Norse words "kelda" and "dalr," meaning spring and valley, and from the Old English word "dæl," meaning valley. The name was given to those from Kendal or Kendale, the name of places in England.

Famous **Bearers:** AMOS KENDALL (1789–1869) of Massachusetts was a newspaper editor, postmaster general, advisor to Andrew Jackson, and business agent of Samuel F.B. Morse. GEORGE WILKINS KENDALL (1809–1867) of New Hampshire was the founder and editor of the *New Orleans Picayune* in 1837. EDWARD CALVIN KENDALL (1886–1972) of Connecticut was a biochemist at the Mayo Clinic in Rochester, Minnesota, where he isolated cortisone and was one of the scientists who successfully used it to treat arthritis. In 1950 he received a Nobel Prize for medicine.

Genealogies: *James Arthello Kendall (1883–1942) of Nephi, UT*, was compiled by Della Kendall Hall and published in Asheville, North Carolina, in 1989. *The Kendall Family History* was compiled by Denise Kelley Mortorff and published in Hercules, California, in 1989.

KENDRICK (S.S. Abbreviation: Kendri)

Ranking: 1124 **S.S. Count:** 39,137

Origin: English, Scottish, Welsh. English: derived from the Middle English first name Ceric, which is derived from the Old English components "cyne" and "ric," meaning royal and power. Irish: derived from the Gaelic name Indreachtach, meaning assailant. Scottish: derived from the name McKendrick, which is derived from a Gaelic cognate to the first name Henry. Welsh: derived from the first name Cyn(w)rig, which is of uncertain etymology.

Famous **Kendricks:** JOHN KENDRICK (1740?–1794) of Massachusetts was a navigator and world trader. He was the first to fly the American flag in Japan. He traded between the Pacific Northwest and the Orient. ASAHEL CLARK KENDRICK (1809–1895) of Vermont was a scholar and classicist. He taught Greek at Colgate University, then at the University of Rochester. He devised a new method for teaching and learning Greek. JOHN BENJAMIN KENDRICK (1857–1933) of Texas was the governor of Wyoming and a U.S. senator.

Genealogies: *The Family of Kendrick, 1782–1991* was compiled by Mary Elizabeth Gunn and published in Arlington, Texas, in 1991. *The Kendrick Kindred* was compiled by Guy Dyson and published in Hammond, Louisiana, in 1973.

KENNEDY (S.S. Abbreviation: Kenned)

Ranking: 120 **S.S. Count:** 242,717

Origin: Irish, Jewish. Irish: derived from the Gaelic name Ó Cinnéidigh, which was derived from the first name Cinnéidigh, which was derived from the words "ceann" and "éidigh," meaning head and armored. The name was given to those with misshapen or unsightly heads. Jewish: cognate to Kennedi, a Hungarian-Jewish surname of unknown origin.

Famous **Kennedys:** ARCHIBALD KENNEDY (1685–1763) of Scotland was a customs official who wrote pamphlets against the Crown's policies. JOHN PENDLETON KENNEDY (1795–1870) of Maryland was a novelist who wrote under the name Mark Littleton. He also served in the House of Representatives and as the secretary of the navy. JOSEPH CAMP GRIFFITH KENNEDY (1813–1887) of Pennsylvania was the head of the 1850 and 1860 censuses and was one of the organizers of the First International Statistical Congress (Brussels, 1853). KATE KENNEDY (1827–1890) of Ireland was a teacher and reformer who believed that equal pay should result from equal work. Because of her efforts, the California legislature passed a law requiring just that for teachers in 1874. JOHN STEWART KENNEDY (1830–1909) of Scotland was a builder of western railroads as J. S. Kennedy and Co. JOHN DOBY KENNEDY (1840–1896) of South Carolina was a Confederate brigadier general who worked to restore white supremacy attitudes and laws after the Civil War. WILLIAM SLOANE KENNEDY (1850–1929) of Ohio was a biographer and anthologist. He was a close friend of Walt Whitman's and the author of *Reminiscences of Walt Whitman* (1896). JOSEPH PATRICK KENNEDY (1888–1969) of Massachusetts was a businessman, banker, and ambassador to Great Britain. He was the father of President John F. Kennedy, U.S. Senator Robert F. Kennedy, and their siblings. SYLVESTER MICHAEL KENNEDY (1894–1973) of Illinois was a businessman in the food industry. He was the chairman of Consolidated Foods Corporation. JOHN FITZGERALD KENNEDY (1917–1963) of Massachusetts, the 35th president of the United States, was the first Roman Catholic and the youngest man to be elected president. He won a Pulitzer Prize for his book *Profiles in Courage* and previously served as a member of Congress and a U.S. senator. He was assassinated. ROBERT FRANCIS KENNEDY (1925–1968) of Massachusetts was the son of Joseph P. Kennedy and the brother of President John F. Kennedy. He served as his brother's attorney general and was a major force in the civil rights unrest of the 1960s. He later served as a U.S. senator from New York and was assassinated during his run for the Democratic presidential nomination.

Genealogies: *Alford-Kennedy Family History* was compiled by Eileen Alford and published in San Antonio, Texas, in 1971. *Ancestors and Kin* was compiled by Mary Kennedy Reynolds and published in Birmingham, Alabama, in 1991.

KENNERLEY, KENNERLY (S.S. Abbreviation: Kenner)

Ranking: 4512 **S.S. Count:** 9921

Origin: English. Uncertain etymology. The names were given to those who came from Kennerleigh, a place in Devonshire, England.

Genealogies: None known.

KENNEY

Ranking: 1078 **S.S. Count:** 40,916

Origin: Irish, Scottish. Irish: derived from the Gaelic name Ó Coinnigh, which is derived from the Old Irish first name Coinneach. Scottish: derived from the Gaelic first name Cionaodha.

Genealogies: *By the Name of Kinne* [also Kenney] was compiled by Basil E. Kinney and published in Belfast, Maine, in 1992.

KENNY

Ranking: 1938 S.S. Count: 23,343
Origin: Irish, Scottish. Transformation of Kenney.
Genealogies: None known.

KENT

Ranking: 705 S.S. Count: 59,940
Origin: English. Uncertain etymology. The name was given to those from the county named Kent, located in England.

Famous **Kents:** JAMES KENT (1763–1847) of New York was a lawyer and one of the contributors to the American system of equity jurisdiction. JOSEPH KENT (1779–1837) of Maryland was a member of Congress, U.S. senator, and governor of Maryland. EDWARD KENT (1802–1877) of Maine was the governor of Maine. CHARLES FOSTER KENT (1867–1925) of New York founded the National Council on Religion in Higher Education. ARTHUR ATWATER KENT (1873–1949) of Vermont was an inventor and radio manufacturer. He founded the Atwater Kent Manufacturing Works in Philadelphia to make electrical devices. ROCKWELL KENT (1882–1971) of New York was an artist who is best remembered for his landscapes and figure paintings that incorporate nature in the composition. WALTER KENT (?–1994) was a songwriter who cowrote "I'll Be Home for Christmas" but is probably best remembered for the World War II anthem "Blue Birds Over the White Cliffs of Dover." Written without Kent's having been to England, the song symbolized the Allied resistance in the early days of the war. He did not visit the cliffs until 1989. WILLIAM KENT (1851–1918) of Pennsylvania was a mechanical engineer and the author of *Mechanical Engineers' Pocket-Book* (1895). AMOS EUGENE KENT (1908–1978) of New York was a mechanical engineer who was responsible for the mechanical systems in many of the office complexes on the east coast, including those of Hartford Hospital, Rutgers University, and Macalester College.

Genealogies: *Kent, Gibson, Jeans* was compiled by Frances E. Caldwell and published in Veneta, Oregon, in 1968.

KENYON

Ranking: 2524 S.S. Count: 17,971
Origin: English. Uncertain etymology. The name was given to those from Kenyon, a place in Lancashire, England.

Famous **Kenyons:** WILLIAM SQUIRE KENYON (1869–1933) of Ohio was a U.S. senator, an effective supporter of farmers' interests, and an active participant in battling the Teapot Dome scandal. JOHN SAMUEL KENYON (1874–1959) of Ohio was a phonetician who was a coauthor of *A Pronouncing Dictionary of American English.* DOROTHY KENYON (1888–1972) of New York was a lawyer and judge who switched interests from social butterflies to social injustice. She served on the national board of directors of the American Civil Liberties Union from 1930 until her death. She was active in New York politics and served as a municipal judge for one year. She was an officer in many women's organizations and was a member of a League of Nations committee to study the status of women worldwide.

Genealogies: *They Came to Find Their Dream in Adams, New York* was compiled by David A. Sinclair and published in Syracuse, New York, in 1983.

KERN

Ranking: 1107 S.S. Count: 39,942
Origin: German, Jewish. Derived from the German word "kern," meaning kernel.

Famous **Kerns:** JOHN WORTH KERN (1849–1917) of Indiana was a U.S. senator and a leader of progressive lawmakers. He fought for social justice. DAVID JEROME KERN (1885–1945) of New York was a composer of musical-comedy and film scores. He wrote, among other songs, "Smoke Gets in Your Eyes."

Genealogies: *The Kearns Family* [also Kern] was compiled by David L. Greene and published in Demorest, Georgia, in 1979.

KERNS

Ranking: 2179 S.S. Count: 21,051
Origin: Uncertain etymology. Most likely a transformation of Kern.
Genealogies: None known.

KERR

Ranking: 655 S.S. Count: 63,886
Origin: English, Scottish. Derived from the Middle English word "kerr," meaning moist ground with dense undergrowth. The name was given to those who lived near such an area.

Famous **Kerrs:** JOHN GLASGOW KERR (1824–1901) of Ohio was a Presbyterian missionary who was a pioneer in proper treatment of the insane in China, where he headed the Medical Missionary Society's hospital. MICHAEL CRAWFORD KERR (1827–1876) of Pennsylvania was a politician best known for his tough stand against monopolies and Reconstruction. WASHINGTON CARRUTHERS KERR (1827–1885) of North Carolina was the geologist who made the state survey map and who advertised the state's resources. WALTER CRAIG KERR (1858–1910) of Minnesota was an engineer and the force behind firms' taking contracts for complete construction projects.

Genealogies: *Christian Frederick Kerr* was compiled by Elaine Ford Eaton and published in Baton Rouge, Louisiana, in 1981. *Heasley, Kerr, Smith, Cook* was compiled by Alice Heasley Dwight and published in Gibson Island, Maryland, in 1983.

KERSEY

Ranking: 3980 S.S. Count: 11,359

Origin: English. Uncertain etymology. Most likely derived from the Old English words "cœrs" and "ēg," meaning watercress and island. The name was given to those from Kersey, a place in Suffolk, England.

Genealogies: *Keirsey, Kiersey, Kersey* was compiled by Martha Keirsey Cooper and published in Maryville, Missouri, in 1988.

KERSTEIN, KERSTEN, KERSTENS (S.S. Abbreviation: Kerste)

Ranking: 4999 S.S. Count: 8968

Origin: Kersten—Dutch, German; Kerstens—German; Kerstein—Jewish. Kersten, Kerstens: cognates to Christian. Kerstein: derived from the German words "kirsch" and "stein," meaning cherry and stone. The name was taken ornamentally.

Genealogies: None known.

KESSEL (ALSO KESSELER, KESSELMAN)

Ranking: 4611 S.S. Count: 9690

Origin: Kesseler—Dutch; Kessel—German; Kesselman—Jewish. Derived from the German word "kessel," meaning kettle. The name was given to those who made copper kettles.

Genealogies: None known.

KESSLER

Ranking: 1047 S.S. Count: 41,812

Origin: German. Transformation of Kessel.

Genealogies: *Abraham Kesler (also Kessler), 1809–1891* was compiled by Richard W. Tobin and published in Gainesville, Florida, in 1982.

KESTER (ALSO KESTERTON)

Ranking: 3345 S.S. Count: 13,548

Origin: Kester—Dutch; Kesterton—English. Kester: 1) uncertain etymology. The name was given to those from Kester, a place in Holland. 2) uncertain etymology. The name was given to those who sold or made boxes. Kesterton: Derived from the Old English words "ceaster" and "tūn," meaning Roman fort and settlement. The name was given to those from Kesterton or Chesterton, the names of several places in England.

Famous Bearers: VAUGHAN KESTER (1869–1911) of New Jersey was a journalist and the author of *The Prodigal Judge.* He was the brother of Paul Kester. PAUL KESTER (1870–1933) of Ohio, a playwright, was the author of *Sweet Nell of Old Drury* (1900) and *When Knighthood Was in Flower* (1901). He was the brother of Vaughan Kester.

Genealogies: None known.

KETCHUM (S.S. Abbreviation: Ketchu)

Ranking: 3816 S.S. Count: 11,820

Origin: Danish/Norwegian?, English? Uncertain etymology. English: possibly a transformation of Kitchen.

Genealogies: None known.

KETTERING (S.S. Abbreviation: Ketter)

Ranking: 4125 S.S. Count: 10,959

Origin: Uncertain etymology. English. The name was given to those who came from Kettering, a place in Northamptonshire, England.

Famous Ketterings: CHARLES FRANKLIN KETTERING (1876–1958) of Ohio was the inventor of the first electric cash register and the co-developer of the first electric starter for automobiles, which was introduced on the 1912 Cadillac. He is probably best known as the co-founder of the Sloan-Kettering Institute for Cancer Research in New York City.

Genealogies: None known.

KEY

Ranking: 980 S.S. Count: 44,730

Origin: English. Transformation of Kay.

Famous Keys: PHILIP BARTON KEY (1757–1815) of Maryland was the uncle of Francis Scott Key and a Loyalist during the Revolution. He remained in America and served as a member of Congress after the war. FRANCIS SCOTT KEY (1779–1843) of Maryland was a lawyer but is probably best remembered as the man who was present at the British bombardment of Fort McHenry in Baltimore in 1814. When dawn broke the following day and the American flag still flew over the fort, he wrote the poem "Defense of Fort M'Henry," which was published in the *Baltimore Patriot.* The poem was later set to the music of John Stafford Smith's song "To Anacreon in Heaven," and the title was changed to "The Star Spangled Banner." It was adopted as the national anthem in 1931. DAVID MCKENDREE KEY (1824–1900) of Tennessee was a Confederate soldier, and, after the war, he served as a U.S. senator, U.S. postmaster general, and U.S. district judge. VALDIMER ORLANDO KEY JR. (1908–1963) of Texas was a political scientist who taught at Yale, Harvard, and Johns Hopkins universities and who wrote several books on the subject.

Genealogies: *Key and Allied Families* was compiled by Janie Warren Lane and published in Macon, Georgia, in 1931. *Key Is My Name* was compiled by Irene Frances Key Padgett and published in Shelby, North Carolina, in 1980.

KEYES

Ranking: 2093 S.S. Count: 21,921

Origin: English, Irish. English: 1) Uncertain etymology.

The name was given to those from Guise, a place in Picardy, France. 2) transformation of Kay. Irish: transformation of McKay.

Famous **Keyeses:** ERASMUS DARWIN KEYES (1810–1895) of Massachusetts was a soldier and businessman and the author of *Fifty Years' Observation of Men and Events* (1884). ELISHA WILLIAMS KEYES (1828–1910) of Vermont was the longtime postmaster of Madison, Wisconsin. EDWARD LAWRENCE KEYES (1843–1924) of South Carolina was a physician and a pioneer in dermatology and male genitourinary surgery. He was the author of an important paper on the treatment of syphilis. FRANCES PARKINSON WHEELER KEYES (1885–1945) of Virginia was a novelist who wrote, among other works, *All That Glitters.*

Genealogies: A History and Genealogy of One Branch of the Keyes Family was compiled by J. K. Messamore and published in Stow, Massachusetts. *By the Name of Keyes* was compiled by Peggy Keyes Gray and published in St. Petersburg, Florida, in 1989.

KEYS

Ranking: 1795 **S.S. Count:** 25,111

Origin: English, Irish. Transformation of Keyes.

Genealogies: *By the Name of Keyes (also Keys)* was compiled by Peggy Keyes Gray and published in St. Petersburg, Florida, in 1989.

KEYSER (ALSO KEYSERS)

Ranking: 4072 **S.S. Count:** 11,106

Origin: English, German. Cognates to and transformations of Kaiser.

Genealogies: *History of the Descendants of Charles Keyser* was compiled by Florence Skinner Miller and published in Baltimore, Maryland, in 1983.

KHAN

Ranking: 3019 **S.S. Count:** 15,054

Origin: Arabic, Persian, Turkish. 1) uncertain etymology. The name was given to innkeepers. 2) the name was given to those who were descended from a lord or to those who exhibited the characteristics of a lord.

Genealogies: None known.

KIDD

Ranking: 993 **S.S. Count:** 44,139

Origin: English, Scottish. English: 1) derived from the Middle English word "kidde," meaning fagot or bundle of branches. The name was given to those who sold fagots. 2) derived from the Middle English word "kid(e)," meaning a young goat. The name was given to goatherds or to those who were playful and lively. Scottish: derived from Kit, which is derived from the name Christopher.

Famous **Kidds:** WILLIAM KIDD (1645?–1701) of Scotland was better known as Captain Kidd, the British pirate who terrorized the American coastline. He was a shipowner and sea captain in New York City and was hired by the British to roust the pirates from the Indian Ocean, but he became one of the outlaws himself. He returned to New England requesting a pardon but was imprisoned in England and hanged. Rumors exist to this day that he buried his treasure along the American coast.

Genealogies: None known.

KIDDER

Ranking: 4808 **S.S. Count:** 9318

Origin: English. Uncertain etymology. The name was given to those who cared for or trained hawks for hunting.

Famous **Kidders:** DANIEL PARISH KIDDER (1815–1891) of New York was a minister who organized the Sunday-school work of his church. ALFRED VINCENT KIDDER (1885–1963) of Michigan was an archaeologist who worked extensively in the American Southwest and at Mayan sites in Central America.

Genealogies: *The Shepard* [also Kidder] *Genealogy* was compiled by Lowell Shepard Blaisdell and published in Arizona in 1952.

KIDWELL (S.S. Abbreviation: Kidwel)

Ranking: 3663 **S.S. Count:** 12,329

Origin: English. Derived from the Old English word "kidel," meaning fish weir. The name was given to those who lived near a fish weir.

Genealogies: *The Kidwell Ancestry in America* was compiled by Will M. Kidwell and published in Twentynine Palms, California, in 1988. *Kidwell Families of Kentucky* was compiled by Harold Kidwell and published in Twentynine Palms, California, in 1990.

KIEFER

Ranking: 2823 **S.S. Count:** 16,151

Origin: German. 1) derived from the Middle High German word "kiffen," meaning to quarrel. The name was given to those who quarreled. 2) derived from the German word "kiefer," meaning pine. The name was given to those who lived near pine trees. 3) derived from the Middle High German word "kifen," meaning to chew. The name was given to those who ate a lot or to sloppy eaters. 4) derived from the German word "kufe," meaning barrel. The name was given to coopers.

Genealogies: None known.

KILGORE (S.S. Abbreviation: Kilgor)

Ranking: 1530 **S.S. Count:** 29,047

Origin: Scottish. Derived from the Gaelic words "coille" and "gobhar," meaning wood and goat. The name was given to those from Kilgour, a place in Fife, Scotland.

Famous **Kilgores:** CARRIE BURNHAM KILGORE (1838–1909) of Vermont was a teacher, lawyer, and advocate of women's rights. After 10 years of vying for admittance to a law school, she was admitted to and was graduated from the University of Pennsylvania Law School, the first woman to do so. She was graduated in 1883, but she was not granted admittance to all courts until 1890.

Genealogies: None known.

KILLIAN (S.S. Abbreviation: Killia)

Ranking: 2689 **S.S. Count:** 16,947

Origin: Irish. Derived from the Gaelic first name Cillín, which was derived from the first name Ceallach, meaning troublesome.

Genealogies: None known.

KILLINGBACK, KILLINGBECK, KILLINGTON (S.S. Abbreviation: Killin)

Ranking: 3451 **S.S. Count:** 13,079

Origin: Killingback, Killingbeck—English; Killington—English. Killingback, Killingbeck: derived from the Old Norse first name Killing and the Old Norse word "bekkr," meaning stream. The name was given to those from Killingbeck, a place in England. Killington: derived from the Old English first name Cylla and the Old English word "tūn," meaning settlement. The name was given to those from Killington, a place in England.

Genealogies: None known.

KILPATRICK (S.S. Abbreviation: Kilpat)

Ranking: 2317 **S.S. Count:** 19,569

Origin: Irish, Scottish. Irish: derived from the Gaelic name Mac Giolla Phádraig, meaning "son of the servant of (St.) Patrick" (H&H). Scottish: derived from the Gaelic phrase "cill Padraig," meaning "church of (St.) Patrick" (H&H). The name was given to those from Kilpatrick, the name of several places in Scotland.

Famous **Kilpatricks:** HUGH JUDSON KILPATRICK (1836–1881) of New Jersey was a West Point soldier who, as a Union cavalry officer, led the raid on the Libbey Prison in Richmond to rescue captured Union soldiers.

Genealogies: *Kilpatrick and Allied Families* was compiled by Edward Floyd Kilpatrick and published in Fort Loudon, Pennsylvania, in 1984.

KIM

Ranking: 369 **S.S. Count:** 104,769

Origin: Korean. Derived from the Korean word meaning gold.

Genealogies: None known.

KIMBALL (S.S. Abbreviation: Kimbal)

Ranking: 1316 **S.S. Count:** 33,812

Origin: English, Welsh. Transformation of Kimble.

Famous **Kimballs:** HEGER CHASE KIMBALL (1801–1868) of Vermont was a leader in the Mormon Church. He was one of the 12 apostles, served as the missionary to England, and was part of the first migration to Utah. He served as one of Brigham Young's confidants. GILMAN KIMBALL (1804–1892) of New Hampshire was a surgeon and a pioneer in gynecological and traumatic surgery. RICHARD BURLEIGH KIMBALL (1816–1892) of New Hampshire was the founder of Kimball, Texas, and the head of the first Texas railroad. NATHAN KIMBALL (1823?–1898) of Indiana served in the Mexican and Civil wars and as the surveyor general of Utah and the postmaster of Ogden, Utah. SUMNER INCREASE KIMBALL (1834–1923) of Maine organized the U.S. Lifesaving Service. WILLIAM WIRT KIMBALL (1848–1930) of Maine was a pioneer in the promotion of submarines and the commander of the first U.S. torpedo-boat flotilla.

Genealogies: *Genealogy of the Kemble* [also Kimball] *Family in America* was compiled by Kemble Stout and published in Pullman, Washington, in 1992. *The Kimble* [also Kimball] *Family from Z to A* was compiled by Seruch Titus Kimble and published in Olney, Maryland, in 1984.

KIMBER, KIMBERLEY, KIMBERLY (S.S. Abbreviation: Kimber)

Ranking: 3616 **S.S. Count:** 12,483

Origin: Kimber—English; Kimberley, Kimberly—English. Kimber: derived from the Old English first name Cyneburh, which was derived from the components "cyne-" and "burh," meaning royal and fortress. Kimberley, Kimberly: derived from various Old English first names and the Old English word "lēah," meaning wood. The name was given to those from Kimberley, the name of several places in England.

Genealogies: None known.

KIMBLE

Ranking: 1708 **S.S. Count:** 26,157

Origin: English, Welsh. English: 1) derived from the British word "cyfyl," meaning border. The name was given to those from Kemble, a place in Gloucestershire, England. 2) derived from the Old English first name Cynebeal(d), which was derived from the components "cyne-" and "beald," meaning royal and bold. Welsh: derived from a Celtic first name that comprises the components "cyn" and "bel," meaning chief and war.

Genealogies: *The Kimble Family from Z to A* was compiled by Seruch Titus Kimble and published in Olney, Maryland, in 1984.

KIMBREW (S.S. Abbreviation: Kimbre)

Ranking: 4247 **S.S. Count:** 10,602

Origin: English. Transformation of Kimbrough.
Genealogies: None known.

KIMBROUGH (S.S. Abbreviation: Kimbrough)
Ranking: 2234 **S.S. Count:** 20,498
Origin: English. Transformation of Kimber.
Genealogies: *Early Kimbroughs* was compiled by Tom F. Carson and published in Auburn, Alabama, in 1968.

KIMMEL, KIMMELFIELD, KIMMELMAN
Ranking: 2740 **S.S. Count:** 16,622
Origin: Jewish. Derived from the German word "kümmel," meaning caraway. The name was given to those who sold caraway seeds.
Famous **Kimmels:** HUSBAND EDWARD KIMMEL (1882–1968) of Kentucky was a naval officer who was the commander of the Pacific Fleet but who was relieved of command after the 1941 attack on Pearl Harbor.
Genealogies: None known.

KINARD
Ranking: 4747 **S.S. Count:** 9435
Origin: English. Derived from the Old English first name Cyneweard, which was derived from the components "cyne-" and "heard," meaning royal and hardy.
Genealogies: *Footprints of Jacob Kynerd, Kinard, Kynard, Kinerd* was compiled by Dan P. Kinard and published in Montgomery, Alabama, in 1986. *Kennard* [also Kinard], *King, Knight, Hardin, Goodin* was compiled by Alta Kennard Patterson and published in Huffman, Texas, in 1988.

KINCAID, KINCAIDIE
Ranking: 1723 **S.S. Count:** 26,003
Origin: Scottish. Uncertain etymology. Most likely derived from the Gaelic words "ceann" and "càithe," meaning top or head and pass. The name was given to those from Kincaid, a place in Scotland.
Genealogies: *A Genealogical History of the Name of Kincaid* was compiled by Eugene Davis Kincaid and published in Uvalde, Texas, in 1987. *Kincaid-Claypool Descendants* was compiled by William Harold Kincaid and published in Ann Arbor, Michigan, in 1991.

KINDER (ALSO KINDERLEHRER, KINDERLERER)
Ranking: 2839 **S.S. Count:** 16,077
Origin: Kinder—English; Kinderlehrer, Kinderlerer—Jewish. Kinder: the name was given to those from Kinder, a place in Derbyshire, England. Kinderlehrer, Kinderlerer: derived from the German words "kinder" and "lehrer," meaning children and teacher. The name was given to those who taught children in a traditional Jewish school.

Genealogies: None known.

KING
Ranking: 32 **S.S. Count:** 621,112
Origin: English. Derived from the Old English word "cyning," meaning king. The name was given to those who exhibited the characteristics of a king.
Famous **Kings:** RUFUS KING (1755–1827), of land that is now part of Maine, was a member of the Continental Congress and the Constitutional Convention and was one of the framers of the Constitution. WILLIAM KING (1768–1852) of Maine was a leader in the movement to separate Maine from Massachusetts. He then served as Maine's first governor. WILLIAM RUFUS DE VANE KING (1786–1853) of North Carolina was a U.S. senator and the vice president of the United States under President Franklin Pierce. He died in office. SAMUEL WARD KING (1786–1851) was governor of Rhode Island. JOHN ALSOP KING (1788–1867) of New York City was the son of Rufus King (1755–1827) and a New York legislator, member of Congress, and governor. CHARLES KING (1789–1867) of New York was the president of Columbia College, now Columbia University, as it began to grow in both curriculum and professional schools. DAN KING (1791–1864) of Connecticut was part of the Rhode Island suffrage movement and the author of *The Life and Times of Thomas Wilson Dorr* (1859). JOHN PENDLETON KING (1799–1888) of Kentucky was a cotton manufacturer and railroad president and a major industrialist in the South after the Civil War. AUSTIN AUGUSTUS KING (1802–1870) of Tennessee was a member of Congress and governor of Tennessee. CHARLES WILLIAM KING (1809?–1845) of New York City spent much of his life in China learning the intricate cultural lifestyles of the people of eastern Asia. JOHN KING (1813–1893) of New York City was the founder of the eclectic school of medicine. RUFUS KING (1814–1876) of New York City was an editor and diplomat. He was the last U.S. Minister to the entity known then as the Papal States, known today as The Vatican. THOMAS STARR KING (1824–1864) of New York City is credited with keeping California loyal to the Union. RICHARD KING (1825–1885) of New York was a rancher who had the largest ranch in the country, in southern Texas, totaling 600,000 acres at the time of his death. SAMUEL ARCHER KING (1828–1914) of Pennsylvania made the first balloon ascent from Philadelphia in 1851. ALBERT FREEMAN AFRICANUS KING (1841–1914) of England came to the United States as a boy. He was a physician who taught obstetrics and was a pioneer in the linkage of the mosquito to malaria. CLARENCE KING (1842–1901) of Rhode Island was a geologist and one of the discoverers of Mount Whitney in California. He also explored the deserts of the Southwest and discovered the first glaciers in the United States. FRANKLIN HIRAM KING (1848–1911) of Wis-

consin was the inventor of the cylindrical tower silo for the storage of silage. GRACE ELIZABETH KING (1853?–1932) of Louisiana was an author who wrote about the grandeur of New Orleans. LOUISA BOYD YEOMANS KING (1863–1948) of New Jersey was one of the founders of the Garden Club of America. She wrote books and articles on the subject of gardening and did much to promote gardening and gardening clubs in America. LIDA SHAW KING (1868–1932) of Massachusetts was a classical scholar and a college administrator. FRANK O. KING (1883–1969) of Wisconsin was a cartoonist and the creator of "Gasoline Alley." CAROL WEISS KING (1895–1952) of New York was a lawyer and a civil libertarian. She mainly worked to help those who could not help themselves, particularly immigrants. She was an influence on her generation of lawyers. E[DWARD] WARD KING (1896–1977) of Tennessee was the founder of the Mason and Dixon Lines, Inc., a trucking company. MARTIN LUTHER KING JR. (1929–1968) of Georgia was a Baptist minister and the unofficial head of the nonviolent civil rights movement. He was awarded a Nobel Peace Prize for his "I Have a Dream" speech. He was assassinated.

Genealogies: *History of the King Family in Flanders & America* was compiled by Robert E. King and published in Pullman, Washington, in 1980. *Kennard, King, Knight, Hardin, Goodin* was compiled by Alta Kennard Patterson and published in Huffman, Texas, in 1988.

KINGSBERG, KINGSBURY (S.S. Abbreviation: Kingsb)

Ranking: 4154 **S.S. Count:** 10,892

Origin: Kingsbury—English; Kingsberg—Jewish. Kingsbury: derived from the Old English component "cyne-" and the Old English word "burh," meaning royal and fortress. The name was given to those from Kingsbury, the name of several places in England. Kingsberg: 1) derived from the Middle High German word "künigesberc," meaning the king's hill. The name was given to those from Königsberg, a place in Germany. 2) derived from the name König.

Famous **Bearers:** SUSAN MYRA KINGSBURY (1870–1949) of California was a pioneer in the field of social research, setting up the first academic department offering advanced training in the field of social services.

Genealogies: None known.

KINGSLEY (S.S. Abbreviation: Kingsl)

Ranking: 3482 **S.S. Count:** 12,953

Origin: English. Derived from the Old English word "cyningesleah," meaning the king's wood. The name was given to those from Kingsley, the name of several places in England.

Famous **Kingsleys:** JAMES LUCE KINGSLEY (1778–1852) of Connecticut was the first professor of languages at Yale

University. NORMAN W. KINGSLEY (1829–1913) of New York was a dentist who specialized in oral deformities. His book *A Treatise on Oral Deformities* (1880) was a standard text.

Genealogies: None known.

KINGSTON (S.S. Abbreviation: Kingst)

Ranking: 4972 **S.S. Count:** 9015

Origin: English. Derived from the Old English word "cyningestūn," meaning the king's settlement. The name was given to those from Kingston or Kingstone, the name of several places in England.

Genealogies: None known.

KINNEY

Ranking: 981 **S.S. Count:** 44,666

Origin: Irish, Scottish. Transformation of Kenney.

Famous **Kinneys:** WILLIAM B. KINNEY (1799–1880) of New Jersey was a journalist and diplomat. He was U.S. chargé d'affaires in Turin, Italy. His wife, ELIZABETH CLEMENTINE DODGE STEDMAN KINNEY (1810–1889) of New York, was a poet and essayist. SELWYNE PEREZ KINNEY (1890–1976) of Utah was a metallurgist and chemical engineer who did extensive research on industrial gas and ventilation in railroad tunnels and in iron blast furnaces, to which he made many innovative improvements.

Genealogies: None known.

KINSEY

Ranking: 2157 **S.S. Count:** 21,268

Origin: English. Derived from an Old English first name that comprised the components "cyne-" and "sige," meaning royal and victory.

Famous **Kinseys:** JOHN KINSEY (1693–1750) of New Jersey was chief justice of the Pennsylvania Supreme Court. He also made the first compilation of New Jersey laws. CHARLES ALFRED KINSEY (1894–1956) of New Jersey was a zoologist at Indiana University. In 1938 he began scientific study of human sexuality; he founded the Institute for Sex Research at Indiana University in 1942 and also served as its director. He published books on both male and female sexuality.

Genealogies: None known.

KIRBY

Ranking: 546 **S.S. Count:** 74,681

Origin: English. Derived from the Old Norse words "kirkja" and "býr," meaning church and settlement. The name was given to those from Kirby, the name of several places in England.

Famous **Kirbys:** EPHRAIM KIRBY (1757–1804) of Connecticut was editor of the first complete published volume of law reports in the United States, *Reports of Cases Adjudged in the Superior Court of Errors of the State of Con-*

necticut, *1785–1788* (1789). His grandson, EDMUND KIRBY-SMITH (1824–1893) of Florida, was a Confederate officer and the last one to surrender (May 26, 1865). After the war, he served as the president of the University of Nashville. ROLLIN KIRBY (1875–1952) of Illinois was a cartoonist. Although he worked for major New York papers, he freelanced his political cartoons after 1942. He is best known for the subjects of Wall Street; "Mr. Dry," the symbol of Prohibition; and his Pulitzer Prize–winning "On the Road to Moscow" cartoons.

Genealogies: *Colonial Settlers and English Adventurers* was compiled by Noel Currier Briggs and published in Baltimore, Maryland, in 1971. *Tidewater Ancestors* was compiled by Louise Niemeyer Fontaine and published in Petersburg, Virginia, in 1991.

KIRCHNER (S.S. Abbreviation: Kirchn)

Ranking: 3287 S.S. Count: 13,798

Origin: German. Derived from the word "kirche," meaning church. The name was given to sextons.

Genealogies: *The Ancestors and Descendants of Herman Buechele and Mary Rehklau and Michael Kirchner* was compiled by Ruth Buchele Doerr and published in Milford, Michigan, in 1991.

KIRK

Ranking: 554 S.S. Count: 73,796

Origin: English, Scottish. Derived from the Old Norse word "kirkja," meaning church. The name was given to those who lived near or worked in a church.

Famous **Kirks:** JOHN FOSTER KIRK (1824–1904), born in Canada, was editor of *Lippincott's Magazine* for 16 years. ALAN GOODRICH KIRK (1888–1963) of Pennsylvania was a naval officer and diplomat. He was the commander of the Western Naval Task Force at Normandy on D-Day, June 6, 1944.

Genealogies: *Southern Kirk and Carrell Families* was compiled by Maudie Marie Holt Marshall and published in Houston, Texas, in 1971. *Farrington and Kirk Family* was compiled by Herschel B. Rochelle and published in Hillsborough, North Carolina, in 1983.

KIRKLAND (S.S. Abbreviation: Kirkla)

Ranking: 1104 S.S. Count: 40,008

Origin: English. Derived from the Middle English words "kirk" and "land," meaning church and land. The name was given to those who lived on land owned by a church.

Famous **Kirklands:** SAMUEL KIRKLAND (1741–1808) of Connecticut was a Congregational missionary with the Iroquois Indians. He was influential in keeping the peace with the Indians. He later served as chaplain to the American troops during the Revolutionary War. JOHN THORNTON KIRKLAND (1770–1840) of New York was the son of Samuel

and the president of Harvard University. CAROLINE MATILDA STANSBURY KIRKLAND (1801–1864) of New York moved to Michigan when it was a frontier. Her written accounts of life on the frontier were the first realistic ones of that kind of life. She wrote under the pen name of Mrs. Mary Clavers. Her son, JOSEPH KIRKLAND (1830–1894) of New York, also a writer, is credited with helping to develop realism in American fiction. His books included *The Captain of Company K* (1891).

Genealogies: *The Kirklands of Ayr Mount* was compiled by Jean Bradley Anderson and published in Chapel Hill, North Carolina, in 1991. *The Kirtland-Kirkland Families* was compiled by Elfrieda A. Kraege and published in New York, New York, in 1979.

KIRKPATRICK (S.S. Abbreviation: Kirkpa)

Ranking: 1139 S.S. Count: 38,582

Origin: Irish, Scottish. Derived from the Middle English word "kirk," meaning church, and St. Patrick. The name was given to those from Kirkpatrick, the name of several places in Ireland and Scotland.

Famous **Kirkpatricks:** ANDREW KIRKPATRICK (1756–1831) of New Jersey was chief justice of the New Jersey Supreme Court for 20 years.

Genealogies: *The Descendants of Valentine Kirkpatrick* was compiled by Willett Douglas Kirkpatrick and published in Montgomery, Alabama, in 1991. *Homestead* was compiled by Jane Kirkpatrick and published in Dallas, Texas, in 1991.

KIRKWOOD (S.S. Abbreviation: Kirkwo)

Ranking: 3934 S.S. Count: 11,468

Origin: Scottish. Derived from the Middle English words "kirk" and "wode," meaning church and wood. The name was given to those from Kirkwood, the name of several places in Scotland.

Famous **Kirkwoods:** SAMUEL JORDAN KIRKWOOD (1813–1894) of Maryland was governor of Iowa, a U.S. senator, and a U.S. secretary of the interior. DANIEL KIRKWOOD (1814–1895) of Maryland, an astronomer, is credited with establishing a connection between comets and meteors.

Genealogies: *Kirkwoods, and their Kin* was compiled by Anna Lee Kirkwood Smith and published in Jarrettsville, Maryland, in 1972.

KIRSCH (ALSO KIRSCHBAUM, KIRSCHBLUM, KIRSCHE, KIRSCHENBAUM)

Ranking: 1601 S.S. Count: 28,020

Origin: Kirsch, Kirsche—German, Jewish; Kirschbaum, Kirschblum, Kirschenbaum—Jewish. Kirsch, Kirsche—German: derived from the German word "kirsch(baum)," meaning cherry (tree). The name was given to those who lived near a cherry tree or orchard. Jewish: derived from the German or Yiddish word "kirsch," meaning cherry. The name was taken ornamentally. Kirschbaum, Kirschblum, Kirschenbaum: derived from the German or Yiddish word "kirsch," meaning cherry, and "baum," meaning tree, or "blum," meaning flower. The name was taken ornamentally.

Genealogies: None known.

KISER
Ranking: 1818 S.S. Count: 24,827
Origin: German. Transformation of Kaiser.
Genealogies: None known.

KISH
Ranking: 3690 S.S. Count: 12,235
Origin: English, Hungarian. English: derived from the Anglo-Norman-French word "cuisse," meaning thigh. The name was given to those who made armor for the leg. Hungarian: derived from the word "kis," meaning small. The name was given to those who were small in stature or who were the younger of two persons of the same name.
Genealogies: None known.

KISSEL
Ranking: 4829 S.S. Count: 9271
Origin: German. Derived from the first name Geisel, meaning staff.
Genealogies: None known.

KITCHENMAN, KITCHEN, KITCHENER (S.S. Abbreviation: Kitche)
Ranking: 1143 S.S. Count: 38,471
Origin: English. Derived from the Latin word "cūcina," meaning kitchen. The name was given to those who worked in kitchens.
Genealogies: The Kitchen Family was compiled by Lennie M. Carter and published in Timonium, Maryland, in 1989.

KITTLE
Ranking: 4657 S.S. Count: 9601
Origin: English. Derived from the Old Norse first name Ketill, which was derived from the component "-ketill," meaning cauldron.
Genealogies: Some Descendants of Four Pioneer Families was compiled by Eleanor R. Lewis and published in Stephentown, New York, in 1972.

KLEIN
Ranking: 319 S.S. Count: 116,602
Origin: Dutch, German, Jewish. Dutch, German: derived from the Middle Dutch and Middle High German word "kleine," meaning small. Jewish: derived from the Yiddish

word "kleyn," meaning small. The name in all cases was given to those who were considered diminutive.

Famous Kleins: JOSEPH FREDERIC KLEIN (1849–1918), born in France but a U.S. resident since childhood, was an engineer who developed the engineering school at Lehigh University. BRUNO OSCAR KLEIN (1858–1911), born in Germany, toured the United States as a pianist, then settled in New York, where he taught and composed music. AUGUST C. KLEIN (1887–1948) of New Jersey, a mechanical engineer who worked on major power plant projects, was project engineer of the Manhattan Project's Oak Ridge, Tennessee, plant.

Genealogies: The Klein Family from Holland was compiled by John Snell and published in Ravenna, Nebraska, in 1986. The Klein Family History was compiled by Harrold A. Weinberger and published in Los Angeles, California, in 1980.

KLINE
Ranking: 660 S.S. Count: 63,630
Origin: Jewish. Transformation of Klein.
Famous Klines: GEORGE KLINE (1757–1820), born in Germany, was a frontier publisher. In 1785 he started The Carlisle (Pennsylvania) Gazette, the first Pennsylvania newspaper published west of the Susquehanna River. FRANZ JOSEPH KLINE (1910–1962) of Pennsylvania was a painter of modern art and a member of the "action painting" branch of abstract expressionism.
Genealogies: The Jacob Snyder [also Kline] Family History was compiled by Loucile Ruth Mayhew Heckman and published in 1991. Cline-Kline Family was compiled by Paul G. Kline and published in Dayton, Virginia, in 1971.

KLING
Ranking: 4228 S.S. Count: 10,669
Origin: German, Jewish. German: 1) derived from the Middle High German word "klinge," meaning sword. The name was given to swordsmiths. 2) Uncertain etymology. The name was given to those who lived near mountain streams.
Genealogies: None known.

KLINGELSMITH (S.S. Abbreviation: Klinge)
Ranking: 1675 S.S. Count: 26,669
Origin: German. Derived from the Middle High German word "klingen," meaning to ring. The name was given to those who made bells.
Famous Klingelsmiths: MARGARET CENTER KLINGELSMITH (1859–1931) of Maine was a lawyer and author who also was law librarian at the University of Pennsylvania.
Genealogies: Klingelsmith, Klingensmith, Klinginsmith, Klingonsmith was compiled by Barbara Klingelsmith Ceisert and published in Marietta, Georgia, in 1979.

KLOTZ

Ranking: 4897 **S.S. Count:** 9129

Origin: German, Jewish. Derived from the German word "klotz," meaning lump. The name was given to those who were clumsy.

Genealogies: *The Descendants of Johann Jacob Klotz in America* was compiled by Ralph Dean Kluttz and published in Salisbury, North Carolina, in 1990.

KNAPP

Ranking: 707 **S.S. Count:** 59,817

Origin: English, German. English: derived from the Old English word "cnæpp," meaning hilltop. The name was given to those from Knapp, the name of several places in England. German: derived from the Middle High German word "knappe," meaning boy. The name was given to squires or servants.

Famous Knapps: HERMAN KNAPP (1832–1911), born in Germany, practiced opthalmology in New York, where he established the *Archives of Opthalmology and Otology*. SEAMAN ASAHEL KNAPP (1833–1911) of New York was an agriculturalist who devised a new method of teaching farming techniques that became the model for the U.S. Department of Agriculture's Farmers Cooperative Demonstration Work program. WILLIAM I. KNAPP (1835–1908) of New York was the first professor of Romance languages at the University of Chicago. PHILIP C. KNAPP (1858–1878) of Massachusetts was a neurologist who published the first treatise in the United States on brain tumors. BRADFORD KNAPP (1870–1938) of Iowa was president of three technical colleges: Oklahoma Agricultural and Mechanical College, Alabama Polytechnic Institute, and Texas Technological College.

Genealogies: *Family History and Genealogy of James McEvers, 1755–1829, Abraham Knapp, Jr., 1759–1809, the Children and Grandchildren* was compiled by Harry B. Zabriskie and published in Midvale, Utah, in 1980.

KNECHT

Ranking: 4998 **S.S. Count:** 8970

Origin: German, Jewish. Cognate to Knight.
Genealogies: None known.

KNIGHT (ALSO KNIGHTLEY, KNIGHTLY, KNIGHTS)

Ranking: 171 **S.S. Count:** 195,677

Origin: Knight, Knights—English; Knightley, Knightly—English. Knight, Knights: derived from the Middle English word "knight," meaning a tenant who served a landholder as a mounted soldier. The name was most likely given to those in the employ of a knight. Knightley, Knightly: derived from the Old English word "cniht" and "leah," meaning servant and wood. The name was given to those from Knightley, the name of several places in England.

Famous Bearers: SARAH KEMBLE KNIGHT (1666–1727) of Massachusetts took a trip on horseback from Boston to New York City and back. Her diary of people she met, swollen rivers, and foods she ate offers an intimate look at colonial America. JONATHAN KNIGHT (1787–1858) of Pennsylvania was a civil engineer who surveyed the route of the Baltimore & Ohio Railroad. JONATHAN KNIGHT (1789–1864) of Connecticut was a founder of Yale University's medical school and of the American Medical Association. MARGARET E. KNIGHT (1838–1914) of Maine was an inventor; among her inventions was a machine that makes square-bottom paper bags. Altogether she received 27 patents and was called the "woman Edison." She was also the first woman ever to receive a patent. DANIEL RIDGEWAY KNIGHT (1840–1924) of Pennsylvania was an internationally recognized artist for his paintings of French life. JOHN SHIVELY KNIGHT (1894–1981) of West Virginia was a newspaper publisher who merged his operation with Ridder Publications to become Knight-Ridder Newspapers, Inc. He also was the recipient of a Pulitzer Prize in 1968 for his weekly column called "Editor's Notebook."

Genealogies: *A Genealogy of Some Early Missouri Settlers* was compiled by Donald Jack Knight and published in Kansas City, Missouri, in 1982. *Kennard, King, Knight, Hardin, Goodin* was compiled by Alta Kennard Patterson and published in Huffman, Texas, in 1988.

KNOLL

Ranking: 3530 **S.S. Count:** 12,783

Origin: English. 1) derived from the Old English word "cnoll," meaning hill. The name was given to those who were short and stout. 2) derived from the Old English word "cnoll," meaning hill. The name was given to those who lived on hills or to those from Knoll, the name of several places in England.

Genealogies: None known.

KNOTT

Ranking: 2320 **S.S. Count:** 19,555

Origin: English, Jewish. English: 1) derived from the Middle English word "knot," meaning small hill. The name was given to those who lived near a small hill. 2) derived from the Old English word "cnotta," meaning knot or lump. The name was given to those who were heavy and lumpy. 3) derived from the Old English first name Knútr. Jewish: cognate to any of several similar-sounding Jewish surnames.

Famous Knotts: ALOYSIUS L. KNOTT (1829–1918) of Maryland was one of the organizers of the Conservative-Democratic Party in 1866. JAMES PROCTOR KNOTT (1830–1911) of Kentucky was governor of Kentucky and a member of Congress.

Genealogies: *Nutt* [also Knott] *Chronicles* was compiled by Irene E. Amato and published in Bountiful, Utah, in 1991. *The Knotts* [also Knott] *Family of Randolph County,*

Arkansas was compiled by Gladys Knotts Reynolds and published in Reyno, Arkansas, in 1981.

KNOTTS (ALSO KNOTTSON)
Ranking: 4610 S.S. Count: 9691
Origin: English. Transformation of Knott.
Genealogies: *The Knotts Family of Randolph County, Arkansas* was compiled by Gladys Knotts Reynolds and published in Reyno, Arkansas, in 1981.

KNOWLES (S.S. Abbreviation: Knowle)
Ranking: 1110 S.S. Count: 39,844
Origin: English. Transformation of Knoll.
Famous **Knowleses:** LUCIUS J. KNOWLES (1819–1884) of Massachusetts invented a steam pump.
Genealogies: *Descendants & Antecedents of Darius Daniel Knowles* was compiled by Beverly Metzger and published in Manly, Iowa, in 1984. *Descendants of John Knowles* was compiled by Virginia Knowles Hufbauer and published in La Jolla, California, in 1979.

KNOWLTON (S.S. Abbreviation: Knowlt)
Ranking: 4033 S.S. Count: 11,228
Origin: English. Transformation of Knoll.
Famous **Knowltons:** CHARLES KNOWLTON (1800–1850) of Massachusetts was a physician who advocated birth control in his book *The Fruits of Philosophy*, for which he was arrested and imprisoned for three months. His became a test case in England; the prosecution lost. MARY HELEN KNOWLTON (1832–1918) of Massachusetts was a painter who is best remembered for her portrait of William Morris Hunt. MARCUS P. KNOWLTON (1839–1918) of Massachusetts was a renowned chief justice of the Massachusetts Supreme Court. FRANK HALL KNOWLTON (1860–1926) of Vermont was a paleontologist and geologist who was a pioneer in the study of prehistoric climates. He was responsible for the discovery of many different fossilized plants.
Genealogies: None known.

KNOX
Ranking: 677 S.S. Count: 62,001
Origin: English, Irish, Scottish. Derived from the Old English word "cnocc," meaning a hill with a rounded top. The name was given to those who lived on the top of a hill or to those from Knock, the name of several places in England and Scotland.
Famous **Knoxes:** HENRY KNOX (1750–1806) of Massachusetts was a Revolutionary War officer and George Washington's successor as commander of the army. He founded the Society of the Cincinnati and served as the U.S. secretary of war. PHILANDER CHASE KNOX (1853–1921) of Pennsylvania was the U.S. attorney general and the creator of the U.S. Department of Commerce and Labor. He served as secretary of state and as a U.S. senator. ROSE MARKWARD

KNOX (1857–1950) of Ohio was the business genius behind the Knox gelatine empire. WILLIAM FRANKLIN KNOX (1874–1944) of Massachusetts, a successful newspaperman, was the unsuccessful vice presidential candidate in 1936. He served as secretary of the navy during World War II.
Genealogies: *Knox Memorial* was compiled by Christine Wood and published in Lubbock, Texas, in 1972. *Pioneers in a Frontier Land* was compiled by Daryl K. Knox and published in Milwaukee, Wisconsin, in 1978.

KNUDSEN (S.S. Abbreviation: Knudse)
Ranking: 3537 S.S. Count: 12,766
Origin: Danish, Norwegian. Cognate to Knott.
Famous **Knudsens:** WILLIAM S. KNUDSEN (1879–1948) of Denmark was an industrialist and an officer in Ford, then Chevrolet, then General Motors corporations. He served his adopted country during World War II as the director of production for the War Department.
Genealogies: None known.

KNUDSON (S.S. Abbreviation: Knudso)
Ranking: 4351 S.S. Count: 10,306
Origin: Danish, Norwegian. Cognate to Knott.
Genealogies: None known.

KNUTSON (S.S. Abbreviation: Knutso)
Ranking: 1976 S.S. Count: 22,940
Origin: Danish, English, Norwegian, Swedish. Uncertain etymology. Most likely a transformation of Knott.
Genealogies: *Paternal Grandfather's Norwegian Genealogy* was compiled by Helen Grace Knutson Farvour and published in Fond du Lac, Wisconsin, in 1971.

KOCH
Ranking: 584 S.S. Count: 70,997
Origin: Czech, German, Jewish. Czech: derived from several first names beginning with "Ko-." German: derived from the German word "koch," meaning cook. Jewish: uncertain etymology.
Famous **Koches:** FRED C. KOCH (1876–1948) of Illinois was a noted biochemist whose laboratory work contributed to the understanding of male hormones. FREDERICK HENRY KOCH (1877–1944) of Kentucky was an educator and founder of many theater groups. He is considered the father of American folk drama. ARNOLD THEODOR KOCH (1900–1979) of New York was the lawyer who represented Herman H. Kind and won in *Herman H. Kind v. Robert F. Kennedy, Attorney General of the United States.*
Genealogies: None known.

KOCHER
Ranking: 4743 S.S. Count: 9442

Origin: German. Transformation of Koch.
Genealogies: None known.

KOEHLER (S.S. Abbreviation: Koehle)

Ranking: 1596 **S.S. Count:** 28,083
Origin: German. Cognate to Collier.
Famous **Koehlers:** SYLVESTER R. KOEHLER (1837–1900) of Germany was curator at the Boston Museum of Fine Arts in Massachusetts, where he is credited with expanding the collection of prints. ROBERT KOEHLER (1850–1917) of Germany was a pioneer art instructor in the American West.
Genealogies: *Keen, Koehler, Kuntzi* was compiled by Ray A. Keen and published in Manhattan, Kansas, in 1983.

KOEHN

Ranking: 4881 **S.S. Count:** 9158
Origin: Jewish. Transformation of Cohen.
Genealogies: *A compilation of the Genealogical and Biographical Record of the Descendants and Relation Circle of Henry B. Koehn* was compiled by Henry B. Koehn and published in North Newton, Kansas, in 1955.

KOENIG

Ranking: 1295 **S.S. Count:** 34,202
Origin: German, Jewish. German: cognate to King. Jewish: translation of the Yiddish first names Meylekh and Elemeylekh, meaning king and "God is my king" (H&H). The name was taken ornamentally.
Famous **Koenigs:** GEORGE A. KOENIG (1844–1913) of Germany taught chemistry and mineralogy in Pennsylvania and Michigan and is credited with the discovery of 13 types species of minerals.
Genealogies: *The Anton and Rosina Koenigh Beck Family* was compiled by Lillie Wasserman and published in Brenham, Texas, in 1979.

KOESTER (S.S. Abbreviation: Koeste)

Ranking: 4249 **S.S. Count:** 10,598
Origin: German. Derived from the German word "küster," which was derived from the Late Latin word "custor," meaning guard. The name was given to church wardens and sextons.
Genealogies: *Most All Our Koester Cousins* was compiled by Marjorie M. Rector and published in Sedalia, Missouri, in 1974.

KOHL

Ranking: 3289 **S.S. Count:** 13,790
Origin: German. 1) transformation of Koehler. 2) derived from the German word "kohl," meaning cabbage. The name was given to those who sold or grew cabbages.

Genealogies: *Ordinary Americans* was compiled by Charles Evans Cole and published in Nashville, Tennessee, in 1981.

KOHLER

Ranking: 1919 **S.S. Count:** 23,557
Origin: German. Transformation of Koehler.
Famous **Kohlers:** KAUFMAN KOHLER (1843–1926) of Bavaria was a rabbi in Michigan and New York and the editor of *Jewish Encyclopedia.* He organized the 1885 conference that adopted the Pittsburgh Platform as a statement of principles for American Reform Judaism. His son, MAX JAMES KOHLER (1871–1934) of Michigan, was a lawyer who was an authority on immigrant law. WALTER JODOK KOHLER (1875–1940) of Wisconsin ran the plumbing-fixtures business that bears his name. He was governor of Wisconsin (1928–1930), and he built the model industrial town of Kohler, Wisconsin.
Genealogies: *The House of von Kohler* was compiled by Arvid Axel Kohler and published in Decorah, Iowa, in 1989.

KOHN

Ranking: 3302 **S.S. Count:** 13,725
Origin: Jewish. Transformation of Cohen.
Genealogies: None known.

KOLB

Ranking: 2756 **S.S. Count:** 16,519
Origin: German?, Jewish? Uncertain etymology. Possibly a cognate to the English name Calf, which was derived from the Old Norse first name Kalfr, meaning calf. The name was given to those who tended calves.
Famous **Kolbs:** DIELMAN KOLB (1691–1756) of Germany was a prominent Mennonite preacher in Pennsylvania who aided in the emigration of many from Germany and Switzerland. REUBEN F. KOLB (1839–1918) of Alabama fought against the tide for progressive democracy in Alabama.
Genealogies: *The Ancestry & Descendants of John Coward* [also Kolbs] was compiled by Kyser Cowart Ptomey and published in New Orleans, Louisiana, in 1984.

KOONTZ

Ranking: 3042 **S.S. Count:** 14,943
Origin: German? Uncertain etymology. Most likely a transformation of the German first name Kunz, which is derived from the name Konrad, which was derived from the Germanic components "kuoni" and "rad," meaning brave and counsel.
Genealogies: *Keen, Koehler, Kuntzi* [also Koontz] was compiled by Ray A. Keen and published in Manhattan, Kansas, in 1983.

KOPP

Ranking: 2871 S.S. Count: 15,851

Origin: German. Cognate to the English name Copp. 1) derived from the Old English word "copp," meaning summit. The name was given to those who lived at the top of a hill. 2) derived from the Middle English word "cop(p)," meaning head. The name was given to those with a large or misshapen head.

Genealogies: *The German Ancestry of William Frederick Heuss and Mary Catherine Kopp* was compiled by John Sanford Heuss and published in Charlotte, North Carolina, in 1983. *Virginia to Ohio and States West* was compiled by Mary Mae Cupp Campbell and published in Lima, Ohio, in 1986.

KOSTER (ALSO KOSTERS)

Ranking: 4815 S.S. Count: 9306

Origin: Dutch, Flemish, German, Jewish. Cognates to Koester.

Genealogies: None known.

KOVACH

Ranking: 3374 S.S. Count: 13,428

Origin: Hungarian. Cognate to Kowalski.

Genealogies: None known.

KOVACS

Ranking: 3595 S.S. Count: 12,550

Origin: Hungarian, Jewish. Cognates to Kowalski.

Genealogies: None known.

KOWALCZYK, KOWALCZYNSKI (S.S. Abbreviation: Kowalc)

Ranking: 4308 S.S. Count: 10,421

Origin: Polish. Transformations of Kowalski.

Genealogies: None known.

KOWALSKI, KOWALSKY

Ranking: 1518 S.S. Count: 29,300

Origin: Jewish, Polish. Derived from the Polish word "kować," meaning to forge, and the surname suffix "-ski."

Genealogies: None known.

KOZAK

Ranking: 4332 S.S. Count: 10,336

Origin: Jewish, Polish. Polish: 1) cognate to Kozlow. 2) the name was given to Cossacks. Jewish: uncertain etymology. Most likely derived from the Polish word "kozak," meaning Cossack. The name was given to those who were merciless.

Genealogies: None known.

KOZLOW (ALSO KOZLOWSKI)

Ranking: 2799 S.S. Count: 16,255

Origin: Kozlow—Jewish; Kozlowski—Jewish, Polish. Derived from the Russian word "kozyol," meaning goat. The name was usually given to those who were stubborn or lascivious or to goatherds.

Genealogies: None known.

KRAEMER, KRAEMERS (S.S. Abbreviation: Kraeme)

Ranking: 4259 S.S. Count: 10,578

Origin: Kraemers—Dutch; Kraemer—Jewish. Transformations of Kramer.

Genealogies: None known.

KRAFT

Ranking: 1496 S.S. Count: 29,729

Origin: Danish, German, Jewish. Derived from the Danish and German words "kraft," meaning strength. The name was given to those who were strong.

Famous **Krafts:** JAMES KEWIS KRAFT (1874–1953) of Canada was the founder of the Kraft Food Co., which was started when Kraft found himself stranded in Chicago with $65 to his name. He bought cheese from a wholesaler and resold it to smaller stores, thereby saving each of the smaller stores a daily trip to the wholesale market and making a profit for himself.

Genealogies: *Kraft Family Genealogy* was compiled by Susan Kaplan Stone and published in St. Louis, Missouri, in 1982. *Schnitz and Plum Pudding* was compiled by Eunice M. Brake and published in Ann Arbor, Michigan, in 1992.

KRAMER (ALSO KRAMERMAN, KRAMERS)

Ranking: 453 S.S. Count: 88,011

Origin: Kramer—German, Jewish; Kramerman—Jewish; Kramers—German. Derived from the Old High German word "crām," meaning trading post. The name was given to shopkeepers.

Genealogies: None known.

KRAUS

Ranking: 1685 S.S. Count: 26,497

Origin: German, Jewish. Derived from the German word "kraus," meaning curly. The name was given to those with curly hair.

Famous **Krauses:** JOHN KRAUS (1815–1896), a German immigrant, helped develop the kindergarten theory of education. He and his wife, MARIA KRAUS-BOELTÉ (1836–1918), who also emigrated from Germany, established early kindergarten model schools in New York.

Genealogies: None known.

KRAUSE (ALSO KRAUSER)

Ranking: 836 S.S. Count: 50,972

Origin: Krause—German; Krauser—Jewish. Transformations of Kraus.

Famous **Bearers:** ALLEN K. KRAUSE (1881–1941) was a physician whose own affliction with tuberculosis helped lead him to become a medical authority on the disease. He edited the *American Review of Tuberculosis.*

Genealogies: None known.

KRAUSS

Ranking: 3956 S.S. Count: 11,429

Origin: German. Transformation of Kraus.

Genealogies: None known.

KREBS

Ranking: 2826 S.S. Count: 16,144

Origin: German. Uncertain etymology. The name means crab. The name was given to those who were considered crabby.

Genealogies: None known.

KREMER (ALSO KREMERMAN, KREMEROV)

Ranking: 4571 S.S. Count: 9773

Origin: Kremer—Dutch, Flemish, German, Jewish; Kremerman—Jewish; Kremerov—Jewish. Cognates to and transformations of Kramer.

Genealogies: None known.

KRESS

Ranking: 4410 S.S. Count: 10,165

Origin: German. Derived from the first name Erasmus.

Famous **Kresses:** SAMUEL HENRY KRESS (1863–1955) of Pennsylvania was the founder of a chain of five-and-dime stores named S. H. Kress & Co.

Genealogies: *The Descendents [sic] of Johann Nicholaus Heinrich Kress* was compiled by Bernard W. Cruse and published in Indian Trail, North Carolina, in 1978.

KRIEGER (S.S. Abbreviation: Kriege)

Ranking: 2509 S.S. Count: 18,079

Origin: German, Jewish. German: 1) derived from the German word "krieger," meaning soldier. The name was given to mercenary soldiers. 2) derived from the German word "krieger," meaning soldier. The name was given to those who were belligerent. Jewish: derived from the German word "krieger" or the Yiddish word "kriger," meaning soldier. The name was given to those who were belligerent.

Genealogies: *Notes on the Two Krieger Families of Wythe County, Virginia* was compiled by Clifford R. Canfield and published in New York, New York, in 1982.

KROLL

Ranking: 2983 S.S. Count: 15,245

Origin: German, Jewish. German: derived from the Middle High German word "krol," meaning curly. The name was given to those with curly hair. Jewish: uncertain etymology. Possibly derived from the Middle High German word "krol," meaning curly or from the Polish word "król," meaning king.

Genealogies: None known.

KRUEGER (S.S. Abbreviation: Kruege)

Ranking: 801 S.S. Count: 52,667

Origin: German, Jewish. Derived from the Old High German word "krugg," meaning jug. The name was given to those who worked making jugs or serving beverages in jugs.

Famous **Kruegers:** WALTER KRUEGER (1881–1967) of Germany was an army officer who served in the Spanish-American War, and as commander of the Third Army in 1941 and the Sixth Army in 1943 in World War II. He retired as a general.

Genealogies: *Krueger Kin and Related Families* was compiled by Bernadette Durben Bittner and published in Green Bay, Wisconsin, in 1977. *Our Four Families* was compiled by Evelyn A. Krueger and published in Clinton, Wisconsin, in 1985.

KRUG

Ranking: 4020 S.S. Count: 11,262

Origin: German, Jewish. Transformation of Krueger.

Famous **Krugs:** EDWARD AUGUST KRUG (1911–1979) of Illinois was an educator and historian who wrote, among other works, *Curriculum Planning* (1950) and *Secondary School Curriculum* (1960).

Genealogies: None known.

KRUGER

Ranking: 2389 S.S. Count: 19,015

Origin: German, Jewish. Transformation of Krueger.

Genealogies: None known.

KRUSE

Ranking: 1659 S.S. Count: 26,977

Origin: Danish, German. Cognate to and transformation of Kraus.

Genealogies: None known.

KUEHN

Ranking: 4290 S.S. Count: 10,464

Origin: German? Uncertain etymology. Most likely a transformation of Koontz.

Genealogies: None known.

KUHLMAN (S.S. Abbreviation: Kuhlma)

Ranking: 3761 S.S. Count: 12,042

Origin: German. Derived from the Middle Low German

word *"kūle,"* meaning hollow. The name was given to those who lived near a hollow or to those from Kuhl, the name of several places in northern Germany.

Genealogies: *A Chronology of Kilmer* [also Kuhlman] was compiled by Lawrence Harold Kilmer and published in San Jose, California, in 1982.

KUHN

Ranking: 948 **S.S. Count:** 45,681

Origin: German. Transformation of Kuehn.

Famous **Kuhns:** JOSEPH E. KUHN (1864–1935) of Kansas was president of the Army War College and commander of the 79th Division during World War I. WALTER FRANCIS KUHN (1877–1949) of New York was a painter known for his bold, unpolished pictures of clowns, showgirls, and acrobats. Later in life he painted still lifes and trees.

Genealogies: *Coon-Cohn* [also Kuhn] *Descendants* was compiled by Frances Davis McTeer and published in Holiday, Florida, in 1979. *The Swiss Connection* was compiled by Gwendolyn Pryor and published in Houston, Texas, in 1991.

KUNKEL

Ranking: 3505 **S.S. Count:** 12,864

Origin: German. Derived from the German word "kunkel," meaning spindle. The name was given to spinners or to those who made spindles.

Genealogies: None known.

KUNTZ

Ranking: 2948 **S.S. Count:** 15,459

Origin: German. Transformation of Koontz.

Genealogies: None known.

KUNZ

Ranking: 3370 **S.S. Count:** 13,459

Origin: German. Transformation of Koontz.

Famous **Kunzes:** GEORGE F. KUNZ (1856–1932) of New York was well known for his expertise in gems and ancient jewelry.

Genealogies: *The Family of Dorothea E. Rueter and Christian David Kunz* was compiled by Gerdena E. Rosenow Koehler and published in Elmwood, Nebraska, in 1973.

KURTZ (ALSO KURTZE)

Ranking: 1371 **S.S. Count:** 32,331

Origin: German. Derived from the Latin word "curtus," meaning curtailed or cut off. The name was given to those who were short.

Famous **Kurtzes:** BENJAMIN KURTZ (1838–1919) of Pennsylvania, a clergyman, was editor of the *Lutheran Observer* for 25 years.

Genealogies: *Lest We Forget* was compiled by Thelma E.

Kurtz and published in Kearney, Missouri, in 1977. *The Jacob S. Kurtz Family* was compiled by Lydia Kurtz Baer and published in Harrisonburg, Virginia, in 1981.

KUYKENDALL (S.S. Abbreviation: Kuyken)

Ranking: 3086 **S.S. Count:** 14,716

Origin: Dutch. Uncertain etymology. The name was given to those who lived in a valley in which chickens were bred.

Genealogies: *A Forest of Many Trees* was compiled by Velma Kuykendall Winn and published in Petaluma, California, in 1976. *Ouders* [also Kuykendall] was compiled by William Arthur Kirkendale and published in Douglaston, New York, in 1981.

KWIATK

Ranking: 4435 **S.S. Count:** 10,107

Origin: Jewish, Polish. Polish: 1) derived from the Polish word "kwiecień," meaning April. The name was given to those who were baptized in the month of April. 2) derived from the first name Kwiatek, which was derived from the Polish word "kwiat," meaning flower. Jewish: 1) derived from the Polish word "kwiat," meaning flower. The name was taken ornamentally. 2) derived from the Polish word "kwiecień," meaning April. The name was given to those whose official surnames were adopted in the month of April.

Genealogies: None known.

KYLE

Ranking: 1839 **S.S. Count:** 24,597

Origin: Irish, Scottish. 1) derived from the name Coel Hen. The name was given to those from Kyle, a region in southwestern Scotland. 2) derived from the Gaelic word "caol," meaning narrows. The name was given to those from Kyle, the name of several places in Scotland.

Famous **Kyles:** JAMES H. KYLE (1854–1901) of Ohio was a U.S. senator from South Dakota and chairman of the National Industrial Commission. DAVID B. KYLE (1863–1916) of Ohio was a laryngologist who wrote a widely used textbook in his field.

Genealogies: *German Burnett Kyle of Logan County, Arkansas* was compiled by Edith Madeline Replogle and published in Pullman, Washington, in 1990.

LABELL, LABELLA, LABELLE, LABELSON (S.S. Abbreviation: Label)

Ranking: 3838 S.S. Count: 11,733

Origin: Labell, Labelle—French; Labella— Italian. Labell, Labelle: derived from the Old French word "beu" or "bel," meaning fair or good-looking. The name was in some cases given ironically to effeminate men. Labella: cognate to Labell. Labelson: uncertain etymology.

Genealogies: None known.

LABOY

Ranking: 4824 S.S. Count: 9283

Origin: Uncertain etymology.

Genealogies: None known.

LACEY

Ranking: 1769 S.S. Count: 25,369

Origin: English, Irish. Derived from the Gaulish first name Lascius and the suffix "-acum." The name was given to those from Lassy, a place in Normandy, France.

Famous Laceys: JOHN F. LACEY (1841–1913) of Virginia was a member of Congress from Iowa. DANIEL D. LACEY (1950–1992) of Pennsylvania was a journalist and author of books, including *The Paycheck Disruption* (1988) and *Your Rights in the Workplace* (1991).

Genealogies: *The Thomas Lacy III (also Lacey) Family* was compiled by Hubert Wesley Lacey and published in Farmville, Virginia, in 1983.

LACKEY

Ranking: 1786 S.S. Count: 25,162

Origin: English, Irish. Uncertain etymology. The name was given to a footman or to those who lived near a rocky area.

Genealogies: *Climbing Our Family Tree* was compiled by Edith Black and published in Baltimore, Maryland, in 1988. *Lackey, Stratton, and Allied Families* was compiled by Harriett I. Pratt and published in Glastonbury, Connecticut, in 1971.

LACROIX (S.S. Abbreviation: Lacroi)

Ranking: 4378 S.S. Count: 10,247

Origin: French. Cognate to Cross.

Genealogies: *Genealogy of the Fayard, Lacroix, Lizana, Dubuisson, and Cuevas Families* was compiled by Ernest Anthony Carvin and published in Belford, New Jersey, in 1974.

LACY

Ranking: 1361 S.S. Count: 32,602

Origin: English, Irish. Transformation of Lacey.

Famous Lacys: ERNEST LACY (1863–1916) of Pennsylva-

nia was instrumental in developing public-speaking and debating programs in Philadelphia public schools.

Genealogies: *The Thomas Lacy III Family* was compiled by Hubert Wesley Lacey and published in Farmville, Virginia, in 1983. *Descendants of Lawrence and Catherine Monaghan Lacy* was compiled by Patricia J. Rezek and published in Glendale, California, in 1981.

LADD

Ranking: 2063 S.S. Count: 22,200

Origin: English. Derived from the Middle English word "ladde," meaning someone of low birth or a servant. The name was given to those who worked as servants.

Famous Ladds: WILLIAM LADD (1778–1841) of New Hampshire was a pacifist and the founder of the American Peace Society. He proposed a congress of nations and an international court that eventually became, respectively, the League of Nations and the World Court. He devoted his life to world peace. WILLIAM S. LADD (1826–1893) of Vermont was an active promoter of transportation and industry in Oregon. GEORGE TRUMBULL LADD (1842–1921) of Ohio was a psychologist and one of the founders of experimental psychology in the United States. CHRISTINE LADD-FRANKLIN (1847–1930) of Connecticut was a psychologist and logician who reduced all syllogisms to a single formula and worked on humans' color sense. EDWIN F. LADD (1859–1925) of Maine was a U.S. senator from North Dakota who campaigned vigorously against adulterated foods. KATE MACY LADD (1863–1945) of New York City was a philanthropist, with her main contribution to society being the establishment of the Josiah Macy Jr. Foundation in New York City, which saw the need for more money to be given to scientific research. She directed that her contribution be used to try to solve medical problems. Her husband set up the Kate Macy Ladd Foundation at the time of her death. CARL E. LADD (1888–1943) of New York, as dean of agriculture and home economics (1932–1943), led Cornell University's prominent agricultural research program. ALAN W. LADD (1913–1964) of Arkansas was a screen actor who was voted most popular male star in a 1943 poll. He starred in the movie *Shane* (1953), and his last movie role was in *The Carpetbaggers* (1964).

Genealogies: *One Ladd's Family* was compiled by Ruth Kline Ladd and published in Naperville, Illinois, in 1974.

LAFFERTY (S.S. Abbreviation: Laffer)

Ranking: 3092 S.S. Count: 14,693

Origin: Irish. Transformation of Laverty. Derived from the Gaelic names Ó Fhlaithbheartaigh and Mac Fhlaithbheartaigh, which were derived from the first name Flaithbheartach, which comprises the components "flaith" and "beartach," meaning prince and "doer of valiant deeds" (H&H).

Genealogies: None known.

LAFLEUR (S.S. Abbreviation: Lafleu)
Ranking: 3856 S.S. Count: 11,692
Origin: French. Uncertain etymology. The name was given to those who worked as servants or soldiers.
Genealogies: None known.

LAFRANÇOIS (S.S. Abbreviation: Lafran)
Ranking: 4803 S.S. Count: 9329
Origin: French. Derived from the French first name Francois, meaning free. The name was given to those who were free.
Genealogies: None known.

LAI
Ranking: 4758 S.S. Count: 9413
Origin: Uncertain etymology.
Genealogies: None known.

LAIRD
Ranking: 1697 S.S. Count: 26,318
Origin: Irish, Scottish. Derived from the Middle English word "laverd," meaning lord. The name was most likely given to a landlord.
Genealogies: *Laird Family* was compiled by Edward Forrest Brouhard and published in Harlan, Iowa, in 1954.

LAKE
Ranking: 1021 S.S. Count: 42,885
Origin: English. Derived from the Old English word "lacu," meaning stream. The name was given to those who lived near a stream or to those from Lake, the name of several places in England.
Famous **Lakes:** SIMON LAKE (1866–1945) of New Jersey was a naval architect. He invented the even-keel type of submarine and a submarine apparatus for recovering sunken ships. KIRSOPP LAKE (1872–1946) of England was a New Testament scholar at Harvard University and an author of many books.
Genealogies: *Forget Me Not* was compiled by Carole Clawson Nation and published in 1980.

LAM
Ranking: 1677 S.S. Count: 26,667
Origin: Danish. 1) cognate to Lamb. 2) derived from the Old Norse word "lami," meaning lame. The name was given to those who were lame.
Genealogies: None known.

LAMAR
Ranking: 2899 S.S. Count: 15,699

Origin: French. Derived from the Old Northern French words "la" and "mare," meaning the pool or pond. The name was given to those from La Mare, the name of several places in Normandy, France.
Famous **Lamars:** MIRABEAU BUONAPARTE LAMAR (1798–1859) of Georgia was a politician who went to Texas, served with Sam Houston at the Battle of San Jacinto, and served as vice president, then president, of the Republic of Texas. He favored annexation to the United States. His nephew, LUCIUS QUINTUS CINCINNATUS LAMAR (1825–1893) of Georgia, served in the Confederate army, in the U.S. House of Representatives, and as an associate justice of the U.S. Supreme Court. JOSEPH RUCKER LAMAR (1857–1916) of Georgia was a lawyer who practiced in Augusta and a member of the state supreme court. In 1911 he became an associate justice of the U.S. Supreme Court.
Genealogies: *Thomas Lamar, The Immigrant* was compiled by Donnis Mott Borchers and published in Omaha, Nebraska, in 1977. *Genealogical Notes on a Branch of the Family of Mayes (also Lamar)* was compiled by Edward Mayes and published in Jackson, Mississippi, in 1928.

LAMB
Ranking: 486 S.S. Count: 83,169
Origin: English, Irish. English: 1) transformation of Lambert. 2) derived from the Old English word "lamb," meaning lamb. The name was given to shepherds or to those who were meek. Irish: derived from the Gaelic name Ó Luain, which was derived from the first name Luan, meaning warrior.
Famous **Lambs:** MARTHA JOANNA READE MASH LAMB (1826–1893) of Massachusetts was an author and historian and is remembered for her historical writings about New York City. ISAAC W. LAMB (1840–1906) of Michigan invented the first successful flat knitting machine designed in the United States. ARTHUR B. LAMB (1880–1952) of Massachusetts was a chemist who, during World War II, worked for the government in developing poison gases and gas masks. He was president of the American Chemical Society for three years and editor of the *Journal of the American Chemical Society* for 32 years. WILLIAM F. LAMB (1883–1952) of New York, an architect, was principal designer of the Empire State Building, in New York City. HORACE RAND LAMB (1892–1977) of Ohio was a lawyer who specialized in corporate and antitrust law. He was general counsel and a director of St. Regis Paper Co.
Genealogies: *The Lambs of Lanarkshire and their Descendants in America* was compiled by Mary Grant Charles and published in Port Huron, Michigan, in 1972. *The Family History of William Faris of Washington County Ohio and the Fraser, McKenzie, Lamb and Graham Families* was compiled by Joy Gibboney and published in 1967.

LAMBERT, LAMBERTI, LAMBERTINI, LAMBERTS, LAMBERTSON (S.S. Abbreviation: Lamber)

Ranking: 261 **S.S. Count:** 140,643

Origin: Lambert—English, French, German; Lamberti, Lambertinii-Italian; Lamberts—German; Lambertson—English. Lambert (English, French, German): derived from the Germanic first name comprising the components "land" and "berht," meaning land and bright. Lambert (English): derived from the Old English words "lamb" and "hierd," meaning lamb and heard. The name was given to shepherds. Lamberti, Lambertini: cognates to the English, French, and German Lambert. Lamberts: cognate to the English, French, and German Lambert. Lambertson: cognate to the English, French, and German Lambert.

Famous **Bearers:** LOUIS A. LAMBERT (1835–1910) of Pennsylvania, a Roman Catholic priest, was editor of the New York *Freeman's Journal* for 16 years.

Genealogies: *History of the Lambert Family from Jugenheim in Rheinhessen* was compiled by Christene Lambert Bertram and published in Elverson, Pennsylvania, in 1993. *The Lambert/Lambeth Family of North Carolina* was compiled by Mary Norton Doggett and published in Greensboro, North Carolina, in 1974.

LAMONT

Ranking: 2723 **S.S. Count:** 16,716

Origin: Irish, Scottish. Derived from the Old Norse first name Logmaðr, which comprises the components "log" and "maðr," meaning law and man.

Famous **Lamonts:** DANIEL S. LAMONT (1851–1905) of New York was private secretary to President Grover Cleveland, secretary of war, and vice president of Northern Pacific Railway Co. HAMMOND LAMONT (1864–1909) of was an editor at the New York *Evening Post* and at *The Nation.* He also wrote the book *English Composition* (1906). THOMAS W. LAMONT (1870–1948) of New York was an investment banker who, while working with J. P. Morgan and Co., was instrumental in offering $6 billion in securities over a 14-year period. HELEN LAMB LAMONT (1906–1975) of Massachusetts was a professor and economist who wrote a number of works on India and Vietnam. A collection of her essays was published posthumously in 1976 as *Studies on India and Vietnam.*

Genealogies: None known.

LAMPKIN (S.S. Abbreviation: Lampki)

Ranking: 4683 **S.S. Count:** 9555

Origin: Uncertain etymology. Possibly a transformation of or cognate to Lambert.

Famous **Lampkins:** DAISY ELIZABETH ADAMS LAMPKIN (1883?–1965) of Washington, D.C., was the vice president of the *Pittsburgh Courier* and the national field secretary of the NAACP.

Genealogies: *Lampkin Genealogy* was compiled by Richard H. Lampkin and published in Bradenton, Florida, in 1989.

LANCASTER, LANCASTLE (S.S. Abbreviation: Lancas)

Ranking: 994 **S.S. Count:** 44,130

Origin: English. Derived from the British river Lune and the Old English word "cæster," meaning Roman fort. The name was given to those from Lancaster, a place in England.

Famous **Lancasters:** HENRY C. LANCASTER (1882–1954) of Virginia was a literary historian who was editor of *Modern Language Notes* for 35 years.

Genealogies: *Lancaster, the John Harrison Lancaster Families* was compiled by Cora Belle Lancaster Kirk and published in Gainesville, Georgia, in 1974.

LANCE

Ranking: 2775 **S.S. Count:** 16,433

Origin: English. Derived from the Germanic first name Lanzo, derived from several compound names with the first component "land," meaning land.

Genealogies: None known.

LAND

Ranking: 1554 **S.S. Count:** 28,652

Origin: English. 1) derived from the Old English word "land," meaning land. The name was given to those from rural areas. 2) derived from the Middle English and Old French word "la(u)nde," meaning glade. The name was given to those who lived in an open area in a forest or to those from Launde, a place in Leicestershire, England.

Famous **Lands:** EDWIN HERBERT LAND (1909–1991) of Connecticut invented the Polaroid Land camera. He also developed a polarizing film that led to the making of polarizing filters for cameras. He was a consultant to the U.S. army during World War II, contributing to the development of optical devices used in warfare.

Genealogies: None known.

LANDER (ALSO LANDERS)

Ranking: 1136 **S.S. Count:** 38,710

Origin: English, German, Jewish. English: transformation of Lavender. German: cognate to Land. The name was given to persons who were indigenous to the area in which they lived or to those from rural areas. Jewish: derived from the Old High German words "lant" and "auwa," meaning land and wet valley. The name was given to those from Landau, the name of places in Germany.

Famous **Bearers:** FREDERICK W. LANDER (1821–1862) of

Massachusetts was a surveying engineer who explored the Pacific Northwest for railroad routes and was a decorated Union officer who died in the line of duty during the Civil War. His wife, JEAN MARGARET DAVENPORT LANDER (1829–1903) of England, was a child actress in New York who played the first "Camille" role in United States. Frederick Lander's brother, EDWARD LANDER (1816–1907) of Massachusetts, was a justice of the supreme court for the Washington territory.

Genealogies: *History of the Landers Family in America* was compiled by Simon Elbert Booner and published in Tuttle, New York, in 1966.

LANDIS

Ranking: 1771 S.S. Count: 25,346

Origin: French. Uncertain etymology. The name was given to those from Landes, a place in France.

Famous **Landises:** KENESAW MOUNTAIN LANDIS (1866–1944) of Ohio was the first commissioner of baseball (1920–1944). He was elected to the Baseball Hall of Fame. His nephew, FREDERICK LANDIS (1912–1990) of Indiana, was a justice of the supreme court of Indiana, then a judge on the U.S. Customs Court. HENRY ROBERT MURRAY LANDIS (1872–1937) of Ohio was a doctor who conducted pioneering research in tuberculosis and other diseases. WALTER SAVAGE LANDIS (1881–1944) was a chemical engineer noted for his contributions to fertilizer production and to the development of synthetic resins. JAMES MCCAULEY LANDIS (1899–1964), born in Japan to missionary parents, was the youngest dean of his time at the Harvard Law School.

Genealogies: *Our Brechbill/Brightbill, Kreider and Landis Ancestors* was compiled by Patricia Shannon Brightbill and published in Fountain Valley, California, in 1980.

LANDON

Ranking: 3879 S.S. Count: 11,626

Origin: English, French. English: transformation of Langdon. French: unknown etymology.

Famous **Landons:** MELVILLE DE LANCEY LANDON (1839–1910) of New York was a prominent journalist and lecturer who also wrote under the pen name of Eli Perkins.

Genealogies: *Landon Family History* was compiled by Joy Deal Lehmann and published in Novato, California, in 1988.

LANDRETH, LANDREY (S.S. Abbreviation: Landre)

Ranking: 4386 S.S. Count: 10,234

Origin: Landreth—English, Scottish; Landrey—French. Landreth: derived from the name Lanreath, which comprises components meaning court and justice. The name was given

to those from Lanreath, a place in Cornwall, England. *Landrey: derived from the first name Landry, which comprises components meaning land and powerful.*

Genealogies: None known.

LANDRUM (S.S. Abbreviation: Landru)

Ranking: 2577 S.S. Count: 17,648

Origin: Scottish. Derived from the Celtic name Lendrum, meaning moor of the ridge.

Famous **Landrums:** PHILIP M. LANDRUM (1907–1990) of Georgia was a member of Congress from Georgia (1952–1977).

Genealogies: *The Landrum Family of Fayette County, Georgia* was compiled by Joel P. Shedd and published in 1972.

LANDRY

Ranking: 862 S.S. Count: 49,835

Origin: French. Transformation of Landrey.

Genealogies: *The Book of Landry* was compiled by Nora Lee Clouatre Pollard and published in New Orleans, Louisiana, in 1979. *Grandpa with a Stick* was compiled by Norma Pontiff Evans and published in Beaumont, Texas, in 1980.

LANE

Ranking: 181 S.S. Count: 187,471

Origin: English, French, Irish. English: derived from the Old English word "lane," meaning a narrow path. The name was given to those who lived in lanes. French: 1) cognate to Land. 2) derived from the Old French word "la(i)ne," meaning wool. The name was given to those who worked in the wool trade. Irish: 1) derived from the Gaelic name Ó Luain, which was derived from the first name Luan, meaning warrior. 2) derived from the Gaelic name Ó Laighin, which was derived from the first name Laighean, meaning spear.

Famous **Lanes:** JOHN LANE (1789–1855) of Virginia was a founder of Vicksburg, Mississippi, as administrator of the estate of his father-in-law, Newet Vick. WILLIAM C. LANE (1789–1863) of Pennsylvania was the first mayor of St. Louis. He later was governor of the New Mexico territory. JOSEPH LANE (1801–1881) of North Carolina was the governor of the Oregon Territory, a member of Congress, U.S. senator, and the vice presidential candidate on a ticket with John Breckinridge in 1860. JOHN LANE (1804–1886) of Vermont was a blacksmith and the inventor of the first steel plow. It was manufactured under the name of John Deere. His son, JOHN LANE (1824–1897), possibly of Illinois, continued his father's business, inventing improvements to the plow. HENRY S. LANE (1811–1881) of Kentucky was a member of Congress and a U.S. senator from Indiana. JAMES HENRY LANE (1814–1866), possibly of Indiana, was a U.S.

senator from Kansas, a supporter of Abraham Lincoln, and a defender of the rights to freedom for the slaves. JAMES HENRY LANE (1833–1907) of Virginia was a Confederate general and then professor of civil engineering at Alabama Polytechnic Institute for 25 years. JONATHAN HOMER LANE (1819–1880) of New York was a physicist and the first to consider the sun to be a gaseous body. ALFRED CHURCH LANE (1863–1948) of Massachusetts was a geologist and the head of the committee to measure geologic time. He founded and directed a group that researched the age of the Earth. FRANKLIN KNIGHT LANE (1864–1921), born in Canada and raised in California, was a highly effective member of the Interstate Commerce Commission and is considered the architect of much of the early regulation of common carriers. He also was secretary of the interior under President Woodrow Wilson. GERTRUDE BATTLES LANE (1874–1941) of Maine was the editor of the *Woman's Home Companion*, which had the largest circulation of any women's magazine at that time. ARTHUR BLISS LANE (1894–1956) of New York was a career U.S. diplomat who served as minister to Nicaragua and Yugoslavia and as ambassador to Poland. He was the author of *I Saw Poland Betrayed* (1948).

Genealogies: *The Lane Robertson Families of Amherst County, Virginia* was compiled by Lyle Keith Williams and published in Fort Worth, Texas, in 1991. *Lain (also Lane), Lowrance, Lorance, and Related Families* was compiled by Nadine Lain and published in Dallas, Texas, in 1978.

LANEY

Ranking: 3184 **S.S. Count:** 14,265

Origin: Uncertain etymology. Most likely derived from the Gaelic name Ó Dubhshláine, which was derived from the first name Dubhshláine, which comprises the components "dubh" and "slán," meaning black and challenge.

Famous **Laneys:** LUCY CRAFT LANEY (1854–1933) of Georgia was born a free Negro in the days before the Civil War because her father, David Laney, born a slave in South Carolina, had learned the carpenter's trade and bought his freedom. He made his living by teaching the slaves of the plantation owners his carpentry skills. Lucy's mother, Louisa, a slave in the Campbell household, was also purchased by her father, but she continued to work in the Campbell home. There Lucy had the run of the library and subsequently fared well in school. She was one of the first to attend and graduate from Atlanta University. She taught in Georgia, eventually opening a school for blacks with the help of Francina E.H. Haines, for whom the school was named. The school eventually became a black high school with one year of college work. She also opened the city of Augusta's first kindergarten. In 1949, the school was closed and razed, and the city of Augusta built the Lucy C. Laney

High School on the spot where the original school had stood.

Genealogies: *Laney: Lineage and Legacy* was compiled by Guy B. Funderburk and published in Monroe, North Carolina, in 1974.

LANG

Ranking: 469 **S.S. Count:** 85,470

Origin: English. Transformation of Long.

Famous **Langs:** LUCY FOX ROBINS LANG (1884–1962), born in Russia, became an anarchist after moving to the United States, but she shifted away from radical politics when she worked with Samuel Gompers at the American Federation of Labor and became an active campaigner for American workers' rights. FRITZ LANG (1890–1976) of Austria was a film director of movies with the theme of terror and death.

Genealogies: *The Lang, Meyer, Longtin, Gousset Lines* was compiled by Gloria Lang Smethers and published in Beatrice, Nebraska, in 1978.

LANGDON (S.S. Abbreviation: Langdo)

Ranking: 3388 **S.S. Count:** 13,361

Origin: English. Derived from the Old English words "lang" and "dūn," meaning long and hill. The name was given to those from Langdon, the name of several places in England.

Famous **Langdons:** JOHN LANGDON (1741–1819) of New Hampshire was a Revolutionary War leader. He was active in the Revolutionary government, serving in the Continental Congress as president, then as governor of New Hampshire, and as a member of the U.S. Senate, where he was the first president pro tempore. He also was one of the financiers of the Revolution. WILLIAM CHAUNCEY LANGDON (1831–1895) of Vermont, a lawyer, was one of the founders of the American Confederation of Y.M.C.A. HARRY PHILMORE LANGDON (1884–1944) of Iowa was a silent-film actor best known for his innocent ways and boyish charm in comedic roles.

Genealogies: None known.

LANGE

Ranking: 1010 **S.S. Count:** 43,301

Origin: German, Norwegian. Cognates to Long.

Famous **Langes:** LOUIS LANGE (1829–1893), born in Germany, was an influential printer and editor in St. Louis. ALEXIS FREDERICK LANGE (1862–1924) of Missouri, a dean at the University of California School of Education, helped begin both the junior high school and junior college movements. DOROTHEA LANGE (1895–1965) of New Jersey was a photographer who is best known for her documentary pictures of victims of the Depression and of Japanese-Americans who were victimized by World War II.

Genealogies: *A Family History: Immigrant Ancestors from Ireland and Germany* was compiled by George L. Williams and published in Port Washington, New York, in 1990.

LANGENDORF, LANGENDORFER, LANGENSCHEIDT, LANGENTHAL (S.S. Abbreviation: Langen)

Ranking: 4360 **S.S. Count:** 10,282

Origin: Langendorf, Langendorfer—German; Langenscheidt—German; Langenthal—Jewish. Langendorf, Langendorfer: derived from German words meaning long village. The name was given to those from Langendorf, a place in Germany. Langenscheidt: derived from the Middle High German words "lang" and "scheide," meaning long and boundary. Langenthal: Uncertain etymology. The name means long valley and was taken ornamentally.

Genealogies: *The Langendorfer Family of Weingarten* was compiled by David V. Agricola and published in Cleveland, Ohio, in 1981.

LANGER (ALSO LANGERMAN)

Ranking: 3865 **S.S. Count:** 11,664

Origin: Langer—German, Jewish; Langerman—Jewish. Cognates to the English name Long.

Famous Bearers: WILLIAM LANGER (1886–1959) of North Dakota was governor of North Dakota, then a U.S. senator. SUZANNE KNAUTH LANGER (1895–1985) of New York City was a philosopher and a teacher of philosophy at Harvard University and Connecticut College. She was noted for her studies of signs, symbols, and feelings in language, art, and psychoanalysis.

Genealogies: None known.

LANGFORD (S.S. Abbreviation: Langfo)

Ranking: 1653 **S.S. Count:** 27,070

Origin: English. Derived from the Old English words "lang" and "ford," meaning long and ford. The name was given to those from Langford, the name of several places in England.

Famous Langfords: NATHANIEL PITT LANGFORD (1832–1911) of New York was an explorer and conservationist. He was one of the organizers and founders of Yellowstone National Park and was its first superintendent. SAMUEL LANGFORD (1883–1956) of Canada became one of the first African-American professional boxers in Boston in 1902. He boxed until 1928.

Genealogies: *The Descendants and Antecedents of John Parham Rose et al. of Warren County, North Carolina* was compiled by Seth Warner and published in Durham, North Carolina, in 1982. *Langfords in America* was compiled by George Shealy Langford and published in College Park, Maryland, in 1977.

LANGLEBEN, LANGLEY (S.S. Abbreviation: Langle)

Ranking: 1157 **S.S. Count:** 37,864

Origin: Langleben—Jewish; Langley—English. Langleben: Uncertain etymology. The name means long life and was teken ornamentally. Langley: 1) derived from the Old Norse feminine first name Langlif, which comprises the elements "lang" and "lif," meaning long and life. 2) derived from the Old English words "lang" and "leah," meaning long and wood. The name was given to those from Langley, the name of several places in England.

Famous Bearers: SAMUEL PIERPONT LANGLEY (1834–1906) of Massachusetts was an astronomer and a pioneer in the airplane industry. He invented a bolometer and worked in the measurement of solar radiation at different wavelengths to chart their effects on the weather. He developed and flew model planes but failed in attempts to fly full-sized planes. KATHERINE GUDGER LANGLEY (1883?–1948) of North Carolina was aide and secretary to her husband John W. Langley when he was a member of the 60th Congress. When he resigned after being convicted of a Prohibition crime, she ran, won and became the seventh woman to serve in that capacity.

Genealogies: *Genealogy of the Nicholson (also Langley) Sisters* was compiled by Eileen E. Langley and published in Ellis, Kansas, in 1986.

LANGLOIS, LANGLOY (S.S. Abbreviation: Langlo)

Ranking: 4122 **S.S. Count:** 10,968

Origin: French. Cognates to the English name English.

Genealogies: None known.

LANGSTON (S.S. Abbreviation: Langst)

Ranking: 1576 **S.S. Count:** 28,316

Origin: English. Derived from the Old English words "lang" and "stan," meaning long and stone. The name was given to those from Langston(e), the name of several places in England.

Famous Langstons: JOHN MERCER LANGSTON (1829–1927) of Virginia was an educator and diplomat. He was the son of Ralph Quarls, a plantation owner, and his slave, Lucy Langston. He became a professor of law and dean at Howard University, a diplomat in Haiti and Santo Domingo, the president of Virginia Normal and Collegiate Institute, and a member of Congress.

Genealogies: *Landon (also Langston) Family History* was compiled by Joy Deal Lehmann and published in Novato, California, in 1988. *Langstons and their Kin* was compiled by Inez M. McClellan and published in 1979.

LANHAM

Ranking: 3469 **S.S. Count:** 13,020

Origin: English. Derived from the Old English words "lang" *and* "hām," *meaning long and homestead (H&H). The name was given to those from Langham, the name of several places in England.*

Famous **Lanhams**: FREDERICK G. (FRITZ) LANHAM (1880–1965) of Texas was a member of Congress from Texas for 28 years.

Genealogies: *Snatched from the Dragon* was compiled by Megan Gabriel Lanham and published in Nashville, Tennessee, in 1990.

LANIER
Ranking: 1578 **S.S. Count:** 28,307
Origin: French. 1) derived from the Old French word "asne," *meaning donkey. The name was given to those who worked transporting goods on donkeys. 2) derived from the Old French word* "la(i)ne," *meaning wool. The name was given to those who worked in the wool trade.*

Famous **Laniers**: SIDNEY LANIER (1842–1881) of Georgia was an American poet. He was a Confederate soldier, first flutist with the Peabody Orchestra in Baltimore, and an English literature lecturer at Johns Hopkins University. He is best known for his poetry. One of his more famous poems is "The Marshes of Glynn."

Genealogies: *The History and Genealogy of the Nances (also Laniers)* was compiled by D. Nance and published in Charlotte, North Carolina, in 1930.

LANKFORD (S.S. Abbreviation: Lankfo)
Ranking: 2643 **S.S. Count:** 17,233
Origin: English. Transformation of Langford.
Genealogies: None known.

LANNIN
Ranking: 3620 **S.S. Count:** 12,456
Origin: Irish. Transformation of Lennon.
Genealogies: None known.

LANTZ
Ranking: 2814 **S.S. Count:** 16,189
Origin: German. Cognate to Lance.
Famous **Lantzes**: WALTER LANTZ (1900–1994) was a cartoonist who developed Woody Woodpecker and other characters. The famous fictional woodpecker was modeled after a pesky real woodpecker that annoyed Lantz and his bride on their honeymoon.
Genealogies: None known.

LAPLANTE (S.S. Abbreviation: Laplan)
Ranking: 3520 **S.S. Count:** 12,809
Origin: French. Derived from the Old French word "plante," *meaning plant. The name was given to those from a place where shrubs and trees were cultivated for transplanting.*

Genealogies: None known.

LAPOINTE (S.S. Abbreviation: Lapoin)
Ranking: 2898 **S.S. Count:** 15,707
Origin: French. Derived from the French word meaning point, especially the point of a sword. The name was given to soldiers or swordsmen.
Genealogies: None known.

LAPORTA, LAPORTE (S.S. Abbreviation: Laport)
Ranking: 3542 **S.S. Count:** 12,748
Origin: Laporta—Catalan, Italian; Laporte—French. Derived from the Latin word "porta," *meaning door. The names were given to those who lived near a town's gates or to those who were the gatekeepers of a town.*
Genealogies: None known.

LARA
Ranking: 1370 **S.S. Count:** 32,334
Origin: Spanish. Uncertain etymology. The name was given to those from Lara, a place in Burgos, Spain.
Genealogies: None known.

LARGE
Ranking: 4706 **S.S. Count:** 9511
Origin: English, French. Derived from the Latin word "largus," *meaning plentiful. The name was given to those who were magnanimous or unselfish.*
Genealogies: None known.

LARKIN (ALSO LARKING)
Ranking: 1056 **S.S. Count:** 41,708
Origin: English, Irish. English: derived from a medieval first name that was derived from the name Lawrence and the Middle English suffix "-kin." *Irish: derived from the Gaelic name Ó Lorcáin, which was derived from the first name Lorcán, which was derived from the word* "lorc," *meaning fierce.*

Famous **Bearers**: JOHN LARKIN (1801–1858) of England was a Catholic priest in Maryland and New York who founded Xavier High School in New York City and was president of Fordham University (1851–1853). THOMAS O. LARKIN (1802–1858) of Massachusetts was an agent for President James Buchanan during the campaign to separate California from Mexico.
Genealogies: None known.

LAROCHE, LAROCHELLE, LAROCHETTE (S.S. Abbreviation: Laroch)
Ranking: 4375 **S.S. Count:** 10,252
Origin: French. Cognates to Roach.
Famous **LaRoches**: RENÉ LAROCHE (1795–1872) of

Pennsylvania wrote extensively on medical subjects. His *Yellow Fever* (1855) is a classic treatise.

Genealogies: None known.

LAROSE

Ranking: 4782 S.S. Count: 9367

Origin: French. Cognate to the English name Rose.

Genealogies: None known.

LARSEN

Ranking: 531 S.S. Count: 76,197

Origin: Danish. Cognate to Lawrence.

Famous **Larsens:** ESPER SIGNIUS LARSEN (1879–1961) of Oregon was a petrologist and a member of the U.S. Geological Survey (1909–1958). He was a professor at Harvard and is best known for his work in radioactive dating and his studies of igneous rocks.

Genealogies: None known.

LARSON

Ranking: 212 S.S. Count: 168,218

Origin: English. Transformation of Lawrence.

Famous **Larsons:** LAURENCE M. LARSON (1868–1938) of Norway grew up in Wisconsin and became an authority on the history of the cultures of northern and western Europe.

Genealogies: *Life in Nebraska and our Heritage* was compiled by Ellen Larson and published in Boelus, Nebraska, in 1983. *The Larson Legacy* was compiled by Lee Grippen and published in Caledonia, Minnesota, in 1978.

LARUE

Ranking: 2731 S.S. Count: 16,668

Origin: French. Derived from the French words "la" and "rue," meaning the and pathway. The name was given to those who lived on a road or path.

Genealogies: *The LaRue Family History* was compiled by Katherine B. LaRue and published in Indiana in 1980. *Collection of Genealogical Data Concerning the La Rue/Rue Families of America* was compiled by Marne H. Dubbs and published in St. Louis, Missouri, in the 1940's.

LASH

Ranking: 4820 S.S. Count: 9295

Origin: German. Derived from the first name Lash, which was derived from the name Lazarus.

Genealogies: *The History of the Descendants of Jacob Lash* was compiled by Dorothy Smith Lathrop and published in Plainfield, New Jersey, in 1969.

LASSITER (S.S. Abbreviation: Lassit)

Ranking: 2484 S.S. Count: 18,248

Origin: English. Derived from Ligore, the Old English name of a tribe, and from the Old English word "cœster,"

meaning Roman fort. The name was given to those from Leicester, the name of a place in England.

Genealogies: None known.

LASTER

Ranking: 3813 S.S. Count: 11,826

Origin: English. Derived from the Middle English word "last," meaning the wooden model of a foot, which was used for repairing and making shoes. The name was given to cobblers.

Genealogies: *The Lasters* was compiled by Letha Irene Laster Sanderson and published in Tulsa, Oklahoma, in 1973.

LATHAM

Ranking: 1489 S.S. Count: 29,811

Origin: English. Derived from the Old Norse word "hlaða," meaning barn. The name was given to those from Latham, the name of several places in England.

Famous **Lathams:** MILTON S. LATHAM (1827–1882) of Ohio was a governor of, member of Congress from, and U.S. senator from California.

Genealogies: *The Ancestry of Arthur Wood Latham* was compiled by Margret Latham Worden and published in Largo, Florida, in 1980.

LATHROP, LATHROPE (S.S. Abbreviation: Lathro)

Ranking: 3901 S.S. Count: 11,555

Origin: English. Uncertain etymology. The name was given to those from Lowthorpe, a place in Yorkshire, England.

Famous **Lathrops:** JOHN HIRAM LATHROP (1799–1866) of New York was president of three universities in Missouri, Wisconsin, and Indiana. FRANCIS A. LATHROP (1849–1909), who was born at sea on a voyage to Hawaii, was a mural painter famous for wall panels and stained-glass windows. His brother, GEORGE P. LATHROP (1851–1898) of Hawaii, was an author and editor who was also a founder of the Catholic Summer School of America. MARY ALPHONSA LATHROP (1851–1926) of Massachusetts was known as Mother Alphonsa. She was born Rose Hawthorne, a daughter of Nathaniel Hawthorne. She was married to George Lathrop, and was the author of poems, stories, and a biography of her father. She founded Servants of Relief for Incurable Cancer, which became the Dominican Congregation of St. Rose of Lima. She served as its mother superior (1900–1926). In 1901 she started the Rosary Hill Home in Hawthorne, New York. JULIA CLIFFORD LATHROP (1858–1932) of Illinois was a social worker and reformer. She was a champion of those who could not defend themselves and spent her life in service to poor, insane, and deliquent children.

Genealogies: *Ancestors and Descendants of the Walker*

Lathrop Family of Chelsea, Vermont was compiled by Maia Gudmundson Walker and published in Portland, Oregon, in 1977. *In This Place* was compiled by Charles Leonard Lathrop and published in Lebanon, Connecticut, in 1976.

LATIMER (S.S. Abbreviation: Latime)
Ranking: 3068 S.S. Count: 14,791
Origin: English. Derived from the Anglo-Norman-French word "latinier," meaning a clerk who kept records in Latin.
Famous **Latimers**: MARY ELIZABETH WORMELEY LATIMER (1822–1904), born in England, emigrated to Maryland and wrote many articles on European history. WENDELL M. LATIMER (1893–1955) of Kansas, a chemist and an authority on temperatures and liquefaction of gases, was the director of a plutonium project at the University of California (1943–1945).
Genealogies: *The Lattimores* [also Latimer] was compiled by Esther Lattimore Jenkins and published in Myrtle Point, Oregon, in 1982.

LAU
Ranking: 2020 S.S. Count: 22,617
Origin: German. Derived from the German word "löwe," meaning lion. The name was given to those who were majestic or courageous.
Genealogies: None known.

LAUDER
Ranking: 3794 S.S. Count: 11,886
Origin: Scottish. Uncertain etymology. The name was given to those from Lauder, a place in Scotland.
Genealogies: *The Lauder Family in America* was compiled by Margaret Emily Lauder and published in Ridgway, Pennsylvania, in 1975.

LAUER
Ranking: 2991 S.S. Count: 15,189
Origin: German, Jewish. German: 1) derived from the Middle High German word "löwære," which was derived from the word "lö," meaning tannin. The name was given to tanners. 2) the name was given to those from Lauer, a place in Franconia, Germany. 3) derived from the Middle High German word "lūre," meaning a cunning, deceptive, or shrewd person. Jewish: uncertain etymology.
Genealogies: None known.

LAUGHLAN, LAUGHLAND, LAUGHLIN (S.S. Abbreviation: Laughl)
Ranking: 1936 S.S. Count: 23,365
Origin: Irish. Derived from the Gaelic name Lochlann, meaning a stranger or Viking settler, which was derived from the the words "loch" and "lann," meaning fjord or lake and land.

Famous **Bearers**: JAMES LAURENCE LAUGHLIN (1850–1933) of Ohio was an economics professor at Harvard University and the author of numerous authoritative works, including *The Principles of Money* (1903). GAIL LAUGHLIN (1868–1952) of Maine was a lawyer, suffragist, feminist, and state legislator. She dedicated her life to righting injustices in existing laws and to tearing down the legal walls to women's emancipation. HARRY H. LAUGHLIN (1880–1943) of Iowa was superintendent of the Eugenics Record Office at Cold Spring Harbor, New York, for 29 years and was an active proponent of sterilization of people with mental and physical handicaps. HENRY ALEXANDER LAUGHLIN (1892–1977) of Pennsylvania was a publisher at Houghton Mifflin, a book publishing company.
Genealogies: *The Laughlin Family* was compiled by Edward Floyd Kilpatrick and published in Fort Loudon, Pennsylvania, in 1986.

LAUREN (ALSO LAURENCE, LAURENSON, LAURENT, LAURENTI)
Ranking: 2555 S.S. Count: 17,782
Origin: Laurence—English; Laurenson—English, Scottish; Lauren—Flemish; Laurent—French, German; Laurenti—Italian. Transformations of and cognates to Lawrence.
Genealogies: *Cooper, Laurence, Dowdle, Smith, Clem and Allied Families* was compiled by Velna Cooper Brown and published in Charleston, Missouri, in 1971.

LAVALLE (S.S. Abbreviation: Lavall)
Ranking: 2710 S.S. Count: 16,776
Origin: French, Italian. Cognates to Vale.
Genealogies: None known.

LAVELL (ALSO LAVELLE)
Ranking: 4685 S.S. Count: 9550
Origin: Irish. Derived from the Gaelic name Ó Maoil Fhábhail, meaning "descendant of the devotee of (St.) Fábhal" (H&H).
Genealogies: None known.

LAVENDER (S.S. Abbreviation: Lavend)
Ranking: 4179 S.S. Count: 10,817
Origin: English. Derived from the Anglo-Norman-French word "lavend(i)er," meaning launderer. The name was given to launderers or washers.
Genealogies: *Lavender & Cavender* was compiled by Lynn Spohr and published in Tulsa, Oklahoma, in 1987. *Tinsley (Lavender) et al.* was compiled by William Eldon Tinsley and published in Pflugerville, Texas, in 1986.

LAVIGNE (S.S. Abbreviation: Lavign)
Ranking: 4254 S.S. Count: 10,588
Origin: French. Cognate to Vine.

Genealogies: None known.

LAVOIE

Ranking: 3384 **S.S. Count:** 13,378
Origin: French. Uncertain etymology. Most likely derived from the French word "voie," meaning way or road.
Genealogies: None known.

LAW

Ranking: 1137 **S.S. Count:** 38,674
Origin: English, Scottish. 1) derived from the Middle English word "law," which was derived from the Old English word "hlāw," meaning hill or burial mound. The name was given to those who lived near a hill. 2) transformation of Lawrence.
Famous **Laws:** JONATHAN LAW (1674–1750) of Connecticut was governor of Connecticut. ANDREW LAW (1748?–1821) of Connecticut published popular hymnals. SALLIE CHAPMAN GORDON LAW (1805–1894) of North Carolina was a nurse who organized and managed Confederate hospitals during the Civil War. GEORGE LAW (1806–1881) of New York was a founder of the U.S. Mail Steamship Co. He also was a well-known politician of the Know-Nothing Party.
Genealogies: *The Law Family of Wanlockhead, Scotland, and Northfield, Minnesota* was compiled by Margaret D. Leslie Lindner and published in Ypsilanti, Michigan, in 1986.

LAWHORN (S.S. Abbreviation: Lawhor)

Ranking: 4905 **S.S. Count:** 9118
Origin: English. Derived from the Old English words "lagu" and "horn," meaning law and horn. The name was given to those from Laughern, a place in Worcestershire, England.
Genealogies: None known.

LAWLER

Ranking: 2225 **S.S. Count:** 20,616
Origin: Irish. Derived from the Gaelic name Ó Leathlobhair, which was derived from the first name Leathlobar, comprising the components "leath" and "lobar," meaning half and ill or leprous.
Famous **Lawlers:** JOSEPH JOHN LAWLER (1901–1977) of Pennsylvania was the Pennsylvania secretary of highways under Governor George Leader. He was named "Father of the Pennsylvania–Canada Highway" by the Pennsylvania Turnpike Commission.
Genealogies: *Lawler Family in America* was compiled by Harold Henry Lawler and pubished in Denver, Colorado, in 1970.

LAWLESS (S.S. Abbreviation: Lawles)

Ranking: 3588 **S.S. Count:** 12,569

Origin: English. Derived from the Old English word "lagu," meaning law, and the suffix "-l(ē)as," meaning lacking. The name was given to those who were intemperate or lawless.
Genealogies: None known.

LAWRENCE, LAWRENSON (S.S. Abbreviation: Lawren)

Ranking: 206 **S.S. Count:** 172,430
Origin: English. Derived from the Middle English and Old French first names Lorens and Laurence.
Famous **Bearers:** JAMES LAWRENCE (1781–1813) of New Jersey was a naval officer who died a hero's death in the War of 1812. He was mortally wounded in a battle between the American ship *Chesapeake* and the British ship *Shannon*. On June 1, 1813, as he was being taken below deck after receiving his injuries, it was reported that he yelled, "Don't give up the ship" to his men. WILLIAM LAWRENCE (1783–1838) of Massachusetts opened the first woolen plant in Lowell, Massachusetts. His brothers, AMOS LAWRENCE (1786–1852) and ABBOTT LAWRENCE (1792–1855), were partners in the founding and development of the town of Lawrence, Massachusetts, as a manufacturing city. Abbott also served as a member of Congress and as a minister to Great Britain. He contributed to Harvard University, where the Lawrence Scientific School was named in his honor. AMOS ADAMS LAWRENCE (1814–1886) of Massachusetts was a sales agent for large textile mills and an independent textile manufacturer who established Lawrence University in Kansas, a forerunner of the state university. His son, WILLIAM LAWRENCE (1850–1941) of Massachusetts was an Episcopal clergyman who was bishop of Massachusetts for 34 years. RICHARD S. LAWRENCE (1817–1892) of Vermont invented machine tools used in manufacturing rifles. FLORENCE LAWRENCE (1886–1938) of Canada was a motion-picture actress. She had a skyrocketing career, with pressures that she was not able to control, and her career and life took a downward turn. She died by her own hand. DAVID LAWRENCE (1888–1973) of Pennsylvania was a journalist and the founder of *U.S. News* in 1933. It became *U.S. News & World Report* in 1947. DAVID L. LAWRENCE (1889–1966) of Pennsylvania was that state's first Catholic governor. GERTRUDE LAWRENCE (1898–1952), born in England, was an actress and singer in New York. She starred in plays such as *Private Lives* (1930) and *The King and I* (1941). ERNESTO ORLANDO LAWRENCE (1901–1958) of South Dakota was the founder and director of the Radiation Laboratory at Berkeley and is considered a pioneer in the field of radioactivity. He received a Nobel Prize for physics in 1939. FREDERICK PORTER LAWRENCE (1911–1975) of West Virginia was a business executive, small-town mayor, and the annual-giving chairman at Princeton University.

Genealogies: *The History of the Bemis, Perkinson, Fay, and Lawrence Families* was compiled by Ted H. Bemis and published in Stroudsburg, Pennsylvania, in 1980. *From the European Continent to American Colonist & Citizen: the 275 Year History of the Lowrance (also Lawrence) Family in America* was compiled by Gayford Rader Lowrance and published in 1986.

LAWS

Ranking: 2291 S.S. Count: 19,876

Origin: English. Transformation of Lawrence.

Famous **Lawses:** SAMUEL SPAHR LAWS (1824–1921) of Virginia was an educator, but his claim to fame was his invention of the stock ticker, circa 1865. ANNIE LAWS (1855–1927) of Ohio was a kindergarten and educational worker. She is best known as a pioneer in nursing, kindergarten, and home economics education.

Genealogies: None known.

LAWSON

Ranking: 223 S.S. Count: 157,745

Origin: English. Transformation of Lawrence.

Famous **Lawsons:** JOHN LAWSON (?–1711), possibly of England, was an English colonist and the surveyor general of North Carolina in 1708. He was one of the early North Carolina settlers and the founder of the town of New Bern, North Carolina. VICTOR FREEMONT LAWSON (1850–1925) of Illinois bought the *Chicago Daily News* and merged it with other Chicago papers to form the *Chicago Herald Record* before he sold it. He is best remembered as a pioneer in developing the availability of foreign news for American papers. THOMAS WILLIAM LAWSON (1857–1925) of Massachusetts was a stock market speculator and a writer of books on the financial market. ANDREW COWPER LAWSON (1861–1952) of Scotland was a geologist and the head of the commission that investigated the 1906 earthquake in California. ERNEST LAWSON (1873–1939) of California was a painter known for his colorful, impressionistic style. ROBERTA CAMPBELL LAWSON (1878–1940) of Oklahoma was the president of the General Federation of Women's Clubs and a student of Indian music and culture. ROBERT R. LAWSON (1892–1957) of New York was an illustrator and author. He wrote and illustrated, among other works, *Ben and Me* (1939) and *The Tough Winter* (1954). STANLEY KING LAWSON (1906–1977) of West Virginia was a judge best noted for granting a court order allowing women to receive laetrile injections.

Genealogies: *The Descendants of John Henry Lawson* was compiled by Mona Gee Lawson and published in Sumner, Washington, in 1991. *The Lawson Golden Book* was compiled by Virginia Ruth Lawson Trent and published in Dubuque, Iowa, in 1990.

LAWTON

Ranking: 2311 S.S. Count: 19,658

Origin: English. Derived from the Old English words "hlāw" and "tūn," meaning hill and settlement. The name was given to those from Lawton, the name of several places in England.

Famous **Lawtons:** ALEXANDER R. LAWTON (1818–1896) of South Carolina was a Confederate general and a Georgia legislator who went on to become U.S. minister to Austria. HENRY WARE LAWTON (1843–1899) of Ohio was a soldier in the Union army during the Civil War. As an Indian fighter, he pursued and captured Geronimo.

Genealogies: *The Descendants of George Lawton* was compiled by Elva Lawton and published in Seattle, Washington, in 1977. *How Grand a Flame* was compiled by Clyde Bresee and published in Chapel Hill, North Carolina, in 1992.

LAY

Ranking: 1960 S.S. Count: 23,105

Origin: English. Transformation of the English name Lee.

Famous **Lays:** HENRY C. LAY (1823–1885) of Virginia was an Episcopal clergyman who served as missionary bishop for Arkansas and the Indian Territory for 10 years. JOHN LOUIS LAY (1832–1899) of New York invented, among other things, an electronically driven torpedo and the launching mechanism for it.

Genealogies: None known.

LAYMAN

Ranking: 3084 S.S. Count: 14,734

Origin: English. Transformation of the first definition of Lee.

Genealogies: *Layman-Lehman Records and Lines* was compiled by Laurine Mae Palmerton Logsdon and published in Spokane, Washington, in 1986.

LAYNE

Ranking: 2554 S.S. Count: 17,797

Origin: English. Transformation of the English name Lane.

Genealogies: None known.

LAYTON

Ranking: 1695 S.S. Count: 26,339

Origin: English. Derived from various first components and the second component "tūn," meaning settlement. The name was given to those from Layton, the name of several places in England.

Genealogies: *The Family and Ancestors of Joseph Anthony Layton* was compiled by Robert F. Layton and published in Cliffside Park, New Jersey, in 1989. *In My Father's House: the Story of the Layton Family and the Rev-*

erend Jim Jones was compiled by Min S. Yee and published in New York, New York, in 1981. *A Leighton (also Layton) Genealogy* was compiled by Perley M. Leighton and published in Boston, Massachusetts, in 1989.

LE
Ranking: 1661 S.S. Count: 26,933
Origin: Chinese. The name means pear tree.
Genealogies: None known.

LEA
Ranking: 3691 S.S. Count: 12,233
Origin: English. Transformation of the English name Lee.
Famous **Leas**: MATHEW CAREY LEA (1823–1897) of Pennsylvania was a chemist who contributed to the advancement of photochemistry and to knowledge about platinum metals. His brother, HENRY C. LEA (1825–1909) of Pennsylvania, was a publisher and historian who wrote many authoritative works, including *A History of the Inquisition of Spain* (1906–1907). HOMER LEA (1876–1912) of Colorado was a soldier and the author of *The Valor of Ignorance*, which predicted the U.S./Japan World War II confrontation. LUKE LEA (1879–1945) of Tennessee founded the *Nashville Tennesseean* in 1907 and was a U.S. senator from Tennessee.
Genealogies: None known.

LEACH
Ranking: 652 S.S. Count: 63,997
Origin: English. 1) derived from the Old English word "lœcc," meaning stream. The name was given to those who lived near a marshy stream. 2) derived from the Old English word "lœce," meaning physician. The name was given to physicians.
Famous **Leaches**: DANIEL DYE LEACH (1806–1891) of Massachusetts, a superintendent of schools in Providence, Rhode Island, wrote many elementary school textbooks. ABBY LEACH (1855–1918) of Massachusetts was a teacher and the head of the Greek Department at Vassar College.
Genealogies: *Leach-Leech Family* was compiled by Anna Laura Griffith and published in Mayfield, Kentucky, in 1985. *William Adams (also Leach), 1594– 1661, of Ipswich, Massachusetts* was compiled by Kenneth L. Bosworth and published in Bowie, Maryland, in 1992.

LEAHY
Ranking: 2926 S.S. Count: 15,565
Origin: Irish. Derived from the Gaelic name Ó Laochdha, which was derived from the first name Laochdh, which was derived from the word "laoch," meaning hero.
Fanous **Leahys**: WILLIAM DANIEL LEAHY (1875–1959) of Iowa was a naval officer, chief of staff to Presidents Franklin D. Roosevelt and Harry S Truman, and admiral of the fleet (1944).
Genealogies: None known.

LEAKE
Ranking: 4661 S.S. Count: 9593
Origin: English. 1) derived from the Old English word "lēac," meaning leek. The name was given to those who sold or grew leeks. 2) derived from the Old Norse word "lœkr," meaning brook. The name was given to those who lived near a brook or to those from Leek or Leak(e), the name of several places in England.
Genealogies: None known.

LEAL
Ranking: 2115 S.S. Count: 21,681
Origin: Portuguese, Spanish. Derived from the Portuguese and Spanish word "leal," meaning loyal. The name was given to those who were trustworthy.
Genealogies: None known.

LEAR
Ranking: 4324 S.S. Count: 10,363
Origin: English. 1) derived from "Leire," possibly the name of a river. The name was given to those from Leire, a place in Leicester, England. 2) derived from the Germanic component "lār," meaning clearing. The name was given to those from several places in France with names that include this component.
Famous **Lears**: TOBIAS LEAR (1762–1816) of New Hampshire was a diplomat. He served as secretary to George Washington, then as U.S. consul at Algiers. WILLIAM POWELL LEAR (1902–1978) of Missouri was the founder of the Lear Jet Corporation. FLOYD RAYMOND LEAR JR. (1911–1975) of Pennsylvania was an industrialist and the president of Industrial Engraving Co. He was one of the people responsible for the development of powderless etching, and Industrial Engraving was the first plant to use the process. He increased his company's involvement in the electronics industry.
Genealogies: None known.

LEARY
Ranking: 2098 S.S. Count: 21,887
Origin: Irish. Derived from the Gaelic name Ó Laoghaire, which was derived from the first name Laoghaire, meaning "Keeper of Calves" (H&H), derived from "loagh," meaning calf.
Famous **Learys**: JOHN LEARY (1837–1905) of Canada moved to the state of Washington and became a leading industrial developer in the Puget Sound area.
Genealogies: *The Leary-Evans, Ohio's Free People of Color* was compiled by Robert Ewell Greene and published in Washington, D.C., in 1979.

LEATHER, LEATHERBARROW, LEATHERMAN, LEATHERS (S.S. Abbreviation: Leathe)

Ranking: 1873 **S.S. Count:** 24,171

Origin: Leather, Leathers—English; Leatherbarrow—English; Leatherman—Jewish. Leather, Leathers: derived from the Middle English word "lether," meaning leather. The name was given to leather workers. Leatherbarrow: derived from the Old Norse word "látr," meaning "lair of a wild animal" (H&H), and the Old English word "bearu," meaning wood or grove. The name was given to those from Latterbarrow, a place in England. Leatherman: a cognate to Leather.

Famous **Bearers:** WALLER S. LEATHERS (1874–1946) of Virginia, as dean of medical schools in Mississippi and Tennessee, contributed greatly to the modernization of practices and standards in the South.

Genealogies: None known.

LEAVITT (S.S. Abbreviation: Leavit)

Ranking: 2718 **S.S. Count:** 16,733

Origin: English. 1) derived from the Old English first name Lēofgēat, which comprises the components "lēof," meaning dear or beloved, and "Gēat," the name of a tribe. 2) Uncertain etymology. The name was given to those from Livet, the name of several places in Normandy, France. 3) derived from the Anglo-Norman-French word "leu," meaning wolf. The name was given to those who were cunning or dangerous.

Famous **Leavitts:** MARY GREENLEAF CLEMENT LEAVITT (1830–1912) of New Hampshire was a teacher and a temperance missionary. She established 86 branches of the Woman's Christian Temperance Union and 24 men's temperance societies in foreign countries. FRANK M. LEAVITT (1856–1928) of Ohio was an inventor who obtained more than 300 patents over a 46-year period. Many of his inventions related to metalworking machinery. HENRIETTA SWAN LEAVITT (1868–1921) of Massachusetts was an astronomer on the staff of Harvard Observatory. She is responsible for the discovery of four novae and 2400 variable stars. FRANK S. LEAVITT (1889–1953) of New York was a wrestler and actor who wrestled as Man Mountain Dean and played bit parts in films.

Genealogies: *An Index of Names of Leavitt* was compiled by Julia Bumpus Berndt and published in North Attleboro, Massachusetts, in 1981.

LEBLANC (S.S. Abbreviation: Leblan)

Ranking: 765 **S.S. Count:** 55,220

Origin: French. Derived from the Old French word "blanc," meaning white. The name was given to those who were pale or whose hair was light or white in color.

Genealogies: None known.

LEBRON

Ranking: 2455 **S.S. Count:** 18,502

Origin: Spanish. Uncertain etymology. The name was given to those who "raised large hares" (ES).

Genealogies: None known.

LECLAIR (S.S. Abbreviation: Leclai)

Ranking: 3177 **S.S. Count:** 14,289

Origin: French. 1) cognate to Clark. 2) Uncertain etymology. The name was given to those with clear skin or to those who were "quick to act" (ES).

Genealogies: None known.

LEDBETTER (S.S. Abbreviation: Ledbet)

Ranking: 1630 **S.S. Count:** 27,554

Origin: English. Derived from the Old English words "lēad" and "bēatan," meaning lead and to strike. The name was given to those who worked with lead.

Famous **Ledbetters:** HUDDIE LEDBETTER (1885–1949) of Louisiana was a singer nicknamed "Ledbelly." Born of African-American and Cherokee stock, he became one of the greatest blues singers of the first half of the 20th century. His most famous recordings are "Good Morning Blues," "Rock Island Line," and "Good Night, Irene."

Genealogies: *Yeiser, Ledbetter and Allied Families* was compiled by Mary Louise Yeiser Wiley and published in Columbia, Tennessee, in 1977.

LEDESMA (S.S. Abbreviation: Ledesm)

Ranking: 3707 **S.S. Count:** 12,177

Origin: Spanish. Uncertain etymology. Possibly derived from a Celtic word meaning "broad" (H&H). The name was given to those from Ledesma, the name of several places in Spain.

Genealogies: None known.

LEDFORD (S.S. Abbreviation: Ledfor)

Ranking: 1798 **S.S. Count:** 25,092

Origin: English. The name was given to those from Lydford, meaning the "ford at the torrent" (ES), or from Leckford, meaning "grove by a river crossing" (ES), the names of several places in England.

Genealogies: *Generations: An American Family* was compiled by John Edgerton and published in Lexington, Kentucky, in 1983.

LEE

Ranking: 26 **S.S. Count:** 661,071

Origin: English, Irish. English: 1) derived from the Old English word "lēah," meaning wood or clearing. The name was given to those from Lee or Lea, the name of several places in England. 2) derived from the Old English word "lēah," meaning wood. The name was given to those who lived near a pasture or meadow. Irish: derived from the Gaelic name Ó Laoidhigh, which was derived from the first name Laoidheach, derived from the word "laoidh," meaning poem. The name was originally given to poets.

Famous Lees: CHARLES LEE (1731–1782) of England was an American soldier who was captured by the British and agreed to work to their benefit in the Revolutionary War. His attempt to retreat instead of attack in the Battle of Monmouth was spoiled by George Washington, who subsequently had him court-martialed. RICHARD HENRY LEE (1732–1794) of Virginia was a Revolutionary War statesman and a defender of colonial rights. He was the Virginia delegate to the Continental Congress and a signer of the Declaration of Independence and the Articles of Confederation. After the Revolutionary War, he served in the U.S. Senate. FRANCIS LIGHTFOOT LEE (1734–1797) of Virginia was a member of the Continental Congress and a signer of the Declaration of Independence. ANN LEE (1736–1784) of England was known as Mother Ann. She was the founder of the Shaker Society in America. ARTHUR LEE (1740–1792) of Virginia was a colonial diplomat. He was involved in arranging a treaty with France in 1778, but charges of disloyalty by another member of the American team led to his being recalled in 1779. As a member of the Continental Congress, he opposed to the adoption of the Constitution. HENRY LEE (1756–1818) of Virginia was known by the name Light-Horse Harry Lee. He was a Revolutionary War hero, governor of Virginia, commander of the troops that halted the Whiskey Rebellion, and the deliverer of the eulogy at the funeral of George Washington. In that eulogy he said the famous line "First in war, first in peace, first in the hearts of his countrymen." Henry was the father of Robert E. Lee. CHARLES LEE (1758–1815) of Virginia was a friend and supporter of George Washington and served as attorney general in his administration. JASON LEE (1803–1845) of Canada was a Methodist missionary in Oregon. He was instrumental in the establishment of the Oregon government and was one of the founders of the school that became Willamette University. ROBERT EDWARD LEE (1807–1870) of Virginia was the son of Henry Lee. He was a professional soldier who left the Union and accepted a command from Jefferson Davis at the beginning of the Civil War. He rose during the war to the position of general of all the armies of the Confederacy. He surrendered to General Ulysses S. Grant at Appomattox Court House on April 9, 1865. After the war he served as the president of the university now named Washington and Lee. SAMUEL PHILLIPS LEE (1812–1897) of Virginia was a Union naval officer during the Civil War. He was the commander of the North Atlantic blockading squadron and the Mississippi squadron. MARY ANN LEE (1823?–1899) of Pennsylvania was one of the first American ballet dancers. She toured the country with George Washington Smith. FITZHUGH LEE

(1835–1905) of Virginia was a Confederate soldier, governor of Virginia, general of volunteers in the Spanish-American War, and the military governor of Havana, Cuba. He also was the nephew of Robert E. Lee. IVY LEDBETTER LEE (1877–1934) of Georgia was the father of public relations as a respectable field because of the honest way he conducted himself in his work in corporate policies. MUNA LEE (1895–1965) of Mississippi was an international affairs specialist who did much to improve relations between the United States and Latin America. ROSE HUM LEE (1904–1964) of Montana was a sociologist who conducted pioneering research into how Chinese-Americans assimilated into the American social structures. She was the first woman of Chinese ancestry to head a department at an American university. MANFRED BENNINGTON LEE (1905–1971) of New York was an author who wrote under the pen names of Ellery Queen and Barnaby Ross. GYPSY ROSE LEE (1914–1970) of Oregon was born Rose Louise Hovick and was a striptease artist who was known for her style and grace. She also acted on Broadway and in motion pictures.

Genealogies: Descendants & Ancestors of Charles & Fanny Crandall Lee was compiled by Earl Lee Smith and published in Middleburg, Pennsylvania, in 1985. Lee of Virginia was compiled by Edmund Jennings Lee and published in Baltimore, Maryland, in 1974. Hezekiah Leigh [also Lee] was compiled by John D. Gifford and published in Springfield, Missouri, in 1980.

LEEPER
Ranking: 4774 S.S. Count: 9381
Origin: English. Derived from the Old English words "lĕap" and "mann," meaning basket and man. The name was given to those who made baskets.
Genealogies: History of the Descendants of Samuel Harper, James Purdy, and James Leeper was published in Philadelphia, Pennsylvania, in 1894.

LEGER
Ranking: 4071 S.S. Count: 11,108
Origin: English. Derived from a Germanic first name comprising the components "liut" and "geri," meaning tribe and spear.
Genealogies: None known.

LEGG
Ranking: 3232 S.S. Count: 14,039
Origin: English. 1) transformation of Leigh. 2) derived from the Middle English word "legg," meaning leg. The name was given to those with malformed or unusual legs.
Genealogies: All in our Family was compiled by Lilla Bullington Brackeen and published in Decatur, Alabama, in 1976.

LEGGET

Ranking: 2454 S.S. Count: 18,503

Origin: English. 1) derived from the Middle English and Old French word "legat," meaning ambassador. The name was given to ambassadors or deputies or possibly to village representatives. 2) derived from a medieval first name comprising the components "liut" and "gard" or "gari," meaning tribe and enclosure or spear.

Genealogies: None known.

LEHMAN (ALSO LEHMANN)

Ranking: 754 S.S. Count: 56,218

Origin: German, Jewish. German: derived from the Middle High German word "lēheman," which comprises the components "lēhen" and "man," meaning "loan(ed land)" (H&H) and man. The name was given to vassals. Jewish: etymology unknown.

Famous **Bearers:** ARTHUR LEHMAN (1873–1936) of New York was instrumental in Lehman Brothers' becoming a prominent investment banking firm. His wife, ADELE LEWISOHN LEHMAN (1882–1965) of New York, was an art collector and philanthropist, much of whose collection was given to the Metropolitan Museum of Art and the Fogg Museum. HERBERT HENRY LEHMAN (1878–1963) of New York, a brother and partner of Arthur Lehman in the Lehman Brothers firm, was governor of New York (1932–1942). Later a U.S. senator, he took a lead in opposing McCarthyism. Another Lehman brother, IRVING LEHMAN (1876–1945) of New York, was a chief justice of the New York State Court of Appeals. LOTTE LEHMANN (1888–1976) of Germany was one of the finest lyric dramatic sopranos in the United States.

Genealogies: *A Tree in a Forest: Linnaeus Sheetz Lehman* was compiled by Thomas R. Lehman and published in Pennsylvania in 1985. *Descendants of John Daniel Lehman* was compiled by Naomi Irene Shaum and published in Leetonid, Ohio, in 1967.

LEHR

Ranking: 4765 S.S. Count: 9395

Origin: German, Jewish. The name was given to those who lived in swampy areas or to those from places with names including the word "lehr," of which there are several in Germany.

Genealogies: *The Lehr Family* was compiled by Stephen J. Kennedy and published in Needham Heights, Massachusetts, in 1978.

LEIGH

Ranking: 3284 S.S. Count: 13,807

Origin: English. Derived from the Old English word "lēah," meaning wood or clearing. The name was given to those from Leigh, the name of several places in England.

Famous **Leighs:** BENJAMIN W. LEIGH (1781–1849) of Virginia was a U.S. senator from Virginia. WILLIAM R. LEIGH (1866–1955) of Virginia was an artist and author whose paintings of the American West are well known. VIVIEN LEIGH (1913–1967), born in India, was an actress in the United States best known as Scarlett O'Hara in *Gone With the Wind* (1939). She was married to the actor Laurence Olivier.

Genealogies: *Hezekiah Leigh (also Lee)* was compiled by John D. Gifford and published in Springfield, Missouri, in 1980.

LEIGHTON (S.S. Abbreviation: Leight)

Ranking: 2623 S.S. Count: 17,329

Origin: English. Derived from the Old English words "lēac" and "tūn," meaning leek and settlement. The name was given to those from Leighton, the name of several places in England.

Famous **Leightons:** WILLIAM LEIGHTON (1825–1868), a glassmaker for New England Glass Co., developed a new formula for ruby glass in the 1840s.

Genealogies: *A Leighton (also Layton) Genealogy* was compiled by Perley M. Leighton and published in Boston, Massachusetts, in 1989.

LEMASTER (S.S. Abbreviation: Lemast)

Ranking: 3377 S.S. Count: 13,400

Origin: French? Uncertain etymology. Possibly a cognate to Master.

Genealogies: None known.

LEMAY

Ranking: 3959 S.S. Count: 11,422

Origin: French. Uncertain etymology. The name was given to those who "set up the maypole" (ES).

Genealogies: None known.

LEMIEUX (S.S. Abbreviation: Lemieu)

Ranking: 4326 S.S. Count: 10,361

Origin: French. Uncertain etymology. The name was given to those who lived along the Loire River in France.

Genealogies: None known.

LEMKE

Ranking: 3194 S.S. Count: 14,211

Origin: German. Cognate to Lambert.

Famous **Lemkes:** PETER H. LEMKE (1796–1882) was a pioneering Catholic priest in Pennsylvania and Kansas. WILLIAM F. LEMKE (1878–1950) of Minnesota was a member of Congress from North Dakota.

Genealogies: *The Lemke Family Heritage* was compiled by Dolores Giese and published in Merrill, Wisconsin, in 1982.

LEMMON

Ranking: 3106 S.S. Count: 14,640

Origin: English. Transformation of the English name Lemon.

Famous **Lemmons**: JOHN G. LEMMON (1832–1908) of Michigan was a botanist who explored large areas of the West and produced reports that were used after his death to prepare forest policy.

Genealogies: *John Lemmon and his Wife, Elizabeth Mickey: Pioneer Settlers of Colonial Pennsylvania* was compiled by Lawrence Clifton Lemmon and published in Bowie, Maryland, in 1983.

LEMON

Ranking: 2256 S.S. Count: 20,234

Origin: English, Irish, Scottish. English: 1) Derived from the Old English words "lēof" and "mann," meaning beloved or dear and man. The name was given to a lover. 2) derived from the Middle English first name Lefman, which was derived from the Old English words "lēof" and "mann," meaning beloved or dear and man. Irish, Scottish: transformation of Lamont.

Genealogies: *The Lemon and Cox Ancestors of Harriet Caroline Lemon* was compiled by Arthur Channing Downs and published in Primos, Pennsylvania, in 1960.

LEMONS

Ranking: 2616 S.S. Count: 17,369

Origin: English. Transformation of Lemon.

Genealogies: *Through the Orchard—Arterberry, Hillsberry, Lemons, Ragsdale* was compiled by Nova A. Lemons and published in Dallas, Texas, in 1989.

LENHARD, LENHARDT, LENHART (S.S. Abbreviation: Lenhar)

Ranking: 4284 S.S. Count: 10,479

Origin: German. Cognates to the English name Leonard.

Genealogies: *Plath (Plaat), Lenhart (also Leonard) & Hankin* was compiled by Marion Plath Peterson and published in 1978.

LENNON

Ranking: 3154 S.S. Count: 14,390

Origin: Irish. 1) derived from the Gaelic name Ó Lonáin, which was derived from the first name Lonán, which was derived from the word "lon," meaning blackbird. 2) derived from the Gaelic name Ó Leannáin, which is derived from the first name Leannán, meaning lover.

Famous **Lennons**: JOHN BROWN LENNON (1850–1923) of Wisconsin was an active labor-union organizer and treasurer of the American Federation of Labor (AFL) for 27 years. JOHN WINSTON LENNON (1940–1980) of England was a songwriter and singer. He was one of the members of the Beatles, the most successful rock 'n' roll group of the 1960s, not only in sales but also in the influence the music had on the musical style of the day. He and fellow Beatle Paul McCartney were the principal writers of nearly all of the Beatles' songs. Lennon also appeared in several movies that were the prelude to the rock music videos of the 1980s. He was living in New York City when he was shot and killed by an obsessed fan on December 8, 1980.

Genealogies: None known.

LENTZ

Ranking: 2184 S.S. Count: 20,991

Origin: German. Uncertain etymology. Most likely a cognate to Lawrence.

Genealogies: *The Diary of Henry Jackson Lentz (1819–1869)* was compiled by Henry Jackson Lentz and published in Tupelo, Mississippi, in 1983. *Lentz Heritage* was compiled by John Paul Lentz and published in Burlington, North Carolina, in 1986.

LENZ

Ranking: 2928 S.S. Count: 15,546

Origin: German, Jewish. German: 1) cognate to Lance. 2) cognate to Lawrence. 3) derived from the German word "lenz," meaning spring (the season). Jewish: unknown etymology.

Genealogies: None known.

LEO

Ranking: 4564 S.S. Count: 9786

Origin: Italian. Cognate to the English name Lyon.

Genealogies: None known.

LEON

Ranking: 1080 S.S. Count: 40,900

Origin: English, French, Italian, Spanish. English, French, Italian: transformation of and cognate to the English name Lyon. Spanish: 1) cognate to Lyon. 2) derived from the Latin word "legio," meaning legion. The name was given to those from León, a place in Spain.

Genealogies: *The Empresario Don Martin de Leon (also Leon)* was compiled by Arthur B.J. Hammett and published in Waco, Texas, in 1973.

LEONARD, LEONARDELLI, LEONARDI, LEONARDINI, LEONARDO (S.S. Abbreviation: Leonar)

Ranking: 269 S.S. Count: 136,807

Origin: Leonard—English, French, Irish, Italian; Leonardelli, Leonardi, Leonardini, Leonardo—Italian. Leonard (English): derived from a Norman first name, which was derived from the Germanic components "leo" and "hard," meaning lion and hardy. Leonard (French, Italian): cognate to the English name Leonard. Leonard (Irish): transformation of Lennon. Leonardelli, Leonardi, Leonardini, Leonardo: cognates to the English name Leonard.

Famous **Bearers:** ZENAS LEONARD (1809–1857) of Pennsylvania was a trapper who wrote about his experiences in his book *Narratives of the Adventures of Zenas Leonard* (1839). CHARLES L. LEONARD (1861–1913) of Massachusetts was a doctor who may have been the first to show kidney stones, using X-rays. He studied and worked extensively with X-rays and used his knowledge to teach others. Eventually, however, overexposure led to cancer on his hands, which led to his death. HARRY W. LEONARD (1861–1915) of Ohio was an electrical engineer who made a number of electrical inventions, including the first electric train-lighting system (1889) and an elevator-control device. WILLIAM ELLERY LEONARD (1876–1944) of New Jersey was a university professor and a poet. BENNY LEONARD (1896–1947) of New York City was born Benjamin Leiner. He was the world lightweight champion in boxing, holding the title from 1917 to 1925, when he retired. EDWOOD EDSON LEONARD JR. (1923–1977) of Massachusetts was a manufacturing and civic leader who worked as the head of the United Way in southeastern New England.

Genealogies: *Grigsby X. Leonard* was compiled by Carroll Mendenhall Leonard and published in Stillwater, Oklahoma, in 1977. *Plath (Plaat), Lenhart (also Leonard) & Hankin* was compiled by Marion Plath Peterson and published in 1978.

LEONE

Ranking: 2269 **S.S. Count:** 20,116
Origin: Italian. Cognate to the English name Lyon.
Genealogies: None known.

LEONG

Ranking: 4903 **S.S. Count:** 9122
Origin: Chinese. Uncertain etymology.
Genealogies: None known.

LERNER

Ranking: 4083 **S.S. Count:** 11,068
Origin: English, German, Jewish. English: Derived from the Middle English word "lern(en)," meaning to learn and to teach (H&H). The name was given to teachers or scholars. German: derived from the German word "lernen," meaning to learn. The name was given to students or apprentices. Jewish: derived from the Yiddish word "lerner," meaning one who studies the Talmud.

Famous **Lerners:** ALAN JAY LERNER (1918–1986) of New York City was a dramatist and librettist. He, as the lyrist, collaborated with Frederick Lowe on such Broadway musicals as *Brigadoon, Paint Your Wagon, My Fair Lady,* and *Camelot.* He received several Academy Awards for his film musicals.
Genealogies: None known.

LEROY

Ranking: 4143 **S.S. Count:** 10,928
Origin: French. Cognate to the name Ray, derived from the Old French word "roy," meaning king.
Genealogies: None known.

LESLIE

Ranking: 1305 **S.S. Count:** 33,936
Origin: Scottish. Uncertain etymology. Possibly derived from the Gaelic phrase "leas celyn," meaning "court, garden of hollies" (H&H). The name was given to those from Leslie, the name of two places in Scotland.

Famous **Leslies:** ELIZA LESLIE (1787–1858) of Pennsylvania went by the nickname Betsy. She was an author and editor especially remembered for writing books on manners. Her brother, CHARLES R. LESLIE (1794–1859), born in England and raised in Pennsylvania, was an artist and author of *A Handbook for Young Painters* (1855) and *Memoirs of the Life of John Constable* (1843). FRANK LESLIE (1821–1880) of England was Henry Carter Leslie until 1857. He was the publisher of *Frank Leslie's Illustrated Newspaper.* His wife, MIRIAM FLORENCE FOLLINE LESLIE (1836–1914) of New York City, edited *Frank Leslie's Lady's Magazine* and took over his operations after his death. In 1882 she legally changed her name to Frank Leslie. AMY LESLIE (1855–1939) of Iowa was an opera singer and drama critic. She was the only female drama critic in Chicago. ANNIE LOUISE BROWN LESLIE (1869–1948) of Maine was a journalist who was better known as Nancy Brown. She wrote an advice column for the *Detroit News* that was very popular in its day.

Genealogies: *Early Leslies in York County, South Carolina* was compiled by Marion Emerson Murphy and published in San Diego, California, in 1976.

LESTER

Ranking: 683 **S.S. Count:** 61,267
Origin: English, Jewish, Scottish. Transformation of Lister.
Genealogies: *Lester, Neal, and Allied Families* was compiled by Shirley Wimpey Ward and published in Anadarko, Oklahoma, in 1987.

LEUNG

Ranking: 3570 **S.S. Count:** 12,630
Origin: Chinese. Uncertain etymology.
Genealogies: None known.

LEVERE (ALSO LEVERENTZ, LEVERENZ, LEVERETT)

Ranking: 3749 **S.S. Count:** 12,081

Origin: Leverett—English; Leverentz, Leverenz—German; Levere—Italian. Leverett: 1) transformation of the English name Lever, which was derived from the the Old French word "levre," meaning hare. The name was given to those who were considered rabbit-like or to those who hunted rabbits. 2) derived from the Middle English first name Lefred, which was derived from the Old English name Lēofrœd, comprising the components "lēof" and "rœd," meaning beloved and counsel. Leverentz, Leverenz: cognates to Lawrence. Levere: derived from the the Old French word "levre," meaning hare. The name was given to those who were considered rabbit-like or to those who hunted rabbits.

Famous **Bearers:** JOHN LEVERETT (1616–1679) of England was a colonial governor in Massachusetts, serving as a member of the Massachusetts general court and council, as the lieutenant governor, and finally as the governor until his death. His grandson, JOHN LEVERETT (1662–1724), possibly of Massachusetts, was the president of Harvard University (1707–1724). FRANK LEVERETT (1859–1943) of Iowa was a geologist and an expert on glacial deposits in the Midwest.

Genealogies: *Genealogy of William Leverett, 1773–1807* was compiled by Erwin James Otis and published in Dearborn, Michigan, in 1960.

LEVESQUE (S.S. Abbreviation: Levesq)

Ranking: 2754 **S.S. Count:** 16,530

Origin: French. Cognate to Bishop.

Genealogies: None known.

LEVIN

Ranking: 1566 **S.S. Count:** 28,497

Origin: Jewish. Derived from the Hebrew first name Levi, meaning "joining" (H&H).

Famous **Levins:** LEWIS C. LEVIN (1808–1860) of South Carolina was a member of Congress from Pennsylvania.

Genealogies: *The History and Record of the Families Levin, Garber, Rymland* was compiled by Marilyn Lane Taylor and published in Milwaukee, Wisconsin, in 1989.

LEVINE

Ranking: 710 **S.S. Count:** 59,388

Origin: Jewish. Transformation of Levin.

Famous **Levines:** LENA LEVINE (1903–1965) of New York was a physician and a pioneer in the field of birth control and marriage counseling.

Genealogies: None known.

LEVINSKY, LEVINSOHN, LEVINSON (S.S. Abbreviation: Levins)

Ranking: 3329 **S.S. Count:** 13,612

Origin: Jewish. Transformations of Levin.

Famous **Bearers:** SALMON OLIVER LEVINSON (1865–1941) of Indiana was a lawyer and peace advocate. He started the "outcry on war" movement and established the William Edgar Borah Outlawry of War Foundation at the University of Idaho.

Genealogies: None known.

LEVY

Ranking: 735 **S.S. Count:** 57,711

Origin: English, French, Jewish. English: derived from the Middle English first name Lefwi. French: derived from the Gallo-Roman first name Laevius, meaning left, and the suffix "-ācum." The name was given to those from Lévy, a place in France. Jewish: transformation of Levin.

Famous **Levys:** URIAH PHILLIPS LEVY (1792–1862) of Pennsylvania was a naval officer. He bought Thomas Jefferson's home, Monticello, and willed it to the nation. The will was contested by his heirs, however, and his wishes were left unfulfilled. JOSEPH L. LEVY (1865–1917) of England was a rabbi in California and Pennsylvania and a leader in Reform Judaism. Brothers LOUIS E. LEVY (1846–1919) of Bohemia and MAX LEVY (1857–1926) of Michigan invented the Levy halftone screen in photochemistry, which was patented in 1893. FLORENCE NIGHTINGALE LEVY (1870–1947) of New York City was an art administrator. Her most important contribution was the founding of the *American Art Annual*, which listed all of the art exhibits and art activities of each year. LIONEL FARADAY LEVY (1884–1978) of Pennsylvania was an engineer who was responsible for several inventions in the photo-engraving company he owned.

Genealogies: *Genealogy of the Goldman, Levy (et al) Families* was compiled by Douglas Edward Goldman and published in San Francisco, California, in 1978.

LEWANDOWSKI (S.S. Abbreviation: Lewand)

Ranking: 2348 **S.S. Count:** 19,328

Origin: Polish. Uncertain etymology. Possibly derived from the Polish first name Lewanda, comprising the components "leo," meaning lion, and the suffixes "-ów" and "-ski." The name was given to those from Lewandów, the name of an estate in Poland.

Genealogies: None known.

LEWIS

Ranking: 21 **S.S. Count:** 713,715

Origin: English, Irish, Jewish, Scottish, Welsh. English: derived from the Norman first names Lowis and Lowowicus, which comprise the Germanic components "hlod" and "wig," meaning fame and war. Irish, Scottish: derived from the Gaelic name Mac Lughaidh, which was derived from the first name Lugaidh, derived from Lugh, the name of a Celtic god meaning "brightness" (H&H). Jewish: transformation of Levin or an Anglicization of similar-sounding Jewish surnames. Scottish: the name was given to those from Lewis, a Hebridean island. Welsh: transformation of the Welsh name Llywelyn, which was probably derived from the word "llyw" meaning leader.

Famous **Lewises:** FRANCIS LEWIS (1713–1803) of Wales came to America in 1738. He was a New York delegate to the Continental Congress and a signer of the Declaration of Independence. ANDREW LEWIS (1720–1781) of Ireland came to America in 1732. He was an American soldier and a brigadier general in the Continental army. MORGAN LEWIS (1754–1844) of New York was a soldier, chief of staff for General Horatio Gates, chief justice of the New York Supreme Court, governor of New York, and a major general in the War of 1812. MERIWETHER LEWIS (1774–1809) of Virginia was private secretary to President Thomas Jefferson. He was appointed by Jefferson to head an expedition into the lands of the Louisiana Purchase and selected William Clark to accompany him. The Lewis and Clark expedition successfully traveled to the Pacific Ocean and brought back information on the plants and animals of the region. He served as the governor of Louisiana (1807–1809). IDA LEWIS (1842–1911) of Rhode Island was a lighthouse keeper and is remembered for her many rescues. EDMONIA LEWIS (1845–1909?) of New York was a sculptor. She was the child of a black father and a Chippewa Indian mother. Her father died when she was three, and she was raised among the Chippewas in upstate New York. Her most important work is probably a piece titled "Forever Free," which is a composition of two slaves, one man and one woman, who are overcome with emotion whem they receive the news of emancipation. ISAAC NEWTON LEWIS (1858–1931) of Pennsylvania was an army officer and inventor. Two of his inventions were an artillery position finder and a machine gun. GILBERT NEWTON LEWIS (1875–1946) of Massachusetts was a pioneer in the field of physical chemistry. JOHN LLEWELLYN LEWIS (1880–1969) of Iowa was the president of the United Mine Workers Union (1920–1960) and the Congress of Industrial Organizations (CIO) (1935–1940). TED LEWIS (1890–1971) of Ohio, a musician born Theodore Friedman, changed his name after a theater manager could not fit the name of his duo act—Lewis and Friedman—on a marquee. The marquee read instead, "Lewis & Lewis." A clarinetist, he earned the nickname Jazz King when he was playing with a quartet in New York City. SINCLAIR LEWIS (1885–1951) of Minnesota was born Harry Sinclair. He

was a journalist and author and was the first American to receive a Nobel Prize for literature. [MYRTLE] TILLIE LEWIS (1901–1977) of New York was the president of Tillie Lewis Foods, a canning business. LEON LEWIS (1904–1977) of Montana was a physician associated with Solano Laboratories at Berkeley, California. MEADE ANDERSON LEWIS (1905–1964) of Illinois went by the name Lux. He was a jazz pianist whose "Honky Tonk Train Blues" was responsible for the boogie-woogie craze that swept the nation in the late 1930s. DOUGLAS RANDOLPH LEWIS (1906–1978) of New York was the founder of Ethylene Corporation, a manufacturer of Teflon.

Genealogies: *Daybreak on Old Fortification Creek: A History of John Lewis* was compiled by Glenn Hodges and published in Hawesville, Kentucky, in 1989. *The Family of John Lewis, Pioneer* was compiled by Irvin Frazier and published in San Antonio, Texas, in 1985. *Genealogy of the James W. Lewis–Susan Clemmer Family* was compiled by Dr. Thomas Ferrell and published in Baltimore, Maryland, in 1978.

LEYVA
Ranking: 3997 **S.S. Count:** 11,314
Origin: Spanish? Uncertain etymology.
Genealogies: None known.

LI
Ranking: 3887 **S.S. Count:** 11,597
Origin: Chinese, Korean. The name means plum or black.
Genealogies: None known.

LIBBY
Ranking: 3026 **S.S. Count:** 15,034
Origin: English. Derived from the first name Elizabeth.

Famous **Libbys:** ORIN GRANT LIBBY (1864–1952) of Wisconsin was a historian whose doctoral thesis, "The Geographical Distribution of the Vote of the Thirteen States on the Federal Constitution, 1787–88," shed much light on the origins of the Constitution. WILLARD FRANK LIBBY (1908–1980) of Colorado was a chemist and a member of the Manhattan Project of World War II. He was awarded a Nobel Prize for chemistry in 1960 for his discovery of the technique of carbon-14 dating.
Genealogies: None known.

LIBERTAL, LIBERTI, LIBERTINI, LIBERTUCCI (S.S. Abbreviation: Libert)
Ranking: 4391 **S.S. Count:** 10,215
Origin: Liberti, Libertini, Libertucci—Italian; Libertal—Jewish. Liberti, Libertini, Libertucci: cognates to Albert. Libertal: transformation of Lieber.
Genealogies: None known.

LICHTENBAUM, LICHTENBERG, LICHTENFELD, LICHTENSTEIN, LICHTENTHAL (S.S. Abbreviation: Lichte)

Ranking: 2912 S.S. Count: 15,605

Origin: Jewish. Derived from the German words "licht," meaning light combined with "baum," meaning tree; "berg," meaning hill; "feld," meaning field; "stein," meaning stone; and "thal," meaning valley. These names were all taken ornamentally.

Genealogies: None known.

LIEBER (ALSO LIEBERMAN, LIEBERMANN, LIEBERMENSCH, LIEBERSON)

Ranking: 2025 S.S. Count: 22,588

Origin: Lieber, Liebermann—German, Jewish; Lieberman—Jewish; Liebermensch—Jewish; Lieberson—Jewish. Derived from the German word "lieb" or the Yiddish word "lib," meaning beloved or dear and, in the case of the compounds, man, "mensch," meaning person, and son. The name was given to those who were amiable.

Famous **Bearers**: FRANCIS LIEBER (1800–1872), born in Germany, was one of the premier political scientists of his time. He was a professor in South Carolina and New York and the author of highly authoritative works, such as *On Civil Liberty and Self-Government* (1853).

Genealogies: None known.

LIGHT

Ranking: 1957 S.S. Count: 23,162

Origin: English. 1) derived from the Old English word "lȳt," meaning little. The name was given to those who were small in stature. 2) derived from the Old English word "lēoht," meaning light (in color) and cheerful. The name was given to those who were of a cheerful disposition. 3) derived from the Old English word "lioht," meaning light (in weight) and quick. The name was given to those who were agile and quick.

Genealogies: *The Light Genealogy in America* was compiled by Moses Light and published in Manheim, Pennsylvania, in 1896.

LIGHTFOOT (S.S. Abbreviation: Lightf)

Ranking: 3456 S.S. Count: 13,065

Origin: English. Derived from the Middle English words "lyght" and "fote," meaning light, as in agile and quick, and foot. The name was given to fast runners.

Genealogies: *The Descendants of Samuel Lightfoot and Rachel Milhous* was compiled by Dorothy Z. Milhous and published in El Monte, California, in 1966. *The History of the Lightfoot and Shirley Families* was compiled by Annie Lightfoot Leith and published in Tampa, Florida, in 1975.

LILES

Ranking: 3079 S.S. Count: 14,762

Origin: English. Uncertain etymology. The name was given to those who lived on an island.

Genealogies: None known.

LILLEY

Ranking: 4042 S.S. Count: 11,200

Origin: English. 1) derived from the Old English word "lilie," meaning lily. The name was given to those with pale hair or skin. 2) derived from the first name Elizabeth. 3) Uncertain etymology. The name was given to those from Lilley, the name of places in England.

Genealogies: None known.

LILLY

Ranking: 1503 S.S. Count: 29,647

Origin: English. Transformation of Lilley.

Famous **Lillys**: JOSIAH KIRBY LILLY (1861–1948) of Indiana was president of the family business known as Eli Lilly and Company, pharmaceutical manufacturers. ELI LILLY (1885–1977) of Indiana inherited the family business started by his grandfather, but he advanced the company by production improvements, time and motion studies, straight line production, and economical lot-size determination. He and his brother started an employee incentive program and suggestion system. The company was responsible for insulin production. THEODORE E. LILLY (1896–1974) of Virginia was a surgical assistant during World War I, then a commissioned officer (major) in World War II, during which he served as chief dental service instructor at several air bases. He also was a prominent dentist in Ohio, where he was active in community service.

Genealogies: *The Lilly Letter* was published in Carbondale, Colorado, in 1977.

LIM

Ranking: 2662 S.S. Count: 17,118

Origin: Chinese?, Korean? Uncertain etymology.

Genealogies: None known.

LIMA

Ranking: 4442 S.S. Count: 10,093

Origin: Portuguese. The name was given to those from the area along the river called Lima. The name was probably of Celtic origin.

Genealogies: None known.

LIN

Ranking: 2355 S.S. Count: 19,245

Origin: Chinese. The name means forest.

Genealogies: None known.

LINCOLN (S.S. Abbreviation: Lincol)

Ranking: 2042 S.S. Count: 22,380

Origin: English. Derived from the British name Lindo, meaning lake, and the Latin word "colōnia," meaning settlement or colony. The name was given to those from Lincoln, a place in England.

Famous **Lincolns:** BENJAMIN LINCOLN (1733–1810) of Massachusetts was a Revolutionary War officer and commander of the troops that suppressed Shays' Rebellion in 1787. LEVI LINCOLN (1749–1820) of Massachusetts was a lawyer and U.S. attorney general who turned down a seat on the U.S. Supreme Court because of failing eyesight. His son, LEVI LINCOLN (1782–1868) of Massachusetts, was governor of Massachusetts, then a member of Congress. ENOCH LINCOLN (1788–1829) of Massachusetts was a member of Congress for the Maine District of Massachusetts, then governor of the state of Maine. ABRAHAM LINCOLN (1809–1865) of Kentucky was the 16th president of the United States. He was elected on an antislavery platform. He issued the Emancipation Proclamation on January 1, 1863, and delivered the Gettysburg Address on November 19, 1863. After being reelected in 1864, he was shot by John Wilkes Booth in Ford's Theater in Washington, D.C., on April 14, 1865. He died the following day. MARY ANN TODD LINCOLN (1818–1882) of Kentucky was the wife of Abraham Lincoln. ROBERT TODD LINCOLN (1843–1926) of Illinois was the U.S. secretary of war, a minister to Great Britain, and the president of the Pullman Co. He also was Abraham Lincoln's son. MARY JOHNSON BAILEY LINCOLN (1844–1921) of Massachusetts was a teacher, writer, and lecturer on cooking. Her *Boston Cook Book* was a bestseller.

Genealogies: *The Ancestry of Abraham Lincoln* was compiled by J. Henry Lea and published in Boston, Massachusetts, in 1909. *The Carrier-Carryer (also Lincoln) and Allied Lines* was compiled by Georgie Carrier Early Armentrout and published in Baltimore, Maryland, in 1985. *The Pioneer and the Prairie Lawyer: Boone and Lincoln Family* was compiled by Willard Mounts and published in Denver, Colorado, in 1992. *Thomas Lincoln of Taunton, and Joseph Kellogg of Hadley, and 144 Related Colonial Families* was compiled by Ruth Lincoln Kaye and published in 1973.

LIND

Ranking: 1992 S.S. Count: 22,764

Origin: Danish, Jewish, Swedish. Danish, Swedish: derived from the Old High German word "linta," meaning lime tree. The name was given to those who lived near a lime tree. Jewish: derived from the German word "linde," meaning lime tree. The name was taken ornamentally.

Famous **Linds:** JOHN LIND (1854–1930) of Sweden was a member of Congress from Minnesota, then governor of Minnesota. He also worked for President Woodrow Wilson to help overthrow the Huerta government in Mexico in 1913.

Genealogies: *Looking Backward to Sweden* was compiled by Marilyn Lind and published in Cloquet, Minnesota, in 1986.

LINDBERG, LINDBERGH (S.S. Abbreviation: Lindbe)

Ranking: 2859 S.S. Count: 15,964

Origin: Swedish. Transformation of Lind combined with "berg(h)," meaning hill. The names were taken ornamentally.

Famous **Bearers:** CHARLES AUGUSTUS LINDBERGH (1902–1974) of Michigan was a pilot and the first to make a solo nonstop flight across the Atlantic Ocean. In 1930 he and Alexis Carrel, a physiologist, devised a system to keep human organs alive outside the body. A 1938 book, *Culture of Organs*, details the system. His autobiography, *The Spirit of St. Louis*, in 1953 won him a Pulitzer Prize.

Genealogies: *Prairie Memories: (Lindberg, Lindbergh families)* was compiled by Algot R. Swanson and published in Tucson, Arizona, in 1974. *Yesterday, a History of Norwegian Ancestry (Lindberg family)* was compiled by Evelyn Hoff and published in Winona, Minnesota, in 1985.

LINDEMAN, LINDEMANN (S.S. Abbreviation: Lindem)

Ranking: 2949 S.S. Count: 15,448

Origin: Lindeman—Danish, Dutch, Flemish, Jewish; Lindemann—German. Cognates to and transformations of Lind.

Famous **Bearers:** EDUARD C. LINDEMAN (1885–1953) of Michigan was instrumental in developing the field of adult education.

Genealogies: None known.

LINDEN (ALSO LINDENBAUM, LINDENBERG, LINDENFELD, LINDENMAN)

Ranking: 2470 S.S. Count: 18,378

Origin: Linden—Dutch, Flemish, German, Swedish; Lindenbaum—German, Jewish; Lindenberg—Jewish; Lindenfeld—Jewish; Lindenman—Jewish. Linden: transformations of and cognates to Lind, combined with words meaning tree, hill, field and man

Genealogies: None known.

LINDER (ALSO LINDERMANN, LINDEROTH, LINDERS)

Ranking: 1718 S.S. Count: 26,059

Origin: Linder—English, German, Swedish; Lindermann—German; Linderoth—Jewish; Linders—Flemish. Linder: cognate to and transformation of Lind. Lindermann: transformation of Lind. Linderoth: cognate to and transfor-

mation of Lind. The name was taken ornamentally. Linders: cognate to the English name Leonard.

Genealogies: *The Linder Family* was compiled by Penny Linder and published in Morgantown, West Virginia, in 1991.

LINDGREN (S.S. Abbreviation: Lindgr)

Ranking: 4027 S.S. Count: 11,242

Origin: Swedish. Transformation of Lind combined with the word "gren," meaning branch. The name was taken ornamentally.

Famous **Lindgrens:** WALDEMAR LINDGREN (1860–1939) of Sweden was a geologist with the U.S. Geological Survey. He was an authority on igneous rocks and wrote *Mineral Deposits*, which became a standard in the geology classroom.

Genealogies: None known.

LINDLEY (S.S. Abbreviation: Lindle)

Ranking: 2785 S.S. Count: 16,373

Origin: English. 1) derived from the Old English words "lind" and "lēah," meaning lime tree and wood. The name was given to those from Lindley, a place in West Yorkshire, England. 2) derived from the Old English words "lin" and "lēah," meaning flax and wood or clearing. The name was given to those from Lindley, another place in West Yorkshire, or to those from Linley, the name of several places in England.

Famous **Lindleys:** JACOB LINDLEY (1774–1857) of Pennsylvania was one of the founders of Ohio State University. DANIEL LINDLEY (1801–1880) of Pennsylvania was a Presbyterian missionary to South Africa. CURTIS H. LINDLEY (1850–1920) of California was a lawyer who was an authority on the law of mines and minerals.

Genealogies: *Jacob Marion Lindley* was compiled by Milam Myrl Ewing and published in Tulsa, Oklahoma, in 1978. *The Lindlys (also Lindley) and Allied Families* was compiled by Horace Lindly and published in Colby, Kansas, in 1970.

LINDNER (S.S. Abbreviation: Lindne)

Ranking: 4304 S.S. Count: 10,427

Origin: German. Transformation of Lind.

Genealogies: *The Lindner & McCarthy Families of Hoboken, Newark, and Elizabethport, New Jersey* was compiled by Florence Lindner McCarthy and published in Baltimore, Maryland, in 1988.

LINDQUIST (S.S. Abbreviation: Lindqu)

Ranking: 2646 S.S. Count: 17,196

Origin: Swedish. Cognate to Lind combined with the word "quist," meaning twig. The name was taken ornamentally.

Genealogies: None known.

LINDSAY (S.S. Abbreviation: Lindsa)

Ranking: 919 S.S. Count: 46,899

Origin: English, Irish, Scottish. English: the name was given to those from Lindsey, a place in Suffolk that was called Lelleseg in Old English, meaning "island of Lelli" (H&H). English, Scottish: derived from the British name Lincoln and the Old English component "ēg," meaning island. The name was given to those from Lindsey, a place in Lincolnshire, England. Irish: derived from various Gaelic names, including Ó Loingsigh, Ó Floinn, and Mac Giolla Fhionntóg.

Famous **Lindsays:** WILLIAM LINDSAY (1835–1909) of Virginia was a U.S. senator from Kentucky. NICHOLAS VACHEL LINDSAY (1879–1931) of Illinois was a poet. He wrote several volumes of poetry. HOWARD LINDSAY (1889–1968) of New York was a playwright, producer, and actor. He co-wrote *The Sound of Music* in 1959.

Genealogies: *The Albemarle Lindseys (also Lindsay) and their Descendants* was compiled by Gordon C. Jones and published in Chesapeake, Virginia, in 1979. *The Descendants of 1. Thomas John Weston Lindsey (also Lindsay) and Mary Kaala Fay and the Descendants of 2. George Kynaston Lindsey (also Lindsay)* was compiled by John Vincent Duey and published in Wailuku, Hawaii, in 1983. *Grandpas, Inlaws, and Outlaws: (a Lindsay Family Genealogy)* was compiled by Kenneth Gene Lindsay and published in Evansville, Indiana, in 1976.

LINDSEY (S.S. Abbreviation: Lindse)

Ranking: 470 S.S. Count: 85,285

Origin: English, Irish, Scottish. Transformation of Lindsay.

Famous **Lindseys:** BENJAMIN BARR LINDSEY (1869–1943) of Tennessee was a jurist and the author of the statute establishing the first juvenile court of the United States in Denver, Colorado. He was responsible for the laws that were established to help youthful offenders, rather than punish them.

Genealogies: *The Albemarle Lindseys and their Descendants* was compiled by Gordon C. Jones and published in Chesapeake, Virginia, in 1979. *The Descendants of 1. Thomas John Weston Lindsey and Mary Kaala Fay and the Descendants of 2. George Kynaston Lindsey* was compiled by John Vincent Duey and published in Wailuku, Hawaii, in 1983. *The Lindseys* was compiled by Ferrell A. Brown and published in Point Lookout, Missouri, in 1970.

LINDSTRAND, LINDSTROM (S.S. Abbreviation: Lindst)

Ranking: 2764 S.S. Count: 16,494

Origin: Swedish. Transformation of Lind combined with the word "strand," meaning shore, and "strom," meaning river. The names were taken ornamentally.

Genealogies: None known.

LING

Ranking: 4794 S.S. Count: 9343

Origin: Chinese, English. Chinese: the name means forest. English: Uncertain etymology. The name was given to those from Lyng, a place in Norfolk, England.

Genealogies: *Ling Surname Index* was compiled by Calvin H. Ling and published in Santa Clara, California, in 1979.

LINK

Ranking: 1479 S.S. Count: 30,135

Origin: English, German, Jewish. English: transformation of the Irish name Lynch, which was derived from the Gaelic name Linseach, which was derived from the Anglo-Norman-French name de Lench. German, Jewish: derived from the German word "linke," meaning left hand. The name was given to those who were left-handed.

Famous **Links:** HENRY C. LINK (1889–1952) of New York was a pioneer in the field of industrial psychology and the author of books such as *Employment Psychology* (1919).

Genealogies: None known.

LINN

Ranking: 2505 S.S. Count: 18,104

Origin: English, Irish, Jewish, Scottish. Transformation of Lynn.

Famous **Linns:** LEWIS F. LINN (1795–1843) of Kentucky was a physician who became an authority on Asiatic cholera. He also was a U.S. senator from Missouri. WILLIAM A. LINN (1846–1917) of New Jersey was editor of the New York *Evening Post*, a newspaper celebrated for the reliability of its news under his leadership.

Genealogies: None known.

LINTON

Ranking: 2414 S.S. Count: 18,779

Origin: English, Scottish. Derived from various first components, including the Old English word "lind," meaning lime tree, and "lin," meaning flax, and the Old English second component "tūn," meaning settlement. The name was given to those from Linton, the name of several places in England and Scotland.

Famous **Lintons:** WILLIAM JAMES LINTON (1812–1897) of England was a wood engraver, reformer, and writer. He wrote several books and had printing presses in New Haven, Connecticut, where he printed *Frank Leslie's Illustrated Newspaper*. His wife, ELIZA LYNN LINTON (1822–1898), birthplace unknown, was a novelist whose works included *Joshua Davidson* (1872). RALPH LINTON (1893–1953) of Pennsylvania was an anthropologist and a pioneer in the field of cultural anthropology. WILLIAM C. LINTON (1888–1977) of Washington, D.C., was a patent attorney and the founder of Fuse Indicator Corporation of Maryland.

Genealogies: *The Linton Heritage, 1637–1981* was compiled by Calvin R. Linton and published in Decorah, Iowa, in 1981. *Some Earlier Americans: Boles-Linton Ancestors* was compiled by Harold W. Boles and published in Kalamazoo, Michigan, in 1986.

LINVILL, LINVILLE (S.S. Abbreviation: Linvil)

Ranking: 4211 S.S. Count: 10,729

Origin: French. Uncertain etymology. The name was given to those from Linivilla, a former place in France.

Genealogies: *The Linville Family in America* was compiled by Alice Eichholz and published in Baltimore, Maryland, in 1982.

LIPSCOMB, LIPSCOMBE (S.S. Abbreviation: Lipsco)

Ranking: 2377 S.S. Count: 19,117

Origin: English. The name was given to those from Letcomb, meaning "ledge in the valley" (ES), or to those from Liscombe, meaning "enclosed valley" (ES). Both are places in England.

Famous **Bearers:** ABNER S. LIPSCOMB (1789–1856) of South Carolina was instrumental in writing the Texas constitution. He later became a justice of the Texas Supreme Court.

Genealogies: *Lipscomb, 300 Years in America* was compiled by Dorothy Garr Helmer and published in Indianapolis, Indiana, in 1979.

LISTER

Ranking: 3960 S.S. Count: 11,422

Origin: English, Jewish, Scottish. English: derived from the Middle English word "litster," meaning dyer. The name was given to dyers. Jewish: etymology unknown. Scottish: derived from the Gaelic name Mac an Fleisdeir, meaning "son of the arrow-maker" (H&H).

Genealogies: None known.

LITTLE (ALSO LITTLEFIELD, LITTLEFORD, LITTLEJOHN, LITTLETON)

Ranking: 161 S.S. Count: 202,588

Origin: Little—English, Irish: Littlefield—English; Littleford—English; Littlejohn—English, Scottish; Littleton—English. Little (English): derived from the Middle English word "littel," meaning little. The name was given to those who were small in stature or to the younger of two persons bearing the same first name. Irish: derived from an Old Norse word meaning strong and big. Littlefield: derived from the Middle English word "littel," meaning little, and the Old English word "feld," meaning field. The name was given to those who lived near a small field in a wood. Littleford: derived from the Old English words "lȳtel" and "ford," meaning little and ford. The name was given to those from Littleford, a former place in England. Littlejohn: the name was given to someone whose first name was John, in order to distinguish him from one or more other persons also called John. Littleton: derived from the Old English words "lӯtel" and "tūn," meaning little and settlement. The name was given to those from Littleton, the name of several places in England.

Famous **Bearers:** CHARLES COFFIN LITTLE (1799–1869) of Maine was a publisher of legal and general works in the firm of Little, Brown & Co. ARTHUR DEHON LITTLE (1863–1935) of Massachusetts was a chemical engineer who invented processes used in the making of chlorates and artificial silk. HENRY (TED) LITTLE (1901–1974) of New York, as president of Campbell-Ewald Co. in Detroit, Michigan, oversaw the advertising account of Chevrolet during the period from 1945 to 1966. WILLIAM L. LITTLE JR. (1910–1968) of Rhode Island was a golfer who won 31 amateur championships, then won the Canadian and U.S. Open tournaments as a professional. Nicknamed Cannonball, he was inducted into the Professional Golfers Hall of Fame in 1961.

Genealogies: *The Little Family: Ancestors and Descendants of Jonas Little Pioneer Settler to Tennessee* was compiled by Dessie Little Simmons and published in Johnson City, Tennessee, in 1975. *A Geneology [sic] of the Little-Odom Family of Georgia and North Carolina* was compiled by Lawrence L. Little and published in Creve Coeur, Missouri, in 1974.

LIU

Ranking: 2678 **S.S. Count:** 17,036
Origin: Chinese. The name means willow and battle-axe.
Genealogies: None known.

LIVELY

Ranking: 3066 **S.S. Count:** 14,810
Origin: English. 1) Uncertain etymology. The name was given to those who were lively or energetic. 2) uncertain etymology. Possibly a transformation of Livesley, which is a transformation of Livesey. 3) derived from the Old Norse word "hlíf," meaning refuge, and the Old English word "ēg," meaning island.
Genealogies: None known.

LIVINGSTON, LIVINGSTONE (S.S. Abbreviation: Living)

Ranking: 657 **S.S. Count:** 63,692
Origin: Livingston—Irish, Jewish, Scottish; Livingstone—Irish, Jewish, Scottish. Irish: derived from the Gaelic names Ó Duinnshléibhe and Mac Duinnshléibhe, which are derived from the first name Duinnsliabh, comprising the components "donn" and "sliabh," meaning brown and mountain. Jewish: derived from the Jewish name Löwenstein. Scottish: the name was given to those from Livingstone, a place in England, the name of which was derived from the Old English first name Lēofwine, comprising the components "lēof" and "wine," meaning beloved or dear and friend.

Famous **Bearers:** ROBERT LIVINGSTON (1654–1728) of Scotland came to America and settled in Albany, New York. He was the secretary of Indian Affairs and a member of the New York provincial assembly. PHILLIP LIVINGSTON (1716–1778) of New York was a merchant and was one of the founders of the university that became Columbia. He was a member of the Continental Congress and one of the signers of the Declaration of Independence. WILLIAM LIVINGSTON (1723–1790) of New York was a member of the Continental Congress and served as the governor of New Jersey. He was a delegate to the Constitutional Convention and a signer of the Constitution. ROBERT R. LIVINGSTON (1746–1813) of New York City was a member of the Continental Congress and one of the five who drew up the Declaration of Independence. He administered the oath of office to President George Washington. His son, EDWARD LIVINGSTON (1764–1836) of New York, moved to New Orleans, where he drew up the Louisiana legal code. He was a member of Congress and a senator from Louisiana, U.S. secretary of state, and minister to France. HENRY BROCKHOLST LIVINGSTON (1757–1823) of New York City served in the Revolutionary army and was an associate justice of the U.S. Supreme Court. BURTON E. LIVINGSTON (1875–1948) of Michigan was a plant physiology professor whose studies shed light on the effect of the environment and climate on vegetation. MILTON STANLEY LIVINGSTON (1905–1986) of Wisconsin was a physicist and the developer of the first atom-smashing device.

Genealogies: *A Biographical History of Clermont, or Livingston Manor* was compiled by Thomas Streatfeild Clarkson and published in Clermont, New York, in 1869.

LLOYD

Ranking: 465 **S.S. Count:** 85,819
Origin: Welsh. Derived from the Welsh word "llwyd," meaning gray. The name was given to those who wore gray or whose hair was gray.

Famous **Lloyds:** EDWARD LLOYD (1779–1834) of Maryland was a member of Congress from, governor of, and U.S. senator from Maryland. HENRY DEMAREST LLOYD (1847–1903) of New York City was a journalist. He was a staff member of the Chicago *Tribune* and is considered one of the first muckrakers. JOHN U. LLOYD (1849–1936) of New York was a pharmacist and chemist who also wrote novels, including *Stringtown on the Pike* (1900). MARSHALL B. LLOYD (1858–1927) of Minnesota invented machinery used to weave wire and wicker. ALICE SPENCER GEDDES LLOYD (1876–1962) of Massachusetts was an educator.She moved to the Kentucky hills, where she founded Caney Junior College. After her death the name of the college was changed to Alice Lloyd College. HAROLD CLAYTON LLOYD (1894–1971) of Nebraska was an actor and producer. He portrayed the little man with glasses and a straw hat in many movies, including *Just Nuts* and *The Kid Brother*. JAMES TURNER LLOYD JR. (1900–1976) of Arkansas was one of the founders of TALO, a sporting goods co-op, which founded Telesport, Inc., a TV production firm that produces "Bill Dance Outdoors." WESLEY PARKINSON LLOYD (1904–1977) of Utah was world renowned as an educator at the college level.

Genealogies: *John and Prudence Lloyd* was compiled by Oliver C. Weaver and published in Birmingham, Alabama, in 1990. *The Lloyds of Southern Maryland* was compiled by Daniel Boone Lloyd and published in 1971.

LOCK

Ranking: 4744 **S.S. Count:** 9441
Origin: English, Scottish. English: 1) derived from the Old English and Old High German word "loc," meaning lock or curl. The name was given to those with thin or fine hair. 2) derived from the Old English word "loc," meaning lock. The name was given to locksmiths. 3) derived from the Old English word "loca," meaning enclosure, which was derived from the Old English word "loc," meaning lock. The name was given to those who lived near an area that was locked. English, Scottish: transformation of Lucas.
Genealogies: None known.

LOCKART (S.S. Abbreviation: Lockar)

Ranking: 4755 **S.S. Count:** 9422
Origin: Scottish. Transformation of Lockhart.
Genealogies: None known.

LOCKE

Ranking: 1168 **S.S. Count:** 37,456
Origin: English. Derived from the Old English word "loc," meaning lock. The name was given to locksmiths.
Famous **Lockes:** JOHN LOCKE (1792–1856) of New Hampshire, a doctor and scientist, invented many instruments used in geological surveying, including the electromagnetic chronograph used to determine longitudes. RICHARD ADAMS LOCKE (1800–1871) of England was a journalist on the staff of the *New York Sun*. He wrote "Moon Hoax," a popular story about discovering men and animals on the moon. DAVID ROSS LOCKE (1833–1888) of New York was a journalist with the pseudonym Petroleum Vesuvius Nasby. He was known for politicial satire and was popular on the lecture circuit. BESSIE LOCKE (1865–1952) of Massachusetts helped to establish more than 3200 kindergartens in the United States. She also was an organizer, then director and executive director, of the National Kindergarten Association. ALAIN LEROY LOCKE (1886–1954) of Pennsylvania was the first black Rhodes

scholar. He encouraged many black artisans and is responsible for the Harlem Renaissance. He wrote many books on African-American art and history in the United States.

Genealogies: *Locke Genealogy* was compiled by Donald P. Hayes and published in Ann Arbor, Michigan, in 1979.

LOCKET (ALSO LOCKETT)

Ranking: 2349 **S.S. Count:** 19,327
Origin: Scottish. Transformation of Lucas.
Genealogies: None known.

LOCKHART (S.S. Abbreviation: Lockha)

Ranking: 1189 **S.S. Count:** 36,833
Origin: Scottish. Uncertain etymology. Most likely derived from a Germanic first name comprising the components "loc" and "hardy," meaning lock and brave or hardy.
Famous **Lockharts:** CHARLES LOCKHART (1818–1905) of Scotland emigrated to the United States and developed a substantial oil business. He built the first major oil refinery and was an early partner in Standard Oil.

Genealogies: *A Lockhart Family in America* was compiled by Anna May Cochrane Gregath and published in 1972.

LOCKLEY (S.S. Abbreviation: Lockle)

Ranking: 2069 **S.S. Count:** 22,166
Origin: English. Derived from the Old English words "loca" and "lēah," meaning enclosure and clearing. Possibly the name was given to those from Lockleywood, a place in Shropshire, England.
Genealogies: None known.

LOCKWOOD (S.S. Abbreviation: Lockwo)

Ranking: 1570 **S.S. Count:** 28,430
Origin: English. Most likely derived from the Old English words "loca" and "wudu," meaning enclosure and wood. The name was given to those from Lockwood, a place in West Yorkshire, England.
Famous **Lockwoods:** RALPH INGERSOLL LOCKWOOD (1798–1858?) of Connecticut was a lawyer who also wrote novels, including *The Insurgents* (1835). BELVA ANN BENNETT LOCKWOOD (1830–1917) of New York was the first woman admitted to practice law before the U.S. Supreme Court (1879). A leader in women's rights, she was nominated by the National Equal Rights Party for president in 1884 and 1888. JAMES B. LOCKWOOD (1852–1884) of Maryland was an Arctic explorer.

Genealogies: *Some Descendants of Edmund Lockwood (1594–1635) of Cambridge, Massachusetts* was compiled by Harriet Woodbury Hodge and published in New York in 1978. *Descendants of Phebe Walters & Isaak Lockwood* was compiled by Nancy Hawlick Stein and published in Wilmette, Illinois, in 1979.

LOFTIN

Ranking: 4654 S.S. Count: 9608
Origin: English? Uncertain etymology. Possibly a transformation of Lofton.
Genealogies: None known.

LOFTIS

Ranking: 4766 S.S. Count: 9389
Origin: English. Transformation of Loftus.
Genealogies: *The Ancestors and Descendants of John Joseph Loftis and Laura May Wolf(e)* was compiled by Sandi Loftis Komosinski and published in Grand Haven, Michigan, in 1983.

LOFTON

Ranking: 2632 S.S. Count: 17,294
Origin: The name was given to those from Lufton, a place in Somerset, England.
Genealogies: None known.

LOFTUS

Ranking: 4015 S.S. Count: 11,275
Origin: English, Irish. English: derived from the Old Norse words "lopt" and "hús," meaning loft or upper level and house. The name was given to those from places in England called Loftus, or Lofthouse, or Loftsome. Irish: derived from the Gaelic names Ó Lachtnáin, which was derived from the first name Lochlann, meaning stranger, and Ó Lochlainn, which was derived from the first name Lachtnán, which was derived from the word "lachtna," meaning gray.
Famous **Loftuses:** CISSIE LOFTUS (1878–1943) of Scotland was an actress and an impersonator. She appeared in the United States in vaudeville.
Genealogies: *The Ancestors and Descendants of John Joseph Loftis [also Loftus] and Laura May Wolf[e]* was compiled by Sandi Loftis Komosinski and published in Grand Haven, Michigan, in 1983.

LOGAN

Ranking: 434 S.S. Count: 91,427
Origin: Irish, Scottish. Irish: derived from the Gaelic name Ó Leocháin, which was derived from the first name Leochán. Irish, Scottish: derived from the Gaelic word "lag," meaning hollow. The name was given to those from Logan, the name of several places in Scotland and Ireland.
Famous **Logans:** JAMES LOGAN (1674–1751) was born in Ireland to Scottish parents. He came to America in 1699 to serve as William Penn's secretary. He served as the mayor of Philadelphia and as chief justice of the Pennsylvania Supreme Court. MARTHA DANIELL LOGAN (1704–1779) of South Carolina was a colonial teacher and gardener. She is best remembered for her horticulture skills and was the "Lady of this Province" who wrote the "Gardener's Kalen-

dar" that was published in the *South Carolina Almanack* for 1752. JAMES LOGAN (1725?–1780) of Pennsylvania was an American Indian leader who had the Indian name Tahgahjute. He befriended the white settlers until his family was massacred in 1774, after which time he sided with the British. GEORGE LOGAN (1753–1821) of Pennsylvania took it upon himself to attempt to smooth relations between the United States and France. His actions were met with disapproval by the U.S. government and prompted the passage of the Logan Act of 1799, which forbids a private citizen from engaging in diplomacy without government approval. He then served as a U.S. senator from Pennsylvania (1801–1807). DEBORAH NORRIS LOGAN (1761–1839) of Pennsylvania was a collector of historical records. It is said that she lived two doors away from the state house in Philadelphia and, at the age of 14, stood on the garden fence to hear the first public reading of the Declaration of Independence, on July 8, 1776. She was related either by blood or marriage to nearly every leading Pennsylvania political figure of the day. In her home she discovered correspondence between William Penn and James Logan, the grandfather of her husband. The letters were in a state of disrepair, so she copied all of the letters and then presented them to the American Philosophical Society, which published them under the title *Memoir*. She is considered one of America's first historians. JOHN ALEXANDER LOGAN (1826–1886) of Illinois was a soldier in the Civil War and one of the founders of the Grand Army of the Republic. He also was the founder of Memorial Day. He was a member of Congress and a senator and the vice presidential candidate in 1884 on a ticket with James G. Blaine. His wife, MARY SIMMERSON CUNNINGHAM LOGAN (1838–1923) of Missouri, was the one who had made the suggestion to him that a day be set aside to decorate the graves of the Union heroes. After her husband's death, she wrote books and magazine articles. OLIVE LOGAN (1839–1909) of New York was an actress, lecturer, and book author; theater stories were some of her best. THOMAS M. LOGAN (1840–1914) of South Carolina developed the railway system that became known as Southern Railway. JAMES HARVEY LOGAN (1841–1928) of Indiana was a lawyer and horticulturist who is best remembered for producing in 1881 a new type of berry that was named the loganberry.
Genealogies: *Historic Families of Kentucky* was compiled by Thomas Marshall Green and published in Baltimore, Maryland, in 1982. *Those Who Have Gone Before* was compiled by Miriam Halbert Bales and published in Muncie, Indiana, in 1976.

LOGSDON, LOGSDEN (S.S. Abbreviation: Logsdo)

Ranking: 3263 S.S. Count: 13,940
Origin: English. Derived from the Old English name Long

and "dūn," meaning hill. The name was given to those from Longsdon or Longstone, the name of places in England.

Genealogies: *Durbin and Logsdon Genealogy with Related Families* was compiled by Betty Jewell Durbin Carson and published in Bowie, Maryland, in 1991. *Logsdons, Roots and Branches* was compiled by Mattie T. Logsdon and published in Ada, Oklahoma, in 1978.

LOGUE
Ranking: 4096 **S.S. Count:** 11,029
Origin: Irish. Derived from the Gaelic name Ó Maol Mhaodhóg, meaning "descendant of the devotee of (St.) Maodhóg" (H&H).
Genealogies: *John Logue of North Carolina* was compiled by Jane Gray Buchanan and published in Oak Ridge, Tennessee, in 1980.

LOHMAN
Ranking: 4884 **S.S. Count:** 9157
Origin: German. Uncertain etymology. The name was given to those from Lohe, the name of several places in Germany, or to those who lived in a wood.
Famous Lohmans: ANN TROW LOHMAN (1812–1878) of England was a notorious New York City abortionist. She practiced under the name Madame Restell and had several encounters with the law.
Genealogies: None known.

LOHR
Ranking: 4712 **S.S. Count:** 9499
Origin: German. Uncertain etymology. The name was given to tanners or to those from Lohr, the name of several places in Germany.
Genealogies: *The Lehr* [also Lohr] *Family* was compiled by Stephen J. Kennedy and published in Needham Heights, Massachusetts, in 1978.

LOMAX
Ranking: 3330 **S.S. Count:** 13,609
Origin: English. Derived from the Old English components "lumm" and "halh," meaning pool and recess or hollow. The name was given to those from Lomac, a place in Lancashire, England.
Famous Lomaxes: JOHN T. LOMAX (1781–1862) of Virginia was the first law professor at the University of Virginia. LUNSFORD L. LOMAX (1835–1913) was a Confederate general and later president of Virginia Agricultural and Mechanical College. His compilation of both Union and Confederate army records was published as *War of the Rebellion* (1885–1899). JOHN AVERY LOMAX (1867–1948) of Mississippi was a folklorist. He collected well over 10,000 folk songs and ballads for the Library of Congress. LOUIS EMANUEL LOMAX (1922–1970) of Georgia, a journalist and

author, was the first African-American television news reporter (1958). He was an author of books on black history, including *The Reluctant African* (1960) and *To Kill a Black Man* (1968).
Genealogies: *Samuel Lomax and his Descendants* was compiled by John B. Lomax and published in Menlo Park, California, in 1991.

LOMBARD, LOMBARDI, LOMBARDO, LOMBARDY
Ranking: 847 **S.S. Count:** 50,393
Origin: Lombard—English, French, Irish, Scottish; Lombardi, Lombardo—Italian; Lombardy—French. The name was given to those from Lombardy, a region of Italy whose name is comprised of components meaning long and beard. The name was given to bankers or money lenders and to Italian immigrants, many of whom were bankers.
Famous Bearers: GUY LOMBARDO (1902–1977) of Canada was a bandleader. Although his band was called the Royal Canadians, he was a U.S. citizen. His New Year's Eve broadcasts became an American tradition, with his music touted as "the sweetest music this side of heaven." CAROLE LOMBARD (1908–1942) of Indiana was a film actress who was married to Clark Gable. She died in a plane crash. VINCENT THOMAS LOMBARDI (1913–1970) of New York was known as Vince. As a football player at Fordham University, he was one of the "Seven Blocks of Granite." As a football coach, he led the Green Bay Packers to five National Football League championships and two Super Bowls.
Genealogies: None known.

LONDON
Ranking: 2121 **S.S. Count:** 21,600
Origin: English, Jewish. English: uncertain etymology. The name was given to Londoners or to those who travelled to London. Jewish: uncertain etymology.
Famous Londons: MEYER LONDON (1871–1926) of Poland was the founder of the Socialist Party in America. He was also a member of Congress. JOHN GRIFFITH LONDON (1876–1916) of California was known as Jack. He was a novelist who wrote 50 books, including *The Call of the Wild* (1903) and *White Fang* (1906).
Genealogies: *200 Years of the London Family in America* was compiled by Opal London Cox and published in Enid, Oklahoma, in 1976. *A Genealogical History of One Branch of the London Family in America Since 1636* was compiled by Hoyt H. London and published in Columbia, Missouri, in 1976.

LONG
Ranking: 81 **S.S. Count:** 322,969
Origin: English, Irish. English: derived from the Old English word "lang" or "long," meaning long or tall. The name

was given to those who were tall. Irish: derived from the Gaelic name Ó Longáin, which was most likely derived from "long," meaning tall.

Famous **Longs**: STEPHEN HARRIMAN LONG (1784–1864) of New Hampshire was an explorer and army officer. He explored the northern United States and was the discoverer of Longs Peak in Colorado. JAMES LONG (1793?–1822), possibly of North Carolina, was an adventurer who went to Texas and formed a republic with himself as president. He was captured and killed in Mexico City. CRAWFORD WILLIAMSON LONG (1815–1878) of Georgia was a physician and the first to use ether as an anesthetic. ARMISTEAD L. LONG (1825–1891) of Virginia was a Confederate general who was military secretary to Robert E. Lee for two years. His book, *Memoirs of Robert E. Lee* (1886), is an authoritative reference. JOHN HARPER LONG (1856–1918) of Ohio was a chemist who wrote a number of textbooks and scientific papers. JOHN LUTHER LONG (1861–1927) of Pennsylvania was a writer. He was the author of the short story "Madame Butterfly," which was adapted for the stage and made into an opera. HUEY PIERCE LONG (1893–1935) of Louisiana was nicknamed the Kingfish. He was the governor of Louisiana, where he started a program of public works and welfare reform. After his governorship, he became a U.S. senator and was assassinated. He was considered by many a radical with his Share the Wealth national program and his trademark slogan, "Every man is king." His tight control over Louisiana was viewed with disapproval by many. His brother, EARL KEMP LONG (1895–1960) of Louisiana, was the governor of Louisiana on and off from 1939 to 1960. PERRIN H. LONG (1899–1965) of Ohio was a doctor and the government's consultant on how to care for the injured in Hawaii after the 1941 attack on Pearl Harbor. He was honored by the U.S., French, and British governments for his work during World War II.

Genealogies: *The Big Long Family in America* was compiled by Harvey Lawrence Long and published in Mt. Morris, Illinois, in 1981.

LONGO

Ranking: 2738 S.S. Count: 16,632
Origin: Italian. Cognate to the English name Long.
Genealogies: None known.

LONGORDIA, LONGORDO (S.S. Abbreviation: Longor)

Ranking: 3272 S.S. Count: 13,866
Origin: Spanish. Uncertain etymology. Possibly derived from words meaning long or lengthy.
Genealogies: None known.

LOOMIS

Ranking: 2141 S.S. Count: 21,393

Origin: English. Transformation of Lomax.

Famous **Loomises**: ELIAS LOOMIS (1811–1889) of Connecticut was a mathematician and astronomer. He was the author of many textbooks. MAHLON LOOMIS (1826–1886) of New York was a dentist and the inventor of a method of communicating over a considerable distance without wires. His device was used between two Virginia mountains that spanned 18 miles. Saddened that he was unable to find financial backing, he died a broken man. ALFRED LEE LOOMIS (1887–1975) of New York established the Loomis Laboratory in New York, at which significant scientific research took place. He also established the Loomis Institute for Scientific Research, which provides assistance in developing other research facilities. Loomis himself was a pioneer in developing navigational systems; he obtained—then assigned to the government—a patent on one long-range navigational system that led to the LORAN system.

Genealogies: *Samuel Lomax* [also Loomis] *and his Descendants* was compiled by John B. Lomax and published in Menlo Park, California, in 1991. *Descendants of Joseph Loomis in America* was compiled by Elias Loomis and published in Fresno, California, in 1981. *Frontier Justice: the Rise and Fall of the Loomis Gang* was compiled by E. Fuller Torrey and published in Utica, New York, in 1992.

LOONEY

Ranking: 2415 S.S. Count: 18,747
Origin: Irish. Derived from the Gaelic name Ó Luanaigh, which was derived from the first name Luanach, which was derived from the word "luan," meaning warrior.

Genealogies: *Looney Family Tree* was compiled by Paul Looney and published in Creswell, Oregon, in 1977.

LOPER

Ranking: 4257 S.S. Count: 10,579
Origin: German. Transformation of Läufer, which was derived from the German word "laufen," meaning to run. The name was given to messengers.

Genealogies: *Loper, Keller, Van Meter and Allied Lines* was compiled by Melba Wood and published in Godfrey, Illinois, in 1969.

LOPES

Ranking: 2261 S.S. Count: 20,194
Origin: Portuguese. Cognate to Lopez.
Genealogies: None known.

LOPEZ

Ranking: 46 S.S. Count: 475,493
Origin: Spanish. Derived from a medieval first name that was possibly derived from the Latin name Lupus, meaning wolf.

Famous **Lopezes:** AARON LOPEZ (1731–1782) of Portugal was a colonial merchant and part owner of a fleet of 30 trading vessels. He made his home in Newport, Rhode Island.

Genealogies: None known.

LORD

Ranking: 1294 **S.S. Count:** 34,223

Origin: English, Irish. English: derived from the Old English word "hlāfweard," meaning keeper of the loaf of bread who was also the leader or lord.

Famous **Lords:** NATHAN LORD (1792–1870) of Maine was a Congregational minister whose support of slavery because he felt that it was a divine gift led to his forced resignation from the pulpit. JOHN LORD (1810–1894) of New Hampshire was the author of *Beacon Lights of History,* which was a series written from 1884 to 1896. ASA DEARBORN LORD (1816–1875) of New York was the superintendent of schools in Columbus, Ohio, and the founder of the first high school there. WILLIAM PAINE LORD (1839–1911) of Delaware was a Union soldier who settled in Oregon in 1868. He became the governor, then a minister to Argentina. He is the "Lord" in *Lord's Oregon Laws* (1910). CHESTER SANDERS LORD (1850–1933) of New York was the managing editor of the New York *Sun* and an educator. With Lord as the managing editor, the *Sun* was considered a learning resource for the journalist. The newspaper's staff became some of the best writers of the time. PAULINE LORD (1890–1950) of California was an actress. Her first love was the stage, and she is remembered for her roles in *Ethan Frome* and *The Glass Menagerie.*

Genealogies: *Fifty New England Colonists and Five Virginia Families* was compiled by Florence Weiland and published in Boothbay Harbor, Maine, in 1966. *The Descendants of Thomas and Mary Lord of Rochdale (Lancashire) England* was compiled by Thomas Henry Lord and published in Baltimore, Maryland, in 1991.

LORENZ (ALSO LORENZETTI, LORENZI, LORENZO, LORENZONI) (S.S. Abbreviation: Lorenz)

Ranking: 936 **S.S. Count:** 46,091

Origin: Lorenz—German, Spanish; Lorenzetti, Lorenzi, Lorenzoni—Italian; Lorenzo—Spanish. Cognates to Lawrence.

Genealogies: None known.

LOTT

Ranking: 1302 **S.S. Count:** 34,097

Origin: English. Derived from a medieval first name of Norman. Uncertain origin.

Genealogies: *Descendants of Cornelius Peter Lott* was compiled by Rhea Lott Vance and published in Lehi, Utah,

in 1973. *The Descendants of Benjamin Franklin through the Bache-Lott-Birt Line* was compiled by Philip S. Hessinger and published in West Caldwell, New Jersey, in 1982.

LOUDERBACK (S.S. Abbreviation: Louder)

Ranking: 4532 **S.S. Count:** 9871

Origin: German. Derived from the name Lauterback, meaning "clear brook" (ES). The name was given to those who lived near a clear brook or to those from Lauterback, the name of several places in Germany.

Genealogies: None known.

LOUIE

Ranking: 4723 **S.S. Count:** 9472

Origin: Chinese, English, French Chinese: the name means thunder. English, French: uncertain eytmology. Possibly a transformation of the English name Lewis.

Genealogies: None known.

LOUIS

Ranking: 2235 **S.S. Count:** 20,495

Origin: English, French. Transformation of and cognate to the English name Lewis.

Famous **Louises:** MORRIS LOUIS (1912–1962) of Maine was an abstract artist. His first successful painting was titled *Veils.*

Genealogies: None known.

LOVE

Ranking: 353 **S.S. Count:** 107,986

Origin: English, Irish, Scottish. English: derived from the Old English first name Lufu, or its masculine counterpart Lufa. English, Scottish: derived from the Anglo-Norman-French word "louve," meaning a female wolf.

Famous **Loves:** ALFRED HENRY LOVE (1830–1913) of Pennsylvania was the founder of the Universal Peace Union (1866). EMANUEL KING LOVE (1850–1900) of Alabama was a leader in the black community as the pastor of the First African Baptist Church in Savannah, Georgia. He was a proponent of educating all blacks. ROBERTUS DONNELL LOVE (1867–1930) of Missouri was a journalist and the author of *The Rise and Fall of Jesse James.*

Genealogies: None known.

LOVEJOY (S.S. Abbreviation: Lovejo)

Ranking: 3913 **S.S. Count:** 11,522

Origin: English. Derived from the Old Engliush word "lēof," and the Middle English word "joie," meaning beloved and joy. The name was given to those who were considered hedonists.

Famous **Lovejoys:** ELIJAH PARISH LOVEJOY (1802–1837) of Maine was an abolitionist and the editor of the *St. Louis Observer.* He used the press for his abolitionist and temperance views, and his presses were vandalized. While defending his property, he was shot and killed by a mob. He was nicknamed "the Martyr Abolitionist." ASA LAWRENCE LOVEJOY (1808–1882) of Massachusetts was the founder of the city of Portland, Oregon. OWEN LOVEJOY (1811–1864) of Maine was a confidant of Abraham Lincoln who urged him to take over the leadership of the new political party (Republican). He also served as a member of Congress from Illinois. OWEN REED LOVEJOY (1866–1961) of Michigan was a minister and reformer. He was a champion of children and traveled the country alerting people to the plight of children who worked under deplorable conditions. He served as the secretary of the Children's Aid Society of New York and as associate director of the American Youth Commission. ESTHER POHL LOVEJOY (1869–1967) of Washington was a physican and feminist. She worked to promote women in medicine and wrote books that told of women in health-related fields. ARTHUR ONCKEN LOVEJOY (1873–1963) of Germany was a philosopher. He was one of the founders of the American Association of University Professors and was a supporter of the 1950s movement to exclude Communists from teaching positions in colleges and universities.

Genealogies: *The Lovejoy Genealogy* was compiled by Lena Lovejoy Clarke and published in Baltimore, Maryland, in 1980.

LOVELACE (S.S. Abbreviation: Lovela)
Ranking: 1402 S.S. Count: 31,678
Origin: English. Derived from the Middle English word "lufelesse," meaning loveless. The name was given to those who were considered philanderers.
Famous **Lovelaces:** FRANCIS LOVELACE (1621–1675) of England was a colonial governor of New York. He worked to improve both land and water transportation, promoted shipbuilding, and was responsible for the first continuous post road to be built between New York City and Boston. While he was in Connecticut, New York City was captured by the Dutch. Governor Lovelace fell out of favor with the English over what they termed negligence. He was imprisoned upon his recall to England.
Genealogies: None known.

LOVELESS (S.S. Abbreviation: Lovele)
Ranking: 3401 S.S. Count: 13,313
Origin: English. Transformation of Lovelace.
Genealogies: *The American Ancestry of Richard Janssen Chalmers Loveless* was compiled by Richard William Loveless and published in Salt Lake City, Utah, in 1991.

LOVELL (ALSO LOVELLI)
Ranking: 1515 S.S. Count: 29,365
Origin: Lovell—English; Lovelli—Italian. Lovell: derived

from the Anglo-Norman-French word "lou," meaning wolf. The name was given to those who were cunning or threatening. Lovelli: cognate to Lovell.

Famous **Bearers:** JAMES LOVELL (1737–1814) of Massachusetts gave the first Boston Massacre speech. He spent a year in an English prison for being a spy. Although pro-American, he opposed Benjamin Franklin and Silas Deane. JOSEPH LOVELL (1788–1836) of Massachusetts was the U.S. surgeon general (1818–1836). He played a key role in William Beaumont's gastric physiology studies and was the creator of a system of weather reports as they related to disease. MANFIELD LOVELL (1822–1884) of Washington, D.C., was the son of Joseph Lovell. He was a civil engineer and served for a time as the New York City street commissioner. He attended West Point and joined the Confederate army as a major general. He was the commander of the garrison at New Orleans that was responsible for the evacuation and loss of the city. He was found innocent of blame by the military court but was given no further commands. JOHN EPY LOVELL (1795–1892) of England came to the United States and started the Lancasterian school in New Haven, Connecticut. He also wrote textbooks, including *The United States Speaker* (1833).

Genealogies: *The Genealogy of the James W. Lovell Family* was compiled by Marshall Wilson Lovell and published in Hermitage, Tennessee, in 1982. *The Lovewell (also Lovell) Family* was compiled by Gloria G. Lovewell and published in North Bend, Oregon, in 1979.

LOVETT
Ranking: 1522 S.S. Count: 29,235
Origin: English, Scottish. English: Derived from the Anglo-Norman-French word "lo(u)vet," meaning a young wolf. The name was given to those who were cunning or threatening. Scottish: derived from the Gaelic words "lobh" and "ait," meaning decay or rot and place. The name was given to those from Lovat, a place in Scotland.
Famous **Lovetts:** ROBERT WILLIAMSON LOVETT (1859–1924) of Massachusetts was an orthopedic surgeon. He is best known for the restoration work he performed on his patients suffering from infantile paralysis (polio). He was the author of the 1923 book *Orthopedic Surgery.* ROBERT MORSS LOVETT (1870–1956) of Massachusetts was an educator and reformer. He was associated with the Hull House settlement and the American Civil Liberties Union. He was the author of textbooks and novels.
Genealogies: None known.

LOVING (ALSO LOVINGER)
Ranking: 3421 S.S. Count: 13,218
Origin: English. Uncertain etymology. The name was given to those from Louvain, a place in Belgium.
Genealogies: *The Loving Family in America* was com-

piled by Carl Read and published in Warner Robins, Georgia, in 1981.

LOW

Ranking: 2913 S.S. Count: 15,604

Origin: English, Jewish, Scottish. English: 1) derived from the Anglo-Norman-French word "lou," meaning wolf. The name was given to those who were cunning or threatening. 2) derived from the Middle English word "lāh," meaning short. The name was given to those who were short. 3) derived from the Old English word "hlāw," meaning hill. The name was given to those who lived near a hill. Jewish: Anglicization of the Jewish name Löwe. Scottish: a short version of Lawrence.

Famous **Lows**: ABIEL ABBOT LOW (1811–1893) of Massachusetts was a merchant and the founder of the firm A. A. Low & Brothers, tea and silk traders with Japan and China. FREDERICK FERDINAND LOW (1823–1894) of Maine was a member of Congress and then a governor of California. He is mostly responsible for the founding of the University of California and the preservation of Golden Gate Park. SETH LOW (1850–1916) of New York was the president of Columbia University, transforming it into the major university that it is today. He also served as the mayor of Brooklyn, then as mayor of New York City, where he expanded public utilities and transportation. JULIETTE MAGILL KINZIE GORDON LOW (1860–1927) of Georgia was the founder of the Girl Scouts of America, in Savannah, Georgia. The organization was founded as Girl Guides in 1912; the name was changed to Girl Scouts the following year.

Genealogies: None known.

LOWE

Ranking: 283 S.S. Count: 126,163

Origin: German, Jewish. German: derived from the German word "löwe," meaning lion. The name was given to those who were courageous or kingly. Jewish: translation of the Yiddish first name Leyb, meaning lion.

Famous **Lowes**: RALPH PHILLIPS LOWE (1805–1883) of Ohio was the governor of Iowa and a justice of the Iowa Supreme Court. CHARLES LOWE (1828–1874) of New York was one of the organizers of the National Conference, American Unitarian Association (1865). THADDEUS SOBIESKI COULINCOURT LOWE (1832–1913) of New Hampshire was an aeronaut and inventor. He made artificial ice, invented a system for the production of water gas (a fuel or illuminate), and built the New Lowe Coke Oven. HELEN T. LOWE-PORTER (1876–1963) of Pennsylvania was the translator of nearly all of Thomas Mann's books from German to English.

Genealogies: *Frasher/Frazier (also Lowe family) Family History and their Kinsmen* was compiled by Harry Leon Sellards and published in Deland, Florida, in 1991. *John Lowe of North Carolina and Indiana* was compiled by Carrie McLain West and published in 1977.

LOWELL

Ranking: 4663 S.S. Count: 9592

Origin: English. Transformation of Lovell.

Famous **Lowells**: JOHN LOWELL (1769–1840) of Massachusetts was the writer of many pamphlets and letters that earned him the nickname of the "Boston Rebel." His fame did not extend past New England. FRANCIS CABOT LOWELL (1775–1817) of Massachusetts was an industrialist. He and Paul Moody built the first complete cotton spinning and weaving mill in the United States. It was built in Waltham, Massachusetts. The town of Lowell, Massachusetts, is named in his honor. JAMES RUSSELL LOWELL (1819–1891) of Massachusetts was a poet, essayist, and diplomat. He served as the minister to Spain, then to Great Britain. MARIA WHITE LOWELL (1821–1853) was the wife of James Russell Lowell and a poet. JOSEPHINE SHAW LOWELL (1843–1905) of Massachusetts was a charity worker and a reformer. She especially worked to help the newly freed slaves and became the major fund raiser of the National Freedman's Relief Association of New York. She spoke out against the deplorable conditions in the jails and almshouses and was subsequently appointed to the State Board of Charities by the governor. She worked to rid the charitable organizations of New York City of waste, which led to the founding of the New York Charity Organization Society. She is remembered as one of the most important people in the charity movement of her time. PERCIVAL LOWELL (1855–1916) of Massachusetts was an astronomer who is best known for his study of Mars and his prediction of the discovery of Pluto. He built an observatory in Flagstaff, Arizona, and wrote books about the Orient and astronomy. ABBOTT LAWRENCE LOWELL (1856–1943) of Massachusetts was a politicial scientist and educator at Harvard University. He also wrote books on the subject of government. AMY LOWELL (1874–1925) of Massachusetts was a poet and critic and a leader of the imagist school. ROBERT TRAILL SPENCE LOWELL JR. (1917–1977) of Massachusetts was a poet and the winner of a Pulitzer Prize in 1946 for "Lord Weary's Castle."

Genealogies: None known.

LOWERY

Ranking: 749 S.S. Count: 56,574

Origin: English, Irish, Scottish. Transformation of Lowry.

Famous **Lowerys**: WOODBURY LOWERY (1853–1906) was a lawyer and legal editor. He wrote *The Spanish Settlements within the Present Limits of the United States.*

Genealogies: None known.

LOWMAN

Ranking: 4425 S.S. Count: 10,129

Origin: English. Transformation of Lemmon.

Genealogies: None known.

LOWRY

Ranking: 1210 S.S. Count: 36,397

Origin: English, Irish, Scottish. English, Scottish: transformation of and cognate to Lawrence. Irish: derived from the Gaelic name Ó Labhradha, which was derived from the first name Labraidh, meaning spokesman (H&H).

Famous **Lowrys:** ROBERT LOWRY (1830–1910) of South Carolina was a Confederate army officer and the governor of Mississippi after the Civil War. THOMAS LOWRY (1843–1909) of Illinois was active in the mass-transit system of Minneapolis. EDITH ELIZABETH LOWRY (1897–1970) of New Jersey was the national director of workers among the agricultural migrants of her day.

Genealogies: *The Lawry (also Lowry) Family of Friendship, Maine* was compiled by A. E. Sutton and published in Camden, Maine, in 1992.

LOY

Ranking: 3700 S.S. Count: 12,204

Origin: German. Derived from the Latin first name Eligius, which was derived from the word "ēligere," meaning to select.

Famous **Loys:** MATHIAS LOY (1828–1915) of Pennsylvania was a Lutheran minister and a leader in the Ohio Synod.

Genealogies: *The Loy Family in America* was compiled by Jennie E. Stewart and published in Baltimore, Maryland, in 1984.

LOYD

Ranking: 2248 S.S. Count: 20,350

Origin: Welsh. Transformation of Lloyd.

Famous **Loyds:** SAMUEL LOYD (1841–1911) of Pennsylvania was an inventor of puzzles and games. His two most popular ones were "Pigs in Clover" and "Parcheesi."

Genealogies: None known.

LOZADA

Ranking: 4032 S.S. Count: 11,229

Origin: Spanish. Derived from the Spanish phrase "en lozar," meaning pavement made from flagstones.

Genealogies: None known.

LOZANO

Ranking: 1417 S.S. Count: 31,368

Origin: Spanish. Derived from the Old Spanish word "loçano," meaning magnificent. The name was given to those who were elegant or vain.

Genealogies: None known.

LUCAS

Ranking: 268 S.S. Count: 137,175

Origin: Dutch, English, Flemish, French, Portuguese, Spanish. Derived from the Latin first name Lucas, which was derived from the Greek name Loucas, meaning "man from Lucania" (H&H), a region of Italy.

Famous **Lucases:** JONATHAN LUCAS (1754–1821) of England emigrated to South Carolina. There he designed tide-mill machinery that enhanced the rice-retrieval process. His contributions to the rice industry are no less important than those Eli Whitney made to the cotton industry. JOHN BAPTISTE CHARLES LUCAS (1758–1842) of France was a member of Congress and a U.S. judge in northern Louisiana. As a judge and commissioner of land titles in Missouri, he acquired a tremendously large amount of land. JONATHAN LUCAS (1775–1832) of England was the son of Jonathan Lucas (1754–1821). He accompanied his father to South Carolina and worked with him in the development of his rice-gathering machinery. ROBERT LUCAS (1781–1853) of Virginia was the governor of Ohio, governor of and superintendent of Indian Affairs in Iowa, and a member of the 1844 Iowa constitutional convention. FREDERIC AUGUSTUS LUCAS (1852–1929) of Massachusetts was a naturalist and the director of the American Museum of Natural History in New York City (1911–1929). ANTHONY FRANCIS LUCAS (1855–1921) of Austria was a geologist and the oilman who was responsible for the famous Spindletop oil strike that took place near Beaumont, Texas, in January 1901. SCOTT WIKE LUCAS (1892–1968) of Illinois was a member of Congress and senator and a representative of the farmer and businessman. He was one of the casualties of McCarthyism.

Genealogies: None known.

LUCE

Ranking: 3328 S.S. Count: 13,620

Origin: English. Derived from the medieval feminine name Lucie, which was derived from the Latin name Lūcia.

Famous **Luces:** STEPHEN BLEEKER LUCE (1827–1917) of New York was responsible for the establishment of the Naval War College and served as its first president. He also was the author of the textbook *Seamanship.* HENRY ROBINSON LUCE (1898–1967) was born in China to American parents. He was an editor and publisher and the co-founder of *Time* magazine, of the monthly *Fortune,* the weekly picture magazine *Life,* and the weekly *Sports Illustrated.* As editor-in-chief of *Time* (1929–1964) he produced the "March of Time" series for radio and a newsreel series for theaters.

Genealogies: *Ancestors and Descendants of James and Althea (Loose) Johnston (also Luce) and Allied Families* was compiled by Aaron Montgomery Johnston and published in Knoxville, Tennessee, in 1983. *The American Descendants of Henry Luce of Martha's Vineyard* was compiled by Martha F. McCourt and published in Vancouver, Washington, in 1985.

LUCERO

Ranking: 1310 **S.S. Count:** 33,848

Origin: Spanish. Derived from the first name Lucero, meaning morning star or the planet Venus.

Genealogies: None known.

LUCIAN (ALSO LUCIANI, LUCIANO)

Ranking: 3213 **S.S. Count:** 14,128

Origin: Lucian—French; Luciani, Luciano—Italian. Derived from the Latin first name Luciānus, which was perhaps derived from the Latin word "lux," meaning light.

Famous **Lucianos:** CHARLES "LUCKY" LUCIANO (1897?–1962) of Italy was a Mafia leader. He was responsible for bootlegging, hijacking, narcotics, and prostitution increases in the United States. He was eventually deported to Italy.

Genealogies: None known.

LUCKETT (S.S. Abbreviation: Lucket)

Ranking: 4463 **S.S. Count:** 10,042

Origin: English. Transformation of Lucas.

Genealogies: *The Lucketts of Georgia* was compiled by Helen Hart Luckett and published in Fort Worth, Texas, in 1976. *Samuel Luckett of Maryland* was compiled by Marcelle Douglass Hoskins and published in Richardson, Texas, in 1990.

LUDWIG

Ranking: 1353 **S.S. Count:** 32,763

Origin: German. Cognate to the English name Lewis.

Genealogies: None known.

LUGO

Ranking: 1447 **S.S. Count:** 30,855

Origin: Spanish. Uncertain etymology. Possibly derived from Lugos, the name of a Celtic god. The name was given to those from Lugo, a place in Spain.

Genealogies: None known.

LUJAN

Ranking: 2522 **S.S. Count:** 17,987

Origin: Spanish. Cognate to Lucian.

Genealogies: None known.

LUKE

Ranking: 2092 **S.S. Count:** 21,942

Origin: English. Transformation of Lucas.

Genealogies: None known.

LUM

Ranking: 4216 **S.S. Count:** 10,706

Origin: English. Transformation of Lumb, which was derived from an Old English word meaning pool. The name was given to those from Lumb, the name of several places in England.

Genealogies: None known.

LUMPKIN, LUMPKINS (S.S. Abbreviation: Lumpki)

Ranking: 2824 **S.S. Count:** 16,147

Origin: English. Transformation of Lambert.

Famous **Lumpkins:** WILSON LUMPKIN (1783–1870) of Virginia was the governor of, then U.S. senator from, Georgia. JOSEPH HENRY LUMPKIN (1799–1867) of Georgia was the chief justice of the Georgia Supreme Court.

Genealogies: None known.

LUNA

Ranking: 817 **S.S. Count:** 51,814

Origin: Jewish, Spanish. Jewish: uncertain etymology. Spanish: derived from the Latin word "lūmina," meaning lights. The name was given to those who lived near a courtyard.

Genealogies: None known.

LUND

Ranking: 1279 **S.S. Count:** 34,558

Origin: Danish, English, Norwegian, Swedish. Derived from the Old Norse word "lundr," meaning grove. The name was given to those who lived near a grove. The Swedish name was most likely taken ornamentally.

Genealogies: None known.

LUNDBERG (S.S. Abbreviation: Lundbe)

Ranking: 3720 **S.S. Count:** 12,147

Origin: Swedish. The name consists of Lund combined with the word "berg," meaning hill. The name was taken ornamentally.

Famous **Lundbergs:** EMMA OCTAVIA LUNDBERG (1881–1954) of Sweden was a social worker. She worked to improve social conditions and welfare provisions for children.

Genealogies: None known.

LUNDGREN (S.S. Abbreviation: Lundgr)

Ranking: 4006 **S.S. Count:** 11,302

Origin: Swedish. The name consists of Lund combined with the word "gren," meaning branch. The name was taken ornamentally.

Genealogies: None known.

LUNDQUIST (S.S. Abbreviation: Lundqu)

Ranking: 4340 **S.S. Count:** 10,324

Origin: Swedish. The name consists of Lund combined with the word "qvist," meaning twig. The name was taken ornamentally.

Genealogies: None known.

LUNDY

Ranking: 2271 S.S. Count: 20,052

Origin: Irish, Scottish. Derived from the Gaelic word "lunnd," meaning marsh. The name was given to those from Lundie, the name of several places in Ireland and Scotland.

Famous **Lundys**: BENJAMIN LUNDY (1789–1839) of New Jersey was an abolitionist and the organizer of the Union Humane Society in Ohio in 1815. It was one of the pioneer antislavery groups in the country. He founded several newspapers as a voice against slavery, and he wrote, traveled, and spoke against slavery in several states.

Genealogies: None known.

LUNSFORD (S.S. Abbreviation: Lunsfo)

Ranking: 1925 S.S. Count: 23,463

Origin: English. Derived from the English river named Lune and "ford," the Old English word meaning a ford in a river. The name was given to those who lived near a ford of the river Lune.

Genealogies: None known.

LUSK

Ranking: 2648 S.S. Count: 17,180

Origin: Polish, Scottish, Ukrainian. Polish, Ukrainian: the name was given to those from Luck, the name of a place in the medieval western Ukraine. Scottish: the name was given to those from Lusk, a place in Dublin, Ireland.

Famous **Lusks**: WILLIAM THOMPSON LUSK (1838–1897) of Connecticut was a Union soldier, an obstetrician, and the author of *The Science and Art of Midwifery* (1882), considered a classic in its field. GRAHAM LUSK (1866–1932) of Connecticut was a researcher in the area of metabolism. He wrote *The Elements of the Science of Nutrition*. GEORGIA LEE WITT LUSK (1893–1971) of New Mexico was an educator and a member of Congress. She is often referred to as "the first lady of New Mexico politics." She was superintendent of Lea County schools, then ran for Congress and became the first woman in New Mexico to become a U.S. representative.

Genealogies: *Ancestors & Friends* was compiled by William Lusk Crawford and published in Dallas, Texas, in 1978. *Lusks, A Pioneer Family* was compiled by Dexter Dixon and published in Blackey, Kentucky.

LUSTER

Ranking: 4531 S.S. Count: 9872

Origin: Norwegian. Uncertain etymology. The name was given to those from Luster, a place in Norway.

Genealogies: None known.

LUTHER

Ranking: 2306 S.S. Count: 19,720

Origin: English, German. English: derived from the Mid-dle English and Old French word "luthier," meaning lute. The name was given to lute players. German: derived from a Germanic first name that comprised the components "liut" and "heri," meaning tribe and army.

Famous **Luthers**: SETH LUTHER (1790?–1850), possibly of Rhode Island, was a campaigner for labor reforms. He spoke against monopolies, capital punishment, debtors' prisons, and the militia. He wrote several papers on these subjects.

Genealogies: *The Luther Family in America* was compiled by Leslie Leon Luther and published in 1976.

LUTTRELL (S.S. Abbreviation: Luttre)

Ranking: 3467 S.S. Count: 13,023

Origin: English. Derived from the Old French word "loutre," meaning otter. The name was given to those who hunted otters or who were considered otter-like.

Genealogies: None known.

LUTZ

Ranking: 932 S.S. Count: 46,286

Origin: German. Cognate to the English name Lewis.

Famous **Lutzes**: FRANK EUGENE LUTZ (1879–1943) of Pennsylvania was an entomologist associated with Carnegie Institution Station for Experimental Evolution, Cold Spring Harbor, New York, and the American Museum of Natural History, New York City, where he served as the curator in his area of expertise and as the editoral director of the scientific publications of the museum. He also was the author of *Field Book of Insects* (1918).

Genealogies: *Johannes Georg Lutz, 1706–1756, and His Descendants* was compiled by Margaret D. Lutes and published in Boise, Idaho, in 1983.

LY

Ranking: 3325 S.S. Count: 13,630

Origin: Vietnamese. The name means a glass, cup, or small quantity.

Genealogies: None known.

LYLE

Ranking: 2424 S.S. Count: 18,698

Origin: Norman English. 1) derived from the Old French word "isle," meaning island, in combination with the definite article "l." The name was given to those from Lille, a city in France. 2) derived from the Old French and Middle English word "isle," meaning island, in combination with the definite article "l." The name was given to those who lived on an island.

Genealogies: *Lyle, Murrell, Nancy, Morton Genealogy* was compiled by Gladys Elizabeth Odil Bracy and published in Nashville, Tennessee, in 1965. *Some Early Families of the Altamaha Delta* was compiled by Bessie Lewis and published in McHenry, Illinois.

LYLES

Ranking: 2094 S.S. Count: 21,905
Origin: English. Transformation of Lyle.
Genealogies: None known.

LYMAN

Ranking: 2771 S.S. Count: 16,465
Origin: English. Transformation of the English name Lee. The name was given to those who lived near a meadow.

Famous **Lymans:** PHINEAS LYMAN (1715–1774) of Connecticut was a Connecticut legislator and the commander of the Connecticut provincial troops in the Seven Years' War. CHESTER SMITH LYMAN (1814–1890) of Connecticut was a Congregational minister and the person whose letter, published in *American Journal of Science and Arts*, was the first reliable account of the gold strike in California. EUGENE WILLIAM LYMAN (1872–1948) of Massachusetts was a theology teacher and the author of *The Meaning and Truth of Religion* (1933). THEODORE LYMAN (1874–1954) of Massachusetts was an experimental physicist. He wrote *The Spectroscopy of the Extreme Ultraviolet.* MARY ELY LYMAN (1887–1975) of Vermont was a theologian. She became a teacher of religion at the college level and a Congregational minister in 1949.

Genealogies: *Genealogy of the Lyman Family* was compiled by Lyman Coleman and published in Albany, New York, in 1872.

LYNCH

Ranking: 215 S.S. Count: 164,738
Origin: English, Irish. English: derived from the Old English word "hlinc," meaning slope. The name was given to those who lived on a slope or the side of a hill. Irish: 1) derived from the Gaelic name Linseach, which was derived from the Anglo-Norman-French name de Lench. 2) derived from the Gaelic name Ó Loingsigh, which was derived from the first name Loingseach, meaning seaman.

Famous **Lynches:** THOMAS LYNCH (1727–1776) of South Carolina was the South Carolina representative to the Stamp Act Congress and a member of both the first and second Continental Congresses. CHARLES LYNCH (1736–1796) of Virginia was a planter and a justice of the peace. After the American Revolution he was judge over the lawless renegades of the area. He convicted the guilty and handed out punishments, usually flogging, which gave rise to the term "lynch law." THOMAS LYNCH (1749–1779) of South Carolina was a member of the second Continental Congress and one of the signers of the Declaration of Independence. He was lost at sea. PATRICK NEESON LYNCH (1817–1882) of Ireland came to the United States as a child, settling in South Carolina. He became a Roman Catholic priest. During the Civil War he carried a letter to Pope Pius IX from Jefferson Davis, expressing his interest

in peace. After the war he worked to smooth relations between the North and the South. JOHN ROY LYNCH (1847–1939) of Louisiana was a lawyer, politician, and army officer. Born a slave, he became a member of Congress from Mississippi and the first black to preside over a Republican National Convention (1884). He was the author of *The Facts of Reconstruction.* ROBERT CLYDE LYNCH (1880–1931) of Nevada was an ear, nose, and throat doctor who developed a sinus operation known as the "Lynch operation." He also made moving pictures of the larynx and vocal cords.

Genealogies: *The Loy (also Lynch) Family in America* was compiled by Jennie E. Stewart and published in Baltimore, Maryland, in 1984. *Scharnhorst, Lynch, Barnett, Thornton* was compiled by Frances Carter and published in Bradenton, Florida, in 1980.

LYNN

Ranking: 816 S.S. Count: 51,845
Origin: English, Irish, Jewish, Scottish. English: Uncertain etymology. Possibly derived from a British word meaning lake. The name was given to those from Lynn, the name of several places in England. Irish: derived from the Gaelic names Mac Fhloinn and Ó Fhloinn, which were derived from the first name Flann, meaning red-complexioned. Jewish: Anglicization of the Jewish surname Lin(n), of unknown etymology. Scottish: derived from the Gaelic word "linne," meaning pool. The name was given to those from Lyne, a place in Scotland.

Genealogies: *Lew Lynn Lineage* was compiled by Billie Allen Jines and published in Detroit, Michigan, in 1980.

LYON

Ranking: 1073 S.S. Count: 41,065
Origin: English, French, Irish. English, French: 1) the name was given to those from Lyon, the name of several places in France. 2) derived from the name Leo(n), which was derived from the Latin word "leo," meaning lion. 3) derived from the Old French and Middle English word "lion," which was derived from the Latin word "leo," meaning lion. The name was given to those who were courageous or kingly. Irish: derived from the Gaelic name Ó Laighin, which was derived from the first name Laighean, meaning spear.

Famous **Lyons:** MATTHEW LYON (1750–1822) of Ireland was a Revolutionary soldier and a legislator from Vermont and Kentucky. He came to America (Connecticut) as an indentured servant and moved to Vermont when freed. He became a leading businessman and was elected to the state legislature, where he and Roger Griswold engaged in a physical encounter, for which he spent four months in jail. He was reelected and cast the decisive vote of Vermont for Thomas Jefferson as president. He moved to Kentucky and was elected to political office there. MARY MASON LYON

(1797–1849) of Massachusetts was an educator and a pioneer in education for women. She founded the school that later became Mount Holyoke College. THEIDATUS TIMOTHY LYON (1813–1900) of New York was a pioneer railroad builder in Michigan. NATHANIEL LYON (1818–1861) of Connecticut was a Civil War Union army officer who captured Jefferson City and Boonville, Missouri. He was killed in action.

Genealogies: *The Ancestors and Descendants of Thomas Lyon Mix* was compiled by Pearl Mix Cox and published in Warrensburg, Missouri, in 1979. *Who's Who in the Lyon Family* was compiled by Burley Frank Lamb and published in Columbus, Ohio, in 1972. *Baldwin/Lyon Family* was compiled by Virginia Baldwin Pomata and published in Baltimore, Maryland, in 1992.

LYONS
Ranking: 316 **S.S. Count:** 117,054
Origin: English, French. Transformation of the English and French Lyon. The name was given to those from Lyon, the name of several places in France.

Famous **Lyonses:** PETER LYONS (1734?–1809) of Ireland was a Virginia lawyer and jurist who served as the attorney for the plaintiff in the "Parsons' Cause," a trial that became an open forum for debate over England's powre over the American colonies.

Genealogies: *Baldwin/Lyon (also Lyons) Family* was compiled by Virginia Baldwin Pomata and published in Baltimore, Maryland, in 1992. *The Ancestry of Nathalie Fontaine Lyons* was compiled by Jo White Linn and published in Salisbury, North Carolina, in 1981.

LYTLE
Ranking: 2419 **S.S. Count:** 18,724
Origin: English, Irish. Transformation of Little.

Famous **Lytles:** WILLIAM HAINES LYTLE (1826–1863) of Ohio was a lawyer and Union officer in the Civil War. Before the war he was an Ohio legislator and the author of *Poems.*

Genealogies: None known.

MAAS

Ranking: 3597 S.S. Count: 12,543
Origin: Dutch, German. 1) uncertain etymology. The name was given to those who lived along the Maas River in Holland and Belgium. 2) derived from the name Thomas.

Famous **Maases**: ANTHONY J. MAAS (1858–1927) of Germany was a Jesuit clergyman of the Roman Catholic faith. He was a well-known seminary professor in the Maryland—New York area.
Genealogies: None known.

MABE

Ranking: 4822 S.S. Count: 9285
Origin: English. Derived from the female first names Mabel and Anabel, both meaning lovable.
Genealogies: None known.

MABRY

Ranking: 2519 S.S. Count: 18,026
Origin: French. The name means "descendant of my daughter-in-law" (ES).
Genealogies: *Yesterday: the Hampton, McCracken, Longwith, Mabry & Wells Families* was compiled by Diana L. Mellen and published in Bowie, Maryland, in 1991.

MACDONA, MACDONALD, MACDONNELL, MACDONOUGH (S.S. Abbreviation: MacDon)

Ranking: 527 S.S. Count: 76,506
Origin: MacDona, MacDonough—Irish, Scottish; MacDonald, MacDonnell—Scottish. MacDona, MacDonagh, MacDonaugh: derived from the Gaelic-Scottish name Mac Donnchaidh and the Gaelic-Irish name Mac Donnchadha, both of which were derived from the first name Donnchadh, which comprises the components "donn" and "cath," meaning brown and battle. MacDonald, MacDonnell: transformations of McDonald.

Famous **Bearers**: THOMAS MACDONOUGH (1783–1825) of Delaware was a naval officer who served in the war against Tripoli. RONALD MACDONALD (1824–1894) of Oregon was an adventurer who ran off to sea and entered Japan. He was captured, and he taught English to his capturers. He was rescued a year later and spent the rest of his life wandering around Australia and North America. JAMES WILSON ALEXANDER MACDONALD (1824–1908) of Ohio was a sculptor best known for a marble bust of Thomas H. Benton. CHARLES BLAIR MACDONALD (1856–1939) of Canada was a golfer and a designer of golf courses. DWIGHT MACDONALD (1902–1982) of New York City was a writer, editor, and film critic. He was the author of *Against the American Grain*. JEANETTE MACDONALD (1907–1965) of Pennsylvania was an actress and

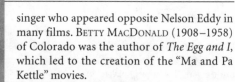

singer who appeared opposite Nelson Eddy in many films. BETTY MACDONALD (1908–1958) of Colorado was the author of *The Egg and I*, which led to the creation of the "Ma and Pa Kettle" movies.
Genealogies: *Adam and Susan Fickas: their Descendants and Allied Families* [also MacDonald] was compiled by Viva Fickas Freeman and published in Santa Ana, California, in 1977. *McDaniel/MacDonald Notes* was compiled by Ellen Byrne and published in Huntsville, Arkansas, in 1971.

MACE

Ranking: 2716 S.S. Count: 16,753
Origin: English. Derived from a medieval first name, of uncertain etymology.
Genealogies: None known.

MACFARLAN, MACFARLAND, MACFARLANE, MACFARLIN (S.S. Abbreviation: MacFar)

Ranking: 4301 S.S. Count: 10,436
Origin: Irish, Scottish. Derived from the Gaelic name Mac Pharthaláin, which was derived from the first name Parthlán.
Genealogies: *Genealogy, History and Biographical Records of Families of Joseph Haney and Sarah Decker, David MacFarlane, et al.* [also MacFarland] was compiled by W. Flora Shepherd and published in Topeka, Kansas, in 1971.

MACHADO (S.S. Abbreviation: Machad)

Ranking: 2421 S.S. Count: 18,715
Origin: Portuguese, Spanish. Derived from the Portuguese and Spanish word "machado," meaning hatchet. The name was given to those who used, made, or sold hatchets.
Genealogies: None known.

MACIAS

Ranking: 1456 S.S. Count: 30,605
Origin: Spanish. Cognate to Matthew.
Genealogies: None known.

MACK

Ranking: 396 S.S. Count: 98,307
Origin: Irish, Scottish. Irish, Scottish: derived from any of a number of names beginning with Mac- or Mc-. Scottish: derived from the old Norse first name Makkr.

Famous **Macks**: NILA MACK (1891–1953) of Kansas was a radio producer, writer, and actress. She was responsible for the production of the children's radio show "Let's Pretend." The Saturday-morning show ran from 1934 to 1954 and was filled with classic stories and fairy tales.
Genealogies: *To Hope, to Labor, and so to Live: Descen-*

dants of John Mack was compiled by Mary P. Engels and published in Forrest City, Arkansas, in 1980.

MACKAY
Ranking: 3238 S.S. Count: 14,024
Origin: Irish, Scottish. Transformation of Mckay.
Famous **MacKays:** JOHN WILLIAM MACKAY (1831–1902) of Ireland came to the United States as a young man and moved to California. He worked as a miner and found gold in the Comstock Lode. He co-founded the Commercial Cable Co. and laid underwater cable between the United States and Europe, thereby breaking the Jay Gould—Western Union monopoly. He also formed the Postal Telegraph Cable Co. in order to break the monopoly held by the Western Union Co. on land. CLARENCE HUNGERFORD MACKAY (1874–1938) of California was the son of John W. MacKay and was his successor in his business dealings. Clarence was responsible for laying the first cables across the Pacific Ocean. He also laid them to southern Europe and Cuba. The consolidation of radio, cable, and telegraph in one company was first implemented by him.
Genealogies: *Family Tree Record* [also MacKay] was compiled by Anthony Steward MacKay Dickins and published in 1974.

MACKENNA, MACKENZIE (S.S. Abbreviation: Macken)
Ranking: 1861 S.S. Count: 24,296
Origin: MacKenna—Scottish; MacKenzie—Scottish. MacKenna: transformation of Kenney. MacKenzie: derived from the Gaelic name Mac Coinnich, which was derived from the first name Coinneach.
Famous **Bearers:** ALEXANDER SLIDELL MACKENZIE (1803–1848) of New York City, born just Alexander Slidell, added the last name to his birth name in 1838. He was the brother of John Slidell. He was a naval officer who stopped a planned mutiny, hanged the three sailors involved, and was acquitted of any wrongdoing in a court of inquiry and court-martial. GEORGE HENRY MACKENZIE (1837–1891) of Scotland was a chess champion who won the American title in 1880 and the world title in 1887. RANDALL SLIDELL MACKENZIE (1840–1889) of New York City was the son of Alexander S. MacKenzie. He was a career army officer, serving in the Union army of the Civil War and as an officer in frontier posts afterward. He retired as a brigadier general. JEAN KENYON MACKENZIE (1874–1936) of Illinois was a missionary and author. She worked as a missionary in Africa and wrote about her experiences there.
Genealogies: None known.

MACKEY
Ranking: 1015 S.S. Count: 43,155
Origin: Irish, Scottish. Transformation of Mckay.

Genealogies: *The MacKeys (variously spelled) and Allied Families* was compiled by Beatrice MacKey Doughtie and published in Decatur, Georgia, in 1957. *Record of Robert MacKey and William MacKey and their Descendants who Lived Mostly in Pennsylvania and/or Maryland* was compiled by Wilmer MacKey Sanner and published in Ellicott City, Maryland, in 1974.

MACKIE
Ranking: 4003 S.S. Count: 11,304
Origin: Irish, Scottish. Transformation of Mckay.
Genealogies: None known.

MACKINTOSH (S.S. Abbreviation: Mackin)
Ranking: 2849 S.S. Count: 16,019
Origin: Scottish. Transformation of Mcintosh.
Genealogies: None known.

MACKLIN, MACKLING (S.S. Abbreviation: Mackli)
Ranking: 4636 S.S. Count: 9645
Origin: Irish. Derived from the first name Flann, meaning ruddy or red.
Famous **Bearers:** MADGE THURLOW MACKLIN (1893–1962) of Pennsylvania was a geneticist and the coiner of the word "genetics." She was a pioneer in the field, working to have courses in genetics and full genetics departments available in many of the North American medical schools. She worked to see that proper controls were used in experiments and research, and she pursued her main interest of hereditary aspects of cancer. She was in favor of eugenics and sterilization for certain types, and she clashed with some of her colleagues. She was never rewarded through promotions in her work, but she received many honors in her lifetime.
Genealogies: *Mechling, Mechlin, Macklin* was compiled by Dorothy Hallarn Mercy and published in Falls Church, Virginia, in 1982. *Our Family Tree Book* [also Macklin] was compiled by Meryl E. Johnson and published in Batavia, Illinois, in 1975.

MACLEAN, MACLEARY, MACLEAVY (S.S. Abbreviation: MacLea)
Ranking: 3797 S.S. Count: 11,881
Origin: MacLean—Irish, Scottish; MacLeary—Irish; MacLeavy—Irish; MacLea—Scottish. MacLean: derived from the Gaelic-Scottish name Mac Gille Eáin and the Gaelic-Irish name Mac Giolla Eóin, both meaning "son of the servant of (St.) John" (H&H). MacLeary: transformation of Cleary. MacLeavy: derived from the first name Duinnsliabh, which comprises the components "donn" and "sliabh," meaning brown and mountain.
Genealogies: None known.

MACLEOD (S.S. Abbreviation: MacLeo)
Ranking: 3758 S.S. Count: 12,048
Origin: Scottish. Transformation of McLeod.
Genealogies: None known.

MACMILLAN, MACMILLEN (S.S. Abbreviation: MacMil)
Ranking: 4724 S.S. Count: 9470
Origin: Scottish. Derived from the Gaelic name Mac Maoláin, which was derived from the first name Maolán, which was derived from the word "maol," meaning shaved-headed or bald. The name was given to those whose heads were partially or entirely shaved.
Genealogies: None known.

MACNEICE, MACNEIL, MACNEILLY (S.S. Abbreviation: Macnei)
Ranking: 6126 S.S. Count: 7174
Origin: MacNeice—Irish; MacNeil—Irish, Scottish; MacNeilly—Irish, Scottish. MacNeice: derived from the Gaelic name Mac Naois, which was derived from the name Mac Aonghuis, meaning "son of Angus" (H&H). MacNeil: transformation of Neil. MacNeilly: derived from the Gaelic name Mac an Fhilidh, meaning "son of the poet" (H&H).
Genealogies: None known.

MACON
Ranking: 4830 S.S. Count: 9266
Origin: French. Cognate to Mason.
Genealogies: *Gideon Macon of Virginia and Some of His Descendants* was compiled by Alethea Jane Macon and published in Washington, Georgia, in 1981.

MACPHEE, MACPHERSON (S.S. Abbreviation: MacPhe)
Ranking: 4300 S.S. Count: 10,436
Origin: MacPhee—Irish, Scottish; MacPherson—Scottish. MacPhee: transformation of the Irish and Scottish name Duffy. MacPherson: derived from the Gaelic name Mac an Phearsain, meaning the parson's son.
Genealogies: None known.

MADDEN (ALSO MADDENS)
Ranking: 886 S.S. Count: 49,019
Origin: Maddens—Flemish; Madden—Irish. Madden: derived from the Gaelic name Ó Madaidhín, which was derived from the first name Madaidhín, which was derived from the word "madadh," meaning hound. Maddens: cognate to the English name Maudling, which was derived from the feminine Greek name Magdalēnē.
Famous **Bearers:** THOMAS M. MADDEN (1907–1976) of New Jersey was chief judge of the U.S. District Court for the New Jersey district (1961–1969).

Genealogies: *We Were Always Free: the Maddens of Culpeper County, Virginia* was compiled by T. O. Madden and published in New York in 1992.

MADDOX
Ranking: 850 S.S. Count: 50,245
Origin: Welsh. Transformation of the Welsh name Madoc, which was derived from the Old Welsh first name Matoc, which was possibly derived from the word "mad," meaning good.
Genealogies: *My Family* [also Maddox] was compiled by Edward Barrett Stanford and published in Roseville, Minnesota, in 1984. *Maddox Family of Virginia & Kentucky* was compiled by Clyde Goddard and published in New Boston, Missouri, in 1973.

MADISON (S.S. Abbreviation: Madiso)
Ranking: 1203 S.S. Count: 36,559
Origin: English. 1) derived from a form of the feminine first name Maud, which was ultimately derived from the Norman first name Mathilde, which comprises the components "maht" and "hild," meaning strength and battle. 2) derived from the feminine first name Magdalen.
Famous **Madisons:** JAMES MADISON (1751–1836) of Virginia was a member of the Virginia legislature and was the fourth president of the United States. He earned the title "father of the U.S. Constitution" for his service as a member of the Continental Congress and as the manager of the Constitutional Convention. DOLLEY PAYNE TODD MADISON (1768–1849) of North Carolina was the wife of James Madison, the fourth president of the United States. She is remembered as the Washington hostess while her husband was secretary of state and then president.
Genealogies: *A Branch of the Madison Tree* was compiled by Ruth Gadbury and published in Austin, Texas, in 1974.

MADRID
Ranking: 2600 S.S. Count: 17,481
Origin: Spanish. Derived from the city name. The name was given to those from Madrid, the capital city of Spain.
Genealogies: None known.

MADRIGAL (S.S. Abbreviation: Madrig)
Ranking: 3802 S.S. Count: 11,868
Origin: Spanish. Uncertain etymology. Most likely derived from the Late Latin word "mātricāle," which was derived from the Latin word "mātrix," meaning womb or bed of a river. The name was given to those from Madrigal, the name of several places in Spain.
Genealogies: None known.

MADSEN
Ranking: 2039 S.S. Count: 22,405

Origin: Danish, Norwegian. Cognate to Matthew.

Genealogies: *Yesterday, a History of Norwegian Ancestry* [also Madsen] was compiled by Evelyn Hoff and published in Winona, Minnesota, in 1985.

MAESTACCI (S.S. Abbreviation: Maesta)

Ranking: 4725 **S.S. Count:** 9469

Origin: Italian. Cognate to Master.

Genealogies: None known.

MAGANA

Ranking: 3355 **S.S. Count:** 13,509

Origin: Uncertain etymology.

Genealogies: None known.

MAGEE

Ranking: 1199 **S.S. Count:** 36,672

Origin: Irish. Transformation of McKay.

Genealogies: *Hill* [also Magee] *Family Cousins of Early Central Texas* was compiled by Yates Michael Hill and published in Poughkeepsie, New York, in 1990. *In Search of Kith and Kin: the History of a Southern Black Family* [also Magee] was compiled by Barnetta McGhee White and published in Baltimore, Maryland, in 1986.

MAGGARD (S.S. Abbreviation: Maggar)

Ranking: 4890 **S.S. Count:** 9139

Origin: English. Uncertain etymology. Possibly derived from the Old English word "maeger," meaning lean.

Genealogies: *Maggard Family Genealogy* was compiled by Kenneth Maggard and published in Glenview, Illinois, in 1969.

MAGGIO (ALSO MAGGIOLI, MAGGIOLINI)

Ranking: 4189 **S.S. Count:** 10,791

Origin: Italian. Derived from the first name Matthew.

Genealogies: None known.

MAGNUS (ALSO MAGNUSON, MAGNUSSEN, MAGNUSSON)

Ranking: 2319 **S.S. Count:** 19,559

Origin: Magnus—Danish, English, Jewish, Norwegian, Swedish; Magnussen—Danish; Magnuson—English; Magnusson—English, Swedish. Magnus (Danish, English, Norwegian, Swedish): derived from the Scandinavian first name Magnús, which was derived from the Latin word "magnus," meaning great. Magnus (Jewish): uncertain etymology. Magnussen: transformation of Magnus. Magnuson: transformation of Magnus. Magnusson: transformation of Magnus.

Genealogies: None known.

MAGUIRE (S.S. Abbreviation: Maguir)

Ranking: 1896 **S.S. Count:** 23,876

Origin: Irish. Derived from the Gaelic name Mag Uidhir, which was derived from the first name Odhar, meaning "sallow" (H&H).

Genealogies: *The Ancestry of Beulah Fogg Maguire of Sanford, Maine* was compiled by Beulah Maguire and published in Saco, Maine, in 1978.

MAHAFFEY (S.S. Abbreviation: Mahaff)

Ranking: 3463 **S.S. Count:** 13,032

Origin: Irish, Scottish. The name means the son of Dubshithe, meaning "the black man of peace" (ES).

Genealogies: *Arthur Ellison of Adams County, Ohio and some of his Descendants and Relatives* [also Mahaffey] was compiled by Floyd Vernon Ellison and published in Middletown, Ohio, in 1979. *Mahaffey Descendants* was compiled by Estelle Kinports Davis and published in Harrisburg, Pennsylvania, in 1914.

MAHAN

Ranking: 2186 **S.S. Count:** 20,980

Origin: Irish. Uncertain etymology. Most likely derived from the Gaelic name Ó Mocháin, which was derived from the first name Mochán, which was derived from the word "moch," meaning early or well timed.

Famous Mahans: ALFRED THAYER MAHAN (1840–1914) of New York was a naval officer. He served in the Civil War and was the president of the Naval War College in Rhode Island. He published many books on the sea and historical battles.

Genealogies: *Genealogy of the Bennington Family* [also Mahan] was compiled by William Kearney Hall and published in Scottsdale, Arizona, in 1991. *Mahan and Allied Families* was compiled by Denise Kay Mahan Moore and published in Gautier, Mississippi, in 1982.

MAHER

Ranking: 1365 **S.S. Count:** 32,457

Origin: Irish. Derived from the Gaelic name Ó Meachair, which was derived from the first name Meachar, meaning cordial and warm.

Genealogies: None known.

MAHON

Ranking: 3275 **S.S. Count:** 13,859

Origin: Irish. 1) transformation of Mahan. 2) derived from the Gaelic first name Mathghamhain, meaning bear.

Genealogies: None known.

MAHONEY (S.S. Abbreviation: Mahone)

Ranking: 666 **S.S. Count:** 62,954

Origin: Irish. Transformation of the second definition of Mahon.

Famous **Mahoneys:** MARY ELIZA MAHONEY

(1845–1926) of Massachusetts was the first black to become a nurse.

Genealogies: None known.

MAIER

Ranking: 2210 S.S. Count: 20,750
Origin: German, Jewish. Transformation of Mayer.
Genealogies: None known.

MAIN

Ranking: 2566 S.S. Count: 17,717
Origin: English. 1) derived from the Anglo-Norman-French word "magne," meaning tall. The name was given to those who were large. 2) derived from the Old French word "main," meaning hand. The name was given to those without a hand or with a misshapen hand. 3) derived from the Germanic first name Maino or Meino, which is derived from several names with a first component derived from "magin," meaning strength. 4) the name was given to those from Maine, the name of a former French province.

Genealogies: *Nimmo, Waddle (Waddell), Gavin Wilson Families Including Mains & Marshall Families of Jasper & Marion Counties, IA* was compiled by Sylvia Nimmo and published in Papillion, Nebraska, in 1988.

MAJOR

Ranking: 1617 S.S. Count: 27,673
Origin: English, Jewish. English: derived from the Norman first name Malg(i)er or Maug(i)er, which comprises the components "madal" and "gari," meaning council and spear. Jewish: transformation of Mayer.

Famous **Majors:** CHARLES MAJOR (1856–1913) of Indiana was a novelist who wrote under the pseudonym Sir Edwin Caskoden. He wrote, among other works, *When Knighthood was in Flower.*

Genealogies: None known.

MAJORS

Ranking: 3483 S.S. Count: 12,948
Origin: English. Transformation of Major.
Genealogies: None known.

MAKI

Ranking: 3152 S.S. Count: 14,398
Origin: Finnish. Derived from the Finnish word "mäki," meaning hill. The name may have been adopted by those living near a hill or taken ornamentally.
Genealogies: None known.

MALAVE

Ranking: 4580 S.S. Count: 9760
Origin: Jewish. Derived from M(e)alave, the Yiddish name for the Polish town called Mława.

Genealogies: None known.

MALCOLM, MALCOLMSON (S.S. Abbreviation: Malcol)

Ranking: 3583 S.S. Count: 12,589
Origin: Scottish. Derived from the Gaelic first name Mael-Colum, meaning a "devotee of (St.) Columba" (H&H).

Famous **Malcolms:** MALCOLM X (1925–1965) of Nebraska was a religious leader. Born Malcolm Little, he converted to the Muslim religion while in jail for robbery, taking his new name after his release in 1952. He rose in the Black Muslim organization to become its first "national minister." He preached black separatism and pride in race. In 1964 he formed his own religion, called Muslim Misque, Inc., and founded the Organization of Afro-American Unity. He converted to Islam and softened his views. He was assassinated.

Genealogies: None known.

MALDONADO (S.S. Abbreviation: Maldon)

Ranking: 410 S.S. Count: 96,691
Origin: Spanish. Derived from the Spanish phrase "mal donado," literally meaning badly given, but also referring to one having an ugly face. The name was given to those who were ugly or obtuse.

Genealogies: None known.

MALINOV, MALINOVITZ, MALINOVSKI, MALINOVSKY, MALINOWSKI (S.S. Abbreviation: Malino)

Ranking: 4018 S.S. Count: 11,269
Origin: Malinov—Bulgarian; Malinovsky—Czech; Malinov, Malinovitz, Malinovski—Jewish; Malinowski—Jewish, Polish. Malinov (Bulgarian): cognate to or transformation of Malinowski. Malinov (Jewish), Malinovitz, Malinovski: transformations of Malinowski. Malinovsky: cognate to Malinowski. Malinowski (Polish): derived from the Polish word "malina," meaning raspberry. The name was given to those from places whose name includes Malin or to those who grew raspberries. Malinowski (Jewish): uncertain etymology. Possibly an ornamental name.

Genealogies: None known.

MALLARD, MALLARMÉ, MALLARMEY, MALLARY (S.S. Abbreviation: Mallar)

Ranking: 4491 S.S. Count: 9980
Origin: Mallard—English; Mallarmé, Mallarmey—French; Mallary—Norman-English. Mallard: 1) derived from the Middle English and Old French word "malard," meaning a drake or male duck. The name was given as a nickname to those who were thought to possess the characteristics of male ducks. 2) derived from the Old French first name Malhard, which comprises the Germanic components "madal" and

"hard," meaning council and brave or hardy. *Mallarmé, Mallarmey:* derived from the Old French words "*mal*" and "*armé*," meaning badly and armed. The name was given to those who were poorly armed. *Mallary:* transformation of *Mallory.*

Genealogies: None known.

MALLET (ALSO MALLETT)

Ranking: 3191 **S.S. Count:** 14,224

Origin: English, French. English: 1) *derived from the Old French word "maleit," meaning doomed. The name was given to those who were not fortunate.* 2) *derived from the medieval feminine first name Malet, which was derived from the first name Mary.* 3) *transformation of Mallard as derived from Malhard. English, French: derived from the Old French word "ma(i)let," which was derived from "ma(i)l," meaning hammer. The name was given to smiths or warriors. French: derived from the first name Malo.*

Genealogies: *Daniel Mallett, 1790–1845* was compiled by Martha V. Mallett Sisler and published in Baltimore, Maryland, in 1980.

MALLORY (S.S. Abbreviation: Mallor)

Ranking: 1840 **S.S. Count:** 24,576

Origin: Norman-English. Derived from the Old French word "malheure," meaning unhappy or unfortunate. The name was given to those who were not lucky.

Famous **Mallorys:** STEPHEN RUSSELL MALLORY (1813?–1873) of Trinidad came to the United States as a child and served as a U.S. senator from Florida (1851–1861). He was the secretary of the navy of the Confederacy (1861–1865).

Genealogies: *The Ancestry of Harvey Dunn* was compiled by Judith Miner Hine Luedemann and published in Chester, Connecticut, in 1972. *The Mallorys of Mystic* was compiled by James P. Baughman and published in Middletown, Connecticut, in 1972.

MALLOY

Ranking: 1948 **S.S. Count:** 23,231

Origin: Irish. 1) *derived from the Gaelic name Ó Maol Aodha, meaning "descendant of the devotee of (St.) Aodh" (H&H).* 2) *derived from the Gaelic name Ó Maol Mhaodhóg, meaning "descendant of the devotee of (St.) Maodhóg" (H&H).* 3) *derived from the Gaelic name Ó Maolmhuaidh, which was derived from the first name Maolmhuadh, which comprises the components "maol" and "muadh," meaning chieftain and proud.*

Genealogies: None known.

MALONE (ALSO MALONEY)

Ranking: 260 **S.S. Count:** 140,838

Origin: Malone—Irish; Maloney—Irish. Malone: derived

from the Gaelic name *Ó Maoil Eoin,* meaning "descendant of the devotee of (St.) John" (H&H). *Maloney:* 1) *derived from the Gaelic name Mac Giolla Dhomhnaigh, meaning "son of the servant of the Church" (H&H). The name was in some cases given to the children of priests, who were illegitimate.* 2) *derived from the Gaelic name Ó Maol Dhomhnaigh, meaning "descendant of the devotee of the Church" (H&H). The name was in some cases given to the children of priests, who were illegitimate.*

Famous **Bearers:** KEMP MALONE (1889–1971) of Mississippi was the co-founder of *American Speech* and etymologist for *American College Dictionary* and *Random House Dictionary.* DUMAS MALONE (1892–1986) of Mississippi was a biographer and an authority on Thomas Jefferson, writing a six-volume biography of him. He edited the *Dictionary of American Biography* and *Political Science Quarterly.*

Genealogies: *Phelan, Malone, Kevill, Stutz & Klaes Families* was compiled by John T. Phelan and published in Baltimore, Maryland, in 1985. *Thrice Three Times Told Tales* [also Malone] was compiled by Mary Waller Shepherd Soper and published in Winchester, Tennessee, in 1979.

MANCHESTER (S.S. Abbreviation: Manche)

Ranking: 4778 **S.S. Count:** 9374

Origin: English. Derived from a first component that was derived from the word "mammā," meaning breast and referring to a hill in the shape of a breast, and the second component "ceaster," meaning Roman fort. The name was given to those from Manchester, a place in England.

Genealogies: None known.

MANCIN (ALSO MANCINELLI, MANCINETTI, MANCINI)

Ranking: 2447 **S.S. Count:** 18,553

Origin: Italian. Transformations of the name Manco, which was derived from the Italian word "manco," meaning left-handed. The name was given to those who were left-handed.

Genealogies: None known.

MANCUSI, MANCUSO (S.S. Abbreviation: Mancus)

Ranking: 3281 **S.S. Count:** 13,835

Origin: Italian. Transformations of Mancin.

Genealogies: None known.

MANDEL (ALSO MANDELBAUM, MANDELBERG, MANDELMAN, MANDELSTAM)

Ranking: 2295 **S.S. Count:** 19,862

Origin: Mandel—Austrian, German, Jewish; Mandel-

baum, Mandelberg, Mandelman, Mandelstam—Jewish. Mandel (Austrian, German): derived from the medieval first name Mann. Mandel (German): derived from the German word "mandel," meaning almond. The name was probably given to those who lived near an almond tree or to those who sold almonds. Mandel (Jewish): derived from the Yiddish word "mandl," meaning almond. Mandelbaum: Mandel combined with "baum," meaning tree. The name was taken ornamentally. Mandelberg: Mandel with "berg," meaning hill. The name was taken ornamentally. Mandelman: Mandel combined with "man," meaning man. The name was given to those who sold almonds. Mandelstam: Mandel combined with "stam(m)," meaning trunk.

Genealogies: None known.

MANESSIER (S.S. Abbreviation: Maness)

Ranking: 3888 S.S. Count: 11,596

Origin: French. Uncertain etymology. Possibly the name was given to those who came from Manens, a place in France.

Genealogies: None known.

MANGAN

Ranking: 2917 S.S. Count: 15,596

Origin: Irish. Derived from the Gaelic name Ó Mongáin, which was derived from the first name Mongán, which was derived from "mong," meaning hair or mane. The name was given to those with thick hair.

Genealogies: None known.

MANGUM

Ranking: 3444 S.S. Count: 13,098

Origin: English, French. Uncertain etymology. 1) given to those who came from Manaccan, a place in England. 2) the name was given to those who worked as butchers.

Genealogies: *The Mangums of Virginia, North Carolina, South Carolina, Georgia, Alabama & Mississippi* was compiled by John T. Palmer and published in Santa Rosa, California, in 1988.

MANLEY

Ranking: 1273 S.S. Count: 34,708

Origin: English. 1) derived from the Middle English word "mannly," meaning manly or virile. The name was given to those who were manly. 2) derived from the Old English words " (ge)mœne" and "lēah," meaning shared and clearing or wood. The name was given to those from Manley, the name of several places in England.

Genealogies: *My Husband's Folks: the Manlys and Galloways and Allied Families* [also Manleys] was compiled by Elizabeth Cate Manly and published in Cleveland, Tennessee, in 1972. *Manley Family: New England and New York, 1650–1950* was compiled by Henry Sackett Manley and published in Strykersville, New York, in 1965.

MANN

Ranking: 331 S.S. Count: 113,684

Origin: English, German, Jewish. English, German: 1) derived from an uncertain Germanic first name. 2) derived from the Middle English and Old High German word "man," meaning man. The name was given to a powerful or savage man. Jewish: uncertain etymology.

Famous **Manns**: HORACE MANN (1796–1859) of Massachusetts was an educator and is considered the father of American public education. He was responsible for organizing the public-school system and for starting the first normal school. MARY TYLER PEABODY MANN (1806–1887) of Massachusetts was the wife of Horace Mann. She was an educator and the author of *Life and Works of Horace Mann* (3 vols., 1865–1868). JAMES ROBERT MANN (1856–1922) of Indiana was a member of the U.S. House of Representatives and was noted for introducing two bills that became law, the Mann-Elkins Act of 1910, and the Mann (or White Slave Traffic) Act of 1910.

Genealogies: *George Adam Mann, 1734–1821: a Family on Four Frontiers, Pennsylvania, Virginia, Kentucky and Ohio* was compiled by Dorothy C. Knoff and published in New Orleans, Louisiana, in 1977. *The Manns of Edwards County, Illinois* was compiled by Betty M. Mann and published in Lansing, Michigan, in 1977.

MANNIN (ALSO MANNING, MANNINGTON, MANNINI, MANNINO)

Ranking: 348 S.S. Count: 109,031

Origin: Manning—English; Mannington—English; Mannin—Irish; Mannini, Mannino—Italian; Manning: transformation of the English name Mann. Mannington: the name was given to those from Merrington, the name of several places in England of different or uncertain etymologies. Mannin: derived from the Gaelic name Ó Mainnín, which was derived from the first name Mainnín, which was ultimately derived from the word "manch," meaning monk. Mannini, Mannino: cognate to the English and German name Mann, derived from an uncertain Germanic first name.

Famous **Bearers**: JAMES MANNING (1738–1791) of New Jersey was a founder and the first president of Brown University. MARIE MANNING (1873?–1945) of Washington, D.C., was a journalist and the originator of the Beatrice Fairfax column, an advice-to-the-lovelorn column.

Genealogies: *The Morgan Manning House, Home of Western Monroe Historical Society* was published in Brockport, New York, in 1971. *Manning Family, Prominent Members of Old Pinhook Church* was compiled by Carl H. Hawkins and published in Richmond, Indiana, in 1970.

MANSFIELD (S.S. Abbreviation: Mansfi)

Ranking: 1646 S.S. Count: 27,143

Origin: English. Uncertain etymology. Most likely derived from the components "mam" and "feld," meaning breast and field. The first component was most likely the name of a hill to which "feld" was later added. The name was given to those from Mansfield, a place in Nottinghamshire, England.

Famous **Mansfields:** JOSEPH KING FENNO MANSFIELD (1803–1862) of Connecticut was an army officer who served in the Mexican and Civil wars. He was killed at Antietam. RICHARD MANSFIELD (1854–1907) was born in Germany to American parents. He became one of the leading stage actors in England and the United States of his time. ARABELLA MANSFIELD (1846–1911) of Iowa was the first woman admitted to the bar in the United States. JAYNE MANSFIELD (1933–1967) of Pennsylvania, born Vera Jayne Palmer, was a Hollywood actress and sex symbol for many years. She made 25 movies in the 1950s and 1960s, one released posthumously, *Single Room Furnished* (1968).

Genealogies: *Mansfield Genealogy* was compiled by Geneva A. Daland and published in Hampton, New Hampshire, in 1980.

MANSON

Ranking: 4260 **S.S. Count:** 10,573

Origin: English, Scottish. English: transformation of the Middle English word "mann," meaning man. The name was given to a savage or powerful man. Scottish: transformation of the name Magnus, which was derived from the Latin word "magnus," meaning great.

Genealogies: None known.

MANUEL (ALSO MANUELE, MANUELI, MANUELLO)

Ranking: 1374 **S.S. Count:** 32,242

Origin: Manuele, Manueli, Manuello—Italian; Manuel—French, Portuguese, Spanish. Cognates to Emanuel.

Genealogies: None known.

MANZANARES, MANZANO (S.S. Abbreviation: Manzan)

Ranking: 4312 **S.S. Count:** 10,411

Origin: Spanish. Derived from the Spanish word "manzano," meaning apple tree. The name was given to those who lived near an apple tree or an apple orchard.

Genealogies: None known.

MAPLES

Ranking: 3089 **S.S. Count:** 14,705

Origin: English. Derived from the Middle English word "mapel," meaning maple tree. The name was given to those who lived near a maple tree.

Genealogies: *The Fifth Commandment: Legend of a Family* [also Maples] was compiled by William Maple and published in 1978. *A Maples Leaf* was compiled by Mary

Ford Southworth and published in Orange, California, in 1968.

MARCAN (ALSO MARCAND, MARCANT, MARCANTEL)

Ranking: 4084 **S.S. Count:** 11,063

Origin: Marcand, Marcant, Marcantel—French; Marcan—Irish. Marcand, Marcant, Marcantel: transformations of Marchant. Marcan: derived from the Gaelic name Ó Marcaigh, which was derived from the first name Marcach, meaning horseman.

Genealogies: None known.

MARCEL (ALSO MARCELEAU, MARCELIN, MARCELINO, MARCELO)

Ranking: 2557 **S.S. Count:** 17,774

Origin: Marcel, Marceleau—French; Marcelo—Portuguese; Marcelin, Marcelino—Portuguese. Marcel, Marceleau: cognates to Marcelo. Marcelo: derived from the first name Marcelo. Marcelin, Marcelino: derived from the the first name Marcelino.

Genealogies: None known.

MARCH

Ranking: 3083 **S.S. Count:** 14,748

Origin: Catalan, English. Catalan: cognate to the English name Mark. English: 1) derived from the Middle English word "march(e)," meaning the month March. The name was given to those born in the month of March or to those with some special connection to the month. 2) derived from the Anglo-Norman-French word "marche," meaning boundary. The name was given to those who lived near a boundary.

Famous **Marches:** FRANCIS ANDREW MARCH (1825–1911) of Massachusetts was one of the founders of modern comparative Anglo-Saxon linguistics. His sons were FRANCIS ANDREW MARCH (1863–1928) of Pennsylvania, a lexicographer, and PEYTON CONWAY MARCH (1864–1955), an army officer who served in World War I as artillery commander in France and as general and chief of staff, 1918–1921. FREDERIC MARCH (1897–1975) of Wisconsin was an actor originally named Frederick McIntyre Bickel. An actor of both the stage and the screen, he won an Academy Award for *The Best Years of Our Lives* (1946).

Genealogies: None known.

MARCHAND, MARCHANT (S.S. Abbreviation: Marcha)

Ranking: 2272 **S.S. Count:** 20,037

Origin: English, French, Jewish. Derived from the Old French and Middle English word "march(e)ant," meaning merchant. The name was given to merchants.

Genealogies: *History of the Henri Marchand II Family in*

America was compiled by Loraine B. Swiger and published in Owensboro, Kentucky, in 1981.

MARCHEL, MARCHELLI, MARCHENT, MARCHESE, MARCHETTI (S.S. Abbreviation: Marche)

Ranking: 1789 S.S. Count: 25,157

Origin: Marchent—English; Marchese—Italian; Marchel, Marchelli, Marchetti—Italian. Marchent: transformation of Marchant. Marchese: cognate to the French name Marquis. Marchel, Marchelli, Marchetti: cognates to the English name Mark.

Genealogies: None known.

MARCHI (ALSO MARCHINI, MARCHIONNE, MARCHISI, MARCHITELLI)

Ranking: 3267 S.S. Count: 13,912

Origin: Italian. Marchi, Marchini, Marchitelli: cognates to the English name Mark, derived from Marcus. Marchisi: cognate to the French name Marquis. Marchionne: cognate to the Dutch and German first name Melchior, which was derived from the Hebrew words "melech" and "or," meaning king and light.

Genealogies: None known.

MARCINIAK, MARCINIEC, MARCINKIEWICZ, MARCINKOWSKI, MARCINOWICZ (S.S. Abbreviation: Marcin)

Ranking: 3433 S.S. Count: 13,147

Origin: Polish. Cognates to Martin.

Genealogies: None known.

MARCOTTE, MARCOTTI (S.S. Abbreviation: Marcot)

Ranking: 4740 S.S. Count: 9448

Origin: Italian. Uncertain etymology. The names are probably descended from ancient Roman names.

Genealogies: None known.

MARCUM

Ranking: 2193 S.S. Count: 20,898

Origin: English, Irish. Transformation of Markham.

Genealogies: *The Way it was with our Ancestors: Markham/Marcum* was compiled by William H. Marcum and published in Fort Myers, Florida, in 1983.

MARCUS

Ranking: 1643 S.S. Count: 27,203

Origin: Danish, Dutch, Flemish, French, German, Norwegian. Cognates to the English name Mark, derived from the Latin first name Marcus.

Genealogies: None known.

MAREK

Ranking: 4424 S.S. Count: 10,138

Origin: Czech. 1) transformation of Martin. 2) derived from the Latin name Mauritius, which was derived from Maurus, which was derived from the Phoenician word "mauharim," meaning eastern. 3) derived from the first name Marek, which is a cognate to Mark.

Genealogies: None known.

MARES

Ranking: 4640 S.S. Count: 9636

Origin: Czech. Transformation of Marek.

Genealogies: None known.

MARGOLIES, MARGOLIOTH, MARGOLIS, MARGOLIUS (S.S. Abbreviation: Margol)

Ranking: 4203 S.S. Count: 10,746

Origin: Jewish. Derived from the Late Latin first name Margarita, meaning pearl. The names were taken ornamentally.

Famous **Bearers:** MAX LEOPOLD MARGOLIS (1866–1932) of Russia was a professor of biblical philology at Dropsie College and editor-in-chief of a translation of the Scriptures from Hebrew to English.

Genealogies: *The Margolis Family* was compiled by Neil Rosenstein and published in Elizabeth, New Jersey, in 1984.

MARIAN

Ranking: 2925 S.S. Count: 15,568

Origin: English. Transformation of the medieval first name Marie.

Genealogies: None known.

MARIN

Ranking: 2049 S.S. Count: 22,320

Origin: French, Jewish. French: 1) derived from the Old French word "marin," meaning sailor. The name was given to sailors. 2) derived from the first name Marin. Jewish: unknown etymology.

Famous **Marins:** FRANCISCO DE PAULA MARIN (1774–1837) of Spain was a horticulturist who moved to the Hawaiian Islands and introduced different plants and methods of agriculture to the islands. JOHN CHERI MARIN (1870–1953) of New Jersey was an American painter who is best remembered for his expressionistic seascapes and scenes of Manhattan. He worked best in watercolors.

Genealogies: None known.

MARINE

Ranking: 2601 S.S. Count: 17,464

Origin: Catalan. Derived from the Latin name Marinus.

Genealogies: None known.

MARINO (ALSO MARINOFF, MARINOLLI, MARINOTTI, MARINOV)

Ranking: 1012 S.S. Count: 43,231

Origin: Marinov—Bulgarian; Marinolli, Marinotti—Italian; Marino—Italian, Spanish; Marinoff—Jewish. Marinov, Marinolli, Marinotti, Marino: derived from the Latin name Marinus. Marinoff: transformation of the Jewish name Marin.

Genealogies: None known.

MARION (ALSO MARIONEAU)

Ranking: 2259 S.S. Count: 20,207

Origin: Marion—English; Marioneau—French. Marion: transformation of Marian. Marioneau: cognate to Marian.

Famous **Bearers:** FRANCIS MARION (1732?–1795) of South Carolina was known as the Swamp Fox. He was an American Revolutionary hero. As a commander of military troops in South Carolina during the Revolutionary War, he attacked the British troops and then escaped into the swamps and forests. He made a death-defying rescue of Americans at Parkers Ferry, South Carolina, in 1781. Before the war he served in the South Carolina Provincial Congress.

Genealogies: None known.

MARK

Ranking: 2550 S.S. Count: 17,813

Origin: English, Jewish. English: 1) derived from the Old English word "mearc," meaning boundary. The name was given to those who lived near or on the boundary of two areas or to those from Mark, the name of several places in England. 2) derived from the Latin first name Marcus. Jewish: 1) Anglization of several Jewish surnames that sound similar. 2) uncertain etymology.

Genealogies: None known.

MARKER

Ranking: 4178 S.S. Count: 10,818

Origin: English, Jewish. English: 1) derived from the Middle English word "mark(en)," meaning to place a mark on something. 2) transformation of Mercer. 3) transformation of the English name Mark, derived from the Old English word "mearc," meaning boundary between two places. Jewish: unknown etymology.

Genealogies: None known.

MARKHAM (S.S. Abbreviation: Markha)

Ranking: 2359 S.S. Count: 19,231

Origin: English, Irish. English: derived from the Old English words "mearc" and "hām," meaning boundary and homestead. The name was given to those from Markham, a place in England. Irish: derived from the Gaelic name Ó Marcacháin, which was derived from the first name Marcach, meaning horseman.

Famous **Markhams:** EDWIN MARKHAM (1852–1940) of Oregon was originally named Charles Edward Anson. He was an educator who gained fame with his poem of social protest, "The Man with the Hoe."

Genealogies: *The Way it was with our Ancestors: Markham/Marcum* was compiled by William H. Marcum and published in Fort Myers, Florida, in 1983.

MARKLE (ALSO MARKLEY)

Ranking: 2344 S.S. Count: 19,351

Origin: Markley—English; Markle—Scottish. Markley: derived from components meaning mark or boundary and wood or clearing. The name was given to those from a wood near a boundary. Markle: derived from components meaning horses and hill. The name was given to those from "the lands of Markle" (ES).

Genealogies: *John Markley Descendants* was compiled by Ruth Markley and published in Baltimore, Maryland, in 1980.

MARKOWICZ, MARKOWITZ, MARKOWSKI, MARKOWSKY (S.S. Abbreviation: Markow)

Ranking: 3138 S.S. Count: 14,463

Origin: Markowicz, Markowitz, Markowsky—Jewish; Markowicz, Markowski—Polish. Cognates to the English name Mark, derived from the Latin first name Marcus.

Genealogies: None known.

MARKS

Ranking: 591 S.S. Count: 70,567

Origin: English, German, Jewish. English: 1) transformation of the English name Mark, derived from the Old English word "mearc." 2) transformation of the English name Mark, derived from the Latin first name Marcus. German: transformation of the German first name Markus, derived from the Latin first name Marcus. Jewish: German cognate to any of several Jewish first names that sound similar.

Famous **Markses:** JOHNNY MARKS (1909–1985) of New York was a composer who is best remembered for his Christmas songs "Rudolph the Red-Nosed Reindeer" and "I Heard the Bells on Christmas Day."

Genealogies: *The LH7 Ranch in Houston's Shadow: the E. H. Marks Legacy from Longhorns to the Salt Grass Trail* was compiled by Deborah Lightfoot Sizemore and published in Denton, Texas, in 1991. *Marks-Barnett Families and their Kin* was compiled by Marion Dewoody Pettigrew and published in Baltimore, Maryland, in 1981.

MARLOW (ALSO MARLOWE)

Ranking: 1676 S.S. Count: 26,669

Origin: English. 1) derived from the English name Marley, which, of uncertain etymology, was given to those from Marley, the name of several places in England. 2) derived from the Old English words "mere" and "lafe," meaning lake and leavings. The names were given to those from Marlow, a place in Buckinghamshire, England.

Famous **Bearers:** JULIA MARLOWE (1866–1950) was born Sarah Jane Frost in England and came to the United States in 1870. She was one of the leading Shakespearean actresses of her time.

Genealogies: *The Marlow Family* was compiled by Odalene Little Ponder and published in 1985.

MARQUAND, MARQUANT, MARQUARDSEN, MARQUARDT (S.S. Abbreviation: Marqua)

Ranking: 2507 S.S. Count: 18,086
Origin: Marquardsen—Danish; Marquand, Marquant—French; Marquardt—German. Marquardsen: cognate to the German name Marquardt. Marquand, Marquant: cognates to Marchant. Marquardt: derived from the words "mark" and "wart," meaning frontier and guard. The name was given to frontier guards.

Famous **Bearers:** JOHN PHILLIPS MARQUAND (1893–1960) of Delaware was a novelist. He is best known for the character of Mr. Moto, a character in his detective series.

Genealogies: None known.

MARQUE (S.S. Abbreviation: Marque)

Ranking: 555 S.S. Count: 73,625
Origin: French. 1) derived from the Old French word "marc," meaning the name of a French coin. The name was given to those who made coins. 2) derived from the Old French word "marque," meaning boundary. The name was given to those who lived near a boundary. 3) derived from the Old French word "marque," meaning mark. The name was given to those who had been scarred through branding or to those with conspicuous birthmarks.

Genealogies: None known.

MARQUIS, MARQUISET (S.S. Abbreviation: Marqui)

Ranking: 3352 S.S. Count: 13,530
Origin: Marquiset—French; Marquis—French, Scottish. Marquiset: transformation of the French last name Marquis. Marquis (French): derived from the Old Northern French word "marquis," meaning the governor of territory on the frontier or border. The name was given to the servants of a marquis or as a nickname to those who acted like a marquis. Marquis (Scottish): derived from the Gaelic name Mac Marcuis, which was derived ultimately from the Latin name Marcus.

Famous **Bearers:** DONALD ROBERT PERRY MARQUIS (1878–1937) of Illinois was known as Don. He was a journalist and humorist known for his column, "The Sun Dial," while on the staff of the New York *Sun.*

Genealogies: None known.

MARR

Ranking: 2999 S.S. Count: 15,154
Origin: English, Scottish. English: the name was given to those from Marr, the name of a place in West Yorkshire, England. Scottish: the name was given to those from Mar, the name of a former county in Scotland.

Genealogies: None known.

MARRERO (S.S. Abbreviation: Marrer)

Ranking: 1230 S.S. Count: 35,999
Origin: Italian. Uncertain etymology. The name was given to those who made and sold hoes.

Genealogies: None known.

MARRON

Ranking: 4590 S.S. Count: 9740
Origin: Irish. Derived from the Gaelic name Ó Mearáin, which was derived from the first name Mearán, which was derived from the word "mear," meaning energetic or full of life.

Genealogies: None known.

MARSH

Ranking: 454 S.S. Count: 87,985
Origin: English. Derived from the Old English word "mersc," meaning marsh. The name was given to those who lived near a marsh.

Famous **Marshes:** GEORGE PERKINS MARSH (1801–1882) of Vermont was a lawyer, diplomat, and philologist. He was a member of Congress, minister to Turkey and then to Italy, a scholar, and a contributor to the *Oxford English Dictionary.* He wrote *The Origin and History of the English Language.* SYLVESTER MARSH (1803–1884) of New Hampshire was an inventor. He invented a special engine capable of moving things up long, steep hills. The inclined railway up Mt. Washington in New Hampshire is one of the best examples of his invention. OTHNIEL CHARLES MARSH (1831–1899) of New York was a paleontologist. He led expeditions to the West in search of fossils and is credited with the discovery of more than 1000. He donated the finds to Yale University, where his uncle, George Peabody, was a professor. He wrote several books dealing with the fossils of North America. MAE MARSH (1895–1968) of New Mexico was a film actress and is best remembered for her role in *Birth of a Nation.* REGINALD MARSH (1898–1954) was born in Paris, France, to American parents. He was an illustrator for New York City magazines and a teacher at several art schools. He is best known for his paintings of New York City scenes.

Genealogies: *The Ancestors and Descendants of F. A. Marsh and Ivy Crites* was compiled by William R. Marsh and published in Baltimore, Maryland, in 1990. *Genealogy of the Family of George Marsh* was compiled by

Eliezer Jewett Marsh and published in Rutland, Vermont, in 1985.

MARSHALL (S.S. Abbreviation: Marsha)

Ranking: 116 S.S. Count: 251,530

Origin: English, Scottish. Derived from the Middle English and Old French word "maresc(h)al," meaning marshall. The name was given to those who cared for horses.

Famous **Marshalls:** CHRISTOPHER MARSHALL (1709–1797) of Ireland was a pharmacist in Philadelphia but is best remembered for the diary he kept during the time of the American Revolution. The published diary is titled *Remembrancer.* THOMAS MARSHALL (1730–1802) of Virginia was a Revolutionary War leader, serving in the Continental army and as a member of the Virginia House of Burgesses. He was the father of John Marshall. JOHN MARSHALL (1755–1835) of Virginia was a Revolutionary War soldier and the main founder of the system of constitutional law in the United States. He was the chief justice of the United States. JAMES WILSON MARSHALL (1810–1885) of New Jersey was the partner of John Sutter, who first discovered the gold at Sutter's Mill that led to the famous California gold rush. CLARA MARSHALL (1847–1931) of Pennsylvania was the dean of the Woman's Medical College of Pennsylvania. THOMAS RILEY MARSHALL (1854–1925) of Indiana was the governor of Indiana and the vice president of the United States (1913–1921) under President Woodrow Wilson. He is credited with saying, "What this country needs is a really good five-cent cigar." LOUIS MARSHALL (1856–1929) of New York was a lawyer who defended the rights of minorities. He was a founder of both the Jewish Welfare Board and the American Jewish Committee. FRANK JAMES MARSHALL (1877–1944) of New York City was a chess champion who won the U.S. title in 1909 and held it until his retirement in 1936. GEORGE CATLETT MARSHALL (1880–1959) of Pennsylvania was a career army officer and the originator in 1947, as U.S. secretary of state, of the European Recovery Program—better known as the Marshall Plan. He received the Nobel Peace Prize in 1953. THURGOOD MARSHALL (1908–1993) of Maryland was the first African American to serve as a justice for the U.S. Supreme Court. His most notable victory came in the 1954 *Brown v. Board of Education* case, in which he successfully argued against "separate but equal" schools.

Genealogies: *Forebears and Descendants of an Early Houston Family* was compiled by Maudie Marie Holt Marshall and published in Houston, Texas, in 1975. *A History of the Marshall and Related Families* was compiled by Wallace Marshall and published in La Fayette, Indiana, in 1922. *Marshall Pioneers and their Descendants Across Canada and the United States* was compiled by Joan Jowsey and published in Aylmer, Quebec, in 1983.

MARTEL (ALSO MARTELET, MARTELL, MARTELLI, MARTELLO)

Ranking: 1386 S.S. Count: 31,937

Origin: Martell—English; Martel—English, French; Martelet—French; Martelli, Martello—Italian. Martell, Martel, Martelet: 1) derived from the Old French word "martel," meaning hammer. The name was given to smiths or to those who were powerful. 2) derived from a medieval first name that was derived from either the name Martin or the name Marthe. Martelli, Martello: cognates to Martel.

Genealogies: None known.

MARTEN (ALSO MARTENS, MARTENSEN, MARTENSSON)

Ranking: 2080 S.S. Count: 22,037

Origin: Marten—English; Martens—Dutch, English, German; Martensen—German; Martensson—Swedish. Transformations of and cognates to Martin.

Genealogies: None known.

MARTIN (ALSO MARTINEAU, MARTINELLI, MARTINETTI, MARTINS)

Ranking: 6 S.S. Count: 1,623,237

Origin: Martin—Czech, Danish, Dutch, English, Flemish, French, German, Irish, Norwegian, Scottish; Martins—English; Martineau—French; Martinelli, Martinetti—Italian. Derived from the first name Martin, which was ultimately derived from Mars, the name of the Roman god of war.

Famous **Martins:** LUTHER MARTIN (1748?–1826) of New Jersey was a lawyer and the first attorney general of Maryland. He was a member of the Revolutionary political groups. As a lawyer, he defended Samuel Chase and Aaron Burr. MARIA MARTIN (1796–1863) of South Carolina was one of the best nature painters of the 19th century. HOMER DODGE MARTIN (1836–1897) of New York was a painter. He is associated with the Hudson River school and later impressionism. LILLIEN JANE MARTIN (1851–1943) of New York was a psychologist. She taught at Stanford University and was the first woman appointed the head of a Stanford department. EDWARD SANDFORD MARTIN (1856–1939) of New York was an editor and writer and a founder of the *Harvard Lampoon.* He also was a member of the editorial staff of *Harper's Weekly.* GEORGIA MAY MADDEN MARTIN (1866–1946) of Kentucky went by the name George. She was an author and an expert on race relations. She wrote *Children in the Mist,* which followed the lives of black children in the South who had to deal daily with the injustices of white neighbors. ANNE HENRIETTA MARTIN (1875–1951) of Nevada was the first woman to run for the U.S. Senate. She ran in 1918 and 1920. Although she was not elected, she was a pioneer in the role of the woman in politics. JOSEPH WILLIAM MARTIN (1884–1968) of Massachusetts was a career politician. He served as a member of Congress

(1925–1967) and as Speaker of the House for several terms. GLENN LUTHER MARTIN (1886–1955) of Iowa was an airplane manufacturer and the founder of one of the first airplane factories in the United States. The plant, located in Santa Ana, California, built B-10 and B-26 planes for World War II.

Genealogies: *Adam Martin (1755–1835) and Thomas Roy Musick (1757–1842), St. Louis County, Missouri, Pioneers* was compiled by Michal Martin Farmer and published in Wolfe City, Texas, in 1989. *Colonial Pioneers: Martin and Bell Families and their Kin* was compiled by Mary Coates Martin and published in Bountiful, Utah, in 1992. *Deacon John Burnham of Ipswich and Ebenezer Martin of Rehoboth, Massachusetts* was compiled by Elisabeth Puckett Martin and published in Baltimore, Maryland, in 1987.

MARTZ

Ranking: 3994 S.S. Count: 11,321

Origin: German? Uncertain etymology. 1) possibly derived from the name Mertz, which was derived from words referring to Mars, the Roman god of war, or meaning famous. 2) The name was possibly given to those who came from Mertz, a place in Germany. 3) the name was possibly given to those who sold trinkets and other small items.

Genealogies: None known.

MARVIN (S.S. Abbreviation: Marvin)

Ranking: 3163 S.S. Count: 14,351

Origin: English. Derived from the first name Marvin, which is comprised of components meaning sea and friend.

Famous **Marvins:** HAROLD M. MARVIN (1893–1977) of Florida was a prominent cardiologist in Connecticut, a professor at Yale University, and the author of *Your Heart—A Handbook for Laymen* (1960).

Genealogies: *An Ormsbee Odyssey* [also Marvin] was compiled by Nora O'Dell Coppage and published in Concord, California, in 1990.

MARX

Ranking: 2691 S.S. Count: 16,928

Origin: German, Jewish. Transformation of Marks.

Famous **Marxes:** THE MARX BROTHERS consisted of a total of five brothers who teamed to become a vaudeville and comedy team. They were JULIUS HENRY MARX (1890–1977), who was known as GROUCHO; LEONARD MARX (1891–1961), who was known as CHICO; ARTHUR MARX, whose original name was ADOLPH (1893–1964) and who was known as HARPO; MILTON MARX (1894–1977), who was known as GUMMO; and HERBERT MARX (1901–1979), who was known as ZEPPO. They were all born in New York City. They played vaudeville, then movie comedies, with Harpo, Chico, and Groucho the three full-time actors.

Gummo left the group after the vaudeville days and was replaced by Zeppo, the youngest, for some of the movies. After their movie career, Groucho hosted a radio, then television, quiz show called "You Bet Your Life."

Genealogies: None known.

MASHBURN (S.S. Abbreviation: Mashbu)

Ranking: 4355 S.S. Count: 9215

Origin: German? Uncertain etymology. Derived from the Old English word "miscian," meaning to mix.

Genealogies: None known.

MASON

Ranking: 135 S.S. Count: 222,112

Origin: English, Scottish. Derived from the Middle English and Old French word "mas(s)on," meaning stone mason. The name was given to stone masons.

Famous **Masons:** JOHN MASON (1588–1635) of England was one of the founders of New Hampshire. JOHN MITCHELL MASON (1770–1829) of New York City was a clergyman and educator and the president of Dickinson College. LOWELL MASON (1792–1872) of Massachusetts was a music teacher who helped to organize the Boston Academy of Music and established the first public-school music program in the United States. WILLIAM MASON (1829–1908) of Massachusetts was a concert pianist and the author of several music books. HENRY MASON (1831–1890) of Massachusetts was a builder of pianos and organs. He co-founded the Mason and Hamlin Organ and Piano Co. DANIEL GREGORY MASON (1873–1953) of Massachusetts was a composer and a music teacher at Columbia University. MAX MASON (1877–1961) of Wisconsin was a mathematician and the inventor of submarine-detection devices. OTIS TUFTON MASON (1838–1908) of Maine was an ethnologist and curator at several museums. LUCY RANDOLPH MASON (1882–1959) of Virginia was a social reformer. She served for many years as the public relations person for the Congress of Industrial Organizations (CIO).

Genealogies: *Yesterday, a History of Norwegian Ancestry* [also Mason] was compiled by Evelyn Hoff and published in Winona, Wisconsin, in 1985. *The Five George Masons* was compiled by Pamela C. Copeland and published in Charlottesville, Virginia, in 1975. *John Mason and Mary Ann Miller* was compiled by Floyd R. Mason and published in Alexandria, Virginia, in 1986.

MASSARI, MASSARINI, MASSARO, MASSAROLLI, MASSARUTTI (S.S. Abbreviation: Massar)

Ranking: 4028 S.S. Count: 11,242

Origin: Italian. The names were given to those who worked as tenant farmers or farm managers.

Genealogies: None known.

MASSEN (ALSO MASSENET, MASSENS)

Ranking: 3514 S.S. Count: 12,833

Origin: Massenet—French; Massen, Massens—German. Massenet: transformation of Thomas. Massen, Massens: transformation of Maas, derived from Thomas.

Genealogies: None known.

MASSEY

Ranking: 552 S.S. Count: 74,105

Origin: English, French. Derived from the Gallo-Roman first name Maccius with the suffix "ācum." The name was given to those from Massey, the name of several places in France.

Genealogies: *Descendants of Arthur Massey, Cheraws District, South Carolina* was compiled by Carmae Massey Smith and published in Owensboro, Kentucky, in 1980. *The Masseys of Grenadier Island* was compiled by Elizabeth C. Meilahn and published in Chetek, Wisconsin, in 1991.

MASSIE

Ranking: 3069 S.S. Count: 14,790

Origin: English, French. Transformation of Massey.

Genealogies: *The Family of John Massie, 1743–c. 1830, Revolutionary Patriot of Louisa County, Virginia* was compiled by Mavis Parrott Kelsey and published in Houston, Texas, in 1979. *A Massie Family History* was compiled by Evelyn Hepworth Massie and published in Kennewick, Washington, in 1972.

MAST

Ranking: 3974 S.S. Count: 11,392

Origin: English, French. Transformation of and cognate to Master.

Genealogies: *The Jacob S. Kurtz Family* [also Mast] was compiled by Lydia Kurtz Baer and published in Harrisonburg, Virginia, in 1981. *Descendants of Emanuel J. Miller and Magdelena Weaver* [also Mast] was compiled by Eli D. Mast and published in Apple Creek, Ohio, in 1970.

MASTER (ALSO MASTERMAN, MASTERS, MASTERSON, MASTERTON)

Ranking: 788 S.S. Count: 53,387

Origin: Master—English, Scottish; Masterman, Masters, Masterson—English; Masterton—Scottish. Master: derived from the Middle English word "maister," meaning master. The name was given to those who were imperious or to those who were master craftsmen. Masterman: derived from Master with "man," meaning "servant of the master" (H&H). Masters, Masterson: transformations of Master. Masterton: derived from the Old English words "maister" and "tūn," meaning master and settlement. The name was given to those who came from Masterton, the name of a place in Scotland.

Famous **Bearers:** SYBILLA MASTERS (pre-1687–1720) of

New Jersey or Bermuda was an inventor whose best-known products were a device for cleaning and curing Indian corn to be used as a medicine for consumption and a second one for the weaving of straw and palmetto leaves into hats and mats. She is believed to have been the first female inventor in America. WILLIAM BARCLAY MASTERSON (1853–1921) of Illinois was known as Bat. He was a peace officer who was associated with Wyatt Earp in Tombstone, Arizona. EDGAR LEE MASTERS (1869–1950) of Kansas was a writer of many books, including *Spoon River Anthology*.

Genealogies: *The Masters Family of Ithaca, N.Y.* was compiled by Arthur C. Downs and published in Primos, Pennsylvania, in 1963.

MASTRO

Ranking: 2445 S.S. Count: 18,573

Origin: Italian. Cognate to Master.

Genealogies: None known.

MATA

Ranking: 2207 S.S. Count: 20,820

Origin: Catalan, Portuguese, Spanish. The name was given to those who lived near an area where trees were cultivated.

Genealogies: None known.

MATHENY (S.S. Abbreviation: Mathen)

Ranking: 2730 S.S. Count: 16,674

Origin: French. Derived from the first name Matto and a component meaning estate. The name was given to those who came from Mathenay, a place in France.

Genealogies: *Matheny Genealogy* was compiled by Dolores E. Matheny Gucciardo and published in Little Rock, Arkansas, in 1980.

MATHER (ALSO MATHERS)

Ranking: 1881 S.S. Count: 24,065

Origin: English. Mather: 1) uncertain etymology. Possibly derived from the Middle English word "mad(d)er," meaning a red dye from a plant root. The name was given to dyers or to those who sold dyes. 2) derived from the Old English word "mœðere," meaning grass or hay. The name was given to a mower or gatherer of grass or hay.

Famous **Bearers:** RICHARD MATHER (1596–1669) of England was a minister who came to America and became the leader of Congregationalism in Massachusetts. He was the author of several books, including *The Bay Psalm Book*. INCREASE MATHER (1639–1723) of Massachusetts was a preacher and the son of Richard. He wrote *Cases of Conscience Concerning Evil Spirits*, which is credited with ending the witchcraft trials of Salem. COTTON MATHER (1663–1728) of Massachusetts was the son of Increase. He was also a clergyman and an opposer of the royal governor. At first he approved of the Salem witch trials, but he later reversed his position. His interest in science led him to speak and write in favor of smallpox innoculations in 1721. However, the populace condemned him for his stand. He was active in the fields of education and charity work. He wrote more than 400 pieces, with *Curiosa Americana* winning him a membership in the Royal Society of London. STEPHEN TYNG MATHER (1867–1930) of California was one of the founders of the Thorkildsen-Mather Borax Co. and the organizer and director of the National Park Service. He was responsible for the organization and establishment of the principles for the continued preservation of the parks.

Genealogies: *The History of King Philip's War* [also Mather] was compiled by Increase Mather and published in Bowie, Maryland, in 1990. *Mather Books & Portraits through Six Early American Generations* was compiled by Franklin P. Cole and published in Portland, Maine, in 1978.

MATHES (ALSO MATHESON)
Ranking: 2220 **S.S. Count:** 20,699
Origin: Mathes—English; Matheson—Scottish. Transformations of Matthew.
Genealogies: None known.

MATHEW (ALSO MATHEWES, MATHEWS, MATHEWSON)
Ranking: 459 **S.S. Count:** 87,222
Origin: English, Scottish. Transformations of Matthew.
Famous **Bearers:** ANN TERESA MATHEWS (1732–1800) of Maryland was the co-founder, with Frances Dickinson, of the first Roman Catholic convent in the United States. SHAILER MATHEWS (1863–1941) of Maine was a leader in the Social Gospel movement. He wrote several books on Christianity. CHRISTOPHER MATHEWSON (1880–1925) of Pennsylvania was a baseball player known as Christy, Matty, and Big Six. He was one of the first players elected to the Baseball Hall of Fame.

Genealogies: *The Mat(t)hews Family* was compiled by John R. Boots and published in Ocala, Florida, in 1970. *A Matthews (also Mathews) Trail from Wales to West Virginia* was compiled by Nelson Elbert Matthews and published in 1990. *Mathews Family History* was compiled by Nathan Mathews and published in Baltimore, Maryland, in 1990.

MATHIAS, MATHIASEN, MATHIASSEN (S.S. Abbreviation: Mathia)
Ranking: 3299 **S.S. Count:** 13,747
Origin: Mathias—English, French, Scottish; Mathiasen, Mathiassen—Danish, Norwegian. Cognates to and transformations of Matthew.

Genealogies: *The Mathias Family of Hardy County, Virginia and West Virginia* was compiled by George R. Griffiths and published in Chicago, Illinois, in 1977.

MATHIE (ALSO MATHIES, MATHIESON, MATHIEU)
Ranking: 3296 **S.S. Count:** 13,759
Origin: Mathies—English; Mathie, Mathieu—French; Mathieson—Scottish. Cognates to and transformations of Matthew.
Genealogies: None known.

MATHIS (ALSO MATHISEN, MATHISON, MATHISSEN)
Ranking: 503 **S.S. Count:** 79,824
Origin: Mathisen, Mathissen—Danish, Norwegian; Mathis—English, French; Mathison—Scottish. Cognates to and transformations of Matthew.
Genealogies: *The Mathis Family of Little Egg Harbor* was compiled by Murray Harris and published in Woodbury, New Jersey, in 1987.

MATLOCK (S.S. Abbreviation: Matloc)
Ranking: 2807 **S.S. Count:** 16,231
Origin: English. Derived from components meaning oak and meeting. The name was given to those from Matlock, a place in England.
Genealogies: None known.

MATOS
Ranking: 1524 **S.S. Count:** 29,174
Origin: Portuguese. Transformation of Mata.
Genealogies: None known.

MATSON
Ranking: 2545 **S.S. Count:** 17,848
Origin: English. Transformation of Matthew.
Genealogies: None known.

MATTER (ALSO MATTERSON)
Ranking: 3262 **S.S. Count:** 13,944
Origin: Matterson—English; Matter—German. Matterson: transformation of Matthew. Matter: cognate to Mead, derived from the Middle Engilsh word "mede," meaning meadow.
Genealogies: None known.

MATTES
Ranking: 3127 **S.S. Count:** 14,542
Origin: English, Jewish. English: transformation of Matthew. Jewish: derived from the Old High German word "maget," meaning maiden, and the possessive suffix "-s."
Genealogies: None known.

MATTHEW (ALSO MATTHEWMAN, MATTHEWS, MATTHEWSON)

Ranking: 178 S.S. Count: 189,048

Origin: Matthew—English, Scottish; Matthewman, Matthews, Matthewson—English. Matthew: derived from the Middle English first name Mathew, which was derived from the Hebrew first name Matityahu, meaning "gift of God" (H&H). Matthewman: derived from Matthew with man, meaning "servant of Matthew" (H&H). Matthews, Matthewson: transformations of Matthew.

Famous **Matthewses:** STANLEY MATTHEWS (1824–1889) of Ohio was a lawyer, U.S. senator, and associate justice of the Supreme Court. [JAMES] BRANDER MATTHEWS (1852–1929) of Louisiana was an author and educator and a professor at Columbia University. VICTORIA EARLE MATTHEWS (1861–1907) of Georgia was born into slavery from an African-American mother and a white father. She was an author and clubwoman and the first president of the Woman's Loyal Union of New York and Brooklyn, and she helped to found the National Federation of Afro-American Women. She also worked to keep young black girls who had recently arrived in New York City from falling into the trap of prostitution because of a lack of funds or housing.

Genealogies: The Mat(t)hews Family was compiled by John R. Boots and published in Ocala, Florida, in 1970. *A Matthews Trail from Wales to West Virginia* [also Mathews] was compiled by Nelson Elbert Matthews and published in 1990. *Mathews Family History* [also Matthews] was compiled by Nathan Mathews and published in Baltimore, Maryland, in 1990.

MATTHIAS, MATTHIESEN, MATTHIS, MATTHISON, MATTHIUS (S.S. Abbreviation: Matthi)

Ranking: 4327 S.S. Count: 10,357

Origin: Matthiesen—Danish, German, Norwegian; Matthias—English, Scottish; Matthis—French; Matthius—German; Matthison—Scottish. Cognates to and transformations of Matthew.

Famous **Bearers:** FRANCIS OTTO MATTHIESEN (1902–1950) of California was a scholar and an English professor at Harvard University.

Genealogies: None known.

MATTIN (ALSO MATTINGLEY, MATTINGLY, MATTINGSON, MATTINSON)

Ranking: 2170 S.S. Count: 21,127

Origin: Mattin, Mattingson, Mattinson—English; Mattingley, Mattingly—English. Mattin, Mattingson, Mattinson: transformations of Matthew. Mattingley, Mattingly: transformation of Matthew. The name was given to those from Mattingley, the name of a place in England.

Genealogies: *The Mattingly Family, Hinckley, Ohio* was compiled by Francis A. LaCroix and published in Maplewood, New Jersey, in 1977.

MATTISON, MATTISSON (S.S. Abbreviation: Mattis)

Ranking: 3416 S.S. Count: 13,242

Origin: Mattison—English; Mattisson—Swedish. Transformations of and cognates to Matthew.

Genealogies: None known.

MATTOX

Ranking: 3164 S.S. Count: 14,347

Origin: English, Welsh. The name means "the son of Madoc" (CB), meaning fortunate.

Genealogies: *Asa Lee Mattox and Nellie Frances Edwards* was compiled by Patricia Eileen Jeski Goodspeed and published in Knightstown, Indiana, in 1983.

MATTSON (S.S. Abbreviation: Mattso)

Ranking: 1922 S.S. Count: 23,491

Origin: English. The name means "son of Matthew" (CB), meaning "gift of Jehovah" (CB).

Genealogies: *Genealogy of the Mattson Family* was compiled by George P. Walmsley and published in Woodbury, New Jersey, in 1983. *Our Family Chronicle* [also Mattson] was compiled by Charyl Mattson and published in Tulsa, Oklahoma, in 1982.

MAULDIN (ALSO MAULDING) (S.S. Abbreviation: Mauldi)

Ranking: 3113 S.S. Count: 14,611

Origin: English. Uncertain etymology. The names possibly mean "son of Magdalene" (CB).

Genealogies: *Ambrose Maulding* [also Mauldin] was compiled by Denzil R. Mauldin and published in Valdez, Alaska, in 1982.

MAUPIN

Ranking: 4557 S.S. Count: 9805

Origin: French? Uncertain etymology. The name was possibly given to those who worked in or near a house with pillars.

Genealogies: None known.

MAURER

Ranking: 1568 S.S. Count: 28,457

Origin: German, Jewish. German: derived from the Latin word "mūrus," meaning wall. The name was given to those who built fortification walls. Jewish: cognate to the German name Maurer. The name was given to bricklayers or masons.

Genealogies: *A Genealogy of Jacob S. Maurer and Wife*

Elisabeth Rickli was compiled by William Benz Maynard and published in Baltimore, Maryland, in 1984.

MAURO

Ranking: 4666 S.S. Count: 9585

Origin: Italian. Derived from the Middle English word "more," meaning moor.

Genealogies: None known.

MAXEY

Ranking: 2906 S.S. Count: 15,670

Origin: English. Derived from the first name Mack and the Old English word "ēg," meaning island. The name was given to those from Maxey, the name of a place in England.

Genealogies: *The Barrens* [also Maxey] was compiled by Emery H. White and published in Glasgow, Kentucky, in 1986. *The Maxeys of Virginia* was compiled by Edythe Maxey Clark and published in Baltimore, Maryland, in 1980.

MAXWELL (S.S. Abbreviation: Maxwel)

Ranking: 430 S.S. Count: 92,476

Origin: Jewish, Scottish. Jewish: transformation of any number of similar-sounding surnames or simple adoptions of the Scottish name. Scottish: transformation of Mackeswell, meaning "spring, stream of Mack" (H&H). The name was given to those from Maxwell, a place in Scotland.

Famous **Maxwells**: ANNA CAROLINE MAXWELL (1851–1929) of New York was a nurse, educator, and superintendent of nursing. ELSA MAXWELL (1883–1963) of Iowa was a syndicated columnist and the hostess of the radio program "Elsa Maxwell's Party Line."

Genealogies: *Ancestors* [Maxwell Family] was compiled by William Maxwell and published in New York, New York, in 1971. *Brandenburg-Maxwell, Brazelton-Lamb, Mitchell-Drake, Sanders-Killen* was compiled by Sarah G. Sitz and published in Manhattan, Kansas, in 1979.

MAY

Ranking: 253 S.S. Count: 143,277

Origin: English, French, German, Jewish. English: 1) derived from the Middle English word "may," meaning a young woman or young man. 2) transformation of Matthew. English, French, German: derived from the Middle English and Old French word "mai," meaning the month May. The name was given in connection with the month of May—for example, to those born during that month. Jewish: derived from the Yiddish word "may," meaning lilac. The name was taken ornamentally.

Famous **Mays**: ABIGAIL WILLIAMS MAY (1829–1888) of Massachusetts was active in the New England Freemen's Aid Society and was a supporter of black institutes of higher learning. ROBERT LEWIS MAY (1905–1976) of New York wrote the story "Rudolph the Red-Nosed Reindeer," on which is based the Johnny Marks song of the same title.

Genealogies: *The Descendants of Claiborne B. May* was compiled by Imogene May Boswell and published in Carrollton, Texas, in 1990. *Ancestors and Descendants of Patty Blackburn Davis (also May Family)* was compiled by Patty Dahm Pascoe and published in Baltimore, Maryland, in 1984.

MAYBERG, MAYBERRY (S.S. Abbreviation: Mayber)

Ranking: 2281 S.S. Count: 19,922

Origin: Mayberry—English; Mayberg—Jewish. Mayberry: uncertain etymology. Most likely a transformation of Maybury. The name was given to those from Maybury, the name of a place in England. Mayberg: derived from the Jewish name May with "berg," meaning hill.

Genealogies: None known.

MAYER

Ranking: 727 S.S. Count: 58,179

Origin: English, German, Jewish. English: derived from the Middle English and Old French word "mair(e)," meaning mayor. The name was given to mayors. German: derived from the Middle High German word "meier," meaning mayor. The name was given to mayors or local officials. Jewish: derived from the masculine Yiddish first name Meyer, which was derived from the Hebrew word "meir," meaning "enlightener" (H&H).

Famous **Mayers**: LOUIS BURT MAYER (1885–1957) of Russia was a motion-picture producer. He founded Metro Pictures Corp. and Louis B. Mayer Pictures Corp. They merged with Goldwyn Corp. to become Metro-Goldwyn-Mayer Corp., or MGM. He developed the star system and had under contract such stars as Clark Gable, Greta Garbo, and Joan Crawford. MARIA GERTRUDE GOEPPERT MAYER (1906–1972), of what was then Germany and is now Poland, was a physicist who was awarded the Nobel Prize in physics in 1963 for studies on nuclear shell structure.

Genealogies: *John Nicholas Mayer and all Known Descendants* was compiled by Sallyann Jean Seaman and published in Owensboro, Kentucky, in 1981.

MAYES

Ranking: 1326 S.S. Count: 33,390

Origin: English. Transformation of May, derived from Matthew.

Genealogies: *Genealogical Notes on a Branch of the Family of Mayes* was compiled by Edward Mayes and published in Jackson, Mississippi, in 1928.

MAYFIELD (S.S. Abbreviation: Mayfie)

Ranking: 1090 S.S. Count: 40,471

Origin: English. Derived from various first components and the Old English word "feld," meaning field. The name was given to those from Mayfield, the name of places in England.

Genealogies: None known.

MAYHEW

Ranking: 3454 **S.S. Count:** 13,068

Origin: English. Derived from the Norman first name Mahieu, a cognate to Matthew.

Famous **Mayhews:** THOMAS MAYHEW (1593–1682) of England came to America and bought Martha's Vineyard, Nantucket, and the Elizabeth Islands. He was the governor of Martha's Vineyard from 1671 until his death. JONATHAN MAYHEW (1720–1746), born on Martha's Vineyard, was the great-great-grandson of Thomas. A Congregational minister, he served as the pastor of West Church in Boston. He was best known for his liberalism in religious doctrine.

Genealogies: *Genealogical History of Nathaniel Mayhew* was compiled by Ralph Danforth Shipp and published in Boulder, Colorado, in 1972. *Mayhew Mixtures* was compiled by Elizabeth Smith Craghead and published in 1989.

MAYNARD (S.S. Abbreviation: Maynar)

Ranking: 866 **S.S. Count:** 49,688

Origin: English, French. Derived from the Germanic first name Mainard, which comprises the components "magin" and "hard," meaning strength and hardy or brave.

Genealogies: *A Genealogy of Jacob S. Maurer (also Maynard Family) and Wife Elisabeth Rickli* was compiled by William Benz Maynard and published in Baltimore, Maryland, in 1984. *The Maynards of East Kentucky* was compiled by Roland B. Maynard and published in Pikeville, Kentucky, in 1979.

MAYO

Ranking: 969 **S.S. Count:** 45,032

Origin: English, Spanish. English: transformation of Mayhew. Spanish: cognate to the English, French, and German name May.

Famous **Mayos:** WILLIAM WORRALL MAYO (1819–1911) of England was a physician who helped the Sisters of St. Francis found St. Mary's Hospital in 1889 in Rochester, Minnesota. WILLIAM JAMES MAYO (1861–1939) of Minnesota was the son of William Worrall Mayo. He developed the Mayo Clinic at St. Mary's Hospital and co-developed the Mayo Foundation for Medical Education and Research with his brother Charles. CHARLES HORACE MAYO (1865–1939) of Minnesota was a surgeon and co-founder with his brother William of the Mayo Foundation. He was also responsible for the modernization of goiter surgery and neurosurgery procedures. KATHERINE MAYO (1867–1940) of Pennsylvania was an author of magazine articles, novels,

and nonfiction. SARA TEW MAYO (1869–1930) of Louisiana was a physician and a surgeon in New Orleans. The hospital where she worked was named in her honor after her death. CHARLES WILLIAM MAYO (1898–1968) of Minnesota was the son of Charles Horace Mayo. Also a surgeon, he was on the Mayo Clinic's board of directors.

Genealogies: *Mayo Genealogy* was compiled by Elna Jean May Mayo and published in Pueblo, Colorado, in 1965.

MAYS

Ranking: 782 **S.S. Count:** 53,864

Origin: English. Transformation of the English name May, derived from Matthew.

Genealogies: *Genealogy and History of Thomas B. Hamrick, John Ray, Seaborn Mays, and E. Warbington* was compiled by Orville O. Ray and published in 1970.

MAZUR

Ranking: 3875 **S.S. Count:** 11,634

Origin: Jewish, Polish. Derived from either Masovia or Masuria, the name of two different Polish provinces.

Genealogies: *It Began with Zade Usher* [also Mazur] was compiled by Yaffa Draznin and published in Los Angeles, California, in 1972.

MAZZA

Ranking: 4231 **S.S. Count:** 10,652

Origin: Italian. Derived from the Italian word "mazzare," meaning to kill. The name was given to those who were destructive.

Genealogies: None known.

MCADAM (ALSO MCADAMS)

Ranking: 2302 **S.S. Count:** 19,816

Origin: Irish, Scottish. Cognates to Adam.

Famous **Bearers:** JOHN LOUDON MCADAM (1756–1836) of Scotland was an engineer and surveyor of roads who devised a way to improve the surfaces of roads by surfacing them with crushed stones. Roads that were so treated were called "macadamized" roads. Today, people in some parts of the United States refer to blacktopped roads as macadam roads.

Genealogies: *Isaac Towell & his Family* [also McAdam] was compiled by Roy H. Towell and published in Beaumont, Texas, in 1990. *My Findings* [also McAdams] was compiled by Lillian Vesta Brown Johnson and published in Smyrna, Tennessee, in 1987.

MCAFEE

Ranking: 2603 **S.S. Count:** 17,456

Origin: Irish. Derived from the Gaelic name Dubhshithe, which comprises components meaning black and peace.

Famous **McAfees:** JOHN A. MCAFEE (1831–1890) of Missouri was co-founder and president of Park College.

Genealogies: *Family of Andrew Hunter McAfee* was compiled by Broadus McAfee and published in Fairfax, Virginia, in 1973.

MCALISH, MCALISTER (S.S. Abbreviation: McAlis)

Ranking: 2780 **S.S. Count:** 16,389

Origin: McAlister—Irish, Scottish; McAlish—Scottish. McAlister: cognate to Alexander. McAlish: transformation of Gillis.

Genealogies: None known.

MCALLISTER (S.S. Abbreviation: McAlli)

Ranking: 1074 **S.S. Count:** 41,039

Origin: Irish, Scottish. Cognate to Alexander.

Famous **McAllisters:** MATTHEW HALL MCALLISTER (1800–1865) of Georgia was a prominent lawyer and legislator in Georgia, then a circuit judge in California. His sons, HALL MCALLISTER (1826–1888) and SAMUEL WARD MCALLISTER (1827–1895), both of Georgia, also were lawyers. Hall McAllister practiced in California, and Samuel Ward McAllister moved to New York City, where he became a social leader. He developed the lists containing "the four hundred," society's elite. CHARLES A. MCALLISTER (1867–1932) of New Jersey was a chief engineer for the U.S. Coast Guard, then president of the American Bureau of Shipping.

Genealogies: None known.

MCALPIN, MCALPINE (S.S. Abbreviation: McAlpi)

Ranking: 4786 **S.S. Count:** 9355

Origin: Scottish. Derived from the name Ailpean, meaning elf.

Famous **Bearers:** WILLIAM JARVIS MCALPINE (1812–1890) of New York City was a civil engineer. He was the chief or consulting engineer for many of the country's bridges.

Genealogies: *McAlpin(e) Genealogies* was compiled by Doris McAlpin Russell and published in Baltimore, Maryland, in 1990.

MCANDREW (S.S. Abbreviation: McAndr)

Ranking: 4991 **S.S. Count:** 8991

Origin: Scottish. Cognate to Andrew.

Famous **McAndrews:** WILLIAM MCANDREW (1863–1937) of Michigan was one of the most colorful and notable public-education administrators in New York City and Chicago.

Genealogies: *Clan McAndrew* was compiled by A. T.

Skeen and published in Winston-Salem, North Carolina, in 1988.

MCARTHUR, MCARTHY (S.S. Abbreviation: McArth)

Ranking: 2534 **S.S. Count:** 17,886

Origin: McArthy—Irish; McArthur—Irish, Scottish. McArthy: transformation of McCarthy. McArthur: cognate to Arthur.

Famous **Bearers:** DUNCAN MCARTHUR (1772–1839) of New York was a general in the army during the War of 1812 and was later governor of Ohio. ARTHUR MCARTHUR (1845–1912) of Massachusetts was an army officer. He served in the Civil War and the Spanish-American War and served as the governor of the Philippines.

Genealogies: None known.

MCATEER (S.S. Abbreviation: McAtee)

Ranking: 4589 **S.S. Count:** 9744

Origin: Scottish. Transformation of McIntyre.

Genealogies: *The William McAteer Family* was compiled by Sallie Stewart Harrison and published in Houston, Texas.

MCBEE

Ranking: 4471 **S.S. Count:** 10,013

Origin: Scottish. Uncertain etymology. The name was probably derived from a word meaning pretty.

Genealogies: *Out of the Wilderness* [also McBee] was compiled by Janice Mercer and published in Excelsior Springs, Missouri, in 1973.

MCBRIDE (S.S. Abbreviation: McBrid)

Ranking: 473 **S.S. Count:** 85,034

Origin: Irish, Scottish. Transformation of the name Kilbride, which was derived from the Gaelic-Irish name Mac Giolla Brighde and the Gaelic-Scottish name Mac Gille Brighde, meaning "son of the servant of (St.) Brigit" (H&H).

Famous **McBrides:** F. SCOTT MCBRIDE (1872–1955) of Ohio was a nationally recognized spokesman for clergymen in opposition to saloons and the drinking of alcohol. HENRY MCBRIDE (1867–1962) of Pennsylvania was a popular, authoritative art critic in New York. He wrote for the New York *Sun* from 1913 to 1950.

Genealogies: *Charles R. McBride Memorial* was compiled by Virginia McBride and published in Honolulu, Hawaii, in 1971. *McBride, Hubbard Family History* was compiled by Peggy Arnold and published in Bloomfield, Iowa, in 1979.

MCCABE

Ranking: 1025 **S.S. Count:** 42,741

Origin: Irish, Scottish. Derived from the Gaelic name Mac Cába, which was derived from the first name Cába, meaning cape.

Famous **McCabes:** JOHN COLLINS MCCABE (1810–1875) of Virginia was an Episcopal clergyman who also wrote frequently for *Southern Literary Messenger*. His son, WILLIAM G. MCCABE (1841–1920) of Virginia, was schoolmaster at the University School, Petersburg, Virginia, for 36 years. CHARLES C. MCCABE (1836–1906) of Ohio was a Methodist clergyman who became widely known through his work as a chaplain during the Civil War.

Genealogies: *The Descendants of James McCabe and Ann Pettigrew* was compiled by Allan Everett Marble and published in Boston, Massachusetts, in 1986. *McCabe-Wisel and Allied Families* was compiled by Julia McCabe Hull and published in Decorah, Iowa, in 1988.

MCCAFFER, MCCAFFERKY, MCCAFFERTY, MCCAFFREY (S.S. Abbreviation: McCaff)
Ranking: 1915 **S.S. Count:** 23,610
Origin: McCafferky, McCafferty—Irish; McCaffer—Irish, Scottish; McCaffrey—Irish, Scottish. McCafferky, McCafferty: derived from the Gaelic name Mac Eachmharcaigh, which was derived from the first name Eachmharcach, which comprises the components "each" and "cach," meaning horse and rider. McCaffer: transformation of the Irish and Scottish name Duffy. McCaffrey: derived from the Gaelic name Mac Gafraidh, which was derived from an Old Norse first name which was comprised of the components "guð" and "fróðr," meaning god and wise.

Famous **Bearers:** JOHN MCCAFFREY (1806–1881) of Maryland, a Catholic clergyman, devoted his working life to Mount St. Mary's College as professor, rector, then governor. He also wrote *Catechism of Christian Doctrine* (1865), which was widely used in elementary schools.

Genealogies: None known.

MCCAIN
Ranking: 1816 **S.S. Count:** 24,834
Origin: Irish. Derived from the first name Eoin, a cognate to John.

Genealogies: *McKean/McCain* was compiled by Elaine Richardson and published in Newton, Iowa.

MCCALL (ALSO MCCALLAN, MCCALLISTER, MCCALLUM, MCCALLY)
Ranking: 428 **S.S. Count:** 92,831
Origin: McCall—Irish, Scottish; McCallister—Irish, Scottish; McCallum—Scottish; McCally—Scottish; McCallan—Scottish. McCall (Irish): derived from the Gaelic name Mac Cathmhaoil, which was derived from the first name Cathmhaol, which comprises the components "cath" and

"maol," meaning battle and chief. McCall (Scottish): derived from the Gaelic name Mac Cathail, which was derived from the first name Cathal, which comprises the components "cad" and "valos," meaning battle and strong. McCallister: cognate to Alexander. McCallum: transformation of McCollum. McCally: 1) derived from the Gaelic name Mac Amhlaidh or Mac Amhlaoibh, both of which were derived from the Old Norse first name Óláfr. 2) derived from the Gaelic name Mac Amhalghaidh. McCallan: derived from the Gaelic name Mac Ailin, which was derived from the word "ail," meaning rock.

Famous **Bearers:** DANIEL C. MCCALLUM (1815–1878), a Scottish immigrant, designed and patented an arched truss bridge. SAMUEL W. MCCALL (1851–1923) of Massachusetts was a member of Congress from, then governor of, Massachusetts. He also wrote books, including *The Life of Thomas Brackett Reed* (1914).

Genealogies: *Campbell and McCall Family History* was compiled by Rachel M. Campbell and published in Baltimore, Maryland, in 1983. *Captain John McCall* was compiled by Clare M. McCall and published in Boston, Massachusetts, in 1985.

MCCANN (ALSO MCCANNA, MCCANNY)
Ranking: 798 **S.S. Count:** 52,756
Origin: Irish. Derived from the Gaelic name Mac Cana, which was derived from the first name Cana, meaning "wolf cub" (H&H).

Famous **Bearers:** WILLIAM P. MCCANN (1830–1906) of Kentucky was a distinguished naval officer who rose to the rank of commodore. ALFRED W. MCCANN (1879–1931) of Pennsylvania was a journalist noted for his advocacy of reforms to make food pure.

Genealogies: *James McCan and Sarah S. Viser* [also McCann] was compiled by Karen McCann Hett and published in Edna, Texas, in 1983.

MCCARRA, MCCARRICK, MCCARRIE, MCCARROLL, MCCARRON (S.S. Abbreviation: McCarr)
Ranking: 2919 **S.S. Count:** 15,595
Origin: McCarrick, McCarroll, McCarron, McCarrie—Irish; McCarra—Scottish. McCarrick: derived from the Gaelic name Mac Concharraige, which was derived from the first name Cúcharraige, which comprises the components "cú" and "carraig," meaning dog and rock. McCarroll: transformation of Carroll. McCarron: derived from the Gaelic name Mac Carrghamhna, which was derived from the first name Corrghamhain, which comprises the components "corr" and "gamhain," meaning sharp or pointed and calf. McCarrie: derived from the Gaelic name Mac Fhearadhaigh, which was derived from the first name Fhearadhach, meaning brave. Mccarra: derived from the Gaelic word "ara," meaning driver.

Famous **Bearers:** JAMES MCCARROLL (1814–1892) of Ireland came to the United States late in life and became a well-known journalist in New York City.

Genealogies: None known.

MCCARTEN, MCCARTER, MCCARTHY, MCCARTNEY, MCCARTY (S.S. Abbreviation: McCart)

Ranking: 154 S.S. Count: 208,963

Origin: McCarthy, McCarty—Irish; McCartney, McCarten—Irish, Scottish; McCarter—Irish, Scottish. McCarthy, McCarty: derived from the Gaelic name Mac Cárthaigh, which was derived from the first name Cárthach, meaning loving. McCartney, McCarten: derived from the Gaelic-Irish name Mac Artnaigh or the Gaelic-Scottish name Mac Artaine, both of which were derived from the first name Art, meaning bear. McCarter: cognate to Arthur.

Famous **Bearers:** CHARLES MCCARTHY (1873–1921) of Massachusetts, a political scientist in Wisconsin, developed the first official library and bill-drafting bureau for legislators in the country in Wisconsin. He also wrote books, including *The Wisconsin Idea* (1912). DANIEL J. MCCARTHY (1874–1958) of Pennsylvania was an internationally prominent neurologist and neuropsychologist. He wrote *Medical Treatment of Mental Disorders: The Toxic and Organic Basis of Psychiatry* (1955). CHARLES L. (CLEM) MCCARTHY (1882–1962) of New York was a popular sports broadcaster well identified with horse racing. He broadcast the first Kentucky Derby ever aired on the radio (1928). JOSEPH VINCENT MCCARTHY (1887–1978) of Pennsylvania was a baseball manager with the New York Yankees. He led them to eight American League pennants and seven World Series. JOSEPH RAYMOND MCCARTHY (1908–1957) of Wisconsin was a U.S. senator from Wisconsin who was responsible for accusing many people of subversive activities, which led to a Senate subcommittee for investigations and hearings. Many citizens were labeled "un-American" by the subcommittee, and careers, mostly of people in the entertainment industry, were ruined. The term "McCarthyism" came to refer to the slandering of a person through such investigations.

Genealogies: *Robert A.B. McCaster: in Navarro County, Texas* [also McCarter] was compiled by Herbert H. McCarter and published in Houston, Texas, in 1979. *The Lindner & McCarthy Families of Hoboken, Newark, and Elizabethport, New Jersey* was compiled by Florence Lindner McCarthy and published in Baltimore, Maryland, in 1988.

MCCASKIE, MCCASKIL, MCCASKILL (S.S. Abbreviation: McCask)

Ranking: 4415 S.S. Count: 10,151

Origin: Irish, Scottish. Cognates to the English name Ashkettle, which was derived from the Old Norse first name Ásketill, which comprises the components "óss" and "ketill," meaning god and kettle.

Genealogies: None known.

MCCASLAN, MCCASLAND, MCCASLINE (S.S. Abbreviation: McCasl)

Ranking: 4922 S.S. Count: 9088

Origin: Irish, Scottish. Derived from the Gaelic name Mac Ausaláin, cognate to the first name Absolom.

Genealogies: None known.

MCCAUL (ALSO MCCAULAY, MCCAULEY, MCCAULL)

Ranking: 1122 S.S. Count: 39,156

Origin: McCaul, McCaull—Irish, Scottish; McCaulay, McCauley—Scottish. McCaul, McCaull: transformations of McCall. McCaulay, McCauley: transformations of McCally.

Famous **Bearers:** MARY LUDWIG MCCAULEY (1754–1832) of New Jersey was known as Molly Pitcher. She was an American Revolutionary War heroine. During the Revolutionary War Battle of Monmouth on June 28, 1778, as she was carrying water out on the battlefield to the soldiers, her husband, George McCauley, was overcome by the heat. She manned his cannon through the rest of the battle, which was won by the colonists.

Genealogies: None known.

MCCLAIN (S.S. Abbreviation: McClai)

Ranking: 643 S.S. Count: 64,805

Origin: Irish. The name means the "son of the servant of St. John" (ES).

Genealogies: None known.

MCCLANACHAN, MCCLANAGHAN, MCCLANNACHAN (S.S. Abbreviation: McClan)

Ranking: 2634 S.S. Count: 17,288

Origin: Scottish. Transformations of McClenaghan.

Genealogies: None known.

MCCLARON (S.S. Abbreviation: McClar)

Ranking: 2713 S.S. Count: 16,760

Origin: Scottish. Transformation of McLaren.

Genealogies: None known.

MCCLEAN, MCCLEANE, MCCLEARY (S.S. Abbreviation: McClea)

Ranking: 2801 S.S. Count: 16,249

Origin: McCleary—Irish; McClean, McCleane—Irish, Scottish. McCleary: transformation of Cleary. McClean, McCleane: transformations of McLean.

Genealogies: None known.

MCCLELLAN, MCCLELLAND (S.S. Abbreviation: McClel)

Ranking: 731 S.S. Count: 57,950

Origin: Irish. Derived from the Gaelic-Irish name Mac Giolla Fhaoláin and the Gaelic-Scottish name Mac Gille Fhaolain, both meaning "son of the servant of (St.) Faolán" (H&H).

Famous **Bearers:** GEORGE BRINTON McCLELLAN (1826–1885) of Pennsylvania was an army officer and the inventor of the McClellan saddle. He was instrumental in keeping Kentucky in the Union during the Civil War. He served during the Civil War as an officer and ran against President Abraham Lincoln for president in the 1864 campaign. He was the governor of New Jersey (1878–1881). HENRY BRAINERD McCLELLAN (1840–1904) of Pennsylvania was a Confederate soldier who entered as a private and rose through the ranks to major. After the war he turned to administration duties at a school. GEORGE BRINTON McCLELLAN (1865–1940) of Saxony, son of George Brinton McClellan (b. 1826), was the president of the New York City Board of Aldermen (1892), a member of Congress from New York, and the mayor of New York City.

Genealogies: *James McClellan, his Progenitors, Descendants and Allied Lines* was compiled by Gerald R. Fuller and published in Bountiful, Utah, in 1991. *Silas and Penelope (Anderson) McClelland and some of their Descendants* [also McClellan] was compiled by Clifton A. McClelland and published in Baltimore, Maryland, in 1987. *McClelland-Harper Settlers in the Wabash Valley* was compiled by Eliza Haddon McClure Brevoort and published in Lawrenceville, Illinois, in 1955.

MCCLENAGHAN, MCCLENNAN (S.S. Abbreviation: McClen)

Ranking: 1299 S.S. Count: 34,161

Origin: McClenaghan—Scottish; McClennan—Scottish. McClenaghan: derived from the Gaelic name Mac Gille Onchon, meaning "son of the servant of (St.) Onchú" (H&H). McClennan: derived from the Gaelic name Mac Gille Fhinneain, meaning "son of the servant of (St.) Fionnán" (H&H), which was derived from the word "fionn," meaning white.

Genealogies: None known.

MCCLINTOCK (S.S. Abbreviation: McClin)

Ranking: 1762 S.S. Count: 25,485

Origin: Irish, Scottish. Derived from the Gaelic-Irish name Mac Giolla Fhiontóg and the Gaelic-Scottish name Mac Gille Ghionndaig, both meaning "son of the servant of (St.) Finndag" (H&H), which was derived from the word "fionn," meaning white.

Famous **McClintocks:** OLIVER McCLINTOCK (1839–1922) of Pennsylvania was a leader in the fight against a corrupt group of Pittsburgh politicians headed by political boss Christopher L. Magee. JAMES HARVEY McCLINTOCK (1864–1934) was commander of one of Teddy Roosevelt's Rough Riders troops.

Genealogies: *Compendium of Family History for the McClintock Surname* was compiled by Maureen L. McClintock Rischard and published in Santa Ana, California, in 1979.

MCCLOSKEY, MCCLOSKY (S.S. Abbreviation: McClos)

Ranking: 2766 S.S. Count: 16,491

Origin: Irish. Transformations of McCluskey.

Famous **Bearers:** JOHN McCLOSKEY (1810–1885) of New York was a Roman Catholic priest and the president of the school that became Fordham University. He was the first American cardinal. WILLIAM GEORGE McCLOSKEY (1823–1909) of New York was a Roman Catholic priest and the first rector at the American College of Rome.

Genealogies: *McClaskeys in Military History* [also McCloskeys] was compiled by Kenneth L. McClaskey and published in Idaho Falls, Idaho, in 1980.

MCCLOUD (S.S. Abbreviation: McClou)

Ranking: 2128 S.S. Count: 21,495

Origin: Scottish. Transformation of McLeod.

Genealogies: None known.

MCCLUNE, MCCLUNG, MCCLUNY (S.S. Abbreviation: McClun)

Ranking: 2860 S.S. Count: 15,963

Origin: McClune—Irish, Scottish; McClung, McCluny—Scottish. McClune: transformation of McLean. McClung, McCluny: derived from the Gaelic name Mac Luinge.

Famous **Bearers:** CLARENCE EDWIN McCLUNG (1870–1946) of Pennsylvania was a zoologist and the man who published a paper suggesting that the X chromosome determines the sex of an individual.

Genealogies: *The McClung Family of Wise County, Texas* was compiled by Jimmy Wayne McClung and published in Santa Clara, California, in 1981. *The McClung Genealogy* was compiled by William McClung and published in Dixon, Illinois, in 1983.

MCCLURE, MCCLURG (S.S. Abbreviation: McClur)

Ranking: 566 S.S. Count: 72,696

Origin: Scottish. McClure: 1) derived from the Gaelic name Mac Gille Dheóradha, meaning "son of the servant of the pilgrim" (H&H). 2) derived from the Gaelic name Mac Gille Uidhir, meaning "son of the servant of (St.) Odhar"

(H&H), meaning sallow. McClurg: derived from the Gaelic name Mac Luirg, which was derived from the first name Lorg.

Famous **Bearers**: JAMES MCCLURG (1746?–1823) of Virginia was the Virginia delegate to the Constitutional Convention who felt that the head of the colonies should be removed from legislative control with life tenure, much like a monarch. GEORGE MCCLURE (1770–1851) of Ireland came to America as a young adult and served as a brigadier general in the War of 1812. He was responsible for the attack on Newark, Canada, for which the British responded by attacking Buffalo, New York. JOSEPH WASHINGTON MCCLURG (1818–1900) of Missouri was a member of Congress from Missouri who stressed carpetbag policies. He was responsible for keeping the Democrats in power in Missouri for 30 years. ALEXANDER KELLY MCCLURE (1828–1909) of Pennsylvania was responsible for switching Pennsylvania's vote at the Republican Convention in 1860 to Abraham Lincoln, which helped Lincoln win the Republican presidential nomination. ALEXANDER CALDWELL MCCLURG (1832–1901) of Pennsylvania was a bookseller and publisher responsible for turning Chicago into the leading book center of the Midwest. SAMUEL SIDNEY MCCLURE (1857–1949) of Ireland was an editor and publisher. He started the first American newspaper syndicate in the United States, the McClure syndicate. He also was the founder of *McClure's Magazine*. ROBERT ALEXIS MCCLURE (1897–1957) of Illinois was a career military officer and chief of intelligence after 1942 and was responsible for security in the invasion of North Africa during World War II.

Genealogies: *Following McCluer Ancestors* [also McClure] was compiled by Leon McCluer and published in Verona, Virginia, in 1974. *The McClure Story* was compiled by Jerry Duane Duncan and published in Alhambra, California, in 1983.

MCCLUSKEY, MCCLUSKIE, MCCLUSKY (S.S. Abbreviation: McClus)

Ranking: 3860 **S.S. Count**: 11,677
Origin: *Irish. Derived from the Gaelic name Mac Bhloscaidhe, which was derived from the first name Bloscadh.*
Genealogies: None known.

MCCOLL (ALSO MCCOLLAM, MCCOLLEY, MCCOLLUM)

Ranking: 905 **S.S. Count**: 47,633
Origin: *McColley—Irish; McColl—Irish, Scottish; McCollam, McCollum—Scottish. McColley: transformation of MacLeavy. McColl: transformation of Quille. McCollam, McCollum: derived from the Gaelic name Mac Coluim, which was derived from the first name Columba, meaning dove.*
Genealogies: None known.

MCCOMB (ALSO MCCOMBE, MCCOMBICH, MCCOMBIE)

Ranking: 2054 **S.S. Count**: 22,285
Origin: *Scottish. Derived from the Gaelic name Mac Thóm, a transformation of the name Thomas.*
Famous **Bearers**: JOHN MCCOMB (1793–1853) of New York City was responsible, as an architect, for much of the traditional colonial architecture evident in the churches and buildings in New York City.
Genealogies: None known.

MCCONNACHIE, MCCONNEL, MCCONNELL (S.S. Abbreviation: McConn)

Ranking: 653 **S.S. Count**: 63,994
Origin: *Irish, Scottish. McConnachie: transformation of McDonagh. McConnel, McConnell (Irish): derived from the Gaelic name Mac Conaill, which was derived from the first name Conall, which comprises the components "con" and "gal," meaning dog and valor. McConnel, McConnell (Scottish): transformations of McDonald.*
Famous **Bearers**: JOHN LUDLUM MCCONNEL (1826–1862) of Illinois was an author whose books give the reader a look at life on the frontier. JOHN FRANCIS MCCONNELL (1871–1953) of Ohio was a Methodist minister and the author of several books. He also served as the president of DePauw University.
Genealogies: *Ancestors and Descendants of Myron and Bessie McConnell* was compiled by Joy L. McConnell and published in Salem, Oregon, in 1985. *The McConnell Family* was compiled by John G. Martin and published in Kingsport, Tennessee, in 1980.

MCCOOL (ALSO MCCOOLE)

Ranking: 4736 **S.S. Count**: 9455
Origin: *Irish, Scottish. Irish, Scottish: transformations of the Irish and Scottish name Cole. Scottish: transformations of McDougall.*
Genealogies: None known.

MCCORD

Ranking: 1830 **S.S. Count**: 24,667
Origin: *Irish. Derived from the Gaelic names Mac Cuairt and MacCuarta.*
Famous **McCords**: DAVID JAMES MCCORD (1797–1855) of South Carolina was the editor of the *Columbia Telescope*. He also edited five volumes of *Statutes at Large of South Carolina*. LOUISA SUSANNAH CHEVES MCCORD (1810–1879) of South Carolina was an author and a defender of the social and economic methods of the antebellum South. JAMES BENNETT MCCORD (1870–1950) of Illinois was a medical missionary in South Africa. He founded a hospital for nonwhites in Durban and worked to break down racial barriers.

Genealogies: *The Story of Commodore Perry McCord and Sarah Elizabeth Smith and their Descendants* was compiled by Forrest Edward Brouhard and published in Harlan, Iowa, in 1972.

MCCORKHILL, MCCORKILL, MCCORKINDALE, MCCORKLE (S.S. Abbreviation: McCork)

Ranking: 3120 **S.S. Count:** 14,566

Origin: Scottish. Cognates to the English name Thirkill, which was derived from the Old Norse first name Porkell, which comprises the components Pórr, meaning Thor, the Scandinavian god of thunder, and "ketill," meaning kettle or cauldron.

Genealogies: *Alexander McCorkle (1722–1800) & his Kin* was compiled by John Hale Stutesman and published in San Francisco, California, in 1983. *From Viking Glory: Notes on the McCorkle Family in Scotland and America* was compiled by Louis W. McCorkle and published in Marceline, Missouri, in 1982.

MCCORMACK, MCCORMICK (S.S. Abbreviation: McCorm)

Ranking: 317 **S.S. Count:** 116,955

Origin: Scottish. Derived from the Gaelic first name Corman, which was derived from the components "corb" and "mac," meaning raven and son.

Famous Bearers: CYRUS HALL MCCORMICK (1809–1884) of Virginia invented a reaping machine. He formed the McCormick Harvesting Machine Co. RICHARD CUNNINGHAM MCCORMICK (1832–1901) of New York City was a war correspondent (1861–1862), the governor of Arizona, and then a territorial delegate to Congress from Arizona. He spoke for the humane treatment of the Indians. NETTIE FOWLER MCCORMICK (1835–1923) of New York was a businesswoman and philanthropist. She was the wife of Cyrus Hall McCormick and the head of his business after his death. SAMUEL BLACK MCCORMICK (1858–1928) of Pennsylvania was the president of the University of Pittsburgh, which he updated and modernized. CYRUS HALL MCCORMICK (1859–1936), son of Cyrus Hall McCormick (1809–1884), took over the company and named it International Harvester Co. EDITH ROCKEFELLER MCCORMICK (1872–1932) of Ohio, daughter of John D. Rockefeller, was a social leader and patron of the arts. She was the founder of the Chicago Zoological Gardens. KATHERINE DEXTER MCCORMICK (1875–1967) of Michigan was a philanthropist. She supported the causes of birth control, women's suffrage, and higher education for women. She was largely responsible for the monetary support given in the development of "the pill." ROBERT RUTHERFORD MCCORMICK (1880–1955) of Illinois was a newspaperman. He was the publisher of the *Chicago Tribune* and the founder of the *New York Daily News*. ANNE ELIZABETH O'HARE MCCORMICK (1880–1954) was born in England and came to the United States as a child. She was a journalist and the first woman to receive a Pulitzer Prize for journalism. JOHN FRANCIS MCCORMACK (1884–1945) of Ireland was a tenor and a well-known concert singer. He is especially remembered for his singing of Irish songs. EDWARD JAMES MCCORMICK (1891–1975) of Michigan was a prominent surgeon who also was a prolific writer and orator. He made speeches in the United States, Europe, Japan, and South America.

Genealogies: *McCormick Genealogy with Related Families* was compiled by B. Dottie McCormick Perkins and published in 1991. *Determined Lives: a Family Odyssey* [McCormick Family] was compiled by Edgar L. McCormick and published in Grantham, New Hampshire, in 1989.

MCCOY

Ranking: 241 **S.S. Count:** 148,717

Origin: Irish, Scottish. Transformation of McKay.

Famous McCoys: ISAAC MCCOY (1784–1846) of Pennsylvania was a Baptist missionary and Indian agent. He proposed a separate state for all of the Indians who inhabited lands east of the Mississippi River. He was responsible for all of Indian lands in Kansas and Oklahoma being surveyed. He wrote *Remarks on the Practicability of Indian Reform* (1827). Needless to say, his Indian state never came to be. JOSEPH GEATING MCCOY (1837–1915) of Illinois established Abilene, Kansas, as the cattle-shipping center of the United States. HORACE MCCOY (1897–1955) of Tennessee was an author who wrote, among other works, *They Shoot Horses, Don't They?* ELIJAH MCCOY (1843–1929) of Canada was an inventor who developed a system of lubricating machinery through automatic, continuous oiling.

Genealogies: *Squirrel Huntin' Sam McCoy* was compiled by Hobert McCoy and published in Pikeville, Kentucky, in 1979. *The McCoys* was compiled by Truda Williams McCoy and published in Pikeville, Kentucky, in 1976.

MCCRACKEN (S.S. Abbreviation: McCrac)

Ranking: 1541 **S.S. Count:** 28,931

Origin: Irish, Scottish. The name means "son of Carrachan," (H&H) which is derived from the Gaelic word "carrach," meaning rough-faced.

Genealogies: *A Record of the Descendants of John McCracken* was compiled by Constable MacCracken and published in Baltimore, Maryland, in 1979. *Virginia Diaspora* [McCracken Family] was compiled by Guida M. Jackson-Laufer and published in Bowie, Maryland, in 1992.

MCCRARY (S.S. Abbreviation: McCrar)

Ranking: 2598 **S.S. Count:** 17,497

Origin: Irish, Scottish. Uncertain etymology.
Genealogies: None known.

MCCRAY

Ranking: 1252   S.S. Count: 35,201
Origin: Irish, Scottish. Derived from the Gaelic name Mag Raith, which was derived from the name Rath, meaning grace and good fortune.
Genealogies: None known.

MCCREA (ALSO MCCREADIE, MCCREADY, MCCREARY, MCCREAVY)

Ranking: 1612   S.S. Count: 27,766
Origin: McCreadie, McCready—Irish; McCreavy—Irish; McCrea—Irish, Scottish; McCreary—Scottish. McCreadie, McCready: derived from the Gaelic name Mac Riada, which was derived from the name Riada, meaning expert. McCreavy: derived from the Gaelic name Riabhach, which was derived from a name meaning gray hair. McCrea: transformation of McCray. McCreary: derived from the Gaelic name Mac Ruidhri, which was derived from the first name Ru(a)idhrí, which is comprised of Celtic components meaning red and rule.

Famous **Bearers:** JANE MCCREA (1752?–1777) of New Jersey was a Revolutionary War martyr. She was scalped and shot by the advance Indians of General John Burgoyne's troops. Her death enraged the Americans and was thus responsible for their victory at Saratoga. JAMES BENNETT MCCREARY (1838–1918) of Kentucky was the governor of and a member of Congress from Kentucky. As governor he worked for reform.
Genealogies: None known.

MCCRORY   (S.S. Abbreviation: McCror)

Ranking: 4574   S.S. Count: 9767
Origin: Irish, Scottish. Derived from the Gaelic first name Ruaidhrí, which is comprised of Celtic components meaning red and rule.
Genealogies: None known.

MCCUE

Ranking: 3815   S.S. Count: 11,821
Origin: Irish, Scottish. Transformation of McKay.
Genealogies: None known.

MCCULLACH, MCCULLAGH, MCCULLOCH, MCCULLOUGH, MCCULLY (S.S. Abbreviation: McCull)

Ranking: 351   S.S. Count: 108,180
Origin: Irish, Scottish. Uncertain etymology. Most likely derived from a Gaelic name that was derived from the word "cullach," meaning wild boar.

Famous **Bearers:** BEN MCCULLOCH (1811–1862) of Tennessee was a soldier in Texas. He was a ranger with Zachary Taylor's army in the Mexican War. JOHN GRIFFITH MCCULLOUGH (1835–1915) of Delaware was a railroad executive and a Vermont politician. CATHARINE GOUGER WAUGH MCCULLOCH (1862–1945) of New York was a lawyer and suffragist. She was the legislative superintendent of the Illinois Equal Suffrage Association. She was responsible for an Illinois bill that granted women equal rights to guardianship of their children. After the adoption of the federal suffrage amendment (1920), she joined the League of Women Voters and served until 1923 in the capacity of chairperson of its Committee on Uniform Laws Concerning Women.
Genealogies: *Descendants of William C. McCullough* was compiled by Edna Hazel McCullough Lowery and published in Falls Church, Virginia, in 1977.

MCCUNE

Ranking: 3305   S.S. Count: 13,699
Origin: Irish. Uncertain etymology. Most likely derived from the Gaelic first name Eógann, which was derived from the Latin name Eugenius.
Genealogies: None known.

MCCURDY   (S.S. Abbreviation: McCurd)

Ranking: 2517   S.S. Count: 18,040
Origin: Irish. Derived from a word meaning navigator.

Famous **McCurdys:** RICHARD ALDRICH MCCURDY (1835–1916) of New York City was a lawyer and insurance executive with Mutual Life Insurance Co.
Genealogies: *The Stone Mountain McCurdys* was compiled by Julius Augustus McCurdy and published in Atlanta, Georgia, in 1979.

MCCURREY, MCCURRIE (S.S. Abbreviation: McCurr)

Ranking: 4245   S.S. Count: 10,607
Origin: Irish. Transformation of McMurray.
Genealogies: None known.

MCCUTCHEN, MCCUTCHEON (S.S. Abbreviation: McCutc)

Ranking: 2249   S.S. Count: 20,327
Origin: Scottish. Derived from the Gaelic name Mac Uisdein, which was derived from the first name Uisdean, which was derived from the Old French name Hugh.

Famous **Bearers:** GEORGE BARR MCCUTCHEON (1866–1928) of Indiana was a novelist and the author of *Brewster's Millions* (1902). JOHN TINNEY MCCUTCHEON (1870–1949) of Indiana was a political cartoonist. He was awarded the Pulitzer Prize for one of his cartoons in 1932.

Genealogies: None known.

MCDADE

Ranking: 4480 S.S. Count: 10,001
Origin: Scottish. Transformation of David.
Genealogies: None known.

MCDANIEL (S.S. Abbreviation: McDani)

Ranking: 274 S.S. Count: 130,678
Origin: Scottish. Transformation of McDonald.
Famous **McDaniels:** HENRY MCDANIEL (1836–1926)
was a Confederate soldier and the governor of Georgia.
During his term he reduced the state debt and tax rate.
WALTON B. MCDANIEL (1871–1978) of Massachusetts was a
prominent professor of Latin and classics at Harvard University, Radcliffe College, the University of Pennsylvania,
and the American Academy in Rome, Italy. He was the
author of several books, including *Roman Private Life and
Its Survivals* (1924) and *Riding a Hobby in the Classical
Lands* (1971). HATTIE MCDANIEL (1895–1952) of Kansas
was an actress and singer. She is best remembered for her
portrayal of "Mammy" in *Gone With the Wind*. Being
black, she was not able to attend the premier showing of
the movie, but she won the Academy Award for best supporting actress, thereby becoming the first black woman to
win an Academy Award.
Genealogies: *Our McDaniel Family* was compiled by
Esta McDaniel Lee and published in Dayton, Ohio, in
1975. *McDaniel/McDonald Notes* was compiled by Ellen
Byrne and published in Huntsville, Arkansas, in 1971.

MCDERMID, MCDERMIT, MCDERMONT, MCDERMOTT (S.S. Abbreviation: McDerm)

Ranking: 883 S.S. Count: 49.097
*Origin: Irish. Derived from the Gaelic first name Difhar-
mait, which was derived from the prefix "di-" and the word
"farmat," meaning not envious.*
Genealogies: None known.

MCDEVITT (S.S. Abbreviation: McDevi)

Ranking: 4626 S.S. Count: 9660
Origin: Irish. Transformation of David.
Genealogies: None known.

MCDONAGH, MCDONALD (S.S. Abbreviation: McDona)

Ranking: 111 S.S. Count: 256,989
*Origin: McDonagh—Irish, Scottish; McDonald—Scot-
tish. McDonagh: transformation of MacDonough. McDonald: derived from the Gaelic name Mac Dhomhnuill, which
was derived from the first name Domhnall, which com-*
*prises the components "dubno" and "val," meaning world
and rule.*
Famous **Bearers:** CHARLES JAMES MCDONALD (1793–
1860) of South Carolina was the governor of Georgia and a
justice of the Georgia Supreme Court. He brought Georgia
through the Panic of 1837, restoring the state's credit. He
favored secession of Georgia from the Union. JOHN
BARTHOLOMEW MCDONALD (1844–1911) of Ireland came to
the United States as a child. A contractor by profession, he
served in that capacity for the Baltimore belt-line railroad
and the first New York City subway. JAMES GROVER
MCDONALD (1886–1964) of Ohio was a diplomat and
internationalist who worked for world peace.
Genealogies: *Kincannon and McDonald of Southwest
Virginia* was compiled by David B. Trimble and published
in Austin, Texas, in 1992. *Never Say Die* [McDonald Fam-
ily] was compiled by Julia Davis and published in Stafford,
Virginia, in 1980.

MCDONNELL (S.S. Abbreviation: McDonn)

Ranking: 2023 S.S. Count: 22,594
Origin: Scottish. Transformation of McDonald.
Genealogies: *Golden Clan: the Murrays, the McDonnells,
and the Irish American Aristocracy* was compiled by John
Corry and published in Boston, Massachusetts, in 1977.

MCDONOUGH (S.S. Abbreviation: McDono)

Ranking: 1397 S.S. Count: 31,764
Origin: Irish, Scottish. Transformation of MacDonough.
Genealogies: *Related Families* [McDonough Family]
was compiled by Carolyn Harris McDonough and published in 1976.

MCDOUGAL, MCDOUGALL (S.S. Abbreviation: McDoug)

Ranking: 1690 S.S. Count: 26,432
*Origin: Scottish. Derived from the Gaelic name Mac
Dhubhghaill, which was derived from the first name Dub-
hghall, which is comprised of the components "dubh" and
"gall," meaning black and stranger or Scandinavian.*
Famous **Bearers:** ALEXANDER MCDOUGALL (1732–1786)
of Scotland came to America in 1738. He served in the
Revolutionary army with the rank of general and succeeded Benedict Arnold as commander of West Point. After
the war he was a member of the Continental Congress.
DAVID STOCKTON MCDOUGAL (1809–1882) of Ohio commanded the USS *Wyoming* on a mission to the Far East
during the Civil War. While there, his ship destroyed Japanese land batteries and armed vessels at one locality after
certain treaty violations by the Japanese. ALEXANDER
MCDOUGALL (1845–1923) of Scotland was a shipbuilder
and inventor. He patented the design for the "whaleback"

freighter and moved his industry to Washington state, where he founded the town of Everett. Forty inventions in the shipbuilding industry are credited to him. WILLIAM McDOUGALL (1871–1938) of England was a psychologist who taught at Harvard and Duke universities and wrote many highly respected books on his work, including *Modern Materialism and Emergent Evolution* (1929).

Genealogies: None known.

MCDOWELL (S.S. Abbreviation: McDowe)

Ranking: 608 **S.S. Count:** 68,693

Origin: Scottish. Transformation of McDougal.

Famous **McDowells:** EPHRAIN McDOWELL (1771–1830) of Virginia was a surgeon and a pioneer in abdominal surgery. It is believed that he performed the first ovarian surgery in 1809. JAMES McDOWELL (1795–1851) of Virginia, a politician and orator, campaigned against slavery because of the dissension it caused. He served as governor of Virginia and member of Congress. ANNE ELIZABETH McDOWELL (1826–1901) of Delaware was an editor and journalist. She is best known as the founder of the weekly paper *Woman's Advocate.* IRVIN McDOWELL (1818–1885) of Ohio was a career soldier. He was the commander of the Union army of the Potomac, his first command, and had the misfortunate to be the commanding officer at the Union's loss in the first battle of Bull Run. Although he was found not guilty of any wrongdoing by a court of inquiry, his career basically ended as General George B. McClellan, who outranked McDowell, took over command of the army. MARY ELIZA McDOWELL (1854–1936) of Ohio was a settlement house director and a social reformer. At Hull House she started a kindergarten, and in 1903 she helped to found the National Women's Trade Union League. KATHERINE SHERWOOD BONNER McDOWELL (1849–1883) of Mississippi was an author who was published in the magazines of her day.

Genealogies: *Historic Families of Kentucky [McDowell Family]* was compiled by Thomas Marshall Green and published in Baltimore, Maryland, in 1982. *McDowells in American* was compiled by Dorothy Kelly MacDowell and published in Baltimore, Maryland, in 1981.

MCDUFF, MCDUFFIE (S.S. Abbreviation: McDuff)

Ranking: 2338 **S.S. Count:** 19,402

Origin: McDuff—Irish, Scottish; McDuffie—Irish, Scottish. McDuff: transformation of Duff. McDuffie: transformation of Duffy.

Famous **Bearers:** GEORGE McDUFFIE (1790?–1851) of Georgia was a South Carolina politician who served as a member of Congress from, U.S. senator from, and governor of that state.

Genealogies: None known.

MCEACHERN, MCEACHIN (S.S. Abbreviation: McEach)

Ranking: 4359 **S.S. Count:** 10,284

Origin: Scottish. Derived from a word with components meaning lord of the house.

Genealogies: *The Family of Daniel and Mary McEachern of Carroll County, Mississippi* was compiled by Sally Stone Trotter and published in Greenville, Mississippi, in 1969.

MCELROY (S.S. Abbreviation: McElro)

Ranking: 1225 **S.S. Count:** 36,048

Origin: Irish. Derived from the Gaelic name Mac Giolla Ruaidh, meaning "son of the red-haired lad" (H&H).

Famous **McElroys:** JOHN McELROY (1782–1877) of Ireland was a Jesuit clergyman and a chaplain during the Mexican War. JOHN McELROY (1846–1929) of Kentucky was a journalist and Union soldier. He wrote *Andersonville* (1879) about his prison experiences. Later in life he was the editor and publisher of the *National Tribune* in Washington, D.C. ROBERT McNUTT McELROY (1872–1959) of Kentucky was a historian, educational director of the National Security League, and supporter of the League of Nations. He wrote biographies of President Grover Cleveland, Vice President Levi P. Morton, and Confederate President Jefferson Davis.

Genealogies: *The Box Book with McElroy and Floyd* was compiled by Mrs. Jeff Wade and published in Bragg City, Missouri, in 1975. *Family Adventures of John Mackelroy of Maryland 1690–1983* [also McElroy] was published in San Antonio, Texas, in 1983.

MCEWEN

Ranking: 4222 **S.S. Count:** 10,684

Origin: Scottish. Cognate to McCune.

Genealogies: *Descendants of Robert McEwen and Sarah Wilcoxson, Stratford, Connecticut* was compiled by Ruth M. Coleman and published in Essex, Connecticut, in 1992.

MCFADDEN (S.S. Abbreviation: McFadd)

Ranking: 1019 **S.S. Count:** 42,933

Origin: Irish, Scottish. Derived from the Gaelic-Irish name Mac Pháidin and the Gaelic-Scottish name Mac Phaid(e)in, both of which were derived from the first name Patrick.

Famous **McFaddens:** LOUIS McFADDEN (1876–1936) of Pennsylvania was a member of Congress and the co-author of the McFadden-Pepper Act (1927), which eased restrictions on national banks.

Genealogies: *A McFadden Chronology* was compiled by William Thomas Skinner and published in Richburg, South Carolina, in 1983.

MCFALL

Ranking: 3216 S.S. Count: 14,094

Origin: Irish, Scottish. Derived from the Irish-Gaelic name Mac Phóil and the Scottish-Gaelic name Mac Pháil, both of which were derived from the first name Paul.

Genealogies: None known.

MCFARLAN, MCFARLAND, MCFARLIN (S.S. Abbreviation: McFarl)

Ranking: 521 S.S. Count: 77,221

Origin: Irish, Scottish. Transformation of Macfarland.

Famous **Bearers:** THOMAS BARD MCFARLAND (1828–1908) of Pennsylvania was a justice of the California Supreme Court. JOHN HORACE MCFARLAND (1859–1948) of Pennsylvania participated in the establishment of the National Parks system. GEORGE BRADLEY MCFARLAND (1866–1942) was born in Siam (Thailand) to American missionary parents. He was educated as a physician in the United States and returned to Siam to found and administer modern hospitals. He also wrote a Thai-English dictionary.

Genealogies: *Clergymen and Chiefs: a Genealogy of the MacQueen and McFarlane Families* [also McFarland] was compiled by Alex M. Quattlebaum and published in Charleston, South Carolina, in 1990. *McFarland Collections* was compiled by Robert H. McFarland and published in Rolla, Missouri, in 1985.

MCGARRAN, MCGARRIGLE, MCGARRITY, MCGARRY (S.S. Abbreviation: McGarr)

Ranking: 2727 S.S. Count: 16,697

Origin: Irish. McGarran: derived from the Gaelic name Mag Eachráin, which was derived from the first name Eachrán. McGarrigle: derived from the Gaelic name Mag Fhearghail, which was derived from the first name Fearghal, which is comprised of the components "fear" and "gal," meaning man and bravery. McGarrity: derived from the Gaelic name Mag Oireachtaigh, which was derived from the name Oireachtach, meaning "member of the assembly" (H&H). McGarry: derived from the Gaelic name Mac Ardghail, which was derived from the first name Ardghal, which is comprised of the components "ard" and "gal," meaning height and bravery.

Genealogies: None known.

MCGEE

Ranking: 385 S.S. Count: 101,082

Origin: Irish, Scottish. Transformation of McKay.

Famous **McGees:** WILLIAM JOHN MCGEE (1853–1912) of Iowa was a geologist and anthropologist. He is best known for his work in Pleistocene geology of the upper Mississippi Valley and work on the Atlantic coastal plain. ANITA NEWCOMB MCGEE (1864–1940) of Washington, D.C., was the founder of the Army Nurse Corps.

Genealogies: None known.

MCGEHEE (S.S. Abbreviation: McGehe)

Ranking: 4809 S.S. Count: 9317

Origin: Uncertain etymology. Possibly a transformation of McKay.

Genealogies: None known.

MCGHEE

Ranking: 1429 S.S. Count: 31,196

Origin: Irish, Scottish. Transformation of McKay.

Famous **McGhees:** CHARLES MCCLUNG MCGHEE (1828–1907) of Tennessee was a Confederate soldier and an executive in the railroad companies of Tennessee.

Genealogies: None known.

MCGILL (ALSO MCGILLAROY, MCGILLICUDDY, MCGILLIGAN, MCGILLIVRAY)

Ranking: 945 S.S. Count: 45,818

Origin: McGill—English; McGillaroy, McGillicuddy—Irish; McGilligan, McGillivray—Irish, Scottish. McGill: transformation of Gall. McGillaroy: derived from the Gaelic name Mac Giolla Ruaidh, meaning "son of the red-haired lad" (H&H). McGillicuddy: derived from the Gaelic name Mac Giolla Chuda, meaning "son of the servant of (St.) Chuda" (H&H). McGilligan—Irish: derived from the Gaelic name Mac Giollagáin, which was derived from the first name Giollagán, which was derived from the word "giolla," meaning servant. McGilligan—Scottish: derived from the Gaelic name Mac Gille Fhaolagain, meaning "son of the servant of (St.) Faolagan," (H&H) which is derived from the word "faol," meaning wolf. McGillivray: derived from the Irish-Gaelic name Mac Giolla Bhraith and the Gaelic-Scottish name Mac Gille Bhrath, both of which were derived from a first name meaning "servant of judgment" (H&H).

Famous **Bearers:** ALEXANDER MCGILLIVRAY (1759?–1793) of Alabama was a Creek Indian chief. Born to a Scottish father and a French/Creek mother, McGillivray was a Loyalist during the American Revolution. Afterward, he sucessfully organized southern Indians to attack frontier settlers in Georgia, Florida, and Tennessee. JOHN MCGILL (1809–1872) of Pennsylvania was a Roman Catholic priest who opposed slavery but was sympathetic to the plight of the southerners. He worked in the reconstuction of his parish after the war. RALPH EMERSON MCGILL (1898–1969) of Tennessee was a journalist with the *Atlanta Constitution* and the recipient of the Pulitzer Prize for his editorial about a synagogue bombing in Atlanta.

Genealogies: *Four Generations of Charles Magill of Ireland* [also McGill] was compiled by Donald Gary Magill and published in Greensboro, Maryland, in 1991.

MCGINLEY (S.S. Abbreviation: McGinl)

Ranking: 4599 S.S. Count: 9721

Origin: Irish. Derived from the Gaelic name Mag Fhion-nghaile, which was derived from the first name Fionnghal, which is comprised of the components "fionn" and "gal," meaning fair and bravery.

Genealogies: None known.

**MCGINN (ALSO MCGINNIS) (S.S.
    Abbreviation: McGinn)**

Ranking: 835 S.S. Count: 50,987

Origin: McGinn—Irish; McGinnis—Irish. McGinn: derived from the Gaelic name Mag Fhionnachtaigh, which was derived from the first name Fionn, meaning white. McGinnis: transformation of McGuinness.

Genealogies: None known.

MCGLOT

Ranking: 4653 S.S. Count: 9610

Origin: Uncertain etymology.

Genealogies: None known.

MCGOVERN (S.S. Abbreviation: McGove)

Ranking: 1929 S.S. Count: 23,409

Origin: Irish. Derived from the Gaelic name Mag Shamhr (adh)áin, which was derived from the first name Samhrad-háin, which was derived from the word "samhradh," meaning summer.

Genealogies: None known.

MCGOWAN (S.S. Abbreviation: McGowa)

Ranking: 921 S.S. Count: 46,849

Origin: Irish, Scottish. Irish, Scottish: derived from the Gaelic-Irish name Mac Gabhann and the Gaelic-Scottish name Mac Gobhan, both of which were derived from names meaning smith. Scottish: derived from the Gaelic name Mac Owein, which was derived from the first name Owen or Ewan, which was derived from the Latin name Eugenius.

Famous **McGowans:** SAMUEL MCGOWAN (1819–1897) of South Carolina was a Confederate officer and a justice of the South Carolina Supreme Court.

Genealogies: *The Ancestry of Thomas W. McGowan* was compiled by Thomas W. McGowan and published in Decorah, Iowa, in 1984.

MCGRATH (S.S. Abbreviation: McGrat)

Ranking: 869 S.S. Count: 49,589

Origin: Irish. Cognate to the usually Scottish name McCray (also McCrae).

Famous **McGraths:** JAMES MCGRATH (1835–1898) of Ireland came to North America as a missionary. He was responsible for the building of the Church of the Immacu-

late Conception in Lowell, Massachusetts, in 1872. MATTHEW J. MCGRATH (1876–1941) of Ireland was a New York City policeman and a U.S. representative to the Olympics in four games between 1908 and 1924. He set the hammer-throw record. JAMES HOWARD MCGRATH (1903–1966) of Rhode Island was the governor of and a U.S. senator from Rhode Island. He then served as the U.S. attorney general and in that capacity was a strong supporter of civil rights.

Genealogies: *Genealogy of the Nicholson Sisters and Related Families: Clennan, Cushing, Keegan, McCormally, McGrath, Ryan, Langley* was compiled by Eileen E. Langley and published in Ellis, Kansas, in 1986.

MCGRAW

Ranking: 1556 S.S. Count: 28,644

Origin: Irish, Scottish. Transformation of McCray.

Famous **McGraws:** JAMES HERBERT MCGRAW (1860–1948) of New York was a book publisher and the head of the McGraw Publishing Co., then the McGraw-Hill Publishing Co. JOHN JOSEPH MCGRAW (1873–1934) of New York was a baseball manager with the New York Giants, during which time the team won the National League pennant 10 times and the World Series three times.

Genealogies: *Dunkin-Reid and Garner-McGraw-Mobley Families of South Carolina, Georgia, and Alabama* was compiled by Dean Smith Cress and published in Alpharetta, Georgia, in 1992. *Early McGraw Families of Arkansas County, Arkansas* was compiled by Carolyn Cloud Stanley and published in Boulder, Colorado, in 1978.

MCGREGOR (S.S. Abbreviation: McGreg)

Ranking: 2033 S.S. Count: 22,469

Origin: Scottish. Derived from the Gaelic name Mac Gri-ogair, which was derived from the first name Gregory.

Genealogies: *McGregor History* was compiled by Howard W. McGregor and published in Utica, Kentucky, in 1984.

MCGREW

Ranking: 3466 S.S. Count: 13,025

Origin: Scottish. Derived from components meaning son of a brewer.

Genealogies: *Descendants of John Simmons and the Allied Families of Hatton, McGrew, Sherwood, Linthicum, and Cathcart* was compiled by Ruth Maxwell Graham and published in Arlington, Virginia, in 1975. *McGrew Genealogy* was compiled by Paul Cornelius McGrew and published in Spokane, Washington, in 1976.

MCGUINNESS (S.S. Abbreviation: McGuin)

Ranking: 4540 S.S. Count: 9844

Origin: Irish. Derived from the Gaelic name Mag Aonghuis, which was derived from the first name Aonghus, which is comprised of the components "aon" and "ghus," meaning one and choice.

Genealogies: None known.

MCGUIRE (S.S. Abbreviation: McGuir)

Ranking: 427 S.S. Count: 93,082

Origin: Irish. Transformation of Maguire.

Famous **McGuires:** CHARLES BONAVENTURE MCGUIRE (1768–1833) of Ireland was a Roman Catholic missionary to the Pittsburgh, Pennsylvania, area. HUNTER HOLMES MCGUIRE (1835–1900) of Virginia was a physician and Stonewall Jackson's chief surgeon. After the Civil War he helped to found the College of Physicians and Surgeons in Richmond, Virginia.

Genealogies: *49er Irish: One Irish Family in the California Mines* [also McGuire] was compiled by F. D. Calhoon and published in Hicksville, New York, in 1977. *The Ancestry of William Gilman Maguire of Sanford, Maine* [also McGuire] was compiled by William Maguire and published in Sanford, Maine, in 1978.

MCHALE

Ranking: 4623 S.S. Count: 9667

Origin: Irish. 1) derived from the Gaelic name Mac Haol, which was derived from Howell. 2) derived from the Gaelic name Mac Céile, which was derived from the first name Céile, meaning companion.

Famous **McHales:** KATHRYN MCHALE (1889–1956) of Indiana was the developer of the McHale Vocational Interest Test for College Women, which was used from 1929 to 1950.

Genealogies: None known.

MCHENRY (S.S. Abbreviation: McHenr)

Ranking: 2758 S.S. Count: 16,517

Origin: Irish, Scottish. Derived from the Irish-Gaelic name Mac Éinrí or Mac Eanraic and the Scottish-Gaelic name Mac Eanruig, both of which were derived from the first name Henry.

Famous **McHenrys:** JAMES MCHENRY (1753–1816) of Ireland was a Revolutionary War patriot. He served as a medic in the Continental army, as private secretary to George Washington and Marie Joseph Paul Yves Roch Gilbert du Motier de Lafayette, as a member of the Continental Congress, and as the Maryland delegate to the Constitutional Convention. Fort McHenry, where "The Star Spangled Banner" was first written as a poem by Francis Scott Key, was named in his honor for his service to his adopted country.

Genealogies: *One Line of the McHenry Clan* was compiled by Shirley McElroy Bucknum and published in Portland, Oregon, in 1976.

MCHUGH

Ranking: 1671 S.S. Count: 26,768

Origin: Irish, Scottish. Transformation of McKay.

Famous **McHughs:** ROSE JOHN MCHUGH (1881–1952) of Michigan was a social worker who had the rare ability to foster cooperation among the local, state, federal, and private agencies in dealing with child welfare issues.

Genealogies: *Some Goodmans and McHughs* was compiled by Matthew Lee McHugh and published in Columbia, South Carolina, in 1968.

MCINNIS (S.S. Abbreviation: McInni)

Ranking: 4210 S.S. Count: 10,730

Origin: Irish. Transformation of McGuinness.

Genealogies: None known.

MCINTIRE (S.S. Abbreviation: McInti)

Ranking: 2897 S.S. Count: 15,719

Origin: Scottish. Transformation of McIntyre.

Famous **McIntires:** SAMUEL MCINTIRE (1757–1811) of Massachusetts was an architect and wood carver. Many examples of his workmanship can be seen in the homes and buildings in the historical town of Salem, Massachusetts. ROSS MCINTIRE (1889–1959) of Oregon was President Franklin D. Roosevelt's private physician, then the head of the Red Cross blood program.

Genealogies: *Charles McIntire of Colonia, Virginia* was compiled by June R. McIntire Taylor and published in Sarasota, Florida, in 1981. *Family History: Ancestors of Robert Harry McIntire and Helen Annette McIntire* was compiled by Robert Harry McIntire and published in Baltimore, Maryland, in 1980.

MCINTOSH (S.S. Abbreviation: McInto)

Ranking: 751 S.S. Count: 56,361

Origin: Scottish. Derived from the Gaelic name Mac an Toisich, meaning "son of the chief, leader, thane" (H&H).

Famous **McIntoshes:** LACHLAN MCINTOSH (1725–1806) of Scotland was a Revolutionary War soldier who wintered with George Washington at Valley Forge. In 1777, in a dispute over a military loss to the British in Florida, he dueled and killed Button Gwinnett, leader of Georgia and a signer of the Declaration of Independence. WILLIAM MCINTOSH (1775–1825) of Georgia was a Creek chief born to an Englishman and a Creek woman in what is present-day Carroll County, Georgia. He was a brigadier general under Andrew Jackson in the Seminole War (1817–1818). He was responsible for a treaty between the Creeks and the Americans; the treaty angered the Upper Creeks, who killed him. MARIA JANE MCINTOSH (1803–1878) of Georgia was the daughter of Lachlan McIntosh. She was an author who wrote under the pen name Aunt Kitty. *Aunt Kitty Tales* is a compilation of all of her children's stories. She also wrote novels and nonfiction works.

Genealogies: *McIntosh* was compiled by Walter H. McIntosh and published in Topsfield, Massachusetts, in 1980.

MCINTYRE (S.S. Abbreviation: McInty)

Ranking: 673 S.S. Count: 62,396

Origin: Scottish. Derived from the Gaelic name Mac an Saoir, meaning "son of the carpenter or mason" (H&H).

Famous **McIntyres:** OSCAR ODD MCINTYRE (1884–1938) of Missouri was a journalist and the author of the column "New York Day by Day," which appeared in more than 500 newspapers. JAMES FRANCIS ALOYSIUS MCINTYRE (1886–1979) of New York City was a priest who was the archbishop of Los Angeles and became a U.S. cardinal in 1953. ALFRED ROBERT MCINTYRE (1886–1948) of Massachusetts was president of the publishing firm Little, Brown & Co. from 1926 to 1948.

Genealogies: *Charles McIntire of Colonia, Virginia* [also McIntyre] was compiled by June R. McIntire Taylor and published in Sarasota, Florida, in 1981. *Family History: Ancestors of Robert Harry McIntire and Helen Annette McIntire* [also McIntyre] was compiled by Robert Harry McIntire and published in Baltimore, Maryland, in 1980.

MCKAY

Ranking: 791 S.S. Count: 53,242

Origin: Irish, Scottish. Derived from the Gaelic name Mac Aodha, which was derived from the first name Aodh, meaning fire or the pagan god of fire.

Famouse **McKays:** DAVID OMAN MCKAY (1783–1970) of Utah was the ninth president of the Church of Jesus Christ of Latter-day Saints. DONALD MCKAY (1810–1880) of Nova Scotia was a shipbuilder in east Boston and is remembered as a designer and builder of the finest and fastest ships of the period 1845–1869. He also built iron ships for the navy. GORDON MCKAY (1821–1903) of Massachusetts was the grandson of Samuel Dexter (b. 1761), a prominent national politician from Massachusetts. He bought the patent for sewing the upper and lower parts of shoes together, then improved the process. He held the contracts for the shoes necessary for the Civil War soldiers. A millionaire after the war, he turned to philanthropic work, including founding a school for the education of African-Americans. CLAUDE MCKAY (1890–1948) of the West Indies was a militant writer of the Harlem Renaissance.

Genealogies: *Archibald McKay, 1720–1797, Scotland to Cumberland County, North Carolina* was compiled by Bettie McKay Fraine and published in Tulsa, Oklahoma, in 1979.

MCKEE

Ranking: 663 S.S. Count: 63,243

Origin: Irish, Scottish. Transformation of McKay.

Famous **McKees:** JOHN MCKEE (1771–1832) of Virginia was a member of Congress from Alabama, a cousin of Sam Houston, and an Indian agent. He managed to keep the peace between the Cherokee and Choctaw Indians during the Creek War. ANDREW IRWIN MCKEE (1896–1976) of Kentucky was a naval officer and an expert on the design and construction of submarines.

Genealogies: *Ancestors of our Children* [McKee Family] was compiled by Wells Laflin Field and published in West Hartford, Connecticut, in 1966.

MCKEEVER (S.S. Abbreviation: McKeev)

Ranking: 4338 S.S. Count: 10,327

Origin: Irish, Scottish. Cognate to the British name Ivor, which was derived from the Old Norse first name Ivarr.

Genealogies: None known.

MCKELVEY, MCKELVIE, MCKELVY (S.S. Abbreviation: McKelv)

Ranking: 3144 S.S. Count: 14,447

Origin: Irish, Scottish. Irish: derived from the Gaelic name Mac Giolla Bhuidhe, meaning "son of the yellow-haired lad" (H&H). Scottish: derived from the Gaelic name Mac Shealbhaigh, which was derived from the first name Sealbhach.

Genealogies: *The Voyage from Ireland* [Mckelvey Family] was compiled by W. Conrad McKelvey and published in Tiburon, California, in 1982.

MCKENNA, MCKENNAN, MCKENNERY, MCKENNY (S.S. Abbreviation: McKenn)

Ranking: 810 S.S. Count: 52,186

Origin: MeKennery—Irish; McKenna, McKennan, McKenny—Scottish; McKennery—Irish. McKenna, McKennan, McKenny: transformations of Kenney. McKennery: derived from the Gaelic name Mac Innéirghe, which was derived from the first name Innéirghe, which may have been derived from the word "éirghe," meaning to ascend.

Famous **Bearers:** THOMAS MCKEAN THOMPSON MCKENNAN (1794–1852) of Delaware was a member of Congress from Pennsylvania and the president of the Hempfield Railroad, which became part of the Baltimore and Ohio. CHARLES HYACINTH MCKENNA (1835–1917) of Ireland was a Roman Catholic missionary. He was instrumental in the growth of the Holy Name Society. JOSEPH MCKENNA (1843–1926) of Pennsylvania was a lawyer, a member of Congress from California, a U.S. attorney general, and an associate justice of the U.S. Supreme Court.

Genealogies: *The MacKennas of Truagh* [also McKennas] was compiled by C. Eugene Swezey and published in Huntington, New York, in 1977. *The American Descendants of James McCourt, John McKenny, Matthew Young and*

Allied Families was compiled by Martha F. McCourt and published in Vancouver, Washington, in 1988.

MCKENZIE (S.S. Abbreviation: McKenz)

Ranking: 572 **S.S. Count:** 72,267

Origin: Scottish. Transformation of Mackenzie.

Famous **McKenzies:** ALEXANDER McKENZIE (1830–1914) of Massachusetts was a Congregational clergyman who preached civic-mindedness. CHARLES W. McKENZIE (1899–1977) of Massachusetts was a noted professor of political science and author of *Party Government in the United States* (1938).

Genealogies: None known.

MCKEON

Ranking: 3886 **S.S. Count:** 11,611

Origin: Scottish. Transformation of McEwen.

Genealogies: None known.

MCKEOWN (S.S. Abbreviation: McKeow)

Ranking: 4266 **S.S. Count:** 10,557

Origin: Scottish. Transformation of McEwen.

Genealogies: None known.

MCKIBBEN, MCKIBBIN, MCKIBBON (S.S. Abbreviation: McKibb)

Ranking: 4637 **S.S. Count:** 9645

Origin: Irish. Cognates to the English name Gibbon.

Genealogies: *The Descendants of William & Mary Simms* [McKibben Family] was compiled by Vivian York Simms and published in Murfreesboro, Tennessee, in 1989.

MCKINLEY (S.S. Abbreviation: McKinl)

Ranking: 1283 **S.S. Count:** 34,475

Origin: Scottish. Derived from the Gaelic name Mac Fhionnlaoich, which was derived from the first name Fionnlaoch, which was comprised of the components "fionn" and "laoch," meaning white and warrior.

Famous **McKinleys:** JOHN McKINLEY (1780–1852) of Virginia was a U.S. senator, member of Congress, and a justice of the U.S. Supreme Court. WILLIAM McKINLEY (1843–1901) of Ohio was the 25th president of the United States. He served in the Civil War, practiced as a lawyer, served as a member of Congress, and was responsible for the McKinley Tariff of 1890. He was the governor of Ohio before becoming president. During his presidency, the United States acquired Cuba, Puerto Rico, and the Philippines and annexed Hawaii, Wake Island, and Samoa. He was assassinated in 1901. IDA SAXTON McKINLEY (1847–1907) of Ohio was the wife of President William McKinley. WILLIAM BROWN McKINLEY (1856–1926) of Illinois was a member of Congress for many years and a spokesman for world peace.

Genealogies: None known.

MCKINNEY, MCKINNON, MCKINNY (S.S. Abbreviation: McKinn)

Ranking: 256 **S.S. Count:** 142,243

Origin: McKinnon—Irish, Scottish; McKinney, McKinny—Scottish. McKinnon: derived from the Gaelic name Mac Fhionghuin, which was derived from a first name meaning "fair born" (H&H). McKinney, McKinny: transformations of Kenney.

Famous **Bearers:** ROSCOE LEWIS McKINNEY (1900–1978) of Washington, D.C., a professor of anatomy, established the first anatomy department at Howard University's medical college. His work was often included in such texts as *Textbook of Histology* and *Gray's Anatomy.*

Genealogies: *Converging Paths* [McKinney Family] was compiled by Thelma D. McKinney and published in Fort Worth, Texas, in 1972. *The Family McKinney* was compiled by Nancy McKinney Sayford and published in North Palm Beach, Florida, in 1983.

MCKNIGHT (S.S. Abbreviation: McKnig)

Ranking: 964 **S.S. Count:** 45,383

Origin: Scottish. Derived from the Gaelic name Mac Neachdainn, which was derived from the first name Neachdán.

Famous **McKnights:** ROBERT McKNIGHT (1789?–1846) of Virginia was a Santa Fe trader who was captured in Mexico without the benefit of a passport and imprisoned for nine years. The United States refused to help, and he settled in Mexico after his release.

Genealogies: *McKnight Genealogy* was compiled by Imogene Linville Millican and published in Oklahoma City, Oklahoma, in 1981. *The McKnight Family and their Descendants* was compiled by Texarado McKnight Peak and published in Austin, Texas, in 1969.

MCLAIN (ALSO MCLAINE)

Ranking: 1739 **S.S. Count:** 25,754

Origin: Irish, Scottish. Transformations of MacLean.

Genealogies: None known.

MCLAUGHLAN, MCLAUGHLANE, MCLAUGHLIN (S.S. Abbreviation: McLaug)

Ranking: 350 **S.S. Count:** 108,682

Origin: Scottish. Derived from the Gaelic name Mac Lachlainn, which was derived from the first name Lachlann, cognate to Laughlan.

Famous **Bearers:** HUGH McLAUGHLIN (1826?–1904) of New York was a political boss with a hold on Brooklyn, New York. JAMES McLAUGHLIN (1842–1923) of Canada was an Indian agent. As a member of the U.S. Indian Service,

Genealogies: None known.

he gained the trust of the Sioux. His 1910 book, *My Friend the Indian*, details many important facts concerning them. ANDREW CUNNINGHAM MCLAUGHLIN (1861–1947) of Illinois was a historian. He headed the newly established Bureau of Historical Research of the Carnegie Institution and wrote several books for which he received national attention. He was awarded a Pulitzer Prize for his *Constitutional History of the United States*.

Genealogies: None known.

MCLAUREN, MCLAURIN (S.S. Abbreviation: McLaur)

Ranking: 3891　**S.S. Count:** 11,591

Origin: Scottish. Derived from the Gaelic name Mac Labhruinn, which was derived from the name Lawrence.

Famous Bearers: ANSELM JOSEPH MCLAURIN (1848–1909) of Mississippi was a U.S. senator from and governor of Mississippi.

Genealogies: *G. G. McLaurin and some of his Kin* was compiled by G. G. McLaurin and pubished in Dillon, South Carolina, in 1970.

MCLEAN

Ranking: 726　**S.S. Count:** 58,314

Origin: Irish, Scottish. Transformation of MacLean.

Famous McLeans: JOHN MCLEAN (1785–1861) of New Jersey was a member of Congress, postmaster general, and associate justice of the Supreme Court, where he dissented in the *Dred Scott* decision. He twice sought unsuccessfully the Republican nomination for the presidency. WILLIAM LIPPARD MCLEAN (1852–1931) of Pennsylvania was the publisher of the *Philadelphia Evening Bulletin*. ROBERT MCLEAN (1891–1980) of Pennsylvania was the son of William Lippard McLean. He succeeded his father as the publisher of the *Evening Bulletin* and was the chairman, then president, of the Associated Press.

Genealogies: *The Way We Were* [also McLean] was compiled by Alethea Mary Wallack McClain and published in Decorah, Iowa, in 1977. *McLean, the Family of Judge Alney and Tabitha McLean of Greenville, Kentucky* was compiled by Sally Stone Trotter and published in Greenville, Mississippi, in 1983.

MCLELLAN, MCLELLAND (S.S. Abbreviation: McLell)

Ranking: 3775　**S.S. Count:** 11,970

Origin: Irish, Scottish. Derived from the Irish-Gaelic name Mac Giolla Fhaoláin and the Scottish-Gaelic name Mac Gille Fhaolain, both meaning "son of the servant of (St.) Faolán" (H&H).

Genealogies: None known.

MCLEMORE (S.S. Abbreviation: McLemo)

Ranking: 3116　**S.S. Count:** 14,602

Origin: Irish?, Scottish? Uncertain etymology.

Genealogies: None known.

MCLENDON (S.S. Abbreviation: McLend)

Ranking: 3507　**S.S. Count:** 12,855

Origin: Irish, Scottish. Irish: the name means son of the servant of Saint Finnian. Scottish: the name means servant of Adaman.

Genealogies: *The McClendon's: the MacLennan, Mackclenden, McClendon & McLendon* was compiled by T. A. McClendon and published in Stockton, California, in 1973.

MCLEOD

Ranking: 1005　**S.S. Count:** 43,568

Origin: Scottish. Derived from the Gaelic name Mac Leóid, which was derived from the Old Norse name Ljótr, meaning unattractive.

Famous McLeods: ALEXANDER MCLEOD (1774–1833) of Scotland was a Reformed Presbyterian minister who was a pastor in New York City. He spoke against slavery. MARTIN MCLEOD (1813–1860) of Canada was a fur trader and one of the pioneers in the history of Minnesota. HUGH MCLEOD (1814–1862) of New York City was raised in Georgia. He was an officer in the army of Texas and is best known for his skirmishes with Sam Houston.

Genealogies: *McLeod, Stovall, Hinkle, and Allied Families* was compiled by Daniel McLeod Peterson and published in Raleigh, North Carolina, in 1978. *Neal McLeod: Emigrant from the Isle of Skye, Scotland* was compiled by Grover Stephen McLeod and published in Wedowee, Alabama, in 1962.

MCMAHAN (S.S. Abbreviation: McMaha)

Ranking: 2246　**S.S. Count:** 20,370

Origin: Irish. Transformation of McMahon.

Genealogies: *The Name & Family McMahan* was compiled by Sara McMahan Fuller and published in Tennessee.

MCMAHON (S.S. Abbreviation: McMaho)

Ranking: 746　**S.S. Count:** 56,886

Origin: Irish. Derived from the Gaelic name Mac Mathghamhna, which was derived from the name Mathghamhain, meaning bear.

Famous McMahons: BERNARD MCMAHON (?–1816) of Ireland came to the United States in 1796 and settled in Philadelphia. He was a horticulturist who opened a seed and nursery business that was well known to the area botanists of the day. He wrote *American Gardener's Calendar* (1806), the first horticultural book of America. BRIEN MCMAHON (1903–1952) of Connecticut was a U.S. senator and the head of the Special Committee on Atomic Energy. He died before his political potential was realized.

Genealogies: None known.

MCMANUS (S.S. Abbreviation: McManu)

Ranking: 1297 S.S. Count: 34,163

Origin: Irish. Derived from the Gaelic name Mac Maghnuis, which was derived from the first name Magnus.

Famous McManuses: GEORGE MCMANUS (1884–1954) of Missouri was a cartoonist and the creator of the comic strip "Bringing up Father."

Genealogies: None known.

MCMASTER, MCMASTERS (S.S. Abbreviation: McMast)

Ranking: 3318 S.S. Count: 13,661

Origin: Scottish. Transformations of Master.

Famous Bearers: JAMES ALPHONSUS MCMASTER (1820–1886) of New York was a journalist who served as the editor of Freeman's Journal, a Catholic paper not associated with the church. JOHN BACH MCMASTER (1852–1932) of New York was a professor at Princeton University and an American historian who wrote about Benjamin Franklin and nine volumes on The History of the People of the United States (1883–1927).

Genealogies: None known.

MCMICHAEL, MCMICHAIL, MCMICHAN, MCMICHIE (S.S. Abbreviation: McMich)

Ranking: 3835 S.S. Count: 11,746

Origin: McMichan—Irish, Scottish; McMichael, McMichie—Scottish. McMichan: derived from the Gaelic name Mac Miadhacháin, which was derived from the first name Miadhachán, which was derived from the word "miadhach," meaning honorable. McMichael: derived from the Gaelic name Mac Mícheil, which was derived from a Gaelic cognate to Michael. McMichie: derived from the Scottish first name Michie, which was derived from Michael.

Famous Bearers: MORTON MCMICHAEL (1807–1879) of New Jersey was a journalist. He was the editor of several magazines and the manager of The North American. He also was involved in local Philadelphia politics, serving as mayor (1866–1869).

Genealogies: None known.

MCMILLAN, MCMILLEN (S.S. ABBREVIAITON: MCMILL)

Ranking: 375 S.S. Count: 102,729

Origin: Scottish. Transformations of MacMillan.

Famous Bearers: JAMES WINNING MCMILLAN (1825–1903) of Kentucky was a Union soldier, organizer of the 21st Indiana Infantry, and a brevet major general of volunteers. JAMES MCMILLAN (1838–1902) of Canada was a manufacturer and U.S. senator. The McMillan Plan named for him outlined physical improvements to be made in the nation's capitol.

Genealogies: Begats, a Chronicle of the McMillan, Preston, Wiggins, and Binford Families was compiled by Mabel E. Preston Wiggins and published in Ellsworth, Maine, in 1979. MacGhillemhaoil: an Account of my Family [also McMillan] was compiled by W. Duncan MacMillan and published in Wayzata, Minnesota, in 1990. Record of McMillan and Allied Families was compiled by Robert H. McMillan and published in Tallahassee, Florida, in 1973.

MCMULLAN, MCMULLEN, MCMULLIN, MCMILLON (S.S. Abbreviation: McMull)

Ranking: 1094 S.S. Count: 40,368

Origin: Scottish. Transformations of McMillan.

Genealogies: None known.

MCMURRAY (S.S. Abbreviation: McMurr)

Ranking: 2102 S.S. Count: 21,867

Origin: Irish. Derived from the Gaelic name Mac Muireadhaigh, which was derived from the first name Muireadhach, which was derived from the word "muir," meaning sea.

Genealogies: The Family History of Wainner, Overton, McMurr(a)y and Interconnecting Lines was compiled by Merle Wainner Jeter and published in Columbia, South Carolina, in 1972. The Tennessee Colony [also McMurray] was compiled by Rhuy K. Williams McMurray and published in Greensburg, Kansas, in 1966.

MCNABB

Ranking: 3344 S.S. Count: 13,549

Origin: Irish, Scottish. Cognate to Abbot.

Genealogies: None known.

MCNAIR

Ranking: 2009 S.S. Count: 22,700

Origin: Irish, Scottish. Irish: derived from the Gaelic name Mac an Mhaoir, meaning "son of the steward, keeper" (H&H). Scottish: 1) derived from the Gaelic name Mac an Oighre, meaning "son of the heir" (H&H). 2) derived from the Gaelic name Mac Iain Uidhir, meaning "son of sallow John" (H&H).

Famous McNairs: LESLEY JAMES MCNAIR (1883–1944) of Minnesota was an army officer who introduced the idea of simulated fighting and battle conditions in the training of new recruits. He also standardized and organized military doctrine. ANDREW H. MCNAIR (1909–1978) of Montana was a geologist and professor who led many expeditions to map places such as the Elizabeth Islands and Canadian Arctic areas.

Genealogies: *A Research Report on John Martin McNair and his Wife Mary Ann Hamill* was compiled by Myrtle Mitchell McNair and published in 1974.

MCNALLY (S.S. Abbreviation: McNall)

Ranking: 1802 **S.S. Count:** 25,008

Origin: Irish. Derived from the Gaelic name Mac an Fhailghigh, meaning "son of the poor man" (H&H).

Genealogies: None known.

MCNAMARA, MCNAMARRA (S.S. Abbreviation: McNama)

Ranking: 1152 **S.S. Count:** 38,089

Origin: Irish. Derived from the Gaelic name Mac Conmara, which was derived from a first name comprised of the components "cú" and "muir," meaning hound and sea.

Genealogies: None known.

MCNAMEE (S.S. Abbreviation: McName)

Ranking: 4891 **S.S. Count:** 9138

Origin: Irish. Derived from the Gaelic name Mac Conmidhe, which was derived from a first name meaning "hound of Meath" (H&H).

Famous McNamees: GRAHAM MCNAMEE (1888–1942) of Washington, D.C., was a radio announcer. He was one of the top radio personalities of his day.

Genealogies: None known.

MCNEAL, MCNEALE, MCNEALL

Ranking: 1465 **S.S. Count:** 30,361

Origin: Irish, Scottish. Transformations of MacNeil.

Genealogies: None known.

MCNEEL (ALSO MCNEELY)

Ranking: 2299 **S.S. Count:** 19,851

Origin: McNeel—Irish, Scottish; McNeely—Irish, Scottish. McNeel: transformation of MacNeil. McNeely: transformation of MacNeilly.

Genealogies: None known.

MCNEIL (ALSO MCNEILL, MCNEILLIE, MCNEILLY)

Ranking: 519 **S.S. Count:** 77,333

Origin: Irish, Scottish. McNeil, McNeill: transformations of MacNeil. McNeillie, McNeilly: transformations of MacNeilly.

Famous Bearers: HECTOR MCNEILL (1728–1785) of Ireland came to Boston as a child. He was a naval officer and commander of the *Boston* in John Manley's squadron in 1777 when he was court-martialed and dismissed for actions taken against the British ship *Rainbow.* DANIEL MCNEILL (1748–1833) of Massachusetts was a privateersman during the Revolutionary War period. He captained

the *General Miffin,* resulting in 13 conquests, after which he was commissioned an officer in the U.S. navy. There he commanded the *Portsmouth* and the *Boston.* WILLIAM GIBBS MCNEILL (1801–1853) of North Carolina was a civil engineer who worked on railroads. JOHN HANSON MCNEILL (1815–1864) of Virginia was a Confederate who organized a group called McNeill's Partisan Rangers that made many successful raids against the Union army. GEORGE EDWIN MCNEILL (1837–1906) of Massachusetts was a labor leader who worked to make the eight-hour day a reality. He wrote *The Labor Movement,* the first book to cover the history of the American labor movement.

Genealogies: *Greer-McNeill Family History* [also McNeil] was compiled by Etta S. Greer and published in Greenville, South Carolina, in 1984. *The McNeill's Ferry Chronicle and Campbell University* [also McNeil] was compiled by Everett McNeill Kivette and published in Burnsville, North Carolina, in 1983.

MCNULTY (S.S. Abbreviation: McNult)

Ranking: 2332 **S.S. Count:** 19,469

Origin: Irish. Derived from the Gaelic name Mac an Ultaigh, meaning "son of the Ulsterman" (H&H).

Famous McNultys: FRANK JOSEPH MCNULTY (1872–1926) of Ireland was the president of the International Brotherhood of Electrical Workers. JOHN AUGUSTINE MCNULTY (1895–1956) of Massachusetts was a journalist with the major New York City newspapers.

Genealogies: *Temple/McNulty* was compiled by Ethel Temple Jensen and published in Omaha, Nebraska, in 1980.

MCNUTT

Ranking: 3333 **S.S. Count:** 13,598

Origin: Scottish. Transformation of McKnight.

Famous McNutts: ALEXANDER MCNUTT (1725?–1811), possibly of Ireland, was a land promoter who participated in a revolt that took place in Nova Scotia. PAUL VORIES MCNUTT (1891–1955) of Indiana was a lawyer and diplomat. He was the governor of Indiana, commissioner of the Philippines, and head of the Federal Security Agency.

Genealogies: None known.

MCPHERSON (S.S. Abbreviation: McPher)

Ranking: 864 **S.S. Count:** 49,777

Origin: Scottish. Transformation of MacPherson.

Famous McPhersons: JAMES BIRDSEYE MCPHERSON (1828–1864) was an army officer in the Civil War. He was the chief engineer on Ulysses S. Grant's staff. EDWARD MCPHERSON (1830–1895) of Pennsylvania was a journalist and a member of Congress from Pennsylvania. He served as the clerk of the House of Representatives and wrote several political books, including *Political Manual* (1866–

1869). AIMEE SEMPLE MCPHERSON (1890–1944) of Canada was born Aimee Elizabeth Kennedy. She was married twice, first to Robert Semple, who died in 1910, then to Harold McPherson. She was a missionary in China and a preacher throughout the United States. Often involved in controversy, she was the founder in 1927 of the International Church of the Foursquare Gospel.

Genealogies: None known.

MCQUEEN, MCQUEENIE (S.S. Abbreviation: McQuee)

Ranking: 1582 S.S. Count: 28,263

Origin: McQueenie—Irish; McQueen—Scottish. McQueenie: transformation of Sweeney. McQueen: derived from the Gaelic name Mac Shuibhne, which was derived from the first name Suibhne, meaning pleasant.

Genealogies: Clergymen and Chiefs: A Genealogy of the MacQueen and MacFarlane Families [also McQueen] was compiled by Alex M. Quattlebaum and published in Charleston, South Carolina, in 1990.

MCQUILLAN, MCQUILLIAM, MCQUILLIAMS, MCQUILLY (S.S. Abbreviation: McQuil)

Ranking: 4583 S.S. Count: 9753

Origin: McQuillan, McQuilly—Irish; McQuilliam, McQuilliams—Scottish. McQuillan: derived from the Gaelic name Mac Uighilín, which was derived from a Gaelic version of the Old French name Huguelin, which was derived from Hugh. McQuilly: 1) derived from the Gaelic name Mac an Choiligh, meaning "son of the cock" (H&H). 2) derived from the Gaelic name Mac Conchoille, meaning "son of Cú Choille" (H&H). The name Cú Choille is comprised of the components "cú" and "coille," meaning hound and wood. McQuilliam, McQuilliams: transformations of McWilliams.

Genealogies: The McQuillan Family of Ulster was compiled by Mildred Irwin Rania and published in Redlands, California, in 1965.

MCRAE

Ranking: 1744 S.S. Count: 25,695

Origin: Irish, Scottish. Transformation of McCray.

Famous McRaes: THOMAS CHIPMAN MCRAE (1851–1929) of Arkansas was a member of Congress from and governor of his home state. In the latter position he streamlined the state government. MILTON ALEXANDER MCRAE (1858–1930) of Michigan was a newspaper publisher in partnership with E. W. Scripps. The Scripps-McRae Press Association became United Press. He also was the author of the 1924 book Forty Years in Newspaperdom.

Genealogies: The Alexander William McRae (1847–1912) Family and Descendants was compiled by Vada McRae Gipson and published in Fort Jones, California, in 1984.

MCREYNOLDS (S.S. Abbreviation: McReyn)

Ranking: 4135 S.S. Count: 10,939

Origin: Irish. Derived from the first name Reginald, meaning powerful.

Famous McReynoldses: JAMES CLARK MCREYNOLDS (1862–1946) of Kentucky was a U.S. attorney general and an associate justice of the U.S. Supreme Court. SAMUEL DAVIS MCREYNOLDS (1872–1939) of Tennessee was a member of Congress and an advocate of limited immigration. He was the chairman of the Foreign Affairs Committee.

Genealogies: None known.

MCVAY

Ranking: 4140 S.S. Count: 10,935

Origin: Scottish. Derived from the Gaelic name Mac Beatha, meaning "son of life" (H&H) or "man of religion" (H&H).

Genealogies: None known.

MCVEY

Ranking: 3573 S.S. Count: 12,624

Origin: Scottish. Transformation of McVay.

Famous McVeys: FRANK LEROND MCVEY (1869–1953) of Ohio was the president of several major universities, the president of the National Association of State Universities, and the author of Financial History of Great Britain.

Genealogies: None known.

MCWHORTER (S.S. Abbreviation: McWhor)

Ranking: 3362 S.S. Count: 13,485

Origin: Irish. Uncertain etymology.

Genealogies: None known.

MCWILLIAM, MCWILLIAMS (S.S. Abbreviation: McWill)

Ranking: 1501 S.S. Count: 29,674

Origin: Scottish. Derived from the Gaelic name Mac Uilleim, which was derived from a Gaelic version of the first name William.

Genealogies: A Family History [also McWilliams] was compiled by George L. Williams and published in Port Washington, New York, in 1990.

MEACHAM (S.S. Abbreviation: Meacha)

Ranking: 4934 S.S. Count: 9072

Origin: English. Derived from the Anglo-Norman-French word "machun," meaning stonemason. The name was given to stonemasons.

Genealogies: Meacham, Mitcham, Mitchum: Families of the South was compiled by Clarence E. Mitcham and published in Mead, Washington, in 1974. The Moses Moroni and Almira Jane Duke Mecham Family [also Meacham] was compiled by Robert Bernard Mecham and published in Provo, Utah, in 1985.

MEAD

Ranking: 1373 **S.S. Count:** 32,294

Origin: English. 1) derived from the Old English word "meodu," meaning mead, the beverage of fermented honey. The name was given to those who made or sold mead. 2) derived from the Middle English word "mede," meaning meadow. The name was given to those who lived near a meadow.

Famous **Meads:** ELIZABETH STORRS BILLINGS MEAD (1832–1917) of Massachusetts was the president of Mount Holyoke College. LARKIN GOLDSMITH MEAD (1835–1910) of New Hampshire was a sculptor whose works include "Ethan Allen" at the Vermont capitol, "Lincoln Monument" in Springfield, Illinois, and "The Father of Waters" in Minneapolis, Minnesota. GEORGE HERBERT MEAD (1863–1931) of Massachusetts was a philosopher who developed the theory of "objective realism" and a psychologist who was a behaviorist who felt that the spoken language contributed greatly to the development of the person. JAMES MICHAEL MEAD (1885–1964) of New York was a U.S. senator and was elected a member of Congress for 10 terms. He held several other offices during his tenure in Washington. MARGARET MEAD (1901–1978) of Pennsylvania was an anthropologist associated with the American Museum of Natural History and Columbia University. Her main interests were in the transition from child to adult within the primitive societies, especially in the Pacific Islands. *Blackberry Winter* (1972) is her autobiography.

Genealogies: *Descendants of John Page (1614–1687) of Hingham and Haverhill, Massachusetts, Together with Genealogical Records of Certain Branches of the Mead, Jeffers and Hunkins Families* was compiled by Theda Page Brigham was published in Haverhill, New Hampshire, in 1972. *Jonathan Mead of Rensselaerwyck and some of his Descendants* was compiled by Cecil Mead Draper and published in Denver, Colorado, in 1972.

MEADE

Ranking: 1498 **S.S. Count:** 29,718

Origin: English. Transformation of Mead.

Famous **Meades:** WILLIAM MEADE (1789–1862) of Virginia was an Episcopal minister who was the person responsible for the renewed interest in the Episcopal church. GEORGE GORDON MEADE (1815–1872) was born in Spain to American parents. He was an artillery officer during the Civil War and is credited with repelling the Confederate army under Robert E. Lee at the Battle of Gettysburg, July 1–4, 1863.

Genealogies: None known.

MEADOR

Ranking: 2335 **S.S. Count:** 19,417

Origin: English, German. 1) the name was given to those who worked with red dyes. 2) the name was given to those who came from Madan, a place in Germany. 3) the name was given to those who mowed or harvested grain.

Genealogies: *The Meaders Family, North Georgia Potters* [also Meador] was compiled by Ralph Rinzler and published in Washington, D.C., in 1980. *Our Meador Families in Colonial America* was compiled by Victor P. Meador and published in Independence, Missouri, in 1983.

MEADOW (ALSO MEADOWS)

Ranking: 693 **S.S. Count:** 60,559

Origin: English. Uncertain etymology. Derived from a form of the Old English word "mōed," meaning meadow. The name was given to those living near a meadow.

Genealogies: *Daniel Meadows and his Descendants* was compiled by Michal Martin Farmer and published in Dallas, Texas in 1976. *History and Genealogical Data of the Poynor, Burns, Meadows, Sudberry, and Conyer Families* was compiled by Marion Joyce Poynor and published in Columbia, Tennessee in 1982.

MEANS

Ranking: 1993 **S.S. Count:** 22,760

Origin: English. The name was given to those who lived near an open area such as a common.

Famous **Meanses:** GASTON BULLOCK MEANS (1879–1938) of North Carolina was a cotton salesman, a German spy in the early part of World War I, then a private investigator. A much-publicized trial took place for the murder of Maude King after she was swindled out of her fortune. Means was acquitted in that case, but he was found guilty of trying to swindle money from Evalyn McLean, with the story that he could recover the kidnapped child of Charles Lindbergh. He spent the rest of his life in prison, where he wrote *The Strange Death of President Harding* (1930) with May Thacker.

Genealogies: *The Means Family of America* was compiled by Elizabeth Cissel Foglesong and published in 1972.

MEARS

Ranking: 3198 **S.S. Count:** 14,193

Origin: English. 1) derived from the Old English word "(ge)mœre," meaning boundary. The name was given to those who lived near a boundary. 2) derived from the Old English word "mere," meaning pond. The name was given to those who lived near a pond.

Famous **Mearses:** OTTO MEARS (1840–1931) of Russia was a Colorado pioneer. HELEN FARNSWORTH MEARS (1872–1916) of Wisconsin was a sculptor. Her best-known work is titled "Genius of Wisconsin."

Genealogies: None known.

MEDEIROS (S.S. Abbreviation: Medeir)

Ranking: 2024 S.S. Count: 22,590

Origin: Portuguese. Derived from the Portuguese word "medeiro," meaning "a place where shocks of maize are gathered" (H&H). The name was given to those from Medeiros, the name of several places in Portugal.

Genealogies: None known.

MEDINA

Ranking: 300 S.S. Count: 120,590

Origin: Spanish. Derived from the Arabic word "medina," meaning city. The name was given to those from Medina, the name of places in Spain.

Genealogies: None known.

MEDLEY

Ranking: 2537 S.S. Count: 17,876

Origin: English. 1) derived from the Middle English and Old French word "medlee," meaning conflict. The name was given to those who were bellicose. 2) derived from the Old English words "middel" and "ēg," meaning middle and island. The name was given to those from Medley or Madeley, the name of several places in England.

Genealogies: None known.

MEDLIN

Ranking: 3031 S.S. Count: 15,004

Origin: English? Uncertain etymology. 1) possibly derived from the Old English word "mæd," meaning meadow. 2) possibly derived from the Old English word "middel," meaning middle.

Genealogies: None known.

MEDRANO (S.S. Abbreviation: Medran)

Ranking: 2701 S.S. Count: 16,834

Origin: Spanish. Uncertain etymology. Possibly derived from the Spanish word "medrar," meaning to thrive or flourish.

Genealogies: None known.

MEEHAN

Ranking: 2085 S.S. Count: 22,010

Origin: Irish. 1) derived from the Gaelic name Ó Maothain, which was derived from the first name Maothán, which was derived from the word "maoth," meaning soft, damp, or weepy. 2) derived from the Gaelic name Ó Miadhacháin, which was derived from the first name Miadhach, meaning esteemed.

Famous **Meehans:** THOMAS MEEHAN (1826–1901) of England was a botanist who settled in Philadelphia and opened nurseries in Upper Germantown. He was also the author of *American Handbook of Ornamental Trees* (1853) and *The Native Flowers and Ferns of the United States* (1878–1880).

Genealogies: None known.

MEEK

Ranking: 2153 S.S. Count: 21,319

Origin: English, Scottish. Derived from the Middle English word "meek," meaning humble. The name was given to those who were meek.

Famous **Meeks:** JOSEPH L. MEEK (1810–1875) of Virginia was an Oregon pioneer whose true abilities were never used. ALEXANDER BEAUFORT MEEK (1814–1865) of South Carolina was a leader in the founding of the Alabama school system. FIELDING BRADFORD MEEK (1817–1876) of Indiana was one of the leading paleontologists of his day.

Genealogies: *The Meek Family of Washington County, Virginia* was compiled by Danny Morris Fluhart and published in Baltimore, Maryland, in 1989.

MEEKER

Ranking: 3626 S.S. Count: 12,416

Origin: English. Uncertain etymology. Probably a transformation of Meek.

Famous **Meekers:** MOSES MEEKER (1790–1865) of New Jersey was a lead miner who worked and developed the mines in Illinois. He was responsible for the building of one of the area's smelting furnaces. JOTHAM MEEKER (1804–1855) of Ohio was a Baptist missionary and a printer. He printed the first pamphlet and book in Kansas. NATHAN COOK MEEKER (1817–1879) of Ohio was a journalist and reformer. He wrote an agricultural column for Horace Greeley's *New York Tribune* and founded Union Colony, a utopian commune in Greeley, Colorado, with the help of Horace Greeley. There he published the *Greeley Tribune*. He was killed by the Ute Indians he was trying to convert from hunters to farmers. EZRA MEEKER (1830–1928) of Ohio was a pioneer of Washington and Oregon. He helped in the marking of the Oregon Trail.

Genealogies: *The Descendants of Timothy Meeker (1708–1798)* was compiled by Kathleen Kirkpatrick and published in Ridgecrest, California, in 1987.

MEEKS

Ranking: 1141 S.S. Count: 38,547

Origin: English, Scottish. Transformation of Meek.

Genealogies: *Descendants of Nathan Meeks and Wife, Sarah C. Jones* was compiled by Sallie Stewart Harrison and published in Fort Worth, Texas, in 1980. *The Meek Family of Washington County, Virginia* [also Meeks] was compiled by Danny Morris Fluhart and published in Baltimore, Maryland, in 1989.

MEIER

Ranking: 1271 S.S. Count: 34,730
Origin: German. Transformation of Meyer.
Genealogies: None known.

MEISTER, MEISTERING (S.S. Abbreviation: Meiste)

Ranking: 4082 S.S. Count: 11,069
Origin: German. Cognates to Master.
Famous **Bearers:** MORRIS MEISTER (1895–1975), born in Poland, organized and served as the first principal of the Bronx (New York) High School of Science, which became world renowned in secondary education.
Genealogies: *A History of the "Meister-Allion" Families, their Emigration to and Settlement in America* was compiled by H. D. Meister and published in Wauseon, Ohio, in 1917.

MEJIAS

Ranking: 1603 S.S. Count: 27,971
Origin: Spanish. Derived from the Greek word "Messias," meaning Messiah.
Genealogies: None known.

MELENDEZ (S.S. Abbreviation: Melend)

Ranking: 647 S.S. Count: 64,380
Origin: Spanish. Transformation of Menendez.
Genealogies: None known.

MELLO

Ranking: 3056 S.S. Count: 14,846
Origin: Italian. Transformation of James.
Genealogies: None known.

MELTON

Ranking: 618 S.S. Count: 67,628
Origin: English. Derived from the Old Norse word "meðal," meaning the middle, and Old English word "tūn," meaning settlement. The name was given to those from Melton, the name of several places in England.
Famous **Meltons:** JAMES MELTON (1904–1961) of Georgia was a tenor and a very popular singing personality in the 1920s and 1930s.
Genealogies: None known.

MELVIN

Ranking: 1623 S.S. Count: 27,622
Origin: Irish, Scottish. Irish: derived from the Gaelic name Ó Maoil Mhin, meaning "a descendant of the devotee of (St.) Min" (H&H). Scottish: 1) derived from the Latin words "mala" and "ville," meaning bad and settlement. The name was given to those who came from Malleville, the name of several places in Normandy. 2) derived from the Gaelic

name Mac Gille Riabhaich, meaning "son of the brindled lad" (H&H).
Genealogies: None known.

MENARD (ALSO MENARDI, MENARDO)

Ranking: 3246 S.S. Count: 13,993
Origin: Menard—French; Menardi, Menardo—Italian. Cognates to Maynard.
Famous **Bearers:** RENÉ MÉNARD (1605–1661) of France was a Jesuit and the first missionary to the Ottawa people of Canada. PIERRE MENARD (1766–1844) of Canada was a fur trader and pioneer. He was one of the organizers of the St. Louis Missouri Fur Co. and the first lieutenant governor of Illinois. MICHEL BRANAMOUR MENARD (1805–1856) of Canada was a fur trader. He eventually settled on Galveston Island, Texas, and founded the town of Galveston. Menard County in Texas is named for him. JOHN WILLIS MENARD (1838–1893) of Illinois was elected to fill a seat as a member of Congress, thereby becoming the first African-American to hold such a position.
Genealogies: *Ancestors of Exzelia Elizabeth Boudreau and Branch Lines of the Boudreau, Senezague, Senet, and Menard Ancestors* was compiled by Betty Lou Madden and published in Hastings, Nebraska, in 1980.

MENDEL (ALSO MENDELEVITZ, MENDELEWICZ, MENDELSOHN, MENDELSON)

Ranking: 3027 S.S. Count: 15,022
Origin: Jewish. Derived from the Yiddish first name Mendl.
Famous **Bearers:** LAFAYETTE BENEDICT MENDEL (1872–1935) of New York was a chemist. He was one of the discoverers of vitamin A and helped with the discovery of vitamin B. ERICH (OR ERIC) MENDELSOHN (1887–1953) of East Prussia was an architect whose works were not given due recognition until after his death. SANUEL MENDELSOHN (1895–1966) of Illinois was the inventor of the three-cell dry battery used by photographers. He also invented microwave components and radar devices.
Genealogies: None known.

MENDENHALL (S.S. Abbreviation: Menden)

Ranking: 3080 S.S. Count: 14,762
Origin: English. Derived from components meaning middle and nook. The name was given to those from Mendenhall, the name of places in England.
Famous **Mendenhalls:** THOMAS CORWIN MENDENHALL (1841–1924) of Ohio was a physicist best known for his research on gravity, seismology, and electricity. CHARLES ELWOOD MENDENHALL (1872–1935) of Ohio was a physicist concerned with gravitational measurements, melting points, and radiation. DOROTHY REED MENDENHALL

(1874–1964) of Ohio was a physician best known for her research on Hodgkin's disease and her work in the area of child care.

Genealogies: *Ancestors and Descendants of Jacob H. Mendenhall and his Wife Hannah W. Newlin* was compiled by Lillian Mendenhall Powell Jacobs and published in Sarasota, Florida, in 1983. *The Mendenhalls: a Genealogy* was compiled by Henry Hart Beeson and published in Long Beach, California, in 1969.

MENDES

Ranking: 4854 S.S. Count: 9219
Origin: Portuguese. Cognate to Menendez.
Famous **Mendeses**: FREDERIC DeSOLA MENDES (1850–1927) of Jamacia was the founder and editor of *American Hebrew Magazine.* HENRY PEREIRA MENDES (1852–1937) of England was the co-founder of the Jewish Theological Seminary of America.
Genealogies: None known.

MENDEZ

Ranking: 456 S.S. Count: 87,844
Origin: Spanish. Transformation of Menendez.
Genealogies: None known.

MENDOZA (S.S. Abbreviation: Mendoz)

Ranking: 416 S.S. Count: 94,895
Origin: Spanish. Derived from the Basque words "mendi" and "otz," meaning mountain and cold. The name was given to those from Mendoza, a place in Spain.
Genealogies: *Shamrocks and Fleurs-de-lis: a Louisiana Genealogy of the O'Brien, Mendoza, Verret, de la Chaise, Chauvin and Allied Families* was compiled by Leland Dudley O'Brien and published in Eunice, Louisiana, in 1983.

MENENDEZ (S.S. Abbreviation: Menend)

Ranking: 4506 S.S. Count: 9942
Origin: Spanish. Derived from the medieval first name Menendo, which was derived from the Visigothic first name Hermenegild, which is comprised of the components "ermen" and "gild," meaning entire and tribute.
Genealogies: None known.

MERCADANTI, MERCADE, MERCADER, MERCADIER, MERCADO (S.S. Abbreviation: Mercad)

Ranking: 679 S.S. Count: 61,476
Origin: Mercade, Mercader—Catalan; Mercadanti—Italian; Mercado—Jewish, Spanish; Mercadier—Provençal. Mercade, Mercader: cognates to Mercadier. Mercadanti: cognate to Marchand. Mercadier: derived from the Old Provençal word "mercadier," meaning a retailer or shopkeeper. Mercado (Jewish): uncertain etymology. Possibly a cognate to the Spanish name Mercado or derived from the Sephardic masculine first name Merkado, meaning "bought" (H&H). *Mercado (Spanish): derived from the Spanish word "mercado," meaning marketplace. The name was given to those who lived by a marketplace.*
Genealogies: None known.

MERCER (ALSO MERCEREAU, MERCERON, MERCEROT)

Ranking: 901 S.S. Count: 48,030
Origin: Mercer—English; Mercereau, Merceron, Mercerot—French. Mercer: derived from the Old French word "mercier," meaning trader. The name was given to traders. Mercereau, Merceron, Mercerot: cognates to Mercer.
Famous **Bearers**: HUGH MERCER (1725?–1777) of Scotland was a Revolutionary War soldier and the commander of the Flying Camp in northern New Jersey. He was killed at the battle of Princeton, January 3, 1777. MABEL MERCER (1900–1984) of England was a cabaret singer best remembered for her unique style of singing. JOHN H. MERCER (1909–1976) of Georgia was called Johnny. He was a songwriter of some of the best-known songs of the 20th century, including "Jeepers Creepers," "You Must Have Been a Beautiful Baby," and "Old Black Magic." He won Acadamy Awards with various co-authors for "On the Atchison, Topeka, and Santa Fe," "In the Cool, Cool, Cool of the Evening," "Moon River," and "Days of Wine and Roses."
Genealogies: *Three Hundred Years in America with the Mercers* was compiled by Dolores Graham Doyle and published in Baltimore, Maryland, in 1991.

MERCHANT

Ranking: 2594 S.S. Count: 17,531
Origin: English. Cognate to and transformation of Marchand.
Genealogies: *Preliminary Record of Gurdon Merchant and his Wife Hannah Van Duzer* was compiled by Mary Gene McCall Middleton and published in South Orange, New Jersey, in 1971.

MERCIER (S.S. Abbreviation: Mercie)

Ranking: 3781 S.S. Count: 11,932
Origin: English, French. Transformation of and cognate to Mercer.
Famous **Merciers**: CHARLES ALFRED MERCIER (1816–1894) of Louisiana was a physician, Creole author, and the founder of the Athenee Louisianais.
Genealogies: None known.

MERCURIO (S.S. Abbreviation: Mercur)

Ranking: 4746 S.S. Count: 9438
Origin: Spanish. Derived from the first name Mercurio, which was derived from the name of the Roman god Mercury.

Genealogies: None known.

MEREDITH (S.S. Abbreviation: Meredi)

Ranking: 1289 S.S. Count: 34,384

Origin: Welsh. Derived from the first name Meredydd, which was derived from the Old Welsh first name Morgetiud, which was derived from an uncertain first component and the second component "udd," meaning lord.

Famous **Merediths**: SAMUEL MEREDITH (1741–1817) of Pennsylvania was a Revolutionary War soldier and the first treasurer of the United States. EDNA C. ELLIOTT MEREDITH (1879–1961) of Iowa was the head of Meredith Publishing Co., which published *Better Homes and Gardens* and *Successful Farming.*

Genealogies: *The Merediths and Selveys of Virginia and West Virginia* was compiled by Joseph N. Meredith and published in Parsons, West Virginia, in 1982. *Your Family and Mine* [also Meredith] was compiled by Mattie Ellen Brown Trube and published in Houston, Texas, in 1973.

MERKEL

Ranking: 4566 S.S. Count: 9780

Origin: German. Cognate to the English name Mark, derived from the Latin name Marcus.

Genealogies: *The Merikle Family, 1710– 1967* [also Merkel] was compiled by Paul V. Merikle and published in Tenafly, New Jersey, in 1975.

MERREL (ALSO MERRELLS)

Ranking: 3850 S.S. Count: 11,711

Origin: Merrel, Merrells—English. Merrel: 1) derived from the Old English components "myrige" and "hyll," meaning pleasant and hill. The name was given to those from Merrill, the name of several places in England. 2) derived from the feminine first name Muriel, which comprises the components "muir" and "gael," meaning sea and bright. Merrells: transformation of Merrel, derived from Muriel.

Genealogies: None known.

MERRICK (S.S. Abbreviation: Merric)

Ranking: 3393 S.S. Count: 13,341

Origin: English, Scottish, Welsh. English: derived from an Old French first name comprised of the components "meri" and "ric," meaning renown and power. Scottish: derived from the Gaelic word "meurach," meaning river or road fork. The name was given to those from Merrick, the name of several places in Scotland. Welsh: derived from the Welsh first name Meuric, which is a form of Maurice.

Famous **Merricks**: CAROLINE ELIZABETH THOMAS MERRICK (1825–1908) of Louisiana was a suffrage and temperance leader in Louisiana. She quietly petitioned the Louisiana constitutional convention and the governor to grant women a limited degree of suffrage and was one of the first women to speak for their sex. Although it appears that she accomplished little, she was the link between the old and the new. Her autobiography is titled *Old Times in Dixie Land: A Southern Matron's Memories* (1901).

Genealogies: *Myrick Family History* [also Merrick] was compiled by Victor R. Myrick and published in Owensboro, Kentucky, in 1980.

MERRIL (ALSO MERRILL, MERRILLS)

Ranking: 950 S.S. Count: 45,635

Origin: English. Merril, Merrill: transformations of Merrel. Merrills: transformation of Merrells.

Famous **Bearers**: SAMUEL MERRILL (1792–1855) of Vermont was the founder of the Bobbs-Merrill Publishing Co. GEORGE PERKINS MERRILL (1854–1929) of Maine was a geologist and is best remembered for his study of meteorites and rock weathering. STUART FITZRANDOLPH MERRILL (1863–1915) of New York was a poet who moved to France and wrote all of his works in French. CHARLES EDWARD MERRILL (1885–1956) of Green Cove Springs, Florida, was the founder of Merrill Lynch and Co. He was one of the founders of *Family Circle* magazine. FRANK DOW MERRILL (1903–1955) of Massachusetts was an army officer who founded a group of volunteers during World War II who trained in jungle warfare and fought behind the Japanese lines in Burma. The volunteers were known as "Merrill's Marauders."

Genealogies: *Some Descendants of Nathaniel Merrill, who was in Newbury, Massachusetts, 1635* was compiled by Winnifred M. Robinson and published in Kingsport, Tennessee, in 1970.

MERRIMAN, MERRIMENT (S.S. Abbreviation: Merrim)

Ranking: 3560 S.S. Count: 12,679

Origin: English. Transformations of the English name Merry, which was derived from the Middle English word "merry," meaning happy. The name was given to those with happy dispositions.

Genealogies: *A History of the Adams and Evarts Families* was compiled by John Merriman Adams and published in Chatham, New York, in 1894.

MERRIT (ALSO MERRITT)

Ranking: 629 S.S. Count: 65,770

Origin: English. 1) derived from the English name Marryat, which was derived from the Middle English first name Meryet, which is comprised of the components "mōer," meaning boundary, and the tribal name Gēat. 2) derived from the English name Marriott, which was derived from the feminine first name Mary. 3) transformation of the English name Merriot, which was derived from the Old English words "(ge)mære" and "geat," meaning boundary and gate. The name was given to those from Merriot, the name of a place in England.

Famous **Bearers:** ISRAEL JOHN MERRITT (1829–1911) of New York City invented a pontoon for use in raising sunken ships. It was an important breakthrough in the salvage business. WESLEY MERRITT (1834–1910) of New York City was an army officer who commanded the first Philippines expedition. ANNA LEA MERRITT (1844–1930) of Pennsylvania was an artist who lived most of her life in England.

Genealogies: *Burris Ancestors* [also Merritt] was compiled by Arthur Price Burris and published in Minneapolis, Minnesota, in 1974. *Historical Perspectives of Charles Merritt, ca. 1652–1718* was compiled by King Merritt and published in Baltimore, Maryland, in 1987.

MERTZ

Ranking: 4103 **S.S. Count:** 11,016
Origin: German. Transformation of and cogate to Martin.
Genealogies: None known.

MESA

Ranking: 4629 **S.S. Count:** 9657
Origin: Spanish. Derived from the Old Spanish word "mesa," meaning plateau. The name was given to those who lived near a mesa or to those from Mesa, the name of several places in Spain.
Genealogies: None known.

MESSER (ALSO MESSERER, MESSERLE, MESSERMAN, MESSERSCHMIDT)

Ranking: 1253 **S.S. Count:** 35,189
Origin: Messer—German, Jewish, Scottish; Messerer, Messerle, Messerschmidt—German; Messerman—Jewish. Messer (German, Jewish): derived from the German word "messer," meaning knife, or its Yiddish cognate "meser." The name was given to cutlers. Messer (German): derived from the Middle High German word "mezzen," meaning to measure. The name was given to the "official in charge of measuring the dues paid in kind by tenants" (H&H). Messer (Scottish): derived from the Old French word "messier," meaning master of the harvest. The name was given to those who stood guard over harvested crops. Messerer, Messerle, Messerschmidt: transformations of the German name Messer, derived from "messer," meaning knife. Messerman: transformation of Messer.

Famous **Bearers:** ASA MESSER (1769–1836) of Massachusetts was the president of Rhode Island College, which, because of the patronage of Nicholas Brown, was changed in name to Brown University.
Genealogies: None known.

MESSICK

Ranking: 4839 **S.S. Count:** 9249
Origin: Uncertain etymology.
Genealogies: None known.

MESSINA, MESSINEO, MESSINESE, MESSINETTI (S.S. Abbreviation: Messin)

Ranking: 1605 **S.S. Count:** 27,946
Origin: Italian. Uncertain etymology. The name was given to those from Messina, a city in Italy.
Genealogies: None known.

METCALF, METCALFE (S.S. Abbreviation: Metcal)

Ranking: 1113 **S.S. Count:** 39,747
Origin: English. Uncertain etymology. Most likely derived from a Middle English word meaning meat calf. The name may have been given to slaughterers or to those thought to resembled a fatted calf.

Famous **Bearers:** THOMAS METCALFE (1780–1855) of Virginia was a member of Congress from, U.S. senator from, and governor of Kentucky. WILLIAM METCALF (1838–1909) of Pennsylvania was a metallurgist and steel manufacturer. He supervised the making of more than 3000 heavy guns that never were known to fail.

Genealogies: *A Study of Metcalfs, Andrews & Smith* was compiled by Clayton G. Metcalf and published in Enterprise, Alabama, in 1979. *Metcalfe & Related Families* was compiled by Annie Walker Burns and published in 1965.

METZ

Ranking: 1534 **S.S. Count:** 29,020
Origin: German, Jewish. German: derived from the German word "messer," meaning knife. The name was given to cutlers. Jewish: the name was given to those from Metz, a city in France.

Famous **Metzes:** CHRISTIAN METZ (1794–1867) of Prussia was a religious leader and the head of the group known as the Community of True Inspiration. The group moved from Buffalo, New York, to Iowa and became the Amana Society.

Genealogies: *Metts Ancestors in America* [also Metz] was compiled by Albert Caswell Metts and published in San Antonio, Texas, in 1984. *Metz Families Research* was compiled by Irene R. Williams Berg and published in Veradale, Washington, in 1982.

METZGER (S.S. Abbreviation: Metzge)

Ranking: 1521 **S.S. Count:** 29,244
Origin: German, Jewish. Derived from the Middle High German word "metziger," meaning slaughterer. The name was given to butchers.
Genealogies: *Germanic Roots of Chicagoans Harvy Met-*

zger Ehlers & Evelynne Meiborg Ehlers was compiled by Harvey Metzger Ehlers and published in Villa Park, Illinois, in 1982. *The Metzger Family History* was compiled by Willodean Rickel Metzger and published in Warsaw, Indiana, in 1981.

METZLE

Ranking: 4931 S.S. Count: 9076
Origin: German? Uncertain etymology. Possibly a transformation of Matthew.
Genealogies: None known.

MEYER

Ranking: 152 S.S. Count: 210,146
Origin: Dutch, German, Jewish. Dutch: cognate to the German name Mayer. German: transformation of the German name Mayer. Jewish: transformation of the Jewish name Mayer.

Famous **Meyers:** LUCY JANE RIDER MEYER (1849–1922) of Vermont was a pioneer in the urban social work and Methodist deaconess movements. ADOLF MEYER (1866–1950) of Switzerland was a psychiatrist who is best known for emphasizing that behavioral disorders were the result of diseases of the nervous system. ANNIE FLORENCE NATHAN MEYER (1867–1951) of New York City was a writer and educator and the cousin of Emma Lazarus, the writer whose poem is inscribed on the base of the Statue of Liberty. She was the founder of Barnard College at Columbia University. AGNES ELIZABETH ERNST MEYER (1887–1970) of New York City was a journalist and one of the first female reporters on the *New York Sun*. Her very wealthy husband purchased the *Washington Post*, and, after his death, she wrote stories and reviews for the *Post*. She generously supported social issues financially. Her autobiography is titled *Out of These Roots.* ANDRÉ MEYER (1898–1979) of France was a financier in New York who was world renowned for his financal genius. Among the corporate shifts he managed was the purchase of Avis Inc. for $7 million and its sale a few years later for $52 million.

Genealogies: *Genealogy of the Meyers Family* [also Meyer] was compiled by I. Austin Meyers and published in Wilmington, Delaware, in 1968. *The Meyer Family: Master Potters of Texas* was compiled by Georgeanna H. Greer and published in San Antonio, Texas, in 1971.

MEYERS (ALSO MEYERSOHN, MEYERSON)

Ranking: 455 S.S. Count: 87,871
Origin: Meyers—Dutch; Meyers—English; Meyers, Meyersohn, Meyerson—Jewish. Meyers (Dutch): cognate to the German name Mayer. Meyers (English): transformation of the English name Mayer. Meyers, Meyersohn, Meyerson: transformations of the Jewish name Mayer.

Genealogies: *A Tale of Two Families: a Biographical*

Genealogy of the Meyers and Sparhawk Families was compiled by Dorothy Hermanne Braithwait and published in Spokane, Washington, in 1981. *Genealogy of the Meyers Family* was compiled by I. Austin Meyers and published in Wilmington, Delaware, in 1968.

MEZA

Ranking: 2685 S.S. Count: 16,985
Origin: Uncertain etymology
Genealogies: None known.

MICHAEL, MICHAELIS, MICHAELS, MICHAELSEN, MICHAELSON (S.S. Abbreviation: Michae)

Ranking: 500 S.S. Count: 80,473
Origin: Michaelsen—Danish, Norwegian; Michael, Michaels, Michaelson—English, Jewish; Michaelis—Italian, Jewish. Michaelsen: cognates to Michael. Michael (English): derived from the Middle English first name Michael, which was derived from the Hebrew name Michaël, meaning "Who is like God?" (H&H). Michael (Jewish): derived from any of several similar sounding Jewish first names. Michaelson: transformations of Michael. Michaels: transformations of Michael. Michaelis: cognate to and transformation of Michael.

Famous **Bearers:** ARTHUR MICHAEL (1853–1942) of New York was a chemist. He is best known as an organic chemist who was more appreciated in Europe than in the United States. LEONOR MICHAELIS (1875–1949) of Germany was a chemist and the assistant to Paul Ehrlich. He is best known for the Michaelis-Menten hypothesis, which dealt with enzyme-catalyzed reactions.

Genealogies: *The Michael, Moad, Mohn Family History of Caldwell Co. Mo.* was compiled by Evelyne K. Michael and published in Shingletown, California, in 1976.

MICHAL (ALSO MICHALEWICZ, MICHALEWSKI, MICHALOPOULOS, MICHALSKI)

Ranking: 1217 S.S. Count: 36,244
Origin: Michal—Czech; Michalopoulos—Greek; Michalewicz, Michalewski, Michalski—Polish. Cognates to Michael.
Genealogies: None known.

MICHAUT, MICHAUX (S.S. Abbreviation: Michau)

Ranking: 2127 S.S. Count: 21,500
Origin: French. Cognates to Michael.
Famous **Bearers:** ANDRÉ MICHAUX (1746–1802) of France came to America to study the trees of North America. His papers were eventually published in 1889. FRANÇOIS ANDRÉ MICHAUX (1770–1855) of France was the

son of André Michauz (1746–1802). He came to America with his father and was the author of *The North American Sylva.* LIGHTFOOT SOLOMON MICHAUX (1885?–1968) of Virginia was a radio personality and evangelical preacher who attracted wealthy supporters.

Genealogies: None known.

MICHEL (ALSO MICHELE, MICHELS, MICHELSEN, MICHELSON)

Ranking: 789 S.S. Count: 53,369

Origin: Michel—Czech, Dutch, Flemish, French, German, Jewish; Michelsen—Danish, German, Norwegian; Michels—Dutch, Flemish, German; Michele—French, Italian; Michelson—Jewish. Cognates to and transformations of Michael.

Famous **Bearers:** WILLIAM MIDDLETON MICHEL (1822–1904) of South Carolina was a physician who founded the Summer Medical Institute of Charleston in 1847. ALBERT ABRAHAM MICHELSON (1852–1931) of Prussia (now Poland) was a physicist who discovered how fast light travels and who invented a device called an interferometer for measuring the length of light waves. He was a pioneer in developing the theory of relativity and was the recipient of the 1907 Nobel Prize for physics.

Genealogies: *The Michels Family Tree* was compiled by Estella Michels and published in Earlville, Iowa, in 1984.

MICKEL (ALSO MICKELSSON)

Ranking: 2708 S.S. Count: 16,791

Origin: Mickel—English; Mickelsson—Swedish. Cognates to and transformations of Michael.

Genealogies: None known.

MICKLE (ALSO MICKLEBRIDE, MICKLEJOHN, MICKLETHWAITE, MICKLEWRIGHT)

Ranking: 4095 S.S. Count: 11,037

Origin: Micklethwaite, Micklewright—English; Micklebride—Irish, Scottish; Mickle, Micklejohn—Scottish. Micklewaite: derived from the Old Norse words "mekil" and "Pveit," meaning large and meadow. The name was given to those from Micklethwaite, the name of several places in England. Micklewright: derived from the Middle English words "mekill" and "wrigt," meaning large and craftsman. Micklebride: transformation of McBride. Mickle: derived from the Scottish word "meikle," meaning large. The name was given to those who were large. Micklejohn: derived from the Scottish word "meikle," meaning large, and the first name John. The name was given to someone whose first name was John in order to distinguish him as the largest or eldest person called John, a common name.

Genealogies: *Genealogy of Willoughby and Susannah Wood Micklethwaite* was compiled by Keith E. Lingenfelter and published in Washington, D.C., in 1973.

MIDDLEBROOK, MIDDLEDITCH, MIDDLEMAN, MIDDLEMASS, MIDDLETON (S.S. Abbreviation: Middle)

Ranking: 556 S.S. Count: 73,451

Origin: Middlebrook, Middleditch, Middleman—English; Middleton—English, Scottish; Middlemass—Scottish. Middlebrook: derived from the Old English words "midel" and "broc" meaning middle and brook. The name was given to those who lived near the middle of a brook. Middleditch: derived from the Old English words "midel" and "dic," meaning middle and ditch or dyke. The name was given to those from Middleditch, a place in England. Middleman: derived from the Old English word "midel" and the Middle English word "man" meaning middle and man. The name was given to those who acted as intermediaries in various ways, including in business. Middlemass: derived from the Middle English word "midelmast," meaning middle part. The name was given to those from Middlemass, a region of England. Middleton: derived from the Old English words "midel" and "tūn," meaning middle and settlement. The name was given to those from Middleton, the name of several places in England and Scotland.

Famous **Bearers:MDNM** ARTHUR MIDDLETON (1681–1737) of South Carolina was a member of the South Carolina House of Commons, acting governor (1725–1731), and the leader in the overthrowing of proprietary control. HENRY MIDDLETON (1717–1784), possibly of South Carolina, was the son of Arthur Middleton. He was a member of the Continental Congress and served as its president for a short period. His son ARTHUR MIDDLETON (1742–1787), possibly of South Carolina, was a member of the Continental Congress and one of the signers of the Declaration of Independence. Arthur's son HENRY MIDDLETON (1770–1846) of South Carolina was the governor of South Carolina, a member of Congress, and minister to Russia. PETER MIDDLETON (?–1781) of Scotland was a physician. He and Dr. John Bard were the first two known in America to dissect a human body for medical study. He was one of the founders of Columbia University and was involved in the conception of New York Hospital (1771). THOMAS COOKE MIDDLETON (1842–1923) of Pennsylvania was a Roman Catholic clergyman and one of the founders of the American Catholic Historical Society.

Genealogies: *The Middletons and Kindred Families of Southern Maryland* was compiled by Daniel B. Lloyd and published in Bethesda, Maryland, in 1975. *A Record of the Descendants of John Brown* [also Middleton] was compiled by Rohease Brown Cook and published in 1973.

MILAM

Ranking: 2735 S.S. Count: 16,664

Origin: English. Derived from components meaning mill and village. The name was given to those from Mileham, a place in Norfolk, England.

Genealogies: *Family: Roots, Ties, and Trails* was compiled by Mary C. Sturgeon and published in Little Rock, Arkansas, in 1991. *Jordan Milam (Milum) and the Descendants of his Son John Milam* was compiled by Eunice Chandler Hockey and published in Springfield, Missouri, in 1978.

MILBURN (S.S. Abbreviation: Milbur)
Ranking: 4161 S.S. Count: 10,867
Origin: English. Derived from the Old English words "mylen" and "burna," meaning mill and stream. The name was given to those from Milburn, a place in England.

Famous **Milburns**: WILLIAM HENRY MILBURN (1823–1903) of Pennsylvania was a Methodist clergyman and chaplain to Congress four times.
Genealogies: None known.

MILES
Ranking: 328 S.S. Count: 114,894
Origin: English, Jewish. English: 1) derived from a shortened Old French version of Michael. 2) derived from the Latin word "miles," meaning soldier. The name was given to servants or employees. 3) derived from the Germanic first name Milo. Jewish: uncertain etymology.

Famous **Mileses**: RICHARD PIUS MILES (1791–1860) of Maryland was a Catholic priest and the first bishop of Nashville, Tennessee. WILLIAM P. MILES (1822–1899) of South Carolina represented a South Carolina district in the U.S. Congress (1857–1860), then in the Confederate Congress throughout its existence. MANLY MILES (1826–1898) of New York was a pioneer in teaching practical agriculture at the college level. He also wrote many books, including *Stock Breeding* (1879) and *Land Drainage* (1892). NELSON A. MILES (1839–1925) of Massachusetts joined the army as a captain as the Civil War began and rose to the rank of brigadier general by May 1864. He continued to advance after the war, commanding troops fighing in the Indian campaigns in the West. He also commanded the force that dealt with the Chicago riots of 1894. The next year, he became senior commander in chief of the army.
Genealogies: *L. D. Miles: his Ancestors and Descendants* was compiled by Carol Bickel Cramer and published in McLean, Virginia, in 1990. *Thomas Hill and Rebecca Miles: Ancestors and Descendants* was compiled by Mary Louise Donnelly and published in Burke, Virginia, in 1984.

MILEY
Ranking: 4558 S.S. Count: 9805
Origin: English. The name means descendent of little Milo or Mile, meaning soldier.
Genealogies: None known.

MILLAN
Ranking: 4741 S.S. Count: 9447

Origin: Spanish. Cognate to the French name Emilien.
Genealogies: None known.

MILLARD (S.S. Abbreviation: Millar)
Ranking: 1622 S.S. Count: 27,626
Origin: English. Derived from the Old English words "mylen" and "weard," meaning mill and guardian. The name was given to those who ran mills.
Genealogies: None known.

MILLER
Ranking: 7 S.S. Count: 1,575,179
Origin: English. Derived from the Middle English word "mille," meaning mill. The name was given to millers.

Famous **Millers**: WILLIAM MILLER (1782–1849) of Massachusetts was a religious leader who believed that the second coming of Christ to Earth would occur in the year 1843 or 1844. He preached from the year 1831 on that this would happen and published works explaining his theories. His followers were called Millerites of Adventists. After the period of Christ's presumed arrival, the Millerites founded the church that came to be known as the Seventh Day Adventists in 1863. SAMUEL FREEMAN MILLER (1816–1890) of Kentucky was an associate justice of the U.S. Supreme Court and was the first to use the 14th amendment in the Slaughterhouse Cases in 1873. ELIZABETH SMITH MILLER (1822–1911) of New York was the inventor of the "bloomer dress," which reached about four inches below the knee with pants to the ankles. HARRIET MANN MILLER (1831–1918) of New York was an ornithologist. She wrote children's books about birds under the name Olive Thorne Miller. CINCINNATUS HINER or HEINE MILLER (1837–1913) of Indiana was a poet who wrote under the pen name Joaquin Miller. He lived the wild life in 19th-century California living in the mining camps and with the Indians. He wrote several books of verse. HENRY JOHN MILLER (1860–1926) of England was an actor and director in New York. Late in life he managed the Henry Miller Theater. EMMA GUFFEY MILLER (1874–1970) of Pennsylvania was a member of the Democratic National Committee of Pennsylvania and worked for the passage of the Equal Rights Amendment. ALICE DUER MILLER (1874–1942) of New York City was an author who wrote, among other titles, *Are Women People?* (1915) and *Women Are People!* (1917). DAVID HUNTER MILLER (1875–1961) of New York City was a lawyer and the legal advisor to the Paris Peace Conference of 1919. BERTHA EVERETT MAHONY MILLER (1882–1969) of Massachusetts was the originator of *Horn Book Magazine*. FREIDA SEGELKE MILLER (1890–1973) of Wisconsin was director of the Women's Bureau, U.S. Department of Labor (1944–1953). Prior to that, she was instrumental in establishing New York's first minimum-wage law. HENRY VALENTINE MILLER (1891–1980) of New

York City was a writer and the author of *Tropic of Cancer* and *Tropic of Capricorn*, which were both banned in the United States because of their sexually explicit content. Other books by him were not banned. GLENN MILLER (1904–1944) of Iowa was one of the greatest American bandleaders of the early 20th century. He was of the big-band era and played "swing music." Two of his best-known songs were "Chattanooga Choo-Choo" and "Moonlight Serenade." He disbanded his own orchestra to join the Army, and died during World War II. PERRY GILBERT EDDY MILLER (1905–1963) of Illinois was a scholar and a historian. He taught at Harvard University and wrote books about the early years of New England history.

Genealogies: *The History and Genealogy of the Miller Family* was compiled by Thelma Ray Miller and published in Seattle, Washington, in 1989. *The Huguenot Millers* was compiled by Margaret Miller White and published in Fulton, Mississippi, in 1986. *The Miller and Simmons Families* was compiled by William Shurtleff and published in Lafayette, California, in 1987.

MILLET (ALSO MILLETT)
Ranking: 3585 **S.S. Count:** 12,576
Origin: Catalan, English, French. Catalan: derived from the Catalan word "millet," meaning millet. The name was given to those who lived near a millet field. English, French: derived from the Old French word "mil," meaning millet. The name was given to those who grew or sold millet. French: transformation of Miles, derived from the first name Milo.
Famous **Bearers:** FRANCIS D. MILLET (1846–1912) of Massachusetts was an artist and journalist whose assignments took him to Europe and the Philippines.
Genealogies: None known.

MILLIGAN, MILLIGEN, MILLIGRAM (S.S. Abbreviation: Millig)
Ranking: 1401 **S.S. Count:** 31,689
Origin: Milligan, Milligen—Irish; Milligram—Jewish. Milligan, Milligen: derived from the Gaelic name Ó Maolagáin, derived from the first name Maolagán, which was derived from the word "maol," meaning bald. Milligram: derived from the Yiddish word "milgrim," meaning pomegranate. The name was taken ornamentally.
Famous **Bearers:** ROBERT MILLIGAN (1814–1875) of Ireland was a professor in Pennsylvania and Ohio, then president of Kentucky University for six years. ROBERT W. MILLIGAN (1843–1909) of Maryland was chief engineer on the USS *Oregon* during a highly publicized cruise around South America in 1898.
Genealogies: *History of the Families Millingas and Millanges of Saxony and Normandy* [also Milligan] was compiled by Gideon Tibbetts Ridlon and published in Lewiston, Maine, in 1907. *Milligan Family of Saratoga Co.,*

N.Y. was compiled by Paul Wesley Prindle and published in Darien, Connecticut, in 1975.

MILLIKEN, MILLIKIN (S.S. Abbreviation: Millik)
Ranking: 3562 **S.S. Count:** 12,674
Origin: Irish. Transformations of Milligan.
Famous **Bearers:** EUGENE D. MILLIKIN (1891–1958) of Ohio was a U.S. senator from Colorado (1942–1956).
Genealogies: None known.

MILLINAIRE, MILLING, MILLINGTON (S.S. Abbreviation: Millin)
Ranking: 4269 **S.S. Count:** 10,539
Origin: Millington, Millinaire—English; Milling—Irish. Millington: derived from the Old English words "mylen" and "tūn," meaning mill and settlement. The name was given to those from Millington, the name of places in England. Millinaire: cognate to Miller. Milling: transformation of the Irish name Mullen.
Genealogies: None known.

MILLS
Ranking: 157 **S.S. Count:** 205,562
Origin: English, Scottish. Derived from the Middle English word "mille," meaning mill. The name was given to those who lived near a mill.
Famous **Millses:** ROBERT MILLS (1781–1855) of South Carolina is considered the first American architect. He designed many Washington, D.C., landmarks, including the Washington Monument. CLARK MILLS (1815–1883) of New York was a sculptor and the first in the United States to use bronze in his work. He is best known for his statue of Andrew Jackson on his horse in Lafayette Square in Washington, D.C. CYRUS T. MILLS (1819–1884) of New York and his wife, SUSAN LINCOLN TOLMAN MILLS (1826–1912) of Vermont, were missionaries and educators who ran Oahu College in Hawaii, then started Mills Seminary in California in 1871. She also was the president (1890–1909) of Mills College, the oldest women's college on the west coast. ANSON MILLS (1834–1924) of Indiana was an army officer who patented the first cartridge belt used by the U.S. army. He also was a surveyor who plotted and named the city of El Paso, Texas. CHARLES K. MILLS (1845–1931) of Pennsylvania was a prominent neurologist and professor and was president of the American Neurological Association for 37 years. He also wrote *The Nervous System and Its Diseases* (1898). ENOS A. MILLS (1870–1922) of Kansas was a naturalist and author who is credited as the founder of Rocky Mountain National Park. CLARENCE ALONZO MILLS (1891–1974) of Indiana was a biochemistry and physiology professor whose study of the climate's effect on human health brought significant results. Part of

his work was confirmed when a leper colony was transferred from Louisiana to Minnesota and the colder climate arrested the disease. FLORENCE MILLS (1895–1927), possibly of Virginia, was a singer and dancer. She and her two sisters were billed as "The Mills Trio" and appeared in vaudeville. CHARLES WRIGHT MILLS (1916–1962) of Texas was a sociologist and the author of *The Power Elite* (1956), among other works.

Genealogies: *The Mills Family of West Virginia and Eastern Kentucky* was compiled by Roger L. Mills and published in Chattanooga, Tennessee, in 1991. *Pamunkey Neighbors of Orange County, Virginia: Transcriptions from the Original Files of County Courts in Virginia, Kentucky, and Missouri of Wills, Deeds, Order Books & Marriages as well as some Family Lines* [also Mills] was published in Baltimore, Maryland, in 1985.

MILLSAP (S.S. Abbreviation: Millsa)

Ranking: 4187 **S.S. Count:** 10,793
Origin: English? Uncertain etymology. Most likely derived from the Middle English word "mille," meaning mill, and another unknown component.
Genealogies: None known.

MILNE

Ranking: 4923 **S.S. Count:** 9088
Origin: English, Scottish. Transformation of Mill(s).
Genealogies: None known.

MILNER

Ranking: 2675 **S.S. Count:** 17,040
Origin: English, German, Jewish. Transformation of and cognate to Miller.
Famous **Milners:** JOHN T. MILNER (1826–1898) of Georgia was one of the founders of the city of Birmingham, Alabama.
Genealogies: None known.

MILTON

Ranking: 1590 **S.S. Count:** 28,135
Origin: English. Derived from the Old English words "middel" and "tūn," meaning middle and settlement. In some cases the first component was derived from the Old English word "mylen," meaning mill. The name was given to those from Milton, the name of several places in England.
Famous **Miltons:** JOHN MILTON (1807–1865) of Georgia was governor of Florida during the Civil War. GEORGE F. MILTON (1894–1955) of Tennessee was an editor and part owner of the *Chattanooga* (Tennessee) *News* and was highly regarded as a historian. Among his books was an authoritative study of Reconstruction, *The Age of Hate: Andrew Johnson and the Radicals* (1930).
Genealogies: None known.

MIMS

Ranking: 1702 **S.S. Count:** 26,267
Origin: English. Uncertain etymology. The name was given to those from Mimms, the name of several places in England.
Genealogies: *Our Mother's People* [also Mims] was compiled by Marie Doan Enderton and published in San Diego, California, in 1972.

MINER

Ranking: 1497 **S.S. Count:** 29,725
Origin: English. Derived from the Middle English and Old French word "mine," meaning mine. The name was given to those who constructed mines.
Famous **Miners:** CHARLES MINER (1780–1865) of Connecticut was a member of Congress from Pennsylvania and was best known as an editor and publisher. He coined the phrase "an axe to grind" in his humor book *Essays from the Desk of Poor Robert the Scribe* (1815). ALONZO AMES MINER (1814–1895) of Massachusetts was president of Tufts College. MYRTILLA MINER (1815–1864) of New York was a pioneer in teacher education for black women. Her school was in Washington, D.C., and provided the only schooling available for blacks other than elementary schooling. The school, named Miner Normal School, became Miner Teachers College, then District of Columbia Teachers College. SARAH LUELLA MINER (1861–1935) of Ohio was a missionary in China. DOROTHY EUGENIA MINER (1904–1973) of New York was a medievalist and the first keeper of the manuscripts at the Walters Art Gallery.

Genealogies: *Fortin and Miner (Monast), French Canadian Families of Vergennes, Vermont, with Notes on Plantier, Gely and Roy Families* was compiled by James Strode Elston and published in Winter Park, Florida. *Thomas Minor* [also Miner], *Descendants* was compiled by John A. Miner and published in Trevett, Maine, in 1981. *The Gardiner-Squires Connection: an Account of the Gardiner Family of Gardiner's Island, Long Island, New York* [also Miner] was compiled by Tiger Gardiner and published in Baltimore, Maryland, in 1989.

MINNICH (S.S. Abbreviation: Minnic)

Ranking: 2621 **S.S. Count:** 17,332
Origin: German. Cognate to Monk.
Genealogies: None known.

MINOR

Ranking: 1070 **S.S. Count:** 41,131
Origin: English. Transformation of Miner.
Famous **Minors:** LUCIAN MINOR (1802–1858) of Virginia was a lawyer and temperance advocate who wrote *Reasons for Abolishing the Liquor Traffic* (1853). His brother, JOHN B. MINOR (1813–1895) of Virginia, was a law

professor credited with establishing a good reputation for the University of Virginia law school. He also wrote books on the law. John Minor's son, RALEIGH C. MINOR (1869–1923) of Virginia, was a lawyer and professor at the University of Virginia who also earned international renown as author of *Conflict of Laws* (1901). BENJAMIN B. MINOR (1818–1905) of Virginia was editor of *Southern Literary Messenger* and president of the University of Missouri. VIRGINIA LOUISA MINOR (1824–1894) of Virginia was a Unionist during the Civil War and was a member of the St. Louis Ladies Union Aid Society, which helped wounded Union soliders and their families. After the war, she was one of the many Missouri suffrage leaders who worked to change the laws of the country concerning women's rights.

Genealogies: *Thomas Minor, Descendants* was compiled by John A. Miner and published in Trevett, Maine, in 1981. *The Gardiner-Squires Connection: an Account of the Gardiner Family of Gardiner's Island, Long Island, New York* [also Minor] was compiled by Tiger Gardiner and published in Baltimore, Maryland, in 1989.

MINTER

Ranking: 3280 **S.S. Count:** 13,841
Origin: English. Derived from the Old English word *"myntere,"* meaning minter. The name was given to those who coined or minted money.
Genealogies: None known.

MINTON

Ranking: 2381 **S.S. Count:** 19,068
Origin: English. Derived from the Welsh word *"mynydd,"* meaning hill, and the Old English word *"tūn,"* meaning settlement. The name was given to those from Minton, a place in England.
Famous Mintons: SHERMAN MINTON (1890–1965) of Indiana was a U.S. senator and a U.S. Supreme Court justice.
Genealogies: None known.

MIRANDA (S.S. Abbreviation: Mirand)

Ranking: 692 **S.S. Count:** 60,625
Origin: Italian, Jewish, Portuguese, Spanish. Uncertain etymology. Most likely derived from the Latin word *"mirandus,"* meaning lovely. The name was given to those from Miranda, the name of many places.
Famous Mirandas: CARMEN MIRANDA (1909–1955), born in Portugal, was a highly popular singer who appeared in many films in the United States, including *Copacabana* (1947).
Genealogies: None known.

MIRELELO (S.S. Abbreviation: Mirele)

Ranking: 4514 **S.S. Count:** 9914

Origin: Italian. Uncertain etymology. Possibly derived from the name Mirella, meaning marvel.
Genealogies: None known.

MITCHEL, MITCHELL, MITCHELMORE, MITCHELSON (S.S. Abbreviation: Mitche)

Ranking: 41 **S.S. Count:** 536,102
Origin: Mitchel, Mitchell, Mitchelson—English, Irish, Scottish; Mitchelmore—Irish, Scottish. Mitchel, Mitchell, Mitchelson: derived from the Middle English and Old French first name Michel, which was derived from Michael. Mitchelmore: derived from the Middle English and Old French first name Michel and the Gaelic word *"mór,"* meaning big. The name was given to someone called Michel who was the largest or eldest among those called Michel.

Famous Bearers: JOHN MITCHELL (?–1768), possibly of Great Britain, was a physician, botanist, and cartographer who lived in Virginia and was successful in treating victims of yellow fever. He drew the "Map of the British and French Dominions in North America" (1755). It was used in many treaty negotiations. ORMSBY MACKNIGHT MITCHELL (1809–1862) of Kentucky was an astronomer who popularized his chosen field. MARIA MITCHELL (1818–1889) of Massachusetts singlehandedly discovered a new comet and became the first woman elected to the American Academy of Arts and Sciences. DONALD GRANT MITCHELL (1822–1908) of Connecticut was an author of novels. SILAS WEIR MITCHELL (1829–1914) of Pennsylvania was a physician and author who served as a physician in the Union army of the Civil War. His medical speciality was in the field of neurological disorders. He also wrote fiction and nonfiction. MARGARET JULIA MITCHELL (1832–1918) of New York City was a comedic actress. JOHN MITCHELL (1870–1919) of Illinois was a miner, then president of the United Mine Workers. LUCY SPRAGUE MITCHELL (1878–1967) of Illinois was an educator. She was the cofounder of the Bureau of Educational Experiments, which was chartered in 1950 as the Bank Street College of Education. She also started a writers' workshop for the writers of children's books so they could better undestand the youngsters for whom they wrote. WILLIAM MITCHELL (1879–1936) was born in France to American parents. He was a career army officer who campaigned vigorously for the use of air power in the military. He was court-martialed because of his criticicsm of how the navy operated. ABBIE MITCHELL (1884–1960) of New York City was a singer and actress and one of the stars of the Pultizer Prize–winning play *In Abraham's Bosom*. MARGARET MUNNERLYN MITCHELL (1900–1949) of Georgia was the novelist who wrote *Gone With the Wind*.

Genealogies: *Descendants of John Mitchell of Drumore Township, Lancaster County, Pennsylvania* was compiled by Warren A. Brannon and published in Baltimore, Maryland, in 1991. *The Mitchell Family of Tipton County, Tennessee* was compiled by Helen Mitchell Goggans and published in Kingsland, Arkansas, in 1990.

MIXON

Ranking: 2653 **S.S. Count:** 17,155

Origin: English. 1) derived from the first name Mick, which was derived from Michael. 2) the name was given to those from Mixon, meaning dunghill, the name of a place in Staffordshire, England.

Genealogies: *The Mixon-Mixson Family* was compiled by John Leslie Mixson and published in Fort Worth, Texas, in 1969.

MIZE

Ranking: 2820 **S.S. Count:** 16,166

Origin: German. Uncertain etymology. The name was given to those who came from Mizell, a place in Germany.

Genealogies: *The Isaac Mize Family of Eastern Kentucky* was compiled by Franklin Miller and published in Gambier, Ohio, in 1985. *Mize Genealogy in America* was compiled by Joel Sanford Mize and published in Athens, Georgia, in 1984.

MIZELL

Ranking: 4900 **S.S. Count:** 9124

Origin: German. Transformation of Mize.

Genealogies: None known.

MOBLEY

Ranking: 1144 **S.S. Count:** 38,465

Origin: English. Derived from the Old English words "(ge)mōt," "burh," and "lēah," meaning assembly, enclosure, and clearing or an enclosure or fortification for meetings that stood in a clearing. The name was given to those from Mobberley, a place in Cheshire, England.

Genealogies: *Dunkin-Reid and Garner-McGraw-Mobley Families of South Carolina, Georgia, and Alabama* was compiled by Dean Smith Cress and published in Alpharetta, Georgia, in 1992.

MOCK

Ranking: 2081 **S.S. Count:** 22,034

Origin: German. Derived from a word meaning corpulent or ungainly. The name was given to those who were awkward or plump.

Genealogies: *The Family History of Walter Raymond Montgomery and Elsie Louise Mock* was compiled by Walter R. Montgomery and published in Virginia Beach, Virginia, in 1975.

MOE

Ranking: 2958 **S.S. Count:** 15,387

Origin: Swedish. Derived from the Swedish word "mo," meaning moor or sand dune. The name was given to those who lived on a moor or sand dune. In some cases, the name was taken ornamentally.

Genealogies: None known.

MOELLER (S.S. Abbreviation: Moelle)

Ranking: 2206 **S.S. Count:** 20,823

Origin: German. Cognate to Miller.

Famous Moellers: HENRY MOELLER (1849–1925) of Ohio was a Catholic priest and the archbishop of Cincinnati for 21 years.

Genealogies: None known.

MOEN

Ranking: 4131 **S.S. Count:** 10,946

Origin: Irish. Derived from the Gaelic name Ó Mocháin, which was derived from the first name Mochán, which was derived from the word "moch," meaning early or well timed.

Genealogies: None known.

MOFFAT (ALSO MOFFATT)

Ranking: 4157 **S.S. Count:** 10,883

Origin: Irish, Scottish. Derived from the Gaelic words "magh" and "fada," meaning field and long. The name was given to those from Moffatt, a former place in Scotland.

Famous Bearers: DAVID HALLIDAY MOFFAT (1839–1911) of New York planned the Moffat Tunnel through the Continental Divide. It was completed in 1920. JAMES MOFFATT (1870–1944) of Scotland was an American theologian connected with Union Theological Seminary. He translated the New and Old Testaments. JAY P. MOFFAT (1896–1943) of New York was a career diplomat who became U.S. minister to Canada in 1940.

Genealogies: *Story of Blooming Grove and the Tribe of Samuel* [also Moffat] was compiled by Hector Moffat and published in Washingtonville, New York, in 1907. *A Moffat Family Record* was compiled by Abbot Low Moffat and published in Princeton, New Jersey, in 1982. *The Moffitt (also Moffat) Family* was compiled by Lorraine Moffat and published in Hesperia, California, in 1988.

MOFFET (ALSO MOFFETT)

Ranking: 2451 **S.S. Count:** 18,523

Origin: Irish, Scottish. Transformation of Moffat.

Famous Bearers: CLEVELAND L. MOFFETT (1863–1926) of New York was the author of many mystery stories and plays. WILLIAM ADGER MOFFETT (1869–1933) of South Carolina was a naval officer. He was the man responsible for the use of dirigibles in the navy. He was killed in the crash of the dirigible *Akron*.

Genealogies: *A Moffat* [also Moffett] *Family Record* was compiled by Abbot Low Moffat and published in Princeton, New Jersey, in 1982. *The Moffitt* [also Moffett] *Family* was compiled by Lorraine Moffat and published in Hesperia, California, in 1988.

MOFFIT (ALSO MOFFITT)
Ranking: 2960 S.S. Count: 15,382
Origin: Irish, Scottish. Transformation of Moffat.
Genealogies: *The Moffitt Family* was compiled by Lorraine Moffat and published in Hesperia, California, in 1988.

MOHR
Ranking: 1785 S.S. Count: 25,168
Famous **Mohrs:** CHARLES T. MOHR (1824–1901) of Germany was a botanist in Alabama whose work culminated in the publication of *Plant Life in Alabama* (1901).
Origin: German. Cognate to the English name Moore.
Genealogies: None known.

MOJICA
Ranking: 3655 S.S. Count: 12,345
Origin: Spanish. Uncertain etymology.
Genealogies: None known.

MOLINA
Ranking: 612 S.S. Count: 68,506
Origin: Spanish. Cognate to Mills.
Genealogies: None known.

MOLL
Ranking: 4473 S.S. Count: 10,009
Origin: Catalan, English, German. Catalan: derived from the Catalan word "moll," meaning soft. The name was given to those who were ineffective. English: derived from the medieval feminine first name Moll(e), which was derived from the feminine first name Mary. German: the name was given to those who were solidly built or sturdy.
Genealogies: None known.

MOLLOY
Ranking: 4357 S.S. Count: 10,291
Origin: Irish. Transformation of Malloy.
Genealogies: None known.

MOLNAR
Ranking: 3657 S.S. Count: 12,344
Origin: Hungarian, Jewish. Cognate to Miller.
Genealogies: None known.

MONACO
Ranking: 4145 S.S. Count: 10,923
Origin: Italian. Cognate to Monk.
Genealogies: None known.

MONAGHAN (S.S. Abbreviation: Monagh)
Ranking: 4265 S.S. Count: 10,558
Origin: Irish. Derived from the Gaelic name Ó Manacháin, which was derived from the first name Manachán, which was derived from the word "manach," meaning monk.
Genealogies: None known.

MONAHAN (S.S. Abbreviation: Monaha)
Ranking: 1962 S.S. Count: 23,071
Origin: Irish. Transformation of Monaghan.
Genealogies: *The Descendants of Lawrence and Catherine Monahan Lacy et al.* was compiled by Patricia J. Rezek and published in Glendale, California, in 1981.

MONK
Ranking: 2869 S.S. Count: 15,862
Origin: English, Irish, Jewish. English: derived from the Middle English word "munk," meaning monk. The name was given to those who acted like or resembled monks or to the servants of a monastery. Irish: translation of Irish-Gaelic names meaning monk. Jewish: uncertain etymology.
Famous **Monks:** MARIA MONK (1816–1849) of Canada was the author of *Awful Disclosures,* an anti-Catholic book about the "secret" lives of priests and nuns. It was deemed a hoax by the intelligent population of the day. THELONIOUS SPHERE MONK (1920–1982) of North Carolina was a musician. He was one of the creators of the "bop" style of music.
Genealogies: *The Monk Family* was compiled by Charles Harwood Bowman and published in Southern Pines, North Carolina, in 1985.

MONROE
Ranking: 539 S.S. Count: 75,276
Origin: Scottish. Transformation of Munro.
Famous **Monroes:** JAMES MONROE (1758–1831) of Virginia was the fifth president of the United States. He was a Revolutionary War soldier, a member of the Continental Congress, a U.S. senator, a governor of Virginia, a major player in the deal for the Louisiana Purchase, minister to various countries, and secretary of state and war. During his presidential administration, Florida was acquired, and the Missouri Compromise and Monroe Doctrine became law. HARRIET MONROE (1860–1936) of Illinois was the founder of the magazine *Poetry: A Magazine of Verse.* PAUL MONROE (1869–1947) of Indiana was a teacher's teacher through his professorship at Teachers College, Columbia University. He also wrote books, including *The Founding of the American Public Education School System* (1940), and was editor for two years of the *Cyclopedia of Education.* MARILYN MONROE (1926–1962) of California was an actress. She was born Norma Jean Mortenson but later used her mother's name, Baker. She took her screen name

in 1946. In her career she was cast as a "sex symbol." She played in 23 movies, including *The Misfits* (1961).

Genealogies: *Munro* [also Monroe] *Family* was compiled by Ronald G. Munro and published in Camden, Maine, in 1989. *History and Genealogy of the Lexington, Massachusetts Munroes* [also Monroes] was compiled by Richard S. Munroe and published in Florence, Massachusetts, in 1985.

MONSON
Ranking: 3540 S.S. Count: 12,753
Origin: Swedish. Transformation of Magnus.
Genealogies: *A Genealogy of Richard Woodworth, 1758 Ireland–1843 Ohio* [also Monson] was compiled by Marie Monson and published in North Bend, Oregon, in 1975.

MONTAG, MONTAGNE, MONTAGU, MONTAGUE, MONTAGUT (S.S. Abbreviation: Montag)
Ranking: 2048 S.S. Count: 22,323
Origin: Montagut—Catalan, French; Montague—English; Montagu—English, Irish; Montagne, Montagnier—French; Montagna, Montagni—Italian. Montagu (English), Montagut, Montague: derived from the Old French words "mont" and "agu," meaning hill and pointed. The names were given to those from a place in La Manche, France. Montagu (Irish): derived from the Gaelic name Mac Taidhg, which was derived from the name Tadhg, meaning poet. Montagne, Montagnier, Montagna, Montagni: derived from the Late Latin word "montānea," meaning moutain. The name was given to those who lived near a hill.
Famous Bearers: HENRY JAMES MONTAGUE (1843–1878), born in England, became a popular actor in leading-man roles in New York. WILLIAM P. MONTAGUE (1873–1953) of Massachusetts was a prominent philosopher and philosophy professor. ANDREW JACKSON MONTAGUE (1862–1937) of Virginia was governor of Virginia, then a member of Congress for 24 years. GILBERT H. MONTAGUE (1880–1961) of Massachusetts was a leading antitrust lawyer who also wrote books, including *Rise and Progress of the Standard Oil Company* (1903).
Genealogies: None known.

MONTALVO (S.S. Abbreviation: Montal)
Ranking: 1250 S.S. Count: 35,256
Origin: Spanish. Derived from the Spanish words "monte" and "albo," meaning hill and white. The name was given to those from Montalbo, the name of places in Spain.
Genealogies: None known.

MONTAN (ALSO MONTANA, MONTANELLI, MONTANER, MONTANIER)
Ranking: 870 S.S. Count: 49,587

Origin: Montaner—Catalan; Montanier—French; Montan, Montanelli—Italian; Montana—Spanish. Montaner: derived from the Catalan word "muntaner," meaning a person who managed a game forest. Montanier, Montan, Montanelli, Montana: transformations of and cognates to Montagne.
Genealogies: *The Ancestors and Descendants of James Montaney* [also Montana] *1799–1857 of Oppenheim, Fulton County, New York* was compiled by Lois Stewart and published in Baltimore, Maryland, in 1982.

MONTEIRO, MONTEITH (S.S. Abbreviation: Montei)
Ranking: 4464 S.S. Count: 10,040
Origin: Monteiro—Portuguese; Monteith—Scottish. Monteiro: cognate to Montero. Monteith: derived from the Gaelic words "mon" and "Teith," meaning hill and the name of a river. The name was given to those from Monteith, a place in Scotland.
Genealogies: None known.

MONTEL, MONTELLI, MONTELLO (S.S. Abbreviation: Montel)
Ranking: 3382 S.S. Count: 13,383
Origin: Montel—French; Montelli, Montello—Italian. Transformations of and cognates to the French name Mont, which was derived from the Old French word "mont," meaning hill. The name was given to those who lived near or on a hill.
Genealogies: None known.

MONTERO (S.S. Abbreviation: Monter)
Ranking: 3064 S.S. Count: 14,812
Origin: Spanish. Derived from the Spanish word "monte," meaning hill or game forest. The name was given to those who assisted at hunts.
Genealogies: None known.

MONTES (ALSO MONTESSANO, MONTESINO, MONTESINOS, MONTESSORI)
Ranking: 1410 S.S. Count: 31,555
Origin: Montessori, Montessano—Italian; Montesino—Jewish; Montes—Portuguese, Spanish; Montesinos—Spanish. Montessori: derived from the Italian words "monte" and "tessoro," meaning hill and treasure. The name was given to those from Montessori, a place in Tuscany, Italy. Montessano, Montesino, Montesinos, Montes: cognates to Montel.
Genealogies: None known.

MONTEZ
Ranking: 4635 S.S. Count: 9646
Origin: Spanish. Transformation of Montes.
Famous Montezes: LOLA MONTEZ (1818–1861) of Ire-

land was a dancer originally named Marie Dolores Eliza Rosanna Gilbert. As the mistress of Louis I of Bavaria, she received the titles of baroness and countess. However, when his regime ended in revolution, she fled the country in 1848. She came to the United States and settled in New York City. She became a popular lecturer and a writer.

Genealogies: None known.

MONTGOLFIER, MONTGOMERIE, MONTGOMERY, MONTGOMRY (S.S. Abbreviation: Montgo)

Ranking: 220 **S.S. Count:** 158,672

Origin: Montgomerie, Montgomery, Montgomry—English, Irish, Scottish; Montgolfier—French. Montgomerie, Montgomery, Montgomry: derived from the Old French word "mont," meaning hill, and a Germanic first name comprising the components "guma" and "ric," meaning man and power. The names were given to those from Montgomery, a place in Calvados, France. Montgolfier: derived from the Old French word "mont," meaning hill, and a Germanic first name comprising the components "wulf" and "heri," meaning wolf and army.

Famous Bearers: RICHARD MONTGOMERY (1736–1775) of Ireland was a Revolutionary War officer. He was killed at the battle of Quebec, December 31, 1775, after he had just led his men in the assault that captured Montreal. EDMUND D. MONTGOMERY (1835–1911) of Scotland was a physician in Texas who wrote *Philosophical Problems in the Light of Vital Organization* (1907). HELEN BARRETT MONTGOMERY (1861–1934) of Ohio was a civic reformer and missionary. JAMES A. MONTGOMERY (1866–1949) of Pennsylvania was an Episcopal clergyman recognized as a scholar of the Old Testament. He also was editor of the *Journal of Biblical Literature*. THOMAS H. MONTGOMERY (1873–1912) of New York was a zoologist and professor who conducted ground-breaking studies of heredity.

Genealogies: *John and Esther Houston Montgomery, 1719–1973* was compiled by Beulah Henry Anderson and published in Maryville, Tennessee, in 1974. *Saying Goodbye: a Memoir for Two Fathers* [also Montgomery] was compiled by M. R. Montgomery and published in New York, New York, in 1989.

MONTOYA (S.S. Abbreviation: Montoy)

Ranking: 913 **S.S. Count:** 47,215

Origin: Spanish. Derived from words meaning mountain fort and horse pasture. The name was given to those from Montoya, a place in Spain, or to those who lived on or near a hill.

Genealogies: None known.

MOODY

Ranking: 451 **S.S. Count:** 88,315

Origin: English. Derived from the Middle English word "modie," meaning angry or impulsive. The name was given to those who were brave or impetuous.

Famous Moodys: LADY DEBORAH MOODY (?–1659?) of England was the founder of Brooklyn, a Long Island, New York settlement. It was the first colonial settlement headed by a woman in America. DWIGHT LYMAN MOODY (1837–1899) of Massachusetts gave up his business to become an evangelist. He founded the North Market Sabbath School, Northfield Seminary for girls, Mount Hermon School for boys, and the school that would become Moody Bible School. He co-published, with organist and composer Ira D. Sankez, books of hymns. WILLIAM HENRY MOODY (1853–1917) of Massachusetts was the special prosecutor in the trial (1893) of Lizzie Borden, who was accused of killing her parents with an axe. JOHN MOODY (1868–1958) of New Jersey was a financial analyst and the founder of *Moody's Magazine* and *Moody's Analysis of Investments*. His business merged with Henry Poor's, and the firm came to be known as Standard and Poor. WILLIAM VAUGHN MOODY (1869–1910) of Indiana was a poet and playwright. His best-known plays were *The Great Divide* (1906) and *The Faith Healer* (1909).

Genealogies: *Francis Moody (1769–1821)* was compiled by Clara Lorene Cammack Park and published in Baltimore, Maryland, in 1984. *The John Wyatt Moody Family* was compiled by E. Grant Moody and published in Tempe, Arizona, in 1985.

MOON

Ranking: 776 **S.S. Count:** 54,121

Origin: Cornish, English, Irish. Cornish: derived from the Cornish word "mon," meaning thin. The name was given to those who were thin. English: 1) derived from the Anglo-Norman-French word "moun," meaning monk. 2) derived from the Gallo-Roman first name Modius and the suffix "-o." The name was given to those from Moyon, a place in La Manche, France. Irish: derived from the Gaelic name Ó Mocháin, which was derived from the first name Mochán, which was derived from the word "moch," meaning early or well timed.

Famous Moons: LOTTIE DIGGES MOON (1840–1912) of Virginia was a Southern Baptist missionary to China. PARKER T. MOON (1892–1936) of New York was a historian who specialized in international affairs and taught at Columbia University.

Genealogies: None known.

MOONEY

Ranking: 786 **S.S. Count:** 53,639

Origin: Irish. Derived from the Gaelic name Ó Maonaigh, which was derived from the first name Maonach, which was derived from the word "maoineach," meaning rich.

Famous Mooneys: JAMES MOONEY (1861–1921) of Indiana was with the Bureau of American Ethnology and wrote several books on the Indians of the South and West. THOMAS JOSEPH MOONEY (1882–1942) of Illinois was a labor leader. He was convicted and sentenced to death for the Preparedness Parade bombing of July 22, 1916, in which nine people were killed and 40 injured.

Genealogies: *Mooney-Garner Ancestry* was compiled by George W. Mooney and published in Glendale, California, in 1980. *The Applings, the Mooneys, Through the Years, 1685–1976* was compiled by Esther Gambrell Deviney and published in Austin, Texas, in 1976.

MOORE

Ranking: 14 S.S. Count: 992,533

Origin: English, Irish, Scottish, Welsh. English: 1) a nickname derived from the Old French word "more," meaning a Moor. The name was given to those who were swarthy. 2) derived from a first name that was derived from the Old French word "more," meaning a Moor. 3) derived from the Middle English word "more," meaning moor or bog. The name was given to those who lived on a moor or bog. Irish: derived from the Gaelic name Ó Mórdha, which was derived from the first name Mórdha, meaning great or dignified. Scottish, Welsh: derived from the Gaelic word "mór" and the Welsh word "mawr," meaning great or big. The name was given to those who were large.

Famous **Moores**: JAMES MOORE (1747–1777) of North Carolina was a leader in the Continental army in North Carolina. He was victorious at Moore's Creek Bridge on February 26, 1776. BENJAMIN MOORE (1748–1816) of New York was an Episcopal priest. He was a Loyalist during the Revolutionary War. He later taught at Columbia University and became its president. ALFRED MOORE (1755–1810) of North Carolina was a Revolutionary War soldier and an associate justice of the U.S. Supreme Court. CLEMENT CLARKE MOORE (1779–1863) of New York City was the author of "A Visit from St. Nicholas," better known as "'Twas the Night Before Christmas." It was published in the Troy, New York, *Sentinel* on December 23, 1823. CLARA SOPHIA JESSUP MOORE (1824–1899) of Pennsylvania was an author and writer on etiquette. Her novels appealed mostly to other women. She published her book *Sensible Etiquette of the Best Society* under the pen name of Mrs. H. O. Ward. Brothers WILLIAM HENRY MOORE (1848–1923) and JAMES HOBART MOORE (1852–1916) were both from New York. They were promoters and players in the stock market and were involved with the Diamond Match Co. and The National Biscuit Co. GEORGE FOOT MOORE (1851–1931) of Pennsylvania was a minister and the author of religious books. HENRY LUDWELL MOORE (1869–1958) of North Dakota was a mathematical pioneer and the founder of econometrics. DANIEL MCFARLAN MOORE (1869–1936) of Pennsylvania was an electrical engineer and inventor. His 100 patents included the neon gas–discharge lamp. ANNE CARROLL MOORE (1871–1961) of Maine was a pioneer in the area of the children's division of the library. Her methods were copied across the country. MARIANNE CRAIG MOORE (1887–1972) of Missouri was a poet, critic, and editor. She won a Pulitzer Prize for her poetry in 1951. DOUGLAS STUART MOORE (1893–1969) of New York was a composer of operas, including *The Devil and Daniel Webster* (1939). JOHN BASSETT MOORE (1860–1947) of Delaware was a professor of international law and a member of the Hague Tribunal, 1912–1928. GRACE MOORE (1901–1947) of Tennessee was an opera singer well acclaimed as a Broadway performer. STANFORD MOORE (1913–1982) of Illinois was a biochemist who is best known for his studies of enzymes. He was the co-recepient of the 1972 Nobel Prize for chemistry.

Genealogies: *The Benjamin Moore Family of Burlington County, New Jersey* was compiled by Edmund E. Moore and published in Woodbury, New Jersey, in 1982. *The Cary-Estes-Moore Genealogy* was compiled by Helen Estes Seltzer and published in Huntington Valley, Pennsylvania, in 1981.

MOORMAN, MOORMANN (S.S. Abbreviation: Moorma)

Ranking: 4239 S.S. Count: 10,637

Origin: Moorman—Dutch, English, Flemish, German; Moormann—German. Transformations of and cognates to the English name Moore, derived from "more," meaning moor or bog.

Genealogies: *Johnson-Moorman Family Connections* was compiled by Jesse Bryan and published in Shaker Heights, Ohio, in 1973.

MORA

Ranking: 1836 S.S. Count: 24,632

Origin: Portuguese, Spanish. Derived from the Spanish word "mora," meaning mulberry or blackberry. The name was given to those who lived near a mulberry or blackberry bush or to those from Mora, the name of several places in Portugal and Spain.

Genealogies: None known.

MORALES (S.S. Abbreviation: Morale)

Ranking: 165 S.S. Count: 199,507

Origin: Spanish. Transformation of Mora.

Genealogies: None known.

MORAN

Ranking: 404 S.S. Count: 96,995

Origin: English, Irish. English: derived from an Old French first name of uncertain etymology. Irish: derived from the Gaelic name Ó Móráin, which was derived from the first name Mórán, meaning large or great.

Famous **Morans**: BENJAMIN MORAN (1820–1886) of Pennsylvania was a diplomat credited with keeping relations with Great Britain from breaking down during the Civil War. Three brothers born in England and who emigrated as children to the United States distinguished themselves as landscape painters: EDWARD MORAN (1829–1901), THOMAS MORAN (1837–1926), and PETER MORAN (1841–1914). MARY NIMMO MORAN (1842–1899) of Scotland was a painter and etcher. Some of her best works are of New Jersey scenes; she and her husband lived there. EUGENE F. MORAN (1872–1961) was chairman for 50 years of the Committee on Rivers, Harbors and Piers of the Maritime Association of the Port of New York.

Genealogies: None known.

MOREAU

Ranking: 3766 **S.S. Count:** 12,028

Origin: French. Cognate to Morrel.

Famous **Moreaus**: LOUIS CASIMIR ELISABETH MOREAU-LISLET (1767–1832), born in Santo Domingo, was a judge and legislator in Louisiana who co-wrote authoritative works on Louisiana law.

Genealogies: None known.

MOREHEAD (S.S. Abbreviation: Morehe)

Ranking: 3967 **S.S. Count:** 11,410

Origin: Scottish. Transformation of the name Muirhead, which was derived from the Middle English words "muir" and "heid," meaning moor and head or end. The name was given to those from Muirhead, the name of several places in Scotland.

Famous **Moreheads**: JOHN M. MOREHEAD (1796–1866) of Virginia was governor of North Carolina. JAMES T. MOREHEAD (1797–1854) of Kentucky was governor of Kentucky, then a U.S. senator. CHARLES S. MOREHEAD (1802–1868) of Kentucky was a member of Congress from Kentucky, then governor when, in 1861, he approved the state's neutrality in the Civil War. JOHN MOTLEY MOREHEAD (1870–1965) of North Carolina was a chemical engineer who developed the first major commercial method of making calcium carbide. He was U.S. minister to Sweden (1930–1933), and he set up the John Motley Morehead Foundation at the University of North Carolina in 1945.

Genealogies: *Muirheid* [also Morehead] *Family Record* was compiled by Nola M. Karr and published in Port Tobacco, Maryland, in 1990. *Tree Top Baby: a Family Tree of Moorhead (Morehead)* was compiled by Susan Moorhead-Nunes and published in Baltimore, Maryland, in 1984.

MOREHOUSE (S.S. Abbreviation: Moreho)

Ranking: 4659 **S.S. Count:** 9597

Origin: English. Derived from the Old English words "mōr" and "hūs," meaning bog and house. The name was

given to those from Moorhouse, the name of several places in England.

Famous **Morehouses**: DANIEL WALTER MOREHOUSE (1876–1941) of Minnesota was an astronomer who was the president and dean of Drake University. A comet was named for him.

Genealogies: None known.

MORELAND (S.S. Abbreviation: Morela)

Ranking: 1809 **S.S. Count:** 24,923

Origin: English, Scottish. Derived from the Old English words "mōr" and "land," meaning bog and land. The name was given to those from Moreland, the name of several places in England and Scotland.

Genealogies: *A Genealogical Record of the Family and Descendants of David E. Moreland* was compiled by John Capron Funk and published in 1966. *Stepping Stones o'er More-land: a History of the Moreland Families* was compiled by P. S. Bennett and published in Hagerstown, Maryland, in 1984.

MORELL (ALSO MORELLET, MORELLI, MORRELLO, MORELLON)

Ranking: 2394 **S.S. Count:** 18,949

Origin: Morell—Catalan, English; Morellet, Morellon—French; Morelli, Morrello—Italian. Transformations of and cognates to Morrel.

Genealogies: None known.

MORENO

Ranking: 376 **S.S. Count:** 102,679

Origin: Jewish, Portuguese, Spanish. Jewish: cognate to the Portuguese and Spanish name Moreno. Portuguese, Spanish: derived from the Portuguese and Spanish word "moreno," meaning dark-haired. The name was given to those with dark hair or a dark complexion.

Genealogies: *Our Family, Facts and Fancies: the Moreno and Related Families* was compiled by Regina Moreno Kirchoff Mandrell and published in Pensacola, Florida, in 1988.

MOREY

Ranking: 2982 **S.S. Count:** 15,252

Origin: Irish. Transformation of Moore.

Famous **Moreys**: SAMUEL MOREY (1762–1843) of Connecticut was an inventor who was among the first to obtain a patent on a combustion engine (1826). He also built steam vessels and claimed that Robert Fulton stole his ideas.

Genealogies: None known.

MORGAN

Ranking: 60 **S.S. Count:** 387,204

Origin: Irish, Scottish, Welsh. Derived from a Celtic first name comprising components meaning sea and bright.

Famous **Morgans:** JOHN MORGAN (1735–1789) of Pennsylvania was the founder of the University of Pennsylvania medical school, which was the first of its kind in colonial America. DANIEL MORGAN (1736–1802) of New Jersey was a Revolutionary War soldier. As a brigadier general, he defeated the British at Cowpens on January 17, 1781, and was a commander in the Whiskey Rebellion. He also served in the U.S. House of Representatives. WILLIAM MORGAN (1774?–1826?) of Virginia was a Freemason who was writing a book about Freemasons. For this he was jailed and murdered to keep the book from being published. The book, *Illustrations of Masonry*, was published anyway in the year of his presumed death. LEWIS HENRY MORGAN (1818–1881) of New York was a lawyer who developed a interest in American Indian culture. He wrote several books on the subject. JOHN HUNT MORGAN (1825–1864) of Alabama was a soldier best remembered for his raids around Cincinnati in July 1863. JOHN PIERPONT MORGAN (1837–1913) of Connecticut was a banker and financier best known for his railroad and industrial reorganizations. He was responsible for forming the United Steel Corporation. ANNA MORGAN (1851–1936) of New York was a teacher of dramatic arts in Chicago. MARY KIMBALL MORGAN (1861–1948) of Wisconsin was a Christian Science educator. She joined the church and her health improved, causing her to believe that her joining had effected her cure. THOMAS HUNT MORGAN (1866–1945) of Kentucky was a geneticist. He made groundbreaking discoveries regarding how and why heredity works. He won a Nobel Prize in 1933. His work was the first to mention genes for specific traits and to indicate that they were located on specific points on the chromosomes. JOHN PIERPONT MORGAN JR. (1867–1943) of New York took over his father's business interests, floating large loans during and after World War I. JULIA MORGAN (1872–1957) of California was a pioneer in the field of architecture, opening the door for women in the field. ANNE TRACY MORGAN, (1873–1952), possibly of New York, was the daughter of J. P. Morgan. She was involved with philanthropy, founding the American Friends for Devastated France, among other organizations. She was the commander of the Legion of Honor and was the first woman ever so honored. ANN HAVEN MORGAN (1882–1966) of Waterford, Connecticut, was a zoologist and ecologist. She wrote several books, including *Field Book of Ponds and Streams: An Introduction to the Life of Fresh Water* (1930) and *Field Book of Animals in Winter*. AGNES FAY MORGAN (1884–1968) of Illinois was a biochemist and nutritionist and a pioneer in the field of home economics. HELEN MORGAN (1900?–1941) of Illinois was a singer and actress. Her greatest role was that of Julie in *Show Boat*.

Genealogies: *The Morgan Family History* was compiled by Alice Helper Morgan and published in Baltimore, Maryland, in 1989. *An American Family: Morgan* was compiled by Patricia Gausnell and published in Roseburg, Oregon, in 1991.

MORIARTY (S.S. Abbreviation: Moriar)

Ranking: 2840 **S.S. Count:** 16,072

Origin: Irish. Derived from the Gaelic first name Muircheartach, comprising the components "muir" and "ceardach," meaning sea and expert, referring to expert navigators.

Genealogies: None known.

MORIN

Ranking: 1188 **S.S. Count:** 36,856

Origin: English, Italian. Transformation of and cognate to the second English definition of the name Moore.

Genealogies: None known.

MORLEY

Ranking: 3055 **S.S. Count:** 14,852

Origin: English. Derived from the Old English words "mōr" and "lēah," meaning bog and wood or clearing. The name was given to those from Morley, the name of several places in England.

Famous **Morleys:** EDWARD WILLIAMS MORLEY (1838–1923) of New Jersey was a chemist and a physicist who conducted atmospheric experiments. MARGARET WARNER MORLEY (1858–1923) of Iowa was a teacher who wrote textbooks on nature, including *Songs of Life* (1891), a book about sex and birth that created a stir. FRANK MORLEY (1860–1937) of England was a prominent mathematician and professor at Harvard and Johns Hopkins universities. CHRISTOPHER DARLINGTON MORLEY (1890–1957) of Pennsylvania was an editor on the staff of the leading magazines of his day and a writer of novels, including *The Trojan Horse* (1937).

Genealogies: *The Morleys—Young Upstarts on the Southwest Frontier* was compiled by Norman Cleaveland and published in Albuquerque, New Mexico, in 1971. *Ancestors and Descendants of Timothy Crosby Jr.* [also Morley] was compiled by Paul Wesley Prindle and published in Orleans, Massachusetts, in 1981.

MORREL (ALSO MORRELL)

Ranking: 2776 **S.S. Count:** 16,431

Origin: English. Transformation of the second English definition of Moore.

Famous **Bearers:** BENJAMIN MORRELL (1795–1839) of New York was a sea captain who wrote of his experiences in *A Narrative of Four Voyages to the South Sea* (1832).

Genealogies: None known.

MORRILL (S.S. Abbreviation: Morril)

Ranking: 4104 S.S. Count: 11,012

Origin: English. Transformation of Morrel.

Famous **Bearers:** DAVID L. MORRILL (1772–1849) of New Hampshire was a clergyman, a doctor, and a politician. He was a U.S. senator from, then governor of, New Hampshire. Brothers ANSON P. MORRILL (1803–1887) and LOT M. MORRILL (1812–1883) of Maine were both governors of Maine, Anson in the mid-1850s and Lot in the late 1850s. Anson also was a member of Congress, and Lot also was a U.S. senator. EDMUND N. MORRILL (1834–1909) of Maine was a member of Congress, then governor of Kansas.

Genealogies: None known.

MORRIS (ALSO MORRISEY, MORRISH, MORRISON, MORRISSEY)

Ranking: 31 S.S. Count: 640,292

Origin: Morris—English, Irish, Jewish, Scottish, Welsh; Morrish, Morrison—English; Morrisey, Morrissey—Irish. Morris (English, Irish, Scottish, Welsh): derived from the Old French first name Maurice, which was ultimately derived from the Phoenician word "mauharim," meaning Eastern. Morris (Jewish): Anglicization of any of several similar-sounding Jewish surnames. Morrish, Morrison: transformations of Morris. Morrisey, Morrissey: derived from the Gaelic name Ó Muirgheas, which was derived from the first name Muirgheasa.

Famous **Bearers:** LEWIS MORRIS (1726–1798), birthplace unknown, was the half-brother of Gouverneur Morris and a signer of the Declaration of Independence. ROBERT MORRIS (1734–1806) of England came to America as a child. He was a signer of the Declaration of Independence and the person who found the finances to purchase the supplies necessary for George Washington's army. He founded and organized the Bank of North America (1782). GOUVERNEUR MORRIS (1752–1816) of New York, the half-brother of Lewis Morris, was a Revolutionary politician and the assistant superintendent of finance. It was his proposal that called for the terms "dollar" and "cent" to be used for U.S. currency. After the war he served as a U.S. senator and as minister to several countries. ELIZABETH MORRIS (1753–1826) of England was a highly successful actress in Philadelphia, associated with the Chestnut St. Theatre. LEWIS RICHARD MORRIS (1760–1825), birthplace unknown, was a member of Congress and the abstainer in the 1800 Thomas Jefferson–Aaron Burr contest for the U.S. presidency. Because Morris did not vote, the election went to Jefferson. GEORGE POPE MORRIS (1802–1864) of Pennsylvania was the founder and editor of the *New York Mirror* and *Ladies' Gazette*. He also dabbled in poetry. ESTHER HOBART McQUIGG SLACK MORRIS (1814–1902) of New York was a justice of the peace in Wyoming and a delegate

from Wyoming to the national suffrage convention in Cleveland in the late 1890s. Statues of her stand in Statuary Hall in the Capitol in Washington, D.C., and at the state house in Cheyenne. WILLIAM MORRIS (1873–1932) of Germany was a theatrical agent and the organizer of the William Morris Agency. He broke the monopoly held by Keith-Albee United Booking Office.

Genealogies: *C.C.'s Clan: Morris, Arms, Mitchell and Related Families* was compiled by Eula Eunice Park Mitchell and published in Utica, Kentucky, in 1984. *The Morris, Arnold and Related Families* was compiled by Louis Arnold Morris and published in Easley, South Carolina, in 1985.

MORROW (ALSO MORROWSON)

Ranking: 511 S.S. Count: 78,472

Origin: Morrow—Irish, Scottish; Morrowson—Irish. Morrow: derived from the Gaelic first name Murchadh, which is comprised of the components "muir" and "cadh," meaning sea and warrior. Morrowson: derived from the Gaelic name Mac Murchadha, which was derived from the first name Murchadha, which is comprised of the components "muir" and "cadh," meaning sea and warrior.

Famous **Bearers:** DWIGHT WHITNEY MORROW (1873–1931) of West Virginia was the organizer of the Kennecott Copper Co., a diplomat, and a U.S. senator from New Jersey. He was the father of Anne Morrow Lindbergh, who married Charles A. Lindbergh.

Genealogies: *The Morrows, and Related Families, 1640–1978* was compiled by J. T. Morrow and published in Baltimore, Maryland, in 1979. *Morrow Cousins* was compiled by Ophelia M. Phillips and published in Tuscaloosa, Alabama, in 1972.

MORSE

Ranking: 702 S.S. Count: 60,220

Origin: English, Jewish. Transformation of Morris.

Famous **Morses:** JEDIDIAH MORSE (1761–1826) of Connecticut was a Congregational minister who published history and geography books in the American colonies. One of his books, *Geography Made Easy*, was the first of its kind published. SAMUEL FINLEY BREESE MORSE (1791–1872) of Massachusetts was the founder and first president of the National Academy of Design. With his interest in the merit of the telegraph, and with the help of Leonard D. Gale, he invented Morse code. Morse sent the first message over the telegraph line, saying, "What hath God wrought?" a comment that also expressed his feelings about the difficulty he was having in trying to secure patent rights. He eventually won his court case. EDWARD SYLVESTER MORSE (1838–1925) of Maine was a zoologist and an authority on Japanese archaeology. CHARLES WYMAN MORSE (1856–1933) of Maine was a business promoter who was tried and convicted of making false banking statements, then redirecting the funds. After his prison term, he reentered the New York financial world. He was tried and acquitted of trying to defraud the government. A civil suit was filed for a judgment against him of $11.5 million.

Genealogies: *Morse Genealogy* was compiled by J. Howard Morse and published in Cloverdale, Oregon, in 1980. *The Ancestors and Descendants of the Rev. Daniel Morse* was compiled by Colleen Morse Elliott and published in Haltom City, Texas, in 1980.

MORTENSEN, MORTENSON (S.S. Abbreviation: Morten)

Ranking: 2362 S.S. Count: 19,205

Origin: Danish, Norwegian. Transformation of Martin.

Genealogies: *Descendants of Hans Jorgen Thomsen and Ane Kjerstine Ditlevsen of Klejs, Denmark* [also Mortensen] was compiled by Frances Hansen Ehrig and published in Richland, Washington, in 1962. *Lie Descendants* [also Mortenson] was compiled by Ingmar Adelbert Lee and published in Minneapolis, Minnesota, in 1968.

MORTIMER, MORTIMOR, MORTIMORE (S.S. Abbreviation: Mortim)

Ranking: 4943 S.S. Count: 9062

Origin: English. Derived from the Old French words "mort(e)" and "mer," meaning dead and sea. The name was given to those from Mortemer, a place in France.

Famous Bearers: MARY MORTIMER (1816–1877) of England was brought to New York City as a child. She was a founder and the first principal of Milwaukee Female College, actually a high school organized like a college.

Genealogies: None known.

MORTON

Ranking: 450 S.S. Count: 88,547

Origin: English, Jewish, Scottish, Swedish. English, Scottish: derived from the Old English words "mōr" and "tūn," meaning bog or moor and settlement. The name was given to those from Mor(e)ton, the name of several places in England and Scotland. Jewish: uncertain etymology. Most likely an Anglicization of any of several similar-sounding Jewish surnames. Swedish: cognate to Martin.

Famous Mortons: THOMAS MORTON (1590?–1647) of England came to America, where his unorthodox lifestyle by Puritan standards and his trading with the Indians earned him a jail sentence in England and again in Boston. He was the author of a satirical book on life in New England, *New England Canaan* (1637). JOHN MORTON (1724?–1777) of Pennsylvania was a member of the Stamp Act Congress and the Continental Congress and was one of the signers of the Declaration of Independence. SARAH WENTWORTH APTHORP MORTON (1759–1846) of Massa-

chusetts was a poet who contributed to the magazines of her day. It is believed that she wrote the book *The Power of Sympathy*. WILLIAM THOMAS GREEN MORTON (1819–1868) of Massachusetts was a dentist and the co-discoverer of the use of sulfuric ether as an anesthesic. The patent was for the use of "letheon." OLIVER HAZARD PERRY THROCK MORTON (1823–1877) of Indiana was the founder of the Republican Party in Indiana. He also served his state as the lieutenant governor, then governor, then U.S. senator. He is known for his great support of the Union cause. LEVI PARSONS MORTON (1824–1920) of Vermont was the vice president of the United States (1889–1893) under President Benjamin Harrison and the governor of New York. JULIUS STERLING MORTON (1832–1902) of New York was the secretary of agriculture and the originator of Arbor Day. JOY MORTON (1855–1934) of Michigan was the founder of the Morton Salt Co. FERDINAND JOSEPH LA MENTHE MORTON (1885–1941) of Louisiana was better known as "Jelly Roll." He was a professional jazz musician who traveled the country with the group Red Hot Peppers. They recorded such songs as "Jelly Roll Blues" and "Black Bottom Stomp."

Genealogies: None known.

MOSBY

Ranking: 4497 S.S. Count: 9966

Origin: English. Uncertain etymology. Possibly derived from the Old English words "mores" and "burh," meaning bog or moor and enclosure and given to those from Mosbrough, a place in Yorkshire, England.

Famous Mosbys: JOHN SINGLETON MOSBY (1833–1916) of Virginia was an American soldier and a Confederate scout for Jeb Stuart. He headed a cavalry unit called Mosby's Rangers that raided federal supply depots. After the war he served the federal government and wrote books about his wartime experiences. He is probably the one who coined the phrase "the solid South."

Genealogies: *Our Noble Heritage: the Mosby Family History* was compiled by James H. Mosby and published in Evansville, Indiana, in 1975.

MOSELEY (S.S. Abbreviation: Mosele)

Ranking: 1645 S.S. Count: 27,151

Origin: English. 1) the name was given to those from several places in England called Moseley. Derived from the Old English words "mos" and "lēah," meaning peat bog and clearing. 2) In both cases, derived from the English word "mūs," meaning mouse.

Famous Moseleys: CORLISS CHAMPION MOSELEY (1894–1974) of Idaho was one of the organizers of Western Air Express, which became Western Air Lines. He achieved notable corporate success in the aviation industry, and another of his companies, Grand Central Corp., trained thousands of people for the U.S. Army Air Force for World War II.

Genealogies: *Epitome of the History of the Moseley Family* was compiled by R. L. Moseley and published in Winter Park, Florida, in 1979.

MOSER

Ranking: 1095 **S.S. Count:** 40,338

Origin: German. Cognate to the English name Moss, derived from "mos," meaning peat bog.

Genealogies: *A Family Letter: Written in Nineteen Thirty-Two by George Moser to his Nephew Arthur Moser* was compiled by George Moser and published in Easthampton, Massachusetts, in 1979.

MOSES

Ranking: 844 **S.S. Count:** 50,455

Origin: English, French, Jewish. Derived from the Hebrew name Moshe (Moses), which is most likely of Egyptian etymology.

Famous Moseses: ANNA MARY ROBERTSON (GRANDMA) MOSES (1860–1961) of New York was a primitive painter.

Genealogies: *Some Ancestors and Descendants of John Frederick Peters and his Wife Maria Louise Moses of Hoosick Falls, New York* was compiled by Dorothy Rudd DuMond and published in Ulster Park, New York, in 1983.

MOSHER

Ranking: 1982 **S.S. Count:** 22,873

Origin: German. Derived from a German word meaning moor or swamp. The name was given to those who lived on or near a moor or swamp.

Famous Moshers: ELIZA MARIA MOSHER (1846–1928) of New York was a physician. She served as the dean of women and the professor of hygiene at the University of Michigan. She was the school's first female faculty member.

Genealogies: *Descendants of Hugh Mosher and Rebecca Maxson through Seven Generations* was compiled by Mildred Mosher Chamberlain and published in Warwick, Rhode Island, in 1980. *The Life Saga and Stories of Harvey, Cisler, Gerstenberger, Mosher, and Some Related Lines* was compiled by Lois Gerstenberger Harvey and published in Decatur, Illinois, in 1979.

MOSIER

Ranking: 4044 **S.S. Count:** 11,193

Origin: French. Uncertain etymology. The name was given to those who raised and sold vegetables.

Genealogies: None known.

MOSKOWICZ, MOSKOWITCH, MOSKOWITS, MOSKOWITZ, MOSKOWSKI (S.S. Abbreviation: Moskow)

Ranking: 4545 **S.S. Count:** 9832

Origin: Moskowicz, Moskowitch, Moskowits, Moskowitz, Moskowski—Jewish. Moskowicz, Moskowitch, Moskowits, Moskowitz: transformations of Moses. Moskowski: uncertain etymology. Possibly derived from the name of the Russian city Moscow. The name was most likely given to those who had traveled to the city, rather than to those from the city.

Famous Bearers: BELLE LINDNER ISRAELS MOSKOWITZ (1877–1933) of New York City was a social worker and longtime supporter of Alfred E. Smith. She served as the director of the Council of Jewish Women, vice president of the Association to Promote Proper Housing for Girls, and a member of the Women's City Club.

Genealogies: None known.

MOSLEY

Ranking: 696 **S.S. Count:** 60,419

Origin: English. Transformation of Moseley.

Genealogies: *Epitome of the History of the Moseley* [also Mosley] *Family* was compiled by R. L. Moseley and published in Winter Park, Florida, in 1979. *Mosley Families of Montgomery and Emanuel Counties* was compiled by John E. Mosley and published in Dunwoody, Georgia, in 1969.

MOSS

Ranking: 366 **S.S. Count:** 105,954

Origin: English, Jewish. English: 1) derived from the first name Moses. 2) derived from the Middle English and Old English word "mos," meaning peat bog. The name was given to those who lived near a peat bog. Jewish: uncertain etymology.

Genealogies: *The David Moss Family* was compiled by Thomas Chester Moss and published in Memphis, Tennessee, in 1968.

MOTLEY

Ranking: 3226 **S.S. Count:** 14,050

Origin: English. Uncertain etymology. The name was given to those who made multicolored cloth.

Famous Motleys: JOHN LOTHROP MOTLEY (1814–1877) of Massachusetts was a diplomat and historian and the author of several books of a historical nature.

Genealogies: *A Bicentennial History of Eleven Pioneer Families* [also Motley] was compiled by Mary M. Beadles and published in Baltimore, Maryland, in 1974. *The Families of Williams, Kenoyer, New, Motley* was compiled by Lola Bernice Frakes and published in Provo, Utah.

MOTT

Ranking: 1847 **S.S. Count:** 24,506

Origin: English. Derived from the Old French and Middle English word "motte," meaning a secured fortress. The name was given to those who lived near a secured fortress.

Famous Motts: LUCRETIA COFFIN MOTT (1793–1880) of

Massachusetts was a reformer. She was the founder of the Philadelphia Female Anti-Slavery Society, the American Equal Rights Association, and the Free Religious Association. She also participated in the Underground Railroad and with Elizabeth Cady Stanton in the organizing of the women's rights convention in Seneca Falls, New York (1848). JOHN RALEIGH MOTT (1865–1966) of New York, a religious leader, was the founder of the World's Student Christian Federation and chairman of the International Missionary Council. He was the co-recepient of the Nobel Prize for peace in 1946. FRANK LUTHER MOTT (1886–1964) of Iowa was a journalist and a Pulitzer Prize winner (1939).

Genealogies: *Mott Street* was compiled by Jordan L. Mott and published in Woodside, California in 1986.

MOULTON (S.S. Abbreviation: Moulto)
Ranking: 2784 S.S. Count: 16,397

Origin: English. Derived from the Old English name Mūla, meaning mule, and the Old English word "tūn," meaning settlement. The name was given to those from Moulton, the name of several places in England.

Famous **Moultons:** LOUISE CHANDLER MOULTON (1835–1918) of Connecticut was an author and literary hostess. She hosted weekly receptions that attracted well-known writers. She became a respected critic and hostess in the United States and England. FOREST RAY MOULTON (1872–1952) of Michigan was an astronomer and the author of many books on astronomy. His area of greatest concern was with the origin of the solar system.

Genealogies: *The Storrs-Moulton-Smith Connection* was compiled by Jessamine Smith Herbst and published in Inglewood, California, in 1981.

MOUNT
Ranking: 3591 S.S. Count: 12,564

Origin: English. Cognate to Montel, which was derived from Mont.

Famous **Mounts:** WILLIAM SIDNEY MOUNT (1807–1868) of New York was a painter of scenes and portraits. Some of his well-known subjects were Daniel Webster and political diplomat Robert Schenck. He is well-known for his paintings of Long Island country life.

Genealogies: *Mount* was compiled by Brent Mount and published in Richardson, Texas, in 1974. *Chronicles of the Mountz-Teeters and Allied Families* [also Mount] was compiled by Margaret Mountz Carroll and published in 1984.

MOWERY
Ranking: 4142 S.S. Count: 10,929

Origin: English. Derived from the Middle English word "mow(en)," meaning to mow. The name was given to those who cut grass for hay.

Genealogies: None known.

MOY
Ranking: 4423 S.S. Count: 10,139

Origin: Chinese. The name means plum flower.

Genealogies: None known.

MOYA
Ranking: 4270 S.S. Count: 10,538

Origin: Catalan. Derived from the Latin name Modius, which was derived from the Latin word "modus," meaning measure.

Genealogies: None known.

MOYE
Ranking: 4460 S.S. Count: 10,049

Origin: Scottish. Derived from a word meaning plain. The name was given to those from Moye, a place in Scotland.

Genealogies: None known.

MOYER
Ranking: 808 S.S. Count: 52,243

Origin: Irish. Derived from a word meaning steward.

Famous **Moyers:** DAVID GEORGE MOYER (1910–1976) of Pennsylvania was a physician in his home state who pioneered in the development of sports medicine.

Genealogies: *History of our Moyer, Finn, Sutton, Russell & Related Families* was compiled by William Finn Moyer and published in Garden City, New York, in 1979.

MUELLER (S.S. Abbreviation: Muelle)
Ranking: 441 S.S. Count: 90,318

Origin: German, Jewish. Cognate to Miller.

Famous **Muellers:** EDWIN WILHELM MUELLER (1911–1977) of Germany was a physicist and the inventor of the field ion microscope, which allowed him to see images of atoms.

Genealogies: *Mueller Genealogy* was compiled by Mrs. George P. Mueller and published in Topeka, Kansas, in 1988. *The Mueller Family Tree and the Meier Family Tree, about 1700–1983, 10 Generations* was compiled by Estella Michels and published in Earlville, Iowa, in 1984. *The Mueller Mystique* was compiled by Ned Mueller and published in Sacramento, California, in 1977.

MUIR
Ranking: 2935 S.S. Count: 15,518

Origin: English, Scottish. Derived from the Middle English word "more," meaning moor. The name was given to those who lived on a moor.

Famous **Muirs:** JOHN MUIR (1838–1914) of Scotland was a naturalist who walked from Indiana to the Gulf of Mexico, during which time he kept a journal of what he saw and how he felt. He then walked to California, studying the Yosemite Valley. He continued to Nevada, Utah, and

Alaska, finally settling in Martinez, California. He and Robert U. Johnson successfully petitioned Congress to set aside land as Yosemite National Park. He also wrote books about his travels through the country.

Genealogies: None known.

MULCAHY (S.S. Abbreviation: Mulcah)

Ranking: 4166 **S.S. Count:** 10,844

Origin: Irish. Derived from the Gaelic name Ó Maolchathaigh, meaning "descendant of the devotee of (St.) Cathach" (H&H).

Genealogies: None known.

MULDER (ALSO MULDERS)

Ranking: 4955 **S.S. Count:** 9038

Origin: Dutch, Flemish. Cognates to Miller.

Genealogies: None known.

MULHOLLAND (S.S. Abbreviation: Mulhol)

Ranking: 4354 **S.S. Count:** 10,299

Origin: Irish. Derived from the Gaelic name Ó Maolcha-lann, meaning "descendant of the devotee of (St.) Calann" (H&H).

Genealogies: None known.

MULL

Ranking: 3396 **S.S. Count:** 13,324

Origin: English, Scottish. English: transformation of Miller. Scottish: derived from words meaning bare rock. The name was given to those from Mull, the name of places in Scotland.

Genealogies: None known.

MULLAN (ALSO MULLANE)

Ranking: 3685 **S.S. Count:** 12,249

Origin: Irish. Transformation of Mullen.

Genealogies: None known.

MULLEN (ALSO MULLENS)

Ranking: 607 **S.S. Count:** 68,736

Origin: English, Irish. English: derived from the Anglo-Norman-French word "mo(u)lin," meaning mill. The name was given to those who lived near a mill. Irish: derived from the Gaelic name Ó Maoláin, which was derived from the first name Maolán, meaning one with a shaved head.

Genealogies: *One Mullins* [also Mullens] *Family* was compiled by Marie R. Justice and published in Pikeville, Kentucky, in 1983.

MULLER

Ranking: 1027 **S.S. Count:** 42,664

Origin: German, Jewish. Cognate to Miller.

Famous Mullers: GERTRUDE AGNES MULLER (1887–

1954) of Indiana was an inventor of child safety products and the founder of the Juvenile Wood Products Co., through which she sold her inventions. HERMANN JOSEPH MULLER (1890–1967) of New York City was a geneticist and the winner of a Nobel Prize (1946) for work on artificial transmutation of a gene by X-rays.

Genealogies: *The Mueller* [also Muller] *Mystique* was compiled by Ned Mueller and published in Sacramento, California, in 1977.

MULLIGAN (S.S. Abbreviation: Mullig)

Ranking: 2111 **S.S. Count:** 21,733

Origin: Irish. Transformation of Milligan.

Genealogies: None known.

MULLIN (ALSO MULLINER, MULLINGER, MULLINGS, MULLINS)

Ranking: 298 **S.S. Count:** 120,661

Origin: Mulliner, Mullinger—English; Mullin, Mullings, Mullins—English, Irish. Mulliner, Mullinger: transformations of the Engish name Mullen. Mullin, Mullings, Mullins: transformations of Mullen.

Famous Bearers: CHARLES J. MULLIN (1914–1975) of Missouri, a physics professor, supervised the expansion of the Physics Department at Notre Dame University from 18 to 30 full-time professors between 1953 and 1960.

Genealogies: *One Mullins Family* was compiled by Marie R. Justice and published in Pikeville, Kentucky, in 1983.

MULLIS

Ranking: 3754 **S.S. Count:** 12,061

Origin: English. Derived from the Middle English words "mulle" and "hus," meaning mill and house. The name was given to those who lived near a mill.

Genealogies: None known.

MUMFORD (S.S. Abbreviation: Mumfor)

Ranking: 4708 **S.S. Count:** 9509

Origin: English. 1) derived from the Norman name Montfort, which was given to those from Mundford, a place in Norfolk, England. 2) uncertain etymology. Possibly derived from the Old English first name Muna and the word "ford." The name may have been given to those who came from Mundford.

Famous Mumfords: MARY ENO BASSETT MUMFORD (1842–1935) of Connecticut was an educator and civic leader. During the Depression she worked with her husband helping children. They organized the Twenty-ninth Ward division of the new Philadelphia Society for Organizing Charity. She also served as one of the founders of the Civic Club of Philadelphia.

Genealogies: None known.

MUNDY

Ranking: 3405 S.S. Count: 13,297

Origin: English, Irish. English: 1) *derived from the Old English word "mōnandœg," meaning "day of the moon" (H&H). The name was given to those who had some special connection to the day Monday. 2) derived from many Old Norse compound names that include the component "mundr," meaning protection. Irish: derived from the Gaelic name Mac Giolla Eoin, meaning "son of the servant of Eoin" (H&H).*

Genealogies: None known.

MUNIZ

Ranking: 1562 S.S. Count: 28,562

Origin: Spanish. *Derived from a first name of uncertain etymology.*

Genealogies: None known.

MUNN

Ranking: 3531 S.S. Count: 12,779

Origin: English. *Transformation of the English name Moon, derived from the Anglo-Norman-French word "moun," meaning monk.*

Famous **Munns**: RALPH WOOD MUNN (1894–1975) of Illinois was director of the Carnegie Library, Pittsburgh, Pennsylvania (1929–1964). The Carnegie Corp. sent him in the 1930s to Australia and New Zealand to study library conditions there and make recommendations for improvements. He was known as the father of the modern library movement in Australia.

Genealogies: None known.

MUNOZ

Ranking: 491 S.S. Count: 82,108

Origin: Spanish. *Transformation of Muniz.*

Genealogies: None known.

MUNRO

Ranking: 4483 S.S. Count: 9997

Origin: Scottish. *Derived from the Gaelic words "mun," meaning the mouth of a river, and Rotha, a river name. The name was given to those from the mouth of the Roe River in Ireland.*

Famous **Munros**: GEORGE MUNRO (1825–1896) of Nova Scotia came to the United States and settled in New York City. He published dime-store novels, including the *Old Sleuth* series and reprints of classics.

Genealogies: *Munro Family* was compiled by Ronald G. Munro and published in Camden, Maine, in 1989. *The Union of our Quigley & Munro Families* was compiled by Eleanor Freeburn and published in Berea, Ohio, in 1982.

MUNSON

Ranking: 1763 S.S. Count: 25,435

Origin: English. *Transformation of Munn.*

Famous **Munsons**: WALTER DAVID MUNSON (1843–1908) of Connecticut was a shipping magnate. Starting with one ship and the New York-to-Havana shipping route, he grew into the largest shipping company in the United States and the Carribean.

Genealogies: None known.

MURDOCH, MURDOCK (S.S. Abbreviation: Murdoc)

Ranking: 1404 S.S. Count: 31,649

Origin: Scottish. *Derived from the Gaelic first name Muire(adh)ach, which was derived from the word "muir," meaning sea.*

Famous **Bearers**: JAMES EDWARD MURDOCK (1811–1893) of Pennsylvania was an actor and best known as a comedian. LOUISE CALDWELL MURDOCK (1858–1915) of New York was an interior designer and art patron. She founded the Twentieth Century Club of Wichita (Kansas) to help women understand the arts.

Genealogies: None known.

MURILL

Ranking: 2591 S.S. Count: 17,561

Origin: English. *Transformation of Morrel.*

Genealogies: None known.

MURPHY

Ranking: 54 S.S. Count: 429,898

Origin: Irish. *Derived from the Gaelic name Ó Murchadha, which was derived from the first name Murchadh, which is comprised of the components "muir" and "cadh," meaning sea and warrior.*

Famous **Murphys**: ISAAC MURPHY (1856–1896) of Kentucky was a jockey and the first to win three Kentucky Derbys. JOHN BENJAMIN MURPHY (1857–1916) of Wisconsin was a specialist in abdominal surgery and the inventor of the Murphy's Button, a device used in surgery. CHARLES FRANCIS MURPHY (1858–1924) of New York City was the head of Tammany Hall. WILLIAM FRANCIS [FRANK] MURPHY (1890–1949) of Michigan was a Michigan politician, governor of the Philippine Islands, and an associate justice of the U.S. Supreme Court. ROBERT DANIEL MURPHY (1894–1978) of Wisconsin was a diplomat and one of the organizers of the Berlin airlift. AUDIE MURPHY (1924–1971) of Texas was the most decorated soldier of World War II. After the war he starred in several war movies.

Genealogies: *The Ancestors and Descendants of Simon Jones and Ann M. (Dorr) Murphy* was compiled by Marjorie Barnes Thompson and published in 1986. *Early Murphys, Murpheys in Pittsylvania County, Virginia, Robertson and Carroll Counties, Tennessee* was compiled by Marion

Emerson Murphy and published in San Diego, California, in 1975.

MURRAY

Ranking: 109 **S.S. Count:** 258,256

Origin: English, Irish, Scottish. English: derived from the Middle English word "merry," meaning happy. The name was given to those with a merry disposition. Irish: 1) derived from the Gaelic name Mac Giolla Mhuire, which was derived from a first name meaning "servant of (the Virgin) Mary" (H&H). 2) derived from the Gaelic name Mac Muire (adh)aigh, which was derived from the word "muir," meaning sea. Scottish: derived from Celtic components meaning sea and settlement. The name was given to those from Moray, a county in Scotland.

Famous **Murrays:** JOHN MURRAY (1741–1815) of England was a clergyman who was a chaplain in the American Revolution and the father of American Universalism. LINDLEY MURRAY (1745–1826) of Pennsylvania was a grammarian and the author of English grammar books for schools. JUDITH SARGENT MURRAY (1751–1820) of Massachusetts was an author and feminist. She wrote about feminist issues. PHILIP MURRAY (1886–1952) of Scotland was a labor leader and the president of the United Mine Workers after John L. Lewis, then president of the United Steel Workers of America. ALAN E. MURRAY (1894–1978) of California, while an ice-skating instructor in Pennsylvania, broke his leg. When it healed, it was shorter than his other leg. He then had surgery to shorten his longer leg and returned to his skating career. He later invented a special skating shoe to help him overcome problems with his feet, and his venture led to the establishment of the Murray Space Shoe Corp. JOHN COURTNEY MURRAY (1904–1967) of New York City was a religious leader and the author of religious books.

Genealogies: *Family Ties of Roy Harold Murray* was compiled by Miriam Adams Cloud Murray and published in Decorah, Iowa, in 1976. *Golden Clan: the Murrays, the McDonnells, and the Irish American Aristocracy* was compiled by John Corry and published in Boston, Massachusetts, in 1977.

MURRELL (S.S. Abbreviation: Murrel)

Ranking: 2895 **S.S. Count:** 15,731

Origin: English. Transformation of Merril.

Famous **Murrells:** JOHN A. MURRELL (or Murrel or Murel) (1804?–1850) of Texas was an outlaw in the old West. He organized bands of criminals to steal goods and arranged for disposal of the stolen property. He was arrested and tried for stealing slaves and received a 10-year sentence. The trial revealed that Murrell had planned to use the stolen slaves to instigate an uprising in the Southwest.

Genealogies: *Lyle, Murrell, Nancy, Morton Genealogy* was compiled by Gladys Elizabeth Odil Bracy and published in Nashville, Tennessee, in 1965.

MURRY

Ranking: 3301 **S.S. Count:** 13,728

Origin: English, Irish, Scottish. Transformation of Murray.

Genealogies: None known.

MUSE

Ranking: 2903 **S.S. Count:** 15,682

Origin: English. The name was given to those who lived on or near a mew or mews.

Genealogies: None known.

MUSGROVE (S.S. Abbreviation: Musgro)

Ranking: 4757 **S.S. Count:** 9417

Origin: English. Derived from the Old English words "mūs" and "grāf," meaning mouse and grove. The name was given to those from Musgrave, the name of places in England.

Famous **Musgroves:** MARY MUSGROVE (1700?–1763?) of Georgia was leader of the Indians in colonial Georgia and was responsible for the friendliness they showed James Oglethorpe and his settlers when they arrived.

Genealogies: None known.

MUSSELMAN (S.S. Abbreviation: Mussel)

Ranking: 3894 **S.S. Count:** 11,584

Origin: English. The name was given to those who sold mussels.

Genealogies: None known.

MUSSER

Ranking: 3592 **S.S. Count:** 12,563

Origin: German. The name was given to those from Mussen, which means swamp, the name of places in Germany.

Genealogies: None known.

MYERS

Ranking: 82 **S.S. Count:** 322,245

Origin: English. Transformation of Mayer.

Famous **Myerses:** WILLIAM I. MYERS (1891–1976) of New York was a noted professor of agricultural economics who also served in a number of government posts dealing with agriculture and world food supply, including as governor of the Farm Credit Administration.

Genealogies: *A Tale of Two Families: a Biographical Genealogy of the Meyers* [also Myers] *and Sparhawk Families* was compiled by Dorothy Hermanne Braithwait and published in Spokane, Washington, in 1981. *Sam Myers, 1805–1883 and Lydia Horner, 1833–1907: their Ancestors* *and Descendants* was compiled by Forrest D. Myers and published in Harrisburg, Pennsylvania, in 1979.

MYLES
Ranking: 2769 **S.S. Count:** 16,476
Origin: English. Transformation of the name Miles.
Genealogies: None known.

MYRICK
Ranking: 2379 **S.S. Count:** 19,087
Origin: English. Derived from the first name Almeric, meaning work or rule.
Genealogies: None known.

NADEAU

Ranking: 2569 S.S. Count: 17,709
Origin: French. Derived from the Old French and Middle englsih word "no(u)el," meaning Christmas.

Genealogies: None known.

NAGEL

Ranking: 2185 S.S. Count: 20,985
Origin: Dutch, Flemish, German, Jewish. Cognate to Naylor.

Genealogies: *Joachim Nagel and His Descendants* was compiled by Marion Nagle Rhoads and published in 1990.

NAGLE

Ranking: 2854 S.S. Count: 15,995
Origin: English, Irish. Derived from the Old French and Middle English word "angle," meaning angle. The name was given to those who lived on a corner of land.

Genealogies: *Joachim Nagel and His Descendants* [also Nagle] was compiled by Marion Nagle Rhoads and published in 1990.

NAGY

Ranking: 2067 S.S. Count: 22,182
Origin: Hungarian, Jewish. Derived from the Hungarian word "nagy," meaning big. The name was given to those who were large.

Genealogies: None known.

NAKAMURA (S.S. Abbreviation: Nakamu)

Ranking: 4428 S.S. Count: 10,127
Origin: Japanese. Derived from components meaning middle and village.

Genealogies: None known.

NANCE

Ranking: 1354 S.S. Count: 32,737
Origin: English. Derived from a word meaning valley. The name was given to those from Nance, a place in Cornwall, England.

Genealogies: *The History and Genealogy of the Nances* was compiled by D. Nance and published in Charlotte, North Carolina, in 1930. *Lyle, Murrell, Nancy, Morton* [also Nance] *Genealogy* was compiled by Gladys Elizabeth Odil Bracy and published in Nashville, Tennessee, in 1965.

NAPIER

Ranking: 1626 S.S. Count: 27,585
Origin: English, French, Scottish. Derived from the Old French word "nappe," meaning tablecloth. The name was given to those who sold table linen or to servants responsible for the linen in a house.

Genealogies: *Doctor Patrick Napier: His Ancestors and Some Descendants* was compiled by John Hawkins Napier and published in Oxford, Mississippi, in 1991.

NAPOLI (ALSO NAPOLIONI, NAPOLITANO)

Ranking: 2510 S.S. Count: 18,076
Origin: Italian. Napoli, Napolitano: ultimately derived from the Greek words "nea" and "polis," meaning new and city. The name was given to those from Naples, a city in Italy. Napolioni: derived from the first name Napoleone, which is of uncertain etymology.

Genealogies: None known.

NASH

Ranking: 495 S.S. Count: 80,974
Origin: English, Jewish. English: derived from the Middle English phrase "atten ash," meaning at the ash. The name was given to those who lived near an ash tree. Jewish: uncertain etymology.

Famous **Nashes**: ABNER NASH (1740?–1786) of Virginia was a Revolutionary War patriot, Speaker of the first North Carolina House of Commons, and Speaker of the North Carolina state senate. He served as governor and was constantly at odds with the legislature over who had the greater amount of power in the state government. FRANCIS NASH (1742?–1777) of Virginia was a Revolutionary War officer who was killed in the Battle of Germantown. Nashville, Tennessee, and Nash County, North Carolina, were named for him. DANIEL NASH (1763–1836) of Massachusetts was an Episcopal missionary in western New York. He was called Father Nash and was the model from which James Fenimore Cooper's "Reverend Mr. Grant" was created in *The Pioneers*. FREDERICK NASH (1781–1858) of North Carolina was a state Supreme Court justice, then a chief justice in the North Carolina state court system. CHARLES SUMNER NASH (1856–1926) of Massachusetts was a Congregational clergyman and the head of the Pacific Theological Seminary. He made the school nondenominational and changed its name to Pacific School of Religion. CHARLES WILLIAMS NASH (1864–1948) of Illinois was an automobile manufacturer. He rose through the Durant-Dort Carriage Co. and took over the troubled Buick Motor Car Co., making it a sound and well-run company. He then performed the same service for General Motors. His style of management was sound but conservative, and he was not well liked by the stockholders. He left and formed his own company, which produced a car brand by his name. The Nash Motors Company was run profitably and efficiently, but when he retired, he gave up the automobile industry and merged his company with the Kelvinator Company and began making appliances. ARTHUR NASH (1870–1927) of Indiana was the originator of the "golden rule" plan of business operation. He was the author of the book *The Golden Rule in Business* (1923). JOHN HENRY NASH (1871–1947) of Canada was a printer. He designed and printed deluxe editions, with Dante's *Divine Comedy* being one of his finest. [FREDERIC] OGDEN NASH (1902–1971) of New York was the author of humorous verse and a writer of many books.

Genealogies: *The History of Five Southern Families* [also Nash] *Family* was compiled by Ethel Evans Albert and published in Baltimore, Maryland, in 1970. *Lives and Times of the Nash Family* was compiled by Gertrude Nash Locke and published in Watertown, Massachusetts, in 1971. *Nash, a Family Genealogy* was compiled by Ralph G. Nash and published in Springfield, Virginia, in 1982.

NATHAN (ALSO NATHANS, NATHANSEN, NATHANSOHN, NATHANSON)

Ranking: 2907 **S.S. Count:** 15,661

Origin: Nathan—English, Jewish; Nathans, Nathansen, Nathansohn, Nathanson—Jewish. Derived from the Hebrew masculine first name Natan, meaning given or given by God and refers to the biblical Nathan.

Famous **Bearers:** MAUD NATHAN (1862–1946) of New York was a social reformer who brought the terrible working conditions for women in retail shops to the attention of the public and brought pressure on those who could change the situation for the better. GEORGE JEAN NATHAN (1882–1958) of Indiana was an editor and critic and the author of books on the American theater.

Genealogies: None known.

NATION (S.S. Abbreviation: Nation)

Ranking: 3310 **S.S. Count:** 13,684

Origin: English. Transformation of Nathan.

Famous **Nations:** CARRY AMELIA MOORE NATION (1846–1911) of Kentucky was a temperance agitator. Struck with the cause of temperance, she smashed saloons in her attempt to eradicate towns of the evil liquor. A hatchet was her trademark, and she sold souvenir replicas to pay the fines she incurred in her 30 arrests for disturbing the peace. Her autobiography was published in 1904.

Genealogies: *House of Nations* was compiled by Verna Nation Jones and published in Riverton, Illinois, in 1979.

NAVA

Ranking: 4009 **S.S. Count:** 11,291

Origin: Spanish. Derived from the Spanish word "nava," meaning a treeless plateau. The name was given to those who lived in such an area.

Genealogies: None known.

NAVARRE, NAVARRETE, NAVARRO (S.S. Abbreviation: Navarr)

Ranking: 570 **S.S. Count:** 72,356

Origin: Navarre—French; Navarrete, Navarro—Spanish. Navarre: cognate to Navarro. Navarrete: derived from the components "Nafar" and "ate," meaning nateive of the Navarre region and pass. The name was given to those from Logroño and Alava, the names of provinces of Spain. Navarro: the name was given to those from the region of Spain called Navarre.

Famous **Bearers:** PIERRE NAVARRE (1790?–1874) of Michigan was a frontiersman and the scout for William Henry Harrison's army (1813–1814).

Genealogies: None known.

NAYLOR (S.S. Abbreviation: Naylor)

Ranking: 1954 **S.S. Count:** 23,182

Origin: English. Derived from the Middle English word "nayl," meaning nail. The name was given to those who made nails.

Genealogies: *Pacific Northwest Grandfathers: Family Lines, Crosby, Martin, Naylor, et al.* was compiled by Alverta Brown Martin and published in Rowland Heights, California, in 1971.

NAZARI (ALSO NAZARIAN)

Ranking: 3447 **S.S. Count:** 13,093

Origin: Nazari—Italian; Nazarian—Armenian. Ultimately derived from the Hebrew Nazareth, of uncertain etymology. The name was originally given to Christians.

Genealogies: None known.

NEAL

Ranking: 289 **S.S. Count:** 124,722

Origin: English. Transformation of Neil.

Famous **Neals:** JOHN NEAL (1793–1876) of Maine was a writer of novels and the first person to speak well of Edgar Allan Poe in print. JOSEPH CLAY NEAL (1807–1847) of New Hampshire was a journalist and humorist and the author of *Charcoal Sketches* (1838) and *Peter Ploddy and Other Oddities* (1844).

Genealogies: *The Neal, Harbison, Snodgrass, Miller, and Related Families* was compiled by Thomas Howe R. Neal and published in Knoxville, Tennessee, in 1971. *Lester, Neal, and Allied Families* was compiled by Shirley Wimpey Ward and published in Anadarko, Oklahoma, in 1987.

NEEDHAM (S.S. Abbreviation: Needha)

Ranking: 2852 **S.S. Count:** 16,059

Origin: English. Derived from the Old English words "nēd" and "hām," meaning need and homestead. The name was given to those from Needham, the name of several places in England.

Famous **Needhams:** JAMES NEEDHAM (?–1673) of England was an explorer. He came to southern Carolina and became a planter on the Ashley River. He searched for a

water route to the Southwest from Petersburg, Virginia. He reached the Cherokee village and is believed to be the first Englishman to have done so.
Genealogies: None known.

NEEL
Ranking: 4271 **S.S. Count:** 10,538
Origin: English, Irish, Scottish. Transformation of Neil.
Genealogies: *The Ancestors of Gregg Livingstone Neel* was compiled by Gregg Livingstone Neel and published in Pittsburgh, Pennsylvania, in 1973.

NEELEY
Ranking: 3445 **S.S. Count:** 13,098
Origin: Irish?, Scottish? Uncertain etymology. Most likely a transformation of Neely.
Genealogies: None known.

NEELY
Ranking: 1292 **S.S. Count:** 34,295
Origin: Irish, Scottish. Transformation of McNeilly.
Famous **Neelys:** THOMAS BENJAMIN NEELY (1841–1925) of Pennsylvania was a Methodist clergyman and bishop and a conservative in his approach to religions and beliefs.
Genealogies: *Borrer: Descendants of Elijah Borrer and Celia Williams Borrer and their Related Families* (also Neely) was compiled by William Otis Hallmark and published in Burnet, Texas, in 1979. *Neely, 200 Years in America* was compiled by Marie Davis Wiles and published in Plattsmouth, Nebraska, in 1974.

NEFF
Ranking: 1348 **S.S. Count:** 32,844
Origin: German. Derived from a word meaning nephew. The name may have been given to the nephew of an important person.
Genealogies: *The Neff-Naf Family* was compiled by William Alfred Neff and published in Princeton Junction, New Jersey, in 1991. *Our Neff Heritage* was compiled by Barbara Neff English and published in Orefino, Idaho, in 1981.

NEGRON (ALSO NEGRONE, NEGRONI)
Ranking: 1169 **S.S. Count:** 37,434
Origin: Negron—Provençal; Negrone, Negroni—Italian. Ultimately derived from the Latin word "niger," meaning the color black. The name was given to those with dark hair or skin.
Genealogies: None known.

NEIL
Ranking: 3475 **S.S. Count:** 12,990

Origin: English, Irish, Scottish. Derived from the Irish-Gaelic first name Niall, which is of uncertain etymology.
Genealogies: None known.

NEILL
Ranking: 3277 **S.S. Count:** 13,857
Origin: English, Irish, Scottish. Transformation of Neil.
Famous **Neills:** WILLIAM NEILL (1778?–1860) of Pennsylvania was a tutor to James Fenimore Cooper and president of Dickinson College. JOHN NEILL (1819–1880) of Pennsylvania was a surgeon who organized military hospitals in that state during the Civil War. His brother EDWARD DUFFIELD NEILL (1823–1893) of Pennsylvania was an author and president of Macalester College. Another brother, THOMAS HEWSON NEILL (1826–1885) of Pennsylvania, was a distinguished army officer and commandant of West Point Military Academy.
Genealogies: None known.

NEILSON (S.S. Abbreviation: Neilso)
Ranking: 4956 **S.S. Count:** 9038
Origin: English, Scottish. Transformation of Neil.
Famous **Neilsons:** WILLIAM ALLEN NEILSON (1869–1946) of Scotland was an English professor and the author of books on literature, especially Shakespeare. He also was the editor-in-chief of *Webster's New International Dictionary, Second Edition* (1934). NELLIE NEILSON (1873–1947) of Pennsylvania was a historian. She taught for nearly 40 years, mostly at the college level. After her retirement she traveled to England, doing research mostly in the area of economic and legal history.
Genealogies: None known.

NELMS
Ranking: 4462 **S.S. Count:** 10,044
Origin: English. Derived from the Middle English phrase "atten elms," meaning at the elm. The name was given to those who lived near an elm tree or grove.
Genealogies: None known.

NELSEN
Ranking: 4737 **S.S. Count:** 9455
Origin: Danish, Norwegian. Cognates to Neil.
Genealogies: None known.

NELSON
Ranking: 35 **S.S. Count:** 588,931
Origin: English. Transformation of Neil.
Famous **Nelsons:** THOMAS NELSON (1738–1789) of Virginia was a member of the Continental Congress, the governor of Virginia, and a signer of the Declaration of Independence. His son, HUGH NELSON (1768–1836) of Virginia, was a member of Congress from Virginia and an

advisor to Thomas Jefferson and James Monroe. SAMUEL NELSON (1792–1873) of New York was an associate justice of the U.S. Supreme Court. His son, RENSSELAER R. NELSON (1826–1904) of New York, was U.S. district judge in Minnesota for 38 years. THOMAS HENRY NELSON (1823–1896) was a founder of the Republican Party in the Midwest, a friend of Abraham Lincoln's, and U.S. minister to Chile and Mexico. His brother, WILLIAM NELSON (1824–1862) of Kentucky, was a Union soldier who, after being promoted to major general, was shot and killed in Louisville, Kentucky, by Jefferson C. Davis, another Union soldier who shared only first and last names with the president of the Confederacy. WILLIAM ROCKHILL NELSON (1841–1915) of Indiana was the founder of the Kansas City *Evening Star.* KNUTE NELSON (1843–1923) of Norway was governor of Minnesota, a member of Congress, and a U.S. senator. NELSON OLSEN NELSON (1844–1922) of Norway grew up in Missouri, where he started N.O. Nelson Manufacturing Co., a firm that grew to be one of the largest building- and plumbing-supplies firms in the world. He introduced profit sharing as a way to ease workers' discontent. HENRY LOOMIS NELSON (1846–1908) of New York was a journalist and editor of *Harper's Weekly.* EDWARD W. NELSON (1855–1934) of New Hampshire was a naturalist who conducted pioneering studies of plant and animal life in many regions of the United States. JULIUS NELSON (1858–1916) of Denmark was a biologist and professor in New Jersey and an authority on oyster culture. ALICE RUTH MOORE DUNBAR NELSON (1875–1935) of Louisiana was an author, teacher, and social worker. She taught in the Wilmington, Delaware, schools for nearly 20 years before becoming the associate editor of the *Wilmington Advocate.* She also was the first black woman to be a member of the Delaware Republican State Committee. BENJAMIN NELSON (1911–1977) of New York City was a sociology and history teacher at the New School for Social Research and was considered an authority on the history of usury and Max Weber.

Genealogies: *Torger and Gertrude Nelson: Their Ancestors, Descendants and Related Families* was compiled by Twila Ruth Eckstrom Schroeder and published in Kanawha, Iowa, in 1976. *Morrison-Wells and Nelson-Watson Families and Collateral Lines* was compiled by Dorothy Nelson Grant and published in Evanston, Illinois, in 1979.

NEMETH

Ranking: 3779 S.S. Count: 11,947

Origin: *Hungarian. Derived from the name Nemchin, meaning German, which was derived from the word "nemoi," meaning dumb or someone who could not be understood. The name was given to Germans or to any foreigners.*

Genealogies: None known.

NESBIT (ALSO NESBITT)

Ranking: 1699 S.S. Count: 26,312

Origin: *English, Scottish. Derived from the Middle English words "nese" and "bit," meaning nose and mouthful or bend (in land or water). The name was given to those from Nisbit or Nesbit(t), the names of several places in England.*

Famous **Bearers:** JOHN M. NESBITT (1730?–1802), an Irish immigrant, helped to establish public credit in 1780 and was the first president of the Insurance Company of North America. ALBERT JOHN NESBITT (1899–1977) of Pennsylvania was the manufacturer of ventilators for classrooms. He also was known for his community service in the Philadelphia area.

Genealogies: *German Burnett (G.B.) Kyle of Logon County, Arkansas, and His Wayne County, Tennessee, Ancestors: Duckworth, Kyle, Nesbitt, et al.* was compiled by Edith Madeline Replogle Raymond and published in Pullman, Washington, in 1990.

NESS

Ranking: 3016 S.S. Count: 15,067

Origin: *English, Scottish. Derived from the Middle English word "ness," meaning headland. The name was given to those who lived near a headland or who were from Ness, the name of some places in England and Scotland.*

Genealogies: None known.

NETHER (ALSO NETHERCOTT, NETHERTON, NETHERWOOD)

Ranking: 4976 S.S. Count: 9008

Origin: *Nethercott, Netherton, Netherwood—English; Nether—German. Nethercott: derived from the Middle English words "nether(e)" and "cot," meaning lower and cottage. The name was given to those who lived in a cottage located at the lower end of a town or settlement. Netherton: derived from the Old English components "neðoera" and "tūn," meaning lower and settlement. The name was given to those from Netherton, the name of several places in England. Netherwood: derived from the Old English words "neðoera" and "wudu," meaning lower and wood. The name was most likely given to those from a place named Netherwood. Nether: derived from the German word "nähen," meaning to sew. The name was given to tailors.*

Genealogies: None known.

NETTLEFIELD, NETTLEFOLD, NETTLETON (S.S. Abbreviation: Nettle)

Ranking: 2309 S.S. Count: 19,679

Origin: *Nettlefield, Nettlefold—English; Nettleton—English. Nettlefield, Nettlefold: derived from the Old English words "netele" and "fal(o)d" or "feld," meaning nettle and enclosure or field. The name was given to those from a former place in England. Nettleton: derived from the Old English* words "netele" and "tūn," meaning nettle and settlement. The name was given to those from Nettleton, the name of places in England.

Famous **Bearers:** ASAHEL NETTLETON (1783–1844) of Connecticut was a Congregational evangelist who preached in eastern Connecticut (1811–1812), then performed his religious deeds in Virginia and England. EDWIN NETTLETON (1831–1901) of Ohio was an engineer who surveyed Greeley, Colorado, and planned the irrigation systems in several Colorado, Wyoming, and Idaho locations.

Genealogies: None known.

NEUBAUER (S.S. Abbreviation: Neubau)
Ranking: 4825 **S.S. Count:** 9283
Origin: German, Jewish. German: derived from the Middle High German words "niuwe" and "gebūre," meaning new and peasant. The name was given to those who were new to an area and who worked in agriculture. Jewish: uncertain etymology.

Genealogies: *The Schwobe Story* [also Neubauer Family] was compiled by Bernadette Durben Bittner and published in Reedsburg, Washington, in 1980.

NEUMAN (ALSO NEUMANN)
Ranking: 1194 **S.S. Count:** 36,762
Origin: Neuman—Jewish; Neumann—German, Jewish. Cognates to Newman.

Famous **Bearers:** JOHN NEPOMUCENE NEUMAN (1811–1860) of Bohemia was a Roman Catholic priest who as an American missionary served in Pittsburgh and Baltimore. He was beatified in 1963. JOHN VON NEUMANN (1903–1957) of Hungary was a mathematician and the coiner of the term "cybernetics."

Genealogies: *William Gottlieb Neumann Genealogy* was compiled by Gertrude Neumann Hinman and published in Detroit, Michigan, in 1958. *The Neumanns: Wisconsin Pioneers, 1848–1978* [also Newman] was compiled by Kathleen Neumann Graber and published in Oshkosh, Wisconsin, in 1978.

NEVARES (S.S. Abbreviation: Nevare)
Ranking: 3825 **S.S. Count:** 11,788
Origin: Spanish. Uncertain etymology. Possibly derived from the Spanish word "nevar," meaning to snow.
Genealogies: None known.

NEVILL (ALSO NEVILLE)
Ranking: 2402 **S.S. Count:** 18,867
Origin: English, Irish. English: derived from the Old French words "neu(f)" and "ville," meaning new and settlement. The name was given to those from Neuville or Néville, the name of places in France. Irish: derived from the Gaelic name Ó Niadh, meaning warrior.

Famous **Bearers:** JOHN NEVILLE (1731–1803) of Virginia was a Revolutionary War soldier and the inspector of survey in the Whiskey Rebellion of 1794. WENDELL CUSHING NEVILLE (1870–1930) of Virginia was a career U.S. marine and the commandant of the corps (1929).

Genealogies: *Westmoreland Nee Neville* was compiled by Olin V. Mapes and published in Bowie, Maryland, in 1992. *A 370-year History of one Neville Family* was compiled by Joseph B. Neville and published in Tempe, Arizona, in 1988.

NEW
Ranking: 2804 **S.S. Count:** 16,243
Origin: English. 1) derived from the Middle English phrase "atten ew," meaning at the yew. The name was given to those who lived near a yew tree. 2) derived from the Middle English word "newe," meaning new. The name was given to newcomers.

Famous **News:** HARRY STEWART NEW (1858–1937) of Indiana was a journalist with the *Indianapolis Journal* and a U.S. senator, then U.S. postmaster general.

Genealogies: *The Families of Williams, Kenoyer, New, Motley* was compiled by Lola Bernice Frakes and published in Provo, Utah. *The Family of New: Genealogy and Descendants of Richard New, Immigrant to Virginia in 1637...* was compiled by Ann Wall Allgood and published in Natchez, Mississippi, in 1981.

NEWBERRY, NEWBERY (S.S. Abbreviation: Newber)
Ranking: 1760 **S.S. Count:** 25,496
Origin: English. Derived from the Old English words "nēowe" and "burh," meaning new and town. The names were given to those from Newberry, the name of several places in England.

Famous **Bearers:** OLIVER NEWBERRY (1789–1860) of Connecticut moved to Detroit and was a merchant and shipbuilder and one of the first to see the future in the location of Chicago, Illinois. He ran a fleet of lake ships from his adopted Midwest home and promoted growth and industry in the Detroit and Chicago areas. He was the brother of Walter. WALTER LOOMIS NEWBERRY (1804–1869) of Connecticut was a merchant who also moved to the Midwest, settling in Detroit, too. He built his fortune as a merchant and a land investor and in railroads and banking. He moved to Chicago and donated heavily to several worthwhile projects, including the Chicago Public Library, which carries his name. JOHN STRONG NEWBERRY (1822–1892) of Connecticut was a geologist and paleontologist. He was the state geologist of Ohio (1869–1874), a student of the fossils of New Jersey and the Connecticut Valley, and the author of *Paleozoic Fishes of North America* (1889). JOHN STOUGHTON NEWBERRY (1826–1887) of New York was a lawyer and the co-owner of the Michigan Car Co. He also was a railroad builder, banker, and real estate investor in Detroit. TRUMAN HANDY NEWBERRY (1864–1945) of Michigan was the son of John Stoughton Newberry and a U.S. senator who was found guilty of conspiracy to violate the Corrupt Practices Act. The Supreme Court narrowly overturned the conviction, but the Senate's investigation of his election practices expressed disapproval of him. He resigned in 1922.

Genealogies: *The Newberry Genealogy* was compiled by Helen Bourne Joy Lee and published in Chester, Connecticut, in 1975.

NEWBY
Ranking: 2841 S.S. Count: 16,072

Origin: English. Derived from the Middle English components "newe" and "by," meaning new and farm. The name was given to those from Newby, the name of several places in England.

Genealogies: *Descendants of Joshua and Ann Newby of West Virginia, 1833– 1904* was compiled by Elizabeth Parcher Walker and published in Manchester, Connecticut, in 1981.

NEWCOMBE, NEWCOME, NEWCOMER (S.S. Abbreviation: Newcom)
Ranking: 1344 S.S. Count: 32,905

Origin: English. Derived from the Middle English words "newe" and "come," meaning new and comer. The name was given to those who were new to an area.

Famous **Bearers**: CHRISTIAN NEWCOMER (1749?–1830) of Pennsylvania was one of the founders of the Church of the United Brethren in Christ.

Genealogies: *The Newcomer Families of Pennsylvania* was compiled by Manley William Mallett and published in Largo, Florida, in 1983. *All Those Newcomer Families of Maryland* was compiled by Manley William Mallett and published in Largo, Florida, in 1982.

NEWELL
Ranking: 953 S.S. Count: 45,620

Origin: English, Irish. Transformation of Nevill.

Famous **Newells**: HARRIET ATWOOD NEWELL (1793–1812) of Massachusetts was a pioneer missionary who, with her husband and other missionaries, was turned away from India by the British East India Co. They sailed on to the Isle of France (Mauritius Island) in the Indian Ocean. She, already weak because of poor health and the premature birth of her only child, died shortly after arrival. She is remembered as the first American to die in a foreign mission. ROBERT NEWELL (1807–1869) of Ohio was an Oregon pioneer. He was the co-author of the Oregon constitution and served as the provisional government's Speaker of the House for two sessions. WILLIAM AUGUSTUS NEWELL (1817–1901) of Ohio was a member of Congress from and governor of New Jersey and the governor of the Washington territory. He was very involved with the U.S. lifesaving service. WILLIAM WELLS NEWELL (1839–1907) of Massachusetts was the founder of the American Folk-Lore Society (1888). FREDERICK HAYNES NEWELL (1862–1932) of Pennsylvania was a hydraulic engineer. He wrote books on water supply and irrigation engineering. PETER SHEAF HERSEY NEWELL (1862–1924) of Illinois was a cartoonist and illustrator for *Harper's Weekly* and *Harper's Bazaar*. He also was the author and illustrator for the *Topsys and Turvys* and *Jungle Jangle*. EDWARD T. NEWELL (1886–1941) of Wisconsin was president for 25 years of the American Numismatic Society, to which he donated a large collection of Greek, Roman, and Byzantine coins.

Genealogies: *A Family Genealogical History* [also Newell] was compiled by Newell Beier Trakel and published in Waukesha, Wisconsin, in 1979. *The Kiehl/Manwarren Genealogy* [also Newell] was compiled by Margery Kiehl Hughes and published in Fort Wayne, Indiana, in 1991.

NEWHOUSE (S.S. Abbreviation: Newhou)
Ranking: 4973 S.S. Count: 9014

Origin: English. Derived from the Old English words "nōewe" and "hūs," meaning new and house. The name was given to those who lived in a new house.

Famous **Newhouses**: SAMUEL NEWHOUSE (1853–1930) of New York City was the force behind the building of the Argo Tunnel in Idaho Springs, Colorado. The tunnel is more commonly referred to as the Newhouse Tunnel. He also was involved in the beautification of Salt Lake City.

Genealogies: None known.

NEWKIRK (S.S. Abbreviation: Newkir)
Ranking: 2941 S.S. Count: 15,479

Origin: Scottish. Derived from the Old English words "nōewe" and "cirice," meaning new and church. The name was given to those who lived near a newly constructed church.

Genealogies: *Newkirk Family in North Carolina with Their Ancestors and Allied Families* was compiled by Elizabeth Newkirk and published in 1958.

NEWLAND, NEWLANDS (S.S. Abbreviation: Newlan)
Ranking: 3930 S.S. Count: 11,479

Origin: English. Derived from the Old English words "nōewe" and "land," meaning new and land. The name was given to those who lived near land newly acquired by a town or newly cultivated. It may also have been given to those from places called Newland.

Famous **Bearers**: FRANCIS GRIFFITH NEWLANDS (1848–

1917) of Mississippi was a politician from Nevada, which he represented in the U.S. House and Senate. He was responsible for the creation of the U.S. Reclamation Service, the Newlands Act, and the Federal Trade Commission.

Genealogies: *Ancestors and Descendants of Jacob H. Mendenhall and his Wife Hannah W. Newlin* [also Newland] *from the first Emigrants, Benjamin Mendenhall, England, and Nathaniel Newlin, Ireland, to Chester County, Pennsylvania, 1683* was compiled by Lillian Mendenhall Powell Jacobs and published in Sarasota, Florida, in 1983.

NEWMAN

Ranking: 249 S.S. Count: 144,937

Origin: English. Derived from the Middle English words "newe" and "man," meaning new and man. The name was given to newcomers.

Famous **Newmans:** HENRY NEWMAN (1670–1743) of Massachusetts was a philanthropist and a benefactor to both Harvard and Yale universities. He was also the colonial agent of New Hampshire. ANGELIA LOUISE FRENCH THURSTON KILGORE NEWMAN (1837–1910) of Vermont was responsible for the enactment of the Edmunds-Tucker Act of 1887, which rescinded Utah's legalization of polygamy. She then created a refuge in Salt Lake City for the cast-off wives and their children of the Mormons and set up the Industrial Christian Home Commission, which obtained congressional monies for the home's expenses. WILLIAM TRUSLOW NEWMAN (1843–1920) of Tennessee was a Confederate soldier, Atlanta attorney, and a U.S. judge of the northern district of Georgia. He was the father of Frances. HENRY RODERICK NEWMAN (1843?–1918) of New York was a painter of architectural pieces. FRANCES NEWMAN (1883–1928) of Georgia was an author and librarian. She was considered one of the up-and-coming authors, her style still developing when she died. She won an O. Henry Award for her short story "Rachel and Her Children." BARNETT NEWMAN (1905–1970) of New York City was an abstract painter of the expressionist movement. In 1948 he co-founded the Subject of the Artist school, which was known for simple forms and large color fields. WILLIAM RICHARD NEWMAN (1906–1977) of Mississippi was a lawyer and insurance company executive.

Genealogies: *The Newman Family: Descendants of Davis and Nancy Newman, 1780, Spartanburg County District, South Carolina* was compiled by William Alton Newman and published in Baltimore, Maryland, in 1992. *The Neumanns: Wisconsin Pioneers, 1848–1978* [also Newman] was compiled by Kathleen Neumann Graber and published in Oshkosh, Wisconsin, in 1978.

NEWSOM (ALSO NEWSOME)

Ranking: 938 S.S. Count: 46,059

Origin: English. Derived from the Old English phrase "nēowan hūsum," meaning at the new houses. The name was given to those from Newsome, the name of several places in England.

Famous **Bearers:** HUGH RAYMOND NEWSOM (1891–1978) was born to American missionary parents in India. He was a composer and concert manager. Some of his works were recorded by him.

Genealogies: *Possums Run over Their Graves* [also Newsom/Newsome] was compiled by Rebecca Newsom Dobson and published in Ozark, Missouri, in 1985. *The Descendants of James Newsome and His Wife Rebeca Illingworth in the United States of America* was compiled by Samuel Hendrixson Newsome and published in Chester, Pennsylvania, in 1976.

NEWTON

Ranking: 379 S.S. Count: 102,185

Origin: English. Derived from the Old English words "nēowe" and "tūn," meaning new and settlement. The name was given to those from Newton, the name of several places in England.

Famous **Newtons:** THOMAS NEWTON (1660–1721) of England was a colonial official. As the attorney general of the Massachusetts Colony, he prosecuted the Salem witchcraft trials. THOMAS NEWTON (1768–1847) of Virginia was a member of Congress from his state of birth. ISAAC NEWTON (1794–1858) of New York was a pioneer steamboat designer who introduced double-deck design and the burning of anthracite coal. ISAAC NEWTON (1800–1867) of New Jersey was responsible for the present-day U.S. Department of Agriculture. JOHN NEWTON (1823–1895) of Virginia was a Union major general in the Civil War but is best remembered as the engineer who was responsible for safe East River (New York City) travel because of the removal of dangerous obstructions. HENRY JOTHAM NEWTON (1823–1895) of Pennsylvania was a pioneer in dry-plate photography. HUBERT ANSON NEWTON (1830–1896) of New York was an astronomer and a pioneer in the study of meteoroids, meteors, and comets. He was an advocate of the use of the metric system. WILLIAM WILBERFORCE NEWTON (1843–1914) of Pennsylvania was an Episcopal preacher best known for his ability to reach children from the pulpit. JOSEPH FORT NEWTON (1876–1950) of Texas was a clergyman and author. He was world renowned as a preacher, servicing churches in both the United States and England. He was also a syndicated columnist.

Genealogies: *The Descendants of James Huston* [also Newton] was compiled by Edith Luella Houston Hurlbutt and published in Faribault, Minnesota, in 1967. *Genealogy of Newton-Forsyth* was compiled by Leo L. Lemonds and published in 1978.

NG

Ranking: 2026 S.S. Count: 22,544
Origin: Chinese. The name means crow and was given to those from Kiangsu, the name of a province of China.
Genealogies: None known.

NGO

Ranking: 4017 S.S. Count: 11,273
Origin: Vietnamese. Uncertain etymology. The name possibly means stupid, dull, to happen, violent, reckless, tough, or undisciplined.
Genealogies: None known.

NGUYEN

Ranking: 330 S.S. Count: 114,519
Origin: Vietnamese. Uncertain etymology. The name possibly means to swear, to pray, the origin, the source, or the cause.
Genealogies: *A Vietnamese Family Chronicle: Twelve Generations on the Banks of the Hat River* was compiled by Trieu Dan Nguyen and published in Jefferson, North Carolina, in 1991.

NICHOLAS, NICHOLES, NICHOLL, NICHOLLS, NICHOLSON (S.S. Abbreviation: Nichol)

Ranking: 76 S.S. Count: 336,895
Origin: Nicholes, Nicholl, Nicholls, Nicholson—English; Nicholas—English, Welsh. Derived from the Greek first name Nikolaos, which was derived from the words "nikān" and "laos," meaning to conquer and people.

Famous **Bearers:** FRANCIS NICHOLSON (1655–1728) of England was the lieutenant governor of Virginia. He was responsible for the establishment of postal service in Virginia and supported the establishment of William and Mary College. He then served the Crown as the governor of Maryland. There he supported education and established the capital in Annapolis. He continued his service to the Crown again as the governor of Virginia, then of South Carolina, but without the good results of the first two governorships. ROBERT CARTER NICHOLAS (1728–1780) apparently of Virginia was a colonial official, a Revolutionary War patriot, and the only man to oppose the adoption of the Declaration of Independence. JAMES NICHOLSON (1736?–1804) of Maryland was a Revolutionary War naval officer and a senior captain in the Continental navy. GEORGE NICHOLAS (1754?–1799) of Virginia was a Revolutionary War soldier and the first attorney general of Kentucky. He was one of the framers of the Kentucky Resolutions (1798) and a member of the committee that approved the first Kentucky constitution. WILSON CARY NICHOLAS (1761–1820) of Virginia was a Revolutionary War soldier, U.S. senator, member of Congress, and gover-

nor of the state of Virginia. JOSEPH HOPPER NICHOLSON (1770–1817) of Maryland was a member of Congress and a leader in the House. He was responsible for settlement in western Pennsylvania, Georgia, and at the new capital of Washington, D.C. ALFRED OSBORNE POPE NICHOLSON (1808–1876) of Tennessee was a promotor of Tennessee railroads. He served as a member of Congress and as a U.S. senator. JAMES WILLIAM AUGUSTUS NICHOLSON (1821–1887) of Massachusetts was active in the suppression of the slave trade in the years before the Civil War. WILLIAM THOMAS NICHOLSON (1834–1893) of Rhode Island was the owner of Nicholson File Co., which was the first company to manufacture machine-made files in the United States. FRANCIS REDDING TILLOU NICHOLLS (1834–1912) of Louisiana was a Confederate brigadier general, lawyer, governor of Louisiana, and chief justice of the state supreme court. ELIZA JANE POITEVENT HOLBROOK NICHOLSON (1849–1896) of Mississippi was a poet, journalist, and the first female publisher in the South of a daily newspaper (the New Orleans *Picayune*). She is credited with adding special sections to the newspaper for women and children, as she wanted the paper to be read by the entire family. In 1879 she added a society column; then she added household hints, fashion, theater news, comics, and even a complaint column, and on Sunday, she ran stories by the noted authors of the day. MEREDITH NICHOLSON (1866–1947) of Indiana was an author of verse and novels and a U.S. minister to several different South and Central American countries. SETH BARNES NICHOLSON (1891–1963) of Illinois was an astronomer and the discoverer of four satellites of Jupiter.

Genealogies: *The Nicholases of Pennsylvania in the Civil War 1861–1865* was compiled by Jerry F. Peter and published in Wilmington, Delaware, in 1968.

NICKEL (ALSO NICKELL, NICKELLS, NICKELS, NICKELSEN)

Ranking: 1420 S.S. Count: 31,329
Origin: Nickel, Nickell, Nickells, Nickels—English; Nickel, Nickell—English, Welsh; Nickelsen—German. Transformations of Nicholas.

Genealogies: *The Story of Benjamin Nickel* was compiled by Phyllis Ferrara and published in Chicago, Illinois, in 1971. *History of the Nickell Family* was compiled by Joe Nickell and published in Topeka, Kansas, in 1932.

NICKERSON (S.S. Abbreviation: Nicker)

Ranking: 1926 S.S. Count: 23,461
Origin: English. Transformation of Nicholas.

Genealogies: *Ancestors and Descendants of Helen Albion Mayhew* [also Nickerson] was compiled by Vernon Roscoe Nickerson and published in Taunton, Massachusetts, in 1971. *The Nickerson Family: The Descendants of William*

Nickerson, 1604–1690, First Settler of Chatham, Mass. was compiled by The Nickerson Family Association and published in 1976.

NICKLE (ALSO NICKLESON, NICKLESS)
Ranking: 4277 S.S. Count: 10,517
Origin: Nickleson—English; Nickle, Nickless—English, Welsh. Transformations of Nicholas.
Genealogies: None known.

NICOLA (ALSO NICOLAI, NICOLAIDES, NICOLAISEN, NICOLAS)
Ranking: 2816 S.S. Count: 16,182
Origin: Nicolas—English, French, Spanish, Welsh; Nicolaisen—Danish, German, Norwegian; Nicolaides—Greek; Nicola, Nicolai—Italian. Transformations of and cognates to Nicholas.
Famous **Bearers:** LEWIS NICOLA (1717–1807) of either France or Ireland was a merchant, editor, and Revolutionary War soldier. He arrived in Philadelphia around 1766 from Ireland. His claim to fame is his proposal to George Washington in May 1782 that the ruling body of the United States be that of a monarchy, with Washington as the king.
Genealogies: None known.

NIEDER (ALSO NIEDERER, NIEDERMAN, NIEDERMANN)
Ranking: 4019 S.S. Count: 11,269
Origin: Nieder—German, Jewish; Niederer, Niedermann—German; Niederman—Jewish. Derived from the German word "nieder," meaning lower. The names were given to those who lived at the lower end of a town.
Genealogies: None known.

NIELSEN (S.S. Abbreviation: Nielse)
Ranking: 728 S.S. Count: 58,150
Origin: Danish, Norwegian. Transformation of Neil.
Famous **Nielsens:** ALICE NIELSEN (1870?–1943) of Tennessee was an opera and concert singer. She sang in England, Italy, Boston, and New York.
Genealogies: *Descendants of Hans Jorgen Thomsen and Ane Kjerstine Ditlevsen of Klejs, Denmark* [also Nielsen] was compiled by Frances Hansen Ehrig and published in Richland, Washington, in 1962.

NIELSON (S.S. Abbreviation: Nielso)
Ranking: 3621 S.S. Count: 12,452
Origin: English. Transformation of Neil.
Genealogies: *Our Norwegian Forefathers and Their American Descendants* [also Nielson] was compiled by Ruby Sather Freid and published in Ingelwood, California, in 1971.

NIEMAN (ALSO NIEMANN)
Ranking: 3516 S.S. Count: 12,830
Origin: Dutch, Flemish. Cognates to Newman.
Genealogies: *The Nieman Family Tree* was compiled by Raymond L. Nodurft and published in Wyoming, Iowa, in 1976.

NIETO
Ranking: 3303 S.S. Count: 13,723
Origin: Spanish. Derived from the Spanish word "nieto," meaning grandson. The name was given to the grandson or descendant of an important person.
Genealogies: None known.

NIEVES
Ranking: 695 S.S. Count: 60,540
Origin: Spanish. Derived from the phrase "Maria de las Nieves," meaning Mary of the Snows, referring to the Virgin Mary.
Genealogies: None known.

NILES
Ranking: 3404 S.S. Count: 13,307
Origin: English. Transformation of Neil.
Famous **Nileses:** SAMUEL NILES (1674–1762) of Rhode Island was a clergyman, historian, and the author of "A Summary Historic Narrative of the Wars in New England with the French and Indians," which is in *Collections of the Massachusetts Historical Society.* NATHANIEL NILES (1741–1828) of Rhode Island was a member of Congress from Vermont. HEZEKIAH NILES (1777–1839) of Pennsylvania was the founder and editor of the *Weekly Register,* a very pro-Union paper of the times. JOHN MILTON NILES (1787–1856) of Connecticut was a U.S. senator from that state. He also served for a short time as the U.S. postmaster general. NATHANIEL NILES (1791–1868) of Vermont was a diplomat who represented the United States in European countries. EMORY HAMILTON NILES (1892–1976) of Maryland was the chief judge of the Supreme Bench of Baltimore. He co-founded and edited *American Maritime Cases* and *United States Aviation Reports.*
Genealogies: *Sixteen Couples: Stories about the Lives and Times of Thirty-Two People* [also Niles] was compiled by P. Parker and published in Boston, Massachusetts, in 1980.

NIX
Ranking: 1321 S.S. Count: 33,687
Origin: English, German. Transformation of and cognate to Nicholas.
Genealogies: *The Descendants of Edward Nix of Oglethorpe County, Georgia and Butler County, Alabama* was compiled by Fern Sulphin Nix and published in Grenville, Alabama, in 1973.

NIXON

Ranking: 804 S.S. Count: 52,367

Origin: English, Irish, Scottish. Derived from the Middle English first name Nik(ke), which was derived from Nicholas.

Famous **Nixons**: JOHN NIXON (1727–1815) of Massachusetts was a Revolutionary War soldier who fought in the battles of Lexington, Concord, and Bunker Hill and was wounded at the last one. JOHN NIXON (1733–1808) of Pennsylvania was a Revolutionary War patriot and the president of the Bank of North America. JOHN THOMPSON NIXON (1820–1889) of New Jersey was a jurist and a U.S. district judge in New Jersey. WILLIAM PENN NIXON (1833–1912) of Indiana was a journalist who edited the Chicago *Inter Ocean*. RICHARD MILHOUS NIXON (1913–1994) of California was the 37th president of the United States. He previously was a member of Congress (1947–1950), U.S. senator (1951–1953), and vice president of the United States (1953–1961) under Dwight D. Eisenhower. Nixon first ran for president in 1960 but lost to John F. Kennedy. He then retired to California, where he ran for governor in 1962. Upon losing this election he lashed out at the press, telling them they wouldn't have Nixon "to kick around any more," then vowed to leave politics forever. In 1968 he returned from political oblivion to win the presidency against vice president Hubert H. Humphrey and governor George C. Wallace of Alabama. In 1972 he was reelected in a landslide, carrying 49 states. Nixon resigned the presidency on August 9, 1974 (the only president to do so), to avoid certain impeachment over the Watergate scandal, then received a full pardon from his successor, president Gerald R. Ford.

Genealogies: *The Ancestry of Richard Milhous Nixon* was compiled by Raymond Martin Bell and published in Washington, Pennsylvania, in 1970. *Nixon Family Memorials* was compiled by Jean White Cox and published in Connellsville, Pennsylvania, in 1970. *The Nixons: An American Family* was compiled by Edwin Palmer Hoyt and published in New York, New York, in 1972.

NOBLE

Ranking: 734 S.S. Count: 57,855

Origin: English, French, Jewish, Scottish. English, French, Scottish: derived from the Middle English and French words "noble," meaning distinguished or high-born. The name was given to those who acted nobly or, ironically, to those of low birth. Jewish: 1) Anglicization of the German name Knöbel, meaning servant. 2) possibly an Anglicization of the name Knobel, meaning garlic.

Famous **Nobles**: JAMES NOBLE (1783–1831) of Virginia was one of the settlers and organizers of the state of Indiana. He represented the state as a U.S. senator (1816–1831). JOHN WILLOCK NOBLE (1831–1912) of Ohio was the initiator of the National Parks policy. FREDERICK ALPHONSO

NOBLE (1832–1917) of Maine was the pastor of the Union Park Church in Chicago (1879–1901). SAMUEL NOBLE (1834–1888) of England came to the United States as a child. The family settled in Georgia. He was the founder and manager of the Woodstock Iron Co. at Anniston, Alabama, a small, rural town near the Georgia-Alabama line. He considered Anniston the "model city" of the new South. He was very generous toward the town in philanthropic works. ALFRED NOBLE (1844–1914) of Michigan was a civil engineer involved with the building of the Panama Canal. GLADWYN KINGSLEY NOBLE (1894–1940) of New York was a biologist who specialized in animal behavior.

Genealogies: *The Roots and Branches of Timothy and Susanna Noble, Delaware County, Iowa, 1650–1987* was compiled by Helen Sue Taylor and published in Hoagland, Indiana, in 1987. *The Russian Rockefellers: The Saga of the Nobel Family and the Russian Oil Industry* [also Noble] was compiled by Robert W. Tolf and published in Stanford, California, in 1976.

NOBLES

Ranking: 2599 S.S. Count: 17,495

Origin: English. Transformation of Noble.

Genealogies: None known.

NOE

Ranking: 2902 S.S. Count: 15,685

Origin: English. Transformation of Noyes.

Genealogies: *Abraham Noe (c. 1755–1803) of New Jersey and His Descendants* was compiled by William Amel Sausaman and published in Springfield, Illinois, in 1973.

NOEL

Ranking: 1290 S.S. Count: 34,312

Origin: English, French. Derived from the Middle English and Old French words "no(u)el," meaning Christmas.

Genealogies: *Eighty Years in America* [Noel Family] was compiled by Leland Noel and published in Salt Lake City, Utah, in 1962. *The Hardys of Louisiana and their Ancestors* [also Noel] was compiled by Grace L. Hardy and published in Baltimore, Maryland, in 1985.

NOLAN

Ranking: 641 S.S. Count: 64,923

Origin: Irish. Derived from the Gaelic name Ó Nualláin, which was derived from the first name Nuallán, which was derived from the word "nuall," meaning famous.

Famous **Nolans**: PHILIP NOLAN (1771?–1801) of Kentucky was a "back alley" horse trader in Texas who was accused by the Mexicans of being a spy. He was killed resisting arrest.

Genealogies: *Descendants of Cornet George Barton in Ireland and the United States with Allied Nolan/Lalor/Kinsella Lines in Ireland and the United States* was compiled by

Louise Egan Peterson and published in Decorah, Iowa, in 1986. *In the Mood for Stardom: The Nolans* was compiled by Kim Treasurer and published in New York, New York, in 1982.

NOLAND

Ranking: 3438 S.S. Count: 13,125
Origin: Irish. Transformation of Nolan.
Famous **Nolands:** EDGAR SMITH NOLAND (1902–1971) of Ohio was an investment banker and bank president.
Genealogies: *The Nolen Story* [also Noland] was compiled by Jewell Nolen and published in Cookeville, Tennessee, in 1976.

NOLEN

Ranking: 2977 S.S. Count: 15,280
Origin: Irish. Transformation of Nolan.
Famous **Nolens:** JOHN NOLEN (1869–1937) of Pennsylvania was a landscape architect and town planner.
Genealogies: *The Nolen Story* was compiled by Jewell Nolen and published in Cookeville, Tennessee, in 1976.

NOLL

Ranking: 3130 S.S. Count: 14,506
Origin: German. Derived from several Germanic names ending with the component "wald," meaning rule.
Genealogies: None known.

NOONAN

Ranking: 2450 S.S. Count: 18,529
Origin: Irish. Derived from the Gaelic name Ó hIonmhaineáin, which was derived from the first name Ionmhaineán, which was derived from the word "ionmhain," meaning beloved.
Famous **Noonans:** FRED J. NOONAN (1893–1937) of Illinois was an aviator and Amelia Earhart's companion on her fateful flight.
Genealogies: None known.

NORDSTROM (S.S. Abbreviation: Nordst)

Ranking: 4978 S.S. Count: 9004
Origin: Swedish. The name means north river.
Genealogies: None known.

NORIEGA (S.S. Abbreviation: Norieg)

Ranking: 4913 S.S. Count: 9108
Origin: Spanish. Uncertain etymology. The name was given to those from Noriega, a place in Spain.
Genealogies: None known.

NORMAN (ALSO NORMAND, NORMANN, NORMANT)

Ranking: 388 S.S. Count: 99,877
Origin: Norman—English, Jewish, Swedish; Normand—English, French; Normant—French; Normann—German. Norman (English): derived from the word "norðmenn," meaning "men from the North" (H&H). The name was given to Scandinavian settlers or to those from Normandy, France. Norman (Jewish): uncertain etymology. Norman (Swedish): cognate to North. Normand: transformation of and cognate to the English Norman. Normant: cognate to the English Norman. Normann: cognate to North.
Famous **Bearers:** JOHN NORMAN (1748–1817) of England was an engraver and publisher and is best remembered as the publisher of *Boston Magazine* and *Boston Directory.* MABEL ETHELREID NORMAND (1893?–1930) of either Rhode Island or Massachusetts was a silent-screen star and comedienne. She appeared with Charlie Chaplin in 11 pictures, including *Mabel's Strange Predicament,* in which his tramp character was first seen. Her career ended with the scandalous death of William Desmond Taylor, a director whom she was the last one to see alive. She retired shortly thereafter.
Genealogies: *Norman Genealogy* was compiled by William Ernest Norman and published in Norfolk, Virginia, in 1976. *The Normans, 1720–1976* was compiled by Maggie Laurie Carson and published in Tuscaloosa, Alabama, in 1976.

NORRIS (ALSO NORRISH)

Ranking: 288 S.S. Count: 124,934
Origin: English, Scottish. 1) derived from the Old English words "norð" and "hūs," meaning north and house. The name was given to those whose houses were on the north side of a town or village. 2) derived from the Old French word "nurice," meaning wet nurse. The name was given to wet nurses. 3) derived from the Old French word "nor(r)eis," meaning northerner. The name was given to those from the north of any given region.
Famous **Bearers:** EDWARD NORRIS (1584–1659) of England was the assistant to Hugh Peter (a religious leader and one of the founders of Harvard University) at the Congregational church in Salem, Massachusetts. ISAAC NORRIS (1671–1735) of England was a member of the Pennsylvania Political Caretakers. He served, among other posts, as the mayor of Philadelphia. ISAAC NORRIS (1701–1766) of Pennsylvania is best remembered as the man who suggested the inscription on the Liberty Bell. WILLIAM NORRIS (1801–1867) of Maryland was a world-renowned builder of locomotives and the co-founder of the American Steam Carriage Co. GEORGE WILLIAM NORRIS (1861–1944) of Ohio was a U.S. senator and member of Congress from Nebraska. He fought for the Tennessee Valley Authority system of dams to be built, and the first was was named Norris Dam in his honor. He was the author of the 20th amendment to the Constitution and the co-author of the

Norris-LaGuardia Act (1932). BENJAMIN FRANKLIN NORRIS (1870–1902) of Illinois went by the name of Frank. He worked as a war correspondent for newspapers and magazines before becoming a novelist. He was considered a pioneer in American naturalism. KATHLEEN THOMPSON NORRIS (1880–1966) of California was a writer of short stories, magazine articles, and novels. Her novels include *The Sea Gull* (1927) and *Through a Glass Darkly* (1955). CHARLES GILMAN NORRIS (1881–1945) was a magazine editor and writer. He was the brother of Frank Norris.

Genealogies: *Descendants of Isaac Patten, Sr., and his Wife, Jane Norris: an Early Pioneer Family in Sullivan County, Indiana* was compiled by Ernest C. Swanson and published in Baltimore, Maryland, in 1985. *Norris, Hackett, Prescott and Allied Families* was compiled by Hugh Albert Johnson and published in Annandale, Virginia, in 1976.

NORTH

Ranking: 1589 **S.S. Count:** 28,152

Origin: English, Irish. English: derived from the Old English word "norð," meaning north. The name was given to those who lived in the northern area of a settlement or north of the settlement itself. Irish: derived from the Gaelic name Mac an Ultaigh, meaning "son of the Ulsterman" (H&H). The name was given to those from Ulster, which is located in the northern part of Ireland.

Famous **Norths:** SIMEON NORTH (1765–1852) of Connecticut was a firearms manufacturer. In 1825 he developed a 10-round repeating rifle and developed interchangeable parts in manufacturing simultneously with Eli Whitney (1798). ELISHA NORTH (1771–1843) of Connecticut established the first eye clinic in the United States in New London, Connecticut, and was the first to publish a study on cerebrospinal meningitis. FRANK JOSHUA NORTH (1840–1885) of New York was a soldier and frontiersman. He moved to Nebraska and learned the customs and language of the Pawnee Indians. He led the Pawnees in raids against other Indians, railroad workers, and U.S. forts. He was a member of Buffalo Bill's Wild West Show and was billed as the best shot with a revolver in the show, as he had beaten "Wild Bill" in competition.

Genealogies: *John North of Farmington, Connecticut, and his Descendants* was compiled by Dexter North and published in Washington, D.C., in 1921.

NORTHCOTE, NORTHCOTT (S.S. Abbreviation: Northc)

Ranking: 3767 **S.S. Count:** 12,028

Origin: English. Derived from the Old English words "norð" and "cot," meaning north and cottage. The name was given to those from Northcott, the name of several places in England.

Genealogies: None known.

NORTHROP, NORTHRUP, NORTHRIP (S.S. Abbreviation: Northr)

Ranking: 3192 **S.S. Count:** 14,222

Origin: English. Derived from the Old English word "norð," meaning north and a word meaning farm. The name was given to those from Northorpe, a place in Lincolnshire, England.

Famous **Bearers:** LUCIUS BELLINGER NORTHROP (1811–1894) of South Carolina was a Civil War soldier who, after being permanently wounded, was given the task of finding food for the southern soldiers and their northern prisoners. Not doing a difficult job well earned him considerable criticism. BIRDSEY GRANT NORTHROP (1817–1898) of Connecticut was involved with the Massachusetts and Connecticut boards of education and was a supporter of Arbor Day and of Japanese-American peace. CYRUS NORTHROP (1834–1922) of Connecticut was the president of the University of Minnesota and received wide recognition for his accomplishments in that capacity. JOHN KNUDSEN NORTHROP (1895–1981) of New Jersey was an engineer who helped to found Lockheed Corp. He was the founder of Avion Corp., Northrop Corp., and Northrop Aircraft.

Genealogies: *Cartwright-Northrip and Allied Families* [also Northrup] was compiled by Lloyd Jay Cartwright and published in 1981.

NORTON

Ranking: 433 **S.S. Count:** 91,573

Origin: English. 1) transformation of the English name Norrington, which was a) derived from the Old English words "norðin tūne," meaning those residing to the north of the principal settlement; or b) given to those from Northampton, meaning north and settlement, water meadow, or high. 2) transformation of the Irish surname Naughton, which was derived from the Gaelic first name Neachtan, meaning the sea god. 3) derived from the Old English words "norð" and "tūn," meaning north and settlement. The name was given to those from Norton, the name of several places in England.

Famous **Nortons:** JOHN NORTON (1606–1663) of England came to America as a Puritan clergyman. He was one of the leaders in the persecution of the Quakers. He also wrote the first Latin book written in America but published in England, called *Responsio ad totam quaestionum syllogen*. ANDREWS NORTON (1786–1853) of Massachusetts was the author of one of the earliest studies of the Bible from a critical viewpoint. CHARLES ELIOT NORTON (1827–1908) of Massachusetts was an author and editor. He founded *The Nation* and lived within the social and literary circle that included Ralph Waldo Emerson and Henry Wadsworth Longfellow. CHARLES HOTCHKISS NORTON (1851–1942) of Connecticut was a mechanical engineer who built the first heavy grinding machine in the United

States. He produced machinery that reduced the price and improved the efficiency of automobiles. ALICE PELOUBET NORTON (1860–1928) of Massachusetts was a teacher of home economics. She was one of the pioneers in elevating the area of home economics from its previously menial position. MARY TERESA HOPKINS NORTON (1875–1959) of New Jersey was a member of Congress from her home state (1925–1951). She chaired the Labor Committee and was responsible for the passage of the Fair Labor Standards Act, which sets minimum wages and maximum working hours for most businesses, and equal pay for equal work as a matter of law. During World War II she worked for federal funds for day-care centers and continued to support them through her backing of the Lanham Act. She is best remembered as a champion of the working class. WILLIAM WARDER NORTON (1891–1945) of Ohio was a book publisher who founded the People's Institute Publishing Co. and W. W. Norton and Company. SKEFFINGTON SANXAY NORTON (1899–1977) of New York was a shipping executive at Norton, Lilly & Co., a merchant and charter sailing company founded in 1841 by John S. Norton.

Genealogies: *Generations Back: Norton & Related Lines* was compiled by Sarah Mills Norton and published in Walhalla, South Carolina, in 1977. *The Nortons from the Norman Conquest through the Settlement of Guilford, Connecticut* was compiled by Harold George Gibboney and published in Athens, Ohio, in 1966.

NORWOOD (S.S. Abbreviation: Norwoo)

Ranking: 1457 **S.S. Count:** 30,554

Origin: English. Derived from the Old English words "norð" and "wudu," meaning north and wood. The name was given to those from Norwood, the name of several places in England.

Famous **Norwoods:** ROBERT WINKWORTH NORWOOD (1874–1932) of Nova Scotia was a well-known Episcopal preacher in Canada, Pennsylvania, and New York City.

Genealogies: *Francis Norwood, Immigrant to Massachusetts, and His Descendants, 1635–1987* was compiled by Maureen Norwood and published in Baltimore, Maryland, in 1987.

NOVAK

Ranking: 849 **S.S. Count:** 50,298

Origin: Czech. Derived from the Czech word "nový," meaning new. The name was given to those who were new to an area or to those who made new shoes.

Genealogies: *The Family of Vaclav Sobotka and Ann Novak in America* was compiled by Margie Sobotka and published in Omaha, Nebraska, in 1978.

NOVOTNY (S.S. Abbreviation: Novotn)

Ranking: 4252 **S.S. Count:** 10,594

Origin: Czech. Transformation of Novak.
Genealogies: None known.

NOWAK

Ranking: 1707 **S.S. Count:** 26,172

Origin: German, Jewish, Polish. Cognates to Novak.
Genealogies: None known.

NOWICK

Ranking: 4676 **S.S. Count:** 9573

Origin: Polish? Uncertain etymology. Most likely a cognate to Novak.
Genealogies: None known.

NOWLIN

Ranking: 4137 **S.S. Count:** 10,938

Origin: Irish. Transformation of Nolan.
Genealogies: None known.

NOYES

Ranking: 3259 **S.S. Count:** 13,594

Origin: English. Derived from the Middle English first name Noye, which was derived from the masculine Hebrew first name Noach (Noah), meaning "long-lived"(H&H).

Famous **Noyeses:** JOHN HUMPHREY NOYES (1811–1886) of Vermont studied to become a minister. He felt that he had reached spiritual perfection and formed a group of Bible communalists in 1836. His beliefs on marriage and free love were against the secular law, and he was arrested in 1846. The group led by him fled to New York state and set up the Oneida Community. The group grew and abandoned their unorthodox ways, supporting themselves through the manufacture of traps and silverware. Noyes later fled to Canada to escape jail for adultery. LA VERNE NOYES (1849–1919) of New York was an inventor who is credited with the wire dictionary holder. He also improved farm machinery and windmills. WILLIAM ALBERT NOYES (1857–1941) of Iowa was the first chief chemist of the U.S. Bureau of Standards. ALEXANDER DANA NOYES (1862–1945) of New Jersey was a financial editor with the New York *Evening Post* who foresaw the crash of 1929 and the Depression as many as three years before the events occurred. WALTER CHADWICK (1865–1926) of Lyme, Connecticut, was a lawyer and a U.S. circuit judge of the second judicial circuit. ARTHUR AMOS NOYES (1866–1936) of Massachusetts was a chemist and the founder of the Laboratory of Physcial Chemistry at California Institute of Technology. He is also known for his work on electrolyte solutions. CLARA DUTTON NOYES (1869–1936) of Maryland was a nurse and the director of the department of nursing services of the American Red Cross.

Genealogies: None known.

NUGENT

Ranking: 2084 S.S. Count: 22,014

Origin: English, Irish. Derived from a Gaulish word meaning new town. The name was given to those from several northern French towns with similar-sounding names.

Famous **Nugents:** JOHN FROST NUGENT (1868–1931) of Oregon was the defense lawyer for W. D. Haywood, a labor union agitator acquitted of the murder of Governor F.R. Steunenberg. He then served as the U.S. senator from Idaho and was a member of the Federal Trade Commission. JOHN CHARLES NUGENT (1878–1947) of Ohio was a vaudeville actor. ELLIOTT NUGENT (1899–1980) of Ohio was the son of John Charles. He was an actor and playwright on Broadway.

Genealogies: None known.

NULL

Ranking: 4275 S.S. Count: 10,525

Origin: German. Derived from a word meaning hill. The name was given to those who lived on or beside a hill.

Genealogies: None known.

NUNES

Ranking: 646 S.S. Count: 64,441

Origin: Portuguese. Uncertain etymology. Derived from a medieval first name of unknown origin.

Genealogies: None known.

NUNLEY

Ranking: 3729 S.S. Count: 12,119

Origin: English. Derived from the Old English words "nunne" aned "lēah," meaning nun and wood or clearing.

Genealogies: None known.

NUNN

Ranking: 2050 S.S. Count: 22,320

Origin: English. Derived from the Old English word "nunn" meaning nun. The name was given to those who were in the employ of a convent or to those who were pious.

Genealogies: *Nunn Families of Northeast Georgia* was compiled by D. C. Nunn and published in Marietta, Georgia, in 1991. *Nunns of the South* was compiled by Alexander Nunn and published in Loachapoka, Alabama, in 1974.

NUTT

Ranking: 4050 S.S. Count: 11,164

Origin: English. Derived from the Middle English word "not(e)," meaning nut. The name was given to those who harvested or sold nuts or to those thought to resemble a nut.

Genealogies: *The Nutt Family through the Years* was compiled by Merle C. Nutt and published in Phoenix, Arizona, in 1973.

NUTTER

Ranking: 3746 S.S. Count: 12,086

Origin: English. 1) derived from the Middle English word "notere," meaning clerk. The name was given to clerks or scribes. 2) derived from the Middle English word "nowt," meaning beast or ox. The name was given to those who kept oxen.

Genealogies: None known.

NYE

Ranking: 2750 S.S. Count: 16,579

Origin: English. Derived from the Middle English phrase "atten (e)ye," meaning "at the river" and "at the island" (H&H). The name was given to those who lived in such places.

Famous **Nyes:** JAMES WARREN NYE (1814–1876) of New York was the territorial governor of Nevada and a U.S. senator from that state. EDGAR WILSON NYE (1850–1896) of Maine was best known as Bill. He was a humorist who went west and founded and edited the *Laramie Boomerang.* His pieces later appeared in books.

Genealogies: *A Genealogy of American Nyes of English Origin* was compiled by Luther Bertram Nye and published in East Sandwich, Massachusetts, in 1980.

OAKES

Ranking: 1810 S.S. Count: 24,911
Origin: English. Transformation of Oaks.
Famous **Oakeses:** URIAN OAKES (1631?–
1681), probably of England, was brought to
America as a boy and became a Congregational
clergyman. He was the leader of the group that ousted an
unpopular Leonard Hoar from the presidency of Harvard
University. He assumed Hoar's position and was eventually
elected to it. GEORGE WASHINGTON OCHS OAKES (1861–
1931) of Ohio was a newspaper editor with the
Chattanooga Daily Times and a civic leader in that city,
serving as its mayor.
Genealogies: *Oakes and Relatives* was compiled by Fred
Arthur Oakes and published in Minneapolis, Minnesota, in
1974. *The Oakes Diaries* was compiled by James Oakes and
published in Rochester, New York, in 1991.

OAKLEY

Ranking: 1864 S.S. Count: 24,278
*Origin: English. Derived from the Old English compo-
nents "āc" and "lēah," meaning oak and clearing. The name
was given to those from Oakley, the name of several places in
England.*
Famous **Oakleys:** THOMAS JACKSON OAKLEY (1783–
1857) of New York was a member of Congress and judge,
then chief justice of the New York City Superior Court.
ANNIE OAKLEY (1860–1926) of Ohio, a frontierswoman,
was originally named Phoebe Anne Oakley Moses. She
toured in vaudeville shows and was one of the stars of Buffalo Bill's Wild West Show.
Genealogies: *The Descendants of William & Mary
Simms: England to Illinois and Beyond* was compiled by
Vivian York Simms and published in Murfreesboro, Tennessee, in 1989.

OAKS

Ranking: 4983 S.S. Count: 8999
*Origin: English. Derived from the Old English word "āc,"
meaning oak. The name was given to those who lived near an
oak tree or a wood of oak.*
Genealogies: None known.

OATES

Ranking: 3057 S.S. Count: 14,841
*Origin: English. Derived from the Middle English first
name Ode, a name that was derived from several first names
of different origin.*
Famous **Oateses:** WILLIAM CALVIN OATES (1835–1910)
of Alabama was a Confederate soldier, a member of Congress from Alabama, and then its governor.
Genealogies: *The Art of Collecting Genealogy and History* was compiled by Addison Ford Oates and
published in 1971. *Oates-Earle and Related
Families* was compiled by William L. Win-
barger and published in Graham, Kentucky, in
1972.

O'BRIEN

Ranking: 207 S.S. Count: 170,087
Origin: Irish. Cognate to Bryan.
Famous **O'Briens:** JEREMIAH O'BRIEN (1744–1818) of
Maine was the leader of 40 Revolutionary War patriots
who overtook and captured the *Margaretta*, a ship of the
royal navy, on June 12, 1775. He was part of the Massachusetts navy until the fall of 1776, when he became a privateer. He was captured by the British and imprisoned in
England, but he escaped and returned to New England to
continue his patriotic deeds. WILLIAM SHONEY O'BRIEN
(1826–1878) of Ireland was a silver-mine operator in
Nebraska. FITZ-JAMES O'BRIEN (1828?–1862) of Ireland was
a writer of plays and stories for magazines. His work was
considered some of the first science fiction. MORGAN
JOSEPH O'BRIEN (1852–1937) was a lawyer and the person
responsible for the New York City Charter revision of 1936.
FREDERICK O'BRIEN (1869–1932) of Maryland was a jour-
nalist and the author of travel books. CECIL STARLING
O'BRIEN (1889–1977) of Indiana was an ophthalmologist
who founded and headed the Department of Ophthalmol-
ogy at the University of Iowa School of Medicine. EDWARD
JOSEPH O'BRIEN (1890–1941) was an author and editor and
the compiler and editor of *The Best Short Stories* and *The
Best British Short Stories.*
Genealogies: *Shamrocks and Fleurs-de-lis: A Louisiana
Genealogy of the O'Brien, Mendoza, Verret, de la Chaise,
Chauvin, and Allied Families* was compiled by Leland Dud-
ley O'Brien and published in Eunice, Louisiana, in 1983.

O'BRYAN

Ranking: 3356 S.S. Count: 13,507
Origin: Irish. Cognate to Bryan.
Genealogies: None known.

OCASIO

Ranking: 2384 S.S. Count: 19,064
*Origin: Italian?, Spanish? Uncertain etymology. Possibly
derived from the Latin word "occasio," meaning without force.*
Genealogies: None known.

OCHOA

Ranking: 1296 S.S. Count: 34,166
*Origin: Spanish. Derived from the Basque first name
Otxoa, which is most likely derived from the Basque word
"otso," meaning wolf.*
Genealogies: None known.

O'CONNELL (S.S. Abbreviation: Oconne)

Ranking: 742 S.S. Count: 57,144

Origin: Irish. Transformation of Connell.

Famous **O'Connells:** SISTER ANTHONY O'CONNELL (1814–1897) of Ireland was christened Mary O'Connell. As is the case with Roman Catholic nuns, her first name was changed to the name of a saint she admired. Sister Anthony worked as a Civil War nurse in the Cincinnati area. WILLIAM HENRY O'CONNELL (1859–1944) of Massachusetts was a Roman Catholic priest who was the rector of the American College in Rome. He rose through the ranks of the church to the position of cardinal (1911).

Genealogies: None known.

O'CONNOLLY, O'CONNOR (S.S. Abbreviation: O'Conno)

Ranking: 347 S.S. Count: 109,253

Origin: Irish. O'Connolly: transformation of Connolly. O'Connor: transformation of Connor.

Famous **Bearers:** CHARLES O'CONNOR (1804–1884) of New York City was a lawyer and the special deputy attorney general for the state of New York in the trial of William M. Tweed. He was nominated for president of the United States by the Straight-Out Democrats (1872). MICHAEL O'CONNOR (1810–1872) of Ireland was the brother of James and also a Roman Catholic priest. He served as the bishop of two dioceses in Pennsylvania before becoming a Jesuit and doing missionary work within the United States. JAMES O'CONNOR (1823–1890) of Ireland was a Roman Catholic priest who was the first bishop of Omaha. He was the brother of Michael. WILLIAM DOUGLAS O'CONNOR (1832–1889) of Massachusetts was a journalist and benefactor of Walt Whitman. [MARY] FLANNERY O'CONNOR (1925–1964) of Georgia was a writer of novels, including *A Good Man Is Hard to Find* (1955).

Genealogies: *The Flow of Time: The Allisons & the Conners, with Related Branches of Southwest Virginia* [also O'Connor] was compiled by Laura Allison Carrothers and published in Fresno, California, in 1989.

ODELL

Ranking: 997 S.S. Count: 43,974

Origin: English. Derived from the Old English words "wād" and "hyll," meaning woad (a kind of plant) and hill. The name was given to those from Odell, a place in England.

Famous **Odells:** JONATHAN ODELL (1737–1818) of New Jersey was a surgeon and a Loyalist during the Revolutionary War. He was one of Benedict Arnold's contacts in correspondence with the British. BENJAMIN BARKER ODELL (1854–1926) of New York was the man who suggested to Theodore Roosevelt that he run for the governorship of New York. He later served well in that same capacity. GEORGE CLINTON DENSMORE ODELL (1866–1949) of New York was an educator and historian of the theater. He

taught at Columbia University and was the author of the 15-volume *Annals of the New York Stage* (1927–1949).

Genealogies: *Through the Hourglass: A History of the Families of Russell Turner Odell and Florence Turner Odell* was compiled by R. T. Odell and published in Champaign, Illinois, in 1980. *Twelve Families, an American Experience* [also O'Dell] was compiled by William F. O'Dell and published in Baltimore, Maryland, in 1981.

ODEN

Ranking: 4167 S.S. Count: 10,844

Origin: English. Transformation of Oates.

Genealogies: None known.

ODOM

Ranking: 910 S.S. Count: 47,400

Origin: English. Derived from the Old English word "āðum," meaning son-in-law. The name was given to those with an important father-in-law.

Genealogies: *My Mother Nancy and her Oldhams* [also Odom] was compiled by Jessye Ann High and published in Sunnyvale, California, in 1978. *A Genealogy of the Little-Odom Family of Georgia and North Carolina* was compiled by Lawrence L. Little and published in Creve Coeur, Missouri, in 1974.

O'DONNELL, O'DONNELLY (S.S. Abbreviation: Odonne)

Ranking: 651 S.S. Count: 64,022

Origin: O'Donnell—Irish, Scottish; O'Donelly—Irish. O'Donnell: transformation of Donald. O'Donnelly: transformation of Donnelly.

Famous **Bearers:** THOMAS JEFFERSON O'DONNELL (1856–1925) of New Jersey was a lawyer who moved to Denver, Colorado, and tried several times to be elected to public office.

Genealogies: *O'Donnell-Miller and Associated Families* was compiled by Dorothy Miller O'Donnell and published in 1980.

OGDEN

Ranking: 1682 S.S. Count: 26,578

Origin: English. Derived from the Old English words "āc" and "denu," meaning oak and valley. The name was given to those from Ogden, the name of places in England.

Famous **Ogdens:** DAVID OGDEN (1707–1798) of New Jersey was a New Jersey councilor, jurist, and Loyalist. UZAL OGDEN (1744–1822) of New Jersey was the first elected Episcopal bishop of New Jersey but was refused consecration and was suspended because of his views. He left the church and became a Presbyterian. AARON OGDEN (1756–1839) of New Jersey was a lawyer, leader of the New Jersey bar, commander of the New Jersey militia in the War of

1812, U.S. senator, and the governor of New Jersey. He was the Ogden of the Supreme Court case of *Gibbons v. Ogden*, in which Chief Justice John Marshall established the principle of freedom of interstate commerce. THOMAS LUDLOW OGDEN (1773–1844) of New Jersey was the grandson of David (1707–1798) and one of the best corporation lawyers in New York City. DAVID BAYARD OGDEN (1775–1849) of New York was a lawyer and is best remembered for his presentations before the Supreme Court. FRANCIS BARBER OGDEN (1783–1857) of New Jersey was the nephew of Aaron and a pioneer in the design of steamboat engines. PETER SKENE OGDEN (1794–1854) of Canada was a fur trader and explorer. He was one of the first white men to visit the Great Salt Lake and was the namesake of the town of Ogden, Utah. WILLIAM BUTLER OGDEN (1805–1877) of New York moved to Chicago and became its first mayor. He also was the first president of the Union Pacific Railroad. HERBERT GOUVERNEUR OGDEN (1846–1906) of New York was a cartographer and topographer with the U.S. Coast and Geodetic Survey. He published three editions of *U.S. Coast Pilot* (1899, 1903, 1904). ROLLO OGDEN (1856–1937) of New York was an editor at the New York *Evening Post* and the *New York Times*.

Genealogies: *A History of the Ogdin Family in America* [also Ogden] was compiled by John V. Kasler and published in St. Petersburg, Florida, in 1988. *Ogden Brothers and Their Descendants* was compiled by Chester Morse Willingham and published in Denver, Colorado, in 1979.

OGLE

Ranking: 2294 **S.S. Count:** 19,867
Origin: Irish, Scottish. Derived from the Old English first name Ocga and the Old English word "hyll," meaning hill. The name was given to those from Ogle, a place in Northumberland, England.
Famous Ogles: SAMUEL OGLE (1702?–1752) of England was a colonial official and proprietary governor of Maryland.
Genealogies: *A Chronicle of Belair* [Ogle Family] was compiled by Shirley Vlasak Baltz and published in Bowie, Maryland, in 1984. *The English Origin of John Ogle, First of the Name in Delaware* was compiled by Francis Hamilton Hibbard and published in Pittsburgh, Pennsylvania, in 1967.

OGLESBEE, OGLESBY (S.S. Abbreviation: Oglesb)

Ranking: 2400 **S.S. Count:** 18,884
Origin: Scottish. Derived from the name Ogilvie, which is of uncertain etymology. Possibly derived from the Old Welsh words "ugl" and "ma" or "ba," meaning high and plain

or hill. The name was given to those from Ogilvie, the name of a place in Scotland.
Famous Bearers: RICHARD JAMES OGLESBY (1824–1899) of Kentucky was a U.S. senator and the governor of Illinois. He was the first person ever elected to three terms as Illinois governor.
Genealogies: None known.

OGLETREE (S.S. Abbreviation: Ogletr)

Ranking: 6604 **S.S. Count:** 6559
Origin: English. The name means "dweller near Odkell's tree" (ES).
Genealogies: None known.

O'GRADY

Ranking: 4456 **S.S. Count:** 10,057
Origin: Irish. Transformation of Grady.
Genealogies: None known.

O'HARA

Ranking: 1464 **S.S. Count:** 30,366
Origin: Irish. Derived from the Gaelic name Ó hEaghra, which was derived from the first name Eaghra, which is of unknown etymology.
Famous O'Haras: JAMES O'HARA (1752–1819) of Ireland was a Revolutionary War soldier, banker in Pittsburgh, and glass manufacturer. THEODORE O'HARA (1820–1867) of Kentucky was a Confederate soldier best remembered for his poem "The Bivouac of the Dead," which recalled the reburial of the Kentucky soldiers killed at the battle of Buena Vista. GEOFFREY O'HARA (1882–1967) of Canada was a composer and songwriter. He wrote many songs, including "K-K-K-Katy." JOHN HENRY O'HARA (1905–1970) of Pennsylvania was a critic and feature writer for newspapers. As a novelist he wrote, among other works, *Butterfield 8*. His newspaper columns are collected in *My Turn* (1966).
Genealogies: None known.

OJEDA

Ranking: 3228 **S.S. Count:** 14,044
Origin: Spanish. Uncertain etymology. Most likely derived from the Latin word "folia," meaning leaves. The name was given to those who lived on the shores of the Ojeda, the name of a Spanish river.
Genealogies: None known.

O'KEEFE

Ranking: 1890 **S.S. Count:** 23,913
Origin: Irish. Transformation of Keefe.
Genealogies: *Anna O'Keefe and Samuel Snedden 1867–1975, Six Generations in California* was compiled by Vir-

ginia Perry Culbert and published in 1975. *The Baron, the Logger, the Miner and Me* was compiled by John H. Toole and published in Missoula, Montana, in 1984.

OLDHAM

Ranking: 2403 S.S. Count: 18,864

Origin: English. Derived from the Middle English words "ald" and "holm," meaning old and island. The name was given to those from Oldham, the name of a place in Lancashire, England.

Famous **Oldhams:** JOHN OLDHAM (1600–1636) of England was one of the first colonists, landing at Plymouth. He explored the Connecticut River and persuaded the colonists to start the first settlements in Connecticut. He was murdered by the Pequot Indians, thus adding fuel which helped to start the Pequot War. WILLIAMSON SIMPSON OLDHAM (1813–1868) of Tennessee was a Confederate senator from Texas. WILLIAM FITZJAMES OLDHAM (1854–1937) of India was a Methodist clergyman who was a pastor in the United States, then a bishop and supervisor of missions in Asia and then in South America.

Genealogies: *My Mother Nancy and her Oldhams* was compiled by Jessye Ann High and published in Sunnyvale, California, in 1978.

OLDS

Ranking: 4059 S.S. Count: 11,134

Origin: English. Derived from the Middle English word "old," meaning old. The name was given to the eldest of two or more persons having the same name or possibly to an old person.

Famous **Oldses:** RANSOM ELI OLDS (1864–1950) of Ohio was an inventor. He founded the Olds Motor Works (1899). It made the Oldsmobile, the first commercially successful car in America. He was also the founder and president of the Reo Motor Car Co. and Oldsmar, a retirement community in Florida. ROBERT EDWIN OLDS (1875–1932) of Minnesota was a Red Cross and government official.

Genealogies: *Letters to Sarah Ann Olds* was compiled by Mary Chalfant Ormsbee and published in Boulder, Colorado, in 1972.

O'LEARY

Ranking: 1412 S.S. Count: 31,480

Origin: Irish. Transformation of Leary.

Famous **O'Learys:** DANIEL O'LEARY (1846?–1933) of Ireland set many records for walking.

Genealogies: *From Ireland, Land of Pain and Sorrow: A Historical Chronicle of Two Cultures* [O'Leary] was compiled by Joseph L. Grady and published in Phoenix, Arizona, in 1984.

OLIVA

Ranking: 3785 S.S. Count: 11,920

Origin: Catalan, Italian, Spanish, Jewish. Derived from the Latin word "oliva," meaning olive. The name was given to those who lived near a grove of olives, to those who harvested or sold olives or olive oil, or to those who extracted olive oil. It may also have been given to those with a yellowish complexion.

Genealogies: None known.

OLIVAR (ALSO OLIVARES, OLIVARI)

Ranking: 2393 S.S. Count: 18,951

Origin: Olivar—Catalan; Olivari—Italian; Olivares—Spanish. Transformations of Oliva.

Genealogies: None known.

OLIVAS

Ranking: 3900 S.S. Count: 11,564

Origin: Spanish. Transformation of Oliva.

Genealogies: None known.

OLIVEIRA (S.S. Abbreviation: Olivei)

Ranking: 3712 S.S. Count: 12,163

Origin: Portuguese. Cognate to Oliva.

Genealogies: None known.

OLIVER (ALSO OLIVERA, OLIVERI, OLIVERIO, OLIVERO)

Ranking: 195 S.S. Count: 181,683

Origin: Oliver—Catalan, English, French, German, Scottish; Oliveri, Oliverio, Olivero—Italian; Olivera—Spanish. Oliver: derived from the Old French first name Olivier, of unknown etymology. Oliveri, Oliverio, Olivero: cognates to Oliver. Olivera: transformation of Oliva.

Famous **Bearers:** ANDREW OLIVER (1706–1774) of Massachusetts was a political leader who was appointed stamp officer to enforce the Stamp Act. The people of Boston damaged his house and hanged him in effigy. He wrote letters back to England describing the colonial unrest and made suggestions of possible remedies, which brought him even more unpopularity among the Bostonians. ANDREW OLIVER (1731–1799) of Massachusetts was a Massachusetts legislator and a scientist who wrote *An Essay on Comets.* HENRY KEMBLE OLIVER (1800–1885) of Massachusetts was the organizer and head of the Massachusetts Bureau of Statistics of Labor (1869). JAMES OLIVER (1823–1908) of Scotland came to the United States as a child. He invented hard-faced plows. They were manufactured by his company, the Oliver Plow Works, in Indiana. PAUL AMBROSE OLIVER (1830–1912) was born at sea. He was the inventor of dynamite and black powder explosives. HENRY WILLIAM OLIVER (1840–1904) of Ireland was one of the founders of the Oliver Iron & Steel Co., which initially manufactured nuts and bolts but grew and branched out into many other areas of the metal industry. GEORGE TENER OLIVER (1848–1919) of Ireland was the publisher of the *Pittsburgh Gazette Times*, a U.S. senator, and an activist for the protective tariff. JOSEPH OLIVER (1885–1938), a jazz musician born in Louisiana, was called King Oliver. At one point in his career he had his own band, called King Oliver's Creole Jazz Band, and Louis Armstrong was his second horn. He moved to New York City, fell on hard times, and died in obscurity. His songs included "Dixieland Blues" and "High Society."

Genealogies: *James Spencer Oliver and his Wife Sarah Elizabeth Bireley* was compiled by Delia Klingler Redman and published in Angola, Indiana, in 1973. *Oliver Genealogical Record, 1750–1970* was compiled by Claude Matthews Oliver and published in Pendleton, Indiana, in 1970.

OLIVIER, OLIVIERI, OLIVIERO (S.S. Abbreviation: Olivie)

Ranking: 3615 **S.S. Count:** 12,490
Origin: Olivier—French; Olivieri, Oliviero—Italian. Transformations of and cognates to Oliver.
Genealogies: None known.

OLIVO

Ranking: 4606 **S.S. Count:** 9705
Origin: Italian. Transformation of Oliva.
Genealogies: None known.

OLMSTED, OLMSTEAD (S.S. Abbreviation: Olmste)

Ranking: 2813 **S.S. Count:** 16,199
Origin: Dutch. The name means "dweller at the homestead where elms grew" (ES).
Famous Bearers: GIDEON OLMSTED (1749–1845) of Connecticut was a sea captain who piloted various privateers (1776–1795). DENISON OLMSTED (1791–1859) of Connecticut was a scientist and inventor who was well known for the study of meteor showers. FREDERICK LAW OLMSTED (1822–1903) of Connecticut was a landscape architect and one of the planners of Central Park in New York City. He also planned the grounds of the nation's capitol, among other things. Reports he wrote for the *New York Times* about the South were collectively published in 1861 as *The Cotton Kingdom*. JOHN CHARLES OLMSTED (1852–1920) of Switzerland was the first president of the American Society of Landscape Architects. ALBERT TEN EYCK OLMSTEAD (1880–1945) of New York was a historian of the Near East civilizations before the Islamic influences. He wrote *Assyrian Historiography* (1916).

Genealogies: *Justice & Umstead Families of Frederick County, Maryland, 1685–1947* [also Olmstead] was compiled by Palmer H. Cushman and published in North Hollywood, California, in 1979. *Anniversary Booklet: Olmsteads in America, 350th Anniversary* was published in 1983.

OLSEN

Ranking: 474 **S.S. Count:** 85,228
Origin: Danish, Norwegian. Derived from the Old Norse first name Øleifr (Olaf), which comprises the components "ans" and "leifr," meaning god and relic.
Genealogies: None known.

OLSON

Ranking: 126 **S.S. Count:** 233,099
Origin: Norwegian, Swedish. Transformation of Olsen.
Famous Olsons: FLOYD BJERSTJERNE OLSON (1891–1936) of Minnesota was the governor of that state (1931–1936). CHARLES JOHN OLSON (1910–1970) of Massachusetts was a poet of the avant-garde school. His poetry was published in *The Maxium Poems* and *The Distances* (both 1960). WILLARD CLIFFORD OLSON (1899–1978) of Minnesota was the dean of the College of Education at the University of Michigan, where he made studies of elementary through high school students, researching them all through their school years. He measured intelligence plus physical characteristics of height, weight, and so on. He then measured dental, carpal, and grip age to obtain the child's organismic age. These data gave the predictability of a pupils' success. His book *Child Development* (1949) details his findings.

Genealogies: *Vart Svenska Urstrung: A Family History of August and Jennie Olson* was compiled by Rosanna Olson and published in White Bear Lake, Minnesota, in 1978. *Johnson-Olson, Hire-Shuck: Ancestors of Maida J. Johnson* was compiled by Bob Gillette and published in Tigard, Oregon, in 1990.

OLVERA

Ranking: 4787 **S.S. Count:** 9353
Origin: Spanish. Uncertain etymology. The name was given to those who came from Olvera, the name of a place in Spain.
Genealogies: *Los Olveras: Journey to America* was compiled by Carlos N. Olvera and published in Baltimore, Maryland, in 1991.

O'MALLEY (S.S. Abbreviation: Omalle)

Ranking: 1897 **S.S. Count:** 23,873
Origin: Irish. Derived from the Gaelic name Ó Máille, which was derived from the word "mál," meaning prince.
Famous O'Malleys: FRANK WARD O'MALLEY (1875–

1932) of Pennsylvania was a highly respected journalist on the staff of the *New York Sun*.

Genealogies: None known.

O'MARA

Ranking: 6914 **S.S. Count:** 6227

Origin: Irish. Derived from the Gaelic name Ó Meadhra, which was derived from the first name Meadhra, which was derived from the word "meadhar," meaning mirth.

Genealogies: None known.

O'MEARA

Ranking: 6650 **S.S. Count:** 6511

Origin: Irish. Transformation of O'Mara.

Genealogies: None known.

O'NEAL

Ranking: 639 **S.S. Count:** 65,080

Origin: Irish. Transformation of Neil.

Famous **O'Neals:** EDWARD ASBURY O'NEAL (1818–1890) of Alabama was a lawyer, Confederate officer, and the governor of Alabama.

Genealogies: *O'Neal* was compiled by Thelma O'Neal Beasley and published in Uvalda, Georgia, in 1989.

O'NEIL

Ranking: 1030 **S.S. Count:** 42,546

Origin: Irish. Transformation of Neil.

Genealogies: None known.

OQUENDO (S.S. Abbreviation: Oquend)

Ranking: 4940 **S.S. Count:** 9065

Origin: Spanish. Derived from words meaning "side of the pasture" (ES). The name was given to those from Oquendo, the name of a place in Spain.

Genealogies: None known.

O'REILLY (S.S. Abbreviation: Oreill)

Ranking: 2901 **S.S. Count:** 15,687

Origin: Irish. Transformation of Reilly.

Famous **O'Reillys:** ALEXANDER O'REILLY (1722–1794) of Ireland was the first Spanish governor of Louisiana. HENRY O'REILLY (1806–1886) of Ireland was a pioneer telegraph line builder who was responsible for the laying of 8000 miles of lines. JOHN BOYLE O'REILLY (1844–1890) of Ireland was sentenced to death by the British for attempting to incite a revolt. His sentence was commuted to 23 years of penal servitude in Australia. He escaped and made his way to the United States, where he became a member of the editorial staff and a part owner of the Boston *Pilot*. He was the author of many poems, including "Songs from the Southern Seas" (1873) and "Songs, Legends and Ballads" (1878). ROBERT MAITLAND O'REILLY (1845–1912) of Penn-

sylvania was the U.S. surgeon general and the personal physician to President Grover Cleveland. LEONORA O'REILLY (1870–1927) of New York City was a labor leader and a reformer. She organized the New York City chapter of the women's local of the United Garment Workers Union and served as a board member of the National Women's Trade Union League. The fire at the Triangle Shirtwaist Factory in March 1911 pushed her into the public eye as she conducted fire-safety surveys and inspections. She was also one of the founders of the National Association for the Advancement of Colored People (NAACP) and served on its general committee.

Genealogies: None known.

ORLANDELLI, ORLANDI, ORLANDINI, ORLANDO, ORLANDONI (S.S. Abbreviation: Orland)

Ranking: 2336 **S.S. Count:** 19,406

Origin: Italian. Cognates to Rowland.

Genealogies: None known.

ORNELAS (S.S. Abbreviation: Ornela)

Ranking: 3695 **S.S. Count:** 12,224

Origin: Spanish. Uncertain etymology.

Genealogies: None known.

O'ROURKE (S.S. Abbreviation: Orourk)

Ranking: 1824 **S.S. Count:** 24,734

Origin: Irish. Transformation of Rourke.

Genealogies: *A Genealogy of the Clifton, Leaton, Rourke, and Secord Families* [also O'Rourke] was compiled by Richard Lee Secord and published in Glendale, Arizona, in 1988.

OROZCO

Ranking: 1971 **S.S. Count:** 22,993

Origin: Basque. Uncertain etymology. The name was given to those from Orozco, a place in the province of Biscay.

Genealogies: None known.

ORR

Ranking: 670 **S.S. Count:** 62,709

Origin: English, Irish, Jewish, Scottish. English: derived from the Old English word "ōra," meaning edge. The name was given to those who lived on a bank or on a hill's edge. English, Irish, Scottish: derived from the Old Norse name Orri, meaning "black-cock" (H&H). Jewish: derived from the Hebrew word "or," meaning light. The name was taken ornamentally.

Famous **Orrs:** HUGH ORR (1715–1798) of Scotland came to America and settled in Massachusetts, where he was a Revolutionary War patriot and the first person to manufacture muskets in the colonies (1748). His business included making muskets and cannons for the Revolutionary soldiers. GUSTAVUS JOHN ORR (1819–1887) of South Carolina was a pioneer school commissioner of Georgia. JAMES LAWRENCE ORR (1822–1873) of South Carolina was against secession until he lost his bid for the Democratic presidential nomination. He then favored secession by South Carolina and became a Confederate senator representing that state. After the war he was governor of South Carolina, a federal judge, and a minister to Russia.

Genealogies: *Ulster Pedigrees: Descendants, in many Lines of James Orr and Janet McClement, Who Emigrated from Scotland to Northern Ireland ca. 1607* was compiled by Ray A. Jones and published in San Francisco, California, in 1977. *William Orr of Ireland, Pennsylvania, and Kentucky and his Descendants* was compiled by Paul J. Ostendorf and published in West Saint Paul, Minnesota, in 1971.

ORTEGA
Ranking: 617   **S.S. Count:** 67,739
Origin: Catalan, Spanish. Uncertain etymology. Possibly derived from the Spanish word "ortiga," meaning nettle, and the local suffix "-eca." The name was given to those from Ortega, the name of several places in Spain.
Genealogies: None known.

ORTIZ
Ranking: 117   **S.S. Count:** 250,812
Origin: Spanish. Cognate to Fort.
Genealogies: None known.

OSBORN (ALSO OSBORNE)
Ranking: 267   **S.S. Count:** 137,218
Origin: English. Derived from the Old Norse first name Ásbjorn, which comprises the components "ás" and "björn," meaning god and bear.
Famous Bearers: CHARLES OSBORN (1775–1850) of North Carolina was an abolitionist and the leader of the abolition movement in Tennessee, Ohio, and Indiana. SELLECK OSBORN (1782?–1826) of Connecticut was a journalist and poet. HENRY FAIRFIELD OSBORN (1857–1935) of Connecticut was the president of the American Museum of Natural History and introduced the idea of instructional museum displays. He wrote many books, including *The Age of Mammals* (1910), *Men of the Old Stone Age* (1915), and *Origins and Evolution of Life* (1917). NORRIS GALPIN OSBORN (1858–1932) of Connecticut was a civil-service and prison reformer and an editor of the *New Haven Evening Register*, then the *New Haven Journal-Courier*. THOMAS BURR OSBORNE (1859–1929) of Connecticut was a biochemist best known for his work with vegetable proteins and vitamins A and B. JAMES WALKER OSBORNE (1859–1919) of North Carolina was a New York district attorney who uncovered scandals at the state capital and

abuses at Sing Sing prison. THOMAS MOTT OSBORNE (1859–1926) of New York was a prison reformer. As chairman of the New York Commission on Prison Reform, he spent a week as a "prisoner." From that experience he wrote *Within Prison Walls* (1914) and then set out to change prison conditions. He founded the Welfare League Association, which provided aid to prisoners once they were freed, and the National Society of Penal Reform. CHASE SALMON OSBORN (1860–1949) of Indiana was a journalist, then governor of Michigan, where he added a workmen's compensation law to the books. [HENRY] FAIRFIELD OSBORN (1887–1969) of New Jersey was a trustee and then president of the New York Zoological Society and the founder of the Conservation Foundation. RILEY RANDOLPH OSBORN (1905–1978) of Missouri was a business executive and the founder of Turnbuckles, Inc. in 1940. E[DWARD] BARTLEY OSBORN (1907–1978) of Minnesota was a businessman who initiated employee programs for grievances plus programs for counseling and treatment of drug-related problems.

Genealogies: *Early Osbornes and Alleys* [also Osborn] was compiled by Rita Kennedy Sutton and published in 1978. *Some Smiths, Osborns, and Allied Families of New England and Ohio* was compiled by Estelle Osborn Watson and published in Skokie, Illinois, in 1964.

OSBURN
Ranking: 4155   **S.S. Count:** 10,886
Origin: English. Transformation of Osborn.
Genealogies: None known.

O'SHEA
Ranking: 3307   **S.S. Count:** 13,692
Origin: Irish. Transformation of Shea.
Famous O'Sheas: MICHAEL VINCENT O'SHEA (1866–1932) was an educator and the author of *Newer Ways with Older Children*.
Genealogies: None known.

OSORIO
Ranking: 3439   **S.S. Count:** 13,121
Origin: Spanish. Uncertain etymology. Possibly ultimately derived from the Greek name Orosios, which was derived from the word "oros," meaning mountain.
Genealogies: None known.

OSTRAND, OSTRANDER (S.S. Abbreviation: Ostran)
Ranking: 3278   **S.S. Count:** 13,852
Origin: Swedish. Uncertain etymology. The name most likely means island or shore.
Genealogies: *Ostrander Family Vital Records: Births, Baptisms and Marriages of the Ostrander Family in New York State and nearby from 1660* was compiled by Barbara

Dahl and published in Decorah, Iowa, in 1989. *The Van Nostrand Family* [also Ostrander] was compiled by Agnes Brinkerhoff Van Nostrand and published in 1966.

OSTROWSKI (S.S. Abbreviation: Ostrow)

Ranking: 3510 S.S. Count: 12,843

Origin: Polish. Derived from the Polish word "ostrów," meaning island in a river or "a water meadow bounded by ditches" (H&H). The name was given to those living in such areas.

Genealogies: None known.

O'SULLIVAN (S.S. Abbreviation: Osulli)

Ranking: 3217 S.S. Count: 14,088

Origin: Irish. Transformation of Sullivan.

Famous O'Sullivans: JOHN LOTUS O'SULLIVAN (1813–1895) of Gibraltar was one of the founders of *United States Magazine* and *Democratic Review* and most likely the originator of the term "manifest destiny." TIMOTHY H. O'SULLIVAN (1840?–1882) of New York City was a photographer who photographed many of the Civil War battles. He also was the chief photographer for the Treasury Department. MARY KENNEY O'SULLIVAN (1864–1943) of Missouri was a labor organizer and reformer. She was the first female president of the American Federation of Labor and co-drafted the structure of the Women's Trade Union League.

Genealogies: None known.

OSWALD

Ranking: 2287 S.S. Count: 19,888

Origin: English, Scottish. Derived from an Old English first name comprising the components "ós" and "weald," meaning god and power.

Famous Oswalds: LEE HARVEY OSWALD (1939–1963) of Louisiana was the presumed assassin of President John F. Kennedy. Oswald spent time in Russia in the years just prior to the killing. He was shot and killed by Jack Ruby as he was being transported from one jail to another two days after the assassination.

Genealogies: None known.

OTERO

Ranking: 1527 S.S. Count: 29,078

Origin: Spanish. Derived from the Spanish word "otero," meaning height or hill. The name was given to those from Otero, the name of places in Spain.

Genealogies: None known.

OTIS

Ranking: 4047 S.S. Count: 11,190

Origin: English. Transformation of Oates.

Famous Otises: JAMES OTIS (1725–1783) of Massachusetts was the king's representative for the collection of taxes in the colonies. When his duties called for him to search houses for evidence of violations of the Sugar Act, he resigned his position and took up the Revolutionary cause. HARRISON GRAY OTIS (1765–1848) of Massachusetts was a member of the U.S. House of Representatives, a member of the Hartford Convention, a U.S. senator, and the mayor of Boston. BASS OTIS (1784–1861) of Connecticut was a painter who did portraits of James Madison and Thomas Jefferson. It is believed that he made the first lithograph in 1818. ELISHA GRAVES OTIS (1811–1861) of Vermont invented a steam elevator (1861) that was the beginning of the Otis Elevator Co. FESSENDEN NOTT OTIS (1825–1900) of New York was a physician who pioneered in the cure of genitourinary diseases. GEORGE ALEXANDER OTIS (1830–1881) of Massachusetts was an army surgeon and the editor of *The Medical and Surgical History of the War of the Rebellion*. HARRISON GRAY OTIS (1837–1917) of Ohio was the owner of the *Los Angeles Times* after 1886. ELWELL STEPHEN OTIS (1838–1909) of Maryland was an army officer, commander of Pacific forces, and the governor of the Philippines.

Genealogies: *The Descendants of John Otis and Margaret Downey of Frankfort, Maine* was compiled by Marian Otis and published in Pound Ridge, New York, in 1981. *A Genealogical Memoir of the Descendants of John Otis, 1797–1873 of Leyden and Denmark, N.Y. and Related Families* was compiled by Erwin James Otis and published in Dearborn, Michigan, in 1964.

O'TOOLE

Ranking: 2994 S.S. Count: 15,170

Origin: Irish. Transformation of Toole.

Genealogies: None known.

OTT

Ranking: 1209 S.S. Count: 36,398

Origin: German. Cognate to Oates.

Famous Otts: ISAAC OTT (1847–1916) of Pennsylvania discovered the hormone of milk secretion and showed that body temperature rises if the corpus striatum is injured. MELVIN THOMAS OTT (1909–1958) of Louisiana was a baseball player and the first to hit 500 home runs in the National League. In 1951 he was elected to the Hall of Fame.

Genealogies: *Utt-Ventures: a Genealogy and History of the Ott-Utt Family in America, 1742–1982* was compiled by Claire Utt and published in Owensboro, Kentucky, in 1982.

OTTO

Ranking: 1422 S.S. Count: 31,309

Origin: Danish, Dutch, Flemish, German, Norwegian. Cognate to Oates.

Famous **Ottos:** BODO OTTO (1711–1787) of Germany was a surgeon in the Continental army. JOHN CONRAD OTTO (1774–1844), birthplace unknown, was the grandson of Bodo Otto. Also a physician, he is best remembered for his description of hemophilia. WILLIAM TOD OTTO (1816–1905) of Pennsylvania was the son of John C. and was the assistant U.S. secretary of the interior.

Genealogies: *The Trummel Family, 1633– 1989 and Related Lines Otto, Gurtner, Ehling* was compiled by Eleanor Clary and published in Astoria, Illinois, in 1990.

OUELLET, OUELLETTE (S.S. Abbreviation: Ouelle)

Ranking: 2137 S.S. Count: 21,423

Origin: French. Uncertain etymology. The name was given to those who lived at the eye of a stream or fountain.
Genealogies: None known.

OUTLAW

Ranking: 3949 S.S. Count: 11,448

Origin: English. Derived from the Old English words "ūt" and "lagu," meaning out and law. The name means descendant of an outlaw, referring to those who failed to appear in court and, as a consequence, are without the protection of the law.
Genealogies: None known.

OVERBY

Ranking: 4784 S.S. Count: 9360

Origin: English. Uncertain etymology. The name was given to those from Overbury, a place in Worcestershire, England.
Genealogies: *The Overbury Story: 500 Years in England and America* [also Overby] was compiled by Libby Overby and published in Baltimore, Maryland, in 1988.

OVERSTREET (S.S. Abbreviation: Overst)

Ranking: 2494 S.S. Count: 18,187

Origin: English. Derived from the Old English words "ofer" and "strēt," meaning over and street. The name was given to those who lived by a road Romans had built near the bank of a river.
Genealogies: *The Grandfathers, a Personal Bicentennial History* [also Overstreet] was compiled by Carrol Carman Hall and published in Springfield, Illinois, in 1981. *Saints and Black Sheep: the Genealogy of B. Z. and Lucy Cheek Overstreet* was compiled by Kenneth E. Crouch and published in Bedford, Virginia, in 1973.

OVERTON (S.S. Abbreviation: Overto)

Ranking: 1726 S.S. Count: 25,996

Origin: English. Derived from the Old English words "ufere," "ōfer," or "ofer" and "tūn," meaning, respectively, upper, river bank, or slope and settlement. The name was given to those from Overton, the name of several places in England.

Famous Overtons: JOHN OVERTON (1766–1833) of Virginia was a Tennessee jurist and an early business partner of Andrew Jackson.

Genealogies: *The American Ancestry and Descendants of Joel Overton, 1779–1844* was compiled by Ernest Clark Overton and published in Albany, New York, in 1970. *The Family History of Wainner, Overton, McMurr(a)y and Interconnecting Lines* was compiled by Merle Wainner Jeter and published in Columbia, South Carolina, in 1972.

OWEN

Ranking: 444 S.S. Count: 90,011

Origin: Welsh. Derived from the Welsh first name Owain, which was possibly derived from the Latin name Eugenius.

Famous Owens: GRIFFITH OWEN (1647?–1717) of Wales was a leader of the Welsh Quakers who led them to a settlement in Lower Merion Township in Pennsylvania. ROBERT DALE OWEN (1801–1877) of Scotland was a resident of Indiana who served as a member of Congress and senator. He introduced the 1844 solution to the Oregon boundary dispute. He also was involved with the founding of the Smithsonian Institution. DAVID DALE OWEN (1807–1860) of Scotland was a geologist and the state geologist of Kentucky, Arkansas, and Indiana. BETHENIA ANGELINA OWENS-ADAIR (1840–1926) of Missouri was a physician, feminist, and social reformer. She worked her way through medical school and also was committed to eradicating the social illnesses brought about by liquor. As a physician, she worked for the mandatory sterilization of those who had been committed and deemed criminally insane. EDWARD THOMAS OWEN (1850–1931) of Connecticut was a pioneer in grammar revision. ROBERT LATHAM OWEN (1856–1947) of Virginia was a U.S. senator from Oklahoma. He was one of the drafters of the Glass-Owen Currency Act (1913), better known as the Federal Reserve Act, and the Farm Loan Act. THOMAS MCADORY OWEN (1866–1920) of Alabama was the founder and director of the Alabama Department of Archives (1901), the first of its kind in the United States.

Genealogies: *A Fair and Happy Land* [Owen family] was compiled by William A. Owens and published in New York, New York, in 1975. *Memories of an Ozarks Mother: 100 Years of Stella Owen* was compiled by Edgar Lyle Owen and published in Branson, Missouri, in 1978. *Owings and Allied Families, 1685– 1985: Genealogy of some of the Descendants of Richard Owings I of Maryland* [also Owen] was compiled by Addison D. Owings and published in Baltimore, Maryland, in 1985.

OWENS

Ranking: 119 **S.S. Count:** 245,442

Origin: Welsh. Transformation of Owen.

Famous **Owenses:** JOHN EDMOND OWENS (1823–1886) of England came to the United States as a child and made his living as an actor. His speciality was in comedic roles. MICHAEL JOSEPH OWENS (1859–1923) of what is now West Virginia was an inventor and manufacturer. He invented an automatic bottle-making machine, which led to the Owens Bottle Machine Co. and the Libbey-Owens Sheet Glass Co. JESSE OWENS (1913–1980) of Alabama was born James Cleveland Owens. He was an Olympic track and field athlete who set three records, tied one, and was awarded four gold medals at the 1936 Olympics.

Genealogies: *A Fair and Happy Land* [Owens family] was compiled by William A. Owens and published in New York, New York, in 1975.

PABON

Ranking: 3710 S.S. Count: 12,165
Origin: French. Cognate to Peacock.
Genealogies: None known.

PACE

Ranking: 779 S.S. Count: 54,026
Origin: English. Derived from the Middle English word "pace," meaning peace. The name was given to those who were temperate and affable.

Famous **Paces**: EDWARD ALOYSIUS PACE (1861–1938) of Starke, Florida, was a Roman Catholic priest and a pioneer in psychology and philosophy.

Genealogies: *Our Ancestors* was compiled by Glen Robert Johnson and published in Baltimore, Maryland, in 1979. *Pace's Smith's, Baucom's* (sic) was compiled by William Carroll Pace and published in Oklahoma City, Oklahoma, in 1990.

PACHECO (S.S. Abbreviation: Pachec)

Ranking: 760 S.S. Count: 55,687
Origin: Portuguese, Spanish. Uncertain etymology. Possibly derived from the first name Francisco.

Famous **Pachecos**: ROMUALDO PACHECO (1831–1899) of California was a governor of California and best known for uniting native Californians with the settlers.

Genealogies: None known.

PACK

Ranking: 1880 S.S. Count: 24,084
Origin: English. Derived from the medieval first name Pack, which is of uncertain etymology.

Famous **Packs**: CHARLES LATHROP PACK (1857–1937) of Michigan was a conservationist who was responsible for the founding of several forestry conservation groups.

Genealogies: *Alexander Stewart, his Scots Ancestry and American Descendants* [also Pack] was compiled by Dorothy Kintigh Sidfrid and published in Orange, California, in 1979. *Descendants of Richard Pack of Maryland 1764–1991* was compiled by Miriam Young Pack and published in Wichita, Kansas, in 1992.

PACKARD (S.S. Abbreviation: Packar)

Ranking: 3306 S.S. Count: 13,694
Origin: English. 1) derived from the Norman first name Pachard or Baghard, which is comprised of the Germanic components "pac" or "bag" and "hard," meaning fight and hardy. 2) derived from the Middle English word "pa(c)k," meaning bundle, and the Anglo-Norman-French suffix "-ard." The name was given to peddlers. 3) derived from the medieval first name Pack, of uncertain etymology.

Famous **Packards**: ELIZABETH PARSONS WARE PACKARD (1816–1897) of Massachusetts was committed by her husband to a mental hospital because her religious beliefs differed from his. She was released, but when her husband tried to have her committed again, she sued him and won in a highly public jury trial. She became a major spokesperson for the rights of married women. SOPHIA B. PACKARD (1824–1891) of Massachusetts was the founder of Spelman College. SILAS SADLER PACKARD (1826–1898) of Massachusetts was the "father of business education." He was the founder of Packard's Business College in New York City and was the one responsible for training women for office work. ALPHEUS SPRING PACKARD (1839–1905) of Maine was the founder and editor-in-chief of *American Naturalist*. An entomologist, he also wrote books, including *The Cave Fauna of North America* (1888). WILLIAM DOUD PACKARD (1861–1923) and JAMES WARD PACKARD (1863–1928), brothers, founded the Packard Electric Co. in 1890 and produced the first Packard car in 1899.

Genealogies: *The Ancestors and Descendants of Daniel Packard* was compiled by Ruth Packard Bartlett and published in Rockport, Maine, in 1982. *Celebration of the Two Hundred and Fiftieth Anniversary of the Landing of Samuel Packard in this Country, August 10, 1638* was compiled by the Packard Memorial Association and published in Brockton, Massachusetts, in 1888.

PACKER

Ranking: 3820 S.S. Count: 11,804
Origin: English, German, Jewish. English: derived from the Middle English word "pack(en)," meaning to pack. The name was given to wool packers. German, Jewish: derived from the German word "pack," meaning bundle. The name was given to wholesalers.

Famous **Packers**: ASA PACKER (1805–1879) of Connecticut was the founder of Lehigh Valley Railroad Co. and Lehigh University. WILLIAM FISHER PACKER (1807–1870) of Pennsylvania was the governor of Pennsylvania and the publisher of the *Lycoming Gazette*.

Genealogies: None known.

PADGET (ALSO PADGETT)

Ranking: 1179 S.S. Count: 37,125
Origin: English. Transformation of Page.

Genealogies: *Padgett Families: Lincoln Co. Ky., 1810–1910* was compiled by Beatrice Padgett Meek and published in Louisville, Kentucky, in 1991. *Scots and Their Kin* [also Padgett] was compiled by Clayton G. Metcalf and published in Enterprise, Alabama, in 1984.

PADILLA (S.S. Abbreviation: Padill)

Ranking: 535 S.S. Count: 75,763
Origin: Spanish. Derived from the Spanish word "padilla," meaning frying pan. The name was given to those from Padilla, the name of several places in Spain.

Genealogies: None known.

PAGAN

Ranking: 955 S.S. Count: 45,578

Origin: English, Italian, Scottish. English, Scottish: uncertain etymology. Possibly derived from the Latin name Pāgānus, which was derived from the word "pāgus," meaning a remote village and referring originally to an unsophisticated or country person. Italian: cognate to Paine.

Genealogies: None known.

PAGANO

Ranking: 4091 S.S. Count: 11,045

Origin: Italian. Cognate to Paine.

Genealogies: None known.

PAGE

Ranking: 321 S.S. Count: 115,738

Origin: English, French. Derived from the Middle English and Old French word "page," meaning a youth who was a servant. The name was given to young servants.

Famous **Pages**: MANN PAGE (1691–1730) of Virginia was the owner of Rosewell, the second-largest home in Virginia. THOMAS JEFFERSON PAGE (1808–1899) of Virginia, a Confederate naval officer, commanded the vessel *Stonewall.* CHARLES GRAFTON PAGE (1812–1868) of Massachusetts was a pioneer in the electric field. WALTER HINES PAGE (1855–1918) of North Carolina was a journalist and a partner in Doubleday, Page & Co., publishers. He also was an ambassador to Great Britain and an author of books, including *The Rebuilding of Old Commonwealths* (1902). LEIGH PAGE (1884–1952) of New Jersey was a physicist whose contribution to the field of physics was the "emission theory of electromagnetism." ORAN THADDEUS ("LIPS") PAGE (1908–1954) of Texas was a trumpet player. He is best known for his recording with Pearl Bailey of "Baby, It's Cold Outside."

Genealogies: *The History and Genealogy of the Robert and Rachael Page Family, c1750–1827: from Goochland County, Virginia, and Spartanburg County, South Carolina* was compiled by Donald W. Page and published in Franklin, North Carolina, in 1992. *Carolina Page's:* (sic) *a Compilation of Genealogical Information on Page Families in the Carolinas Beginning in 1521 to Present Time* was compiled by Robert E. Page and published in Cullman, Alabama, in 1990.

PAIGE

Ranking: 1764 S.S. Count: 25,414

Origin: English. Transformation of Page.

Genealogies: *Carolina Page's:* (sic) *(also Paige) a Compilation of Genealogical Information on Page Families in the Carolinas Beginning in 1521 to Present Time* was compiled by Robert E. Page and published in Cullman, Alabama, in 1990.

PAINE

Ranking: 3532 S.S. Count: 12,779

Origin: English. Derived from the Middle English first name Pain(e), which was derived from the Latin name Pāgānus, which was derived from the word "pāgus," meaning a remote village and referring originally to an unsophisticated or country person.

Famous **Paines**: ROBERT TREAT PAINE (1731–1814) of Massachusetts was one of the signers of the Declaration of Independence. He was a delegate to the Continental Congress and the first attorney general of Massachusetts. As a lawyer, he was associate prosecuting attorney in the "Boston Massacre" trial. He also was one of the founders of the American Academy of Arts and Sciences. His son, also ROBERT TREAT PAINE (1773–1811), of Massachusetts, was a poet whose works brought him social ostracism and physical abuse. THOMAS PAINE (1737–1809) of England was a pamphleteer and agitator. He was the author of *Common Sense*, a pamphlet that urged the colonies to declare their independence from England. He joined George Washington's army and wrote the first of a series of pamphlets called *Crisis*. It began with the famous sentence "These are the times that try men's souls." He fell out of favor politically and died in poverty. Although he was buried in the United States, his remains were unearthed and returned to England in 1819 by William Cobbett. ELIJAH PAINE (1757–1842) of Connecticut was one of the first settlers of Williamstown, Vermont. CHARLES PAINE (1799–1853) of Vermont was a railroad promoter and the governor of Vermont. ROBERT TREAT PAINE (1835–1910) of Massachusetts was the founder of the Associated Charities of Boston. JOHN KNOWLES PAINE (1839–1906) of Maine was responsible for the development of the first really "American" music. ALBERT B. PAINE (1861–1937) of Massachusetts was an editor and author. His works include *Mark Twain, a Biography* (1912).

Genealogies: *The Paynes of Virginia* [also Paine] was compiled by Brooke Payne and published in Harrisonburg, Virginia, in 1977.

PAINTER (S.S. Abbreviation: Painte)

Ranking: 1440 S.S. Count: 30,990

Origin: English. Derived from the Middle English and Old French word "peinto(u)r," meaning painter. The name was given to painters.

Famous **Painters**: GAMALIEL PAINTER (1743–1819) of Connecticut was a Vermont pioneer who was instrumental in the development of Middlebury, Vermont, and who was one of the founders of Middlebury College. WILLIAM

PAINTER (1838–1906) of Maryland was an engineer and the inventor of the "Crown Cork," which is still in use today.

Genealogies: None known.

PAK

Ranking: 4550 S.S. Count: 9817
Origin: Korean. Uncertain etymology.
Genealogies: None known.

PALACIN, PALACIO, PALACIOS (S.S. Abbreviation: Palaci)

Ranking: 2177 S.S. Count: 21,061
Origin: Spanish. Palacin: derived from the Old Spanish word "palacin," meaning "of the palace" (H&H). The name was given to those in the employ of a noble or royal court or to those who were courteous. Palacio, Palacios: derived from the Spanish word "palacio," meaning palace. The names were given to those who lived near a palace or who were employed in one.

Genealogies: None known.

PALAZZETTI, PALAZZI, PALAZZO, PALAZZOLI, PALAZZOTTO (S.S. Abbreviation: Palazz)

Ranking: 4398 S.S. Count: 10,201
Origin: Italian. Cognates to Palacio.
Genealogies: None known.

PALERMI, PALERMO (S.S. Abbreviation: Palerm)

Ranking: 3882 S.S. Count: 11,622
Origin: Italian. Derived from the name of a town in Sicily, Italy, called Palermo, which is of Phoenician origin. The name was given to those from Palermo.

Genealogies: None known.

PALM

Ranking: 4411 S.S. Count: 10,161
Origin: Danish, Swedish. Cognates to Palmer.
Genealogies: *Ancestors and Descendants of James and Althea (Loose) Johnston and Allied Families* [also Palm] was compiled by Aaron Montgomery Johnston and published in Knoxville, Tennessee, in 1983. *Tock sa Mecka: Swedish Pioneer Life on the Prairie, Experienced by the Palm Family* was compiled by Esther Palm Gayman and published in Galesburg, Illinois, in 1978.

PALMA

Ranking: 4759 S.S. Count: 9412
Origin: Italian, Portuguese, Spanish. Cognates to Palmer.
Genealogies: None known.

PALMER (ALSO PALMERI, PALMERIN, PALMERINI, PALMERO)

Ranking: 139 S.S. Count: 217,480
Origin: Palmer—Catalan, English, Swedish; Palmeri, Palmerin, Palmerini—Italian; Palmero—Spanish. Cognates to the English name Palmer, which was derived from the Middle English and Old French word "palmer," which was derived from the Latin word "palma," meaning palm tree. The name was given to those who had made a pilgrimage to the Holy Land or to those who lived near palm trees.

Famous **Bearers:** TIMOTHY PALMER (1751–1821) of Massachusetts was a pioneer bridge builder, known especially for Permanent Bridge over the Schuylkill River in Pennsylvania. PHOEBE WORRALL PALMER (1807–1874) of New York City was an evangelist and an author of religious books. She was the founder of the Five Points Mission in New York City. JAMES SHEDDEN PALMER (1810–1867) of New Jersey was a naval officer who commanded the *Iroquois* and later the *Hartford* during the Civil War. FRANCES FLORA BOND PALMER (1812–1876) of England was a draftsman and lithographer and one of the better artists on the Currier & Ives staff. JOHN MCCAULEY PALMER (1817–1900) of Kentucky was governor of Illinois, then a U.S. senator and presidential candidate. ERASTUS D. PALMER (1817–1904) of Massachusetts was a sculptor whose best-known works include busts of Washington Irving and Erastus Corning. POTTER PALMER (1826–1902) of New York operated the Chicago, Illinois, store that was the forerunner of Marshall Field & Co. He was instrumental in building up the city of Chicago, and he was the builder of the Palmer House hotel. HORATIO R. PALMER (1834–1907) of New York was a music teacher and composer of church hymns, including "Yield Not to Temptation." LIZZIE PITTS MERRILL PALMER (1838–1916) of Maine was a philanthropist whose donation founded the Merrill-Palmer Institute in Detroit. GEORGE H. PALMER (1842–1933) of Massachusetts was a scholar and author. His books include *The Field of Ethics* (1901) and *Autobiography of a Philosopher* (1930). His wife, ALICE ELVIRA FREEMAN PALMER (1855–1902) of New York, was a professor at, then president of, Wellesley College, then dean of women at the University of Chicago. DANIEL D. PALMER (1845–1913), born in Canada, developed and practiced chiropractic in Iowa. He also wrote *Textbook of the Science, Art and Philosophy of Chiropractic* (1910) and *The Chiropractor* (1914). BERTHA HONORE PALMER (1849–1918) of Kentucky was a Chicago society leader and a patron of the arts. SOPHIE FRENCH PALMER (1853–1920) of Massachusetts was a nurse. She was the founder and administrator of the nursing program at the Garfield Memorial Hospital in Washington, D.C. (1889). In 1896 she did the same as superintendent of the Rochester (New York) City (General) Hospital and Training School. She was responsible for the passage of the first state (New York, in 1903) laws requiring state supervision of nursing programs and graduated nurses. A five-nurse committee, the Board of Nurse Examiners, was initiated with Palmer as its first chairperson. CHARLES S. PALMER (1858–1939) of Illinois was a chemist who invented the basic process for obtaining gasoline from oil. AUSTIN N. PALMER (1859–1927) developed the Palmer method of handwriting that has been taught extensively in American schools. ALEXANDER M. PALMER (1872–1936) of Pennsylvania was a member of Congress, then attorney general of the United States. In that capacity, he led government action against radicals during the "Red Scare" of the early 1920s.

Genealogies: *Freeman-Palmer and Related Families* was compiled by Mary Ann Palmer-Schrepfer and published in Yakima, Washington, in 1972. *A Genealogy of Palmers* was compiled by Andrew Stillman and published in 1985. *Memoirs: With Histories of Pound-Murphy-Willingham-Palmer-Pitts Families* was compiled by Jerome B. Pound and published in Miami Beach, Florida, in 1949.

PALMIERI, PALMIERO (S.S. Abbreviation: Palmie)

Ranking: 4713 S.S. Count: 9497
Origin: Italian. Cognates to Palmer.
Genealogies: None known.

PALUMBERI, PALUMBIERI, PALUMBO (S.S. Abbreviation: Palumb)

Ranking: 2955 S.S. Count: 15,403
Origin: Italian. Cognates to the Spanish name Palomo, which was derived from the Spanish word "palomo," meaning pigeon. The name was given to those who kept pigeons or who were mild.
Genealogies: None known.

PANNELL (S.S. Abbreviation: Pannel)

Ranking: 3885 S.S. Count: 11,612
Origin: English. 1) transformation of Paine. 2) uncertain etymology. The name was given to those who made panels for saddles.
Genealogies: None known.

PAPPAS

Ranking: 1725 S.S. Count: 25,998
Origin: Greek. The name means priest.
Genealogies: None known.

PAQUET (ALSO PAQUETEAU, PAQUETOT, PAQUETTE)

Ranking: 3023 S.S. Count: 15,041
Origin: French. 1) derived from the Old French word

"pacquet," meaning bundle. The name was given to those who sold or collected kindling or firewood. 2) derived from the medieval first name Pascal, ultimately derived from the Hebrew word "Pesach," meaning Passover.
Genealogies: None known.

PARADIS, PARADISE, PARADISO (S.S. Abbreviation: Paradi)

Ranking: 2618 S.S. Count: 17,366
Origin: Paradis, Paradise—French; Paradiso—Italian. Paradis, Paradise: derived from the late Latin word "paradis(us)," meaning paradise. The names were given to those who played the role of Paradise in a mystery play. Paradiso: derived from the late Latin word "paradis(us)," meaning paradise. The name was given to those who lived near an orchard or flower garden.
Genealogies: None known.

PAREDES (S.S. Abbreviation: Parede)

Ranking: 3855 S.S. Count: 11,695
Origin: Portuguese, Spanish. Derived from the Spanish word "pared," meaning wall. The name was given to those who lived in a shed attached to the side of a building.
Genealogies: None known.

PARENT (ALSO PARENTE, PARENTEAU, PARENTI, PARENTIN)

Ranking: 1812 S.S. Count: 24,896
Origin: Parent—English, French; Parentin, Parenteau—French; Parente, Parenti—Italian. Parent: 1) derived from the Middle English and Old French word "parent," meaning notable. The name was given to those whose appearance was considered remarkable. 2) derived from the Middle English and Old French word "parent," meaning parent or relative. The name was given to those who were related to an important person.
Genealogies: None known.

PARHAM

Ranking: 2065 S.S. Count: 22,196
Origin: English. Derived from the Old English words "pere" and "hām," meaning pear and homestead. The name was given to those from Parham, the name of several places in England.
Genealogies: *In a Pear Tree: the Story of some of the Parhams in that Tree* was compiled by Marjorie Parham Hailey and published in Edinburg, Texas, in 1987.

PARIS

Ranking: 2031 S.S. Count: 22,479
Origin: English, Spanish. English: transformation of Parish. Spanish: transformation of the Spanish first name Aparicio, derived from the Spanish word "aparición," mean-

ing appearance or manifestation. *The name was given to those born on the feast of the Epiphany.*

Famous **Parises**: WALTER PARIS (1842–1906) of England was an architect and watercolor painter. He lived in the United States after 1872.

Genealogies: None known.

PARISH

Ranking: 2228 **S.S. Count**: 20,576

Origin: *English. 1) derived from the medieval first name Paris, which is of uncertain etymology. 2) derived from the name of the French city, Paris, which was derived from the name of a Gaulish tribe. The name was given to those from Paris, a city in France.*

Famous **Parishes**: ELIJAH PARISH (1762–1825) of Connecticut was a Congregational clergyman and a co-author with Jedidiah Morse of geographies.

Genealogies: None known.

PARISI (ALSO PARISIANI, PARISINI, PARISIO, PARISIUS)

Ranking: 3603 **S.S. Count**: 12,533

Origin: *Parisius—German; Parisi, Parisiani, Parisini, Parisio—Italian. Cognates to Parish.*

Genealogies: None known.

PARK

Ranking: 664 **S.S. Count**: 63,156

Origin: *English. 1) ultimately derived from the Greek name Petros, which was derived from the word "petros," meaning rock. 2) derived from the Middle English and Old French word "parc," meaning park. The name was given to those who worked in a park or who lived near a park.*

Famous **Parks**: WILLIAM HALLOCK PARK (1863–1939) of New York City was a bacteriologist and health officer. He was the man who worked long and hard to isolate the bacterium that caused diphtheria. He was eventually able to isolate it, develop an antitoxin, and create an immunity test. Mass immunization followed, and the once-deadly disease was nearly eliminated from New York City. His program was quickly adopted throughout the nation and world. He worked on other diseases and was in the forefront in the sanitation of milk. ROBERT EZRA PARK (1864–1944) of Pennsylvania, a sociologist who worked as secretary to Booker T. Washington, was an authority on African-Americans and on human ecology. He was an author of books, including *Race and Culture* (1950) and *Human Communities* (1952). MAUD MAY WOOD PARK (1871–1955) of Massachusetts founded several women's suffrage groups and was the first president of the National League of Women Voters.

Genealogies: *Moses Park (1738–1828)* was compiled by Clara Lorene (Cammack) Park and published in Balti-more, Maryland, in 1991. *Park/e/s and Bunch on the Trail West, with Allied Families* was compiled by Alice Crandall Park and published in Baltimore, Maryland, in 1974. *The Parke Family: Earliest Pioneers of New Jersey with Later Generations who Pioneered in Old Frederick Co., Va. & on into Ohio & Indiana* [also Park] was compiled by Dorothy Robertson Becker and published in Fort Worth, Texas, in 1979.

PARKER

Ranking: 50 **S.S. Count**: 458,871

Origin: *English, Jewish. English: derived from the Middle English and Old French word "parc," meaning park. The name was given to gamekeepers of parks. Jewish: Anglicization of any of several similar-sounding Jewish names.*

Famous **Parkers**: JAMES PARKER (1714?–1770) of New Jersey was a partner of Benjamin Franklin in a New York printing business. His business in Woodbridge, New Jersey, was the first permanent printing business in New Jersey. JOHN PARKER (1729–1775) of Massachusetts was commander of the Minutemen in the Battle of Lexington on April 19, 1775. CYNTHIA ANN PARKER (1827?–1864?) of Illinois was captured by the Indians at the age of nine and became part of the wildest sect of the Comanches. She learned their culture and language and eventually married Nocona, a war chief. Three children were born to them. In 1860 white men raided a small party of women who were gathering food. All were killed except for Cynthia Ann and her toddler daughter, Topsannah. She was returned to her white family but cried for her husband and two sons. When her daughter died, she gave up all hope and died. Her son Pecos and husband died soon after, but her last son, Quanah, became a great war chief. He had taken her maiden name as the family name and had had a painting done from the only photograph of her that was known to exist. Hearing the story of her life and death, he searched until he found her grave, then had her remains moved to his home in what is now Oklahoma. The next year he, too, died and was buried beside her. In 1957 the site of the burial was needed by Fort Sill. The remains were removed for reburial, with Cynthia Ann's great-grandsons as pallbearers. Her great-great-granddaughter and her namesake placed a wreath at her grave. In 1965 the remains of Topsannah were discovered and reburied with those of her mother, Cynthia Ann, known as the "White Commanche." ELY SAMUEL PARKER (1828–1895) of New York was a Union officer whose claim to fame is the fact that he handwrote the official copies of the terms of surrender at Appomattox as the secretary to General Ulysses S. Grant. FRANCIS W. PARKER (1837–1902) of New Hampshire was the founder of Chicago (Illinois) Institute, which became the University of Chicago School of Education. GEORGE S. PARKER (1863–1937) of Wisconsin was the founder of the Parker

Pen Company and the inventor of the modernized fountain pen that was sold under the name "Lucky Curve." HORATIO W. PARKER (1863–1919) of Massachusetts, dean of the Yale University Music School, composed oratorios, operas, and other musical works. He also wrote the book *Music and Public Entertainment* (1911). JULIA SARFIELD O'CONNOR PARKER (1890–1972) of Massachusetts was a labor leader and one of the nine women on the Boston Telephone Operator's Union committee who were able to attain enough power to be included in the negotiations after the threatened telephone strike of 1913. DOROTHY ROTHSCHILD PARKER (1893–1967) of New Jersey was a writer who worked on the staff of *Vogue* and *Vanity Fair* and had verse and short stories published in collections. She also collaborated on the screenwriting of *A Star Is Born* and on the writing of plays. CHARLIE (BIRD) PARKER (1920–1955) of Kansas was the premier jazz alto saxophonist and improviser of his time and beyond. A leader in the bebop movement in jazz, he influenced many future musicians.

Genealogies: *Direct Ancestors of the Parker and Gray Families* was compiled by Elizabeth Gray Parker and published in Boston, Massachusetts, in 1967. *Parker in America, 1630–1910* was compiled by Augustus G. Parker and published in Buffalo, New York, in 1911. *Parker Pathways* was compiled by Katherine Jane Parker Brown and published in Genoa, Illinois, in 1986.

PARKIN (ALSO PARKINS, PARKINSON)
Ranking: 2209 **S.S. Count:** 20,757
Origin: Parkin, Parkins, Parkinson—English; Parkins— Jewish. Parkin, Parkins, Parkinson: derived from the Middle English first name Perkin, which was derived from the first name Peter with the suffix "-kin." Parkins: uncertain etymology. Possibly an Anglicization of similar-sounding Jewish names.

Famous **Bearers:** THOMAS IGNATIUS PARKINSON (1881–1959) of Pennsylvania was offered a position in President Franklin D. Roosevelt's administration. He declined and became a critic of Roosevelt's New Deal program.

Genealogies: *Timothy Parkinson and Ann Fielding* was compiled by Virginia Parkinson and published in Utah in 1972.

PARKS
Ranking: 296 **S.S. Count:** 121,681
Origin: English. Transformation of Park, derived from Peter.

Famous **Parkses:** WILLIAM PARKS (1698?–1750), possibly of England, was a printer and newspaper publisher. He is credited with setting up his shop in Williamsburg, Virginia, and founding the *Maryland Gazette* and the *Virginia*

Gazette. Many of the books he printed are of invaluable historical importance.

Genealogies: None known.

PARNELL
Ranking: 2314 **S.S. Count:** 19,632
Origin: English. Ultimately derived from Petrōnius, the name of a Roman family of uncertain etymology.

Genealogies: None known.

PARR
Ranking: 1964 **S.S. Count:** 23,059
Origin: English, German. English: derived from an Old English word meaning enclosure. The name was given to those from Parr, the name of a place in Lancashire, England. German: derived from the Middle Low German word "parre," meaning parish or district.

Famous **Parrs:** SAMUEL WILSON PARR (1857–1931) of Illinois was a chemist and inventor who advanced the use of coal through analysis of heat values of the various types of coal.

Genealogies: *The Descendants of Richard Parr: Pioneers of Licking County, Ohio* was compiled by Mariam Parr and published in Palo Alto, California, in 1983. *The Parr Family: Stephen of Delaware, some of his Descendants and Allied Families* was compiled by Lucille Parr and published in Parsons, West Virginia, in 1974.

PARRA
Ranking: 2712 **S.S. Count:** 16,767
Origin: Spanish. Derived from the Old Spanish word "parra," meaning trellis or arbor. The name was given to those who lived near an enclosure with a trellis.

Genealogies: None known.

PARRIS (ALSO PARRISH, PARRISIUS)
Ranking: 477 **S.S. Count:** 84,646
Origin: Parris, Parrish—English; Parris—French; Parrisius—German. Parris, Parrish: transformations of Parish. Parris, Parrisius: cognates to Parish, derived from Paris, referring to the French city.

Famous **Bearers:** SAMUEL PARRIS (1653–1719?) of England was a clergyman who was the pastor in Salem, Massachusetts, during the witch trials of 1689–1696. He did a thorough job of ferreting out the "witches" and condemning them. ANNE PARRISH (1760–1800) of Pennsylvania was the founder of a school in Philadelphia for poor girls and a place of employment for poor women. ALEXANDER PARRIS (1780–1852) of Maine was an architect responsible for many of the buildings in the Boston area, including David Sears House (1816) and St. Paul's Church (1819). ALBION KEITH PARRIS (1788–1857) of Maine was the governor of, a U.S. senator from, and a justice of the supreme court of

Maine. CELESTIA SUSANNAH PARRISH (1853–1918) of Virginia was a southern educator and one of the pioneers of progressive education. She was the founder of the first Parent-Teacher Cooperative Club in Georgia. She moved to northern Georgia, where she assumed the responsibilities of the state supervisor of rural schools for the North Georgia district. On her gravestone in Clayton, Georgia, is the inscription "Georgia's Greatest Woman." MAXFIELD PARRISH (1870–1966) of Pennsylvania was an artist and illustrator. He was one of the top illustrators for magazines and one of the best in illustrating children's classics. But he is best known for the millions of rural landscape prints made from his paintings that hang over the sofas in many of the homes of middle-class America today.

Genealogies: Ancestors & Descendants, Samuel Parrish, 1847 was published in Logan, Utah, in 1981. *A Portrait of our Ancestors: Jury, Troxell, Shisler & Parrish* was compiled by Irene Parrish Baker and published in Elk Rapids, Michigan, in 1986.

PARROT (ALSO PARROTT)

Ranking: 2120 S.S. Count: 21,606

Origin: English. Parrott: 1) derived from the river name Parret. The name was given to those from Perrott, the name of towns in Somerset, England. 2) derived from the Middle English first name Perot or Parot, which was ultimately derived from the Greek word "petra," meaning rock. Parrot: transformation of Parrott, derived from Peter.

Famous **Bearers:** ROBERT PARKER PARROTT (1804–1877) of New Hampshire invented a method to make cast-iron guns stronger, and his guns were used by Union troops during the Civil War. ENOCH GREENFEADE PARROTT (1815–1879) of New Hampshire was a naval officer and the one who made the first Union capture of a Confederate ship in the Civil War, on June 3, 1861.

Genealogies: Benjamin Parrott, c. 1795–1839 and Lewis Stover, 1781–1850/60, of Overton County, Tennessee and their Descendants was compiled by Mavis Parrott Kelsey and published in 1979. *The Popejoy (also Parrott family) Family in America, 1700–1976: William Popejoy Immigrant from England and his Descendants* was compiled by Charles Luther Popejoy and published in Juneau, Alaska, in 1976.

PARRY

Ranking: 3282 S.S. Count: 13,831

Origin: French, Welsh. French: cognate to Parish, derived from Paris, referring to the French city. Welsh: derived from the Welsh patronymic component "ap" and the first name Harry.

Famous **Parrys:** CHARLES CHRISTOPHER PARRY (1823–1890) of England came to the United States as a boy and became a botanist. He journeyed through the West meticulously cataloguing the plants that he discovered, which

numbered in the hundreds. JOHN S. PARRY (1843–1876) of Pennsylvania was a gynecologist and obstetrician noted for his work at Philadelphia Hospital and his authorship of *Extra-Uterine Pregnancy* (1875).

Genealogies: Eagon-Parry Family was compiled by Herbert B. Eagon and published in Delaware, Ohio, in 1981.

PARSONS (S.S. Abbreviation: Parson)

Ranking: 344 S.S. Count: 110,607

Origin: English. Derived from the Middle English and Old French word "persone," meaning parson. The name was given to the servants or the child of a parish priest.

Famous **Parsonses:** THEOPHILUS PARSONS (1750–1813) of Massachusetts, chief justice of the Massachusetts Supreme Court, was instrumental in establishing English common law as the traditional legal system in the United States. His son, THEOPHILUS PARSONS (1797–1882) of Massachusetts, a Boston lawyer and Harvard University law professor, wrote extensively on the law, with works including *Elements of Mercantile Law* (1856). LEWIS E. PARSONS (1817–1895) of New York was a lawyer and Unionist in Alabama during the Civil War. He served as provisional governor in 1865. EMILY ELIZABETH PARSONS (1824–1880) of Massachusetts was a Civil War nurse who overcame many handicaps and illnesses to assist those in need. ALBERT A. PARSONS (1848–1887) of Alabama was a Confederate soldier, then an anarchist. He edited the anarchist newspaper *The Alarm* in Chicago and was hanged after being convicted of murder in connection with the Haymarket riots. WILLIAM BARCLAY PARSONS (1859–1932) of New York was a civil engineer who was involved in many high-profile projects, including the New York City subway system and Cape Cod Canal. He also wrote *An American Engineer in China* (1900), *The American Engineers in France* (1920), and *Robert Fulton and the Submarine* (1922). ELSIE WORTHINGTON CLEWS PARSONS (1875–1941) of New York, an anthropologist, specialized in feminist sociological studies. Among the books she wrote were *Religious Chastity* and *The Old Fashioned Woman*, both of which were published in 1913 under the pseudonym John Main. LOUELLA OETTINGER PARSONS (1893–1972) of Illinois wrote the first newspaper column about movies in the United States. She wrote for the *Chicago Record-Herald*. A rival of Hedda Hopper, she also wrote a gossip column that was syndicated in more than 400 newspapers through Hearst. TALCOTT PARSONS (1902–1979) of Colorado, a sociologist, wrote of his theoretical system for analysis of society in *Structure of Social Action* (1937) and subsequent books.

Genealogies: The Parsons Family: Descendants of Cornet Joseph Parsons (c. 1618–1683), Springfield, Mass. was compiled by Gerald James Parsons and published in Baltimore, Maryland, in 1984. *Parsons Family History* was compiled by

American Genealogical Research Institute and published in Washington, D.C., in 1977.

PARTINGTON (S.S. Abbreviation: Partin)

Ranking: 3492 S.S. Count: 12,915

Origin: English. Derived from Peartingtūn, the Old English name of a town, meaning the settlement of Pearta's people. The name was given to those from Partington, a place in Greater Manchester, England.

Genealogies: None known.

PARTRICHE, PARTRICK, PARTRIDGE (S.S. Abbreviation: Partri)

Ranking: 3141 S.S. Count: 14,451

Origin: English, Irish. English: derived from the Middle English word "pertriche," meaning partridge. The names were given to those who hunted partridge, to those who lived in a house that bore the sign of the partridge, or to those who somehow resembled the bird. English, Irish: transformations of Patrick.

Famous **Bearers:** ALDEN PARTRIDGE (1785–1854) of Vermont is recognized as the founder of elementary and secondary military schools. He first opened a military academy in Norwich, Vermont, that became Norwich University; then he opened other, similar academies in four other states. JAMES R. PARTRIDGE (1823–1884) of Maryland was a Maryland lawyer, a Unionist, and U.S. minister to Latin American countries. WILLIAM O. PARTRIDGE (1861–1930), born in France of American parents, was a sculptor and author. Among his best-known sculpture works were statues of Ulysses S. Grant and Horace Greeley. Among his books was *Art for America* (1894).

Genealogies: *Partridge Genealogy, Descendants of George Partridge of Duxbury, Massachusetts* was compiled by George Henry Partridge and published in Norwood, Massachusetts, in 1915.

PASCHAL (S.S. Abbreviation: Pascha)

Ranking: 2971 S.S. Count: 15,309

Origin: French. Cognate to the English name Pascall, which was derived from the medieval first name Pascal, ultimately derived from the Hebrew word "Pesach," meaning Passover.

Famous **Paschals:** GEORGE WASHINGTON PASCHAL (1812–1878) of Georgia was a jurist and a staunch Unionist in Texas.

Genealogies: None known.

PASQUA (ALSO PASQUALE, PASQUALI, PASQUALINI, PASQUATO)

Ranking: 3336 S.S. Count: 13,586

Origin: Italian. Pasqua, Pasuato: cognates to the English name Pask, which was derived from the Middle English word

"paske," meaning Easter. The name was given to those born on or around Easter or to those who had some special connection to Easter. Pasquale, Pasquali, Pasqualini: cognates to Paschal.

Genealogies: None known.

PASTOR (ALSO PASTORE, PASTORELLI, PASTORI, PASTORINI)

Ranking: 2541 S.S. Count: 17,863

Origin: Pastor—Catalan, Dutch, English, French, German, Jewish, Spanish; Pastore, Pastorelli, Pastori, Pastorini—Italian. Pastor (Dutch, German): derived from numerous words meaning shepherd. Pastor (Catalan, English, French, Spanish): derived from the Latin word "pastor," meaning shepherd, which was derived from the word "pascere," meaning to graze. The name was given to shepherds. Pastor (Jewish): unknown etymology. Pastore, Pastorelli, Pastori, Pastorini: cognates to Pastor.

Famous **Bearers:** ANTONIO PASTOR (1837–1908) of New York, an actor and theater owner, helped make vaudeville respectable for family entertainment in New York City.

Genealogies: None known.

PATE

Ranking: 1098 S.S. Count: 40,243

Origin: English, Scottish. 1) derived from the Middle English word "pate," meaning skull or head. The name was given to those who were bald. 2) derived from the first name Pat(t), which was derived from Patrick.

Famous **Pates:** MAURICE PATE (1894–1965) of Nebraska was the first executive director of the United Nations Children's Fund (UNICEF, formerly United Nations International Children's Emergency Fund), which he helped to establish in 1948.

Genealogies: *The Pate Pioneers* was published in Buffalo, Texas, in 1986.

PATEL

Ranking: 946 S.S. Count: 45,700

Origin: French, Hindi. French: the name meaning one who sold cakes or tarts. Hindi: the name means the village chief or head.

Genealogies: None known.

PATRIC (ALSO PATRICE, PATRICIO, PATRICK, PATRICOT)

Ranking: 493 S.S. Count: 81,309

Origin: Patrick—English; Patric, Patrice, Patricot—French; Patricio—Portuguese. Patrick: derived from the first name Patrick, which was derived from the Latin name Patricius, meaning the son of a patrician or noble. Patric, Patrice, Patricio, Patricot: cognates to Patrick.

Famous **Bearers:** MARY MILLS PATRICK (1850–1940) of

New Hampshire was president of Istanbul Woman's College, Istanbul, Turkey, 1890–1924, and the author of several books, including *Sappho and the Island of Lesbos* (1912). MASON M. PATRICK (1863–1942) of West Virginia held several strategic commands in the U.S. Army Corps of Engineers and was an early chief of the Army Air Corps. EDWIN (TED) PATRICK (1901–1964) of New Jersey was editor of *Holiday* magazine, to which he attracted top writers and which he made consistently profitable.

Genealogies: *Patrick's Corner* was compiled by Sean Patrick and published in 1992. *Precious Bonds* [also Patrick] was compiled by S. J. Patrick and published in Alden, Iowa, in 1984.

PATTEN (ALSO PATTENDEN)

Ranking: 2503 **S.S. Count:** 18,122

Origin: English. Patten: 1) derived from the Middle English word "paten," meaning clog. The name was given to those who made, sold, or wore clogs. 2) transformation of Pate, derived from Patrick. Pattenden: derived from the name of an Old English town meaning the "swine pasture. associated with Peatta" (H&H). The name was given to those from Pattenden, a place in Kent, England.

Famous **Bearers:** SIMON N. PATTEN (1852–1922) of Illinois was an economist and professor who wrote *The Development of English Thought* (1899) and *The New Basis of Civilization* (1907). JAMES A. PATTEN (1852–1928) of Illinois was a grain dealer in Chicago noted for his success in commodity futures. GILBERT PATTEN (1866–1945) of Maine wrote more than 200 adventure stories based on the fictional character Frank Merriwell. He used the pseudonym Burt L. Standish.

Genealogies: *Descendants of Isaac Patten, Sr., and his Wife, Jane Norris: an Early Pioneer Family in Sullivan County, Indiana* was compiled by Ernest C. Swanson and published in Baltimore, Maryland, in 1985. *Allied Genealogies: Pattenden, Cunnings, Donaldson and Hamilton* was compiled by Donald C. Keller and published in Lancaster, New York, in 1969.

PATTERSON (S.S. Abbreviation: Patter)

Ranking: 98 **S.S. Count:** 282,181

Origin: English, Scottish. Transformation of Pate, derived from Patrick.

Famous **Pattersons:** ROBERT M. PATTERSON (1832–1911) of Pennsylvania was an authority on ecclesiastical law. He was editor of *The Presbyterian*, then editor of *The Presbyterian Journal*. JAMES K. PATTERSON (1833–1922), born in Scotland and raised in Indiana, was president of State College of Kentucky, later the University of Kentucky, for 41 years. JOHN HENRY PATTERSON (1844–1922) of Ohio turned a failing business into the prosperous National Cash Register Co. by using modern sales techniques and direct-mail

advertising. HANNAH JANE PATTERSON (1879–1937) of Pennsylvania was a suffragist and a defense official in World War I. She served as one of President Woodrow Wilson's 11 members of the Woman's Committee of the Council of National Defense. JOSEPH M. PATTERSON (1879–1946) of Illinois, a journalist, was co-editor with his cousin Robert McCormick of the *Chicago Tribune* before he and McCormick founded the New York *Daily News*. His sister, ELEANOR MEDILL PATTERSON (1884–1948), was owner and publisher of the Washington (D.C.) *Herald* and the Washington *Times*, two newspapers she combined into the *Times-Herald*. RICHARD C. PATTERSON JR. (1886–1966) of Nebraska was a corporate executive with many firms and was a diplomat who served in Yugoslavia, Guatemala, and Switzerland. ALICIA PATTERSON (1906–1963) of Illinois was a newspaper publisher and editor and the daughter of Joseph M. Patterson. She was the founder of *Newsday*.

Genealogies: None known.

PATTON

Ranking: 438 **S.S. Count:** 90,901

Origin: English, Scottish. Transformation of Pate, derived from Patrick.

Famous **Pattons:** FRANCIS L. PATTON (1843–1932), born in Bermuda, was president of the College of New Jersey (now Princeton University), from 1888 to 1902. When he retired, he nominated his own successor, Woodrow Wilson, later the 28th president of the United States. GEORGE S. PATTON (1885–1945) of California was called "Old Blood and Guts" because of his experience and leadership as an army officer. He commanded troops in various parts of the world during World War II, including the Third Army during its campaign across France and Germany. His military experiences are recalled in his posthumously published memoirs, *War As I Knew It* (1947).

Genealogies: *Descendants of Isaac Patten, Sr., and his Wife, Jane Norris: an Early Pioneer Family in Sullivan County, Indiana* [also Patton] was compiled by Ernest C. Swanson and published in Baltimore, Maryland, in 1985. *Days of Vintage, Years of Vision* was compiled by Midge Sherwood and published in San Marino, California, in 1982. *Alexander Patton of Haw Old Field Progeny* was compiled by Jack Randolph Howard and published in Towson, Maryland, in 1980.

PAUL

Ranking: 423 **S.S. Count:** 93,918

Origin: Dutch, English, Flemish, French, German. Derived from the first name Paul, which was derived from the Latin name Paulus, meaning small.

Famous **Pauls:** ALICE PAUL (1885–1977) of New Jersey devoted her life to campaigning for women's rights. She was a founder of the Congressional Union for Woman Suffrage. That group became the National Woman's Party, which she served as chairperson. ELLIOT H. PAUL (1891–1958) of Massachusetts was the author of a variety of works, including novels and screenplays, such as *Rhapsody in Blue* (1946). JOSEPHINE BAY PAUL (1900–1962) of Iowa was the first woman to be chairperson of a large steamship company in the United States and the first woman to be president and chairperson of a member firm of the New York Stock Exchange.

Genealogies: *Your Desert and Mine* was compiled by Nina Paul Shumway and published in Palm Springs, California, in 1979. *Philip Paul of Stocklinch, Somerset, England and some of his Descendants in Old Gloucester County, New Jersey and Elsewhere* was compiled by Gordon W. Paul and published in Albuquerque, New Mexico, in 1983.

PAULEY

Ranking: 3183 S.S. Count: 14,266
Origin: English. Transformation of Paul.
Genealogies: *Ancestors and Kin* [also Pauley] was compiled by Robert Walden Coggeshall and published in Spartanburg, South Carolina, in 1988.

PAULIN (ALSO PAULING, PAULINO)

Ranking: 3489 S.S. Count: 12,934
Origin: Pauling—English; Paulin—French; Paulino—Portuguese. Cognates to and transformations of Paul.
Genealogies: None known.

PAULSEN (S.S. Abbreviation: Paulse)

Ranking: 2759 S.S. Count: 16,511
Origin: Danish, German, Norwegian. Cognate to and transformation of Paul.
Genealogies: None known.

PAULSON (S.S. Abbreviation: Paulso)

Ranking: 1649 S.S. Count: 27,093
Origin: English. Transformation of Paul.
Genealogies: None known.

PAXTON

Ranking: 2724 S.S. Count: 16,704
Origin: English, Scottish. Derived from the Old English town name Pœccestūn, meaning "settlement of Pœcc" (H&H). The name was given to those from Paxton, the name of several places in England and Scotland.
Genealogies: None known.

PAYNE (ALSO PAYNELL, PAYNES)

Ranking: 173 S.S. Count: 194,020
Origin: English. Transformations of Paine.
Famous Bearers: JOHN H. PAYNE (1791–1852) of New York, an actor and playwright, was an author, translator, or adaptor of more than 60 plays. He also was U.S. consul at Tunis for four years. HENRY B. PAYNE (1810–1896) of New York was a member of Congress, then a U.S. senator from Ohio. His son, OLIVER H. PAYNE (1839–1917) of Ohio, was a prominent capitalist, involved with companies such as Standard Oil and American Tobacco. A nephew of Henry B. Payne, SERENO ELISHA PAYNE (1843–1914) of New York was a member of Congress from New York.

Genealogies: *The Paynes of Virginia* was compiled by Brooke Payne and published in Harrisonburg, Virginia, in 1977. *Descendants of Sanford Payne* was compiled by Madge Starliper Payne and published in Baltimore, Maryland, in 1992. *Foxworth, Bush, Payne, Bledsoe & Allied Lineages* was compiled by Sarah Payne Foxworth and published in Dallas, Texas, in 1985.

PAYTON

Ranking: 1466 S.S. Count: 30,337
Origin: English. Derived from the Old English first name Pœga and the Old English word "tūn," meaning settlement. The name was given to those from Payton, the name of a place in Sussex, England.
Genealogies: *Yelverton Payton* was compiled by Mary Evelyn Cook Treadway and published in Shipman, Virginia, in 1984.

PAZ

Ranking: 4941 S.S. Count: 9065
Origin: Jewish, Portuguese, Spanish. Portuguese, Spanish: cognates to Pace. Jewish: derived from the Hebrew word "paz," meaning pure gold. The name was taken ornamentally.
Genealogies: None known.

PEACE

Ranking: 3908 S.S. Count: 11,540
Origin: English. Transformation of Pace.
Genealogies: None known.

PEACOCK, PEACOCKE (S.S. Abbreviation: Peacoc)

Ranking: 1470 S.S. Count: 30,298
Origin: English. Derived from the Middle English word "pē," meaning peacock. The name was given to those who were vain or to fops.
Genealogies: *The Sharp Family of Southern New Jersey* [also Peacock] was compiled by Albert Stirling Adams and published in Vincentown, New Jersey, in 1981. *The Peacock, Rueff, Kittle, Van Deusen, Quackenbos, McCarn, Kayser, and Related Families in New Netherland, 1623–1759* was compiled by Earle Franklin Peacox and published in Webster, New York, in 1970.

PEAK

Ranking: 4054 S.S. Count: 11,159

Origin: English. Derived from the Old English word "pēac," meaning pointed hill. The name was given to those who lived near a pointed hill or to those from the district called Peak, in Derbyshire, England.

Genealogies: *The Peak-Peake Family History* was compiled by Cyrus Henderson Peake and published in Claremont, California, in 1975.

PEARCE (ALSO PEARCEY)

Ranking: 961 S.S. Count: 45,442

Origin: English. Pearce: derived from the Middle English first name Piers, which was derived from Peter. Pearcey: transformation of Percy, which was derived from the Gallo-Roman first name Persius and the suffix "-acum." The name was given to those from Percy, the name of several places in northern France.

Famous **Bearers**: JAMES A. PEARCE (1805–1862) of Virginia was a member of Congress, then a U.S. senator, from Maryland. RICHARD M. PEARCE (1874–1930), born in Canada, was a doctor who was named to the first chair of research medicine in the United States at the University of Pennsylvania, in 1910. As director of the Division of Medical Education for the Rockefeller Foundation (1920–1930), he guided the placement of substantial funds to improve medical education around the world. LOUISE PEARCE (1885–1959) of Massachusetts was a pathologist and physician and one of the developers of tryparsamide, a drug to control African sleeping sickness.

Genealogies: *Pearce, Bartlett, Matthews, Smart, and Allied Families* was compiled by James Alonzo Matthews Jr. and published in Midland, Texas, in 1983. *Pearce Pioneers in Kentucky* was compiled by Marvin James Pearce and published in El Cerrito, California, in 1969.

PEARL

Ranking: 4115 S.S. Count: 10,977

Origin: English, Jewish. English: derived from the Middle English and Old French word "perle," meaning pearl. The name was given to those who traded in pearls.

Famous **Pearls**: RAYMOND PEARL (1879–1940) of New Hampshire, a biologist and professor, founded two scientific journals, *Quarterly Review of Biology* and *Human Biology*. He also wrote *Introduction to Medical Biometry and Statistics* (1923).

Genealogies: *The Francis, Pearl, and White Families* was compiled by Larry A. James and published in Neosho, Missouri, in 1984.

PEARSON (S.S. Abbreviation: Pearso)

Ranking: 254 S.S. Count: 142,596

Origin: English. Transformation of Pearce.

Famous **Pearsons**: FRED STARK PEARSON (1861–1915) of Massachusetts was an engineer and an expert in the field of electric streetcars. He introduced streetcars to Brooklyn, New York, and formulated the plans for the subway system of New York City. He died at sea aboard the *Lusitania*. LEONARD PEARSON (1868–1909) of Indiana was a veterinarian who conducted the first tuberculin test in the Americas. THOMAS GILBERT PEARSON (1873–1943) of Illinois was a wildlife conservationist who worked for the protection of wildlife and the environment. ANDREW R. (DREW) PEARSON (1897–1969) of Illinois was a newspaper columnist known for exposing scandals in the nation's capital. His column, which he wrote first with Robert Allen, then with Jack Anderson, was named after the exposé book he and Allen wrote, *The Washington Merry-Go-Round* (1931).

Genealogies: *Northern Neck Families: the Ancestors of Susan Frances Chapman*: Alexander, Chapman, and Pearson was compiled by Brian Joe Lobley Berry and published in 1990. *100 Years of Pearsons: the Descendants of John and Johanna Pearson who Emigrated from Sweden to America in April, 1889* was compiled by Frederick John Pearson and published in Houston, Texas, in 1976.

PEASE

Ranking: 2382 S.S. Count: 19,066

Origin: English. Derived from the Middle English word "pese," meaning peas. The name was given to those who grew or sold peas or to persons who were small or deemed unimportant.

Famous **Peases**: ELISHA MARSHALL PEASE (1812–1883) of Connecticut was a Texas politician who held many offices, including that of governor. In retrospect, he was an excellent governor, reducing the debt and setting up a school fund, but he was not appreciated while in office. FRANCIS G. PEASE (1881–1938) of Massachusetts was an astronomer noted for photographs and spectrograms of stars, the moon, and planets and for designs of telescopes.

Genealogies: *The Ancestors and Descendants of the Honorable Calvin Pease and Laura Grant Risley Pease, his Wife, of Suffield, CT., Rutland, VT., and Warren, OH.* was compiled by Allene Beaumont Duty and published in Cleveland, Ohio, in 1979. *A Genealogical and Historical Record of the Descendants of John Pease, Sen., Last of Enfield, Conn.* was compiled by David Pease and published in Monticello, Kentucky, in 1983.

PECK

Ranking: 723 S.S. Count: 58,509

Origin: English. 1) transformation of Peak. 2) derived from the Middle English word "pekke," meaning peck, a former measure of dry goods. The name was given to those who worked in weights and measures.

Famous **Pecks**: CHARLES HORTON PECK (1833–1917)

of New York studied the fungi that were native to North America. He identified 2500 new species. GEORGE W. PECK (1840–1916) of New York was mayor of Milwaukee and governor of Wisconsin. ANNIE SMITH PECK (1850–1935) of Rhode Island climbed Mt. Huascarán in Peru, which, with an altitude of 21,812 feet, was the highest point in the Americas reached by an American at that time. She also wrote books, including *Search for the Apex of America* (1911). LILLIE PECK (1888–1957) of New York was a settlement house leader and one of the leaders of the National Settlements of the South conferences of 1936.

Genealogies: *Klein-Peck: Prairie Milestones* was compiled by Philip Cuthbert Biddle and published in Logan, Utah, in 1990. *A Sense of Place, Northwest Ohio* was compiled by Mary Mae Campbell and published in Evansville, Indiana, in 1985.

PEDERSEN (S.S. Abbreviation: Peders)
Ranking: 890 **S.S. Count:** 48,860
Origin: Danish, Norwegian. Cognate to Peter.
Genealogies: None known.

PEEBLES (S.S. Abbreviation: Peeble)
Ranking: 3577 **S.S. Count:** 12,608
Origin: Scottish. Uncertain etymology. Possibly derived from the Welsh word "pebyll," meaning tent or pavilion. The name was given to those from Peebles, a place in Scotland.
Genealogies: *The 'Peebles' Family Tree Grows* was compiled by Leslie Arthur Peebles and published in Marathon, New York, in 1974.

PEEK
Ranking: 2974 **S.S. Count:** 15,291
Origin: English, German. English: transformation of Peak. German: transformation of Pike.
Famous **Peeks:** GEORGE NELSON PEEK (1873–1943) of Illinois was a leader in the farm industry who tried politically to end the depression that hit farmers after World War I.
Genealogies: *Descendants of Robert Peek, 1802–1974* was compiled by Zola Nethken Pointer and published in Baltimore, Maryland, in 1975. *Janes-Peek Family History* was compiled by Reba Neighbors Collins and published in Claremore, Oklahoma, in 1981.

PEEL
Ranking: 4727 **S.S. Count:** 9467
Origin: English. Derived from the Anglo-Norman-French word "pel," meaning stake or pole. The name was given to those who were tall and slim or to those who lived near a stake fence.
Genealogies: None known.

PEEPLES (S.S. Abbreviation: Peeple)
Ranking: 4285 **S.S. Count:** 10,476
Origin: Scottish. Transformation of Peebles.
Genealogies: None known.

PELLEGRIN, PELLEGRINELLI, PELLEGRINI, PELLEGRINO, PELLEGRINOTTI (S.S. Abbreviation: Pelleg)
Ranking: 2409 **S.S. Count:** 18,797
Origin: Pellegrin—French; Pellegrinelli, Pellegrini, Pellegrino, Pellegrinotti—Italian. Cognates to the English name Pilgrim, which was ultimately derived from the Latin word "peregrinus," meaning traveler. The names were given to those who had made a pilgrimage to the Holy Land.
Genealogies: None known.

PELLETIER (S.S. Abbreviation: Pellet)
Ranking: 1546 **S.S. Count:** 28,862
Origin: French. Derived from the Old French word "pelletier," meaning furrier, which was derived from the word "pel," meaning skin. The name was given to furriers.
Genealogies: None known.

PEMBERTON (S.S. Abbreviation: Pember)
Ranking: 2699 **S.S. Count:** 16,842
Origin: English. Derived from the British component "penn," meaning head or hill, and the Old English words "bere" and "tūn," meaning barley and settlement. The name was given to those from Pemberton, a place in Greater Manchester, England.
Famous **Pembertons:** ISRAEL PEMBERTON (1715–1779) of Pennsylvania was responsible for keeping peace with the Indians. He spent time in prison for failing to swear an oath of allegiance to Pennsylvania in 1777. JAMES PEMBERTON (1723–1809) of Pennsylvania was the founder of the Society for the Relief of Free Negroes (1775) and the president of a group that worked to abolish slavery. He was the brother of Israel Pemberton. JOHN C. PEMBERTON (1814–1881) of Pennsylvania resigned from the U.S. army to enter the Confederate army. He was commander at Vicksburg when General Ulysses S. Grant forced a Confederate surrender there on July 4, 1863.
Genealogies: *The Hottest Water in Chicago: on Family, Race, Time, and American Culture* was compiled by Gayle Pemberton and published in Boston, Massachusetts, in 1992.

PEÑA
Ranking: 588 **S.S. Count:** 70,802
Origin: Spanish. derived from the Spanish word "peña," meaning crag. The name was given to those who lived near a steeply projecting mass of rock.
Genealogies: None known.

PENCE

Ranking: 2642 S.S. Count: 17,235

Origin: German. Derived from the first name Benzo.

Genealogies: *Genealogy and History of the Pense and Allied Families* [also Pence] was compiled by Beverly Pense and published in Cane Hill, Arkansas, in 1987. *A Guide to the Pence Families of America* was compiled by Richard Allen Pence and published in Fairfax, Virginia, in 1982.

PENDER (ALSO PENDERGAST, PENDERGRASS, PENDERGRAST)

Ranking: 1385 S.S. Count: 31,953

Origin: English. Pender: transformation of Pinder, derived from the Middle English word "pind(en)," meaning to enclose. The name was given to those who corralled stray animals and took them to the pound. Pendergast, Pendergrass, Pendergrast: transformations of Prendergast.

Famous Bearers: WILLIAM DORSEY PENDER (1834–1863) of North Carolina was a Confederate soldier and the commander of the North Carolina brigade under General A. P. Hill at the Seven Days' Battle at Chancellorsville. HAROLD PENDER (1879–1959) of North Carolina was an engineer who proved in 1903 that a magnetic field existed around a moving, electrically charged body. He also wrote *Principles of Electrical Engineering* (1911).

Genealogies: *Pendergrass of Virginia and the Carolinas, 1669–1919* was compiled by Allen Pendergrast and published in Sedona, Arizona, in 1977.

PENDLEBURY, PENDLETON

Ranking: 1508 S.S. Count: 29,493

Origin: English. Pendlebury: derived from the name of the hill called Pendle, which is comprised of the British component "penn," meaning hill or head, and the Old English word "hyll," also meaning hill; and the Old English word "burh," meaning town. The name was given to those from Pendlebury, a place in Greater Manchester, England. Pendleton: derived from the name of the hill called Pendle and the Old English word "tūn," meaning settlement. The name was given to those from Pendleton, the name of places in England.

Famous Bearers: EDMUND PENDLETON (1721–1803) of Virginia was a member of the Continental Congress and governor of Virginia. His great-grandnephew, GEORGE HUNT PENDLETON (1825–1889) of Ohio, was a member of Congress and a U.S. senator. He was instrumental in the passage in 1883 of the act that set up the Civil Service Commission. JOHN B. PENDLETON (1798–1866) of New York City was the first to produce lithographs in the United States. They were first done in Boston in 1825. EDMUND MONROE PENDLETON (1815–1884) of Georgia was an agricultural chemist and the founder of a company that was the first to manufacture fertilizer on a large scale. The company also was the first to use cotton seeds as a fertil-

izer ingredient. ELLEN FRITZ PENDLETON (1864–1936) of Rhode Island was president of Wellesley College (1911–1936).

Genealogies: None known.

PENN

Ranking: 1666 S.S. Count: 26,853

Origin: English. 1) derived from the British component "pen," meaning hill. The name was given to those from Penn, the name of several places in England. 2) transformation of Parnell. 3) derived from the Middle English word "penn," meaning pen, referring to a pen for keeping sheep. The name was given to shepherds.

Famous Penns: WILLIAM PENN (1644–1718) of England was the founder of Pennsylvania and of a public grammar school in Philadelphia called the William Penn Charter School. He also envisioned as early as 1697 a central government for the colonies as one united group. HANNAH CALLOWHILL PENN (1671–1726) of England was the second wife of William Penn (1644–1718). Because of their age difference, much of the running of the Penn estate fell to her, as a series of strokes had left him unable to administer the affairs at hand. Because of her, Pennsylvania remained whole and the colonists at peace. Her branch of the Penn family remained in control of the colony until the Revolution. THOMAS PENN (1702–1775) of England was the son of William Penn. He was willed 25 percent of the proprietary interests in Pennsylvania and acquired another 50 percent. He managed his affairs from England, as he was disliked by the colonists and Indians. The Indians disliked him mostly for his "walking purchase" of the forks of the Delaware (1737). JOHN PENN (1729–1795) of Pennsylvania was the grandson of William and Hannah Penn. He inherited 25 percent of the proprietary rights in Pennsylvania (1771). He served Pennsylvania as a politician, settling boundary disputes with Connecticut, Virginia, and Maryland. He also mediated differences between the frontiersmen and the Indians. RICHARD PENN (1735–1811) of England was the grandson of William Penn. He served as the lieutenant governor of Pennsylvania and was Congress's messenger in the deliverance of the "Olive Branch" petition to the king in 1775. He died in England. JOHN PENN (1740–1788) of Virginia was a Revolutionary patriot, a member of the Continental Congress, and one of the signers of the Declaration of Independence.

Genealogies: *The Storm Gathering: the Penn Family and the American Revolution* was compiled by Lorett Treese and published in University Park, Maryland, in 1992. *The Penn Ancestors of Corine Penn Christian: Descendant of Abram Penn, 2nd of the Penn Family of Virginia* was compiled by Mary Christian and published in Paducah, Kentucky, in 1992.

PENNELL, PENNELLA, PENNELLI (S.S. Abbreviation: Pennel)

Ranking: 4305 **S.S. Count:** 10,426

Origin: Pennell—English; Pennella, Pennelli—Italian. Pennell: transformation of Parnell. Pennella, Pennelli: cognates to Peña.

Famous **Bearers:** ELIZABETH ROBINS PENNELL (1855–1936) of Pennsylvania was an author and art critic. She wrote *Life of Mary Wollstonecraft*, part of a famous women's series. Combining her writing with her husband's illustrations, she published a series of books of their adventures, among them *Our Sentimental Journey through France and Italy* (1888) and *Over the Alps on a Bicycle* (1898). JOSEPH PENNELL (1857–1926) of Pennsylvania was an artist known for illustrating articles published in contemporary journals. He was the husband of Elizabeth Robins Pennell.

Genealogies: None known.

PENNINCK, PENNING, PENNINGTON, PENNINI, PENNINO (S.S. Abbreviation: Pennin)

Ranking: 708 **S.S. Count:** 59,734

Origin: Penninck—Dutch, Flemish; Penning—Dutch, English, German; Pennington—English; Pennini, Pennino—Italian. Penninck, Penning: transformations of and cognates to Penny. Pennington: derived from the Old English words "pening" and "tūn," meaning penny and settlement. The name was given to those from Pennington, the name of places in England. Pennini, Pennino: cognates to Peña.

Famous **Bearers:** WULLIAM SANDFORD PENNINGTON (1757–1826) of New Jersey was a Revolutionary soldier, New Jersey judge, governor of New Jersey, and federal district and state supreme court judge. WILLIAM PENNINGTON (1796–1862) of New Jersey was governor of New Jersey, then a member of and the Speaker of the U.S. House of Representatives. MARY ENGLE PENNINGTON (1872–1952) of Tennessee was a chemist and an expert on the refrigeration of perishable foods. JAMES W.C. PENNINGTON (1809–1870) of Maryland was an escaped slave who came to be known as an accomplished preacher. He wrote *The Fugitive Blacksmith* (London, 1849).

Genealogies: *With their own Bloos: a Saga of Southwestern Pioneers* [also Pennington] was compiled by Virginia Culin Roberts and published in Fort Worth, Texas, in 1992. *Ancestors & Descendants of Wheeler Pennington: Monroe County, West Virginia* was compiled by Richard Allan Blake and published in Londonderry, New Hampshire, in 1993.

PENNY

Ranking: 3363 **S.S. Count:** 13,482

Origin: English. Derived from the Old English word "peni(n)g," meaning penny, a silver coin of great value.

Famous **Pennys:** JAMES CASH PENNY (1875–1971) of Missouri was the founder of the J.C. Penny chain of department stores.

Genealogies: None known.

PEOPLE (ALSO PEOPLES)

Ranking: 1813 **S.S. Count:** 24,852

Origin: English. Derived from the Old French first name Pepis, which is of uncertain etymology.

Genealogies: *Cook, Caldwell, Peoples, Stuart, and other Families* was compiled by David Stuart Peoples and published in Baltimore, Maryland, in 1990. *Priester-Peeples Lives and Legends* [also Peoples] was compiled by Jane Priester Hawkins and published in Aiken, South Carolina, in 1987.

PEPPER (ALSO PEPPERALL, PEPPERELL)

Ranking: 1907 **S.S. Count:** 23,746

Origin: English, Jewish. English: derived from the Middle English word "peper," meaning pepper, the spice. The name was given to spicers. Jewish: derived from the German word "pfeffer," meaning pepper. The name was taken ornamentally.

Famous **Bearers:** SIR WILLIAM PEPPERELL (1696–1759) of Maine was an army officer who was made a baronet after he commanded an American force cooperating with the British in capturing a French fortress on Cape Breton. He was the firt American-born person so honored.

Genealogies: *The History of the Pepper Family in America and Allied Lines* was compiled by Florence Pepper Raya and published in Fort Madison, Iowa, in 1973. *The Descendants and some Ancestors of Luther Marvin Smith and his Wife, Ada Penn Pepper of Lincoln County, Mississippi* was compiled by Charlie Rabb Ashford and published in Starkville, Mississippi, in 1971.

PERALES (S.S. Abbreviation: Perale)

Ranking: 3983 **S.S. Count:** 11,355

Origin: Spanish. Cognate to the English name Pear, which was ultimately derived from the Latin word "pirum," meaning pear. The name was given to those who sold or grew pears.

Genealogies: None known.

PERALTA (S.S. Abbreviation: Peralt)

Ranking: 3107 **S.S. Count:** 14,632

Origin: Portuguese, Spanish. Derived from the Latin phrase "petra alta," meaning high rock. The name was given to those from Peralta, the name of several places in Spain and Portugal.

Famous **Peraltas:** PEDRO DE PERALTA (1584–1666) was the governor of New Mexico and the founder of the city of Santa Fe.

Genealogies: *Luis Maria Peralta and his Adobe* was compiled by Frances L. Fox and published in San Jose, California, in 1975.

PERDUE

Ranking: 1958 S.S. Count: 23,161
Origin: English. Derived from the Old French phrase "par Dieu," meaning by God.
Genealogies: *James A. Perdue and Descendants, 1822–1984* was compiled by Gervaise Wynn-Perdue and published in Warner Robins, Georgia, in 1984. *Our Family Heritage: the Perdues of the Eastern Shore of Maryland, 1563 to Present* was compiled by Edward M. Perdue and published in Baltimore, Maryland, in 1988.

PEREIRA (S.S. Abbreviation: Pereir)

Ranking: 1991 S.S. Count: 22,771
Origin: Spanish. Transformation of Perales.
Famous Pereiras: IRENE RICE PEREIRA (1907–1971) of Massachusetts was a painter of the 1930s and 1940s who specialized in the geometric abstract style of art.
Genealogies: None known.

PEREZ

Ranking: 57 S.S. Count: 415,764
Origin: Spanish. Cognate to Peter.
Genealogies: *Children of the Hummingbird: Perez and Najera of Mexico and Texas* was compiled by Robert McAlear and published in Nice, California, in 1984. *Tales of an Italian-American Family* [also Perez] was compiled by Joseph F. Perez and published in New York, New York, in 1991.

PERKIN (ALSO PERKINS)

Ranking: 190 S.S. Count: 183,743
Origin: English. Transformation of Parkinson.
Famous Bearers: ELIZABETH PECK PERKINS (1735–1807) of Massachusetts was a businesswoman, philanthropist, and one of the founders of the Boston Female Asylum. ELISHA PERKINS (1741–1799) of Connecticut was a medical charlatan and fraud. He used pieces of metal over the body in an attempt to draw out sickness. The practice was referred to as Perkinism. JACOB PERKINS (1766–1849) of Massachusetts was an inventor whose patents included one of the first refrigerating machines. THOMAS H. PERKINS (1764–1854) of Massachusetts made a fortune as a merchant and gave some of it to medical establishments in Massachusetts. He left his home to the New England Asylum for the Blind, which became the Perkins Institute and Massachusetts School for the Blind. FREDERIC BEECHER PERKINS (1828–1899) of Connecticut was a pioneer in the area of library science. GEORGE CLEMENT PERKINS (1839–1923) of Maine was a ship owner with the Pacific Coast Steamship Co. He served as both governor of and U.S. senator from California. CHARLES ELLIOTT PERKINS (1840–1907) of Ohio was the president of the Burlington & Quincy Railroad and responsible for most of the improvements made to the company. GEORGE WALBRIDGE PERKINS (1862–1920) of Illinois was the chairman of the Y.M.C.A. finance committee. Through it he raised $2 million for World War I welfare projects. LUCY FITCH PERKINS (1865–1937) of Indiana was an author of children's books, including *The Puritan Twins* (1921) and *The American Twins of the Revolution* (1926). DWIGHT HEALD PERKINS (1867–1941) of Tennessee was an architect influential in the Chicago school of architecture. FRANCES PERKINS (1882–1965) of Massachusetts, as U.S. secretary of labor (1933–1945), oversaw the implementation of New Deal legislation. She was the first female cabinet member in the government of the United States. MAXWELL E. PERKINS (1884–1947) of New York, an editor and vice president at Charles Scribner's Sons publishing company, advanced the careers of many well-known writers, including F. Scott Fitzgerald, Ernest Hemingway, and Thomas Wolfe.

Genealogies: *Ancestors of Charles Brush Perkins and Maurice Perkins* was compiled by Charles Brush Perkins and published in Baltimore, Maryland, in 1976. *Genealogy and History of One Branch of the Perkins Family in America, Originating with Edward Perkins, Immigrant to America and to New Haven, Connecticut* was compiled by Paul M. Perkins and published in Minerva, Ohio, in 1980.

PERRIN (ALSO PERRINEAU, PERRINET, PERRING, PERRINO)

Ranking: 1651 S.S. Count:
Origin: Perring—English; Perrin—English, French; Perrineau, Perrinet—French; Perrino—Italian. Perring, Perrin, Perrineau, Perrinet: derived from the Middle English and Old French first name Perrin, which was derived from Peter. Perrino: cognate to Perrin.
Famous Bearers: ETHEL PERRIN (1871–1962) of Massachusetts was a physical education specialist. She wrote several books on the subject and believed in "play for its own sake."
Genealogies: *The John Perrin Family of Rehoboth, Massachusetts* was compiled by Stanley Ernest Perin and published in Baltimore, Maryland, in 1974.

PERRON (ALSO PERRONE, PERRONEAU, PERRONEL, PERRONI)

Ranking: 3005 S.S. Count: 15,116
Origin: Perron—English; Perroneau, Perronel—French; Perrone, Perroni—Italian. Perron: derived from the French first name Perron, which was derived from Pierre. Perroneau, Perronel: transformations of Pierre. Perrone, Perroni: cognates to Peter.
Genealogies: *The Perrons: French-Canadian Pioneers of Minnesota* was compiled by Ronald F. Eustice and published in 1990.

PERRY

Ranking: 92 S.S. Count: 303,193

Origin: English, Jewish, Welsh. English: derived from the Middle English word "per(r)ie," meaning pear. The name was given to those who lived near a pear tree. Jewish: derived from the Hebrew word "peri," meaning fruit. The name was taken ornamentally. Welsh: derived from the Welsh patronymic component "ap" and the medieval first name Herry, which was derived from Henry.

Famous **Perrys:** OLIVER HAZARD PERRY (1785–1819) of Rhode Island was a naval officer and the brother of Matthew Perry. He fought in the Battle of Lake Erie, where his ship, the *Lawrence*, was so damaged in the fighting that he rowed to the *Niagara* to continue the fight. There he was able to emerge victorious over the British. His message to their commander, "[w]e have met the enemy and they are ours," remains well remembered to this day. MATTHEW CALBRAITH PERRY (1794–1858) of Rhode Island was a naval officer and a pioneer in the belief that steamships would be a positive addition to the navy. He was the commander of the *Fulton*. STUART PERRY (1814–1890) of New York was an inventor who made improvements to the gas engine. EDWARD AYLESWORTH PERRY (1831–1889) of Massachusetts was a Confederate officer and the governor of Florida. EDWARD BAXTER PERRY (1855–1924) of Massachusetts was a blind concert pianist who gave more than 3000 recitals. BLISS PERRY (1860–1954) was editor of the *Atlantic Monthly* and author of many books, including *The American Spirit in Literature* (1918). ROLAND HINTON PERRY (1870–1941) of New York City was a portrait painter and a sculptor. One of his statues is "Fountain of Neptune" in the Library of Congress. MARIE ANTOINETTE PERRY (1888–1946) of Colorado was an actress and director and a founder of the American Theatre Wing, whose Tony Award is named after her.

Genealogies: *Dibblee-Perry and Allied Families* was compiled by Alice Izalle Dibblee Conlon and published in Portland, Oregon, in 1983. *The Family Tree of Daniel Perry, 1704–1970* was compiled by Hubert L. Perry and published in Caldwell, Texas, in 1970.

PERRYMAN (S.S. Abbreviation: Perrym)

Ranking: 3649 S.S. Count: 12,366

Origin: English. Transformation of the English name Perry.

Genealogies: None known.

PERSON

Ranking: 1713 S.S. Count: 26,126

Origin: Swedish. Cognate to Peter.

Genealogies: *10 Years of Pearsons: the Descendants of John and Johanna Pearson who Emigrated from Sweden to America in April, 1889* [also Person] was compiled by

Frederick John Pearson and published in Houston, Texas, in 1976. *Personotes* was compiled by Dorothy Wooldridge Person and published in Battle Ground, Washington, in 1991.

PETER

Ranking: 3692 S.S. Count: 12,232

Origin: Dutch, English, Flemish, German. Derived from the first name Peter, which was derived from the Greek word "petros," meaning rock.

Famous **Peters:** HUGH PETER (1598–1660) of England was one of the founders of Harvard University. SARAH ANNE WORTHINGTON KING PETER (1800–1877) of Ohio was a leader in charitable work in Cincinnati and Philadelphia. She was responsible for bringing different groups of Catholic nuns to the Cincinnati area to administer to the poor, sick, and needy.

Genealogies: *Genealogical Record of the Peter Families which Originally Settled in Heidelberg Township Northampton, Now Lehigh County, Pennsylvania* was compiled by Beulah Peter Klotz and published in Allentown, Pennsylvania, in 1941.

PETERMANN (S.S. Abbreviation: Peterm)

Ranking: 3354 S.S. Count: 13,524

Origin: German. Transformation of Peter.

Genealogies: None known.

PETERS (ALSO PETERSE, PETERSEN, PETERSON)

Ranking: 27 S.S. Count: 655,983

Origin: Petersen—Danish, Dutch, Flemish, Norwegian; Peters—Dutch, English, Flemish, German; Peterse—Dutch, Flemish; Peterson—English. Transformations of and cognates to Peter.

Famous **Bearers:** SAMUEL ANDREW PETERS (1735–1826) of Connecticut was a Loyalist who moved to England in 1774 and did not return to the United States until 1805. He returned only to lay claim to land along the Mississippi River, a claim rejected by Congress. He wrote *A General History of Connecticut* (1781), in which he wrote about the blue laws that dated back to the first days of New Haven Colony. RICHARD PETERS (1744–1828) of Pennsylvania was a Revolutionary patriot and a federal judge in Pennsylvania. ABSOLOM PETERS (1793–1869) of New Hampshire was one of the founders of the American Home Missionary Society (1826) and the Union Theological Seminary. RICHARD PETERS (1810–1889) of Pennsylvania was the grandson of Richard Peters (1744–1828) and one of the founders and organizers of Atlanta, Georgia. HENRY PETERSON (1818–1891) of Pennsylvania was the longtime editor of the *Saturday Evening Post*. CURTIS ARNOUX (ARNO) PETERS (1904–1968) of New York City was a satirical cartoonist whose works appeared in *The New Yorker* magazine.

Genealogies: *Genealogical Chronolog of John Peter Snyder, 1729–1807 and his Wife Mary Catharine Elizabeth (Stentz) Snyder, 1739–1782 and their Descendants* [also Peters] was compiled by Howard W. Stentz and published in Coos Bay, Oregon, in 1989. *Some Ancestors and Descendants of John Frederick Peters and his Wife Maria Louise Moses of Hoosick Falls, New York* was compiled by Dorothy Rudd DuMond and published in Ulster Park, New York, in 1983. *From Norway to North America: the Descendants in Canada and the United States of Olaf and Caroline Pederson who came from Norway about 1867 to Manitoba and North Dakota* was compiled by Jean E. Peterson and published in Dubuque, Iowa, in 1981.

PETRIE (ALSO PETRIELLO)
Ranking: 3599 **S.S. Count:** 12,542
Origin: Petriello—Italian; Petrie—Scottish. Petriello: cognate to Peter. Petrie: 1) transformation of Patrick. 2) transformation of Peter.
Genealogies: *The Mohawk Valley Petries and Allied Families* was compiled by Hazel Patrick and published in Herkimer, New York, in 1979.

PETRON (ALSO PETRONI)
Ranking: 4719 **S.S. Count:** 9473
Origin: Petron—French; Petroni—Italian. Petron: derived from the Old French word "pestel," meaning pestle. The name was given to grocers or apothecaries. Petroni: cognate to Peter.
Genealogies: None known.

PETROSELLI, PETROSIAN (S.S. Abbreviation: Petros)
Ranking: 3853 **S.S. Count:** 11,699
Origin: Petrosian—Armenian; Petroselli—Italian. Cognates to Peter.
Genealogies: None known.

PETTER (ALSO PETTERS, PETTERSSON)
Ranking: 4469 **S.S. Count:** 10,017
Origin: Petter—English; Petter, Petters—German; Pettersson—Swedish. Petter—English: derived from the Old French word "peter," meaning to expel intestinal gas. The name was given to those who were flatulent. Petter, Petters: transformations of Peter. Pettersson: cognate to Peter.
Genealogies: None known.

PETTIGREE, PETTIGREW (S.S. Abbreviation: Pettig)
Ranking: 3883 **S.S. Count:** 11,620
Origin: Scottish. Uncertain etymology. Most likely derived

from the Old French words "petit" and "cru," meaning small and growth. The name was given to those who were small in stature.

Famous Bearers: CHARLES PETTIGREW (1743–1807) of Pennsylvania was one of the founders of the University of North Carolina. JAMES JOHNSTON PETTIGREW (1828–1863) of North Carolina was a Confederate officer who was the commander at Petersburg and one of the commanders at Gettysburg. RICHARD FRANKLIN PETTIGREW (1848–1926) of Wisconsin was a U.S. senator from South Dakota.
Genealogies: None known.

PETTIS
Ranking: 4560 **S.S. Count:** 9798
Origin: English. Transformation of Pettit.
Genealogies: *The Petty-Pettis Genealogy: Descendants of John Petty of Springfield, Massachusetts, 1668* was compiled by Robert Joseph Curfman and published in Kansas City, Missouri, in 1974.

PETTIT (ALSO PETTITT)
Ranking: 1533 **S.S. Count:** 29,034
Origin: English. Derived from the Anglo-Norman-French word "petit," meaning small. The names were given to those who were small in stature or to those who were younger than other persons bearing the same name.
Famous Bearers: CHARLES PETTIT (1736–1806) of New Jersey was a colonial official of New Jersey and Pennsylvania and was the one responsible for Pennsylvania's adopting the U.S. Constitution. KATHERINE PETTIT (1868–1936) of Kentucky was a settlement worker in the mountains of Kentucky. There she was one of the directors of the Pine Mountain Settlement School.
Genealogies: None known.

PETTY
Ranking: 899 **S.S. Count:** 48,100
Origin: English. Transformation of Pettit.
Genealogies: *The Petty-Pettis Genealogy: Descendants of John Petty of Springfield, Massachusetts, 1668* was compiled by Robert Joseph Curfman and published in Kansas City, Missouri, in 1974. *Petty: a Genealogy Record and Short History of the Descendants of John Petty and Loveday Kent Petty* was compiled by George Bell and published in Newell, Iowa, in 1984. *Petty, of England & Virginia* was compiled by Gerald McKinney Petty and published in Columbus, Ohio, in 1973.

PEYTON
Ranking: 3158 **S.S. Count:** 14,377
Origin: English. The name means "Paega's homestead" (ES) and was given to those from Peyton, a place in Suffolk, England.

Famous **Peytons:** JOHN NEWTON PEYTON (1885–1975) of Minnesota was a banker and one of the organizers of the Citizens State Bank in Minnesota, which became the Pioneer National Bank of Duluth in 1927.

Genealogies: *The Peytons of Virginia* was compiled by Peyton Society of Virginia and published in Stafford, Virginia, in 1976. *Yelverton Payton* [also Peyton] was compiled by Mary Evelyn Cook Treadway and published in Shipman, Virginia, in 1984.

PFAFF

Ranking: 4924 **S.S. Count:** 9088
Origin: German. The name means priest and was given to priests or to those who in manner resembled a priest.
Genealogies: None known.

PFEIFER (S.S. Abbreviation: Pfeife)

Ranking: 2072 **S.S. Count:** 22,121
Origin: German. Cognate to Piper.
Genealogies: None known.

PHAM

Ranking: 2123 **S.S. Count:** 21,591
Origin: Vietnamese. Uncertain etymology. The name could mean gluttonous, greedy, or to commit.
Genealogies: None known.

PHAN

Ranking: 4447 **S.S. Count:** 10,079
Origin: Vietnamese. Uncertain etymology. The name could mean to say, to complain, or to betray.
Genealogies: None known.

PHELAN

Ranking: 2956 **S.S. Count:** 15,398
Origin: Irish. Transformation of Whelan.
Famous **Phelans:** JAMES PHELAN (1856–1891) of Mississippi was a member of Congress from Tennessee who was known as a champion of African-Americans. JAMES JUVAL PHELAN (1861–1930) of California was a California politician and the initiator of the "Burnham Plan," the beginnings of the San Francisco civic center. He also served his state as the mayor of San Francisco and as a U.S. senator.
Genealogies: *Phelan, Malone, Kevill, Stutz & Klaes Families* was compiled by John T. Phelan and published in Baltimore, Maryland, in 1985.

PHELPS

Ranking: 562 **S.S. Count:** 72,941
Origin: English. Transformation of Philip.
Famous **Phelps:** ALMIRA HART LINCOLN PHELPS (1793–1884) of Connecticut was an educator and a writer of textbooks, including *Familiar Lectures on Botany.* JOHN WOL-

COTT PHELPS (1813–1885) of Vermont was a soldier in the Union army who organized the first Negro troops in New Orleans. When the federal government ordered the troops disbanded and the men used as laborers instead of as soldiers, he resigned. ELIZABETH WOOSTER STUART PHELPS (1815–1952) of Massachusetts was a novelist. Her book *The Sunny Side; or, The Country Minister's Wife* (1851) marked the beginning of her career. WILLIAM LYON PHELPS (1865–1943) of Connecticut was an educator at Yale University and a social critic.

Genealogies: *Phelps Family from Z to A* was compiled by William Herald Swango and published in South Charleston, West Virginia, in 1986. *Phelps-Marshall Kinship* was compiled by Nancy G. McBride and published in Verona, Virginia, in 1977.

PHILIP (ALSO PHILIPEAU, PHILIPPE, PHILIPPS, PHILIPPSON)

Ranking: 1930 **S.S. Count:** 23,384
Origin: Philip—Danish, Dutch, English, Flemish, French, Norwegian; Philippson—English; Philipeau, Philippe—French. Philip: derived from the Greek name Philippos, which comprises the components "philein" and "hippos," meaning to love and horse. Philippson, Philipeau, Philippe: transformations of Philip.
Famous **Bearers:** PHILIP (?–1676) of Rhode Island was an Indian leader. He was the son of Massassoit and also went by the names King Philip, Po-Metacom, and Metacomet. In 1662 he became the chief of the Wampanoags. Relations between the Indians and the colonists were peaceful until 1671. From 1671 to 1675 he plotted against the colonists; the scheme was revealed by Philip's secretary, Sassamon, whom Philip then had killed. This led to the King Philip War of 1675. Philip and his allies, the Nipmucks, were responsible for the deaths of many colonists and the burning of their towns. Having endured all that they could, the colonists changed tactics and started capturing the women and children of Philip's tribe, destroying the Indian crops, and offering amnesty to all who would desert Philip and side with the colonists. These tactics forced the downfall of Philip. He hid in a swamp near Mount Hope and was killed by an Indian who served with Captain Benjamin Church's troops. JOHN WOODWARD PHILIP (1840–1900) of New York was a naval officer. He is credited with the statement "Don't cheer, men, those poor devils are dying" as he captained the USS *Texas* in the 1898 Battle of Santiago Bay.
Genealogies: None known.

PHILLIP, PHILLIPPS, PHILLIPS, PHILLIPSON, PHILLIS (S.S. Abbreviation: Philli)

Ranking: 42 **S.S. Count:** 514,517

Origin: Phillips, Phillipson, Phillis—English; Phillipps—English, German; Phillip—English, Jewish. Phillips, Phillipson, Phillis, Phillipps, Phillip: transformations of Philip. Phillip—Jewish: Anglicization of of any of several similar-sounding Jewish surnames.

Famous **Bearers:** ADELAIDE PHILLIPPS (1833–1882) of England was an actress, opera singer, and America's first prima donna. JOHN SANBURN PHILLIPS (1861–1949) of Iowa was an editor and publisher of magazines. He is considered the force behind the success of *McClure's Magazine.* FRANK PHILLIPS (1873–1950) of Nebraska and his brother Lee E. Phillips were the founders of the Phillips Petroleum Co. LENA MADESIN PHILLIPS (1881–1955) of Kentucky was the founder of the National and International Federations of Business and Professional Women's Clubs. IRMA PHILLIPS (1901–1973) of Illinois was a radio and television writer who was referred to as the "Queen of the Soap Operas." AUSTAVE PAUL PHILLIPS JR. (1903–1975) of Georgia was the founder of the A. P. Phillips Co. in Orlando, Florida, an advertising and public relations firm, and the A. P. Phillips Co., Inc., a real estate and business brokerage.

Genealogies: Descendants of William and Elizabeth (Iser) Phillips of Columbiana County, Ohio was compiled by Rita Hineman Townsend and published in Garden City, Kansas, in 1986. *Hatfield and Phillips Families of Eastern Kentucky and Southwestern Western Virginia* was compiled by Harry Leon Sellards and published in DeLand, Florida, in 1993.

PHILPOTT (S.S. Abbreviation: Philpo)

Ranking: 3338 **S.S. Count:** 13,560

Origin: English. Derived from the name Philip.

Genealogies: English and American Backgrounds of a Philpott Family Line of Virginia and Maryland U.S.A. was compiled by Charles H. Philpott and published in Durham, North Carolina, in 1970.

PHIPPS

Ranking: 1411 **S.S. Count:** 31,503

Origin: English. Transformation of Philip.

Famous **Phippses:** HENRY PHIPPS (1839–1930) of Pennsylvania was a bookkeeper and steel manufacturer in association with Andrew Carnegie.

Genealogies: Halcyon Days: an American Family through Three Generations [also Phipps] was compiled by Peggie Phipps Boegner and published in New York, New York, in 1986. *A History of the Ireson/Phipps and Allied Families* was published in 1990.

PIAZZA

Ranking: 4000 **S.S. Count:** 11,311

Origin: Italian. Cognate to Place, derived from the Mid-

dle English and Old French word "place," meaning public square.

Genealogies: None known.

PICARD (ALSO PICARDI, PICARDINO, PICARDO)

Ranking: 3652 **S.S. Count:** 12,354

Origin: Picard—French; Picardi, Picardino, Picardo—Italian. Picard: cognate to Pickard and Pike. Picardi, Picardino, Picardo: cognates to Pickard.

Genealogies: None known.

PICKARD (S.S. Abbreviation: Pickar)

Ranking: 3136 **S.S. Count:** 14,465

Origin: English. Uncertain etymology. The name was given to those from Picardy, a region of northern France.

Famous **Pickards:** SAMUEL THOMAS PICKARD (1828–1915) of Massachusetts was a printer, journalist, and the co-editor of the *Portland* [Maine] *Transcript.*

Genealogies: The Pickard Family was compiled by Dorothy Weller and published in 1970.

PICKEN (ALSO PICKENS)

Ranking: 1787 **S.S. Count:** 25,159

Origin: English. Derived from the Middle English word "pi(c)k," meaning pick or pickaxe. The name was given to those who used or made pickaxes.

Famous **Bearers:** ANDREW PICKENS (1739–1817), who was born in Pennsylvania and made his home in South Carolina, was a Revolutionary War officer who served his country well and was responsible for the American victory at Augusta, Georgia. After the war he served as a member of Congress. ISRAEL PICKENS (1780–1827) of North Carolina was one of the founders of the University of Alabama. FRANCIS WILKINSON PICKENS (1805–1869) of South Carolina was the grandson of Andrew Pickens. He was a leader in the secessionist movement and served as the governor of South Carolina after that state became part of the Confederacy. LUCY PETWAY HOLCOMBE PICKENS (1832–1899) of Tennessee was a Confederate hostess and a member of the Mount Vernon Ladies' Association.

Genealogies: The John Pickens Family was compiled by Nellie Pickens Anderson and published in Baltimore, Maryland, in 1981. *Thomas Boone Pickens, 1928–* was compiled by Lois K. Nix and published in Dallas, Texas, in 1989.

PICKERDEN, PICKERELL, PICKERILL, PICKERIN, PICKERING (S.S. Abbreviation: Picker)

Ranking: 1756 **S.S. Count:** 25,546

Origin: English. Pickerden: uncertain etymology. Possibly a transformation of Pickard. Pickerell, Pickerill: derived from the Middle English word "pykerell," meaning a young pike. The name was given to those who were crafty and aggressive. *Pickerin, Pickering:* derived from the Old English name of a tribe, Piceringas. The names were given to those from Pickering, a place in North Yorkshire, England.

Famous **Bearers:** TIMOTHY PICKERING (1745–1829) of Massachusetts was a general in the Continental army and held the following political positions after the war: postmaster general, secretary of war, secretary of state, senator, and member of Congress. His son, JOHN PICKERING (1777–1846), possibly of Massachusetts, was the author of the first dictionary of Americanisms. CHARLES PICKERING (1805–1878), birthplace unknown, was a naturalist. He was the chief zoologist on Charles Wilkes's expedition to Antarctica and the Pacific Northwest. He was the grandson of Timothy Pickering. EDWARD CHARLES PICKERING (1846–1919), birthplace unknown, was the director of the Harvard Observatory. He was the inventor of the meridian photometer and the one who established the *Harvard Photometry* (1884). He was the great-grandson of Timothy Pickering. Edward's brother, WILLIAM HENRY PICKERING (1858–1938), was also an astronomer. He was the discoverer of Phoebe, the ninth satellite of Saturn, and the predicter of the discovery of Pluto, the ninth planet.

Genealogies: *Gleanings on the Pickerell Line* was compiled by Ann Arnold and published in Bakersfield, California, in 1977.

PICKETT (S.S. Abbreviation: Picket)

Ranking: 1000 **S.S. Count:** 43,734

Origin: English. Derived from the Middle English and Old French first name Picot, which was derived from the first name Pic, meaning pointed.

Famous **Picketts:** GEORGE EDWARD PICKETT (1825–1875) of Virginia was the Confederate commander in the decisive Battle of Gettysburg at Cemetery Ridge. His loss of more than 3000 men and the battle is considered the turning point of the war. JOSEPH PICKETT (1848–1918) of Pennsylvania began painting at age 65. His works were landscapes of the New Hope, Pennsylvania, area. His art was not discovered until he had been dead for more than a decade.

Genealogies: *Pickett Cousins: a 350 Year History* was compiled by Patricia F. Hunter and published in Knoxville, Tennessee, in 1991.

PICKLE, PICKLES, PICKLESS

Ranking: 4775 **S.S. Count:** 9379

Origin: English. Derived from the Middle English word "pigh(t)el," meaning paddock. The names were given to those who lived near a paddock.

Genealogies: *The Pickle Family Circus* was compiled by

Terry Lorant and published in San Francisco, California, in 1986.

PIEPER (ALSO PIEPERS)

Ranking: 4801 **S.S. Count:** 9330

Origin: German. Cognates to Piper.

Genealogies: None known.

PIERCE (ALSO PIERCEY)

Ranking: 169 **S.S. Count:** 196,386

Origin: English. Pierce: transformation of Pearce. Piercey: transformation of Pearcey.

Famous **Bearers:** SARA PIERCE (1767–1852) of Connecticut was an educator. She was the founder of the Litchfield Female Academy. FRANKLIN PIERCE (1804–1869) of New Hampshire was the 14th president of the United States. His tenure brought the country the newly created court of claims, the Gadsden Purchase, the Kansas-Nebraska Act, and the opening of the Pacific Northwest for settlement. JANE MEANS APPLETON PIERCE (1806–1863) of New Hampshire was the wife of Franklin Pierce, 14th president of the United States. The death of her 11-year-old son, Benjamin, shortly before her husband was elected, forced her into a state of mental withdrawal. She declined to perform many of the duties of first lady. GILBERT ASHVILLE PIERCE (1839–1901) of New York was the governor of the Dakota territory and the first U.S. senator from North Dakota. He also was the author of plays and novels. GEORGE WASHINGTON PIERCE (1872–1956) of Texas was a physicist and the inventor of the Pierce oscillator.

Genealogies: *Eslick-Pierce Family History* was compiled by Jacqueline R. Burt and published in Baltimore, Maryland, in 1990. *Fifty New England Colonists and Five Virginia Families* [also Pierce] was compiled by Florence Weiland and published in Boothbay Harbor, Maine, in 1966.

PIERRE (ALSO PIERREPOINT, PIERREPONT)

Ranking: 2339 **S.S. Count:** 19,394

Origin: Pierrepoint, Pierrepont—English, French; Pierre—French. Pierrepoint, Pierrepont: derived from the Old French words "pierre" and "pont," meaning stone and bridge. The names were given to those from Pierrepont, the name of several places in France. Pierre: derived from the French first name Pierre, which is a cognate to Peter.

Famous **Bearers:** EDWARDS PIERREPONT (1817–1892) of Connecticut was the U.S. attorney general and an ambassador to England.

Genealogies: None known.

PIERSON (S.S. Abbreviation: Pierso)

Ranking: 1091 **S.S. Count:** 40,453

Origin: English. Transformation of Pearce.

Famous **Piersons**: ABRAHAM PIERSON (1609–1678) of England came to Massachusetts as a Puritan. He and his followers set up a colony in Southampton, on Long Island. He felt that the church and the state should act as one body, and that only members of the church should be considered freemen. When Southampton joined with Connecticut, he moved his congregation to Branford, part of the New Haven Colony. There they remained for 20 years until the New Haven Colony joined Connecticut. He then moved his group to Newark, New Jersey, in 1667 and remained there.

Genealogies: *Pierson Genealogical Records* was compiled by Lizzie Benedict Pierson and published in 1878.

PIKE

Ranking: 1159 **S.S. Count**: 37,689

Origin: *English. 1) derived from the Middle English word "pic," meaning pike or a pole with a sharp metal point at one end that was used as a weapon. The name was given to soldiers who carried pikes. 2) derived from the Middle English word "pike," meaning a type of fish with a pointed jaw. The name was given to those who fished for pike. 3) derived from the Old French word "pic," meaning woodpecker. 4) derived from the Old English word "pic," meaning a sharp point. The name was given to those who lived near a sharp, pointed hill. 5) derived from the Middle English word "pike," meaning a pointed and sharp gardening tool.*

Famous **Pikes**: ROBERT PIKE (1616?–1708) of England was a colonial official. He spoke out against the Salem witch trials. NICHOLAS PIKE (1743–1819) of New Hampshire was the author of *A New and Complete System of Arithmetick, Composed for the Use of the Citizens of the United States* (1788). He was the first American to write an arithmetic textbook to be used in the schools. ZEBULON MONTGOMERY PIKE (1779–1813) of New Jersey was an explorer who is credited with the discovery of Pikes Peak. His report on the Santa Fe area led to more movement into Texas. ALBERT PIKE (1809–1891) of Massachusetts was the first reporter of the Arkansas Supreme Court, the commander of a troop in the Mexican War, and the author of *Hymns to the Gods*, published in *Blackwood's Magazine* in 1939. MARY HAYDEN GREEN PIKE (1824–1908) of Maine was an author of books and considered a crusading novelist who followed in the path laid down by Harriet Beecher Stowe.

Genealogies: *Some Descendants of James Pike of Charlestown and Reading, Massachusetts* was compiled by Ruth G. Pike.

PIMENTA, PIMENTEL, PIMENTHAL

Ranking: 2732 **S.S. Count**: 16,663

Origin: *Pimenthal—Jewish; Pimentel—Jewish, Portuguese; Pimenta—Portuguese. Derived from the Portuguese word "pimenta," meaning red pepper. The names were given to those who grew peppers.*

Genealogies: None known.

PIÑA

Ranking: 3308 **S.S. Count**: 13,688

Origin: *Portuguese, Spanish. Spanish: 1) cognate to Pine. 2) transformation of Peña. Portuguese: cognate to Peña.*

Genealogies: None known.

PINE

Ranking: 4651 **S.S. Count**: 9616

Origin: *English. Derived from the Middle English word "pine," meaning pine tree. The name was given to those who lived in a pine forest or near a prominent pine tree.*

Famous **Pines**: ROBERT EDGE PINE (1730–1788) of England was a portrait and subject painter. He painted many of the well-known people of his time, including George Washington and his family.

Genealogies: None known.

PIÑEDA

Ranking: 2997 **S.S. Count**: 15,159

Origin: *Spanish. Cognate to Pine.*

Genealogies: None known.

PINKERTON

Ranking: 3400 **S.S. Count**: 13,314

Origin: *Irish, Scottish. Uncertain etymology. The name was given to those from Pinkerton, the name of a place in Scotland.*

Famous **Pinkertons**: ALLAN PINKERTON (1819–1884) of Scotland came to the United States and settled in Illinois. He founded and owned the famed Pinkerton Agency, a private-detective firm. His achievements ranged from the solving of the Adams Express robbery to the successful guarding of generals and presidents. He was the author of several books detailing his work.

Genealogies: None known.

PINKNEY (S.S. Abbreviation: Pinkne)

Ranking: 4806 **S.S. Count**: 9320

Origin: *English. Derived from the Germanic first name Pincino, which is of uncertain etymology. The name was given to those from Picquigny, a place in Somme, France.*

Famous **Pinkneys**: WILLIAM PINKNEY (1764–1822) of Maryland was a politician who served as U.S. minister to Great Britain and Russia, attorney general, and as a member of Congress and U.S. senator.

Genealogies: None known.

PINKSTON, PINKSTONE (S.S. Abbreviation: Pinkst)

Ranking: 3582 S.S. Count: 12,593

Origin: English. Derived from a first element meaning "edge of the woods" (ES) and the Old English word "tūn," meaning settlement. The names were given to those from Pinxton, a place in England.

Genealogies: None known.

PIÑO

Ranking: 4577 S.S. Count: 9763

Origin: Spanish. Cognate to Pine.

Genealogies: None known.

PINSON

Ranking: 4045 S.S. Count: 11,193

Origin: English, French, Jewish. English, French: 1) derived from the Old French word "pinson," meaning pincers. The name was given to those who used pincers. 2) derived from the Old French word "pinson," meaning finch. Jewish: derived from the masculine Yiddish first name Pinkhes.

Genealogies: None known.

PINTO

Ranking: 2500 S.S. Count: 18,138

Origin: Italian, Jewish, Portuguese, Spanish. Derived from the word "pinto," meaning mottled. The name was given to those who had a mottled complexion or hair.

Famous **Pintos**: ISAAC PINTO (1720–1791), birthplace unknown, was a Sephardic Jew who is best known for being the first to translate the Jewish Prayer Book into English.

Genealogies: None known.

PIPER

Ranking: 1463 S.S. Count: 30,462

Origin: English. Derived from the Middle English word "pipere," meaning piper. The name was given to those who played the pipes.

Famous **Pipers**: LEONORE EVELINA SOMONDS PIPER (1859–1950) of New Hampshire was a medium, tested by the noted researchers of the day who concurred that she was a true bridge between the living and the dead. CHARLES VANCOUVER PIPER (1867–1926) of Canada was an agronomist who discovered Sudan grass growing in the South and published *Sudan Grass, a New Drought-resistant Hay Plant* (1913). Sudan grass is a forage grass similar to Johnson grass.

Genealogies: *Scruggs Piper Connections* was compiled by Jane Melonie Scruggs Piper and published in Houston, Texas, in 1992.

PIPKIN

Ranking: 4393 S.S. Count: 10,212

Origin: Uncertain etymology.

Genealogies: None known.

PIPPIN

Ranking: 3822 S.S. Count: 11,798

Origin: English. Derived from the Old French first name Pepis, which is of uncertain etymology.

Famous **Pippins**: HORACE PIPPIN (1888–1946) of Pennsylvania was wounded and partially disabled in World War I. He began painting and is considered one of the great "naïve" painters of the country. He was also the first great black painter. His art is an example of American history and folklore in paint.

Genealogies: None known.

PITMAN

Ranking: 4124 S.S. Count: 10,963

Origin: English. Transformation of Pitt.

Famous **Pitmans**: BENN PITMAN (1822–1910) of England founded Phonographic Institute of Cincinnati.

Genealogies: *Sills & Cliburn & Pitman* was compiled by Isom L. Stephens and published in Provo, Utah, in 1972. *Descendants of William Pitman, 1647–1700, of Boston, Mass. & Portsmouth, N.H.* was compiled by Harold Minot Pitman and published in 1953. *Ancestors and Descendants of Flower Wilkins and George Pitman: Somersetshire, England, 1796 to the United States, 1985* was compiled by Oscar Truman Johnson and published in Springfield, Virginia, in 1985.

PITT

Ranking: 3674 S.S. Count: 12,283

Origin: English. Derived from the Old English word "pytt," meaning hollow. The name was given to those who lived near a pit or hollow.

Genealogies: None known.

PITTMAN (S.S. Abbreviation: Pittma)

Ranking: 581 S.S. Count: 71,172

Origin: English. Transformation of Pitt.

Famous **Pittmans**: KEY PITTMAN (1872–1940) of Mississippi was a U.S. senator from Nevada and the author of the Pittman Act (1918), the silver agreement that was devised at the World Economic Conference (1933), and the Silver Purchase Act (1934).

Genealogies: *Sills & Cliburn & Pitman* [also Pittman] was compiled by Isom L. Stephens and published in Provo, Utah, in 1972. *Ancestors and Descendants of Flower Wilkins and George Pitman: Somersetshire, England, 1796 to the United States, 1985* [also Pittman] was compiled by Oscar Truman Johnson and published in Springfield, Virginia, in 1985.

PITTS

Ranking: 594 S.S. Count: 70,325

Origin: English. Transformation of Pitt.

Famous **Pittses:** HIRAM AVERY PITTS (1800?–1860) of Illinois was an inventor of threshers and fanning mills. He manufactured "Chicago-Pitts" threshers in Chicago. ZASU PITTS (1898?–1963) of Kansas was an actress and comedian.

Genealogies: Memoirs-With Histories of Pound-Murphy-Willingham-Palmer-Pitts Families was compiled by Jerome B. Pound and published in Miami Beach, Florida, in 1949. *Pitts Family History, 1643–1985* was compiled by Josephine Pitts Gambill and published in Marceline, Missouri, in 1985. *Portraits of Eight Generations of the Pitts Family* was compiled by The Detroit Institute of Arts and published in Detroit, Michigan, in 1959.

PIZARRO (S.S. Abbreviation: Pizarr)
Ranking: 4068 S.S. Count: 11,113
Origin: Spanish. Derived from the Spanish word "pizarra," meaning slate. The name was given to those who worked in or lived near a slate quarry.
Genealogies: None known.

PLACE
Ranking: 4376 S.S. Count: 10,250
Origin: English, French. 1) derived from the Middle English and Old French word "pleis," meaning a "quickset fence" (H&H). The name was given to those who lived near a "quickset fence" (H&H). 2) derived from the Middle English and Old French word "place," meaning a public square. The name was given to those who lived near the public square of a town. 3) derived from the Middle English and Old French word "plaise," meaning a flat fish. The name was given to those who sold fish.
Genealogies: The Place Family was compiled by Shirley McElroy Bucknum and published in Portland, Oregon, in 1983.

PLANTE
Ranking: 4100 S.S. Count: 11,020
Origin: English. Derived from the Middle English word "plant," meaning a sapling or herb. The name was given to those who worked as gardeners.
Genealogies: None known.

PLATT
Ranking: 1517 S.S. Count: 29,310
Origin: English, Jewish. English: derived from the Old French word "plat," meaning flat. The name was given to those who were slender. Jewish: uncertain etymology.
Famous **Platts:** ORVILLE HITCHCOCK PLATT (1827–1905) of Connecticut was a U.S. senator and the author of the Platt Amendment (1901). THOMAS COLLIER PLATT (1833–1910) of New York was a member of Congress and

U.S. senator and a nominee for U.S. vice president in 1900.

Genealogies: The Plattsburgh Platts was compiled by Margaret Myers Byrne and published in Plattsburgh, New York, in 1991. *The Story of Mrs. Eliza Platt Stoddard of Succasunna, Morris County, New Jersey* was compiled by Edwin W. Hancock and published in New York, New York, in 1978.

PLEASANCE, PLEASANTS, PLEASAUNCE (S.S. Abbreviation: Pleasa)
Ranking: 3491 S.S. Count: 12,921
Origin: English. 1) derived from the Latin word "placere," meaning to please. The name was given to those from Piacenza, a place in Italy. 2) derived from the medieval feminine first name Plaisance, which was derived from the Latin word "placere," meaning to please.

Famous **Bearers:** JAMES PLEASANTS (1769–1836) of Virginia was a member of Congress, a U.S. senator, and the governor of Virginia. He was Thomas Jefferson's cousin. JOHN HAMPDEN PLEASANTS (1797–1846) of Virginia was the founder and editor of the Richmond *Whig*. He was killed in a duel with Thomas Ritchie Jr., the editor of the Richmond *Enquirer*.

Genealogies: Pleasants and Allied Families: an Historical (sic) *Genealogy of the Descendants of John Pleasants (1644/5–1698) of Henrico County, Virginia* was compiled by Norma Carter Miller and published in DeKalb, Illinois, in 1980. *Our Families from the Atlantic Coast Colonies of 1665 to the California Pacific of 1974* was compiled by Carroll Evan Edmiston and published in Danville, Kentucky, in 1974.

PLUMLEE, PLUMLEY (S.S. Abbreviation: Plumle)
Ranking: 4821 S.S. Count: 9295
Origin: English. Derived from the Old English words "plūme" and "lēah," meaning plum and wood or clearing. The name was given to those from Plumley, the name of several places in England.

Genealogies: The Plumlee Family was compiled by Robert D. Plumlee and published in Clearwater, Florida, in 1979. *The Plum(ly, lee, ley, blee) Family* was compiled by Millard Quentin Plumblee and published in Salisbury, North Carolina, in 1982.

PLUMMER (S.S. Abbreviation: Plumme)
Ranking: 1237 S.S. Count: 35,786
Origin: English. 1) derived from the Anglo-Norman-French word "plom(b)," meaning lead. The name was given to those who worked with lead or made lead pipes. 2) derived from the Old English word "plūme," meaning plum. The name was given to those who lived near a plum tree. 3)

derived from the Middle English word "plume," meaning feather. The name was given to those who traded in feathers.

Famous **Plummers**: HENRY PLUMMER (?–1864), birthplace unknown, was a murderer, gang leader, and bandit. He was the marshal of Nevada City, California, when he was arrested, tried, and convicted of the murder of his lover's husband. Telling the prison officials that he was dying of tuberculosis, he managed an escape and began a life of crime. In 1862 he had settled in Montana, where he was elected sheriff. There he rounded up a group of outlaws with whom he secretly rode, terrorizing the local residents and killing 100 men in the space of a dozen weeks. A group of townspeople acting as vigilantes captured his gang, who exposed him. He was hanged in the true style of western justice. MARY WRIGHT PLUMMER (1856–1916) of Indiana was a librarian. She was a student of Melvil Dewey and a teacher in her own right in the training of new librarians. She was the preisdent of the New York Library Club and the New York State Library Association. HENRY STANLEY PLUMMER (1874–1936) of Minnesota was a physician and a member of the Mayo Clinic staff. He was responsible for introducing a new method of thyroid disease classification.

Genealogies: *Out of the Depths; or, the Triumph of the Cross (Plummer family)* was compiled by Nellie Arnold Plummer and published in Hyattsville, Maryland, in 1927. *Plummer Families History* was compiled by Leonard Lowell Plummer and published in Lake Quivira, Kansas, in 1991.

PLUNKET, PLUNKETT (S.S. Abbreviation: Plunke)

Ranking: 3012 **S.S. Count**: 15,085

Origin: English, Irish. 1) derived from the Middle English word "blaunket," meaning blanket. The name was given to those who sold or made blankets. 2) derived from the possibly Breton word "plou," meaning parish, and the first name Guenec, which is of uncertain etymology. The name was given to those from Plouquenet, a place in Brittany, France.

Famous **Bearers**: CHARLES PESHALL PLUNKETT (1864–1931) of Washington, D.C., was a naval officer on the western front (1918).

Genealogies: *Ten Thousand Plunketts; a Partially Documented Record of the Families of Charles Plunkett of Newbery County, South Carolina* was compiled by Emma Plunkett Ivy and published in Athens, Georgia, in 1974.

POE

Ranking: 1390 **S.S. Count**: 31,901

Origin: English. Transformation of Peacock.

Famous **Poes**: ELIZABETH ARNOLD HOPKINS POE (1787?–1811) of England was an actress, but is best known as the mother of Edgar Allan Poe. EDGAR ALLAN POE (1809–1849) of Massachusetts was a writer of poetry and short stories. He is best known as the creator of the American Gothic tale. ORLANDO METCALFE POE (1832–1895) of Ohio was a soldier and an engineer who served as an engineer under General William T. Sherman.

Genealogies: *Poe Genealogy* was compiled by Walter R. McCarley and published in Greenwich, Ohio, in 1979. *Poe Pages* was compiled by Anne Long and published in Grangeville, Idaho, in 1986.

POGUE

Ranking: 4369 **S.S. Count**: 10,261

Origin: English. Derived from the feminine first name Margaret, meaning pearl.

Genealogies: *Pogue, Pollock, Polk Genealogy: as Mirrored in History, from Scotland to Northern Ireland/Ulster, Ohio, and Westward* was compiled by Lloyd Welch Pogue and published in Baltimore, Maryland, in 1990.

POHL

Ranking: 4994 **S.S. Count**: 8983

Origin: German. Uncertain etymology.

Genealogies: *Ancestral Report for George A. Pohl* was compiled by George A. Pohl and published in Penfield, New York, in 1985.

POINDEXTER (S.S. Abbreviation: Poinde)

Ranking: 2828 **S.S. Count**: 16,123

Origin: English. Derived from words meaning right and fist. The name was given to those who lived near the "sign of the poindexter" (ES).

Famous **Poindexters**: GEORGE POINDEXTER (1779–1853) of Virginia was a Mississippi politician who served as a member of Congress, U.S. senator, and governor. MILES POINDEXTER (1868–1946) of Tennessee was a member of Congress, then a senator representing Washington state.

Genealogies: *A Poingdestre-Poindexter Genealogy: an Account of the Lineage of the Houston, Texas Branch of the Family* was compiled by John D. Poindexter and published in 1980.

POINTEL, POINTER (S.S. Abbreviation: Pointe)

Ranking: 4476 **S.S. Count**: 10,003

Origin: English. Pointel: derived from the the Roman name Pontius, which is of uncertain etymology. Pointer: derived from the Middle English word "pointer," meaning point maker. The name was given to those who made point, a type of lace.

Genealogies: *Zola's Family and Friends: Harrison County, Missouri* [also Pointer] was compiled by Zola Pointer and published in Baltimore, Maryland, in 1989.

POIRIER (S.S. Abbreviation: Poirie)

Ranking: 3499 S.S. Count: 12,885

Origin: French. Cognate to the English name Pear, which was derived from the Middle English word "pe(e)re," meaning pear. The name was given to those who sold or grew pears.

Genealogies: None known.

POLAND

Ranking: 3943 S.S. Count: 11,454

Origin: English. Uncertain etymology. 1) The name was given to those who made or sold a type of long, pointed shoe worn in the 14th century. 2) the name was given to those who lived on a settlement through which a stream flowed or on which there was a pool.

Famous **Polands:** LUKE POTTER POLAND (1815–1887) of Vermont was a U.S. senator, member of Congress, and chairman of a House committee that investigated the Ku Klux Klan; he was also responsible for the revision of U.S. statutes (1867–1875).

Genealogies: None known.

POLING

Ranking: 4313 S.S. Count: 10,405

Origin: English. Uncertain etymology. The name was given to those from Poling, a place in Sussex, England.

Genealogies: *History and Genealogy of the Poling Family* was compiled by Clerissa H. Tatterson and published in Parsons, West Virginia, in 1978.

POLK

Ranking: 1201 S.S. Count: 36,568

Origin: German. 1) Uncertain etymology. The name was given to those who came from Poland. 2) derived from a Slavic first name that was derived from the components "bole" and "slav," meaning great and glory.

Famous **Polks:** JAMES KNOX POLK (1795–1849) of North Carolina was the 11th president of the United States. His term was responsible for settling the Oregon-Canada boundary dispute, passing the Walker Tariff Act, and winning the Mexican War, which added California and the Southwest to the United States. SARAH CHILDRESS POLK (1803–1891) of Tennessee was the wife of James K. Polk, the 11th president of the United States. LEONIDAS POLK (1806–1864) of North Carolina was the founder of the University of the South at Sewanee, Tennessee, and the cousin of James K. Polk, the 11th president of the United States.

Genealogies: *The Genealogical Study of David Reese: with Allied Families: Polk, et al.* was compiled by Cynthia Jones Reese and published in Wichita Falls, Texas, in 1990. *The Seed of Sally Good'n: a Black Family of Arkansas (also Polk family), 1833–1953* was compiled by Ruth Polk Patterson and published in Lexington, Kentucky, in 1985.

POLLACK (S.S. Abbreviation: Pollac)

Ranking: 3139 S.S. Count: 14,460

Origin: German, Jewish. Derived from the Slavic component "pole," meaning field, and the suffix "-ak," which indicates the subject is a person. The name was given to those from Poland or to those from another Slavic country.

Genealogies: None known.

POLLARD (S.S. Abbreviation: Pollar)

Ranking: 854 S.S. Count: 50,144

Origin: English. 1) derived from Paul. 2) derived from the Middle English word "poll," meaning head, and the suffix "-ard." The name was given to those with a large or oddly shaped head.

Genealogies: *Colonel John Pollard and Juliet Jeffries* was compiled by Elizabeth Pollard Cox Johnson and published in 1976. *Rudd-Pollard-Youngblood and Related Families* was compiled by Margaret Rudd Youngblood and published in Houston, Texas, in 1980.

POLLOCK (S.S. Abbreviation: Polloc)

Ranking: 1284 S.S. Count: 34,452

Origin: German, Jewish, Scottish. German, Jewish: transformation of Pollack. Scottish: uncertain etymology. Possibly derived from a British word meaning pool. The name was given to those from Pollock, a place in Scotland.

Famous **Pollocks:** PAUL JACKSON POLLOCK (1912–1956) of Wyoming was a painter best known for his style of dripping or pouring paints onto a canvas.

Genealogies: None known.

POMEROY (S.S. Abbreviation: Pomero)

Ranking: 4134 S.S. Count: 10,941

Origin: English. Derived from the Old French word "pommeroie," meaning apple orchard. The name was given to those from towns named with this word that are located in France.

Famous **Pomeroys:** SETH POMEROY (1706–1777) of Massachusetts was a maker of guns and a soldier in the French and Indian War. He was named the first brigadier general of the Continental army. SAMUEL CLARKE POMEROY (1816–1891) of Massachusetts was a Kansas politician who was elected to the U.S. Senate. He opposed Abraham Lincoln and was responsible for the distribution of the "Pomeroy Circular," which favored Salmon P. Chase for the presidency in 1864. Charges of bribery ended his political career, although he was cleared by a Senate committee. JOHN NORTON POMEROY (1828–1896) of New York was a newspaper editor and publisher. He was known by the name "Brick" Pomeroy.

Genealogies: None known.

PONCE

Ranking: 2006 S.S. Count: 22,711

Origin: French, Spanish. Cognates to Pointel.
Genealogies: None known.

POND

Ranking: 3731 S.S. Count: 12,113

Origin: English. Derived from the Middle English word "pond," meaning a still body of water, usually one made artificially. The name was given to those who lived near a pond.

Famous **Ponds**: PETER POND (1740–1807) of Connecticut was a fur trader and an explorer and one of the first to explore the Athabaska River. On his Northwest travels, he mapped out the territory, which proved to be an invaluable geography project. SAMUEL WILLIAM POND (1808–1891) of Connecticut was a missionary among the Dakota Indians. He wrote a Dakota grammar book and dictionary for their use. JAMES BURTON POND (1838–1903) of New York was a manager of lecturers. He managed, among others, Samuel Clemens and Sir Arthur Conan Doyle. FREDERICK EUGENE POND (1856–1925) of Wisconsin was a sports writer who used the pen name Will Wildwood. IRVING KANE POND (1857–1929) of Michigan was an architect who contributed to the rebirth of Chicago's architecture.

Genealogies: None known.

PONDER

Ranking: 2922 S.S. Count: 15,575

Origin: English. Transformation of Pond.

Genealogies: *The Family of Abner Ponder* was compiled by Jerry Ponder and published in Doniphan, Missouri, in 1989. *Kentucky Ponders* was compiled by Patricia Saupe and published in Moores Hill, Indiana, in 1983.

POOL

Ranking: 2215 S.S. Count: 20,736

Origin: Dutch, English, Jewish. Dutch, Jewish: cognate to Pollack. English: 1) transformation of Paul. 2) derived from the Old English word "pōl," meaning pool. The name was given to those who lived near a pond or pool.

Famous **Pools**: JOHN POOL (1826–1884) of North Carolina was a U.S. senator who was responsible for initiating legislation against the Ku Klux Klan. JUDITH GRAHAM POOL (1919–1975) of New York was a physiologist. Her main field of interest was the investigation of blood coagulation.

Genealogies: *Early North Carolina Pool Clan of Bladen, Anson, Rowan & Davidson Counties* was compiled by William Lee Poole and published in Macon, Georgia, in 1983. *Genealogy and Family History of John Pool(e) in America, 1630–1981* was compiled by Harry M. Hutchinson and published in La Crosse, Wisconsin, in 1982.

POOLE

Ranking: 526 S.S. Count: 76,563

Origin: English. Transformation of Pool.

Famous **Pooles**: WILLIAM FREDERICK POOLE (1821–1894) of Massachusetts was a librarian and the deviser of *Poole's Index to Periodical Literature*. ERNEST COOK POOLE (1880–1950) of Illinois was an author and the winner of the first Pulitzer Prize ever awarded for fiction.

Genealogies: *Early North Carolina Pool Clan of Bladen, Anson, Rowan & Davidson Counties* [also Poole] was compiled by William Lee Poole and published in Macon, Georgia, in 1983. *Genealogy and Family History of John Poole(e) in America, 1630–1981* was compiled by Harry M. Hutchinson and published in La Crosse, Wisconsin, in 1982.

POORE

Ranking: 3830 S.S. Count: 11,763

Origin: English, Irish. Transformation of Power.

Famous **Poores**: BENJAMIN PERLEY POORE (1820–1887) of Massachusetts was an author and journalist. He was responsible for the editing and publishing of catalogues for the U.S. government.

Genealogies: *Descendants of Samuel Poore, 1620–1683, and his Wife, Rebecca, of Newberry, Massachusetts, through Five Generations* was compiled by C. Danford Smith and published in Newburyport, Massachusetts, in 1991.

POPE

Ranking: 460 S.S. Count: 86,837

Origin: English. Derived from the Middle English word "pope," meaning the bishop of Rome and the head of the Roman Catholic church. The name was given to those who were pretentious or self-important.

Famous **Popes**: FRANKLIN LEONARD POPE (1840–1894) of Massachusetts was a partner of Thomas Edison (1869–1870). ALBERT AUGUSTUS POPE (1843–1909) of Massachusetts was a manufacturer who made his fortune after the Civil War in the manufacture of shoes, bicycles, and electric- and gasoline-powered automobiles. JOHN RUSSELL POPE (1874–1937) of New York City was the architect who designed the National Gallery of Art in Washington, D.C.

Genealogies: *The Barrens: a Family History of South Central Kentucky* [also Pope] was compiled by Emery H. White and published in Glasgow, Kentucky, in 1986. *Pabst, Bobst, Pobst, Pope Family in the South* was compiled by Jennings Bland Pope and published in Austin, Texas, in 1978.

POPP

Ranking: 3610 S.S. Count: 12,511

Origin: German, Jewish. German: derived from the Germanic first name Poppo, which is of uncertain etymology. Jewish: derived from the Old High German phrase "Frankena furt," meaning "Ford of the Franks" (H&H). The name was given to those from Frankfurt, the name of two cities in Germany.

Genealogies: None known.

PORTER (ALSO PORTERAT, PORTEREAU)

Ranking: 124 **S.S. Count:** 234,898

Origin: Porter—English; Porterat, Portereau—French. Porter: 1) derived from the Old French word "porteo(u)r," meaning someone who carried loads to earn a living. The name was given to porters. 2) derived from the Middle English word "porter," meaning a gatekeeper. The name was given to gatekeepers or to those attending the door of a great house. Porterat, Portereau: cognates to Porter, meaning gatekeeper.

Famous **Bearers:** DAVID PORTER (1780–1843) of Massachusetts was a naval officer and the first to command the *Essex* in the Pacific in the War of 1812. DAVID DIXON PORTER (1813–1891) of Pennsylvania was the son of David Porter (1780–1843). He also was a career military officer and was the superintendent of the U.S. Naval Academy. DAVID RITTENHOUSE PORTER (1788–1867) of Pennsylvania was a longtime state politician and the governor of Pennsylvania. RUFUS PORTER (1792–1884) of Massachusetts was the founder of *Scientific American.* ELIZA EMILY CHAPPELL PORTER (1807–1888) of New York was a teacher and a Civil War relief worker. She was the director of the Northwestern Sanitary Commission of Chicago, which gathered contributions of food, medical concerns, and other necessary supplies for hospital use in the Civil War. NOAH PORTER (1811–1892) of Connecticut was the president of Yale University and the editor-in-chief of *Webster's Unabridged Dictionary,* among other publications. SARAH PORTER (1813–1900) of Connecticut was the founder of Miss Porter's School in Farmington, Connecticut, a highly acclaimed women's boarding school. ALBERT GALLATIN PORTER (1824–1897) of Indiana was the law partner of President Benjamin Harrison and the governor of Indiana. JAMES DAVIS PORTER (1828–1912) was a Confederate soldier, a governor of Tennessee, a foreign diplomat, and one of the founders of the college that became George Peabody College for Teachers. CHARLOTTE ENDYMION PORTER (1857–1942) of Pennsylvania was the co-founder of *Poet Lore* magazine. WILLIAM SYDNEY PORTER (1862–1910) of North Carolina was a writer of short stories who was better known as O. Henry. After years of dead-end jobs and a short stint behind bars, he took up writing. His stories are best known for their surprise endings. ELEANOR HODGMAN PORTER (1868–1920) of New York was an author and the creator of the little girl Pollyanna and the stories about her life. EDWIN STANTON PORTER (1870–1941) of Pennsylvania was the director/photographer of Thomas Edison's films *Life of an American Fireman* and *The Great Train Robbery.* COLE ALBERT PORTER (1891–1964) of Indiana was an American composer. He wrote "In the Still of the Night" (1937) and "I Love Paris" (1953), among others.

Genealogies: *Edward Culver, John Porter and Mary Estey: a Line of Descent from Two Puritans and a Salem Witch, with Allied Families* was compiled by Marilyn V. Squires Mills and published in Cullman, Alabama, in 1988. *A Family History, William Porter, Jr. of Rockbridge County, Virginia (1740–1804)* was compiled by Mary E. Porter and published in El Reno, Oklahoma, in 1984.

PORTILLA, PORTILLO (S.S. Abbreviation: Portil)

Ranking: 4505 **S.S. Count:** 9944

Origin: Spanish. Uncertain etymology. Most likely a transformation of Laporta.

Genealogies: None known.

POSEY

Ranking: 1621 **S.S. Count:** 27,634

Origin: English. Uncertain etymology. 1) the name means those who lived by a post near an enclosure. 2) the name was given to those from Poce, the name of a place in France.

Famous **Poseys:** THOMAS POSEY (1750–1818) of Virginia was a Revolutionary War soldier and the governor of Louisiana and the Indiana territory. ALEXANDER LAWRENCE POSEY (1873–1908) was knowledgeable in Indian affairs and was the editor of *Indian Journal.*

Genealogies: *The Posey Family in America* was compiled by Lloyd Franklin Posey and published in Hattiesburg, Mississippi, in 1971. *The History of the Posey Family in Europe and the United States* was compiled by R. H. Posey and published in Flora, Mississippi, in 1969.

POST

Ranking: 1336 **S.S. Count:** 33,095

Origin: German, Jewish. German: ultimately derived from the Latin word "postis," meaning a pole or post. The name was given to those who lived near an important or boundary post or pole. Jewish: uncertain etymology.

Famous **Posts:** GEORGE PROWNE POST (1837–1913) of New York was an architect responsible for many of the buildings in New York City, including the College of the City of New York. He also is considered a pioneer in modern-day hotel design. CHARLES WILLIAMS POST (1854–1914) of Illinois was the founder of the Postum Cereal Company. He also founded the Texas town of Post. EMILY PRICE POST (1872–1960) of Maryland was an advisor on etiquette. She wrote several books on the subject and was considered the guru in the world of fine china and manners. MARJORIE MERRIWEATHER POST (1887–1973) of Illinois was the daughter of Charles Williams Post, who founded the Postum Cereal Company, and the heir to the family business. She was responsible for the corporation's buying Birdseye because she saw a "future" in frozen foods. WILEY POST (1899–1935) of Texas flew around the world with Harold Gatty. After the journey he wrote the book *Around the World in Eight Days.* He also made the first solo flight around the world. He died in the same airplane crash that killed Will Rogers.

Genealogies: None known.

POSTON
Ranking: 3146 S.S. Count: 14,442

*Origin: English. Derived from an uncertain first compo-
nent and the Old English word "tūh," meaning settlement.
The name was given to those from Poston, the name of a place
in England.*

Famous Postons: CHARLES DEBRILL POSTON (1825–
1902) of Kentucky was the first Arizona delegate to Congress.

Genealogies: *Those Who Have Gone Before* [also Pos-
ton] was compiled by Miriam Halbert Bales and published
in Muncie, Indiana, in 1976.

POTTER
Ranking: 374 S.S. Count: 102,868

*Origin: English. Potter: derived from the Middle English
word "pot," meaning a vessel for storage or drinking. The
name was given to potters.*

Famous Potters: ALONZO POTTER (1800–1865) of New
York was an Episcopal clergyman and the founder of an
Episcopal hospital and divinity school in Philadelphia.
ELISHA REYNOLDS POTTER (1811–1882) of Rhode Island was
a member of Congress and the commissioner of public
schools who did much to improve the quality of the educational system in Rhode Island. EDWARD CLARK POTTER
(1857–1923) of Connecticut was a sculptor best known for
his pieces with animals as the subjects. WILLIAM BANCROFT
POTTER (1863–1934) of Connecticut was an electrical engineer who invented the "series parallel controller" for electric railway motors.

Genealogies: *Descendants of Deacon Samuel Potter
(1671–1756), Connecticut Farms (now Union), N.J.* was
compiled by Helen Potter Alleman and published in Harmony, New Jersey in 1975. *Descendants of Nicholas Potter of
Lynn, Massachusetts* was compiled by Frank Elwood Potter
and published in Baltimore, Maryland, in 1991.

POTTS
Ranking: 773 S.S. Count: 54,412

*Origin: English. Transformation of Philpott, which is of
uncertain etymology.*

Famous Pottses: JONATHAN POTTS (1745–1781) of
Pennsylvania was a physician who served as the medical
officer at Lake George and the director of hospitals in various locations during the Revolutionary War. BENJAMIN
FRANKLIN POTTS (1836–1887) of Ohio was a Union army
officer and the governor of Montana territory.

Genealogies: *Thomas Potts (Shield): and Related Families* was compiled by Gloria (Potts) Stracke and published

in San Francisco, California, in 1980. *My O'Bryand-Potts-
Cowan Family of Union County, Kentucky* was compiled by
Marscena Frakes and published in Owensboro, Kentucky,
in 1977.

POULIN
Ranking: 4108 S.S. Count: 11,003

*Origin: French. Derived from the Old French word
"poule," meaning chicken. The name was given to those who
raised chickens or to those who were fearful.*

Genealogies: None known.

POUNDS
Ranking: 4485 S.S. Count: 9990

*Origin: English. Derived from the Middle English word
"p(o)und," meaning an enclosure in which animals are
trapped or kept. The name was given to those who lived near
a pound or to those whose job it was to corral stray animals.*

Genealogies: *The Family History of Christopher Overmiller (1813) and Anderson Pounds (1845)* was compiled by
Carol Jean Detwiler Overmiller and published in Smith
County, Kansas, in 1978. *Pioneer Pond People Plus Robinson
and Allied Families* [also Pounds] was compiled by Betty
Pond Snyder and published in Foster City, California, in
1992.

POWELL
Ranking: 90 S.S. Count: 304,573

*Origin: English, Welsh. English: transformation of Paul.
Welsh: derived from the Welsh patronymic component "ap"
and the first name Hywel, the name of a great Welsh king and
meaning distinguished.*

Famous Powells: WILLIAM HENRY POWELL (1823–1879)
of New York City was a painter of historical scenes. His
Discovery of the Mississippi River by DeSoto is in the
Rotunda of the Capitol in Washington, D.C., and *Oliver
Hazard Perry at the Battle of Lake Erie* is in the Ohio state
capitol. JOHN WESLEY POWELL (1834–1902) of New York was
a geologist and a pioneer explorer of the Colorado and
Green rivers. He published the first book on Indian languages. MAUD POWELL (1868–1920) of Illinois was a violinist. LOUISE MATHILDE POWELL (1871–1943) of Virginia was a
nursing educator. She was the first superintendent of the
University of Minnesota School of Nursing. GEORGE
HAROLD POWELL (1872–1922) of New York was a pioneer in
the preservation and transportation of perishable food.
ADAM CLAYTON POWELL JR. (1908–1972) of Connecticut was
a member of Congress from New York who introduced
many social reforms to the House. In 1967 he was barred
from the House for misuse of funds, but his constitutents
reelected him. EARL (BUD) POWELL (1924–1966) of New
York City was a pioneer in the musical style of "bebop" jazz.

Genealogies: *James Ball and Colvin Powell Connections*

was compiled by Grace Powell Harms and published in Baltimore, Maryland, in 1983. *Jerry Basham and Ellen Higgs* [also Powell] was compiled by Omegene Powers Powell and published in Utica, Kentucky, in 1986.

POWER

Ranking: 2155 **S.S. Count:** 21,289

Origin: English, Irish. English: derived from the Middle English and Old French word "povre," meaning poor. The name was given to those who were impoverished or, in irony, to misers. English, Irish: uncertain etymology. Most likely derived from the Old French word "pois," meaning fish. The name was given to those from Pois, the name of a place in Picardy, France.

Famous **Powers:** FREDERICK BELDING POWER (1853–1927) of New York was a chemist and pharmacist who made great advances in plant research. FREDERICK TYRONE POWER (1869–1931) of England came to the United States as a boy. He was a well-known actor who played the romantic hero. He dropped his first name professionally. His son, TYRONE EDMUND POWER (1914–1958) of Ohio also was an actor. He succeeded in motion pictures as a leading man. His films included *Lloyd's of London* (1936) and *The Razor's Edge* (1946).

Genealogies: *A Genealogical Record of the Powers(s) [i.e. Power(s)] Families* was compiled by Franklin E. Powers and published in Aurora, Colorado, in 1974. *Descendants of Alexander Power of Laurens County, South Carolina* was compiled by Lucien L. McNees and published in Lexington, Mississippi, in 1967.

POWERS

Ranking: 281 **S.S. Count:** 128,619

Origin: English, Irish. Transformation of Power.

Famous **Powerses:** HIRAM POWERS (1805–1873) of Vermont was a sculptor. He is known for his statues of Benjamin Franklin and Thomas Jefferson that stand in the U.S. Capitol.

Genealogies: *A Genealogical Record of the Powers(s) [i.e. Power(s)] Families* was compiled by Franklin E. Powers and published in Aurora, Colorado, in 1974. *Descendants of Alexander Power of Laurens County, South Carolina* was compiled by Lucien L. McNees and published in Lexington, Mississippi, in 1967. *Parke-Reitz and Erwin-Powers Families of Kansas* was compiled by Elva Griffith Reitz and published in Sun City, Arizona, in 1977.

PRADO

Ranking: 3833 **S.S. Count:** 11,751

Origin: Italian, Spanish. Ultimately derived from the Latin word "prātum," meaning meadow. The name was given to those who lived near a meadow.

Genealogies: None known.

PRATER

Ranking: 1825 **S.S. Count:** 24,728

Origin: English. Ultimately derived from the Latin word "praetor," the title of a Roman official.

Genealogies: None known.

PRATHER (S.S. Abbreviation: Prathe)

Ranking: 2001 **S.S. Count:** 22,744

Origin: Welsh. Derived from the first name Rhydderch, meaning "the reddish-brown one" (ES).

Genealogies: *Robert and Marshall, the Prather Family in Louisiana, from Wales, England, Virginia, Maryland* was compiled by Dudley Austin Tatman and published in Opelousas, Louisiana, in 1982. *Nellie B.: Tales of a Texan* [also Prather] was compiled by Angela Morgan Burton and published in Kansas City, Missouri, in 1970.

PRATT

Ranking: 475 **S.S. Count:** 84,733

Origin: English. Derived from the Old English word "prœtt," meaning trick. The name was given to those who were tricksters.

Famous **Pratts:** THOMAS WILLIS PRATT (1812–1875) of Massachusetts was the inventor of the "Pratt truss," a bridge and roof support. FRANCIS ASHBURY PRATT (1827–1902) of Vermont was the co-founder of the machine-tool company Pratt & Whitney in Hartford, Connecticut. CHARLES PRATT (1830–1891) of Massachusetts co-founded Charles Pratt & Co., an oil refinery that eventually was acquired by John D. Rockefeller. He founded Pratt Institute in New York City and the first free library in Brooklyn or New York City. RICHARD HENRY PRATT (1840–1924) of New York started the first school for Indians that was not on a reservation. The school became the Carlisle Indian Industrial School. SILAS GAMALIEL PRATT (1846–1916) of Vermont was the founder of the Pratt Institute of Music and Art in Pittsburgh. ANNA BEACH PRATT (1867–1932) of New York was a social worker and a member of the board of education of Philadelphia.

Genealogies: *Ancestors and Descendants of Paul Pratt of New Vineyard, Maine* was compiled by Joan Pratt and published in Searsport, Maine, in 1988. *Descendants of Thomas Horton of Spingfield: and Including Some Descendants of Phineas Pratt* was compiled by Carl W. Fischer and published in Bayside, New York, in 1976.

PRENDEGAST, PRENDEGUEST, PRENDERGAST, PRENDERGRASS, PRENDERGRAST (S.S. Abbreviation: Prende)

Ranking: 4928 **S.S. Count:** 9080

Origin: English. Uncertain etymology. Possibly given to those from a former place in Flanders called Brontegeest.

Famous **Bearers:** MAURICE BRAZIL PRENDERGAST (1859–1924) of Newfoundland was a painter best known for his watercolor scenes of Boston.

Genealogies: None known.

PRENTICE, PRENTIS, PRENTISS (S.S. Abbreviation: Prenti)

Ranking: 3059 **S.S. Count:** 14,828

Origin: Prentice—English, Irish, Scottish; Prentis, Prentiss—English, Scottish. Prentice (English, Scottish): derived from the Middle English and Old French word "aprentis," meaning apprentice. Prentice (Irish): derived from the Gaelic name Ó Pronntaigh (H&H). Prentis, Prentiss: transformations of the English and Scottish Prentice.

Famous **Bearers:** GEORGE DENNISON PRENTICE (1802–1870) was born in an unknown location in New London County, Connecticut, and moved to Kentucky, where he was a newspaper publisher whose paper, the *Louisville Daily Journal*, became a nationally known Whig paper. He also was the main reason Kentucky did not secede from the Union. ELIZABETH PAYSON PRENTISS (1818–1879) of Maine was the author of children's literature. She was the author of the *Little Suzy* books, but her greatest success came from *Stepping Heavenward*, an autobiographical peek at herself. It was serialized in the *Chicago Advance*. HENNING WEBB PRENTIS JR. (1884–1959) of Missouri was a businessman who was the chairman of the National Association of Manufacturers (1941).

Genealogies: *Valentine Prentice* was compiled by Linus Joseph Dewald and published in Bowie, Maryland, in 1992.

PRESCOT, PRESCOTT (S.S. Abbreviation: Presco)

Ranking: 1934 **S.S. Count:** 23,374

Origin: English. Derived from the Old English words "prēost" and "cot," meaning priest and cottage. The name was given to those from Prescott, the name of several places in England.

Famous **Bearers:** WILLIAM PRESCOTT (1726–1795) of Massachusetts was a Minuteman and the commander at the Battle of Bunker Hill. SAMUEL PRESCOTT (1751–1777?) of Massachusetts was a Revolutionary patriot who traveled with Paul Revere on the night of his famous ride. Prescott escaped when Revere was captured and continued on to warn the colonists in Concord. WILLIAM HICKLING PRESCOTT (1796–1859) of Massachusetts was a historian who, through an accident and illness, lost the majority of his vision. He nonetheless published several volumes on different aspects of European and North American history.

Genealogies: *European Ancestry of the Prescott Family of America* was compiled by Doris Cline Ward and published in Allegan, Michigan, in 1977. *Leaves from the Prescott Fam-*

ily Tree was compiled by Bertha Klicka Mannen and published in San Diego, California, in 1985.

PRESTO (ALSO PRESTON)

Ranking: 620 **S.S. Count:** 67,158

Origin: Preston—English; Presto—Italian. Preston: derived from the Old English words "prēost" and "tūn," meaning priest and settlement. The name was given to those from Preston, the name of many places in England. Presto: cognate to Priest.

Famous **Bearers:** WILLIAM CAMPBELL PRESTON (1794–1860) of Pennsylvania was a South Carolina politician and a supporter of states' rights. JOHN SMITH PRESTON (1809–1881) of Virginia was a South Carolina politician who favored states' rights. He was the superintendent of the Confederate Bureau of Conscription (1863–1865). ANN PRESTON (1813–1872) of Pennsylvania was the dean of the Women's Medical College of Pennsylvania. She was the first woman so appointed. MARGARET JUNKIN PRESTON (1820–1897) of Pennsylvania was a southern poet and novelist who wrote of the pain and sorrow felt by families split by the consequences of the Civil War.

Genealogies: *Begats, a Chronicle of the McMillan, Preston, Wiggins, and Binford Families* was compiled by Mabel E. Preston Wiggins and published in Ellsworth, Maine, in 1979. *The Prestons of Smithfield and Greenfield in Virginia* was compiled by John Frederick Dorman and published in Louisville, Kentucky, in 1982.

PREWIT (ALSO PREWITT)

Ranking: 3982 **S.S. Count:** 11,356

Origin: English. Derived from the Middle English word "prou(s)," meaning brave. The name was given to a valiant man or warrior.

Genealogies: *Prewitt-Light, Ringler-Hollowell and Allied Families* was compiled by Lester Dee Prewitt and published in Fairfield, Iowa, in 1970. *Michael Prewitt, Sr., and his Descendants, 1720–1970* was compiled by Richard A. Prewitt and published in Des Moines, Iowa, in 1971. *Prewitt-Pruitt Records of Virginia* [also Prewitt] was compiled by Richard A. Prewitt and published in Grimes, Iowa, in 1988. *The Pruett (Pruitt) Family* [also Prewitt] was compiled by Haskell Pruett and published in Stillwater, Oklahoma, in 1975.

PRICE

Ranking: 83 **S.S. Count:** 321,106

Origin: English, Jewish, Welsh. English: uncertain etymology. Possibly derived from the Middle English and Old French word "pris," meaning prize or price. Jewish: derived from Prūsen, the name of a Baltic tribe. The name was given to those from Prussia, a former state of Germany. Welsh: derived from the Old Welsh first name Rīs, meaning "fiery Warrior" (H&H).

Famous **Prices:** ELI KIRK PRICE (1797–1884) of Pennsylvania was a Pennsylvania politician responsible for the Consolidation Act (1854), which streamlined the city government of Philadelphia. BRUCE PRICE (1845–1903) of Maryland was an architect whose best-known work is Georgian Court in Lakewood, New Jersey. It is now the site of a private college. JOSEPH PRICE (1853–1911) of Virginia was responsible for elevating the level of medical care available for women at the Philadelphia Dispensary. He is considered a pioneer in surgery connected with pregnancy. THOMAS FREDERICK PRICE (1860–1919) of North Carolina was the first native-born North Carolina resident to become a Roman Catholic priest. ELI KIRK PRICE (1860–1933) of Pennsylvania was responsible for the building of the Philadelphia Museum of Art. He was the grandson of Eli Kirk Price (1797–1884). GEORGE MOSES PRICE (1864–1942) of Russia emigrated to the United States in 1882. He was responsible for monitoring the sanitary conditions in the International Ladies' Garment Workers Union. He also founded the Union Health Center. GEORGE EDWARD MCCREADY PRICE (1870–1963) of Canada was a fundamentalist advocate and a geologist. He preached against evolution and for the "new catastrophism." FLORENCE BEATRICE SMITH PRICE (1888–1953) of Arkansas was a composer and instrumentalist and the first black symphonic composer in the United States.

Genealogies: *Ancestors and Descendants of John Price: Immigrant to Virginia, 1610– 11* was compiled by Wina Chandler Price and published in Baltimore, Maryland, in 1988. *The George Jacob Price Family History* was compiled by Janice Gartman Lee and published in West Columbia, South Carolina, in 1986.

PRIDE

Ranking: 4795 S.S. Count: 9340

Origin: English, Welsh. English: 1) derived from the Old English word "prȳde," meaning pride. 2) uncertain etymology. The name was given to those from Priddy, the name of a town in Somerset, England. Welsh: 1) derived from the first name Predyr, referring to a knight of the Round Table in Arthurian legend. 2) derived from the Welsh word "prydudd," meaning bard. The name was given to bards.

Genealogies: *My Colbert County Families: Lanes, Prides, Goodloes, Rutlands, & Bartons* was compiled by Mary Alexander Lollar and published in Tuscumbia, Alabama, in 1974.

PRIDGEON (S.S. Abbreviation: Pridge)

Ranking: 4620 S.S. Count: 9670

Origin: English, French. Uncertain etymology. Possibly derived from the French word "preauxjean," meaning wise, brave John.

Genealogies: None known.

PRIEST (ALSO PRIESTER, PRIESTLEY, PRIESTLY, PRIESTMAN)

Ranking: 1472 S.S. Count: 30,281

Origin: Priest, Priestley, Priestly, Priestman—English; Priester—Jewish. Priest: derived from the Middle English word "pr(i)est," meaning a minister of the church. The name was given to those considered priest-like or to the servant of a priest. Priestman: derived from the Middle English word "pr(i)est," meaning a minister of the church, and "man," meaning man. The name was given to the servant of a priest. Priestley, Priestly: derived from the Old English words "prēost" and "lēah," meaning priest and wood or clearing. Priester: cognate to Priest. Uncertain etymology. Possibly given pejoratively to a rabbi.

Famous **Bearers:** JOSEPH PRIESTLEY (1733–1804) of England was a scientist who wrote *The History and Present State of Electricity* (1767). He also wrote about the rings (Priestley rings) that result from electrical discharges on metal surfaces. EDWARD DWIGHT PRIEST (1861–1931) of Massachusetts was an electrical engineer and the inventor of a motor for use on elevated trains.

Genealogies: *Descendants of Dwight Solomon Priest of Massachusetts and John Henry Linville of North Carolina* was compiled by Thomas Merriam Linville and published in Schenectady, New York, in 1978. *Priester-Peeples Lives and Legends* [also Priest] was compiled by Jane Priester Hawkins and published in Aiken, South Carolina, in 1987.

PRIETO

Ranking: 3647 S.S. Count: 12,369

Origin: Spanish. Derived from the Old Spanish word "prieto," meaning dark. The name was given to those who were of dark hair or complexion.

Genealogies: None known.

PRINCE

Ranking: 681 S.S. Count: 61,292

Origin: English, French, Jewish. English, French: derived from the Middle English and Old French word "prince," meaning a nobleman. Jewish: uncertain etymology. Possibly given to those who were princely in demeanor.

Famous **Princes:** THOMAS PRINCE (1687–1758) of Massachusetts was a scholar and the author of *A Chronological History of New England in the Form of Annals* (1736). He attempted to keep the history of New England in its truest form. His library, thought to be considerable at the time, is now housed in the Boston Public Library. WILLIAM PRINCE (1766–1842) of New York was a nurseryman and the one who introduced "Isabella" grapes to New York wineries. His son, WILLIAM PRINCE (1725–1802) of New York was a nurseryman and a pioneer in breeding new types of plum trees. In the next generation of this family, WILLIAM ROBERT PRINCE (1795–1869) of New York was a nurseryman and the author of gardening publications. LE BARON BRADFORD PRINCE (1840–1922) of New York was chief justice, then the governor, of New Mexico. He is responsible for the first public-school code in New Mexico and the founding of the University of New Mexico. MORTON PRINCE (1854–1929) of Massachusetts was an expert in the field of abnormal psychology. He founded the *Journal of Abnormal Psychology*. FREDERICK HENRY PRINCE (1859–1953) of Massachusetts was a businessman and the chairman of the executive committee of Armour and Co., which he built into a financially secure business.

Genealogies: *Prince and Davis of Tennessee* was compiled by Robert W. Layton and published in Baltimore, Maryland, in 1988. *Prince Family Prince: the Story of 1400 Princes across America* was compiled by Pete Prince and published in Morristown, Tennessee, in 1982.

PRINGLE (S.S. Abbreviation: Pringl)

Ranking: 2511 **S.S. Count:** 18,069

Origin: English, Scottish. Derived from the Middle English word "hop," meaning enclosed valley, and an Old Norse name comprising components meaning peg and ravine. The name was given to those from Pringle, a place in Scotland.

Famous **Pringles:** CYRUS GUERNSEY PRINGLE (1838–1911) of Vermont was a horticulturist who bred plants and created the herbarium at the University of Vermont. ELIZABETH VATIES ALLSTON PRINGLE (1845–1921) of South Carolina was a rice planter and an author in South Carolina. Her books tell of life on the southern plantation in the antebellum South. HENRY FOWLES PRINGLE (1897–1958) of New York was a journalist, biographer, and the author of a Pulitzer Prize–winning biography of Theodore Roosevelt.

Genealogies: None known.

PRIOR

Ranking: 4817 **S.S. Count:** 9301

Origin: English. Derived from the Middle English word "prior," meaning a monastic official ranking just below an abbot. The name was given to priors or to those who served a prior.

Famous **Priors:** MARGARET BARRETT ALLEN PRIOR (1773–1842) of Virginia was a charity worker. Having her own children all die at a very young age led her to adopt those unwanted by others. She is best remembered for her charitable work toward all in need.

Genealogies: None known.

PRITCHARD, PRITCHATT, PRITCHET, PRITCHETT (S.S. Abbreviation: Pritch)

Ranking: 684 **S.S. Count:** 61,292

Origin: Pritchatt, Pritchet, Pritchett—English; Pritchard—Welsh. Pritchard: derived from the first name Richard, a Germanic name comprising the components "ric"

and "hard," meaning power and brave. Pritchatt, Pritchet, Pritchett: derived from the Middle English word "prik(e)," meaning prick or point. The name was given to those who made tools with points or to those who were tall and slender.*

Famous Bearers: HENRY SMITH PRITCHETT (1857–1939) of Missouri was an astronomer and the first president of the Carnegie Foundation for the Advancement of Teaching, 1905–1930. JETER CONNELLY PRITCHARD (1857–1921) of Tennessee was a U.S. senator from Tennessee and a judge for the fourth circuit court of appeals.

Genealogies: *My Folks: Pritchard, Vaught, Beasley, Sargent* was compiled by Thelma Sargent and published in Mesa, Arizona, in 1984. *A History and Genealogy of the Pritchett, Rimmer, Jacobs, Hamilton, [et al.] Families* was compiled by Dorothy Symmonds and published in Bellaire, Texas, in 1989.

PROCTOR (S.S. Abbreviation: Procto)

Ranking: 877 **S.S. Count:** 49,331

Origin: English. Ultimately derived from the Latin words "pro" and "cūrāre," meaning for and to deal with. The name was given to stewards.

Famous **Proctors:** WILLIAM COOPER PROCTOR (1862–1934) of Ohio was the president of Procter & Gamble after 1907. He was responsible for the employee programs of profit sharing, stock ownership, and pensions. He also gave employees a guarantee of 48 weeks of work each year. HENRY HUGH PROCTOR (1868–1933) of Pennsylvania was a Congregational clergyman and black leader. He was one of the first leaders of the interracial movement.

Genealogies: *Free Men in an Age of Servitude: Three Generations of a Black Family* [also Proctor] was compiled by Lee H. Warner and published in Lexington, Kentucky, in 1992. *The Proctor Connection* was compiled by Shirley Brodersen Ross and published in Jefferson, Iowa, in 1978.

PROFFIT, PROFFITT (S.S. Abbreviation: Proffi)

Ranking: 3257 **S.S. Count:** 13,956

Origin: English, Scottish, French. 1) derived from the Middle English word "prophete," meaning prophet. The name was given to those who played the part of the prophet in medieval pageants. 2) uncertain etymology. The name was given to those who were wealthy.

Genealogies: None known.

PROSSER (S.S. Abbreviation: Prosse)

Ranking: 3836 **S.S. Count:** 11,745

Origin: Welsh. Derived from the Welsh first name Rhosier, a cognate to Roger.

Famous **Prossers:** CHARLES SMITH PROSSER (1860–1916) of New York was a geologist who served as the head of Ohio State University's department of geology (1901–1916).

Genealogies: *Bachelder of Alamo (also Prosser family)* was compiled by Glen L. Bachelder and published in East Lansing, Michigan, in 1992.

PROVEN (ALSO PROVENÇAL, PROVENSAL, PROVENZA, PROVENZANO)

Ranking: 2837 **S.S. Count:** 16,078

Origin: Provençal, Provensal—French; Provenza, Provenzano—Italian; Proven—Scottish. Provençal, Provensal, Provenza, Provenzano: cognates to the English name Province, which was derived from the Latin word "prōvincia," meaning province or sphere of office. The name was given to those from Provence, a region in southern France. Proven: derived from the Middle English word "provend," meaning an area of land that generated revenue for a religious office-holder. The name was given to those from Provan, a place in Scotland.

Genealogies: None known.

PROVOST (S.S. Abbreviation: Provos)

Ranking: 3817 **S.S. Count:** 11,819

Origin: English. Derived from the Middle English word "provost," which was derived from the Latin word "prōpositus," which was derived from "praepositus," meaning to place in charge. The name was given to those who were in charge of a religious chapter or educational institution or to those who behaved like headmasters.

Famous Provosts: Etienne Provost (1782?–1850) of Canada was a hunter and a guide and is considered the first white person to see Great Salt Lake. The discovery of South Pass has also been credited to him by some historians.

Genealogies: None known.

PRUETT

Ranking: 2318 **S.S. Count:** 19,560

Origin: English. Transformation of Prewit.

Genealogies: *The Pruett (Pruitt) Family* was compiled by Haskell Pruett and published in Stillwater, Oklahoma, in 1975. *Pruett Past & Present* was compiled by Dorothy Sturgis Pruett and published in Macon, Georgia, in 1982.

PRUITT

Ranking: 724 **S.S. Count:** 58,444

Origin: English. Transformation of Prewit.

Genealogies: *The Pruett (Pruitt) Family* was compiled by Haskell Pruett and published in Stillwater, Oklahoma, in 1975. *Prewitt-Pruitt Records of Virginia* was compiled by Richard A. Prewitt and published in Grimes, Iowa, in 1988.

PRYOR

Ranking: 1134 **S.S. Count:** 13,795

Origin: English. Transformation of Prior.

Famous Pryors: Nathaniel Pryor (1775?–1831) of Vir-

ginia was a member of the Lewis and Clark expedition. Roger Atkinson Pryor (1828–1919) of Virginia was the founder of the pro-southern newspaper *The South* and a member of Congress from Virginia. He was "honored" by his fellow southerners by being offered the chance to fire the first shot at Fort Sumter. He refused the offer in favor of another. After the Civil War he practiced law in New York City and became a justice of the New York State Supreme Court. Sara Agnes Rice Pryor (1830–1912) of Nebraska was an author and southern leader. She was a founder of the National Society of the Daughters of the American Revolution and was the first regent of the New York City chapter. Arthur W. Pryor (1870–1942) of Missouri was a trombone player well known at the turn of the century. He is best known for his recording of "The Whistler and his Dog."

Genealogies: *The Pryors, American Pioneers* was compiled by John H. Cunningham and published in Cullman, Alabama, in 1989. *A Study in Lineage of the Wiley Pryor Family of the Carolinas* was compiled by Melvin B. Johnson and published in Dearborn, Michigan, in 1992. *A Wilson-Pryor Lineage* was compiled by Gloria Stracke and published in San Francisco, California, in 1982.

PRZYBYLAK, PRZYBYLOWSKI, PRZYBYLSKI, PRZYBYSZ, PRZYBYSZEWSKI

Ranking: 4346 **S.S. Count:** 10,315

Origin: Polish. Derived from the Polish word "przybysz," meaning newcomer. The name was given to those who were new to an area.

Genealogies: None known.

PUCKETT (S.S. Abbreviation: Pucket)

Ranking: 1138 **S.S. Count:** 38,648

Origin: English. Derived from the name Puca, meaning goblin.

Genealogies: *Some Pucketts and Their Kin* was compiled by Hester Elisabeth Garrett and published in Lansing, Michigan, in 1978.

PUENTE (ALSO PUENTES)

Ranking: 3770 **S.S. Count:** 12,017

Origin: Spanish. The name means bridge.

Genealogies: None known.

PUGH

Ranking: 730 **S.S. Count:** 57,959

Origin: Welsh. Derived from the Welsh first name Hugh, which is derived from several Germanic names with the first component derived from "hug," meaning "heart, mind, spirit" (H&H).

Famous Pughs: Ellis Pugh (1656–1718) of North

Wales was the author of *Annerch ir Cymru* (1721), the first Welsh book printed in America. SARAH PUGH (1800–1884) of Virginia was a teacher, abolitionist, and a supporter of suffrage for women. She traveled as the companion of Lucretia Mott, thereby allowing Miss Mott, with her advanced age, to still attend the meetings and rallies of the day.

Genealogies: *Chapman and Pugh Family History and Allied Lines* was compiled by Minnie May Pugh and published in Birmingham, Alabama, in 1976.

PULLEN

Ranking: 2938 **S.S. Count:** 15,482

Origin: English. Derived from the Old French word "poulain," meaning colt. The name was given to those who were frisky and to those who raised horses.

Genealogies: *Minnie Mallory Boyett and Mallory, Hagan, Pullen, Radford, Goggans, Peterson, and Richardson Kin* was compiled by Woodrow W. Boyett and published in Tuscaloosa, Alabama, in 1987.

PULLEY

Ranking: 4168 **S.S. Count:** 10,843

Origin: English, Scottish. Uncertain etymology. English: the name was given to those who lived near a pool in a wood or on an island. Scottish: the name was given to those from Pulhay Burn, a place in Scotland.

Genealogies: None known.

PULLIAM (S.S. Abbreviation: Pullia)

Ranking: 2739 **S.S. Count:** 16,629

Origin: Welsh. Uncertain etymology. Probably derived from the name William.

Genealogies: None known.

PURCEL (ALSO PURCELL, PURCELLI)

Ranking: 1352 **S.S. Count:** 32,782

Origin: Purcell—English; Purcelli—Italian; Purcel—Romanian. Purcell: derived from the Old French word "pourcel," meaning piglet. The name was given to those who kept or herded pigs. Purcelli, Purcel: cognates to Purcell.

Genealogies: None known.

PURDY

Ranking: 1975 **S.S. Count:** 22,958

Origin: English. Derived from the Anglo-Norman-French oath "pur die," meaning by God. The name was given to those who used this oath frequently.

Famous **Purdys:** CORYDON TYLER PURDY (1859–1944) of Wisconsin was a structural engineer. Seeing the benefits of steel construction of buildings, he was one of the first to build steel skyscrapers. He was the engineer of the Marquette Building in Chicago and the Fuller Building (popularly known as the Flatiron Building) and the Metropolitan Life Insurance Tower in New York City. LAWSON PURDY (1863–1959) of New York was a tax and zoning expert. As president of the New York Tax Reform Association, he began the New York City requirement for publishing assessment rolls.

Genealogies: *Descendants of Francis Purdy of Fairfield, Connecticut* was compiled by Louis E. Beiringer and published in Larchmont, New York, in 1978. *Family Records of Sigismond Hugget, 1744–1810, and his Wife Susanne Marguerite Pichonnet, with Related Families, Especially Purdy Spinning* was compiled by Georgie A. Hill and published in Bernardsville, New Jersey, in 1943. *Gabriel Purdy* was compiled by Clayton C. Purdy and published in Baton Rouge, Louisiana, in 1983.

PURNELL (S.S. Abbreviation: Purnel)

Ranking: 3843 **S.S. Count:** 11,724

Origin: English. Transformation of Parnell.

Famous **Purnells:** BENJAMIN PURNELL (1861–1927) of Kentucky was the religious leader of the communal group called the House of David. His followers referred to him as "King." The colony was located in Benton Harbor, Michigan.

Genealogies: *Lambie Genealogy* [also Purnell] was compiled by Hugh J. Purnell and published in 1968.

PURVIS

Ranking: 1984 **S.S. Count:** 22,844

Origin: English, Scottish. Derived from the Middle English word "purveys," meaning provisions. Uncertain etymology. The name was most likely given to those in charge of provisioning a great house or monastery.

Genealogies: *The Purvis Family, by George!: the Descendants of George Purvis of Virginia and their Kin* was compiled by Virginia J. Murphy and published in Manchester, Tennessee, in 1991. *The Purvis Family in Virginia and their Kin* was compiled by Alice Lee Simpson Oliver and published in Shipman, Virginia, in 1969.

PUTMAN

Ranking: 3407 **S.S. Count:** 13,273

Origin: English. Transformation of Pitt.

Genealogies: *The Putman Family, New York and Beyond* was compiled by Warren Thomas Putman and published in Rio Linda, California, in 1989.

PUTNAM

Ranking: 1696 **S.S. Count:** 26,322

Origin: English. Derived from the Old English name Putta, meaning kite, and the Old English word "ham," meaning homestead. The name was given to those who came from Puttenham, the name of places in England.

Famous **Putnams:** ISRAEL PUTNAM (1718–1790) of Massachusetts was a soldier who served in the French and Indian, Pontiac's, and the Revolutionary wars. RUFUS PUTNAM (1738–1824) of Massachusetts, the cousin of Israel Putnam, also was a Revolutionary War soldier. He also organized the Ohio Co. and colonized the area north of the Ohio River. He laid out the town of Marietta, and he was the first to settle a town in the Northwest Territory. GEORGE PALMER PUTNAM (1814–1872) of Maine was a publisher. He was the founder of G. P. Putnam & Sons and *Putnam's Monthly Magazine.* FREDERIC WARD PUTNAM (1839–1915) of Massachusetts was an anthropologist and one of the curators at the Peabody Museum at Harvard University. He was responsible for the organization of the anthropological part of the 1893 exposition in Chicago, which was the basis for the Field Museum of Natural History. ALICE HARVEY WHITING PUTNAM (1841–1919) of Illinois was a pioneer in the education of kindergarteners. [GEORGE] HERBERT PUTNAM (1861–1955) of New York was the director of the Library of Congress. Under him the library grew in size and prestige. EMILY JAMES SMITH PUTNAM (1865–1944) of New York was an author and the first dean of Barnard College. BERTHA HAVEN PUTNAM (1872–1960) of New York City was a historian and an expert in the area of medieval English legal and economic history.

Genealogies: *The Putman Family, New York and Beyond* [also Putnam] was compiled by Warren Thomas Putman and published in Rio Linda, California, in 1989. *A Brief History of the Family of Nathan Allen and Mary Putnam* was compiled by Augustus L. Allen and published in Poughkeepsie, New York, in 1895. *A Family Tree in America: Being a Genealogical Story of the Families of Deane, Putnam, Boynton, Gager, Bull, and Allied Families from the Year 1630* was compiled by Frank Putnam Deane and published in Richmond, Virginia, in 1979.

PYLE

Ranking: 2017 **S.S. Count:** 22,634

Origin: English. Derived from the Middle English word "pile," meaning a stake used as a landmark. The name was given to those who lived near such a stake or post.

Famous **Pyles:** HOWARD PYLE (1853–1911) of Delaware was an author and illustrator of children's books. He is best known for *The Merry Adventures of Robin Hood* (1883) and *Otto of the Silver Hand* (1888). ROBERT PYLE (1877–1951) of Pennsylvania was an authority on roses. He was the founder of the American Association of Botanical Gardens and Arboretums. CHARLES C. "CASH AND CARRY" PYLE (1882?–1939), birthplace unknown, was a sports promoter. He managed football players, started the first professional tennis tours, and started the "Bunion Derby," a transcontinental walking race. ERNEST TAYLOR (EARNIE) PYLE (1900–1945) of Indiana was a journalist who was famous for writing columns about ordinary soldiers in World War II.

Genealogies: *A Genealogical History of Bloss-Pyles-Ross-Sellards and their Kinsmen* was compiled by Harry Leon Sellards and published in DeLand, Florida, in 1990. *The Pyle-Pile Family in America, 1642–1980: also Pyles-Piles* was compiled by Howard Thornton Pyle and published in Kokomo, Indiana, in 1981.

PYLES

Ranking: 4041 **S.S. Count:** 11,201

Origin: English. Transformation of Pyle.

Genealogies: *The Pyle-Pile Family in America, 1642–1980: also Pyles-Piles* was compiled by Howard Thornton Pyle and published in Kokomo, Indiana, in 1981.

QUALLS

Ranking: 2939 S.S. Count: 15,481
Origin: Uncertain etymology.
Genealogies: None known.

QUARLES (S.S. Abbreviation: Quarle)

Ranking: 3346 S.S. Count: 13,545
Origin: English. Derived from the Old English word "hwerflas," meaning circles. The name was given to those who came from Quarles, a place in Norfolk, England.

Famous **Quarleses:** LOUIS QUARLES (1883–1972) of Wisconsin was a corporate and patent lawyer. DONALD AUBREY QUARLES (1894–1959) of Arkansas served as a U.S. deputy secretary of defense and was one of the organizers of the Defense Reorganization Act, the National Aeronautics and Space Administration (NASA), and the Federal Aviation Agency.

Genealogies: None known.

QUEEN

Ranking: 1874 S.S. Count: 21,145
Origin: English. Derived from the Old English word "cwēn," meaning woman, wife or queen. The name was given to those who worked for a queen or played the part of a queen in a pageant or play.

Genealogies: *The Ancestors and Descendants of Charles Jerningham Queen, Prince Georges County, Maryland* was compiled by Mary Elizabeth Jensen and published in Hicksville, New York, in 1982.

QUICK

Ranking: 1309 S.S. Count: 33,865
Origin: Cornish, English. Cornish: derived from the Cornish word "gwyk," meaing wood. The name was given to those who lived in the woods. English: 1) derived from the Old English words "cū" and "wīc," meaning cow and remote settlement. The name was given to those who dwelled on a remote dairy farm. 2) derived from the Middle English word "quik," meaning lively. The name was given to those who were considered spirited. 3) derived from the Old English word "cwice," meaning couch grass. The name was given to those who lived near couch grass. 4) derived from the Old English word "cwicbēam," meaning poplar tree. The name was given to those who lived near poplar trees. 5) derived from the Old English word "cwictrēow," meaning aspen tree. The name was given to those who lived near aspen trees.

Famous **Quicks:** ARMAND JAMES QUICK (1894–1978) of Wisconsin was a medical researcher. Partially paralyzed from the age of four, he became a professor of pharmacology and biochemistry, then a research professor at Hemostasis Research Laboratory at Marquette, which became the Medical College of Wisconsin. There he developed the Quick Test for liver function. He also developed, among other tests, the aspirin tolerance test, which showed that aspirin could extend bleeding, and he showed evidence of a new vitamin he named "Q," a necessary ingredient in the clotting of blood.

Genealogies: *Quicks of East Fork* was compiled by Howard Wilbert Quick and published in Milwaukee, Wisconsin, in 1978.

QUIGLEY (S.S. Abbreviation: Quigle)

Ranking: 1852 S.S. Count: 24,419
Origin: Irish. Derived from the Gaelic name Ó Coigligh, which was derived from the first name Coigleach.

Genealogies: *The Union of our Quigley and Munro Families* was compiled by Eleanor Freeburn and published in Berea, Ohio, in 1982.

QUILES

Ranking: 3653 S.S. Count: 12,348
Origin: Catalan. Derived from the first name Quilico, which was derived from the name Quirico.

Genealogies: None known.

QUINLAN (S.S. Abbreviation: Quinla)

Ranking: 3137 S.S. Count: 14,464
Origin: Irish. 1) derived from the Gaelic name Ó Conailláin, which was derived from the first name Conall, which is of uncertain etymology. 2) derived from the Gaelic name Ó Caoindealbháin, which was derived from the name Caoindealbhán, which comprises the components "caoin" and "dealbh," meaning fair and shape.

Genealogies: *The De May, Quinlin, and Jorgensen Families* [also Quinlan] was compiled by Ida De May Wilson and published in Saint Helena, California, in 1986.

QUINN

Ranking: 356 S.S. Count: 107,448
Origin: Irish. Derived from the Gaelic name Ó Cuinn, which was derived from the name Conn, meaning leader.

Genealogies: None known.

QUINONES (S.S. Abbreviation: Quinon)

Ranking: 784 S.S. Count: 53,709
Origin: Spanish. Derived from the Latin word "quinque," meaning five. The name was given to those who lived and worked on a shared piece of land.

Genealogies: None known.

QUINTANA, QUINTANILLA, QUINTAS (S.S. Abbreviation: Quinta)

Ranking: 1046 S.S. Count: 41,934
Origin: Quintana—Catalan, Spanish; Quintanilla—

Spanish; *Quintas—Portuguese. Derived from the Catalan and Spanish word "quintana," meaning a fifth. The name was given to those who lived on a piece of land that owed one-fifth of its yield as rent.*
Genealogies: None known.

QUINTER (S.S. Abbreviation: Quinte)
Ranking: 2016 **S.S. Count:** 22,638
Origin: French. Derived from the Latin word "quinque," meaning five. The name was given to those who managed the merchandise of a hospital or church and to whom one-fifth of its revenues were paid.
Genealogies: None known.

QUIRK
Ranking: 4957 **S.S. Count:** 9036

Origin: Irish, Manx. Derived from the Gaelic name Ó Cuire, which was derived from the name Corc, which was derived from either the word "corc," meaning heart, or the word "curc," meaning clump of hair.
Genealogies: None known.

QUIROZ
Ranking: 4112 **S.S. Count:** 10,981
Origin: Spanish. Uncertain etymology. 1) the name was given to those who came from Quiros, a place in Spain. 2) the name was given to those who lived near the plant heather.
Genealogies: None known.

RABINOV, RABINOVICH, RABINOVITCH, RABINOWICZ, RABINOWITZ (S.S. Abbreviation: Rabino)

Ranking: 4457 S.S. Count: 10,057

Origin: Jewish. Derived from the Polish word "rabin," meaning rabbi, which was ultimately derived from the Hebrew word "rav," meaning rabbi.

Genealogies: None known.

RADCLIFF, RADCLIFFE (S.S. Abbreviation: Radcli)

Ranking: 2965 S.S. Count: 15,341

Origin: English. Derived from the Old English words "rēad," and "clif," meaning red and cliff. The name was given to those from Radcliffe, the name of several places in England.

Famous **Bearers:** JACOB RADCLIFF (1764–1844) of New York was the mayor of New York City and one of the founders of Jersey City, New Jersey.

Genealogies: The Descendants of Joseph Ratcliff of Bienville Parish, Louisiana [also Radcliff] was compiled by Jane Clancy Debenport and published in Midland, Texas, in 1988. *Isaac and Mary (Presnall) Ratcliff of Henry County, Indiana and their Descendants* [also Radcliffe] was compiled by Richard P. Ratcliff and published in Dublin, Indiana, in 1979.

RADER

Ranking: 1979 S.S. Count: 22,893

Origin: German. 1) derived from a word meaning moor. The name was given to those from Raden, a place in Germany. 2) derived from the first name Radheri. 3) uncertain etymology. The name was given to those who used reed to thatch roofs. 4) uncertain etymology. The name was given to wheelwrights. 5) uncertain etymology. The name was given to aldermen.

Genealogies: Henry Rader and his Descendants was compiled by Cecile Rhodes Cannon and published in Lenoir, North Carolina, in 1987. *Raders-Schmitt Genealogy* [also Radetr] was compiled by Irene Doll and published in Lena, Illinois, in 1979.

RADFORD, RADFORTH (S.S. Abbreviation: Radfor)

Ranking: 2582 S.S. Count: 17,638

Origin: English. Derived from the Old English words "rēad" and "ford," meaning red and ford. The name was given to those from Radford or Radforth, the name of several places in England.

Genealogies: Minnie Mallory Boyett and Mallory, Hagan, Pullen, Radford, Goggans, Peterson, and Richardson Kin was compiled by Woodrow W. Boyett and published in Tuscaloosa, Alabama, in 1987.

RAFFERTY (S.S. Abbreviation: Raffer)

Ranking: 3470 S.S. Count: 13,016

Origin: Irish. Derived from the Gaelic name Ó Rabhartaigh, which was derived from the first name Robhartach, meaning "wielder of prosperity" (H&H).

Genealogies: Raffety's (Rafferty's) in America was compiled by Charles E. Raffety and published in 1975.

RAGAN

Ranking: 2992 S.S. Count: 15,180

Origin: German. Derived from the first name Ragin, meaning counsel.

Genealogies: The Lineage of the Amos Ragan Family was compiled by Elizabeth H. Ragan and published in Greensboro, North Carolina, in 1976.

RAGLAN, RAGLAND

Ranking: 2625 S.S. Count: 17,322

Origin: English, Welsh. The name was given to those from Raglan, the name of a place in England.

Genealogies: The Raglands: The history of a British-American family was compiled by Charles J. Ragland and published in Winston-Salem, North Carolina, in 1987. *Early Ragland Families of Middle Tennessee* was compiled by Hobert Daniel Ragland and published in Watonga, Oklahoma, in 1966.

RAGSDALE (S.S. Abbreviation: Ragsda)

Ranking: 2539 S.S. Count: 17,864

Origin: English. 1) derived from words meaning "valley at the pass" (ES). The name was given to those from Ragdale, a place in Leicestershire, England. 2) the name was given to those who lived in a lichen-covered valley.

Genealogies: Elijah Ragsdale: Born Virginia, November 1, 1778 to South Carolina was compiled by June Hart Wester and published in Canton, Georgia, in 1975. *Through the Orchard: Arterberry, Hillsberry, Lemons, Ragsdale* was compiled by Nova A. Lemons and published in Dallas, Texas, in 1989.

RAINES

Ranking: 1544 S.S. Count: 28,890

Origin: English, French, Jewish, Scottish. English: derived from the feminine medieval first name Reine, which was ultimately derived from the Latin word "rēgina," meaning queen. English, French: 1) derived from the Old French word "raine," meaning frog. 2) derived from the Germanic first name Ragin, meaning counsel; or from other names that had Ragin as a first component. Jewish: derived from the feminine Yiddish first name Rayne, meaning queen. Scottish: derived from the Gaelic phrase "rath cháin," meaning ford of the tax. The name was given to those from Raine, the name of a former place in Scotland.

Famous **Raineses:** JOHN RAINES (1840–1909) of New York was the New York state senator responsible for the "Raines Law," which controlled liquor traffic.

Genealogies: . . . and the Raines Came was compiled by Fredna Raines Threatt and published in Dallas, Texas, in 1967.

RAINEY
Ranking: 1406 S.S. Count: 31,610
Origin: Irish, Scottish. Derived from various Germanic first names with the first component "rand," meaning shield, or "ragin," meaning counsel.

Famous **Raineys:** JOSEPH HAYNE RAINEY (1832–1887) of South Carolina was the first black member of Congress. He was known as a champion of civil rights. HENRY THOMAS RAINEY (1860–1934) of Illinois was a member of Congress and Speaker of the House (1933–1934). GERTRUDE PRIDGETT RAINEY (1886–1939) of Georgia was a black blues singer who recorded "See See Rider" and "Trust No Man." She was known as Ma Rainey.

Genealogies: *Middletown Upper Houses* [also Rainey] was compiled by Charles Collard Adams and published in Canaan, New Hampshire, in 1983.

RAINS
Ranking: 2757 S.S. Count: 16,519
Origin: English, Scottish. Transformation of Raine.

Famous **Rainses:** GABRIEL JAMES RAINS (1803–1881) of North Carolina was a Confederate officer and an expert in the use of explosives. GEORGE WASHINGTON RAINS (1817–1898) of North Carolina was the brother of Gabriel James Rains. He also served as a Confederate soldier and was an expert in the field of explosives. Following the Civil War he served as a professor and dean at the Medical College of Georgia. CLAUDE RAINS (1889–1967) of England was an actor of stage and screen. His best-known role was that of the prefect of police in *Casablanca.*
Genealogies: None known.

RAINWATER, RAINWATERS (S.S. Abbreviation: Rainwa)
Ranking: 4697 S.S. Count: 9525
Origin: English. The name was given to those who lived near an area of poor drainage where rain collects in a pool.
Genealogies: None known.

RALPH
Ranking: 3918 S.S. Count: 11,509
Origin: English. Derived from an Old Norse first name comprising the Germanic components "rad" and "wolf," meaning counsel and wolf.

Famous **Ralphs:** JAMES RALPH (1695?–1762), possibly of New Jersey, was both a political and a literary writer. He wrote the first American play to be viewed in England.
Genealogies: None known.

RALSTON (S.S. Abbreviation: Ralsto)
Ranking: 2501 S.S. Count: 18,137
Origin: English? Uncertain etymology. Possibly derived from the Old Norse first name Hrølf, comprising the components "hrōd" and "wulf," meaning fame and wolf, and the Old English word "tūn," meaning settlement. The name was given to those from Rowlston or similarly named places in England.

Famous **Ralstons:** WILLIAM CHAPMAN RALSTON (1826–1875) of Ohio was a banker in California. Using the bank's funds for his personal financial dealings ultimately caused his downfall. After being asked to resign, he was found drowned. SAMUEL MOFFETT RALSTON (1857–1925) of Ohio was a governor of, then a U.S. senator from, Indiana.
Genealogies: *Trails Trod by Holloway and Ralstons* was compiled by Orella Chadwick and published in Tillamook, Oregon, in 1980.

RAMBO
Ranking: 4556 S.S. Count: 9807
Origin: German. The name was given to those who came from places with similar-sounding names in Germany.
Genealogies: *The Rambo Family Tree* was compiled by Beverly J. Rambo and published in Decorah, Iowa, in 1987.

RAMEY
Ranking: 1509 S.S. Count: 29,489
Origin: French. Derived from the Old French word "ra(i)m," meaning branch. The name was given to those who lived near a wood.
Genealogies: *Robert Ryburn and Martha Ramey* was compiled by Loubeth Ramey Hames and published in State University, Arkansas, in 1977.

RAMIREZ (S.S. Abbreviation: Ramire)
Ranking: 118 S.S. Count: 248,727
Origin: Spanish. Derived from a Germanic first name comprising the components "ragin" and "meri," meaning counsel and fame.
Genealogies: None known.

RAMOS
Ranking: 167 S.S. Count: 198,672
Origin: Portuguese, Spanish. Cognate to Ramey.
Genealogies: None known.

RAMSAY
Ranking: 3869 S.S. Count: 11,652

Origin: Scottish. 1) *derived from the Old English name Ram(m). The name was given to those from Ramsey, the name of a place in Scotland.* 2) *derived from the Old English words "hramsa" and "ēg," meaning wild garlic and island. The name was given to those from Ramsey, the name of several places in Scotland.*

Famous **Ramsays:** NATHANIEL RAMSAY (1741–1817) of Pennsylvania was a Revolutionary War soldier who excelled at the Battle of Monmouth. ALEXANDER RAMSAY (1754?–1824) of Scotland was an anatomist who came to America and wandered the country teaching and lecturing. ERSKINE RAMSAY (1864–1953) of Pennsylvania was an engineer and inventor. He and his father, Robert Ramsay, were the inventors of coal-mining tools and techniques. He was a pioneer in the use of coal by-products and the founder of Pratt Consolidated Coal Co. and the Alabama By-Products Co.

Genealogies: None known.

RAND
Ranking: 3111 **S.S. Count:** 14,624
Origin: English. 1) *derived from the Old English word "rand," meaning rim. The name was given to those who lived on the shores of a river.* 2) *derived from the Middle English first name Rand(e), derived from various Germanic first names that included the first component "rand," meaning shield.*

Famous **Rands:** JAMES HENRY RAND (1859–1944) of New York was an inventor and the founder of the Rand Ledger Co., which later merged with Remington Typewriter to become the Remington-Rand Co. under the leadership of his son, James Henry Rand Jr. MARIE GERTRUDE RAND (1886–1970) of New York was one of the leading researchers in the field of optics. She, who professionally used her maiden name, and her husband, Clarence Errol Ferree, who had been her teacher during her doctoral work, experimented with the effects of light on one's perception of color and developed measuring devices relating these perceptions to the retina. This led to the Ferree-Rand perimeter, which was used in recognizing vision problems. She was the first woman elected a member of the Illuminating Engineering Society, and she was also the first woman to be awarded the Edgar D. Tillyer Medal of the Optical Society of America. SALLY RAND (1904–1979) of Missouri was originally named Helen Gould Beck. She was an acrobat in carnivals and Hollywood but is best remembered as a fan dancer first seen at the 1933 Chicago World's Fair. AYN RAND (1905–1982) of Russia came to the United States in 1926. She was the author of such novels as *Capitalism: The Unknown Ideal* (1966) and *The New Left* (1971).

Genealogies: *Rand Ramblings: from the arrival of Francis Rand, Strawbery Banke, New Hampshire, 1630, to the 90th birthday anniversary of Margaret Rand Keen, Topeka,*

Kansas, 1985 was compiled by Ray A. Keen and published in Manhattan, Kansas, in 1985.

RANDALL (S.S. Abbreviation: Randal)
Ranking: 533 **S.S. Count:** 75,999
Origin: English. Derived from the Middle English first name Randel, which was derived from the first name Rand, derived from various Germanic first names that include the first component "rand," meaning shield.

Famous **Randalls:** ROBERT RICHARD RANDALL (1750?–1801), possibly of New Jersey, was a philanthropist whose fortune was at least partly due to privateerism. He left his fortune for an asylum for seamen that was first built in Sailors Snug Harbor, Staten Island, New York, then moved to Sea Level, North Carolina. ALEXANDER WILLIAMS RANDALL (1819–1872) of New York was the governor of Wisconsin and a supporter of Abraham Lincoln. He served as the postmaster general (1866–1869). SAMUEL JACKSON RANDALL (1828–1890) of Pennsylvania was a member of Congress (1863–1890) and the Speaker of the House (1876–1881). JAMES RYDER RANDALL (1839–1908) of Maryland was the author of the song "Maryland, My Maryland." JAMES GARFIELD RANDALL (1881–1953) of Indiana was a historian and an authority on the Civil War and Abraham Lincoln. CLARENCE BELDEN RANDALL (1891–1967) of New York was the president and chairman of the board of Inland Steel Co. He was the recipient of the Presidential Medal of Freedom in 1963.

Genealogies: *Ancestors and Descendants of Snow Randall, the Quaker, 1609–1973* was compiled by Robert Ferris Randall and published in Eden, New York, in 1973. *A Randall Family of Long Island, New York, 1667–1989* was compiled by Genevieve Randall Lanyon and published in 1989. *The Rundle, Rendel, Randle, Randol, Randall, Rundall, Rundell, Runnell Ancestry of Long Island and Greenwich, 1667–1992* was published in Decorah, Iowa, in 1991.

RANDAZZO (S.S. Abbreviation: Randaz)
Ranking: 4762 **S.S. Count:** 9409
Origin: Italian. The name was given to those from Randazzo, a place in Italy.

Genealogies: None known.

RANDLE (ALSO RANDLEMAN, RANDLES)
Ranking: 1913 **S.S. Count:** 23,633
Origin: English. Transformations of Randall.

Genealogies: *Randleman, Rendleman, Rintelman Reunion, 1981* was compiled by Billee Snead Webb and published in Corvallis, Oregon, in 1983.

RANDOLPH (S.S. Abbreviation: Randol)
Ranking: 703 **S.S. Count:** 60,166
Origin: English. Derived from a Germanic first name

comprising the components "rand" and "wolf," meaning shield and wolf.

Famous **Randolphs:** WILLIAM RANDOLPH (1651?–1711) of England was a colonist and a plantation owner in Virginia. He was one of the founders of the College of William and Mary. SIR JOHN RANDOLPH (1693–1736?) of Virginia was a lawyer and scholar. He served as the Speaker of the House of Burgesses and was considered an intellectual of the day. PEYTON RANDOLPH (1721?–1775) of Virginia was the first president of the Continental Congress. EDMUND JENNINGS RANDOLPH (1753–1813) of Virginia was a colonial politician and one of the ones who refused to sign the Constitution. As a lawyer he represented Aaron Burr in his 1807 trial for treason. JOHN RANDOLPH (1773–1833) of Virginia was also known as John Randolph of Roanoke. He was a colonial politician and a champion of states' rights. He was involved in a duel with Henry Clay. THOMAS JEFFERSON RANDOLPH (1792–1875) of Virginia was a grandson of Thomas Jefferson and the keeper of Monticello, the family home. JACOB RANDOLPH (1796–1848) of Pennsylvania was a surgeon who introduced lithotripsy to America. GEORGE WYTHE RANDOLPH (1818–1867) of Virginia, brother of Thomas Jefferson Randolph, was a grandson of Thomas Jefferson and was born at the ancestral home, Monticello. He served as the Confederate secretary of war until ill health and ill will toward Jefferson Davis forced his resignation. THEODORE FITZ RANDOLPH (1826–1883) of New Jersey was the governor of New Jersey and a U.S. senator from his home state. SARAH NICHOLAS RANDOLPH (1839–1892) of Virginia, daughter of Thomas Jefferson Randolph, was the author of biographies about Stonewall Jackson and Thomas Jefferson, her great-grandfather. ASA PHILIP RANDOLPH (1889–1979) of Florida was the founder of *The Messenger,* a paper that encouraged an aggresive approach by African-Americans in pursuing job opportunities and improving working conditions. He founded and was president of the Brotherhood of Sleeping Car Porters and was the force behind President Franklin D. Roosevelt's creation of the Fair Employment Practices Committee. He also was the director of the August 1963 March on Washington for Jobs and Freedom, which was the largest civil rights event to that date in the history of the United States.

Genealogies: *Edward Fitz Randolph Branch Lines, Allied Families, and English and Norman Ancestry* was compiled by Oris Hugh Fitz Randolph and published in Anamosa, Iowa, in 1976. *The Randolphs of Virginia* was compiled by Jonathan Daniels and published in Garden City, New York, in 1972.

RANEY
Ranking: 3650 **S.S. Count:** 12,359
Origin: Irish, Scottish. Transformation of Rainey.

Famous **Raneys:** GEORGE PETTUS RANEY (1845–1911) of Florida was active in the Florida court system, serving as the state attorney general and on the state supreme court as both an associate justice and the chief justice.
Genealogies: None known.

RANGEL
Ranking: 1758 **S.S. Count:** 25,521
Origin: Spanish. Uncertain etymology.
Genealogies: None known.

RANKIN (ALSO RANKINE, RANKING)
Ranking: 909 **S.S. Count:** 47,444
Origin: English, Scottish. Derived from the name Rand, which was derived from various Germanic first names that include the first component "rand," meaning shield.

Famous **Bearers:** WILLIAM BIRCH RANKINE (1858–1905) of New York was responsible for the Niagara Falls power project and is considered the "father of Niagara power." JEANNETTE PICKERING RANKIN (1880–1973) of Montana was the first woman elected to the House of Representatives and the only member of Congress to vote against the entry of the United States into both World War I and II. JOHN ELLIOT RANKIN (1882–1960) of Mississippi was a member of Congress who co-sponsored the bill that created the Tennessee Valley Authority.

Genealogies: *Selections from a Van Rensselaer Family Library: 1536–1799* [also Rankin] was compiled by Joyce Jackson and published in Albany, New York, in 1979.

RANSOM (ALSO RANSOME)
Ranking: 1742 **S.S. Count:** 25,718
Origin: English. Transformations of Rand, derived from the Middle English first name Rand(e).

Famous **Bearers:** MATT WHITAKER RANSOM (1826–1904) of North Carolina was a Confederate soldier and a U.S. senator after the Civil War. He was instrumental in bringing about a peaceful end to the war with the Compromise of 1876–1877. THOMAS EDWARD GREENFIELD RANSOM (1834–1864) of Illinois was a Union soldier and was considered one of the best Union volunteers. He died in action. FREDERICK LESLIE RANSOME (1868–1935) of England came to the United States as a small child and settled in California. He was considered one of the best geologists of his time. JOHN CROWE RANSOM (1888–1974) of Tennessee was a poet and teacher. He wrote several volumes of poetry and verse and taught English at Vanderbilt University.
Genealogies: None known.

RAPP
Ranking: 2213 **S.S. Count:** 20,740
Origin: German, Jewish, Swedish. German, Jewish: cognate to the English name Raven, which was derived from the

Middle English word "raven," meaning the bird. The name was given to those with dark hair or to thieves. Swedish: derived from the Swedish word "rapp," meaning quick. The name was given to soldiers.

Famous **Rapps**: GEORGE RAPP (1757–1847) of Germany was a religious leader who started the group known as the Harmonites or Rappites. Their law of celibacy led to their demise.

Genealogies: *The Rapp Tree, 1801–1973* was compiled by Gladys Mack and published in Tomah, Wisconsin, in 1973.

RASH

Ranking: 4198 **S.S. Count**: 10,759
Origin: English, Jewish. English: derived from the Middle English phrase "atter ashe," meaning "at the ash tree" (H&H). Jewish: uncertain etymology.

Genealogies: None known.

RASMUS (ALSO RASMUSSEN)

Ranking: 813 **S.S. Count**: 51,967
Origin: Rasmussen—Dano-Norwegian; Rasmus—German. Derived from the first name Erasmus, which is derived from the Greek word "erasmos," meaning loved.

Genealogies: *Hans and Sofie Rasmussen* was compiled by Maynard LeRoy May and published in Phillips, Nebraska, in 1982.

RATCLIFF, RATCLIFFE (S.S. Abbreviation: Ratcli)

Ranking: 2191 **S.S. Count**: 20,915
Origin: English. Transformations of Radcliff.

Genealogies: *The Descendants of Joseph Ratcliff of Bienville Parish, Louisiana* was compiled by Jane Clancy Debenport and published in Midland, Texas, in 1988. *Isaac and Mary (Presnall) Ratcliff of Henry County, Indiana and their Descendants* was compiled by Richard P. Ratcliff and published in Dublin, Indiana, in 1979.

RATHBUN, RATHBURN (S.S. Abbreviation: Rathbu)

Ranking: 3419 **S.S. Count**: 13,233
Origin: English. Uncertain etymology. Most likely derived from the Old English words "hrēod" and "burna," meaning reeds and stream. The names were given to those from places in England called Radbourn or variations thereof.

Famous **Bearers**: RICHARD RATHBUN (1852–1918) of New York was a zoologist who wrote about marine invertebrates and was considered an authority on the economics of marine biology.

Genealogies: *A Partial History of Certain Mastin-Rathbun-Dye Families* was compiled by Victor E. Mastin and published in Des Moines, Iowa, in 1974.

RATLIFF, RATLIFFE (S.S. Abbreviation: Ratlif)

Ranking: 1101 **S.S. Count**: 40,145
Origin: English. Transformations of Radcliff.

Genealogies: *My Ratliff Family, 1730's–1990* was compiled by Ralph H. Ratliff and published in Princeton, West Virginia, in 1991. *Ratliff-Keller* was compiled by Carl M. Ratliff and published in Decorah, Iowa, in 1980.

RAU

Ranking: 3903 **S.S. Count**: 11,547
Origin: German, Jewish, Italian. German, Jewish: transformation of Rauch. Italian: derived from the name Rou(l).

Famous **Raus**: CHARLES RAU (1826–1887) of Belgium was an archaeologist and curator at the U.S. National Museum. He was considered a pioneer in recognizing the importance of the study of aboriginal peoples and their technology.

Genealogies: *The Rau Family Chronicle* was published in Marao, Illinois.

RAUCH

Ranking: 3593 **S.S. Count**: 12,561
Origin: German, Jewish. Derived from the German word "rauch," meaning rough. The name was given to an untidy person.

Famous **Rauches**: JOHN HENRY RAUCH (1828–1894) of Pennsylvania was a physician and the first president of the Illinois State Board of Health.

Genealogies: *Oliphant-Rauch-Doty Genealogy* was compiled by Eva Emery Doty and published in Lawrence, Indiana, in 1977.

RAUSCH (ALSO RAUSCHER)

Ranking: 2789 **S.S. Count**: 16,333
Origin: German. 1) the names were given to those who were excitable. 2) the names were given to those who lived near rushes.

Genealogies: *Rauscher Family History* was compiled by Donald Ralph Campolongo and published in Wescosville, Pennsylvania, in 1983.

RAWLIN (ALSO RAWLING, RAWLINGS, RAWLINGSON, RAWLINS)

Ranking: 1700 **S.S. Count**: 26,308
Origin: English. Transformation of Ralph.

Famous **Bearers**: JOHN AARON RAWLINS (1813–1869) of Illinois was a Union soldier and an aide to General Ulysses S. Grant. MARJORIE KINNAN RAWLINGS (1896–1953) of Washington, D.C., was a writer for newspapers. She wrote a syndicated piece called, "Songs of a Housewife" (1925–1927). Although she tried many times, her attempts at writing novels proved unsuccessful. In 1928, the Rawlingses bought property in North Florida in Cross Creek, near the town of Hawthorne. There, away from the cold of the North, she wrote. She was published in *Scribner's Magazine* and noticed by Maxwell Perkins, an editor at Scribner's. With him guiding her unique abilities to capture the rural spirit of the people of northern Florida, she began writing a series of novels, beginning in 1933. Her finest literary accomplishment was *The Yearling*, which won a Pulitzer Prize in 1939.

Genealogies: None known.

RAWLS

Ranking: 2884 **S.S. Count:** 15,796

Origin: English. Derived from the French name Raoul, a cognate to Ralph.

Genealogies: None known.

RAY

Ranking: 187 **S.S. Count:** 184,312

Origin: English, Jewish. English: 1) derived from the Middle English word "ray," meaning a female roe deer. The name was given to those who were timid. 2) transformation of Rea. 3) transformation of Wray. 4) derived from the Old French word "roy," meaning king. The name was given to those who were regal.

Famous Rays: CHARLES BENNETT RAY (1807–1886) of Massachusetts was one of the first black journalists. He published the *Colored American* (1838–1842). ISAAC RAY (1807–1881) of Massachusetts was a psychiatrist who was considered a top man in his field. MAN RAY (1890–1976) of Pennsylvania, originally named Emmanuel Rudnitsky, was a painter, photographer, and filmmaker. He was part of the Dadaist and surrealist movements in both New York City and Paris. He was the developer of "cameraless" pictures called "rayographs."

Genealogies: *Bound for the Promised Land: History of the Ray and Armstrong Families* was compiled by Joan Cervenka Cobb and published in Midland, Texas, in 1992. *The Wests and the Rays and Allied Lines: Southern Families from the Colonies to Texas* was compiled by Nan Overton West and published in Lubbock, Texas, in 1991.

RAYBURN (S.S. Abbreviation: Raybur)

Ranking: 3858 **S.S. Count:** 11,684

Origin: English, Scottish. English: the name was given to those from Ripponden, a place in Yorkshire, England. Scottish: the name was given to those from Ryburn, a former place in Scotland.

Famous Rayburns: SAMUEL TALIAFERRO RAYBURN (1882–1961) of Tennessee was a member of the U.S. House of Representatives (1913–1961), serving as Speaker of the House on and off for 16 years. He was the force behind the passage of President Franklin D. Roosevelt's New Deal.

Genealogies: None known.

RAYMOND, RAYMONT (S.S. Abbreviation: Raymon)

Ranking: 783 **S.S. Count:** 53,864

Origin: English, French. Derived from the Norman first name Raimund, comprising the Germanic components "ragin" and "mund," meaning counsel and protection.

Famous Bearers: BENJAMIN WRIGHT RAYMOND (1801–1883) of New York was the mayor of Chicago during an economic depression. Because of the economic conditions of the time, he donated his salary to the unemployed. Later he was responsible for laying out the town of Lake Forest. HENRY JARVIS RAYMOND (1820–1869) of New York was one of the founders of the *New York Times*. He also dabbled in politics and was the author of several biographies. PERCY EDWARD RAYMOND (1879–1952) of Connecticut was the curator of the Museum of Comparative Zoology at Harvard University (1912–1945). ALEXANDER GILLESPIE RAYMOND (1919–1956) of New York was a cartoonist who created "Flash Gordon," "Jungle Jim," and "Rip Kirby."

Genealogies: *Raymond Genealogy* was compiled by Samuel Edward Raymond and published in Seattle, Washington, in 1972.

RAYNOR

Ranking: 4218 **S.S. Count:** 10,700

Origin: English. Derived from the Norman first name Rainer, which comprises the Germanic components "ragin" and "hāri," meaning counsel and army.

Genealogies: None known.

REA

Ranking: 2512 **S.S. Count:** 18,064

Origin: English. 1) derived from the Middle English phrase "atter eye," meaning at the river. The name was given to those who lived near a river. 2) derived from the Middle English phrase "atter ye," meaning at the island. The name was given to those who lived on an island or in a swampy area.

Genealogies: *Ancestors of Joseph Bolen & Mary Read* was compiled by Todd Bolen and published in Wheaton, Illinois, in 1983.

READ

Ranking: 1806 **S.S. Count:** 24,934

Origin: English. 1) the name was given to those from Read, the name of several places in England of varying etymology. 2) derived from the Old English word "ried," meaning clearing. The name was given to those who lived in a clearing. 3) derived from the Middle English word "re(a)d," meaning red. The name was given to those with red hair or a ruddy complexion.

Famous Reads: JOHN READ (1679?–1749) of Connecticut was an outstanding lawyer of his time and was instrumental in the founding of the New England legal system. CHARLES READ (1713?–1774) of Pennsylvania was a political figure in colonial New Jersey. He is credited with being a pioneer in the bog-iron industry. GEORGE READ (1733–1798) of Maryland was a Revolutionary leader and one of the signers of the Declaration of Independence. DANIEL READ (1757–1836) of Massachusetts was a musician and composer and the author of *The American Singing Book*. He edited *The American Musical Magazine*, the first of its kind in America. THOMAS BUCHANAN READ (1822–1872) of Pennsylvania was a painter and poet. He is remembered for two pieces of poetry, "Drifting" and "Sheridan's Ride." His paintings did not survive the test of time. OPIE PERCIVAL or POPE READ (1852–1939) of Tennessee was a writer of journals and books set mostly in the South. He was the founder of *Arkansas Traveler*, a weekly periodical.

Genealogies: *A Read Genealogy* was compiled by Hugh S. Austin and published in West Palm Beach, Florida, in 1973. *The Read Family History, 1740 to 1978* was compiled by Mildred Edgington and published in Grinnell, Iowa, in 1980. *The Reads, an American Saga* was compiled by Dorothy Lutomski and published in De Pere, Wisconsin, in 1980.

REAGAN

Ranking: 2040 **S.S. Count:** 22,402
Origin: Irish. Transformation of Regan.

Famous Reagans: JOHN HENNIGER REAGAN (1818–1905) of Tennessee was a member of Congress from Texas in the years before the Civil War. He served as the Confederate postmaster general during the Civil War. Noting the writing on the wall, he told Texans to accept the outcome of the war and award civil rights to the newly freed slaves. He eventually returned to the U.S. Congress as a Texas representative, then served as a senator. As a politician he cosponsored the bill that led to the creation of the Interstate Commerce Commission (1887). RONALD WILSON REAGAN (1911–) of Illinois was the 40th president of the United States. He also is a former actor who appeared in about 50 movies.

Genealogies: *Smoky Mountain Clans* [also Reagan] was compiled by Donald B. Reagan and published in Knoxville, Tennessee, in 1983. *The Way I See It: An Autobiography* was compiled by Patti Davis and published in New York, New York, in 1992. *The Invincible Irish: Ronald Wilson Reagan— Irish Ancestry and Immigration to America* was compiled by Patricia Meade White and published in Santa Barbara, California, in 1981.

REARDON (S.S. Abbreviation: Reardo)

Ranking: 2202 **S.S. Count:** 20,837

Origin: Irish. Transformation of Riordan.
Genealogies: None known.

REAVES

Ranking: 2169 **S.S. Count:** 21,173
Origin: English. Transformation of Reeves.

Genealogies: *The Reaves Family Tree* was compiled by Timothy O. Reaves and published in Greeneville, Tennessee, in 1983. *The Revis Family of Madison County, North Carolina* [also Reaves] was compiled by David H. Reece and published in Asheville, North Carolina, in 1983.

RECTOR

Ranking: 2254 **S.S. Count:** 20,262
Origin: English. The name was given to those in charge of a parish or church.
Genealogies: None known.

REDD

Ranking: 2630 **S.S. Count:** 17,301
Origin: English. Transformation of Read, meaning the color red.
Genealogies: None known.

REDDEN

Ranking: 3644 **S.S. Count:** 12,373
Origin: Scottish. Derived from words meaning "raven dell" (ES). The name was given to those from Redden, a place in Scotland.
Genealogies: None known.

REDDICH, REDDICK (S.S. Abbreviation: Reddic)

Ranking: 3043 **S.S. Count:** 14,937
Origin: Reddich—German; Reddick—Irish, Scottish. Reddich: derived from the German word "rettich," meaning radish. The name was given to those who grew or sold radishes. Reddick: the name was given to those from Rerrick, the name of a former place in Scotland.
Genealogies: None known.

REDDIN (ALSO REDDING, REDDINGTON)

Ranking: 1687 **S.S. Count:** 26,485
Origin: Redding, Reddington—English; Reddin—Irish. Redding: 1) derived from the Old English word "ryding," meaning a clearing. The name was given to those who lived near a clearing. 2) derived from the Old English word "Rēadingas," meaning "people of Rēad(a)" (H&H), which was derived from the Middle English word "re(a)d," meaning red. Reddington: uncertain etymology. Possibly Redding with the Old English word "tūn," meaning settlement. Reddin:

derived from the Gaelic name Ó Rodáin, which was derived from a first name meaning spirited.

Genealogies: None known.

REDMAN

Ranking: 2439 S.S. Count: 18,610

Origin: English, Jewish. English: transformation of Read, meaning red. Jewish: Anglicization of Roth, meaning red.

Famous **Redmans:** JOHN REDMAN (1722–1808) of Pennsylvania was a physician and teacher of medicine at Pennsylvania Hospital and at the College of Physicians of Philadelphia. BEN RAY REDMAN (1896–1961) of New York was an author and editor who worked with many of the major newspapers and magazines of the day.

Genealogies: None known.

REDMON (ALSO REDMOND)

Ranking: 1064 S.S. Count: 41,423

Origin: Redmon—English; Redmond—Irish. Redmon: transformation of Redman. Redmond: cognate to Raymond.

Genealogies: None known.

REECE

Ranking: 1378 S.S. Count: 32,115

Origin: Welsh. Transformation of the Welsh name Price.

Genealogies: *The Reeces of Worcester, Mass.* was compiled by Louise Elise Jackson Wilder and published in Worcester, Massachusetts, in 1973.

REED

Ranking: 62 S.S. Count: 382,400

Origin: English. Transformation of Read, meaning red.

Famous **Reeds:** JOSEPH REED (1741–1785) of New Jersey was a Revolutionary leader and military secretary to George Washington. THOMAS BRACKETT REED (1839–1902) of Maine was the member of Congress who was responsible for Reed's Rules, which gave the Speaker of the House power. WALTER REED (1851–1902) of Virginia was a member of the Army Medical Corps. He was the one who linked the mosquito to the spread of yellow fever and was then able to eradicate the disease. The military hospital in Washington, D.C., is named in his honor. MARY REED (1854–1943) of Ohio was a missionary to India and the head of the leper asylum at Chandag (1891–1943). JAMES A. REED (1861–1944) of Ohio was a U.S. senator from Missouri. MYRTLE REED (1874–1911) of Illinois wrote many romance novels, including *Lavender and Old Lace* (1902). DAVID AIKEN REED (1880–1953) of Pennsylvania was the U.S. senator who was responsible for the introduction of the Reed-Johnson Immigration Act, which set immigration quotas based on the percentage of nationalities living in the United States in 1920. This heavily favored the countries of northern Europe and was considered prejudical against those in Mediterranean Europe and all of Asia. In retrospect, this act is considered one of the factors leading to the U.S./Japan World War II involvement. JOHN REED (1887–1920) of Oregon was a poet, journalist, and the founder of the Communist Labor Party in the United States.

Genealogies: *Dunkin-Reid and Garner-McGraw-Mobley Families of South Carolina, Georgia, and Alabama* [also Reed] was compiled by Dean Smith Cress and published in Alpharetta, Georgia, in 1992. *The Read Family History, 1740 to 1978* [also Reed] was compiled by Mildred Edgington and published in Grinnell, Iowa, in 1980. *The Reads, an American Saga* [also Reed] was compiled by Dorothy Lutomski and published in De Pere, Wisconsin, in 1980.

REEDER

Ranking: 1658 S.S. Count: 26,978

Origin: English. Derived from the Middle English word "rēd(en)," meaning to cover with reeds. The name was given to those with roofs thatched with reeds.

Famous **Reeders:** ANDREW HORATIO REEDER (1807–1864) of Pennsylvania had the governorship of the Kansas Territory taken away from him because of lack of ability and involvment in land speculation.

Genealogies: *The Reader/Reeder Family* was compiled by Florence Reader Thilly and published in Danville, Pennsylvania, in 1988.

REEDY

Ranking: 2818 S.S. Count: 16,168

Origin: English, Irish, Scottish. English: derived from the Middle English word "readi," meaning prepared. The name was given to those who were frugal. Irish: derived from the Gaelic name Ó Rodaigh, which was derived from the first name Rodach, which is of uncertain etymology. Scottish: the name was given to those from Reedie, a former county in Scotland.

Genealogies: None known.

REES

Ranking: 2548 S.S. Count: 17,830

Origin: Welsh. Transformation of Price.

Famous **Reeses:** JAME REES (1821–1889), born in Wales and raised in Pennsylvania, was a boat builder who made many improvements in steamboat construction and made the stern-wheeler more popular. JOHN K. REES (1851–1907) of New York was a noted astronomer and director of the observatory at Columbia University.

Genealogies: None known.

REESE

Ranking: 378 S.S. Count: 102,341

Origin: Welsh. Transformation of Price.

Famous **Reeses:** JOHN J. REESE (1818–1892) of Pennsylvania was a toxicologist and author of *A Text Book of Medical Jurisprudence and Toxicology* (1884). Three brothers who emigrated to Pennsylvania from Wales—ISAAC REESE (1821–1908), JACOB REESE (1825–1907), and ABRAM REESE (1829–1908)—were notable inventors. Isaac, a brick manufacturer, invented the Reese Silica Brick, which is capable of holding up to extremely high temperatures without shrinking. Jacob, a metallurgist, developed the open-hearth steel process. Abram, a machinery manufacturer, held many patents, including one for a universal steel-rolling mill. LIZETTE WOODWORTH REESE (1856–1935) of Maryland was a teacher in the Baltimore schools and a poet who wrote several books of lyric verse. CHARLES LEE REESE (1862–1940) of Maryland, a chemist, was director of the Du Pont company's research laboratory for 29 years.

Genealogies: The Genealogical Study of David Reese was compiled by Cynthia Jones Reese and published in Wichita Falls, Texas, in 1990. *Some German-American Families* [also Reese family], *1460–1975* was compiled by Harriet R. Frische and published in Scottsdale, Arizona, in 1975.

REEVES

Ranking: 339 **S.S. Count:** 112,030

Origin: English: 1) derived from the Middle English word "reeve," meaning a steward or bailiff. 2) derived from the Middle English phrase "atter eaves," meaning at the edge. The name was given to those who lived on the edge of a wood.

Famous **Reeveses:** JOSEPH M. REEVES (1872–1948) of Illinois was a naval officer who is credited with developing and conducting the training that shaped early aircraft-carrier flight crews.

Genealogies: Those Reeves Girls was compiled by Christine Wood and published in Lubbock, Texas, in 1973.

REGAN

Ranking: 1437 **S.S. Count:** 31,103

Origin: Irish. Derived from the Gaelic name Ó Ríagáin, which was derived from the name Riagán, which is of uncertain etymology.

Famous **Regans:** AGNES G. REGAN (1869–1943) of California, through her leadership in the National Council of Catholic Women and the National Catholic School of Social Service, was a recognized expert on social legislation.

Genealogies: The Invincible Irish: Ronald Wilson Reagan--Irish Ancestry and Immigration to America [also Regan] was compiled by Patricia Meade White and published in Santa Barbara, California, in 1981. *The Lineage of the Amos Ragan Family* was compiled by Elizabeth H. Ragan and published in Greensboro, North Carolina, in 1976.

REGISTER (S.S. Abbreviation: Regist)

Ranking: 3601 **S.S. Count:** 12,538

Origin: English. The name was given to those who kept records.

Genealogies: The Registers and our Kin was compiled by J. Lamar Wells and published in Baltimore, Maryland, in 1989.

REICH

Ranking: 2495 **S.S. Count:** 18,165

Origin: German, Jewish. Cognates to Rich, meaning wealthy.

Genealogies: None known.

REICHARDT, REICHARTZ, REICHARZ (S.S. Abbreviation: Reicha)

Ranking: 4368 **S.S. Count:** 10,263

Origin: German. Transformations of Richard.

Genealogies: None known.

REICHE (ALSO REICHEL, REICHENBACH, REICHENBAUM, REICHER)

Ranking: 1553 **S.S. Count:** 28,658

Origin: Reiche, Reichel, Reicher—German; Reichenbach—German, Jewish; Reichenbaum—Jewish. Reiche, Reichel: cognates to Rich. Reicher: 1) cognate to Rich, meaning wealthy. 2) cognate to Richer. Reichenbach: derived from the Old High German words "rihhi" and "bah," meaning rich and stream. The name was given to those from Reichenbach, the name of several towns in Germany. Reichenbaum: cognate to Rich.

Genealogies: None known.

REID

Ranking: 244 **S.S. Count:** 147,646

Origin: English. Transformation of Read, meaning red.

Famous **Reids:** SAMUEL CHESTER REID (1783–1861) of Connecticut was a naval officer and the designer of the American flag in its present-day form. His wife, Mary, sewed the first one that was flown at the U.S. Capitol. It was raised April 12, 1818. DAVID S. REID (1813–1891) of North Carolina was a member of Congress from, governor of, then U.S. senator from North Carolina. WHITELAW REID (1837–1912) of Ohio was a journalist and a war correspondent during the Civil War. He was editor of the *New York Tribune*, then later served as a European diplomat. His son, OGDEN MILLS REID (1882–1947) of New York, was the editor and publisher of the *New York Tribune*. He and his wife, HELEN MILES ROGERS REID (1882–1970), the *Tribune's* advertising director, acquired the *New York Herald* and merged the two into the New York *Herald Tribune*. She succeeded him as publisher. She was single-handedly responsible for having more female staff members on the *Herald*

Tribune than on any other paper in the United States. IRA DE AUGUSTINE REID (1901–1968) of Virginia was a leader in the New York Urban League and a prominent researcher into living and working conditions of African-Americans in the United States. His study, *Negro Membership in American Labor Unions* (1930), was an early authoritative reference on African-Americans in the workplace.

Genealogies: *Dunkin-Reid and Garner-McGraw-Mobley Families of South Carolina, Georgia, and Alabama* was compiled by Dean Smith Cress and published in Alpharetta, Georgia, in 1992. *The Nathan Reids of Virginia in the March of Freedom* was compiled by Elizabeth Reid Austin and published in Tuscaloosa, Alabama, in 1976. *Reid Family, 1776–1974* was compiled by Maude Reid Tomlinson and published in Shelbyville, Illinois, in 1974.

REILLY

Ranking: 699 **S.S. Count:** 60,359

Origin: Irish. Derived from the Gaelic first name Raghailleach.

Famous **Reillys:** MARION REILLY (1879–1928) was a prominent suffragist and dean of Bryn Mawr College.

Genealogies: *Reilly of Ballintlea* was compiled by Joseph F. Reilly and published in Hartland, Vermont, in 1981.

REIMER (ALSO REIMERS, REIMERT)

Ranking: 2795 **S.S. Count:** 16,289

Origin: German. Reimer, Reimers: derived from a Germanic first name comprising the components "ragin" and "meri," meaning counsel and fame. Reimert: Derived from the Old French first name Rainbert, comprising the Germanic components "ragin" and "behrt," meaning counsel and famous.

Genealogies: None known.

REINER (ALSO REINERS, REINERT, REINERTS)

Ranking: 2650 **S.S. Count:** 17,172

Origin: Reiners—Dutch, Flemish, German; Reiner—Dutch, English, French, German, Jewish; Reinert, Reinerts—German. Reiner (Dutch, English, French, German): derived from the Norman first name Rainer, which comprises the Germanic components "ragin" and "hari," meaning counsel and army. Reiner (Jewish): derived from the German word "rein" or the Yiddish word "reyn," both meaning pure. Reiners: transformation of or cognate to Reiner, derived from the Norman first name Rainer. Reinert, Reinerts: derived from a Germanic first name comprising the components "ragin" and "hard," meaning counsel and brave.

Famous **Bearers:** FRITZ REINER (1888–1963) of Hungary was a musician and conductor who directed in Philadelphia, Pittsburgh, and Chicago.

Genealogies: *Ancestors and Descendants of Johann Jacob*

Reiner and Elsbeth Hitz and Allied Lines was compiled by Helen A. Reiner Reed and published in Sturgeon Bay, Wisconsin, in 1984.

REINHARD, REINHARDT, REINHART (S.S. Abbreviation: Reinha)

Ranking: 1235 **S.S. Count:** 35,807

Origin: German. Transformations of Reinert.

Famous **Bearers:** BENJAMIN F. REINHART (1829–1885) of Pennsylvania was a prominent genre and portrait painter. His nephew, CHARLES S. REINHART (1844–1896) of Pennsylvania, also was a genre painter, and he was also a highly respected illustrator. AURELIA ISABEL HENRY REINHARDT (1877–1948) of California was president of Mills College for 27 years. ADOLF FREDERICK REINHARDT (1913–1967) of New York was an abstract expressionist painter in the 1940s. He is best known for his monochrome paintings, with his last pieces done in black.

Genealogies: None known.

REINKE (ALSO REINKEN, REINKENS)

Ranking: 4769 **S.S. Count:** 9386

Origin: German. Cognates to the English and French name Raines, derived from the Germanic first name Ragin.

Genealogies: None known.

REIS

Ranking: 3312 **S.S. Count:** 13,676

Origin: German, Jewish, Portuguese. German: derived from the Middle High German word "ris," meaning brushwood. The name was given to those who lived in an area of dense undergrowth. Jewish: uncertain etymology. Portuguese: cognate to Ray, meaning king.

Genealogies: None known.

REISS

Ranking: 4164 **S.S. Count:** 10,657

Origin: Jewish. Transformation of the Jewish name Reis.

Genealogies: *The Unterreiner-Reiss Families* was compiled by Shirley Robinson Bryant and published in St. Louis, Missouri, in 1984.

REITER

Ranking: 3100 **S.S. Count:** 14,657

Origin: German. Transformation of Reuter, meaning clearing.

Genealogies: None known.

REITZ

Ranking: 4366 **S.S. Count:** 10,271

Origin: German. 1) derived from the first name Ragizo, which was derived from the word "ragin," meaning counsel. 2) the name was given to those from Ragizo, a place in Germany.

Genealogies: Parke-Reitz and Erwin-Powers Families of Kansas was compiled by Elva Griffith Reitz and published in Sun City, Arizona, in 1977. *Supplement to Parke-Reitz and Erwin-Powers Families of Kansas* was compiled by Louis Powers Reitz and published in Sun City, Arizona, in 1982.

RENDON
Ranking: 4227 **S.S. Count:** 10,672
Origin: Spanish. The name was given to those who lived near a border or boundary.
Genealogies: None known.

RENFRO
Ranking: 1757 **S.S. Count:** 25,538
Origin: Scottish. Derived from words meaning "flowing brook" (ES). The name was given to those from Renfrew, a place in Scotland.
Genealogies: *William Renfro, 1734–1830* was compiled by Josie Baird and published in Rotan, Texas, in 1973.

RENNER (ALSO RENNERT)
Ranking: 2296 **S.S. Count:** 19,860
Origin: Renner—English, German; Rennert—German. Renner: 1) transformation of Reiner, derived from the Norman first name Rainer. 2) derived from the Middle English and Middle High German word "rennen," meaning to run. The name was given to those who were mounted messengers, usually employed in the military. Rennert: transformation of Reinert.
Genealogies: None known.

RENO
Ranking: 3547 **S.S. Count:** 12,725
Origin: Spanish. The name was given to those who lived near the "sign of the reindeer" (ES).
Famous Renos: JESSE LEE RENO (1823–1862) of West Virginia was an army officer during the Civil War. Reno, Nevada, is named in his honor. MILO RENO (1866–1936) of Iowa was a leader in the farm union movement. He organized the group that struck in 1932 for higher farm prices; the strike prompted legislation in farmers' favor.
Genealogies: None known.

RENTER
Ranking: 3521 **S.S. Count:** 12,809
Origin: English?, French? Uncertain etymology. Most likely given to those who worked as rent gatherers.
Genealogies: None known.

RESENDE (S.S. Abbreviation: Resend)
Ranking: 4846 **S.S. Count:** 9230
Origin: Portuguese. Derived from a Visigothic first name comprising the components "rēðs" and "sinðs," meaning counsel and path. The name was given to those from Resende, the name of places in Portugal.
Genealogies: None known.

REUTER (ALSO REUTERS)
Ranking: 4196 **S.S. Count:** 10,761
Origin: German, Jewish. German: 1) derived from the Middle High German word "riutœr," meaning highwayman. 2) derived from the Middle High German word "(ge)riute," meaning clearing. The name was given to those who lived near a clearing or to those who cleared woods. Jewish: uncertain etymology.
Genealogies: None known.

REYES
Ranking: 208 **S.S. Count:** 169,707
Origin: Spanish. Cognate to Ray, meaning king.
Genealogies: None known.

REYNA
Ranking: 2158 **S.S. Count:** 21,253
Origin: Spanish. The name was given to those from Reina, meaning "queen's place" (ES), a place in Spain.
Genealogies: None known.

REYNOLD, REYNOLDS, REYNOLDSON (S.S. Abbreviation: Reynol)
Ranking: 99 **S.S. Count:** 278,796
Origin: English. Derived from a Germanic first name comprising the components "ragin" and "wald," meaning counsel and rule.
Famous Bearers: JOHN REYNOLDS (1713–1788), possibly of England, was the first royal governor of Georgia. He called the colonists "lawless, antimonarchal people" and felt that military force was needed to control them. JOHN REYNOLDS (1788–1865) of Pennsylvania was the governor of, then U.S. senator from, Illinois. CHARLES ALEXANDER REYNOLDS (1842?–1876) of Kentucky was a Union soldier and scout. He was known by the nickname "Lonesome Charley." He was the scout used by George Armstrong Custer in the Black Hill expedition (1874) and at Little Big Horn (1876). WILLIAM NEAL REYNOLDS (1863–1951) of Virginia was a member of the R. J. Reynolds Tobacco Co. family and an executive with the company when the first mass-produced and -marketed cigarette, the Camel, was made in 1913. Some of his fortune was used to further education at universities in North Carolina. RICHARD SAMUEL REYNOLDS SR. (1881–1955) of Tennessee was a member of the R. J. Reynolds Tobacco Co. family. He started his oun company, the U.S. Foil Co., which became the Reynolds Metals Company. QUENTIN JAMES REYNOLDS (1902–1965) of New York was a World War II correspon-

dent and the author of the well-received *The Wounded Don't Cry* (1941).

Genealogies: *The Gilded Leaf: triumph, tragedy, and tobacco: three generations of the R. J. Reynolds family and fortune* was compiled by Patrick Reynolds and published in Boston, Massachusetts, in 1989. *Lambshead before Interwoven: a Texas range chronicle, 1848–1878* [also Reynolds] was compiled by Frances Mayhugh Holden and published in College Station, Texas, in 1982.

REYNOSO (S.S. Abbreviation: Reynos)
Ranking: 4468 **S.S. Count:** 10,023
Origin: Spanish. Uncertain etymology. Possibly derived from the Spanish word "rey," meaning king.
Genealogies: None known.

RHEA
Ranking: 3925 **S.S. Count:** 11,492
Origin: Welsh. The name was given to those who lived near the Rea River in Wales or to those who lived near a rapids.
Famous Rheas: JOHN RHEA (1753–1832) of Ireland came to America and settled in Tennessee. He represented his adopted state as a member of Congress.
Genealogies: *Ray-Rhea: a family book of history and genealogy for Rhea and related families* was compiled by Joseph C. Rhea and published in Naperville, Illinois, in 1969.

RHINEHARD, RHINEHART (S.S. Abbreviation: Rhineh)
Ranking: 4963 **S.S. Count:** 9026
Origin: Uncertain etymology.
Genealogies: None known.

RHOADES (S.S. Abbreviation: Rhoade)
Ranking: 1717 **S.S. Count:** 26,067
Origin: English. Transformation of Rhodes.
Genealogies: *Rhoades, Trowbridge, and Related Families* was compiled by Myrtle Savage Rhoades and published in East Orange, New Jersey, in 1975.

RHOADS
Ranking: 2330 **S.S. Count:** 19,475
Origin: English. Transformation of Rhodes.
Famous Rhoadses: CORNELIUS PACKARD RHOADS (1898–1959) of Massachusetts was a scientist and physician and is best remembered as one of the best researchers in the area of cancer. He served as the director of the Sloan-Kettering Institute for Cancer Research.
Genealogies: *The Rhoads Family of Pennsylvania* was compiled by S. Castner and published in Philadelphia, Pennsylvania, in 1901.

RHODES
Ranking: 291 **S.S. Count:** 123,582
Origin: English. Derived from the Old English word "rod," meaning a clearing in a wood. The name was given to those who lived in a clearing in a wood.
Famous Rhodeses: JAMES FORD RHODES (1848–1927) of Ohio was a historian and the author of several books on different aspects of American history.
Genealogies: *Carry Me Back—: the story of the Roddens, Rawdens, Rodens, and allied families* [also Rhodes] was compiled by Paul G. Rodden and published in High Point, North Carolina, in 1980. *Rhodes-Barnett and Mitchusson-Ingram* was compiled by Norma Rhodes Ladd and published in Calvert City, Kentucky, in 1991.

RICCI
Ranking: 2943 **S.S. Count:** 15,470
Origin: Italian. Derived from the Italian word "ricco," meaning curly. The name was given to those with curly hair.
Genealogies: None known.

RICE
Ranking: 147 **S.S. Count:** 211,617
Origin: Welsh. Transformation of Price.
Famous Rices: THOMAS DARTMOUTH RICE (1808–1860) of New York City was a minstrel and the originator of the "Jim Crow" song-and-dance routine. He is considered the father of the American minstrel. HENRY MOWER RICE (1816–1894) was a Minnesota pioneer and one of the founders of the territory of Minnesota. WILLIAM MARSH RICE (1816–1900) of Massachusetts was a merchant and philanthropist in Houston, Texas. His fortune, left to Houston for educational uses, was the financial foundation for Rice University, which opened in 1912. VICTOR MOREAU RICE (1818–1869) of New York was the organizer and first superintendent of the New York State Department of Public Instruction. His most-remembered accomplishment was the establishment of free education for all. DAN[IEL MCLAREN] RICE (1823–1900) of New York City was the most famous circus clown of his day. ISAAC LEOPOLD RICE (1850–1915) of Bavaria was a financier, inventor, and prominent railroad attorney. GEORGE SAMUEL RICE (1866–1950) of New Hampshire was a mining engineer and is credited with the implementation of many techniques that made mining safer. ALICE CALDWELL HEGAN RICE (1870–1942) of Kentucky was a novelist. She wrote several books, including *Mrs. Wiggs of the Cabbage Patch* (1901) and *My Pillow Book* (1937). [HENRY] GRANTLAND RICE (1880–1954) of Tennessee was a sportswriter who was considered the best in the business at the time. He is the one who nicknamed Notre Dame's backfield "The Four Horsemen." JOHN ANDREW RICE (1888–1968) of South Carolina was the founder of the now-defunct Black Mountain College in

North Carolina, which had a reputation as a creative, artistic college. ELMER RICE (1892–1967) of New York was a playwright and novelist. With 50 plays to his credit, he received a Pulitzer Prize for *Counsellor-at-Law* (1931). He was a pioneer in the use of the stage for social criticism.

Genealogies: *A Genealogical Register of Edmund Rice Descendants* was compiled by Ray Lowther Ellis and published in Rutland, Vermont, in 1970. *Henry Rice (1717–1818), the Pioneer Tennessee Gristmiller and his Twelve Children* was compiled by Melvin Weaver Little and published in Arlington, Virginia, in 1984.

RICH
Ranking: 623 S.S. Count: 67,079
Origin: English. 1) transformation of Richard. 2) derived from the Middle English word "riche," meaning wealthy. The name was given to those who were rich. 3) the name was given to those from Riche, a former place in England.

Famous **Riches:** OBADIAH RICH (1783–1850) of Massachusetts was a bookseller whose specialty section of early American manuscripts made him a favorite with the historians of his day. ISAAC RICH (1801–1872) of Massachusetts was a fish merchant and real estate owner. He left his estate to Boston University. ROBERT RICH (1883–1968) of Pennsylvania was a member of Congress from Pennsylvania. He is best remembered as a strong opponent of the New Deal. He was part of the Woolrich Woolen Mills family.

Genealogies: *Holway-Rich Heritage: a history and genealogy of two Cape Cod families* was compiled by Richard Thomas Holway and published in Baltimore, Maryland, in 1988. *Stephens Ancestors and Pioneer Relatives: the Stewart, Rich,* [et al.] *and other Families of the 1800's* was compiled by Clyde S. Stephens and published in Alva, Florida, in 1982.

RICHARD, RICHARDEAU, RICHARDS, RICHARDSON, RICHARDSSON (S.S. Abbreviation: Richar)
Ranking: 37 S.S. Count: 588,362
Origin: Richard—Dutch, English, Flemish, French, German; Richards, Richardson—English; Richardeau—French; Richardsson—Swedish. Richard: derived from a Germanic first name that comprises the components "ric" and "hard," meaning power and brave or hardy. Richards, Richardson, Richardeau, Richardsson: cognates to or transformations of Richard.

Famous **Bearers:** GABRIEL RICHARD (1767–1832) of France was a Roman Catholic clergyman sent to the Detroit area as a missionary to work with both the Indians and the newer settlers of the area. He civilized the area, spoke out against the evils of drink, and was responsible for the organization of educational facilities in the area, co-founding the University of Michigan in 1817. He energized the local economy by obtaining a printing press and spinning wheels and looms from the East and started the first Detroit-printed newspaper, the *Essai du Michigan*. He died comforting the victims of a cholera epidemic. WILLIAM RICHARDS (1793–1847) of Massachusetts was a Congregational missionary in the Hawaiian Islands. He was responsible for helping to set up Hawaii's government and for promoting the recognition of its independent status by the European powers. ZALMON RICHARDS (1811–1899) of Massachusetts was one of the founders of and served as first president of the National Teachers' Association. The name of the organization was later changed to the National Education Association. THOMAS ADDISON RICHARDS (1820–1900) of England came to the United States as a boy. He was a painter and illustrator and a member of the Hudson River school. HENRY HOBSON RICHARDSON (1838–1886) of Louisiana was an architect who was considered a pioneer in American architecture. LAURA ELIZABETH HOWE RICHARDS (1850–1943) of Massachusetts was the author of children's books and biographies. For the biography of her sister Julia Ward Howe, which she co-wrote with her sister Maud Howe Elliott, a Pulitzer Prize was awarded. JOSEPH WILLIAM RICHARDS (1864–1921) of England came to the United States as a boy and was the first to graduate from Lehigh University with a Ph.D. (1893). He was considered an expert as a metallurgist. THEODORE WILLIAM RICHARDS (1868–1928) of Pennsylvania was a chemist and the recipient of the 1914 Nobel Prize for chemistry. DICKINSON WOODRUFF RICHARDS (1895–1973) of New Jersey was a physician and one of the winners of a 1956 Nobel Prize in medicine for a cardiac catheter that enabled medical personnel to monitor a patient's blood pressure. VINCENT RICHARDS (1903–1959) of New York was a tennis player who won many national and international matches. He was instrumental in founding the Professional Lawn Tennis Association of the United States and in elevating the game to the status of a professional sport.

Genealogies: *American Patriot vs. Hessian Mercenary: fourteen generations of the Arnolds, the Maughts, the Richards and related families* was compiled by Lynda Alexander-Fonde and published in Trenton, New Jersey, in 1991. *Ball Cousins: descendants of John and Sarah Ball and of William and Elizabeth Richards of Colonial Philadelphia Co., Penna.* was compiled by Margaret Biser Kinsey and published in Baltimore, Maryland, in 1981. *Minnie Mallory Boyett and Mallory, Hagan, Pullen, Radford, Goggans, Peterson, and Richardson Kin* was compiled by Woodrow W. Boyett and published in Tuscaloosa, Alabama, in 1987.

RICHER
Ranking: 4144 S.S. Count: 10,928
Origin: English. Derived from a Germanic first name that

comprises the components "ric" and "heri," meaning power and army.

Genealogies: None known.

RICHEY

Ranking: 1844 S.S. Count: 24,531

Origin: English, Scottish. Transformation of and cognate to Richard.

Genealogies: None known.

RICHIE

Ranking: 4761 S.S. Count: 9410

Origin: English, Scottish. Transformation of and cognate to Richard.

Genealogies: None known.

RICHMAN (S.S. Abbreviation: Richma)

Ranking: 4416 S.S. Count: 10,149

Origin: English. 1) transformation of Rich. 2) transformation of Richmond.

Genealogies: None known.

RICHMOND, RICHMONT (S.S. Abbreviation: Richmo)

Ranking: 858 S.S. Count: 50,055

Origin: English. The names comprise the Old French components "riche" and "mont," meaning rich and hill. The names were given to those from Richmond, the name of several places in France and England.

Famous **Bearers:** JOHN LAMBERT RICHMOND (1785–1855) of Massachusetts was a physician who reportedly performed the first cesearean section operation, in Ohio (1827). DEAN RICHMOND (1804–1866) of Vermont was one of the leaders in the "Barnburner" movement and was considered a "soft" Democrat, willing to compromise on the issue of slavery. MARY ELLEN RICHMOND (1861–1928) of Illinois was a social worker and one of the first to suggest that special training was necessary for the field of social work. CHARLES WALLACE RICHMOND (1869–1932) of Wisconsin was considered the leading ornithologist of his time.

Genealogies: *Reminiscences of the Baylies and Richmond Families* was compiled by Mary Richmond Baylies Allen and published in Boston, Massachusetts, in 1875.

RICHTER, RICHTERING, RICHTERS (S.S. Abbreviation: Richte)

Ranking: 1040 S.S. Count: 42,110

Origin: Richter—German, Jewish; Richtering, Richters—German. Richter (German): derived from the German occupational title richter, meaning a judge. The name was given to a judge or to those who settled disputes. Richter (Jewish): translation of the Hebrew word "dayan," meaning a rabbinic

judge. *Richtering, Richters: transformations of the German name Richter.*

Famous **Bearers:** GISELA MARIE AUGUSTA RICHTER (1882–1972) of England was an archaeologist and a curator of the Metropolitan Museum of Art in New York City. HANS RICHTER (1888–1976) of Germany was a painter and filmmaker. He is best known as a pioneer in abstract animation. CONRAD MICHAEL RICHTER (1890–1968) of Pennsylvania was a bestselling novelist and the winner of a Pulitzer Prize for *The Town* (1950), the third book of a trilogy called *The Awakening Land*. It was published as a set in 1966. CHARLES FRANCIS RICHTER (1900–1985) of Ohio was a seismologist and the creator of the Richter scale, which measures earthquake strength.

Genealogies: *Richter Genealogy: the Ohio branch* was compiled by Charles Boardman Richter and published in Iowa City, Iowa, in 1974.

RICKARD, RICKARDES, RICKARDS, RICKARDSSON (S.S. Abbreviation: Rickar)

Ranking: 2929 S.S. Count: 15,539

Origin: Rickard, Rickardes, Rickards—English; Rickardsson—Swedish. Transformations of and cognates to Richard.

Famous **Bearers:** GEORGE LEWIS RICKARD (1871–1929) of Missouri was a boxing promoter. He was known by the name "Tex." He promoted Jack Dempsey.

Genealogies: *Ellen Virginia Kauffman (Rickard)* was compiled by Patricia Jean Minger Vorenberg and published in Lexington, Massachusetts.

RICKER (ALSO RICKERD, RICKERS, RICKERT, RICKERTSEN)

Ranking: 1917 S.S. Count: 23,572

Origin: Rickerd, Rickers—English; Rickertsen—German; Ricker, Rickert—English, German. Rickers: transformation of Richer. Rickerd, Rickert, Rickertsen: transformations of Richard. Ricker: 1) transformation of Richard. 2) transformation of Richer.

Famous **Bearers:** [MARTHA] EDITH RICKERT (1871–1938) of Ohio was an educator and novelist.

Genealogies: *The Descendants of John and Sally (Guile) Rickerd: with notes on the ancestors and the so-called Palatine migration* was compiled by Barbara Rickerd Thompson and published in Grosse Pointe Farms, Michigan, in 1980. *German Pioneers, Dhonau, Rickert, and Related Families* was compiled by Robert Will-Fred Dhonau and published in Little Rock, Arkansas, in 1979.

RICKET (ALSO RICKETT, RICKETTS)

Ranking: 2074 S.S. Count: 22,107

Origin: English. Transformations of Rich, derived from Richard.

Famous **Bearers:** HOWARD TAYLOR RICKETTS (1871–

1910) of Ohio was a pathologist and the discoverer of ticks as the transmitters of Rocky Mountain spotted fever and body lice as the transmitters of tabardillo. The organisms responsible for both illnesses were named *rickettsia*.

Genealogies: *The Descendants of John and Sally (Guile) Rickerd: with notes on the ancestors and the so-called Palatine migration* [also Ricketts] was compiled by Barbara Rickerd Thompson and published in Grosse Pointe Farms, Michigan, in 1980. *German Pioneers, Dhonau, Rickert, and Related Families* [also Ricketts] was compiled by Robert Will-Fred Dhonau and published in Little Rock, Arkansas, in 1979. *Truth and Honor: a history of the Ricketts family* was compiled by Robert Daniel Ricketts and published in Axton, Virginia, in 1981.

RICKMAN (S.S. Abbreviation: Rickma)

Ranking: 4416 **S.S. Count:** 10,149

Origin: English. The name means a servant of a person called Rick, a transformation of Richard.

Genealogies: None known.

RICKS

Ranking: 1947 **S.S. Count:** 23,235

Origin: English, German. Transformation of and cognate to Richard.

Genealogies: *John Hastle Tynes and Associated Families* [also Ricks] was compiled by Valerie Fields Harris and published in Apollo, Pennsylvania, in 1988.

RICO

Ranking: 4274 **S.S. Count:** 10,535

Origin: Spanish. Cognate to Rich, meaning wealthy.

Genealogies: None known.

RIDDICK (S.S. Abbreviation: Riddic)

Ranking: 3985 **S.S. Count:** 11,346

Origin: Irish, Scottish. Transformation of Reddick.

Genealogies: None known.

RIDDLE

Ranking: 879 **S.S. Count:** 49,201

Origin: English, Scottish. 1) derived from the Norman first name Ridel, which is of uncertain etymology. 2) the name means the valley of the river. It was given to those from Ryedale, the name of a region of England.

Genealogies: *Descendants of Hampton and Nancy Riddle, 1814–1972* was compiled by Norma Simpson and published in Baltimore, Maryland, in 1973. *A Partial History of the Riddle-Beavers Families: of Botetourt County, Virginia, Highland County, Ohio, Decatur and Page Counties, Iowa* was compiled by Andree Sieverin Hoeman and published in Dallas Center, Iowa, in 1981.

RIDENOUR (S.S. Abbreviation: Rideno)

Ranking: 3910 **S.S. Count:** 11,533

Origin: German. Derived from words meaning a reedy meadow. The name was given to those from Rietenau, a place in Germany.

Genealogies: None known.

RIDER

Ranking: 2015 **S.S. Count:** 22,641

Origin: English. 1) derived from the Old English word "ried," meaning clearing in a wood. The name was given to those who lived in a clearing in a wood. 2) derived from the Old English word "ridere," meaning a mounted messenger or fighter.

Famous Riders: FREMONT RIDER (1885–1962) of New Jersey was an editor and publisher. As a librarian, he invented microcards, the book truck, and stack shelving.

Genealogies: *The Gorman Family History: including the genealogy of their Rider and Armstrong ancestors* was compiled by Edith Lynn Mlaker and published in Decorah, Iowa, in 1984.

RIDGE

Ranking: 4649 **S.S. Count:** 9617

Origin: English, Irish. English: derived from the Middle English word "rigge," meaning ridge. The name was given to those who lived on a ridge. Irish: derived from the Gaelic name Mac Con Iomaire, which was derived from a first name meaning "Hound" (i.e., watchdog) of the Ridge (i.e., border) (H&H).

Famous Ridges: MAJOR RIDGE (1771–1839) of Tennessee was an Indian leader. It was he who signed the treaty giving up all lands east of the Mississippi River and agreeing that all Cherokees would move to its western side. For this he was murdered.

Genealogies: None known.

RIDGEWAY, RIDGEWELL (S.S. Abbreviation: Ridgew)

Ranking: 3725 **S.S. Count:** 12,127

Origin: English. Ridgeway: derived from the Old English words "hrycg" and "weg," meaning ridge and path. The name was given to those who lived on a path beside a ridge. Ridgewell: derived from the Old English words "hrēod" and "well(a)," meaning reed and spring. The name was given to those from Ridgewell, a place in England.

Genealogies: None known.

RIDLEY

Ranking: 2797 **S.S. Count:** 16,258

Origin: English. The name was given to those from Ridley, the name of several places in England.

Genealogies: *Genealogy of John Ranks of England and*

his Descendants: including the Ridley genealogy of his wife Annie Ridley was compiled by Emma Clement Ranks and published in Springfield, Massachusetts, in 1974. *Ridley of Southampton* was compiled by Lyndon H. Hart and published in Pensacola, Florida, in 1992.

RIEDEL
Ranking: 4585 S.S. Count: 9749
Origin: German. Derived from any of several Germanic first names with the first component "hrod," meaning fame.
Genealogies: None known.

RIES
Ranking: 4559 S.S. Count: 9805
Origin: Jewish. Derived from the German word "riese," meaning giant. The name was given to those who were tall or heavy.
Genealogies: None known.

RIGGIN (ALSO RIGGINS)
Ranking: 2513 S.S. Count: 18,061
Origin: English. Derived from the first name Riggs, which was derived from Richard.
Genealogies: *Jackson: Hefton-Dobbins-Riggins/Reagon-Cooper genealogy and family history* was compiled by Naomi Ruth Jackson Chasteen and published in Miami, Oklahoma, in 1988.

RIGGLESFORD (S.S. Abbreviation: Riggle)
Ranking: 4914 S.S. Count: 9108
Origin: English. The name was given to those from Wrigglesworth, the former name of a place in England, now called Woodlesford.
Genealogies: None known.

RIGGS
Ranking: 915 S.S. Count: 47,109
Origin: English. Transformation of Ridge.
Famous **Riggses:** JOHN MANKEY RIGGS (1810–1885) of Connecticut was a dentist whom some considered an expert in the area of pyorrhea. Using nitrous oxide gas as an anesthetic, he removed a tooth from his patient's mouth. This is rumored to have been the first such operation.
Genealogies: *Genealogical Notes on a Branch of the Family of Mayes* [also Riggs] was compiled by Edward Mayes and published in Jackson, Mississippi, in 1928. *More about the Riggs Family, 1590–1973* was compiled by Clara Nichols Duggan and published in Holtland, Tennessee, in 1974.

RIGSBY
Ranking: 4656 S.S. Count: 9603
Origin: English. The name means settlement on a ridge

and was given to those from Rigsby, a place in Lincolnshire, England.
Genealogies: None known.

RILEY
Ranking: 194 S.S. Count: 182,231
Origin: English, Irish. English: derived from the Old English words "ryge" and "lēah," meaning rye and clearing. The name was given to those from Ryley, a place in Lancashire, England. Irish: transformation of Reilly.
Famous **Rileys:** BENNET RILEY (1787–1853) of Maryland was the provisional governor of California and the one responsible for the first California constitution and the state's admission into the Union. CHARLES VALENTINE RILEY (1843–1895) of England was a well-respected entomologist of his time. JAMES WHITCOMB RILEY (1849–1916) of Indiana was a poet known as the Hoosier poet. He wrote many poems, including "The Old Swimmin' Hole" and "When the Frost Is on the Pumpkin."
Genealogies: *Reilly of Ballintlea* [also Riley] was compiled by Joseph F. Reilly and published in Hartland, Vermont, in 1981. *Petty, of England & Virginia; Wright, of Virginia, Kentucky & Missouri; Riley, of Maryland, Kentucky & Missouri* was compiled by Gerald McKinney Petty and published in Columbus, Ohio, in 1973. *Indiana Kindred: a record of the Riley family and their kinfolk of Boone & Switzerland Counties, Indiana* was compiled by Frederick Glenn Riley and published in Decatur, Illinois, in 1967.

RINALDELLI, RINALDI, RINALDINI, RINALDO, RINALDUCCI (S.S. Abbreviation: Rinald)
Ranking: 3642 S.S. Count: 12,377
Origin: Italian. Cognates to Reynold.
Genealogies: *The Rinaldos from Poland* [also Rinaldi] was compiled by Peter M. Rinaldo and published in Briarcliff Manor, New York, in 1984.

RINEHART (S.S. Abbreviation: Rineha)
Ranking: 2303 S.S. Count: 19,788
Origin: German. Transformations of Reinert.
Famous **Rineharts:** MARY ROBERTS RINEHART (1876–1958) of Pennsylvania was an author and founder of the "had I but known" school of novels about crime. Her son, STANLEY MARSHALL RINEHART JR. (1897–1969) of Pennsylvania, was a publisher with Holt, Rinehart & Winston.
Genealogies: *The Rineharts of Perry Co. Ohio* was compiled by Bruce Anderson and published in Lancaster, Ohio, in 1981.

RING
Ranking: 2199 S.S. Count: 20,860
Origin: Danish, English, German, Norwegian, Swedish.

Derived from the Old English and Old High German word "hring," meaning ring. The name was given to those who made rings as jewelry or for other items.

Genealogies: *Ancestors, Descendants, and Other Relatives of Joseph Henry Ring and Sarah Ann Combs* was compiled by Elma A. Ring and published in Wichita, Kansas, in 1971. *Nathaniel Ring* was compiled by Donald Levi McClure and published in Bloomington, Indiana.

RIORDAN (S.S. Abbreviation: Riorda)
Ranking: 4176 **S.S. Count:** 10,822
Origin: Irish. Derived from the Gaelic name Ó Rioghbhárdáin, which was derived from the first name Ríoghbhárdán, comprising the components "ríogh" and "bárd," meaning royal and poet.
Genealogies: None known.

RIOS
Ranking: 545 **S.S. Count:** 74,777
Origin: Portuguese, Spanish. Ultimately derived from the Latin word "rivus," meaning stream. The name was given to those who lived by a stream.
Genealogies: None known.

RIPLEY
Ranking: 3544 **S.S. Count:** 12,739
Origin: English. Derived from the Old English words "ripel" and "lēah," meaning "strip of land" (H&H) and clearing. The name was given to those from Ripley, the name of places in England.
Famous Ripleys: GEORGE RIPLEY (1802–1880) of Massachusetts was trained as a minister but left that calling to work with the Transcendental movement. He founded *Harper's New Monthly Magazine* and the *Dial* and co-edited *New American Cyclopaedia.* EDWARD PAYSON RIPLEY (1845–1920) of Massachusetts restored the Atchison, Topeka & Santa Fe Railroad as an executive in the company. WILLIAM ZEBINA RIPLEY (1867–1941) of Massachusetts was an anthropologist and economist. He wrote several books, including *Races of Europe* (1899). He also drew up the plans for the Interstate Commerce Commission. [ROBERT] LEROY RIPLEY (1893–1949) of California was a cartoonist specializing in sports cartoons. He is best known for his syndicated "Believe It or Not" column, which he started in 1918.
Genealogies: *With Pen or Sword: lives and times of the remarkable Rutland Ripleys* was compiled by Robert G. Steele and published in New York, New York, in 1979.

RITCHEY (S.S. Abbreviation: Ritche)
Ranking: 3211 **S.S. Count:** 14,136
Origin: English, Scottish. Transformation of Rich, derived from Richard.

Famous Ritcheys: GEORGE WILLIS RITCHEY (1864–1945) of Ohio was an astronomer. He was the co-inventor of an aplanatic reflecting telescope and the inventor of a fixed vertical universal reflecting telescope and a cellular type of optical mirror.
Genealogies: *Genealogy of the Descendants of Samuel Diehl and Margaretha Ritchey, his Wife, of Loudoun County, Va. and Bedford County, Pa., 1740–1828* was published in Holidaysburg, Pennsylvania, in 1976.

RITCHIE (S.S. Abbreviation: Ritchi)
Ranking: 1083 **S.S. Count:** 40,866
Origin: English, Scottish. Transformation of Rich, derived from Richard.
Famous Ritchies: THOMAS RITCHIE (1778–1854) of Tappahannock, Virginia, was the founder and editor of the Richmond *Enquirer* and made it a leading U.S. paper of its era. ALBERT CABELL RITCHIE (1876–1936) of Virginia was the attorney general, then the governor, of Maryland.
Genealogies: *Genealogy of the Descendants of Samuel Diehl and Margaretha Ritchey, his Wife, of Loudoun County, Va. and Bedford County, Pa., 1740–1828* [also Ritchie] was published in Holidaysburg, Pennsylvania, in 1976. *Descendants of Isaac Ritchie of Virginia* was compiled by Vergie Ruth Carr Lantz and published in Bridgewater, Virginia in 1983. *Singing Family of the Cumberlands* [also Ritchie] was compiled by Jean Ritchie and published in Lexington, Kentucky, in 1955.

RITTENBERG, RITTENHOUSE (S.S. Abbreviation: Ritten)
Ranking: 3963 **S.S. Count:** 11,418
Origin: German. Rittenberg: the name means "stronghold among reeds" (ES). It was given to those from Rittenberg, a place in Germany. Rittenhouse: the name was given to those who lived on a reed-covered slope.
Famous Bearers: WILLIAM RITTENHOUSE (1644–1708) of Russia came to America and started the first paper mill in the colonies. His great-grandson DAVID RITTENHOUSE (1732–1796) of Pennsylvania was an astronomer and is thought to have been the maker of the first American-made telescope. He also invented a collimating telescope and used spider webs as reticle in the telescope eyepiece. He served as the first director of the U.S. Mint. JESSIE BELLE RITTENHOUSE (1869–1948) of Virginia was one of the leading poets and critics in the early part of the 20th century.
Genealogies: None known.

RITTER (ALSO RITTERMAN, RITTERS)
Ranking: 852 **S.S. Count:** 50,185
Origin: Ritter—German, Jewish; Ritterman—Jewish; Ritters—German. Cognates to Rider, meaning to ride.
Famous Bearers: FREDERIC LOUIS RITTER (1834–1891)

of Germany founded the Cecelia Society and the Cincinnati orchestra. WILLIAM EMERSON RITTER (1856–1944) of Wisconsin was responsible for the establishment of Scripps Institute of Oceanography, the Foundation for Population Research in Ohio, and Science Service, a science news agency. JOSEPH ELMER RITTER (1892–1967) of Indiana was a Roman Catholic priest responsible for five centers for black children and for establishing integration within the Catholic schools. He became a cardinal and authorized the first U.S. Mass that was said in English instead of Latin, in St. Louis, 1965.

Genealogies: None known.

RIVAS
Ranking: 1320 **S.S. Count:** 33,704
Origin: Spanish. Ultimately derived from the Latin word "ripa," meaning river. The name was given to those who lived by a river or lake.
Genealogies: None known.

RIVERA
Ranking: 51 **S.S. Count:** 458,369
Origin: Spanish. Cognate to Rivers.
Genealogies: None known.

RIVERS
Ranking: 855 **S.S. Count:** 50,141
Origin: English. Derived from the Old French word "rivière," meaning river. The name was given to those from Rivières, the name of several places in northern France.
Famous Riverses: THOMAS MILTON RIVERS (1888–1962) of Georgia was the chairman of the virus research committee at the National Foundation for Infantile Paralysis. His administrative dedication gave Jonas Salk and Albert Sabin the ways and means to develop their polio vaccines. LUCIUS MENDEL RIVERS (1905–1970) of North Carolina was a member of Congress elected in 1940. He served for 32 years in that capacity as an outspoken southerner. He favored better and better weapons and stronger military installations but spoke against the all-volunteer army. His district included Charleston, South Carolina.
Genealogies: The Revis Family of Madison County, North Carolina [also Rivers] was compiled by David H. Reece and published in Asheville, North Carolina, in 1983.

RIZZO
Ranking: 1807 **S.S. Count:** 24,933
Origin: Italian. Transformation of Ricci.
Genealogies: None known.

ROACH
Ranking: 640 **S.S. Count:** 64,951
Origin: English. Derived from the Middle English and Old French word "roche," meaning outcrop. The name was given to those who lived by a crag.
Famous Roaches: JOHN ROACH (1813–1887) of Ireland was a shipbuilder. He was one of the first to realize that shifting from wooden to iron ships was inevitable. He is considered the "father of iron shipbuilding in America."
Genealogies: The Descendants of Simpson-Roach Families of South Carolina was compiled by Max Perry and published in Midland, Texas, in 1974. A Roach Family History was compiled by Frank W. Medley and published in Lubbock, Texas, in 1974.

ROARK
Ranking: 2387 **S.S. Count:** 19,017
Origin: English. The name was given to those who lived near a rock.
Genealogies: None known.

ROBB
Ranking: 2354 **S.S. Count:** 19,246
Origin: English. Transformation of Robert.
Genealogies: Robb Miscellanea was compiled by Ruth Flesher Robb and published in Ft. Myers, Florida, in 1987.

ROBBIN (ALSO ROBBINS)
Ranking: 342 **S.S. Count:** 111,029
Origin: English. Derived from the medieval first name Robin, a transformation of Robert.
Famous Bearers: THOMAS ROBBINS (1777–1856) of Connecticut was the librarian of the Connecticut Historical Society (1844–1854).
Genealogies: The Hardys of Louisiana and their Ancestors was compiled by Grace L. Hardy and published in Baltimore, Maryland, in 1985. The Robbins Family of Scott County, Tennessee was compiled by Robert Lee Bailey and published in 1992.

ROBERSON (S.S. Abbreviation: Robers)
Ranking: 499 **S.S. Count:** 80,530
Origin: English. Transformation of Robert.
Genealogies: None known.

ROBERT (ALSO ROBERTIS, ROBERTO, ROBERTS, ROBERTSON)
Ranking: 20 **S.S. Count:** 740,805
Origin: Robert—Catalan, Dutch, English, French, German; Robertson—English; Roberts—English, German; Robertis, Roberto—Italian. Robert: derived from a Germanic first name that comprises the components "hrōd" and "berht," meaning renown and fame or bright. Robertis, Roberto, Roberts, Robertson: Cognates to and transformations of Robert.
Famous Bearers: JAMES ROBERTSON (1742–1814) of Vir-

ginia was a pioneer and the leader of the group that settled Nashville, Tennessee. BENJAMIN STONE ROBERTS (1810–1875) of Vermont was the inventor of one type of breech-loading rifle. ORAN MILO ROBERTS (1815–1898) of South Carolina moved to Texas and served as a judge and as governor of Texas. He improved Texas's financial status and founded the University of Texas. HENRY MARTYN ROBERT (1837–1923) of South Carolina was the author of *Pocket Manual of Rules of Order.* They are better known as "Robert's Rules of Order." OWEN JOSEPHUS ROBERTS (1875–1955) of Pennsylvania was a U.S. Supreme Court justice. MARY MAY ROBERTS (1877–1959) of Michigan was a nurse and the editor of the *American Journal of Nursing.* LYDIA JANE ROBERTS (1879–1965) of Michigan was a nutritionist and a home economics educator. She wrote *Nutrition Work with Children,* considered a classic. ELIZABETH MADDOX ROBERTS (1881–1941) of Kentucky was a novelist whose stories told of nature and its effect on people. KENNETH LEWIS ROBERTS (1885–1957) of Maine was an author best known for his novel *Northwest Passage.* GLENN ROBERTS (1927–1964) of Florida was a race car driver. He was nicknamed "Fireball" and was the inventor of "drafting." He died in a car crash while racing in the Charlotte, North Carolina, World 600.

Genealogies: *Three Pioneer Rapides Families* [also Robert] was compiled by George Mason Graham Stafford and published in Baton Rouge, Louisiana, in 1946. *Roberts-Allen Families* was compiled by Merritt E. Roberts and published in Los Olivos, California, in 1985. *Children of Nashville* [also Robertson] was compiled by Sarah Foster Kelley and published in Nashville, Tennessee, in 1973.

ROBICHAUD (S.S. Abbreviation: Robich)

Ranking: 4354 **S.S. Count:** 10,327

Origin: French. Uncertain etymology. Most likely a transformation of Robert.

Genealogies: None known.

ROBINEAU, ROBINET (S.S. Abbreviation: Robine)

Ranking: 2611 **S.S. Count:** 17,392

Origin: French. Cognates to Robbin.

Genealogies: None known.

ROBINS (ALSO ROBINSON)

Ranking: 22 **S.S. Count:** 710,382

Origin: Robins—English; Robinson—English, Jewish. Robins: transformation of Robbin. Robinson (English): transformation of Robbin. Robinson (Jewish): derived from the Polish word "rabin," meaning rabbi.

Famous Bearers: EDWARD ROBINSON (1794–1863) of Connecticut was a scholar and is considered the father of biblical geography. SOLON ROBINSON (1803–1880) of Connecticut was the driving force behind the formation of the U.S. Agricultural Society. CHARLES ROBINSON (1818–1894) of Massachusetts was a physician and the governor of Kansas. His administration was marred by impeachment proceedings brought about because of questions over state bond sales. WILLIAM ROBINSON (1840–1921) of Ireland came to the United States as a child. He was the inventor of the railroad block-signal. THEODORE ROBINSON (1852–1896) of Vermont was one of the founders of the Art Students League. He studied the impressionists in France and influenced American artists in this new style. JAMES HARVEY ROBINSON (1863–1936) of Illinois was one of the founders of the New School for Social Research in New York City. MARGARET DRIER ROBINS (1868–1945) of New York was a social reformer and the president of the National Women's Trade Union League. BOARDMAN ROBINSON (1876–1952) of Nova Scotia was a painter and illustrator. He published political cartoons and founded the Colorado Springs Fine Arts Center. BILL (ORIGINALLY LUTHER) ROBINSON (1878–1949) of Virginia, known as "Bojangles," was a tap dancer. He played clubs and Hollywood. He was best known for his roles in the Shirley Temple movies *The Little Colonel* (1935), *The Littlest Rebel* (1935), and *Rebecca of Sunnybrook Farm* (1937). EDWIN ARLINGTON ROBINSON (1869–1935) of Maine was a poet best remembered for his stories set in New England. He won a Pulitzer Prize for "Tristram" in 1927. RAYMOND ROBINS (1873–1954) of New York was a social worker in Chicago and a member of the Red Cross team that traveled to Russia in 1917, and again in 1933, to help stabilize the Russian government. CLAUDE EVERETT ROBINSON (1900–1961) of Oregon was an associate of George Gallup in researching public opinion. He started *Public Opinion Index for Industry* and Gallup and Robinson, a research company. JACKIE ROBINSON (1919–1972) of Georgia, originally John Roosevelt Robinson, was a baseball player and the first black to play for the major leagues. He was awarded the Rookie of the Year and the Most Valuable Player awards. He retired in 1956 and was elected to the Hall of Fame in 1962. RUBYE DORIS SMITH ROBINSON (1942–1967) of Georgia was a civil rights reformer who was a leader in the Student Non-Violent Coordinating Committee. She died at the age of 25 from natural causes.

Genealogies: *Descendants of John Craig, Esquire and John Robinson, Senior, Scotch-Irish Immigrants to Lancaster County, South Carolina* was compiled by Eloise Craig and published in 1988. *Pioneer Pond People Plus Robinson and Allied Families* was compiled by Betty Pond Snyder and published in Foster City, California, in 1992. *Robinson and Related Families (1700–1990): Carolinas, Georgia, Alabama* was compiled by Delton D. Blalock and published in Cullman, Alabama, in 1990.

ROBISON (S.S. Abbreviation: Robiso)

Ranking: 1043 S.S. Count: 42,025
Origin: English. Transformation of Robbin.
Genealogies: None known.

ROBLES

Ranking: 778 S.S. Count: 54,038
Origin: Spanish. Ultimately derived from the Latin word "robur," meaning oak. The name was given to those who lived near a prominent oak tree or in an oak grove.
Genealogies: None known.

ROBSON

Ranking: 3783 S.S. Count: 11,922
Origin: English. Transformation of Robert.
Famous **Robsons**: [HENRY] STUART ROBSON (1836–1903) of Maryland was an actor and a partner in a comedy team with William H. Crane. MAY ROBSON (1858–1942) of Australia, originally Mary Jeanette Robison, was an actress who starred in several films, including *Bringing Up Baby*.
Genealogies: None known.

ROBY

Ranking: 3604 S.S. Count: 12,533
Origin: English, Scottish. 1) derived from the Old Norse words "rá" and "býr," meaning boundary mark and settlement. The name was given to those from Roby, a place in Lancashire, England. 2) transformation of Robert.
Genealogies: *A Genealogical History of the Robie Family in England and America* [also Roby] was compiled by Eva Barbara Robie Schwarting and published in New York, New York, in 1956. *Meschack Turner III, his Wife Sarah Robey Tucker* [also Roby] was compiled by Lucille R. Maddox and published in Baltimore, Maryland, in 1976.

ROCHA

Ranking: 1487 S.S. Count: 29,865
Origin: Portuguese. Cognate to Roach.
Genealogies: None known.

ROCHE

Ranking: 1683 S.S. Count: 26,533
Origin: French. Cognate to Roach.
Famous **Roches**: JAMES JEFFREY ROCHE (1847–1908) of Ireland came to the United States via Canada and settled in Boston. He was the editor of the Catholic newspaper the *Pilot*. In later years he served as consul in Italy, then Switzerland.
Genealogies: None known.

ROCK

Ranking: 1731 S.S. Count: 25,921
Origin: English. 1) derived from the Middle English

phrase *"atter oke," meaning at the oak. The name was given to those who lived near a large oak tree. 2) derived from the Middle English word "rocc," meaning rock. The name was given to those who lived near a prominent outcrop. 3) derived from the Middle English word "rok," meaning distaff. The name was given to those who made distaffs or spun wool.*
Famous **Rocks**: JOHN ROCK (1890–1984) of Massachusetts was an obstetrician-gynecologist who was the founder of a fertility clinic in the Boston area. He was one of a team of doctors that successfully fertilized a human egg *in vitro* in 1944.
Genealogies: None known.

ROCKWELL (S.S. Abbreviation: Rockwe)

Ranking: 2631 S.S. Count: 17,297
Origin: English. The name was given to those from Rockwell, the name of places in England of which the first component is derived from the Old English word "hrōc," meaning rook.
Famous **Rockwells**: ALPHONSO DAVID ROCKWELL (1840–1933) of Connecticut was a surgeon and a pioneer in the field of electrotherapeutics. NORMAN ROCKWELL (1894–1978) of New York City was a painter and illustrator who was made famous by his *Saturday Evening Post* covers. His style was uniquely American. GEORGE LINCOLN ROCKWELL (1918–1967) of Illinois was the founder of the American Nazi Party.
Genealogies: *1150 Years of Continuous Rockwell Families Descent* A.D. *827 to 1977* was compiled by Ross Robert Rockwell and published in Binghamton, New York, in 1976. *A History and Genealogy of the Rockwell and Thayer Families* was compiled by Willard Frederick Rockwell and published in Pittsburgh, Pennsylvania, in 1984. *Rockwell Families from the Beginning of Time and Forever* was compiled by Ross Robert Rockwell and published in Binghamton, New York, in 1975.

RODDY

Ranking: 4692 S.S. Count: 9538
Origin: Irish. Transformation of Reedy.
Genealogies: None known.

RODERICK (S.S. Abbreviation: Roderi)

Ranking: 3922 S.S. Count: 11,501
Origin: English, Welsh. English: derived from the Germanic first name Hrōdric, comprising the components "hrōd" and "ric," meaning renown and power. Welsh: derived from the first name Rhydderch.
Genealogies: *Rothrock Genealogy, 1684–1978: Rodrock-Rotruck-Roderick-Roadrock* was compiled by Henry Shirley Rothrock and published in Wilmington, Delaware, in 1979.

RODGER (ALSO RODGERS, RODGERSON)

Ranking: 349 S.S. Count: 108,758

Origin: English. Transformation of Rogers.

Famous **Bearers:** JOHN RODGERS (1773–1838) of Maryland was a naval officer who fought the Barbary pirates off the North African coast. He later fought valiantly against the British in the War of 1812. JAMES (JIMMIE) CHARLES RODGERS (1897–1933) of Mississippi was a country-and-western singer who was nicknamed the "Singing Brakeman." After he contracted tuberculosis and retired from the railroad, he recorded more than 100 songs, many with a railroad theme. RICHARD RODGERS (1902–1979) of New York City was a composer who worked with Lorenz Hart and Oscar Hammerstein in the writing of songs for Broadway musicals. He is credited with writing the music for *Oklahoma, Carousel, The Sound of Music, Flower Drum Song,* and *South Pacific.* He won Pulitzer Prizes for songs in many all of his musicals.

Genealogies: None known.

RODRIGO, RODRIGUE, RODRIGUES, RODRIGUEZ (S.S. Abbreviation: Rodrig)

Ranking: 18 S.S. Count: 789,535

Origin: Rodrigue—Jewish; Rodrigo—Italian, Spanish; Rodrigues—Jewish, Portuguese; Rodriguez—Jewish, Spanish. Cognates to the English name Roderick.

Genealogies: *Descendants of Jean Rodrigue and Anne Le Roy of Portugal, Canada, U.S.A. (Louisiana)* was compiled by Wilma Boudreaux and published in 1990. *Our Rodriquez Family: descendants of Manuel Rodriguez and Isabel Ortega Alvarez of Spain* was compiled by B. M. Rodriquez and published in Metairie, Louisiana, in 1983.

RODRIQUES (S.S. Abbreviation: Rodriq)

Ranking: 800 S.S. Count: 52,721

Origin: Jewish. Cognate to the English name Roderick.

Genealogies: None known.

ROE

Ranking: 1262 S.S. Count: 34,938

Origin: English. Transformation of Ray, meaning female roe deer.

Famous **Roes:** FRANCIS ASBURY ROE (1823–1901) of New York was a naval officer and a hero at the Battle of New Orleans. EDWARD PAYSON ROE (1838–1888) of New York was a bestselling novelist of his day. His works include *A Knight of the Nineteenth Century* (1877).

Genealogies: *Some Descendants of Hugh Roe, an Immigrant to the Massachusetts Bay Colony from England, ca. 1642* was compiled by Frank Chapman Roe and published in Kennett Square, Pennsylvania, in 1972. *A Supplement of Roe/Rowe Additions and Corrections to the 1972 Record of Some Descendants of Hugh Roe* was compiled by Frank Chapman Roe and published in Kennett Square, Pennsylvania, in 1978.

ROEDER

Ranking: 4429 S.S. Count: 10,127

Origin: German. 1) the name was given to those who lived on newly cleared land. 2) derived from the first name Rothari, comprising components meaning fame and army.

Genealogies: None known.

ROGERS (ALSO ROGERSON)

Ranking: 55 S.S. Count: 422,837

Origin: English. Derived from a Germanic first name comprising the components "hrōd" and "geri," meaning renown and spear.

Famous **Bearers:** MOSES ROGERS (1779–1821) of Connecticut was commander aboard the first ocean voyage of a steamship, the *Phoenix*, on its trip around the New Jersey shore to the Delaware River. He also commanded the steamship *Savannah* on her first transatlantic voyage. ISAIAH ROGERS (1800–1869) of Massachusetts was an architect whose speciality was hotels. He designed the Tremont, Boston, and the Astor House, New York, and is referred to as the "father of the modern hotel." HENRY HUTTLESTON ROGERS (1840–1909) of Massachusetts invented machinery that separated naphtha from crude oil and originated the concept of transporting oil by pipeline. He also was an executive with Standard Oil and a financial advisor to Samuel Clemens (Mark Twain). JAMES GAMBLE ROGERS (1867–1947) of Kentucky was an architect who specialized in buildings on college campuses. He was responsible for the main buildings at Yale University. BRUCE ROGERS (1870–1987) of Indiana was a printer and book designer who was an advisor to both Cambridge University Press and Harvard University Press. He also designed two typefaces, Montaigne and Centaur. WILL ROGERS (1879–1935) of Oklahoma was an actor and humorist noted for his monologues. He starred in movies, including *A Connecticut Yankee* (1931), wrote a syndicated newspaper column, and wrote books, including *The Cowboy Philosopher on Prohibition* (1919). He died in a plane crash. EDITH NOURSE ROGERS (1881–1960) Maine was a member of Congress from Massachusetts. She served in that capacity for 35 years, the longest tenure of any woman. MOTHER MARY JOSEPH ROGERS (1882–1955) of Massachusetts was the founder of the Maryknoll Sisters of St. Dominic. CARL RANSOM ROGERS (1902–1987) of Illinois, a psychologist, was a founder or pioneer of several movements or techniques, including humanistic psychology and encounter-group therapy. He also wrote books, including *Client-Centered Therapy* (1951). Four brothers from Pennsylvania—JAMES BLYTHE ROGERS (1802–1852),

WILLIAM BARTON ROGERS (1804–1882), HENRY DARWIN ROGERS (1808–1866), and ROBERT EMPIE ROGERS (1813–1884)—were notable scientists and educators. Henry was a leading geologist whose survey of Pennsylvania contributed to the understanding of mountains. Henry and William, also a geologist, together wrote *On the Physical Structure of the Appalachian Chain* (1842). William also helped establish and served as the first president of the Massachusetts Institute of Technology. James and Robert, both chemists, published *A Text Book on Chemistry* (1846).

Genealogies: *1699–Rogers–1991: descendants and ancestors* was compiled by Marie Rogers Sittler and published in Miami, Oklahoma, in 1991. *Ancestors of Reeks and Rogers, Christchurch, Dorset* was compiled by Lindsay S. Reeks and published in Baltimore, Maryland, in 1989. *Branching out from Stephen Graves* [also Rogers] was compiled by Jessie Wagner Graves and published in Knoxville, Tennessee, in 1991.

ROHDE

Ranking: 4488 S.S. Count: 9987

Origin: Danish, German, Norwegian. Danish, Norwegian: 1) cognate to Roth, meaning clearing. 2) cognate to Roth, meaning red. German: cognate to Rhodes.

Famous **Rohdes**: RUTH BRYAN OWEN ROHDE (1885–1954) of Illinois was a member of Congress who concentrated on feminist issues and was the first woman appointed to serve on a major committee, the Foreign Affairs Committee.

Genealogies: None known.

ROHRBACH, ROHRBACHER, ROHRBACK (S.S. Abbreviation: Rohrba)

Ranking: 4479 S.S. Count: 10,002

Origin: German. Derived from words meaning reedy stream. The name was given to those from Rohrbach, the name of several places in Germany, or to those who lived on or near the Rohrbach, the name of many rivers in Germany.

Genealogies: *Family History of the Rohrbachs of Moniteau County, Missouri* was compiled by Glen E. Mutti and published in Marceline, Missouri, in 1979. *Rohrbach Genealogy* was compiled by Lewis Bunker Rohrbaugh and published in Philadelphia, Pennsylvania, in 1982.

ROHRER

Ranking: 4502 S.S. Count: 9945

Origin: German. Derived from the German word "rohr," meaning reed. The name was given to those who lived in a reed-covered area.

Genealogies: *The Rohrer Families* was compiled by Wickliffe B. Neal and published in Arlington, Kentucky, in 1991.

ROJAS

Ranking: 1004 S.S. Count: 43,669

Origin: Spanish. Derived from the word "rojo," meaning red.

Genealogies: None known.

ROLAND (ALSO ROLANDEAU, ROLANDI, ROLANDINO)

Ranking: 1648 S.S. Count: 27,112

Origin: Roland, Rolandeau—French; Rolandi, Rolandino—Italian. Cognates to Rowland, a Norman first name.

Genealogies: *The Roland and Spicer Families of Maryland and Dorset, England* was compiled by Charles Thomas Roland and published in Bethel Park, Pennsylvania, in 1983.

ROLDAN

Ranking: 3552 S.S. Count: 12,703

Origin: Spanish. Cognate to Rowland, a Norman first name.

Genealogies: None known.

ROLLERSON (S.S. Abbreviation: Roller)

Ranking: 3533 S.S. Count: 12,777

Origin: English. Transformation of the English name Rollo, which was derived from the Norman name Rou(l), comprising components meaning fame and wolf.

Genealogies: None known.

ROLLIN (ALSO ROLLINGS, ROLLINGSON, ROLLINS, ROLLINSON)

Ranking: 757 S.S. Count: 56,065

Origin: Rollings, Rollingson, Rollins, Rollinson—English; Rollin—English, French. Transformations of and cognates to Rollerson.

Famous **Bearers**: WILLIAM ROLLINSON (1762–1842) of England was an engraver who worked with bank notes, making improvements in the process. JAMES SIDNEY ROLLINS (1812–1888) of Kentucky was a Missouri politician and one of the reorganizers of the University of Missouri. EDWARD HENRY ROLLINS (1824–1889) of New York was one of the founders of the Republican Party in New Hampshire and a U.S. senator from that state. HYDER E. ROLLINS (1889–1958) of Texas was a longtime English professor at Harvard University and an editor of books, including *Old English Ballads* (1920) and *The Letters of John Keats* (1957).

Genealogies: None known.

ROLON

Ranking: 4942 S.S. Count: 9063

Origin: French. Cognate to Rollerson.

Genealogies: None known.

ROMAN

Ranking: 501 S.S. Count: 80,316

Origin: Belorussian, Catalan, English, French, Polish, Romanian, Ukrainian. Catalan, English, French: 1) the name was given to those from Rome or Italy, either as an ethnic or regional name. 2) the name was given to those with some special connection to Rome. Belorussian, Catalan, English, French, Polish, Romanian, Ukrainian: derived from the Latin first name Rōmānus.

Famous **Romans:** ANDRÉ BIENVENU ROMAN (1795–1866) of Louisiana was a governor of Louisiana who worked to improve flood control and the public-school system.

Genealogies: *Pioneer Families* [also Roman] was compiled by Becky Hardin and published in Mooresville, Indiana, in 1982.

ROMANO

Ranking: 974 S.S. Count: 44,904

Origin: Italian. Transformation of Roman.

Genealogies: None known.

ROMEO

Ranking: 4295 S.S. Count: 10,447

Origin: Italian. Transformation of Romero.

Genealogies: None known.

ROMERO

Ranking: 327 S.S. Count: 115,207

Origin: Italian, Spanish. 1) the name was given to pilgrims, originally to pilgrims from the Roman Empire passing through the Byzantine Empire on their way to the Holy Land. 2) derived from the Latin name Rōmaeus. The name was given to those from Rome or Italy as an ethnic or regional name.

Genealogies: None known.

ROMINE

Ranking: 3569 S.S. Count: 12,638

Origin: Russian. Derived from the surname Romanov, which was the surname of a Russian royal family.

Genealogies: None known.

ROMO

Ranking: 3297 S.S. Count: 13,759

Origin: Spanish. Derived from the Spanish word "romo," menaing blunt. The name was given to those who were snub-nosed.

Genealogies: None known.

ROOKS

Ranking: 4691 S.S. Count: 9541

Origin: English. Derived from the Old English word "hrōc," meaning a kind of bird. The name was given to those with dark hair.

Genealogies: *The Final Irony* [Rooks family] was compiled by Katherine Lane Nichols and published in 1975. *Thatcher, Buckmaster and Rooks Genealogy, and Allied Families* was compiled by Nellie Thatcher and published in Detroit, Michigan, in 1971.

ROONEY

Ranking: 1995 S.S. Count: 22,758

Origin: Irish. Derived from the Gaelic name Ó Ruannaidh, which was derived from the first name Ruannaidh, meaning champion.

Genealogies: None known.

ROOT

Ranking: 1535 S.S. Count: 29,013

Origin: Dutch, English. Dutch: derived from the Dutch word "ro(o)ten," meaning to ret or rot. The name was given to those who lived near an area set aside for retting. English: 1) derived from the Middle English word "rote," meaning a medieval stringed instrument. The name was given to those who played the rote. 2) derived from the Middle English word "rote," meaning glad. The name was given to those with a sunny disposition.

Famous **Roots:** JESSE ROOT (1736?–1822) of Connecticut was a Revolutionary War soldier and politician, then chief justice of the Connecticut Superior Court. ERASTUS ROOT (1773–1846) of Connecticut was a member of Congress from New York. ELISHA KING ROOT (1808–1865) of Massachusetts was president of the Colt Armory and the inventor of the drop hammer, which is used in die forging. GEORGE F. ROOT (1820–1895) of Massachusetts composed several Civil War songs, including "Battle Cry of Freedom" and "Tramp, Tramp, Tramp, the Boys are Marching." ELIHU ROOT (1845–1937) of New York was a prominent diplomat and a U.S. senator from New York who won the Nobel Peace Prize in 1912. JOHN WELLBORN ROOT (1850–1891) of Georgia was an architect who designed several buildings in Chicago, including the Montauk and Monadnock buildings.

Genealogies: *Pioneers of Vernon, Oneida County, New York, and the Root Family* was compiled by Ferne Kitson Patterson and published in Interlaken, New York, in 1985. *The Root Family of Bolivar, New York* was compiled by William A. Paquette and published in Baltimore, Maryland, in 1991.

ROPER

Ranking: 1669 S.S. Count: 26,762

Origin: English, French. English: derived from the Old English word "rāp," meaning rope. The name was given to those who made or sold rope. French: transformation of Robert.

Famous Ropers: DANIEL CALHOUN ROPER (1867–1943) of South Carolina was a businessman and public official. He held high positions in the post office and the U.S. Tariff Commission, and he became the commissioner of the Internal Revenue Service.

Genealogies: *The Roper Family Bible Record* was compiled by Mary Waller Shepherd Soper and published in Winchester, Tennessee, in 1982.

ROSA

Ranking: 1193 **S.S. Count:** 36,771

Origin: Catalan, Czech, Italian, Polish. Catalan, Italian: cognate to Rose, meaning the flower. Czech, Polish: uncertain etymology. Possibly derived from the Czech and Polish word "rosa," meaning dew.

Famous Rosas: EDWARD BENNETT ROSA (1861–1921) of New York was a physicist who worked with the law of conservation of energy.

Genealogies: None known.

ROSADO

Ranking: 848 **S.S. Count:** 50,365

Origin: Portuguese, Spanish. Derived from the Portuguese and Spanish word "rosado," meaning pink. The name was given to those with an especially pink complexion.

Genealogies: None known.

ROSALES (S.S. Abbreviation: Rosale)

Ranking: 1599 **S.S. Count:** 28,044

Origin: Spanish. Derived from the Spanish word "rosal," meaning a rosebush. The name was given to those who lived near a rosebush.

Genealogies: None known.

ROSARIO (S.S. Abbreviation: Rosari)

Ranking: 650 **S.S. Count:** 64,076

Origin: Portuguese. Derived from the word "rosário," meaning rosary. The name was frequently given to those born on the feast of Our Lady of the Rosary, which is held the first Sunday of October.

Genealogies: None known.

ROSAS

Ranking: 2682 **S.S. Count:** 17,022

Origin: Catalan, Portuguese, Spanish. Portuguese, Spanish: cognates to Rose, meaning the flower. Catalan: the name was given to those from Roses, a place in the province of Gerona in Spain.

Genealogies: None known.

ROSE

Ranking: 159 **S.S. Count:** 203,280

Origin: English, French, German, Jewish. English: derived from the medieval feminine first name Rose, which was derived from a Germanic first name comprising the components "hrōd" and "haid(is)," meaning fame and sort. English, French, German: derived from the Middle English and Old French and Middle High German word "rose," meaning the flower. The name was given to those who lived in a house that bore the sign of the rose, to those with an especially pink complexion, or to those who lived near wild roses. Jewish: the name was given ornamentally and derived either from the Yiddish word "royz," meaning rose, the flower, or from the feminine Yiddish first name Royze, which was ultimately derived from the name of the flower rose.

Famous Roses: EDWARD ROSE (?–1834), birthplace unknown, was the child of a white trader and a part–Cherokee Indian, part-black mother. He made his living as a guide and interpreter. JOSEPH NELSON ROSE (1862–1928) of Indiana was a botanist with the U.S. Department of Agriculture. His speciality was the flora of Mexico. MARY DAVIES SWARTZ ROSE (1874–1941) of Ohio was a nutritionist and the author of the books *Feeding the Family* (1916) and *The Foundations of Nutrition* (1927). BILLY ROSE (1899–1966), born William Rosenburg in New York, was a prominent figure in entertainment in New York. He produced many shows and composed more than 400 songs, including "Me and My Shadow" and "Barney Google."

Genealogies: *Descendants of Robert Rose of Wethersfield and Branford, Connecticut: who came on the ship "Francis" in 1634 from Ipswich, England* was compiled by Christine Rose and published in San Jose, California, in 1983. *William Rose of Surry County, Virginia* was compiled by Eunice Brooks Freese and published in 1976.

ROSEN

Ranking: 1177 **S.S. Count:** 37,142

Origin: Swedish. Cognate to Rose, meaning the flower.

Genealogies: *Henry Roosen-Rosen: to Pennsylvania 1765* was compiled by Peggy S. Joyner and published in Portsmouth, Virginia, in 1980. *Search for the Family: a chronicle of the Tzvi Hirsh Shulkin and Gelye Devorah Rosen Family* was compiled by Sallyann Amdur Sack and published in Bethesda, Maryland, in 1980.

ROSENBAUM, ROSENBERG, ROSENBLOOM, ROSENBLUM, ROSENBUSH (S.S. Abbreviation: Rosenb)

Ranking: 415 **S.S. Count:** 95,234

Origin: Rosenbaum, Rosenbloom, Rosenblum, Rosenbush—Jewish; Rosenberg—Jewish, Swedish. Cognates to Rose, meaning the flower. Rosenbaum: the name means rose tree. Rosenbloom, Rosenblum: the names mean rose flower and rose leaf, respectively. Rosenbush: the name means rosebush. Rosenberg: the name means rose hill.

Famous Bearers: HENRY ROSENBERG (1824–1893) of

Switzerland came to the United States and settled in Texas. He was a merchant and banker who left the bulk of his estate to the city of Galveston. ABRAHAM HAYYIM ROSENBERG (1838–1925) of Russia was a rabbi who came to the United States in 1891 and wrote *Ozar ha-shemoth*, a book of Hebrew literature. PAUL ROSENBERG (1881–1959) of France was the owner of prestigious art galleries in Paris. With the Nazi invasion of Paris, Rosenberg fled to the United States and opened his gallery in New York City, staying in New York after the war ended. ETHEL ROSENBERG (1915–1953) and JULIUS ROSENBERG (1918–1953), husband and wife and both of New York City, were American spies during World War II. They were the first American non-military personnel executed for espionage.

Genealogies: *The Rosenbaum-Rosenbalm Family of Southwest Virginia* was compiled by Clifford R. Canfield and published in Carlsbad, California, in 1990.

ROSENFARB, ROSENFELD, ROSENFELDER, ROSENFIELD, ROSENFRUCHT (S.S. Abbreviation: Rosenf)

Ranking: 3128 S.S. Count: 14,542

Origin: Jewish. *Cognates to Rose, meaning the flower. The names were taken ornamentally. Rosenfarb: the name means rose color. Rosenfeld, Rosenfelder, Rosenfield: the names mean rose field. Rosenfrucht: the name means rose fruit.*

Famous **Bearers:** MORRIS ROSENFELD (1862–1923) of Poland came to New York City and worked in the sweatshops for 14 years. He then edited and contributed to some of the Yiddish newspapers of the time. He wrote *Die Glocke* (1888) and *Songs from the Ghetto* (1898).

Genealogies: None known.

ROSENSCHEIN, ROSENSHINE, ROSENSHTEIN, ROSENSTEIN, ROSENSTOCK (S.S. Abbreviation: Rosens)

Ranking: 4833 S.S. Count: 9261

Origin: Jewish. *Cognates to Rose, meaning the flower. The names were taken ornamentally. Rosenschein, Rosenshine: the names mean rose shine. Rosenshtein, Rosenstein: the names mean rose stone. Rosenstock: the names mean rose bush.*

Genealogies: None known.

ROSENTHAL, ROSENTHALL (S.S. Abbreviation: Rosent)

Ranking: 1495 S.S. Count: 29,740

Origin: German, Jewish. *German: derived from the German word "rose," meaning rose and the word "thal," meaning valley. The name was given to those who came from Rosenthal, the name of several places in Germany. Jewish: derived from the Yiddish word "royze," meaning flower and the word*

"thal," meaning valley. The name was taken ornamentally and by those who lived in valleys known for roses.

Famous **Bearers:** HERMAN ROSENTHAL (1843–1917) of Russia was a promoter of agricultural colonies for Russian Jews. He was also on the editorial staff of the *Jewish Encyclopedia*. JEAN ROSENTHAL (1912–1969) of New York City was a lighting designer considered a pioneer in her field.

Genealogies: None known.

ROSS

Ranking: 80 S.S. Count: 324,600

Origin: English, German, Jewish, Scottish. *English, German: derived from the Germanic first name Rozzo, a shortening of any of several compound names with the first component "hrōd," meaning fame. English, Scottish: 1) uncertain etymology. Possibly, in some cases, derived from the Welsh word "rhós," meaning moorland. The name was given to those from Ross or Roos(e), the name of several places in England and Scotland. 2) the name was given to those from Rots, a place in Normandy, France. German: derived from the German word "ross," meaning horse. The name was given to those who kept or raised horses. Jewish: 1) Anglicization of similar-sounding Jewish surnames. 2) cognate to the German name Ross, meaning horse.*

Famous **Rosses:** GEORGE ROSS (1730–1779) of Delaware was one of the signers of the Declaration of Independence. ELIZABETH (BETSY) GRISCOM ROSS (1752–1836) of Pennsylvania is considered to have been the person who sewed the first American flag that was accepted by the Continental Congress as the official United States emblem, on June 14, 1777. JOHN ROSS (1790–1866) of Tennessee was an Indian chief whose birth name was either Coowescoowe or Kooweskoowe. He was the chief of the United Cherokee Nation, 1839–1866. EDMUND GIBSON ROSS (1826–1907) of Ohio was a journalist at the *Kansas Tribune*, a U.S. senator from Kansas, and, in later years, the governor of the territory of New Mexico. EDWARD ALSWORTH ROSS (1866–1951) of Illinois was the founder of American sociology. NELLIE TAYLOR ROSS (1876–1977) of Missouri was the first female governor of Wyoming and the first female director of the U.S. Mint. HAROLD WALLACE ROSS (1892–1951) of Colorado was the founder of *The New Yorker* magazine. He was responsible for the one-line cartoon format that is considered a standard in today's magazine cartoons.

Genealogies: *The Baron, the Logger, the Miner, and Me* was compiled by John H. Toole and published in Missoula, Montana, in 1984. *Crossroads in Kansas: a Stearns-Ross Genealogy* was compiled by Phyllis Ross Kostner and published in Pretty Prairie, Kansas, in 1982. *History of the Clan Ross* was compiled by Alexander M. Ross and published in Morgantown, West Virginia, in 1983.

ROSSER

Ranking: 4174 S.S. Count: 10,830

Origin: English. Transformation of Roger.

Famous **Rossers**: THOMAS LAFAYETTE ROSSER (1836–1910) of Virginia was attending West Point at the outbreak of the Civil War. He left to become an officer in the Confederate army. After the war he worked as an engineer with the Northern Pacific and the Canadian Pacific railroads before retiring to become a gentleman farmer.

Genealogies: *The Descendants of Benjamin Rosser (1814–1864) and Sarah Griffiths (1820–1895)* was compiled by John C. Rosser and published in San Francisco, California, in 1972.

ROSSI

Ranking: 1244 S.S. Count: 35,508

Origin: Italian. Cognate to Rouse.

Genealogies: *Descendants of Nicola Dall'Ava Including Related Families, Viale and Rossi, of Vicenza, Italy and Berkshire County, Massachusetts* was compiled by Phyllis Walker Johnson and published in Arlington, Virginia, in 1977.

ROTH

Ranking: 488 S.S. Count: 82,823

Origin: English, German, Jewish. English, German: transformation of and cognate to Rhodes, meaning clearing. German: derived from various Germanic names with the first component "hrōd," meaning fame. German, Jewish: derived from the German word "rot," meaning red. The name was given to those with red hair, or, in some cases, the name was taken ornamentally.

Genealogies: *Patrimony: a true story* was compiled by Philip Roth and published in New York, New York, in 1991.

ROTHENBERG, ROTHENBERGER (S.S. Abbreviation: Rothen)

Ranking: 4341 S.S. Count: 10,323

Origin: Jewish. Derived from the Old High German words "rōt" and "berg," meaning red and hill. The name was given to those from Rothenberg, a place in Germany.

Genealogies: None known.

ROTHER (ALSO ROTHERAM, ROTHERFORTH, ROTHERHAM)

Ranking: 4948 S.S. Count: 9055

Origin: Rotheram, Rotherham—English; Rother—German; Rotherforth—Scottish. Rotheram, Rotherham: derived from the name of a British river called Rother and the Old English word "hām," meaning homestead. The name was given to those from Rotherham, a place in Yorkshire, England. Rother: transformation of Roth, meaning red. Rotherforth: transformation of Rutherford.

Genealogies: None known.

ROTHMAN, ROTHMANN (S.S. Abbreviation: Rothma)

Ranking: 4739 S.S. Count: 9451

Origin: Rothman—Jewish; Rothmann—German, Jewish. Rothman: transformation of Roth, meaning red. Rothmann (Jewish): transformation of Roth, meaning red. Rothmann (German): 1) transformation of Roth. 2) derived from the German word "rat," meaning counsel. The name was given to those who were counselors or who gave sage advice.

Genealogies: None known.

ROUNDS

Ranking: 4901 S.S. Count: 9124

Origin: English. Derived from the Middle English and Old French word "rond," meaning fat. The name was given to those who were chubby.

Genealogies: *The John Round Family of Swansea and Rehoboth, Massachusetts* [also Rounds] was compiled by H. L. Peter Rounds and published in Baltimore, Maryland, in 1983.

ROUNTREE

Ranking: 4221 S.S. Count: 10,687

Origin: English. Derived from the Middle English words "rown" and "tree," meaning rowan tree or mountain ash. The name was given to those who lived near a rowan.

Genealogies: None known.

ROUSE

Ranking: 1238 S.S. Count: 35,772

Origin: English. Derived from the Middle English and Old French word "rous," meaning red. The name was given to those with red hair.

Genealogies: *Rouse Hill House and the Rouses* was compiled by Caroline Rouse Thornton and published in 1988. *Rouse, Stevens Ancestry and Allied Families* was compiled by Dolly Bottens and published in Carthage, Missouri, in 1970.

ROUSH

Ranking: 2920 S.S. Count: 15,581

Origin: German. 1) transformation of Raush. 2) the name means rush or intoxication.

Genealogies: *Rev. James Johnson England, his Wife, Sarah Roush, and Descendants: Delaware Co., Ohio to Edgar Co., Ill.* was compiled by Virginia Biddle Those and published in Tuscola, Illinois, in 1982.

ROUSSEAU, ROUSSEAUX, ROUSSEL, ROUSSELL (S.S. Abbreviation: Rousse)

Ranking: 2301 S.S. Count: 19,843

Origin: Roussel—English, French, Irish, Scottish; Roussell—English, Irish, Scottish; Rousseau, Rousseaux—French. Transformations of and cognates to Russell.

Famous **Bearers:** LOVELL HARRISON ROUSSEAU (1818–1869) of Kentucky was the U.S. representative who accepted the title to Alaska from the Russians. HARRY HARWOOD ROUSSEAU (1870–1930) of New York was an engineer involved with the construction and design of the Panama Canal.

Genealogies: *The Roussel Register* was compiled by Robert Louis Leo Roussel and published in Arlington, Massachusetts, in 1973.

ROWAN

Ranking: 2376 **S.S. Count:** 19,118

Origin: Irish. Derived from the Gaelic name Ó Ruadháin, derived from the first name Ruadhán, which was derived from the word "ruadh," meaning red.

Genealogies: *The Rowan Story: from Federal Hill to My Old Kentucky Home* was compiled by Randall Capps and published in Bowling Green, Kentucky, in 1976. *The Rev. John Rowan Family* was compiled by Mabel Phillips Baker and published in Baltimore, Maryland, in 1980.

ROWE

Ranking: 407 **S.S. Count:** 96,852

Origin: English. 1) derived from the medieval first name Row, which was derived either from the Norman first name Rou(l) or from Rowland. 2) derived from the Middle English word "row," meaning row. The name was given to those who lived in a row of attached houses or to those who lived near a hedgerow.

Famous **Rowes:** LEO STANTON ROWE (1871–1946) of Iowa was an economist and diplomat specializing in Latin America. LYNWOOD THOMAS ROWE (1912–1961) of Texas was a baseball pitcher. He played in three World Series, winning the Series in 1935.

Genealogies: *The Marriage of Catherine & David: a history of southwestern Pennsylvania families* was compiled by LaVonne R. Hanlon and published in Laurel, Maryland, in 1982. *The Families of Johann Martin Rau and Johann Conrad Bohne* [also Rowe] was compiled by Nancy Ann Dietrich and published in Clarendon Hills, Illinois, in 1976.

ROWELL

Ranking: 2277 **S.S. Count:** 22,020

Origin: English. 1) transformation of Rowe, derived from the medieval first name Row. 2) derived from the Old English words "rūh" and "hyll," meaning rough and hill. The name was given to those from Rowell, a place in England. 3) derived from Old English words meaning clearing and well or spring. The name was given to those from Rowell, the name of several places in England.

Famous **Rowells:** GEORGE PRESBURY ROWELL (1838–1908) of Vermont was the advertising agent who founded

Printer's Ink (1888), a periodical. CHESTER HARVEY ROWELL (1867–1948) of Illinois was a journalist at the *Fresno (California) Republican* and the *San Francisco Chronicle.*

Genealogies: None known.

ROWLAND, ROWLANDS, ROWLANDSON (S.S. Abbreviation: Rowlan)

Ranking: 785 **S.S. Count:** 53,648

Origin: English. 1) derived from the Old Norse words "rá" and "lundr," meaning roebuck and wood. The name was given to those from Rowland, the name of places in England. 2) derived from the Norman first name Rol(l)ant, which comprises the components "hrōd" and "wald," meaning fame and rule.

Famous **Bearers:** MARY WHITE ROWLANDSON (1635?–1678), possibly of England, was an Indian captive and an author. She was captured and held for 11 weeks by the Indians who burned the town of Lancaster, Massachusetts. After being traded back she wrote *The Sovereignty & Goodness of God, Together with the Faithfulness of His Promises Displayed, etc.* It was an account of her weeks of captivity and was a bestseller, of sorts, in the early colonial days. THOMAS FITCH ROWLAND (1831–1907) of Connecticut was the boat builder who constructed the original *Monitor* for John Ericsson. HENRY AUGUSTUS ROWLAND (1848–1901) of Pennsylvania was the first physics instructor at Johns Hopkins University.

Genealogies: *John C. Rowland, Missouri Pioneer and his Kin* was compiled by Vaden R. Mayers and published in Woodside, California, in 1983. *Sons of Frontiersmen: history & genealogy of Rowland, Whitmire and associated families* was compiled by Billie Louise Owens and published in Canon City, Colorado, in 1976.

ROWLEY

Ranking: 2277 **S.S. Count:** 19,953

Origin: English. Derived from the Old English words "rūh" and "lēah," meaning rough and clearing. The name was given to those from Rowley, the name of places in England.

Genealogies: *The Shepard Genealogy* [also Rowley] was compiled by Lowell Shepard Blaisdell and published in 1952. *One Branch of the Tree: Rowley 1630–1986* was compiled by Ralph Duane Rowley and published in Brookings, Oregon, in 1986.

ROY

Ranking: 614 **S.S. Count:** 68,007

Origin: English, French, Scottish. English: transformation of Ray, meaning king. French: transformation of Ray, meaning king. Scottish: derived from the Gaelic word "ruadh," meaning red. The name was given to those with red hair.

Genealogies: None known.

ROYAL

Ranking: 2270 S.S. Count: 20,111

Origin: English. Derived from the Old English words "rā" and "hyll," meaning roe deer and hill. The name was given to those from Royle, a place in Lancashire, England.

Genealogies: *Ancestry of William Henry Wright and Wife Polly Ann Royal and their Descendants* was compiled by Watie Delfa Wright Ellis and published in San Jose, California, in 1991. *The Royal Way West* was compiled by Violet Coe Mumford and published in Baltimore, Maryland, in 1988.

ROYER

Ranking: 3087 S.S. Count: 14,708

Origin: French. Derived from the Old Provençal word "rode," meaning wheel. The name was given to wheelwrights or to those who lived near a waterwheel.

Genealogies: None known.

ROYSTER (S.S. Abbreviation: Royste)

Ranking: 4111 S.S. Count: 10,985

Origin: English. The name was given to those who were blustering and swaggering.

Famous **Roysters:** JAMES FINCH ROYSTER (1880–1930) of North Carolina was a dean of the college of liberal arts at the University of North Carolina, then dean of the graduate school. He also taught at other major American universities.

Genealogies: None known.

RUBENS

Ranking: 4470 S.S. Count: 10,016

Origin: Dutch, Flemish, Jewish. Dutch, Flemish: transformation of Robert. Jewish: derived from the Hebrew first name Reuven, comprising the components "reu" and "ben," meaning behold and son.

Genealogies: None known.

RUBIN

Ranking: 1246 S.S. Count: 35,458

Origin: Jewish. Transformation of Rubens.

Famous **Rubins:** ISIDOR CLINTON RUBIN (1883–1958) of Austria was the leading gynecologist of his day. He specialized in the area of fertility. He was the first to discover how eggs travel through the Fallopian tubes.

Genealogies: *Yesterday, Today and Tomorrow. A history of the Rottenberg, Rubin, Goldstein et al.* families was compiled by Dan Rottenberg and published in Philadelphia, Pennsylvania, in 1977. *A Link with the Future: a history of the Rottenberg, Rubin, Goldstein,* [et al.] *Families* was compiled by Dan Rottenberg and published in Chicago, Illinois, in 1969.

RUBINO (ALSO RUBINOV, RUBINOVISCH, RUBINOWICH, RUBINOWITZ)

Ranking: 4650 S.S. Count: 9617

Origin: Rubino—Italian; Rubinov, Rubinovisch, Rubinowich, Rubinowitz—Jewish. Rubino: 1) derived from the first name Rubino, which was derived from the name Cherubini, meaning cherub. 2) the name was given to those with red hair or a ruddy complexion. 3) derived from the Latin word "rube(us)," meaning red. The name was given to those who traded in rubies. Rubinov, Rubinovisch, Rubinowich, Rubinowitz: transformations of Rubens.

Genealogies: None known.

RUBIO

Ranking: 2079 S.S. Count: 22,046

Origin: Spanish. Ultimately derived from the Latin word "rubeus," meaning red. The name was given to those with red hair or a ruddy complexion.

Genealogies: None known.

RUBY

Ranking: 3559 S.S. Count: 12,687

Origin: English. 1) the name was given to those from Roubaix, a place in France. 2) derived from the name Ruby, a transformation of Reuben. 3) the name was given to those who dealt in rubies, the precious red stones.

Famous **Rubys:** JACK L. RUBY (1911–1967) of Illinois shot and killed Lee Harvey Oswald. In 1963, as Oswald, the man who was charged with assassinating President John F. Kennedy, was being transferred to a jail with tighter security, Ruby shot him at point-blank range. The event was captured on television. His reason for the act, he said, was to spare Jacqueline Kennedy, widow of the president, the ordeal of a trial having to do with her husband's assassination. Ruby died of cancer in jail while awaiting a second trial after the first one's guilty verdict had been reversed on appeal. Innuendoes and rumors suggested a conspiracy and that Ruby had been sent to kill Oswald as a way to permanently silence him, but this was never proven.

Genealogies: None known.

RUCKER

Ranking: 1196 S.S. Count: 36,733

Origin: English. Transformation of Rock, meaning distaff.

Famous **Ruckers:** GEORGE "NAP" RUCKER (1884–1970) of Georgia was a baseball player. He excelled as a left-handed Brooklyn Dodgers pitcher.

Genealogies: *The Rucker Family of South Carolina, 1752–1983* was compiled by Brent Holcomb and published in Greenville, South Carolina, in 1983.

RUDD

Ranking: 2322 **S.S. Count:** 19,543

Origin: English, Jewish. English: derived from the Middle English word "rudde," meaning red or ruddy. The name was given to those with red hair or a ruddy complexion. Jewish: a shortened form of any of several Jewish surnames that begin with Rud-.

Genealogies: *The Landings Scatter* [also Rudd] was compiled by Helen Greenli Swenson and published in Bismarck, North Dakota, in 1972. *Rudd-Pollard-Youngblood and Related Families* was compiled by Margaret Rudd Youngblood and published in Houston, Texas, in 1980. *Some Ancestors and Descendants of Joseph Rudd, Jr., 1740–1818, and his Wife, Sarah Story, 1744–1842, of Bennington, Vermont* was compiled by Dorothy Rudd DuMond and published in Ulster Park, New York, in 1982.

RUDOLPH (S.S. Abbreviation: Rudolp)

Ranking: 1613 **S.S. Count:** 27,766

Origin: English, German. Derived from the Middle English first name Rolf, comprising the Germanic components "hrōd" and "wulf," meaning fame and wolf.

Genealogies: None known.

RUDY

Ranking: 4371 **S.S. Count:** 10,255

Origin: Ukrainian. Derived from the Russian name Rudak, meaning a man with red hair.

Genealogies: *John Rudy and Mary Gahman* was compiled by Marie Peer and published in Craig, Colorado, in 1990. *The Rudys of God's House and Related Families* was compiled by William Osborne Wingeard and published in Baltimore, Maryland, in 1986.

RUFF

Ranking: 2151 **S.S. Count:** 21,324

Origin: English. Transformation of Rudolph.

Genealogies: *The Ruff Family Album* was compiled by Bonner Ruff and published in Jonesboro, Arkansas, in 1982. *Look Behind your Mirror: some descendants of Michael Rugh* [also Ruff] was compiled by J. C. Rugh and published in Belleville, Illinois, in 1975.

RUFFIN (ALSO RUFFINELLI, RUFFINI, RUFFINO, RUFFINONI)

Ranking: 1665 **S.S. Count:** 26,872

Origin: Ruffin—French; Ruffinelli, Ruffini, Ruffino, Ruffinoni—Italian. Ruffin: derived from a first name that was ultimately derived from the Latin first name Rūfus, meaning a redhead. Ruffinelli, Ruffini, Ruffino, Ruffinoni: cognates to Ruffin.

Famous Bearers: THOMAS RUFFIN (1787–1879) of Virginia was a lawyer and a justice of the North Carolina Supreme Court. EDMUND RUFFIN (1794–1865) of Virginia was an agriculturist and a writer. He was able to devise a method of replenishing worn-out soils through the application of certain chemicals and minerals. He wrote about his theories in a book entitled *An Essay on Calcareous Manures* (1832).

Genealogies: None known.

RUGGIER, RUGGIERI, RUGGIERO (S.S. Abbreviation: Ruggie)

Ranking: 2893 **S.S. Count:** 15,739

Origin: Italian. Cognates to Roger, derived from a Germanic first name.

Genealogies: None known.

RUIZ

Ranking: 295 **S.S. Count:** 121,706

Origin: Spanish. Cognate to the English name Roderick.

Genealogies: None known.

RUNYAN

Ranking: 4971 **S.S. Count:** 9016

Origin: English. Uncertain etymology. The name was given to a mangy, sickly person.

Genealogies: *The Ancestors, and their Children of Enoch M. Runyon (1824–1908) of New Jersey and Illinois and his Known Descendants* [also Runyan] was compiled by Melba Marie Runyon Aaron and published in 1975. *Tracking Barefoot Runyan: descendants of Isaac Barefoot Runyan: tracing the path of these Runyans from the Shenandoah Valley through Tennessee and Alabama on their journey westward* was compiled by Marie Runyan Wright and published in Baltimore, Maryland, in 1980.

RUNYON

Ranking: 3555 **S.S. Count:** 12,694

Origin: English. Transformation of Runyan.

Famous Runyons: [ALFRED] DAMON RUNYON (1884–1946) of Kansas was a sportswriter for the *New York American*. He later wrote the syndicated columns "Both Barrels" and "The Brighter Side," the latter appearing in the Sunday comics. Movie scripts credited to him were those for *The Lemon Drop Kid* and *Little Miss Marker*.

Genealogies: *The Ancestors, and their Children of Enoch M. Runyon (1824–1908) of New Jersey and Illinois and his Known Descendants* was compiled by Melba Marie Runyon Aaron and published in 1975.

RUPERT (ALSO RUPERTI, RUPERTO)

Ranking: 3672 **S.S. Count:** 12,288

Origin: Rupert—German; Ruperti, Ruperto—Italian. Transformations of and cognates to Robert.

Genealogies: None known.

RUPP

Ranking: 2861 S.S. Count: 15,932

Origin: German. Transformation of Robert.

Famous **Rupps:** ISRAEL DANIEL RUPP (1803–1878) of Pennsylvania was a historian and the author of *History of Lancaster County* (1844). ADOLF FREDERICK RUPP (1901–1977) of Kansas, nicknamed "the Baron," was a basketball coach at the University of Kentucky (1930–1972). He led the teams to four national titles.

Genealogies: None known.

RUSH

Ranking: 790 S.S. Count: 53,361

Origin: English, Irish. English: derived from the Middle English word "rush," meaning the marshy plant. The name was given to those who lived near a mass of rushes. Irish: derived from the Gaelic name Ó Ruis, which was derived from the first name Ros.

Famous **Rushes:** BENJAMIN RUSH (1745–1813) of Pennsylvania was a physician, a signer of the Declaration of Independence, and the man who started the first free clinic in America. WILLIAM RUSH (1756–1833) of Pennsylvania was a sculptor and wood carver. He was well known as the carver of ship figureheads and the statue of George Washington in Philadelphia's Independence Hall. He was one of the founders of the Pennsylvania Academy of Fine Arts and is considered the first American-born sculptor. RICHARD RUSH (1780–1859) of Pennsylvania was the son of Benjamin Rush and a U.S. diplomat. JAMES RUSH (1786–1869) of Pennsylvania was the founder of the Ridgway Branch Library Company in Philadelphia.

Genealogies: *Haese History (also Rush family)* was compiled by Lora Rabenhorst Klug and published in Greenleaf, Wisconsin, in 1980.

RUSHING (S.S. Abbreviation: Rushin)

Ranking: 1608 S.S. Count: 27,840

Origin: German. 1) derived from the first name Rusch, meaning rose. 2) the name was given to those who lived near a pear or elm tree.

Genealogies: *Family Histories: Rushing, Morris, Bradford, Estes, Day* was compiled by Merle Virginia Morris Hayes Day and published in Oceanside, California, in 1988.

RUSS

Ranking: 2172 S.S. Count: 21,097

Origin: English. Transformation of Rouse.

Famous **Russes:** JOHN DENNISON RUSS (1801–1881) of Massachusetts was a pioneer in the teaching of the blind. He was one of the founders of the New York Institution for the Blind.

Genealogies: *Russ Family Genealogy* was compiled by Herbert M. Russ and published in Teague, Texas, in 1989.

The Johannes Russ Family in Germany and America and their Contemporaries, the Mellenthins, 1837–1985 was compiled by Ruth Clara Binkley Arthurs and published in Cullman, Alabama, in 1985.

RUSSEL (ALSO RUSSELL, RUSSELLO)

Ranking: 88 S.S. Count: 311,247

Origin: Russel, Russell—English, Irish, Scottish; Russello—Italian. Derived from the Anglo-Norman-French name Rousel, meaning a person with red hair.

Famous **Bearers:** JOSEPH RUSSELL (1719?–1804) of Massachusetts was the ship owner whose vessel the *Rebecca* was the first to round Cape Horn on a whaling expedition in the Pacific Ocean. BENJAMIN RUSSELL (1761–1845) of Massachusetts was a journalist and the founder of *The Massachusetts Centinel.* After 1790 the paper was called the *Columbian Centinel.* WILLIAM HEPBURN RUSSELL (1812–1872) of Vermont was the founder of the Pony Express. OSBORNE RUSSELL (1814–1865?) of Maine was a trapper, a pioneer in the Pacific Northwest, and a chronicler of his travels in the book *Journal of a Trapper, Or Nine Years in the Rocky Mountains, 1834–1843.* It was not published until 1914. JOHN HENRY RUSSELL (1827–1897) of Maryland was the leader of the group that attacked and burned the Confederate privateer the *Judah.* MOTHER MARY BAPTIST RUSSELL (1829–1898) of Ireland was the founder of the Sisters of Mercy in California. CHARLES TAZE RUSSELL (1852–1916) of Pennsylvania founded *The Watchtower* and preached the second coming of Christ. He said that the world would end in 1914. His followers, under the leadership of his successor, Joseph Franklin Rutherford, became the Jehovah's Witnesses. IRWIN RUSSELL (1853–1879) of Mississippi was considered a pioneer in the field of black dialect poetry. His one volume was published after his death. LILLIAN RUSSELL (1861–1922), born Helen Louise Leonard in Iowa, was a singer and actress. NORRIS RUSSELL (1877–1957) of New York was an astronomer and the first to show the amount of hydrogen present in stars. MORGAN RUSSELL (1886–1953) of New York City was a painter and the co-founder of the art movement called synchronism. RICHARD JOEL RUSSELL (1895–1971) of California was a geologist best remembered for his work along the coastlines. CHARLES ELLSWORTH "PEE WEE" RUSSELL (1906–1969) of Missouri was a clarinet player who gained national attention as a jazz musician. JANE ANNE RUSSELL (1911–1967) of California was a biochemist and endocrinologist and a pioneer in the area of hormone research.

Genealogies: *Descendants of William Russell of Salem, Mass., 1674* was compiled by George Ely Russell and published in Middletown, Maryland, in 1989. *Odyssey of the Barkers and the Russells* was compiled by Don W. Barker and published in Baltimore, Maryland, in 1984. *Long, Long Ago, 1776–1976: a genealogical record of the Farris, Wells,*

Keltner, Wynne, Russell, Roberts Families in America was compiled by Harriett Farris Boozer and published in Sandy Springs, Georgia, in 1976.

RUSSO

Ranking: 627 S.S. Count: 66,325
Origin: Italian. Cognate to Rouse.
Genealogies: None known.

RUST

Ranking: 2720 S.S. Count: 16,728
Origin: English, Scottish. Derived from the Old English word "rūst," meaning rust. The name was given to those with red hair or a ruddy complexion.

Famous **Rusts**: JOHN DANIEL RUST (1892–1954) of Texas was the co-inventor, with his brother Mack, of a cotton-picking machine in 1931. It was not manufactured until after World War II because he did not want to take work away from migrant workers.

Genealogies: *Back When and Now: history of the family of Agnes Rust Gordon Smith* was compiled by Agnes Rust Gordon Smith and published in San Angelo, Texas, in 1976. *Rust: a history of the Clark County, Ohio pioneer family* was compiled by William Lester Griffin and published in Chicago, Illinois, in 1973.

RUTH

Ranking: 2160 S.S. Count: 21,245
Origin: English. Derived from the Middle English word "reuthe," meaning pity. The name was given to those who were charitable or, ironically, to those who were contemptible.

Famous **Ruths**: GEORGE HERMAN (BABE) RUTH (1895–1948) of Maryland was also known by the names Bambino and the Sultan of Swat. He was a baseball player with a grand total of 714 home runs during his career. He was elected to the Baseball Hall of Fame (1936).

Genealogies: *Family History of the Warren, Stone, Dayton, Routh, Wurster, Daggett, and Young Families* [also Ruth] was compiled by Candy Daggett Young and published in Baltimore, Maryland, in 1983. *The Routh (also Ruth) Family in America* was compiled by Ross Holland Routh and published in El Paso, Texas, in 1976. *The Rouths (also Ruth) of Randolph County, N.C.* was compiled by Lawrence W. Routh and published in North Carolina in 1978.

RUTHERFURD, RUTHERFURD (S.S. Abbreviation: Ruther)

Ranking: 1081 S.S. Count: 40,899
Origin: Scottish. Derived from the Old English words "hryðer" and "ford," meaning cattle and ford. The name was given to those from Rutherford, a place in Scotland.

Famous **Bearers**: LEWIS MORRIS RUTHERFURD (ALSO RUTHERFORD) (1816–1892) of New York was an astrophysi-cist and a pioneer in the field of photographing the stars. JOSEPH FRANKLIN RUTHERFORD (1869–1942) of Missouri, known as Judge Rutherford, was a religious leader with the group that changed its name to the Jehovah's Witnesses (1931).

Genealogies: *Genealogical History of our Ancestors* [also Rutherford] was compiled by William Kenneth Rutherford and published in Lexington, Missouri, in 1989. *Rutherford Gleanings* was compiled by William A. Yates and published in Murray, Utah, in 1977.

RUTKOWSKI (S.S. Abbreviation: Rutkow)

Ranking: 4286 S.S. Count: 10,475
Origin: Polish. Uncertain etymology. Possibly derived from the first name Rudek, which either means red-haired or is a short form of any of several names beginning with the component "rudy," meaning red.
Genealogies: None known.

RUTLEDGE (S.S. Abbreviation: Rutled)

Ranking: 1183 S.S. Count: 37,025
Origin: English, Scottish. Unknown etymology.

Famous **Rutledges**: JOHN RUTLEDGE (1739–1800) of South Carolina was a Revolutionary leader who was president, then governor, of South Carolina. His brother, EDWARD RUTLEDGE (1749–1800) of South Carolina, was also a Revolutionary leader, a signer of the Declaration of Independence, and the governor of South Carolina. ANN RUTLEDGE (1813–1835) of Illinois was the daughter of Abraham Lincoln's landlord in Illinois and is the woman who incorrectly was rumored to be the fiancée of Lincoln. WILEY BLOUNT RUTLEDGE JR. (1894–1949) of Kentucky was an associate justice of the U.S. Supreme Court.

Genealogies: *A Record of John Rutledge and his Descendants* was compiled by Houston Odell Rutledge and published in 1966.

RUTTER (ALSO RUTTERFORD))

Ranking: 4287 S.S. Count: 10,474
Origin: Rutter—English; Rutterford—Scottish. Rutter: 1) derived from the Old French word "ro(u)tier," meaning highwayman or robber. The name was given to those without scruples. 2) transformation of Root, meaning a stringed medieval instrument. Rutterford: transformation of Rutherford.
Genealogies: None known.

RYAN

Ranking: 164 S.S. Count: 199,637
Origin: Irish. 1) derived from the Gaelic name Ó Riain, meaning "descendant of Rian or Riaghan" (H&H), a first name of uncertain etymology. 2) derived from the name Mulryan, which was derived from the Gaelic name Ó

Maolchaoine, meaning "*descendant of the devotee of (St.) Ríaghan*" *(H&H), a name of uncertain etymology.*

Famous **Ryans:** EDWARD GEORGE RYAN (1810–1880) of Ireland was the chief justice of the Wisconsin Supreme Court. ABRAM JOSEPH RYAN (1838–1886) of Maryland was a clergyman with the Confederate army who is best remembered for his poetry. Some of his best-known poems are "The Conquered Banner" and "The Sword of Robert E. Lee." THOMAS FORTUNE RYAN (1851–1928) of Virginia was a financier involved with the New York City railway systems and the American Tobacco Co. ANNE RYAN (1889–1954) of New Jersey was an artist whose main contribution was as a visual artist, especially in the area of collage. ELIZABETH RYAN (1892–1979) of California was a tennis player of international prominence.

Genealogies: *Cordell-Ryan, Hicks-Bradford Families* was compiled by John Cordell Hicks and published in Van Nuys, California, in 1978. *Irish Roots* [also Ryan] was compiled by Mary Zacchaeus Ryan and published in Faribault, Minnesota, in 1980.

RYDER
Ranking: 2217 **S.S. Count:** 20,724
Origin: English. Transformation of Rider.
Famous **Ryders:** ALBERT PINKHAM RYDER (1847–1917) of Massachusetts was a painter known for his *Macbeth and the Witches* and *Toilers of the Sea.*
Genealogies: None known.

SAAVEDRA (S.S. Abbreviation: Saaved)

Ranking: 4935 **S.S. Count:** 9071
Origin: Spanish. Derived from the words "saa" and "vedra," meaning hall and old. The name was given to those from Saavedra, a place in Spain.
Genealogies: None known.

SABO

Ranking: 3391 **S.S. Count:** 13,346
Origin: Hungarian. The name means those who made outer clothing and was given to tailors.
Genealogies: None known.

SACCO

Ranking: 4763 **S.S. Count:** 9407
Origin: Italian. Ultimately derived from the Greek word "sakkos," meaning bag. The name was given to those who made sacks.
Genealogies: None known.

SACHS

Ranking: 3976 **S.S. Count:** 11,368
Origin: German, Jewish. German: derived from the name of a Germanic tribe. The name was given to those from the region of Saxony or Sachsen in Germany. Jewish: uncertain etymology. Possibly a cognate to the German name Sachs or derived as an acronym from the Hebrew phrase Zera Kodesh Shemo, meaning "his name is of the seed of holiness" (H&H).
Famous **Sachses:** CURT SACHS (1881–1959) of Germany was a musicologist and the founder of modern organology.
Genealogies: *Scattered Seeds: the descendants of Rabbi Israel, one of the martyrs of Rozanoi, who perished on the second day of Rosh Hashanah 5420* [also Sachs] was compiled by George I. Sackheim and published in Skokie, Illinois, in 1986. *The Wernecke Family (also Sachs family)* was compiled by Gretchen Ann Wernecke Warda and published in Decorah, Iowa, in 1984.

SADLER

Ranking: 1519 **S.S. Count:** 29,299
Origin: English, German. Derived from the Middle English and Middle Low German word "sadel," meaning saddle. The name was given to those who made saddles.
Genealogies: None known.

SADOWSKI, SADOWSKY (S.S. Abbreviation: Sadows)

Ranking: 4353 **S.S. Count:** 10,301
Origin: German, Jewish, Polish. Derived from the Polish word "sad," meaning orchard, and the possessive suffix "-ów." The name was given to those from places named with these components.

Genealogies: None known.

SAENZ

Ranking: 2055 **S.S. Count:** 22,280
Origin: Spanish. Transformation of Sanchez.
Genealogies: None known.

SAGE

Ranking: 3051 **S.S. Count:** 14,881
Origin: English, French. Derived from the Middle English and Old French word "sage," meaning wise. The name was given to those who were learned.
Famous **Sages:** RUSSELL SAGE (1816–1906) of New York was a financier and politician who left his $70 million estate to his wife, MARGARET OLIVIA SLOCUM SAGE. She used the money for philanthropic work, founding the Russell Sage Foundation for the betterment of living conditions in the United States and giving freely to educational seats of higher learning.
Genealogies: *Sages: past and present: descendants of David Sage, 1639* was compiled by Florence Sage Nylin and published in Platteville, Wisconsin, in 1971.

SAGER

Ranking: 3115 **S.S. Count:** 14,605
Origin: German, Jewish. Cognates to Sawyer.
Genealogies: *The Saeger Family* [also Sager] was compiled by Elizabeth S. Daniel and published in South Glastonbury, Connecticut, in 1982. *The Sagers Clan* was compiled by Ella Sager Swanson and published in Tucson, Arizona, in 1980.

ST. CLAIR, ST. CLARE (S.S. Abbreviation: St. Cla)

Ranking: 2194 **S.S. Count:** 20,898
Origin: English, French. Transformations of Sinclair.
Famous **Bearers:** ARTHUR ST. CLAIR (1736–1818), born in Scotland, purchased a sizable tract of land in western Pennsylvania and became a controversial figure in the development of that area for many years.
Genealogies: None known.

ST. JOHN (S.S. Abbreviation: St. Joh)

Ranking: 2133 **S.S. Count:** 21,471
Origin: English. Derived from the name John. The name was given to those from St. Jean, the name of several places in France.
Famous **St. Johns:** JOHN PIERCE ST. JOHN (1833–1916) of Indiana was governor of Kansas (1879–1883) and a Prohibition Party presidential candidate in 1884. CHARLES EDWARD ST. JOHN (1857–1935) of Michigan was an astronomer noted for his studies of the sun.
Genealogies: *St. John and Harries, the Ancestors and*

Descendants of Theodore Edgar St. John was compiled by Ben LeGrande Cash and published in Albuquerque, New Mexico, in 1973.

ST. PIERRE (S.S. Abbreviation: St. Pie)
Ranking: 3495 S.S. Count: 12,894
Origin: French. Derived from the name Pierre, a cognate to Peter. The name was given to those from St. Pierre, the name of several places in France whose churches were dedicated to St. Peter.
Genealogies: None known.

SALAS
Ranking: 1255 S.S. Count: 35,050
Origin: Spanish. Derived from the word "sala," meaning hall. The name was given to those who worked at a manor house.
Genealogies: None known.

SALAZAR (S.S. Abbreviation: Salaza)
Ranking: 518 S.S. Count: 77,479
Origin: Portuguese, Spanish. Derived from the words "sala" and "zahar," meaning hall and old. The name was given to those from Salazar, the name of places in Spain and Portugal.
Genealogies: None known.

SALCEDO (S.S. Abbreviation: Salced)
Ranking: 4951 S.S. Count: 9051
Origin: Spanish. Ultimately derived from the Latin word "salix," meaning a willow tree. The name was given to those who lived near a willow tree.
Genealogies: None known.

SALDANA (S.S. Abbreviation: Saldan)
Ranking: 2417 S.S. Count: 18,727
Origin: Spanish. Uncertain etymology. The name was given to those from Saldana, a place in Spain.
Genealogies: None known.

SALERNO (S.S. Abbreviation: Salern)
Ranking: 3461 S.S. Count: 13,038
Origin: Italian. Uncertain etymology. The name was given to those from Salerno, a city and province in Italy.
Genealogies: None known.

SALES
Ranking: 4427 S.S. Count: 10,128
Origin: Catalan, English, Portuguese. Catalan, English: Uncertain etymology. The name was given to those who lived near a sallow tree. Portuguese: 1) the name was given in honor of St. Francis of Sales. 2) the name was given to those from Sales, a place in Portugal whose name is of uncertain etymology.

Genealogies: None known.

SALGADO (S.S. Abbreviation: Salgad)
Ranking: 2540 S.S. Count: 17,864
Origin: Spanish. Uncertain etymology. The name was given to those who lived near a place where mountain spinach was growing.
Genealogies: None known.

SALINAS (S.S. Abbreviation: Salina)
Ranking: 959 S.S. Count: 45,472
Origin: Spanish. Derived from the Spanish word "salinas," meaning saltworks. The name was given to those who lived near or worked in a saltworks.
Genealogies: None known.

SALISBERRY, SALISBURY (S.S. Abbreviation: Salisb)
Ranking: 2467 S.S. Count: 18,400
Origin: English. 1) derived from the Old English words "salh" and "burh," meaning willow and manor. The name was given to those from Salesbury, a place in Lancashire, England. 2) the name was given to those from Salisbury, a place in Wiltshire, England, that is of unknown etymology.
Genealogies: *Travels Around America* [Salisbury family] was compiled by Harrison Evans Salisbury and published in New York, New York, in 1976.

SALMON (ALSO SALMOND, SALMONE, SALMONI, SALMONOV)
Ranking: 1885 S.S. Count: 23,985
Origin: Salmon—English, French, Irish, Jewish; Salmond—English; Salmone, Salmoni—Italian; Salmonov— Jewish. Salmon (English, French): ultimately derived from the Hebrew word "shalom," meaning peace. Salmon (Irish): derived the Gaelic name Ó Bradáin, which was derived from the first name Bradán, meaning salmon. Salmon (Jewish): derived from the masculine Yiddish first name Zalmen, which was ultimately derived from the Hebrew word "shalom," meaning peace. Salmond, Salmone, Salmoni: transformations of and cognates to the English and French name Salmon.
Genealogies: *The Descendants of Michael & Catharine Salmon* was compiled by Robert James Salmon and published in 1978. *Salmon Chronicles* was compiled by H.J.D. Salmon.

SALTER (ALSO SALTERS)
Ranking: 1942 S.S. Count: 23,281
Origin: English. Salter: 1) derived from the Middle English and Old French word "saltere," meaning psaltery. The name was given to those who played the psaltery, a stringed instrument. 2) derived from the Old English word "s(e)alt," meaning salt. The name was given to those who extracted and

sold salt. Salters: same derivation as in 2 above. The name was given to those who were employed in a saltworks, to those who lived near one, or to those who lived in a place named for a saltworks.

Genealogies: *Salter-Hemann-Suhre Family Histories* was compiled by Ellen Salter Dal Pozzo and published in Staunton, Illinois, in 1982.

SALVATOR, SALVATORE, SALVATORELLI, SALVATORELLO, SALVATORI (S.S. Abbreviation: Salvat)

Ranking: 3135 **S.S. Count:** 14,490
Origin: Italian. Derived from the Latin name Salvātor, meaning savior and referring to Christ.
Genealogies: None known.

SALYER

Ranking: 2663 **S.S. Count:** 17,114
Origin: English, French. Derived from the French surname Sallier. The name was given to those who came from places in France with similar-sounding names.
Genealogies: *The Salyer Family: genealogy & Records of their first 250 years in America* was compiled by Elisabeth L.W. Salyer and published in Stuart, Florida, in 1982.

SAM

Ranking: 4937 **S.S. Count:** 9069
Origin: English. Transformation of Samson.
Genealogies: None known.

SAMMONDS, SAMMONS (S.S. Abbreviation: Sammon)

Ranking: 3361 **S.S. Count:** 13,487
Origin: English. Transformations of the English and French name Salmon.
Genealogies: None known.

SAMPLE

Ranking: 1500 **S.S. Count:** 29,685
Origin: English, Irish, Scottish. Uncertain etymology. The name was given to those from places in Normandy named for St. Paul.
Genealogies: None known.

SAMPSON (S.S. Abbreviation: Sampso)

Ranking: 830 **S.S. Count:** 51,235
Origin: English. Transformation of Samson.
Famous Sampsons: DEBORAH SAMPSON (1760–1827) of Massachusetts enlisted in the Continental army and fought side by side with the male soldiers, as she had disguised herself as one of them. It was not until she was wounded and hospitalized that her gender was revealed. She was discharged by General Knox. She was awarded a pension from the state of Massachusetts and eventually from the United States because of her service to her country. WILLIAM THOMAS SAMPSON (1840–1902) of New York was the commander in chief of the North Atlantic Squadron in the Spanish-American War. He and his squadron destroyed a Spanish fleet.

Genealogies: *Abraham Sampson in America* was compiled by Elizabeth Newman Hutchinson and published in Salt Lake City, Utah, in 1970. *Descendants of John and Elizabeth Sansom* [also Sampson] was compiled by Van Edwin Turner and published in North Ridgeville, Ohio, in 1982.

SAMS

Ranking: 2192 **S.S. Count:** 20,915
Origin: English. Transformation of Samuel.
Genealogies: *The Sams Family of Virginia* was compiled by Crawford F. Sams and published in Atherton, California, in 1981. *The Sams Family* was compiled by Elizabeth Manuel and published in Evansville, Indiana, in 1974.

SAMSON (ALSO SAMSONOV, SAMSONOVICH, SAMSONOVITZ)

Ranking: 3607 **S.S. Count:** 12,513
Origin: Samson—Dutch, English, Flemish, French, German, Jewish; Samsonov, Samsonovich, Samsonovitz—Jewish. Samson: derived from the biblical name Samson, which was derived from the Hebrew name Shimshon, which was derived from the word "shemesh," meaning sun. Samsonov, Samsonovich, Samsonovitz: transformations of Samson.
Genealogies: None known.

SAMUEL (ALSO SAMUELLI, SAMUELS, SAMUELSEN, SAMUELSON)

Ranking: 668 **S.S. Count:** 62,757
Origin: Samuelsen—Danish, Norwegian; Samuel—English, French, German, Jewish; Samuels, Samuelson—English; Samuelli—Italian. Samuelsen: cognate to Samuel. Samuel: derived from the biblical masculine first name Samuel, which was derived from the Hebrew name Shemuel, meaning "name of God" (H&H). Samuels, Samuelson, Samuelli: transformations of and cognates to Samuel.
Genealogies: *Samuels Searcher* was published in Anchorage, Alaska.

SANBORN (S.S. Abbreviation: Sanbor)

Ranking: 3170 **S.S. Count:** 14,325
Origin: English. Uncertain etymology. The name was given to those from Sambourn, a place in Warwickshire, England.
Famous Sanborns: FRANKLIN BENJAMIN SANBORN (1831–1917) of New Hampshire was a journalist. He is best remembered as a writer of biographies or memoirs of Henry David Thoreau, John Brown, and Ralph Waldo Emerson. He also co-founded the Concord School of Phi-

losophy. JAMES S. SANBORN (1835–1903) of Maine was the founder of Chase & Sanborn, today known as a brand of coffee.

Genealogies: *Supplement to Genealogy of the Sanborn Family* was compiled by Nathan Sanborn and published in Bath, Maine, in 1982. *The English Ancestry of the American Sanborns* was compiled by Victor Channing Sanborn and published in 1916.

SANCHES, SANCHEZ (S.S. Abbreviation: Sanche)

Ranking: 78 S.S. Count: 330,754
Origin: Portuguese, Spanish. Derived from the medieval first name Sancho, which is of uncertain etymology.
Genealogies: None known.

SANDBERG (S.S. Abbreviation: Sandbe)

Ranking: 3494 S.S. Count: 12,896
Origin: Jewish, Swedish. The name means sand hill and was taken ornamentally.
Genealogies: None known.

SANDER (ALSO SANDERING, SANDERMAN, SANDERS, SANDERSON)

Ranking: 71 S.S. Count: 355,962
Origin: Sander—English, German, Scottish; Sanderman, Sanders, Sanderson—English; Sandering—German. Sander: derived from the medieval first name Sander, which is a transformation of Alexander. Sandering, Sanderman, Sanders, Sanderson: transformations of Sander.
Famous **Bearers:** HARLAND (COLONEL) SANDERS (1890–1980) of Indiana was the owner of Sanders' Café in Corbin, Kentucky, where his speciality was fried chicken. He expanded and founded the Colonel Sanders Kentucky Fried Chicken Corporation.
Genealogies: *Ancestors and Descendants of Henry Simeon Saunders (also Sanders)* was compiled by R. S. Sanders and published in McAllen, Texas, in 1983. *Sanders Saga* was compiled by Catherine S. McConnell and published in 1972. *James & Alvin Sanders, Livestock Journalists of the Midwest* was compiled by Richard Bryan Helmer and published in Bryn Mawr, Pennsylvania, in 1985.

SANDLIN (S.S. Abbreviation: Sandli)

Ranking: 3892 S.S. Count: 11,589
Origin: Irish?, Scottish. Derived from the Celtic word "cellt," meaning flintstone, which was used to make war clubs.
Genealogies: *The Sandlin Clan* was compiled by Dale S. Sandlin and published in Jones Creek, Texas, in 1970.

SANDOVAL, SANDOVIC (S.S. Abbreviation: Sandov)

Ranking: 662 S.S. Count: 63,337

Origin: Sandovic—Croatian; Sandoval—Spanish. Sandovic: cognate to Sander. Sandoval: derived from the Latin words "saltus" and "novālis," meaning wood and land that was newly cleared. The name was given to those from Sandoval, a place in Burgos, Spain.
Genealogies: None known.

SANDS

Ranking: 1729 S.S. Count: 25,967
Origin: English. Derived from the Middle English word "sand," meaning sand. The name was given to those who lived in a sandy area.
Genealogies: *Osbourne and Sands* was compiled by Elizabeth Jane Osbourne Sands and published in Port Charlotte, Florida, in 1986.

SANFORD (S.S. Abbreviation: Sanfor)

Ranking: 826 S.S. Count: 51,401
Origin: English. Derived from the Old English words "sand" and "ford," meaning sand and a shallow place in a river. The name was given to those from Sandford, the name of places in England.
Famous **Sanfords:** EDWARD TERRY SANFORD (1865–1930) of Tennessee was a lawyer and an associate justice of the U.S. Supreme Court.
Genealogies: *Indians in our Trees* [Sanford family] was compiled by Mary Lokken and published in San Antonio, Texas, in 1989. *President John Sanford of Boston, Massachusetts and Portsmouth, Rhode Island, 1605–1965* was compiled by Jack Minard Sanford and published in Rutland, Vermont, in 1966. *The Sandford/Sanford Families of Long Island* was compiled by Grover Merle Sanford and published in Baltimore, Maryland, in 1975.

SANSON (ALSO SANSONE, SANSONETTI, SANSONI)

Ranking: 4543 S.S. Count: 9833
Origin: Sanson—French; Sansone, Sansonetti, Sansoni—Italian. Transformations of and cognates to Samson.
Genealogies: *Legacy of Death* [Sanson family] was compiled by Barbara Levy and published in Englewood Cliffs, New Jersey, in 1973.

SANTANA (S.S. Abbreviation: Santan)

Ranking: 743 S.S. Count: 57,031
Origin: Catalan, Portuguese, Spanish. Derived from the name Ana. The name was given to those from places in Spain and Portugal whose churches were dedicated to St. Anne.
Genealogies: None known.

SANTIAGO (S.S. Abbreviation: Santia)

Ranking: 213 S.S. Count: 166,618
Origin: Portuguese, Spanish. Derived from the name

Jaime. The name was given to those from places in Spain and Portugal whose churches were dedicated to St. James.
Genealogies: None known.

SANTILLI, SANTILLO (S.S. Abbreviation: Santil)

Ranking: 4183 **S.S. Count:** 10,802
Origin: Italian. Derived from the Latin word "sanctus," meaning holy. The name was given to those who were pious.
Genealogies: None known.

SANTORELLI, SANTORI, SANTORIELLO, SANTORINI, SANTORO (S.S. Abbreviation: Santor)

Ranking: 2237 **S.S. Count:** 20,488
Origin: Italian. Derived from the Italian word "santoro," which was derived from the Latin phrase "sanctorum (omnium dies festus)" (H&H), meaning All Saints' Day. The name was given to those born on All Saints' Day.
Genealogies: None known.

SANTOS

Ranking: 412 **S.S. Count:** 95,732
Origin: Portuguese, Spanish. Cognate to Santilli.
Genealogies: None known.

SAPP

Ranking: 1552 **S.S. Count:** 28,683
Origin: German. Derived from the first name Sabbe, a shortened version of names beginning with Sache, meaning "legal action" (ES).
Genealogies: *Early Families of Blount County, Alabama* [also Sapp] was compiled by Carolina Nigg and published in Cullman, Alabama, in 1982.

SARGENT, SARGENTSON (S.S. Abbreviation: Sargen)

Ranking: 1126 **S.S. Count:** 39,094
Origin: Sargent—French; Sargentson—English. Derived from the Middle English and Old French word "sergent," meaning servant. The names were given to those who worked as servants.
Famous **Sargents:** WINTHROP SARGENT (1753–1820) of Massachusetts was a Revolutionary War soldier, one of the founders of Marietta, Ohio, and the first governor of the Mississippi territory. CHARLES SPRAGUE SARGENT (1841–1927) of Massachusetts was a dendrologist and the first director of the Arnold Arboretum. He also edited books about the trees of North America. JOHN SINGER SARGENT (1865–1925) was born in Italy to American parents. He was an artist who spent much of his time in Paris and London. He was responsible for causing quite a scandal by titling a portrait of Madame Gautreau *Madame X.* His

murals can be seen as the murals at the Boston Public Library and the Boston Museum of Fine Arts.
Genealogies: *The Story of Captain Redford Webster Sargent, 1844–1901* was compiled by Cecilia Vennard Sargent and published in Camden, Maine, in 1971. *Descendants of William Sargent (1624–1716) of England & Gloucester, MA* was compiled by Clifton R. Sargent and published in Yarmouth, Maine, in 1980.

SARVER

Ranking: 4860 **S.S. Count:** 9209
Origin: English, French. Derived from the Old French word "serveir," meaning servant.
Genealogies: None known.

SASSER

Ranking: 4588 **S.S. Count:** 9745
Origin: English, German. Uncertain etymology. English: possibly derived from the Old English word "sasse," meaning a lock in a river. German: the name was possibly given to those who came from places in Germany with similar-sounding names.
Genealogies: None known.

SATTERFIELD, SATTERLEY, SATTERTHWAITE, SATTERWHITE (S.S. Abbreviation: Satter)

Ranking: 1166 **S.S. Count:** 37,531
Origin: English. Satterfield: derived from an uncertain first component and the Old English word "feld," meaning field. 1) the name was given to those who lived near a hill pasture. 2) the name was given to those who lived in a field where robbers convened. 3) the name was given to those who lived in a hut in an open area, remote from a settlement. Satterley: the name means robber's clearing and was given to those from Satterleigh, a place in Devonshire, England. Satterthwaite, Satterwhite: derived from the Old English word "sætr," meaning shepherd's hut, and the Old Norse word "þveit," meaning pasture. The name was given to those from Satterthwaite, a place in England.
Genealogies: *Satterlee-ley-ly & Allied Families* was compiled by Goldie Satterlee Moffatt and published in Perris, California, in 1970.

SAUCED

Ranking: 2345 **S.S. Count:** 19,345
Origin: English? Uncertain etymology. The name may have been given to those who worked preparing sauces.
Genealogies: None known.

SAUER

Ranking: 2164 **S.S. Count:** 21,224
Origin: German, Jewish. Derived from the German word

"sauer," meaning sour. The name was given to those who were ill tempered.

Famous **Sauers:** CARL ORTWIN SAUER (1889–1975) of Missouri was a geographer and an expert on deserts, the tropics, crops of the Americas, and Native Americans.

Genealogies: None known.

SAUL

Ranking: 4690 **S.S. Count:** 9542

Origin: English, French, German, Italian. Derived from the first name Saul, which was derived from the Hebrew name Shaul, meaning "asked-for (child)" (H&H) and referring to the biblical figure Saul.

Genealogies: *A Tale of Two Families: Inez Gibbs, Twig Sauls (also Saul), whose ancestors were in Florida even when it was a Spanish territory* was compiled by Byron T. Sauls and published in St. Petersburg, Florida, in 1976.

SAUNDER, SAUNDERS, SAUNDERSON (S.S. Abbreviation: Saunde)

Ranking: 384 **S.S. Count:** 101,294

Origin: English, Scottish. Transformations of Sander.

Genealogies: *Ancestors and Descendants of Henry Simeon Saunders* was compiled by R. S. Sanders and published in McAllen, Texas, in 1983. *James & Alvin Sanders, Livestock Journalists of the Midwest* [also Saunders] was compiled by Richard Bryan Helmer and published in Bryn Mawr, Pennsylvania, in 1985. *Loomis Legacies and a Saga of Sanders* [also Saunders] was compiled by Lorell Loomis and published in Ferriday, Louisiana, in 1989.

SAVAGE

Ranking: 611 **S.S. Count:** 68,567

Origin: English. Derived from the Middle English word "salvage," meaning wild. The name was given to those who were unrefined or crude.

Famous **Savages:** EDWARD SAVAGE (1761–1817) of Massachusetts was a portrait painter who is best remembered for his paintings of George and Martha Washington. JAMES SAVAGE (1784–1873) of Massachusetts was involved in the incorporation of one of the first savings banks in the colonies, was the founder of the Boston Athenaeum, and published *Genealogical Dictionary of the First Settlers of New England* (1860–1862). THOMAS STAUGHTON SAVAGE (1804–1880) of Connecticut was the first Episcopal missionary sent to Africa. He worked in Liberia. Upon his return to the United States, he wrote about gorillas that were unknown to the civilized world, the social habits of chimpanzees, and the termites of Africa. ARTHUR WILLIAM SAVAGE (1857–1938) of Jamaica was the founder of the Savage Arms Co. of New York. He also invented a dirigible torpedo. AUGUSTA CHRISTINE SAVAGE (1892–1962) of Green Cove Springs, Florida, was a black sculptor who excelled in her field despite the difficulties created by poverty and racism.

Genealogies: *America's First Family, the Savages of Virginia* was compiled by August Burghard and published in Philadelphia, Pennsylvania, in 1974. *Savage-Stillman-Rogers-Lindsey-Dever and Related Families with Magna Carta and Royal Lines* was compiled by Myrtle Savage Rhoades and published in East Orange, New Jersey, in 1971. *We Are the Savages: descendants of Ensign Thomas Savage of Jamestown* was compiled by Jacob Cochran Savage and published in Wurtland, Kentucky, in 1974.

SAVOY

Ranking: 4954 **S.S. Count:** 9047

Origin: French. The name means Savoie, the name of a region of France, and was given to those from this area.

Genealogies: *Savoy Heritage, 1621 to the Present* was compiled by Louis Germain Savoy and published in Smithtown, New York, in 1983.

SAWYER (ALSO SAWYERS)

Ranking: 537 **S.S. Count:** 75,531

Origin: English. Derived from the Middle English word "saghier," meaning those who worked sawing wood. The name was given to those who were lumberjacks.

Famous **Bearers:** LEMUEL SAWYER (1777–1852) of North Carolina was a member of Congress from North Carolina. SYLVANUS SAWYER (1822–1895) of Massachusetts was an inventor of machinery. One particular machine split rattan. WALTER HOWARD SAWYER (1867–1923) of Connecticut was a hydraulic and sanitary engineer. He invented different types of machinery to help in this field. WILBUR AUGUSTUS SAWYER (1879–1951) of Wisconsin was responsible, as the director of the West African Yellow Fever Commission, for the isolation of the yellow-fever virus. RUTH SAWYER (1880–1970) of Massachusetts was a writer of children's stories.

Genealogies: *Four Generations of the Descendants of William Sawyer of Newbury, Massachusetts, in 1644* was compiled by Noreen C. Pramberg and published in Newburyport, Massachusetts, in 1992. *A Genealogical Dictionary of the Early Sawyer Families of New England, ca 1632–1900* was compiled by Fred E. Sawyer and published in American Falls, Idaho, in 1983.

SAXON

Ranking: 4440 **S.S. Count:** 10,094

Origin: English. 1) derived from the medieval first name Saxon, which was originally given to those from Saxony, a region of Germany. 2) transformation of Saxton, meaning Saxons.

Genealogies: None known.

SAXTON

Ranking: 3643 S.S. Count: 12,376

Origin: English. 1) transformation of sexton. 2) derived from the Old English words "seuxe" and "tūn," meaning Saxons and settlement.

Famous **Saxtons**: JOSEPH SAXTON (1799–1873) of Pennsylvania was an inventor of equipment used by the U.S. Mint in the weighing of currency. He also invented a thermometer used in the deep sea and other sea-related instruments. EUGENE FRANCIS SAXTON (1884–1943) of Maryland was an editor at Harper & Brothers.

Genealogies: None known.

SAYERS

Ranking: 4206 S.S. Count: 10,740

Origin: English. 1) derived from the Middle English word "say," meaning a kind of cloth. The name was given to those who made or sold a kind of cloth called say. 2) derived from the Middle English word "assayer," which was derived from the word "assay," meaning test or trial. The name was given to those who tasted food or to those who assayed or analyzed metals. 3) derived from the Middle English word "say(en)," meaning to say. The name was given to those who recited as a profession. 4) derived from the Middle English word "saghier," meaning those who worked sawing wood. The name was given to those who were lumberjacks. 5) derived from the Middle English first name Saher, which is of uncertain etymology.

Genealogies: None known.

SAYLOR

Ranking: 1910 S.S. Count: 23,686

Origin: English. Derived from the Old French word "sailleor," meaning an acrobat. The name was given to those who were acrobats or dancers.

Genealogies: *Saylor-Carter and Moulden and Kindred Families* was compiled by Elizabeth Saylor Moore and published in Knoxville, Tennessee, in 1973. *Saylor Family Footprints: being the family and descendants of Solomon & Sarah Saylor of Harlan County, Kentucky* was compiled by Holly Fee and published in Harlan, Kentucky, in 1987.

SAYRE

Ranking: 3927 S.S. Count: 11,491

Origin: English, Welsh. English: transformation of Sayer. Welsh: transformation of the Welsh name Sayer, which was derived from the Welsh word "saer," meaning carpenter. The name was given to carpenters or wrights.

Famous **Sayres**: LEWIS ALBERT SAYRE (1820–1880) of New Jersey was a surgeon and the organizer of Bellevue Hospital Medical College. He was a pioneer in the fields

of orthopedic surgery and disorders having to do with curvature of the spine. His son, REGINALD HALL SAYRE (1859–1929) of New York City, followed in his father's footsteps and served as a surgeon and lecturer at Bellevue Hospital Medical College. ROBERT HEYSHAM SAYRE (1824–1907) of Pennsylvania was a civil engineer involved in the development of the Lehigh Valley Railroad system.

Genealogies: *Brown and Sayre Ancestry: three centuries in Northern New Jersey* was compiled by Mortimer Freeman Sayre and published in Columbus, Ohio, in 1971.

SCALES

Ranking: 2426 S.S. Count: 18,688

Origin: English. Derived from the Middle English word "scale," meaning shed. The name was given to those who lived in a primitive hut or shed or to those from places called Scales in England.

Genealogies: None known.

SCANLON (S.S. Abbreviation: Scanlo)

Ranking: 2556 S.S. Count: 17,776

Origin: Irish. Derived from the Gaelic name Ó Scannail, which was derived from the first name Scannal, meaning controversy or rivalry.

Genealogies: None known.

SCARBOROUGH (S.S. Abbreviation: Scarbo)

Ranking: 2205 S.S. Count: 20,826

Origin: English. Derived from the Old Norse name Skarði and the Old Norse word "borg," meaning town. The name was given to those from Scarborough, the name of a place in North Yorkshire, England.

Famous **Scarboroughs**: WILLIAM SAUNDERS SCARBOROUGH (1852?–1926) of Georgia was born a slave, was graduated from college, and taught the classics at Wilberforce University in Ohio. LEE RUTLAND SCARBOROUGH (1870–1945) of Louisiana was a Baptist minister and president of Southwestern Baptist Theological Seminary. DOROTHY SCARBOROUGH (1878–1935) of Texas was an authority on folklore.

Genealogies: *Jacob Miller and Jane Scarborough Kith 'n' Kin'* was compiled by Flavil R. Miller and published in Newcomerstown, Ohio, in 1971. *Some Quaker Families: Scarborough/Haworth* was compiled by Roger S. Boone and published in Wichita, Kansas, in 1991.

SCARBRO, SCARBROUGH (S.S. Abbreviation: Scarbr)

Ranking: 3452 S.S. Count: 13,073

Origin: English. Transformations of Scarborough.

Famous **Bearers**: WILLIAM SCARBROUGH (1776–1838)

of South Carolina was a merchant and planter in Savannah, Georgia. He was one of the backers of the transatlantic ship the *Savannah*. It traveled to Europe and back in 1819.

Genealogies: None known.

SCHACHTER (S.S. Abbreviation: Schach)

Ranking: 3870 S.S. Count: 11,650

Origin: Jewish. Derived from the Hebrew word "shachat," meaning to slaughter. The name was given to those who were ritual slaughterers.

Genealogies: None known.

SCHAEFER (S.S. Abbreviation: Schaef)

Ranking: 479 S.S. Count: 84,429

Origin: German. Transformation of Schafer, meaning shepherd.

Genealogies: None known.

SCHAFER (S.S. Abbreviation: Schafe)

Ranking: 1332 S.S. Count: 33,216

Origin: German, Jewish. German: derived from the German word "schaf," meaning sheep. The name was given to shepherds. Jewish: uncertain etymology. Possibly the name refers to the 23rd Psalm, "The Lord is my Shepherd" (H&H); or, possibly, to King David, who was a shepherd.

Genealogies: None known.

SCHAFFER, SCHAFFERLIN, SCHAFFNER (S.S. Abbreviation: Schaff)

Ranking: 1022 S.S. Count: 42,839

Origin: Schafferlin, Schaffner—German; Schaffer—German, Jewish. Schaffer—German: derived from the German word "schaffen," meaning to manage. The name was given to stewards or bailiffs. Schaffer—Jewish: transformation of the Jewish name Schafer. Schaffler: derived from the German word "schäffl," meaning cooper. The name was given to coopers. Schafferlin, Schaffner: transformations of Schaffer, meaning to manage.

Genealogies: None known.

SCHALL (ALSO SCHALLER)

Ranking: 2578 S.S. Count: 17,644

Origin: German. Uncertain etymology. 1) the name means a garrulous person. 2) the name was given to those who lived near a prominent or important stone slab. 3) the name was given to those who were servants.

Famous **Bearers**: THOMAS DAVID SCHALL (1877–1935) of Michigan was a lawyer who became a member of Congress, then a U.S. senator. He overcame the problems associated with his blindness with the help of his wife.

Genealogies: *Schaller and Allied Families from Monroe County, Wisconsin* was compiled by Alice Schaller and published in Cashton, Wisconsin, in 1983.

SCHARF (ALSO SCHARFE, SCHARFF, SCHARFHERZ, SCHARFMAN)

Ranking: 3693 S.S. Count: 12,230

Origin: Scharfe, Scharff—German; Scharf—German, Jewish; Scharfherz, Scharfman—Jewish. Cognates to Sharp.

Genealogies: None known.

SCHATZ (ALSO SCHATZBERG, SCHATZER, SCHATZL, SCHATZLER)

Ranking: 3635 S.S. Count: 12,395

Origin: Schatzer, Schatzler, Schatzl—German; Schatz—German, Jewish; Schatzberg—Jewish. Schatz (German): derived from the German word "schatz," meaning treasure. The name was given to those who were employed as treasurers. Schatz (Jewish): derived from the Hebrew phrase "sheliach-tsibur," meaning "emissary of the congregation" (H&H), referring to the cantor. Schatzer, Schatzler, Schatzl: transformations of Schatz, meaning treasurer. Schatzberg: elaboration of the Jewish surname Schatz, meaning treasure hill. The name was taken ornamentally.

Genealogies: *The Schaetz Family in the Netherlands (1400–1652) and in America (1652–1983)* [also Schatz] was compiled by John T. Palmer and published in Hancock, Michigan, in 1983.

SCHAUBER (S.S. Abbreviation: Schaub)

Ranking: 4237 S.S. Count: 10,641

Origin: German. Derived from the Middle High German word "schouwen," meaning to inspect. The name was given to official inspectors.

Genealogies: None known.

SCHEEL (ALSO SCHEELE)

Ranking: 4947 S.S. Count: 9057

Origin: German. Transformation of Schiller.

Genealogies: *Memories that Never Fade Away* [Scheeler family] was compiled by Aman Scheeler and published in Glen Ellyn, Illinois, in 1983.

SCHEERER (S.S. Abbreviation: Scheer)

Ranking: 4246 S.S. Count: 10,603

Origin: German. Cognate to Shearer.

Genealogies: None known.

SCHEFF (ALSO SCHEFFEL, SCHEFFER, SCHEFFERS, SCHEFFLER)

Ranking: 3636 S.S. Count: 12,391

Origin: Scheff, Scheffel, Scheffers, Scheffler—German; Scheffer—Jewish. Scheff: derived from the Middle Low Ger-

man word "schief," meaning crooked. The name was given to those with a deformity. Scheffel, Scheffler: transformations of Schaffler. Scheffers: transformation of Schaffer. Scheffer: transformation of Schafer.

Genealogies: None known.

SCHEIB (ALSO SCHEIBE, SCHEIBEL, SCHEIBLE)

Ranking: 4197 **S.S. Count:** 10,761

Origin: German. Uncertain etymology. 1) the names were given to those who lived near the sign of a straw bundle. 2) the names were given to those who lived on a round field. 3) the names were given to those who lived near a round structure or object.

Genealogies: None known.

SCHEIDER, SCHEIDLER, SCHEIDT (S.S. Abbreviation: Scheid)

Ranking: 2684 **S.S. Count:** 17,001

Origin: German. Derived from the Middle High German word "scheide," meaning boundary. The names were given to those who lived near a boundary or to those from any of several places named with "scheide."

Genealogies: None known.

SCHELL (ALSO SCHELLER, SCHELLIG, SCHELLINCK, SCHELLING)

Ranking: 1293 **S.S. Count:** 34,276

Origin: Schellinck—Dutch; Schell, Schellig, Schelling—German; Scheller—German, Jewish. Schellinck, Schelling: cognates to and transformations of Schilling. Schell, Schellig, Scheller: derived from the Middle High German word "schel," meaning noisy. The names were given to those who were unruly.

Famous Bearers: AUGUSTUS SCHELL (1812–1884) of New York was a politician and businessman in the railroad and banking business. FELIX EMANUEL SCHELLING (1858–1945) of Indiana was an editor of plays and the writer of books that dealt with English literature. He also taught at the University of Pennsylvania. ERNEST HENRY SCHELLING (1876–1939) of New Jersey was a conductor and composer specializing in the piano.

Genealogies: None known.

SCHENCK, SCHENCKE (S.S. Abbreviation: Schenc)

Ranking: 4542 **S.S. Count:** 9837

Origin: German. Transformations of Schenk.

Famous Bearers: ROBERT CUMMING SCHENCK (1809–1890) of Ohio was a member of Congress from Ohio and a U.S. minister to Brazil. NICHOLAS MICHAEL SCHENCK (1881–1969) of Russia was one of the founders of Palisades Amusement Park, Fort Lee, New Jersey.

Genealogies: None known.

SCHENK (ALSO SCHENKE)

Ranking: 2612 **S.S. Count:** 17,387

Origin: German. Derived from the Old High German word "scenken," meaning to pour out or to serve. The names were given to those who served wine or to cup bearers.

Genealogies: None known.

SCHERER (S.S. Abbreviation: Schere)

Ranking: 2411 **S.S. Count:** 18,793

Origin: German. Cognate to Shearer.

Genealogies: None known.

SCHICK (ALSO SCHICKE, SCHICKEL, SCHICKELE, SCHICKER)

Ranking: 3614 **S.S. Count:** 12,498

Origin: Schicke, Schickel, Schickele, Schicker—German; Schick—German, Jewish. Schicke, Schickel, Schickele, Schicker: transformations of Schick. Schick (German): derived from the German word "schick," meaning polished and courteous. The name was given to those who were refined or who had polished manners. Schick (Jewish): uncertain etymology.

Famous Bearers: BELA SCHICK (1877–1967) of Hungary was a physician who discovered the test for diphtheria known as the Schick test.

Genealogies: None known.

SCHIFF (ALSO SCHIFFER, SCHIFFMAN, SCHIFFMANN)

Ranking: 2546 **S.S. Count:** 17,847

Origin: Schiff, Schiffer—German; Schiffmann—German, Jewish; Schiffman—Jewish. Cognates to Shipman, meaning mariner.

Famous Bearers: JACOB HENRY SCHIFF (1847–1920) of Germany was a banker and philanthropist. He made his money in banking and speculation and gave it away to hospitals, settlement houses, museums, the Red Cross, and universities.

Genealogies: None known.

SCHILLER, SCHILLING, SCHILLOGA, SCHILLOK (S.S. Abbreviation: Schill)

Ranking: 880 **S.S. Count:** 49,173

Origin: Schilling, Schilloga, Schillok—German; Schiller—German, Jewish. Schilling, Schilloga, Schillok: derived from the German word "schilling," meaning a coin called a schilling. Schiller (German): derived from the Middle High German word "schilhen," meaning to squint. The name was given to those with a squint. Schiller (Jewish): transformation of Schuler.

Genealogies: *The Schiller-Vallier and Related Families* was compiled by Katherine Schiller Mulanax and published in Manhattan, Kansas, in 1974.

SCHINDEL, SCHINDELMAN, SCHINDL, SCHINDLER (S.S. Abbreviation: Schind)

Ranking: 2565 S.S. Count: 17,718

Origin: Schindel, Schindl—German; Schindler—German, Jewish; Schindelman—Jewish. Derived from the Middle English word "schingle," meaning shingle. The names were given to those who shingled roofs.

Famous **Bearers:** KURT SCHINDLER (1882–1935) of Germany was a musician and composer and the organizer of the MacDowell Chorus (1909). RUDOLPH MICHAEL SCHINDLER (1887–1953) of Austria moved to California and worked as an architect. He is best remembered for his homes designed of wood and stucco with a central theme of outdoor living.

Genealogies: *The Descendants of Christian Sexauer and Caroline Schindler of Baden, Germany, 1806– 1980* was compiled by Yvonne Spahr Erickson and published in Fair Oaks, California, in 1982. *Genealogy of Georg Friedrich & Maria Barbara Hamm Schindel* was compiled by William Richard Shindle and published in Baltimore, Maryland, in 1985.

SCHLEGEL, SCHLEGL (S.S. Abbreviation: Schleg)

Ranking: 4051 S.S. Count: 11,161

Origin: German. Derived from the Middle High German word "slegel," meaning sledgehammer. The names were given to those who were employed as smiths or to those who were powerful.

Genealogies: *John Christian Schlegel of Berks County, Pennsylvania and Descendants* was compiled by Mary Irene Savage and published in Baltimore, Maryland, in 1991. *Linse-Schlegel/Schlagel: from Germany with love to— Ontario, Wisconsin, South Dakota, Washington* was compiled by Bette Schlagel Rogers and published in Yakima, Washington, in 1984.

SCHLEICH, SCHLEICHER, SCHLEIER, SCHLEIFER, SCHLEIN (S.S. Abbreviation: Schlei)

Ranking: 2695 S.S. Count: 16,883

Origin: Schleich, Schleicher, Schleier—German; Schleifer—German, Jewish; Schlein—Jewish. Schleich, Schleicher: derived from the German word "schleichen," meaning to creep soundlessly. The name was given to those who were secretive or covert. Schleier: derived from the German word "schleier," meaning veil. The name was given to those who made or sold veils. Schleifer (German): derived from the German word "schleifen," meaning to grind or polish. The name was given to those who polished armor and swords or to

grinders of diamonds and knives. Schleifer (German, Jewish): Uncertain etymology. Probably the same derivation as German definition. The name was given to those from Schleife, a place in Germany. Schlein: derived from the Yiddish word "shlayn," meaning tench, a type of fish. The name was given to those who fished tenches or it was taken ornamentally.

Genealogies: *A History and Genealogy of Hans Ulric Schleich of Wiesloch, Germany and South Carolina* was compiled by Yancey J. Dickert and published in Midland, Michigan, in 1988.

SCHLESINGER, SCHLESSINGER (S.S. Abbreviation: Schles)

Ranking: 4519 S.S. Count: 9910

Origin: Schlessinger—German; Schlesinger—Jewish. Derived from the Germanic tribal name Silingae. The names were given to those from Silesia, a region of Germany.

Famous **Bearers:** FRANK SCHLESINGER (1871–1943) of New York was an astronomer who worked with the Yerkes Observatory, as director of the Allegheny Observatory at the University of Pittsburgh, and as director of the Yale University observatory. He died shortly after retirement from Yale at his home in Old Lyme, Connecticut. BENJAMIN SCHLESINGER (1876– 1932) of Lithuania was the driving force behind the Jewish labor movement and was the president of the International Ladies Garment Workers Union.

Genealogies: None known.

SCHLICH, SCHLICHT, SCHLICHTER, SCHLICK, SCHLICKMANN (S.S. Abbreviation: Schlic)

Ranking: 3945 S.S. Count: 11,452

Origin: Schlich, Schlicht, Schlichter, Schlickmann—German; Schlick—German, Jewish. Schlicht, Schlichter: 1) derived from the Old High German word "sleht," meaning flat. The name was given to those from Schlect, the name of several places in Germany. 2) derived from the Middle High German word "sleht," meaning direct. The name was given to those who were candid or direct. Schlich, Schlickmann: transformations of Schlick, meaning bog. Schlick (German): 1) derived from the Middle Low German word "slik," meaning bog. The name was given to those who lived in a boggy area. 2) derived from the Middle High German word "slicken," meaning to swallow greedily. The name was given to gluttons. Schlick (Jewish): uncertain etymology. Possibly derived from the German word "schlick," meaning mud, and given pejoratively to Jewish persons by someone in the government.

Genealogies: None known.

SCHLOSS, SCHLOSSBERG, SCHLOSSER, SCHLOSSHAUER, SCHLOSSMANN (S.S. Abbreviation: Schlos)

Ranking: 2761 S.S. Count: 16,500

Origin: Schlosser, Schlosshauer, Schlossmann—German; Schloss—German, Jewish; Schlossberg—Jewish. Schlosser, Schlossmann: transformations of Schloss. Schlosshauer: transformation of Schloss, meaning castle. Schloss (German): 1) derived from the German word "schloss," meaning castle. The name was given to those who lived near or who worked at a castle. 2) derived from the German word "schloss," meaning lock. The name was given to locksmiths. Schloss (Jewish): uncertain etymology. Possibly a transformation of Schloss, meaning lock. Schlossberg: derived from the German words "schloss" and "berg," meaning castle and hill. The name was given to those from Schlossberg, the name of several places in Germany with castles situated on hills.

Genealogies: None known.

SCHMAL, SCHMALT, SCHMALZ, SCHMALZER, SCHMALZL (S.S. Abbreviation: Schmal)

Ranking: 3443 **S.S. Count:** 13,106

Origin: Schmal, Schmalt, Schmalzl—German; Schmalz—German, Jewish; Schmalzer—Jewish. Schmal: cognate to Small. Schmalt, Schmalzl: transformations of Schmalz. Schmalz (German): derived from the German word "schmalz," meaning fat or grease. The name was given to chandlers. Schmalz (Jewish): uncertain etymology. Possibly derived from the Yiddish word "shmalts," meaning animal fat. Schmalzer: transformation of Schmalz.

Genealogies: None known.

SCHMELING (S.S. Abbreviation: Schmel)

Ranking: 3907 **S.S. Count:** 11,541

Origin: German. Cognate to Small.

Genealogies: None known.

SCHMID (ALSO SCHMIDT)

Ranking: 125 **S.S. Count:** 234,234

Origin: German, Jewish. Cognates to Smith.

Famous Bearers: FRIEDRICH AUGUST SCHMIDT (1837–1928) of Germany came to Missouri as a child. He was a Lutheran minister who taught theology in several seminaries. ARTHUR PAUL SCHMIDT (1846–1921) of Germany founded a music publishing firm in Boston. He was known for publishing the works of composers who had not yet achieved success. CARL LOUIS AUGUST SCHMIDT (1885–1946) of South Dakota was a biochemist who did research with bile, proteins, and amino acids and used the data in immunology research.

Genealogies: *Descendants of John Schmidt and Magdalena Kopfenstein was compiled by Bertha Louise Schmidt Krause and published in Ridgefield, Washington, in 1989. Johan (John) Schmidt and Six Generations of his Descendants, 1850 to 1987 was compiled by Damon Purinton*

Collins and published in Modesto, California, in 1987. *Sixteen Maryland Families* [also Schmidt] *was compiled by Richard Gary Schmidt and published in Baltimore, Maryland, in 1981.*

SCHMIED, SCHMIEDEL, SCHMIEDER, SCHMIEDLE (S.S. Abbreviation: Schmie)

Ranking: 4518 **S.S. Count:** 9911

Origin: Schmied, Schmiedel, Schmiedle—German; Schmieder—German, Jewish. Schmied: cognate to Smythe, meaning to forge. Schmiedel, Schmiedle: cognates to Smith. Schmieder (German): cognate to Smythe, meaning to forge. Schmieder (Jewish): cognate to Smith.

Genealogies: None known.

SCHMITT, SCHMITZ (S.S. Abbreviation: Schmit)

Ranking: 449 **S.S. Count:** 88,731

Origin: German. Cognates to Smith.

Genealogies: *Immigration to St. Joseph County, Indiana* [Schmitt family] *was compiled by Howard John Schmitt and published in Benton Harbor, Michigan, in 1983. Family Tree: Schmitz, Burbach, and related families was compiled by Helen Schmitz Fischels and published in Independence, Iowa, in 1974.*

SCHNEIDER, SCHNEIDERMAN, SCHNEIDERMANN, SCHNEIDERS, SCHNEIDMAN (S.S. Abbreviation: Schnei)

Ranking: 226 **S.S. Count:** 155,642

Origin: Schneidermann, Schneiders—German; Schneider—German, Jewish; Schneiderman, Schneidman—Jewish. Derived from the German word "schneider" or the Yiddish word "shnayder," both meaning tailor. The names were given to tailors.

Famous Bearers: THEODORE SCHNEIDER (1703–1764) of Germany was a Roman Catholic priest who came to Philadelphia as a missionary to the German people. BENJAMIN SCHNEIDER (1807–1877) of Pennsylvania was a missionary to Turkey. GEORGE SCHNEIDER (1823–1905) of Bavaria was a journalist, banker, and supporter of Abraham Lincoln. ALBERT SCHNEIDER (1863–1928) of Illinois was a bacteriologist and a professor at several universities. HERMAN SCHNEIDER (1872–1939) of Pennsylvania was an engineer who taught at the university level. He was involved in developing the "cooperative system" of technological education in Cincinnati, which gave students a mix of theoretical and shop experience.

Genealogies: *Notes on the Ancestors and Descendants of Robert Isaac Schneider, Born 14 May 1903, Bethel, Berks Co., Pa. was compiled by Schuyler C. Brossman and published in Reading, Pennsylvania, in 1974. Remember: a book to honor the family I never knew* [also Schneiderman] *was* compiled by Isidore C. Myers and published in Newport Beach, California, in 1992.

SCHNELL, SCHNELLER, SCHNELLI, SCHNELLMANN (S.S. Abbreviation: Schnel)

Ranking: 3060 S.S. Count: 14,825

Origin: Schnell, Schnelli, Schnellmann—German; Schneller—Jewish. Schnelli: cognate to Snow. Schnell, Schnellmann, Schneller: cognates to Snell.

Famous **Bearers:** GEORGE OTTO SCHNELLER (1843–1895) of Germany was an inventor of a machine that made and inserted brass corset eyelets.

Genealogies: None known.

SCHOEN (ALSO SCHOENBACH, SCHOENBAUM, SCHOENBERG, SCHOENFELD)

Ranking: 704 S.S. Count: 60,008

Origin: Schoen—Dutch, Jewish; Schoenbach, Schoenbaum, Schoenberg, Schoenfeld—Jewish. Schoen (Dutch): derived from the German word "schuh," meaning shoe. The name was given to those who made or repaired shoes. Schoen (Jewish): The name was taken ornamentally. Derived from the German word "schön," meaning lovely or nice. Schoenbach, Schoenbaum, Schoenberg, Schoenfeld: all ornamental compounds derived from the German word "schön," meaning lovely, combined with "bach," meaning stream, "baum," meaning tree, "berg," meaning hill, and "feld," meaning field. The names was taken ornamentally.

Famous **Bearers:** ARNOLD FRANZ WALTER SCHOENBERG (1874–1951) of Vienna was one of the finest composers of the 20th century. He mostly used a 12-tone method of composition, a method he invented, and is believed to have been the first composer to use the atonal method (1908).

Genealogies: None known.

SCHOFIELD (S.S. Abbreviation: Schofi)

Ranking: 2589 S.S. Count: 17,583

Origin: English. Derived from the Middle English words "sc(h)ole" and "feld," meaning hut and pasture. The name was given to those from Schofield, the name of places in England.

Famous **Schofields:** JOHN MCALLISTER SCHOFIELD (1831–1906) of New York was an army officer in the Civil War. He was one of the three commanders in General William T. Sherman's march to the sea. WILLIAM HENRY SCHOFIELD (1870–1920) of Canada was an English professor at Harvard University.

Genealogies: None known.

SCHOLL

Ranking: 2588 S.S. Count: 17,590

Origin: German, Jewish. German: transformation of Schell. German, Jewish: derived from the German word "scholle," meaning clod of dirt. The name was given to those who were lumpy. Jewish: derived from an acronym derived from the Hebrew phrase "shevach leel," meaning "praise to God" (H&H).

Genealogies: *Shull [also Scholl]: John W. and Martha Mosk, descendants* was compiled by Elizabeth K. Glover and published in Gilbert, South Carolina, in 1971.

SCHOOLCRAFT, SCHOOLEY, SCHOOLFIELD, SCHOOLMAN, SCHOOLS (S.S. Abbreviation: School)

Ranking: 2595 S.S. Count: 17,518

Origin: English. All the names' first components were derived from the Old English words "sc(h)ole" or the Old English word "scōl," meaning hut and school. Schoolcraft: the name was given to those who lived in a hut in a field. Schooley: the name was given to those who lived in a hut in a grove. Schoolfield: the name was given to those who lived in a hut in field. Schoolman: the name was given to those who worked in a school or to teachers. Schools: the name was given to those from Scholes, a place in Yorkshire, England.

Famous **Bearers:** HENRY ROWE SCHOOLCRAFT (1793–1864) of New York was an ethnologist and the author of *Historical and Statistical Information Repecting the History, Condition and Prospects of the Indian Tribes of the United States.* It was illustrated with engravings done from the paintings of Seth Eastman.

Genealogies: *Schoolfield Family Tree: genealogy of the Schoolfield family* was compiled by Cleopatra Doss Schoolfield and published in Shreveport, Louisiana, in 1968.

SCHOON (ALSO SCHOONMAKER)

Ranking: 2405 S.S. Count: 18,839

Origin: Schoonmaker—Dutch; Schoon—German. Schoonmaker: 1) Uncertain etymology. The name was given to those who made and sold shoes. 2) Uncertain etymology. The name was given to those who cleaned up and swept. Schoon: derived from the German word "schön," meaning fine, lovely, or nice. The name was given to persons who were attractive or nice.

Genealogies: *The Schoonmaker Family* was compiled by Ruth P. Heidgerd and published in New Paltz, New York, in 1974.

SCHOTT (ALSO SCHOTTE, SCHOTTLANDER, SCHOTTLE, SCHOTTLER)

Ranking: 2652 S.S. Count: 17,164

Origin: Schott, Schottle—German; Schotte, Schottler—German, Jewish; Schottlander—Jewish. Schott, Schottle: cog-

nates to Scott. Schotte (German): 1) cognate to Scott. 2) derived from the Middle High German word "schüssel(e)," meaning a small bowl of wood. The name was given to turners. Schotte (Jewish): derived from the German word "schussel," meaning dish. Schottler: transformation of the Jewish name Schotte, as well as of the German name Schotte, meaning small bowl of wood. Schottlander: cognate to the English name Scotland, an ethnic name given to those from Scotland.

Famous **Bearers:** CHARLES ANTHONY SCHOTT (1826–1901) of Germany was a geodesist and the chief of the computing division with the U.S. Coast Survey.

Genealogies: None known.

SCHRADER (S.S. Abbreviation: Schrad)

Ranking: 1804 S.S. Count: 24,947

Origin: German. Transformation of Schroeder.

Genealogies: None known.

SCHRAMM, SCHRAMME, SCHRAMMEL (S.S. Abbreviation: Schram)

Ranking: 2222 S.S. Count: 20,652

Origin: Schramme, Schrammel—German; Schramm—German, Jewish. Schramme, Schrammel: transformations of Schramm. Schramm: derived from the German word "schramme" and the Yiddish word "scram," both meaning scar. The name was given to those with a conspicuous scar.

Genealogies: *Haatvedt-Schram Genealogy* [also Schramm] was compiled by Eleanor Delong and published in Vista, California, in 1981.

SCHRECK, SCHRECKE (S.S. Abbreviation: Schrec)

Ranking: 4316 S.S. Count: 10,398

Origin: German, Polish. Uncertain etymology. 1) the name was given to those who were timid. 2) the name was given to those who lived at a "broad place" (ES). 3) the name was given to those who frightened persons by jumping out at them.

Genealogies: None known.

SCHREIBER, SCHREIER, SCHREINER (S.S. Abbreviation: Schrei)

Ranking: 1017 S.S. Count: 43,001

Origin: Schreiner—German; Schreiber, Schreier—German, Jewish; Schreiner: derived from the German word "schreiner," meaning joiner. The name was given to those who worked joining pieces of wood together. Schreiber (German): derived from the German word "schreiben," meaning to write. The name was given to clerks. Schreiber (Jewish): derived from the German word "schreiber" and the Yiddish word "shrayber," both meaning writer. Schreier (German): derived from the German word "schreien," meaning to shout. The name was given to those who were loud or to the town crier.

Schreier (Jewish): derived from the German word "schreier" and the Yiddish word "shrayer," both meaning shouter. Uncertain etymology. The name was given either to those who were loud or to those who called Jews to worship.

Genealogies: None known.

SCHROCK, SCHROCKER (S.S. Abbreviation: Schroc)

Ranking: 4813 S.S. Count: 9312

Origin: German. The name was given to those from Schrock, the name of places in Germany, meaning a slippery area.

Genealogies: *Family History of Joni Miller and his Descendants* [also Schrock] was compiled by Emanuel Jeremiah Miller and published in Topeka, Indiana, in 1992. *The Schrock Family* was compiled by Thomas S. Reed and published in Chillicothe, Missouri, in 1965. *The Schrock Family: with First supplement to the Schrock family* was compiled by Thomas S. Reed and published in Purdin, Missouri, in 1980.

SCHROEDER (S.S. Abbreviation: Schroe)

Ranking: 368 S.S. Count: 104,788

Origin: German. Derived from the Middle Low German word "schröten," meaning to cut. The name was given to tailors.

Famous **Schroeders:** RUDOLPH WILLIAM SCHROEDER (1886–1952) of Illinois was an aviation pioneer and one of the first to fly in the stratosphere.

Genealogies: None known.

SCHUBEL, SCHUBERT, SCHUBLER (S.S. Abbreviation: Schube)

Ranking: 2282 S.S. Count: 19,922

Origin: Schubel, Schubler—German; Schubert—German, Jewish. Schubel, Schubler: uncertain etymology. Possibly derived from the Middle High German word "schubel," meaning tuft. Schubert: derived from the Middle High German words "schuoch" and "würhte," meaning shoe and maker. The name was given to shoemakers.

Genealogies: *The Shuberts of Broadway* was compiled by Brooks McNamara and published in New York, New York, in 1990.

SCHUETT, SCHUETTE (S.S. Abbreviation: Schuet)

Ranking: 3050 S.S. Count: 14,885

Origin: Dutch. Uncertain etymology. The name was given to those who lived near a hedge or fence.

Genealogies: None known.

SCHULE (ALSO SCHULER)

Ranking: 1973 S.S. Count: 22,982

Origin: Schule—German; Schuler—German, Jewish.

Schule: derived from the German word "*schuh*," meaning shoe. The name was given to those who made or repaired shoes. *Schuler* (German): derived from the German word "*schule*," meaning school. The name was given to those who were scholars or to those studying to be priests. *Schuler* (Jewish): derived from the Yiddish word "*shul*," meaning synagogue. The name was given to scholars of the Talmud or to synagogue sextons.

Genealogies: *The Philip Schuler Family, 1822–1983, from Stotternheim, Saxony-Weimar, Germany* was compiled by Ilagene Mertens Salzman and published in Shawano, Wisconsin, in 1984.

SCHULMAN, SCHULMEISTER (S.S. Abbreviation: Schulm)

Ranking: 4961 **S.S. Count:** 9028

Origin: Schulman—German; Schulmeister—Jewish. Schulman: transformation of the German name Schuler. Schulmeister: derived from the German word "schulmeister," meaning schoolmaster. The name was given to those who taught in Jewish schools.

Genealogies: None known.

SCHULTE, SCHULTEN, SCHULTING, SCHULTZ, SCHULTZE (S.S. Abbreviation: Schult)

Ranking: 183 **S.S. Count:** 185,445

Origin: Schulte—Dutch, German; Schulten, Schulting, Schultze—German; Schultz—German, Jewish. Schulte, Schulten, Schulting, Schultze: cognates to and transformations of the German surname Schultz. Schultz (German): derived from the Middle High German word "schulteize," meaning the person in charge of collecting payments on behalf of the lord of a manor. The name was given to the head man of a village. Schultz (Jewish): uncertain etymology. Possibly given to rabbis.

Genealogies: *The House by the Dvina: a Russian-Scottish childhood* [also Schultz] was compiled by Eugenie Fraser and published in New York, New York, in 1984. *Matthias Shultz and his Descendants* was compiled by Carlyle W. Bennett and published in Owensboro, Kentucky, in 1980. *The Walker County Schultz Family History* was compiled by Eva Regina Swindle and published in Cullman, Alabama, in 1083.

SCHULZ (ALSO SCHULZE)

Ranking: 898 **S.S. Count:** 48,104

Origin: German. Transformations of Schultz.

Genealogies: None known.

SCHUMACHER, SCHUMANN (S.S. Abbreviation: Schuma)

Ranking: 729 **S.S. Count:** 58,004

Origin: Schumann—German; Schumacher—German, Jewish. Schumann: 1) transformation of Schule. 2) derived from the Middle High German word "schiur(e)," meaning barn. The name was given to those who lived near a barn where agricultural produce was collected for an obligatory payment to some authority. The name may also have been given to the person in charge of taking in the produce. Schumacher: transformation of Schule.

Famous Bearers: ELIZABETH SCHUMANN (1885–1962), born in Germany, was a soprano opera singer in the United States.

Genealogies: None known.

SCHUSTER, SCHUSTERL, SCHUSTERMAN, SCHUSTL (S.S. Abbreviation: Schust)

Ranking: 1746 **S.S. Count:** 25,629

Origin: Schusterl, Schustl—German; Schuster—German, Jewish; Schusterman—Jewish. Schusterl, Schustl, Schusterman: transformations of Schuster. Schuster: derived from the German word "schuster" or the Yiddish word "shuster," both meaning shoemaker or shoe repairman, to whom the name was given.

Famous Bearers: MAX LINCOLN SCHUSTER (1897–1970) was born in Austria of American parents. He was the co-founder of Simon and Schuster, a book-publishing firm.

Genealogies: None known.

SCHUTT (ALSO SCHUTTE)

Ranking: 2669 **S.S. Count:** 17,080

Origin: German. Transformations of Schutze.

Genealogies: *Browne-Schutt Ancestral Lines* was compiled by Jessie Bruce Smith Ornes and published in Los Angeles, California, in 1979.

SCHUTZ (ALSO SCHUTZE, SCHUTZER, SCHUTZMAN)

Ranking: 4404 **S.S. Count:** 10,185

Origin: Schutze—German; Schutz—German, Jewish; Schutzer, Schutzman—Jewish. Schutze: derived from the German word "schütze," meaning bowman, to whom the name was given. Schutz (German): derived from the German word "schützen," meaning to guard. The name was given to watchmen. Schutz (Jewish): uncertain etymology. Schutzer, Schutzman: transformations of Schutz.

Genealogies: None known.

SCHWAB (ALSO SCHWABE, SCHWABEL, SCHWABLE)

Ranking: 1628 **S.S. Count:** 27,561

Origin: Schwab, Schwabel, Schwable—German, Jewish; Schwabe—Jewish. Derived from Schwaben, the name of a region of Germany that is called Swabia in English. The names were given to those from Swabia.

Famous **Bearers:** CHARLES MICHAEL SCHWAB (1862–1939) of Pennsylvania was an industrialist in the steel industry. JOHN CHRISTOPHER SCHWAB (1865–1916) of New York City was an economist and librarian and the author of *The Confederate States of America, 1861–1865: A Financial and Industrial History* (1901).

Genealogies: *The Swope Family Book of Remembrance; a history of the origins of the first Schwab, Schwob, Swope families in early Lancaster County, Pennsylvania* was compiled by Emily Swope Morse and published in Provo, Utah, in 1972.

SCHWALB, SCHWALBE, SCHWALBLE (S.S. Abbreviation: Schwal)

Ranking: 4498 **S.S. Count:** 9965

Origin: Schwalble—German; Schwalb, Schwalbe—German, Jewish. The name refers to a swallow (the bird) and was given to people considered to have swallowlike qualities.

Genealogies: None known.

SCHWAN (ALSO SCHWAND, SCHWANDER, SCHWANDT)

Ranking: 3041 **S.S. Count:** 14,955

Origin: German. Schwan: cognate to the name Swan, referring to the bird called swan. Schwand, Schwander, Schwandt: derived from the Middle High German word "schwand," meaning clearing. The name was given to those who lived in a clearing.

Genealogies: None known.

SCHWARD, SCHWART, SCHWARTZ, SCHWARTZKOPF, SCHWARZ (S.S. Abbreviation: Schwar)

Ranking: 203 **S.S. Count:** 173,508

Origin: Schward, Schwart—German; Schwartz, Schwartzkopf, Schwarz—German, Jewish. Schward, Schwart, Schwartz, Schwarz: derived from the German word "schwarz" or the Yiddish word "shvarts," both meaning dark. The names were given to those with black hair or to those with a dark complexion. Schwartzkopf: derived from the German words "schwarz" and "kopf," meaning black and head. The name was given to those with black or dark hair.

Famous **Bearers:** EUGENE AMANDUS SCHWARZ (1844–1928) of Germany was an entomologist with the U.S. Department of Agriculture. DELMORE DAVID SCHWARTZ (1913–1966) of New York was a writer. His best work was *In Dreams Begin Responsibilities.* He was a national success and continued writing and teaching at the university level. His life was the subject of Saul Bellow's novel *Humboldt's Gift* (1975).

Genealogies: *The Descendants of Samuel Aaron Schwartz of Monroe County, Ohio* was compiled by Miriam K. Berlekamp Frankhauser and published in Green Springs, Ohio, in 1992. *The Schwartz Family of El Paso: the story of a pioneer Jewish family in the Southwest* was compiled by Floyd S. Fierman and published in El Paso, Texas, in 1980.

SCHWEIGER, SCHWEITZER, SCHWEIZER (S.S. Abbreviation: Schwei)

Ranking: 1112 **S.S. Count:** 39,765

Origin: German, Jewish. Schweiger: derived from the German word "schweigen" or the Yiddish word "shvaygn," both meaning to be silent. The name was given to those who were laconic or brooding. Schweitzer, Schweizer: derived from the German word "Schweizer," meaning a Swiss person. The names were given to those from Switzerland.

Genealogies: *The Schweitzer Family from Eschelbronn, Baden, Germany and Rahway, New Jersey, U.S.A.* was compiled by Regina F. Schweitzer and published in Rahway, New Jersey, in 1985.

SCHWEN (ALSO SCHWENDE, SCHWENDLER, SCHWENKE, SCHWENNSEN)

Ranking: 2936 **S.S. Count:** 15,509

Origin: German. Schwen, Schwennsen: cognates to Swain. Schwende, Schwendler: transformations of Schwand. Schwenke: cognate to the name Swan, referring to the bird called swan.

Genealogies: None known.

SCHWERTLEIN, SCHWERMANN (S.S. Abbreviation: Schwer)

Ranking: 4281 **S.S. Count:** 10,493

Origin: German. Schwertlein: Uncertain etymology. The name was given to those who used or made small swords. Schwermann: the name means father-in-law.

Genealogies: None known.

SCHWINN (S.S. Abbreviation: Schwin)

Ranking: 3606 **S.S. Count:** 12,519

Origin: German. Derived from the German word "schwein," meaning hog. The name was given to those who tended, raised, or sold swine.

Genealogies: None known.

SCOFIELD (S.S. Abbreviation: Scofie)

Ranking: 4760 **S.S. Count:** 9411

Origin: English. Derived from the Middle English words "sc(h)ole" and "feld," meaning hut and field. The name was given to those from Schofield, the name of places in England.

Genealogies: *A Scofield Survey* was compiled by Harriet Scofield and published in High Point, North Carolina, in 1972.

SCOGGIN, SCOGGINS (S.S. Abbreviation: Scoggi)

Ranking: 3243 S.S. Count: 14,011

Origin: English. The names were given to the son of a fool or flatterer.

Genealogies: None known.

SCOTT

Ranking: 38 S.S. Count: 587,567

Origin: English, Scottish. Uncertain etymology. The name is possibly an ethnic name given to those from Scotland or to those who spoke Gaelic in Scotland.

Famous **Scotts**: CHARLES SCOTT (1739?–1813) of Virginia was a Revolutionary War officer and the governor of Kentucky. WINFIELD SCOTT (1786–1866) of Pennsylvania was an army officer known by the nickname "Fuss and Feathers." DRED SCOTT (1795?–1858) of Virginia was a runaway slave and the subject of the U.S. Supreme Court case that resulted in the famous *Dred Scott* decision. ORANGE SCOTT (1800–1847) of Vermont was an abolitionist and a Methodist minister. He headed in 1843 a convention at which the Wesleyan Methodist Connection of America had its beginning. HUGH LENOX SCOTT (1853–1934) of Kentucky was an expert on the Plains Indians. WALTER EDWARD SCOTT (1870–1954) of Kentucky was a performer with Buffalo Bill's Wild West Show and a teller of wild tales, such as finding gold in Death Valley. For this he earned the nickname "Death Valley Scotty." EMMETT JAY SCOTT (1873–1957) of Texas was the private secretary to Booker T. Washington and the co-founder, with Washington, of the National Negro Business League. During World War I he was the advisor on black soldiers to the secretary of war. ALLEN CECIL SCOTT (1882–1964) of Nebraska was the inventor of the parachute for humans. His design is still in use today.

Genealogies: *Fullers, Sissons, and Scotts, our Yeoman Ancestors: 46 New England and New York families* was compiled by Carol Clark Johnson and published in Mobile, Alabama, in 1976. *Hand, Sisson, and Scott: More Yeoman Ancestors* was compiled by Carol Clark Johnson and published in 1981. *John Scott, 1761–1843: an American Revolutionary veteran* was compiled by Kenneth R. Scott and published in Greenwood, Indiana, in 1975.

SCRIBNER (S.S. Abbreviation: Scribn)

Ranking: 4819 S.S. Count: 9296

Origin: English. Derived from the Old French word "escrivein," meaning scribe or writer. The name was given to those who were copyists or clerks.

Famous **Scribners**: CHARLES SCRIBNER (1821–1871) of New York City was the co-founder of the publishing firm Baker & Scribner. Upon the death of his partner, the name of the company changed to his name only. His son,

CHARLES SCRIBNER (1854–1930) of New York City, took over his father's business. His son, CHARLES SCRIBNER (1890–1952), also of New York, joined the family business which, by now, was called Charles Scribner's Sons. He expanded the reference department, adding *The Dictionary of American History* (1940).

Genealogies: None known.

SCROGGIN, SCROGGINS (S.S. Abbreviation: Scrogg)

Ranking: 2651 S.S. Count: 17,167

Origin: English. Uncertain etymology. The names were given to those who lived near a copse or a "stunted undergrowth" (ES).

Genealogies: *Scrogin, Scroggin, Scroggins* was compiled by Arthur Evander Scroggins and published in Dodge City, Kansas, in 1964.

SCRUGGS (S.S. Abbreviation: Scrugg)

Ranking: 2018 S.S. Count: 22,629

Origin: English. Uncertain etymology. 1) the name was given to those who were bony and lean. 2) the name was given to those who lived near dwarfish bushes.

Genealogies: *Scruggs Piper Connections* was compiled by Jane Melonie Scruggs Piper and published in Houston, Texas, in 1992. *Diary of Allen Franklin Scruggs 1803–1902* was compiled by Allen Franklin Scruggs and published in Bothell, Washington, in 1974.

SCULLY

Ranking: 3556 S.S. Count: 12,693

Origin: Irish. Derived from the Gaelic name Ó Scolaidhe, meaning "descendant of the scholar" (H&H).

Genealogies: None known.

SEAL

Ranking: 3839 S.S. Count: 11,730

Origin: English. 1) derived from the Middle English word "sele," meaning seal, the aquatic mammal. The name was given to those who were thickset or clumsy. 2) derived from the Middle English and Old French word "seel," meaning a seal that is used to stamp an impression on a surface. The name was given to those who made seals or signet rings. 3) derived from the Old French word "seele," meaning saddle. The name was given to those who made saddles.

Genealogies: *A Seale Anthology* [also Seal] was compiled by Nancy L. Kuehl and published in 1985. *The Seale Family from the Northern Neck of Virginia to Greene County, Alabama* [also Seal] was compiled by Joyce Ellison Graf and published in Baltimore, Maryland, in 1984. *The Seale (also Seal) Family of Old Virginia* was compiled by Deborah A. Sprouse and published in 1981.

SEALS

Ranking: 2265 S.S. Count: 20,160

Origin: English. Transformation of Seal, referring to the mammal.

Genealogies: *The Seals Family History* was compiled by Elmer D. Scalf and published in Glendora, California, in 1984.

SEAMAN

Ranking: 1855 S.S. Count: 24,404

Origin: English. 1) derived from the Old English words "sæ" and "mann," meaning sea and man. The name was given to sailors. 2) derived from the Old English first name Sæmann, which is comprised of the components "sæ" and "mann," meaning sea and man.

Famous **Seamans:** ELIZABETH COCHRANE SEAMAN (1865?–1922) of Pennsylvania was a journalist better known by her byline name, Nellie Bly.

Genealogies: *A Copy of an Account Written by Jordan Seaman of Jericho* was compiled by Jordan Seaman and published in New York, New York, in 1860. *Descendants of William Seaman of Washington County, Pennsylvania* was compiled by Helen Elizabeth Vogt and published in Brownsville, Pennsylvania, in 1981. *The Ancestors and Descendants of Fletcher de la Seaman* was compiled by Ferne Davidson Hill and published in Glendale, California, in 1975.

SEARCY

Ranking: 3230 S.S. Count: 14,042

Origin: English. Derived from the first name Cercious and a component meaning estate. The name was given to those from Cercy or Cerisy, the names of places in France.

Genealogies: None known.

SEARLE (ALSO SEARLES)

Ranking: 2972 S.S. Count: 15,294

Origin: English. Derived from the Norman first name Serlo, which is of uncertain etymology. The name is possibly derived from a word meaning armor.

Genealogies: *The Searle Family* was compiled by Elishu Blackman and published in 1897.

SEARS

Ranking: 958 S.S. Count: 45,493

Origin: English. Transformation of Sayers.

Famous **Searses:** ISAAC SEARS (1730–1786) of Massachusetts was a Revolutionary patriot and the leader of the colonists against the Stamp Act in New York City. EDMUND HAMILTON SEARS (1810–1876) of Massachusetts was the author of the hymns "It Came Upon a Midnight Clear" and "Calm in the Listening Ear of Night." RICHARD DUDLEY SEARS (1861?–1943) of Massachusetts was the first winner of the U.S. national amateur lawn tennis championship in Newport, Rhode Island. He also won the U.S. national court tennis championship in New York City in 1892. RICHARD WARREN SEARS (1863–1914) of Minnesota started a mail-order business that became Sears, Roebuck & Co. ELEONORA RANDOLPH SEARS (1881–1968) of Massachusetts was the first national squash champion and was considered a pioneer in the area of women in sports.

Genealogies: None known.

SEATON

Ranking: 3584 S.S. Count: 12,582

Origin: English, Scottish. Derived in most cases from the Old English words "sæ" and "tūn," meaning sea and settlement. The name was given to those from Seaton, the name of several places in England and Scotland.

Famous **Seatons:** WILLIAM WINSTON SEATON (1785–1866) of Virginia was a journalist and the co-editor with his brother-in-law, Joseph Gales, of the *National Intelligencer*, the official federal government newspaper in Washington, D.C.

Genealogies: None known.

SEAY

Ranking: 2273 S.S. Count: 20,017

Origin: English. Uncertain etymology. 1) the name was given to those from Sai, meaning Saius' estate, a place in Normandy, France. 2) derived from the Old English word "sæ," meaning sea. The name was given to those who lived near the sea. 3) the name was given to those who were sage.

Genealogies: *Descendants of Abraham Seay* was compiled by Burwell Warren Seay and published in Richmond, Virginia, in 1966. *Seay and Allied Lines of Western Washington County, Arkansas* was compiled by Billie Allen Jines and published in Springdale, Arkansas, in 1986.

SEBASTIAN, SEBASTIANELLI, SEBASTIANI, SEBASTIANO, SEBASTIEN (S.S. Abbreviation: Sebast)

Ranking: 3237 S.S. Count: 14,026

Origin: Sebastien—French; Sebastian—German, Provençal, Spanish; Sebastianelli, Sebastiani, Sebastiano— Italian. Derived from the Latin name Sebastiānus, which was at one time an ethnic name given to those from Sebastia, a town in the ancient region of Pontus in Asia Minor whose name was derived from the Greek word "sebastos," meaning revered.

Famous **Bearers:** BENJAMIN SEBASTIAN (1745?–1834), birthplace unknown, was a lawyer and Revolutionary soldier. He moved from Virginia to Kentucky and was a rising figure in politics until it was discovered that he was a Spanish informant. This revelation ended his political career.

Genealogies: *The Chronicle of a Southern Family*

[Sebastian family] was compiled by William Hobart Sebastian and published in 1972.

SEE

Ranking: 4215 S.S. Count: 10,711

Origin: English. Derived from the Middle English word "see," meaning lake or sea. The name was given to those who lived along a sea or by a lake.

Famous Sees: HORACE SEE (1835–1909) of Pennsylvania was a naval architect responsible for designs in the "new navy."

Genealogies: *The History and Genealogy of the See and Related Families* was compiled by Joseph Benjamin See and published in Grinnell, Iowa, in 1969.

SEELEY

Ranking: 2805 S.S. Count: 16,241

Origin: English. Derived from the Middle English word "seely," meaning happy. The name was given to those who were genial.

Genealogies: *The Seeley-Seely-Seelye Family of Connecticut and Ohio* was compiled by Helene Bromwell Ault and published in Redding, Connecticut, in 1940. *Descendants of Robert Seeley: Robert Seeley, born 1600/01, England, died October 1667, New York City, N.Y.* was compiled by Esther Hogg Houtz and published in Allenspark, Colorado, in 1977.

SEGAL

Ranking: 4035 S.S. Count: 11,224

Origin: French, Jewish. French: derived from the Old French word "segal," meaning rye. The name was given to those who sold or grew rye. Jewish: derived as an acronym from the Hebrew phrase "segan levia" (H&H), meaning "second-rank Levite" (H&H).

Genealogies: None known.

SEGURA

Ranking: 3132 S.S. Count: 14,496

Origin: Catalan, Provençal. Derived from the Latin word "sēcūrus," meaning free of worries. The name was given to those from Segura, a place in Spain.

Genealogies: None known.

SEIBER (ALSO SEIBERLICH, SEIBERS, SEIBERT, SEIBERTZ)

Ranking: 2304 S.S. Count: 19,765

Origin: German. Seiber, Seibers, Seibert, Seibertz: transformations of Siebert. Seiberlich: derived from the German word "sauber," meaning clean. The name was given to those who were clean and neat.

Genealogies: *Lest We Forget: John Clark of Wythe County, Virginia* [also Seibert] was compiled by Ella Rae Wilson Coleman and published in Decorah, Iowa, in 1990. *Memoirs of the Seibert Family* was compiled by Charles Herman Seibert and published in Birmingham, Alabama, in 1964. *A Genealogical Postscript; notes on Baskin, Seibert, Wotring, Bell* was compiled by Raymond Martin Bell and published in Washington, Pennsylvania, in 1970.

SEIDEL (ALSO SEIDELMANN)

Ranking: 3410 S.S. Count: 13,269

Origin: German. Seidel: 1) transformation of Siegel, a Germanic first name. 2) Uncertain etymology. The name was given to those from Seidel, a place in Germany. 3) Uncertain etymology. The name was given to those who lived near the "sign of the beer mug" (ES). Seidelmann: 1) Uncertain etymology. The name was given to those from Seidel, a place in Germany. 2) Uncertain etymology. The name was given to those who traded in silks.

Famous Bearers: GEORGE LUKAS EMIL SEIDEL (1864–1947) of Pennsylvania was a wood carver and the mayor of Milwaukee, serving one term. He was the first socialist mayor elected in a major city.

Genealogies: None known.

SEIFER (ALSO SEIFERLIN, SEIFERT)

Ranking: 2683 S.S. Count: 17,018

Origin: Seiferlin, Seifert—German; Seifer—German, Jewish. Seiferlin, Seifert: transformations of Siegfried. Seifer (German): transformation of Siegfried. Seifer (Jewish): cognate to Soper.

Genealogies: None known.

SEILER

Ranking: 4065 S.S. Count: 11,125

Origin: English, German, Jewish. English: transformation of Saylor. German: derived from the German word "seil," meaning rope. The name was given to those who made rope. Jewish: uncertain etymology.

Famous Seilers: CARL SEILER (1849–1905) of Switzerland was a physician who specialized in laryngology.

Genealogies: None known.

SEITZ

Ranking: 2525 S.S. Count: 17,966

Origin: German. Derived from any of several Germanic first names that include the first component "sigi," meaning victory.

Famous Seitzes: DON CARLOS SEITZ (1862–1935) of Ohio was a journalist with the *New York World*, which he made a powerful, liberal paper of its time. He also wrote biographies of noted men of the day.

Genealogies: *Genealogical Records of the Seitz-Sites Family* was compiled by John V. Beck and published in Bloomington, Indiana, in 1984.

SELBY

Ranking: 2704 **S.S. Count:** 16,830

Origin: English. Derived from the Old Norse word "selja," meaning willow. The name was given to those from Selby, a place in England.

Famous **Selbys:** WILLIAM SELBY (1739?–1798), possibly of England, was a popular organist in Boston after 1771. NORMAN SELBY (1873–1940) of Indiana was a boxer who went by the name Kid McCoy. He is best remembered for his tricks and deceitful ways in the boxing ring.

Genealogies: *The Merediths and Selveys of Virginia and West Virginia* [also Selbys] was compiled by Joseph N. Meredith and published in Parsons, West Virginia, in 1982. *Selby Families of Colonial America* was compiled by Donna Valley Russell and published in Middletown, Maryland, in 1990.

SELF

Ranking: 1453 **S.S. Count:** 30,664

Origin: English. Derived from the Middle English first name Saulf, which was derived from the Old English name Sœwulf, comprising the components "sœ" and "wulf," meaning sea and wolf.

Genealogies: *Lizzie's Legacy and our Coffey Cousins* [also Self] was compiled by Mary Elizabeth Coffey Self and published in Kiowa, Oklahoma, in 1984. *Self Heritage* was compiled by Larry Brown and published in Cullman, Alabama, in 1984.

SELL

Ranking: 3094 **S.S. Count:** 14,673

Origin: English, Hungarian. English: derived from the Middle English word "selle," meaning a primitive hut usually used for housing animals. The name was given to those who lived in such huts. Hungarian: derived from the Hungarian word "szel," meaning wind. The name was given to those who lived in a windy area.

Genealogies: *Tax Records, Selected Family Names (also Sell family), Franklin County, Pennsylvania, 1796–1847* was compiled by Robert F. Cell and published in Edinburg, Texas, in 1990.

SELLAR (ALSO SELLARO, SELLAROLI, SELLARS)

Ranking: 4272 **S.S. Count:** 10,538

Origin: Sellar, Sellars—English; Sellaro, Sellaroli—Italian. Sellar, Sellars: transformations of Seller. Sellaro, Sellaroli: cognates to Seller, meaning saddle or seat.

Genealogies: None known.

SELLER (ALSO SELLERET, SELLERS)

Ranking: 716 **S.S. Count:** 58,864

Origin: Seller, Sellers—English, Scottish; Selleret—French. Seller, Sellers: 1) derived from the Middle English word "sellen," meaning to sell. The names were given to merchants. 2) derived from the Anglo-Norman-French word "celler," meaning cellar. The names were given to those who worked in the cellars of a monastery or important house. 3) derived from the Anglo-Norman-French word "seller," meaning saddler. The names were given to those who made, sold, or repaired saddles. 4) transformation of the English name Sell, meaning a primitive hut usually used for housing animals. Selleret: cognate to Seller, meaning saddler.

Famous **Bearers:** ISAIAH SELLERS (1802–1864) of North Carolina was a pioneer steamboat pilot on the Mississippi River and was the first to use "Mark Twain" as a pen name in articles appearing in the New Orleans *Daily Picayune*. WILLIAM SELLERS (1824–1905) of Pennsylvania was a toolmaker and the inventor of the spiral-geared planer. COLEMAN SELLERS (1827–1909) of Pennsylvania was an engineer who contributed to the design of the Niagara Falls hydroelectric power development. MATTHEW BACON SELLERS (1869–1932) of Maryland was a pioneer in the field of aerodynamics.

Genealogies: *Descendants of Hezekiah Sellards* [also Sellers] was compiled by Clayton R. Cox and published in Baltimore, Maryland, in 1977. *A Backward Glance* [also Sellers] was compiled by Jane Parker McManus and published in Pineville, Louisiana, in 1986. *Cradled by the Massanutten: the Zellers/Sellers family* was compiled by Mary Marie Koontz Arrington and published in Baltimore, Maryland, in 1986.

SELLS

Ranking: 4066 **S.S. Count:** 11,119

Origin: English. Transformation of Seller, meaning saddler.

Genealogies: None known.

SEPULVEDA (S.S. Abbreviation: Sepulv)

Ranking: 2260 **S.S. Count:** 20,206

Origin: Spanish. The name was given to those from Sepulveda, the name of places in Spain.

Genealogies: None known.

SERNA

Ranking: 3081 **S.S. Count:** 14,762

Origin: Spanish. Derived from the Spanish word "serna," meaning those who worked land belonging to a manor lord.

Genealogies: None known.

SERRANO (S.S. Abbreviation: Serran)

Ranking: 732 **S.S. Count:** 57,949

Origin: Italian, Portuguese, Spanish. Derived from the Latin word "serra," meaning saw. The name was given to those who lived on or beside a series of hills.

Genealogies: None known.

SESSIONS (S.S. Abbreviation: Sessio)

Ranking: 3339 S.S. Count: 13,560

Origin: English. The name was given to those from Soissons, a place in northern France named for a Gaulish tribe that formerly inhabited the area.

Famous Sessionses: HENRY HOWARD SESSIONS (1847–1915) of New York was a builder of railroad cars and the inventor of the enclosed entrances at the ends of railroad passenger cars. KATE OLIVIA SESSIONS (1857–1940) of California was a horticulturist and the contributor of many new plant varieties to San Diego. ROGER HUNTINGTON SESSIONS (1896–1985) of New York City was a composer who received two Pulitzer Prizes for his work, in 1974 and 1981.

Genealogies: None known.

SETTLE

Ranking: 2000 S.S. Count: 22,746

Origin: English. Derived from the Old English word "setl," meaning seat. The name was given to those from Settle, a place in Yorkshire, England.

Genealogies: *The Settle-Suttle Family* was compiled by William Emmet Reese and published in Palm Beach, Florida, in 1974.

SEVERS (ALSO SEVERSON)

Ranking: 2744 S.S. Count: 16,599

Origin: English. Derived from the first name Saefaru, meaning sea way.

Genealogies: None known.

SEWARD

Ranking: 2989 S.S. Count: 15,199

Origin: English, Irish. English: 1) derived from the Old English words "sū" and "hierde," meaning pig and herdsman. The name was given to those who herded swine. 2) derived from the names Siward and Seward. The former has the first component "sige," meaning victory, and the latter has the first component "sæ," meaning sea; both have a second component of "weard," meaning guard. Irish: derived from the Gaelic name Ó Suaird, which was derived from the first name Suart, comprising the components "sige" and "weald," meaning victory and guard.

Famous Sewards: WILLIAM HENRY SEWARD (1801–1872) of New York was a governor of New York, U.S. senator, and secretary of state. In his capacity as secretary of state, he negotiated the deal with Russia to buy Alaska.

Genealogies: *Seward and Related Families* was compiled by George C. Seward and published in Scarsdale, New York, in 1987. *We Remember Carroll* [also Seward] was published in Scarsdale, New York, in 1992.

SEWELL

Ranking: 1442 S.S. Count: 30,951

Origin: English. 1) derived from the Old English words "seofon" and "wella," meaning seven and spring. The name was given to those from Sewell, Showell, Seawell, or Sywell, the names of places in England. 2) derived from the Middle English first names Siwal(d) or Sewal(d). The former comprises the components "sige" and "weald," meaning victory and rule; the latter comprises the components "sæ" and "weald," meaning sea and rule.

Famous Sewells: WILLIAM JOYCE SEWELL (1835–1901) of Ireland was the head of the Pennsylvania railroad lines in New Jersey and a state senator in, then U.S. senator from, New Jersey. EDNA BELLE SCOTT SEWELL (1881–1967) of Indiana was the first director of the Associated Women of the American Farm Bureau Federation.

Genealogies: *History of One Sewell Family in America* was compiled by Franklin Comer Sewell and published in Anniston, Alabama, in 1978.

SEXTON

Ranking: 756 S.S. Count: 56,146

Origin: English, Irish. English: derived from the Middle English word "sexteyn," meaning sexton. The name was given to those in charge of the maintenance of a church or to the warden of a church. Irish: derived from the Gaelic name Ó Seastnáin, which was derived from the first name Seastnán, which is of uncertain etymology.

Famous Sextons: ANNE HARVEY SEXTON (1928–1974) of Massachusetts was a poet and the winner of a Pulitzer Prize for the poem "Live or Die" (1966).

Genealogies: *The Sexton Family of Scott County, Tennessee* was compiled by Robert Lee Bailey and published in Huntsville, Tennessee, in 1992.

SEYMOUR, SEYMOURE (S.S. Abbreviation: Seymou)

Ranking: 1240 S.S. Count: 35,654

Origin: English. 1) derived from the Old English words "sæ" and "mere," meaning sea and lake. The names were given to those from Seamer, the name of places in England. 2) Uncertain etymology. The names were given to those from Saint-Maur-des-Fossés, a place in northern France.

Famous Bearers: THOMAS HART SEYMOUR (1807–1868) of Connecticut was the governor of Connecticut and a U.S. minister to Russia. HORATIO WINSLOW SEYMOUR (1854–1920) of New York was a journalist best known for his eye-catching headlines. DAVID SEYMOUR (1911–1956) of Poland was a photojournalist best remembered for his photographs taken for UNESCO (the United Nations Educational, Scientific, and Cultural Organization) of children in World War II. He was killed covering the Arab-Israeli War.

Genealogies: *Puritan Migration to Connecticut: the saga*

of the Seymour family, 1129–1746 was compiled by Malcolm Seymour and published in Canaan, New Hampshire, in 1982. *Mallory Family* [also Seymour] was published in 1973.

SHACKEL, SHACKELL (S.S. Abbreviation: Shacke)

Ranking: 2407 S.S. Count: 18,835

Origin: English. 1) derived from the medieval first name Schackel, which was derived from the Old Norse name Skokull, meaning "wagon-pole" (H&H). 2) derived from the Middle English word "schackel," meaning chain. The names were given to those who made shackles.

Genealogies: None known.

SHACKLE, SHACKLES, SHACKLETON, SHACKLOCK (S.S. Abbreviation: Shackl)

Ranking: 4816 S.S. Count: 9304

Origin: English. Shackle: transformation of Shackel. Shackles: transformation of Shackel, meaning "wagon-pole." Shackleton: derived from Old English components meaning "tongue of land" (H&H) and settlement. The name was given to those from Shackleton, the name of places in England. Shacklock: derived from the Middle English word "shaklock," meaning shackles. The name was given to jailers.

Genealogies: *The Shackletons* was compiled by Bernice Close Shackelton and published in Pittsburg, Kansas, in 1972.

SHADE

Ranking: 4670 S.S. Count: 9581

Origin: English, Scottish. 1) derived from the Middle English word "schade," meaning shadow. The name was given to those who were extremely slim. 2) derived from the Old English word "scēad," meaning divider. The name was given to those who lived near a border.

Genealogies: None known.

SHAFER

Ranking: 1220 S.S. Count: 36,194

Origin: German. Transformation of Schafer, meaning shepherd.

Famous **Shafers:** HELEN ALMIRA SHAFER (1839–1894) of New Jersey was the president of Wellesley College.

Genealogies: *Families of Frenches, Williamsons, Shafers, Braswells in America 1710–1972* was compiled by Irene French Braswell and published in Gilmer, Texas, in 1973. *Our Illustrious Shaffer, Shafer Family* was compiled by Robert N. Ungerer and published in Wooster, Ohio, in 1980. *The First Three Generations of the Frederick Shafer Family in America, 1817–1965* was compiled by Thomas J.S. Heim and published in West Chester, Pennsylvania, in 1966.

SHAFFER (S.S. Abbreviation: Shaffe)

Ranking: 483 S.S. Count: 83,575

Origin: German. Transformation of Schafer, meaning shepherd.

Genealogies: *Our Illustrious Shaffer, Shafer Family* was compiled by Robert N. Ungerer and published in Wooster, Ohio, in 1980. *The First Three Generations of the Frederick Shafer Family in America, 1817–1965* [also Shaffer] was compiled by Thomas J.S. Heim and published in West Chester, Pennsylvania, in 1966. *A History of the Shaffer-Miller Schrawder Families* was compiled by Lois Green Schoffstall and published in Hollis, New Hampshire, in 1982.

SHAH

Ranking: 2800 S.S. Count: 16,250

Origin: Hindi, Persian, Turkish. The name means king or sovereign was given to those attached to a royal house.

Genealogies: None known.

SHANAHAN (S.S. Abbreviation: Shanah)

Ranking: 4029 S.S. Count: 11,241

Origin: Irish. Transformation of Shane, derived from Ó Seanaigh.

Genealogies: None known.

SHANE

Ranking: 4770 S.S. Count: 9386

Origin: Irish. 1) derived from the Gaelic name Ó Seanaigh, which was derived from the first name Seanach, meaning wise or old. 2) derived from the Gaelic name Mac Seáin, which was derived from the first name Seán, a cognate to John.

Genealogies: *The Family of James and Elizabeth Shane* was compiled by Vivian L. Snyder and published in Steubenville, Ohio, in 1984.

SHANK

Ranking: 2452 S.S. Count: 18,522

Origin: English, Scottish. Transformation of Shanks.

Genealogies: *Schenck, Shenk, Shank* was compiled by Thomas L. Shank and published in Baltimore, Maryland, in 1985.

SHANKLIN (S.S. Abbreviation: Shankl)

Ranking: 3864 S.S. Count: 11,667

Origin: English. The name means "leg hill" (ES) and was given to those from Shanklin, a place in England.

Genealogies: None known.

SHANKS

Ranking: 2702 S.S. Count: 16,833

Origin: English, Scottish. Derived from the Old English

word *"sceanca,"* meaning leg. *The name was given to those with an unusual walk or to those with long legs.*

Genealogies: None known.

SHANNON (S.S. Abbreviation: Shanno)
Ranking: 645 **S.S. Count:** 64,560

Origin: Irish. Transformation of Shane, meaning old or wise.

Genealogies: *My Byers-Bonar-Shannon and Allied Families* was compiled by Marion Stark Craig and published in Little Rock, Arkansas, in 1977. *Shannon Family and Connections* was compiled by William G. Shannon and published in Columbia, South Carolina, in 1973.

SHAPIRO (S.S. Abbreviation: Shapir)
Ranking: 1100 **S.S. Count:** 40,169

Origin: Jewish. Uncertain etymology. 1) the name was given to those from Speyer, a place in Germany. 2) Perhaps derived from the Hebrew word "shapir," meaning fair.

Genealogies: None known.

SHARKEY (S.S. Abbreviation: Sharke)
Ranking: 3704 **S.S. Count:** 12,197

Origin: Irish. Derived from the Gaelic name Ó Searcaigh, which was derived from the first name Searcach, meaning beloved.

Famous Sharkeys: WILLIAM LEWIS SHARKEY (1798–1873) of Tennessee moved to Mississippi and entered politics. He was an active antisecessionist in his state.

Genealogies: *Louth to Louisiana: the story of the Sharkey family and their kindred* was compiled by Nicholas Russell Murray and published in Hammond, Louisiana, in 1974. *The Sharkey Family* was compiled by Margaret Sharkey Welch and published in Medford, Oregon, in 1991.

SHARP
Ranking: 357 **S.S. Count:** 107,287

Origin: English. Derived from the Middle English word "scharp," meaning quick or acute. The name was given to those who were quick.

Famous Sharps: WILLIAM GRAVES SHARP (1859–1922) of Ohio was a member of Congress from Ohio and the U.S. ambassador to France. KATHERINE LUCINDA SHARP (1865–1914) of Illinois was the founder of the Illinois State Library School.

Genealogies: *A Brief History of our Cook Family and our Sharp Family* was compiled by Violet Sharp Cook and published in Pacifica, California, in 1985. *The Family of John Sharpe, Revolutionary Soldier* [also Sharp] was compiled by Mildred J. Miller and published in 1976. *Descendants of Andrew Caldwell and Ruth Reese Sharpe* [also Sharp] was compiled by Archibald Henderson Caldwell and published in Mill Valley, California, in 1977.

SHARPE
Ranking: 1020 **S.S. Count:** 42,931

Origin: English. Transformation of Sharp.

Famous Sharpes: HORATIO SHARPE (1718–1790) of England was the colonial goveror of Maryland and probably the one who suggested the Stamp Act as a means of taxation. He was removed from office in 1769 and returned to England in 1773.

Genealogies: *The Family of John Sharpe, Revolutionary Soldier* was compiled by Mildred J. Miller and published in 1976. *Descendants of Andrew Caldwell and Ruth Reese Sharpe* was compiled by Archibald Henderson Caldwell and published in Mill Valley, California, in 1977.

SHAUGHNESSY (S.S. Abbreviation: Shaugh)
Ranking: 4797 **S.S. Count:** 9337

Origin: Irish. Derived from the Gaelic name Ó Seachnasaigh, meaning "descendant of Seachnasach," which is of uncertain etymology.

Famous Shaughnessys: CLARK DANIEL SHAUGHNESSY (1892–1970) of Minnesota was a football coach for universities, then professional teams. He was the developer of the "T" formation.

Genealogies: None known.

SHAVER
Ranking: 1640 **S.S. Count:** 27,435

Origin: German. Transformation of Schafer, meaning shepherd.

Famous Shavers: DOROTHY SHAVER (1897–1959) of Arkansas was an illustrator by trade. Through her training in the arts she became associated with the Lord & Taylor department store. She rose through the ranks to the level of president, becoming the highest-paid female executive in the country. Unfortunately, her salary was only one-fourth of a man's salary for the same position.

Genealogies: None known.

SHAW
Ranking: 137 **S.S. Count:** 220,529

Origin: English, Irish, Scottish. English: derived from the Old English word "sceaga," meaning copse. The name was given to those who lived near a thicket or to those from places called Shaw in England. Irish, Scottish: derived from the Gaelic first name Sithech, meaning wolf.

Famous Shaws: HENRY WHEELER SHAW (1818–1885) of Massachusetts was a humorist who wrote under the name Josh Billings. THOMAS SHAW (1838–1901) of Pennsylvania was an inventor of 200 devices, including the spring-lock nut washer, a pile driver, and the Shaw gas tester. PAULINE AGASSIZ SHAW (1841–1917) of Switzerland was a financial supporter of kindergartens and vocational training in Boston. EDWARD RICHARD SHAW (1850–1903) of New York was one of the founders of the college of education at New York University. MARY SHAW (1854–1929) of Massachusetts was an actress. She appeared in Henrik Ibsen's *Ghost*. [WARREN] WILBER SHAW (1902–1954) of Indiana was a race car driver and the winner of the Indianapolis 500 in 1937, 1939, and 1940. He became the president of the raceway after World War II. He was killed in a plane crash.

Genealogies: *Beacon Hill's Colonel Robert Gould Shaw* was compiled by Marion Whitney Smith and published in New York, New York, in 1986. *Eight Generations of the Family of John Shaw, 1788–1858 and his Wife, Nancy Worthy Shaw, 1788–1846 of North Carolina, South Carolina, and Mississippi* was compiled by William David McCain and published in Hattiesburg, Mississippi, in 1974. *Isaac Towell & his Family* [also Shaw] was compiled by Roy H. Towell and published in Beaumont, Texas, in 1990.

SHAY

Ranking: 3535 **S.S. Count:** 12,769
Origin: English. Transformation of the English name Shaw.

Genealogies: *Shay Families with Roots in Lebanon County, Pennsylvania* was compiled by Thomas P. Shay and published in Henderson, Nevada, in 1991.

SHEA

Ranking: 853 **S.S. Count:** 50,183
Origin: Irish. Derived from the Gaelic name Ó Séaghdha, which was derived from the first name Séaghdha, meaning lucky or admirable.

Famous **Sheas:** JOHN DAWSON GILMARY SHEA (1824–1892) of New York City was an editor and historian. To his credit are *Discovery and Exploration of the Mississippi Valley* (1852), *History of the Catholic Missions Among the Indian Tribes of the United States* (1854), and *History of the Catholic Church in the United States* (1886–1892).

Genealogies: *Shay Families with Roots in Lebanon County, Pennsylvania* [also Shea] was compiled by Thomas P. Shay and published in Henderson, Nevada, in 1991.

SHEARER, SHEARES (S.S. Abbreviation: Sheare)

Ranking: 1686 **S.S. Count:** 26,494
Origin: Sheares—English; Shearer—English, Scottish. Sheares: derived from the Middle English word "scher," meaning bright or fair. The name was given to those who were attractive or fair-haired. Shearer: derived from the Middle English word "schere(n)," meaning to shear. The name was given to those who sheared sheep or to those who trimmed fabric with shears.

Famous **Bearers:** [EDITH] NORMA SHEARER (1900?–1983) of Canada was an actress who successfully made the transition from silent films to the talkies. She won an Academy Award for her role in the *The Divorcee* (1930).

Genealogies: None known.

SHEEHAN (S.S. Abbreviation: Sheeha)

Ranking: 1125 **S.S. Count:** 39,118
Origin: Irish. Derived from the Gaelic name Ó Síodhacháin, which was derived from the first name Síodhachán, which was derived from the word "síodhach," meaning peaceful.

Genealogies: None known.

SHEETS

Ranking: 1505 **S.S. Count:** 29,618
Origin: English. 1) the name was given to those from Sheat or Sheet, meaning park, the name of places in England. 2) Uncertain etymology. The name was given to those who lived near a corner or protuberance. 3) Uncertain etymology. The name was given to those who lived on or near a precipitous hill.

Genealogies: None known.

SHEFFIELD (S.S. Abbreviation: Sheffi)

Ranking: 1705 **S.S. Count:** 26,183
Origin: English. Derived from Sheaf, the name of a river, and the Old English word "feld," meaning field. The name was given to those from Sheffield, the name of a place in Yorkshire, England.

Famous **Sheffields:** JOSEPH EARL SHEFFIELD (1793–1882) of Connecticut was a merchant, financier, and philanthropist to Yale University. The science department was renamed in his honor the Sheffield Scientific School.

Genealogies: None known.

SHELBY

Ranking: 2777 **S.S. Count:** 16,401
Origin: English. Transformation of Selby.

Famous **Shelbys:** EVAN SHELBY (1719–1794) of Wales came to America as a teenager. He was a frontier soldier. His son, ISAAC SHELBY (1750–1826) of Maryland, was also a soldier and served in Dunmore's War under his father's command. He was the first governor of Kentucky.

Genealogies: *Chasin' Shelby's* (sic) was compiled by Janet Schonert and published in Decatur, Illinois, in 1971. *Our Ancestors and Kinsmen: the Shelbys, Polks, et al.* was compiled by Max W. Camp and published in Detroit, Michigan, in 1976.

SHELDON (S.S. Abbreviation: Sheldo)

Ranking: 1631 **S.S. Count:** 27,545
Origin: English. Uncertain etymology. Possibly a transformation of Shelton. The name was given to those from Sheldon, the name of several places in England.

Famous **Sheldons:** EDWARD AUSTIN SHELDON (1823–1897) of New York was the founder of the Oswego Primary Teachers' Training School, the first of its kind in the United States. CHARLES MONROE SHELDON (1857–1946) of New York was a Congregational clergyman and the author of *In His Steps,* a bestseller at the time.

Genealogies: *Sheldons at Bicentennial* was compiled by Keith M. Sheldon and published in Bay Village, Ohio, in 1979.

SHELL

Ranking: 2536 **S.S. Count:** 17,880

Origin: English. The name means bank and was given to those from Shell, a place in Worcestershire, England, or to those who lived on a bank.

Genealogies: None known.

SHELLEY (S.S. Abbreviation: Shelle)

Ranking: 1692 **S.S. Count:** 26,389

Origin: English. Derived from the Old English words "scylf" and "lēah," meaning shelf and clearing. The name was given to those from Shelley, the name of places in England.

Genealogies: None known.

SHELTON (S.S. Abbreviation: Shelto)

Ranking: 297 **S.S. Count:** 120,803

Origin: English. Uncertain etymology. Most likely derived from the Old English words "scylf" and "tūn," meaning shelf and settlement. The name was given to those from Shelton, the name of several places in England.

Famous **Sheltons:** FREDERICK WILLIAM SHELTON (1815–1881) of New York was a clergyman and an author. He wrote *The Trollopiad* (1837) and articles published in *Knickerbocker Magazine* (1838–1845).

Genealogies: *Sheldons at Bicentennial* [also Sheltons] was compiled by Keith M. Sheldon and published in Bay Village, Ohio, in 1979. *Descendants of Jessee Shelton and some Related Families* was compiled by Cecil Shelton and published in Fresno, California, in 1977. *Ralph Shelton Family in Early Virginia* was compiled by Frank H. Shelton and published in Colorado Springs, Colorado, in 1982.

SHEPARD (S.S. Abbreviation: Shepar)

Ranking: 764 **S.S. Count:** 55,396

Origin: English. Transformation of Sheppard.

Famous **Shepards:** THOMAS SHEPARD (1605–1649) of England was a preacher in the early days of New England. He also wrote books, including *The Sincere Convert* (1641). His diary was published in 1747 and entitled *Autobiography.* WILLIAM SHEPARD (1737–1817) of Massachusetts was a Revolutionary War soldier and one of the leaders who quelled Shays' Rebellion.

Genealogies: *The History of the Shepherd Family* [also Shepard] was compiled by Robert Sidney Shepherd and published in Cullman, Alabama, in 1990. *The Shepard Genealogy* was compiled by Lowell Shepard Blaisdell and published in 1952. *William G. Shepherd (also Shepard) Family Story and Genealogy* was compiled by Ralph W. Hedrick and published in Parkersburg, West Virginia, in 1970.

SHEPHARD (S.S. Abbreviation: Shepha)

Ranking: 4938 **S.S. Count:** 9069

Origin: English. Transformation of Sheppard.

Genealogies: None known.

SHEPHEARD, SHEPHERD, SHEPHERDSON (S.S. Abbreviation: Shephe)

Ranking: 482 **S.S. Count:** 83,662

Origin: English. Transformations of Sheppard.

Famous **Bearers:** ALEXANDER ROBEY SHEPHERD (1835–1902) of Washington, D.C., was the territorial governor of the District of Columbia and the man responsible for many of the improvements made to the city. J. CLINTON SHEPHERD (1888–1975) of Iowa toured the West as a rodeo performer in his youth, then became a prominent artist as an adult. Among his most notable works is the sculpture "The Doughboy," a bronze statue of a World War I soldier. He also was well known as a muralist.

Genealogies: *The History of the Shepherd Family* was compiled by Robert Sidney Shepherd and published in Cullman, Alabama, in 1990. *Thrice Three Times Told Tales* [Shepherd family] was compiled by Mary Waller Shepherd Soper and published in Winchester, Tennessee, in 1979. *William G. Shepherd Family Story and Genealogy* was compiled by Ralph W. Hedrick and published in Parkersburg, West Virginia, in 1970.

SHEPPARD, SHEPPARDSON (S.S. Abbreviation: Sheppa)

Ranking: 833 **S.S. Count:** 51,142

Origin: English. Derived from the Old English words "scēap," meaning sheep, and either "hierde" or "weard," meaning, respectively, herdsman and guardian. The names were given to shepherds.

Famous **Bearers:** JOHN MORRIS SHEPPARD (1875–1941) of Texas was the author of the 18th amendment to the U.S. Constitution, which introduced Prohibition. He continued to favor it even after it was repealed. SAMUEL EDWARD SHEPPARD (1882–1948) of England was a chemist and part of the Kodak Research Laboratory. He was responsible for more than 60 patents.

Genealogies: *My North Carolina Ancestors* [Sheppard family] was compiled by Jennifer M. Sheppard and published in Williamston, North Carolina, in 1990. *Sheppard-*

Marshall and Allied Families was compiled by Lillian A. Sheppard and published in San Jose, California, in 1974.

SHERIDAN (S.S. Abbreviation: Sherid)

Ranking: 1381   S.S. Count: 32,040

Origin: Irish. Derived from the Gaelic name Ó Sirideáin, meaning "descendant of Sirideán" (H&H).

Famous **Sheridans**: PHILIP HENRY SHERIDAN (1831–1888) of New York was a Union soldier who rose through the ranks and, as commander of the Shenandoah troops, was possibly most responsible for General Robert E. Lee's defeat and subsequent surrender.

Genealogies: None known.

SHERMAN, SHERMANN (S.S. Abbreviation: Sherma)

Ranking: 383   S.S. Count: 101,512

Origin: Sherman—English, Jewish; Shermann—Jewish. Sherman (English): derived from the Middle English word "shereman," meaning shearer. The name was given to those who sheared sheep or to those who trimmed finished fabric. Sherman (Jewish): derived from the Yiddish words "sher" and "man," meaning scissors and man. The name was given to tailors. Shermann: transformation of the Jewish name Sherman.

Famous **Bearers**: ROGER SHERMAN (1721?–1793) of Massachusetts was one of the signers of the Declaration of Independence, which he helped to draft. WILLIAM TECUMSEH SHERMAN (1820–1891) of Ohio was a Union soldier and the man responsible for the famous "march to the sea" of the Civil War. His reason for the march, he said, was to destroy goods, not lives, so as to bring about a quicker end to the war. JOHN SHERMAN (1823–1900) of Ohio was the brother of William Tecumseh Sherman. He was a politician who was involved in the Antitrust and Silver Purchase Acts of 1890. FREDERICK CARL SHERMAN (1888–1957) of Michigan was a naval officer and the commander of the carrier *Lexington* in the Pacific. FORREST PERCIVAL SHERMAN (1896–1951) of New Hampshire was a naval officer in World War II. He was the captain of the carrier *Wasp*.

Genealogies: *A Genealogical History of the Hatfield and Sherman Families of Utica, N.Y.* was compiled by John Bennett Hatfield and published in 1981. *Sherman Directory* was compiled by John H. Sherman and published in Baltimore, Maryland, in 1991. *Sherman Genealogy* was compiled by Thomas Townsend Sherman and published in Bethany, Oklahoma, in 1985.

SHERRIDAN, SHERRIFF, SHERRIFFS, SHERRILL, SHERRINGTON (S.S. Abbreviation: Sherri)

Ranking: 1797   S.S. Count: 25,094

Origin: Sherriff, Sherriffs, Sherrill, Sherrington—English; Sherridan—Irish. Sherriff, Sherriffs: derived from the Old

English words "scir" and "(ge)refa," meaning shire and reeve. The names were given to sheriffs. Sherrill: the name was given to those from Shirwell, meaning clear spring, a place in Devonshire, England. Sherrington: derived from the Old English town name Scīringtūn, meaning "settlement associated with Scira" (H&H), a first name meaning comely and luminous. Sherridan: transformation of Sheridan.

Genealogies: *Jacob Sherrill* was compiled by William Andrew Sherrill and published in Mesa, Arizona, in 1983.

SHERROD (S.S. Abbreviation: Sherro)

Ranking: 3260   S.S. Count: 13,946

Origin: English. 1) derived from the first name Scirheard, meaning bright and hard. 2) transformation of Sherwood.

Genealogies: None known.

SHERRY

Ranking: 4418   S.S. Count: 10,144

Origin: Irish. Derived from the first name Searrach, meaning colt and flighty.

Genealogies: None known.

SHERWOOD (S.S. Abbreviation: Sherwo)

Ranking: 1488   S.S. Count: 29,851

Origin: English. Derived from the Old English words "scir" and "wudu," meaning either shire or luminous and wood. The name was given to those from Sherwood, a place in England.

Famous **Sherwoods**: ADIEL SHERWOOD (1791–1879) of New York was a Baptist clergyman and the president of several universities. His son, THOMAS ADIEL SHERWOOD (1834–1918) of Georgia, was a justice of the Missouri Supreme Court. ISAAC RUTH SHERWOOD (1835–1925) of New York was a soldier and a member of Congress from Ohio. He opposed the U.S. entry into World War I. MARY ELIZABETH WILSON SHERWOOD (1826–1903) of New Hampshire was an author who wrote books and contributed to newspapers and magazines. WILLIAM HALL SHERWOOD (1854–1911) of New York was a pianist and the founder of Sherwood Music School in Chicago. ROBERT EMMET SHERWOOD (1896–1955) of New York was a writer of plays and magazine reviews. He wrote the book *Roosevelt and Hopkins: An Intimate History*, for which he was awarded a Pulitzer Prize.

Genealogies: *Sherwood Family Group Sheets* was compiled by Donald F. Notley and published in Tulsa, Oklahoma, in 1985. *Sherwood Family Papers* was compiled by William Lounsbury Sherwood and published in Salt Lake City, Utah, in 1990.

SHIELD (ALSO SHIELDS)

Ranking: 557   S.S. Count: 73,389

Origin: English, Irish. English: 1) derived from the Old

English word "scieldu," meaning shallows. The names were given to those who lived by the shallow area of a river. 2) derived from the Middle English word "schēle," meaning shed. The names were given to those from Shield, the name of places in England. 3) Uncertain etymology. The names were given to those who made armor. Irish: derived from the Gaelic name Ó Siaghail, meaning "descendant of Siadhal" (H&H), a name of uncertain etymology.

Famous **Bearers:** JAMES SHIELDS (1806–1879) of Ireland was a soldier and politician. He served as the governor of the Oregon Territory, as a U.S. senator from Illinois, then as a U.S. senator from Minnesota. He died in office as the senator from Missouri after the Civil War. JOHN KNIGHT SHIELDS (1858–1934) of Tennessee was a U.S. senator from Tennessee. THOMAS EDWARD SHIELDS (1862–1921) of Minnesota was a Roman Catholic clergyman and the founder of the *Catholic Educational Review*.

Genealogies: *Brookes's Book: Ancestry of Brooke Shields* was compiled by Daniel MacGregor and published in Chicago, Illinois, in 1986. *Shields Family* was published in Lenoir City, Tennessee, in 1980. *Irish Origins of the Shields Family* was compiled by John Edgar Shields and published in Gaithersburg, Maryland, in 1975.

SHIFFLETT (S. S. ABBREVIATION: SHIFFL)
Ranking: 3488 **S.S. Count:** 12,935
Origin: Uncertain etymology.
Genealogies: None known.

SHILLING, SHILLINGFORD, SHILLITO (S.S. Abbreviation: Shilli)
Ranking: 4212 **S.S. Count:** 10,720
Origin: English. Shilling: cognate to Schilling. Shillingford: Uncertain etymology. The name was given to those from Shillingford, the name of places in England. Shillito: uncertain etymology.
Genealogies: None known.

SHINN
Ranking: 3898 **S.S. Count:** 11,576
Origin: English, Norwegian. English: transformation of Skinner. Norwegian: uncertain etymology.
Famous **Shinns:** ASA SHINN (1781–1853) of New Jersey was one of the founders of the Methodist Church. EVERETT SHINN (1876–1953) of New Jersey was a painter and illustrator who advanced the concept of urban realism in American Art. Many of his illustrations were published in *Harper's Magazine*. In 1951 he was elected to the American Academy of Arts and Letters.
Genealogies: None known.

SHIPLEY (S.S. Abbreviation: Shiple)
Ranking: 1537 **S.S. Count:** 28,981

Origin: English. Derived from the Old English words "scēap" and "lēah," meaning sheep and clearing or wood. The name was given to those from Shipley, the name of places in England.

Famous **Shipleys:** RUTH BIELASKI SHIPLEY (1885–1966) of Maryland was a career government worker whose greatest achievements were seen in her reorganization and cleanup of the passport operations at the U.S Stated Department. Her efficiency made possible the capture of the Communist Party leader Earl Browder and the Nazi spy Gunther Rumrich.

Genealogies: *The Shipleys of Maryland, 1968; a study of the descendants of Adam Shipley, of Yorkshire, England, who came to Annapolis, Maryland, in 1668* was published in Baltimore, Maryland, in 1971. *Ten Generations of Descendants of Fisherman David Shapley of Marblehead, Mass.* [also Shipley] was compiled by Brian Joe Lobley Berry and published in McKinney, Texas, in 1991.

SHIPMAN (S.S. Abbreviation: Shipma)
Ranking: 2188 **S.S. Count:** 20,974
Origin: English. 1) derived from the Middle English word "schipman," meaning mariner. The name was given to mariners or to those who built boats. 2) derived from the Old English words "scēap" and "mann," meaning sheep and man. The name was given to shepherds.
Genealogies: *Mount Hope* [Shipman family] was compiled by Pauline Callaway Sheriff and published in Hollis, Oklahoma, in 1982.

SHIPP
Ranking: 2825 **S.S. Count:** 16,145
Origin: English. Transformation of Shipman, meaning mariner.
Famous **Shipps:** SCOTT SHIPP (1839–1917) of Virginia was a Confederate soldier and an 1859 graduate of Virginia Military Institute. He was credited with leading the charge of the cadets against the Union forces at New Market, May 1864.
Genealogies: *The Shipp Family Genealogy* was compiled by Ralph D. Shipp and published in Baltimore, Maryland, in 1975. *Family Affiliation of Abraham Shippee* [also Shipp] was compiled by Lenn Alan Bergsten and published in 1977.

SHIRLEY (S.S. Abbreviation: Shirle)
Ranking: 1187 **S.S. Count:** 36,970
Origin: English. Derived from the Old English words "scīr" and "lēah," meaning luminous and wood or clearing. The name was given to those from Shirley, the name of several places in England.
Famous **Shirleys:** WILLIAM SHIRLEY (1694–1771) of England was a colonial official and one of the negotiators

at the Paris meeting that decided the boundary between French North America and New England.

Genealogies: *The History of the Lightfoot and Shirley Families* was compiled by Annie Lightfoot Leith and published in Tampa, Florida, in 1979.

SHIVELY (S.S. Abbreviation: Shivel)

Ranking: 3931 **S.S. Count:** 11,479

Origin: German. Uncertain etymology. 1) the name was given to those who sold or made shovels. 2) the name was given to those who lived on a circular and even area of land.

Genealogies: *Across the Blue Ridge* [also Shively] was compiled by Billie Redding Lewis and published in Lake Wales, Florida, in 1984.

SHIVER

Ranking: 2832 **S.S. Count:** 16,110

Origin: French. Uncertain etymology. The name was given to goatherds.

Genealogies: None known.

SHOCKLEY (S.S. Abbreviation: Shockl)

Ranking: 2520 **S.S. Count:** 17,995

Origin: English. The name was given to those from Shocklach, meaning "goblin stream" (ES), a place in Cheshire, England.

Genealogies: *Shockley* was compiled by Nancy Miller and published in Dallas, Texas, in 1987.

SHOEMAKER (S.S. Abbreviation: Shoema)

Ranking: 842 **S.S. Count:** 50,612

Origin: German. Transformation of Schule.

Genealogies: *Shoemaker Pioneers* was compiled by Benjamin H. Shoemaker and published in Germantown, Pennsylvania, in 1975. *Uncle Billy: the ancestors and descendants of William B. Shoemaker, Sr., of Jasper County, Mississippi* was compiled by Mattie Shoemaker Holliday and published in Vidor, Texas, in 1987.

SHOOK

Ranking: 1970 **S.S. Count:** 23,022

Origin: German. Derived from the first name Cak, meaning expectation.

Famous Shooks: ALFRED MONTGOMERY SHOOK (1845–1923) of Tennessee was the superintendent and general manager of the Tennessee Coal, Iron & Railroad Co. He enlarged the company and led the company into the manufacture of steel, thus opening the South to industrial development.

Genealogies: None known.

SHORE

Ranking: 3229 **S.S. Count:** 14,044

Origin: English, Jewish. English: 1) derived from the Old English word "scora," meaning bank. The name was given to those who lived on a bank or slope. 2) derived from the Middle English word "schore," meaning shore. The name was given to those who lived by the shore of a sea. Jewish: Anglicization of the surnames S(c)hor(r) and Szor, which were ultimately derived from the Hebrew word "shor," meaning ox.

Genealogies: *Ancestors and Descendants of Frederick Shore: Switzerland, 1570– Surry County, North Carolina, 1750* was compiled by Leo Jane Shore and published in Kansas City, Missouri, in 1983. *History of the Benjamin Shore Family* was compiled by Alice Brumfield and published in Greensboro, North Carolina, in 1984.

SHORES

Ranking: 4182 **S.S. Count:** 10,803

Origin: English. Transformation of Shore.

Genealogies: None known.

SHORT

Ranking: 509 **S.S. Count:** 78,743

Origin: English, Irish. English: derived from the Old English word "sceort," meaning short. The name was given to those who were of short stature. Irish: derived from the Gaelic name Mac an Ghirr, meaning "son of the short man" (H&H).

Famous Shorts: WILLIAM SHORT (1759–1849) of Virginia was one of the founders of Phi Beta Kappa. CHARLES WILKINS SHORT (1794–1863) of Kentucky was a botanist and a collector of plants from the lands west of the Alleghenies. WALTER CAMPBELL SHORT (1880–1949) of Illinois was the army officer in charge at Pearl Harbor in 1941. Accused of negligence, he was later vindicated.

Genealogies: *Baxter-Short, Miller-Gill, and Related Families* was compiled by Mary Cynthia Baxter Harrell and published in St. Petersburg, Florida, in 1989. *Descendants of Wingate Short* was compiled by Lucille Day English and published in Houston, Texas, in 1991.

SHORTEN, SHORTER, SHORTERS (S.S. Abbreviation: Shorte)

Ranking: 3389 **S.S. Count:** 13,361

Origin: Shorter, Shorters—English; Shorten—Irish. Shorter: transformation of Short. Shorters: derived from the Middle English words "schort" and "hose," meaning short and hose. The name was given to those who dressed oddly. Shorten: ultimately derived from the Middle English words "schort" and "halse," meaning short and neck.

Famous Bearers: JOHN GILL SHORTER (1818–1872) of Georgia was the governor of Alabama.

Genealogies: None known.

SHOWALTER (S.S. Abbreviation: Showal)
Ranking: 3939 S.S. Count: 11,463
Origin: German. Uncertain etymology. 1) the name was given to schoolmasters. 2) the name was given to those who lived in a wood.
Genealogies: None known.

SHRADER (S.S. Abbreviation: Shrade)
Ranking: 4646 S.S. Count: 9626
Origin: German. Transformation of Schroeder.
Genealogies: *A History of the Shrader, Schrader, Schrater Family of Pendleton County, West Virginia* was compiled by Walter L. Eye and published in Harrisonburg, Virginia, in 1980.

SHREVE
Ranking: 4238 S.S. Count: 10,641
Origin: English. Transformation of Sheriff.
Famous **Shreves**: HENRY MILLER SHREVE (1785–1851) of New Hampshire was a steamboat captain. He started fur trading between St. Louis and Philadelphia, made steamship travel on the Mississippi River possible, and designed the first steam snagboat to clear debris from rivers. Shreveport, Louisiana, is named in his honor.
Genealogies: None known.

SHULER
Ranking: 2988 S.S. Count: 15,208
Origin: German. Transformation of Schuler.
Genealogies: *The David and Elizabeth Shuler Dantzler Family* was compiled by David Heber Dantzler and published in Orangeburg, South Carolina, in 1970. *The History of the Shuler Family* was compiled by Christine Weaver Shuler and published in Savannah, Georgia, in 1974.

SHULL
Ranking: 3428 S.S. Count: 13,166
Origin: German. Uncertain etymology. The name was given to a rowdy fellow or thug.
Famous **Shulls**: GEORGE HARRISON SHULL (1874–1954) of Ohio was a plant geneticist. He was the developer of hybrid corn, one of the greatest agricultural achievements of the 20th century.
Genealogies: *Shull: John W. and Martha Mosk, Descendants* was compiled by Elizabeth K. Glover and published in Gilbert, South Carolina, in 1971.

SHULTZ
Ranking: 1782 S.S. Count: 25,233
Origin: German. Transformation of Schultz.
Genealogies: *Matthias Shultz and his Descendants* was compiled by Carlyle W. Bennett and published in Owensboro, Kentucky, in 1980.

SHUMAKER (S.S. Abbreviation: Shumak)
Ranking: 3190 S.S. Count: 14,228
Origin: German. Transformation of Schule.
Genealogies: None known.

SHUMAN
Ranking: 3498 S.S. Count: 12,887
Origin: German. Transformation of Schule.
Genealogies: None known.

SHUMATE (S.S. Abbreviation: Shumat)
Ranking: 3738 S.S. Count: 12,103
Origin: French. Uncertain etymology. The name was given to those who lived on a plateau without trees.
Genealogies: *The Ancestry and Descendants of William Riley Shumate, 1777–1979* was compiled by Norma Pontiff Evans and published in Beaumont, Texas, in 1979.

SIBLEY
Ranking: 3465 S.S. Count: 13,027
Origin: English. Derived from the feminine medieval first name Sibley, which was ultimately derived from the Greek word "sibylla," the title of female prophetesses in ancient Greece and Rome.
Famous **Sibleys**: HIRAM SIBLEY (1807–1888) of Massachusetts was the founder of the Western Union Telegraph Co. HENRY HASTINGS SIBLEY (1811–1891) of Michigan was a fur trader and a Minnesota pioneer. He served as Minnesota's first governor. JOSEPH CROCKER SIBLEY (1850–1936) of New York was a member of Congress from Pennsylvania.
Genealogies: *The Sibley Family in America, 1629–1972* was compiled by James Scarborough Sibley and published in Honolulu, Hawaii, in 1972. *The Sibley Family in America, 1629–1972: with data compiled by 1982* was compiled by James Scarborough Sibley and published in Midlothian, Texas, in 1982.

SICKLE
Ranking: 4572 S.S. Count: 9772
Origin: English, German. Derived from the Old English word "sicol," meaning sickle. 1) the name was given to those who harvested with a sickle. 2) the name was given to those who lived near "the sign of the sickle" (ES).
Genealogies: None known.

SIDES
Ranking: 4105 S.S. Count: 11,102
Origin: English, German. English: the name means slope and was given to those from Syde, a place in Gloucestershire, England, or to those who lived on a slope. German: transformation of Seitz.
Genealogies: None known.

SIEBERT, SIEBERTZ (S.S. Abbreviation: Sieber)

Ranking: 2946 S.S. Count: 15,463

Origin: German. Derived from a Germanic first name comprising the components "sigi" and "berht," meaning victory and luminous.

Genealogies: None known.

SIEGEL (ALSO SIEGELMAN)

Ranking: 1191 S.S. Count: 36,775

Origin: Siegel—German, Jewish; Siegelman—Jewish. Siegel (German): 1) derived from various compound names with the first component "sigi," meaning victory. 2) a cognate to Seal, referring to a seal that is used to stamp an impression on a surface. Siegel (Jewish): transformation of the Jewish name Segal. Siegelman: transformation of Siegel.

Genealogies: None known.

SIERRA

Ranking: 1704 S.S. Count: 26,203

Origin: Spanish. Transformation of Serrano.

Genealogies: None known.

SIEVERS, SIEVERSEN, SIEVERT, SIEVERTS, SIEVERTSEN (S.S. Abbreviation: Siever)

Ranking: 3440 S.S. Count: 13,116

Origin: German. Transformations of Siegfried.

Genealogies: None known.

SIGLER

Ranking: 3719 S.S. Count: 12,149

Origin: German. Cognates to Stamper. 1) the name was given to makers of rubber stamps. 2) the name was given to those who made and sold seals that were used for documents.

Genealogies: None known.

SIKES

Ranking: 3148 S.S. Count: 14,431

Origin: English. Transformation of Sykes.

Famous **Sikeses**: WILLIAM WIRT SIKES (1836–1883) of New York was a journalist and a folklorist.

Genealogies: None known.

SILBER (ALSO SILBERBAUM, SILBERFELD, SILBERSHEIN, SILBERSTEIN)

Ranking: 2747 S.S. Count: 16,586

Origin: Silber—German; Silberbaum, Silberfeld, Silberman, Silberstein—Jewish. Silber: cognate to Silver. Silberbaum, Silberfeld, Silberman, Silberstein: Cognates to Silver, combined with "baum," meaning tree, "feld," meaning field, "shein," meaning shine, and "stein," meaning stone. The names were taken ornamentally.

Genealogies: None known.

SILER

Ranking: 4037 S.S. Count: 11,217

Origin: German. Transformation of Seiler.

Genealogies: None known.

SILLS

Ranking: 4555 S.S. Count: 9809

Origin: English. Derived from a medieval first name, a transformation of Silvester.

Famous **Sillses**: MILTON SILLS (1882–1930) of Illinois was an actor and one of the founders of the Academy of Motion Picture Arts and Sciences.

Genealogies: *Sills & Cliburn & Pitman* was compiled by Isom L. Stephens and published in Provo, Utah, in 1972. *Sills Family and Related Lines* was compiled by Louise Jelks Sills and published in Orangeburg, South Carolina, in 1969.

SILVA

Ranking: 336 S.S. Count: 112,603

Origin: Portuguese, Spanish. Derived from the Old Portuguese and Old Spanish word "silva," meaning wood. The name was given to those who lived in a wood.

Genealogies: *Silva Descendants: Portuguese Genealogy* was compiled by Henrietta Mello Mayer and published in 1978.

SILVER (ALSO SILVERMAN, SILVERS, SILVERTON, SILVERWOOD)

Ranking: 395 S.S. Count: 98,480

Origin: Silverton, Silverwood—English; Silver—English, Jewish; Silverman—Jewish; Silvers. Silver (English): 1) derived from the Middle English word "silver" meaning the color silver. The name was given to those who lived near a silvery stream. 2) same derivation as 1. The name was given to those who were wealthy or to those with silver hair. Silver (Jewish): derived from the German word "silber," meaning silver. The name was taken ornamentally. Silverman: cognate to Silver. Silvers: transformation of Silver. Silverton: uncertain etymology. Silverwood: uncertain etymology. The name may have been given to those from Silver Wood, a place in Yorkshire, England.

Famous **Bearers**: THOMAS SILVER (1813–1888) of New Jersey was the inventor of a marine engine governor. SIME SILVERMAN (1873–1933) of New York was the editor and publisher of *Variety* after 1905. LOUIS SILVERS (1889–1954) of New York was the composer of the song "April Showers." He also wrote the music for *The Jazz Singer* (1927), *It Happened One Night* (1934), and *One Night of Love* (1934), for which he won an Academy Award. ABBA HILLEL SILVER (1893–1963) of Lithuania was a rabbi and Zionist leader and the leader of "The Temple," his congregation in Cleveland, Ohio.

Genealogies: *Silver, our Pioneer Ancestors* was compiled by John Silver Harris and published in Boca Raton, Florida, in 1988. *The Silver Family Lineage of Anna, Charles, Mary and Elisabeth Silver* was compiled by Arthur E. Silver and published in Upper Montclair, New Jersey, in 1966. *Our Silver Heritage* was compiled by Benjamin Stump Silver and published in Gatesville, Texas, in 1976.

SILVESTER, SILVESTRELLI, SILVESTRINI, SILVESTRO, SILVESTRONI (S.S. Abbreviation: Silves)

Ranking: 3755 **S.S. Count:** 12,060

Origin: Silvester—English, German; Silvestrelli, Silvestrini, Silvestro, Silvestroni—Italian. Silvester: derived from the Latin name Silvester, which was derived from the word "silva," meaning wood. Silvestrelli, Silvestrini, Silvestro, Silvestroni: cognates to Silvester.

Genealogies: None known.

SIMMER

Ranking: 4981 **S.S. Count:** 9001

Origin: German. Transformation of Zimmerman.

Genealogies: None known.

SIMMON (ALSO SIMMOND, SIMMONDS, SIMMONITE, SIMMONS)

Ranking: 97 **S.S. Count:** 286,750

Origin: Simmond, Simmonds, Simmonite, Simmons— English; Simmon—English, German. Simmonds, Simmonite, Simmons, Simmon: transformations of Simon. Simmond: derived from the Germanic words "sigi" and "mund," meaning victory and protection.

Famous Bearers: GEORGE HENRY SIMMONS (1852–1937) of England was a physician and the editor of the *Journal,* the magazine of the American Medical Association. EDWARD EMERSON SIMMONS (1852–1931) of Massachusetts was a painter best remembered for his murals at the Library of Congress and the Massachusetts State House in Boston. FURNIFOLD MCLENDEL SIMMONS (1854–1940) of North Carolina was a member of Congress, then U.S. senator, from North Carolina. ROSCOE CONKLING MURRAY SIMMONS (1878–1951) of Mississippi was a black journalist who, as a columnist for the *Chicago Defender,* made its circulation the largest of any minority paper. WILLIAM JOSEPH SIMMONS (1880–1945) of Alabama was the founder of the "revived" Ku Klux Klan. JAMES STEVENS SIMMONS (1890–1954) of North Carolina was a bacteriologist with various government medical services. While attached to the National Research Council, he was one of the first to research the use of DDT.

Genealogies: *Reluctant Gentile: the life and times of Andrew Montom Simmonds, 1844–1925* was compiled by A. J. Simmonds and published in Trenton, Utah, in 1980.

SIMMS

Ranking: 1205 **S.S. Count:** 36,531

Origin: English. Transformation of Simpson.

Famous Simmses: WILLIAM GILMORE SIMMS (1806–1870) of South Carolina was an author who wrote novels and serials for magazines. WILLIAM ELLIOTT SIMMS (1822–1898) of Kentucky was a member of Congress from Kentucky, then a Confederate member of Congress during the Civil War. DAISY FLORENCE SIMMS (1873–1923) of Indiana was one of the leaders in the Young Women's Christian Association (Y.W.C.A.). RUTH HANNA SIMMS MCCORMICK (1880–1944) of Ohio was the first woman in the United States to win a statewide election when she was elected as member of Congress-at-large from Illinois.

Genealogies: *The Descendants of William & Mary Simms: England to Illinois and Beyond* was compiled by Vivian York Simms and published in Murfreesboro, Tennessee, in 1989. *Sims Kin* [also Simms] was compiled by Billie Louise Owens and published in Canon City, Colorado, in 1982.

SIMON

Ranking: 400 **S.S. Count:** 97,698

Origin: Czech, Dutch, English, Flemish, French, German, Hungarian, Jewish. Uncertain etymology. Derived from the Hebrew first name Shimòn, which was possibly derived from the word "shamà," meaning to hearken.

Famous Simons: RICHARD LEO SIMON (1889–1960) of New York City was a publisher. With Max Schuster he founded the publishing firm of Simon and Schuster.

Genealogies: None known.

SIMONE (ALSO SIMONEAU, SIMONEL, SIMONELLI, SIMONETTI)

Ranking: 1887 **S.S. Count:** 23,965

Origin: Simoneau, Simonel—French; Simone, Simonelli, Simonetti—Italian. Transformations of and cognates to Simon.

Genealogies: None known.

SIMONS (ALSO SIMONSEN, SIMONSOHN, SIMONSON, SIMONSSON)

Ranking: 777 **S.S. Count:** 54,088

Origin: Simons—Dutch, English, Flemish, German, Jewish; Simonsen—Danish, German, Norwegian; Simonsohn— Jewish; Simonson—English, Jewish; Simonsson—Swedish. Transformations of and cognates to Simon.

Famous Bearers: ALGIE MARTIN SIMONS (1870–1950) of Wisconsin was a socialist and a journalist and the author of *Packingtown* (1899). LEE SIMONSON (1888–1967) of New York City was a set designer and the author of several books on set designing. HENRY CALVERT SIMONS (1899–1946) of Illinois was an economist. He also was the author of *Personal Income Taxation* (1938).

Genealogies: *The Ancestors and Descendants of Ephraim Simmons (also Simons), 1769– 1837, of Little Compton, Rhode Island, Cleveland, and Peru, Ohio* was compiled by Allene Beaumont Duty and published in Cleveland, Ohio, in 1977. *Descendants of John Simmons* [also Simons] was compiled by Ruth Maxwell Graham and published in Arlington, Virginia, in 1975.

SIMPKIN, SIMPKINS, SIMPKINSON, SIMPKISS (S.S. Abbreviation: Simpki)
Ranking: 2703 **S.S. Count:** 16,832
Origin: English. Derived from the Middle English first name Simkin, ultimately a transformation of Simon.
Genealogies: *The Ancestors of Simpkins & Snowden* was compiled by Lorna K. Simpkins and published in 1978.

SIMPSON (S.S. Abbreviation: Simpso)
Ranking: 133 **S.S. Count:** 222,646
Origin: English. Derived from the medieval first name Sim, a transformation of Simon.
Famous Simpsons: STEPHEN SIMPSON (1789–1854) of Pennsylvania was an editor and reformer and the first person to run for Congress on the Labor ticket. MATTHEW SIMPSON (1811– 1884) of Ohio was the president of DePauw University and one of the most influential Methodist ministers of his day. He delivered the eulogy at Abraham Lincoln's funeral. JAMES HERVEY SIMPSON (1813– 1883) of New Jersey was a soldier and explorer. The reports he wrote of his explorations have significant historical content. WILLIAM DUNLAP SIMPSON (1823–1890) of South Carolina was the governor of South Carolina, then the chief justice of the South Carolina Supreme Court. JEREMIAH SIMPSON (1842–1905) of Canada was a member of Congress who went by the nickname Sockless Jerry. WALLIS WARFIELD SIMPSON (1896–1986) of Pennsylvania was the Duchess of Windsor. In order to marry her, King Edward VIII of England gave up his throne and family. Together they led an international social life.
Genealogies: *The Descendants of Simpson-Roach Families of South Carolina* was compiled by Max Perry and published in Midland, Texas, in 1973. *Look Back with Pride* [also Simpson] was compiled by Dorothea Simpson Meriwether and published in Chicago, Illinois, in 1988. *Simpson, a Family of the American Frontier* was compiled by John Worth Simpson and published in Baltimore, Maryland, in 1983.

SIMS
Ranking: 231 **S.S. Count:** 152,973
Origin: English. Transformation of Simpson.
Famous Simses: JAMES MARION SIMS (1813–1883) of South Carolina was a gynecologist and a pioneer in medical surgery. WINFIELD SCOTT SIMS (1844–1918) of New York City was an inventor of torpedo propulsion devices. WILLIAM SOWDEN SIMS (1858–1936) of Canada was a naval officer who led efforts to improve the operating efficiency of the U.S. Navy.
Genealogies: *Sims Kin* was compiled by Billie Louise Owens and published in Canon City, Colorado, in 1982. *Ancestors & Descendants of Thomas Sims of Culpeper County, Virginia* was compiled by Lela (Wolfe) Prewitt and published in Fairfield, Iowa, in 1972.

SINCLAIR, SINCLAIRE (S.S. Abbreviation: Sincla)
Ranking: 1236 **S.S. Count:** 35,796
Origin: English, French, Scottish. English, Scottish: the name was given to those from Saint-Clair-sur-Elle, or Saint-Clair-l'évêque, places in France whose churches were dedicated to St. Clarus. French: the name was given to those from places in France whose churches were dedicated to St. Clarus.
Famous Bearers: HARRY FORD SINCLAIR (1878–1956) of West Virginia was the founder of the Sinclair Oil and Refining Company. UPTON BEALL SINCLAIR JR. (1878–1968) of Maryland was a journalist and novelist who wrote *The Jungle* (1906), among others. Many of his works were bestsellers.
Genealogies: *The Sinclair Family of Virginia* was compiled by Jefferson Sinclair Selden and published in Hampton, Virginia, in 1964. *They Came to Find their Dream in Adams, New York: ancestors of the Sinclairs* was compiled by David A. Sinclair and published in Syracuse, New York, in 1983.

SINGER (ALSO SINGERS)
Ranking: 1116 **S.S. Count:** 39,620
Origin: Singers—English; Singer—German. Derived from words meaning to sing. The names were given to those who sang often or to choristers.
Famous Bearers: ISAAC MERRIT SINGER (1811–1875) of New York was the inventor of the first household sewing machine, which was simply referred to as a "Singer." ISRAEL JOSHUA SINGER (1893–1944) of Poland was a Yiddish novelist and the author of *East of Eden* (1939).
Genealogies: *Johann David Singer Family Book* was compiled by J. W. Singer and published in Stamping Ground, Kentucky, in 1972. *Singer Family Tree* was compiled by John Singer and published in Springfield, Ohio, in 1980.

SINGH
Ranking: 2101 **S.S. Count:** 21,873
Origin: Indian. Uncertain etymology.
Genealogies: None known.

SINGLETON (S.S. Abbreviation: Single)
Ranking: 401 **S.S. Count:** 97,619

Origin: English. Derived from the Old English words "scingel" and "tūn," meaning shingle and settlement. The name was given to those from Singleton, a place in Lancashire, England.

Famous **Singletons:** JAMES WASHINGTON SINGLETON (1811–1892) of Virginia was a member of Congress from Illinois.

Genealogies: None known.

SIPE

Ranking: 4975 **S.S. Count:** 9010

Origin: English. Uncertain etymology. The name was given to those who sold sieves.

Genealogies: *Paul Sipe, Palatine Immigrant, 1752* was compiled by Mildred Sipe Dickey and published in Midwest City, Oklahoma, in 1978.

SIPES

Ranking: 4776 **S.S. Count:** 9379

Origin: English. Transformation of Sipe.

Genealogies: None known.

SISCO

Ranking: 4199 **S.S. Count:** 10,755

Origin: Italian. Derived from the first name Francesco, meaning free.

Genealogies: None known.

SISK

Ranking: 2677 **S.S. Count:** 17,039

Origin: Irish?, German? Uncertain etymology.

Genealogies: *Some Early Pioneers of Western Kentucky* was compiled by Helen E. Hart Peyton and published in Decorah, Iowa, in 1990.

SISSON (ALSO SISSONS)

Ranking: 2773 **S.S. Count:** 16,447

Origin: English. Derived from the medieval first name Sisley, which was derived from the Latin feminine first name Caecilia, which was ultimately derived from the word "caecus," meaning blind.

Genealogies: *Hand, Sisson, and Scott: more yeoman ancestors* was compiled by Carol Clark Johnson and published in 1981. *Yankee Heritage, a Sisson Ancestry* was compiled by Brian Joe Lobley Berry and published in McKinney, Texas, in 1991.

SIZEMORE (S.S. Abbreviation: Sizemo)

Ranking: 1779 **S.S. Count:** 25,279

Origin: English. 1) derived from a first name meaning great victory. 2) Uncertain etymology. The name was given to those who lived on the wasteland of the Saxons.

Genealogies: *Sizemore: the descendants of Wesley Dudley and Ann Elizabeth* was compiled by Ann Bunch and published in 1976.

SKAGGS

Ranking: 1854 **S.S. Count:** 24,407

Origin: English, Swedish. Derived from the Old Norse name Skegg, meaning beard. The name was given to those with a beard.

Genealogies: *A Perspective on the Family Skaggs* was compiled by Lucille Sparks-Edwards and published in Lima, Ohio, in 1978. *Skaggs: the right to be proud* was compiled by Ida M. Lancaster and published in Amarillo, Texas, in 1992.

SKELTON (S.S. Abbreviation: Skelto)

Ranking: 2144 **S.S. Count:** 21,366

Origin: English. Transformation of Shelton. The name was given to those from Skelton, the name of places in England.

Genealogies: *Nine Generations of the Skelton Family* was compiled by Zenobia Bell Callahan and published in Anniston, Alabama, in 1964. *Rogers-Skelton and Allied Families* was compiled by Helen Rogers Skelton and published in Baltimore, Maryland, in 1987.

SKIDMORE (S.S. Abbreviation: Skidmo)

Ranking: 2987 **S.S. Count:** 15,214

Origin: English. Uncertain etymology.

Famous **Skidmores:** LOUIS SKIDMORE (1897–1962) of Indiana was an architect who designed the 1939 World's Fair; Oak Ridge, Tennessee, the town built for the people who worked on the Manhattan Project; and the U.S. Air Force Academy, Colorado Springs, Colorado.

Genealogies: *The Scudamores of Upton, Scudamore: a Knightly Family in Medieval Wiltshire, 1086–1382* [also Skidmores] was compiled by Warren Skidmore and published in Akron, Ohio, in 1982. *Skidmore: Rickmansworth, England–Delaware–North Carolina and West* was compiled by Warren Skidmore and published in Akron, Ohio, in 1983. *Thomas Skidmore (Scudamore), 1605–1684, of Westerleigh, Gloucestershire, and Fairfield, Connecticut* was compiled by Warren Skidmore and published in Akron, Ohio, in 1980.

SKINNER (S.S. Abbreviation: Skinne)

Ranking: 549 **S.S. Count:** 74,313

Origin: English. Derived from a word meaning skin. The name was given to those who prepared skins.

Famous **Skinners:** JOHN STUART SKINNER (1799–1851) of Maryland was traveling with Francis Scott Key during the bombing of Fort McHenry. It was he who arranged to have "The Star Spangled Banner" published. He also founded several magazines, including *American Farmer*, the first continuously published agricultural magazine in the United States. HALCYON SKINNER (1824–1900) of Ohio was the inventor of a carpet-weaving machine. AARON NICHOLS SKINNER (1845–1918) of Massachusetts was an astronomer with the U.S. Naval Observatory. OTIS SKINNER (1858–1942) of Massachusetts was a correspondent for the New York *Dramatic News* and an actor of the stage. ALANSON BUCK SKINNER (1886–1925) of New York was an anthropologist and ethnologist and an authority on the Algonquian and Siouan Indians.

Genealogies: *Descendants of Richard Alexander Skinner of Loudoun County, Virginia* was compiled by Lester Granville Holcombe and published in Bourbonnais, Illinois, in 1972. *"The Tishomingo County Connection"* [also Skinner] was compiled by Esther Welch Adams and published in Crump, Tennessee, in 1981.

SKIPPER (S.S. Abbreviation: Skippe)
Ranking: 3293 **S.S. Count:** 13,783
Origin: English. 1) derived from the Middle English word "skipp(e)," meaning basket. The name was given to those who made baskets. 2) derived from the Middle English word "skip(en)," meaning to jump. The name was given to acrobats or to those who were lively. 3) derived from the Middle English word "skipper," meaning a ship's master.
Genealogies: None known.

SLACK
Ranking: 2397 **S.S. Count:** 18,925
Origin: English. 1) derived from the Middle English word "slack," meaning careless. The name was given to those who were lazy. 2) derived from the Middle English word "slack," meaning a valley that was not deep. The name was given to those who lived in such a valley.
Genealogies: *6,474 Slack Relatives* was compiled by Roscoe C. Keeney and published in Parsons, West Virginia, in 1984. *Adjusting Branches of the Lane, Slack, Bush, et al. Family Trees* was compiled by Doris Christine Blummer Jackson and published in Annapolis, Maryland, in 1988.

SLADE
Ranking: 2666 **S.S. Count:** 17,103
Origin: English. Derived from the Old English word "slæd," meaning a little valley. The name was given to those who lived in a small dell.
Famous **Slades:** WILLIAM SLADE (1786–1859) of Vermont was the governor of Vermont and the founder of the state's public-school system.
Genealogies: *Slade-Babcock Genealogy* was compiled by Carl Boyer and published in Newhall, California, in 1970.

SLAGLE
Ranking: 3680 **S.S. Count:** 12,255

Origin: German. Uncertain etymology. The name was given to those who were in charge of the keys at a prison.
Genealogies: None known.

SLATER
Ranking: 962 **S.S. Count:** 45,397
Origin: English. Derived from the Middle English word "s(c)late," meaning slate. The name was given to those who slated roofs.
Famous **Slaters:** SAMUEL SLATER (1768–1835) of England is credited with founding the cotton-spinning industry in America. Unable to produce textile machinery legally, Slater memorized the structural components, slipped out of England, and had the Rhode Island firm of Almy and Brown reproduce the machinery, and then formed the company Almy, Brown and Slater to build their first factory.
Genealogies: *The Slaters from St. Albans* was compiled by Keith Slater and published in Berkeley Heights, New Jersey, in 1966.

SLATTER, SLATTERY (S.S. Abbreviation: Slatte)
Ranking: 3201 **S.S. Count:** 14,161
Origin: Slatter—English; Slattery—Irish. Slatter: transformation of Slater. Slattery: derived from the Gaelic name Ó Slat(ar)ra, which was derived from the first name Slatra, meaning hardy.
Famous **Bearers:** CHARLES LEWIS SLATTERY (1867–1930) of Pennsylvania was an Episcopal minister and the head of the committee to revise the Book of Common Prayer.
Genealogies: None known.

SLAUGHTER (S.S. Abbreviation: Slaugh)
Ranking: 1085 **S.S. Count:** 40,774
Origin: English. 1) derived from the Old English word "sloghtre," meaning a muddy patch. The name was given to those who lived in a muddy place. 2) derived from the Old English word "sloahtreow," meaning a sloe tree. The name was given to those who lived near a sloe tree. 3) derived from the Middle English word "slahter," meaning slaughter. The name was given to those who slaughtered animals.
Genealogies: *History of a Missouri Farm Family* [Slaughter family] was compiled by Stephen S. Slaughter and published in Harrison, New York, in 1978. *Slaughter and Price Genealogy* was compiled by Raymond D. Slaughter and published in Columbus, Ohio, in 1990. *The Slaughter Ranches & their Makers* was compiled by Mary Whatley Clarke and published in Austin, Texas, in 1979.

SLAYTON, SLAYTOR (S.S. Abbreviation: Slayto)
Ranking: 4732 **S.S. Count:** 9461

Origin: English. Slayton: Uncertain etymology. The name was given to those who lived on a grass-covered slope. Slaytor: transformation of Slaughter, meaning slaughterer of animals.

Genealogies: The Slaten Bunch [also Slayton] was compiled by Joe J. Slaten and published in Riverside, California, in 1992. *The Slaton (also Slayton) Family, ab Antiquitas* was compiled by Arthur J. Slaton and published in Los Angeles, California, in 1967.

SLEDGE

Ranking: 4074 S.S. Count: 11,100
Origin: English. The name was given to those who used a sledge, unclear if meaning a sleigh or a hammer.

Genealogies: Boone, Eller, Sledge, Vaughn and Related Families was compiled by Jesse H. Boone and published in Middleboro, Massachusetts, in 1970.

SLOAN

Ranking: 682 S.S. Count: 61,288
Origin: Irish, Scottish. Derived from the Gaelic first name Sluaghadhán, which was derived from the word "sluaghadh," meaning raid.

Famous **Sloans:** RICHARD ELIHU SLOAN (1857–1933) of Ohio was the governor of Arizona. JOHN FRENCH SLOAN (1871–1951) of Pennsylvania was an artist who developed an urban realism concept in American art. JAMES FORMAN SLOAN (1874–1933) of Indiana was a professional jockey known as Tod. He developed a new style of riding seat that others quickly adopted. ALFRED PRITCHARD SLOAN JR. (1875–1966) of Connecticut was a philanthropist and one of the benefactors of the Sloan-Kettering Institute for Cancer Research.

Genealogies: Hugh Russell Sloan and Margaret Violet Reid Sloan Family Newsletter was published in Granada Hills, California, in 1964.

SLOCUM

Ranking: 3162 S.S. Count: 14,363
Origin: English. Derived from the Old English words "slāh" and "cumb," meaning sloe tree and valley. The name was given to those from Slocum, a place in England.

Famous **Slocums:** FRANCES SLOCUM (1773–1847) of Rhode Island was captured by the Indians at the age of five. Although she lived peacefully with her Indian family until her death, her family searched for her for 59 years until she and her sisters and brothers were reunited. She was known as the "White Rose of the Miamis." The Frances Slocum State Forest in Indiana is named in her honor. SAMUEL SLOCUM (1792–1861) of Rhode Island invented of a stapling machine that pinned papers together for packaged sale. HENRY WARNER SLOCUM (1827–1894) of New York was a major general in the Union army. After the Civil War he served as a member of Congress from New York. JOSHUA

SLOCUM (1844–1910) of Canada sailed around the world in 1895. He wrote *Sailing Alone Around the World* (1900). He died at sea.

Genealogies: None known.

SLONE

Ranking: 3117 S.S. Count: 14,601
Origin: Irish, Scottish. Transformation of Sloan.
Genealogies: None known.

SMALL

Ranking: 621 S.S. Count: 67,121
Origin: English. Derived from the Middle English word "smal," meaning thin. The name was given to those who were slim or petite.

Famous **Smalls:** ALBION WOODBURY SMALL (1854–1926) of Maine was a sociologist and the founder of *American Journal of Sociology.*

Genealogies: Buxton Forbes Laurie of Southcote [also Small] was compiled by N. J. Vine Hall and published in Sydney, New Jersey, in 1976. *Descendants of Margry Lemond and James Nicholas Small* was compiled by Haskell Pruett and published in Stillwater, Oklahoma, in 1983.

SMALLE (ALSO SMALLEN, SMALLES, SMALLEY)

Ranking: 2477 S.S. Count: 18,310
Origin: Smalle—Dutch; Smalles, Smalley—English; Smallen—Irish. Smalle, Smalles: cognates to and transformations of Small. Smalley: derived from the Old English words "smœl" and "lēah," meaning small and clearing. The name was given to those from Smalley, the name of places in England. Smallen: transformation of the Irish name Spillane, which was derived from the Gaelic name Ó Spealáin, which was derived from the first name Spealán, which was derived from the word "speal," meaning scythe.

Famous **Bearers:** GEORGE WASHBURN SMALLEY (1833–1916) of Massachusetts was a war correspondent during the Austro-Prussian War (1866) and thought to have been the first to send a cabled news story to his paper.

Genealogies: None known.

SMALLS (ALSO SMALLSHAW))

Ranking: 3161 S.S. Count: 14,366
Origin: English. Smalls: transformation of Small. Smallshaw: derived from the Old English words "smœl" and "sceaga," meaning narrow and thicket. The name was given to those from Smallshaw, a place in Yorkshire, England.

Famous **Bearers:** ROBERT SMALLS (1839–1915) of South Carolina was a black Union soldier and a member of Congress from South Carolina after the Civil War.

Genealogies: None known.

SMALLWOOD (S.S. Abbreviation: Smallw)

Ranking: 1796 **S.S. Count:** 25,106

Origin: English. Derived from the Old English words "smœol" and "wudu," meaning narrow and wood. The name was given to those from Smallwood, a place in England.

Famous Smallwoods: WILLIAM SMALLWOOD (1732–1792) of Maryland was a Revolutionary War soldier and the governor of Maryland.

Genealogies: *The Smallwood Family of Maryland and Virginia* was compiled by Mildred A. McDonnell and published in 1970.

SMART

Ranking: 1334 **S.S. Count:** 33,147

Origin: English. Derived from the Middle English word "smart," meaning quick or energetic. The name was given to those who were lively or quick.

Famous Smarts: DAVID ARCHIBALD SMART (1892–1952) of Nebraska was the founder of the David A. Smart Publishing Co., which published *Gentleman's Quarterly* as its first magazine. It also published the first edition of *Esquire: The Magazine for Men.*

Genealogies: *The Descendants of William Smart, Sr., 1720–c1795* was compiled by Richard Eugene Smart and published in Cullman, Alabama, in 1986.

SMILEY

Ranking: 1691 **S.S. Count:** 26,418

Origin: Scottish. Uncertain etymology. 1) Possibly derived from the Middle English word "smile," meaning grin. 2) possibly derived from the Middle English word "smil," meaning smell.

Genealogies: *Mohonk, Its People and Spirit* [also Smiley] was compiled by Larry E. Burgess and published in New Paltz, New York, in 1980.

SMITH

Ranking: 1 **S.S. Count:** 3,376,494

Origin: English. Derived from the Middle English word "smith," meaning a metalworker. The name was given to metalworkers.

Famous Smiths: JOHN SMITH (1579?–1631) of England was an adventurer even before sailing with the Virginia Co. colonists. He landed in Jamestown in 1607. In one of his food-gathering expeditions he was taken prisoner by the Indians, condemned to death, and then rescued by Pocahontas. He returned to England after an administrative period as president of the Jamestown settlement, then explored New England for England, bringing back fish, furs, and maps of the new lands. He also wrote about his explorations. He died in England. DANIEL SMITH (1748–1818) of Virginia was a Revolutionary War soldier and the maker of the first map of Tennessee. He also served as a U.S. senator from Tennessee. DANIEL B. SMITH (1792–1883) of Pennsylvania was one of the founders of the Philadelphia College of Pharmacy. SOPHIA SMITH (1796–1870) of Massachusetts was the founder of Smith College. ABBY HADASSAH SMITH (1797–1878) and her sister JULIA EVELINA SMITH (1792–1886), both of Connecticut, were women's rights advocates. They refused to pay taxes without the right to vote. Although their property and livestock were seized for nonpayment of taxes, they held steadfast in their beliefs toward taxation without representation until they died. Their actions came to be the first stone removed in the wall barring women from equal rights. ELIZA ROXEY SNOW SMITH (1804–1887) of Massachusetts is called the "Mother of Mormonism." EMMA HALE SMITH (1804–1879) of Pennsylvania was the wife of Joseph Smith, the Mormon prophet. JOSEPH SMITH (1805–1844) of Vermont was a Mormon prophet and the founder of the Church of Jesus Christ of Latter-day Saints. He was killed by an angry mob in Carthage, Illinois. His son, JOSEPH SMITH (1832–1914) of Ohio, served as the president of the church in Utah. ERMINNIE ADELLE PLATT SMITH (1836–1886) of New York was an expert on the language, customs, and myths of the Iroquois Indians. VIRGINIA THRALL SMITH (1836–1903) of Connecticut was a pioneer in the area of child care in Connecticut. Children's Services of Connecticut and Newington Hospital grew out of her work on behalf of children. FRANCIS MARION SMITH (1846–1931) of Wisconsin was co-founder of the Pacific Coast Borax Co., which bought the rights to the colemanite deposits in Death Valley, from which borax is made. It was "trucked" out of the desert to Mojave, California, by mules. Thus the advertising slogan "20 mule-team Borax" was born. EDGAR FAHS SMITH (1854–1928) of Pennsylvania was a pioneer in the area of electrochemistry. ALFRED EMANUEL SMITH (1873–1944) of New York City was the governor of New York and the first Roman Catholic ever to be nominated for presidency, by the Democratic Party in 1928. LUCY HARTH SMITH (1888–1955) of Virginia was a schoolteacher and the first woman to serve as the president of the Kentucky Negro Education Association. BESSIE SMITH (1894–1937) of Tennessee was a blues singer and was called the "Empress of the Blues." ALBERT MERRIMAN SMITH (1913–1970) of Georgia was a journalist and the author of several books on the U.S. presidency. He was awarded a Pulitzer Prize for his coverage of the assassination of President John F. Kennedy.

Genealogies: *Andrew M. and O. S. Smith, Sons of Maine and Nebraska Homesteaders* was compiled by Claude R. Wiegers and published in Lincoln, Nebraska, in 1979. *Kinfolk of Henry Smith (1846–1887)* was published in Philip, South Dakota, in 1993. *Pioneer Heritage: the Smith family* was compiled by Marguerite Esther Smith and published in New York, New York, in 1977.

SMITHE (ALSO SMITHER, SMITHERMAN, SMITHERS)

Ranking: 2721 S.S. Count: 16,721

Origin: English. Smithe: transformation of Smythe. Smither, Smitherman, Smithers: transformations of Smith.

Genealogies: *Tanglewood Chronicles (also Smithers family)* was compiled by Debra Winfield Smithers and published in Baltimore, Maryland, in 1983.

SMITHSON (S.S. Abbreviation: Smiths)

Ranking: 4675 S.S. Count: 9577

Origin: English. Transformation of Smith.

Genealogies: None known.

SMOOT

Ranking: 3522 S.S. Count: 12,806

Origin: Dutch. The name was given to those who made lard.

Famous Smoots: REED OWEN SMOOT (1862–1941) of Utah was a U.S. senator and the co-author of the Smoot-Hawley Tariff Act. He also served as an official of the Mormon church.

Genealogies: None known.

SMOTHERMAN, SMOTHERS (S.S. Abbreviation: Smothe)

Ranking: 3197 S.S. Count: 14,194

Origin: English. Transformations of Smith.

Genealogies: None known.

SMYTH

Ranking: 3326 S.S. Count: 13,626

Origin: English. Uncertain etymology. 1) most likely a transformation of Smythe. The name was given to those who lived near the forge of a smith. 2) possibly a transformation of Smith.

Famous Smyths: ALEXANDER SMYTH (1765–1830) of Ireland came to America as a child. As an officer in the War of 1812 he attempted to invade Canada at Black Rock, New York. After the war he served as a member of Congress from Virginia. JOHN HENRY SMYTH (1844–1908) of Virginia was the son of a slave father and a free black woman. He attended the Pennsylvania Academy of Fine Arts, served as the U.S. minister to Liberia, and founded the Virginia Manual Labor School. HENRY DEWOLF SMYTH (1898–1986) of New York was a professor of physics and one of the builders of the first atomic bomb.

Genealogies: None known.

SNEAD

Ranking: 3020 S.S. Count: 15,048

Origin: English. Derived from the Old Norse word

"sneið," meaning a portion of land. The name was given to those from Snaith, a place or former place in England.

Famous Sneads: THOMAS LOWNDES SNEAD (1828–1890) of Virginia was a Confederate officer and the author of studies about the Civil War.

Genealogies: *Snead Notebook* was compiled by Elizabeth Cowan Snead Shue and published in Baltimore, Maryland, in 1991. *"Your Heritage": Bush-Sneed* [also Snead] was compiled by Estelle Clark Herdeg and published in Gowanda, New York, in 1983. *Snead, Sneed, Sneyde Genealogical Workbook* was published in North Bend, Oregon.

SNEED

Ranking: 1876 S.S. Count: 24,126

Origin: English. Transformation of Snead.

Genealogies: *"Your Heritage": Bush-Sneed* was compiled by Estelle Clark Herdeg and published in Gowanda, New York, in 1983. *Snead, Sneed, Sneyde Genealogical Workbook* was published in North Bend, Oregon.

SNELL

Ranking: 1413 S.S. Count: 31,472

Origin: English. Derived from the Middle English word "snell," meaning quick. The name was given to those who were energetic or lively.

Famous Snells: BERTRAND HOLLIS SNELL (1870–1958) of New York was a member of Congress and the chairman of the House Rules Committee in the 1920s.

Genealogies: *The Snell Family* was compiled by Jane Lawrence Stone and published in Nashville, Tennessee, in 1974.

SNIDER (ALSO SNIDERMAN, SNIDERS)

Ranking: 966 S.S. Count: 45,186

Origin: Sniders, Sniderman—English; Snider—English, Jewish. Cognates to and transformations of Schneider.

Famous Bearers: DENTON JAQUES SNIDER (1841–1925) of Ohio was an original member of the St. Louis Philosophical Society.

Genealogies: None known.

SNIPES

Ranking: 3915 S.S. Count: 11,513

Origin: English. Derived from a word meaning bog or swamp. The name was given to those from Snipe, a place in Northumberland, England or to those from a swampy area.

Genealogies: *The Descendants & Ancestors of Young Snipes* was compiled by Earl A. Truett and published in Reston, Virginia, in 1982.

SNODGRASS (S.S. Abbreviation: Snodgr)

Ranking: 2241 S.S. Count: 20,460

Origin: Scottish. Derived from the Middle English words "snod" and "grass," meaning smooth and grass. The name was given to those from Snodgrass, a place or former place in Scotland.

Genealogies: The Neal, Harbison, Snodgrass, Miller, and Related Families was compiled by Thomas Howe R. Neal and published in Knoxville, Tennessee, in 1971. *Oregon Pioneers of 1852 and 1853: the Snodgrass, Deckard, and Moore families* was compiled by Willetta Moore Smith and published in Corvallis, Oregon, in 1970.

SNOOK
Ranking: 4528 S.S. Count: 9888
Origin: English. Derived from the Middle English word "snoke," meaning a protruding area of land. The name was given to those who lived on such a piece of land.

Genealogies: Some Snoke Families [also Snook] was compiled by Frank McElwain Snoke and published in Pittsburgh, Pennsylvania, in 1979.

SNOW
Ranking: 665 S.S. Count: 63,039
Origin: English, Jewish. English: derived from the Old English word "snāw," meaning snow. The name was given to those of very fair complexion or to those with white hair. Jewish: Anglicization of any of several names, including compound names, with a first component meaning snow.

Famous **Snows:** JESSE BAKER SNOW (1868–1947) of Massachusetts was an engineer involved in the construction of the tunnels for the New York subways. CARMEL WHITE SNOW (1887–1961) of Ireland was the editor of *Vogue* magazine and the one responsible for changing the magazine's format. Through the magazine she also made the names Christian Dior and Balenciaga common in the United States.

Genealogies: The Family of Mrs. J. B. Snow was compiled by T. D. Boaz and published in McLean, Virginia, in 1974. *James Middleton Snow* was compiled by Dorothy May Snow-Nelson and published in New York, New York, in 1992.

SNOWDEN (S.S. Abbreviation: Snowde)
Ranking: 2830 S.S. Count: 16,120
Origin: English. Derived from the Old English words "snāw" and "dūn," meaning snow and hill. The name was given to those from Snowden, the name of places in England.

Famous **Snowdens:** JAMES SNOWDEN (1809–1878) of Pennsylvania was the director of the U.S. Mint in Philadelphia. THOMAS SNOWDEN (1857–1930) of New York was a naval officer and the military governor of Santo Domingo.

Genealogies: The Descendants of Joseph Snowden was compiled by Virginia Whitman Snowden and published in Baltimore, Maryland, in 1981. *Montpelier & the Snowden Family* was compiled by William Grover Cook and published in Laurel, Maryland, in 1976.

SNYDER (ALSO SNYDERS)
Ranking: 127 S.S. Count: 232,854
Origin: Snyders—English; Snyder—English, Jewish. Cognates to and transformations of Schneider.

Famous **Bearers:** SIMON SNYDER (1759–1819) of Pennsylvania was the governor of Pennsylvania and the first of German descent to hold that position. HOWARD MCCRUM SNYDER (1881–1970) of Wyoming was an army physician and a pioneer in medicine related to sports and military injuries.

Genealogies: Barth and Schneider (Snyder) Families was compiled by Jack Frederick Snyder and published in Muncie, Indiana, in 1978. *The Jacob Snyder Family History* was compiled by Loucile Ruth Mayhew Heckman and published in 1991.

SOARES
Ranking: 4147 S.S. Count: 10,920
Origin: English, Portuguese. English: derived from the Anglo-Norman-French word "sor," meaning chestnut. The name was given to those with hair the color of chestnut. Portuguese: derived from a Germanic medieval name with a second component meaning army.

Genealogies: None known.

SOKOLOF, SOKOLOV, SOKOLOVIC, SOKOLOW, SOKOLOWSKI (S.S. Abbreviation: Sokolo)
Ranking: 3792 S.S. Count: 11,891
Origin: Sokolof, Sokolovic, Sokolow—Jewish; Sokolowski—Polish; Sokolov—Jewish, Russian. Sokolowski, Sokolov (Russian): Derived from the word "sokol," meaning falcon. The name was given to falconers or to those who were thought to resemble a falcon. Sokolof, Sokolovic, Sokolow, Sokolov (Jewish): derived from a word meaning falcon. The names were taken ornamentally.

Genealogies: None known.

SOLANO
Ranking: 4562 S.S. Count: 9793
Origin: Spanish. Derived from the Old Spanish word "solano," meaning a sunny area. The name was given to those from Solano, the name of several places in Spain.

Genealogies: None known.

SOLIS
Ranking: 1181 S.S. Count: 37,051
Origin: English, Jewish. English: derived from a medieval

first name that was derived from the Middle English word "solace," meaning consolation. The name was given to those born after a sister or brother had died. Jewish: etymology unknown.

Genealogies: None known.

SOLOMON (S.S. Abbreviation: Solomo)

Ranking: 678 **S.S. Count:** 61,942

Origin: Danish, English, French, German, Hungarian, Jewish, Norwegian, Polish. Derived from the Hebrew masculine first name Shelomo, which was derived from the word "shalom," meaning peace.

Famous **Solomons:** HANNAH GREENEBAUM SOLOMON (1858–1942) of Illinois was the founder of the National Council of Jewish Women. SIDNEY L. SOLOMON (1902–1975) of Massachusetts was the first person not a member of the founding families to assume the presidency of the Abraham & Straus department store chain. Under his leadership, the company established such employee benefits as the 37.5-hour work week and scholarships for employees' children.

Genealogies: None known.

SOMERS (ALSO SOMERSCALES, SOMERSCHEIN, SOMERSET)

Ranking: 2654 **S.S. Count:** 17,146

Origin: Somers, Somerscales, Somerset—English; Somerschein—Jewish. Somers, Somerschein: transformations of Summer, meaning the season of summer. Somerscales: derived from the Old Norse words "sumar" and "skáli," meaning summer and hut. The name was given to those who lived in huts built for summer habitation. Somerset: derived from the Old English phrase "Sumor(tūn)sœ," meaning "dwellers at the summer settlement" (H&H).

Famous **Bearers:** RICHARD SOMERS (1778–1804) of New Jersey was a naval officer on board the *Intrepid* in Tripoli harbor. An explosion caused his death.

Genealogies: *The Story of My Life* [also Somers] was compiled by Emma Etta Somers Miller and published in 1991.

SOMERVILLE (S.S. Abbreviation: Somerv)

Ranking: 4533 **S.S. Count:** 9867

Origin: Irish, Scottish. Irish: derived from the Gaelic name Ó Somacháin, which was derived from the name Somachán, which was derived from a word meaning fat. Scottish: 1) derived from the Germanic first name Sigimar and the Old French word "ville," meaning settlement. 2) uncertain etymology. Possibly given to those from a place called Somerville.

Genealogies: *The Families Somerville, Somervaill, Summerall, Summerell, Summerill, et al.* was compiled by James H. Hines and published in Houston, Texas, in 1981.

SOMMER (ALSO SOMMERFELD, SOMMERMAN, SOMMERS, SOMMERSETT)

Ranking: 1034 **S.S. Count:** 42,327

Origin: Sommer—Danish, English, German, Norwegian; Sommers, Sommersett—English; Sommerfeld, Sommerman—Jewish. Sommer, Sommerfeld, Sommerman, Sommers: cognates to and transformations of Summer, meaning the season of summer. Sommersett: transformation of Somerset.

Genealogies: *Lineage and Descendants of Joseph Sommer and Elisabeth Barbe Garber* was compiled by Grace Hildy and published in Provo, Utah, in 1991. *The Sommer, Sommers, Somers, and Summers that Missed the Boat* was compiled by William Clark Summers and published in Billings, Montana, in 1979.

SOPER

Ranking: 4771 **S.S. Count:** 9385

Origin: English. Derived from the Middle English word "sōpe," meaning soap. The name was given to those who made soap.

Genealogies: *The New Soper Compendium* was compiled by Earl F. Soper and published in Berne, New York, in 1989.

SORENS (ALSO SORENSEN, SORENSON, SORENSSON)

Ranking: 739 **S.S. Count:** 57,266

Origin: Sorens, Sorensen—Danish, Norwegian; Sorenson—Jewish; Sorensson—Swedish. Sorens, Sorensen, Sorensson: derived from the Latin first name Severus, meaning austere. Sorenson: derived from the Yiddish feminine first name Sore, which was derived from the Hebrew name Sara, meaning princess.

Genealogies: *The Descendants of Soren Ottersen and Marie Andersdatter: a Sorenson family history* was compiled by Elva Sorenson Steffenson and published in Iowa in 1979.

SORIANO (S.S. Abbreviation: Sorian)

Ranking: 4529 **S.S. Count:** 9885

Origin: Jewish, Spanish. Uncertain etymology. The name was given to those from Soria, the name of a place in Castile, Spain.

Genealogies: None known.

SORREL (ALSO SORRELL)

Ranking: 2027 **S.S. Count:** 22,539

Origin: English. Transformation of Soares, meaning chestnut.

Genealogies: *Notes on the Family History of the Sorelle Family of the South* [also Sorrel] was compiled by Vivian Sorelle and published in New York, New York, in 1950.

SOSA

Ranking: 2140 S.S. Count: 21,409
Origin: Spanish. Cognate to Sousa.
Genealogies: None known.

SOTO

Ranking: 466 S.S. Count: 85,800
Origin: Spanish. Derived from the Latin word "saltus," meaning grove. The name was given to those who lived near a grove or wood.
Genealogies: None known.

SOUDER (ALSO SOUDERS)

Ranking: 3849 S.S. Count: 11,715
Origin: French. Derived from the Old French word "sol-dure," meaning to solder. The names were given to welders or solderers.
Genealogies: *Charles P. Skouras Family History* [also Souder] was compiled by Florence Louise Souders Skouras and published in Los Angeles, California, in 1979. *Family History of Nathaniel Z. Martin, 1841–1971* [also Souder] was compiled by Richard B. Martin and published in Gordonville, Pennsylvania, in 1971.

SOUSA

Ranking: 2879 S.S. Count: 15,811
Origin: Portuguese. Uncertain etymology. Possibly derived from the words "sausa" and "agua," meaning salty and water. The name was given to those from Sousa, the name of several places in Portugal.
Famous **Sousas**: JOHN PHILIP SOUSA (1854–1932) of Washington, D.C., was a composer and bandmaster. He is responsible for the marching music and the national interest in high school marching bands. Among his compositions are "Stars and Stripes Forever."
Genealogies: None known.

SOUTH

Ranking: 3002 S.S. Count: 15,125
Origin: English. Derived from the Middle English word "s(o)uth," meaning south. The name was given to those from the south of any area.
Genealogies: None known.

SOUTHALL, SOUTHAM, SOUTHAN (S.S. Abbreviation: Southa)

Ranking: 2371 S.S. Count: 19,144
Origin: English. Southall: derived from the Old English words "sūð" and "halh," meaning south and recess. The name was given to those from Southall, the name of various places in England. Southam: derived from the Old English words "sūð" and "hām," meaning south and homestead. The name
was given to those from Southam, the name of places in England. Southan: transformation of South.
Famous **Bearers**: JAMES COCKE SOUTHALL (1828–1897) of Virginia was a journalist with the *Richmond Enquirer* and the author of *The Recent Origin of Man* (1875).
Genealogies: None known.

SOUTHEE, SOUTHERIN, SOUTHERN, SOUTHEY (S.S. Abbreviation: Southe)

Ranking: 1564 S.S. Count: 28,536
Origin: English. Southee, Southey: derived from the Old English words "sūð" and "(ge)hœg," meaning south and enclosure. The names were given to those from Southey or Southee, the name of places in England. Southerin, Southern: transformations of South.
Genealogies: None known.

SOUTHWARD, SOUTHWELL, SOUTHWOOD, SOUTHWORTH (S.S. Abbreviation: Southw)

Ranking: 2579 S.S. Count: 17,644
Origin: English. Southward, Southworth: derived from the Old English words "sūð" and "worð," meaning south and enclosure. The names were given to those from Southworth, a place in England. Southwell: derived from the Old English words "sūð" and "well(a)," meaning south and spring. The name was given to those from Southwell, a place in England. Southwood: derived from the Old English words "sūð" and "wudu," meaning south and wood. The name was given to those from Southwood, a place in Norfolk, England.
Famous **Bearers**: ALBERT SANDS SOUTHWORTH (1811–1894) of Vermont was a photographer, with Josiah Johnson Hawes, of some of the well-known personalities of his day. EMMA DOROTHY ELIZA NEVITTE SOUTHWORTH (1819–1899) of Washington, D.C., was a novelist. Her most well-received novel was *The Hidden Hand* (1959).
Genealogies: *Ancestors and Descendants of Micajah and Martha Southard* [also Southworth] was compiled by Ralph Kimball Potter and published in Lakewood, New Jersey, in 1976. *Early Southards* [also Southworths] of New York and New Jersey was compiled by Ralph Kimball Potter and published in 1974.

SOUZA

Ranking: 1777 S.S. Count: 25,281
Origin: Portuguese. Transformation of Sousa.
Genealogies: None known.

SOWELL

Ranking: 3349 S.S. Count: 13,536
Origin: English. Transformation of Southwell.
Genealogies: None known.

SOWERS (ALSO SOWERSBY)

Ranking: 3044 S.S. Count: 14,936

Origin: Sowersby—English; Sowers—German, Jewish. Sowersby: derived from the Old Norse words "saurr" and "býr," meaning sour land and settlement. The name was given to those from Sowerby, the name of places in England. Sowers: derived from the Middle High German word "sūr," meaning sour. The name was given to those with sour dispositions.

Genealogies: *The Christopher Sauers: courageous printers who defended religious freedom in early America* [also Sowers] was compiled by Steve Longenecker and published in Elgin, Illinois, in 1981. *A Thousand Doors: the history of Philip Sauer (Sowers) and his 14 children* was compiled by Ruth Sowers Owen and published in Lexington, North Carolina, in 1971. *Sowers-Martin Genealogy of Floyd County, Virginia* was compiled by Erma C. Sowers and published in 1979.

SPAIN

Ranking: 2887 S.S. Count: 15,774

Origin: English, Irish. 1) an ethnic name given to those from Spain. 2) derived from the Old French word "espine," meaning bush of thorns. The name was given to those from Espinay, a town in Brittany, France.

Genealogies: None known.

SPALDING (S.S. Abbreviation: Spaldi)

Ranking: 11,089 S.S. Count: 1684

Origin: English. Derived from the Old English tribe called Spaldingas, meaning "people of the district called Spald" (H&H). The name was given to those from Spalding, the name of a place in Lincolnshire, England.

Famous Spaldings: THOMAS SPALDING (1774–1851) of Frederica, Georgia, was one of the first to introduce Sea-Island cotton to the South, and the first to grow sugar cane and manufacture sugar in Georgia. LYMAN SPALDING (1775–1821) of New Hampshire was the founder of the U.S. Pharmacopeia (1820). CATHERINE SPALDING (1793–1858) of Maryland was the founder and head of the Sisters of Charity of Nazareth. HENRY HARMON SPALDING (1801?–1874) of New York was a missionary with the Indians. He built the first white home, school, and church in Idaho and founded the first printing press in the Pacific Northwest. JOHN LANCASTER SPALDING (1840–1916) of Kentucky was one of the founders of Catholic University of America in Washington, D.C. ALBERT GOODWILL SPALDING (1850–1915) of Illinois was a baseball player, then the founder of A. G. Spalding & Brothers, a sporting-goods store, which he started with his brother, JAMES WALTER SPALDING (1856–1931). Albert was elected to the Baseball Hall of Fame in 1939. ALBERT SPALDING (1888–1953) of Illinois was the first American violinist to achieve international renown.

Genealogies: None known.

SPANGLER (S.S. Abbreviation: Spangl)

Ranking: 1602 S.S. Count: 28,013

Origin: German. Uncertain etymology. The name was given to tinkers.

Famous Spanglers: HENRY WILSON SPANGLER (1858–1912) of Pennsylvania was an engineer and the author of textbooks on thermodynamics.

Genealogies: *The Spanglers* was compiled by Theresa Spangler Lowe and published in Shelby, North Carolina, in 1983.

SPANN

Ranking: 2873 S.S. Count: 15,836

Origin: German. The name was given to those from Spann, the name of settlements in Germany, or to those from Spahn, the name of a place in Germany.

Genealogies: *A History of the Spann Family* was compiled by Joseph Earle Steadman and published in Batesburg, South Carolina, in 1968. *A Spann Line, 1724–1982: North Carolina, South Carolina, Arkansas* was compiled by Ruby Emma Herman and published in North Little Rock, Arkansas, in 1982.

SPARKMAN (S.S. Abbreviation: Sparkm)

Ranking: 4592 S.S. Count: 9733

Origin: English. Derived from the Old English word "spearca," meaning to spark, as in to animate. The name was given to those who were lively.

Genealogies: None known.

SPARKS

Ranking: 467 S.S. Count: 85,656

Origin: English. Derived from the Old Norse name Sparkr, meaning witty and lively.

Famous Sparkses: JARED SPARKS (1789–1866) of Connecticut was a historian and editor and the author of biographies of the people of the early days of the United States. WILLIAM ANDREW JACKSON SPARKS (1828–1904) of Indiana was a member of Congress from Illinois.

Genealogies: *William & Mary Hoare: British-American families* [also Sparks] was compiled by Bernice Ruth Hoare Sparks and published in Rockville, Maryland, in 1974.

SPARROW (S.S. Abbreviation: Sparro)

Ranking: 4138 S.S. Count: 10,938

Origin: English. Derived from the Middle English word "sparewe," meaning the bird sparrow. Uncertain etymology. The name was possibly given to those who were small or whose voice was thought to resemble a sparrow's.

Famous Sparrows: WILLIAM SPARROU (1801–1874) of

Massachusetts was an Episcopal minister and the head of several theological seminaries.

Genealogies: *James Sparrow and Eliza Payne Morse of Boardman and Lower Salem, Ohio* was compiled by Ruth Varney Held and published in San Diego, California, in 1979. *Sparrow Family* was compiled by Ruth Mary Varney Held and published in San Diego, California, in 1965.

SPAULDING (S.S. Abbreviation: Spauld)
Ranking: S.S. Count: 26,506

Origin: English. Transformation of Spalding.

Famous **Spauldings:** GILBERT R. SPAULDING (1811–1880), birthplace unknown, was the inventor of "The Floating Palace," a floating circus aboard a steamboat that docked along the Mississippi and Ohio rivers, bringing the circus to the people. He was also the first to use the railroad as a means of transportation.

Genealogies: None known.

SPEAR
Ranking: 2343 S.S. Count: 19,355

Origin: English. Derived from the Middle English word "spere," meaning spear. The name was given to those who were tall and slim like a spear, or to those who hunted with a spear.

Famous **Spears:** WILLIAM THOMAS SPEAR (1834–1913) of Ohio was a justice of the Ohio Supreme Court.

Genealogies: None known.

SPEARMAN (S.S. Abbreviation: Spearm)
Ranking: 4039 S.S. Count: 11,211

Origin: English. 1) derived from the Old Engish first name Spereman, which was given to those who hunted with a spear. 2) derived from the Middle English words "spere" and "man," meaning spear and man. The name was given to soldiers with spears.

Genealogies: None known.

SPEARS
Ranking: 797 S.S. Count: 52,783

Origin: English. Transformation of Spear.

Genealogies: *The Families of Ruebsamen, Spear, et al.* was compiled by Neil N. Ruebsamen and published in Baltimore, Maryland, in 1987. *John E. and Noah Spears in Kentucky, Missouri, Kansas, Texas & Oklahoma* was compiled by L. K. Gillespie and published in Kansas City, Missouri, in 1987.

SPECK
Ranking: 4641 S.S. Count: 9633

Origin: English, German. English: derived from the Middle English word "spek(e)," meaning a woodpecker. German: derived from the German word "speck," meaning bacon. The name was given to those who sold or butchered pork.

Famous **Specks:** FRANK GOULDSMITH SPECK (1881–1950) of New York was an ethnologist and the author of *Naskapi: Savage Hunters of the Labrador Peninsula* (1935) and *Penobscot Man* (1940).

Genealogies: None known.

SPEED
Ranking: 4522 S.S. Count: 9906

Origin: English, Irish. English: 1) derived from the Middle English word "sped," meaning prosperity or success. The name was given to fast runners. 2) derived from the Middle English word "sped," meaning prosperity or success. The name was given to those who prospered. Irish: derived from the Gaelic name Ó Fuada, which was derived from the first name Fuada, which was derived from the word "fuad," meaning swiftness.

Famous **Speeds:** JAMES SPEED (1812–1887) of Kentucky was Abraham Lincoln's advisor on the affairs of Kentucky and his attorney general during his presidency.

Genealogies: None known.

SPEER
Ranking: 2645 S.S. Count: 17,203

Origin: English, Irish. Transformation of Spear.

Famous **Speers:** WILLIAM SPEER (1822–1904) of Pennsylvania was a missionary. He organized the first Presbyterian mission in Canton, China. EMORY SPEER (1848–1918) of Georgia was a member of Congress from Georgia and a federal judge in that state. EMMA BAILEY SPEER (1872–1961) of Pennsylvania was an administrator within the Y.W.C.A., serving as president of the association (1915–1932).

Genealogies: None known.

SPEIGHT (S.S. Abbreviation: Speigh)
Ranking: 3905 S.S. Count: 11,545

Origin: English. Derived from the Middle English word "speght," meaning woodpecker.

Genealogies: None known.

SPELLMAN (S.S. Abbreviation: Spellm)
Ranking: 4089 S.S. Count: 11,057

Origin: English. Derived from the Middle English word "spell(en)," meaning to tell. The name was given to those who recited.

Famous **Spellmans:** FRANCIS JOSEPH SPELLMAN (1889–1967) of Massachusetts was a Roman Catholic clergyman who rose through the ranks and became one of the most powerful officials of the American Catholic church.

Genealogies: *The Spillman Family of Lawrence Co., Ky.* [also Spellman] was compiled by Lennie M. Carter and published in Timonium, Maryland, in 1987.

SPENCE (ALSO SPENCER)

Ranking: 128 S.S. Count: 230,820

Origin: English. Derived from the Middle English word "spense," meaning storeroom. The names were given to those who were servants in the storeroom of an important house.

Famous **Bearers:** AMBROSE SPENCER (1765–1848) of Connecticut was a politician in the early days of the United States and the brother-in-law of DeWitt Clinton, a governor of New York. CHRISTOPHER MINER SPENCER (1833–1922) of Connecticut was an inventor and patenter of the Spencer self-loading rifle. It was used during the Civil War. He also founded the Spencer Automatic Machine Screw Co. in Windsor, Connecticut. BRENT SPENCE (1874–1967) of Kentucky was a member of Congress from Kentucky. He was one of the founders of the Small Business Administration. ANNA CARPENTER GARLIN SPENCER (1851–1931) of Massachusetts was the first female minister in Rhode Island.

Genealogies: *Darnall, Spence, Steers, Spangler, Stuckey, Sill* was compiled by Erma D. Stuckey and published in Piper City, Illinois, in 1983. *The Spencer Family History* was compiled by O. M. Richards and published in 1980.

SPERRY

Ranking: 4243 S.S. Count: 10,621

Origin: English. Derived from the first name Sperri, meaning spear.

Famous **Sperrys:** NEHEMIAH D. SPERRY (1827–1911) of Connecticut was a member of Congress from Connecticut. ELMER A. SPERRY (1860–1930) of New York was an inventor who owned more than 400 patents. One of his most widely used inventions was the gyroscopic compass for ships and airplanes. WILLARD L. SPERRY (1882–1954), as dean of Harvard Divinity School, opened the institution to a variety of denominations. He also wrote *Religion in America* (1946).

Genealogies: *Anson and Thyrza Sperry* was compiled by Dorothy Hodgman and published in 1977. *The Sperry Family Line of Jeremiah Aperry of Minnesota, 1802–1870* was compiled by Rodney Prestage Homer and published in 1969.

SPICER

Ranking: 1780 S.S. Count: 25,275

Origin: English. Derived from the Middle English word "spic(i)er," meaning a seller of spices. The name was given to those who worked as such.

Genealogies: *Descendants of Nathan Spicer* was compiled by Florence LeVan Spicer and published in Eugene, Oregon, in 1980.

SPIEGEL, SPIEGELMAN, SPIEGELMANN (S.S. Abbreviation: Spiege)

Ranking: 3854 S.S. Count: 11,699

Origin: Spiegelmann—German; Spiegel—German, Jewish; Spiegelman—Jewish. Derived from the German word "spiegel" and the Yiddish word "shpigl," meaning those who made or sold mirrors.

Genealogies: *The Coffelt History Notebook* [also Spiegel] was compiled by Robert K. Coffelt and published in Clifton, Texas, in 1991.

SPILLER (S.S. Abbreviation: Spille)

Ranking: 4055 S.S. Count: 11,151

Origin: English. 1) derived from the Middle English word "spill(en)," meaning to waste. The name was given to those who were profligate. 2) derived from the Middle English word "spill(en)," meaning to play. The name was given to jesters.

Genealogies: None known.

SPINELLA, SPINELLI, SPINELLO (S.S. Abbreviation: Spinel)

Ranking: 4452 S.S. Count: 10,067

Origin: Italian. Derived from the Latin word "spina," meaning a spiny bush. The names were given to those who lived near a thorny bush.

Genealogies: None known.

SPIRES

Ranking: 4768 S.S. Count: 9387

Origin: English. Derived from the Middle English word "spir," meaning stalk. The name was given to those who were thin.

Genealogies: None known.

SPITZER (S.S. Abbreviation: Spitze)

Ranking: 4508 S.S. Count: 9928

Origin: German, Jewish. German: derived from the German word "spitz," meaning pointed. The name was given to those who lived near a hill with a point or by a field with a sharp angle. Jewish: uncertain etymology. Possibly a cognate to the German name Spitzer.

Genealogies: *All Our Yesterdays* [also Spitzer] was compiled by Evelyn Spitzer Drinnen and published in Knoxville, Tennessee, in 1982.

SPIVEY

Ranking: 1604 S.S. Count: 27,967

Origin: Scottish. Uncertain etymology. The name was given to those who were deformed or lame.

Genealogies: *Spivey Family* was compiled by Odis Mae Spivey Dunagin and published in Biloxi, Mississippi, in 1974.

SPOONER (S.S. Abbreviation: Spoone)

Ranking: 3984 S.S. Count: 11,353

Origin: English. Derived from the Middle English word "spoon," meaning splinter. The name was given to roofers.

Famous **Spooners:** LYSANDER SPOONER (1808–1887) of Massachusetts was a lawyer and the author of *Unconstitutionality of Slavery* (1845) and *Essay on the Trial by Jury* (1852). JOHN COIT SPOONER (1843–1919) of Indiana was a U.S. senator from Wisconsin.

Genealogies: None known.

SPRADLEY (S.S. Abbreviation: Spradl)

Ranking: 2410 **S.S. Count:** 18,797

Origin: English. Uncertain etymology. The name was given to those from Sproatley, a place in Yorkshire, England.

Genealogies: None known.

SPRAGUE (S.S. Abbreviation: Spragu)

Ranking: 1356 **S.S. Count:** 32,732

Origin: English. Transformation of Sparks.

Famous **Spragues:** HOMER BAXTER SPRAGUE (1829–1918) of Massachusetts was president of Mills College, then president of the University of North Dakota. WILLIAM SPRAGUE (1830–1915) of Rhode Island was governor of, then U.S. senator from, Rhode Island. CHARLES EZRA SPRAGUE (1842–1912) of New York, a banker, was one of the first to qualify as a certified public accountant. He also taught accounting and was the author of textbooks on the subject. FRANK JULIAN SPRAGUE (1857–1934) of Connecticut was an inventor. His multiple-unit control mechanism for trains was adopted by subway, elevated, and suburban rail systems. CHARLES A. SPRAGUE (1887–1969) of Kansas was editor and publisher of the Oregon *Statesman* for 40 years and governor of Oregon from 1938 to 1942.

Genealogies: *Ancestors of Moses Belcher Bass, Born in Boston, July 1735, died January 31, 1817* [also Sprague] was compiled by Susan Augusta Smith and published in Boston, Massachusetts, in 1896. *One Branch of the Sprague Family* was compiled by Gordon Harvey Sprague and published in Paris, Illinois, in 1972.

SPRIGG (ALSO SPRIGGS)

Ranking: 3940 **S.S. Count:** 11,461

Origin: English. Derived from the Middle English word "sprigge," meaning twig. The names were given to those who were tall and slender.

Genealogies: None known.

SPRING (ALSO SPRINGATE, SPRINGER, SPRINGETT, SPRINGFIELD)

Ranking: 515 **S.S. Count:** 77,801

Origin: Springer—Dutch, English, German, Jewish; Spring, Springate, Springett, Springfield—English. Spring, Springate, Springett: uncertain etymology. Possibly derived from a first name that was derived from the word "springan," meaning to leap. Springer (Dutch, English, German, Jewish): derived from the Middle English and German word "srin-

gen," the Middle Dutch word "springhen," and the Yiddish word "shpringen," all meaning to leap. The name was given to those who were energetic. Springer (English): derived from the Middle English word "spring," meaning the source of a brook or river. The name was given to those who lived near springs. Springfield: derived from the Middle English word "spring" and the Old English word "feld," meaning pasture. The name was given to those from Springfield, a place in Essex, England.

Famous **Bearers:** GARDINER SPRING (1785–1873) of Massachusetts, as pastor of Brick Presbyterian Church in New York City, was an influential person in the city for many years. WILLIAM M. SPRINGER (1836–1903) of Indiana was a member of Congress from Illinois who introduced the bills making Washington, Montana, and the Dakotas states. LEVERETT W. SPRING (1840–1917) of Vermont was a Congregational clergyman who wrote the nonpartisan book *Kansas: The Prelude to the War for the Union* (1885). FRANK SPRINGER (1848–1927) of Iowa was a prominent attorney in New Mexico with an avocation in paleontology that led to the publication of works on fossil crinoids.

Genealogies: *The Springer Families from Adam to Present* was compiled by Joseph R. Armentrout and published in Peoria, Illinois, in 1984. *A Springer Family History* was compiled by Ruth Beckey Irwin and published in Columbus, Ohio, in 1987.

SPRINKEL, SPRINKLE (S.S. Abbreviation: Sprink)

Ranking: 4347 **S.S. Count:** 10,313

Origin: English. The name was given to soldiers responsible for a springalde, a weapon of medieval warfare.

Genealogies: *They Came to Warrick County, Indiana* was compiled by J. Oscar Phillips.

SPROUSE (S.S. Abbreviation: Sprous)

Ranking: 3923 **S.S. Count:** 11,497

Origin: Uncertain eytmology.

Genealogies: None known.

SPRUILL, SPRUILLE (S.S. Abbreviation: Spruil)

Ranking: 4294 **S.S. Count:** 10,451

Origin: English. Uncertain etymology. The name was given to those who were nimble and fast.

Genealogies: *Gabriel Spruill of Carroll County, Georgia* was compiled by Clarice S. Cox and published in Carrollton, California, in 1984.

SPURGE

Ranking: 4373 **S.S. Count:** 10,254

Origin: English. Derived from the Old French word "(E)spurge," the name of a plant thought to clean away warts. The name was given to those who lived near the plant and to those who were thought to have the plant's cleansing characteristic.

Genealogies: *The Spurgeon Story* was compiled by Bee Dee Abbott Spurgeon and published in Orange, California, in 1971.

SPURLOCK (S.S. Abbreviation: Spurlo)
Ranking: 2881 **S.S. Count:** 15,805

Origin: English. Derived from the Old English words "spearwa" and "luh," meaning sparrow and lake. The name was given to those who lived near a lake overrun with spar-rows.

Genealogies: None known.

SQUIRE (ALSO SQUIRES)
Ranking: 1674 **S.S. Count:** 26,685

Origin: English. Derived from the Old French word "esquier," meaning one who bore a shield. The names were given to those members of the social rank immediately below a knight.

Famous **Bearers:** WATSON C. SQUIRE (1838–1926) of New York was territorial governor of, then U.S. senator from, Washington.

Genealogies: *The Gardiner-Squires Connection: an account of the Gardiner family of Gardiner's Island, Long Island, New York, and the Squires family of Squiretown, Long Island, New York and West Haven, Connecticut* was compiled by Tiger Gardiner and published in Baltimore, Maryland, in 1989. *Musgrave to Mosgrave, 1066– 1979, with Allied Families of Squire, et al.* was compiled by Glenna James Mosgrove and published in Mansfield, Illinois, in 1979.

STACEY
Ranking: 3541 **S.S. Count:** 12,752

Origin: English. Derived from the masculine medieval first name Stace, which was ultimately derived from the Greek name Eustakhios, meaning prolific.

Genealogies: None known.

STACK
Ranking: 2746 **S.S. Count:** 16,593

Origin: English. Derived from the Middle English word "stack," meaning haystack. The name was given to those who were strong and of substantial build.

Genealogies: None known.

STACY
Ranking: 1837 **S.S. Count:** 24,616

Origin: English. Transformation of Stacey.

Famous **Stacys:** WALTER P. STACY (1884–1951) of North Carolina was chief justice of the North Carolina Supreme

Court. Also, four consecutive U.S. presidents (Calvin Coolidge, Herbert Hoover, Franklin D. Roosevelt, and Harry S Truman) appointed him as a mediator in labor disputes.

Genealogies: *Simon Stacy and his Descendants* was compiled by Virginia Meadows McCann and published in Decorah, Iowa, in 1978. *Stacy, a Record of some of the Descendants of William Stacy of Hawkins County, Tennessee* was compiled by Mary Scott and published in Salina, Kansas, in 1985.

STAFFORD (S.S. Abbreviation: Staffo)
Ranking: 644 **S.S. Count:** 64,569

Origin: English. The name was given to those from Stafford, the name of many places in England of which the second component is "ford," meaning ford.

Genealogies: *Stafford: descendants of Abraham and Frances Melissa Dearman Stafford* was compiled by Zuma Fendlason Magee and published in Franklinton, Louisiana, in 1967. *The Staffords of North Carolina* was compiled by Charles Warner Stafford and published in Stuart, Florida, in 1973.

STAGGS
Ranking: 3589 **S.S. Count:** 12,568

Origin: English. Derived from the Old English word "stagga," meaning a male deer. The name was given to those who somehow resembled a stag.

Genealogies: None known.

STAHL
Ranking: 1409 **S.S. Count:** 31,569

Origin: German. Cognate to Steel.

Genealogies: None known.

STALEY
Ranking: 1857 **S.S. Count:** 24,381

Origin: English. Derived from the Middle English word "stalward," meaning stalwart. The name was given to those who were uncompromising and sturdy.

Famous **Staleys:** CADY STALEY (1840–1928) of New York was a civil engineer who was president of Union College and Case School of Applied Science.

Genealogies: None known.

STALLING, STALLINGS (S.S. Abbreviation: Stalli)
Ranking: 1722 **S.S. Count:** 26,005

Origin: English. Derived from a word meaning stallion. The names were given to those from Stalling, a place in Yorkshire, England.

Famous **Bearers:** LAURENCE TUCKER STALLINGS (1894–1968) of Georgia was a writer of screenplays from book adaptations and the author of *The Doughboys* (1963), a history of U.S. participation in World War I.

Genealogies: None known.

STALLWOOD, STALLWORTH, STALLWORTHY (S.S. Abbreviation: Stallw)

Ranking: 4495 **S.S. Count:** 9972

Origin: English. Transformations of Staley.

Genealogies: *Stallworth, 1785–1985* was compiled by T. A. Stallworth and published in Chester, South Carolina, in 1985.

STAMPER (S.S. Abbreviation: Stampe)

Ranking: 2636 **S.S. Count:** 17,287

Origin: English. Derived from the Old English word "stempan" meaning to pound. The name was given to those who stamped, pounded, or printed.

Genealogies: None known.

STAMPS

Ranking: 4526 **S.S. Count:** 9894

Origin: English. Derived from the Old English word "stempan" meaning to pound. The name was given to those from Étampes, a place in France.

Genealogies: *A Patterson Family: also Darby and Stamps* was compiled by Noel Douglas Patterson and published in Dallas, Texas, in 1966. *The Stamps Family History and Lineage* was compiled by Charles Thomas Stamps and published in Clinton, Utah, in 1979.

STANCIL, STANCILL (S.S. Abbreviation: Stanci)

Ranking: 4966 **S.S. Count:** 9021

Origin: German, Polish. Derived from the first name Stanislaus, which is comprised components meaning become and fame.

Genealogies: *Richard Arrow Smith of Wake Co., North Carolina* [also Stancil] was compiled by Rebecca L. Blackwell and published in Bowie, Maryland, in 1993.

STANDIDGE, STANDING, STANDISH (S.S. Abbreviation: Standi)

Ranking: 3638 **S.S. Count:** 12,389

Origin: English. Standidge, Standish: derived from the Old English words "stān" and "edisc," meaning stone and pasture. The names were given to those from Standish, a place in England. Standing: derived from the Old English words "stān" and "denu," meaning stone and valley. The name was given to those from Standen or Standing, the names of places in England.

Famous Bearers: MYLES STANDISH (1584?–1656) of England was hired by the Pilgrims to accompany them on their voyage to America. He was their guide, as he was knowledgeable in camping, fortification erection, and methods of defense. His dealings with the Indians probably kept the Pilgrims alive, as he was considered an expert in negotations with them.

Genealogies: *Standish Families Compendium for Mayflower Research* was compiled by Walter H. McIntosh and published in Topsfield, Massachusetts, in 1981.

STANFIELD, STANFILL (S.S. Abbreviation: Stanfi)

Ranking: 2250 **S.S. Count:** 20,323

Origin: English. Derived from the Old English words "stān" and "feld," meaning stone and field. The names were given to those from Stanfield, the name of a place in Norfolk, England.

Genealogies: *Descendants of Sampson Stanfield, Who went from Anson County, North Carolina, via East Tennessee into Knox County, Kentucky in the Early 1800s* was compiled by Goldie Smith Hieronymus and published in Arlington, Virginia, in 1981.

STANFORD (S.S. Abbreviation: Stanfo)

Ranking: 1532 **S.S. Count:** 29,046

Origin: English. Derived from the Old English words "stān" and "ford," meaning stone and ford. The name was given to those from Stanford, the name of places in England.

Famous Stanfords: AMASA LELAND STANFORD (1824–1893) of New York was a builder of railroads, governor of California, and U.S. senator. As governor in 1861, he had as his chief responsibility keeping California secure in the Union. He also had the opportunity to amass a great fortune through his railroad building because of his position as governor. He and his wife, JANE ELIZA LATHROP STANFORD (1828–1905) of New York, as a memorial to their son, Leland Stanford Jr., who had died as a teenager, co-founded Stanford University in 1885.

Genealogies: *Goin' Home* [also Stanford] was compiled by Timeri Murari and published in New York, New York, in 1980. *Moses Stanford, Minuteman* was compiled by Lois Remington Smith and published in Roseville, Minnesota, in 1984.

STANGER (S.S. Abbreviation: Stange)

Ranking: 4208 **S.S. Count:** 10,736

Origin: English, Jewish. English: Uncertain etymology. Possibly derived from the Middle English word "stang," meaning pole. Jewish: Uncertain etymology.

Genealogies: None known.

STANISLAV, STANISLAVSKY, STANISLAWSKI (S.S. Abbreviation: Stanis)

Ranking: 4718 **S.S. Count:** 9480

Origin: Stanislav—Czech; Stanislavsky—Jewish, Russian;

Stanislawski—Polish. Derived from the first name Stanislaw, comprising the Slavic components "stan," "slav," and "-ski," meaning become and fame, and a surname suffix.

Genealogies: None known.

STANLEY (S.S. Abbreviation: Stanle)

Ranking: 279 **S.S. Count:** 129,172

Origin: English. Derived from the Old English words "stān" and "lēah," meaning stone and clearing. The name was given to those from Stanley, the name of several places in England.

Famous **Stanleys:** HENRY MORTON STANLEY (1841–1904) of Wales was a journalist and explorer. He was a traveling newspaper correspondent with the *New York Herald* and is credited with finding David Livingstone, a Scottish missionary who had been working in the African village of the Ujiji. It was then that Stanley said to him the immortal words "Dr. Livingstone, I presume?" He explored the headwaters of the Nile, Lake Tanganyika, and the Congo River. Because of him, the Congo Free State was formed. FRANCIS EDGAR STANLEY (1849–1918) of Maine was an inventor and manufacturer. He invented photographic equipment that he sold to Eastman. He was co-founder of the Stanley Motor Carriage Co. AUGUSTUS OWSLEY STANLEY (1867–1958) of Kentucky was a member of Congress and the head of the investigation of U.S. Steel, which led to the Clayton Antitrust Act. He then served his state first as governor, then as U.S. senator. LOUISE STANLEY (1883–1954) of Tennessee was the first woman to head a bureau in the U.S. Department of Agriculture. FRANK LESLIE STANLEY (1906–1974) of Illinois was the longtime publisher of the Louisville (Kentucky) *Defender*, a community newspaper that won numerous national awards under his leadership. He also was a syndicated columnist and a civil rights leader.

Genealogies: *Sands Stanley of the Pee Dee Valley* was compiled by Haywood A. Stanley and published in Marion, South Carolina, in 1978. *Stanley Families of America* was compiled by Harold S. Langland and published in Bloomington, Minnesota, in 1978. *Whither Thou Goest: a story of the Stanley family in Virginia, North Carolina, Kansas and Oklahoma* was compiled by Elnora Stanley Flaherty and published in Irving, Texas, in 1973.

STANSBERRY, STANSBURY (S.S. Abbreviation: Stansb)

Ranking: 3340 **S.S. Count:** 13,557

Origin: English. Derived from the Old English words "stān" and "burh," meaning stone and fort. The names were given to those from Stanbury, meaning stone fort, a place in England.

Famous **Bearers:** JOSEPH STANSBURY (1742–1809) of England was a Loyalist and the man who acted as go-between in the treason proposal Benedict Arnold sent to the British. HOWARD STANSBURY (1806–1863) of New York was a civil engineer, explorer, and soldier. He was responsible for the survey of the Great Salt Lake region (1849).

Genealogies: *Kindred: Davis-Stansbury Lines* was compiled by Helen E. Davis and published in Philadelphia, Pennsylvania, in 1977.

STANTON (S.S. Abbreviation: Stanto)

Ranking: 873 **S.S. Count:** 49,517

Origin: English. Derived from the Old English words "stān" and "tūn," meaning stone and settlement. The name was given to those from Stanton, the name of many places in England.

Famous **Stantons:** HENRY BREWSTER STANTON (1805–1887) of Connecticut was a journalist, reformer, husband of Elizabeth Cady Stanton, and author of *Random Recollections* (1887). EDWIN MCMASTERS STANTON (1814–1869) was a lawyer, a political figure, and an appointee to the U.S. Supreme Court by President Ulysses S. Grant. He died before taking his seat. ELIZABETH CADY STANTON (1815–1902) of New York was a women's rights leader. In her marriage ceremony to Henry Stanton, she refused to have the word "obey" included. She was the president of the Woman Suffrage Association, the author of numerous newspaper articles, co-author of *History of Woman Suffrage*, and the author of *Eighty Years and More* (1898), her autobiography. FRANK LEBBY STANTON (1857–1927) of South Carolina was one of the first newspaper columnists, writing for the *Atlanta Constitution*.

Genealogies: *A Record, Genealogical, Biographical, Statistical, of Thomas Stanton, of Connecticut* was compiled by William A. Stanton and published in Bethany, Oklahoma, in 1985. *A Williams Genealogy: ancestors and descendants of Luke Stanton Williams and his Wife, Olive Miller Williams* was compiled by Olin E. Williams and published in Pittsburgh, Pennsylvania, in 1976.

STAPLE (ALSO STAPLES, STAPLETON, STAPLEY)

Ranking: 815 **S.S. Count:** 51,862

Origin: Staple, Staples, Stapley—English; Stapleton—English, Irish. Staple, Staples: derived from the Middle English word "staple," meaning a boundary marker. The names were given to those who lived near a staple. Stapleton: derived from the Old English words "stapol" and "tūn," meaning post and settlement. The name was given to those from Stapleton, the name of places in England and Ireland. Stapley: derived from the Old English words "stapol" and "lēah," meaning post and clearing. The name was given to those from Stapeley or Stapely, the name of places in England.

Famous **Bearers:** WILLIAM READ STAPLES (1798–1868) of Rhode Island was a historian and the author of *Annals of* the Town of Providence (1843) and *Rhode Island in the Continental Congress* (1870). WALLER REDD STAPLES (1826–1897) of Virginia was a judge on the Virginia Supreme Court of Appeals who was involved in the Coupon Case of 1878. This case led to the forming of the Readjuster Party.

Genealogies: *Descendants of Jeffery and John Staple of Weymouth, Massachusetts* was compiled by James Courtenay Staples and published in Orlando, Florida, in 1978.

STARK
Ranking: 717 S.S. Count: 58,708
Origin: English, Scottish. Derived from the Middle English word "stark," meaning firm. The name was given to those who were powerful or resolute.

Famous **Starks:** JOHN STARK (1728–1822) of New Hampshire was a colonial and Revolutionary soldier who fought from Bunker Hill to the Battle of Springfield, New Jersey, 1780. As a major general he was on the board of officers who tried Major John André. EDWARD JOSEF STARK (1858–1918) of Austria came to the United States as a young boy. He was a composer of synagogue music. LOUIS STARK (1888–1954) of Hungary was a newspaper correspondent. His coverage of the split of the American Federation of Labor (AFL) into the AFL-CIO won him a Pulitzer Prize.

Genealogies: *James Stark of Stafford County, Virginia* was compiled by Mary Kathryn Harris and published in Fort Worth, Texas, in 1985. *John Stark of Wurttemberg and Long Island* was compiled by Thomas M. Stark and published in Riverhead, New York, in 1972.

STARKE (ALSO STARKEL, STARKER, STARKEY)
Ranking: 1548 S.S. Count: 28,850
Origin: Starkey—English; Starke—Flemish, German; Starker, Starkel—German. Cognates to or transformations of Stark.

Genealogies: *The Starkey Family of Saybrook (Essex) Connecticut* was compiled by Margaret Buckridge Bock and published in Tacoma, Washington, in 1981.

STARKS
Ranking: 1712 S.S. Count: 26,130
Origin: Flemish? Uncertain etymology. Most likely a transformation of Starke.

Famous **Starks:** EDWIN CHAPIN STARKS (1867–1932) of Wisconsin was an authority on the osteology of fishes. He was the curator of zoology at Stanford University after 1901 until the year of his death.

Genealogies: None known.

STARLING (S.S. Abbreviation: Starli)
Ranking: 3123 S.S. Count: 14,559

Origin: English. Derived from the Middle English word "starling," meaning the bird called starling. The name was given to those who somehow resembled a starling.

Genealogies: None known.

STARNES (S.S. Abbreviation: Starne)
Ranking: 2010 S.S. Count: 22,698
Origin: English. 1) Derived from the Old English word "styrne," meaning stern. The name was given to those who were stern. 2) Derived from the Old English word "steorra," meaning star. The name was given to those who lived near the "sign of the stars" (ES).

Genealogies: None known.

STARR
Ranking: 1048 S.S. Count: 41,797
Origin: English. Derived from the Old English word "steorra," meaning star.

Famous **Starrs:** BELLE STARR (1848–1889) of Missouri was known as the "Bandit Queen" of the Southwest. She was the subject of unauthorized biographies that were mostly fiction, but she was, however, if one is known by the company one keeps, a woman on the wrong side of the law. ELLEN GATES STARR (1859–1940) of Illinois was the cofounder of Hull House, a cultural and educational center in Chicago.

Genealogies: *Starr Tracks: Belle and Pearl Starr* was compiled by Phillip W. Steele and published in Gretna, Louisiana, in 1989. *They Followed the Sun: the story of James Penn Starr and Georgian Theus* was compiled by Marguerite Starr Crain and published in Dallas, Texas, in 1971.

STATEN
Ranking: 4534 S.S. Count: 9863
Origin: English. Uncertain etymology. The name was given to those who lived on a settlement near a wharf.

Genealogies: None known.

STATON
Ranking: 2423 S.S. Count: 18,702
Origin: English. Transformation of Staten.

Genealogies: *Staton History* was compiled by John Samuel Staton and published in Charlotte, North Carolina, in 1982.

STAUFFER (S.S. Abbreviation: Stauff)
Ranking: 2119 S.S. Count: 21,627
Origin: German. 1) derived from the German word "stauf," meaning beaker, and referring to hills shaped like beakers. The name was given to those from Stauffer, the name of places in Germany. 2) derived from the German word "stauf," meaning beaker. The name was given to those who made or sold beakers or mugs.

Famous **Stauffers:** DAVID MCNEELY STAUFFER (1845–1913) of Pennsylvania was a civil engineer and the author of *American Engravers upon Copper and Steel.*

Genealogies: *Genealogical Study of Henry Stauffer* was compiled by Elsie Stauffer and published in Spencer, Iowa, in 1974. *The Stauffer Families of Switzerland, Germany, and America* was compiled by Richard Warren Davis and published in Provo, Utah, in 1992. *Stauffer-Sauder Genealogy* was compiled by Margorie Ladd Holbrook and published in Ann Arbor, Michigan, in 1978.

STEADMAN (S.S. Abbreviation: Steadm)
Ranking: 4394 **S.S. Count:** 10,211
Origin: English. Derived from the Middle English word "steed," meaning a stallion. The name was given to those who cared for stallions or to those who were vigorous.
Genealogies: None known.

STEARN (ALSO STEARNE, STEARNS)
Ranking: 1937 **S.S. Count:** 23,353
Origin: English. Transformations of the English name Stern.
Famous **Bearers:** GEORGE LUTHER STEARNS (1809–1867) of Massachusetts was an abolitionist and the recruiter of blacks for the Union army. IRVING ARIEL STEARNS (1845–1920) of New York was a mining engineer who made improvements in mining processes. FREDERIC PIKE STEARNS (1851–1919) of Maine designed and implemented the water system of the Boston metropolitan area. FRANK BALLOU STEARNS (1878–1955) of Ohio was an inventor and manufacturer of cars and engines. He was the founder of the F. B. Stearns Co. (1898), which manufactured Stearns-Knight cars.
Genealogies: *From the Puritan Migration to the Ohio River and Indiana* [also Stearns] was compiled by Frances Kutchback Eisan and published in Hanover, Indiana, in 1991.

STEBBING, STEBBINGS, STEBBINS (S.S. Abbreviation: Stebbi)
Ranking: 4507 **S.S. Count:** 9934
Origin: English. Derived from the Middle English word "stebbing," meaning clearing. The name was given to those who lived in a clearing in a wooded area.
Famous **Bearers:** RUFUS PHINEAS STEBBINS (1810–1885) of Massachusetts was the first president of the Meadville (Pennsylvania) Theological School and the president of the American Unitarian Association. His cousin, HORATIO STEBBINS (1821–1902) of Massachusetts, was the Unitarian minister in San Francisco for 35 years. He was instrumental in the formation of the University of California, Stanford University, and Lick Observatory.
Genealogies: *A Genealogy and History of some Stebbins Lines* was compiled by John Alfred Stebbins and published in California in 1953.

STEED
Ranking: 3637 **S.S. Count:** 12,391
Origin: English. 1) transformation of Steadman. 2) derived from the Old English word "stede," meaning estate. The name was given to those from Stead, a place in England.
Genealogies: None known.

STEEL
Ranking: 4188 **S.S. Count:** 10,792
Origin: English, Scottish. Derived from the Middle English word "stele," meaning steel. The name was given to those who were employed in a foundry or to those who were thought to exhibit the qualities of steel.
Genealogies: *The Steele Family in America* [also Steel] was compiled by Steele Barnett and published in Tulsa, Oklahoma, in 1935.

STEELE
Ranking: 307 **S.S. Count:** 119,531
Origin: English, Scottish. Transformation of Steel.
Famous **Steeles:** JOHN STEELE (1764–1815) of North Carolina was a member of Congress from North Carolina, then comptroller of the U.S. Treasury. FREDERICK STEELE (1819–1868) of New York was a Civil War soldier. DANIEL STEELE (1824–1914) of New York was a leader in the Methodist church. WILBUR DANIEL STEELE (1886–1970) of North Carolina was a writer whose stories appeared in many of the magazines of the time. He was the winner of the O. Henry Award 12 times. He died in Essex, Connecticut.
Genealogies: *The Steele Family in America* was compiled by Steele Barnett and published in Tulsa, Oklahoma, in 1935. *The Moody-Steele and Allied Families* was compiled by Ruby Moody Gamble and published in Cullman, Alabama, in 1985. *Steele and Related Family Ancestry* was compiled by Lewis L. Neubacher and published in Berkeley, California, in 1988.

STEEN
Ranking: 2462 **S.S. Count:** 18,415
Origin: German, Scottish, Swedish. German, Swedish: cognates to Stone. Scottish: transformation of Stein.
Genealogies: None known.

STEFAN (ALSO STEFANEK, STEFANELLI, STEFANI, STEFANO)
Ranking: 1502 **S.S. Count:** 29,653
Origin: Stefan—Czech; Stefanelli, Stefani, Stefano—Italian; Stefanek—Polish. Cognates to Stephen.
Genealogies: None known.

STEFFEN, STEFFENS, STEFFENSEN (S.S. Abbreviation: Steffe)

Ranking: 1266 S.S. Count: 34,846

Origin: Steffensen—Danish, German, Norwegian; Steffen, Steffens—English, German. Cognates to and transformations of Stephen.

Famous **Bearer:** LINCOLN STEFFENS (1866–1936) of California was a journalist who wrote for the *New York Evening Post*, the New York *Commercial Appeal*, and *McClure's Magazine* on muckraking and civic corruption.

Genealogies: None known.

STEGALL (S.S. Abbreviation: Stegal)

Ranking: 4422 S.S. Count: 10,140

Origin: English, German. Derived from the Old English word "stigol," meaning climb. The name was given to those who lived near a steep passage up a hill.

Genealogies: *William Jasper Stigall* [also Stegall] was compiled by William Jasper Stigall and published in Scarborough, New York, in 1980.

STEIGER (S.S. Abbreviation: Steige)

Ranking: 4331 S.S. Count: 10,343

Origin: German. 1) derived from the Middle High German word "stec," meaning a "plank bridge" (H&H). The name was given to those who lived near such a bridge. 2) derived from the German word "steig," meaning a steep path. The name was given to those who lived near a steep path going up a hill.

Genealogies: None known.

STEIN

Ranking: 624 S.S. Count: 66,763

Origin: German, Jewish, Scottish. German, Jewish: cognates to Stone. Scottish: transformation of Stephen.

Famous **Steins:** GERTRUDE STEIN (1874–1946) of Pennsylvania was an author and the subject of many portraits done by the great artists of the day, including Picasso.

Genealogies: *From Switzerland to Sonnenberg: the story of the Steiner, Amstutz, and Zuercher families from Wayne County, Ohio* [also Stein] was compiled by Clayton Steiner and published in Goshen, Indiana, in 1976. *Poets, Painters, Paupers, Fools: Indiana's Stein Family* was compiled by Robert C. Kriebel and published in West Lafayette, Indiana, in 1990. *Stein Stammbaum* was compiled by Bachrach of Reichensachsen and published in Cincinnati, Ohio, in 1975.

STEINBACH, STEINBAUM, STEINBERG, STEINBERGER (S.S. Abbreviation: Steinb)

Ranking: 1006 S.S. Count: 43,532

Origin: Jewish. The names are cognates to stone combined with "bach," meaning stream, "baum," meaning tree, and "berg(er)," meaning hill. The names were taken ornamentally.

Genealogies: None known.

STEINECKE, STEINEKE, STEINEMANN, STEINER, STEINERT (S.S. Abbreviation: Steine)

Ranking: 1131 S.S. Count: 38,918

Origin: Steiner—English, German, Jewish; Steinecke, Steineke, Steinemann, Steinert—German. Steiner (English): derived from the Middle English word "steyn(en)," meaning to stain. The name was given to those who dyed glass. Steiner (German, Jewish), Steinecke, Steineke, Steinemann, Steinert: cognates to Stone.

Famous **Bearers:** LEWIS HENRY STEINER (1827–1892) of Maryland was a physician and the first librarian of the Enoch Pratt Free Library, Baltimore. His son, BERNARD CHRISTIAN STEINER (1867–1926) of Connecticut, followed his father as the librarian of Enoch Pratt Free Library. He also wrote on the history of Maryland and Connecticut.

Genealogies: *My Lathberry-Harding-Iszard Ancestry* [also Steiner] was compiled by Frances Lathberry Steiner and published in New Jersey in 1992.

STEINHARD, STEINHARDT, STEINHERTZ, STEINHERZ, STEINHORN (S.S. Abbreviation: Steinh)

Ranking: 2613 S.S. Count: 17,379

Origin: Jewish. The names are cognates to Stone combined with "hard(t)," meaning hard, "her(t)z," meaning heart, and "horn," meaning horn. The names were taken ornamentally.

Famous **Bearers:** LAURENCE ADOLPH STEINHARDT (1892–1950) of New York was a lawyer and behind-the-scenes diplomat in the two decades before his death. He was killed in a plane crash returning to New York from Canada, where he was serving as the U.S. ambassador.

Genealogies: None known.

STEINKE (S.S. Abbreviation: Steink)

Ranking: 3549 S.S. Count: 12,712

Origin: German. Cognate to Stone.

Genealogies: None known.

STEINMAN, STEINMANN, STEINMASSEL, STEINMEISSEL, STEINMETZ (S.S. Abbreviation: Steinm)

Ranking: 2019 S.S. Count: 22,625

Origin: Steinmann, Steinmassel, Steinmeissel—German; Steinmetz—German, Jewish; Steinman—Jewish. Steinmann, Steinman: cognates to Stone. Steinmassel, Steinmeissel, Steinmetz: derived from the German word "steinmetz," meaning stonemason. The names were given to those who were masons.

Famous **Bearers:** CHARLES PROTEUS STEINMETZ (1865–1923) of Germany was a genius in the area of mathematics and electrical engineering. DAVID BARNARD STEINMAN (1886–1960) of New York was an engineer and the designer of bridges. His company is credited with designing the George Washington Bridge (1931), the Thousand Islands International Bridge (1938), and the Mackinac Strait Bridge (1957).

Genealogies: *Ancestors of Charles A. Stymus and his Wife Ella C. Smith: Orleans County New York* [also Steinmetz] was compiled by Marion Reed Page and published in Leesburg, Florida, in 1989.

STENGEL, STENGELE, STENGER (S.S. Abbreviation: Stenge)

Ranking: 4581 **S.S. Count:** 9759

Origin: Stenger—French, German. Stengel, Stengele—German. Stengel, Stengele: Derived from word meaning stake. The names were given to those who lived near a stake or pole. Stenger: Uncertain etymology. The name was given to those who were tall and slim.

Famous **Stengels:** ALFRED STENGEL (1868–1939) of Pennsylvania was a physician and the president of the American College of Physicians, which he reorganized for the better. CHARLES DILLON (CASEY) STENGEL (1890?–1975) of Missouri was a baseball player and manager. He was the manager of the New York Yankees when they appeared in 10 American League pennant games and 7 World Series. His unique use of the American language was dubbed "Stengelese." He was elected to the Baseball Hall of Fame in 1966.

Genealogies: None known.

STEPHAN, STEPHANELLI, STEPHANELLO, STEPHANO, STEPHANSEN (S.S. Abbreviation: Stepha)

Ranking: 2728 **S.S. Count:** 16,688

Origin: Stephansen—Danish, Norwegian; Stephan—French; Stephanelli, Stephanello, Stephano—Italian. Cognates to Stephen.

Genealogies: None known.

STEPHEN, STEPHENS, STEPHENSEN, STEPHENSON (S.S. Abbreviation: Stephe)

Ranking: 103 **S.S. Count:** 272,396

Origin: Stephensen—Danish, Norwegian; Stephen, Stephens, Stephenson—English. Stephensen: a cognate to Stephen. Stephen, Stephens, Stephenson: derived from the Middle English first name Stephen, which was ultimately derived from the Greek name Stephanos, meaning crown.

Famous **Bearers:** JOHN STEPHENSON (1809–1893) of Ire-

land came to the United States as a small boy, settling in New York City. He designed and built the first bus in New York (1931). He also designed and built the first streetcar in the world. ALEXANDER HAMILTON STEPHENS (1812–1883) of Georgia was a lawyer, member of Congress, and governor of Georgia. URIAH SMITH STEPHENS (1821–1882) of New Jersey was one of the founders of the Garment Cutters' Association of Philadelphia and the Noble Order of Knights of Labor. BENJAMIN FRANKLIN STEPHENSON (1823–1871) of Illinois was the founder of the Grand Army of the Republic at Decatur, Illinois. ISAAC STEPHENSON (1829–1918) of Canada was a member of Congress and a U.S. senator from Wisconsin.

Genealogies: *John Steevens of Guilford, Connecticut* [also Stephens] was compiled by Claude W. Barlow and published in Rochester, New York, in 1976. *Stephens-Stevens and Stevenson-Stephenson* was compiled by A. Maxim Coppage and published in Owensboro, Kentucky, in 1980.

STEPP

Ranking: 3160 **S.S. Count:** 14,368

Origin: English. Transformation of Stephen.

Genealogies: *Johnston Stepp and Allied Families* was compiled by Jennie F. Downing Crow and published in North Platte, Nebraska, in 1980. *The Stepp Family Chronicles* was compiled by William Wayne Stepp and published in Independence, Missouri, in 1984.

STERLING (S.S. Abbreviation: Sterli)

Ranking: 1363 **S.S. Count:** 32,547

Origin: Scottish. Uncertain etymology. The name was given to those from Stirling, the name of a place in Scotland.

Famous **Sterlings:** JAMES STERLING (1701?–1763) of Ireland was a colonial clergyman. JOHN WHALEN STERLING (1816–1885) of Pennsylvania was one of the forces behind the growth of the University of Wisconsin. JOHN WILLIAM STERLING (1844–1918) of Connecticut was a lawyer who left the bulk of his estate to Yale University. Sterling Library is named in his honor. GEORGE STERLING (1869–1926) of New York was a poet and a leader of the art colony in Carmel, California.

Genealogies: None known.

STERN

Ranking: 1164 **S.S. Count:** 37,591

Origin: English, German, Jewish. English: derived from the Middle English word "stern(e)," meaning harsh or strict. The name was given to those who were austere. German, Jewish: cognates to Starr.

Famous **Sterns:** JOSEPH WILLIAM STERN (1870–1934) of New York City was a songwriter and publisher of music in the early 20th century. OTTO STERN (1888–1969) of Germany was an associate of Albert Einstein and the winner of the Nobel Prize for physics in 1943 for a series of experiments on dormant molecular-beam methods. CATHERINE BRIEGER STERN (1894–1973) of Germany was an innovative pioneer in the field of elementary education. She specialized in reading and mathematics. KURT GUENTHER STERN (1904–1956) of Germany was a biochemist who reserved the characteristics of heavy metals.

Genealogies: *Crossroads in Kansas: a Stearns– Ross Genealogy* [also Sterns] was compiled by Phyllis Ross Kostner and published in Preety Prairie, Kansas, in 1982. *Of Them That Left a Name Behind: a history of the Starnes family's first 125 years and beyond in America* [also Sterns] was compiled by H. Gerald Starnes and published in Baltimore, Maryland, in 1983.

STERNE

Ranking: 4570　**S.S. Count:** 9774

Origin: English. Transformation of Stern.

Famous Sternes: SIMON STERNE (1839–1901) of Pennsylvania was a lawyer and civic reformer. He specialized in common carrier law and worked to improve the rights of people being served by the carriers. MAURICE STERNE (1878–1957) of Latvia was an artist. He painted murals for the library of the Department of Justice.

Genealogies: None known.

STEVEN (ALSO STEVENEL, STEVENIN, STEVENS, STEVENSON)

Ranking: 68　**S.S. Count:** 359,841

Origin: Stevens—Dutch, English, Flemish, German; Stevenson—English; Steven—English, German; Stevenel, Stevenin—French. Cognates to and transformations of Stephen.

Famous Bearers: JOHN STEVENS (1749–1838) of New York City was an engineer and an inventor. He built a practical steamboat and ran it between Philadelphia and Trenton, New Jersey. He also built the first American-made steam locomotive. He proposed bridges across and tunnels under the Hudson River connecting New York City and Hoboken, New Jersey, and an elevated railway in New York City. ROBERT LIVINGSTON STEVENS (1787–1856) of New Jersey was the son of John Stevens (1749–1838). He was involved with his father in the building of the steam locomotive, and he engineered the first one that ran in New Jersey, in Bordentown. His brother, EDWIN AUGUSTUS STEVENS (1795–1868) of New Jersey, was an engineer and the endower of lands and finances for the building of Stevens Institute of Technology. THADDEUS STEVENS (1792–1868) of Vermont was vehemently opposed to slavery and, as a lawyer, defended escapees without a fee. He served in the political arena and was constantly at odds with President Andrew Johnson. His temper and hateful ways, unfortunately, will be the best-remembered part of him. JOHN

WHITE STEVENSON (1812–1886) of Virginia was the governor of and U.S. senator from Kentucky. ISAAC INGALLS STEVENS (1818–1862) of Massachusetts was the governor of the Washington territory and a Washington delegate to Congress. A major general in the Civil War, he was killed in action. JOHN HARRINGTON STEVENS (1820–1900) of Canada was a Minnesota pioneer and the builder of the first home in Minneapolis. ADLAI EWING STEVENSON (1835–1914) of Kentucky was the vice president of the United States (1893–1897) under President Grover Cleveland. He also served as a member of Congress from Illinois. He was the grandfather of Adlai Ewing Stevenson II (1900–1965). JAMES STEVENSON (1840–1888) of Kentucky is believed to have been the first white man to climb to the top of the Grand Teton, in 1872. JOHN FRANK STEVENS (1853–1943) of Maine was a civil engineer and a pioneer in international railroad building. NETTIE MARIA STEVENS (1861–1912) of Vermont was a biologist and geneticist whose most important research dealt with chromosomes and heredity. She was the person who discovered that the sex of a being was determined by a chromosome. She also identified the chromosomes as the X and the Y. She also discovered in her studies of flies and mosquitoes that chromosomes were paired. WALLACE STEVENS (1879–1955) of Pennsylvania was one of the major poets of the 20th century. His book *Collected Poems* (1954) won a Nobel Prize in 1955. ADLAI EWING STEVENSON II (1900–1965) was the governor of Illinois and a behind-the-scenes politician through most of his life. He was the Democratic nominee for president in 1952 and 1956, and he was the grandson of Adlai Ewing Stevenson (1835–1914).

Genealogies: *Stevens & Anderson Kinsmen of American Descendant* (sic) was compiled by J. B. Bell and published in Hernando, Mississippi, in 1987. *A Stevens Genealogy* was compiled by Janet Evelyn Savage Cornell and published in Baltimore, Maryland, in 1992. *The Stevens Tree* was compiled by Joe M. Clark and published in Marceline, Missouri, in 1982.

STEWARD, STEWARDSON, STEWART, STEWARTSON (S.S. Abbreviation: Stewar)

Ranking: 48　**S.S. Count:** 467,779

Origin: Scottish. Derived from the Middle English word "stiward," meaning an administrative official. The names were given to those who worked as such.

Famous Bearers: ALVIN STEWART (1790–1849) of New York was the founder of the New York Anti-Slavery Society. ANDREW STEWART (1791–1872) of Pennsylvania was a member of Congress from Pennsylvania and was nicknamed "Tariff Andy" because of his views. PHILO PENFIELD STEWART (1798–1868) of Connecticut was the co-founder of Oberlin College and the inventor of the Oberlin stove (1834). ALEXANDER TURNEY STEWART (1803–1876) of Ireland was a New York City merchant who took his profits and built the town of Garden City, Long Island, New York. IRA STEWARD (1831–1883) of Connecticut was a leader in the fight for the eight-hour work day. ISABEL MAITLAND STEWART (1878–1963) of Canada was responsible for raising the standards in the field of nursing. JULIAN H. STEWARD (1902–1972) of Washington, D.C., was an anthropologist and an authority on cultural evolution.

Genealogies: The Sampson Stewarts was compiled by Morris Monroe Stewart and published in Monroe, Louisiana, in 1989. *The Family of Thomas Stewart of Madison County, Alabama* was compiled by Mary Bivins Geron Countess and published in Huntsville, Alabama.

STICKLES (S.S. Abbreviation: Stickl)
Ranking: 3659 S.S. Count: 12,337
Origin: English. 1) derived from the Old English word "stigel," meaning stile. The name was given to those who lived near a stile. 2) derived from the Old English word "stigol," meaning a steep climb or path. The name was given to those who lived near a steep path.
Genealogies: None known.

STIDHAM (S.S. Abbreviation: Stidha)
Ranking: 4631 S.S. Count: 9655
Origin: English. The name was given to those from Stedham, the name of a place in Sussex, England, meaning an area where stallions grazed.
Genealogies: None known.

STILES
Ranking: 1469 S.S. Count: 30,307
Origin: English. Transformation of Stickle.
Famous Stileses: EZRA STILES (1727?–1795) of Connecticut was a Congregational clergyman and a scholar. He was instrumental in the founding of Brown University. He was a supporter of the Revolution and the rights of the American. CHARLES WARDELL STILES (1867–1941) of New York was a zoologist and health expert. He is best remembered as the man who discovered the hookworm and the diseases with which it is associated.
Genealogies: A History of the David Stiles Family was compiled by Lois Ogden Stiles Sparks and published in Murray, Kentucky, in 1980.

STILL
Ranking: 2671 S.S. Count: 17,063
Origin: English, German. English: derived from the Middle English word "still," meaning a fish trap. The name was given to those who lived near a fish trap in a river. English, German: derived from the Middle English and Middle High German word "still," meaning quiet. The name was given to those who were calm.

Famous Stills: WILLIAM STILL (1821–1902) of New Jersey was a black leader and reformer. He was the author of *The Underground Railroad* (1872). ANDREW TAYLOR STILL (1828–1917) of Virginia was the founder of osteopathy. WILLIAM GRANT STILL (1895–1978) of Mississippi was a conductor and the first black man to conduct a symphony orchestra. CLYFFORD STILL (1904–1980) of North Dakota was an abstract expressionist painter. He was most influential on the modern artists.
Genealogies: Chatelain, Stahly, Still, Hunter, Tears et al. was compiled by Elvin J. Chatelain and published in Manhattan, Kansas. *Olof Stille in New Sweden* [also Still] was compiled by Fritz Nordstrom and published in Winter Park, Florida, in 1987.

STILLWELL (S.S. Abbreviation: Stillw)
Ranking: 3558 S.S. Count: 12,688
Origin: English. Derived from the Old English words "stille" and "well(a)" meaning constant and well. The name was given to those who lived near a spring that flowed without interruption.
Genealogies: Stillwell Heritage in Arkansas, 1798–1976 was compiled by Robert Will-Fred Dhonau and published in Little Rock, Arkansas, in 1976. *Ash, Ashe, Stillwell* was compiled by John Reid Ashe and pubilshed in Greensboro, North Carolina, in 1977.

STILWELL (S.S. Abbreviation: Stilwe)
Ranking: 4810 S.S. Count: 9317
Origin: English. Transformation of Stillwell.
Famous Stilwells: SILAS MOORE STILWELL (1800–1881) of New York City was a New York legislator and the one credited with introducing the legislation that ended debtors' prison in New York. JOSEPH WARREN STILWELL (1883–1946) of Florida was raised in New York and was a career army officer and a West Point graduate. He was nicknamed Uncle Joe and Vinegar Joe and became an expert on the affairs of China.
Genealogies: None known.

STINE
Ranking: 3072 S.S. Count: 14,784
Origin: German. Transformation of Stein.
Famous Stines: CHARLES MILTON ALTLAND STINE (1882–1954) of Connecticut was an industrial chemist. He was one of the first organic chemists and was involved in the making of TNT.
Genealogies: None known.

STINNES (S.S. Abbreviation: Stinne)
Ranking: 3468 S.S. Count: 13,022
Origin: German. Cognate to Austin.
Genealogies: None known.

STINSON (S.S. Abbreviation: Stinso)

Ranking: 1226 S.S. Count: 36,044

Origin: English. Transformation of Stephen.

Genealogies: *A History of the Stinson Family: in Scotland, Northern Ireland, New Hampshire and Illinois* was compiled by William S. Stinson and published in Elmhurst, Illinois, in 1984. *Our Stinson's (sic)* was compiled by Ulery Stinson and published in Columbia, Tennessee, in 1981. *The Stinson Family* was compiled by Leroy David Lillie and published in Ames, Iowa, in 1971.

STIVER (ALSO STIVERSON)

Ranking: 4791 S.S. Count: 9346

Origin: English. Derived from the first name Stever, a transformation of Stephen.

Genealogies: *Stover, Stoever, Staver, Stiver: an account of the ancestry and descendants of Johann Caspar Stoevar of Pennsylvania* was compiled by Vernon Stiver and published in Loveland, Ohio, in 1992. *The Stivers in the Ball-Stivers Line and Allied Families* was compiled by Dorothy Stivers Brown and published in Lewisburg, Pennsylvania, in 1976.

STOCK

Ranking: 2715 S.S. Count: 16,759

Origin: English. 1) derived from the Old English word "stocc," meaning tree trunk or stump. 2) uncertain etymology. Proabably given to those who lived near a prominent tree stump or trunk.

Famous **Stocks**: FREDERICK AUGUST STOCK (1872–1942) of Germany was the conductor of the Chicago Symphony Orchestra.

Genealogies: *Stock Family History* was compiled by Margaret Reynolds Stock and published in Cody, Wyoming, in 1972.

STOCKE (ALSO STOCKEN, STOCKER)

Ranking: 3375 S.S. Count: 13,428

Origin: Stocke—English; Stocken, Stocker—English, German. Transformations of and cognates to Stock.

Genealogies: None known.

STOCKMAN, STOCKMANN (S.S. Abbreviation: Stockm)

Ranking: 4513 S.S. Count: 9918

Origin: Stockman—Dutch, Flemish; Stockmann—German. Cognates to Stock.

Genealogies: *Stockman-Gallison Ancestral Lines: 114 lines of early New England Settlers* was compiled by Katherine Dickson and published in Henniker, New Hampshire, in 1984. *The Stockman Story* was compiled by Katherine Dickson and published in Henniker, New Hampshire, in 1992.

STOCKS

Ranking: 4126 S.S. Count: 10,958

Origin: English. Transformation of Stock.

Genealogies: None known.

STOCKTON (S.S. Abbreviation: Stockt)

Ranking: 2436 S.S. Count: 18,641

Origin: English. Derived from the Old English words "stocc" or "stoc" and "tūn," meaning tree trunk, subordinate and settlement. The name was given to those from Stockton, the name of several places in England.

Famous **Stocktons**: RICHARD STOCKTON (1730–1781) of New Jersey was a Revolutionary War soldier, a member of the Continental Congress, and a signer of the Declaration of Independence. His son, RICHARD STOCKTON (1764–1828) of New Jersey, was a U.S. senator from New Jersey. His son, ROBERT FIELD STOCKTON (1795–1866) of New Jersey, was a naval officer in the War of 1812 and a U.S. senator from New Jersey, in which capacity he fought for the abolition of naval flogging. During the war he proclaimed California to be a U.S. territory. FRANCIS (FRANK) RICHARD STOCKTON (1834–1902) of Pennsylvania was the author of fiction about local history that was published in magazines and books.

Genealogies: *The Estes Family of Virginia, Southern Kentucky, Iowa, Missouri and Kansas and their Ancestor Families—Yates, Marshall, Stockton* was compiled by Lucille Alexander and published in Wayne, New Jersey, in 1990. *Families and Kin of Elias Stockton, Moses Dickey, and James Upchurch, Cherokee County, Texas, Pioneers* was compiled by Mae Gean Pettit and published in Baltimore, Maryland, in 1991. *A House Called Morven* [also Stockton] was compiled by Alfred Hoyt Bill and published in Princeton, New Jersey, in 1978.

STOCKWELL (S.S. Abbreviation: Stockw)

Ranking: 4878 S.S. Count: 9169

Origin: English. Derived from the Old English words "stocc" and "well(a)," meaning tree trunk and stream. The name was given to those from Stockwell, a place in England.

Famous **Stockwells**: JOHN NELSON STOCKWELL (1832–1920) of Massachusetts was an astronomer whose primary contribution was the theory about the moon's motion and its eclipses.

Genealogies: *The Stockwell Family* was compiled by Irene Dixon Stockwell and published in Janesville, Wisconsin, in 1982. *The Stockwell Genealogy* was compiled by Mabel Stockwell Kennedy and published in Chelsea, Vermont, in 1983.

STODDARD, STODDART (S.S. Abbreviation: Stodda)

Ranking: 2203 S.S. Count: 20,829

Origin: English. Derived from the Old English words "stōd" or "stott" and "hierde," meaning a horse kept for breeding, a horse not greatly valued, and herdkeeper. The names were given to those who raised horses.

Famous **Bearers:** JOSHUA C. STODDARD (1814–1902) of Vermont was the inventor of the steam calliope. WILLIAM OSBORN STODDARD (1835–1925) was the author of *Inside the White House in War Times* (1890) and 76 stories for young boys. JOSEPH MARSHALL STODDART (1845–1921) of Pennsylvania was the first American publisher.

Genealogies: *The Wheel of Truth* [also Stoddard, Stoddart] was compiled by Gertrude S. Lowry and published in Hicksville, New York, in 1977. *The Story of Mrs. Eliza Platt Stoddard of Succasunna, Morris County, New Jersey* was compiled by Edwin W. Hancock and published in New York, New York, in 1978.

STOKES
Ranking: 484 S.S. Count: 83,453
Origin: English. Uncertain etymology. The name was given to those from Stoke, the name of places in England.

Famous **Stokeses:** MONTFORT STOKES (1762–1842) of Virginia was the governor of North Carolina and a U.S. Indian commissioner and agent. ISAAC NEWTON PHELPS STOKES (1867–1944) of New York City was an architect and a housing reformer. He was a pioneer in the building of housing in New York. THOMAS LUNSFORD STOKES JR. (1898–1958) of Georgia was a journalist who was responsible for uncovering corruption in the Works Progress Administration in Kentucky. Because of his investigative reporting, the Hatch Act (1938) was passed. He received a Pulitzer Prize for his story.

Genealogies: *The Mills, Stokes, and Forrester Families of Primarily Greenville, Co., S.C.* was compiled by Lorene Burton Ambrose and published in Greer, South Carolina, in 1979. *The Stokes Family of Pitt County, N.C.* was compiled by Taney Brazeal and published in Fairhope, Alabama, in 1974. *The Andrews, Clapp, Stokes, Wright, Van Cleve Genealogies* was compiled by Alred S. Andrews and published in Fort Lauderdale, Florida, in 1975.

STOLL
Ranking: 2961 S.S. Count: 15,829
Origin: German. Uncertain etymology. 1) the name was given to those who lived near a mine shaft. 2) the name was given to those who lived near a pole.

Genealogies: *Descendants of Michael Stohler Sr. and Maria Schwanger* [also Stoll] was compiled by Charles H. Saunders and published in Anderson, Indiana, in 1979.

STOLTZ (ALSO STOLTZE, STOLTZEL)
Ranking: 3294 S.S. Count: 13,771
Origin: German. Derived from the German word "stolz,"

meaning haughty. The names were given to those who were arrogant.
Genealogies: None known.

STONE
Ranking: 145 S.S. Count: 213,852
Origin: English. Derived from the Old English word "stān," meaning stone. The name was given to those who lived in a stony area, near stone markers, to masons, or to those from any of several places called Stone.

Famous **Stones:** SAMUEL STONE (1602–1663) of England came to America with Thomas Hooker. Stone purchased the present-day site of Hartford, Connecticut, from the Indians and settled there in 1636. He was the minister of the church there until his death. THOMAS STONE (1743–1787) of Maryland was a member of the Continental Congress and a signer of the Declaration of Independence and worked on the committee for the Articles of Confederation. DAVID STONE (1770–1818) of North Carolina was the governor of, then U.S. senator from, North Carolina. LUCY STONE (1818–1893) of Massachusetts was a supporter of suffrage for women who kept her maiden name in protest of the unequal laws that applied to women. She came to be known as Mrs. Stone. MELVILLE ELIJAH STONE (1848–1929) of Illinois was the founder of the *Chicago Daily News*, the first penny daily newspaper in Chicago. CHARLES AUGUSTUS STONE (1867–1941) of Massachusetts was the co-founder of Stone & Webster Engineering Corp. HARLAN FISKE STONE (1872–1946) of New Hampshire was the chief justice of the United States.

Genealogies: *The Andrew Hicks and Charles Stone Families* was compiled by Lucile Kaufmann Novak and published in Nashua, New Hampshire, in 1977. *Descendants of Henry Stone and Tabitha Tuttle* was compiled by Eva Laughlin LeBlanc and published in Baltimore, Maryland, in 1986.

STONEBRIDGE (S.S. Abbreviation: Stoneb)
Ranking: 4603 S.S. Count: 9710
Origin: English. Derived from the Old English words "stān" and "briycg," meaning stone and bridge. The name was given to those who lived near a bridge of stone.
Genealogies: None known.

STONER
Ranking: 1845 S.S. Count: 24,524
Origin: English. Transformation of Stone.
Genealogies: None known.

STOREY
Ranking: 2331 S.S. Count: 19,470
Origin: English. Derived from the Old Norse name Stóri, which was derived from the word "storr," meaning large.

Genealogies: None known.

STORM

Ranking: 3490 S.S. Count: 12,930

Origin: Danish, Dutch, English, Flemish, German, Norwegian. Derived from the Old English word "storm" or the Old Norse word "stormr," both meaning storm. The name was given to those of stormy disposition.

Genealogies: *Descendants of John Springs (Springsteen) and Sophia Gassaway of Mecklenburg County, North Carolina* [also Storm] was compiled by Max Perry and published in Midland, Texas, in 1988. *Kin of My Grandchildren* [Storm family] was compiled by Noble K. Littell and published in Franklin, North Carolina, in 1990.

STORY

Ranking: 1644 S.S. Count: 27,179

Origin: English. Transformation of Storey.

Famous Storys: JOSEPH STORY (1779–1845) of Massachusetts was a U.S. Supreme Court justice. His son, WILLIAM WETMORE STORY (1819–1895) of Massachusetts, was a sculptor and author.

Genealogies: *Some Ancestors and Descendants of Joseph Rudd, Jr., 1740–1818, and his Wife, Sarah Story, 1744–1842, of Bennington, Vermont* was compiled by Dorothy Rudd DuMond and published in Ulster Park, New York, in 1982.

STOUT

Ranking: 700 S.S. Count: 60,332

Origin: English. 1) derived from the Old Norse name Stútr, meaning gnat. The name was given to those who were considered unimportant. 2) derived from the Middle English word "stout," meaning loyal.

Famous Stouts: WILLIAM BUSHNELL STOUT (1880–1956) of Illinois was an engineer and the owner of the company that built the first all-metal airplane and was active in the budding airplane industry. REX TODHUNTER STOUT (1886–1975) of Indiana was a writer of detective stories whose central character was Nero Wolfe.

Genealogies: *James Pindall Stout, 1819–1903* was compiled by Kemble Stout and published in Pullman, Washington, in 1975. *Richard Stout Descendants in West Virginia* was compiled by Russel Ray Stout and published in Lyndhurst, Virginia, in 1966. *Some Stout Families of Central Illinois* was compiled by Littleton P. Bradley and published in St. Louis, Missouri, in 1972.

STOVALL (S.S. Abbreviation: Stoval)

Ranking: 1951 S.S. Count: 23,219

Origin: English. The name was given to those from Esteville, a place in France whose name means east village.

Famous Stovalls: PLEASANT ALEXANDER STOVALL (1857–

1935) of Georgia was the editor of the *Savannah Press* and was a U.S. minister to Switzerland.

Genealogies: *The Stovall Family* was compiled by Lyle Keith Williams and published in Fort Worth, Texas, in 1984. *The Stovall Family in America* was compiled by Carmae Massey Smith and published in Houston, Texas, in 1979.

STOVER

Ranking: 1264 S.S. Count: 34,860

Origin: German. 1) transformation of Stauffer. 2) the name was given to those from Stove, a place in Germany. 3) the name was given to those who managed a public bath.

Genealogies: *Stover, Stoever, Staver, Stiver: an account of the ancestry and descendants of Johann Caspar Stoevar of Pennsylvania* was compiled by Vernon Stiver and published in Loveland, Ohio, in 1992. *Benjamin Parrott, c. 1795–1839 and Lewis Stover, 1781–1850/60, of Overton County, Tennessee* was compiled by Mavis Parrott Kelsey and published in 1979. *The Stover/Stauffer Connection* was compiled by Raymond M. Stover and published in Lewiston, Idaho, in 1991.

STOWE

Ranking: 3028 S.S. Count: 15,020

Origin: English, Jewish. English: derived from the Old English word "stōw," meaning a gathering place. The name was given to those from Stow, the name of several places in England. Jewish: Anglicization of any of several similar-sounding Jewish surnames.

Famous Stowes: CALVIN ELLIS STOWE (1802–1886) of Massachusetts was the author of *Report on Elementary Instruction in Europe* (1837) and the husband of Harriet Elizabeth Beecher Stowe. HARRIET ELIZABETH BEECHER STOWE (1811–1896) of Connecticut was the author of *Uncle Tom's Cabin.*

Genealogies: *Genealogy of the Stow (Stowe) Family in America* was compiled by Aber Stowe Wiester and published in Baltimore, Maryland, in 1933. *The Stowe Family: descendants of William and Mary Stowe, from Virginia to North Carolina* was compiled by Rachel Hanna Hoke and published in Myrtle Beach, South Carolina, in 1977.

STRAIN (ALSO STRAINGE)

Ranking: 3424 S.S. Count: 13,188

Origin: Strainge—English; Strain—Scottish. Strainge: transformation of Strange. Strain: uncertain etymology. Possibly derived from the Gaelic words "srath" and "eachain," meaning valley and foal. The name was given to those from Strachan, a place in Scotland.

Famous Bearers: ISAAC G. STRAIN (1821–1857) of Pennsylvania was the naval officer in charge of the expedition which decided that a ship canal was not possible at the Isthmus of Darien, 1853.

Genealogies: *The Strain Family: a genealogy of the descendants of Andrew Strain, Sr., of North Carolina* was compiled by James C. Parker and published in Toccoa, Georgia, in 1985.

STRAIT
Ranking: 4444 **S.S. Count:** 10,090
Origin: English. Derived from the Middle English word "strecchen," meaning to stretch. 1) the name was given to those who lived near a Roman road. 2) the name was given to those who has good posture.
Genealogies: None known.

STRAND (ALSO STRANDBERG)
Ranking: 2165 **S.S. Count:** 21,207
Origin: Strand—Danish, Norwegian, Swedish; Strandberg—Swedish. Strand: derived from the Old Norse word "strond," meaning shore. The name was given to those who lived by the sea. Strandberg: derived from the words "strand" and "berg," meaning shore and hill.
Famous Bearers: PAUL STRAND (1890–1976) of New York City was a photographer of still and motion pictures. He also published photographic books, including *Little Egypt* (1969).
Genealogies: None known.

STRANG (ALSO STRANGE, STRANGER, STRANGEWAY, STRANGMAN)
Ranking: 1473 **S.S. Count:** 30,238
Origin: English. Strang, Strangman: transformations of Strong. Strange, Stranger: derived from the Middle English word "strange," meaning foreign. The name was given to those who were new to an area. Strangeway: derived from the Old English words "strang," and "(ge)wæesc," meaning strong and current. The name was given to those from Strangeways, place in England.
Famous Bearers: JAMES JESSEE STRANG (1813–1856) of New York was a Mormon leader and the founder of a Mormon sect.
Genealogies: None known.

STRASSER, STRASSLER, STRASSMANN, STRASSNER (S.S. Abbreviation: Strass)
Ranking: 3946 **S.S. Count:** 11,450
Origin: Strassner—German; Strasser, Strassler, Strassmann—German, Jewish. Cognates to Street.
Genealogies: None known.

STRATTON (S.S. Abbreviation: Stratt)
Ranking: 1343 **S.S. Count:** 32,914
Origin: English. Derived from the Old Engish words "stræt" and "tūn," meaning Roman road and settlement. The name was given to those from Stratton, the name of several places in England.
Famous Strattons: CHARLES SHERWOOD STRATTON (1838–1883) of Connecticut was "General Tom Thumb" of P. T. Barnum's museum. SAMUEL WESLEY STRATTON (1861–1931) of Illinois was a physicist and the first director of the U.S. Bureau of Standards.
Genealogies: *Lackey, Stratton, and Allied Families* was compiled by Harriett I. Pratt and published in Glastonbury, Connecticut, in 1971. *The Stratton Clan* was compiled by Gertrude Kratzer Rosenkild and published in Mason City, Iowa, in 1982. *I'm Claiming the Promise* [also Stratton] was compiled by David C. Stratton and published in Salem, Ohio, in 1977.

STRAUB (ALSO STRAUBER, STRAUBLE)
Ranking: 2753 **S.S. Count:** 16,551
Origin: Straub, Strauble—German; Strauber—Jewish. Derived from the Middle High German word "strūp," meaning slovenly. The name was given to those whose hair was unkempt.
Genealogies: *Johann Reibenspies and his Descendants* [also Straub] was compiled by Elaine Farrell Summers and published in 1985.

STRAUS (ALSO STRAUSS, STRAUSSLE, STRAUSSMAN, STRAUSSMANN)
Ranking: 1287 **S.S. Count:** 34,401
Origin: Straussle—German; Strauss, Straussman, Straussmann—German, Jewish; Straus—Jewish. Straussle: transformation of the German name Strauss. Straus: transformation of the Jewish name Strauss. Strauss, Straussman, Straussmann (German): 1) derived from the German word "strauss," meaning ostrich. The names were given to those whose house bore the sign of an ostrich. 2) derived from the German word "strauss," meaning complaint. The names were given to those who were quick-tempered or aggressive. Strauss, Straussman, Straussmann (Jewish): derived from the German word "strauss," meaning ostrich. The names were taken ornamentally.
Famous Bearers: LEVI STRAUSS (1829?–1902) of Germany came to the United States, then joined the settlers of California. He sold prospectors pants made from his tent material. They became known as "blue jeans," or "Levi's," and his company came to be known as Levi Strauss & Company. ISADOR STRAUS (1845–1912) of Bavaria was co-owner of Macy's department store. He also owned Abraham and Straus department store. His brother, NATHAN STRAUS (1848–1931) of Bavaria, was his partner in the Macy's stores. He was also a pioneer in the area of public

health. JOSEPH BAERMANN STRAUSS (1870–1938) of Ohio was a bridge engineer. His best-known bridge is San Francisco's Golden Gate Bridge. PERCY SELDEN STRAUS (1876–1944) of New York City worked in the family's Macy's department store business. He initiated training programs for clerks and executives. ROGER WILLIAMS STRAUS (1891–1957) of New York City was the husband of Gladys Guggenheim. He helped to found the National Conference of Christians and Jews.

Genealogies: *The Waltz Emperors: the life and times and music of the Strauss family* was compiled by Joseph Wechsberg and published in New York, New York, in 1973.

STREET (ALSO STREETE, STREETER, STREETLY, STREETS)

Ranking: 871 S.S. Count: 49,551

Origin: English. Street: derived from the Old English word "stræt," meaning Roman road. The name was given to those from Street, the name of several places in England. Streetly: derived from the Old English words "stræt" and "lēah," meaning Roman road and wood or clearing. The name was given to those from Streetly or Streatley, the name of places in England.

Famous **Bearers:** JOSEPH MONTFORT STREET (1782–1840) of Virginia was a frontier journalist and Indian agent for the Winnebago. AUGUSTUS RUSSELL STREET (1791–1866) of Connecticut was a benefactor of Yale University. Street Hall is named for him. GEORGE LINIUS STREETER (1873–1948) of New York was an embryologist and the author of *Handbook on Human Embryology.*

Genealogies: *Our Streets* was compiled by Lawrence M. Bichell and published in Edgewater, Maryland, in 1973.

STRICKLAND

Ranking: 294 S.S. Count: 121,867

Origin: English. Derived from the Old English words "steorc" and "land," meaning steer and land. The name was given to those from Strickland, a place in England.

Famous **Stricklands:** WILLIAM STRICKLAND (1787?–1854) of Pennsylvania was an architect who was responsible for the design of the U.S. Customs House in Philadelphia.

Genealogies: *Strickland Genealogy and Family History* was compiled by Naomi Ruth Jackson Chasteen and published in Miami, Oklahoma, in 1987. *The Strickland Story* was compiled by Kathleen S. Bell and published in Arkansas in 1993.

STRING (ALSO STRINGER, STRINGFELLOW)

Ranking: 1173 S.S. Count: 37,246

Origin: English. String, Stringer: derived from the Middle English word "string," meaning string. The name was given to those who made string. Stringfellow: derived from the Middle

English words *"streng" and "felaw,"* meaning strong and fellow. The name was given to those who were strong.

Famous **Bearers:** FRANKLIN STRINGFELLOW (1840–1913) of Virginia was the chief of scouts in the Army of Northern Virginia. ARTHUR JOHN ARBUTHNOTT STRINGER (1874–1950) of Canada was a writer of adventure novels, including *Heather of the High Hand* (1937).

Genealogies: None known.

STROBEL (S.S. Abbreviation: Strobe)

Ranking: 4389 S.S. Count: 10,222

Origin: German. Transformation of Straub.

Famous **Strobels:** CHARLES LOUIS STROBEL (1852–1936) of Ohio was a civil engineer and a pioneer in the use of steel framing in skyscrapers. EDWARD HENRY STROBEL (1855–1908) of South Carolina was a diplomat specializing in southeast Asia.

Genealogies: None known.

STROM

Ranking: 3420 S.S. Count: 13,228

Origin: Swedish. Derived from the Swedish word "ström," meaning river. The name was given to those who lived near a river or was taken ornamentally.

Genealogies: *The Stroms of South Carolina, 1765–1983* was compiled by Samuel T. Strom and published in Union, South Carolina, in 1984.

STRONG (ALSO STRONGE)

Ranking: 672 S.S. Count: 62,475

Origin: English. Derived from the Middle English word "strong," meaning strong. The names were given to those who were strong or, ironically, to those who were not strong.

Famous **Bearers:** CALEB STRONG (1745–1819) of Massachusetts was one of Massachusetts's first two U.S. senators and an early governor of the state. WILLIAM STRONG (1808–1895) of Connecticut was an associate justice of the U.S. Supreme Court. WILLIAM L. STRONG (1837–1914) of Ohio was a mayor of New York City. He appointed a future president, Theodore Roosevelt, to the position of police commissioner. JOSIAH STRONG (1847–1916) of Illinois was a clergyman and author whose popular books *Our Country* (1885) and *The New Era* (1893) offered religious solutions to social and industrial problems. ANNA LOUISE STRONG (1885–1970) of Nebraska was a journalist on labor-union newspapers in the United States before becoming founding editor of the English-language *Moscow Daily News* in Russia. Russian officials expelled her in 1949 for alleged spying, and she moved to China, where she wrote *Letters from China* (1961–1970). RICHARD P. STRONG (1872–1948) of Virginia was a physician, a professor of medicine, and a widely recognized authority on tropical diseases. WILLIAM D. STRONG (1899–1962) of Oregon was an anthropologist who was an expert on Indians of the Americas. Among his books was *Cross Sections of New World Prehistory* (1943).

Genealogies: *American Ancestors and Cousins of the Princess of Wales* [also Strong] was compiled by Gary Boyd Roberts and published in Baltimore, Maryland, in 1984. *Strong Family of Virginia* was compiled by James Robert Rolff and published in Oak Forest, Illinois, in 1982. *True Tales from the Early Days of Long Island* [also Strong] was compiled by Kate W. Strong and published in Bay Shore, New York, in 1940.

STROTHER, STROTHERS (S.S. Abbreviation: Stroth)

Ranking: 3360 **S.S. Count:** 13,228

Origin: English. Derived from words meaning boggy and meadow. The names were given to those from a marshy area and to those who came from Strother, the name of a place in Northumberland, England.

Famous **Bearers:** DAVID H. STROTHER (1816–1888) of West Virginia was a popular writer and illustrator for *Harper's New Monthly Magazine.*

Genealogies: *Strother Families* was compiled by Harold Heard and published in Amarillo, Texas, in 1974.

STROUD

Ranking: 1298 **S.S. Count:** 34,163

Origin: English. Derived from the Old English component "strōd," meaning marshy area covered with a dense undergrowth. The name was given to those from Stroud, the name of places in England.

Famous **Strouds:** ROBERT STROUD (1890–1963) of Washington became an authority on bird diseases and on canaries while imprisoned for murder at California's Alcatraz Prison. His nickname was the Birdman of Alcatraz.

Genealogies: *Strode and Stroud Families in England and America* was compiled by James Strode Elston and published in Rutland, Vermont, in 1976. *Scattered Chips from the Woodpile* [also Stroud] was compiled by Marcella Pickerel Headrick and published in Utica, Kentucky, in 1982. *No Beginning, No Ending* [also Stroud] was compiled by Logan Drexel Wilson and published in Dallas, Texas, in 1972.

STROUP (ALSO STROUPE)

Ranking: 3103 **S.S. Count:** 14,647

Origin: German. Uncertain etymology. The names were given to those with shaggy hair or to those with coarse, stiff hair.

Genealogies: *Stroope/Stroop Family History* [also Stroup] was compiled by Connie Stroope Brooks and published in Lovington, New Mexico, in 1988.

STRUNK

Ranking: 4268 **S.S. Count:** 10,541

Origin: German. Cognate to Stock. The name was given to those who lived near or were surrounded by tree stumps.

Genealogies: None known.

STUART

Ranking: 828 **S.S. Count:** 51,362

Origin: Scottish. Transformation of Stewart.

Famous **Stuarts:** GILBERT C. STUART (1755–1828) of Rhode Island was a premier portrait painter, perhaps best known for his several portraits of George Washington. JOHN TODD STUART (1807–1885) of Kentucky was Abraham Lincoln's law partner and a member of Congress from Illinois. JAMES E.B. STEWART (1833–1864) of Virginia, known as Jeb Stuart, was a Confederate army general who had several successes against the Union army until he was defeated and killed in Virginia. GRANVILLE STUART (1834–1918) of Virginia was a pioneer in Montana who wrote of his experiences in *Montana As It Is* (1865) and, with his brother James Stuart, in *Forty Years on the Frontier* (1925). RUTH M. STUART (1849–1917) of Louisiana was a short-story writer whose works were published in volumes after they appeared in periodicals. She described post-Civil War African-Americans within their own environments, and she was particularly skillful at dialect.

Genealogies: *Alexander Stewart, his Scots Ancestry and American Descendants* [also Stuart] was compiled by Dorothy Kintigh Sidfrid and published in Orange, California, in 1979. *Stewart Family History, 1821–1982* [also Stuart] was compiled by Ruth Ann Reiser Stewart and published in Waverly, Illinois, in 1982.

STUBBLEFIELD (S.S. Abbreviation: Stubbl)

Ranking: 3365 **S.S. Count:** 13,477

Origin: English. Transformation of Stock combined with the Old English word "feld," meaning field. The name was given to those who lived in a newly cleared field in which the stumps of the trees remained.

Genealogies: None known.

STUBBS

Ranking: 1670 **S.S. Count:** 26,775

Origin: English. Derived from the Old English word "stub(b)," meaning tree stump. The name was given to those near a prominent tree stump or to those thought to have the physical build of a tree stump.

Famous **Stubbses:** WALTER R. STUBBS (1858–1929) of Indiana was governor of Kansas from 1909 to 1913.

Genealogies: *Galveston was their Home: genealogy of the Kauffman-Stubbs-Brotherson families* was compiled by Sara Ellen Stubbs and published in 1977.

STUCKE (ALSO STUCKER, STUCKEY)

Ranking: 2138 **S.S. Count:** 21,411

Origin: Stuckey—English; Stucke, Stucker—German. Stuckey: derived from the Old English word "stocc," meaning tree trunk. The name was given to those who were stocky and stout. Stucke, Stucker: transformation of and cognate to Stock. 1) the names were given to those who lived near a tree stump. 2) the names were given to those from Stuck, the name of a place in Germany.
Genealogies: *Stuckey-Huffman Cousins was compiled by Opal L. Streiff and published in Burwell, Nebraska, in 1978. The Stuckeys of Somerset was compiled by Michael Churchman and published in Kansas City, Missouri, in 1961.*

STULL
Ranking: 3497 **S.S. Count:** 12,888
Origin: German. Transformation of Stoll.
Genealogies: None known.

STUMP
Ranking: 2313 **S.S. Count:** 19,636
Origin: English. Derived from the Middle English word "stump," meaning tree stump. The name was most likely given to those who lived near a significant or large tree stump or to those whose physical build was thought to resemble that of a tree stump.
Genealogies: *The Inheritance of Friedrich Schremmel [also Stump] was compiled by Mary L. Doerflein and published in Seattle, Washington, in 1982. Michael Stump, Sr. of Virginia, 1709–1768 was compiled by Thurman Stump and published in Parsons, West Virginia, in 1975. Stump was compiled by Robert H. Knotts and published in Salisbury, North Carolina, in 1985.*

STUMPF
Ranking: 4329 **S.S. Count:** 10,347
Origin: German. Cognate to Stump.
Genealogies: None known.

STURDIVANT (S.S. Abbreviation: Sturdi)
Ranking: 4395 **S.S. Count:** 10,210
Origin: English? Uncertain etymology. Most likely derived from the Middle English word "stert(en)" and the Anglo-Norman-French word "avaunt," meaning forward. The name was probably given to those who were considered speedy.
Genealogies: None known.

STURGE (ALSO STURGEON, STURGES, STURGESS)
Ranking: 2352 **S.S. Count:** 19,298
Origin: English. Sturge, Sturges, Sturgess: derived from the Old Norse first name Þorgils, which comprises the components "Þorr," the name of a deity, and "gils," meaning hostage.

Sturgeon: meaning the name of a fish called sturgeon. The name was given to those who sold fish.
Famous Bearers: PRESTON STURGES (1898–1959) of Illinois was a playwright, director, and producer. He wrote the screenplay for and directed *The Great McGinty* (1940), which won an Academy Award for writing.
Genealogies: *Family: roots, ties, and trails (Sturgeon family) was compiled by Mary C. Sturgeon and published in Little Rock, Arkansas, in 1991. The Rev. Daniel Sturges Story was compiled by Dorothy Sturgis Pruett and published in Macon, Georgia, in 1983.*

STURGIS (S.S. Abbreviation: Sturgi)
Ranking: 2418 **S.S. Count:** 18,725
Origin: English. Transformation of Sturgess.
Famous Sturgises: RUSSELL STURGIS (1836–1909) of Maryland was an architect of the Greek Revival and Victorian Gothic styles. He also was published as a critic of art and architecture in *Nation* and *Scribner's*.
Genealogies: *Cousins by the Dozen: Sturgis, Thrasher, Carlton, Mitchell, Branch was compiled by Dorothy Sturgis Pruett and published in Macon, Georgia, in 1975. Our Parents [Sturgis family] was compiled by Robert Sturgis Ingersoll and published in Boyertown, Pennsylvania, in 1973.*

STURM
Ranking: 3331 **S.S. Count:** 13,603
Origin: German, Jewish. Cognate to or transformation of Storm.
Genealogies: None known.

SUAREZ
Ranking: 941 **S.S. Count:** 45,978
Origin: Spanish. Cognate to the Portuguese name Soares.
Genealogies: *The Suarez Family, 1798–1980 was compiled by Dicy Villar Bowman and published in Pensacola, Florida, in 1980.*

SUGGS
Ranking: 2475 **S.S. Count:** 18,327
Origin: English. Derived from the Old English word "augu," meaning sow. 1) the name was given to those who were thought to resemble a sow. 2) the name was given to those who lived in a house that bore the sign of a sow.
Genealogies: None known.

SULLIVAN (S.S. Abbreviation: Sulliv)
Ranking: 85 **S.S. Count:** 312,785
Origin: Irish. Derived from the Gaelic name Ó Súileabháin, which was derived from a first name comprising the components "súil" and "dubh," meaning eye and dark.
Famous Sullivans: JOHN SULLIVAN (1740–1795) of New

Hampshire was a Revolutionary War officer and statesman. He served as a member of both the first and second Continental Congresses, as an active participant in the Revolutionary War, and as governor, among other political appointments, of New Hampshire after the war, and as a U.S. district judge in New Hampshire. LOUIS HENRI SULLIVAN (1856–1924) of Massachusetts, an architect, is known as the father of modern architecture and the founder of the "Chicago school." JOHN LAWRENCE SULLIVAN (1858–1918) of Massachusetts was a boxer known as the "Great John L" or the "Boston Strong Boy." He was the heavyweight champion from 1882 to 1892, winning the title from Paddy Ryan and losing it to James Corbett. JAMES EDWARD SULLIVAN (1860–1914) of New York City was a publisher of the *Sporting Times* and a sports promoter. TIMOTHY DANIEL SULLIVAN (1862–1913) of New York City was known as "Big Tim" and was involved in the political corruption of New York at the turn of the century. MARK SULLIVAN (1874–1952) of Pennsylvania was known as a "muckraker" journalist of the first half of the 20th century. MARY JOSEPHINE QUINN SULLIVAN (1877–1939) of Indiana was one of the founders of the Museum of Modern Art in New York. FRANCIS JOHN SULLIVAN (1892–1976) of New York was a comedian and the creator of the character Mr. Arbuthnot. EDWARD VINCENT SULLIVAN (1902–1974) of New York City was a gossip columnist for the New York *Daily News* and a television personality with his own variety show named after him.

Genealogies: Wild Bill Sullivan, King of the Hollow was compiled by Ann Hammons and published in Jackson, Mississippi, in 1980. *Adam's Ancestors* [also Sullivan] was compiled by Thomas Nathan Clark and published in Naperville, Illinois, in 1984.

SUMMER (ALSO SUMMERFIELD, SUMMERHILL, SUMMERS, SUMMERVILLE)

Ranking: 361 **S.S. Count:** 106,989

Origin: Summerhill, Summers—English; Summer—English, Irish; Summerfield—Jewish, Scottish; Summerville—Scottish. Summer (English): 1) transformation of Sumner. 2) transformation of Sumpter. 3) derived from the Middle English word "sum(m)eer," meaning the season summer. The name was given to those with a cheery disposition. Summer (Irish): derived from the Gaelic name Ó Samhraidh, which was derived from the first name Samhradh, meaning the season summer. Summerfield (Jewish): Anglicization of Sommerfeld, meaning summer and field. Summerfield (Scottish): transformation of the Scottish surname Somerville. Summerhill: derived from the Old English components "somer" and "hyll," meaning summer and hill. The name was possibly given to those from a former place called Summerhill. Summers: transformation of Summer, meaning the season sum-

mer. Summerville: transformation of the Scottish surname Somerville.

Famous Bearers: THOMAS OSMOND SUMMERS (1812–1882) of England was a Methodist clergyman responsible for the founding of the Texas and Alabama church administrative regions.

Genealogies: Carolina Summers was compiled by Mildred J. Miller and published in Winston-Salem, North Carolina, in 1980. *The Sommer, Sommers, Somers, and Summers that Missed the Boat* was compiled by William Clark Summers and published in Billings, Montana, in 1979.

SUMNER

Ranking: 1664 **S.S. Count:** 26,905

Origin: English. Derived from the Middle English word "sumner," meaning summoner. The name was given to court officials who served summonses.

Famous Sumners: CHARLES SUMNER (1811–1874) of Massachusetts was a U.S. senator who vehemently opposed slavery. He was the deliverer of the famous "crimes against Kansas" speech in 1856 and is best remembered as the man who woke the conscience of the American people to the barbarism of slavery. WILLIAM GRAHAM SUMNER (1840–1910) of New Jersey was a social scientist and the one who coined the phrase "the forgotten man."

Genealogies: The Benson Family Records [also Sumner] was compiled by Fred Harvey Benson and published in Syracuse, New York, in 1920. *Sumner Family History and Genealogy* was compiled by George W. Moore and published in Seattle, Washington, in 1983.

SUMPTER (S.S. Abbreviation: Sumpte)

Ranking: 4310 **S.S. Count:** 10,418

Origin: English. Derived from the Middle English word "sum(p)ter," meaning those who carried goods on pack animals. The name was given to people who did so.

Genealogies: None known.

SUNDERHAUF, SUNDERLAND, SUNDERMAN, SUNDERMEIER, SUNDERMEYER (S.S. Abbreviation: Sunder)

Ranking: 3733 **S.S. Count:** 12,108

Origin: Sunderland—English; Sunderhauf, Sunderman, Sundermeier, Sundermeyer—German. Uncertain etymology. Sunderland: 1) the name was given to those who lived on separate or private land. 2) the name was given tho those from Sunderland, the name of several places in England. Sunderhauf: the name was given to those from Sinderhauf, a place in Germany whose name means cinder pile. Sunderman: the name was given to those from places in Germany called Sundern, meaning muddy ground. Sundermeier, Sundermeyer: the names were given to those who farmed in a muddy area.

Famous **Bearers:** LAROY SUNDERLAND (1804–1885) of Rhode Island was a clergyman who organized the first antislavery group associated with the Methodist Church. He also was the *Zion's Watchman*'s first editor. ELIZA JANE READ SUNDERLAND (1839–1910) of Illinois was a reformer in the areas of temperance, education, and women's rights.

Genealogies: None known.

SUTHERBY, SUTHERLAND, SUTHERN (S.S. Abbreviation: Suther)

Ranking: 971 **S.S. Count:** 45,029

Origin: Sutherby, Suthern—English; Sutherland—Scottish. Sutherby: derived from the Old Norse phrase "suðr í bý," meaning "south in the village" (H&H). The name was given to those who lived at the south of a village. Suthern: transformation of South. Sutherland: derived from the Old Norse words "suðroen" and "land," meaning southern and land. The name was given to those from the former region of Sutherland in Scotland.

Famous **Bearers:** GEORGE SUTHERLAND (1862–1942) of England was a justice of the U.S. Supreme Court. EARL WILBUR SUTHERLAND JR. (1915–1974) of Kansas was a pharmacist and a physiologist and the winner of a Nobel Prize for his discovery of cyclic adenosine monophosphate.

Genealogies: *Uriah Sutherland Family* was compiled by Logan Sutherland and published in Windsor, Missouri, in 1971. *The Seven Sutherland Sisters* was compiled by Clarence O. Lewis and published in Lockhart, New York, in 1965.

SUTTER (ALSO SUTTERER, SUTTERLE, SUTTERLIN)

Ranking: 2639 **S.S. Count:** 17,248

Origin: German. Derived from the Middle High German word "sûter," meaning a cobbler or shoemaker. The name was given to those who worked as such.

Famous **Bearers:** JOHN AUGUSTUS SUTTER (1803–1880) of Switzerland came to California and settled an area on the American River near the junction with the Sacramento River. He called his lands Nueva Helvetia. When gold was discovered on his land on January 24, 1848, he was overrun with squatters. He lost everything, went bankrupt, and was eventually awarded a pension from the state of California of $250 a month from 1864 to 1878.

Genealogies: None known.

SUTTLE (ALSO SUTTLES)

Ranking: 3911 **S.S. Count:** 11,530

Origin: English. Uncertain etymology. 1) the names were given to those who were clever. 2) the names were given to those who lived at a southern hill.

Genealogies: *The Settle-Suttle Family* was compiled by

William Emmet Reese and published in Palm Beach, Florida, in 1974.

SUTTON

Ranking: 292 **S.S. Count:** 123,261

Origin: English. Derived from the Old English words "sūð" and "tūn," meaning south and settlement. The name was given to those from Sutton, the name of many places in England.

Famous **Suttons:** WALTER STANBOROUGH SUTTON (1877–1916) of New York was a geneticist who first showed that chromosomes carry a person's inherited traits and come in pairs (1902–1903). WILLIAM FRANCIS SUTTON JR. (1901–1980) of New York was better known by his nicknames Willie Sutton or Willie the actor. He was a bank robber whose use of disguises earned him his nickname. Once caught he continued with his disguises in his jail-break attempts. Most were unsuccessful.

Genealogies: *The Fruit of this Tree* [also Sutton] was compiled by Dorothy Sutton Nicolaysen and published in Stockton, California, in 1981. *History of our Moyer, Finn, Sutton, Russell & Related Families* was compiled by William Finn Moyer and published in Garden City, New York, in 1979.

SWAFFORD (S.S. Abbreviation: Swaffo)

Ranking: 3496 **S.S. Count:** 12,892

Origin: English. Derived from the tribal name Swaefas. The name was given to those who lived near the river crossing of the Swaefas.

Genealogies: None known.

SWAIN

Ranking: 1280 **S.S. Count:** 34,549

Origin: English. 1) derived from the Old Norse first name Sweinn, meaning servant. 2) derived from the Middle English word "swein," meaning servant. The name was given to those employed as servants.

Famous **Swains:** DAVID LOWERY SWAIN (1801–1868) of North Carolina was a governor of North Carolina who did not favor secession but who nonetheless stood by his state during the war. He was an advisor to President Andrew Johnson on Reconstruction. CLARA A. SWAIN (1834–1910) of New York was a pioneer missionary in India. A graduate of the Woman's Medical College, Philadelphia, she did much to help the Indian people. GEORGE FILLMORE SWAIN (1857–1931) of California was a pioneer in modern engineering techniques.

Genealogies: *John Quigg, Jr. (1779–1814), Immigrant 1802, his Ancestors and Descendants* [also Swain] was compiled by Sylvia Cecilia Fuson Ferguson and published in Oxford, Ohio, in 1977. *Old European Progenitors and Mayflower Ancestors of the A. T. F. and Mary Swain Fuller*

Family was compiled by Jean Fuller Butler and published in Ironton, Ohio, in 1990.

SWAN

Ranking: 1415 **S.S. Count:** 31,414
Origin: English. 1) transformation of Swain, meaning servant. 2) derived from the Old English word "swan," meaning swan, the aquatic bird. The name was given to those who were thought to resemble a swan.

Famous **Swans:** TIMOTHY SWAN (1758–1842) of Massachusetts was a writer of psalms. He composed "China" in 1790.

Genealogies: *The Black Swan: the story of Edward Hornsby, alias Swan, and his descendants* was compiled by Wendy E. Nunan and published in 1989. *Records of the Families of Brothers, Swan, Bonar/Reeves, Beardsley* was compiled by William P. Brothers and published in Palo Alto, California, in 1990. *The Affinity and Consanguinity of my "Swans"* was compiled by L. P. Fauskee and published in Santa Barbara, California, in 1987.

SWANK

Ranking: 4093 **S.S. Count:** 11,041
Origin: German. Cognate to Swan, meaning the aquatic bird.

Famous **Swanks:** JAMES MOORE SWANK (1832–1914) of Pennsylvania was a statistician with the American Iron and Steel Association.

Genealogies: *The John Swank Genealogy Line* was compiled by Gladys Rae Swank and published in Lewiston, Idaho, in 1976. *Some Descendants of John Swank and his Wife Rosannah Summit* was compiled by Williams Johnson Swank and published in Jupiter, Florida, in 1982.

SWANN

Ranking: 2672 **S.S. Count:** 17,062
Origin: English. Transformation of Swan.

Famous **Swans:** THOMAS SWANN (1806?–1883) of Virginia was a mayor of Baltimore, governor of Maryland, and member of Congress from Maryland. He opposed Reconstruction.

Genealogies: *Richard Swan and Some of his Descendants* [also Swann] was compiled by Frank H. Swan and published in 1927.

SWANSON (S.S. Abbreviation: Swanso)

Ranking: 338 **S.S. Count:** 112,247
Origin: English. 1) transformation of Swan. 2) transformation of Swain.

Famous **Swansons:** CLAUDE AUGUSTUS SWANSON (1862–1939) of Virginia was a member of Congress from, governor of, and U.S. senator from Virginia. He served as a member of the House Ways and Means Committee and worked for free rural delivery of mail.

Genealogies: *Prairie Memories: a history of the Swanson, Erickson, and Lindgerg families of North Dakota* was compiled by Algot R. Swanson and published in Tucson, Arizona, in 1974. *I Remember* [also Swanson] was compiled by D. Verner Swanson and published in Golden, Colorado, in 1981.

SWARTZ

Ranking: 1002 **S.S. Count:** 43,718
Origin: Dutch, German. Cognate to and transformation of Schwartz.

Genealogies: *The Descendants of John Swartz, Sr., 1760–1817, of Saumsville, Shenandoah County, Virginia* was compiled by Benjamin Kinsell Swartz and published in Muncie, Indiana, in 1970.

SWEARINGEN, SWEARINGIN (S.S. Abbreviation: Sweari)

Ranking: 3506 **S.S. Count:** 12,864
Origin: German. The name means swamp water and was given to those from Schweringen, a place in Germany.

Genealogies: *American Pilgrimage for Lesans, Blanchards, Swearingens* was compiled by Ruth Blanchard Knudson and published in Albion, Iowa, in 1974. *Some Descendants of Garrett Vansweringen (also Swearingen) of St. Mary's, Maryland* was compiled by Frances C.T. Daniels and published in Baltimore, Maryland, in 1983.

SWEAT

Ranking: 3776 **S.S. Count:** 11,969
Origin: English. Transformation of Sweet.

Genealogies: *Sweat Families of the South* was compiled by Erbon W. Wise and published in Sulphur, Louisiana, in 1983.

SWEENEY (S.S. Abbreviation: Sweene)

Ranking: 550 **S.S. Count:** 74,263
Origin: Irish. Derived from the Gaelic name Mac Suibhne, which was derived from the first name Suibhne, meaning agreeable.

Famous **Sweeneys:** MARTIN LEONARD SWEENEY (1885–1960) of Ohio was a member of Congress elected as an independent.

Genealogies: *The Descendants of Redmond Peter Fahey and Cecelia Haverty and John Sweeney and Mary Dineen, 1810–1984* was compiled by Verne Raymond Spear and published in West Springfield, Massachusetts, in 1984.

SWEET

Ranking: 1071 **S.S. Count:** 41,112
Origin: English. Derived from the Middle English word

"swete," *meaning pleasant or sweet. The name was given to those who were well liked.*

Famous **Sweets:** JOHN EDSON SWEET (1832–1916) of New York was a mechanical engineer and a pioneer in the building of high-speed trains.

Genealogies: *Sweat Families of the South* [also Sweet] was compiled by Erbon W. Wise and published in Sulphur, Louisiana, in 1983.

SWENSON (S.S. Abbreviation: Swenso)

Ranking: 1405　**S.S. Count:** 31,613

Origin: English. Transformation of Swain.

Famous **Swensons:** DAVID FERDINAND SWENSON (1876–1940) of Sweden was an expert in philosophy and an authority on Søren Kierkegaard.

Genealogies: *The Search for Ancestors: a Swedish-American family saga* [also Swenson] was compiled by Hildor Arnold Barton and published in Carbondale, Illinois, in 1979. *The Swenson Saga and the SMS Ranches* was compiled by Mary Whatley Clarke and published in Austin, Texas, in 1976.

SWIFT

Ranking: 1307　**S.S. Count:** 33,930

Origin: English, Irish. English: derived from the Old English word "swift," meaning rapid or nimble. The name was given to those who were swift runners. Irish: derived from the Gaelic name Ó Fuada, which was derived from a first name meaning rapidity.

Famous **Swifts:** ZEPHANIAH SWIFT (1759–1823) of Massachusetts was a member of Congress from Connecticut and a judge of the state superior court. He was the author of the first American law book, *A System of the Laws of the State of Connecticut* (1795, 1796). GUSTAVUS FRANKLIN SWIFT (1839–1903) of Massachusetts was a meat packer. He developed products from the animal parts that previously had been discarded and was the founder of Swift & Co. in 1885. HOMER FORDYCE SWIFT (1881–1953) of New York was a physician who treated victims of syphilis, rheumatic fever, streptococcus infections, and trench fever. He co-developed the Ellis-Swift treatment for a type of syphilis.

Genealogies: None known.

SWINDLEHURST (S.S. Abbreviation: Swindl)

Ranking: 4873　**S.S. Count:** 9181

Origin: English. Swindlehurst: uncertain etymology. Possibly derived from the Old English words "swin," "hyll," and "hyrst," meaning pig, hill, and wooded crest, and given to those who lived in a wooded valley in which swine were raised.

Genealogies: None known.

SWISHER (S.S. Abbreviation: Swishe)

Ranking: 3368　**S.S. Count:** 13,461

Origin: English. Derived from the country name Switzerland. The name was given to those from Switzerland.

Genealogies: *Early Swisher and Switzer Families in Virginia and West Virginia* was compiled by Bob Swisher and published in Richmond, Virginia, in 1979. *The Swisher Family of Harrison and Lewis Counties, West Virginia* was compiled by Robert Edward Swisher and published in Richmond, Virginia, in 1974.

SWOPE

Ranking: 3774　**S.S. Count:** 11,974

Origin: German. Transformation of Schwab.

Famous **Swopes:** GERALD SWOPE (1872–1957) of Missouri was the author of the "Swope Plan" (1931), which was used by the National Industrial Recovery Act (1933). He was the first president of International General Electric. HERBERT BAYARD SWOPE (1882–1958) was a journalist and the winner of the first Pulitzer Prize ever given for journalism. As an editor, he was the first to use an "Op Ed" page (*op*posite the *ed*itorial page) in the paper.

Genealogies: *History of the Swope Family and Descendants of Rockingham County, Virginia* was compiled by The Swope Family History Committee and published in Verona, Virginia, in 1971. *The Swope Family Book of Remembrance* was compiled by Emily Swope Morse and published in Provo, Utah, in 1972.

SYKES

Ranking: 1158　**S.S. Count:** 37,777

Origin: English. Derived from the Middle English word "syke," meaning a swampy stream. The name was given to those who lived in a wet, low-lying area or near a stream in a swampy area.

Famous **Sykeses:** GEORGE SYKES (1822–1880) of Delaware was a Union major general who commanded troops at Gettysburg.

Genealogies: None known.

SYLVEST, SYLVESTER, SYLVESTRE (S.S. Abbreviation: Sylves)

Ranking: 1611　**S.S. Count:** 27,781

Origin: Sylvest—Danish, Norwegian; Sylvester—English; Sylvestre—French. Cognates to and transformations of Silvester.

Famous **Bearers:** JAMES JOSEPH SYLVESTER (1814–1897) of England was a mathematician and probably one of the greatest of all time. He was refused a degree because he was Jewish, taught at the University of Virginia but left and returned to England because of problems with discipline, and taught at Oxford University for the remainder of his days. He edited the *American Journal of Mathematics* (1878–1884).

Genealogies: *The Francis Sylvest Story* was compiled by Vince Sylvest and published in Baton Rouge, Louisiana, in 1968. *Pedigree Chart of Sara Natalie Sylvester* was published in 1978.

SZABO

Ranking: 4200 **S.S. Count:** 10,755
Origin: Hungarian. Derived from the Hungarian word "szabó," meaning tailor. The name was given to tailors.
Genealogies: None known.

SZYMANCZYK, SZYMANEK, SZYMANIAK, SZYMANOWICZ, SZYMANOWSKI (S.S. Abbreviation: Szyman)

Ranking: 3022 **S.S. Count:** 15,047
Origin: Polish. Cognates to Simon.
Genealogies: None known.

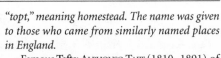

TABER

Ranking: 4031 S.S. Count: 11,233
Origin: English. Transformation of Tabor.
Famous **Tabers**: JOHN TABER (1880–1965) of
New York was a member of Congress from New
York and a conservative influence on the federal
budget for many years. THOMAS T. TABER (1899–1975) of
New York was an insurance executive who was instrumen-
tal in advancing public mass transportation in the New Jer-
sey-New York-Connecticut area. The Tom Taber Express, a
former Erie-Lackawanna Railroad commuter train, was
named in his honor.
Genealogies: None known.

TABOR

Ranking: 2181 S.S. Count: 21,033
*Origin: English, Jewish. English: derived from the Middle
English and Old French word "tabo(u)r," meaning drum. The
name was given to those who played drums. Jewish: derived
from the Hebrew name Tavor. The name was taken ornamen-
tally.*
Famous **Tabors**: HORACE A.W. TABOR (1830–1899) of
Vermont was a prospector who was among the first to rush
Pikes Peak in Colorado in 1859. He built Tabor Grand
Opera House in Denver.
Genealogies: *A Tabor Saga* was compiled by Clifford
Clark Tabor and published in Asheville, North Carolina, in
1981. *The Tabors* was compiled by Myrtle F. Bartolini and
published in Knoxville, Tennessee, in 1983.

TACKET (ALSO TACKETT)

Ranking: 1949 S.S. Count: 23,288
*Origin: French? Uncertain etymology. Possibly derived
from the Old French words "tache" or "teche," meaning spot
or stain. The names were probably given to those who bore a
distinguishing mark or scar.*
Genealogies: *The Tackett-Fletcher Pioneers and Supplement* was compiled by Mae Elizabeth Lang and published
in St. Joseph, Illinois, in 1970. *The Tacketts in Kanawha
County Virginia* was compiled by Erna Young Johnson and
published in Charleston, West Virginia, in 1969.

TAFOYA

Ranking: 4840 S.S. Count: 9,245
*Origin: Spanish. Uncertain etymology. Possibly derived
from the Middle High German word "toufen," meaning to
dip. The name was given to those who were Anabaptists.*
Genealogies: None known.

TAFT

Ranking: 3565 S.S. Count: 12,646
Origin: English. Derived from the Old Norman word
"topt," meaning homestead. The name was given
to those who came from similarly named places
in England.
Famous **Tafts**: ALPHONSO TAFT (1810–1891) of
Vermont was a prominent national politician
and diplomat. He served as U.S. secretary of
war and U.S. attorney general before becoming minister
to Austria-Hungary and to Russia. His son, WILLIAM
HOWARD TAFT (1857–1930) of Ohio, was the 27th president of the United States. Prior to becoming president, he
was a lawyer and judge in Ohio, then a U.S. circuit judge.
He was the first governor of the Philippine Islands under
American control (1901–1904), U.S. secretary of war
(1904–1908) under President Theodore Roosevelt, then
U.S. president (1909–1913). When he ran for a second
term in 1912, his opponents were Woodrow Wilson and
former President Roosevelt. Wilson was elected, and Taft
was later appointed chief justice of the United States by
Wilson's successor, President Warren G. Harding, in 1921.
His wife, HELEN HERRON TAFT (1861–1943), was the
woman behind the man. In retrospect, without her guidance, he probably never would have been president. Their
son, ROBERT ALPHONSO TAFT (1889–1953), a U.S. senator
from Ohio, sponsored the Taft-Hartley Labor Relations
Act of 1947. LORADO ZADOC TAFT (1860–1936) of Illinois
was a sculptor and art teacher who had a lasting effect on
the development of midwestern sculpture. Among his
sculptural works are "Columbus Memorial Fountain" in
Washington, D.C., and "Fountain of Time" in Chicago,
Illinois.
Genealogies: *Taft Family Gathering* was compiled by
Beatrice Taft Aldridge and published in Rockland, Massachusetts, in 1979. *A Meeting of the Descendants of Ebenezer
and Mary Howard Taft* was compiled by Charlotte E.
McShea and published in New York in 1979.

TAGGART (S.S. Abbreviation: Taggar)

Ranking: 3334 S.S. Count: 13,595
*Origin: Irish, Scottish. Derived from the Gaelic name Mac
an t-Sagairt, which was derived from the word "sagart,"
meaning priest.*
Famous **Taggarts**: THOMAS TAGGART (1856–1929) of
Ireland emigrated to the United States as a child and
became a major figure in Indiana politics. He was mayor of
Indianapolis and later a U.S. senator.
Genealogies: None known.

TALBERT (S.S. Abbreviation: Talber)

Ranking: 2719 S.S. Count: 16,731
*Origin: English. Uncertain etymology. 1) the name may
mean descended from Talbot. 2) the name may mean "pil-
lager or bandit" or "dweller at the sign of the talbot" (ES).*

Genealogies: *Some Southern Talberts* was compiled by Eugene Talbert Aldridge and published in Provo, Utah, in 1975.

TALBOT

Ranking: 1380 **S.S. Count:** 32,056

Origin: English. Uncertain etymology. Possibly derived from the Germanic words "tal" and "bod," meaning destroy and message.

Famous **Talbots:** ETHELBERT TALBOT (1848–1928) of Missouri was an Episcopal missionary in Wyoming and Idaho who wrote of his experiences in *My People of the Plains* (1906). ARTHUR NEWELL TALBOT (1857–1942) of Illinois was an engineer and professor who was instrumental in establishing the world's first engineering experiment station at the University of Illinois in 1904. FRANCIS XAVIER TALBOT (1889–1953) of Pennsylvania was a prominent Roman Catholic priest who was president of Loyola College and author of a number of books.

Genealogies: *Some Southern Talberts* [also Talbot] was compiled by Eugene Talbert Aldridge and published in Provo, Utah, in 1975. *New England Colonial Families* was compiled by Helen H. Lane and published in Newhall, California, in 1981.

TALLEY

Ranking: 1084 **S.S. Count:** 40,866

Origin: Irish. Transformation of the second definition of Tully.

Genealogies: None known.

TALLMADGE (S.S. Abbreviation: Tallma)

Ranking: 3880 **S.S. Count:** 11,626

Origin: English. The name means "one who carried a knapsack" (ES).

Famous **Tallmadges:** BENJAMIN TALLMADGE (1754–1835) of New York was a Revolutionary War officer and the head of George Washington's secret service. He later was a member of Congress from Connecticut. JAMES TALLMADGE (1778–1853) of New York was the member of Congress who introduced legislation that would prohibit any more slaves from being introduced into Missouri, and those born there would gradually be freed. After serving as the lieutenant governor of New York, he was a founder of the New York University.

Genealogies: None known.

TAM

Ranking: 4863 **S.S. Count:** 9205

Origin: Vietnamese. The name is derived from a first name meaning heart.

Genealogies: None known.

TAN

Ranking: 4439 **S.S. Count:** 10,095

Origin: Chinese. The name means several things, among them 1) to boast, 2) to gossip, and 3) to accept responsibility.

Genealogies: None known.

TANAKA

Ranking: 4584 **S.S. Count:** 9753

Origin: Japanese. The name means rice field or middle (ES).

Genealogies: None known.

TANG

Ranking: 3557 **S.S. Count:** 12,691

Origin: Chinese, Dutch, Flemish. Chinese: the name means many things, among them 1) a hall, 2) to boast or to be boastful, 3) rude, 4) soup, and 5) gravy. Dutch, Flemish: derived from the Old English word "tang(e)," meaning tongs. The name was given to those who made or used tongs.

Genealogies: None known.

TANNER

Ranking: 661 **S.S. Count:** 63,549

Origin: English, Finnish, German, Jewish. English: derived from the Old English word "tanner," meaning tanner—as in the occupation. The name was given to those who worked tanning animal skins. Finnish: derived from the word "tanner," meaning open field. The name was given to those who lived near an open field. German: derived from the Middle High German word "tan," meaning forest. The name was given to those who lived in a forest. Jewish: uncertain etymology.

Famous **Tanners:** HENRY SCHENCK TANNER (1786–1858) of New York was a cartographer and is credited with *A New American Atlas* (1818–1823). JAMES TANNER (1844–1927) of New York was a Union soldier known as Corporal Tanner and was considered an inept commissioner of pensions. HENRY OSSAWA TANNER (1859–1937) of Pennsylvania was an artist known for his paintings of a religious nature.

Genealogies: *Sidney Tanner: His Ancestors and Descendants* was compiled by Elizabeth De Brouwer and published in Salt Lake City, Utah, in 1982. *Three Pioneer Rapides Families: A Genealogy* [also Tanner] was compiled by George Mason Graham Stafford and published in Baton Rouge, Louisiana, in 1968. *Genealogies of the Tracy-Tanner Families, and Other Genealogies* was compiled by Mathew J. Tracy and published in Indiana in 1903.

TAPIA

Ranking: 2163 **S.S. Count:** 21,230

Origin: Spanish. Derived from the Spanish word "tapia,"

meaning mud wall. The name was given to those who lived near a mud wall, or to those who came from Tapia, the name of several places in Spain.
Genealogies: None known.

TARANTELLA, TARANTELLI, TARANTINO
(S.S. Abbreviation: Tarant)
Ranking: 4851 **S.S. Count:** 9224
Origin: Italian. Tarantella, Tarantelli: 1) the names mean "the lively dancing man" (ES). 2) the names mean "one who dances the tarantella," a dance used to counteract the venom of the tarantula (ES). Tarantino: uncertain etymology. Most likely the same as in 1. The name was given to those who came from Taranto, Italy (ES).
Genealogies: None known.

TARR
Ranking: 4625 **S.S. Count:** 9661
Origin: English. 1) probably derived from the Old English word "te(o)ru," meaning tar. The name was given to those who worked with tar in keeping ships waterproof. 2) the name may have been given to those who lived in or near a tower.
Famous **Tarrs:** RALPH STOCKTON TARR (1864–1912) of Massachusetts was a geologist and geographer who worked with the U.S. Geological Survey and taught at various seats of higher learning.
Genealogies: *The Ancestry and Descendants of Josiah Mendum Tarr and Mary Delia Sawyer* was compiled by Hugh A. Johnson and published in Annandale, Virginia, in 1976.

TARVER
Ranking: 3703 **S.S. Count:** 12,198
Origin: English. Derived from words meaning shack made from sod. The name was given to those who came from Torver, the name of a place in England.
Genealogies: None known.

TATE
Ranking: 91,746 **S.S. Count:** 431
Origin: English. Derived from the Old English personal name Tāta.
Famous **Tates:** ALLEN TATE (1899–1979) of Kentucky was a poet, editor, and biographer. His books included *Stonewall Jackson* (1928) and *Robert E. Lee* (1932).
Genealogies: *Tate and Allied Families of Robertson County, Tennessee* was compiled by Evelyn Yates Carpenter and published in Clarksville, Tennessee, in 1987. *Taylors and Tates of the South* was compiled by Ann K. Blomquist and published in Baltimore, Maryland, in 1993. *Van Buren Tate: Ancestors, Descendants* was compiled by Rachel Tate Smith and published in Austin, Texas, in 1976.

TATUM
Ranking: 1366 **S.S. Count:** 32,457
Origin: English. Derived from the Old English first name Tāta and the word "hām," meaning homestead. The name was given to those who came from Tatham, a place in North Lancashire, England.
Famous **Tatums:** ART TATUM (1910–1956) of Ohio was a jazz pianist who was blind in one eye. His career started when he sang on the radio as a child. As an adult, he formed his own group and toured the country.
Genealogies: *Rising in the West: The True Story of an 'Okie' Family* was compiled by Dan Morgan and published in New York, New York, in 1992. *The Name and Family of Tatum or Tatham* was compiled by Media Research Bureau and published in Yoakum, Texas, in 1973.

TAVARES (S.S. Abbreviation: Tavare)
Ranking: 2995 **S.S. Count:** 15,169
Origin: Portuguese. Uncertain etymology. Probably derived from the pre-Roman first name Talavus. The name was given to those who came from Tavares, the name of several places in Portugal.
Genealogies: None known.

TAYLOR
Ranking: 13 **S.S. Count:** 1,000,062
Origin: English. Derived from the Old French word "tailleur," meaning to cut. The name was given to those who worked as tailors.
Famous **Taylors:** GEORGE TAYLOR (1716–1781), born in Ireland, was an iron manufacturer in Pennsylvania and a signer of the Declaration of Independence. ZACHARY TAYLOR (1784–1850) of Virginia was the 12th president of the United States. Nicknamed Old Rough and Ready, he served in many capacities and in many locations in the U.S. army before being elected president. He died in office. MARGARET MACKALL SMITH TAYLOR (1788–1852) of Maryland was the wife of President Zachary Taylor. CHARLOTTE DE BERNIER TAYLOR (1806–1861) of Georgia was an entomologist whose published research concentrated on the agricultural significance of entomology. JOHN TAYLOR (1808–1887), born in England, emigrated to Utah and became active in territorial government and Mormon affairs. He succeeded Brigham Young as head of the Mormons but was forced into exile to manage the church's affairs because U.S. agents wanted to arrest him. WILLIAM TAYLOR (1821–1902) of Virginia was a Methodist missionary who traveled extensively in the United States and the world. He was missionary bishop to Africa (1884–1896). JAMES BAYARD TAYLOR (1825–1878) of Pennsylvania was a writer who traveled the world and wrote of his experiences. He was published in periodicals such as the *Saturday Evening Post* and in books, such as *A Visit to India, China, and Japan* (1855).

Lucy Beaman Hobbs Taylor (1833–1910) of New York was the first American woman to receive a degree in dentistry. Alfred A. Taylor (1848–1931) of Tennessee was a Republican governor of that state. His brother, Robert L. Taylor (1850–1912) of Tennessee, was twice a Democratic governor of the state and later a U.S. senator. David W. Taylor (1864–1940) of Virginia was a naval officer who set up and directed the country's first ship-model testing center in Washington, D.C. A marine architect, he developed the Taylor Standard Series Method, by which a ship hull's resistance to water can be determined. He also designed U.S. navy ships and aircraft, including the navy's first plane to fly the Atlantic Ocean, the NC-4. Bert L. Taylor (1866–1921) of Massachusetts was a columnist for the Chicago *Daily Tribune* and the author of novels and short stories. Joseph D. Taylor (1885–1966) of New York was a journalist, author, and composer. He wrote music for several Broadway plays, and his books include *Some Enchanted Evenings: The Story of Rodgers and Hammerstein* (1953). Robert Taylor (1911–1969) of Nebraska was an actor with Metro-Goldwyn-Mayer for 24 years (1934–1958), starring in such films as *A Yank at Oxford* (1938). He later starred in the television series "The Detectives," and he was host and sometimes actor in "Death Valley Days."

Genealogies: *The Forebearers and Descendants of William Taylor and Mahala Cromwell* was compiled by Carrie Cathern Carte and published in Parsons, West Virginia, in 1980. *From Log Cabins to the White House: A History of the Taylor Family* was compiled by Mary Taylor Brewer and published in Wooton, Kentucky, in 1985.

TEAGUE
Ranking: 1322 **S.S. Count:** 33,672

Origin: Cornish, Irish. Cornish: derived from the word "tek," meaning beautiful. The name was given to those who were beautiful or handsome. Irish: derived from the Gaelic name Ó Taidhg, meaning poet.

Famous **Teagues:** Walter Dorwin Teague (1883–1960) of Indiana was instrumental in establishing industrial design as a career in the United States. His own designs include the interior of the Boeing 707 airplane and many exhibits for the 1939 New York World's Fair.

Genealogies: *History and Genealogy on Teague Pioneers of Christian County, Kentucky* was compiled by Agnes Teague Cunningham and published in Nortonville, Kentucky, in 1971.

TEAL
Ranking: 3764 **S.S. Count:** 12,034

Origin: English. Derived from the Middle English word "tele," meaning teal. The name was given to those who had teal-like characteristics.

Genealogies: None known.

TEDESCO (S.S. Abbreviation: Tedesc)
Ranking: 3953 **S.S. Count:** 11,439

Origin: Italian, Jewish. Italian: derived from the Italian word "tedesco," meaning German. The name was given to those who were of German origin or to those who spoke German. Jewish: the name was used by Ashkenazic Jews living in Italy, or by those who had traveled there.

Genealogies: None known.

TEEL
Ranking: 4240 **S.S. Count:** 10,633

Origin: English. Transformation of Teal.

Genealogies: None known.

TEETER (ALSO TEETERS)
Ranking: 3829 **S.S. Count:** 11,773

Origin: German. 1) derived from the name Dieter, which means people or army. 2) derived from the name Dietrich, a cognate to the English name Derrick.

Genealogies: *Chronicles of the Mountz-Teeters and Allied Families* was compiled by Margaret Mountz Carroll and published in 1984. *Teter* [also Teeters] *Descendants of Hans Jorg and Maria Dieter* was compiled by Eva A. Teter Winfield and published in Baltimore, Maryland, in 1992.

TEMPLE
Ranking: 744 **S.S. Count:** 56,999

Origin: English, French, Scottish. English, French: derived from the Middle English and Old French word "temple," meaning temple. The name was usually given to those who worked in or lived near a house founded by a crusading order called the Knights of Templar (H&H).

Famous **Temples:** William G. Temple (1824–1894) of Vermont was a distinguished Union naval officer during the Civil War.

Genealogies: *The Rise of the Temples* was compiled by Albert R. Temple and published in Cincinnati, Ohio, in 1974. *The Temple Family of Wake County, North Carolina, and Related Families* was compiled by Eunice Temple Kirkpatrick and published in Durham, North Carolina, in 1978. *William Temple of Prince George County, Virginia and His Descendants* was compiled by Lucy Temple and published in Richmond, Virginia, in 1978.

TENNANT (S.S. Abbreviation: Tennan)
Ranking: 3826 **S.S. Count:** 11,784

Origin: English. Derived from the Middle English and Old French word "tenant," meaning tenant. The name was given to tenant farmers.

Genealogies: None known.

TENNEY
Ranking: 4852 **S.S. Count:** 9220

Origin: English. Derived from the medieval first name *Den(n)is,* which is ultimately derived from the Greek name *Dionysios,* meaning follower of the god *Dionysos.*

Famous **Tenneys:** TABITHA GILMAN TENNEY (1792–1837) of New Hampshire was an author of several stories, including the satirical "Female Quixotism" (1801). WILLIAM JEWETT TENNEY (1811–1883) of Rhode Island was the editor of *Appleton's Cyclopaedia* (1861–1883) and a contributor to *Rise and Fall of the Confederate Government* (1881).

Genealogies: *Our Tenney Family (of Upshur County, West Virginia)* was compiled by Patty Webb Eubanks and published in Oklahoma City, Oklahoma, in 1980.

TERREL (ALSO TERRELL)

Ranking: 903 **S.S. Count:** 47,848

Origin: English, Irish. Transformations of *Tyrrell.*

Famous **Bearers:** MARY ELIZA CHURCH TERRELL (1863–1954) of Tennessee was the daughter of a house slave of the pre–Civil War days. She became a social reformer and lecturer and a writer on black history for newspapers and magazines, publishing the book *A Colored Woman in a White World* (1940).

Genealogies: None known.

TERRY

Ranking: 329 **S.S. Count:** 114,737

Origin: English, Irish, Provençal. Derived from the Norman first name *T(h)erry,* which was derived from Germanic elements meaning people and power. Irish: derived from the Gaelic name *Mac Toirdhealbhaigh,* which was derived from the components *Tor* and "*dealbhach,*" meaning Thor and resemble. Provençal: derived from the Old Provençal word "*terrin,*" meaning clay vase. The name was given to those who worked as potters.

Famous **Terrys:** ELI TERRY (1772–1852) of Connecticut achieved notable commercial success as a clockmaker in Connecticut with his own "Terry clock." ALFRED HOWE TERRY (1827–1890) of Connecticut was an army officer who was commander of the campaign in which George Custer was killed. MARSHALL ORLANDO TERRY (1848–1914) of New York was a physician and the surgeon general of the New York State National Guard.

Genealogies: *All About Terrys: A Genealogy of the Surname Terry* was compiled by Paul Terry Thompson and published in Turlock, California, in 1991. *The Story of a Family* [also Terry] was compiled by Henry Vernon Hall and published in Salt Lake City, Utah, in 1974. *Terry and Allied Families of Virginia, Kentucky, Illinois, Texas* was compiled by Frances Terry Ingmire and published in Creve Coeur, Missouri, in 1976.

TESTA

Ranking: 4165 **S.S. Count:** 10,845

Origin: Italian. Derived from the Old French word "*teste,*" meaning head. The name was given to those who had an unusually unattractive or oversized head.

Genealogies: None known.

THACKER, THACKERAY, THACKEREY, THACKERY (S.S. Abbreviation: Thacke)

Ranking: 1577 **S.S. Count:** 28,309

Origin: English. Thacker: derived from the Middle English word "*thack,*" meaning thatch. The name was given to those who worked thatching roofs. Thackeray, Thackerey, Thackery: derived from the Old Norman words "*pak*" and "*(v)rá,*" meaning reeds and corner or cranny. The names were given to those who came from Thackray, the name of a place in England.

Genealogies: *Thomas Thacher, 1620–1678, Boston Branch, Progenitors and Descendants* was compiled by Elwood James Thacher and published in Winter Haven, Florida, in 1978.

THAMES

Ranking: 4684 **S.S. Count:** 9553

Origin: English, Irish? Derived from the Old Celtic word "*tám,*" meaning still water, and the ending "*es,*" which was derived from the Gaelic and Irish word "*uisge,*" meaning water. The name was given to those who lived by the Thames, a river in England.

Genealogies: None known.

THARP

Ranking: 2325 **S.S. Count:** 19,527

Origin: English. Transformation of *Thorpe.*

Genealogies: *Tharp Genealogy* was compiled by Elaine Tharp Dean and published in Hastings, Nebraska, in 1976.

THATCHER (S.S. Abbreviation: Thatch)

Ranking: 3322 **S.S. Count:** 13,653

Origin: English. Derived from the Middle English word "*thach(en),*" meaning to thatch. The name was given to those who worked thatching roofs.

Famous **Thatchers:** HENRY KNOX THATCHER (1806–1880) of Maine was a naval officer and part of the North Atlantic Blocking squadron. BENJAMIN BUSSEY THATCHER (1809–1840) of Maine was in favor of colonizing Africa. He was also the author of *Indian Biography* (1832). MAHLON DANIEL THATCHER (1839–1916) of Pennsylvania was a banking pioneer in Colorado.

Genealogies: None known.

THAYER

Ranking: 1867 **S.S. Count:** 24,246

Origin: English. Derived from the name Thaider, meaning army or people.

Famous **Thayers:** GIDEON FRENCH THAYER (1793–1864) of Massachusetts was the founder of the Chauncy-Hall School, Boston (1828). SYLVANUS THAYER (1785–1872) of Massachusetts, as superintendent of the U.S. Military Academy at West Point, New York (1817–1833), set military and academic standards that in principle are still being used today. He also founded and endowed the Thayer School of Engineering at Dartmouth College. JOHN MILTON THAYER (1820–1906) of Massachusetts was a Union officer, U.S. senator from Nebraska, governor of the Wyoming territory, and governor of the state of Nebraska. ABBOTT HENDERSON THAYER (1849–1921) of Massachusetts was an artist popular for his paintings of figures and landscapes. He is credited with "Thayer's Law" of colorization. ERNEST LAWRENCE THAYER (1863–1940) of Massachusetts was the poet who wrote "Casey at the Bat" (1888). WILLIAM SYDNEY THAYER (1864–1932) of Massachusetts was a physician who made strides in the study of the circulatory system and studied the blood in its relation to leukemia, typhoid fever, and malaria. TIFFANY ELLSWORTH THAYER (1902–1959) of Illinois was the author of novels termed "smutty." The first, *Thirteen Men* (1930), was a bestseller.

Genealogies: A History and Genealogy of the Rockwell and Thayer Families was compiled by Willard Frederick Rockwell and published in Pittsburgh, Pennsylvania, in 1984. *Ancestors of Adelbert P. Thayer, Florine Thayer McCray and Geo. Burton Thayer, Children of John W. Thayer and Adaline Burton* was compiled by George B. Thayer and published in Hartford, Connecticut, in 1894. *Nearly 500 Years of Thayer Ancestry* was compiled by Hugh A. Johnson and published in Colorado in 1990.

THEODORAKIS, THEODORE, THEODORIDIS (S.S. Abbreviation: Theodo)

Ranking: 4818 **S.S. Count:** 9229

Origin: Theodore—French; Theodorakis, Theodoridis—Greek. Derived from the first name Théodore or Theodōros, which were derived from the Greek words "theos" and "dōron," meaning God and gift.

Genealogies: None known.

THERIAULT, THERIOT (S.S. Abbreviation: Theria)

Ranking: 4930 **S.S. Count:** 9079

Origin: French. Cognates to Theodore.

Genealogies: None known.

THERRIAULT (S.S. Abbreviation: Therri)

Ranking: 4811 **S.S. Count:** 9315

Origin: French? Uncertain etymology. 1) probably a cognate to Theodore. 2) possibly a cognate to the name Terry.

Genealogies: None known.

THIBAUD, THIBAUDET (S.S. Abbreviation: Thibau)

Ranking: 4919 **S.S. Count:** 9097

Origin: French. Derived from a Germanic first name composed of an uncertain component, possibly "þeudō", meaning people, and the word "bald," meaning brave.

Genealogies: None known.

THIBOD, THIBODEAU, THIBEDIAU, THIBIDEAU (S.S. Abbreviation: Thibod)

Ranking: 1490 **S.S. Count:** 29,792

Origin: French. Cognates to Thibaud.

Genealogies: None known.

THIEL

Ranking: 3477 **S.S. Count:** 12,989

Origin: German. Derived from the Norman first name T(h)erry, which was derived from an uncertain Germanic component, possibly "þeudō," meaning people, and the component "ric," meaning power.

Genealogies: None known.

THIELE (ALSO THIELECK, THIELEKE, THIELEMANN, THIELEN, THIELENS)

Ranking: 4067 **S.S. Count:** 11,119

Origin: German. Cognates to Terry.

Genealogies: None known.

THIGPEN (S.S. Abbreviation: Thigpe)

Ranking: 3519 **S.S. Count:** 12,813

Origin: German. 1) derived from the name Thigfuns, meaning thrive and swift. The name means "descendant of Thigfuns" (ES). 2) the name means "one who begged for coins" (ES). 3) the name means "dweller at, or near, Thyga's enclosure or hill" (ES).

Genealogies: None known.

THOMAS (ALSO THOMASEN, THOMASON)

Ranking: 12 **S.S. Count:** 1,005,052

Origin: English, Danish/Norwegian, Dutch/Flemish, French, German. Derived from a medieval first name meaning twin.

Famous **Bearers:** ISAIAH THOMAS (1749–1831) of Massachusetts was a standard-setting printer in colonial America. He printed *The Power of Sympathy* (1789), written by W. H. Brown, the first novel by a native-born American. ROBERT BAILEY THOMAS (1766–1846) of Massachusetts was founder and editor of *The Farmer's Almanac* (1792–1846). SETH THOMAS (1785–1859) of Connecticut started and ran the Seth Thomas Clock Co. in Plymouth Hollow, Connecticut. His son, SETH THOMAS (1816–1888), continued the business in that town, which later was named Thomaston. AUGUSTUS THOMAS (1857–1934) of Missouri wrote or adapted about 70 plays and was noted for such titles as *The Hoosier Doctor* (1897) and *Arizona* (1899). MARTHA CAREY THOMAS (1857–1935) of Maryland was the first female president of Bryn Mawr College. NORMAN MATTOON THOMAS (1884–1968) of Ohio was a founder of the American Civil Liberties Union and a Socialist candidate for U.S. president. LOWELL J. THOMAS (1892–1981) of Ohio wrote more than 50 books, mostly on travel and adventure, and was a popular radio newscaster. He was the host of the television show "Lowell Thomas Remembers" (1976–1979). GEORGE ALLISON THOMAS (1911–1968) of New York was an Onondaga Indian chief and spiritual leader who promoted the Onondaga Indian culture.

Genealogies: *Ancestors and Kin . . .* was compiled by Robert Walden Coggeshall and published in Spartanburg, South Carolina, in 1988. *The Descendants of William Thomas* was compiled by Francis Marion Ammon and published in Richton Park, Illinois, in 1975. *Thomas Ancestors: A History of a Thomas Family* was compiled by Mark Everett Thomas and published in San Jose, California, in 1983.

THOMPSON (S.S. Abbreviation: Thomps)
Ranking: 17 **S.S. Count:** 901,758
Origin: English, Scottish. Cognate to Thomas.

Famous **Thompsons:** BENJAMIN THOMPSON (1753–1814) of Massachusetts was a scientist and philanthropist and known by the name "Count Rumford." His scientific work centered on cooling air masses. SMITH THOMPSON (1768–1843) of New York was an associate justice of the U.S. Supreme Court. DAVID THOMPSON (1770–1857) of England was one of the best geographers and surveyors of North America. DANIEL PIERCE THOMPSON (1795–1868) of Massachusetts was a historical novelist and the author of *The Green Mountain Boys* (1839). WILLIAM TAPPAN THOMPSON (1812–1882) of Ohio was a journalist and humorist who was founder and editor of the *Savannah* (Georgia) *Morning News* (1850–1882). MARY HARRIS THOMPSON (1829–1895) of New York was one of the top physicians in the Midwest, the first woman to perform surgery in Chicago, and one of the organizers of the Northwestern University Woman's Medical School. J. WALTER THOMPSON (1847–1928) of Massachusetts established an advertising agency bearing his name and developed it into a highly successful firm. JOHN TALIAFERRO THOMPSON (1860–1940) of Kentucky was co-inventor, with John N. Blish, of the Thompson submachine gun. DOROTHY THOMPSON (1894–1961) of New York was a journalist, columnist, and author. Her books include *New Russia* (1928) and *The Courage to Be Happy* (1957). HELEN MULFORD THOMPSON (1908–1974) of Illinois was instrumental in the founding of symphony orchestras across the United States in the 20th century.

Genealogies: *Edgewood, The Story of a Family and Their House* [also Thompson] was compiled by James Wooldridge Powell and published in Kansas City, Missouri, in 1978. *The Family of William Taliaferro Thompson, Jr., and His Wife, Anne Claiborne McIlwaine* was compiled by Ben Lacy Rose and published in Richmond, Virginia, in 1982. *Dixie's Diverse Destiny* was compiled by Margery Thompson Lockhart and published in Huntsville, Alabama, in 1979.

THOMSEN (S.S. Abbreviation: Thomse)
Ranking: 4080 **S.S. Count:** 11,074
Origin: German. Cognate to Thomas.
Genealogies: *Descendants of Hans Jorgen Thomsen and Ane Kjerstine Ditlevsen of Kleis, Denmark* was compiled by Frances Hansen Ehrig and published in Richland, Washington, in 1962.

THOMSON (S.S. Abbreviation: Thomso)
Ranking: 1247 **S.S. Count:** 35,411
Origin: English. Cognate to Thomas.

Famous **Thomsons:** WILLIAM THOMSON (1727–1796), possibly of Pennsylvania, was a South Carolina planter who, during the Revolutionary War, blocked, with his rangers, the British from landing at Sullivan's Island, near Charleston. CHARLES THOMSON (1729–1824) of Ireland was the secretary of the Continental Congress. MORTIMER NEAL THOMSON (1831–1895) of New York, who went by the name Q. K. Philander Doesticks, was a humorist and a staff member of the New York *Tribune*. ELIHU THOMSON (1853–1937) of England was an inventor and an electrical engineer. His electrical company, the Thomson-Houston Electric Co., merged with Thomas Edison's company to form the General Electric Co. He was the inventor of more than 700 devices that revolutionized his business.

Genealogies: *Thomson, A Family History* was compiled by Kathryn Blevins and published in Cameron, North Carolina, in 1993.

THORN
Ranking: 3210 **S.S. Count:** 14,138
Origin: Danish, English, German. Danish, English: derived from the Old English and Old Norman word "þorn," meaning bush with thorns. The name was given to those who lived near a thorn bush or who came from Thorne, Thorns, or other places containing this word. Danish, German: derived from the Middle Low German word "torn," meaning tower. The name was given to those who lived near a tower. German: derived from the Middle High German word "torn," meaning tower. The name was given to those who came from Thorn, now called Toruń, a city in Poland.
Genealogies: None known.

THORNBERRY, THORNBOROUGH, THORNBURG, THORNBURGH, THORNBURY ET AL. (S.S. Abbreviation: Thornb)

Ranking: 2385 S.S. Count: 19,049

Origin: English. Derived from the Old English word "þorn," meaning bush with thorns, and either "berg," meaning hill, or "burh," meaning fort. The names were given to those who came from Thornborough or Thornbrough, the names of places in England.

Genealogies: *Forebears of the Thornburg and Hockett Families was compiled by Velma Hockett Bosworth and published in Lacey, Washington, in 1987.*

THORNE (ALSO THORNELL, THORNER, THORNES)

Ranking: 1536 S.S. Count: 29,007

Origin: Thorne, Thornell, Thornes—English; Thorner—German. Thorne, Thornes: transformations of Thorn. Thornell: transformation of Thornhill. Thorner: transformation of Thorn.

Famous **Bearers:** CHARLES ROBERT THORNE (1814–1893) of New York City was a theater manager. His son, CHARLES ROBERT THORNE (1840–1883) of New York City was an actor best known for his heroic roles in melodramas.

Genealogies: *None known.*

THORNHILL (S.S. Abbreviation: Thornh)

Ranking: 4517 S.S. Count: 9912

Origin: English. Derived from the Old English words "þorn" and "hyll," meaning bush with thorns and hill. The name was given to those who came from Thornell of Thornhill, the names of places in England.

Genealogies: *Thornhill: Genealogy and Family History was compiled by Naomi Ruth Jackson Chasteen and published in Cullman, Alabama, in 1986. Isreal [sic] Thornell, Planter, Woodbridge, New Jersey and His Descendants was compiled by Jay W. Thornall and published in Princeton, New Jersey, in 1982.*

THORNTON (S.S. Abbreviation: Thornt)

Ranking: 334 S.S. Count: 112,908

Origin: English, Irish, Scottish. English, Scottish: derived from the Old English words "þorn" and "tūn," meaning bush with thorns and settlement. The name was given to those who came from Thornton, the name of many places in England and Scotland. Irish: a translation of the Gaelic first name Mac Sceadháin, which was derived from the Gaelic word "sceach," meaning bush with thorns.

Famous **Thorntons:** MATTHEW THORNTON (1714?–1803) of Ireland was a physician involved in the activities of the Revolution. He was a signer of the Declaration of Independence and a member of the Continental Congress.

WILLIAM THORNTON (1759–1828) of the British West Indies was an architect well known in the Washington, D.C., area. He also was the inventor of firearm innovations. JESSY QUINN THORNTON (1810–1888) of West Virginia was an Oregon pioneer and co-founder of the Oregon government. JOHN WINGATE THORNTON (1818–1878) of Maine was one of the founders of the New England Historic Genealogical Society and of the Prince Society.

Genealogies: *Scharnhorst, Lynch, Barnett, Thornton was compiled by Frances Carter and published in Bradenton, Florida, in 1980.*

THORP

Ranking: 4601 S.S. Count: 9714

Origin: English. Transformation of Thorpe.

Famous **Thorps:** JOHN THORP (1784–1848) of Massachusetts was the inventor of the ring spinning machine, which improved the spinning and twisting of cotton.

Genealogies: *None known.*

THORPE

Ranking: 1513 S.S. Count: 29,397

Origin: English. 1) derived from the Old Norman component "Porp," meaning village. 2) derived from the Old English word "Prop," meaning village. The name in both cases was given to those who came from Thorpe, the name of many places in England.

Famous **Thorpes:** THOMAS BANGS THORPE or THORP (1815–1878) of Massachusetts was a newspaper publisher in New Orleans and Baton Rouge, Louisiana, and the author of humorous stories. ROSE ALNORA HARTWICK THORPE (1850–1939) of Indiana was a poet and the author of "Remember the Alamo." JAMES FRANCIS THORPE (1886–1953) of Oklahoma was an athlete and the winner of 1912 Olympic games. He was the first president of the National Football League.

Genealogies: *Genealogy of Some Early Families in Grant and Pleasant Districts, Preston County, West Virginia, also the Thorpe Family of Fayette County, Pennsylvania was compiled by Edward Thorp King and published in Baltimore, Maryland, in 1977. Facts & Anecdotes of Turnersville, Texas was compiled by Laura A. Tharp and published in Waco, Texas, in 1973. Sifting Through the Ashes for the Althorp, Allentharpe, Tharp, Tharpe [also Thorpe] Family and Connections was compiled by Eleanor Davis McSwain and published in Macon, Georgia, in 1989.*

THORSON (S.S. Abbreviation: Thorso)

Ranking: 4733 S.S. Count: 9460

Origin: Norwegian, Swedish. Derived from the Swedish name Thor, meaning the god of thunder, and the word "son" or "sen," meaning son.

Genealogies: *Asle Thorson, Immigrant Ancestor of Asle-*

son, Thorson, and Thorsen: A Family Genealogy was compiled by Duane Wee Thorsen and published in Oconomowoc, Wisconsin, in 1971.

THRASHER (S.S. Abbreviation: Thrash)
Ranking: 1819 **S.S. Count:** 24,808

Origin: English, German, Jewish. English: derived from the Middle English word "threser," meaning to thresh—separating grain from shaft. German: derived from the German word "drescher," meaning thresher. The name was given to those who worked as threshers. Jewish: derived from the Yiddish word "dresher," meaning to thresh. The name was given to those who worked as threshers.

Famous **Thrashers:** JOHN SIDNEY THRASHER (1817–1879) of Maine was a journalist and adventurer and an active participant in the purchase of Cuba.

Genealogies: *A History of the Thrasher Family Traced Through the Eighteenth and Nineteenth Centuries in England and America* was compiled by Marion Thrasher and published in San Francisco, California, in 1895. *Cousins by the Dozens: Sturgis, Thrasher, Carlton, Mitchell, Branch* was compiled by Dorothy Sturgis Pruett and published in Macon, Georgia, in 1975.

THURMAN, THURMAND (S.S. Abbreviation: Thurma)
Ranking: 1389 **S.S. Count:** 31,903

Origin: English. Derived from the Middle English first name Thurmond or the Old Norman name Pormundr, which was derived from the name Pórr, the Swedish god of thunder, and the word "mundr," meaning protection.

Famous **Bearers:** ALLEN GRANBERRY THURMAN (1813–1895) of Virginia was a member of Congress, a member of the Ohio Supreme Court, leader of the "Peace Democrats" during the Civil War, and a U.S. senator after the war. He was the author of the Thurman Act and twice an unsuccessful candidate for the vice presidency.

Genealogies: *Descendants of Arthur Massey, Cheraws District, South Carolina, 1769, with Allied Lines of Thurman and Tucker* was compiled by Carmae Massey Smith and published in Owensboro, Kentucky, in 1980. *The Stroms of South Carolina* [also Thurman] was compiled by Samuel T. Strom and published in Union, South Carolina, in 1984. *The Thurmond Family: A Black Lineage* [also Thurman] was compiled by Sameera V. Thurmond and published in 1991.

THURMOND (S.S. Abbreviation: Thurmo)
Ranking: 4573 **S.S. Count:** 9769

Origin: English. Cognate to Thurman.

Genealogies: *Thurmond-Thurmon, From Georgia to Louisiana, 1781–1982* was compiled by Mary Edith Thurmon Freudendorf and published in Monroe, Louisiana, in 1983. *The Thurmond Family: A Black Lineage* was compiled by Sameera V. Thurmond and published in 1991. *The Thurmonds of Virginia* was compiled by Walter Robert Thurmond Witschey and published in Richmond, Virginia, in 1978.

THURSTAN, THURSTON (S.S. Abbreviation: Thurst)
Ranking: 2099 **S.S. Count:** 21,881

Origin: English. 1) derived from a medieval first name that was derived from the Old Norman name Porsteinn, which was derived from the name Pórr and the word "steinn," meaning the Swedish god of thunder and stone. 2) derived from the Old Norman first name Pori which was derived from the Swedish name Thor and the Old English word "tūn," meaning settlement. The name was given to those from Thurston, the name of a place in England.

Famous **Bearers:** ROBERT LAWTON THURSTON (1800–1874) of Rhode Island was a pioneer manufacturer of steam engines. HOWARD THURSTON (1869–1936) of Ohio was a magician and best remembered for his illusion of a floating woman. LORRIN ANDREWS THURSTON (1858–1931) of Hawaii was the drafter of the 1893 proclamation that was presented to Washington, D.C., to annex Hawaii as part of the United States. MATILDA THURSTON (1875–1958) of Connecticut was the founder of Ginling College for Women in China.

Genealogies: None known.

TIBBETT, TIBBETTS (S.S. Abbreviation: Tibbet)
Ranking: 3809 **S.S. Count:** 11,850

Origin: English. Derived from the medieval first names Tebald and Tibalt, which were derived from a Germanic first name comprising components meaning people and brave.

Famous **Bearers:** LAWRENCE M. TIBBETT (1896–1960) of California was an opera singer who worked in the Metropolitan Opera in New York and in films and on Broadway.

Genealogies: *The Tippit Family of Louisiana and the Related Families of Bass, O'Bryant, Sellars/Smith and Groves/Nash* [also Tibbetts] was compiled by Jane Parker McManus and published in New Orleans, Louisiana, in 1972. *Mary Tibbetts Dennison, 1877–1970, Her Genealogical Lines* was compiled by Bertie Holmes Boodry and published in Beaumont, Texas, in 1982.

TIBBS
Ranking: 4616 **S.S. Count:** 9674

Origin: English. Derived from the medieval first names Tebald and Tibalt, which were probably derived from words meaning people and brave.

Genealogies: None known.

TICE

Ranking: 3218 S.S. Count: 14,086

Origin: English, German. 1) the name means "descendant of Tica" (H&H), meaning pleasant. 2) derived from the name Matthias, which means Jehovah's gift.

Genealogies: *Family History of John V. Tice, Including His Immediate Ancestors and His Descendants* was compiled by Crist Swartzentruber and published in Berlin, Pennsylvania, in 1962. *The Tice Families in America: Theis, Thyssen, Tyssen, Deis* was compiled by James Strode Elston and published in Rutland, Vermont, in 1972.

TIDWELL (S.S. Abbreviation: Tidwel)

Ranking: 1588 S.S. Count: 28,182

Origin: English. Derived from the name Tidi and the word "well," meaning stream or well. The name was given to those who came from Tidwell, the name of a place in Derbyshire, England.

Genealogies: None known.

TIERNEY (S.S. Abbreviation: Tierne)

Ranking: 2300 S.S. Count: 19,847

Origin: Irish. Derived from the Gaelic name Ó Tighearnaigh, which means descended from Tighearnach, a name meaning lord (H&H).

Famous Tierneys: RICHARD HENRY TIERNEY (1870–1928) of New York was a Roman Catholic clergyman and the editor of *America* (1914–1925).

Genealogies: *Genealogical Charts of Descendants of John Tierney and of the Related Families* was compiled by Raymond Moran Tierney and published in Oceanport, New Jersey.

TILLER

Ranking: 2028 S.S. Count: 22,505

Origin: English. Derived from the Middle English word "til(l)er," which was derived from the Old English word "tilian," meaning to till. The name was given to those who worked tilling soil.

Genealogies: *Deep East Texas Folk: The Tillers, Crenshaws, Woodleys, Goldens, and Other Related Families of Panola and Harrison Counties* was compiled by Terry G. Jordan and published in Dallas, Texas, in 1976.

TILLEY

Ranking: 2147 S.S. Count: 21,345

Origin: English. 1) derived from either the Gallo-Roman first name Tilius with the suffix "-acum" or from the first name Attilius with the suffix "-acum." The name was given to those who came from places named Tilly in northern France. 2) derived from the Old English words "telg(e)" and "lēah," meaning branch and clearing. The name was given to those who came from Tilley, the name of a place in Shropshire, England. *3) derived from the Middle English word "tilie," meaning tiller of earth. The name was given to those who worked tilling soil. 4) derived from the medieval first name Till, which was a shortened form of Matilda.*

Genealogies: *The Tilley Treasure* was compiled by James B. King and published in Point Lookout, Missouri, in 1984.

TILLMAN (S.S. Abbreviation: Tillma)

Ranking: 1092 S.S. Count: 40,425

Origin: English. Transformation of Tiller.

Famous Tillmans: BENJAMIN R. TILLMAN (1847–1918) of South Carolina was a governor of, then U.S. senator from, South Carolina.

Genealogies: None known.

TILTON

Ranking: 3798 S.S. Count: 11,881

Origin: English. Derived from the name Tila and the word "tūn," meaning settlement. The name was given to those who came from Tilton, the name of a place in Leicestershire, England.

Famous Tiltons: JAMES TILTON (1745–1822) of Delaware was an army surgeon during the Revolutionary War. THEODORE TILTON (1835–1907) of New York was a journalist and a friend of Henry Ward Beecher's, whom he sued over an allegedly adulterous relationship between his wife and Beecher. The trial lasted 112 days and resulted in a hung jury. Ruined by the scandal, he left the country in 1883. EDWARD LIPPINCOTT TILTON (1861–1933) of New York was an architect and the designer of the immigration processing building at Ellis Island.

Genealogies: *Tilton Territory: A Historical Narrative, Warren Township, Jefferson County, Ohio, 1775–1838* was compiled by Robert H. Richardson and published in Philadelphia, Pennsylvania, in 1977.

TIMM

Ranking: 3622 S.S. Count: 12,442

Origin: English, German. English: uncertain etymology. Possibly derived from an Old English first name related to the Germanic name Timmo. German: derived from a shortened version of the medieval first name Dietmar.

Famous Timms: HENRY CHRISTIAN TIMM (1811–1892) of Germany was a musician and one of the first members of the New York Philharmonic Society, serving as its president from 1848 to 1863.

Genealogies: None known.

TIMMER (ALSO TIMMERMAN, TIMMERMANN, TIMMERMANS)

Ranking: 2896 S.S. Count: 15,726

Origin: Timmerman, Timmermans—Dutch, Flemish;

Timmer, Timmermann—German; Timmerman, Timmermann—Jewish. Transformations of Zimmerman.

Genealogies: *Descendants of Lieut. Henry Timmerman of Herkimer County, New York* was compiled by Carolyn Timmerman Sidenius and published in Little Falls, New York, in 1988.

TIMMONS (S.S. Abbreviation: Timmon)

Ranking: 1627 S.S. Count: 27,579

Origin: *English, Irish. English: derived from the first name Timm. Irish: 1) derived from the Gaelic name Mac Toimín, meaning son of Toimín, which was derived from the name Tomás. 2) derived from the Gaelic name Ó Tiomadín, meaning descendant of Tiomán, which was derived from the word "tiom," meaning soft. 3) derived from the Gaelic name Ó Tiománaidhe, meaning descendant of Tiománaidhe.*

Genealogies: *The Timms of Waterloo County: A Chronicle* [also Timmons] was compiled by Barbara Timm Arndt and published in Cleveland, Ohio, in 1991. *Timms-Weir: The Ancestry of William Robert Tims of Augusta, Texas* [also Timmons] was compiled by Janet Scott Weir and published in Maryville, Missouri, in 1988.

TINDAL (ALSO TINDALE, TINDALL)

Ranking: 3821 S.S. Count: 11,802

Origin: *English. Tindale: derived from the name of the river called Tina, which was probably derived from the Celtic word meaning to flow, and the Old English word "dœl," meaning valley. Tindal, Tindall: transformations of Tindale.*

Genealogies: None known.

TINGLE (ALSO TINGLER, TINGLEY)

Ranking: 3464 S.S. Count: 13,028

Origin: *English. Derived from the Middle English word "tingle," meaning a small nail or tack. The names were given to those who made nails.*

Famous **Bearers**: KATHERINE AUGUSTA WESTCOTT TINGLEY (1847–1929) of Massachusetts was the founder of the town of Point Loma, California.

Genealogies: *The Tingley Family Revised* was compiled by Marian McCauley Frye and published in Falls Church, Virginia, in 1970.

TINSLEY (S.S. Abbreviation: Tinsle)

Ranking: 2013 S.S. Count: 22,679

Origin: *English. Derived from an Old English first name, possibly Tynni, and the word "hlāw," meaning hill. The name was given to those who came from Tinsley, the name of a place in England.*

Genealogies: *From Totopotomoy to Transylvania: A Descendancy Line of the Tinsley Family in America Since 1638* was compiled by Jim Bob Tinsley and published in Ocala, Florida, in 1976.

TIPTON

Ranking: 1282 S.S. Count: 34,495

Origin: *English. Derived from an unknown Old English first name and the word "tūn," meaning settlement. The name was given to those who came from Tipton, the name of a place in England.*

Famous **Tiptons**: JOHN TIPTON (1730–1813) of Maryland was a Virginia and Tennessee legislator. His nephew, JOHN TIPTON (1786–1838) of Tennessee, was a U.S. senator from Indiana.

Genealogies: *We Tiptons and Our Kin* was compiled by Ervin Charles Tipton and published in San Rafael, California, in 1975.

TIRADO

Ranking: 2717 S.S. Count: 16,744

Origin: *Spanish. Uncertain etymology. 1) probably derived from the word "tirado," meaning stretched. The name may have been given to those who had long limbs. 2) possibly derived from the word 'éstirado," meaning aloof. The name may have been given to those who were aloof.*

Genealogies: None known.

TISDALE (S.S. Abbreviation: Tisdal)

Ranking: 3285 S.S. Count: 13,802

Origin: *English. Possibly derived from the Old English first name Tissi, which was derived from the components "tid" and "sige," meaning season and victory, and the word "dœl," meaning valley. The name was given to those who came from a now-unknown place in England.*

Genealogies: *The Descendants of John Tisdale (1614–1675) Colonial Massachusetts* was compiled by Robert L. Tisdale and published in 1981. *Meet the Tisdales: Descendants of John Tisdale of Taunton, Mass., 1634–1980* was compiled by Rosa D. Tisdale and published in Baltimore, Maryland, in 1981.

TITUS

Ranking: 2134 S.S. Count: 21,465

Origin: *English. The name means "descendant of Titus" (ES).*

Genealogies: *A History of the Titus and Related Families* was compiled by Elroy Wilson Titus and published in Columbus, Ohio, in 1984. *Saga of Two North American Families: Andrews-Titus* was compiled by John Alva Titus and published in South Paris, Maine, in 1987. *A Titus Family* was compiled by Ianthe Hebel and published in Daytona Beach, Florida, in 1968.

TOBIAS

Ranking: 2508 **S.S. Count:** 18,085

Origin: English, French, German, Jewish. Derived from a Greek version of the Hebrew male first name Tovya, meaning Jehovah is good (H&H).

Famous **Tobiases:** CHANNING HEGGIE TOBIAS (1882–1961) of Georgia was a civic leader and the first black director of the Phelps-Stokes Foundation. He was the author of *To Secure These Rights* (1947).

Genealogies: None known.

TOBIN

Ranking: 1678 **S.S. Count:** 26,663

Origin: English, Irish. English: derived from the first name Tobias. Irish: derived from the Gaelic name Tóibín.

Famous **Tobins:** DANIEL JOSEPH TOBIN (1875–1955) of Ireland was a labor leader and one of the founders of the International Brotherhood of Teamsters, Chauffeurs, Warehousemen, and Helpers of America, serving as its president from 1907 to 1952. MAURICE JOSEPH TOBIN (1901–1953) of Massachusetts was the governor of that state, mayor of Boston, and a member of the Massachusetts House of Representatives. He was responsible for a bill to end discrimination in the state of Massachusetts.

Genealogies: None known.

TODD

Ranking: 392 **S.S. Count:** 98,726

Origin: English. Derived from the Middle English word "tod(de)," meaning fox. The name was given to those who exhibited the characteristics of a fox.

Famous **Todds:** THOMAS TODD (1763–1845) of Virginia was an associate justice of the U.S. Supreme Court. ELI TODD (1769–1833) of Connecticut was a pioneer in the modern approach to the treatment of alcoholics and mental illness. MABEL LOOMIS TODD (1856–1932) of Massachusetts was the first editor of Emily Dickinson's poems. After Dickinson's death, she edited more than 800 poems found by the family that Dickinson had packed away in a box. The editing consisted of translating difficult handwriting and choosing between different versions of the poem that had been scribbled in the margins of the papers. Todd also was an author in her own right and the founder of the Amherst Historical Society.

Genealogies: *A Todd Family History and Genealogy, 1749–1987* was compiled by Frederick Becker and published in Decorah, Iowa, in 1987. *My Family: The Young-Todd Genealogy, 1754–1972* was compiled by Lois Young and published in Anderson, South Carolina, in 1972. *Todds in Early Lawrence and Monroe Counties, Indiana* was compiled by Nancie Todd Weber and published in Vienna, Virginia, in 1979.

TOLBERT (S.S. Abbreviation: Tolber)

Ranking: 1438 **S.S. Count:** 31,089

Origin: English, French. Derived from a Germanic first name comprising an unknown first component and the word "berht," meaning famous.

Genealogies: None known.

TOLEDO

Ranking: 3386 **S.S. Count:** 13,376

Origin: Spanish, Jewish. Spanish: uncertain etymology. The name was given to those who came from Toledo, the name of a city in Spain. Jewish: uncertain etymology. Possibly derived from the Hebrew word "toledot," meaning generations.

Genealogies: None known.

TOLER

Ranking: 3446 **S.S. Count:** 13,094

Origin: English. Derived from the Old English word "toln," both meaning tax. The name was given to those who worked collecting taxes or tolls.

Genealogies: None known.

TOLIVER (S.S. Abbreviation: Tolive)

Ranking: 4311 **S.S. Count:** 10,417

Origin: Italian. The name was given to those who worked with iron.

Genealogies: None known.

TOLLIVER (S.S. Abbreviation: Tolliv)

Ranking: 3071 **S.S. Count:** 14,785

Origin: Italian. Cognate to Toliver.

Genealogies: None known.

TOM

Ranking: 3814 **S.S. Count:** 11,826

Origin: Czech. Cognate to Thomas.

Genealogies: None known.

TOMLIN

Ranking: 857 **S.S. Count:** 50,064

Origin: English. Cognate to Thomas.

Famous **Tomlins:** BRADLEY WALKER TOMLIN (1899–1953) of New York was an artist who specialized in abstract paintings, such as *Tension by Moonlight* (1948).

Genealogies: None known.

TOMPKIN, TOMPKINS (S.S. Abbreviation: Tompki)

Ranking: 1243 **S.S. Count:** 35,522

Origin: English. Cognates to Thomas.

Famous **Bearers:** DANIEL D. TOMPKINS (1774–1825) of

New York was a governor of that state and vice president of the United States (1817–1825) under President James Monroe. SALLY LOUISA THOMPKINS (1833–1916) of Virginia was the head of Robertson Hospital in Richmond, Virginia, during the Civil War. She was commissioned by Jefferson Davis as a captain in the cavalry as a means to keep her hospital open because all private hospitals were being closed. She accepted no payment for her services. The hospital remained open for the duration of the war and recorded only 73 deaths—very low because of the degree of cleanliness with which she ran the hospital.

Genealogies: *The 7th U.S. Cavalry's Own Colonel Tommy Tompkins: A Military Heritage and Tradition* was compiled by John M. Carrol and published in Mattituck, New York, in 1984. *Travels in Search of an Ancestor: with Genealogies of the Tompkins, Kingsley, Kirkland, (et al) Families* was compiled by Grace Tompkins Walker and published in Fairield, Connecticut, in 1975.

TONEY

Ranking: 1906 **S.S. Count:** 23,747

Origin: English. Derived from the medieval first name Ton(e)y, a shortened form of Anthony.

Genealogies: *The Toney Family History* was compiled by Elma Henning and published in Baltimore, Maryland, in 1979.

TOOLE

Ranking: 4894 **S.S. Count:** 9132

Origin: English, Irish. English: derived from the Middle English and Old English first name Toll, or from the Old Norman name Tóli, which was probably derived from the compound name Þórleifr, which comprised the name Þórr and the word "leifr," meaning god of thunder and relic.

Famous Tooles: EDWIN WARREN TOOLE (1839–1905) of Missouri was a pioneer lawyer in Montana Territory. His brother and law partner, JOSEPH KEMP TOOLE (1851–1929) of Missouri, was the territorial delegate to Congress from Montana. The brothers had moved to the Montana territory to open their practice.

Genealogies: None known.

TOOMEY

Ranking: 3992 **S.S. Count:** 11,324

Origin: Irish. Derived from the Gaelic name Ó Tuama, meaning descendant of Tuama (H&H), which was probably derived from the word "tuaim," meaning hill.

Genealogies: *The Ancestry & Descendants of John Cowart* [also Toomey], *1816– 1882* was compiled by Kyser Cowart Ptomey and published in New Orleans, Louisiana, in 1984. *The Ptomey Family of Alabama and the Allied Families of Blakenship, Melton, Kyser, and Cowart* [also Toomey] was compiled by Kyser Cowart Ptomey and published in New Orleans, Louisiana, in 1983.

TORO

Ranking: 4484 **S.S. Count:** 9992

Origin: Italian, Spanish. Italian: derived from medieval names such as Victor and Salvātor. Italian, Spanish: derived from the Italian and Spanish word "toro," meaning bull.

Genealogies: None known.

TORRENCE, TORRENS, TORRENT, TORRENTE, TORRENTS (S.S. Abbreviation: Torren)

Ranking: 3748 **S.S. Count:** 12,082

Origin: Torrent—French; Torrence—Irish, Scottish; Torrens—Irish, Provençal, Scottish; Torrente, Torrents—Spanish. Torrence: derived from the Gaelic word "torran," meaning hill. The name was given to those who came from Torrence, the name of places in Ireland or Scotland. Torrens (Irish, Scottish): derived from the Gaelic word "torran," meaning hill. The name was given to those who came from Torrence, the name of places in Ireland or Scotland. Torrens (Provençal): cognate to Torrente. Torrent, Torrente, Torrents: derived from the Spanish word "torrente," meaning flood stream, which was derived from the Latin word "torrēre," meaning to seethe. The names were given to those who lived near a stream prone to flooding.

Famous Bearers: FREDERICK RIDGELY TORRENCE (1875–1950) of Ohio was a poet and poetry editor who wrote many volumes of verse. He also wrote plays.

Genealogies: None known.

TORRES (ALSO TORRESE, TORRESI)

Ranking: 77 **S.S. Count:** 333,045

Origin: Torres—Catalan, Jewish, Provençal; Torrese, Torresi—Italian. Derived from the Old French word "tūr," meaning tower. The names were given to those who lived near some type of tower.

Genealogies: None known.

TORREZ

Ranking: 2762 **S.S. Count:** 16,500

Origin: Spanish. Uncertain etymology. Most likely a cognate to Torres.

Genealogies: None known.

TOTH

Ranking: 1547 **S.S. Count:** 28,861

Origin: German. 1) derived from the Middle High German word "tōt," meaning death. 2) derived from the Middle High German word "tote," meaning godfather.

Genealogies: None known.

TOTTEN

Ranking: 4662 S.S. Count: 9593

Origin: English. Derived from the name Toton, meaning Tofi's home. The name was given to those who came from Toton or Totten, the names of places in England.

Genealogies: None known.

TOVAR

Ranking: 3376 S.S. Count: 13,408

Origin: Spanish. Derived from the Old Spanish word "tovar," meaning pumice stone or pumice stone quarry. The name was given to those who lived near pumice stone quarries.

Genealogies: None known.

TOWNE

Ranking: 4710 S.S. Count: 9505

Origin: English, Irish. English: derived from the Middle English words "tune" and "tone," which were derived from the Old English word "tūn," meaning settlement. The name was given to those who lived in villages. Irish: derived from the Gaelic first name Ó Tomhrair, which was derived from the word "tomhra(r)," meaning protection.

Famous **Townes**: BENJAMIN TOWNE (?–1793) of England was the publisher of the *Pennsylvania Evening Post*, the first evening newspaper in Philadelphia and the only paper that was continuously published throughout the Revolutionary War. LAURA MATILDA TOWNE (1825–1901) of Pennsylvania was the founder of the Penn School on the Sea Islands of South Carolina. There she taught slaves that had been abandoned by their owners during the Civil War. HENRY ROBINSON TOWNE (1844–1924) of Pennsylvania was co-manufacturer, with Linus Yale, of locks. They formed the Yale Lock Manufacturing Co. Towne also was a pioneer in the building of cranes.

Genealogies: None known.

TOWNS

Ranking: 4148 S.S. Count: 10,918

Origin: English, Irish. Transformation of Towne.

Famous **Townses**: GEORGE WASHINGTON BONAPARTE TOWNS (1801–1854) of Georgia was a governor of Georgia who improved the slavery code, initiated the "ad valorum" tax, completed the railroad, and improved education.

Genealogies: None known.

TOWNSEND (S.S. Abbreviation: Townse)

Ranking: 402 S.S. Count: 97,211

Origin: English. Derived from the Middle English words "tone" and "tune," both meaning village, and the word "end," meaning end. The name was given to those who lived at the outskirts of a village.

Famous **Townsends**: Brothers JOB TOWNSEND (1699–1765) and CHRISTOPHER TOWNSEND (1701–1773) of Rhode Island started a family business whose name has become synonymous with fine craftsmanship in cabinetmaking. With the Goddard family, the brothers and their descendants formed the Goddard-Townsend group of cabinetmakers and are credited with setting standards in case furniture characterized by block fronts and decorative carved shells. FRANCIS E. TOWNSEND (1867–1960) of Illinois was a physician who originated and managed the Old-Age Revolving Pensions, Ltd., a plan that generated support for starting a federal social security program. WILLIAM SAXBY TOWNSEND JR. (1895–1957) of Ohio was the founder and first president of the Red Caps (1936). The organization was remaned the United Transport Service Employees in 1940. He was the first black seated on the executive council of the Congress of Industrial Organizations (CIO).

Genealogies: *Allen Townsend of Madison County, Florida: A Genealogy* was compiled by Joseph T. Burval and published in Charleston, West Virginia, in 1991. *Master Craftsmen of Newport: The Townsends and Goddards* was compiled by Michael Moses and published in Tenafly, New Jersey, in 1984. *I'm Claiming the Promise, A History and Genealogy of the Wm. Henry and Edith* [also Townsend] *Stratton Family* was compiled by David C. Stratton and published in Salem, Ohio, in 1977.

TRACEY

Ranking: 4086 S.S. Count: 11,060

Origin: English, Irish. English: derived from the Gallo-Roman first name Thracius, which was derived from the Latin names Thrax or Thracis, and the suffix "eium." The name was given to those who came from places with similar-sounding names in France. Irish: derived from the Gaelic name Ó Treasaigh, meaning descendant of Treasach (H&H), which means warlike.

Genealogies: None known.

TRACY

Ranking: 1060 S.S. Count: 41,648

Origin: English, Irish. Transformation of Tracey.

Famous **Tracys**: JOSEPH TRACY (1793–1874) of Vermont was one of the founders of Liberia College and the director of the American Colonization Society. SPENCER BONAVENTURE TRACY (1900–1967) of Wisconsin was an actor who starred in more than 60 movies. He won Academy Awards for his performances in *Captains Courageous* (1937) and *Boys' Town* (1938). His most famous co-star was Katharine Hepburn.

Genealogies: *Genealogies of the Tracy-Tanner Families, and Other Genealogies* was compiled by Mathew J. Tracy and published in Indiana in 1903. *An Ormsbee* [also Tracy]

Odyssey: The Ancestry of Reverend Oliver Amos Ormsbee of Plato, Texas Co., Missouri was compiled by Nora O'Dell and published in Concord, California, in 1990.

TRAHAN
Ranking: 2711 S.S. Count: 16,775

Origin: French?, Welsh? Uncertain etymology. French: 1) possibly derived from the Celtic word "traon," meaning river valley. 2) possibly derived from the medieval word "trahant," meaning a stick used to clean stables. Welsh: possibly derived from the first name Trahaearn, which was derived from the components "tra" and "haearn" or "haiairn," meaning very and iron.

Genealogies: *The St. Jean and Trahan Families* was compiled by William St. John and published in Brattleboro, Vermont, in 1983.

TRAINOR (S.S. Abbreviation: Traino)
Ranking: 4293 S.S. Count: 10,458

Origin: English, Irish, Scottish. English, Scottish: derived from the Middle English word "train(e)," meaning to trap, which was derived from the Old French word "trainer," meaning to draw into. The name was given to those who worked as trappers. Irish: derived from the Gaelic name Mac Thréinfhir, meaning champion.

Genealogies: None known.

TRAMMEL, TRAMMELL (S.S. Abbreviation: Tramme)
Ranking: 2189 S.S. Count: 20,927

Origin: English?, Welsh? Uncertain etymology. Possibly derived from the Cornish and Welsh word "tre," meaning village, and the Cornish word "mel(l)an" or the Welsh word "melin," both meaning mill. The names were given to those who lived near a village or estate having a mill.

Genealogies: *Descendants of Thomas Trammell, Revolutionary Soldier* was compiled by Charles S. McCleskey and published in Baton Rouge, Louisiana, in 1972. *Duty, Patience, and Endurance: The Trammells of Meriwether and Harris* was compiled by W. Winston Skinner and published in Luthersville, Georgia, in 1977.

TRAN
Ranking: 766 S.S. Count: 54,895

Origin: Vietnamese. The name means 1) serious, 2) intelligent, 3) beautiful, or 4) generous.

Genealogies: None known.

TRAPP
Ranking: 3580 S.S. Count: 12,599

Origin: English, German. English: derived from the Old English word "træppe," meaning trap. The name was given to those who worked as trappers. German: derived from the

Middle High German word "trappe," meaning bustard, a type of bird. The name was given to those who were considered stupid.*

Genealogies: None known.

TRAVERS (S.S. Abbreviation: Traver)
Ranking: 2211 S.S. Count: 20,750

Origin: English, French, Irish. English, French: derived from the Old French word "traverser," meaning to cross. The name was given to those who lived near a bridge or who collected tolls. Irish: derived from the Gaelic name Ó Treabhair, a name meaning industrious or prudent (H&H).

Famous **Traverses:** JEROME DUNSTAN TRAVERS (1887–1961) of New York was a golfer who won numerous amateur championships and who won the professional U.S. Open in 1915.

Genealogies: *Southern Travis, Travers, Traverse Families from Lancashire and Post-Elizabethan Ireland* was compiled by Albert Eugene Casey and published in Birmingham, Alabama, in 1978.

TRAVIS
Ranking: 933 S.S. Count: 46,263

Origin: English. Transformation of Travers.

Famous **Travises:** WILLIAM BARRET TRAVIS (1809–1836) of South Carolina was commander of the Texas forces destroyed by the Mexican army at the Alamo in 1836. WALTER JOHN TRAVIS (1862–1927), born in Australia, emigrated to the United States as a child and became the first American golfer to win the British Amateur championship.

Genealogies: *Southern Travis, Travers, Traverse Families From Lancashire and Post-Elizabethan Ireland* was compiled by Albert Eugene Casey and published in Birmingham, Alabama, in 1978. *The Travis Family Today and Yesterday* was compiled by Berdyne D. Travis and published in Ionia, Michigan, in 1969. *A Travis Tree on Me and Mine* was compiled by Harold Gilbert Travis and published in Weston, Massachusetts, in 1969.

TRAYLOR (S.S. Abbreviation: Traylo)
Ranking: 2544 S.S. Count: 17,850

Origin: English. 1) the name means "one who constructed trellis work" (ES). 2) the name means "one who travels on foot, sometimes with long trailing garments" (ES).

Famous **Traylors:** MELVIN ALVAH TRAYLOR (1878–1934) of Kentucky was a lawyer and banker and the president of the First National Bank after 1925.

Genealogies: None known.

TREADWELL (S.S. Abbreviation: Treadw)
Ranking: 2429 S.S. Count: 18,669

Origin: English. Derived from the Old English word

"tredan," meaning tread, and the word "well," meaning well. The name was given to those who worked as fullers.

Famous **Treadwells**: DANIEL TREADWELL (1791–1872) of Massachusetts invented a printing press that was very popular in its time.

Genealogies: None known.

TREJO

Ranking: 3630 S.S. Count: 12,407
Origin: Spanish? Uncertain etymology.
Genealogies: None known.

TREMBLAY, TREMBLE, TREMBLEY, TREMBLY (S.S. Abbreviation: Trembl)

Ranking: 2872 S.S. Count: 15,843
Origin: English, French, Scottish. English, Scottish: 1) derived from an Old English first name, possibly Trumbeald, which comprised the components "trum" and "beald," meaning strong and brave. 2) uncertain etymology. The name was given to those who came from Trimley, the name of a place in Suffolk, England. French: derived from the Old French word "tremble," meaning quiver. The name was given to those who lived near aspen trees.
Genealogies: None known.

TRENT

Ranking: 1793 S.S. Count: 25,139
Origin: English. Uncertain etymology. 1) the name may have been given to those known for travelling (H&H). 2) the name may have been given to those who lived near one of the various rivers named Trent in England. 3) the name may have been given to those who came from a town named Trent in Dorset, England.

Famous **Trents**: WILLIAM TRENT (1715–1787?) of Pennsylvania was an Indian trader and land speculator. He and several others were responsible for securing a large tract of land from the Iroquois Indians. The land was called Indiana. WILLIAM PETERFIELD TRENT (1862–1939) of Virginia was a teacher of literature and a historian.

Genealogies: *The Lawson Golden Book* was compiled by Virginia Ruth Lawson Trent and published in Dubuque, Iowa, in 1990.

TREVINO (S.S. Abbreviation: Trevin)

Ranking: 928 S.S. Count: 46,386
Origin: Spanish. The name means "dweller near a boundary stone touching three districts" (ES).
Genealogies: None known.

TRICE

Ranking: 3972 S.S. Count: 11,396
Origin: German. The name means maker or seller of small bells, or one who lived nearby or on a dormant field (ES).

Genealogies: *The Trices of North Carolina, Georgia and Alabama* was compiled by Olive Lynn Trice Jackson and published in Fairhope, Alabama, in 1988.

TRIMBLE (S.S. Abbreviation: Trimbl)

Ranking: 1983 S.S. Count: 22,868
Origin: Irish. Derived from an Old English first name comprising the components "trum" and "beald," meaning strong and brave.

Famous **Trimbles**: ROBERT TRIMBLE (1777–1828) of Virginia was an associate justice of the U.S. Supreme Court. ALLEN TRIMBLE (1783–1870) of Virginia was the governor of Ohio.

Genealogies: *American Beginings* was compiled by David B. Trimble and published in San Antonio, Texas, in 1974. *Southwest Virginia Families* [also Trimble] was compiled by David B. Trimble and published in San Antonio, Texas, in 1974. *Trimble Families of America* was compiled by John Farley Trimble and published in Parsons, West Virginia, in 1973.

TRINIDAD (S.S. Abbreviation: Trinid)

Ranking: 4877 S.S. Count: 9176
Origin: Spanish. Uncertain etymology.
Genealogies: None known.

TRIPLET, TRIPLETT, TRIPLETTE (S.S. Abbreviation: Triple)

Ranking: 1791 S.S. Count: 25,144
Origin: English. The name means "one of three born at one birth, a triplet" (ES).
Genealogies: None known.

TRIPP

Ranking: 1791 S.S. Count: 25,144
Origin: English. 1) derived from the Old French word "triper" and the Old English word "treppan," both meaning to tread. The name was given to dancers or to those who walked with an unusual step. 2) derived from the Middle English and Old French word "trip(p)e," meaning tripe. The name was given to those who worked as butchers.

Famous **Tripps**: BARTLETT TRIPP (1842–1911) of Maine was the chief justice of the territorial supreme court of the Dakotas and presided over the first territorial constitutional convention. GUY EASTMAN TRIPP (1865–1927) of Maine was the chairman of the board of Westinghouse Electric & Manufacturing Co.

Genealogies: *John Heron Trippe, Senior, Husband of Sarah Ann Jones, Their Ancestors and Descendants* was compiled by Helen A. Ball and published in Horton, Michigan, in 1986. *Tripp Trails* was compiled by Julie A. Hendricks and published in Spokane, Washington, in 1976.

TROMBLAY, TROMBLEY, TROMBLY (S.S. Abbreviation: Trombl)

Ranking: 3804 S.S. Count: 11,864

Origin: English. Transformations of Tremble.

Genealogies: None known.

TROTTER (S.S. Abbreviation: Trotte)

Ranking: 1720 S.S. Count: 26,040

Origin: English, German, Scottish. English, Scottish: derived from the Old French word "troter," meaning to walk rapidly. The name was given to those who worked as messengers. German: derived from the Middle High German word "trot(t)e," meaning winepress. The name was given to those who worked crushing grapes to make wine.

Genealogies: *The Guardian of Boston: William Monroe Trotter* was compiled by Stephen R. Fox and published in New York, New York, in 1970. *Troutman Family History* [also Trotter] was compiled by Flodene Parks Troutman and published in Marion, Illinois, between 1961 and 1967.

TROUT

Ranking: 2474 S.S. Count: 18,328

Origin: English. Derived from the Old English word "trūht," both meaning trout. The name was given to those who worked as fishermen, or those who were thought to resemble a trout in some way.

Genealogies: *250 Year History of My Trout Family* was compiled by George E. Trout and published in Buena Park, California, in 1991. *The Trouts From London: William Trout Branch* was compiled by Peter M. Rinaldo and published in 1988.

TROUTMAN (S.S. Abbreviation: Troutm)

Ranking: 2909 S.S. Count: 15,624

Origin: English. Transformation of Trotter.

Genealogies: *Troutman Family History* was compiled by Flodene Parks Troutman and published in Marion, Illinois, between 1961 and 1967.

TROWBRIDGE (S.S. Abbreviation: Trowbr)

Ranking: 4342 S.S. Count: 10,322

Origin: English. Derived from the Old English words "trēow" and "brycg," meaning tree and bridge. The name was given to those who came from Trowbridge, the name of a place in Wiltshire, England.

Famous **Trowbridges**: JOHN T. TROWBRIDGE (1827–1926) of New York was the author of a series of novels for boys, in addition to plays, poetry, and an autobiography. JOHN TROWBRIDGE (1843–1923) of Massachusetts was a physicist and author of *What Is Electricity?* (1896).

Genealogies: *Rhoades, Trowbridge, and Related Families* was compiled by Myrtle Savage Rhoades and published in East Orange, New Jersey, in 1975.

TROXEL (ALSO TROXELL)

Ranking: 3988 S.S. Count: 11,334

Origin: German. The name means "one who fashioned objects on a lathe, a turner" (ES).

Genealogies: *Troxel(l) Trails* was compiled by Richard M. Troxel and published in Baltimore, Maryland, in 1977.

TROY

Ranking: 3950 S.S. Count: 11,447

Origin: Irish, Jewish. Irish: derived from the Gaelic name Ó Troighthigh, meaning foot soldier (H&H). Jewish: uncertain etymology. Probably derived from similar-sounding names.

Genealogies: None known.

TROYER

Ranking: 4614 S.S. Count: 9685

Origin: Irish?, Jewish? Uncertain etymology. Possibly a cognate to Troy.

Genealogies: *A Brief History of Jonathan S. Miller and Mary J. Troyer* was compiled by Jonas E. Miller and published in Millersburg, Ohio, in 1958. *Descendants of David C. Troyer and Lydia Speicher, 1870–1971* was compiled by Amanda Sommers Coblentz and published in Hartville, Ohio, in 1971. *A History of the Miller Family* [also Troyer] *with a Complete Record of the Descendants of Daniel B. Miller* was compiled by J. Virgil Miller and published in Bluffton, Ohio, in 1970.

TRUE

Ranking: 4048 S.S. Count: 11,190

Origin: Provençal. Derived from the Old Provençal word "t(r)uc," meaning hill. The name was given to those who lived on or next to a hill.

Famous **Trues**: ALFRED CHARLES TRUE (1852–1929) of Connecticut was instrumental in what became the Association of Land Grant Colleges and Universities. His brother, FREDERICK WILLIAM TRUE (1858–1914) of Connecticut, was curator of the National Museum.

Genealogies: *Genealogy of the True & Bevers* was compiled by Odessa Morrow Isbell and published in Gainesville, Texas, in 1983. *The True Family: Some Henry True Descendants on the Frontier* was compiled by Charles Wesley True and published in San Antonio, Texas, in 1991.

TRUESDALE (S.S. Abbreviation: Truesd)

Ranking: 4162 S.S. Count: 10,856

Origin: English. Derived from the name Trucedale, meaning trout pool. The name was given to those who came from Trouts Dale, the name of a place in Yorkshire, England.

Genealogies: *The Truesdale Family History* was compiled by P. G. Hansen and published in Richland Center, Wisconsin, in 1970.

TRUITT (ALSO TRUITTE)

Ranking: 3208 S.S. Count: 14,143

Origin: English. 1) *the name means "the dear, beloved friend" (ES).* 2) *the name was derived from the name Trewhitt, meaning "dry resinous meadow" (ES). The name was given to those who came from Trewhitt, the name of a place in Northumberland, England.*

Genealogies: *Truitt Tracings* was compiled by Myrtis Irene Siddon and published in 1982.

TRUJILLO (S.S. Abbreviation: Trujil)

Ranking: 818 S.S. Count: 51,707

Origin: Spanish. Derived from the Latin name Turgalium. The name was given to those who lived in Trujillo, the name of places in Spain.

Genealogies: None known.

TRUONG

Ranking: 3683 S.S. Count: 12,250

Origin: Vietnamese. The name means 1) *page, as in page of a book,* 2) *tapestry or wall hanging, or* 3) *unit of ten feet.*

Genealogies: None known.

TUBBS

Ranking: 2707 S.S. Count: 16,794

Origin: English. Derived from the Middle English first name Tubbe.

Genealogies: *The Tubbs and Quinton Families of Pulaski County, Kentucky* was compiled by Sharon Minor Schermerhorn and published in Olympia, Washington, in 1983. *Daniel Tubb, 1794– 1882, of South Carolina, Tennessee, Alabama, and Descendants* was compiled by Dianne Lollar and published in Cullman, Alabama, in 1982.

TUCK

Ranking: 3298 S.S. Count: 13,756

Origin: English. Derived from the Old Norman first name Tóki, which was possibly derived from the name Thirkill, which was derived from the Old Norman first name Porkell, which was derived from the name Thor, referring to the god of thunder, and the word "ketill," meaning pot.

Famous **Tucks:** AMOS TUCK (1810–1879) of Maine was an abolitionist and one of the founders of the Republican Party.

Genealogies: *John and Edward Tuck of Halifax County, Virginia, and Some of Their Descendants* was compiled by Alethea Jane Macon and published in Greenville, Alabama, in 1978.

TUCKER

Ranking: 129 S.S. Count: 229,838

Origin: English, Jewish. English: 1) *derived from the Middle English word "tuck(en)," meaning to shrink and stretch wool, and the Old English word "tūcian," meaning to torment. The name was given to those who worked as fullers of cloth.* 2) *uncertain etymology. Possibly derived from the Old French words "tout" and "coeur," meaning all and heart. The name was possibly given to those who displayed valor or generosity. Jewish: derived from the Polish name Tokarz, which was derived from the word "tokarz," meaning turner.*

Famous **Tuckers:** ST. GEORGE TUCKER (1752?–1827) of Bermuda was a Revolutionary War soldier and a state supreme court of appeals judge in Virginia. SOPHIE TUCKER (1884–1966) of Russia was an actress and entertainer in the first half of the twentieth century. RICHARD TUCKER (1913–1975) of New York was a popular and successful opera singer associated with the New York Metropolitan Opera for 30 years.

Genealogies: *Descendants of Arthur Massey, Cheraws District, South Carolina, 1769, with Allied Lines of Thurman and Tucker* was compiled by Carmae Massey Smith and published in Owensboro, Kentucky, in 1980. *The Descendants of William Tucker of Throwleigh, Devon* was compiled by Robert Dennard Tucker and published in Spartanburg, South Carolina, in 1991. *Genealogy & Ancestry of Descendants of Tom & Martha Clark: Also the Families of Young, Tucker & Stalnaker* was compiled by W. S. Ross and published in Missouri in 1979.

TUGGLE (ALSO TUGGLES)

Ranking: 4552 S.S. Count: 9813

Origin: English. Derived from the name Tughall, meaning Tucga's corner. The names were given to those who came from Tughall, the name of a place in Northumberland, England.

Genealogies: *The Tuggle Family of Virginia* was compiled by Vivian S. Tuggle and published in Baltimore, Maryland, in 1970.

TULLY

Ranking: 3632 S.S. Count: 12,400

Origin: Irish. 1) *derived from the Gaelic name Ó Taithlagh, meaning quiet and peaceful (H&H).* 2) *derived from the Gaelic name Ó Maol Tuile, meaning "descendant of the devotee of (St.) Tuile" (H&H), which was derived from the word "toil," meaning will, as in will of God.*

Famous **Tullys:** WILLIAM TULLY (1785–1859) of Saybrook Point, Connecticut, was a graduate of Yale University and considered one of the most learned physicians of his time. JIM TULLY (1891–1947) of Ohio was a writer who held various jobs, such as publicist for Charlie Chaplin and staff member on movie magazines. He was often jailed for vagrancy. His books included *Beggars of Life* (1924).

Genealogies: None known.

TURK

Ranking: 3219 S.S. Count: 14,082

Origin: English, Scottish. English: 1) derived from the Middle English and Old French word *"turc,"* of unknown origin. The name was given to those who were considered unruly, or to those who lived at a sign of a Turk, or to those who fought in the war against the Turks. 2) derived from a medieval name, probably a form of *Thirkill.* Scottish: derived from the Gaelic name *Mac Torc,* meaning son of and boar.

Genealogies: None known.

TURLEY

Ranking: 3266 **S.S. Count:** 13,920

Origin: Irish. Derived from the Gaelic name *Mac Toirdhealbhaigh,* which was derived from the first name *Toirdhealbhach,* which comprised the name *Tor,* meaning god of thunder, and the word *"dealbhach,"* meaning like, as in similar.

Genealogies: *Turley Family Records* was compiled by Beth Mitchell and published in Alexandria, Virginia, in 1981.

TURNBULL (S.S. Abbreviation: Turnbu)

Ranking: 3681 **S.S. Count:** 12,254

Origin: English, Scottish. Derived from the Old English word *"turnian,"* meaning to turn, and *"bul(l)e,"* meaning bull. The name was given to those who were thought capable of turning back charging bulls.

Famous **Turnbulls:** ANDREW TURNBULL (1718?–1792) of Scotland was one of the founders of New Smyrna, Florida, an unsuccessful colony for Greeks, Italians, and Minorcan immigrants. ROBERT JAMES TURNBULL (1775–1883) of Florida was a planter in South Carolina and an opponent of national consolidation under the doctrine of implied constitutional power. WILLIAM TURNBULL (1800–1857) of Pennsylvania was responsible for the design and construction of the Potomoc Aquaduct.

Genealogies: *American Beginnings* [also Turnbull] was compiled by David B. Trimble and published in Texas in 1974. *The Texas Turnbo's* [also Turnbull] was compiled by Charles Alton Turnbo and published in Wichita Falls, Texas, in 1977.

TURNER

Ranking: 47 **S.S. Count:** 473,966

Origin: English, Jewish, Scottish. English, Scottish: 1) derived from the Anglo-Norman-French word *"torner,"* meaning to turn, as in turning a lathe. The name was given to those who worked making objects on a lathe. 2) uncertain etymology. Possibly derived from the Middle English word *"turn,"* meaning turn. The name was given to those who worked as translators or tumblers or in other occupations having to do with turning. 3) derived from the Middle English words *"turnen"* and *"hare,"* meaning to turn and rabbit. The name was given to those who could run fast. 4) derived

from the Old French word *"tornei,"* meaning to turn. The name was given to those who worked as officials at tournaments. Jewish: 1) derived from a pronounciation of the Yiddish name *Torner,* which was derived from the name *Torne.* The name was given to those who came from Tarnów, a city Spain. 2) derived from similar-sounding Jewish surnames.

Famous **Turners:** EDWARD TURNER (1778–1860) of Virginia was one of the drafters of the Mississippi constitution. NAT TURNER (1800–1831) of Virginia was a slave who led an uprising, killed his master's family and other people, then was captured and hanged. HENRY MCNEAL TURNER (1834–1915) of South Carolina was the first black to be appointed army chaplain (1863). CHARLES Y. TURNER (1850–1918) of Maryland was an artist best known for his figure paintings and murals. FREDERICK J. TURNER (1861–1932) of Wisconsin was a historian who helped promote the significance of the West in American history.

Genealogies: *Gibson, McCormick, Turner Genealogy* was compiled by F. McCormick Moore and published in Pennsylvania in 1980. *Meshack Turner III, His Wife Sarah Robey Tucker* was compiled by Lucille R. Maddox and published in Baltimore, Maryland, in 1976. *Book I, Descendants of Benjamin Turner, Mariner, 1721–1985 and Book II, Allied Ancestors and Cousins* were compiled by Susan Hewitt Pierson and published in St. James, Minnesota, in 1985.

TURNEY

Ranking: 4866 **S.S. Count:** 9201

Origin: English. Derived from the pre-Roman first name *Turnus,* probably meaning height or eminence (H&H), and the suffix *"acum."* The name was given to those who came from Tournai, Tournay, and Tourny, the names of places in France.

Famous **Turneys:** PETER TURNEY (1827–1903) of Tennessee was a justice and chief justice of the Tennessee Supreme Court. He also served as the governor of Tennessee.

Genealogies: None known.

TURPIN

Ranking: 2844

Origin: English, French. Derived from a Norman French version of the Old Norman first name *Porfinnr,* which is derived from the name *Pórr,* meaning god of thunder, and the name *Finnr.* **S.S. Count:** 16,049

Famous **Turpins:** BEN TURPIN (1869?–1940) of Louisiana was a slapstick comedian. He was known on stage as the "Happy Hooligan."

Genealogies: None known.

TUTTLE

Ranking: 1120 **S.S. Count:** 39,289

Origin: English. Derived from the Old Norman first name

Porkell, which was derived from the name Pórr, meaning god of thunder, and the word "ketill," meaning pot.

Famous **Tuttles**: CHARLES WESLEY TUTTLE (1829–1881) of Maine was an astronomer who explained the "dusky" ring around Saturn.

Genealogies: Andrew Hull Tuttle, 177–1845: His Ancestry and Descendants was compiled by Joyce Bruner Whitman and published in Lenoir, North Carolina, in 1985. *"Shipwreck" John Tuttle, Ancestor of the New Hampshire Tuttles* was compiled by Alva M. Tuttle and published in Keno, Oregon, in 1992. *Tuttle-Tuthill Lines in America* was compiled by Alva M. Tuttle and published in Columbus, Ohio, in 1968.

TYLER

Ranking: 464 **S.S. Count:** 86,431

Origin: English. Derived from the Middle English word "tile," which was derived from the Old English word "tigele," both meaning tile. The name was given to those who worked making or installing tiles.

Famous **Tylers**: JOHN TYLER (1747–1813) of Virginia was governor of Virginia and a strong judge in colonial America. His son, JOHN TYLER (1790–1862) of Virginia, was the 10th president of the United States. Prior to becoming president, he was a member of Congress from, governor of, and U.S. senator from Virginia. He then served as U.S. vice president and was the first to succeed to the presidency upon the death of a president (William Henry Harrison in 1841). LYON G. TYLER (1853–1935) of Virginia, son of President John Tyler, was president of the College of William and Mary and author of several books of a historical nature.

Genealogies: The Descendants of Job Tyler Since 1619 was compiled by Charles R. Tyler and published in East Grand Rapids, Michigan, probably in 1980. *Tyler-Browns of Brattleboro* was compiled by Dorothy Sutherland Melville and published in New York, New York, in 1973.

TYNER

Ranking: 4575 **S.S. Count:** 9764

Origin: German. Derived from the name Tinnen. The name was given to those who came from Tinnen, the name of a place in Germany.

Genealogies: John Kendig Barr: His Ancestors and His Descendants [also Tyner] was compiled by Mary Alice Burchfield and published in Bavard, Nebraska, in 1984. *The Tyner Family and Some Other Relatives* was compiled by Max R. Tyner and published in McAllen, Texas, in 1979.

TYREE

Ranking: 3534 **S.S. Count:** 12,775

Origin: Scottish. 1) derived from the name Tyrie, meaning land. The name was given to those who came from Tyrie, the name of a place in Perthshire, Ireland. 2) derived from the Gaelic name Mac an Toisich, meaning son of the carpenter or mason (H&H).

Genealogies: A Tyree Genealogy was compiled by Forrest Hill Tyree and published in Nashville, Tennessee, in 1983. *The Tyree Trail with Allied Lines of Adams and Blair* was compiled by Ella Rae Wilson Coleman and published in Port St. Lucie, Florida, in 1987. *The Tyree Tree* was compiled by Dorothy Chambers Watts and published in Albuquerque, New Mexico, in 1978.

TYRRELL (S.S. Abbreviation: Tyrrel)

Ranking: 4898 **S.S. Count:** 9128

Origin: English, Irish. Uncertain etymology. Probably derived from the Old French word "tirer," meaning to pull. The name was probably used to refer to a stubborn person.

Genealogies: None known.

TYSON

Ranking: 1148 **S.S. Count:** 38,160

Origin: English. 1) transformation of Dyson. 2) derived from the Old French word "tison," which was derived from the Latin word "titio," both meaning hot-tempered person. The name was given to those who were considered high-spirited.

Famous **Tysons**: GEORGE TYSON (1829–1906) of Red Bank, New Jersey, was a whaling captain and the hero of a six-month drift on an ice floe in the arctic. LAWRENCE DAVIS TYSON (1861–1929) of North Carolina served in the Spanish-American war, as publisher of the Knoxville *Sentinel*, and as a U.S. senator from Tennessee.

Genealogies: Cornelius Tyson Descendants, 1652–1986 was compiled by Genevieve A. Kerr-Tyson and published in Pennsylvania in 1987. *The Tyson Family History, Compiled 1963–19`65* was compiled by Elsie Tyson Hughes and published in Bartleville, Oklahoma, in 1965.

ULMER

Ranking: 3889 **S.S. Count:** 11,593

Origin: English, French, German. 1) the name was given to those who came from Ulm, the name of many places in Germany. 2) the name was given to those who lived near marshes. 3) derived from the name Ulmar, which was derived from components meaning owl and fame. 4) derived from the name Othalmar, which was derived from components meaning homeland and fame.

Genealogies: None known.

ULRICH

Ranking: 1870 **S.S. Count:** 24,213

Origin: German. Derived from the Old High German first name Odalric, which was derived from the components "odal" and "ric," meaning fortune and power.

Famous Ulrichs: EDWARD O. ULRICH (1857–1944) of Ohio was one of the top geologists and paleontologists of his time.

Genealogies: *Uhrich, A History and Genealogy* [also Ulrich] was compiled by Thomas Vincent Uhrich and published in 1982. *The Family History of Frederich H. Ulrich* was compiled by Esther Urich Bender and published in Twentynine Palms, California, in 1976.

UNDERHILL (S.S. Abbreviation: Underh)

Ranking: 4520 **S.S. Count:** 9908

Origin: English. Derived from the Middle English words "under" and "hill," meaning under and hill. The name was given to those who lived at the bottom of a hill.

Famous Underhills: FRANK P. UNDERHILL (1877–1932) of New York was a pharmacologist and toxicologist who was instrumental in organizing the U.S. Army Chemical Warfare Service.

Genealogies: *Underhill Genealogy* was compiled by Josephine C. Frost and published in Baltimore, Maryland, in 1980.

UNDERWOOD (S.S. Abbreviation: Underw)

Ranking: 514 **S.S. Count:** 77,889

Origin: English, Scottish. Derived from the Middle English words "under" and "wood," meaning under and wood. The name was given to those who lived near woods and to those who came from places in England with the words "under" and/or "wood" in their names.

Famous Underwoods: FRANCIS H. UNDERWOOD (1825–1894) was instrumental in the development of *Atlantic Monthly* magazine and was an author of books, including *Quabbin, the Story of a Small Town* (1893). LUCIEN MARCUS UNDERWOOD (1853–1907) of New York was a botanist and professor recognized as an authority on ferns and hepaticae.

JOHN THOMAS UNDERWOOD (1857–1937), born in England, introduced the Underwood typewriter in the United States in 1896. He headed Underwood Typewriter Co. (1896–1927). OSCAR W. UNDERWOOD (1862–1929) of Kentucky was a member of Congress and U.S. senator from Kentucky.

Genealogies: *Isaac W. Underwood: His Ancestors and Descendants* was compiled by Willie Bruce Underwood and published in Baltimore, Maryland, in 1988. *The Underwood Families of America* was compiled by Lucien Marcus Underwood and published in Baltimore, Maryland, in 1976.

UNGER

Ranking: 2174 **S.S. Count:** 21,084

Origin: Czech, German, Jewish. The name was given to those who came from Hungary.

Genealogies: None known.

UPCHURCH (S.S. Abbreviation: Upchur)

Ranking: 3364 **S.S. Count:** 13,481

Origin: English. The name means "the higher or farther inland church" (ES). It was given to those who came from Upchurch, the name of a place in England.

Famous Upchurches: JOHN J. UPCHURCH (1820–1887) founded the Ancient Order of United Workmen, a lodge that opposed trade unionism in the beginning but eventually became a prototype of fraternal benefit societies.

Genealogies: *Families and Kin of Elias Stockton, Moses Dickey, and James Upchurch, Cherokee County, Texas, Pioneers* was compiled by Mae Gean Pettit and published in Alto, Texas, in 1991.

UPSHAW

Ranking: 4679 **S.S. Count:** 9561

Origin: English. 1) the name was given to those who lived at the upper of two groves. 2) the name was given to those who lived near the head of a brook.

Famous Upshaws: WILLIAM D. UPSHAW (1866–1952) of Georgia was a member of Congress from Georgia and a Prohibition Party presidential candidate in 1932.

Genealogies: *Captain William Upshaw, Gent., Planter of Virginia* was compiled by Sophie W. Upshaw and published in Baltimore, Maryland, in 1975.

UPTON

Ranking: 2350 **S.S. Count:** 19,310

Origin: English. Derived from the Old English words "up" and "tūn," meaning upper and settlement. The name was given to those who came from Upton, the name of several places in England.

Famous **Uptons:** GEORGE PUTNAM UPTON (1834–1919) of Massachusetts was a journalist, music critic, and author of several books. EMORY UPTON (1839–1919) of New York was an army officer and author of books on military tactics.

Genealogies: None known.

URBAN

Ranking: 1550 **S.S. Count:** 28,723

Origin: Belorussian, Czech, English, French, Jewish, Polish. Derived from the Latin word "urbānis," meaning one who lives in a city.

Famous **Urbans:** JOSEPH URBAN (1872–1933) of Austria directed the Boston Opera Company and designed sets for many productions, including the Ziegfeld Follies.

Genealogies: None known.

URIBE

Ranking: 4079 **S.S. Count:** 11,075

Origin: Basque. Derived from the Basque words "uri" and "be(h)e," meaning settlement and lower part. The name was given to those who lived at the bottom part of a village.

Genealogies: None known.

USHER

Ranking: 4630 **S.S. Count:** 9657

Origin: English, Irish, Scottish. Derived from the Middle English word "usher," meaning janitor or gatekeeper. The name was given to those who worked as gatekeepers or who had official ceremonial duties at court.

Famous **Ushers:** JOHN P. USHER (1816–1889) of New York was a U.S. secretary of the interior. NATHANIEL R. USHER (1855–1931) of Indiana, the nephew of John P. Usher, was a distinguished officer in the U.S. navy. He was commandant of the Brooklyn (New York) Navy Yard during World War I.

Genealogies: *Ushers in America through Twelve Generations* was compiled by Avis Hedrix Nelson and published in Chadron, Nebraska, in 1977.

UTLEY

Ranking: 4367 **S.S. Count:** 10,265

Origin: English. Derived from the Old English name Utta and the Old English word "leah," meaning wood. The name was given to those who came from Utley, a place in Yorkshire, England.

Genealogies: *Descendants of William Utley and Elizabeth Turner of Wake County, North Carolina* was compiled by C. Joan Brink and published in Auburn, Washington, in 1992.

Famous **Utleys:** GEORGE B. UTLEY (1876–1946) of Connecticut, a librarian, was a leader in the American Library Association for many years.

Genealogies: None known.

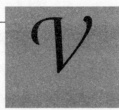

VACCARELLI, VACCARI, VACCARINO, VACCARO (S.S. Abbreviation: Vaccar)

Ranking: 3742 **S.S. Count:** 12,095

Origin: Italian. Derived from the Italian word "vaccaro," meaning cattle herder. The names were given to those who worked herding cows.

Genealogies: None known

VAIL

Ranking: 3124 **S.S. Count:** 14,554

Origin: English. Derived from the Anglo-Norman-French word "veil," meaning watch. The name was given to those who worked as guards.

Famous **Vails:** ALFRED LEWIS VAIL (1807–1859) of New Jersey provided financing for Samuel F.B. Morse's last stages of development of the telegraph. He was the receiver of Morse's 1844 message, "What hath God wrought!" His cousin, THEODORE NEWTON VAIL (1845–1920) of Ohio, was the incorporator of American Telephone & Telegraph Co. (1885) and the developer of the first transcontinental telephone line.

Genealogies: *Joe Vail's Civil War* was compiled by Joe Vail and published in Sparta, Wisconsin, in 1989.

VAILLANT (S.S. Abbreviation: Vailla)

Ranking: 7115 **S.S. Count:** 6010

Origin: French. Derived from the Old French word "vail(l)ant," meaning brave. The name was given to those who were considered courageous.

Famous **Vaillants:** GEORGE C. VAILLANT (1901–1945) of Massachusetts was an archaeologist associated with the American Museum of Natural History in New York who made significant progress in the understanding of Mexican archaeology.

Genealogies: None known.

VALADEZ (S.S. Abbreviation: Valade)

Ranking: 3848 **S.S. Count:** 11,719

Origin: Spanish. Derived from the Germanic first name Baldo, which was derived from the Germanic word "bald," meaning bold.

Genealogies: None known.

VALDES

Ranking: 2195 **S.S. Count:** 20,894

Origin: Portuguese. Cognate to Valadez.

Genealogies: None known.

VALDEZ

Ranking: 542 **S.S. Count:** 74,827

Origin: Spanish. Cognate to Valadez.

Genealogies: None known.

VALENCIA, VALENCIANO (S.S. Abbreviation: Valenc)

Ranking: 1467 **S.S. Count:** 30,335

Origin: Spanish. Derived from the Latin name Valens, which is derived from the Latin word "valēre," meaning to be healthy. The name was given to those who came from Valencia, a region in Spain.

Genealogies: None known.

VALENTE, VALENTIN, VALENTINE, VALENTINELLI, VALENTINO ET AL. (S.S. Abbreviation: Valent)

Ranking: 322 **S.S. Count:** 115,735

Origin: Valentin, Valentine—English, Scottish; Valentin, Valentinelli, Valentino—Italian; Valente—Italian, Portuguese; Valenti—Jewish. Valentin, Valentine, Valentinelli, Valentino: derived from the Latin first name Valentīnus, which was derived from the Latin word "valēre," meaning to be healthy. Valente, Valenti: derived from the medieval first name Valente, which was derived from the Latin word "valēre," meaning to be healthy.

Famous **Bearers:** EDWARD V. VALENTINE (1838–1930) of Virginia was a sculptor whose works include the figure of Robert E. Lee in the Lee Mausoleum at Washington and Lee University. LILA HARDAWAY MEADE VALENTINE (1865–1921) of Virginia was an educator and the person responsible for introducing kindergartens and vocational training classes to the Richmond (Virginia) schools. RUDOLPH VALENTINO (1895–1926) of Italy was a prominent actor in the United States, starring in such films as *The Sheik* (1921) and *Son of the Sheik* (1926).

Genealogies: *History of the Bill(s) Family and Allied Lines* [and Valentine] was compiled by Everett James Hubbard and published in Long Beach, California, in 1979.

VALENZA, VALENZANI, VALENZANO, VALENZI, VALENZUELA ET AL. (S.S. Abbreviation: Valenz)

Ranking: 1318 **S.S. Count:** 33,792

Origin: Spanish. Derived from the Latin word "valēre," meaning to be healthy. The names were given to those who came from Valencia, the name of several places in Spain.

Genealogies: None known.

VALERI (ALSO VALERIA, VALERIAN, VALERIANI, VALERIANO, VALERIO, VALERIUS)

Ranking: 3661 **S.S. Count:** 12,333

Origin: Valerian—French; Valeri—French, Jewish; Valerius—German; Valeriani, Valeriano, Valeria—Italian. Derived from the Latin surname Valērius, which was most likely derived from the Latin word "valēre," meaning to be healthy.

Genealogies: None known.

VALLE

Ranking: 2289 S.S. Count: 19,881

Origin: English, French, Italian, Portuguese, Spanish. Derived from the Latin word "vallis," meaning valley. The name was given to those who lived in valleys.

Genealogies: None known.

VALLEJO (S.S. Abbreviation: Vallej)

Ranking: 3373 S.S. Count: 13,438

Origin: Spanish. Cognate to Valle.

Famous **Vallejos**: MARIANO GUADELUPE VALLEJO (1808–1890) of California was a soldier and politician who helped establish California's separation from Mexico, then its submission as a state.

Genealogies: None known.

VALLES (ALSO VALLESE, VALLESI)

Ranking: 4586 S.S. Count: 9749

Origin: Vallese, Vallesi—Italian; Valles—Italian, Spanish. Cognates to Valle.

Genealogies: None known.

VAN DE BRINK, VAN DE KAMP, VAN DE LOO, VAN DE MEY ET AL. (S.S. Abbreviation: Van De)

Ranking: 1265 S.S. Count: 34,858

Origin: Dutch, Flemish. The prefix "Van de" means one who lived at or one who came from and was attached to existing surnames. Some common examples are: Van de Brink, Van de Loo, Van de Mey—Dutch; and Van de Kamp—Flemish. Van de Brink: cognate to Brink. Van de Kamp: derived from the Old French word "champ," meaning empty land. The name was given to those who lived near or on empty land. Van de Loo: derived from the Middle Low German and Middle Dutch name "lō" and the Old English "leah," meaning wood. The name was given to those who lived in a clearing. Van de Mey: cognate to May.

Genealogies: *A Partial Genealogy of the Van Deman and Mothershead Families in America* was compiled by Wilma E. Van Deman and published in Washington, D.C., in 1970.

VANCE

Ranking: 671 S.S. Count: 62,638

Origin: English. Derived from the Old English word "fenn," meaning swamp. The name was given to those who lived in a swampy area.

Famous **Vances**: ZEBULON BAIRD VANCE (1830–1894) of North Carolina was a member of Congress from, governor

of, and U.S. senator from that state. LOUIS J. VANCE (1879–1933) of Washington, D.C., was a novelist. His books include *The Lone Wolf* (1914) and *The Lone Wolf's Son* (1931). AP MORGAN VANCE (1854–1915) of Tennessee was Kentucky's first doctor who was exclusively a surgeon. ARTHUR C. (DAZZY) VANCE (1891–1961) of Iowa was a baseball pitcher who led the National League in strikeouts for seven years. He won 15 consecutive games for the Brooklyn Robins in 1924. He was elected to the Baseball Hall of Fame in 1955.

Genealogies: *The Vance Family of Piedmont, North Carolina* was compiled by Vance Voss Smith and published in Kernersville, North Carolina, in 1981. *The Rich Heritage: Being the Story of Harry and Annie Vance* was compiled by Joseph Harvey Vance and published in Lombard, Illinois, in 1957.

VAN CLEAVE, VAN CLEEF, VAN CLEVE (S.S. Abbreviation: Vancle)

Ranking: 4959 S.S. Count: 9030

Origin: Dutch. The prefix "Van" means one who lived at or one who came from and was attached to existing surnames. In this case the names were derived as follows: 1) the names were given to those who came from Cleve, a city and area in Germany. 2) the names were given to those who lived near a cliff.

Genealogies: *The Van Cleef Family* was compiled by Wilson V. Ledley and published in New Orleans, Louisiana, in 1976. *Our Jolly Grandpas* was compiled by Mrs. Iver Longeteig and published in Craigmont, Idaho, in 1974.

VANDENBERG, VAN DEN BERGH, VAN DEN BURG, VANDENCAMP, VAN DEN WALL ET AL. (S.S. Abbreviation: Vanden)

Ranking: 1801 S.S. Count: 25,016

Origin: Dutch. The prefix "Van den" means one who lived at or one who came from and was attached to existing surnames. Some common examples are: Vandenberg, Van den Bergh, Van den Burg, Vandencamp, Van den Horn. Vandenberg, Van den Bergh, Van den Burg: 1) the names were given to those who came from Berg, the name of places in Holland. 2) the names were given to those who lived on or near an incline or hill. Vandencamp: derived from the Old French word "champ," meaning field. The name was given to those who lived in open areas. Van den Wall: derived from the Old English word "w(e)all," meaning wall. The name was given to those who lived near a town wall.

Famous **Bearers**: ARTHUR VANDENBERG (1884–1951) of Michigan was a U.S. senator from that state who led passage of the Marshall Plan and the North Atlantic Treaty Organization (NATO). HOYT S. VANDENBERG (1899–1954) of Wisconsin was the first chief of staff for the U.S. Air Force.

Genealogies: *Gysbert and Claes Van Den Bergh and One Line of Their Descendants* was compiled by Edward C. Vandenburgh and published in Dubuque, Iowa, in 1990. *Van den Bergh Genealogy* was compiled by Edward C. Vandenburgh and published in Dubuque, Iowa, in 1992.

VANDERBILT, VANDERBORNE, VAN DER LINDE, VAN DER POST ET AL. (S.S. Abbreviation: Vander)

Ranking: 286 **S.S. Count:** 125,929

Origin: *Vanderbilt, Van der Post—Dutch; Van der Linde—Dutch, Flemish; Vanderborne—Flemish. The prefix "Van der" means one who lived at or one who came from and was attached to existing surnames. Some common examples include the following. Vanderbilt: derived from the Middle Low German word "bilt," meaning mound. The name was given to those who lived on or near a hill or incline. Vanderborne: derived from the Old English word "burna," meaning stream. The name was given to those who lived near a stream. Van der Linde: derived from the Old High German word "linta," meaning lime tree. The name was given to those who lived near a lime tree. Van der Post: derived from the Middle Low German word "post," meaning post. The name was given to those who lived near a post.*

Famous **Bearers:** CORNELIUS VANDERBILT (1794–1877) of New York, known as Commodore Vanderbilt, started one of the country's most visible economic empires by working as a ferryman in New York. His business grew around steamers and railroads into a substantial transportation and financial empire. His descendants include a son, WILLIAM H. VANDERBILT (1821–1885) of New Jersey. He headed the transportation business after his father's death. William's four sons were CORNELIUS VANDERBILT (1843–1899) of New York, who headed the family business after 1885; WILLIAM K. VANDERBILT (1849–1920) of New York, who worked in the family business; FREDERICK W. VANDERBILT (1856–1938) of New York, a railroad executive; and GEORGE W. VANDERBILT (1862–1914) of New York, who moved to Asheville, North Carolina, and built the Biltmore Estate, a country mansion surrounded by a model agricultural center.

Genealogies: *Commodore Vanderbilt and His Family* was compiled by Dorothy Kelly and published in Hendersonville, North Carolina, in 1989. *Fortune's Children: The Fall of the House of Vanderbilt* was compiled by Arthur T. Vanderbilt and published in New York, New York, in 1989. *Some Descendants of Jan Aertsen Vanderbilt* was compiled by Jean M. Rand and published in Baltimore, Maryland, in 1991.

VANDIVER (S.S. Abbreviation: Vandiv)

Ranking: 4607 **S.S. Count:** 9703

Origin: *Dutch. The name was given to those who came from Vere, the name of a place in Holland.*

Genealogies: None known.

VAN DYK (ALSO VAN DYKE)

Ranking: 1842 **S.S. Count:** 24,559

Origin: *Van Dyk—Dutch; Van Dyke—Dutch, English. The prefix "Van" means one who lived at or one who came from and was attached to existing surnames. In this case, the name was derived from the Middle English words "diche" and "dike" and the Old English word "dic," all meaning work done with the earth. The names were given to those who lived near a dike.*

Famous **Bearers:** NICHOLAS VAN DYKE (1738–1789) and his son, NICHOLAS VAN DYKE (1770–1826), were early political leaders of Delaware. HENRY VAN DYKE (1852–1933) of Pennsylvania was a Presbyterian minister, U.S. minister to the Netherlands and Luxembourg, and author of several books, including *Fisherman's Luck* (1899). His brother, PAUL VAN DYKE (1859–1933) of New York, also was a Presbyterian clergyman and author. He wrote *Catherine de Medicis* (1922), an internationally acclaimed history of France's religious wars. JOHN C. VAN DYKE (1856–1932) of New Jersey was a prominent art critic and author of books on art and nature.

Genealogies: *Van Dyke: Over Three Hundred Years of One Line* was compiled by E. F. Baty and published in Cottage Grove, Oregon, in 1991.

VANG

Ranking: 3902 **S.S. Count:** 11,550

Origin: *Danish, Norwegian. Derived from the Low German and Austrian/Bavarian word "wang," meaning someone who lived near a field.*

Genealogies: None known.

ONAME: VAN HOORN (S.S. Abbreviation: Vanhoo)

Ranking: 2962 **S.S. Count:** 15,369

Origin: *Dutch. The prefix "Van" means one who lived at or one who came from and was attached to existing surnames. In this case, the name is a cognate to Horn.*

Genealogies: None known.

VAN HORN (S.S. Abbreviation: Vanhor)

Ranking: 2053 **S.S. Count:** 22,294

Origin: *Dutch. The prefix "Van" means one who lived at or one who came from and was attached to existing surnames. In this case, the name is a cognate to Horn.*

Genealogies: *A New Jersey Dutch Lineage to Christian Barentsen Van Horne* was compiled by Jean Baber and published in 1975. *Our Dutch Ancestors* was compiled by Ralph H. Dean and published in Woodland, California, in 1978.

The Reverend William Van Horne: His Ancestors and Descendants was compiled by William E. Van Horne and published in Columbus, Ohio, in 1990.

VAN METER (S.S. Abbreviation: Vanmet)
Ranking: 3686 S.S. Count: 12,246
Origin: Dutch. The prefix "Van" means one who lived at or one who came from and was attached to existing surnames. In this case, the name was given to those who came from Meteren, the name of places in France and Holland.

Famous **Van Meters:** JOHN B. VAN METER (1842–1930) of Pennsylvania was a Methodist clergyman who was one of the founders of the Woman's College of Baltimore.

Genealogies: *Loper, Keller, Van Meter* [and] *Allied Lines* was compiled by Melba Wood and published in Godfrey, Illinois, in 1969.

VANN
Ranking: 2262 S.S. Count: 20,192
Origin: English. Transformation of Vance.
Genealogies: None known.

VANOVER (S.S. Abbreviation: Vanove)
Ranking: 4554 S.S. Count: 9810
Origin: Dutch?, Flemish? Uncertain etymology. The prefix "Van" means one who lived at or one who came from and was attached to existing surnames. In this case, the name was probably a combination of this prefix and a surname derived from the Old English word "ōfer," meaning shore, as in by the sea or river. The name was most likely given to those who lived in such a place.
Genealogies: None known.

VAN PELT (S.S. Abbreviation: Vanpel)
Ranking: 4655 S.S. Count: 9606
Origin: Dutch. The prefix "Van" means one who lived at or one who came from and was attached to existing surnames. In this case, the name is a cognate to Pelletier.
Genealogies: None known.

VAN SICKLE, VAN SICKEL (S.S. Abbreviation: Vansic)
Ranking: 4380 S.S. Count: 10,246
Origin: Dutch. The prefix "Van" means one who lived at or one who came from and was attached to existing surnames. In this case, the name was given to those who lived on or near land shaped like a sickle.
Genealogies: None known.

VAN WINCKEL (S.S. Abbreviation: Vanwin)
Ranking: 3975 S.S. Count: 11,373
Origin: Flemish. The prefix "Van" means one who lived at or one who came from and was attached to existing sur-

names. In this case, the name was derived from the Middle High German word "winkel," meaning corner. The name was given to those lived on a corner and to those who owned a corner store.

Genealogies: *The Van Winkle Family* was compiled by Marilyn Larner Hicks and published in Wolfe City, Texas, in 1990.

VAN ZANDEN (S.S. Abbreviation: Vanzan)
Ranking: 4107 S.S. Count: 11,005
Origin: Dutch. The prefix "Van" means one who lived at or one who came from and was attached to existing surnames. In this case, the name was derived from the Danish, German, Middle English, and Swedish word "sand." The name was given to those who lived on sandy land.
Genealogies: None known.

VARELA
Ranking: 2914 S.S. Count: 15,600
Origin: Spanish. Derived from the Late Latin word "vara," meaning forked stick. The name was sometimes given to those who kept animals or to those who used a stick to command.
Genealogies: None known.

VARGAS
Ranking: 413 S.S. Count: 95,709
Origin: Portuguese, Spanish. Derived from the Spanish and Portuguese word "varga," meaning shack, incline, or soggy winter field. The name was given to those who lived or worked in or near such places.
Genealogies: None known.

VARGO
Ranking: 4073 S.S. Count: 11,101
Origin: Hungarian? Uncertain etymology. The name was possibly given to those who worked as cobblers or shoemakers.
Genealogies: None known.

VARNERIN, VARNERINI (S.S. Abbreviation: Varner)
Ranking: 1856 S.S. Count: 24,399
Origin: Italian. Cognates to Warner.
Genealogies: None known.

VARNEY
Ranking: 3899 S.S. Count: 11,573
Origin: English, French. Derived from the Gaulish word "ver(n)," meaning alder, and the local suffix "-acum." The name was given to those who lived in Saint-Paul-du-Varnay, the name of several places in northern France.

Genealogies: *Charles Varney and Rachel Parker of Berwick, Maine: Their Ancestors and Descendants* was compiled by Ruth Varney Held and published in San Diego, California, in 1976.

VASQUES (S.S. Abbreviation: Vasque)
Ranking: 364 S.S. Count: 106,533
Origin: Portuguese. Cognate to Velasco.
Genealogies: None known.

VAUGHAN (S.S. Abbreviation: Vaugha)
Ranking: 715 S.S. Count: 58,931
Origin: Irish, Welsh. Irish: derived from the Anglicized version of Gaelic last names such as Mohan, which is derived from the word "moch," meaning timely. Welsh: transformation of Baugh.

Famous **Vaughans:** BENJAMIN VAUGHAN (1751–1835), born in Jamaica, was a propagandist associated with Benjamin Franklin during the American Revolution. DANIEL VAUGHAN (1818–1879), born in Ireland, was recognized as a scientific genius in astronomy, math, and chemistry. VICTOR C. VAUGHAN (1851–1929) of Missouri was a biochemist who was a pioneer in the teaching of bacteriology at the University of Michigan. THOMAS W. VAUGHAN (1870–1952) was a geologist, paleontologist, and oceanographer who became an authority on stratigraphy. WAYNE W. VAUGHAN (1913–1969) of Texas, as president of Vaughan Interior Walls, Inc., in California, was a pioneer in the development of the interior wallboard. He is credited with the concept of movable partitions.

Genealogies: *John Vaughan Settled Newport, Rhode Island, 1638* was compiled by Herman Vaughan Griffin and published in Rutland, Vermont, in 1976. *Vaughan Pioneers: William and Fereby Vaughan of Russell County, Virginia* was compiled by Lewis Elmo Vaughan and published in Baltimore, Maryland, in 1979. *Vaughans in Wales & America* was compiled by James E. Vaughan and published in Salem, Massachusetts, in 1990.

VAUGHN
Ranking: 301 S.S. Count: 120,544
Origin: Irish, Welsh. Transformation of Vaughan.
Genealogies: *The Vaughn/Cross Family Book* was compiled by James E. Coles and published in Paducah, Kentucky, in 1989. *Boone, Eller, Sledge, Vaughn and Related Families* was compiled by Jesse H. Boone and published in Middleboro, Massachusetts, in 1970.

VAUGHT
Ranking: 3323 S.S. Count: 13,638
Origin: Irish?, German? Uncertain etymology.
Genealogies: *My Folks: Pritchard, Vaught, Beasley, Sargent* was compiled by Thelma Sargent and published in Mesa, Arizona, in 1984.

VAZQUEZ (S.S. Abbreviation: Vazque)
Ranking: 341 S.S. Count: 111,335
Origin: Spanish. Cognate to Velasco.
Genealogies: None known.

VEAL
Ranking: 4405 S.S. Count: 10,183
Origin: English. 1) derived from the Anglo-Norman-French word "viel," meaning old. The name was given to elderly men. 2) derived from the Anglo-Norman-French word "ve(d)l," meaning calf. The name was given to those who worked as calf herders or who were thought to have calflike qualities.
Genealogies: None known.

VEGA
Ranking: 558 S.S. Count: 73,348
Origin: Spanish. Uncertain etymology. Derived from a pre-Roman word possibly having to do with the irrigation of the land. The name was given to those who lived near a meadow.
Genealogies: None known.

VELA
Ranking: 2736 S.S. Count: 16,633
Origin: Spanish. 1) derived from a now-unknown Germanic medieval first name, a component of which was the Germanic word "wig," meaning war. 2) cognate to the English definition of Veil.
Genealogies: None known.

VELASCO (S.S. Abbreviation: Velasc)
Ranking: 3258 S.S. Count: 13,955
Origin: Spanish. Derived from a common medieval first name (Basque in origin) that was derived from the word "bela," meaning crow, and the suffix "-sko," meaning small.
Genealogies: None known.

VELASQUEZ (S.S. Abbreviation: Velasq)
Ranking: 1312 S.S. Count: 33,827
Origin: Spanish. Uncertain etymology. Most likely a transformation of Velasco.
Genealogies: None known.

VELAZQUEZ (S.S. Abbreviation: Velazq)
Ranking: 942 S.S. Count: 45,925
Origin: Spanish. Transformation of Velasco.
Genealogies: None known.

VELEZ
Ranking: 534 S.S. Count: 75,882
Origin: Spanish. Transformation of Vela.
Genealogies: None known.

VENABLES (S.S. Abbreviation: Venabl)

Ranking: 2915 **S.S. Count:** 15,599

Origin: English. Uncertain etymology. Probably derived from the Late Latin word "vēnābulum," meaning hunting area. The name was given to those who came from Venables, the name of a place in England.

Genealogies: None known.

VENTUR (ALSO VENTURA, VENTURE, VENTURELLA, VENTURELLI, VENTURINI ET AL.)

Ranking: 2090 **S.S. Count:** 21,978

Origin: Ventur, Venture—English; Ventura—Catalan, Italian (sometimes Jewish), Portuguese, Spanish; Venturella, Venturelli, Venturini—Italian. Ventur, Venture: derived from the Middle English and Middle French word "aventure," meaning to chance. Ventura, Venturella, Venturelli, Venturini: cognates to Venture. Venturi, Venturini: transformations of Ventura. Derived from the medieval first name Bonaventura, meaning good fortune.

Genealogies: None known.

VERA

Ranking: 2916 **S.S. Count:** 15,598

Origin: Spanish. Derived from the Spanish word "vera," meaning river bank. The name was given to those who lived by a river bank or to those who came from a place with the word "vera" in its name.

Genealogies: None known.

VERMILION, VERMILLION (S.S. Abbreviation: Vermil)

Ranking: 4450 **S.S. Count:** 10,072

Origin: French? Uncertain etymology. The names probably refer to the color vermillion and were most likely given to those with ruddy complexions.

Genealogies: None known.

VERNON

Ranking: 1892 **S.S. Count:** 23,890

Origin: English, French. Derived from the Gaulish word "ver(n)," meaning alder, and the Gallo-Roman ending "-o." The name was given to those who came from places named Vernon in England and France.

Famous Vernons: SAMUEL VERNON (1683–1737) of Rhode Island was a silversmith in Newport noted for his craftsmanship and design. His son, WILLIAM VERNON (1719–1806), was a distinguished naval officer in the developing American navy.

Genealogies: None known.

VEST

Ranking: 2933 **S.S. Count:** 15,525

Origin: Norwegian. Cognate to West.

Famous Vests: GEORGE G. VEST (1830–1904) of Kentucky was a U.S. senator from Missouri.

Genealogies: *The Reverend J. J. Vest and Some of His Kinfolk* was compiled by Lora Smith Cooper Ross and published in Melbourne, Alaska, in 1985.

VETTER (ALSO VETTERLE)

Ranking: 3508 **S.S. Count:** 12,855

Origin: German. Derived from the Middle High German word "vete(r)," meaning uncle.

Genealogies: None known.

VICK

Ranking: 2305 **S.S. Count:** 19,723

Origin: English, Frisian. English: derived from the Anglo-Norman-French word "léveske," meaning "the Bishop" (H&H). Frisian: transformation of Frederick.

Famous Vicks: JAMES VICK (1818–1882) of England was a horticulturist, publisher, and businessman. He was publisher of *Vick's Monthly Magazine*, and he developed one of the largest mail-order seed companies in the United States.

Genealogies: *Reverend Newit Vick, Founder of Vicksburg, Mississippi* was compiled by James Morris Perrin and published in Hammond, Louisiana, in 1990. *The Vick Family, 1880–1983* was compiled by James Bailey Parker and published in 1983.

VICKER (ALSO VICKERS, VICKERY)

Ranking: 986 **S.S. Count:** 44,487

Origin: English. Derived from the Middle English word "vicare," meaning priest. Vicker, Vickery: the names were given to those who worked as priests or who carried out pastoral duties in the absence of a priest. Vickers: the name was given to those who worked as servants for priests or who were the sons of priests.

Famous Bearers: HOWARD L. VICKERY (1892–1946) of Ohio was a naval officer who supervised the building of more than 5500 ships during World War II.

Genealogies: *Wiley Vickers: Pioneer of Coffee County, Ga* was compiled by Jessie H. and Delma (Wilson) Paulk and published in Tallahassee, Florida, in 1991.

VICTOR (ALSO VICTORSON)

Ranking: 1952 **S.S. Count:** 23,204

Origin: French. Derived from the Latin first name Victor, meaning conquerer.

Famous Bearers: FRANCES AURETTA FULLER VICTOR (1826–1902) of New York and METTA VICTORIA FULLER VICTOR (1831–1885) of New York were sisters who married brothers. They were both writers: Frances wrote poetry and Metta wrote novels. Frances also became a top authority on the history of the Pacific Northwest. ORVILLE JAMES VICTOR

(1827–1910) of Ohio, husband of Metta, was an editor who specialized in producing inexpensive books and magazines.

Genealogies: None known.

VIDAL

Ranking: 3431 S.S. Count: 13,161
Origin: Italian, Jewish. Transformation of Vitale.
Genealogies: None known.

VIEIRA

Ranking: 4333 S.S. Count: 10,336
Origin: Portuguese. Derived from the Late Latin word "veneria," a version of the word for the goddess Venus, and the Portuguese word "vieira," meaning shell. The name was given as a first name, and to those who came from places marked by scallop shell-like depressions.
Genealogies: None known.

VIERA

Ranking: 3971 S.S. Count: 11,399
Origin: Italian?, Portuguese? Uncertain etymology. Italian: possibly a cognate to Oliver. Portuguese: possibly a cognate to Vieira.

VIGIL

Genealogies: None known.
Ranking: 1584 S.S. Count: 28,253
Origin: Spanish. 1) the name means "descendant of Vigil" (ES). 2) the name means "one born on the feast of the nativity" (ES).
Genealogies: None known.

VILLA

Ranking: 1709 S.S. Count: 26,156
Origin: Italian. Cognate to Ville (French). Derived from the Old French word "ville," meaning settlement. The name was given to those who lived in villages or towns.
Genealogies: None known.

VILLALBA, VILLALOBOS (S.S. Abbreviation: Villal)

Ranking: 1573 S.S. Count: 28,420
Origin: Spanish. Villalba: derived from "villa" and "alba," meaning settlement and white. The name was given to those who came from Villabia, the name of places in Spain. Villalobos: derived from the Late Latin word "villa" and the name Lupus, meaning settlement and wolf. The name was given to those who came from places in Zamora, Spain.
Genealogies: None known.

VILLAN (ALSO VILLANEAU, VILLANELLO, VILLANOVA, VILLANUEVA ET AL.)

Ranking: 972 S.S. Count: 44,928

Origin: Villaneau, Villanello—English, French; Villanova, Villanueva—Spanish. Villaneau, Villanello: derived from the Middle English and Old French words "vilein" and "vilain," meaning feudal serf. The names were given to serfs and peasants who served lords. Villanova, Villanueva: derived from the Spanish words "villa" and "nueva," meaning settlement and new. The names were given to those who lived in places so named.
Genealogies: None known.

VILLAR (ALSO VILLARD, VILLAREL, VILLARET, VILLARS ET AL.)

Ranking: 642 S.S. Count: 64,849
Origin: English, French. Derived from the Late Latin word "villare," meaning remote farm. The name was given to those who lived in many of the similarly named places in France.
Genealogies: None known.

VILLEGAS (S.S. Abbreviation: Villeg)

Ranking: 1940 S.S. Count: 23,303
Origin: Spanish. Derived from the Spanish word "villa," meaning settlement, and the first name "Egas."
Genealogies: None known.

VINCENDEAU, VINCENDET, VINCENT, VINCENTI ET AL. (S.S. Abbreviation: Vincen)

Ranking: 583 S.S. Count: 71,064
Origin: Vincent—English, French, Irish; Vincendeau, Vincendet—French; Vincenti—Italian. English, French, Italian: derived from the medieval first name Vincent, which came from the Latin name Vincentius, a derivative of "vincere," meaning to conquer. Irish: derived from the Gaelic name Mac Dhuibhinse, which is derived from the first name Duibhinse, which is derived from the words "dubh" and "inis," meaning black and island.

Famous **Bearers:** MARY ANN VINCENT (1818–1887), born in England, emigrated to Massachusetts and became a successful Boston actress. A hospital was founded in her memory. JOHN H. VINCENT (1832–1920) of Alabama was a Methodist clergyman who developed a uniform Sunday-school program that was adopted by Protestant churches around the world. FRANK VINCENT (1848–1916) of New York was a world traveler and collector who wrote the book *The Land of the White Elephant* (1874). GEORGE E. VINCENT (1864–1941) of Illinois was president of the University of Minnesota, then president of the Rockefeller Foundation.

Genealogies: *The Vincent Family: Descendants of Adrian Vincent* was compiled by Anna M. Vincent and published in Millbrook, New York, in 1959. *The Vincent Family Genealogy* was compiled by Clyde W. and Ida C. Vincent and published in 1975. *Vincent Family Records* was compiled by Sheridan Eugene Vincent and published in Rochester, New York, in 1977–1979.

VINES

Ranking: 3412 **S.S. Count:** 13,256

Origin: English. Derived from the Middle English word "vine," meaning vine. The name was given to those who lived near vineyards.

Genealogies: None known.

VINSON

Ranking: 1248 **S.S. Count:** 35,292

Origin: English, French. Cognate to Vincent.

Famous **Vinsons:** CARL VINSON (1883–1981) of Georgia was a member of Congress from his home state for 50 years (1914–1964), one of the longest tenures ever in the U.S. House of Representatives. FREDERICK M. VINSON (1890–1953) of Kentucky was chief justice of the U.S. Supreme Court (1946–1953).

Genealogies: None known.

VITALE

Ranking: 2694 **S.S. Count:** 16,890

Origin: Italian, Jewish. Derived from the Latin name Vitālis, a derivative of "vita," meaning life. Jewish: derived from the Jewish/Hebrew name Chayim, meaning life.

Famous **Vitales:** FERRUCCIO VITALE (1875–1933), born in Italy, came to the United States as a diplomat. He later resided in New York and developed a practice in landscape architecture, and he is credited with advancing the status of his profession as a fine art.

Genealogies: None known.

VOGEL

Ranking: 1009 **S.S. Count:** 43,302

Origin: Dutch/Flemish, German, Jewish. Dutch/Flemish, German: derived from the German name Vogel, meaning bird. The name was given to those who worked as bird catchers or who were timid. Jewish: transformation of the modern German name Vogel, meaning bird.

Genealogies: *The Putzier-Vogel and Groth-Nielsen Families* was compiled by Clifford R. Putzier and published in Strafford, Missouri, in 1983.

VOGT

Ranking: 1761 **S.S. Count:** 25,489

Origin: German. Derived from the Middle High German word "voget," meaning farm manager or bailiff. The name was given to those who worked as such.

Genealogies: *The Astronom's Passengers: The Vogt Family in Southern Illinois* was compiled by Ann L. Nilsson and published in Ames, Iowa, in 1989.

VOIGT

Ranking: 4343 **S.S. Count:** 10,319

Origin: German. Cognate to Vogt.

Genealogies: None known.

VOLK

Ranking: 3708 **S.S. Count:** 12,170

Origin: German, Jewish. German: derived from a Germanic medieval first name with the component "folk," meaning people. Jewish: derived from the German word "folk," meaning people, or possibly from the Polish word "wilk," meaning wolf.

Famous **Volks:** LEONARD WELLS VOLK (1828–1895) of New York was a sculptor known for his accurate portraiture and his works of Abraham Lincoln.

Genealogies: *The Volk Family, 1700–1972 From Pfullingen, Wurttemberg, Germany* was compiled by Bernice Close Shackelton and published in Pittsburg, Kansas, in 1973.

VOLLMER, VOLLMERT (S.S. Abbreviation: Vollme)

Ranking: 4436 **S.S. Count:** 10,102

Origin: German. Derived from the first name Folkmar, which is derived from "folk" and "meri/mari," meaning people and famous.

Genealogies: None known.

VOLPE

Ranking: 4026 **S.S. Count:** 11,254

Origin: Italian, Jewish. Italian: Derived from "volpe," meaning fox. Jewish: derived from the Yiddish name of a town in Belorussia called Volpe.

Genealogies: None known.

VOORHEES (S.S. Abbreviation: Voorhe)

Ranking: 4597 **S.S. Count:** 9724

Origin: Dutch. The name was given to those who lived near Hees, the name of places in Holland.

Famous **Voorheeses:** DANIEL W. VOORHEES (1827–1897) of Ohio was a member of Congress and a U.S. senator from Indiana. EDWARD B. VOORHEES (1856–1911) of New Jersey was an agriculturist who, as director of the New Jersey Experiment Station, developed short courses for farmers. He also wrote books on his specialty, including *Fertilizers* (1898).

Genealogies: *Through a Dutch Door: 17th Century Origins of the Van Voorhees Family* was compiled by the Van Voorhees Association and published in Wilmington, Delaware, in 1992.

VOSS

Ranking: 1563 **S.S. Count:** 28,539

Origin: English, German. English: derived from the Old

English word "foss" and the Old French word "fosse," meaning ditch. German: cognate to the English definition of Fox.
Genealogies: None known.

VU
Ranking: 4204 **S.S. Count:** 10,745
Origin: Vietnamese? Uncertain etymology.
Genealogies: None known.

WACHTE, WACHTEL, WACHTER
(S.S. Abbreviation: Wachte)
Ranking: 4349 S.S. Count: 10,309
Origin: German, Jewish. Wachtel (German): derived from the Middle High German word "wachtele" and the Old High German word "wahtala," both meaning quail. The name was given to those who were timid. Wachtel (Jewish): derived from the German word "wachtel" or the Yiddish word "vakhtl," both meaning quail. Wachter (German): derived from the Middle High German word "wachte," meaning watch. The name was given to those who worked as watchmen. Wachter (Jewish): derived from the German word "wachter," meaning watchman. The name may have been given to those who worked in synagogues as beadles.
Genealogies: None known.

WADDEL, WADDELL (S.S. Abbreviation: Waddel)
Ranking: 1430 S.S. Count: 31,188
Origin: Scottish. Possibly derived from the Old English word "wedd" and the Old English word "dœl," meaning pledge and valley. The names were given to those who came from Wedale, a place near Edinburgh, Scotland.
Famous Bearers: HUGH WADDELL (1734?–1773) of Ireland was a colonial soldier who built and commanded Fort Dobbs on the Rowan County frontier in North Carolina. He was the leader of the group opposing the Stamp Act in North Carolina. MOSES WADDEL (1770–1840) of North Carolina was a schoolmaster whose pupils included the 19th-century politician John C. Calhoun. JAMES IREDELL WADDELL (1824–1886) of North Carolina was commander of the Confederate ship *Shenandoah* during the Civil War and the first Confederate naval commander to sail around the world. ALFRED MOORE WADDELL (1834–1912) of North Carolina was a member of Congress from North Carolina and the mayor of Wilmington, North Carolina. JOHN ALEXANDER LOW WADDELL (1834–1938) of Canada was a civil engineer best known as a bridge builder. He was responsible for the South Halsted Street Bridge, Chicago (1893).
Genealogies: None known.

WADE
Ranking: 273 S.S. Count: 130,765
Origin: English. 1) derived from the Middle English first name Wade and/or the Old English name Wada, which is derived from the verb "wadan," meaning to go. 2) derived from the Old English word "(ge)woed," meaning to go.
Famous Wades: BENJAMIN FRANKLIN WADE (1800–1878) of Ohio was a U.S. senator who was vehemently opposed to Abraham Lincoln and his Reconstruction plan. He was the cosponsor of the Wade-Davis Bill, which would have coun-teracted Reconstruction. After Lincoln's death he worked for the impeachment of President Andrew Johnson. As president pro tempore of the U.S. Senate, he would have assumed the presidency had Johnson been convicted and removed from office. He was so confident that that would happen that he selected his cabinet before the proceedings were over. Unsuccessful in both his presidential hopes and his reelection bid to the Senate, he returned to Ohio and his law practice.
Genealogies: *Pushed Back to Strength: A Black Woman's Journey Home* was compiled by Gloria Wade-Gayles and published in Boston, Massachusetts, in 1993. *Wade-Waid-Waide* was compiled by Ophelia Richardson Wade and published in Bragg City, Missouri, in 1975.

WADSWORTH (S.S. Abbreviation: Wadswo)
Ranking: 3206 S.S. Count: 14,151
Origin: English. Transformation of Wordsworth. Derived from the Old English first name Wœddi and the word "word," meaning enclosure. The name was given to those who came from Wadsworth, a place in West Yorkshire, England.
Famous Wadsworths: JEREMIAH WADSWORTH (1743–1804) of Connecticut was a member of the Continental Army and a member of Congress. He was one of the founders of the Bank of North America. PELEG WADSWORTH (1748–1829) of Massachusetts was a general in the Revolutionary War and a member of Congress from Maine. JAMES WADSWORTH (1768–1844) of Connecticut was a land developer in the area of Geneseo, New York. His son, JAMES SAMUEL WADSWORTH (1807–1864) of New York, was the general of volunteers in the Civil War. He died from wounds he received at the Battle of the Wilderness. JAMES WOLCOTT WADSWORTH JR. (1877–1952) of New York was a major figure in the politics of New York at both the state and national level. He was one of the framers of the Selective Service Act of 1940.
Genealogies: *George Allen Wadsworth—Pilley to Panaca* was compiled by Helen Free VanderBeek and published in Idaho Falls, Idaho, in 1983. *The Wadsworth Family in America, 1632–1985* was compiled by Mary Jane Fry Wadsworth and published in Utica, Kentucky, in 1985.

WAGGONER (S.S. Abbreviation: Waggon)
Ranking: 2130 S.S. Count: 21,485
Origin: German. Transformation of Wagner.
Genealogies: *The Descendants of Michael Wagoner, ca. 1774–1826* [also Waggoner] was compiled by Margaret M. Wagner and published in Cedar Rapids, Iowa, in 1976.

WAGNER
Ranking: 138 S.S. Count: 217,575
Origin: German, Jewish. Derived from the Middle High

German word "wagen," meaning cart. The name was given to those who worked with or drove wagons.

Famous **Wagners:** WILLIAM WAGNER (1796–1885) of Pennsylvania was a student of geology and mineralogy and the founder of Wagner Free Institute of Science (1855). WEBSTER WAGNER (1817–1882) of New York was the designer of sleeping cars and drawing-room cars for the New York Central Railroad. JOHN PETER (HONUS) WAGNER (1874–1955) of Pennsylvania is considered one of the best all-around baseball players ever. As shortstop with the Pittsburgh Pirates for 17 years, he was the National League's batting champion for eight years, and he led the league in stolen bases for five years. ROBERT F. WAGNER (1877–1953), born in Germany, was a U.S. senator from New York who introduced a number of social reform acts, including the Social Security Act and the National Labor Relations Act.

Genealogies: *Wagners Wagons Westward* was compiled by Thelma Behimer Wagner and published in Boulder, Colorado, in 1984. *John Wagner and His Twelve Children of Harrison County, Ohio and Surrounding Counties, 1776–1984* was compiled by Audrey L. Wagner Woodruff and published in Independence, Missouri, in 1984. *The Descendants of Michael Wagoner, ca. 1774–1826* was compiled by Margaret M. Wagner and published in Cedar Rapids, Iowa, in 1976.

WAGONER (S.S. Abbreviation: Wagone)

Ranking: 2243 **S.S. Count:** 20,444
Origin: German, Jewish. Cognate to Wagner.
Genealogies: *The Descendants of Michael Wagoner, ca. 1774–1826* was compiled by Margaret M. Wagner and published in Cedar Rapids, Iowa, in 1976.

WAHL

Ranking: 2433 **S.S. Count:** 18,650
Origin: Jewish, Swedish. Jewish: derived from the German word "wahl," meaning election. The name was taken by those who "claimed descent from Saul Katzenellenbogen" (H&H), believed to be king of Poland at one time in Jewish folklore. Swedish: transformation of Wall.
Famous **Wahls:** WILLIAM HENRY WAHL (1848–1909) of Pennsylvania was a metallurgist and the discoverer of the thermit process.
Genealogies: None known.

WAINWRIGHT (S.S. Abbreviation: Wainwr)

Ranking: 4568 **S.S. Count:** 9778
Origin: English. Derived from the Middle English word "wain" and the Old English word "wyrhta," meaning wagon and craftsman. The name was given to those who made wagons.
Famous **Wainwrights:** JONATHAN MAYHEW WAINWRIGHT (1792–1854) was an Episcopal clergyman who was bishop

of New York and a founder of New York University. His son, JONATHAN MAYHEW WAINWRIGHT (1821–1863) of New York, was a Union naval commander during the Civil War who was instrumental in reducing Confederate strength on the Mississippi River. RICHARD WAINWRIGHT (1817–1862) of Massachusetts was a navy commander whose tours of duty included the helm of David Farragut's flagship, the *Hartford.* His son, RICHARD WAINWRIGHT (1849–1926) of Washington, D.C., was commander of the *Gloucester* during the battle of Santiago Bay. JONATHAN MAYHEW WAINWRIGHT (1883–1953) of Washington was an army officer who was a prisoner of war for much of World War II, until he was rescued by parachutists. He succeeded Douglas MacArthur as commander of the Fourth Army.

Genealogies: None known.

WAITE

Ranking: 1989 **S.S. Count:** 22,784
Origin: English. Derived from the Anglo-Norman-French word "waite," meaning watch. The name was given to those who worked as watchmen.
Famous **Waites:** MORRISON R. WAITE (1816–1888) of Connecticut was a chief justice of the U.S. Supreme Court. His written opinions totaled more than a thousand.
Genealogies: *Corbin-Waite-Cooper of Baltimore County and City* was compiled by Dorothy Cooper Knoff and published in East Sandwich, Massachusetts, in 1983. *Six Generations of Descendants from Sylvestor Craig, Timothy Walker, Martin Waite, Sr., and Nathan Hough* was compiled by Dorothy Marsh Brunka and published in 1979.

WAKEFIELD (S.S. Abbreviation: Wakefi)

Ranking: 2264 **S.S. Count:** 20,180
Origin: English. Derived from the Old English words "wacu" and "feld," meaning country fair and field. The name was given to those who came from Wakefield, a place in West Yorkshire, England.
Genealogies: None known.

WALDEN

Ranking: 1276 **S.S. Count:** 34,681
Origin: English. Derived from the Old English words "wealh" and "denu," meaning stranger or serf and field. The name was given to those who came from Walden, the name of several places in England.
Famous **Waldens:** JOHN MORGAN WALDEN (1831–1914) of Ohio was a journalist in Illinois and Kansas and worked for the betterment of conditions for blacks.
Genealogies: None known.

WALDMAN, WALDMANN (S.S. Abbreviation: Waldma)

Ranking: 4658 **S.S. Count:** 9599

Origin: English, German, Jewish. English, German: derived from the Old English word "w(e)ald" and the Old High German word "wald." The names were given to those who lived in or near woods. Jewish: uncertain etymology. The name was probably given to those who lived near woods or worked with wood.

Genealogies: None known.

WALDRON (S.S. Abbreviation: Waldro)

Ranking: 1033 **S.S. Count:** 42,345

Origin: English. 1) derived from a Germanic first name comprising the words "walh" and "hrafn," meaning foreigner and raven. 2) derived from the Old English words "w(e)ald" and "œrn," meaning woods and home. The name was given to those who lived in Waldron, a place in Sussex, England.

Genealogies: None known.

WALKER

Ranking: 23 **S.S. Count:** 702,429

Origin: English, Scottish. 1) derived from the Old English word "wealcere," meaning to cleanse or thicken cloth. The name was given to those who worked with cloth. 2) derived from the Middle English words "wall" and "kerr," meaning wall and swamp. The name was given to those who came from a place in Northumberland, England.

Famous **Walkers:** AMASA WALKER (1799–1875) of Connecticut was an economist and professor, a member of Congress from Massachusetts, and author of *The Science of Wealth* (1866). His son, FRANCIS AMASA WALKER (1840–1897) of Massachusetts, also was an economist. He was chief of the U.S. Bureau of Statistics and superintendent of the ninth and tenth U.S. censuses. He also served as president of Massachusetts Institute of Technology. ROBERT J. WALKER (1801–1865) of Pennsylvania was a U.S. senator from Mississippi who was instrumental in establishing the U.S. Department of the Interior. WILLIAM WALKER (1824–1860) of Tennessee was a notorious filibuster. His escapades included invasion of lower California and declaring himself president of an independent republic, plus the capture and election to the presidency of Granada. He later was shot in Honduras. MARY EDWARDS WALKER (1832–1919) of New York, a physician, was a nurse, then assistant surgeon with the Union army during the Civil War. She was awarded the Medal of Honor in 1865, which was rescinded but restored in 1977. She was an outspoken advocate of women's rights who adopted men's clothing as her attire. SARAH BREEDLOVE WALKER (1867–1919) of Louisiana was a black businesswoman and millionaire. She developed a hair-care system for black women called "The Walker Method," preparing it in her kitchen sink. She moved her company to Colorado and sold her product door-to-door. She used her earnings in philanthropic work. EDWARD P. ("MICKEY") WALKER (1901–1981) of New

Jersey was a professional boxer who won 99 bouts and lost 11. He also wrote an autobiography, *The Will to Conquer* (1953).

Genealogies: *Ancestors and Descendants of the Walker Lathrop Family of Chelsea, Vermont* was compiled by M. Gudmundson Walker and published in Portland, Oregon, in 1977. *The Genealogy of the Families Formon-Boisclair, Walker, Beers, Lacy* was compiled by Mary W. Meadows and published in Columbia, South Carolina, in 1980. *Genealogy of the Vale, Walker, Littler and Other Related Families* was compiled by George Walker Vale and published in Winter Park, Florida, in 1973.

WALL

Ranking: 520 **S.S. Count:** 77,326

Origin: English, Irish, Swedish. English: 1) derived from the Old English word "w(e)all," meaning wall. The name was given to those who lived near a stone wall. 2) derived from the Middle English word "wall(e)," meaning stream or spring. The name was given to those who lived near a brook or spring. Irish: derived from the Middle English word "vale," meaning valley. The name was given to those who lived in valleys. Swedish: derived from the words "wall" and "vall," meaning field.

Genealogies: *The Walls of Walltown* was compiled by Anne Wall Thomas and published in North Carolina in 1969. *A George Willard Wall Memorial* was compiled by Juliette (Wall) Pope and published in 1959.

WALLACE, WALLACH (S.S. Abbreviation: Wallac)

Ranking: 101 **S.S. Count:** 274,071

Origin: Wallace—English, Irish, Scottish; Wallach—Czech. Wallace: derived from the Anglo-Norman-French word "waleis," which meant foreign but usually referred to a Celt. Wallach: derived from the word "vlach," meaning Italian or stranger.

Famous **Bearers:** WILLIAM A.A. WALLACE (1817–1899) of Texas was a frontiersman, a protector of life and property from Indian attacks, deliverer of the mail between San Antonio and El Paso, and a neutralist in the Civil War. WILLIAM ROSS WALLACE (1819–1881) of Kentucky was a poet and lawyer and the author of the famous line "And the hand that rocks the cradle, is the hand that rules the world." HENRY AGARD WALLACE (1888–1965) of Iowa was the developer of the first hybrid corn suitable for human consumption. DEWITT WALLACE (1889–1981) of Minnesota founded and published *Reader's Digest* magazine, which was the largest-circulation periodical in the world the year he died. KARL R. WALLACE (1905–1973) of New York was a prominent educator in the discipline of speech and communication. He taught at several universities and was either writer or editor of numerous books in his field.

LURLEEN BURNS WALLACE (1926–1968) of Alabama was the governor of Alabama, succeeding her husband, George C. Wallace, because Alabama law at that time did not allow him to succeed himself. She was only the third woman elected governor in the United States, but she is best known for continuing her husband's policies.

Genealogies: *Wallace-Frierson and Allied Families* was compiled by Charles Hamilton Young and published in Kyle, Texas, in 1982. *The McKnight Families and their Descendants, also, The Wallace and Alexander Families* was compiled by Texarado McKnight Peak and published in Austin, Texas, in 1965.

WALLEN

Ranking: 3003 S.S. Count: 15,123
Origin: Swedish. Transformation of Wall.
Genealogies: *Elisha Wallen: the Longhunter* was compiled by Carolyn D. Wallin and published in Johnson City, Tennessee, in 1990. *A Wallen/Walling Genealogy* was compiled by Maribelle H. Wilder and H. Bruce Wilder Jr. and published in Baltimore, Maryland, in 1985.

WALLER

Ranking: 809 S.S. Count: 52,189
Origin: English. 1) transformation of Wall. 2) the name was given to those who worked as masons. 3) derived from the Middle English word "well(en)," meaning to boil. The name was given to those who extracted salt from ocean water by boiling. 4) derived from the Anglo-Norman-French word "wall(i)er," which was derived from the Old French word "galer," meaning to be festive.

Famous **Wallers:** THOMAS M. WALLER (1840?–1924) of New York was the mayor of New London, Connecticut, and the governor of Connecticut. FREDERIC WALLER (1886–1954) of New York was an inventor of camera equipment for the motion-picture industry, including the first automatic printer and timer and first optical printer. He won an Academy Award for his invention of Cinerama (1954). JUDITH CARY WALLER (1889–1973) of Illinois was a pioneer in the field of radio broadcasting. She was manager of WMAQ radio station in Chicago. THOMAS W. WALLER (1904–1943) of New York was a jazz pianist known as "Fats" Waller. His first successful composition was "Ain't Misbehavin' " (1929). He also composed "Honeysuckle Rose."

Genealogies: None known.

WALLIN (ALSO WALLINGTON, WALLINS)

Ranking: 1750 S.S. Count: 25,601
Origin: Wallington—English; Wallin, Wallins—Swedish. Wallington: derived from the Old English words "wealh" and "tūn," meaning stranger and settlement. The name was given to those who came from Wallington, the name of several places in England. Wallin: Transformation of Wall.

Genealogies: None known.

WALLIS

Ranking: 2531 S.S. Count: 17,906
Origin: English, Irish, Scottish. Transformation of Wallace.

Famous **Wallises:** SEVERN TEACKLE WALLIS (1816–1894) of Maryland was a lawyer, reformer, and leader in the Maryland bar. WILSON DALLAM WALLIS (1886–1970) of Maryland was an anthropologist noted for studying religion and science among Native American tribes.

Genealogies: *The Tennesseans; Family History of Dr. James Deval Wallis 1830–1904* was compiled by Gertrude Morton Price Katz and published in Valley Stream, New York, in 1972.

WALLS

Ranking: 780 S.S. Count: 53,895
Origin: English. Transformation of Wall.
Genealogies: *The Descendants of John May, Sr. and Sarah Jane (Phillips) May* [also Walls] *1760–1967* was compiled by Mrs. Howard Walker Woodruff and published in Kansas City, Missouri, in 1967. *The Walls Family of Delaware* was compiled by Lewis Kiehn and published in Folsom, California, in 1988.

WALSH

Ranking: 235 S.S. Count: 150,531
Origin: English, Irish. English: derived from the Middle English word "walsche," meaning stranger or Celtic person. Irish: transformation of the Gaelic name Breathnach, meaning Briton or Welshman.

Famous **Walshes:** THOMAS JAMES WALSH (1849–1933) of Wisconsin was a U.S. senator from Montana. THOMAS JOSEPH WALSH (1873–1952) of Pennsylvania was a Roman Catholic clergyman and the archbishop of New Jersey. He was known as the Bishop of Charity and Education. EDWARD AUGUSTINE WALSH (1881–1959) of Pennsylvania, known as "Big Ed," was a baseball player, pitching for the Chicago White Sox. He was best known for his "spitball." EDWARD ALOYSIUS WALSH (1885–1956) of Massachusetts was a Roman Catholic clergyman and the founder of the School of Foreign Services. RAOUL WALSH (1887–1980) of New York directed more than 100 movies, including *Thief of Baghdad* (1924) and *High Sierra* (1941).

Genealogies: *Patrick Walsh of Seward County and Related Families* was compiled by Edward V. Walsh and published in Seward, Nebraska, in 1981.

WALTER

Ranking: 144 S.S. Count: 215,054

Origin: English. Derived from a Germanic first name, which was derived from the words "wald" and "heri" or "hari," meaning reign and armed forces.

Famous **Walters:** THOMAS USTICK WALTER (1804–1887) of Pennsylvania was a master bricklayer and in charge of the wings, the dome, and the center extensions of the U.S. Capitol (1851–1865). FRANCIS E. WALTER (1894–1963) of Pennsylvania was a member of Congress from Pennsylvania who specialized in immigration laws and "un-American" activities. BRUNO WALTER (1876–1962) of Germany was conductor of the Metropolitan Opera in New York and the New York Philharmonic Symphony.

Genealogies: *Families of Eliza Walters & Benjamin Franklin Johnson of Orange Co., Indiana* [also Walter] was compiled by James Walters Johnson and published in Baltimore, Maryland, in 1977. *My Cooley-Walters ancestry in from Fairchance, Penna., and Surrounding Areas* [also Walter] was compiled by Kathryn Mercedes Cooley Miller and published in Houston, Texas, in 1987.

WALTHER (S.S. Abbreviation: Walthe)
Ranking: 4207 **S.S. Count:** 10,740
Origin: German. Cognate to Walter.

Famous **Walthers:** CARL FERDINAND WILHELM WALTHER (1811–1887) of Saxony came to the United States as a Lutheran clergyman and was the most influential clergyman in the Lutheran church of his time.

Genealogies: *Walther Family Recollections* was compiled by Emma Gene Seale and published in Austin, Texas, in 1976.

WALTON
Ranking: 386 **S.S. Count:** 100,340
Origin: English. Derived from any of the Old English words "wealh," "w(e)ald," " w(e)all," or "wœll(a)," meaning stranger or British person, woods, bulwark, and brook. The name was given to those who came from Walton, the name of several places in England.

Famous **Waltons:** GEORGE WALTON (1741–1804) of Virginia was a Revolutionary patriot and a signer of the Declaration of Independence. LESTER AGLAR WALTON (1882–1965) of Missouri was editor of *New York Age* and a writer for the *New York World* and the *New York Herald Tribune.*

Genealogies: *A Brief Historical and Genealogical Account of the Walton Family* was compiled by Hattie E. Walton and published in 1972. *Kith and Kin of Willie Adam Walton and Ethel Mae King* was compiled by June Roper Walton and published in Four Oaks, North Carolina, in 1991. *The Waltons of Brunswick County, Virginia* was compiled by Joe C. Tinney and published in Waco, Texas, in 1983.

WALTZ
Ranking: 4553 **S.S. Count:** 9812

Origin: German. Transformation of Walter.
Genealogies: None known.

WALZ
Ranking: 4579 **S.S. Count:** 9762
Origin: German. Transformation of Walter.
Genealogies: *The Walz Genealogical Record* was compiled by Roy Walz and published in Elmira, New York, in 1977.

WANG
Ranking: 1974 **S.S. Count:** 22,978
Origin: Chinese, German, Jewish. Chinese: the name means any of the following: 1) the prince or king, 2) grand, 3) flourishing, 4) hope or expect, 5) prestige. German: derived from the Low German and Austrian and Bavarian word "wang." The name was given to those who lived near a field. Jewish: 1) a cognate to the German name Wang. 2) the name was given to Jews who came from Hungary.
Genealogies: None known.

WARD
Ranking: 66 **S.S. Count:** 364,274
Origin: English, Irish, Jewish. English: derived from the Old English word "weard," meaning sentinel. Irish: derived from the Gaelic name Mac an Bhaird. Jewish: transformation of the Jewish name Warszawski. The name was given to those who came from Warsaw, Poland.

Famous **Wards:** ARTEMUS WARD (1727–1800) of Massachusetts was second in command in the Revolutionary army under George Washington. He later was a member of the Continental Congress, then a member of Congress from Massachusetts. NANCY WARD (1738?–1822) of Tennessee was a Cherokee leader and called the "Pocahontas of the West." She was a friend of the white settlers, warning them several times of danger. In East Tennessee folklore, she is called "Granny" Ward. JOHN Q.A. WARD (1830–1910) of Ohio was a sculptor. His "Indian Hunter" was one of the first statues placed in New York City's Central Park. His works are highly regarded today and are on display throughout government buildings. AARON MONTGOMERY WARD (1843–1913) of New Jersey was the co-founder of a mail-order business in Illinois that escalated into a big business known as Montgomery Ward & Co. His wife, ELIZABETH J. COBB WARD (1857–1926), established a medical and dental school in his memory at Northwestern University. GEORGE GRAY WARD (1844–1922) of England was responsible for the first cable across the Pacific Ocean. ARCH BURDETTE WARD (1896– 1955) of Illinois was a sportswriter and the one who came up with the idea for the all-star baseball and football games.

Genealogies: *Ward: A Genealogical Record of the Wards of Big Sandy* was compiled by Billie Edyth Ward and published in Boons Camp, Kentucky, in 1987. *A Scattered People: An American Family Moves West* was compiled by Gerald W. McFarland and published in New York in 1985. *The Noble Family of Ward* was compiled by James Mayfield Ward and published in 1975.

WARDEN
Ranking: 2885 **S.S. Count:** 15,784

Origin: English. 1) derived from the Anglo-Norman-French word "wardein," which was derived from the Germanic word "warder," meaning to protect. The name was given to those who worked as watchmen. 2) derived from the Old English words "weard" and "dūn," meaning guard and incline. The name was given to those who came from Warden, the name of several places in England.

Genealogies: None known.

WARE
Ranking: 610 **S.S. Count:** 68,633

Origin: English. 1) derived from the Old English words "wœr" and "wer," meaning river and dam. The name was given to those who lived near a river dam. 2) same derivation as in 1. The name was given to those who came from Ware, the name of several places in England. 3) derived from the Old English word "(ge)wœr," meaning cautious. The name was given to those who were careful.

Famous **Wares:** HENRY WARE (1764–1845) of Massachusetts started a divinity school that became Harvard Divinity School. ASHUR WARE (1782–1873) of Massachusetts was an authority on maritime law. EDMUND ASA WARE (1837–1885) of Massachusetts was the superintendent of schools of Georgia and one of the founders of Atlanta University.

Genealogies: *Descendants and Related Families of David Samuel Ware and Amanda Roselee Chesteen Ware* was compiled by Sarah Hattie Hazel Delgado and published in Oxnard, California, in 1985. *Garrett, Catlett, Ware, and Related Families* was compiled by Sunie Garrett Talbert Elliott Fisher and published in Cullman, Alabama, in 1989. *Genealogy of the Descendants of Joseph Ware of Fenwick Colony, England, 1675; His Successors in Florida* was compiled by Franklin Ware and published in Tampa, Florida, in 1969.

WARFIELD (S.S. Abbreviation: Warfie)
Ranking: 3990 **S.S. Count:** 11,332

Origin: English. Derived from the Old English words "wœr" and "feld," meaning fishing dam and pasture land. The name was given to those who came from Warfield, a place in England.

Famous **Warfields:** SOLOMON DAVIES WARFIELD (1859–1927) of Maryland was the postmaster of Baltimore, founder of the Continental Trust Co., and head of the

Seaboard Air Line Railway. He was responsible for the merger of the Baltimore utilities.

Genealogies: *Warfield Records* was compiled by Evelyn Ballenger and published in Annapolis, Maryland, in 1970.

WARNER
Ranking: 323 **S.S. Count:** 115,675

Origin: English. 1) derived from a Germanic first name that was derived from the Germanic words "war(in)" and "heri" or "hari," meaning sentinel and militia. 2) derived from Warrener, a transformation of Warren.

Famous **Warners:** SETH WARNER (1743–1784) of Connecticut was a Revolutionary soldier who aided Ethan Allen and Benedict Arnold in the Battle of Ticonderoga (1775) and was captured at Crown Point. He led a group of Green Mountain Boys and fought in the Battle of Bennington (1777), which is said to have been the turning point in the the Revolution in favor of the colonists. HIRAM WARNER (1802–1881) of Massachusetts was chief justice of the Georgia Supreme Court. JONATHAN TRUMBULL WARNER (1807–1895) of Connecticut was a California pioneer who settled in the Los Angeles area. OLIN LEVI WARNER (1844–1896) of Connecticut was a sculptor responsible for the doors of the Library of Congress. GLENN SCOBEY (POP) WARNER (1871–1954) of New York was a football coach at Carlisle Indian School in Pennsylvania, where he gained fame for his ability to use the plays and the players to their fullest advantage. The youth football teams across the nation are named for him. HARRY MORRIS WARNER (1881–1958) of Poland was the financial manager of Warner Bros. Pictures, Inc., founded in 1923. The "brothers" consisted of four brothers and a sister, with Harry as the president of the business.

Genealogies: *Warner Family History* was compiled by Verle M. Arnold and published in Decorah, Iowa, in 1991. *Ecroyd, Warner, and Morris Genealogy* was compiled by Lewis Ecroyd Morris and published in Earlham, Iowa, in 1976.

WARREN
Ranking: 148 **S.S. Count:** 211,447

Origin: English. 1) derived from a Gaulish word probably having to do with sand. 2) derived from the Anglo-Norman-French word "warrene," meaning an area used for animal cultivation.

Famous **Warrens:** JOSEPH WARREN (1741–1775) of Massachusetts was a physician and Revolutionary patriot who was killed assembling troops for the Battle of Bunker Hill. FRANCIS EMORY WARREN (1844–1929) of Massachusetts was a Wyoming pioneer. He was the first territorial governor and the first governor of the state. He also served as the U.S. senator from Wyoming for more than 30 years.

Genealogies: *Family History of the Warren, Stone, Day-*

ton, Routh, Wurster, Daggett, and Young Families was compiled by Candy Daggett Young and published in Ferriday, Louisiana, in 1983. *Genealogy of Elihue Warren: a descendant of Richard of the Mayflower and of William Sumner, with allied families* was compiled by Racola Ford Cooke and published in Twin Falls, Idaho, in 1981.

WARRIN (ALSO WARRINER)

Ranking: 4419   S.S. Count: 10,144

Origin: English. Transformation of the second definition of Warren.

Genealogies: *The Colonial and European Ancestry of Julia Adelaide Warriner (1853– 1883)* was compiled by Richard L. Dickson and published in Salem, Massachusetts, in 1991.

WASHBURN, WASHBURNE (S.S. Abbreviation: Washbu)

Ranking: 1516   S.S. Count: 29,339

Origin: English. Derived from the Old English first name Walc and the word "burna," meaning brook. The names were given to those who lived by the side of the river Washburn in England.

Famous Bearers: ICHABOD WASHBURN (1798–1868) of Massachusetts was the co-founder of Washburn & Moen, a manufacturer of wire. He was the first to make galvanized iron telegraph wire. ISRAEL WASHBURN (1813–1883) of Maine was a leader of the Republican Party and is rumored to have suggested that the party be called "Republican." He was the governor of Maine and ranks historically as one of the best northern governors. CADWALLADER COLDEN WASHBURN (1818–1882) of Maine was a member of Congress from, then governor of, Wisconsin. After his political career he became a manufacturer of flour, revolutionizing the industry with a new process of milling. He was one of the founders of Washburn, Crosby & Co. (1877). MARGARET F. WASHBURN (1871–1939) of New York City was an experimental psychologist and considered the one who made Vassar College one of the leading psychological centers in the country.

Genealogies: *Nathaniel Washburn: An American Pioneer* was compiled by Catherine Lutes Gowdy and published in Novato, California, in 1988. *Our Washburn Heritage* was compiled by Elaine Washburn Olney and published in Manhattan, Kansas, in 1986. *The Washburn Family in America* was compiled by Brenton P. Washburne and published in Buena Park, California, in 1983.

WASHINGTON (S.S. Abbreviation: Washin)

Ranking: 134   S.S. Count: 222,294

Origin: English. Derived from the Old English first name Wassingatūn, which was derived from the name Wassa and the word "tūn," meaning settlement. The name was given to those who lived in Washington, the name of several places in England.

Famous **Washingtons**: GEORGE WASHINGTON (1732–1799) of Virginia was a planter, soldier, and the first president of the United States. MARTHA DANDRIDGE CUSTIS WASHINGTON (1731– 1802) of Virginia was the wife of George Washington. BOOKER TALIAFERRO WASHINGTON (1856–1915) of Virginia was born into slavery. He worked his way through college and is considered a black educational leader who worked to improve the educational lot of African-Americans. He wrote several books, including *The Future of the American Negro* (1899) and *Up From Slavery* (1901). DINAH WASHINGTON (1924–1963) of Alabama was a singer and pianist known by the nicknames "Queen of the Blues" and "Queen of the Jukeboxes." Her biggest ballad was "What a Difference a Day Makes."

Genealogies: *Wright-Washington and Allied Families* was compiled by Myrtle Viola Sears Steiner and published in Chillicothe, Missouri, in 1967. *Augustine Washington's Descendants* was compiled by John A. Washington and published in 1964. *The Ancestry of Mayor Harold Washington (1922–1987)* was compiled by Curtis G. Brasfield and published in Bowie, Maryland, in 1993.

WASSER (ALSO WASSERMAN, WASSERSTROM)

Ranking: 2874   S.S. Count: 15,831

Origin: Wasser—German, Jewish; Wasserman—Jewish; Wasserstrom—Swedish. Wasser: derived from the Old English word "wœter," meaning water. The name was given to those who lived near water. Wasserman: the name was given to those who worked carrying water. Wasserstrom: cognate to Strom.

Genealogies: None known.

WASSON

Ranking: 3581   S.S. Count: 12,594

Origin: English, Scottish. Transformation of the Norman first name Wazo, which was derived from a Germanic name containing the word "wad," meaning to proceed.

Genealogies: *A Genealogy of the McCullah-Wasson Families* was compiled by Willis Austin McCullah and published in 1990. *Wassons* was compiled by Nellie Mae Conklin and published in Shawnee, Oklahoma, in 1992. *Through the Generations: A Genealogy of the Coffin Family. . . Shockney Family. . . Wasson Family. . .* was compiled by Judith Stoleson and published in 1989.

WATERMAN, WATERMANN (S.S. Abbreviation: Waterm)

Ranking: 2521   S.S. Count: 17,988

Origin: Waterman—English, Flemish/Dutch, Jewish; Watermann—German. Waterman (English): transformation of Walter. Waterman (English, Flemish/Dutch), Wattermann: derived from the Old English word "wœter," meaning water. The name was given to those who lived near water or to those who worked carrying water or with boats. Waterman (Jewish): transformation of Wasserman.

Famous **Bearers:** LEWIS EDSON WATERMAN (1837–1901) of New York obtained the first patent and marketed the first fountain pen under the Ideal Pen Co.

Genealogies: *A Genealogy of the Paine and Waterman Families* was compiled by Robert John Paine and published in 1975. *Descendants of Roger Williams* [also Waterman] was published in Baltimore, Maryland, in 1991.

WATERS

Ranking: 411 **S.S. Count:** 96,427

Origin: English, Irish. English: 1) transformation of Walter. 2) derived from the Old English word "wœter," meaning water. The name was given to those who lived near water. Irish: derived from the Gaelic name Ó Fuarisc(e), meaning descended from people with the last name Fuarisc(e).

Famous **Waterses:** DANIEL WATERS (1731–1816) of Massachusetts was a naval officer in the Continental navy. He was the captain of the *Thorn*, which defeated the British privateers *Governor Tryon* and *Sir William Erskine* on Christmas Day, 1779. ETHEL WATERS (1896–1977) of Pennsylvania was a stage actress on Broadway and a singer noted for songs such as "Heat Wave" and "Stormy Weather." MUDDY WATERS (1915–1983), born McKinley Morganfield in Mississippi, was a blues musician who influenced more than a generation of blues and rock musicians. He led the first electronically amplified blues-rock band and is known for songs such as "Hoochie Coochie Man" and "Got My Mojo Working."

Genealogies: *A Genealogical History of the Farrow, Waters, and Rlated Families* was compiled by Audrey Doris Goolsby Farrow and published in Ripley, Mississippi, in 1973. *One Waters Family* was compiled by Jean Waters Strong and published in Los Altos Hills, California, in 1980. *Waters in Depth, 1648–1978* was compiled by Marjory McGillivray Waters and published in Darien, Connecticut, in 1978.

WATKIN (ALSO WATKINS)

Ranking: 201 **S.S. Count:** 175,249

Origin: English, Scottish. Watkin: derived from the Middle English first name Wat(t), a shortened version of Walter. Watkins: transformation of Watt.

Famous **Bearers:** GEORGE CLAIBORNE WATKINS (1815–1872) of Kentucky was the chief justice of the Arkansas Supreme Court. JOHN ELFRETH WATKINS (1852–1903) of Virginia was the curator of mechanical technology at the U.S. National Museum, Washington, D.C.

Genealogies: *Ancestors and Descendants of George*

Watkins was compiled by George Watkins Anderson Jr. and published in Pleasanton, California, in 1987. *Henry Watkins of Henrico County* was compiled by Jane McMurtry Allen and published in Baltimore, Maryland, in 1985. *James Watkins and Catherine Hen and Their Descendants* was compiled by Austin E. Dwight and published in Downers Grove, Illinois, in 1990.

WATSON

Ranking: 74 **S.S. Count:** 342,015

Origin: English, Scottish. Transformation of Watt.

Famous **Watsons:** ELKANAH WATSON (1758–1842) of Massachusetts was the father of the "agricultural county fairs" in America by sponsoring the first "cattle show" in 1810. THOMAS AUGUSTUS WATSON (1854–1934) of Massachusetts was Alexander Graham Bell's assistant in his telephone experiments. He was the first research and technical head of the Bell Telephone Co. CHARLES ROGER WATSON (1873–1948) was born in Egypt of American missionary parents. He was one of the founders of what became the American University in Cairo and served as its president from 1920 to 1945. THOMAS JOHN WATSON (1874–1956) of New York was the founder of International Business Machines (IBM) Corporation (1924). JOHN BROADUS WATSON (1878–1958) of South Carolina was a psychologist and one of the founders of the school of behavioral psychology, which had as its basis the stimulus-response method of behavior modification. He also was president of the American Psychological Association.

Genealogies: *The American Family of John Watson of the Narragansett Country, Rhode Island* was compiled by George C. Davis and published in Kingston, Rhode Island, in 1983. *Ancestors and Descendants of John and Hannah (Goodwin) Watson of Hartford, Connecticut and Associated Families* was compiled by Ralph Arthur Watson and published in Alexandria, Virginia, in 1985. *Genealogy and History of the Watson Family* was compiled by Samuel E. Watson and published in Santa Rosa, California, in 1988.

WATT

Ranking: 2117 **S.S. Count:** 21,643

Origin: English, Scottish. Derived from the Middle English first name Wat(t), a shortened version of Walter.

Genealogies: *Some Descendants of John Watts of Virginia* [also Watt] was compiled by Soule J. Watt and published in Birmingham, Alabama, between 1943 and 1960.

WATTER (ALSO WATTERS, WATTERSON)

Ranking: 2113 **S.S. Count:** 21,721

Origin: English. Transformations of Walter.

Famous **Bearers:** HARVEY MAGEE WATTERSON (1811–1891) of Tennessee was a member of Congress from Tennessee, then editor of the *Washington Union*. He was a

Unionist and remained loyal to the country throughout the Civil War. His son, HENRY WATTERSON (1840–1921) of Washington, D.C., was a journalist, serving as editor of several newspapers.

Genealogies: None known.

WATTS

Ranking: 304 **S.S. Count:** 120,229

Origin: English, Scottish. Derived from the Middle English first name Wat(t), a transformation of Walter.

Genealogies: *A History of the Watts Family* was compiled by George B. Watts? and published in Garden City, New York, in 1981. *Thomas Watts and Alexander McElwain: Their Ancestors, Descendants, and Related Families* was compiled by Dorothy Claybroke Watts Brooks and published in Camden, Tennessee, in 1980. *Watts, 1687–1975: Ancestry and Descendants of Ridley Watts* was compiled by Harriet Mott Stryker-Rodda and published in New Orleans, Louisiana, in 1975.

WAUGH

Ranking: 2877 **S.S. Count:** 15,814

Origin: English, Scottish. Uncertain etymology. Possibly derived from the Old English word "salh," meaning alien.

Famous Waughs: FREDERICK JUDD WAUGH (1861–1940) of New Jersey was an artist best known as a painter of seascapes.

Genealogies: None known.

WAY

Ranking: 2238 **S.S. Count:** 20,485

Origin: English. Derived from the Old English word "weg," meaning thoroughfare or pathway. The name was given to those who lived next to a thoroughfare, or to those who came from a place with the word "way" in its name.

Genealogies: *Descendants of Robert and Hannah Hickman Way of Chester County, Pennsylvania* was compiled by D. Herbert Way and published in Woodstown, New Jersey, in 1975–1978. *Hezekiah Hiatt & Sarah Davison Way: Their Ancestors and Descendants* was compiled by Mary Elizabeth Way and published in Marinez, California, in 1967.

WAYNE

Ranking: 3241 **S.S. Count:** 14,019

Origin: English. Derived from the Middle English word "wain," meaning wagon. The name was given to those who worked with wagons.

Famous Waynes: ANTHONY WAYNE (1745–1796) of Pennsylvania was a Revolutionary soldier. He was responsible for preventing West Point from falling to the British when Benedict Arnold tried to surrender the fort to them. JAMES MOORE WAYNE (1790?–1867) of Georgia was a justice of the Supreme Court.

Genealogies: None known.

WEATHER, WEATHERTHILL, WEATHERILL, WEATHERITT, WEATHERS ET AL. (S.S. Abbreviation: Weathe)

Ranking: 563 **S.S. Count:** 72,824

Origin: English. Weather, Weathers: derived from the Middle English word "wether," meaning castrated ram. The name was given to those men who resembled a castrated male sheep in sexual ability. The name may also have been given to those who worked as sheep herders. Weatherhill, Weatherill, Weatheritt: derived from the name Wetheral, which was derived from the Old English words "weðð er" and "halh," meaning castrated male sheep and indentation. The name was given to those who came from Wetheral, a place in Cumberland, England.

Genealogies: *Black Seeds in the Blue Grass* was compiled by Jacqueline Annette Sue and published in Corte Madera, California, in 1983. *Descendants of John Martin Weatherford (1814–1892) and Adeline Mobrey Weatherford (1817–1904)* was compiled by Robert E. Weatherford and published in 1992.

WEAVER (ALSO WEAVERS)

Ranking: 176 **S.S. Count:** 189,720

Origin: English. 1) derived from the Middle English word "weven," meaning to weave. The name was given to those who worked as weavers. 2) derived from the Old English word "wēfer(e)," meaning twisting brook. The name was given to those who lived near the river Weaver in Cheshire, England.

Famous Bearers: PHILIP WEAVER (1791–1861) of Rhode Island, with his brothers, was one of the first operators of a cotton mill in the Spartanburg, South Carolina, area. JAMES BAIRD WEAVER (1833–1912) of Ohio was a Union soldier, member of Congress from Iowa, and unsuccessful candidate for president of the United States.

Genealogies: *Henry B. Weaver's Descendants* was compiled by Elizabeth W. Shirk and published in Lititz, Pennsylvania, in 1981. *The George Philip Williams of Craig Co. Virginia and Aylett Weaver of Monroe Co. West Virginia* was compiled by Herman Joseph Williams and published in Portsmouth, Ohio, in 1981. *Virginia to Ohio and States West: Descendants of Peter Weaver and J. Jacob Kopp* was compiled by Mary Mae Cupp Campbell and published in Lima, Ohio, in 1986.

WEBB

Ranking: 130 **S.S. Count:** 229,177

Origin: English, Jewish. English: derived from the Old English word "webba," meaning weaver. The name was given to those who worked as weavers. Jewish: transformation of the Jewish names Web(b)er(man), Webman, and Webb, all cognates to Weaver.

Famous **Webbs:** THOMAS SMITH WEBB (1771–1819) of Massachusetts was a printer and the founder of the the American Masonry system. He also founded the Handel and Haydn Society, Boston. CHARLES HENRY WEBB (1834–1905) of New York was a journalist who worked as a war correspondent during the Civil War. A close friend of Bret Harte's and Mark Twain's, he was the founder and editor of *The Californian* and the publisher of Twain's first book, *The Celebrated Jumping Frog of Calaveras County*. CLIFTON WEBB (1893–1966) of Indiana was a singer, actor, and dancer. He mostly appeared in plays and comedies done for children. He was nominated for an Oscar for his role in *Laura* (1944).

Genealogies: *Webb Families of the Virginias* was compiled by Ronald R. Turner and published in Fairview Park, Ohio, in 1983. *Webb Family of Bearwallow Ridge* was compiled by David G. Webb Jr. and published in Summerville, South Carolina, in 1983.

WEBBER

Ranking: 1197 **S.S. Count:** 36,726

Origin: English, Jewish. Cognate to Weaver and Webb.

Famous **Webbers:** CHARLES WILKINS WEBBER (1819–1856) of Kentucky fought in the Texas war for independence and became a journalist in New York City. He died on an expedition in Nicaragua at the battle of Rivas. HERBERT JOHN WEBBER (1865–1946) of Michigan was a plant physiologist specializing in subtropical horticulture.

Genealogies: *The Dutch Webbers of Indiana and Illinois* was compiled by Ercel Virginia Webber Hunt and published in Deerfield, Illinois, in 1980.

WEBER

Ranking: 234 **S.S. Count:** 150,623

Origin: Dutch, Flemish, Jewish. Cognate to Weaver.

Famous **Webers:** JOSEPH MORRIS WEBER (1867–1942) of New York was a burlesque comedian and teammate of Kewis Maurice Fields. Their routine consisted of blackface, song and dance, and slapstick. MAX WEBER (1881–1961) of Russia was an artist and a pioneer in the genre of cubism and futurism.

Genealogies: *Leonard Weber and His Progeny* was compiled by Jerome F. Weber and published in Utica, New York, in 1982. *A Genealogical Report of the Direct Blood Line Descendants of Peter Sr. and Katharina, nee Schowalter, Weber, 1806–1970* was compiled by Olga Krebill Hirschler and published in 1972.

WEBSTER (S.S. Abbreviation: Webste)

Ranking: 390 **S.S. Count:** 99,014

Origin: English. Cognate to Webb.

Famous **Websters:** PELATIAH WEBSTER (1726–1795) of Connecticut was a Philadelphia merchant, Congregational clergyman, and economist who urged through his writings that the Revolution be supported through taxation, not loans. His essays are collected in *Political Essays on the Nature and Operation of Money, etc.* NOAH WEBSTER (1758–1843) of Connecticut was the maker of dictionaries, including *A Compendious Dictionary of the English Language* and *An American dictionary of the English Language*. His books were considered the very best of their kind. DANIEL WEBSTER (1782–1852) of New Hampshire was a member of Congress, a U.S. senator, twice a secretary of state, and a lawyer. He is best remembered as an orator and lawyer for several Supreme Court cases.

Genealogies: *The Family of William Webster of Rhode Island: A Genealogical History* was compiled by Leo H. Garman and published in Elmhurst, Illinois, in 1982. *Indian Hollow Road: A 19th Century American Family, Their Letters, Their Story* was compiled by JoAnne Meade Webster and published in Louisville, Kentucky, in 1984. *A Webster Genealogy* was compiled by Myrna V. Sandwall and published in Westlake Village, California, in 1978.

WEDDLE

Ranking: 4944 **S.S. Count:** 9061

Origin: Scottish. Derived from the name Wedale, which is of uncertain etymology. The name was given to those who came from Wedale, a place in Scotland.

Genealogies: *Kinfolks, Weddle, Sullivan, Gable, and Roach* was compiled by Elizabeth Weddle Mueting and published in Ventura, California, in 1984.

WEED

Ranking: 3909 **S.S. Count:** 11,534

Origin: English, German. Derived from the name Wido. The name was given to those who lived close to an area characterized by having weeds.

Famous **Weeds:** LEWIS HILL WEED (1886–1952) of Ohio was an anatomist and medical administrator; trustee of the Carnegie Institution of Washington and the Institute for Advanced Study, Princeton; and chief of the medical division of the National Research Council of the National Academy of Sciences. He was a major researcher for the war efforts of the country.

Genealogies: *History of the Weed and Allied Families* was compiled by Charles Allison Weed and published in Baltimore, Maryland, in 1971. *Southern Weeds and Allied Families* was compiled by Louie Clarence Weed and Louie Gordon Weed and published in Baltimore, Maryland, in 1991.

WEEKS

Ranking: 720 **S.S. Count:** 58,565

Origin: English. Transformation of Wick.

Famous **Weekses:** JOSEPH DAME WEEKS (1840–1896) of

Massachusetts was a technical journalist with the *American Manufacturer* and was responsible for initiating the first wage scale for employees.

Genealogies: *Geo. Weekes: Genealogy of the Family of George Weekes, of Dorchester, Mass., 1635– 1650* [also Weeks] was compiled by Robert Dodd Weekes and published in Newark, New Jersey, in 1885. *The Weeks Family of Southern New Jersey* was compiled by Elmer Garfield Van Name and published in Haddonfield, New Jersey, in 1967. *Family Reminiscences* was compiled by Minnie Marcella Feinberg and published in 1992.

WEEMS

Ranking: 3300 **S.S. Count:** 13,743

Origin: *Scottish. Derived from the Old Gaelic word "uaim," meaning cavern, and the plural suffix "s." The name was given to those who came from Weems or Weemyss, places in Scotland.*

Famous **Weemses:** MASON LOCKE WEEMS (1759–1825) of Maryland was an author who wrote *The Life and Memorable Action of George Washington* (1800?). It was in its fifth edition, 1806, that the "hatchet and cherry tree" story first appeared. TED WEEMS (1901–1963) of Pennsylvania was a composer and bandleader. He and his brother Art had several hits, including, "Somebody Stole My Gal," "My Gal Sal," "You're the Cream in My Coffee," and "Heartaches."

Genealogies: None known.

WEGNER

Ranking: 3965 **S.S. Count:** 11,411
Origin: *German. Cognate to Wagner.*
Genealogies: None known.

WEIDNER (S.S. Abbreviation: Weidne)

Ranking: 4025 **S.S. Count:** 11,255

Origin: *German. Derived from the Old High German word "weida," meaning stalking or tracking. The name was given to those who lived near an area used for hunting.*

Famous **Weidners:** REVERE FRANKLIN WEIDNER (1851–1915) of Pennsylvania was the first president of the Chicago Lutheran Seminary.

Genealogies: *Heinrich Weidner, 1717–1792, Catharina Mull Weidner, 1733–1804: Through Four Generations* was compiled by Anne Williams McAllister and published in Lenoir, North Carolina, in 1992.

WEIGEL

Ranking: 4408 **S.S. Count:** 10,170

Origin: *German. Derived from the Germanic first name Wigant, which was derived from the word "wigan," meaning to battle.*

Famous **Weigels:** GUSTAVE WEIGEL (1906–1964) of New

York was an expert in Protestant theology and a pioneer in promoting ecumenism in the United States.

Genealogies: None known.

WEIL

Ranking: 4087 **S.S. Count:** 11,060

Origin: *German, Jewish. German: derived from the Latin word "villa," meaning country dwelling or group of dwellings. The name was given to those who came from various places in Germany. Jewish: uncertain etymology. Probably a transformation of the German name.*

Famous **Weils:** RICHARD WEIL (1876–1917) of New York was a physician and considered an international expert on serology of cancer and immunity. He was the founder of the *Journal of Cancer Research.*

Genealogies: *Strangers in the Land; the Story of Jacob Weil's Tribe* was compiled by Moses Rountree and published in Philadelphia, Pennsylvania, in 1969.

WEILER

Ranking: 4434 **S.S. Count:** 10,114

Origin: *German, Jewish. German: derived from the Late Latin word "villāre," meaning country dwelling. Jewish: transformation of Weil.*

Genealogies: None known.

WEIMER

Ranking: 3600 **S.S. Count:** 12,542

Origin: *German. 1) the name was given to those who came from Weimar, meaning swamp, a place in Thuringia, Germany. 2) the name was given to those who lived near churches. 3) the name means descended of Wigmar.*

Genealogies: *The Weimer Family as Known to 1974* was compiled by Robert E. Weimer and published in Albuquerque, New Mexico, in 1975. *Weimer History* was compiled by Ruth F. Rickert and published in Rockville Centre, New York, in 1983.

WEINBERG, WEINBERGER (S.S. Abbreviation: Weinbe)

Ranking: 1849 **S.S. Count:** 24,491

Origin: *Weinberg—German, Jewish; Weinberger—Jewish. Derived from the Middle High German word "winberc," which was derived from the words "win" and "berc," meaning vine and mound. The names were given to those who lived on a mountainside where grapevines were grown, or to those who worked in vineyards. Jews sometimes took the names ornamentally.*

Genealogies: None known.

WEINER

Ranking: 1609 **S.S. Count:** 27,832
Origin: *German, Jewish. German: derived from the Mid-*

dle High German word "win," meaning vine or wine. The name was given to those who worked as a vendor or manufacturer of wine. Jewish: the name was taken ornamentally.

Genealogies: None known.

WEINGARDT, WEINGART, WEINGARTEN, WEINGARTER, WEINGARTNER ET AL. (S.S. Abbreviation: Weinga)

Ranking: 4895 S.S. Count: 9130

Origin: Weingardt, Weingarter, Weingartner—German; Weingart, Weingarten—Jewish. Weingardt, Weingarter, Weingartner: derived from the Old English words "win" and "geard," meaning wine or vine and garden. The names were given to those who worked in vineyards. Weingart, Weingarten: same derivation as above. The names were sometimes taken ornamentally.

Genealogies: A Walk Through the Vineyards: Ishmael and His Descendants (the Weingarten family) was compiled by Thomas Daniel Knight and published in Birmingham, Alabama, in 1990.

WEINSTEIN, WEINSTEINER, WEINSTOCK (S.S. Abbreviation: Weinst)

Ranking: 1581 S.S. Count: 28,281

Origin: Jewish. Weinstein, Weinsteiner: derived from the Middle High German word "win" and the Old English word "stān," meaning wine or vine and stone. Weinstock: derived from the Middle High German word "win," meaning wine, and the word "stock" (in this case the meaning of the name is "wine stone").

Genealogies: Memoirs of Harry Weinstein and Family Reflections was compiled by Harry Weinstein and published in 1979.

WEIR

Ranking: 1575 S.S. Count: 28,340

Origin: English, Irish, Scottish. English: transformation of Ware. Irish: Anglicized version of several Gaelic names such as Mac an Mhaoir, meaning "son of the steward" (H&H). Scottish: cognate to Ware, of Old Norman derivation.

Famous **Weirs:** ROBERT FULTON WEIR (1838–1927) of New York was a surgeon considered an expert in operating on joints and intestines. He was the first to recognize duodenal ulcers. JOHN FERGUSON WEIR (1841–1926) of New York was an artist and part of the Hudson River School. He was the first director of the School of Fine Arts at Yale University.

Genealogies: The Normans, 1720–1976, and Information on the Walker, Clayton and Weir Families of Mississippi was compiled by Maggie Laurie Carson and published in Tuscaloosa, Alabama, in 1976. Tims-Weir: The Ancestry of William Robert Tims of Augusta, Texas was compiled by Janet Weir Scott and published in Maryville, Missouri, in

1988. *Weir/Wear Families: From Here & There to the White House* was compiled by Olga Jones Edwards and published in Tuscon, Arizona, in 1990.

WEIS

Ranking: 3545 S.S. Count: 12733

Origin: English, German. English: derived from the Old English word "wis," meaning wise. The name was given to those who were considered wise. German: cognate to White.

Genealogies: The Ancestry of the Children of John Peter Carl Weis and Georgina Lewis was compiled by Frederick Lewis Weis and published in Lincoln, Rhode Island.

WEISEN (S.S. Abbreviation: Weisen)

Ranking: 4546 S.S. Count: 9823

Origin: German? Uncertain etymology. Possibly derived from the German word "weiss," meaning white.

Genealogies: None known.

WEISS

Ranking: 481 S.S. Count: 84,386

Origin: German, Jewish. Cognate to White.

Famous **Weisses:** JOHN WEISS (1818–1879) of Massachusetts introduced German literature to New England. EHRICH WEISS (1874–1926) of Wisconsin was the real name of the magician Harry Houdini, best known for his sensational escapes from seemingly impossible predicaments. SOMA WEISS (1899–1942) of Hungary was a professor of medicine and an authority on the flow of human blood.

Genealogies: Mayflower Lines of Our Grandchildren was compiled by Frederick Lewis Weis and published in Dublin, New Hampshire, in 1958.

WELBORN (S.S. Abbreviation: Welbor)

Ranking: 4318 S.S. Count: 10,384

Origin: English. The name means water that flows from a spring or well. The name was given to those who came from Welborne, the name of a place in England.

Genealogies: None known.

WELCH

Ranking: 236 S.S. Count: 150,337

Origin: English, Irish. Cognate to Walsh.

Famous **Welches:** ASHBEL WELCH (1809–1882) of New York was a civil engineer who worked on the canals and railroads of New Jersey. PHILIP HENRY WELCH (1849–1889) of New York was a journalist and humorist and is best remembered for his anonymous "question and answer" jokes that were carried in the *Sun* and most magazines of the day. WILLIAM HENRY WELCH (1850–1934) of Connecticut was the founder and editor of *The Journal of Experimental Medicine.*

Genealogies: *"The Tishomingo County Connection": History of Skinner-Welch, Adams-Seago and Allied Families of Tishomingo County, Mississippi* was compiled by Esther Welch Adams and published in Crump, Tennessee, in 1981. *The Welsh (also Welch) Family from the Revolution to the Bicentennial, 1776– 1976* was compiled by Mrs. Berne Chamberlin and published in Wooster, Ohio. *Welch* was compiled by Jeff D. Welch and published in Dallas, Texas, in 1950.

WELDON

Ranking: 2266 **S.S. Count:** 20,146
Origin: English. Derived from the Old English words "well(a)" and "dūn," meaning stream and hill. The name was given to those who came from Weldon, a place in Northamptonshire, England.
Genealogies: *The Welden-Weldon Connection* was compiled by Lloyd Washington Welden and published in Morgantown, West Virginia, in 1983.

WELKER

Ranking: 3828 **S.S. Count:** 11,777
Origin: German. The name was given to those who worked fulling cloth.
Famous Welkers: HERMAN WELKER (1906– 1957) of Idaho was a U.S. senator and part of Senator Joseph McCarthy's Internal Security Subcommittee. Welkner's participation led to his failure to win reelection.
Genealogies: None known.

WELLER

Ranking: 1902 **S.S. Count:** 23,821
Origin: English. Derived from the Old English word "well(a)," meaning stream or spring. The name was given to those who lived near a stream or spring.
Famous Wellers: JOHN B. WELLER (1812– 1875) of Ohio was in charge of the commission to outline the boundary between the United States and Mexico. He also served as U.S. senator, governor of California, and minister to Mexico.
Genealogies: *Many Descendants From Philipp Weller (1615–1671/85)* was compiled by Margaret Mighell Weller and published in Pullman, Washington, in 1970. *The Weller Family* was compiled by Ralph H. Weller and published in New York, New York, in 1982.

WELLING, WELLINGS, WELLINGTON (S.S. Abbreviation: Wellin)

Ranking: 3098 **S.S. Count:** 14,663
Origin: English. Welling, Wellings: derived from the Old English word "well(a)," meaning stream or spring. The names were given to those who lived near a stream or spring. Wellington: uncertain etymology. The name was given to those who came from Wellington, the name of several places in England.
Famous Bearers: JAMES CLARKE WELLING (1825–1894) of New Jersey was a journalist and educator. Before becoming the president of George Washington University, he was the editor-in-chief of the *Daily National Intelligencer* in Washington, D.C.
Genealogies: None known.

WELLMAN, WELLMANN (S.S. Abbreviation: Wellma)

Ranking: 2815 **S.S. Count:** 16,183
Origin: Wellman—English; Wellmann—German. Derived from the Old English word "well(a)," meaning stream or spring. The names were given to those who lived near a stream or spring.
Famous Bearers: SAMUEL THOMAS WELLMAN (1847– 1919) of Massachusetts was an engineer and the inventor of machinery used in the manufacture of iron and steel. WALTER WELLMAN (1858–1934) of Ohio was the founder of the *Cincinnati Post*.
Genealogies: *A Genealogical Record of Some Descendants of Bennett Wellman of Maryland, Virginia, West Virginia, Kentucky, and North Carolina* was compiled by Herbert V. Lane and published in Bradenton, Florida, in 1978. *In Memory of Abijah Joslyn Wellman, 1836 to 1889* was compiled by the Friendship Landmark Society and published in Friendship, New York, in 1974.

WELLS

Ranking: 121 **S.S. Count:** 241,098
Origin: English. Derived from the Old English word "well(a)," meaning stream or spring. The name was given to those who lived near a stream or spring.
Famous Wellses: WILLIAM HENRY WELLS (1812–1885) of Connecticut was the superintendent of schools, Chicago, and the founder of the first high school in that city. He also initiated a grading system that was quickly adopted across the country. HORACE WELLS (1815–1848) of Vermont was a dentist who suggested that nitrous oxide be used as an anesthetic in tooth extraction. Publication of the use of ether by W.T.G. Morton two months before Wells's use of nitrous oxide as an anesthetic went public, coupled with the superiority of ether, left Wells despondent. He committed suicide.
Genealogies: *The Ancestors, Life, Times and Descendants of Ephraim Wells, 1675– 1988* was compiled by William A. Wells and published in Decorah, Iowa, in 1988. *The Descendants of Governor Thomas Welles of Connecticut, 1590–1658, and His Wife Alice Tomes* was compiled by Donna Holt Siemiatkoski and published in Baltimore, Maryland, in 1990. *A History of the Warman and Related Families* [including Wells] was compiled by

Elroy Wilson Titus and published in Columbus, Ohio, in 1972.

WELSH

Ranking: 998 S.S. Count: 43,905

Origin: English, Irish. Cognate to Walsh.

Famous **Welshes:** JOHN WELSH (1805–1886) of Pennsylvania was one of the developers of the Fairmount Park system and the financial manager for the Philadelphia Centennial Exhibition.

Genealogies: None known.

WENDEL (ALSO WENDELL)

Ranking: 2996 S.S. Count: 15,163

Origin: German. The names mean "descendant of little Wendimar" (ES), a first name that is derived from words meaning wander and famous.

Famous **Bearers:** BARRETT WENDELL (1855–1921) of Massachusetts was the first professor at Harvard University to offer American literature as a program of study.

Genealogies: None known.

WENDT

Ranking: 2488 S.S. Count: 18,210

Origin: German. The name was given to Wends, a Slavic people from eastern Germany.

Genealogies: *Our Family* was compiled by John W.W. Wendt and published in Salt Lake City, Utah, in 1964.

WENGER

Ranking: 3077 S.S. Count: 14,769

Origin: German, Czech, Jewish. Cognate to Unger.

Genealogies: *History of Michael S. Wenger (1819–1900)* was compiled by Eli D. Wenger and published in Manheim, Pennsylvania, in 1960. *The Men from Wengen and America's Agony: The Wenger-Winger-Wanger History* was compiled by John E. Fetzer and published in Kalamazoo, Michigan, in 1971.

WENTWORTH (S.S. Abbreviation: Wentwo)

Ranking: 3762 S.S. Count: 12,039

Origin: English. Uncertain etymology. Probably derived from the Old English name Winter and the word "worð," meaning winter and enclosure. The name was given to those who lived in places in Cambridgeshire and South Yorkshire, England.

Famous **Wentworths:** BENNING WENTWORTH (1696–1770) of New Hampshire was the first royal governor of New Hampshire province. He was succeeded in that position by his nephew, JOHN WENTWORTH (1737–1820) of New York. JOHN WENTWORTH (1815–1888) of New Hampshire was editor, then owner, of the weekly paper the *Chicago Democrat.* He also represented Illinois as a member of Congress, then served as the mayor of Chicago.

Genealogies: None known.

WENTZ

Ranking: 3961 S.S. Count: 11,420

Origin: German. Cognate to Warner.

Genealogies: None known.

WENZEL

Ranking: 2709 S.S. Count: 16,781

Origin: German. Derived from the Middle High German first name Wenze, which is of Czech and Slavic origin.

Genealogies: None known.

WERNER

Ranking: 824 S.S. Count: 51,431

Origin: German. Cognate to Warner.

Genealogies: *Henry Werner's Posterity—With Its Twigs and Branches* was compiled by Ione F. Palmer and published in 1975. *Werner Family History* was compiled by Mrs. Robert Schmid and published in Columbus, Nebraska, in 1979. *Country Carpenter: Josiah C. Werner, 1863–1926* was compiled by Catherine M. Rhoads and published in Baltimore, Maryland, in 1991.

WERTZ

Ranking: 3737 S.S. Count: 12,105

Origin: German. Cognate to Warner.

Genealogies: *The Wertz Family* was compiled by Mrs. Robert N. Ungerer and published in Wooster, Ohio, in 1978. *Wertz, Wirt, Wuertz, etc. Families of Pennsylvania, 1400's–1990* was compiled by Carolyn Cell Choppin and published in Bowie, Maryland, in 1990.

WESLEY

Ranking: 1514 S.S. Count: 29,390

Origin: English. Derived from the Old English words "west" and "lēah," meaning west and clearing. The name was given to those who came from the many places having names comprising the components "west" and "lēah."

Genealogies: *Memoirs of the Wesley Family* was compiled by Adam Clarke and published in New York, New York. *Ancestors and Descendents [sic] of Francis Wesley and Lucinda Elmira (Shearer) Cornbower* was compiled by Harry A. Diehl and published in Wilmington, Delaware, in 1982.

WESSEL (ALSO WESSELS)

Ranking: 2453 S.S. Count: 18,517

Origin: Frisian. Cognate to Warner.

Genealogies: None known.

WEST

Ranking: 108 S.S. Count: 262,809

Origin: English, German. Derived from the Middle English and Middle High German word "west," meaning west. The name was given to those who lived west of an inhabited place or to those who came from places to the west.

Famous Wests: JOSEPH WEST (?–ante 1692) of England was a South Carolina pioneer and official. He was governor several different times and was instrumental in the settlement and expansion of Charleston. SAMUEL WEST (1730–1807) of Massachusetts was a Congregational chaplin in the Revolutionary War and the one who broke the code in the treason letter sent by Dr. Benjamin Church to the British (1775). He also convinced John Hancock to vote in favor of the federal constitution. BENJAMIN WEST (1738–1820) of Pennsylvania was a painter. He is best known for *Penn's Treaty with the Indians,* which hangs in Independence Hall, Philadelphia.

Genealogies: A Chart of Some Ancestors of Benjamin Holmes West, 1861–1919 was compiled by William J. Harrison and published in Bloomfield, New Jersey, in 1970. *Hill-West, Fisher-Beauchamp and Related Families* was compiled by Olive M. Fisher and published in Baltimore, Maryland, in 1983. *Some Descendants of Anthony West of Accomack, Virginia* was compiled by Elmer D. West and published in Silver Spring, Maryland, in 1980.

WESTBROCK, WESTBROOK, WESTBROOKE (S.S. Abbreviation: Westbr)

Ranking: 1485 S.S. Count: 29,931

Origin: English. Derived from the Old English words "west" and "brōc," meaning west and brook. The names were given to those who came from Westbrock, Westbrook, or Westbrooke, the names of several places in England.

Genealogies: The Westbrook Family of New York was compiled by William Edward Westbrooke and published in San Francisco, California, in 1969. *McNames, Names, McNamish* was compiled by Sue Gunter and published in Cheney, Washington, in 1990. *Davis, Westbrook, Hill, Smith, Echols, and Cave Families Miscellany* was compiled by Carl Forrest Greenway and published in New York.

WESTCOATE, WESTCOT, WESTCOTE, WESTCOTT (S.S. Abbreviation: Westco)

Ranking: 4888 S.S. Count: 9148

Origin: English. Derived from the Old English words "west" and "cot," meaning west and cottage. The names were given to those who came from Westcoate, Westcot, Westcote, or Westcot, the names of places in England.

Famous Bearers: THOMPSON WESTCOTT (1820–1888) of Pennsylvania was the co-author of *History of Philadelphia* (1884). EDWARD NOYES WESTCOTT (1846–1898) of New York was the author of the bestselling novel *David Harcum.*

Genealogies: Seaboard, Lake country, and West: A Genealogy of Certain Branches of the Families Finley-Kelley, . . . Westcott, (et al) was compiled by Howard J. Finley and published in Weedsport, New York, in 1983.

WESTER (ALSO WESTERBERG, WESTERLIND, WESTERLING, WESTERMAN, WESTERMANN ET AL.)

Ranking: 949 S.S. Count: 45,639

Origin: Wester, Westerman—English, German; Westermann, Westerling—German; Westerberg, Westerlind—Swedish. Weste, Westerman, Westermann, Westerling: transformations of West. Westerberg, Westerlind: cognates to West.

Genealogies: None known.

WESTFAL, WESTFALL (S.S. Abbreviation: Westfa)

Ranking: 2401 S.S. Count: 18,868

Origin: German. 1) the name was given to those who came from Westphalia. 2) the name was given to those who lived "at the western clearing" (ES).

Genealogies: None known.

WESTMORLAND, WESTMORELAND (S.S. Abbreviation: Westmo)

Ranking: 3024 S.S. Count: 15,041

Origin: English. Derived from the Old English name Westmōringaland, meaning "territory of the people living west of the moors" (H&H). The names were given to those who came from the former country of Westmoringaland.

Genealogies: Westmoreland Nee Neville was compiled by Olin V. Mapes and published in Bowie, Maryland, in 1992. *The Westmores of Hollywood* was compiled by Frank Westmore and published in Philadelphia, Pennsylvania, in 1976.

WESTON

Ranking: 1278 S.S. Count: 34,573

Origin: English, Scottish. Derived from the Old English words "west" and "tūn," meaning west and settlement. The name was given to those who came from Weston, the name of a place in England.

Famous Westons: EDWARD WESTON (1850–1936) of England was an electrical engineer and through his company, Weston Dynamo Electric Company, a major manufacturer of electroplating dynamos. EDWARD HENRY WESTON (1886–1958) of Illinois was a photographer of Hollywood celebrities and the first photographer to be a recepient of a Guggenheim fellowship.

Genealogies: *Lower Richland Planters: Hopkins, Adams, Weston, and Related Families of South Carolina* was compiled by Laura Jervey Hopkins and published in Hopkins, South Carolina, in 1976.

WESTPHAL (S.S. Abbreviation: Westph)
Ranking: 3979 S.S. Count: 11,360
Origin: German. The name was given to those who came from Westphalen, the name of a place in Germany.
Genealogies: None known.

WETHERALL, WETHERBEE, WETHERBY, WETHERILL, WETHERSPOON ET AL.
(S.S. Abbreviation: Wether)
Ranking: 3378 S.S. Count: 13,400
Origin: Wetherall, Wetherbee, Wetherby, Wetherill—English; Wetherspoon—Scottish. Wetherall, Wetherill: derived from the Old English words "weðer" and "halh," meaning castrated ram and nook. The names were given to those who came from several places named Wetheral in Cumberland, England. Wetherbee, Wetherby: derived from the Old Norman words "veðr" and "býr," meaning castrated ram and settlement. The name was given to those who came from Wetherby, a place in West Yorkshire, England. Wetherspoon: uncertain etymology. Probably derived from the Middle English words "ewther" and "spong" or "spang," meaning castrated ram and narrow piece of land.
Famous **Bearers**: SAMUEL WETHERILL (1736–1816) of New Jersey was a maker of white lead and a civic leader in Philadelphia. Because of his support for colonial causes, the Society of Friends removed him from their congregation. He then helped to found the Free or Fighting Quakers. SAMUEL WETHERILL (1821–1890) of Pennsylvania invented a way to remove white zinc oxide from ore. CHARLES MAYER WETHERILL (1825–1871) of Pennsylvania was a chemist and the first scientist connected with the U.S. Department of Agriculture.
Genealogies: *John Wetherbee of Marlboro and Stow, Massachusetts* was compiled by Ethel Wetherbee Mazza and published in Somersworth, New Hampshire, in 1991. *If Our Earthly House Dissolve; A Story of the Wetherby-Hagadorn Family of Almond, NY* was compiled by Helene C. Phelan and published in Almond, New York, in 1973. *History and Genealogy of the Witherell/Wetherell/Witherill Family of New England* was compiled by Peter Charles Witherell and published in Baltimore, Maryland, in 1976.

WETZEL
Ranking: 2056 S.S. Count: 22,251
Origin: German. Transformation of Wenzel.
Famous **Wetzels**: LEWIS WETZEL (1764–1808?) of Pennsylvania was a scout consumed with hatred for the Native Americans.

Genealogies: *Recollections of Lewis Bonnett, Jr. (1778–1850) and the Bonnett and Wetzel Families* was compiled by Jared C. Lobdell and published in Bowie, Maryland, in 1991.

WHALEN
Ranking: 1285 S.S. Count: 34,435
Origin: Irish. Transformation of Whelan.
Famous **Whalens**: GROVER ALOYSIUS WHALEN (1886–1962) of New York City was the police commissioner and the founder of the New York City Police Academy.
Genealogies: None known.

WHALEY
Ranking: 1443 S.S. Count: 30,948
Origin: English. Derived from the Old English words "hwealf" and "lēah," meaning arch or hill and clearing. The name was given to those who came from Whalley in Lancashire or Whaley in Derbyshire, England.
Genealogies: *Heritage, the History and Genealogy of the Donaldson and Whaley Families of Bath County, Kentucky, and Their Descendants* was compiled by O. Clyde Donaldson and published in Hopkins, Minnesota, in 1979. *Consignments to El Dorado* [also Whaley] was compiled by Thomas Whaley and published in New York, New York, in 1972.

WHARTON (S.S. Abbreviation: Wharto)
Ranking: 2688 S.S. Count: 16,950
Origin: English. Derived from the Old English words "wœfre" and "tūn," meaning wandering and settlement. The name was given to those who came from Wharton, the name of several places in England.
Famous **Whartons**: JOSEPH WHARTON (1826–1909) of Pennsylvania was the first commercially successful smelter in the United States and the manufacturer of nickel. He was the founder of Swarthmore College and the person responsible for establishing the Wharton School of Finance at the University of Pennsylvania. EDITH NEWBOLD JONES WHARTON (1862–1937) of New York was an author. She wrote *The Age of Innocence*, for which she won a Pulitzer Prize.
Genealogies: None known.

WHATLEY (S.S. Abbreviation: Whatle)
Ranking: 2853 S.S. Count: 16,005
Origin: English. Transformation of Wheatley.
Genealogies: *Samuel Whatley (Rev. Sol.) 1762–1826* was compiled by Frederick S. Mulder and published in New York, New York, in 1975.

WHEAT
Ranking: 2891 S.S. Count: 15,742

Origin: English. Derived from the Old English word "hwæte," meaning wheat. The name was given to those who worked growing or selling wheat.

Genealogies: *Wheat Genealogy: The Story of a Family of the Old South* was compiled by Dan D. Wheat and published in Lafayette, Indiana, in 1983. *Wheat Family* was compiled by Christine R. Brown and published in Lenoir City, Tennessee, in 1978.

WHEATLY, WHEATLEY (S.S. Abbreviation: Wheatl)

Ranking: 2561 **S.S. Count:** 17,745
Origin: English. Derived from the Old English words "hwæte" and "lēah," meaning wheat and clearing. The names were given to those who came from Wheatley and Whatley, the names of several places in England.

Famous **Bearers:** PHILLIS WHEATLEY (1753?–1784) of Africa was a black poet who was purchased "off the boat" by John Wheatley in Boston. She was purchased as a child and was given the run and use of the house. She wrote poetry and had a book published called *Poems on Various Subjects, Religious and Moral.*

Genealogies: *Genealogy of the Wheatley or Wheatleigh Family* was compiled by Hannibal Parish Wheatley and published in Farmington, New Hampshire, in 1902. *Henry Sharp (c. 1737–1800) of Sussex County, New Jersey and Fayette County, Pennsylvania, and His Wife Lydia Morgan, and Some of Their Descendants, Including Chalfant, Depuy, Silverthorn, and Wheatley Families* was compiled by Elizabeth Cobb Stewart Eastwood and published in Cleveland, Ohio, in 1975.

WHEATON (S.S. Abbreviation: Wheato)

Ranking: 3763 **S.S. Count:** 12,038
Origin: English. Uncertain etymology. Possibly derived from the Old English words "hwæte" and "tūn," meaning wheat and settlement. The name was probably given to those who came from places named Wheaton in England.

Famous **Wheatons:** HENRY WHEATON (1785–1848) of Rhode Island was a diplomat and an authority on international law. He was the author of the well-received book *Elements of International Law* (1836). NATHANIEL SHELDON WHEATON (1792–1862) of Connecticut was the rector of Christ Church, Hartford, Connecticut, and the president of what is now Trinity College, Hartford.

Genealogies: None known.

WHEELER (S.S. Abbreviation: Wheele)

Ranking: 199 **S.S. Count:** 175,377
Origin: English. Derived from the Middle English word "whele," meaning wheel. The name was given to those who worked making wheels.

Famous **Wheelers:** CANDACE THURBER WHEELER (1827–

1923) of New York was a pioneer in the area of textile and interior design. EVERETT PEPPERRELL WHEELER (1840–1925) of New York City was a lawyer and the founder of the New York Bar Association. GEORGE POST WHEELER (1869–1956) of New York was the first American career diplomat, serving in Europe and Asia.

Genealogies: *Ancestors of Our Grandchildren and Their Cousins, 1742–1977* was compiled by Harriet R. Frische and published in Scottsdale, Arizona, in 1977. *The Genealogy of Samual North Wheeler and Theodora La Barre of Hancock, N.Y.* was compiled by Thomas J. Wheeler and published in Ithaca, New York, in 1980. *Bond-Wheeler Genealogy with Related Families* was compiled by Lorene Bond Prewitt and published in Dallas, Texas, in 1972.

WHELAN

Ranking: 2865 **S.S. Count:** 15,895
Origin: Irish. Derived from the Gaelic first name Ó Faoláin, which was derived from the word "faol," meaning wolf.

Genealogies: *Wheeland/Wieland/Wheland/Weyland and Allied Families (also Whelan family)* was compiled by Alvin L. Anderson and published in Canton, Ohio, in 1984. *Heirs of Eleanor Abell & Thomas Greenwell, Robert Abell & Margaret Mills to Ann Adele Greenwell & Charles Joseph Whelan, Elias Richard Ray & Martha Ellen Buckman* was compiled by Tillie Whelan Onischak and published in Sacramento, California, in 1974.

WHETSTONE (S.S. Abbreviation: Whetst)

Ranking: 4864 **S.S. Count:** 9204
Origin: English. The name was given to those who came from Whitstone, the name of a place in England.

Genealogies: *Whetstone Family of Wilkinson County, Mississippi* was compiled by Levi Jackson Horlacher and published in Lexington, Kentucky, in 1977.

WHIPPLE (S.S. Abbreviation: Whippl)

Ranking: 2391 **S.S. Count:** 18,975
Origin: English. Uncertain etymology.
Genealogies: *The Antecedents and Descendants of Noah Whipple of the Rogerene Community at Quakertown, Connecticut* was compiled by Robert W. Merriam and published in Ithaca, New York, in 1971.

WHISEN

Ranking: 4224 **S.S. Count:** 10,679
Origin: Uncertain etymology.
Genealogies: None known.

WHITAKER (S.S. Abbreviation: Whitak)

Ranking: 543 **S.S. Count:** 74,801
Origin: English. Derived from the Old English words

"hwit" or "hwæte," meaning white and wheat, and the word "æcer," meaning land that is cultivated. The name was given to those who came from Whitaker, the name of several places in England.

Famous **Whitakers**: ALEXANDER WHITAKER (1585–1616?) of England was an Anglican clergyman who baptized Pocahontas. He also was the author of *Good News from Virginia* (1613).

Genealogies: *Dr. John McCaa of Camden, South Carolina, 1793– 1859, His Descendants* [also Whitaker] was compiled by John McCaa and published in Anniston, Alabama, in 1975. *Genealogy: Spaid, Anderson, Whitacre, and a Number of Allied Families* [also Whitaker] was compiled by Rual Purcell Anderson and published in Strasburg, Virginia, in 1975. *Higdon-Whitaker* [various spellings] *and Allied Families* was compiled by Bettina Pearson Higdon and published in Cullman, Alabama, in 1982.

WHITCOMB, WHITCOMBE (S.S. Abbreviation: Whitco)

Ranking: 3574 **S.S. Count:** 12,612

Origin: English. Derived from the Old English words "hwit" and "cumb," meaning white and valley. The names were given to those who came from Whitcomb or Whitcombe, the names of several places in England.

Famous **Bearers**: JAMES WHITCOMB (1795–1852) of Vermont was the governor of, then U.S. senator from, Indiana. SELDEN LINCOLN WHITCOMB (1866–1930) of Iowa was a professor of English and the author of *Chronological Outlines of American Literature* (1894).

Genealogies: *The John Whitcomb Family in Indiana, and Interrelated Branches, 1830– 1978* was compiled by Margaret Whitcomb Baird and published in Santa Ana, California, in 1978. *Yankee Heritage, a Sisson Ancestry* [also Whitcomb] was compiled by Brian J.L. Berry and published in McKinney, Texas, in 1991.

WHITE

Ranking: 16 **S.S. Count:** 907,387

Origin: English, Irish, Scottish. English, Irish, Scottish: derived from the Old English word "hwit" or the last name Hwit, both meaning white. The name was given to those who had white hair or pale skin. Irish, Scottish: derived from the Gaelic components "bán" and "fionn," meaning white and fair.

Famous **Whites**: WHITE EYES (?–1778) was a Delaware Indian chief and the chief sachem of the Delaware nation (1776). He signed a treaty with the colonists that was misrepresented to him, and he was killed leading the colonists in battle. JAMES WHITE (1747–1821) of North Carolina was a Revolutionary soldier who settled in Tennessee, laid out the town of Knoxville, and helped to frame the Tennessee constitution. THOMAS WILLIS WHITE (1788–1843) of Vir-

ginia was the founder of the *Southern Literary Messenger*, the magazine edited by Edgar Allan Poe. CANVASS WHITE (1790–1834) of New York, a civil engineer, was principal designer of the locks on the Erie Canal. He also patented waterproof cement in 1820. ELLEN GOULD HARMON WHITE (1827–1915) of Maine was the co-founder of the Seventh Day Adventist Church. ANNA WHITE (1831–1910) of New York was an elder in the Shaker community. ANDREW DICKSON WHITE (1832–1918) of New York was the organizer of Cornell University. JAMES CLARKE WHITE (1833–1916) of Maine was the co-founder of the first dermatological clinic in America, circa 1860. ALFRED TREDWAY WHITE (1846–1921) of New York inspired the passage of tenement reform legislation in New York City in 1895 by building model tenements in Brooklyn. STANFORD WHITE (1853– 1906) of New York was an architect and the designer of the original Madison Square Garden in New York City. HELEN MAGILL WHITE (1853–1944) of Rhode Island was the first American woman to earn a Ph.D. ALMA BRIDWELL WHITE (1862–1946) of Kentucky was the founder and bishop of the Pillar of Fire Church. WILLIAM ALLEN WHITE (1868–1944) of Kansas was a newspaper editor and author. He wrote the famed editorial "What's the matter with Kansas?" and stories for magazines. An opponent of the New Deal and of the Ku Klux Klan, he was the epitome of small-town America. BENJAMIN FRANKLIN WHITE (1873–1958) of Canada was a breeder and trainer of harness horses. His success in his field resulted in his being nicknamed the "Dean of the Colt Trainers." CLARENCE CAMERON WHITE (1880–1960) of Tennessee was a violinist, composer, and educator. He taught music at the college level and collected black music, concentrating on American and Caribbean life. PEARL WHITE (1889–1938) of Missouri was an actress and the star of *The Perils of Pauline*. EDWARD HIGGINS WHITE II (1930–1967) of Texas was an astronaut and the pilot of the *Gemini IV* mission. Named to the first *Apollo* flight, he died in a fire in the *Apollo* simulator.

Genealogies: *The Ancestors of Daniel White, 1777– 1836 and His Wife, Sarah Ford* was compiled by Paula Porter Griffin and published in Evansville, Indiana, in 1979. *Ancestral Chronological Record of the William White Family, from 1607–8 to 1895* was compiled by Thomas and Samuel White and published in 1965. *Family Ties of Roy Harold Murray: Ancestors and Descendants of the Murray, White, Waybright Families* was compiled by Miriam Adams Cloud Murray and published in Decorah, Iowa, in 1976.

WHITED

Ranking: 4524 **S.S. Count:** 9898

Origin: English. Derived from the name Whitehead.
Genealogies: None known.

WHITEHEAD, WHITEHORN, WHITEHORNE, WHITEHOUSE (S.S. Abbreviation: Whiteh)

Ranking: 448 S.S. Count: 88,957

Origin: Whitehouse—English; Whitehead—English, Irish, Scottish; Whitehorn, Whitehorne—Scottish. Whitehouse: derived from the Middle English words "whit" and "hous," meaning white and house. The name was given to those who came from Whitehouse, the name of several places in England. Whitehead (English, Scottish): derived from the Middle English words "whit" and "heved," meaning white and head. The name was given to those with light-colored or white hair. Whitehead (Irish): mistaken translation of the name Canavan. Whitehorn, Whitehorne: derived from the Old English words "hwīt" and "œrn," meaning white and house. The names were given to those who came from Whitehorn or Whiterhorne, the names of places in Scotland.

Famous **Bearers**: WILLIAM ADEE WHITEHEAD (1810–1884) of New Jersey was a historian and an expert in the history of New Jersey. FREDERIC COPE WHITEHOUSE (1842–1911) of New York was an archaeologist especially interested in Egypt and the flood waters of the Nile River. ALFRED NORTH WHITEHEAD (1861–1947) of England was a philosopher and the author of *The Concept of Nature* (1920). WILBUR CHERRIER WHITEHEAD (1866–1931) of Ohio was an expert in the game of bridge. He was the founder of the Cavendish Club.

Genealogies: *The Family Tree* was compiled by Thomas Wayne Whitehead and published in Shannon, Mississippi, in 1980. *The Reverend William W. Whitehead, Mississippi Pioneer: His Antecedents and Descendants* was compiled by E. Grey Diamond and published in St. Louis, Missouri, in 1985.

WHITELAW, WHITELEY, WHITELL, WHITELOCK, WHITELY ET AL. (S.S. Abbreviation: Whitel)

Ranking: 3347 S.S. Count: 13,538

Origin: Whiteley, Whitell, Whitelock, Whitely—English; Whitelaw—English, Scottish. Whiteley, Whitely: derived from the Old English words "hwīt" and "lēah," meaning white and clearing. The name was given to those who came from Whiteley or Whitley, the names of several places in England. Whitell: derived from the Old English words "hwīt" and "well(a)," meaning white and spring. The name was given to those who came from places named Whitell, the name of several places in England. Whitelock: derived from the Middle English words "whit" and "lock," meaning white and curl. The name was given to those with light-colored or white hair.

Genealogies: *A Family History of Williams, Eaton, McBroom, Whiteley, and Related Lines* was compiled by E. Derl Williams and published in Wichita, Kansas, in 1991. *Joseph Whiteley, Sr. and His Descendants in America, 1751–1990*

was compiled by Dorris Easley Estes and published in Baltimore, Maryland, in 1990.

WHITEMAN, WHITEMORE (S.S. Abbreviation: Whitem)

Ranking: 3884 S.S. Count: 11,619

Origin: English. Whiteman: derived from the Middle English words "whit" and "man," meaning white and man. The name was given to those who had white hair or pale skin or to those who worked as servants for people nicknamed White. Whitemore: 1) derived from the Old English words "hwīt" and "mōr," meaning white and moor. The name was given to those who came from Whitmore, the name of several places in England. 2) possibly derived from the name Whittimere, the name of a place in England, which might mean "pool associated with someone called Hwīta" (H&H).

Famous **Bearers**: PAUL SAMUEL "POPS" WHITEMAN (1890–1967) of Colorado was a bandleader. He was known as the "King of Jazz" and is associated with George Gershwin's "Rhapsody in Blue." He became the musical director of the Blue Network, the beginning company of the American Broadcasting Co., serving as the vice president of ABC.

Genealogies: None known.

WHITEN

Ranking: 4214 S.S. Count: 10,715

Origin: English. Transformation of Whitten.

Genealogies: None known.

WHITES (ALSO WHITESIDE, WHITESMITH, WHITESON)

Ranking: 1606 S.S. Count: 27,887

Origin: Whitesmith—English; Whites, Whiteson—English, Irish, Scottish; Whiteside—English, Scottish. Whitesmith: transformation of Smith. Whites, Whiteson: transformations of White. Whiteside: derived from the Old English words "hwīt" and "side," meaning white and hill slope. The name was probably given to those who came from Whiteside, the name of several places in England.

Famous **Bearers**: ARTHUR DARE WHITESIDE (1882–1960) of New York was the incorporator of National Credit, R. G. Dun and Bradstreet Co. into Dun and Bradstreet, Inc., 1933, serving as its president.

Genealogies: None known.

WHITFIELD (S.S. Abbreviation: Whitfi)

Ranking: 1069 S.S. Count: 41,135

Origin: English. Derived from the Old English words "hwīt" and "feld," meaning white and open field. The name was given to those who came from Whitfield, the name of several places in England.

Famous **Whitfields**: HENRY WHITFIELD (1597–1657?) of England was one of the founders of the town of Guilford,

Connecticut. He worked as a missionary to area Indians. ROBERT PARR WHITFIELD (1828–1910) of New York was a paleontologist, the chief illustrator for the New York Geological Survey, and curator of geology, American Museum of Natural History, New York City.

Genealogies: *Whitfield History and Genealogy of Tennesse* was compiled by Vallie Jo Fox Whitfield and published in Pleasant Hill, California, in 1979. *Virginia History and Whitfield Biographies* was compiled by Vallie Jo Fox Whitfield and published in Pleasant Hill, California, in 1976.

WHITING, WHITINGTON (S.S. Abbreviation: Whitin)

Ranking: 1997 **S.S. Count:** 22,755

Origin: English. *Whiting: transformation of White. Whitington: uncertain etymology. Probably derived from the Old English name Wsitantūn, meaning "settlement associated with Hwita" (H&H). The name was given to those who came from Whitington, the name of several places in England.*

Famous Bearers: WILLIAM HENRY CHASE WHITING (1824–1865) of Mississippi was a major general in the Confederate army. Considered a hero and described by General T. J. Jackson as a "matchless display of valor," he guarded Fort Fisher and made the Cape Fear River a safe harbor for blockade runners in the war.

Genealogies: *Genealogy of Evans, Nivin, and Allied Families* [also Whiting] was compiled by Septimus Evans Nivin and published in Philadelphia, Pennsylvania, in 1930. *Genealogy of the William Whiting Family, 1724–1936* was compiled by Gregory C. Schwarz and published in Lebanon, New Hampshire, in 1978.

WHITLEY (S.S. Abbreviation: Whitle)

Ranking: 1170 **S.S. Count:** 37,357

Origin: English. Transformation of Whiteley.

Genealogies: *A Family History of William, Eaton, McBroom, Whiteley (also Whitley), and Related Lines* was compiled by E. Derl Williams and published in Wichita, Kansas, in 1991. *The George Whitley Family* was compiled by Walter Charles Whitley and published in Little Rock, Arkansas, in 1974. *Joseph Whiteley, Sr. and His Descendants in America, 1751–1990* [also Whitley] was compiled by Dorris Easley Estes and published in Baltimore, Maryland, in 1990.

WHITLOCK (S.S. Abbreviation: Whitlo)

Ranking: 1249 **S.S. Count:** 35,265

Origin: English. 1) derived from the Middle English words "whit" and "lock," meaning white and curl. The name was given to those who had light-colored or white hair. 2) derived from an Old English first name that was derived from the elements "wiht" and "lāc," meaning creature and play.

Famous **Whitlocks:** BRAND WHITLOCK (1869–1934) of Ohio was a writer and diplomat who served as ambassador to Belgium and was the author of *A Personal Record* (1919), his best-known work.

Genealogies: None known.

WHITMAN (S.S. Abbreviation: Whitma)

Ranking: 1511 **S.S. Count:** 29,413

Origin: English. Derived from the Middle English words "whit" and "man," meaning white and man. The name was given to those who had light-colored or white hair, or to those who worked for those named White.

Famous **Whitmans:** EZEKIEL WHITMAN (1776–1866) of Massachusetts was chief justice of the Maine Supreme Court. NARCISSA PRENTISS WHITMAN (1808–1847) of New York was a missionary to the Indians in the Pacific Northwest. WALT WHITMAN (1819–1892) of New York was a poet best remembered for his "Leaves of Grass" and "Democratic Vistas." CHARLES OTIS WHITMAN (1842–1910) of Maine was a biologist and the first director of the Woods Hole (Massachusetts) Marine Biological Laboratory. ALBERY ALLSON WHITMAN (1851–1901) of Kentucky was born into slavery and became one of the best of the nation's black poets. ROYAL WHITMAN (1857–1946) of Maine was a pioneer in the field of orthopedic surgery.

Genealogies: *The History of Alfred & Sarah Andrews Whitman: Their Ancestors & Descendants* was compiled by Herbert S. Whitman and published in Rutland, Vermont, in 1979.

WHITMIRE (S.S. Abbreviation: Whitmi)

Ranking: 4253 **S.S. Count:** 10,592

Origin: English. The name was given to those who lived near the white lake (ES).

Genealogies: *The Families of the Sons of Christopher Columbus Whitmire, Sr., 1774–1842* was compiled by Haskell Pruett and published in Stillwater, Oklahoma, in 1986. *Sons of Frontiersmen: History & Genealogy of Rowland, Whitmire and Associated Families* was compiled by Billie Louise Owens and published in Canon City, Colorado, in 1976. *The Whitmer Family Genealogy* was compiled by Dallis Whitmer and published in 1976.

WHITMORE (S.S. Abbreviation: Whitmo)

Ranking: 2043 **S.S. Count:** 22,367

Origin: English. 1) derived from the Old English words "hwit" and "mōr," meaning white and moor. The name was given to those who came from Whitmore, the name of several places in England. 2) possibly a misspelling of Whittimere, which might mean "pool associated with someone called Hwita" (H&H).

Famous **Whitmores:** WILLIAM HENRY WHITMORE (1836–1900) of Massachusetts was a merchant who was a records commissioner and city registrar. FRANK CLIFFORD WHITMORE (1887–1947) of Massachusetts was an organic chemist and considered an authority in his field.

Genealogies: *Wetmore History and Some Maternal Lines* (also Whitmore) was compiled by Kathryn Lee Wetmore and published in Ann Arbor, Michigan, in 1970.

WHITNEY (S.S. Abbreviation: Whitne)

Ranking: 822 **S.S. Count:** 51,513

Origin: English. Uncertain etymology. The first component was possibly derived from the Old English name Hwita or the word "hwit," both meaning white. The second component is derived from the Old English word "ēg," meaning island. The name was given to those who came from Whitney, the name of a place in Hertfordshire, England.

Famous Whitneys: ELI WHITNEY (1765– 1825) of Massachusetts was the inventor of the cotton gin and the maker of rifles with interchangeable parts, the first of their kind. CASPAR WHITNEY (1861–1929) of Massachusetts was a sportswriter and the originator of the idea for an All-American Football Team (1889). WILLIS RODNEY WHITNEY (1868–1958) of New York was a chemist and the developer of the GEM lamp filament, the modern X-ray tube, and the "gas-filled" lamp. GERTRUDE VANDERBILT WHITNEY (1875–1942) of New York was a sculptor, art patron, and the founder of the Whitney Museum of American Art.

Genealogies: *Whitney Genealogy* was compiled by Fred F. Whitney and published in Rutland, Vermont, in 1980. *The Whitneys: an Informal Portrait, 1635–1975* was compiled by Edwin P. Hoyt and published in New York, New York, in 1976. *Family of Ruth Whitney Lawrence* was compiled by Georgene Sones and published in 1977.

WHITSON (S.S. Abbreviation: Whitso)

Ranking: 3512 **S.S. Count:** 12,841

Origin: English. Transformation of White.
Genealogies: None known.

WHITT

Ranking: 2104 **S.S. Count:** 21,822

Origin: English. Transformation of White.
Genealogies: None known.

WHITTA (ALSO WHITTAKER, WHITTAMORE)

Ranking: 1767 **S.S. Count:** 25,383

Origin: Whitta: derived from the Middle English word "whit," meaning white. The name was given to those who worked as a whitewasher or with bleach. Whittaker: derived from the Old English words "hwits" or "hwœte," meaning white and wheat, and the word "œcer," meaning land that is cultivated. The name was given to those who came from

Whittaker, the name of several places in England. Whittamore: transformation of the first definition of Whitmore.
Genealogies: None known.

WHITTE (ALSO WHITTELL, WHITTEMORE, WHITTERS, WHITTEY ET AL.)

Ranking: 1088 **S.S. Count:** 40,624

Origin: English. Whitte: transformation of White. Whittell: derived from the Old English words "hwit" and "well(a)," meaning white and stream. The name was given to those who came from Whittell, the name of several places in England. Whittemore: transfromation of the first definition of Whitmore. Whitters: transformation of Whitehouse. Whittey: uncertain etymology. 1) derived from the Old English words "hwit" and "(ge)hœg," meaning white and enclosure. 2) derived from the Middle English words "whit" and "eye," meaning white and eye. The name was given to those who had abnormally light-colored eyes.

Famous Bearers: AMOS WHITTEMORE (1759–1828) of Massachusetts invented a machine that made cotton and wool cards used in textile manufacturing. THOMAS WHITTEMORE (1800–1861) of Massachusetts was the editor and owner of the *Trumpet and Universalist Magazine*. His grandson, THOMAS WHITTEMORE (1871–1950) of Massachusetts, was an archaeologist who is best known for uncovering the mosaics in the Byzantine churches located in Constantinople.

Genealogies: *Genealogy of Whittemore Family* was compiled by D. S. Zimmer and published in the 1940s in the United States. *The Whittemore Family in America* was compiled by Bradford Adams Whittemore and published in Massachusetts in the 1950s. *McLean, the Family of Judge Alney and Tabitha McLean of Greenville, Kentucky* [also Whittemore] was compiled by Sally Stone Trotter and published in Greenville, Mississippi, in 1989.

WHITTIER, WHITTIMORE, WHITTING, WHITTINGHAM, WHITTINGTON ET AL. (S.S. Abbreviation: Whitti)

Ranking: 1382 **S.S. Count:** 32,028

Origin: Whittier, Whittimore, Whittington—English; Whittingham—English, Scottish; Whitting—English, Irish, Scottish. Whittier: derived from the Old English words "whit" and "taw(i)er," meaning white and prepare. The name was given to those who worked dressing white leather. Whittimore: transformation of the first definition of Whitmore. Whittington: uncertain etymology. Possibly derived from the Old English name Hwita and the word "tūn," meaning settlement. The name was given to those who came from Whittington, the name of many places in England. Whittingham: derived from the Old English last name Hwita and the word "hām," meaning white and homestead. The name was given to those who came from Whittingham, the name of several places in England. Whitting: transformation of White.

Famous **Bearers:** WILLIAM ROLLINSON WHITTINGHAM (1805–1879) of New York was an Episcopal minister and the rector of St. Luke's Church in New York City. JOHN GREENFEAF WHITTIER (1807–1892) of Massachusetts was a poet and abolitionist. "Snow-Bound" is considered his best work.

Genealogies: None known.

WHITTLE, WHITTLEY (S.S. Abbreviation: Whittl)

Ranking: 3288 S.S. Count: 13,796

Origin: English. Whittle: derived from the Old English words "hwit" and "hyll," meaning white and hill. The name was given to those who came from Whittle, the name of several places in England. Whittley: transformation of Whiteley.

Genealogies: None known.

WHITWORTH (S.S. Abbreviation: Whitwo)

Ranking: 3369 S.S. Count: 13,461

Origin: English. Derived from the Old English words "hwit" and "worð," meaning white and enclosure. The name was given to those who came from Whitworth, the name of several places in England.

Famous **Whitworths:** GEORGE FREDERIC WHITWORTH (1816–1907) of England was a Presbyterian minister who founded churches in Portland, Oregon. Whitworth College in Washington state is named for him.

Genealogies: *Isaac Towell & His Family: Including Towell, McAdams, Whitworth, Shaw, Fitzgerald & Others, 1764–1990* was compiled by Roy H. Towell and published in Beaumont, Texas, in 1990.

WICK

Ranking: 3772 S.S. Count: 12,003

Origin: English. Derived from the Old English word "wic," which was derived from the Latin "vicus," meaning settlement. The name was given to those who came from a settlement on the outskirts of a large village.

Genealogies: None known.

WICKER (ALSO WICKERT)

Ranking: 2200 S.S. Count: 20,848

Origin: Wicker—English; Wickert—French. Wicker: transformation of Wick. Wickert: derived from a Germanic personal name that was derived from the words "wig" and "hard," meaning war and brave.

Genealogies: *Gleanings in the Family Field: A Study of the Wicker Family and Related Lines in the South* was compiled by Mary-Helen Sears Foxx and published in Glendale, Arizona, in 1976. *The Wicker Family of the South* was

compiled by Mary-Helen Sears Foxx and published in Glendale, Arizona, in 1992.

WICKHAM (S.S. Abbreviation: Wickha)

Ranking: 4390 S.S. Count: 10,220

Origin: English. Derived from the Old English words "wic" and "ham," meaning settlement and homestead. The name was given to those who came from Wickham, the name of several places in England.

Famous **Wickhams:** JOHN WICKHAM (1763–1839) of New York was a lawyer and a pleader. He successfully argued that the Supreme Court has appellate jurisdiction over state courts.

Genealogies: *Descendants of Noyes Wickham* was compiled by Evelyn Wickham Hale and published in Southbury, Connecticut, in 1973.

WICKS

Ranking: 3459 S.S. Count: 13,046

Origin: English. Transformation of Wick.

Genealogies: None known.

WIENER

Ranking: 4548 S.S. Count: 9819

Origin: German, Jewish. German: derived from the German name Wien. The name was given to those who came from Wien, the name of the city (Vienna) in Austria. Jewish: derived from the Yiddish name Vin. The name was given to those who came from Vin, the name of the city (Vienna) in Austria.

Famous **Wieners:** LEO WIENER (1862–1939) of Poland was a scholar of Slavic languages and a cultural historian of Arabic, Germanic, African, and American Indian cultures. NORBERT WIENER (1894–1964) of Missouri was a mathematician and the author of *Cybernetics* (1948).

Genealogies: None known.

WIESE

Ranking: 3543 S.S. Count: 12,747

Origin: German. Derived from the Old High German word "wisa," meaning piece of land in a meadow. The name was given to those who lived on a piece of land in a meadow.

Genealogies: *In Search of Familie Wiese* was compiled by Irma Wiese Whipple and published in Rohnert, California, in 1983.

WIGGINS (S.S. Abbreviation: Wiggins)

Ranking: 541 S.S. Count: 75,024

Origin: English. Derived from the Breton first name Wiucon, which comprised components meaning worthy and noble.

Famous **Wigginses:** CARLETON WIGGINS (1848–1932) of New York was a landscape and animal painter who studied under George Inness. He was a member of the National Academy of Design, 1906.

Genealogies: *Begats, A Chronicle of the McMillan, Preston, Wiggins, and Binford Families* was compiled by Mamel E. Preston Wiggins and published in Ellsworth, Maine, in 1979. *Descenenendants & Antecedents of Darius Knowles, 1829–1881, and His Wife Rhoda Ann Wiggins, 1831–1915* was compiled by Beverly Knowles Metzger and published in Manly, Iowa, in 1984. *The Gardiner-Squires Connection* [also Wiggins] was compiled by Tiger Gardiner and published in Baltimore, Maryland, in 1989.

WILBAN (ALSO WILBANKS)
Ranking: 4146 **S.S. Count:** 10,921
Origin: English? Uncertain etymology. Possibly a cognate to Wallbank, derived from the Middle English words "wall" and "bank," meaning wall and slope. The name was given to those who lived by a slope with a wall built on it.
Genealogies: *Wilbanks-Willbanks in America* was compiled by Eileen Sheffield and published in Texas in 1968.

WILBERT (S.S. Abbreviation: Wilber)
Ranking: 3085 **S.S. Count:** 14,728
Origin: English. Derived from a Germanic first name that comprised the components "wil" and "berht," meaning desire and famous.
Genealogies: None known.

WILBUR (ALSO WILBURN)
Ranking: 1251 **S.S. Count:** 35,237
Origin: English. Wilbur: the name signifies a descendant of named Wilburh or Wilburg. Wilburn: 1) the name was given to those who lived near brooks beside which stood willow trees. 2) the name was given to those who came from Welborne, the name of many places in England.
Genealogies: None known.

WILCOX
Ranking: 471 **S.S. Count:** 85,280
Origin: English. Derived from the medieval first name Will with the suffix "cock," which was derived from the Middle English word "cok," meaning bird.
Famous Wilcoxes: STEPHEN WILCOX (1830–1893) of Rhode Island was an inventor and engineer. He designed a safety water-tube boiler (1856) and a steam generator (1867). With George Babcock he founded Babcock and Wilcox Co., which made boilers and steam engines. ROY C. WILCOX (1891–1975) of Connecticut was a treasurer, then lieutenant governor, of Connecticut, who lost clout when he called out the National Guard to quell a labor disturbance during the governor's absence from the state. He then became an internationally respected nature photographer and filmmaker.

Genealogies: *Descendants of Elisha Bacon Wilcox of Middletown, Connecticut* was compiled by Albert Wilcox Savage and published in Las Vegas, Nevada, in 1990. *The Wilcox Families: Descended from John Wilcockson and David Alonzo Wilcox* was compiled by Donald H. Wilcox and published in Sparta, Wisconsin, in 1988. *Wilcox/Wilcoxson Families of New England* was compiled by Martha Scott Osborne and published in Bowie, Maryland, in 1990.

WILD
Ranking: 4013 **S.S. Count:** 11,282
Origin: English. 1) derived from the Old English word "wilde," meaning wild. The name was given to those who were violent or uncontrolled. 2) the name was given to those who lived on a piece of land in its natural, untamed state.
Genealogies: *The Shepard Genealogy* [also Wild] was compiled by Lowell Shepard Blaisdell and published in Arizona in 1952.

WILDE
Ranking: 3350 **S.S. Count:** 13,535
Origin: English. Transformation of Wild.
Famous Wildes: RICHARD HENRY WILDE (1789–1847) of Ireland came to America as a child and was raised in Georgia, where he served as attorney general and which he represented as a member of Congress. It was he, in his travels through Europe, who discovered Giotto's portrait of Dante in the Bargello in Florence, Italy.
Genealogies: None known.

WILDER
Ranking: 920 **S.S. Count:** 46,852
Origin: English, German, Jewish. English: transformation of Wild. German, Jewish: cognate to Wild.
Famous Wilders: MARSHALL PINCKNEY WILDER (1798–1886) of New Hampshire was one of the founders of the Continental Union party and the Massachusetts Institute of Technology. He was a leading agriculturist of the day, developing several varieties of fruits and flowers. JOHN THOMAS WILDER (1830–1917) of New York was a Union brigadier general and the leader of "Wilder's Lightning Brigade." After the war he settled in Tennessee, founded the Roane Iron Works, and built one of the South's first blast furnaces. LAURA INGALLS WILDER (1867–1957) of Wisconsin was the author of *Little House on the Prairie* (1935), *On the Banks of Plum Creek* (1937), and *The Long Winter* (1940), among others. She did not publish her books until the age of 65. RUSSELL SAGE WILDER (1885–1959) of Ohio was an authority on the treatment of diabetes and was one of the first to use insulin in such treatment.
Genealogies: *The Descendants of Harvey Wilder and His Ancestors to 1485 in England* was compiled by Justin E. Wilder and published in Winona Lake, Indiana, in 1974.

Lucy Jane Wylder: Kith and Kin [also Wilder] was compiled by Jessye Ann High and published in California in 1976. *The Book of the Wilders (Revised)* was compiled by Edwin M. Wilder and published in Goshen, Indiana, in 1979.

WILES

Ranking: 2535 S.S. Count: 17,881

Origin: English. Derived from the Old English words "wil" and "mann," meaning trick and man. The name was given to those who worked as hunters or trappers, or those who were untrustworthy.

Genealogies: *Wiles: 300 Years in America* was compiled by Marie Davis Wiles and published in 1976.

WILEY

Ranking: 603 S.S. Count: 68,888

Origin: English. 1) the name was given to those who came from Wylye, the name of a place in England. 2) the name was given to those who lived near the river Wylye or Wiley in England. 3) the name was given to those who lived near mills.

Famous Wileys: HARVEY WASHINGTON WILEY (1844–1930) of Indiana was a chemist who campaigned to have the Pure Food and Drugs Act (1906) made into law. ANDREW WILEY (1862–1931) of Delaware was an irrigation engineer and a consultant on the major dams built after 1902. ALEXANDER WILEY (1884–1967) of Wisconsin was a U.S. senator (1939–1963).

Genealogies: *Days of Old: The History of the Wileys and Other Early Settlers of Saxtons River, Vermont, 1783–c.1850* was compiled by Ruth M. Buxton and published in Bellows Falls, Vermont, in 1980. *Descendants of Hezekiah Sellards (Father of Jenny Wiley)* was compiled by Clayton R. Cox and published in Baltimore, Maryland, in 1977. *The White, Hill, Wiley, & Kuns Cousins* was compiled by Opal L. Streiff and published in Callaway, Nebraska, in 1986.

WILHELM, WILHELMS, WILHELMSEN, WILHELMSSON (S.S. Abbreviation: Wilhel)

Ranking: 1350 S.S. Count: 32,839

Origin: Wilhelmsen—Danish, German, Norwegian; Wilhelm—Dutch; Wilhelms—German; Wilhelmsson—Swedish. Transformations of William.

Genealogies: *Genealogy and Family Histories of the Lighter and Wilhelm Families* was compiled by Edward H. Lighter and published in Rapid City, South Dakota, in 1935.

WILHITE (S.S. Abbreviation: Wilhit)

Ranking: 4190 S.S. Count: 10,789

Origin: German? Uncertain etymology.

Genealogies: None known.

WILKE

Ranking: 4097 S.S. Count: 11,025

Origin: English, German. English: derived from a medieval first name that was derived from the name Wilkin. German: transformation of Will.

Genealogies: None known.

WILKENS (S.S. Abbreviation: Wilken)

Ranking: 3624 S.S. Count: 12,426

Origin: English, German. English: transformation of Wilkins. German: transformation of Will.

Genealogies: None known.

WILKERSON (S.S. Abbreviation: Wilker)

Ranking: 635 S.S. Count: 65,236

Origin: English. Transformation of Wilkin.

Genealogies: *Our Wilkersons: From Burke to Rutherford to Polk, 1760–1980* was compiled by Blanche W. Culbreth and published in Columbus, North Carolina, in 1980.

WILKES

Ranking: 1719 S.S. Count: 26,042

Origin: English. Derived from a medieval first name that was a transformation of the name Wilkin.

Famous Wilkeses: CHARLES WILKES (1798–1877) of New York was a naval officer and explorer. On an expedition to the Antarctic, Pacific Islands, and the Northwest Pacific coast, he stopped the British ship *Trent* and removed two Confederate agents against their will. This resulted in the "Trent Affair." He was court-martialed (1864) and he later retired as rear admiral (1866). GEORGE WILKES (1817–1885) of New York was co-founder of the *National Police Gazette*. He also was the first to introduce pari-mutuel betting and to promote prizefighting.

Genealogies: *Wilks and Young Families, Texas Pioneers* [also Wilkes] was compiled by Doris Ross Brock Johnston and published in Irving, Texas, in 1984.

WILKIE

Ranking: 4356 S.S. Count: 10,297

Origin: English. Derived from a medieval first name that was a transformation of the name Wilkin.

Famous Wilkies: FRANC BANGS WILKIE (1832–1892) of New York was the head *New York Times* war correspondent during the Civil War. He wrote *Personal Reminiscences of Thirty-five Years of Journalism* (1891).

Genealogies: *The Jonathan Tree; or, A Wilkey Genealogy* [also Wilkie] was compiled by Hubert Weldon Wilkey and published in Kentucky in 1970. *The Wilkie/Wilkey Family* was compiled by Hubert Weldon Wilkey and published in Baltimore, Maryland, in 1976.

WILKIN, WILKINS, WILKINSON (S.S. Abbreviation: Wilkin)

Ranking: 219 **S.S. Count:** 158,968

Origin: English. Wilkin: derived from a medieval first name that was derived from of the name Will with the suffix "kin."

Famous **Bearers:** JEMIMA WILKINSON (1752–1819) of Rhode Island preached that she was possessed by spirits. She moved to New York, founding the colony of Jerusalem and serving as its leader. DAVID WILKINSON (1771–1852) of Rhode Island was an inventor and manufacturer. He was the co-founder of David Wilkinson & Co., a maker of iron and textile machinery. WILLIAM WILKINS (1779–1965) of Pennsylvania was a U.S. senator, a minister to Russia, and secretary of war.

Genealogies: *The Descendants of the Rev. Christopher Wilkinson of Queen Anne's County, Maryland was compiled by George B. Wilson* and published in Baltimore, Maryland, in 1973. *The Gaston, Howard, and Wilkinson Families* was compiled by Kathleen Wilkinson Wood and published in Baltimore, Maryland, in 1976. *Pioneers and Patriots: A History of the John Wilkins and Some Related Families of Virginia* [also Wilkinson] was compiled by James Richard Wilkins and published in Winchester, Virginia, in 1980.

WILKS

Ranking: 3723 **S.S. Count:** 12,134

Origin: English. Derived from a medieval first name that was a transformation of the name Wilkin.

Genealogies: *Wilks and Young Families, Texas Pioneers* was compiled by Doris Ross Brock Johnston and published in Irving, Texas, in 1984.

WILL

Ranking: 2802 **S.S. Count:** 16,249

Origin: English, Scottish. 1) derived from the medieval first name Will, a shortened form of the name William. Also possibly derived from other medieval names with the component Will-, such as Wilbert and Willard. 2) derived from the Middle English word "will," meaning stream. The name was given to those who lived near a stream.

Genealogies: None known.

WILLARD (S.S. Abbreviation: Willar)

Ranking: 1393 **S.S. Count:** 31,846

Origin: English. Derived from a Germanic first name comprising the words "wil" and "hard," meaning desire and strong or courageous.

Famous **Willards:** SIMON WILLARD (1605–1676) of England was a fur trader, colonist, and the co-founder, with Peter Bulkely, of Concord, Massachusetts. SIMON WILLARD (1753–1848) of Massachusetts was a clockmaker and

inventor. He is best remembered for the "Willard Patent Timepiece," or the "Banjo clock." SOLOMON WILLARD (1783–1861) of Massachusetts was a sculptor and architect famous for his Bunker Hill Monument. JOSIAH FLINT WILLARD (1869–1907) of Wisconsin was a writer who used the name Josiah Flynt. He wrote about vagrants and criminology. HOBARD H. WILLARD (1881–1974) of Pennsylvania was a nationally prominent chemist and an author of numerous research papers and books, including the text *Instrumental Methods of Analysis*, which has been published in several editions. FRANK HENRY WILLARD (1893–1958) of Illinois was a cartoonist and the creator of "Moon Mullins."

Genealogies: *History of Valuable Pioneers* [also Willard] *of the State of Arizona* was compiled by Sally Munds Williams and published in Chino Valley, Arizona, in 1987. *The Gump Family in America, 1732–1983 (also Willard family)* was compiled by Arlo K. Gump and published in Fort Wayne, Indiana, in 1983. *The Family of Stephen Franklin Willard, Wethersfield, Connecticut* was compiled by Stephen Franklin Willard and published in Wollaston, Massachusetts, in 1960.

WILLET (ALSO WILLETT)

Ranking: 1638 **S.S. Count:** 27,459

Origin: English. Transformations of the first definition of Will.

Famous **Bearers:** MARINUS WILLETT (1740–1830) of New York was a merchant and Revolutionary soldier and a Son of Liberty in New York. After the war, he served as the sheriff of New York City and county and mayor of New York City.

Genealogies: *The Willett Families of North America* [also Willet] was compiled by Albert James Willett and published in Easley, South Carolina, in 1985. *The Willett Family of Maryland: Colonial Pewterers, Kentucky Pioneers* was compiled by Mary Louise Donnelly and published in Burke, Virginia, in 1983.

WILLEY

Ranking: 2316 **S.S. Count:** 19,599

Origin: English. 1) derived from the Old English words "wilig" and "lēah," meaning willow and clearing. The name was given to those who came from places named Willey in Cheshire, Herefordshire, Shropshire, and Warwickshire, England. 2) derived from the Old English word "wēoh," meaning pagan church. The name was given to those who came from places named Willey in Surrey, England.

Famous **Willeys:** WAITMAN THOMAS WILLEY (1811–1900) of West Virginia was a U.S. senator from Virginia, then West Virginia after the latter state was created. The Willey Admendment called for the gradual abolition of slavery. SAMUEL HOPKINS WILLEY (1821–1914) of New Hampshire was a clergyman and one of the founders of the College of California at Berkeley (1855).

Genealogies: *Some Descendants of Waitman Willey* was compiled by Helen McBroom Mayo and published in Edina, Minnesota, in 1981. *A Sketch of the Destruction of the Willey Family by the White Mountain Slide* was compiled by Edward Melcher and published in Lancaster, New Hampshire, in 1880. *Willey, Core, Bennett, and Other Ancestors* was compiled by Leroy Ellis Willie and published in Baton Rouge, Louisiana, in 1982.

WILLIAM, WILLIAMS, WILLIAMSON (S.S. Abbreviation: Willia)

Ranking: 3   **S.S. Count:** 2,307,467

Origin: English. Derived from the Norman version of an Old French first name comprising the Germanic words "wil" and "helm," meaning will and helmet.

Famous Bearers: ROGER WILLIAMS (1603–1682), born in England, was a minister in the Massachusetts Colony who was openly critical of Puritanism and its effect on government. Banished from Massachusetts, he founded Providence, Rhode Island. He secured from England a patent for Providence Plantations in 1644. He served three terms as president of the Rhode Island colony. HUGH WILLIAMSON (1735–1819) of Pennsylvania was a member of the Continental Congress, a signer of the U.S. Constitution, and a member of Congress from North Carolina. ALPHEUS S. WILLIAMS (1810–1878) of Connecticut was a high-ranking Union army officer during the Civil War, U.S. minister to Salvador in the late 1860s, then a member of Congress from Michigan. HENRY SHALER WILLIAMS (1847–1918) of New York was a paleontologist who developed the commonly used photographic method of fossil illustration. He also was an editor with the *Journal of Geology* and the *American Journal of Science*. FANNIE BARRIER WILLIAMS (1855–1944) of New York, after experiencing racial discrimination as a teacher, became a highly visible spokeswoman for African-American civil rights. DANIEL HALE WILLIAMS (1858–1931) of Pennsylvania is probably the most famous African-American doctor in U.S. history. A charter member of the American College of Surgeons, he performed the first successful closure of a wound of the heart and pericardium in 1893. He also perfected the suture for stopping a hemorrhage of the spleen. CHARLES R. WILLIAMS (1853–1927) of New York was editor of the *Indianapolis News* (1892–1911) and is credited with setting high standards in language style for Midwest newspapers. He also was a biographer of President Rutherford B. Hayes. EDWARD (NED) WILLIAMSON (1857–1895) of Pennsylvania was a professional baseball player who set a record for single-season home runs in 1884, a record that stood until Babe Ruth broke it in 1919. BERT WILLIAMS (1876–1922) of the Bahamas was a highly successful actor on stage and in vaudeville productions. He was the lead comedian in the Ziegfeld Follies for a while, and he and George Walker formed a vaudeville team and produced musical comedies with all–African-American casts in New York and London. His work helped to establish a foundation for African-Americans in the American theater. GLUYAS WILLIAMS (1888–1982) of California was a cartoonist who was published in periodicals such as *Collier's* and *The New Yorker*, in addition to daily newspapers. BEN AMES WILLIAMS (1889–1953) of Mississippi was a writer who had almost 600 pieces published in periodicals, including almost 180 in the *Saturday Evening Post*. His novels included the best-selling *House Divided* (1947), about the Civil War. AUBREY W. WILLIAMS (1890–1965) of Alabama was one of Franklin Roosevelt's New Deal administrators noted for his liberalism and outspokenness on civil rights and social justice. Later, as publisher of the *Southern Farmer* and as president of the Southern Conference Education Fund, he continued to speak out on civil rights, in opposition to many southern whites' determination to maintain segregation. MARY LOU WILLIAMS (1910–1981) of Pennsylvania was an influential jazz musician, composer, and arranger. TENNESSEE WILLIAMS (1911–1983) of Mississippi, born Thomas Lanier Williams, was a playwright who achieved fame with such works as *The Glass Menagerie* (1944) and *A Streetcar Named Desire* (1947), for which he was awarded a Pulitzer Prize. JOHN LEE (SONNY BOY) WILLIAMSON (1914–1948) of Tennessee was a blues musician who exercised great influence in harmonical and vocal styles. HANK WILLIAMS (1923–1953) of Alabama was a country music singer known for standards in his field, such as "Cold, Cold Heart," "Jambalaya," and "Your Cheatin' Heart." His death at age 29 was attributed to alcohol and drugs. His son, Hank Williams Jr., has had his own success as a country music singer.

Genealogies: *The Ancestors and Descendants of Ebenezer and Martha Porter Williams of Painesville, Ohio* was compiled by Percy Williams Lewis and published in La Grange, Illinois, in 1974. *The Ancestor; The World of William Williams* was compiled by John Francis Williams and published in Philadelphia, Pennsylvania, in 1971. *Diamonds in the Desert: The Family History of Bill and Gertie Williams* was compiled by Billie Williams Yost and published in Flagstaff, Arizona, in 1987.

WILLIFORD (S.S. Abbreviation: Willif)

Ranking: 3877   **S.S. Count:** 11,628

Origin: English. 1) the name was given to those who came from Wilford, the name of places in England. 2) the name was given to those who lived near willows that grew by the side of a river.

Genealogies: None known.

WILLING, WILLINGS (S.S. Abbreviation: Willin)

Ranking: 1966 S.S. Count: 23,041

Origin: German. Cognates to the first definition of Will.

Famous Bearers: THOMAS WILLING (1731–1821) of Pennsylvania was a banker, serving as president of the Bank of North America and the first bank of the United States, the mayor of Philadelphia, justice of the Pennsylvania Supreme Court, and a member of the second Continental Congress.

Genealogies: None known.

WILLIS

Ranking: 197 S.S. Count: 181,063

Origin: English. Transformation of the first definition of Will.

Famous Willises: NATHANIEL WILLIS (1780–1870) of Massachusetts started the first religious newspaper, the *Boston Recorder* (1816). His son, NATHANIEL PARKER WILLIS (1806–1867) of Maine, was considered one of the most sought-after periodical writers of his time. Nathaniel's son, BAILEY WILLIS (1857–1949) of New York, was a geologist who made progress in the studies of faults, seismology, and earthquakes. HENRY PARKER WILLIS (1874–1937) of New York was an economist and one of the first to foretell the stock market crash of 1929.

Genealogies: *The Family History of Nathaniel Purdue Willis of Eason, Oklahoma Territory* was compiled by Kathryn S. Carter and published in Tecumseh, Oklahoma, in 1979. *Some Willis Families of New England* was compiled by Aurie Willis Morrison and published in Massachusetts in 1973.

WILLOUGHBY (S.S. Abbreviation: Willou)

Ranking: 1994 S.S. Count: 22,760

Origin: English. Derived from the Old English word "wilig" and the Old Norman word "býr," meaning willow and farm. Also possibly derived from the word "wilig" and the Old English word "bēag," meaning willow and ring. The name was given to those who came from Willoughby, the name of several places in England.

Famous Willoughbys: WESTEL WOODBURY WILLOUGHBY (1867–1945) of Virginia was the founder of political science as a discipline. He was the editor of *American Political Science Review* and advisor to the Chinese government.

Genealogies: *The Willoughbys of Connecticut* was compiled by Miranda Goodrie Willoughby and published in Riverside, Connecticut, in 1976. *The Willoughby Family of New England* was compiled by Issac J. Greenwood and published in New York in 1876.

WILLS

Ranking: 1099 S.S. Count: 40,210

Origin: English. Transformation of Will.

Famous Willses: CHILDE HAROLD WILLS (1878–1940) of Indiana was a designer and manufacturer of automobiles. At first a designer with Henry Ford and an active participant in the design of the Model T, he left Ford Motor Co. in 1919 to produce his own car, named the Wills-St. Claire motor car. A car with four-wheel brakes and made of molybdenum steel stayed in production only until 1926 because of costs and design changes by Wills. HARRY WILLS (1889?–1958) of Louisiana was a boxer who was never able to fight Jack Dempsey for the heavyweight championship because of his being black. He was elected to the Boxing Hall of Fame in 1970.

Genealogies: *Tueth: Other Families, Hart, Fields, Newkirk, Wills* was compiled by Doris E. Wastradowski and published in 1983.

WILLSON (S.S. Abbreviation: Willso)

Ranking: 3639 S.S. Count: 12,389

Origin: English. Transformation of Will.

Famous Willsons: AUGUSTUS EVERETT WILLSON (1846–1931) of Kentucky was the governor of that state (1907–1911).

Genealogies: *Descendants in Canada and the United States of Benjamin and Sarah Willson* was compiled by Thomas B. Wilson and published in Madison, New Jersey, in 1967. *Willson, Wilson, and Allied Lines* was compiled by Clotilde Wilson Blower and published in Dunedin, Florida, in 1972.

WILMOT

Ranking: 3147 S.S. Count: 14,435

Origin: English. Transformation of William.

Genealogies: None known.

WILSON

Ranking: 10 S.S. Count: 1,119,446

Origin: English. Transformation of Will.

Famous Wilsons: JAMES WILSON (1742–1798) was born in Scotland and lived in Pennsylvania as an adult. He was a member of the Continental Congress, a signer of the Declaration of Independence, and a delegate to the Constitutional Convention. Later, he was an associate justice of the U.S. Supreme Court, then the first law professor at the University of Pennsylvania. ALEXANDER WILSON (1766–1813) of Pennsylvania was an ornithologist who catalogued birds of the eastern United States in seven volumes of *American Ornithology* (1808–1813). SAMUEL WILSON (1766–1854) of Massachusetts was the inspiration for the phrase "Uncle Sam" as a representation of the U.S. government. He was a meat packer in Troy, New York, where he was known simply as Uncle Sam. However, during the War of 1812 he stamped meat for a government contractor with the initials U.S., meaning "United States," and from then on U.S. and

Uncle Sam were synonymous. HENRY WILSON (1812–1875) of New Hampshire was a U.S. senator from Massachusetts and a U.S. vice president under President Ulysses S. Grant. He died in office. WILLIAM LYNE WILSON (1843–1900) of Virginia was a member of Congress from West Virginia, then U.S. postmaster general. He led the startup of rural free delivery of mail. He later was president of Washington and Lee University. ROBERT BURNS WILSON (1850–1916) of Pennsylvania was a poet and novelist who wrote the poem "Remember the Maine" (1898), which provided the slogan for the Spanish-American War. WOODROW WILSON (1856–1924) of Virginia was the 28th president of the United States (1913–1921). He was president of Princeton University and governor of New Jersey prior to becoming president. ELLEN LOUISE AXSON WILSON (1860– 1914) of Savannah, Georgia, was the first wife of President Woodrew Wilson. She died during her husband's presidency. EDITH BOLLING GALT WILSON (1872–1961) of Virginia was the second wife of President Woodrow Wilson. Edith was the granddaughter, seven times removed, of Pocahontas. WILLIAM BAUCHOP WILSON (1862–1934), born in Scotland, worked in Pennsylvania coal mines and was one of the organizers of the United Mine Workers of America. He later was a member of Congress, then the first U.S. secretary of labor. HALSEY WILLIAM WILSON (1868–1954) of Vermont founded the publishing firm of H. W. Wilson Co. and compiled many common references of today, including *Cumulative Book Index*, *Reader's Guide to Periodical Literature*, and *Book Review Digest*. J. FINLEY WILSON (1881–1952) of Tennessee founded, edited, and published the *Washington Eagle* in Washington, D.C. He also was president of the Colored Voters League in 1933. CHARLES ERWIN WILSON (1890–1961) of Ohio was president of General Motors (1941–1953), then U.S. secretary of defense (1953–1957). He reduced the defense budget by $5 billion and the civilian workforce by 40,000 people.

Genealogies: *A Brief Account of the Wilsons* was compiled by Emery Small Wilson and published in Camilla, Georgia, in 1970. *The DeMay Family and the Wilson Family* was compiled by Ida DeMay Wilson and published in Angwin, California, in 1974. *The Family of Samuel & Jean Love Wilson* was compiled by Sara Stewart Hinckley and published in Clarion, Pennsylvania, in 1984.

WILT

Ranking: 3942 **S.S. Count:** 11,456
Origin: German. The name means "descendant of Willihard" (ES).
Genealogies: None known.

WIMBERLY, WIMBERLEY (S.S. Abbreviation: Wimber)

Ranking: 2940 **S.S. Count:** 15,481

Origin: English. The names were given to those who came from Wimboldsley, a place in England.

Genealogies: *Wimberly Family History* was compiled by Vera Meek Wimberly and published in Houston, Texas, in 1979. *The Descendants of Joseph Ratcliff of Bienville Parish, Louisiana: Including the Families of Jeter, Wimberly, Davis, Dubberly, Wood, Hardy, Carmichael, Mathews, Norris, McKinney* was compiled by Jane Clancy Debenport and published in Midland, Texas, in 1988.

WIMMER (ALSO WIMMERS)

Ranking: 4925 **S.S. Count:** 9088
Origin: English. 1) derived from the Middle English first name Wymer, which was derived from the Old English name Wigmœr, which was derived from the Old English words "wig" and "mœr," meaning war and famous. 2) derived from the Old Breton first name Wiumarch, which comprised the words "uuiu" and "march," meaning worthy and horse.

Famous Bearers: BONIFACE WIMMER (1809–1887) of Bavaria was a Roman Catholic Benedictine clergyman and the founder of the Benedictine Order in the United States by establishing the first abbey in Westmoreland County, Pennsylvania (1846).

Genealogies: None known.

WINCHESTER (S.S. Abbreviation: Winche)

Ranking: 2052 **S.S. Count:** 22,297
Origin: English. Derived from the Romano-British name Venta, of unknown etymology, and the Old English word "ceaster," meaning Roman village. The name was given to those who came from Winchester, the name of a place in Hampshire, England.

Famous Winchesters: JAMES WINCHESTER (1752–1826) of Maryland was a U.S. senator from Tennessee. He was the founder of Memphis, Tennessee. OLIVER FISHER WINCHESTER (1810–1880) of Massachusetts invented a new way to manufacture shirts (1848). He founded the New Haven Arms Co., which later became the Winchester Repeating Arms Co. (1857).

Genealogies: *John Winchester 1616–1694, A Settler of New England, and One Line of His Descendants* was compiled by George Rogers Presson and published in San Francisco and Oakland, California, in 1897.

WINDER

Ranking: 4283 **S.S. Count:** 10,480
Origin: English. 1) derived from the Middle English word "wind(en)," meaning to wind. The name was given to those who worked as winders of wool. 2) derived from the Old English words "vinder" and "erg," meaning wind and shelter. The name was given to those who came from Winder, the name of several places in England.

Famous **Winders**: Levin Winder (1757–1819) of Maryland was the governor of Maryland. William Henry Winder (1775–1824) of Maryland was a soldier in the War of 1812 and the commander at the Battle of Bladensburg who was blamed for the defeat of the Americans that left Washington, D.C., vunerable to attack by the British. How much of the fiasco was his fault is still in question. His son, John Henry Winder (1800–1865) of Maryland, was a Confederate soldier who was also commander of several military prisons. He was defended by Jefferson Davis for his decisions during command.

Genealogies: None known.

WINDHAM (S.S. Abbreviation: Windha)

Ranking: 3178 **S.S. Count:** 14,289

Origin: English, Irish. English: 1) derived from the Old English first name Winda and the Old English word "hamm," meaning wet meadow. The name was given to those from Wyndham, a place in western Sussex, England. 2) derived from the Old English first name Wigmund and the Old English word "hām," meaning homestead. The name was given to those who came from Wymondham, the name of places in England. Irish: derived from the Anglicized versions of Gaelic names that were derived from the Gaelic word "gaoith," meaning wind.

Genealogies: None known.

WINDSOR (S.S. Abbreviation: Windso)

Ranking: 4233 **S.S. Count:** 10,650

Origin: English. Derived from an Old English word, probably "windels," meaning windlass, and the word "ōra," meaning bank. The name was given to those who came from Windsor, the name of several places in England.

Genealogies: *Early Pioneers of Piedmont North Carolina Where Yadkin, Wilkes, & Iredell Meet: The Descendants of Isaac Windsor, 1753–1821, Eight Generations* was compiled by Gerald Wilson Cook and published in Fancy Gap, Virginia, in 1992. *Descendants of Roger Williams (also Windsor family)* was compiled by Roger Williams Family Association and published in Baltimore, Maryland, in 1991.

WINFIELD (S.S. Abbreviation: Winfie)

Ranking: 4004 **S.S. Count:** 11,304

Origin: English. Uncertain etymology. Probably derived from the Old English words "wynn" and "feld," meaning meadow and open field. The name was given to those who came from Winfield (now Wingfield), the name of several places in England.

Genealogies: *Tanglewood Chronicles: A Pedigree of Branches of the Smithers, Kelley, Winfield, Johnson, and Allied Families* was compiled by Debra Winfield Smithers and published in Corpus Christi, Texas, in 1983.

WINFREE, WINFREY (S.S. Abbreviation: Winfre)

Ranking: 3528 **S.S. Count:** 12,791

Origin: English. The name was given to those who came from Winfrith, the name of a place in England.

Genealogies: *The Winfrey Family* was compiled by James Clifton Winfrey and published in Littleton, Colorado, in 1982.

WING

Ranking: 2340 **S.S. Count:** 19,385

Origin: English. 1) uncertain etymology. Probably derived from a word meaning protector.

Famous **Wings**: Joseph Elwyn Wing (1861–1915) of New York was an Ohio farmer and an agricultural journalist who favored the introduction of alfalfa in the eastern half of the country.

Genealogies: *Reuben Wing, Senior, Of "Old Winthrop"* was compiled by Harold C. Perham and published in West Paris, Maine, in 1968.

WINGATE (S.S. Abbreviation: Wingat)

Ranking: 3852 **S.S. Count:** 11,708

Origin: English, Scottish. Derived from the Old English words "wind" and "geat," meaning wind and gate. The name was given to those who came from Wingate, the name of several places in England.

Famous **Wingates**: Paine Wingate (1739–1838) of Massachusetts was a member of Congress and a U.S. senator from New Hampshire, then a judge of the New Hampshire superior court.

Genealogies: None known.

WINGER (ALSO WINGERT)

Ranking: 3571 **S.S. Count:** 12,629

Origin: Winger—English; Wingert—German. Winger: the name means "descendant of Winegar" (ES). Wingert: derived from the English words "win" and "geard," meaning wine and yard. The name was given to those who lived near or worked in a vineyard.

Genealogies: None known.

WINGFIELD (S.S. Abbreviation: Wingfi)

Ranking: 4871 **S.S. Count:** 9186

Origin: English. Transformation of Winfield.

Famous **Wingfields**: Edward Maria Wingfield (?–1613), birthplace unknown, was one of Virginia's first settlers and a grantee of the Virginia charter (1606).

Genealogies: None known.

WINKEL

Ranking: 3265 **S.S. Count:** 13,929

Origin: Dutch, German. Derived from the Old High Ger-

man word "winkil," meaning corner. The name was given to those who owned a corner store, or who lived on a street corner, or who lived on a corner of land in the country.

Genealogies: None known.

WINKLE (ALSO WINKLER)

Ranking: 1038 S.S. Count: 42,149

Origin: Winkle, Winkler—Dutch, German. Transformations of Winkel.

Famous **Bearers:** Edwin Theodore Winkler (1823–1883) of Savannah, Georgia, was a Confederate chaplin, editor of the *Southern Baptist* and *Alabama Baptist*, and pastor of churches in Charleston, South Carolina. His greatest concern was the welfare of blacks.

Genealogies: None known.

WINN

Ranking: 1449 S.S. Count: 30,742

Origin: English. Derived from the Old English name Wine, meaning friend.

Famous **Winns:** Richard Winn (1750–1818) of Virginia was a Revolutionary soldier and a captain in the defense of Forth McIntosh, Georgia (1777). After the war he served as a member of Congress from South Carolina.

Genealogies: *The Winns of Fairfield County: Colonel John Winn, William Winn, General Richard Winn* was compiled by Buford S. Chappell and published in Columbia, South Carolina, in 1975.

WINSLOW (S.S. Abbreviation: Winslo)

Ranking: 2286 S.S. Count: 19,893

Origin: English. Derived from the Old English name Wine and the word "hlāw," meaning hill. The name was given to those who came from Winslow, a place in Buckinghamshire, England.

Famous **Winslows:** Edward Winslow (1595–1655) of England was an explorer and the father of Josiah Winslow. Josiah Winslow (1629?–1680) of Massachusetts was the commander of the Plymouth Colony, succeeding Myles Standish. He is credited with starting the first school at Plymouth. As the chief of the United Colonies' forces, he became the first native-born commander of an American army. He was the commander who won in the battle against Narragansett (1675). John Flack Winslow (1810–1892) of Vermont was an industrialist in association with Erastus Corning. Their firm, Corning & Winslow, made the iron plates for the Union ironclad the *Monitor*.

Genealogies: *The Quaker and Southern Winslows* was compiled by Elizabeth Doherty Herzfeld and published in Spartanburg, South Carolina, in 1991. *Tracing Shadows: The Record of a 19th Century Vermont Family, Their Ancestors and Descendants* [also Winslow] was compiled by Eliz-

abeth Sharpe Lincoln and published in East Greenwich, Rhode Island, in 1978. *The Winslows of Careswell in Marshfield* was compiled by Betty Magoun Bates and published in Marshfield, Massachusetts, in 1992.

WINSTEAD (S.S. Abbreviation: Winste)

Ranking: 3460 S.S. Count: 13,041

Origin: English. The name was given to those who came from Winstead, the name of a place in England.

Genealogies: None known.

WINSTON (S.S. Abbreviation: Winsto)

Ranking: 3460 S.S. Count: 29,514

Origin: English, Jewish. English: 1) derived from an Old English first name, comprising the words "wynn" and "stān," meaning joy and stone. 2) derived from various Old English first names and the Old English words "tūn" or "stān," meaning settlement and stone. Jewish: Anglicized version of Weinstein.

Famous **Winstons:** Joseph Winston (1746–1815) of Virginia was Patrick Henry's cousin, a member of Congress from North Carolina, and the namesake of the town of Winston (now Winston-Salem), North Carolina. John Anthony Winston (1812–1871) of Alabama was the governor of Alabama before the Civil War and elected U.S. senator afterward. By his refusal to take the oath of allegiance, he was denied the office.

Genealogies: *The Winstons of Hanover County, Virginia and Related Families, 1666–1992* was compiled by Alfred Sumner Winston III and published in Hilton Head, South Carolina, in 1992.

WINTER

Ranking: 302 S.S. Count: 120,513

Origin: Danish/Norwegian, English, German, Irish, Jewish. Danish/Norwegian, English, German: derived from the Danish/Norwegian and Old English word "winter," the Old High German word "wintar," or the Old Norman word "vetr," all meaning winter. The name was given to those who were of cold or gloomy disposition. Irish: derived from the Gaelic name Mac Giolla Gheimhridh, meaning winter. Jewish: derived from the German word "winter," meaning winter. The name was assigned or taken ornamentally.

Famous **Winters:** William Winter (1836–1917) of Massachusetts was a drama critic and historian of stage roles and actors. He lived in the Greenwich Village section of New York City, and his 1909 *Old Friends* about that time is considered an excellent journal on the life and times of that period.

Genealogies: None known.

WIRTH

Ranking: 3189 S.S. Count: 14,231

Origin: German, Jewish. German: derived from the Middle High German word "wirt," meaning provider. The name was given to men who were heads of families or heads of households. German and Jewish: derived from the Middle High German word "wirt," meaning host. The name was given to those who worked as innkeepers.

Genealogies: None known.

WISE
Ranking: 419 **S.S. Count:** 94,491
Origin: English, German, Jewish. English: derived from the Old English word "wis," meaning wise. The name was given to those who were considered to be wise, or who were considered to have mystical ability. German, Jewish: Anglicized version Weiss, a cognate to White.

Famous Wises: AARON WISE (1844–1896) of Hungary was one of the founders of the Jewish Theological Seminary of New York (1886). His son, STEPHEN SAMUEL WISE (1874–1949) of Hungary, was brought to New York City as an infant. He was a fighter of injustices, co-founding the National Association for the Advancement of Colored People (1909) and the American Civil Liberties Union (1920). He was the founder of the Jewish Institute of Religion (1922), a training school for rabbis. JOHN WISE (1808–1879) of Pennsylvania was a balloonist responsible for the balloon safety feature of the rip panel, which he invented. He was the holder of the long-distance record of 809 miles set in 1859.

Genealogies: *History of the Wise and Wyse Families of South Carolina* was compiled by Sybil Harmon and published in Dallas, Texas, in 1992. *Looking Back: A Family History and Genealogy of and by Hazel Wise Huffman* was compiled by Hazel Wise Huffman and published in 1985. *The Wise Family Chronicles* was compiled by Ronnie W. Wise and published in Cleveland, Mississippi, in 1985.

WISEMAN (S.S. Abbreviation: Wisema)
Ranking: 1703 **S.S. Count:** 26,204
Origin: English. Transformation of Wise.
Genealogies: *The Wiseman Family and Allied Lines* was compiled by Eugene M. Wiseman and published in Franklin, North Carolina, in 1991.

WISNIEWSKI (S.S. Abbreviation: Wisnie)
Ranking: 2171 **S.S. Count:** 21,124
Origin: Jewish, Polish. Jewish: 1) derived from the Polish word "wiśnia," meaning cherry tree. The name was taken ornamentally. 2) cognate to the Polish definition. Polish: derived from the Polish word "wiśnia," meaning cherry tree, and the suffix "-ak." The name was given to those who came from Wiśniewo, a place in Poland.
Genealogies: None known.

WITHER (ALSO WITHERS, WITHERSPOON)
Ranking: 1063 **S.S. Count:** 41,456
Origin: Wither, Withers—English; Witherspoon—Scottish. Wither: 1) derived from the Old Norman first name Víðarr, which was derived from the words "víð" and "árr," meaning wide and messenger. 2) derived from the Middle English word "wyth(e)," meaning willow tree. The name was given to those who lived near willow trees. Withers: transformation of Wither. Witherspoon: uncertain etymology. Possibly derived from the Middle English words "wither" and "spong" or "spang," meaning ram and thin piece of land.

Famous **Bearers:** JOHN WITHERSPOON (1723–1794) of Scotland was the president of Princeton University, breathing new life into the school with more money, faculty, and students. He was a member of the Continental Congress and a signer of the Declaration of Independence. SARAH WITHER (1761–1804) of Pennsylvania kept a diary covering the period from September 1777 to June 1778, when the British occupied Philadelphia. FREDERICK CLARKE WITHERS (1828–1901) of England was an architect whose work can be seen in many of the churches and buildings of New York City, including the Jefferson Market Police Court in the Greenwich Village section.

Genealogies: None known.

WITHROW (S.S. Abbreviation: Withro)
Ranking: 3862 **S.S. Count:** 11,673
Origin: English. The name was given to those who lived on a road that passed through willow trees.
Genealogies: None known.

WITT
Ranking: 977 **S.S. Count:** 44,817
Origin: English, Irish, German, Scottish. English, Irish, Scottish: transformation of White. German: cognate to White.
Genealogies: *Our Ancestors Witt and Copeland* was compiled by Forrest E. Witt and published in Hastings, Nebraska, in 1976. *Witt-Bates Connections, 1976* was compiled by Mrs. J. M. Harris and published in Denton, Texas, in 1976. *Witty-Todd Genealogy* was compiled by Carl Dean Witty and published in Athens, Alabama, in 1983.

WITTE
Ranking: 3418 **S.S. Count:** 13,236
Origin: English, Irish, German, Scottish. English, Irish, Scottish: transformation of White. German: cognate to White.
Famous **Wittes:** EDWIN EMIL WITTE (1887–1960) of Wisconsin was the author of *The Government in Labor Disputes* (1932) and the head of President Franklin D. Roosevelt's Committee on Economic Security, which was responsible for the Social Security Act of 1935.
Genealogies: None known.

WITTEN

Ranking: 3576 S.S. Count: 12,609
Origin: German. Cognate to White.
Genealogies: *Greenup, Witten, Cecil* was compiled by Elise Greenup Jourdan and published in Knoxville, Tennessee, in 1989.

WITTMAN (S.S. Abbreviation: Wittma)

Ranking: 4799 S.S. Count: 9332
Origin: English. Transformation of Whitman.
Genealogies: None known.

WOFFORD (S.S. Abbreviation: Woffor)

Ranking: 3705 S.S. Count: 12,191
Origin: English. The name means "enclosure for protection against wolves" (ES). The name was given to those who came from Wolford, the name of a place in England.
Genealogies: *The Homecoming: A Celebration of the Wofford, Lottie, and Brinker Families* was compiled by Dorothy Wofford Witherspoon and published in Kansas City, Missouri, in 1990.

WOJCIECH, WOJCIEHOWICZ, WOJCIEDHOWSKI, WOJCIESZEK (S.S. Abbreviation: Wojcie)

Ranking: 4704 S.S. Count: 9512
Origin: Polish. Derived from the Czech first name Vojtech, which was derived from the words "noi" and "tech," meaning soldier and comfort.
Genealogies: None known.

WOJCIK

Ranking: 4149 S.S. Count: 10,914
Origin: Polish. Derived from the Polish word "wójt," meaning town chief, which was derived from the German word "vogt," meaning farm boss or bailiff.
Genealogies: None known.

WOLF

Ranking: 394 S.S. Count: 98,549
Origin: English, German, Irish, Jewish. English, German: derived from names having the word "wolf," meaning wolf, as the first component. Irish: translation of the Gaelic name Ó Faoláin, which was derived from the Gaelic word "faol," meaning wolf. Jewish: derived from the Yiddish first name Volf, which is derived from the Hebrew first name Binyamin.
Famous **Wolfs**: GEORGE WOLF (1777–1840) of Pennsylvania was a member of Congress, then governor of Pennsylvania. SIMON WOLF (1836–1923) of Bavaria was the founder and president of Hebrew Orphan's Home, Atlanta, Georgia.
Genealogies: *Jacob Wolf, Burnet County Pioneer* was

compiled by R. S. Crawford and published in Waco, Texas, in 1969. *Jacob Wolf History* was compiled by Merritt W. Wolfe and published in Akron, Ohio, in 1982. *Descendants of Leonard Wolf Sr. and Catharine Cripe, 1755–1984* was compiled by Ardelta Delores Wolfe Baker and published in Wichita, Kansas, in 1985.

WOLFE

Ranking: 313 S.S. Count: 117,809
Origin: English, German, Jewish. Cognate to Wolf. The name was sometimes given to those who had wolflike qualities.
Famous **Wolfes**: THOMAS CLAYTON WOLFE (1900–1938) of North Carolina was a novelist. His first book, *Look Homeward, Angel* (1929), was autobiographical. He died before his six-volume series was finished. Three books were released from his unfinished works: *The Web and the Rock* (1939), *You Can't Go Home Again* (1940), and *The Hills Beyond* (1941).
Genealogies: *The Wolf, Wolfe, Wolff Families of Pennsylvania* was compiled by Raymond Alvin Wolff and published in Baltimore, Maryland, in 1971. *Joe Garrett: A Pictorial and Written History of the Joseph Luther Garrett Family, 1860–1935* [also Wolfe] was published in Conroe, Texas, in 1980. *The Wolfe Family in Raleigh* was compiled by Richard Walser and published in Raleigh, North Carolina, in 1976.

WOLFF

Ranking: 1357 S.S. Count: 32,705
Origin: Danish/Norwegian, Jewish. Danish/Norwegian: cognate to Wolf. Jewish: transformation of the Jewish definition of Wolf.
Famous **Wolffs**: KURT AUGUST PAUL WOLFF (1887–1963) of Germany was a publisher who was responsible for the publication of *Born Free* and *Dr. Zhivago*.
Genealogies: *The Wolf, Wolfe, Wolff Families of Pennsylvania* was compiled by Raymond Alvin Wolff and published in Baltimore, Maryland, in 1971.

WOLFORD (S.S. Abbreviation: Wolfor)

Ranking: 2979 S.S. Count: 15,265
Origin: English. Derived from the Old English first name Wulfweard, derived from the words "wulf" and "weard," meaning wolf and guardian. The name was given to those who came from Wolford, a place in Warwickshire, England.
Genealogies: None known.

WOLTER

Ranking: 3675 S.S. Count: 12,269
Origin: German. Cognate to Walter.
Genealogies: None known.

WOMACK

Ranking: 1218 S.S. Count: 36,235

Origin: English. The name was given to those who lived near a twisted or hollowed oak tree.

Genealogies: *Womack Genealogy* was compiled by Maxine Hulse Tinkham and published in 1979.

WONG

Ranking: 457 S.S. Count: 87,758

Origin: Chinese, English. Chinese: 1) the name means royal or king. 2) the name means yellow. 3) the name means wide, as in wide ocean. English: cognate to/transformation of the German definition of Wang.

Famous **Wongs:** ANNA MAY WONG (1907–1961) of California was an actress who broke the ethnic barrier that previous minority performers had accepted to be hired at all in Hollywood. First appearing in *The Thief of Baghdad* (1924), she went on to star in many films made about the Orient. The 1933 movie *A Study in Scarlett* was one of her best.

Genealogies: None known.

WOO

Ranking: 4123 S.S. Count: 10,967

Origin: Chinese? Uncertain etymology.

Genealogies: None known.

WOOD

Ranking: 70 S.S. Count: 356,012

Origin: English, Scottish. 1) derived from the Old English word "wudu," meaning wood. The name was given to those who worked as woodcutters or those who lived near woods. 2) derived from the Old English word "wād," meaning crazed or crazy. The name was given to those who were considered mad or violent.

Famous **Woods:** JETHRO WOOD (1774–1834) of either New York or Massachusetts was the inventor of a cast-iron plow (1819). FERNANDO WOOD (1812–1881) of Pennsylvania was the mayor of New York City and a leader in Tammany Hall. His contribution to society was helping to organize Central Park. JAMES RUSHMORE WOOD (1813–1882) of New York was the co-founder of Bellevue Hospital. WALTER ABBOTT WOOD (1815–1892) of New Hampshire was the maker of farm mowers, reapers, and binders. DAVID DUFFLE WOOD (1838–1910) was blind from his youth. He taught himself music, then taught it at the Pennsylvania Institution for the Instruction of the Blind and organ instructor at the Philadelphia Musical Academy. JAMES J. WOOD (1856–1928) of Ireland came to the United States as a boy and was raised in Connecticut. He invented electrical devices, for which he received 240 patents. One of his inventions was the floodlighting system used to illuminate the Statue of Liberty. LEONARD WOOD (1860–1927) of New Hampshire was a surgeon in the military and a close friend of Teddy Roosevelt's. He helped Roosevelt organize the Rough Riders. MARY ELIZABETH WOOD (1861–1931) of New York was the founder of the Boone Library School, China (1920).

Genealogies: *The Davis-Wood Family of Gadsden County, Florida and Their Forebears [sic]* was compiled by Fenton Garnett Davis Avant and published in Easley, South Carolina, in 1979. *Descendants of John Wood, A Mariner, Who Died in Portsmouth, Rhode Island, in 1655* was compiled by Dorothy Wood Ewers and published in Colorado Springs, Colorado, in 1978. *The Michael Woods– Mary Campbell Family in America* was compiled by Patsy Young Woods and published in Eagar, Arizona, in 1984.

WOODALL (S.S. Abbreviation: Woodal)

Ranking: 2059 S.S. Count: 22,227

Origin: English, Scottish. Derived from the Old English words "wudu" and "hall," meaning wood and hall or manor. The name was given to those who came from Woodall, the name of several places in England.

Genealogies: None known.

WOODARD (S.S. Abbreviation: Woodar)

Ranking: 676 S.S. Count: 62,014

Origin: English. 1) derived from an Old English first name, probably Wuduheard. 2) derived from the Old English words "wudu" and "hierde," meaning wood and herder of animals. 3) transformation of Woodward.

Genealogies: *Ancestors of Dr. Franklin Columbus Woodard and his Descendants, 1757–1982* was compiled by Jewell Daphne Gerron Woodard and published in Fort Worth, Texas, in 1982.

WOODBURN, WOODBURY (S.S. Abbreviation: Woodbu)

Ranking: 3341 S.S. Count: 13,557

Origin: Woodburn—English, Scottish; Woodbury—English. Woodburn: derived from the Old English words "wudu" and "burna," meaning wood and stream. The name was given to those who came from Woodburn, the name of several places in England. Woodbury: the name means built of wood or located in the woods. The name was given to those who came from Woodbury or Woodborough, the name of places in England.

Famous **Bearers:** LEVI WOODBURY (1789–1851) of New Hampshire was the governor of New Hampshire, a member of Congress, Speaker of the House, U.S. senator from New Hampshire, and a justice of the U.S. Supreme Court. DANIEL PHINEAS WOODBURY (1812–1864) of New Hampshire was a Union soldier and engineer and a builder of several forts, including Fort Laramie, Wyoming. CHARLES JEPTHA HILL WOODBURY (1851–1916) was an expert in fire prevention and an executive with Mutual Fire Insurance Co. HELEN LAURA SUMNER WOODBURY (1876–1933) of Wisconsin was a pioneer in the field of labor problems and social legislation in that area.

Genealogies: None known.

WOODCOCK (S.S. Abbreviation: Woodco)

Ranking: 3944 S.S. Count: 11,453

Origin: English. 1) derived from the Old English words "wudu" and "cocc," meaning wood and bird. The name was given to those who were stupid or foolish. 2) derived from the Old English words "wudu" and "cot," meaning wood and cottage. The name was given to those who came from Woodcott or Woodcock, the names of places in England.

Genealogies: None known.

WOODEN

Ranking: 4481 S.S. Count: 10,000

Origin: English. 1) the name was given to those who came from Wooden, meaning valley of wolves, the name of a place in England. 2) the name was given to those who lived at the end of the woods.

Genealogies: None known.

WOODFORD (S.S. Abbreviation: Woodfo)

Ranking: 4748 S.S. Count: 9432

Origin: English, Scottish. Derived from the Old English words "wudu" and "ford," meaning wood and ford. The name was given to those who came from Woodford, the name of several places in England.

Famous Woodfords: WILLIAM WOODFORD (1734–1789) of Virginia was a Revolutionary War patriot who fought in the battles of Monmouth, Brandywine, and Germantown and wintered at Valley Forge. He was captured in Charleston, South Carolina, and died as a prisoner of war. STEWART LYNDON WOODFORD (1835–1913) of New York City was a Union soldier, lawyer, and diplomat. He served politically in New York City and as the minister to Spain.

Genealogies: Descendants of James and Jane Stokes Woodford was compiled by George Woodford Weston and published in Aurora, Illinois, in 1971.

WOODLEY (S.S. Abbreviation: Woodle)

Ranking: 3926 S.S. Count: 11,492

Origin: English. Derived from the Old English words "wudu" and "lēah," meaning wood and clearing. The name was given to those who came from Woodley or Woodleigh, the names of places in England.

Genealogies: Deep East Texas Folk: The Tillers, Crenshaws, Woodleys, Goldens, and Other Related Families of Panola and Harrison Counties was compiled by Terry G. Jordan and published in Dallas, Texas, in 1976.

WOODMAN (S.S. Abbreviation: Woodma)

Ranking: 4291 S.S. Count: 10,462

Origin: English, Scottish. 1) transformation of Wood. The name was given to those who worked as woodcutters. 2) possibly derived from the Old English first name Wudumann, which was derived from the words "wudu" and "mann," meaning wood and man.

Genealogies: The Woodmans of Rhode Island: Descendants of John Woodman of Little Compton, Rhode Island was compiled by Helen Denny Woodman and published in St. Petersburg, Florida, in 1989.

WOODRUFF (S.S. Abbreviation: Woodruff)

Ranking: 1041 S.S. Count: 42,065

Origin: English. Derived from the Old English word "wudurofe," meaning woodruff. The name was given to those who lived on land with woodruff growing on it.

Famous Woodruffs: WILLIAM EDWARD WOODRUFF (1795–1885) of New York was the founder of the Arkansas Gazette and the Arkansas Democrat. WILFORD WOODRUFF (1807–1898) of Connecticut was the official historian and one of the apostles appointed by Brigham Young in the Morman religion. He was responsible for the Mormon "Manifesto" (1890), which outlawed plural marriages. THEODORE TUTTLE WOODRUFF (1811–1892) of New York was an inventor of the seat and couch railway cars. He also worked on railway sleeping cars, a coffee-hulling machine, and a steam plow.

Genealogies: Tall Trees in the Forest: The Woodruff Family of Virginia, Alabama, and Missouri was compiled by Mrs. Howard Woodruff and published in Kansas City, Missouri, in 1966. Woodfuff-Rardin Families was compiled by Audrey Lee Wagner Woodruff and published in Kansas City, Missouri, in 1968.

WOODS

Ranking: 122 S.S. Count: 238,204

Origin: English, Scottish. Transformation of the first definition of Wood.

Famous Woodses: WILLIAM BURNHAM WOODS (1824–1887) of Ohio was a justice of the U.S. Supreme Court. WILLIAM ALLEN WOODS (1837–1901) of Tennessee was an Indiana Supreme Court justice and is best known for the case of United States v. Debs, in which he sentenced Eugene Debs to prison.

Genealogies: Let the Deed Shaw: A Pictorial and Historical Record of the Fleming, Edwards and Woods Families was compiled by James R. Fleming and published in Palos Verdes Estates, California, in 1981. The Michael Woods-Mary Campbell Family in America was compiled by Patsy

Woods Young and published in Eagar, Arizona, in 1984. *The Woods Family: Colonial Days to 1979* was compiled by Willa Woods Hiltner and published in Wenatchee, Washington, in 1979.

WOODSON (S.S. Abbreviation: Woodso)
Ranking: 1838 S.S. Count: 24,609
Origin: English. 1) derived from the Old Englsh word "wudu," meaning wood. The name means houses in the woods. The name was given to those who came from Woodsome, the name of a place in England. 2) the name means "the son of Wuda" (ES), which is derived from the Old English word "wudu," meaning wood.

Famous Woodsons: CARTER GODWIN WOODSON (1875–1950) of Virginia was the child of people born into slavery. Hard work on his part gave him the opportunity to attend school and earn his degree. He became a historian and an author of books about blacks, including *The Negro in Our History* (1922).

Genealogies: *The Sable Curtain (Woodson family)* was compiled by Minnie Shumate Woodson and published in Washington, D.C., in 1987.

WOODWARD (S.S. Abbreviation: Woodwa)
Ranking: 771 S.S. Count: 54,596
Origin: English. 1) derived from the Old English words "wudu" and "weard," meaning wood and guardian. The name was given to those who worked as foresters. 2) uncertain etymology. Possibly derived from the Old English first name Wuduweard, which was derived from "wudu" and "weard," meaning wood and guardian.

Famous Woodwards: HENRY WOODWARD (1646?–1686?) of the West Indies was the first English settler in South Carolina in the Cape Fear area. SAMUEL BAYARD WOODWARD (1787–1850) of Connecticut was one of the founders of the Connecticut Retreat for the Insane in Hartford (1824). JOSEPH JANVIER WOODWARD (1833–1884) of Pennsylvania was the physician who attended President James A. Garfield between the time he was shot and his death in 1881. ROBERT SIMPSON WOODWARD (1849–1924) of Michigan was an engineer and mathematical physicist and the editor of *Science Magazine* (1884–1924). WILLIAM WOODWARD (1876–1953) of New York City was the breeder of race horses, including Gallant Fox and Omaha, both of whom won the "Triple Crown."

Genealogies: None known.

WOODWORTH (S.S. Abbreviation: Woodwo)
Ranking: 3383 S.S. Count: 13,382
Origin: English. Derived from the Old English words "wudu" and "worð," meaning wood and worth. The name was given to those who lived on a homestead in or near a forest.

Famous Woodworths: SAMUEL WOODWORTH (1784–1842) of Massachusetts was a journalist and the author of three satires, *New Haven* (1809), *Beasts of Law* (1811), and *Quarter-Day* (1812). JAY BACKUS WOODWORTH (1865–1925) of New York was a pioneer in seismology and was the founder of the Harvard seismological station, one of the nation's first.

Genealogies: *From the Old Colony of New Plymouth to Nebraska, 1620–1920: The History and Genealogy of the Family of Mildred Woodworth* was compiled by Leopold H. Hoppe and published in Gladstone, Missouri, in 1992. *Some Descendants of Robert Porter, Farmington, Connecticut, 1640: With Female Lines* [also Woodworth] was compiled by Margaret Porter Miller and published in Easton, Maryland, in 1986. *A Genealogy of Richard Woodworth, 1758 Ireland–1843 Ohio* was compiled by Marie Monson and published in North Bend, Oregon, in 1975.

WOODY
Ranking: 1822 S.S. Count: 24,788
Origin: English. 1) the name was given to those who lived in an enclosed area in a forest. 2) the name was given to those who came from Woodhay, the name of places in England.
Genealogies: None known.

WOOLDRIDGE (S.S. Abbreviation: Wooldr)
Ranking: 3912 S.S. Count: 11,529
Origin: English. Derived from the Middle English first name Wol(f)rich or the Old English name Wulfric, which were derived from the words "wulf" and "ric," meaning wolf and power.

Genealogies: *John Wooldridge, Blacksmith* was compiled by Laurence B. Gardiner and published in Troutville, Virginia, in 1980. *The Descendants of Josiah and Keziah Nichols Wooldridge and Their Ancestors* was compiled by Wright W. Frost and published in Knoxville, Tennessee, in 1973.

WOOLEY
Ranking: 4647 S.S. Count: 9619
Origin: English. Transformation of Woolley.
Famous Wooleys: EDGAR MONTILLION "MONTY" WOOLEY (1888–1963) of New York City was an actor who starred in the 1939 play and 1942 movie *The Man Who Came to Dinner*. He received Oscar nominations for his roles in *The Pied Piper* (1942) and *Since You Went Away* (1944).

Genealogies: None known.

WOOLLEY (S.S. Abbreviation: Woolle)
Ranking: 3981 S.S. Count: 11,359
Origin: English. 1) derived from the Old English words "wulf" and "lēah," meaning wolf and clearing. The name was given to those who came from Woolley, the name of several

places in England. 2) derived from the Middle English words "woll" or "wull," meaning stream. The name was given to those who came from Woolley, the name of several places in England.

Famous **Woolleys:** CELIA PARKER WOOLLEY (1848–1918) of Ohio was a settlement worker. She founded and lived in Frederick Douglass Center in Chicago. MARY EMMA WOOL-LEY (1863–1947) of Connecticut was an advocate of women's rights and the president of Mount Holyoke College (1901–1937).

Genealogies: None known.

WOOLSEY (S.S. Abbreviation: Woolse)

Ranking: 4644 S.S. Count: 9628

Origin: English. Derived from the Old English first name Wulfsige, which was derived from the words "wulf" and "sige," meaning wolf and victory.

Famous **Woolseys:** THEODORE DWIGHT WOOLSEY (1801–1889) of New York City was the president of Yale University and one of the foremost political scientists of his time. SARAH CHAUNCY WOOLSEY (1835–1905) of Ohio was an author of children's stories. She wrote under the name Susan Coolidge and was the author of *What Katy Did* (1872) and *Letters of Jane Austen* (1892).

Genealogies: *Ancestry of Sarah Fowler* [also Woolsey] was compiled by Harriette Grace Lewis and published in 1979. *One Branch of the Woolsey Family* was compiled by Grace Woolsey Nelson and published in Onamia, Minnesota, in 1976.

WOOTEN

Ranking: 1039 S.S. Count: 42,126

Origin: English. Derived from the Old English words "wudu" and "tūn," meaning wood and settlement. The name was given to those who came from Wooten, the name of several places in England.

Genealogies: None known.

WORDEN

Ranking: 3430 S.S. Count: 13,164

Origin: English. Uncertain etymology. Probably derived from the Old English words "wer" and "denu," meaning weir and valley. The name was given to those who came from Worden, the name of several places in England.

Famous **Wordens:** JOHN LORIMER WORDEN (1818–1897) of New York was the commander of the *Monitor* in battle with the *Merrimack* in the Civil War.

Genealogies: None known.

WORKMAN (S.S. Abbreviation: Workma)

Ranking: 1075 S.S. Count: 41,017

Origin: English. Derived from the Old English words "weord" and "mann," meaning work and man. The name was given to those who worked as laborers.

Famous **Workmans:** FANNY BULLOCK WORKMAN (1859–1925) of Massachusetts was an explorer and the holder in 1906 of the woman's mountaineering record.

Genealogies: *Some Branches of the Workman Tree* was compiled by Ralph Hall Sayre and published in Baltimore, Maryland, in 1979. *Workman Family History* was compiled by Thelma C. Anderson and published in Salt Lake City, Utah, in 1962.

WORLEY

Ranking: 1274 S.S. Count: 34,698

Origin: English. Uncertain etymology. 1) possibly derived from the Old English words "wyrt" and "lēah," meaning plant and clearing. The name was given to those who came from Worley or Wortley, the names of places in England. 2) possibly derived from the name Warley, which was derived from the Old English words "wœr" or "wer" and "lēah," meaning weir and clearing. The name was given to those who came from Warley or Worley, the names of places in England. 3) possibly derived from the name Warley, which was derived from the Old English words "weorf" and "lēah," meaning yoke oxen and clearing. The name was given to those who came from Warley or Worley, the names of places in England.

Genealogies: *300th Anniversary of Worleys in America, 1682–1982* was compiled by Carolyn Worley and published in Elberton, Georgia, in 1981.

WORRELL (S.S. Abbreviation: Worrel)

Ranking: 2808 S.S. Count: 16,231

Origin: English. Derived from the Old English words "wir" and "halh," meaning bog myrtle, a shrub, and nook. The name was given to those who came from Worrall, a place in South Yorkshire, England.

Genealogies: *Ancestors & Descendants of Jonathan Worrell, 1833–1915* was compiled by Donna Kelly and published in Fallston, Maryland, in 1991.

WORTH

Ranking: 4007 S.S. Count: 11,298

Origin: English. Derived from the Old English word "worð," meaning enclosed area. The name was given to those who came from Worth, the name of several places in England.

Famous **Worths:** JONATHAN WORTH (1802–1869) of North Carolina was the governor of that state (1865–1868).

Genealogies: *A Genealogical History of the Clark & Worth Families and Other Puritan Settlers in the Massachusetts Bay Colony* was compiled by Carol Clark Johnson and published in Cygnet, Ohio, in 1970.

WORTHINGTON (S.S. Abbreviation: Worthi)

Ranking: 2116 S.S. Count: 21,659

Origin: English. Uncertain etymology. 1) possibly derived from the Old English name Wurð and the word "tūn," meaning settlement. 2) possibly derived from the Old English word "word" and "tūn," meaning enclosure and settlement. The name in both cases was given to those who came from Worthington, the name of several places in England.

Famous **Worthingtons:** THOMAS WORTHINGTON (1773–1827) of Virginia was a U.S. senator from and governor of Ohio. HENRY ROSSITER WORTHINGTON (1817–1880) of New York City was a hydraulic engineer and the inventor of improvements for canal-boat engines.

Genealogies: A Genealogical Sketch of the Worthington and Plaskitt Families with Others was compiled by J. Plaskitt and published in Baltimore, Maryland, in 1886.

WORTHY

Ranking: 3832 S.S. Count: 11,754
Origin: English. 1) derived from the Old English word "word," meaning enclosed place. The name was given to those who came from Worthy, the name of several places in England. 2) derived from the Old English word "weord," meaning value. The name was given to people who were especially respected.

Genealogies: None known.

WOZNIACKI, WOZNIAK, WOZNIAKIEWICZ
(S.S. Abbreviation: Woznia)

Ranking: 3633 S.S. Count: 12,399
Origin: Polish. 1) derived from the Polish word "wozić," meaning to carry. The name was given to those who worked as drivers of carts or coaches. 2) derived from either of the Polish words "woźny," meaning bailiff, or "wozić," meaning to carry out. The names were given to those who worked as bailiffs.

Genealogies: None known.

WRAY

Ranking: 2176 S.S. Count: 21,068
Origin: English. Derived from the Old Norman word "vrá," meaning corner. The name was given to those who came from Wray, the name of several places in England.

Genealogies: Kit, Kin, & Kaboodle of Wilkins Wray was compiled by Bob Milner and published in Bardwell, Kentucky, in 1990.

WREN

Ranking: 3090 S.S. Count: 14,704
Origin: English, Irish. English: derived from the Old English words "wrenna" or "wrænna," meaning wren. The name was sometimes given to those who were small in stature. Irish: transformation of the Gaelic first name Ó Rinn, which was derived from the word "rinn," meaning star.

Genealogies: None known.

WRIGHT

Ranking: 33 S.S. Count: 618,980
Origin: English, Scottish. Derived from the Old English word "wyrhta," meaning craftsperson, which was derived from the word "wyrcan," meaning to make or to work. The name was given to those who worked making objects or with machinery.

Famous **Wrights:** JOSEPH WRIGHT (1756–1793) of New Jersey was the first draftsman and die-sinker in the U.S. Mint and is believed to be the designer of the first U.S. coins. LAURA MARIA SHELDON WRIGHT (1809–1886) of Vermont was a missionary to the Seneca Indians of western New York. JAMES LENDREW WRIGHT (1816–1893) of Ireland came to the United States as a boy. He was the founder of the Noble Order of the Knights of Labor (1869). HORATIO GOUVERNEUR WRIGHT (1820–1899) of Clinton, Connecticut, was a graduate of West Point. He was chief engineer at Bull Run. A career soldier, he attained the rank of general before retiring in 1884. GEORGE GROVER WRIGHT (1820–1896) of Indiana was chief justice of the United States (1855–1870). HENRY WRIGHT (1835–1895) of England came to the United States as an infant and settled in New York City. He was the organizer of the Cincinnati Red Stockings, managing the team and playing center field. His brother, GEORGE WRIGHT (1847–1937) of New York City, was a professional baseball player. He was the shortstop with the Cincinnati Red Stockings, the first professional team. He was considered the home-run king of the day with 59 homers in 52 games. After leaving baseball he opened a sporting goods store called Wright & Ditson in Boston where he introduced the town to the game of golf. RICHARD ROBERT WRIGHT (1853–1947) of Georgia was born a slave. He founded the Georgia State Teachers' Association, founded and served as the principal of the state's first high school for blacks in Augusta, and served as the head of the State Industrial College in Savannah. FRANK LLOYD WRIGHT (1867–1959) of Wisconsin was an architect. He was the head of group of architects called the Prairie School who envisioned buildings and their inhabitants' melding with the natural surroundings, working together, not against each other. ORVILLE WRIGHT (1871–1948) of Ohio and WILBUR WRIGHT (1867–1912) of Indiana were brothers, inventors, and pioneers in aviation. Their flight at Kitty Hawk, North Carolina, is considered the first stable airborne flight in history. RICHARD NATHANIEL WRIGHT (1908–1960) of Mississippi was a novelist who, against all odds, became a writer of stories, including *Native Son* (1940).

Genealogies: Wright's 400 Years—Plus: 13 Generation Family was compiled by Larry C. Wright and published in Amarillo, Texas, in 1984. *Ancestry of William Henry Wright and Wife Polly Ann Royal and Their Descendants* was compiled by Watie Delfa Wright Ellis and published in San

Jose, California, in 1991. *Captain William Upshaw, Gent., Planter of Virginia* was compiled by Sophie W. Upshaw and published in Baltimore, Maryland, in 1975.

WU
Ranking: 2692 **S.S. Count:** 16,922
Origin: Chinese. 1) the name means warlike. 2) the name means company. 3) the name means province of Kiangsu.
Genealogies: None known.

WUNDER (ALSO WUNDERLICH)
Ranking: 4319 **S.S. Count:** 10,384
Origin: German, Jewish. German: 1) Wunder: derived from the Old High German word "wundar," meaning marvel. 2) Wunderlich: derived from the Middle High German word "wunderlich," meaning unpredictable or whimsical. Jewish: 1) possibly derived from the Yiddish word "vunderlekh," meaning wonderful. 2) possibly derived from the German word "wunderlich," meaning unpredictable or whimsical.
Genealogies: None known.

WYATT
Ranking: 577 **S.S. Count:** 71,366
Origin: English. Derived from the Old English first name Wigheard, which was derived from the words "wig" and "heard," meaning war and hardy or brave.
Famous **Wyatts:** FRANCIS WYATT (1588–1644) of England was the governor of Virginia and was responsible for the "Convention Assembly" (1625).
Genealogies: *The Wiatt Family of Virginia* [also Wyatt] was compiled by Alexander Lloyd Wiatt and published in Virginia in 1980. *A Reasearch Report About Our Wyatt-Mitchell & Allied Families* was compiled by E. Myrtle Mitchell and published in 1974.

WYLIE
Ranking: 2523 **S.S. Count:** 16,028
Origin: English. Transformation of Wiley.
Famous **Wylies:** SAMUEL BROWN WYLIE (1773–1852) of Ireland was a Presbyterian clergyman and the first to be ordained in the United States. ROBERT WYLIE (1839–1877) of England was a painter of landscapes. ELINOR MORTON HOYT WYLIE (1885–1928) of New Jersey was a poet and novelist. She wrote, among other works, *The Orphan Angel*.
Genealogies: None known.

WYMAN
Ranking: 2847 **S.S. Count:** 16,028
Origin: English. Derived from the Old English first name Wigmund, which was derived from the words "wig" and "mund," meaning war and protection.
Famous **Wymans:** SETH WYMAN (1784–1843) of New Hampshire was a burglar and the author of *Life and Adventures* (1843). JEFFRIES WYMAN (1814–1874) of Massachusetts was an anatomist who studied the gorilla and the blind fish in Mammoth Cave. He was considered the finest anatomist of his day. HORACE WYMAN (1827–1915) of Massachusetts was an inventor of loom machinery at Compton & Knowles Loom Works. He invented the first American "dobby" loom (1879).
Genealogies: *Genealogy of the Wyman Family From Its First Settlement in America* was compiled by Thomas Bellows Wyman and published in Burlington, Iowa, in 1880.

WYNN
Ranking: 1105 **S.S. Count:** 40,000
Origin: English. Transformation of Winn.
Famous **Wynns:** ED WYNN (1886–1966) of Pennsylvania was born Isaiah Edwin Leopold Wynn. He was an actor and comedian who left home at age 15 to join the Thurber-Nash Repertoire Co. He appeared in vaudeville, with the Ziegfeld Follies, and in movies. He appeared with his son, Keenan, in the television program "Requiem for a Heavyweight." He also appeared in *Mary Poppins* (1964).
Genealogies: *A Family History of the Wynns (Winn, Wynne) of Virginia, South Carolina, and Georgia* was compiled by Charles Arthur Wynn and published in Panama City Beach, Florida, in 1991.

WYNNE
Ranking: 3182 **S.S. Count:** 14,273
Origin: English. Transformation of Winn.
Genealogies: *A Family History of the Wynns (Winn, Wynne) of Virginia, South Carolina, and Georgia* was compiled by Charles Arthur Wynn and published in Panama City Beach, Florida, in 1991.

WYRICK
Ranking: 4875 **S.S. Count:** 9177
Origin: Uncertain etymology.
Genealogies: None known.

YAGER
Ranking: 4328 S.S. Count: 10,356
Origin: German. Transformation of Yeager.
Genealogies: None known.

YAMAMOTO (S.S. Abbreviation: Yamamo)
Ranking: 4911 S.S. Count: 9110
Origin: Japanese. The name means mountain, or base of a mountain.
Genealogies: None known.

YANCEY
Ranking: 2323 S.S. Count: 19,533
Origin: French. 1) the name was given to those who came from England. 2) the name means Englishman.
Famous Yanceys: WILLIAM LOUNDES YANCEY (1814–1863) of Georgia was a lawyer and member of Congress from Alabama. After Abraham Lincoln's election to the presidency, he wrote the Ordinance of Secession. He served as the Confederate minister to France and England (1861–1862), returned to Alabama, and served in its congress, where he fought centralized government as he had in the U.S. Congress before the war. JAMES EDWARD YANCEY (1894?–1951) of Illinois was a jazz musician and the one who started the boogie-woogie style of piano music.
Genealogies: None known.

YANEZ
Ranking: 4219 S.S. Count: 10,695
Origin: Spanish. Cognate to John.
Genealogies: None known.

YANG
Ranking: 1831 S.S. Count: 24,666
Origin: Chinese. The name means any of the following: 1) the sun, 2) masculine principle in nature, 3) to admire, 4) to raise.
Genealogies: None known.

YARBOROUGH (S.S. Abbreviation: Yarbor)
Ranking: 4344 S.S. Count: 10,317
Origin: English. Transformation of Yarbrough.
Genealogies: None known.

YARBROUGH (S.S. Abbreviation: Yarbro)
Ranking: 1213 S.S. Count: 36,331
Origin: English. Derived from the Old English words "eorð" and "burh," meaning soil and fortress. The name was given to those who came from Yarborough, a place in Lincolnshire, England.
Genealogies: None known.

YATES
Ranking: 468 S.S. Count: 85,585
Origin: English. Derived from the Old English word "geat," meaning gate. The name was given to those who worked as gatekeepers or who lived near a gate.
Famous Yateses: ABRAHAM YATES (1724–1796) of New York was the head of the committee that drafted New York state's first constitution. He served his state as both state senator and as mayor of Albany. ROBERT YATES (1738–1801) of New York was a justice of the New York Supreme Court. RICHARD YATES (1815–1873) of Kentucky was a member of Congress from, then governor of, Illinois. He gave Ulysses S. Grant his first Civil War commission. HERBERT JOHN YATES (1880–1966) of New York was the co-founder of Republic Film Laboratories (1917). He then started Consolidated Film Industries, which became the largest such company in films.
Genealogies: None known.

YAZZIE
Ranking: 3165 S.S. Count: 14,343
Origin: Uncertain etymology.
Genealogies: None known.

YBARRA
Ranking: 1918 S.S. Count: 23,569
Origin: Spanish. Derived from the Basque word "ibar," meaning meadow, and the definite article "a." The name was given to those who lived near meadows.
Genealogies: None known.

YEAGER
Ranking: 1360 S.S. Count: 32,625
Origin: German. The name given to those who were hunters.
Famous Yeagers: JOSEPH YEAGER (1792–1859) of Pennsylvania was an engraver, a publisher of children's books, and the president of Harrisburg and Lancaster Railroad Co. (1848).
Genealogies: None known.

YEE
Ranking: 1846 S.S. Count: 24,522
Origin: Chinese. The name means I, as in the first person singular.
Genealogies: None known.

YI
Ranking: 3140 S.S. Count: 14,459
Origin: Chinese. The name means any of the following: 1) one, 2) whole, 3) appearance, 4) smooth, 5) happy, joyful.
Genealogies: None known.

YOCUM

Ranking: 4738 **S.S. Count:** 9455
Origin: Dutch. The name means descended from Jojakim.
Genealogies: None known.

YODER

Ranking: 1185 **S.S. Count:** 36,996
Origin: German. 1) the name means descended from Joder, meaning "gift of God" (ES). 2) The name was a cognate to Theodor. 3) cognate to Jodocus, a name meaning "the just" (ES).
Genealogies: *History of the Yoder Family in North Carolina* was compiled by Fred Roy Yoder and published in Ann Arbor, Michigan, in 1970. *The Christian J. Yoder and Catherine Bacher Yoder Family Genealogy* was compiled by Richard J. Yoder and published in Wooster, Ohio, in 1988. *Descendants of Jacob Yothers, Bucks County, Pennsylvania* [also Yoder] was compiled by Richard J. Yothers and published in Boston, Massachusetts, in 1984.

YORK

Ranking: 596 **S.S. Count:** 70,078
Origin: English. Uncertain etymology. Possibly derived from the name Eburācum, meaning "yew-tree place" (H&H), which was derived from the Old English words "eofor" and "wic," meaning wild boar and settlement. The name was given to those who came York, the name of several places in England.
Famous **Yorks:** ALVIN CULLUM YORK (1887–1964) of Tennessee was an expert shot but religiously opposed to killing and had applied unsuccessfully for conscientious objector status. As a soldier in World War I he shot and killed 25 enemy soldiers with 25 rounds of ammunition during the Meuse-Argonne offensive. The Germans, fearing the worst, surrendered to York and his seven foxhole buddies. One hundred thirty-two Germans were delivered to the authorities as prisoners of war. York received the Congressional Medal of Honor and France's Croix de Guerre and was the subject of the film *Sergeant York* (1941).
Genealogies: None known.

YOST

Ranking: 1662 **S.S. Count:** 26,919
Origin: German. The name means descendant of Yost, which is a nickname for the first names Jodocus and Justinius, both meaning just.
Famous **Yosts:** CASPER YOST (1864–1941) of Missouri was a journalist, the founder of the American Society of Newspaper Editors, and the author of the book *The Principles of Journalism* (1924). FIELDING HARRIS YOST (1871–1946) of West Virginia was a football coach at a number of universities, each one producing a championship team. He coached for more than 20 years at the University of Michigan and earned the nickname "Hurry up" for his approach to how plays should be executed.
Genealogies: None known.

YOUNG

Ranking: 29 **S.S. Count:** 650,782
Origin: English. Derived from the Old English word "geong," meaning young. The name was given to the younger of two relatives with the same first name.
Famous **Youngs:** THOMAS YOUNG (1731?–1777) of New York was a Revolutionary patriot and physician who suggested the name "Vermont" for the state between New York and New Hampshire. He died in service to his country as a surgeon in the Continental army. EWING YOUNG (?–1841) of Tennessee was a trapper and pioneer. He helped to open the Santa Fe Trail, led Kit Carson across the desert into California, explored California, and eventually settled in the area of Chehalem, Oregon. BRIGHAM YOUNG (1801–1877) of Vermont was the leader of the first people to settle Utah and was the second president of the Mormon Church. ANN ELIZA WEBB YOUNG (1844–1908) of Illinois was the 27th wife of Brigham Young and a writer and speaker against the Mormon practice of polygamy. She wrote a book entitled *Wife No. 19, or The Story of a Life in Bondage.* SAMUEL HALL YOUNG (1847–1927) of Pennsylvania was a Presbyterian clergyman and the founder of the first Protestant and the first American church in Alaska (1879). ELLA FLAGG YOUNG (1845–1918) of New York was the superintendent of schools, Chicago, and the first woman elected president of the National Education Association. LAFAYETTE YOUNG (1848–1926) of Iowa nominated Theodore Roosevelt for vice president at the Republican National Convention in 1900. ART YOUNG (1866–1943) of Illinois was a cartoonist who is known for his satire in the periodical *The Masses.* DENTON TRUE "CY" YOUNG (1867–1955) of Ohio was a baseball player whose record of 509 wins and 316 losses was one of the best. He was elected to the Baseball Hall of Fame (1937). An award given each year to an outstanding baseball player is named the Cy Young Award in his honor. OWEN D. YOUNG (1874–1962) of New York was the organizer of RCA and one of the founders of NBC. STARK YOUNG (1881–1963) of Connecticut was a novelist and playwright and the author of the 1934 bestseller *So Red the Rose.* STANLEY YOUNG (1906–1975) of Indiana was a prominent book publishing executive in New York, holding such positions as managing director of Farrar, Straus and Young (later Farrar, Straus & Giroux). He also is credited with advancing the arts through his position as an executive with the American National Theater and Academy. LESTER YOUNG (1909–1959) of Mississippi, know as "pres," was a jazz saxophone player. WHITNEY MOORE YOUNG JR. (1921–1971) of Kentucky was a civil

rights leader, dean of the School of Social Work at Atlanta University, and director of the National Urban League. He also was the author of several books.

Genealogies: *Biographical Dictionary of the Youngs (born 1653–1870)* was compiled by Louise Ryder Young and published in Bowie, Maryland, in 1990. *Descendants of Jacob Young of Shelby County, Kentucky, Including President Harry S. Truman* was compiled by Elsie Spry Davis and published in Coronado, California, in 1980. *Genealogy and Letters of the Strudwick, Ashe, Young and Allied Families* was compiled by Betsy Lawson Willis and published in Alexandria, Virginia, in 1971.

YOUNGBLOOD (S.S. Abbreviation: Youngb)

Ranking: 1512 **S.S. Count:** 29,405

Origin: German, Swedish. 1) the name means heather plant or leaf. 2) transformation of the German name Jungblut.

Genealogies: *Jeremiah Youngblood: A Genealogy* was compiled by Dorothy Morris Quaife and published in Fountain Valley, California, in 1991. *Rudd-Pllard-Youngblood and Related Families* was compiled by Margaret Rudd Youngblood and published in Houston, Texas, in 1980. *The Youngblood Family: Some Descendants of Three Generations* was compiled by Reba Holmes Brown and published in Port Arthur, Texas, in 1973.

YOUNGE (ALSO YOUNGER)

Ranking: 2665 **S.S. Count:** 17,112

Origin: English. Younge: transformation of Young. Younger: 1) transformation of Young. 2) derived from the Middle Dutch words "jong(h)" and "herr," meaning young and lord. The name was given to nobility who had not yet been knighted.

Famous **Youngers:** THOMAS COLEMAN "COLE" YOUNGER (1844–1916) of Missouri was a bandit who rode with the Jesse James gang, then with his brothers and others in what was called the Younger Brothers gang. He was captured in 1876 and sentenced to life imprisonment. He was paroled in 1901 and pardoned in 1903. MAUD YOUNGER (1870–1936) of California, a suffragist and campaigner for labor unions, delivered the keynote speech at the convention at which the National Woman's Party was founded in 1966.

Genealogies: None known.

YOUNGS, YOUNGSON, YOUNGSTROM (S.S. Abbreviation: Youngs)

Ranking: 4827 **S.S. Count:** 9280

Origin: Youngs, Youngson—English; Youngstrom—Swedish. English: 1) Youngs: transformation of Young. 2) Youngson: the name means the younger of the sons.

Famous **Bearers:** JOHN YOUNGS (1623–1698) of England was a colonial official and the magistrate from Southold, New York, a town on the eastern end of Long Island, to New Haven, Connecticut.

Genealogies: None known.

YOUNT

Ranking: 4136 **S.S. Count:** 10,939

Origin: English? Uncertain etymology.

Famous **Younts:** GEORGE CONCEPCION YOUNT (1794–1865) of North Carolina was a farmer, trapper, and California pioneer. On a land grant from Mexico he settled a large tract of land in the Napa Valley.

Genealogies: *A Brief Sketch of the Origin of the Yount Family in America* was compiled by William Calvin Yount in 1936.

YU

Ranking: 2533 **S.S. Count:** 17,890

Origin: Chinese?, Japanese? Uncertain etymology. The name could mean any of the following: 1) to float, 2) more, 3) to be in opposition, 4) surplus, 5) joyful.

Genealogies: None known.

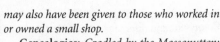

ZACHARY (S.S. Abbreviation: Zachar)

Ranking: 2628 S.S. Count: 17,305

Origin: English, Jewish, Polish. Derived from the Hebrew first name Zecharya, which was derived from the words "zachar" and "ya," meaning to remember and God.

Genealogies: None known.

ZAMBRANO (S.S. Abbreviation: Zambra)

Ranking: 4861 S.S. Count: 9208

Origin: Spanish. The name was given to those who came from Zambrano, a place in Spain.

Genealogies: None known.

ZAMORA

Ranking: 1387 S.S. Count: 31,937

Origin: Spanish. Uncertain etymology. Probably derived from the word "azemur," of Arabic origin, meaning wild olive. The name was given to those who came from Zamora, the name of a place in Spain.

Genealogies: None known.

ZAPATA

Ranking: 2617 S.S. Count: 17,369

Origin: Spanish. Derived from the word "zapato," meaning shoe. The name was given to those who manufactured or sold shoes.

Genealogies: None known.

ZAVALA

Ranking: 2587 S.S. Count: 17,602

Origin: Spanish. Uncertain etymology.

Genealogies: None known.

ZAYAS

Ranking: 3608 S.S. Count: 12,513

Origin: Jewish, Spanish. Jewish: derived from the Hebrew word "zayit," meaning olive. The name was taken ornamentally. Spanish: the name was given to those who came from Zayas, a place in Spain.

Genealogies: None known.

ZEIGLER (S.S. Abbreviation: Zeigle)

Ranking: 2328 S.S. Count: 19,488

Origin: German. Variation of Ziegler.

Genealogies: None known.

ZELLER

Ranking: 2442 S.S. Count: 18,602

Origin: German, Jewish. Derived from the Middle High German word "zelle," meaning cell. The name was given to those who lived near a shrine or hermit's dwelling. The name may also have been given to those who worked in or owned a small shop.

Genealogies: *Cradled by the Massanutten: The Zellers/Sellers Family* was compiled by Mary Marie Koontz Arrington and published in Broadway, Virginia, in 1986. *From A B to Z: A Genealogy* [also Zeller] was compiled by Margaret Zeller Garrett and published in Burlington, Kansas, in 1975.

ZEPEDA

Ranking: 3609 S.S. Count: 12,512

Origin: Spanish. Uncertain etymology.

Genealogies: None known.

ZIEGLER (S.S. Abbreviation: Ziegle)

Ranking: 1211 S.S. Count: 36,393

Origin: German, Jewish. Derived from the Old High German word "ziagal," meaning roof tile. The name was given to those who worked tiling roofs, or possibly to those who worked with bricks.

Famous **Zieglers**: DAVID ZIEGLER (1748–1811) of Germany was a soldier in the Revolutionary War and was active in the settlement affairs of Cincinnati, Ohio. WILLIAM ZIEGLER (1843–1905) of Pennsylvania was one of the founders of the Royal Chemical Co., manufacturers of Royal Baking Powder.

Genealogies: *Roots and Branches of a Ziegler Family Tree, 1767–1980, Georg Michael Ziegler* was compiled by Alta Buckingham Drasser and published in Sargent, Nebraska, in 1981. *The Ziegler Family and Related Families in Pennsylvania* was compiled by Gertrude Mohlin Ziegler and published in Zelienople, Pennsylvania, in 1978. *Genealogical Chronolog of John Peter Snyder, 1729–1807 and His Wife Mary Catharine Elizabeth (Stentz) Snyder, 1739–1782 and Their Descendants* [also Ziegler] was compiled by Howard W. Stentz and published in Coos Bay, Oregon, in 1989.

ZIELENIEWICZ, ZIELENIEWSKI, ZIELENKIEWICZ (S.S. Abbreviation: Zielen)

Ranking: 2793 S.S. Count: 16,291

Origin: Jewish, Polish. Polish: derived from the Polish word "zielony," meaning green. The name was probably given to those who had sickly complexions, or to those who were inexperienced. Jewish: same derivation as in the Polish. The name was usually taken ornamentally.

Genealogies: None known.

ZIMMER (ALSO ZIMMERMAN, ZIMMERMANN)

Ranking: 237 S.S. Count: 150,097

Origin: Zimmer—German; Zimmerman—Jewish; Zim-

mermann—German, Jewish. Zimmer: transformation of Zimmermann. Zimmerman: transformation of Zimmermann. Zimmermann: derived from the Middle High German words "zimber" or "zimmer" and "mann," meaning wood and man. The name was given to those who worked as carpenters.

Famous **Bearers:** EUGENE ZIMMERMAN (1862–1935) of Switzerland was a cartoonist who came to the United States as a child. His career began with the magazine *Puck* and grew as he became the cartoonist on the staff of *Judge* (1885–1913). HENRY "HEINIE" ZIMMERMAN (1896–1960) of New York was a baseball player considered to be the best third baseman in the National League. He was traded to another team that made it to the World Series. There he performed his infamous "bonehead" play in the last game of the series and "chased Eddie Collins across the plate," which the *New York Times* called "one of the stupidest plays that has ever been seen in a world's series." He was suspended for intentionally swaying the outcome of games in 1919, and his career ended.

Genealogies: *Genealogical History of Our Ancestors* was compiled by William Kenneth Rutherford and published in Lexington, Missouri, in 1989. *The Family of Henry Zimmerman of Pennsylvania and Ohio: A Genealogical History* was compiled by Leo H. Garman and published in Elmhurst, Illinois, in 1985.

ZINK

Ranking: 3768 **S.S. Count:** 12,023
Origin: German. Derived from the Old High German word "zinko," meaning point. The name was given to those

who lived near a pointed lot of land, or to men who had pointed noses.

Genealogies: *The Making of an American Family (including Zink family)* was compiled by Ann Zink Beck and published in Montvale, New Jersey, in 1977. *Sink Descendants, Jacob Zinck Pioneer: Zinck, Zink, and Sink* was published in Lexington, North Carolina, in 1979.

ZUCKER

Ranking: 3453 **S.S. Count:** 13,071
Origin: German, Jewish. German: 1) derived from the Middle High German word "zucker," meaning sugar. The name was given to those who worked as confectioners or sugar dealers. 2) derived from the Middle High German word "zuckœre," meaning thief, which was derived from the Old High German word "zucchen," meaning to pull (as in to snatch). The name was given in a derogatory manner to those who were believed to be thieves. Jewish: derived from a last name derived from the German word "zucker" or the Yiddish word "zuker," both meaning sugar. The name was taken ornamentally or given to those who worked as confectioners or sugar dealers.

Genealogies: *Zucker Family, Nine Generations* was compiled by Kaye Kole and published in Savannah, Georgia, in 1988.

ZUNIGA

Ranking: 2201 **S.S. Count:** 20,846
Origin: Spanish? Uncertain etymology.
Genealogies: None known.

SOURCES

In addition to Philip Slepian's files, the following sources were consulted:

Bardsley, Charles. *Dictionary of English and Welsh Surnames*. Baltimore: Genealogical Publishing Company, Inc., 1967. (Cited in the text as CB)

Concise Dictionary of American Biography, Fourth Edition. New York: Charles Scribner's Sons, 1990.

Dictionary of American Biography. New York: Charles Scribner's Sons. (Multiple editions and publication dates.)

Fucilla, Joseph G. *Our Italian Surnames*. Baltimore: Genealogical Publishing Company, Inc., 1987.

Hanks, Patrick, and Flavia Hodges. *A Dictionary of Surnames*. Oxford: Oxford University Press, 1988. (*primary source; cited in the text as H&H)

Harrison, Henry. *Surnames of the United Kingdom*. Baltimore: Genealogical Publishing Company, Inc., 1969.

Hook, Julius. *Family Names*: how our surnames came to America. London: MacMillan, 1982.

James, Edward T., editor. *Notable American Women, 1607–1950*. Cambridge, Mass.: Belknap Press of Harvard University Press, 1971.

Jones, George. *German-American Names*. Baltimore: Genealogical Publishing Company, Inc., 1990.

Jones, Russell. *Chinese Names*: the use and meanings of Chinese surnames in Singapore and Malaysia. Petaling Jaya, Selangor, and Durul Ehsan, Malaysia: Pelanduk Publishing, 1989.

Maduell Jr., Charles R. *Romance of Spanish Surnames*. New Orleans: Charles Maduell, Jr., 1967.

Morlet, Marie-Th'er'ese. *Dictionnaire Etymologique des noms de Famille*. Paris: Perrin, 1991.

National Cyclopedia of American Biography. Clifton, N.J.: James T. White Co. (Multiple editions and publication dates.)

Reaney, Percy, and R. M. Wilson. *A Dictionary of English Surnames*. 3d Edition. London: Routledge, 1991.

Sicherman, Barbara, and Carol Hurd Green, editors. *Notable American Women, The Modern Period*. Cambridge, Mass.: Belknap Press of Harvard University Press, 1980.

Smith Elsdon. *A New Dictionary of American Family Names.* New York: Harper and Row, 1972. (*secondary source; cited in the text as ES)

Unbegaun, Boris. *Russian Surnames.* Oxford: Clarendon Press, 1972.

Webster's American Biographies. Springfield, Mass.: Merriam-Webster, 1975.

Webster's New Biographical Dictionary. Springfield, Mass.: Merriam-Webster, 1988.

Who Was Who in America. New Providence, N.J.: Marquis Who's Who, Reed Reference Publishing Co. (Multiple editions and publication dates.)